THIRD EDITION

ORGANIZATION THEORY & DESIGN

AN INTERNATIONAL PERSPECTIVE

Richard L. Daft

Jonathan Murphy & Hugh Willmott

CENGAGE
Learning·

Australia • Brazil • Mexico • Singapore • United Kingdom • United States

Organization Theory and Design, 3rd edition
Richard L. Daft, Jonathan Murphy, Hugh Willmott

Publisher: Annabel Ainscow

Editorial Assistant: Lauren Cartridge

Content Project Manager: Sue Povey

Manufacturing Manager: Eyvett Davis

Marketing Manager: Vicky Pavlicic

Typesetter: Lumina Datamatics, Inc.

Cover design: Adam Renvoize

For product information and technology assistance,
contact **emea.info©cengage.com.**
For permission to use material from this text or product,
and for permission queries,
email **emea.permissions@cengage.com.**

British Library Cataloguing-in-Publication Data
A catalogue record for this book is available from the British Library.

ISBN: 978-1-4737-2638-3

Cengage Learning EMEA
Cheriton House, North Way, Andover, Hampshire, SP10 5BE
United Kingdom

Cengage Learning products are represented in Canada by Nelson Education Ltd.

For your lifelong learning solutions, visit **www.cengage.co.uk**

Purchase your next print book, e-book or e-chapter at **www.cengagebrain.com.**

Printed in China by RR Donnelley
Print Number 02   Print Year 2018

BRIEF CONTENTS

CONTENTS

PART I

INTRODUCTION TO ORGANIZATIONS   1

PART II

ORGANIZATIONAL PURPOSE AND STRUCTURAL DESIGN   49

PART III

OPEN SYSTEM DESIGN ELEMENTS   137

5   THE EXTERNAL ENVIRONMENT   138

6   INTERORGANIZATIONAL RELATIONSHIPS   179

7   DESIGNING ORGANIZATIONS FOR THE INTERNATIONAL ENVIRONMENT   214

PART IV

INTERNAL DESIGN ELEMENTS   253

PART V

MANAGING DYNAMIC PROCESSES   371

12   INNOVATION AND CHANGE   410

13   DECISION-MAKING PROCESSES   450

14   CONFLICT, POWER AND POLITICS   494

INTEGRATIVE CASES

FEATURES

A LOOK INSIDE

Philips NV

Philips was one of the world's first genuine multinationals. Founded in Eindhoven, Netherlands by Gerard Philips in 1891, the company initially manufactured light bulbs, seizing the opportunity of widespread home and business electrification. Electricity soon brought opportunities for inventing and selling further electrical devices, and during much of the twentieth century, no European company seized market opportunities better than Philips. The relatively small size of Holland's domestic market pushed the company to seek new markets on the continent and eventually beyond. By the mid-1980s, the company was active in 14 different divisions ranging from the original lighting sector to large appliances and the new field of computers. Philips' product development laboratories were unparalleled, developing cutting-edge electrical equipment across the company's vast product range.

But as is often the case in business, at the height of Philips' success, storm clouds were forming on the horizon. Several different factors were beginning to work against the company as it approached its second century.

One issue was the very loose organizational structure that the company was forced to adopt when it internationalized. Before the great era of trade and market liberalization that began in the 1970s, it was simply not possible to centralize functions globally. Indeed, during the Second World War, when Holland was occupied by the German Nazis, international branches of Philips basically operated entirely independently. Even in normal times, companies wishing to enter different countries' markets were typically forced to set up fully functional national units, with their own manufacturing, marketing and distribution systems.

The national units that had to be set up tended to become autonomous power bases. In theory this could have been beneficial, if innovative approaches were developed and tested in one country and then rolled out internationally, as was the case for example for the Anglo-Dutch consumer products firm, Unilever.[1] But consumer electronics are different from household products; they are costly to develop, and generally don't require tailoring to individual markets; thus centralized product development tends to be the preferred approach. Autonomy sometimes reached extremes, for example when Philips in North America decided to manufacture early video recorders based on a competitor's product.

Another problem was bureaucracy and inefficiency. Philips was so successful, for so long, that workers and managers began to see their positions as jobs-for-life. Employment grew and grew, ultimately Philips had over 300 000 employees worldwide. Eindhoven itself was every bit the company town; Philips took on numerous social projects ranging from the Philips library and theatre to the PSV Eindhoven football team, which under Philips' benevolent sponsorship became one of the giants of European club soccer. The Philips product development division seemed to lose its knack for creating products that fit customer needs. Its early forays into computers, in particular, were not competitive with either the American giants like IBM and later Compaq, or the emerging brands from the Far East.

By the 1980s, Japan had emerged from its early post-war avatar as producer of cheap copies of Western consumer goods. In motorcycles, then the automobile industry, and fatefully for Philips, in electronics, Japan began producing flashy, competitively priced but well-made products. The Matsushita conglomerate, in particular, with brands such as Toshiba, as well as Sony Corporation, began to develop the same kind of positive reputation amongst consumers that Philips once enjoyed, whereas Philips products started to be viewed as expensive and behind the times.

Philips' bottom line suddenly turned red. Despite fitful efforts to cut costs in the late '80s, by 1990 the company had run up an accumulated deficit of $2.6 billion. PSV Eindhoven had won the European Cup in 1988, but on the eve of its hundredth anniversary, its sponsor Philips was in real danger of disappearing underneath this sea of red ink.[2]

Philips turned to a new company president, Jan Timmer, who slashed the company's workforce by 50 000, got out of the computer business altogether, terminated a number of unprofitable joint ventures and reoriented the company towards Asian production facilities in place of increasingly costly Europe. Timmer's hard-nosed strategy stemmed some but not all the bleeding. In 1996, Sony, Philips'

A Look Inside cutting-edge examples of organization theory in practice within a wide range of organizations

BOOKMARK 3.0

Have you read this book?

Managing Sceptically: A Critique of Organizational Fashion

BY HARVIE RAMSAY

In *Managing Sceptically*, Harvie Ramsay takes a close look at various 'innovations' in organization theory and management practice, and finds many of them to be fads that are quickly forgotten and replaced by other new, but often shallow ideas. Some past fads that Ramsay identifies include:

- *Quality circles*: this idea was imported from Japan in the 1970s, and saw its greatest popularity in the early 1980s. The idea was for groups of workers to get together to discuss ways to improve the production process. Within a few years researchers found that any short-term gains were quickly lost. Corporate productivity is embedded in a whole range of social relationships that extend into wider society, and in most cases productivity cannot be fundamentally improved by adopting a single idea from another country.
- *Total Quality Management*: a combination of American systems theory and Japanese meticulousness, TQM was intended to ensure organization-wide quality management, resulting in improved products for consumers, as well as better return to shareholders. TQM seems to have been successful mainly when combined with incentive bonuses, suggesting that it did not succeed in improving intrinsic employee motivation. By the mid-1990s, TQM seemed to be reaching the end of its life cycle.
- *Change management*: an approach that aims to structure the change process in an organization from current practices to an improved future. There are numerous change management models, which might include stages such as developing a change management strategy, enrolling senior managers as change leaders, communicating the need for change, training employees in the changed systems, coaching employees to accept and support change and approaches to sustaining the change. However, Ramsay cites one large-scale study that showed only one-third of organizations undertaking change management achieved lasting organizational strengthening.

Ramsay considers different explanations for why organizations continue to seize on new fads and fashions, given the singular lack of evidence for their success. These include the inherent contradiction in business organizations between the means to achieve improved productivity which is largely through building employee commitment, and the appropriation by shareholders of the resultant increased profits. He concludes that there is a tendency for fads to oscillate between 'rationalist' approaches such as Taylorism and 'normative' approaches, each of which generates dysfunctionalities that lead to oscillating paradigm shifts between the two norms.

Ramsay's work is several years old, but the pattern of management fads continues unabated. A highly influential and long-lasting fad for private-public partnerships was generated by David Osborne and Ted Gaebler's 1992 *Reinventing Government*. Although Osborne and Gaebler intended to strengthen public service provision, the result of applying their ideas was often state capture by private interests and the loss of universal public services. Many of the private finance schemes set up as part of the 'reinventing government' movement have proven poor value for money, and a number collapsed during the 2007–2009 global economic crisis, leaving the taxpayer holding the tab.

Source: Faranak Miraftab (2004), 'Public–Private Partnerships: The Trojan Horse of Neoliberal Development?', *Journal of Planning Education and Research*, 24, 89–101; Warwick Funnell, Robert Jupe and Jane Andrew (2009), *In Government We Trust: Market-Failure and the Delusions of Privatisation*, London, Pluto; David Walker (2008), 'Out with the outsourcers?' *Prospect*, November 20.

'Managing Sceptically: A Critique of Organizational Fashion', is Chapter Nine in Stewart Clegg and Gill Palmer (1996), *The politics of management knowledge*, London, Sage.

Bookmark short reviews of books highlighting key issues that impact modern management

IN PRACTICE

W. L. Gore & Associates

When Jack Dougherty began work at W. L. Gore & Associates, Inc., he reported to Bill Gore, the company's founder, to receive his first assignment. Gore told him, 'Why don't you find something you'd like to do'. Dougherty was shocked at the informality but quickly recovered and began interrogating various managers about their activities. He was attracted to a new product called Gore-Tex, a membrane that was waterproof but breathable when bonded to fabric. The next morning, he came to work dressed in jeans and began helping feed fabric into the maw of a large laminator. Five years later, Dougherty was responsible for marketing and advertising in the fabrics group.

Bill Gore died in 1986, but the organization he designed still runs in the same informal way as before. One of the key tenets of the organization is that employees (called associates) figure out what they want to do and where they think they can make a contribution. Instead of bosses, associates can choose to work with 'leaders' who emerge organically in the process of addressing work's regular challenges. The company has over 9000 associates in 45 locations around the world. The plants are kept small – up to 200 people – to maintain a family atmosphere. 'It's much better to use friendship and love than slavery and whips', Bill Gore said. Several professional associates are assigned to act as 'sponsors' for new product development, but the administrative structure is lean. Good human relations is a more important value than is internal efficiency. The company has seven times been named one of *Fortune* magazine's '100 Best Companies to Work For in America'. In 2009 it was listed twelfth on the '50 Best Large Workplaces in Europe' list, and in 2012, in the top ten workplaces in the world named by the Great Place to Work Institute. The company was featured in Malcolm Gladwell's famous book *The Tipping Point*, to illustrate how small sized plants and mutual familiarity make for positive and efficient working teams. It has also been featured in Frederick Laloux's 2014 book, *Reinventing Organizations*, as a "teal" organization: one that fosters its members' abilities to self-manage and self-organize.[4] Gore continues to grow and prosper.[5] (see Counterpoint 2.2).

Carrefour

Carrefour is one of the giants in today's global retailing. In 1963, Carrefour pioneered the concept of the *hypermarché*, or hypermarket in English, a concept bringing together the traditional food-based supermarket with the full-range department store, carrying items from clothes to house paint to computers: 'everything under the same roof'. The company, based in France but by 2016 operating in 28 different national markets from China to Argentina, is the world's second largest by retail sales after Wal-Mart, with over 10 000 stores worldwide, on four continents. Although in some markets Carrefour operates a number of other chains ranging from convenience stores to cash and carry warehouses, these operations are driven by the supply and distribution systems established for the hypermarket operations. Its hypermarkets all contain the same product mix of about 60 per cent food and 40 per cent non-food, with the specific products sold tailored, of course, to national tastes. Where Carrefour has expanded through purchasing existing chains, such as Spain's Continente chain, it has usually moved quickly to rebrand the purchased properties with the name, logo, and 'look and feel' of the Carrefour group.

Carrefour's success has been built on following its basic model quite rigidly across national markets. The company's managers are drawn from all its operating countries, but management training places a strong emphasis on creating common corporate values and understanding amongst both managers and shop-floor employees, enabling it to avoid some of the differing visions that so hampered Philips, discussed in the previous chapter.[6]

Not-for-Profit Organizations and Charities

Many nonprofit organizations (NGOs) rely heavily on public and other external funding. NGOs in the arts sector, for example, can rarely earn enough money from ticket sales to cover even their expenses, despite having a small staff complement who are

In Practice practical illustrations of the text's surrounding theory in practice

LEADING BY DESIGN

Shazam – It's Magic!

Many people have had the experience of hearing a song they like on the radio or in a dance club and waiting in vain for the DJ to identify it. Shazam, a mobile-phone music service launched in the United Kingdom in August 2002, has come to the rescue. The next time a mobile phone user hears that mystery tune, all he or she has to do is dial a four-digit number on the mobile phone, let the music play into the handset, and moments later receive a text message with the artist and song title. The user can forward a 30-second clip of the track to friends, or even download the song directly to his or her phone. The song can then be legally copied from the mobile phone to a PC and shared between multiple devices.

Shazam's magic happens through the use of a pattern-recognition software algorithm developed by the company's chief scientist. The algorithm picks out the salient characteristics of a tune and matches them against a massive music database. The company, founded by Californian entrepreneur Chris Barton, calls the process 'tagging', and by 2012 Shazam claimed that worldwide its users had 'tagged' five billion songs, TV shows and advertisements. Users can go online and see a list of all the songs they've tagged.

Shazam's success depends on collaborative partnerships with mobile phone companies, major record labels, software companies and others. A partnership with Swiss-based SDC (Secure Digital Container) AG provides the technology that enables a complete 'tag to download' in three simple steps, allowing users to purchase music on the move. A strategic alliance with MTV Japan helped Shazam expand to about 40 million mobile phone subscribers in Japan. Deals with international mobile operators and media companies throughout the United States, Europe and Asia make Shazam's service available to more than 1 billion mobile phone users worldwide. By 2013 Shazam claimed it had 300 million users.

The mobile phone companies offer tagging as a premium service to their customers and pay Shazam a cut of the profits. Since tagging promises to drive up call times, most mobile phone companies are interested. And the record labels' interests are served by getting new music in front of consumers. Word-of-mouth recommendations are a powerful means of driving music sales, so the idea of people

Leading by Design cutting-edge examples of organizations undergoing major change within the turbulent global environment

Online Counterpoint additional counterpoints can be found on the associated online platform. Look out for this icon in the margin.

Briefcase insights on analyzing cases and managing organizations, are given on the online platform. Look for this icon in the margin.

Summary and Interpretation

In established thinking, organizations tend to be regarded as 'closed systems' – as autonomous and separate, trying to outdo other companies. In contrast, in more recent, 'open systems' thinking, organizations are seen as part of an ecosystem. An organization may span several industries and be positioned in a dense web of relationships with other companies and agencies. Collaboration then comes to be regarded as a weapon in the armoury of competition. Organizations may compete and collaborate at the same time depending on the location and issue. In this business ecosystem, management include the development of horizontal relationships with other organizations.

Four perspectives have been developed to explain relationships among organizations. The resource-dependence perspective argues that organizations try to avoid excessive dependence on other organizations. In this view, considerable effort is devoted to controlling the environment to ensure ample resources while maintaining independence; and managers in powerful organizations gain advantage by exploiting the dependence of weaker organizations. In the collaborative-network perspective, organizations welcome collaboration and interdependence with other organizations to enhance value for both. Many executives are changing mindsets away from independence toward collaboration, often with former corporate enemies.

? ONLINE COUNTERPOINT 4.10

The population-ecology perspective explains why organizational diversity continuously increases with the appearance of new organizations filling niches left open by established companies. This perspective suggests that large companies usually cannot adapt to meet a changing environment; hence, new companies emerge with the appropriate form and skills to serve new needs. Through the process of variation, selection and retention, some organizations survive and grow while others perish. Executives may develop a generalist or specialist strategy to survive in the population of organizations.

The institutional perspective argues that interorganizational relationships are significantly shaped by the quest for legitimacy. Structures and activities are favoured that are perceived as valid, proper and up-to-date by external stakeholders. Techniques are copied with the consequence that organizations begin to look very similar. There are three core mechanisms that explain increasing organizational homogeneity: mimetic forces, which result from responses to uncertainty; coercive forces, which stem from power differences and political influences; and normative forces, which result from common training and professionalism.

The four perspectives offer distinct ways of making sense of organizations which may be adopted by managers to address challenges of change, competition and collaboration. Managers in organizations may be seen to struggle to reduce dependence and vulnerability; to engage in collaborative relationships with others; to capitalize on others' slowness to adapt by seizing upon openings for new organizations to flourish; and to be enabled and constrained by the requirement to secure legitimacy from the external environment.

Summary highlight the key learning points and how they can be applied to organizational settings

COUNTERPOINT 4.6

Although these problems may arise from 'structural deficiency' that can be corrected by the technical fix of structural redesign, the problems may also be endemic to capitalist work organizations. Decision-making may be delayed because senior managers anticipate that their jobs or career prospects are threatened by change. Innovation may be slow because it poses a threat to established 'empires' within the organization. Declines in employee performance may be associated with frustration and dissatisfaction in, ultimately, being treated as a disposable commodity or, at least, with insufficient dignity as changes are introduced (or imposed) without genuine consultation or adequate understanding of their counterproductive effects. Conflicts between individuals, groups, departments and divisions may arise from the basic understanding that responding to the demands of shareholders and/or customers is not necessarily compatible with improving the wages and conditions (e.g. pensions) of particular groups of employees.

Counterpoint deliberately provocative viewpoints that generate debate and encourage multiple perspectives for rounded learning

KEY CONCEPTS

centralized	horizontal grouping	organization structure	teams
decentralized	horizontal linkage	outsourcing	vertical information system
departmental grouping	horizontal structure	process	vertical linkages
divisional grouping	hybrid structure	product matrix	virtual network grouping
divisional structure	integrator	re-engineering	virtual network structure
functional grouping	liaison role	symptoms of structural deficiency	virtual team
functional matrix	matrix structure	task force	
functional structure	multifocused grouping		

Key Concepts highlighted throughout with a detailed glossary at the back of the text

Discussion Questions

1 What is the definition of *organization structure*? Does organization structure appear on the organization chart? Explain.

2 How do rules and plans help an organization achieve vertical integration?

3 When is a functional structure preferable to a divisional structure?

4 Large corporations tend to use hybrid structures. Why?

5 What are the primary differences between a traditional organization designed for efficiency and a more contemporary organization designed for learning?

6 What is the difference between a task force and a team? Between a liaison role and an integrating role? Which of these provides the greatest amount of horizontal coordination?

7 What conditions usually have to be present before an organization should adopt a matrix structure?

8 The manager of a consumer products firm said, 'We use the brand manager position to train future executives'. Do you think the brand manager position is a good training ground? Discuss.

9 Why do companies using a horizontal structure have cultures that emphasize openness, employee empowerment and responsibility? What do you think a manager's job would be like in a horizontally organized company?

10 Describe the virtual network structure. Why do you think this is becoming a good structural alternative for some of today's organizations?

Discussion Questions carefully prepared questions help tease out the key issues

Chapter 2 Workbook Measuring Dimensions of Organizations

Analyze two organizations along the dimensions shown below. Indicate where you think each organization would fall on each of the scales. Use an X to indicate the first organization and an * to show the second.

You may choose any two organizations you are familiar with, such as your place of work, the university, a student organization, your local community organization or church, or your family.

Workbook experiential exercises encourage team learning and skills development

CASE FOR ANALYSIS 4.1

Organization Structures

Scotia University

Scotia University is located in Scotland and, like most organizations, periodically re-structures its organization to better align its structure to its strategy. Universities are no different to any other organization but tend to use different terminology when it comes to organization structures. Senate is the senior academic body of the university. Legally and constitutionally it is responsible for the academic activity of the university which is teaching and research. Senate is also responsible for student conduct. The University Court is involved in the development of, and ultimately approves, the university's strategic plan. It approves any major financial decisions, such as whether or not to borrow money; it also approves the university's proposed budget.

The principal divisions are normally termed colleges, faculties or schools, with colleges being an overarching structure with direct responsibility to the University Executive or Senior Management Team. The Scotia University College of Arts contains: the School of Humanities; the School of Critical Studies; the School of Culture & Creative Arts; the School of Modern Languages & Cultures; and its graduate school. The College of Medical, Veterinary and Life Sciences contains: the School of Life Sciences; the School of Medicine; the School of Veterinary Medicine; its graduate school and seven research institutes. The College of Science and Engineering contains: the School of Chemistry; the School of Computing Science; the School of Engineering; the School of Geographical & Earth Sciences; the School of Mathematics & Statistics; the School of Physics & Astronomy; the School of Psychology; and its graduate school. The College of Social Sciences contains: the Business School; the School of Education; the School of Interdisciplinary Studies; the School of Law; the School of Social & Political Sciences; and its graduate school.

The chief executive of a Scottish university has the title Principal and Vice-Chancellor and the Chancellor is a lay-member of the university (not an employee). The Senior Management Group advises the Principal as chief executive officer of the University on matters of policy. It also advises Court and Senate on matters of strategic policy (academic and resource), and acts on a day-to-day basis to implement the policies of Court and Senate. The Senior Management Group (SMG) comprises: the Principal; Vice-Principals; Heads of Colleges; Secretary of Court; and the Director of Finance. The SMG has responsibility for ensuring that the university policies are effectively implemented and that this is done in a coordinated way across the Colleges and University Services. It has a role in developing corporate initiatives and policies, for consideration by Senate and Court. SMG maintains a watching brief on the university strategy and in particular on progress against the strategic key performance indicators (KPIs) and it takes action as required to ensure that the university is positioned to meet them. SMG also has an ongoing responsibility to monitor, assess and address risk, and in liaison with Court, update the strategic risk list annually.

The Court is the governing body of the university, and is sometimes compared to the Board of Directors of a company. Its powers have been defined over a number of years and are set out in a series of Acts of Parliament, the Universities (Scotland) Acts 1858–1966, and subsidiary regulations and ordinances. The Court has ultimate responsibility for the deployment of resources in the university and for the strategic plans of the institution. It also has a monitoring role in relation to the overall performance of the university, and it holds the Principal accountable for the effective and efficient management of the university. It is responsible for the well-being of staff. With the Senate, it is responsible for the well-being of students and for the reputation of the university. The Rector is elected by the students of the university to represent their interests. He or she is also, ex-officio, the Chairperson of the University Court, the body which administers the resources of the university. The Rector is not active in university strategy or policy-making. The role is principally as spokesperson and representative for student issues. The Rector's participation in events is entirely voluntary and depends on availability and personal choice.

Case Study Questions

1 Describe and explain the structure of Scotia University in terms of its vertical structure and illustrate with an organization chart of the Colleges.

Case for Analysis chapter-ending cases provide real-world settings for analysis and assessment

1.0 **INTEGRATIVE CASE 1.0**

Luxurious Goat Milk Products: Working with Local Culture – RojaAHP

Kim Maya Sutton
Jade Hochschule Wilhelmshaven, Germany

This case study is fictional for educational purposes. All people except President Rouhani are fictional; RojaAHP is also fictional. Any likeness to persons or organizations is purely coincidental.

Hannah woke up with a start that morning in September of 2016, convinced she'd slept in. She had to get up, get ready, meet the Abdarschi, find a taxi, make it to town and all of that in just … wait – only 5am? She sighed and placed her head back on the linen sheet she used to fend off some of the night heat. In the last five years, the one thing she had not gotten used to was the heat.

Hannah Williams (*14 October 1984 in Al Fashir, Sudan)

Born to US American parents, a general logistician and a nurse who both worked for Doctors Without Borders, Hannah Williams was more of a miracle than anything else, said her grandmother Dotty: 'Your parents always met so briefly. He clearly heard my wish for another little one in the family to whom I could tend.' Hannah grew up with Dotty in her old plantation house in Kentucky and until she turned 5, she only saw her mum and dad on special occasions. One dismal day in 1989, her world turned into a whirlwind that had not stopped since. Dotty died, and her mother showed up to home-school her while working part-time in the field. They lived in foreign countries on 9-12 month assignments. (MSF UF, 2016)

Hannah got used to this lifestyle, learned languages quickly, and was particularly fascinated with Middle Eastern cultures. The beauty of Damascus with the strong bazaar colours and smells, the strange sizzling noises at the Dead Sea and the beautiful ruins of Karnak Temple in Luxor sparked an interest in her. This is where she would live when she was an adult, she decided. When her parents retired to a quiet life back on the Old Plantation, Hannah went to Cologne, Germany, to study pharmaceutical chemistry. At a student party in 2004, she met her later husband, Philip, and their future business partner, Ali, who studied engineering and management.

Ali Turani (* 02 April 1984 in Tehran, Iran)

Ali grew up with the traditional Persian values. He was also very interested in everything Western. When in 1994, the opportunity arose to stay with a distant uncle in Germany, his parents gave him as much money and jewellery as they could spare and sent their only son to study, knowing he'd come back and bring new knowledge to help his country later. Ali learned German easily, soaked up all the information like a sponge, and concluded German high school with honors. He worked in a Persian restaurant to earn his living and took up internships where he could. With very structured days, he knew exactly when to study, work, enjoy culture. As a Shiite, he did not consume alcohol and was always a role model for his fellow students. It was tough for Philip to convince his friend to join the party in the first place.

Integrative Cases longer cases integrate learning by addressing themes and concepts from across the text

PREFACE

Our vision for this third edition of *Organization Theory and Design: An International Perspective*, is to explore contemporary issues in organization design using both classic ideas and contemporary theories while also mobilizing some critical thinking. Our aim is to help students understand different approaches to management. In the first EMEA edition, published in 2010, Jonathan Murphy and Hugh Willmott joined Richard Daft to incorporate many significant changes and additions to the enormously successful sole-authored *Organization Theory and Design* by Professor Daft, and now in its 11th US edition. In the second edition, the counterpoint feature was updated, and new case examples and book reviews were added. In this third edition, every chapter has been updated, taking into account developments in both corporate life and the wider economy since the last edition went to press.

Throughout this new edition, examples are drawn from global sources, reflecting different issues and best practices faced by managers working in national and international business, public sector, and nonprofit environments around the world.

Changing World – Changing Organizations

The international crisis that has rocked economic activity around the world for the past decade since 2007, has raised fundamental questions about the international economic order, and it has challenged earlier assumptions about organizational design. The period of US dominance of the world economy, in place since the end of the Second World War, is in the process of dissolution. New economic powers like China and India have grown rapidly and may well overtake the former economic powers in America, Europe and Japan within the next generation, although their economies too have not escaped unscathed from international economic instability. Many major multinational corporations are in decline, a phenomenon that has been brought home in striking fashion through bankruptcy and reorganization of companies as large as General Motors. Large multinational companies will continue to exist in some form, but it is clear that US-headquartered manufacturing MNCs are no longer unrivalled in organizational innovation and entrepreneurial dynamism. It is not only in the auto industry but, more crucially, in other areas, notably electronics, that new and powerful competitors have emerged, particularly from the Asia-Pacific region. There has also been a shift – particularly within the advanced economies – away from manufacturing and towards services, particularly tied to the dramatic development of information technology. This third EMEA edition of *Organization Theory and Design* keeps up-to-date this changing business environment, with greater focus on service-delivering organizations, as well as further geographic diversity in the organizations we discuss and explore.

The economic changes that have been occurring since the 1970s – brought to a head by the post-2007 economic crisis – reflect the decline of a form of production based on large multinationals whose sheer size and available resources enabled them to set the standard for business practice throughout their industries. International economic liberalization combined with advances in information and communication technologies means that companies do not need to be enormous in order to compete internationally. We explore in the text how numerous smaller, more agile companies, often based in emerging economies, have been able to grow rapidly, and have in many cases outstripped the former market leaders in the established developed countries. These companies are embedded in distinctive (frequently non-Western) cultures and they incorporate practices that have proven highly effective. These newcomers have often humbled many industry giants, although at the same time other well-established companies have adapted and flourished in new conditions nurtured by globalization and market liberalization.

These developments have served to underscore the key, yet repeatedly overlooked, insight that *there is no single, effective way of designing and managing an organization*. When we look around the world, we find very different organizations, designed on highly divergent principles and philosophies, succeeding in both national and international markets. British firms controlled by private equity funds with a very short term profit-maximizing perspective operate cheek-by-jowl with Japanese companies that plan generations ahead. Western multinational corporations that are constantly looking to sell off 'non-core' assets compete against sprawling Asian conglomerates that are happy to incorporate an ever-burgeoning range of apparently disconnected product ranges; extending for example from tomato paste to air conditioners. Similarly, organizations with very different management styles coexist in the global business environment. Many successful companies have highly developed human resource departments, where hiring is carried out on the basis of 'scientific' assessments including batteries of psychometric tests and rigorous multi-stage hiring panels, and where every staff member has a multi-faceted, multi-year development plan. In other, equally competitive corporations, new employees may be brought onboard through connections with the founding family, or a short interview with the CEO, who relies entirely on intuition in making key hiring decisions. While there is no doubt that some information important to organizations can be gathered and analyzed systematically and scientifically, many other factors will remain unknowable, or even more significantly, subject to very different cultural interpretations.

Differing interpretations, and the uncertainties that they cause, affect the contemporary organization not only in terms of its own planning and decision-making, but also in how it is perceived from the outside, which in turn has a substantial effect on the resources available to the organization and the possibilities of it achieving its objectives. As we have seen in several boom and bust cycles of the 'dot-com' sector, the valuation of companies and their ability to raise capital can soar and plunge within days or weeks, whereas the actual work being carried out by the company, and the quality of its technicians and engineers, is unchanged. Perceptions, therefore, change material reality for organizations no less than the reality of organizations, including their strengths and weaknesses, drives changes in society including perceptions of organizations.

But what does this mean for managers? First of all, it is extremely important to be able to stand back, take stock, be self-reflective. How we see things is often quite different from the way others see things, and the way we see ourselves is different from the way others see us. The better that this lesson is learned, the more likely we will be able to organize people and technologies effectively. Secondly, our efforts to exert control over our internal and external environments are likely to be partially successful at best. The potency and scope of management control should not be exaggerated, as unexpected and unscheduled developments and events disrupt the best laid plans. Appreciating the limits of executive intervention and control encourages the development of a more agile, facilitating and adaptable, rather than controlling, approach. It can also help reduce stress levels as the unforeseen becomes less surprising and threatening. Thirdly, it points to the importance of developing an ability to understand more intuitively and respond more skillfully to change, rather than relying upon techniques and procedures which hold out the overblown promise of rendering the future predictable.

How have these new insights been incorporated in this textbook? First of all, we have tried to avoid one-size-fits-all answers. Students often hope to find a single simple answer (if nothing else, it promises to reduce uncertainties and stress associated with writing assignments and revising for exams). But, as we have stressed, there is no single best way to design an organization, and no single best way to manage. These are *contingent* on circumstances, capacities, and in no small measure, on chance – which should come as no great surprise as the same (il)logic applies to our own life-histories and 'choices'. We have sought to provide some, necessarily partial, illumination of how different organizations have dealt with diverse issues, as well as the pros and cons of their decisions, again bearing in mind that every situation is distinctive and dynamic.

In line with this way of looking at organizational practices and problems this EMEA edition again includes a Counterpoints feature. Its purpose is to challenge conventional wisdom and thereby stimulate reflection. The main body of the text concentrates primarily upon 'mainstream' or traditional ways of looking at organizations. As you will encounter these established ideas and recipes as a practitioner, as well as in other courses you are taking, it is important to understand traditional management thinking and theories. The Counterpoints, some available within the text, others in the companion material online, are intended to signal the existence of alternative ways of looking at organization theory and design – recall what we said earlier about different perceptions and perspectives. By providing brief commentaries on traditional management perspectives, we highlight their (inevitable) limitations as a reliable basis for advancing, or significantly broadening, your understanding of organization design. Our hope is that the Counterpoints will serve as an inviting bridge between a traditional approach to studying organization and management, in which a single view of 'best practice' tends to be emphasized, and newer, diverse and flexible ways of looking at issues. Our intention is to facilitate ways of approaching problems in a more open way that does not presuppose what is 'right' and 'wrong'. In organizations, the most demanding decisions are made based on differing and sometimes conflicting assessments, and the Counterpoint feature is consistent with an acknowledgement of the value of the differences of understanding encountered in real-life organizations. The Online Counterpoints hosted on the associated online platform are labelled independently and are identifiable by the margin icon shown here.

Major challenges currently face the senior executives of corporations. Not least of these is the role of corporations in relation to the sustainability of the contemporary economic order. Climate change will increasingly disrupt supply chains and economic security – problems that reach to the core of corporate activity. The bigger picture is one of material questions about sustainability. How are business leaders going to address and reconcile the spread of an affluent, resource-depleting lifestyle to emerging economies? And how is this to be achieved with the finite availability of natural resources? Corporations are eagerly entering and developing emerging markets but can improved material well-being be enabled without a corresponding, radical shift in consumption patterns in the affluent, developed world? What roles – benign or malevolent – will corporations play in attending to sustainability issues – issues that are of such key importance to the welfare of future generations? To what extent can the pursuit of profitable growth – which is what corporations are traditionally designed to deliver – be reconciled with demands for 'global justice' in the form of a more equitable and sustainable distribution of wealth? The first EMEA edition was published in 2010 when the depth and longevity of the global economic crisis was becoming apparent. Four years later, the second edition appeared in the wake of internationally widespread citizen resistance to conventional, austerity-driven responses to the continuing crisis, manifested in the Occupy Wall Street Movement, the Arab Spring revolutions, and countless other challenges to the post-war, corporate-friendly international order. This third edition's publication coincides with existential challenges to the global order, with economic and political blocs such as the European Union facing unparalleled centrifugal forces, mass refugee movements, and a series of terrorist attacks.

These are not questions that this text addresses directly. Indeed, there is a chasm between traditional thinking about organization design and the question of how corporations might be (re) designed to make them 'fit' for social responsibility mandates such as achieving ecological efficiency (e.g. attaining a zero carbon footprint) or the systematic alleviation of poverty. We have taken a small step in this direction in the Counterpoints feature insofar as this is responsive to mounting criticisms of the ethics of business. These criticisms have become more pointed in the light of corporate malfeasance which contributed to, and has been exposed by, recent economic crises. The reputation and credibility of corporations and their leaders has been badly damaged and it is not easy to see how it will be restored. A number of Counterpoints identify practices where the corporate interest (for example, in data gathering on customers) is poorly aligned with

?

ONLINE
COUNTERPOINT

public and customer expectations of business conduct and public good. But, beyond these issues, there is the larger question of whether corporations will contribute to the solution, or simply exacerbate the problem of climate change and sustainability. Is the mantra of corporate social responsibility (CSR) a superficial response to a deepening crisis of trust in corporations or is it the beginning of a reinvention of corporations – will the leopard evolve to change its spots? There are few clear cut answers to such key issues – notably the tensions between profitable growth and public service, and between ecologically sustainable growth and pressures for business expansion. As this third edition goes to print, the economic and political outlook facing organizations and their leaders is more uncertain than it has been for several decades. Globalization has created tremendous opportunities to expand cross-national business activities by making the world a smaller and more interconnected place. At the same time, it has also removed the insulation from instabilities, that national borders and economic zones once provided. The product cycle has accelerated enormously; when we put together the first EMEA edition in 2010, Nokia was easily the biggest global handset maker; by 2016 it was no longer even in the business. The illusion that global business activity could somehow be carried out in isolation from political and social stresses has been thoroughly exploded; a globalized economy cannot peacefully sustain extreme divergences of income and wealth, or provide freedom for capital movements while forcefully restricting human migration. Leaders of organizations in both private and public sectors must become increasingly attuned to demands for economic and social justice in both their own organizations and in wider society. These challenges and responsibilities that we all face as members and leaders of organizations are what make the study of organization design both intellectually rewarding and of critical practical importance.

Distinguishing Features of *Organizational Theory and Design: An International Perspective*

Many students on a typical organization theory course do not have extensive work experience, especially at the middle and upper management levels, where organization theory tends to be consciously applied. Therefore, to help engage students in the world of organizations, this book contains a number of special learning features: A Look Inside chapter introductions, Bookmarks, the Leading by Design feature, In Practice examples, end-of-chapter and integrative cases for student analysis, as well as the Counterpoint feature discussed in the previous section.

A Look Inside   The A Look Inside feature introduces chapters by exploring examples of companies that have faced the organizational design issues featured in that chapter. Many of the A Look Inside organizations have enjoyed success, but others have struggled despite imaginative responses to organizational challenges. These cases show that in a turbulent business environment, failure may be due to factors outside the control of management, rather than because of bad decisions or poor management skills. A Look Inside examples include companies from around the world such as Philips NV, Starbucks, Nokia, H&M, Interpol, Boots PLC, Toyota and Lenovo.

Bookmarks   Bookmarks are a unique feature of the *Organization Theory and Design* texts. The Bookmarks are short reviews of books that address current issues of concern for managers. They offer an introduction into the wider management literature that addresses real-life challenges of contemporary organizations, encouraging students and practical managers to extend their reading on organizational theory and design.

Updated Case Examples   This third edition contains a balance of case examples from different parts of the world as well as numerous examples to illustrate theoretical concepts in today's context. All the examples are based on real organizations, and have been thoroughly updated up to the time of publication. We look at companies from emerging economies, like South Africa's *Transnet, Johor Corporation* of Malaysia, Chile's *Codelco,* and India's *Tata Group*. European organizations are a particular focus, with discussion of corporations such as Sweden's *H&M*, Germany's *Continental*, Britain's *Virgin Group*, Spain's *Zara*, and the European *EADS* aerospace consortium. The success of – and challenges facing – Asia-Pacific organizations is also examined, through numerous examples such as *Toyota* and *Sony* of Japan, Korea's *Samsung* and *SK Telecom,* and Australia's *Oroton*.

Leading by Design   The Leading by Design feature highlights organizations that have applied new design ideas, based both on contemporary management thinking and the availability of new information and communication technologies. Typically, these organizations have undergone a major shift in organization design, strategic direction, values, or culture as they strive to be more competitive in today's turbulent global environment. Many of the Leading by Design examples illustrate company transformations toward knowledge sharing, empowerment of employees, new structures, new cultures, the breaking down of barriers between departments and organizations, and the joining together of employees in a common mission. Once again, the Leading by Design examples for this edition have been drawn from across the world, with up-to-date exploration of organizational structure and performance. Cases include the *Rolling Stones, Acer Computers* and *Singapore Airlines*.

In Practice   These cases illustrate theoretical concepts in organizational settings. In Practice cases have been thoroughly revised and updated, and include *Apotex, Inc.* of Canada, *Lopez Holdings* from Phillipines, UK's *Bedlam Puzzles* and the Anglo-Dutch *Unilever*.

Manager's Briefcase   This feature, which is located on the associated online platform, tells students how to use concepts to analyze cases and manage organizations.

BRIEFCASE

Text Exhibits   Frequent exhibits are used to help students visualize organizational relationships, and the artwork has been redrawn to communicate concepts more clearly.

Summary and Interpretation   The summary and interpretation section tells students how the chapter points are important in the broader context of organizational theory.

Case for Analysis   A number of cases have been commissioned for the EMEA edition from prominent business scholars, mainly from leading European business schools. These are tailored to chapter concepts and provide a vehicle for student analysis and discussion.

Integrative Cases   The integrative cases at the end of the text, commissioned especially for the EMEA Edition, are positioned to encourage student discussion and involvement, and cover cross-cutting themes that have been addressed in the text. Particular attention has been paid to selecting integrative cases from a diverse range of geographical and organizational settings, from profiling the sequence of potentially avoidable errors that led to the Nimrod disaster (when a military aircraft caught fire tragically killing the crew), to a dispute on a New Zealand farm which highlights the inherent tensions and challenges faced when a business moves from a family-run to a corporate organization.

ABOUT THE AUTHORS

RICHARD L. DAFT

Richard L. Daft, PhD, is the Brownlee O. Currey, Jr, Professor of Management in the Owen Graduate School of Management at Vanderbilt University, Nashville, USA. Professor Daft has served on the editorial boards of *Academy of Management Journal, Administrative Science Quarterly, and Journal of Management Education.* He was the Associate Editor-in-Chief of *Organization Science* and served for three years as associate editor of *Administrative Science Quarterly.*

Professor Daft has authored or co-authored numerous books, including *Management* (Cengage/South-Western, 2010), *The Leadership Experience* (Cengage/South-Western, 2008), and *What to Study: Generating and Developing Research Questions* (Sage, 1982). He also published *Fusion Leadership: Unlocking the Subtle Forces That Change People and Organizations* (Berrett-Koehler, 2000, with Robert Lengel). He has authored dozens of scholarly articles, papers and chapters.

Professor Daft has been involved in management development and consulting for many companies and government organizations, including the American Banking Association, Bell Canada, National Transportation Research Board, NL Baroid, Nortel, TVA, Pratt & Whitney, State Farm Insurance, Tenneco, the United States Air Force, the United States Army, J. C. Bradford & Co., Central Parking System, Entergy Sales and Service, Bristol-Myers Squibb, First American National Bank and the Vanderbilt University Medical Center.

JONATHAN MURPHY

Jonathan Murphy is Senior Lecturer in International Management and Organizational Analysis at Cardiff University, Wales, UK and has held visiting academic posts in Denmark, India, South Africa and Finland. For 20 years, Jonathan has combined academic study of management with professional practice in the areas of democracy and good governance. Jonathan is author of *The World Bank and Global Managerialism* (Sage, 2008), and co-editor with Virpi Malin and Marjo Siltaoja of *Getting Things Done: Practice in Critical Management Studies* (Emerald, 2013), as well as numerous articles and book chapters on international management, nonprofit sector and international development issues. He holds a doctorate in management from the Judge Business School at Cambridge University, UK.

Jonathan has a worldwide reputation as a leading consultant in the area of democratic development, with clients including the United Nations, the World Bank, USAID, Britain's Department for International Development and the European Union. Jonathan is frequently called upon to deliver international training around the world on management and development of democratic institutions. He has worked as a development and democracy expert in over 20 countries on four continents and is globally acknowledged for his expertise in parliamentary development.

Jonathan's current main research focus is studying the development of global norms in organizational practice, as well as the challenges of dialogue in social and organizational transformation.

HUGH WILLMOTT

Hugh Willmott joined Cass Business School in 2014 as a Professor of Management and also holds a position of Professor of Organization Studies at Cardiff Business School. He has previously held professorial appointments at Cambridge (Judge Business School) and UMIST (now Manchester Business School) and visiting appointments at Copenhagen Business School, University of Sydney and Uppsala University.

Hugh's research interests span the sub-fields of management organization studies. He has co-authored two major textbooks, including Introducing *Organizational Behaviour & Management* (co-edited with David Knights, Cengage Learning 2017) and, additionally, has published over 20 books and contributed to a wide range of management and social science journals. He is particularly interested in the development and application of management theory by drawing upon the resources of critical social science. Substantively, his research has contributed to the areas of professionalization, teamwork, regulation, business ethics, management learning, accounting policy and practice, organizational culture, financialization and the management of higher education. With Jeroen Veldman, Senior Research Fellow at Cass, he is currently engaged in study of comparative models of corporate governance [http://themoderncorporation.wordpress.com/]. Hugh is an Associate Editor on The Academy of Management Review, having previously served an equivalent role on the journal Organization. He has been a board member of numerous other journals including Administrative Science Quarterly, Journal of Management Studies, and Organization Studies. He was appointed to the Business and Management Panel for the UK Research Assessment Exercise 2008 and was also a member of the 2014 REF Panel. He is a member of the British Academy and in 2011 he was awarded an honorary doctorate at Lund University. Full details can be found on his homepage: https://sites.google.com/site/hughwillmottshomepage

ACKNOWLEDGEMENTS

Textbook writing is a team enterprise, and no more so than this text which is a thorough revision of Richard Daft's original *Organization Theory and Design*, focused on the requirements of students studying within Europe, the Middle East and Africa. The extensive revisions were carried out by Jonathan Murphy and Hugh Willmott. In addition to the three authors, the three respective EMEA editions have integrated ideas and hard work from many people to whom we are grateful. Robin Klimecki of Cardiff University greatly aided the process by cross-checking data accuracy and identifying potential new cases. Reviewers made an important contribution that has greatly strengthened the book. They praised many features, were critical of things that didn't work well, and offered valuable suggestions.

Dirk Akkermans, Assistant Professor, Department of International Economics and Business, Faculty of Economics and Business, University of Groningen (Netherlands)

John Cullen, Department of Business & Law, National University of Ireland Maynooth (ROI)

Robert Finnigan, Associate Lecturer, Bradford University School of Management (UK)

Hugo Gaggiotti, Senior Lecturer, Bristol Business School (UK)

Anni Hollings, Principal Lecturer, Staffordshire University Business School (UK)

Theo Lynn, Lecturer, DCU Business School, Dublin City University (ROI)

Thomas Pawlik, Professor of Maritime Management, University of Applied Sciences, Bremen (Germany)

Henrik B. Sørensen, Associated Professor, Department of Economics and Management, University of Aarhus (Denmark)

Jawad Syed, Professor of Organizational Behaviour and Diversity Management, University of Huddersfield (UK)

Patricia Plackett, Assistant Professor, Copenhagen Business School (Denmark)

Menno de Lind van Wijngaarden, Senior Lecturer, HU University of Applied Sciences Utrecht (Netherlands)

We would also like to thank the team of international academics that contributed case studies and new integrative cases prepared specifically for this textbook:

Mehdi Boussebaa, University of Bath (UK)

Helga Drummond, University of Liverpool (UK)

Kate Kenny, Queen's University Belfast (UK)

Glenn Morgan, University of Warwick (UK)

Yuri Narayen, VU University Amsterdam (Netherlands)

Cliff Oswick, Queen Mary University of London (UK)

Tuomo Peltonen, University of Oulu (Finland)

Craig Prichard, Massey University (NZ)

Maxine Robertson, Queen Mary University of London (UK)

Renee Scheerman, VU University Amsterdam (Netherlands)

Henrik B. Sørensen, University of Aarhus (Denmark)

Brian Tjemkes, VU University Amsterdam (Netherlands)

Anni Hollings, Staffordshire University Business School (UK)

Kim Maya Sutton, Jade University of Applied Sciences (Germany)

Patricia Plackett, Copenhagen Business School (Denmark)

Dr Bobby Mackie, University of West Scotland (UK)

Neil Coade, Regent's University London (UK)

The team at Cengage UK deserves special mention: Lauren Cartridge, Jenny Grene, Sue Povey, Vicky Pavlicic and Eyvett Davis. We owe them all a huge 'thank you' for making this third edition happen – by keeping us on track and by handling problems so skilfully and effectively.

The publisher also thanks the various copyright holders for granting permission to reproduce material throughout the text. A credits page with full details is provided at the back of the book.

CENGAGE

Teaching & Learning Support Resources

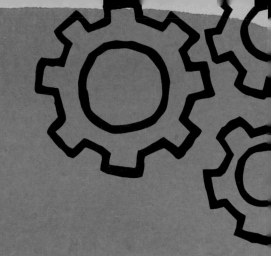

Cengage's peer reviewed content for higher and further education courses is accompanied by a range of digital teaching and learning support resources. The resources are carefully tailored to the specific needs of the instructor, student and the course. Examples of the kind of resources provided include:

- A password protected area for instructors with, for example, a testbank, PowerPoint slides and an instructor's manual.

- An open-access area for students including, for example study questions.

Lecturers: to discover the dedicated lecturer digital support resources accompanying this textbook please register here for access: login.cengage.com.

Students: to discover the dedicated student digital support resources accompanying this textbook, please search for **Organization Theory & Design** on: cengagebrain.co.uk.

BE UNSTOPPABLE

INTRODUCTION TO ORGANIZATIONS

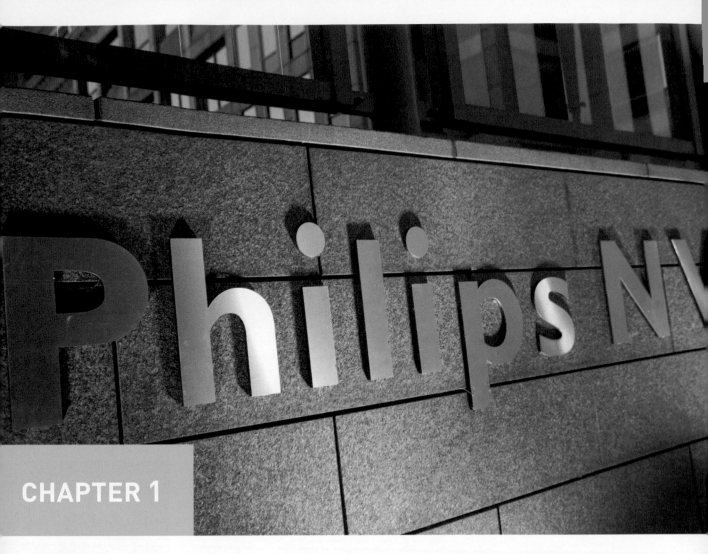

WHAT ARE ORGANIZATIONS?

A LOOK INSIDE

Philips NV

Philips was one of the world's first genuine multi-nationals. Founded in Eindhoven, Netherlands by Gerard Philips in 1891, the company initially manufactured light bulbs, seizing the opportunity of widespread home and business electrification. Electricity soon brought opportunities for inventing and selling further electrical devices, and during much of the twentieth century, no European company seized market opportunities better than Philips. The relatively small size of Holland's domestic market pushed the company to seek new markets on the continent and eventually beyond. By the mid-1980s, the company was active in 14 different divisions ranging from the original lighting sector to large appliances and the new field of computers. Philips' product development laboratories were unparalleled, developing cutting-edge electrical equipment across the company's vast product range.

But as is often the case in business, at the height of Philips' success, storm clouds were forming on the horizon. Several different factors were beginning to work against the company as it approached its second century.

One issue was the very loose organizational structure that the company was forced to adopt when it internationalized. Before the great era of trade and market liberalization that began in the 1970s, it was simply not possible to centralize functions globally. Indeed, during the Second World War, when Holland was occupied by the German Nazis, international branches of Philips basically operated entirely independently. Even in normal times, companies wishing to enter different countries' markets were typically forced to set up fully functional national units, with their own manufacturing, marketing and distribution systems.

The national units that had to be set up tended to become autonomous power bases. In theory this could have been beneficial, if innovative approaches were developed and tested in one country and then rolled out internationally, as was the case for example for the Anglo-Dutch consumer products firm,

Unilever.[1] But consumer electronics are different from household products; they are costly to develop, and generally don't require tailoring to individual markets; thus centralized product development tends to be the preferred approach. Autonomy sometimes reached extremes, for example when Philips in North America decided to manufacture early video recorders based on a competitor's product.

Another problem was bureaucracy and inefficiency. Philips was so successful, for so long, that workers and managers began to see their positions as jobs-for-life. Employment grew and grew, ultimately Philips had over 300 000 employees worldwide. Eindhoven itself was every bit the company town; Philips took on numerous social projects ranging from the Philips library and theatre to the PSV Eindhoven football team, which under Philips' benevolent sponsorship became one of the giants of European club soccer. The Philips product development division seemed to lose its knack for creating products that fit customer needs. Its early forays into computers, in particular, were not competitive with either the American giants like IBM and later Compaq, or the emerging brands from the Far East.

By the 1980s, Japan had emerged from its early post-war avatar as producer of cheap copies of Western consumer goods. In motorcycles, then the automobile industry, and fatefully for Philips, in electronics, Japan began producing flashy, competitively priced but well-made products. The Matsushita conglomerate, in particular, with brands such as Toshiba, as well as Sony Corporation, began to develop the same kind of positive reputation amongst consumers that Philips once enjoyed, whereas Philips products started to be viewed as expensive and behind the times.

Philips' bottom line suddenly turned red. Despite fitful efforts to cut costs in the late '80s, by 1990 the company had run up an accumulated deficit of $2.6 billion. PSV Eindhoven had won the European Cup in 1988, but on the eve of its hundredth anniversary, its sponsor Philips was in real danger of disappearing underneath this sea of red ink.[2]

Philips turned to a new company president, Jan Timmer, who slashed the company's workforce by 50 000, got out of the computer business altogether, terminated a number of unprofitable joint ventures and reoriented the company towards Asian production facilities in place of increasingly costly Europe. Timmer's hard-nosed strategy stemmed some but not all the bleeding. In 1996, Sony, Philips'

▶

biggest competitor, generated sales of $43 billion with 150 000 employees, while Philips managed only $37 billion with almost twice as many workers. In 1996, and once again in 2001, the company changed its top management, but the same cycle of job cuts, divestments, market upticks and then disappointing losses continued. In 2001 the company lost €2.5 billion on sales, down 15 per cent from the previous year.[3] The competitive situation was even more dire, as Korean brands like LG had joined the Japanese giants as global competitors, cleaning up the cost-conscious market segment where Sony and Toshiba had a stranglehold on the most affluent customers.

The enigma of Philips was that while the company's engineers brought many of electronic technology's most important innovations to market (for example the audio cassette, the compact disc *and* the DVD), it didn't seem able to take commercial advantage of the breakthroughs, with Far Eastern companies quickly adopting the most important inventions, and making money out of them where Philips seemed incapable. In the early years of the new millennium, Philips resolved to move away from being a manufacturing-driven company towards one that would be customer-driven, a change in direction that involved a much greater focus on what insiders called 'The Marketing Journey'.[4] Building from this approach, Philips developed the slogan, 'Sense and Simplicity', reflecting not only an external marketing tool but also a new ethos of product development. Products would be innovative, but they also needed to be simple and easy to use. Right across the product spectrum, from mass-market consumer products like electric toothbrushes to the most sophisticated medical equipment like the cardiovascular X-ray, Philips would apply this same approach. Simplicity didn't mean basic, however, but rather well-designed. The company tried innovative approaches like appointing a 'simplicity board' that brought in renowned designers to help the company think 'outside the box' in product development.[5]

From 2004 onwards, Philips' fortunes seemed to be on the upswing. Finally, the company seemed to be doing well with its innovations. Medical systems and consumer electronics sales were up 9 per cent and 10 per cent respectively, but temporary growth blips like that had been seen before. What was more important, sales from newly introduced products rose sharply. In the medical area, 70 per cent of sales were of products introduced in the previous two years,

unusual for a field with typically long product cycles. Company-wide, the proportion of sales derived from products introduced in the previous two years rose from one-quarter in 2003 to over half in 2006.

From 2005 to 2007, the company won numerous awards for its products from its main dealers, companies like Wal-Mart in the US, Dixons in Britain and Carrefour in Europe. The bottom line picked up too.[6] Group revenues rose an average of over 6 per cent per year between 2003 and 2007, and earnings were up 9 per cent annually in the same period. Share price easily outperformed the Dow Jones index between 2003 and 2007. Finally, brand valuation, a crucial indication of how well a company is able to manage and valorize its intellectual property, rose by 60 per cent to nearly $8 billion in the three years to 2007.

In 2008, Philips moved to simplify its organizational structure, establishing three core divisions of consumer, healthcare and lighting, which helped to focus the company on its best-performing product lines. New CEO, Frans van Houten, who arrived in mid-2011, took this focused strategy to a new level, by ruthlessly eliminating 'sunset' products, particularly in the globally cut-throat home entertainment sector, where convergence between the computer and entertainment segments can wipe out whole product categories overnight while creating new 'must haves' such as tablets. Televisions, long the company's talisman products, have been ditched altogether, along with video players, another declining segment.

Van Houten is acutely aware that in a sprawling company such as Philips, wayward units can lose touch with market trends and eventually end up hurting the overall bottom line. So in conjunction with the CFO, van Houten designed a 'Dashboard' computer programme allowing senior managers to look at performance across the company and its different geographic and product operations, and quickly check performance and trends.

This has helped Philips to develop a more sophisticated and forward-looking product focus. For example, in Western markets with their affluent, ageing populations, the company is focusing particularly on consumer healthcare products, while in emerging markets it is tailoring its product design and marketing to meet the needs of new and discriminating consumers. For example, in the Russian market it adapted its vegetable choppers so that they could produce vegetable cubes, popular in that market, while Philips tailored its marketing to appeal to Chinese consumers by hiring the popular Taiwanese actor Godfrey Gao to endorse its electric shavers.

Moves like this helped the company to slowly increase its emerging economy share of revenues from 33 per cent to 35 per cent between 2011 and 2013. Stock prices in 2013 rose to a three year high, earnings per share were above competitors such as Siemens and GE, and several market analysts rated the company a 'buy'. All a far cry from the early 2000s.[7]

However, Philips still has its detractors. It had poor results again in 2014.[8] The company doesn't have a 'segment killer' product like Apple's iPhone and iPad, nor does it dominate a single product area such as Apple and Samsung in the smartphone and tablet segments. Some analysts still argue the company has too many brands and thus doesn't leverage a single global name like Apple for example. In response the company decided in 2014 to spin-off its lighting division into a separate company, yet another shift in its institutional design. The spin-off was to be completed by mid-2016. The next few years will start to tell whether Philips has weathered the storm of the last years of its first century, and can move from strength to strength in its next century, or whether its recent successes are more like rearranging the deckchairs on the *Titanic*. Philips' trajectory is similar to that of many other companies in today's volatile environment, where companies constantly revisit their organizational design in order to address changing consumer preferences and business environments.

Organization Theory in Action

Topics

Many of the topics covered in this book are illustrated in the Philips case. Consider, for example, the company's failure to respond to, or control, competitors and customers in the fast-paced external environment; its difficulties implementing strategic and structural changes to attain effectiveness; difficulties coping with the problems of large size and bureaucracy; lack of adequate cost controls; challenges associated with an outmoded corporate culture that stifled innovation and change, and its repeated efforts to redesign itself in order to address these challenges. These are illustrative of the issues with which organization theory is concerned (but see the Counterpoint, below, for another viewpoint on organizational design).

COUNTERPOINT 1.1

Note how these topics tend to take a managerial focus and also to assume that problems are the same for everyone. Those who lost their jobs at Philips might well question this view. They might challenge the legitimacy of a system that resulted in such poor performance. What about the accountability of executives to their employees as well as to their shareholders? Employees bore the brunt of the poor decision-making; but they had little input into the strategic decision-making process. Organization theory extends beyond a managerial perspective to ask more fundamental questions about how and why organizations are designed the way that they are, who creates and authorizes the design, and may also explore alternative designs. Design is not reducible to a technical matter; it is an inherently political one that involves the distribution of power and opportunity. Whatever design is calculated to be most appropriate, efficient or effective, it will reflect the values and priorities of its architects. Implementation of the design will be contingent upon the political will to implement and the capacity to overcome resistance to it.

Of course the application of organization theory is not limited to firms like Philips. All companies and other organizations – from the largest to struggling start-ups – undergo changes that can be illuminated and informed by theories of organization and its design. Organization theory is no less relevant to public sector and nonprofit organizations, including

BRIEFCASE 1.1

central and local government departments, non-governmental organizations (NGOs), arts organizations, charities and so on. In different ways, people responsible for the design and development of organizations as well as everyone working in them face challenges comparable to Philips, even if they are accountable to politicians or trusts rather than shareholders, and are generally more influenced by an ethos of public or charitable service rather than private gain.

The story of Philips is important because it demonstrates that organizing involves continuous challenges in the face of uncertainty and change. No organization – not even tax departments or undertakers – are protected from changes of technologies, conventions, customer preferences, availability of supplies, etc. Organizing is a fraught and vulnerable process. Lessons are not learned automatically. Designs are only as strong – ethically as well as economically and technically – as the decision-makers who take primary responsibility for shaping structures and cultures. Organizations (see Counterpoint 1.2) are not static. There is a continuous process of adaptation in response to changes beyond the organization. Managers of change endeavour to exploit or control those changes and, in so doing, contribute to the changes which affect the other organizations. Surveys of top executives indicate that coping with rapid change is the most common problem facing managers and organizations.[9] Organizations face the challenge of finding ways of changing themselves or changing their environments to become technically, economically and ethically more responsive and effective. Of course, it is important to acknowledge that organizational design is only one factor that can help a company to succeed. Conversely, if a company is successful, it doesn't necessarily mean that this was because of good organizational design, and therefore others should emulate the organizational structure. Perhaps the company's software engineers just came up with a killer app, for example!

COUNTERPOINT 1.2

The term 'organizations' is repeatedly used in everyday life as well as in this text. How are we to interpret it? When we say 'organizations face challenges' or 'the company failed to ...' we probably do not mean all the people who work in that organization or company. In fact, organizations are often very diverse, with different departments and factions pulling in different directions as well as attempting to cooperate with each other.

Organizations are often also hierarchical and undemocratic. That means that it is only a handful of people who actually determine how 'challenges' are to be 'faced' or how 'failure' is to be addressed. In corporations, executive decision-makers are typically accountable primarily to the owners, or shareholders and creditors. Decisions that they make may pay attention to other stakeholders insofar as they are relevant for the profitable growth of the business. These decisions may also be coloured by executives' own priorities and preferences, including any material or career advantages that flow from the decisions they make.

When reading this book, therefore, it is relevant to take acount of what may be termed the 'political economy' of organizations.

The political economy of organizations is defined by Zald and Hasenfeld as 'a theoretical framework that focuses on two key components of organizations and their interaction: the polity and the economy of organizations. The polity, or political system of organizations, is the constitution, or fundamental norms, of the organization and the system of authority, power and influence. The economy is the economic structures and processes of the organization; that is, the system for processing and transforming raw materials into the goods and services that the organization produces.'[10]

Current Challenges

Some specific challenges are dealing with globalization, maintaining high standards of ethics and social responsibility, responding rapidly to environmental changes and customer needs, managing the digital workplace and supporting diversity.

Globalization   With rapid advances in technology and communications, the time it takes to exert influence around the world from even the most remote locations has been reduced from years to only seconds. Markets, technologies and organizations are becoming increasingly interconnected.[11] It is now more feasible to locate different parts of an organization wherever it makes the most business sense: top leadership in one country, technical brainpower and production in other locales, depending upon calculations of where is best for cutting costs, generating revenues and thereby increasing the return on capital invested to shareholders. A related trend is to contract out some functions to organizations in other countries or to partner with foreign organizations to gain global advantage. India's Wipro Ltd used to sell cooking oils; by 2016, the company had 170 000 employees in over 50 countries, who develop sophisticated software applications, design semiconductors and manage back-office solutions for giant companies from all over the world. In 2013, the company decided to demerge all of its 'old' non-IT units from the main company, helping the company focus on its IT core.[12] Many of Intel's new chip circuits are designed by companies in India and China. These organizations can often do the job 50 to 60 per cent more cheaply than companies based in more developed, but more expensive, capitalist economies, creating new advantages as well as increased competitive pressures.[13] Companies large and small are searching for the structures and processes that can help them reap the advantages of global interdependence and minimize the disadvantages.

Ethics and Social Responsibility   Issues of ethics and social responsibility – relating to concerns about ecological sustainability, and not just corporate survival – are becoming increasingly important; and corporations, in particular, are being expected to take a lead on addressing these issues. At the same time, the list of executives and major corporations involved in financial and ethical scandals casts a shadow over corporate life. The sordid story of high-flying Enron Corporation, where managers admitted they inflated earnings and hid debt through a series of complex partnerships, was hardly unprecedented but has, hopefully, been a loud wake-up call. Executives profited handsomely from the fraud at Enron, but when the company collapsed, employees and average investors lost billions. Arthur Andersen LLP, the company's auditor, was found guilty of obstruction of justice for improperly shredding documents related to the Enron investigation. Elsewhere, the UK's flagship defence contractor, BAE, became embroiled in a multi-billion pound corruption scandal that precipitated a diplomatic crisis and diverted attention away from the company's business activities.[14] Lax financial and management controls at France's giant Société Générale financial services company allowed a junior trader to gamble away over a billion euros in company funds.[15] In 2016, the release of the so-called Panama Papers detailing the efforts many major corporations have made to avoid taxation caused a major stir and raised questions about the overall ethical foundations of capitalism.[16] Scandals are not confined to corporations. Britain's Revenue and Customs agency managed to lose personal data on 25 million citizens – nearly half the entire population – somewhere in the mail system.[17] Pick up any major newspaper on almost any day, and there will be a story about some corporation, government department or even entire administration embroiled in some form of 'sleaze' or wilful incompetence.

While executives and officials are inclined to insist that it is a few bad apples or a single junior employee involved in all the wrongdoing, the ordinary citizen is quickly forming the opinion that all executives and senior managers are crooks.[18] The public is disillusioned with such 'leadership', and leaders – corporate and political – are under pressure to hold their organizations and employees to higher standards of ethics and competency.

Responsiveness   A third significant challenge for organizations is to respond quickly and decisively to environmental changes, organizational crises and shifting customer expectations. For much of the period between the end of the Second World War in 1945 and the onset of the global financial crisis, organizations operated in relatively stable conditions. There was little need to search for new ways to cope with increased competition,

ONLINE
COUNTERPOINT 1.1

volatile environmental shifts or changing customer demands. Today, globalization and advancing technology have accelerated the pace at which organizations in all industries must adapt their internal structures and systems in order to keep rolling out new products and services that are sufficiently competitive.

Companies that relied on mass production and distribution techniques have had to adjust to customer demands, often fuelled by leaner and more nimble competitors, for the tailoring of products and services to their specific requirements. Reflecting the importance attributed to 'customization' and branding, the financial basis of today's economy is *information*, not machines and factories. Intangible assets, including corporations' investments in people as well as financial products, become increasingly important relative to tangible assets. In the mid-1900s tangible assets represented 73 per cent of the assets of nonfinancial corporations in the United States. By 2002, the percentage had shrunk to about 53 per cent, and it continues to decline.[19,20] Knowledge involved in designing and coordinating the manufacture of products and the delivery of services becomes increasingly important. In this process, it becomes clearer that, ultimately, it is employees and their knowledge, not the means of production or of service delivery, who provide the best chance of organizational prosperity. (See Counterpoint 1.3). At the same time, as demonstrated by the Enron and Société Générale scandals, among many others that continue to come to light as a result of the global financial crisis that began in 2007, the line between making appropriate use of knowledge and indulging in out-and-out gambling with other people's money, or even illegal schemes, has become ever more blurred.[21]

COUNTERPOINT 1.3

If this point about employees being the most precious resources is accepted, why do you think that employees are typically able to exert so little influence over key corporate decision-making and what are the implications of this for organizational theory and design?

The Digital Workplace   Many traditional managers find it difficult to keep up with today's technology-driven workplace. Organizations have been flooded by information technology that affects how they are designed and managed. In today's workplace, many employees perform much of their work on computers and may work in virtual teams, connected electronically to colleagues around the world. In addition, organizations are becoming enmeshed in electronic networks. More and more business takes place by digital processes over a computer network rather than in physical space. End-to-end digital supply-chain networks are used to keep in touch with customers, take orders, buy components from suppliers, coordinate with manufacturing partners and ship customized products directly to consumers. This trend towards *disintermediation* – eliminating the middleman often by consuming the unpaid time of the customer who, for example, experiences the frustration of waiting for, and dealing with, responses from call centres – is affecting every industry.[22] These developments mean that a pressing requirement of leadership in organizations is to become technologically savvy in addition to managing a web of relationships that reaches far beyond the boundaries of the physical organization to employees, suppliers, contract partners and customers.[23]

Diversity   In advanced capitalist societies, today's average worker is older, and many more women, ethnic minorities and immigrants are seeking job and advancement opportunities. This development brings a variety of challenges, including fully recognizing and embracing diversity, balancing work and family concerns and coping with the differences associated with varying cultural styles. People from diverse ethnic and cultural backgrounds offer varying styles of interacting and working; and managing diversity may be one of the most rewarding challenges for organizations competing on a global basis. Consider the consulting firm McKinsey & Co. In the

1970s most consultants were American, but by the turn of the twenty-first century McKinsey's chief partner, Rajat Gupta, was Indian, and 60 per cent of consultants were from outside the US, coming from 40 different countries.[24] But diversity is often the exception rather than the rule. Research has indicated that women's style of working may hold important lessons for success in the emerging global world of the twenty-first century, but the glass ceiling which keeps women from reaching positions of top leadership remains in place.[25]

LEADING BY DESIGN

The Rolling Stones

They may be old, but they keep on rocking and rolling after more than 50 years in the music business. Indeed, in November and December 2012 the company embarked on a highly lucrative four-concert 50th anniversary tour, with Mick Jagger, 69, Keith Richards, 68, Ronnie Wood, 65 and Charlie Watts, 71 joined for the first time in 20 years by former members Bill Wyman and Mick Taylor. Tickets sold out in minutes despite an eye-watering starting price of over $150. The Rolling Stones have enjoyed phenomenal commercial success in recent decades, generating billions of dollars in revenue from record sales, song rights, concert tickets, sponsorships and merchandising. In 2016 the Stones famously accompanied President Obama in his historic visit to Cuba, performing in front of 200 000 fans in the country's biggest ever rock concert.

The Rolling Stones group has been cited as one of the world's ten most enduring organizations, according to a study commissioned by the consulting firm Booz Allen Hamilton. One reason for the Stones' success is that the band operates like an effective global business organization. The Stones have set up a solid organizational structure, with different divisions to run different aspects of the business, such as touring or merchandising. At the top of the organization is a core top management team made up of the four band members: Mick Jagger, who acts as a sort of CEO, Keith Richards, Charlie Watts and Ronnie Wood. This core team manages a group of somewhat autonomous yet interlocking companies that include Promotour, Promopub,

Promotone and Musidor, each dedicated to a particular part of the overall business. At times, depending on what's happening in the organization, each company might employ only a few dozen people. When the band is touring, on the other hand, head count goes way up – on a concert night sometimes reaching 350 – and the organization resembles a flourishing start-up company. Jagger himself keeps a close eye on the market price range for concert tickets so that the band can keep their prices competitive. That sometimes means cutting costs and increasing efficiency to make sure the organization turns a profit.

The Stones also recognize the importance of inter-organizational partnerships, cutting sponsorship deals with big companies such as Sprint, Anheuser-Busch, Microsoft and E*Trade, which sponsored their Licks tour. They hire lawyers, accountants, managers and consultants to keep in touch with changes in the environment and manage relationships with customers (fans), partners, employees, record companies, promoters and tour sites. Key among their advisers is the financier Prince Rupert Loewenstein, co-owner of a small merchant bank, who originally came on board as a consultant but soon quit banking to work full time for the band. Jagger learned from the early days that creativity and talent aren't enough to ensure success – in the mid-1960s, the band was selling millions of records but still living hand to mouth. Effective control systems and widespread information sharing make sure that doesn't happen today. The band's controversial decision to take up residency outside the UK to avoid heavy taxation on the advice of Prince Loewenstein, certainly helped the band members' bottom line!

'You don't start to play your guitar thinking you're going to be running an organization that will maybe generate millions', Jagger says. Yet by understanding and applying organization theory, the Rolling Stones have become one of the most successful

▶

organizations ever in the music industry – and the wealthiest rock 'n' roll band on the planet, even if a recent biographer has claimed that these days, they are just in it for the money!

Sources: Andy Serwer, 'Inside the Rolling Stones Inc.', *Fortune* (September 30, 2002), 58–72; and William J. Holstein, 'Innovation, Leadership, and Still No Satisfaction', *The New York Times* (December 19, 2004), Section 3, 11. Alexis Petridis (26 November, 2012), The Rolling Stones, O2, London – review, *The Guardian*. *Daily Telegraph* (26 November,

2012), 'The Rolling Stones celebrate 50 years with sold-out O2 show'. Lynn Barber (17 February, 2013) Rock royalty; 'He hated their music, but financial wizard Prince Rupert Loewenstein saved the Rolling Stones', *The Sunday Times*. "Rolling Stones are a 'bitter married couple' just in it for the money", Daily Telegraph, April 1 2016, accessed at www.telegraph.co.uk/music/news/rolling-stones-are-a-bitter-married-couple-just-in-it-for-the-mo/, Jonathan Watts, "Rolling Stones play rock'n'roll diplomats in Cuba's 'biggest concert ever'", March 25 2016, accessed at www.theguardian.com/world/2016/mar/25/rolling-stones-cuba-historic-concert-diplomacy.

Purpose of this Chapter

The remainder of this chapter explores the nature of organizations and organization theory today. The next section provides a formal definition of organization. It then introduces some basic concepts for describing and analyzing organizations before noting the diversity of types of organizations and outlining their contemporary importance. The chapter closes with a brief overview of the themes to be covered in this book.

What is an Organization?

Organizations are hard to see. We see a tall building, a computer workstation or a friendly employee; but 'the organization' is an abstract notion. Physically, it may be scattered among several locations in different continents. We live in a world so populated by organizations that we tend to take their existence for granted. We hardly notice that we are born in a hospital, have our birth records registered in a government agency, are educated in schools and universities, are raised on food produced in factory farms, are treated by doctors engaged in a joint practice, buy a house built by a construction company, borrow money from a bank, turn to police and fire departments when trouble erupts, receive an array of benefits from government agencies and so on.[26]

Definition

Organizations as diverse as a church, a hospital and a giant corporation like Philips have characteristics in common (see Counterpoint 1.4).

COUNTERPOINT 1.4

When it is claimed that 'organizations … have characteristics in common' it is important to reflect on what we are doing. We are attributing specific, ostensibly shared characteristics to very diverse phenomena. It is rather like saying that all employees have 'characteristics in common' – that is, they all receive payment for their contribution and, therefore, they can be analyzed in the same way. But the nature and the meaning of this payment will likely differ – for example, between a cooperative where the employees co-own and co-control the organization and a privately owned company where most employees have at best a very minimal ownership stake and no significant control. This approach risks overlooking the diversity of organizations. *They are diverse both in their composition and the conditions of their operation.* Diversity tends to be overlooked when it is assumed that one 'model' of organization is equally relevant and successful for grasping the salient features of very different kinds of organization. Or that one, 'dominant' model is readily applicable to all organizations.

The definition used in this book to describe organizations is as follows: organizations are (1) social entities that (2) are goal-directed, (3) are designed as deliberately structured and coordinated activity systems, and (4) are linked to the external environment. In the light of Counterpoint 1.4 (above), it is worth bearing in mind the particularity of this definition. Like all definitions it has limits that flow from the assumptions that are made – for example, with respect to the extent that goals are rationally determined or broadly shared. Another way to think of a 'goal' is as a notion invoked by executives to convince employees that objectives are shared and rationally deliberated rather than politically defined though struggles and coalition building (see Counterpoint 1.5).

The key element of an organization is not a building or a set of policies and procedures; organizations are made up of people and their relationships with one another. An organization exists when people interact with one another. The importance of people and their interactions is evident in a growing emphasis upon empowering employees by increasing opportunities to learn and to contribute as they work together toward ostensibly 'common' goals.

Managers deliberately structure and coordinate organizational resources to achieve *'the organization's purpose'* (see Counterpoint 1.5). However, even though work may be structured into separate departments or sets of activities, there is a trend towards improving horizontal coordination of work activities, often using teams of employees from different functional areas to work together on projects. Boundaries between departments, as well as those between organizations, are becoming more flexible and diffuse as companies face the need to respond more rapidly to changes. Today, many companies are even cooperating with their competitors, sharing information and technology to their mutual advantage, in joint ventures and other collaborative arrangements.

COUNTERPOINT 1.5

It is worth stressing that this is simply one possible definition of organization(s) that is potentially misleading as well as illuminating.

Social entities This is a key point as it indicates that organizations are cultural and political as well as economic phenomena. They are 'social' all-the-way-down. To regard organizations as equivalent to machines or as technologies is to invite disaster. Organizations comprise people who, in contrast to material entities, interpret their situations and are capable of ignoring or resisting, collectively and individually, often in subtle and difficult-to-control ways, demands that are made of them.

Goal-directed This element of the definition emphasizes how activity in organizations is highly instrumental (e.g. to get paid, acquire a skill or gain in status) rather than intrinsically meaningful. That is to say, such activity is strongly influenced by calculations concerning the most effective means of achieving ends or 'goals', whatever these may be. The idea that organizations are 'goal-directed' may be taken to imply that there is a single, consensually agreed goal. This is misleading in circumstances where there are considerable conflicts between stakeholders and between senior executives about the goal, or goals, that an organization is, or should be, pursuing. To suggest that organizations are goal-directed tends to conceal the extent to which these goals are contested and that whatever goal is attributed to an organization is the outcome of processes of negotiation and struggle that result in specific goals being privileged or 'hegemonized', at least for the time being. For this reason, it is necessary to place scare quotes[27] around the idea of 'common' goals or the shared 'purpose' attributed to an organization.

Designed as deliberately structured and coordinated activity systems In contrast to other human 'activity systems', such as the family, it is likely that the division and coordination of labour in work organizations will be more 'deliberately structured'. For example, there will likely be formal job descriptions and reporting procedures. It would be a mistake, however, to assume that such designs are necessarily effective, or that an intended design is what operates in practice. Designs are frequently a product of ideals and/or compromises that incorporate fondly held beliefs, and they involve more or less participation in their design and cooperation in their operation from those who are expected to make the 'structures' work.

Linked to the external environment It is important to appreciate that organizations exist within a wider context or set of conditions. The idea of being 'linked' to the environment does not necessarily grasp the extent to which organizations are part-and-parcel of their 'environments' rather than simply connected to them. The so-called environment is shaped and changed by the organizations that comprise it. It is therefore necessary to place scare quotes around 'external environment'.

Types of Organizations

Some organizations are large, multinational corporations. Others are small, family-owned businesses. Some manufacture products such as automobiles or computers, whereas others provide services such as legal representation, banking or medical services. Later in this text, Chapter 8 will look at the distinctions between manufacturing and service technologies. Chapter 10 discusses size and life cycle and describes some differences between small and large organizations.

A further important distinction is between for-profit businesses and *nonprofit organizations*. With the proviso entered in Counterpoint 1.5, the topics in this text are of relevance to nonprofit organizations (also known as non-governmental organizations; NGOs), although there are some important differences to keep in mind. The primary one is that the activities of managers in for-profit organizations are directed primarily at producing goods and services in a way that retains the confidence of shareholders. Managers in nonprofits do not face this particular constraint. They may, however, encounter many other challenges. These include the difficulty of securing funding or raising capital or competing with profit-making businesses. The distinctive characteristics of nonprofit organizations created by this difference present unique challenges for their organizational leaders.[28]

Financial resources for nonprofits typically come from sources such as government grants, private foundation grants and donations, rather than from the sale of products or services to customers. In businesses, managers focus on developing and positioning the organization's products and services in ways that are intended to increase sales revenues. Nonprofit organizations are responsive to demands that are inadequately met by markets. In nonprofits, services are typically provided to nonpaying clients, and a major problem for many organizations is securing a steady stream of funds as well as staff or volunteers to continue operating. Nonprofit managers are often committed to serving a large pool of potential clients with limited income. To serve these clients, they are obliged to keep organizational costs as low as possible and, in order to secure funding, must demonstrate a highly efficient use of resources.[29] As they do not have a conventional 'bottom line', it is more difficult or inappropriate for nonprofits to measure their performance in terms of returns on capital invested, for example. Nonprofits have, instead, to measure intangible goals such as 'improve public health' or 'make a difference in the lives of the disenfranchised'.

With these considerations in mind, many organization design concepts discussed throughout this book – such as setting goals and measuring effectiveness, coping with environmental uncertainty, implementing effective control mechanisms, satisfying multiple stakeholders and dealing with issues of power and conflict – are of relevance for nonprofit organizations. As in the case of for-profit businesses, the concepts and theories must be assessed, adapted and continuously revisited in relation to an assessment of distinct challenges and operating circumstances.

Importance of Organizations

Only a century ago, there were comparatively few organizations of any size or importance.[30] *Bookmark 1.0* examines the rise of the corporation and its contemporary significance. Why have organizations become so important? Exhibit 1.1 lists seven reasons.

EXHIBIT 1.1 Importance of Organizations

Organizations are credited with:

1. *Bringing together resources to achieve desired goals and outcomes*

2. *Producing goods and services*

3. *Facilitating innovation*

4. *Harnessing modern manufacturing, service and information technologies*

5. *Adapting to and influencing a changing environment*

6. *Creating value*

7. *Accommodating ongoing challenges of diversity, ethics and the motivation and coordination of employees*

BOOKMARK 1.0

Have you read this book?

The Company: A Short History of a Revolutionary Idea

BY JOHN MICKLETHWAIT AND ADRIAN WOOLDRIDGE

'The limited liability corporation is the greatest single discovery of modern times', is one conclusion of the concise and readable book, *The Company: A Short History of a Revolutionary Idea* by John Micklethwait and Adrian Wooldridge. Companies are so ubiquitous today that we take them for granted, so it may come as a surprise that the company as we know it is a relatively recent innovation. Although people have joined together in groups for commercial purposes since ancient Greek and Roman times, the modern company has its roots in the late nineteenth century. The idea of a *limited liability company* that was legally an 'artificial person' began with the Joint Stock Companies Act, enacted by the London Board

of Trade in 1856. Today the company is seen as 'the most important organization in the world'. Here are a few reasons why:

■ The corporation was the first autonomous legal and social institution that was within society yet independent of the central government.

■ The concept of a limited liability company unleashed entrepreneurs to raise money because investors could lose only what they invested. Increasing the pool of entrepreneurial capital spurred innovation and generally enriched the societies in which companies operated.

■ The company is the most efficient creator of goods and services that the world has ever known. Without a company to harness resources and organize activities, the cost to consumers for almost any product we know today would be impossible to afford.

■ Historically, the corporation has been a force for civilized behaviour and provided people with worthwhile activities, identity and community, as well as a paycheck.

■ The Virginia Company, a forerunner of the limited liability corporation, helped introduce the revolutionary concept of democracy to the American colonies.

▶

■ The modern multinational corporation began in Britain in the third quarter of the 1800s with the railroads, which built rail networks throughout Europe by shipping into each country the managers, materials, equipment and labour needed.

Large companies have been reviled throughout modern history – consider the robber barons at the beginning of the twentieth century. Nevertheless, during the past few years, it seems that large corporations have been increasingly in conflict with societies' interests. The key to ensuring that companies benefit the population through the business they do is that they remain accountable; not merely to shareholders but to all their stakeholders including workers, customers, and broader society.

The Company: A Short History of a Revolutionary Idea, by John Micklethwait and Adrian Wooldridge, is published by The Modern Library.

First, organizations bring together resources to generate wealth from the production of goods and services purchased by customers – an often complex process which could not be so readily accomplished by individuals acting on their own or in smaller units. To take a rather extreme example, putting together an aircraft carrier for use by the military involves 47 000 tons of precision-welded steel, more than 1 million distinct parts, 900 miles of wire and cable, about 40 million skilled-worker hours and more than 7 years of hard work by the organization's 17 800 employees.[31] Companies are continuously under pressure from shareholders to develop innovative ways of producing and distributing desirable goods and services. Two ways are through e-business and through the use of computer-based manufacturing technologies. Redesigning organizational structures and management practices can also contribute to reducing costs and thereby increasing profitability, at least in the short term.

Consider Google, provider of the internet's most popular search engine, which continues to adapt and evolve along with the evolving internet. Rather than being a rigid service, Google is continually adding technological features that create an enhanced offer by accretion. At any time, Google's site features several technologies in development so that engineers can get ideas and feedback from users at virtually no cost.[32] Some large businesses have entire departments charged with monitoring the 'external environment' and finding ways either to influence demand for its products and services or adapt to changes created by its competitors. Organizations such as Philips, AES Corporation, Heineken Breweries and IBM are involved in strategic alliances and partnerships with companies around the world. They are also engaged in lobbying governments and regulators and committing enormous sums to initiatives to strengthen the organization's position, the promotion of their brands or the avoidance of taxes (e.g. through transfer pricing and use of tax havens) in an effort to influence the environment, compete on a global scale, and thereby ensure that their stock remains attractive to investors.

Through all of these activities, organizations create value for owners as they deliver goods and services to customers, and provide employment to their staff. Managers are hired to analyze which parts of the operation create value and which parts do not. Ultimately it is this preoccupation that gives shape to how organizations cope with, and accommodate, today's challenges of workforce diversity, growing concerns over ethics and social responsibility, and address the question of how to motivate employees in conditions where job security may be absent or under threat. The challenge is to understand organizations in ways that are capable of analyzing and addressing such issues.

Framework for the Book

What topic areas are relevant to organization theory and design? How does a course in management or organizational behaviour differ from a course in organization theory? The topics within the field of organization theory are interrelated. Chapters are presented so that major ideas unfold in logical sequence. The framework that guides the organization of the book is shown in Exhibit 1.2.

EXHIBIT 1.2 Framework for the Book

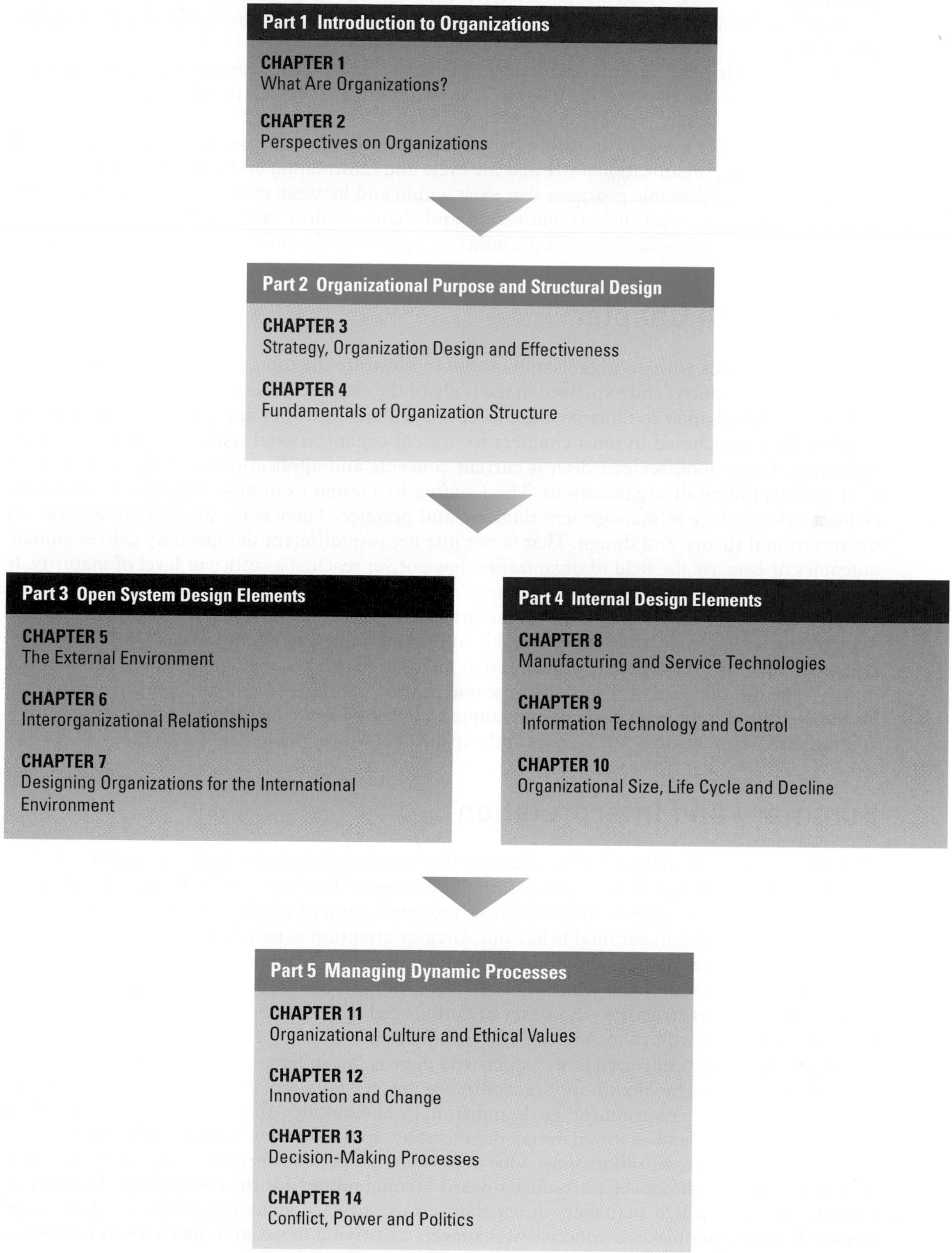

Part 1 Introduction to Organizations

CHAPTER 1
What Are Organizations?

CHAPTER 2
Perspectives on Organizations

Part 2 Organizational Purpose and Structural Design

CHAPTER 3
Strategy, Organization Design and Effectiveness

CHAPTER 4
Fundamentals of Organization Structure

Part 3 Open System Design Elements

CHAPTER 5
The External Environment

CHAPTER 6
Interorganizational Relationships

CHAPTER 7
Designing Organizations for the International
Environment

Part 4 Internal Design Elements

CHAPTER 8
Manufacturing and Service Technologies

CHAPTER 9
Information Technology and Control

CHAPTER 10
Organizational Size, Life Cycle and Decline

Part 5 Managing Dynamic Processes

CHAPTER 11
Organizational Culture and Ethical Values

CHAPTER 12
Innovation and Change

CHAPTER 13
Decision-Making Processes

CHAPTER 14
Conflict, Power and Politics

Part 1 introduces the basic idea of organizations as social systems and the nature of organization theory.

Part 2 is about strategic management, goals and effectiveness, and the fundamentals of organization structure.

Part 3 considers the various open system elements that influence organization structure and design, including the external environment, interorganizational relationships and the global environment.

Part 4 describes how organization design is related to such factors as manufacturing and service technology, organizational size and life cycle and information and control systems.

Part 5 shifts to dynamic processes that exist within and between major organizational departments and includes topics such as innovation and change, culture and ethical values, decision-making processes, managing intergroup conflict and power and politics.

Plan of Each Chapter

Each chapter begins with an organizational case to illustrate the topic to be covered. Theoretical concepts are introduced and explained in the body of the chapter. Several *In Practice* segments are included in each chapter to illustrate the concepts and show how they apply to real organizations. *Bookmarks* are included in most chapters to present organizational issues that managers face right now. These book reviews discuss current concepts and applications to deepen and enrich your understanding of organizations. The *Leading by Design* examples illustrate the dramatic changes taking place in management thinking and practice. There is no single 'right answer' in organizational theory and design. That is not just because different designs may deliver similar outcomes or because the field of organization has not yet reached a sufficient level of maturity. It is because whatever is counted as a 'right answer' implicitly appeals to some particular set of values (and, often, particular actors within the firm). An alternative set of values might view a very different answer as 'right', and it not possible to provide values with a rational warrant. Counterpoints are included throughout, which present alternative perspectives on issues discussed in the book. There are two sets of Counterpoints; one printed within the book and the other available on the dedicated online platform accompanying the text. Each chapter closes with a 'Summary and Interpretation' section that reviews and explains important theoretical concepts.

Summary and Interpretation

The primary focus of analysis for organization theory is not the psychology of individual employees but, rather, their activities as organizational members. That is why this book is less directly concerned with topics such as supervision or the motivation of employees which are the mainstay of courses on organizational behaviour. Greater attention is paid here to how behaviour in organizations, which includes the supervision and motivation of employees, is shaped within the structure of social relations in which it occurs. Accordingly, our focus is upon the characteristics and dynamics of this structure – how they are influenced by the wider environment, and how key decision-makers attempt to manage their environment by designing effective structures. Students of this structure have conceived of its aspects and dimensions in terms of degrees of formalization, specialization, hierarchy of authority, centralization, professionalism, personnel ratios, size, organizational technology, environment, goals and strategy and culture. All of them have been invoked to offer conceptual handles for analyzing organizations and informing actions within them.

Many types of organizations exist. One important distinction is between for-profit businesses, in which managers direct their activities toward earning money for the company, and nonprofit organizations, in which managers direct their efforts toward generating some kind of social impact. It is commonplace to conceive of managers as striving to design organizations to achieve what they deem to be effective or efficient. But the meaning of what is 'effective and efficient', let alone the purpose of their pursuit, is often contested because different stakeholders have different priorities that they want the organization to satisfy. In the end, the priorities that are pursued will reflect the outcomes of negotiations between stakeholders, with the most privileged and well resourced of these – owners and creditors in corporations – being able to exert the greatest influence upon how organizational goals are defined and pursued. There is nothing natural or inevitable about this but a significant change – for example, in the direction of social enterprise, mutuality and sustainability – would require a shift in the balance of power accompanying organized resistance to entrenched forms of organization.

KEY CONCEPTS

organization theory   organizations

Discussion Questions

1   Any definition of organization provides a way of 'not seeing' as well as a way of 'seeing'. Discuss.

2   How do the challenges facing managers and employees within organizations influence one another?

3   Identify some key differences between organizations and consider how the challenges affect them in different ways.

4   Illustrate and explore how we live in an organizational world.

Notes

1. Geoffrey Jones (2005), *Renewing Unilever: Transformation and Tradition,* Oxford, OUP.
2. 'After three years of painful effort, Europe's biggest electronics company is still struggling to get fit', *The Economist*, April 7, 1990, Pg. 99.
3. G. Mahesh and S. Chaudhuri (2004), 'Philips: Restructuring to Make Things Better', ICFAI Business School Case Study 304-330-1, Hyderabad.
4. Sean Meehan (2007), 'The Philips Marketing Journey', IMD Case Study IMD-5-0729.
5. Kerry Capell (2006), 'Thinking Simple At Philips: A panel of outside experts is helping the electronics giant reinvent itself', *Business Week*, December 11.
6. S. Govind and S. George (2007), 'Philips, Making Sense of Simplicity', ICFAI Case Study 507-085-1.
7. Sara Webb (2013) 'Philips turns off TV in turnaround', Reuters.com, 12 February.
8. Toby Sterling, 'St. Louis Today, Royal Philips NV to split into two separate companies', September 23, 2014, accessed at http://www.stltoday.com/business/local/royal-philips-nv-to-split-into-two-separatecompanies/article_32778739-85ce-5031-a1ee-ccd6c7299348.html
9. Harry G. Barkema, Joel A. C. Baum and Elizabeth A. Mannix, 'Management Challenges in a New Time', *Academy of Management Journal* 45, no. 5 (2002), 916–930. Eileen Davis, 'What's on American Managers' Minds?' *Management Review* (April 1995), 14–20.
10. Zald, M. and Hasenfeld, Y. (2008), 'Political economy of organizations', In S. Clegg, and J. Bailey (Eds), *International Encyclopedia of Organization Studies*, pp. 1250–1252).
11. Harry G. Barkema, Joel A. C. Baum and Elizabeth A. Mannix, 'Management Challenges in a New Time', *Academy of Management Journal* 45, no. 5 (2002), 916–930. Eileen Davis, 'What's on American Managers' Minds?' *Management Review* (April 1995), 14–20.
12. 'Top five takeaways from Wipro Q3 earnings', *Economic Times of India*, January 18, 2016, accessed at articles.economictimes.indiatimes.com/2016-01-18/news/69870252_1_wipro-ltd-interim-dividend-march-quarter
13. http://www.wipro.com/about-wipro/ accessed on September 15, 2013.
14. Craig Unger, 'House of cards: From 9/11 to BAE, the Saudis have turned the purchase of political power into a fine art', *The Guardian*, April 15, 2008, Pg. 28; Robert Baer, 'The Saudis do not give up their secrets, Mr Blair', *The Independent on Sunday*, April 13, 2008, Pg. 50; Jane Wardell, 'Calls to reopen UK inquiry into BAE-Saudi arms deal', Associated Press Worldstream, April 11, 2008; Nick Clark and Stephen Foley, 'BAE chief detained as US turns up heat in bribes case', *The Independent*, May 19, 2008, Pg. 36.
15. 'After JK; Société Générale', *The Economist*, May 31, 2008; Peter Robison, 'When traders go bad; The Société

Générale scandal is following a familiar script', *Ottawa Citizen* January 26, 2008, Pg. E3; 'Societe Generale boss admits faults in control systems', *Agence France Presse*, June 10, 2008.

16. Jean-Pierre Lehmann, 'Panama—The Coming Crash of Capitalism', *Forbes*, April 6, 2016 accessed at www.forbes.com/sites/jplehmann/2016/04/06/panama-the-coming-crash-of-capitalism/#34eacbf956fd

17. Joe Willis, '"Woeful" – Scandal of Lost Data Discs', *The Northern Echo*, June 26, 2008, Pg. 1.

18. David Wessel, 'Venal Sins: Why the Bad Guys of the Boardroom Emerged en Masse', *The Wall Street Journal* (June 20, 2002), A1, A6.

19. Greg Ip, 'Mind Over Matter – Disappearing Acts: The Rapid Rise and Fall of the Intangible Asset', *The Wall Street Journal* (April 4, 2002), A1, A6.

20. Leila E. Davis, 'Financialization and the nonfinancial corporation: an investigation of firmlevel investment behavior in the U.S., 1971–2011', Working Paper 2013-08, University of Massachusetts Amherst Department of Economics, accessed at https://www.umass.edu/economics/publications/2013-08.pdf

21. Jim Davis (2003), 'Speculative Capital in the Global Age', *Race and Class*, 44, 1–22; Anita Hawser, 'Mergers and Acquisitions: A Dangerous Game', *Global Finance Magazine*, May, 2007, Pg. 4.

22. Bernard Wysocki Jr., 'Corporate Caveat: Dell or Be Delled', *The Wall Street Journal* (May 10, 1999), A1.

23. Andy Reinhardt, 'From Gearhead to Grand High Pooh-Bah', *BusinessWeek* (August 28, 2000), 129–130.

24. G. Pascal Zachary, 'Mighty is the Mongrel', *Fast Company* (July 2000), 270–284.

25. Debra E. Meyerson and Joyce K. Fletcher, 'A Modest Manifesto for Shattering the Glass Ceiling', *Harvard Business Review* (January–February 2000), 127–136; Annie Finnigan, 'Different Strokes', *Working Woman* (April 2001), 42–48; Joline Godfrey, 'Been There, Doing That', *Inc.* (March 1996), 21–22; Paula Dwyer, Marsha Johnston and Karen Lowry Miller, 'Out of the Typing Pool, into Career Limbo', *BusinessWeek* (April 15, 1996), 92–94.

26. Howard Aldrich, *Organizations and Environments* (Englewood Cliffs, NJ: Prentice-Hall, 1979), 3.

27. Scare quotes are defined by Oxford dictionaries as 'quotation marks placed round a word or phrase to draw attention to an unusual or arguably inaccurate use' Oxford Dictionaries, accessed at http://oxforddictionaries.com/definition/english/scare-quotes

28. This section is based largely on Peter F. Drucker, *Managing the Non-Profit Organization: Principles and Practices* (New York: HarperBusiness, 1992); and Thomas Wolf, *Managing a Nonprofit Organization* (New York: Fireside/Simon & Schuster, 1990).

29. Christine W. Letts, William P. Ryan and Allen Grossman, *High Performance Nonprofit Organizations* (New York: John Wiley & Sons, Inc., 1999), 30–35.

30. Robert N. Stern and Stephen R. Barley, 'Organizations and Social Systems: Organization Theory's Neglected Mandate', *Administrative Science Quarterly* 41 (1996): 146–162.

31. Philip Siekman, 'Build to Order: One Aircraft Carrier', *Fortune* (July 22, 2002), 180[B]–180[J].

32. Schlender, 'The New Soul of a Wealth Machine', and Keith H. Hammonds, 'Growth Search', *Fast Company* (April 2003), 75–80.

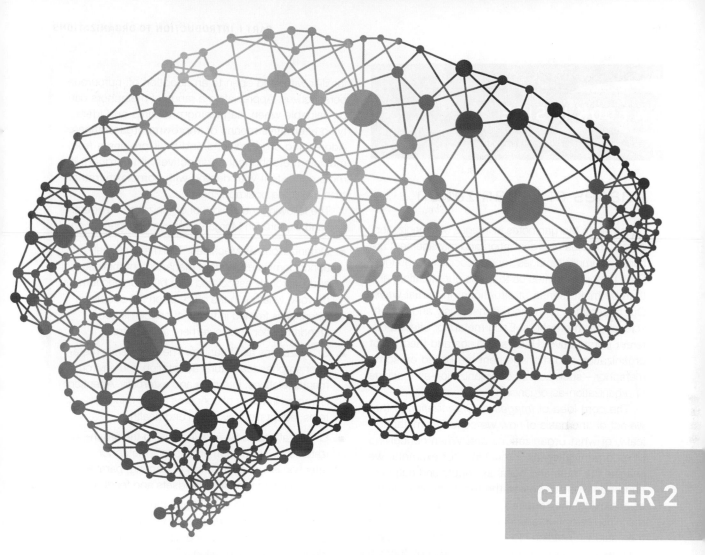

PERSPECTIVES ON ORGANIZATIONS

Images of Organization

As Gareth Morgan notes in Images of Organization, 'All theories of organization and management are based on implicit images', and associated languages. Each metaphor invites us to frame our attention, and thereby make sense of situations, in partial ways. Our experience is framed, consciously and unconsciously, by metaphors. Each metaphor offers a different perspective. Understandings and theories of organization and management are based on some metaphor – such as that of organization-as-machine or organization-as-organism.

The core idea of *Images of Organization* is that we act on the basis of how we conceive, metaphorically, of what organizations are. When conceiving of an organization as a machine, for example, we imagine the 'nuts and bolts' as 'inputs and outputs', and endeavour to design the most efficient means of achieving the required 'throughput'. Using the machine metaphor, elements of the organization are then said to 'run like clockwork' so long as people operate as 'cogs in the machine' and do not 'throw a spanner in the works'.

When thinking or communicating about organization(s), the use of metaphors may be more or less explicit. Each metaphor provides some illumination of organization(s). But their use can also be restrictive – in the sense that they limit as well as enable us to make sense of our world. They can be helpful but they may also be misleading.

An appreciation of the role of metaphors in making sense of organizations and acting within enables a better appreciation of how our understanding and behaviour is governed by taken-for-granted images and metaphors. An awareness of the extent to which we are confined by our use of just a few metaphors may, in turn, invite consideration of alternative metaphors which offer different ways of thinking and acting.

Advocates of the use of metaphors contend that adopting just one or two metaphors is restrictive and inflexible. They suggest that it is important to be familiar with, and open to an adoption of, numerous perspectives. Appreciating a range of metaphors can be valuable when diagnosing problems and identifying alternative means of improving organizations. Addressing organisations and their problems from multiple metaphorical perspectives, it is argued, is more consistent with dealing with complexity rather than trivializing or simplifying it.

The following metaphors of organization are identified and explored in Morgan's *Images of Organization*:

- **Organizations as Machines.** The machine metaphor dominates modern management thinking and is strongly associated with bureaucratic forms of work, whether in the office or on the shopfloor. Attention is framed in terms of concerns about standardization, measurement and control.

- **Organizations as Organism.** The organismic metaphor emphasizes natural adaptation and environmental relations, internally and externally. Attention is framed in terms of concerns about living systems, adaptation, evolution and health.

- **Organizations as Brain.** When using the organizations as information processors metaphor attention is framed in terms of learning, parallel information processing, mindsets and feedback.

- **Organization as Culture.** When the culture metaphor is deployed, attention to organization is framed in terms of concerns about values, ideology, rituals and vision.

- **Organizations as Political.** When conceived as political, attention is framed in terms of power, interests, alliances and conflict management.

- **Organizations as Psychic Prisons.** When the psychic prison metaphor is deployed, people seem to be trapped by others' perspectives and agendas. This metaphor frames attention in terms of concerns about unconscious processes, repression, defence mechanisms and projection.

- **Organizations as Flux and Transformation.** Using this metaphor, attention is framed in terms of concerns about complexity, self-organization, emergent properties and paradox.

- **Organizations as Instruments of Domination.** When conceived as instruments of domination, emphasis is placed on the imposition of the will of one group upon others. Attention is framed in terms of concerns about alienation, discrimination imposing and exploitation.

Morgan's *Images of Organizations* is very helpful in reminding us that our knowledge is always partial and perspectival. We never 'see' what 'is'. Instead, we apprehend 'it' within a particular frame of reference in which a frame-specific metaphor tends to dominate. Morgan's emphasis upon the importance of metaphors helpfully recalls the existence of numerous, counterveiling ways of understanding organization(s), and the behaviour within them. In this text, the Counterpoint feature is intended to refresh and stimulate this awareness.

Source: Gareth Morgan (1986/2006), *Images of Organization,* Sage. For a good summary of the eight metaphors, see http://www.systems-thinking.ca/myfiles/ GarethMorgan.pdf

How we approach and work in organizations will depend upon how we make sense of them. If the organization already exists, then it contains a legacy of the earlier sense-making involved in establishing it and developing it. Managers and employees acquire and apply different ways of making sense of organization(s) – that is, different perspectives for designing them and interpreting what goes on in them. Their perspective may be narrow or broad, rigid or flexible, singular or multiple, static or dynamic. They are important because they enable us to build and navigate the world of organizations. Perspectives may be shared or divergent – producing harmony or discord, a capacity to contemplate alternatives that allow for change and adaptation, or a view that 'there is no alternative'. For these reasons, it is relevant to consider the existence of different perspectives on organizations, and to appreciate how, over time, different perspectives become embedded or subjected to questioning and replacement.

Purpose of this Chapter

In this chapter, the scope and nature of organization theory are discussed more fully. Succeeding sections examine the structural and contextual dimensions of organization design, the history of organization theory, the development of new organizational forms in response to change and how organization theory can be helpful in managing organizations in a period of massive challenges associated with rapid changes. There are various ways of thinking about organizations. Two important perspectives are the open-systems approach and the organizational-configuration framework.

From Closed to Open Systems

A significant development in the study of organizations is the distinction between a closed and an open systems perspective.[1] A closed-system perspective focuses exclusively upon the organization. Minimal consideration is given to its dependencies upon, or capacities to influence, elements that lie beyond it ('the environment'). From a closed systems perspective, organizations are conceived as self-contained, effectively sealed off from the outside world. Early management philosophies tended to be closed system in approach. Taking the wider context as a given, it was assumed that the organization could be made more effective through internal design. Managerial attention is then appropriately focused upon how to refine existing structures in order to address increases in scale, for example, rather than adapting them to a changing situation.

Open system thinking pays attention to the (open) boundary between the organization and its context. Developing a design that effectively manages the exchanges – of raw materials, people, products, etc. – across this boundary is, in an open systems perspective, key to survival and prosperity (see Counterpoint 2.1). Organizations are conceived as consumers of resources (inputs, such as raw materials) and exporters of resources (outputs, such as services). In order to survive and prosper they are impelled, according to an open-system perspective, to adapt to, or attempt to control, a changing environment. It is necessary to find and obtain needed resources, interpret and act on environmental change, dispose of outputs and control and coordinate internal activities in the face of environmental disturbances and uncertainty. In organizations, it can happen – surprisingly easily – that particular divisions, departments and especially top managers forget that they are part of an open system. They may, for example, isolate themselves within a self-referential culture – a 'bubble' – as they fail to pay attention to what is going on with their employees, customers, suppliers and competitors. It would seem that in our example in the first chapter, Philips suffered through a lack of attention to environmental changes in addition to weak responsiveness to new product opportunities. The relevance of open-systems thinking and designs has been underscored in recent years with regard to changes relating to the explosion of the internet and e-business; growing diversity of the workforce; and the opening up of low wage labour economies, such as China and India, and the participation of even newer (and lower-cost) entrants in the global economy like Vietnam and Bangladesh.

COUNTERPOINT 2.1

Open-systems thinking is helpful in reminding us of the interdependencies both between subsystems (e.g. 'production' and 'maintenance') as well as between the organization and what exists beyond its boundaries.

A major limitation of this thinking is that it presents an excessively neat picture of how organizations operate and relate to elements of their environment. It is worth recalling that organizations comprise people who are not necessarily willing to be compliant tools of systems. Nor are the designers of these systems necessarily able to make employees operate according to apparently rational specifications.

In practice, organizing, like politics, is 'the art of the possible' based upon available capacities and capabilities, and always at the mercy of 'events'. How people 'fulfil' the 'needs' attributed to subsystems will inevitably depend upon their **own values, priorities and preconceptions**. If a set of subsystems were designed that perfectly met the 'needs' of their system, this would be achieved only by transforming employees into automatons – that is, perfectly formed cogs in a smooth-running machine. That is perhaps the ambition of designs based upon systems thinking but its failure to deal with the practicalities of organizing means that it is unrealized except in the most regimented and oppressive of corporations. And where it is nearly realized, it can be counterproductive as automatons are usually better at following procedures than responding creatively to unexpected events.

Exhibit 2.1 illustrates an open system. Inputs to an organization system include employees, raw materials and other physical resources, information and financial resources. The transformation process changes these inputs into something of value that can be exported back to the environment. Outputs include specific products and services for customers and clients. Outputs may also include employee satisfaction, pollution and other by-products of the transformation process.

In systems thinking, each system is understood to comprise several subsystems, as illustrated at the bottom of Exhibit 2.1. These subsystems are identified in relation to the specific functions they are conceived to perform for organizational survival – such as production, boundary spanning, maintenance, adaptation and management. In a systems perspective, the production subsystem is understood to produce the product and service outputs of the organization. Boundary subsystems are deemed responsible for enabling exchanges with the external environment. They include activities such as purchasing supplies or marketing products. Maintaining the smooth operation and upkeep of the organization's physical and human elements is understood to be performed by the maintenance subsystem. The adaptive subsystems are said to be responsible for organizational change and adaptation. Management is a distinct subsystem, responsible for coordinating and directing the other subsystems of the organization (see Counterpoint 2.1).

EXHIBIT 2.1 An Open System and its Subsystems

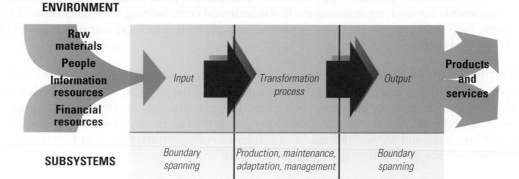

Organizational Configuration

Systems thinking conceives of different parts of an organization being designed to perform the key subsystem functions as illustrated in Exhibit 2.1. As there are limitations with this thinking (see Counterpoint 2.3), it is necessary to keep these firmly in mind when adopting an approach that is reliant upon it. One configuration framework proposed by Henry Mintzberg suggests that every organization has five parts.[2] These parts, illustrated in Exhibit 2.2, include the technical core, top management, middle management, technical support and administrative support. The five parts may vary in size and importance depending on an organization's particular environment, its technology and other factors.

BRIEFCASE 2.1

Technical Core The technical core includes diverse support staff who do the basic work of the organization. It performs the production subsystem function and produces the product and service outputs of the organization. This is where the primary transformation from inputs to outputs takes place. The technical core is the production department in a manufacturing firm, the teachers and classes in a university and the medical activities in a hospital. This core is complemented by other parts that provide technical and administrative support.

EXHIBIT 2.2 Five Basic Parts of an Organization

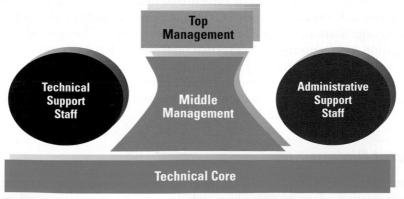

Source: Based on Henry Mintzberg, *The Structuring of Organizations* (Englewood Cliffs, NJ: Prentice-Hall, 1979), 215–297; and Henry Mintzberg, 'Organization Design: Fashion or Fit?' Harvard Business Review 59 (January-February 1981): 103–116.

Technical Support   Technical support employees, such as engineers and researchers, scan the environment for problems, opportunities and technological developments. Technical support is responsible for creating innovations in the technical core, helping the organization change and adapt. Technical support includes departments such as technology, research and development (R&D) and marketing research.

Administrative Support   The administrative support function is responsible for the smooth operation and upkeep of the organization, including its physical and human elements. This includes human resource activities such as recruiting and hiring, establishing compensation and benefits, and employee training and development, as well as maintenance activities such as cleaning of buildings and service and repair of machines. Administrative support functions include the human resource department and maintenance staff.

ONLINE
COUNTERPOINT 2.1

Management – Top and Middle   Management is a function responsible for directing and coordinating other parts of the organization. Top management provides direction, strategy, goals and policies for the entire organization or major divisions. Middle management is responsible for implementation and coordination at the departmental level. In traditional organizations, middle managers are responsible for mediating between top management and the technical core, such as implementing rules and passing information up and down the hierarchy.

In real-life organizations, the five parts are not readily distinguishable and they may serve more than one subsystem function. For example, managers coordinate and direct other parts of the system, but they may also be involved in administrative and technical support. In addition, several of the parts are involved in the *boundary spanning* function mentioned in the previous section. For example, in the administrative support realm, human resource departments are responsible for interacting with external as well as internal labour markets to find quality employees; and members of R&D departments work directly with outside organizations to learn about new technological developments. Moreover, with increasing pressures to deliver short-term shareholder value, there has been a preoccupation with cutting costs by off-shoring, outsourcing and generally hollowing out organizations so that the middle stata in Mintzberg's schema is shrunk and the 'technical core' is limited to activities that are assessed to be 'core'.

Dimensions of Organization Design

The systems view pertains to dynamic, ongoing activities within organizations. The next step for understanding organizations is to look at dimensions that describe specific organizational design traits.

Organizational dimensions can be categorized in two types: structural and contextual, illustrated in Exhibit 2.3. Structural dimensions provide labels to distinguish some key, internal characteristics of an organization, such as the degree of formalization. They provide a basis for comparing the composition of organizations. Contextual dimensions characterize both the organization as a whole, including its size, technology, etc. and the broader organizational setting. To understand and evaluate organizations, it is important to examine both structural and contextual dimensions.[3] These dimensions of organization design interact with one another and can be adjusted to accomplish the purposes listed earlier in Exhibit 2.1.

Structural Dimensions

1   *Formalization* refers to the reliance upon written documentation in the organization. Such documentation relates to procedures, job descriptions, regulations and policy manuals. Larger organizations tend to score high on formalization because they have written rules to

EXHIBIT 2.3 Interacting Contextual and Structural Dimensions of Organization Design

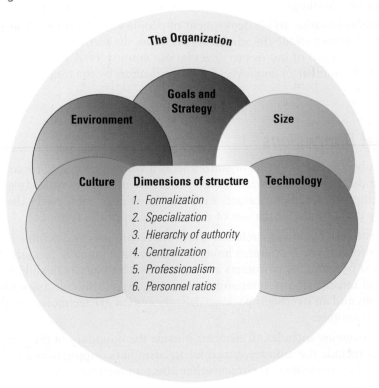

authorize and control a wide range of activity. A small, family-owned business, in contrast, may have almost no written rules and would be considered 'informal' even if the personal control exercised by its head is rigid and all-encompassing.

2 *Specialization* is the degree to which organizational tasks are subdivided into separate jobs. If specialization is extensive, each employee performs only a narrow range of tasks. High levels of specialization are found on production lines, where each worker is expected to become highly adept at repeatedly performing a narrow set of skills. Likewise, the division of labour amongst managers may be highly specialized.

BRIEFCASE 2.2

3 *Hierarchy of authority* describes who reports to whom and the span of control for each manager. The hierarchy is related to span of control (the number of employees reporting to a supervisor). When spans of control are narrow, specialization is high and the hierarchy tends to be tall. When spans of control are wide, the hierarchy of authority will be shorter.

4 *Centralization* refers to the hierarchical level that has authority to make a decision. When decision-making is kept at the top level, the organization is centralized. When decisions are delegated to lower organizational levels, it is decentralized. Organizational decisions that might be centralized at head office or decentralized to a particular division or operating unit may include the purchasing of certain types of equipment or the hiring of particular grades of employee.

5 *Professionalism* is the term used to describe the level of formal education and training of employees. Professionalism is considered high when employees require long periods of training to hold jobs in the organization. The average number of years of education of

employees is one measure of professionalism, which could be as high as 20 in a medical practice and less than ten in a construction company in a country with fewer years of mandatory schooling.

6 *Personnel ratios* refer to the deployment of people to various functions and departments. Personnel ratios include the administrative ratio, the clerical ratio, the professional staff ratio and the ratio of indirect to direct labour employees. A personnel ratio is measured by dividing the number of employees in a classification by the total number of organizational employees.

Contextual Dimensions

1 *Size* can be measured for the organization as a whole or for specific components, such as a plant or division. As organizations are social systems, size is typically measured by the number of employees. Other measures such as total sales or total assets also reflect magnitude, but they do not indicate the size of the human part of the system.

2 *Organizational technology* refers to the tools, techniques and actions used to transform inputs into outputs. It concerns how the organization actually produces the products and services it provides for customers and includes such things as flexible manufacturing, advanced information systems and the internet. An automobile assembly line, a college classroom and an overnight package delivery system are technologies, although they differ from one another.

3 The *environment* includes all elements outside the boundary of the organization. Key elements include the industry, government, customers, suppliers and the financial community. The environmental elements that affect an organization the most are often other organizations.

4 The organization's *goals and strategy* define the purpose and competitive techniques that set it apart from other organizations. Goals are often written down as an enduring statement of company intent (which should not be confused with actual practice). A strategy is the plan of action that describes resource allocation and activities for dealing with the environment and for reaching the organization's 'goals'. Goals and strategies notionally define the scope of operations and the relationship with employees, customers and competitors.

5 An organization's *culture* is the underlying set of key values, beliefs, understandings and norms shared by employees. These underlying values may pertain to ethical behaviour, commitment to employees, efficiency or customer service, and they provide the glue to hold organization members together. An organization's culture is unwritten but can be observed in its stories, slogans, ceremonies, dress and office layout.

The contextual and structural dimensions discussed above are understood to interact with, and to influence, each other. For example, large organization size, a routine technology and a stable environment all tend to be associated with organizations that have greater formalization, specialization and centralization. More detailed relationships among the dimensions are explored in later chapters of this book.

These dimensions also provide a basis for measurement and analysis of organizational characteristics. Consider, for example, the dimensions of W. L. Gore & Associates compared with those of European supermarket chain Carrefour and non-governmental organizations (NGOs).

IN PRACTICE

W. L. Gore & Associates

When Jack Dougherty began work at W. L. Gore & Associates, Inc., he reported to Bill Gore, the company's founder, to receive his first assignment. Gore told him, 'Why don't you find something you'd like to do'. Dougherty was shocked at the informality but quickly recovered and began interrogating various managers about their activities. He was attracted to a new product called Gore-Tex, a membrane that was waterproof but breathable when bonded to fabric. The next morning, he came to work dressed in jeans and began helping feed fabric into the maw of a large laminator. Five years later, Dougherty was responsible for marketing and advertising in the fabrics group.

Bill Gore died in 1986, but the organization he designed still runs in the same informal way as before. One of the key tenets of the organization is that employees (called associates) figure out what they want to do and where they think they can make a contribution. Instead of bosses, associates can choose to work with 'leaders' who emerge organically in the process of addressing work's regular challenges. The company has over 9000 associates in 45 locations around the world. The plants are kept small – up to 200 people – to maintain a family atmosphere. 'It's much better to use friendship and love than slavery and whips', Bill Gore said. Several professional associates are assigned to act as 'sponsors' for new product development, but the administrative structure is lean. Good human relations is a more important value than is internal efficiency. The company has seven times been named one of *Fortune* magazine's '100 Best Companies to Work For in America'. In 2009 it was listed twelfth on the '50 Best Large Workplaces in Europe' list, and in 2012, in the top ten workplaces in the world named by the Great Place to Work Institute. The company was featured in Malcolm Gladwell's famous book *The Tipping Point*, to illustrate how small sized plants and mutual familiarity make for positive and efficient working teams. It has also been featured in Frederick Laloux's 2014 book, *Reinventing Organizations*, as a "teal" organization:

one that fosters its members' abilities to self-manage and self-organize.[4] Gore continues to grow and prosper.[5] (see Counterpoint 2.2).

Carrefour

Carrefour is one of the giants in today's global retailing. In 1963, Carrefour pioneered the concept of the *hypermarché*, or hypermarket in English, a concept bringing together the traditional food-based supermarket with the full-range department store, carrying items from clothes to house paint to computers: 'everything under the same roof'. The company, based in France but by 2016 operating in 28 different national markets from China to Argentina, is the world's second largest by retail sales after Wal-Mart, with over 10 000 stores worldwide, on four continents. Although in some markets Carrefour operates a number of other chains ranging from convenience stores to cash and carry warehouses, these operations are driven by the supply and distribution systems established for the hypermarket operations. Its hypermarkets all contain the same product mix of about 60 per cent food and 40 per cent non-food, with the specific products sold tailored, of course, to national tastes. Where Carrefour has expanded through purchasing existing chains, such as Spain's Continente chain, it has usually moved quickly to rebrand the purchased properties with the name, logo, and 'look and feel' of the Carrefour group.

Carrefour's success has been built on following its basic model quite rigidly across national markets. The company's managers are drawn from all its operating countries, but management training places a strong emphasis on creating common corporate values and understanding amongst both managers and shopfloor employees, enabling it to avoid some of the differing visions that so hampered Philips, discussed in the previous chapter.[6]

Not-for-Profit Organizations and Charities

Many nonprofit organizations (NGOs) rely heavily on public and other external funding. NGOs in the arts sector, for example, can rarely earn enough money from ticket sales to cover even their expenses, despite having a small staff complement who are typically poorly paid, overwhelmed with rules and regulations (usually imposed by the external funders) and swamped by paperwork. Chronically under-staffed organizations are caught in a perpetual cycle of justifying funding to outside granting agencies. Being that they are typically very small, they have very little power to assert themselves over their environments. For example, they usually receive support in small amounts from a number of different funders, each of which has different reporting expectations. This is an extremely inefficient way of doing business (and a waste of the funders' money and the arts organizations' energies). Further, government often dictates particular artistic priorities (such as for example, the insistence of the Government of Wales, UK, that funded arts activities must be targeted to 'disadvantaged' people) even though government officials may have very little practical understanding of the artistic field and even less idea about how 'impact' might be measured.

However, even though almost all small arts NGOs are in the same situation, faced with unreasonable or impossible demands, they are also in competition with each other for very limited funds, and it is notoriously difficult for them to band together and demand a more coherent approach on the part of the funders.

Small NGOs such as those in the arts sector can still impact their environments through a variety of strategies. They can attempt to broaden their funding base so that they are not so dependent on government grants; most have done this in recent years by seeking out corporate sponsorship, expanding the range of revenue-generating activities (for example, some arts organizations, such as the Manchester-based Act on Info have begun offering team-building workshops for companies based on producing a 'play-in-a-day'), and operating cafes and restaurants from their facilities.

An alternative strategy has been to set aside competitive rivalries and work with other arts organizations. This can take various forms. It can involve, for example, sharing services and space, as has occurred in Birmingham, England. This involves working with 'Organizational Technology' as described in the Contextual Dimensions of Organization Design in this chapter.

On a more 'political' level it can involve acting collectively to challenge unfair and unreasonable government policies. When the government-appointed Arts Council of Wales decided to carry out an 'Investment Portfolio Review' in 2010/2011, it essentially decided to force all Welsh arts organizations to compete with each other for a smaller pot of money, with criteria determined on the basis of political priorities established by the Welsh government. Thirty-two organizations were slated to lose their funding altogether, putting the future of most in jeopardy. Whether coincidentally or not, the result of the initial review was that funding became more concentrated in areas from which the political party in power drew most of its support, on the grounds that these were of 'greatest need', while the Arts Council's own bureaucracy was not assessed and downsized as part of the review. Arts organizations worked together, with local governments and politicians, to pressure the Arts Council to reconsider. Although the bulk of the funding cuts were upheld, several were reversed, and alternative funding identified for many organizations. Most importantly, the transparency and accountability of the funding process came under unprecedented scrutiny, and subsequent funding processes and decisions have become more consultative and collegial. This is an example of even very small organizations finding ways both to adapt to, and sometimes to change, their environments in order to improve their performance and chances of survival.[7]

COUNTERPOINT 2.2

W. L. Gore[8] is probably one of the most celebrated 'good guys' in corporate history (See *In Practice*, above). Not only does the company treat its employees very well in comparison to most international firms, its product line is synonymous with quality and healthy living. In addition, the breathable membrane which forms the basis of the company's waterproof clothing is increasingly being used in cutting-edge healthcare applications, giving the company's products a further positive gloss.

However, Gore has come under increasing criticism for its business practices, especially what is claimed are its efforts to hamper competition. Due to its dominant position in the market for waterproof clothing, competitor companies often find it difficult to secure investment to develop their own products. That is part of business life, but some competitors claim that Gore goes further, demanding that companies it contracts to produce the garments sign exclusivity deals with the company. Also, some clothing brands that use Gore-Tex cloth in their garments have complained that they too are put under pressure not to use any competitive products, at the risk of losing the ability to use any Gore-Tex cloth in their garments. A Columbia Sportswear spokesman said, 'This is the worst kept secret in our industry. Our brands have experienced the exclusionary conduct directly, but we also have numerous written communications from other brands and manufacturers that they believe Gore dictates what waterproof breathable technologies they are allowed to offer to consumers.'

Gore strongly denies the claims: 'The waterproof, breathable category is highly competitive with a number of membranes available', a spokesman said. 'Gore's business practices do not foreclose competitors from selling products'. However, both the European Commission and the US Federal Trade Commission take the issues seriously. Both have launched anti-trust probes.

The criticism of Gore – whether ultimately proven justified or not – underlines a number of issues. First, even for major market players, the external environment is difficult to control; in fact, it can often be unlawful to try to control it. Second, companies need to be very careful to ensure that organizational culture is reflected not only in how people treat each other within the company, but also the company's external relationships with suppliers, retailers, etc. Finally, the most difficult position to hold is at the top – all other actors are monitoring your every move, whether to assure that it is lawful, or to identify a weakness or mistake that can be exploited!

Exhibit 2.4 provides a pictorial illustration of a number of the structural and contextual dimensions of Gore & Associates, Carrefour and the Wales Millennium Centre, a nonprofit UK regional arts centre. Gore & Associates, a medium-sized manufacturing organization, ranks low with respect to formalization, specialization and centralization. A number of professional staff are assigned to nonworkflow activities to do the R&D needed to stay abreast of changes in the

EXHIBIT 2.4 Characteristics of Three Organizations

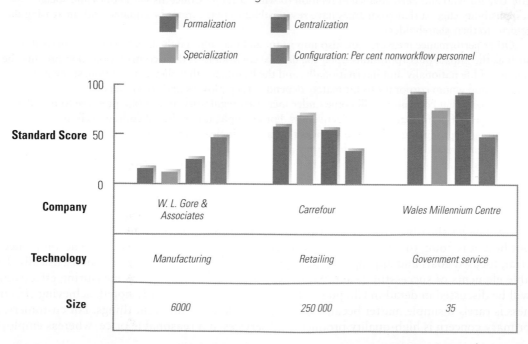

fibre industry. Carrefour is much more formalized, specialized and centralized. Cost-cutting to protect market share and increase profitability are of key importance and this is accomplished through standardization and economies of scale: 'growing market share can only be achieved on a consistent basis, if we are always locally the price leader'. The percentage of nonworkflow personnel is kept to a minimum. The structure of the Wales Millennium Centre, in contrast to the other organizations, reflects its dependent status within the nonprofit sector. The organization has to comply with many rules and procedures and different stakeholder demands that are imposed upon it. Most employees are assigned to workflow activities, although a substantial amount of staff time is consumed in providing administration and clerical support.

Performance and Effectiveness Outcomes

BRIEFCASE 2.3

For many analysts and designers of organizations the only point of understanding varying perspectives and the structural and contextual dimensions of organizations is to create and develop the organization in such a way as to achieve high performance and effectiveness (see Counterpoint 2.3). It would, of course, be difficult to justify the resources devoted to organizations if the purpose or outcome was low performance and ineffectiveness. In principle, managers are hired to adjust structural and contextual dimensions and organizational subsystems to most efficiently and effectively transform inputs into outputs and provide value. Efficiency refers to the amount of resources used to achieve the organization's goals. It is based on the quantity of raw materials, money and employees necessary to produce a given level of output. Effectiveness is a broader term, meaning the degree to which an organization achieves its goals. However, the pursuit of high performance and effectiveness can compromise or undermine what makes it possible – such as morale and cooperation. In any event, it is questionable whether slavish pursuit of such objectives is consistent with human flourishing or sustainability.

COUNTERPOINT 2.3

When reference is made to such things as 'high performance and effectiveness', it is worth asking: effective for who and performance in relation to what criteria? Concerns with ethics and social responsibility suggest that companies have responsibilities that cannot be equated with increasing the returns to their shareholders.

Other performance measures are also important and may ultimately affect their very survival – such as the impact of corporations upon the natural environment, their contribution to improving the quality of life nationally and internationally, and the legitimacy that they enjoy amongst the general public upon whom corporations ultimately depend – as employees and consumers.

It is likely that companies will come under increased regulatory and public pressure to broaden their criteria of performance and effectiveness. For example, it may be asked how well they are performing in producing goods and services that are ecologically enhancing and sustainable rather than destructive and degrading, or how they are performing in returning the wealth generated by companies to the communities from where their resources – material and social – are drawn.

ONLINE
COUNTERPOINT 2.2

Whatever the objective ascribed to an organization, it is relevant to take care in working out how it is going to be achieved. A clear, consensually determined objective accompanied by clear, focused goals and appropriate strategies for their attainment, are commonsensically desirable elements of successful design. Strategy, goals and approaches to measuring effectiveness will be discussed in detail in Chapter 3. However, as we have already noted, achieving effectiveness is rarely a simple matter because different people want different things. For customers, the primary concern is high-quality products and services at a reasonable price, whereas employees are mostly concerned with adequate pay, good working conditions, promotion prospects and job satisfaction. Managers are faced with competing demands when setting goals and striving for effectiveness. The idea of balancing the preferences of different groups has been characterized as a stakeholder approach. Its claim is to integrate diverse organizational activities by taking account of the various organizational stakeholders and considering what they want from the organization. A stakeholder is any group within or outside of the organization that has a stake in the organization. The satisfaction level of each group can be assessed as an indication of the organization's performance and effectiveness.[9]

Exhibit 2.5 illustrates various stakeholders and indicates what each group may want from the organization. Organizations frequently struggle to satisfy the demands of all groups. A business might have high customer satisfaction, but the organization might have difficulties with creditors, or supplier relationships might be poor. Consider the American-headquartered retail chain Wal-Mart. Customers love its efficiency and low prices, but the low-cost emphasis the company uses with suppliers and in relation to employees has caused friction. Some activist groups argue that Wal-Mart's tactics are unethical because they force suppliers to lay off workers, close factories and outsource to manufacturers from low-wage countries operating facilities with poor working conditions. One supplier has said clothing is being sold at Wal-Mart so cheaply that suppliers from developed countries in Europe and North America couldn't compete even if they paid their workers nothing! The challenges of managing such a huge organization have also led to strains in relationships with employees and other stakeholder groups, as evidenced by recent gender discrimination suits and complaints about low wages.[10] And then there are other groups affected by company actions – such as communities from where the raw materials used in products sold by Wal-Mart are sourced – that do not even appear in Exhibit 2.5.

Stakeholder interests often conflict. In nonprofit organizations, the priorities of clients sometimes conflict with restrictions on use of government funds or contributions from donors. In companies, there is conflict when unions campaign for improved conditions or wage increases that might hurt shareholders' financial returns or prompt a switch to lower-cost suppliers.

EXHIBIT 2.5 Major Stakeholder Groups and What They Expect

OWNERS AND SHAREHOLDERS
• *Financial return*

EMPLOYEES
• *Satisfaction*
• *Pay*
• *Supervision*

CUSTOMERS
• *High-quality goods, services*
• *Service*
• *Value*

SUPPLIERS
• *Satisfactory transactions*
• *Revenue from purchases*

CREDITORS
• *Creditworthiness*
• *Fiscal responsibility*

COMMUNITY
• *Good corporate citizen*
• *Contribution to community affairs*

ORGANIZATION

MANAGEMENT
• *Efficiency*
• *Effectiveness*

UNION
• *Employee pay*
• *Benefits*

GOVERNMENT
• *Obedience to laws and regulations*
• *Fair competition*

IN PRACTICE

Conflict and Compromise in the Forest Products Industry

The forest products industry literally underpins our part of the homes we live in, especially if our houses are of wood frame construction as in much of Europe and North America. Even if they have an outer shell of brick or concrete, much of the internal framing and finishing is likely to be wood-based. Despite the growth of electronic media, most of us still access much of our information by picking up books and newspapers, again produced from wood pulp. At the same time, many of us are shocked by visions of some of the world's great forests being logged, whether teak from the Burmese rain forest, or old growth cedar trees in British Columbia, on Canada's west coast. Wood and wood products are a crucial part of our daily lives.

Nowhere are the debates about the forest industry more heated, or the stakes higher, than in Canada. The forest industry is a major job creator in the country, accounting for more than 300 000 jobs directly and 600 000 indirectly. The industry is worth 3 per cent of Canada's GDP annually, and whole communities are entirely dependent on forestry.[11] In 2008 the town of Mackenzie in northern British Columbia faced complete closure when forest products giant, Abitibi Bowater, indefinitely closed the community's two saw mills and a pulp mill.[12]

At the same time, Canada is home not merely to vast expanses of pristine wilderness, but also one of the world's most active and sometimes militant environmental movements. Greenpeace, the world's best known environmental group, was founded in Canada. During the 1990s, proposals to log old growth forest in Clayoquot Sound in British Columbia led to the largest campaign of civil disobedience in Canadian history, with over 800 environmentalists arrested.[13] In addition to the conflicting perspectives of forest industry companies and workers and environmentalists, much of the country's usable timber is located on lands claimed by the country's indigenous peoples, who tend to share environmentalists' concerns about damage to their homelands, while also wanting to ensure that any development benefits their populations which are easily the poorest in Canada's generally affluent society.[14] Canada's forest products industry, therefore, is working in an extraordinarily complex environment.

After the great conflicts over Clayoquot Sound, some of Canada's more forward looking forest companies decided on a different approach from simply relying on property rights and contract enforcement through the courts. In the late 1990s, MacMillan Bloedel (MacBlo), now part of Weyerhauser, had been running into financial difficulties, caused by decline in Asian markets due to the 'Asian flu' economic downturn, a softwood lumber trade dispute with the US, and difficulty selling to Europe because of environmentalists' pressure on European buyers to guarantee that all their wood came from sustainable sources. In 1997 MacBlo's new CEO, Tom Stephens, decided that the only way he would be able to provide value to his shareholders would be if he adopted a stakeholder approach. Stephens charged his managers to come up with a strategy that would respond to concerns about sustainability by moving to selective logging, reducing the impact of logging on forest land biodiversity, and signing up to the sustainable forestry certification scheme run by the Forest Stewardship Council (FSC). He developed long-term dialogue and partnerships with environmental groups, effectively widening the company's sphere of accountability to include both environmental groups and First Nations communities, as well as its workforce.[15]

Tom Stephens' approach turned out to be the only game in town. Since 2000, the area of forest land certified as managing sustainably has risen tenfold, and major retailers in Europe and North America from B&Q to Hallmark Cards have committed to use wood products sourced exclusively or almost exclusively from independently certified sources like FSC.[16] Although frictions continue between environmental organizations and the forest products industry, these are increasingly seen on both sides as part of the process of negotiating compromises that will allow forest companies to contribute to the economy while helping to protect the planet for future generations.

▶

The next major challenge will be ensuring that sustainable practices become the norm across the world, and not merely in the wealthiest countries. In fact, with globalization, if sustainable practices are not implemented globally, damage to the environment in the West is simply going to be replaced by damage to the environment in emerging economies. In the forest stewardship sector, the FSC is supporting some positive practices, although too much logging in developing countries remains unregulated and unsustainable.

One positive example is in Madagascar, where the FSC's certification contractor GFA Consulting Group worked with an ambitious local forestry company, VIMA Wood Industry, to help the company secure FSC certification. Two key aspects of the certification process were assuring that the cutting cycle was sustainable while also delivering the different types of wood needed in the local and international market (including wood for charcoal, pallets, as well as finished lumber for building), and ensuring that work was created for local employees. This latter is an important aspect of FSC certification because unless sustainable practices benefit local communities, illegal and unsustainable logging will be inevitable as local populations are desperate for income. 'We are creating employment for indigenous populations, notably in the security of the forest from illegal cutting, but also in maintaining the forest. We are recruiting forest wardens continuously', said company spokesperson, Fanjavola Beboarimisa. The company is planning to invest in further mechanization to increase the efficiency of production.[17]

Demands made by stakeholders other than shareholders and senior executives are likely to meet resistance unless they can be reconciled with increased financial returns – for example, by tying in wage increases to productivity gains or improving reliability from suppliers in return for better treatment. In reality, it is unreasonable to assume that all stakeholders can be equally satisfied or even equally treated. However, if an organization fails to manage the expectations and/or meet the demands of stakeholder groups, it is likely risking its longer term survival – by becoming a takeover target or simply going out of business – as well as failing to live up to its claims to care for its employees and customers as well as its stockholders. Research has shown that the assessment of multiple stakeholder groups is a strong indicator of organizational effectiveness, especially with respect to organizational adaptability.[18] As profit and nonprofit organizations are generally (but not universally) concerned about their reputations amongst customers, creditors and regulators, they also put considerable resources into shaping and controlling the part of the environment comprising stakeholders' perceptions of their performance.[19]

Failure to attend to stakeholders – or, at least, the more powerful ones – invites disruption and loss of reputation which is likely to prove damaging. Satisfying multiple stakeholders can be challenging, particularly as goals and priorities change.

The Evolution of Organization Theory and Design

Organization theory is not a collection of facts or an operation manual; it is a way of thinking about, and informing action within, organizations. 'Facts' are, in this sense, contingent upon the particular kind of thinking that goes into specific theories of organization. Different theories of organization – for example, closed systems theories and open systems theories – provide alternative ways to represent and analyze organizations. Each theory makes its own claims about the accuracy and depths of its analysis relative to commonsense views or alternative theories. Drawing upon different theories, organization scholars point to, or suggest the relevance of, diverse features, patterns and regularities which they make available to the rest of us. For this reason, the specific 'facts' generated from the research are not, in practice, as important as the general patterns and insights into the realities of organizing and organizations.

Historical Perspectives

Organization design and management practices have varied over time in response to changes in the larger society.

The modern era of management theory began with the classical management perspective in the late nineteenth and early twentieth century. The emergence of capitalism brought with it the development of the factory system which posed problems that earlier organizations had not encountered. Factories became a new source of wealth creation. Enclosing large numbers of workers in factories, where their productive activity could be more readily controlled, made it possible to extract significant surpluses from their labour. That was because workers could be supervised closely as they performed repetitive but highly productive tasks. By combining workers in factories, goods could be mass produced to reach a mass market, with the prospect of earning a handsome profit on each item sold as a consequence of the long hours and low wages of factory workers. This was not a recipe for good industrial relations; and an outcome was the formation of unions and the development of ideologies that demanded fairer treatment and less autocratic forms of control. In turn, the scale of the factories and the competition between producers stimulated interest in how to design and manage work in order to better incentivize cooperation as a means of further increasing productivity and profitability.

The so-called 'classical perspective' sought to apply rational calculations to turn organizations into efficient, well-oiled machines. This perspective is associated with the development of extended hierarchies and bureaucratic procedures of control. Pioneered by Frederick Winslow Taylor, his principles of scientific management postulate that decisions about organizations and job design should be based on a precise, 'scientific' study of individual situations to determine which method of doing a job delivers the greatest output.[20] On this basis, managers standardize procedures for doing each job, select workers with the most appropriate abilities, train them to follow the standard procedures, carefully plan work and provide wage incentives to increase output. Favouritism and amateurism were to be replaced by careful research, meritocracy and standardization.

For example, Taylor, an engineer by training, studied the unloading of iron from railcars and reloading finished steel for the Bethlehem Steel plant in Pennsylvania, USA, in 1898. He calculated that with 'correct' movements, tools and sequencing, each man was capable of loading 47.5 tons per day instead of the typical 12.5 tons. He also worked out an incentive system that paid each man $1.85 per day for meeting the new standard, an increase from the previous rate of $1.15. Finally, he devised a means of identifying the workers most capable – 'morally' as well as physically – of maximizing their earnings using this system – that is, what Taylor calls his 'first class man'. In Taylor's view, workers sought employment for one reason alone – to earn money. So, he believed that by enabling them to be more productive – by linking output directly to payment – he could reconcile the demands of two key stakeholders: employees who obtained substantially improved wages, and shareholders who received massively increased surpluses, while ensuring that the basis of this reconciliation was impartial and therefore fair.

However, Taylor's scientific management was based upon closed systems thinking. He overlooked how employees develop a sense of identity and meaning outside of the workplace. Despite a strong interest in earning money from their employment, many were unwilling to accept their treatment as living machines who simply executed repetitive tasks conceived by others and incentivized to work as rapidly as possible by piecework payments systems (see Exhibit 2.6). Nor, when economic conditions changed, were workers willing to accept cuts in their pay in order to preserve surpluses for the owners. An unintended consequence of Taylor's treatment of workers as human machines programmed to be maximally productive was to facilitate their solidarity in opposition to management. Workers, it turned out, would not necessarily do what they were told.

Another version of the classical perspective took a broader look at the organization. Whereas scientific management focused primarily on the technical core and its immediate support functions – on the organization of work performed on the shop floor – a focus on administrative principles considered the design and functioning of the organization as a whole. For example, Henri Fayol

EXHIBIT 2.6 Scientific Management

'Scientific management, the charge went, pitted workers against one another, made them claw at each other for the privilege of being one of Taylor's 'first class men'. It broke up the comradely fellow-feeling, the respect of one man for his brother, that lay behind the labour movement at its best...

Scientific management was degrading. In reducing work to instructions and rules, it took away your knowledge and skill. In standing over you with a stopwatch, peering at you, measuring you, rating you, it treated you like a side of beef. You weren't supposed to think. Whatever workmanly pride you might once have possessed must be sacrificed on the altar of efficiency, your role only to execute the will of other men paid to think for you. You were a drone, fit only for taking orders.'

Source: R. Kanigel (1997), *The One Best Way: Frederick Winslow Taylor and the Enigma of Efficiency*, New York: Little, Brown and Company, p. 534.

proposed 14 principles of management, such as 'each subordinate receives orders from only one superior' (unity of command) and 'similar activities in an organization should be grouped together under one manager' (unity of direction). These principles have formed the foundation for many aspects of modern management practice and organization design.

The scientific management and administrative principles approaches provided potent ideas for establishing high productivity and increasing prosperity. Administrative principles in particular contributed to the development of bureaucratic organizations, which emphasized designing and managing organizations on an impersonal, ostensibly rational basis by establishing clearly defined authority and responsibility, formal record keeping and uniform application of standard rules. Although the term *bureaucracy* has taken on negative connotations, the introduction of bureaucratic characteristics into the sphere of work revolutionized its organization. Notably, at its best, it replaced nepotism and other forms of favouritism with impartial processes that were in principle indifferent to rank, gender, colour and so on. It is worth recalling how it is often 'red tape' and tedious procedure that ensures that people – customers and suppliers as well as employees – are treated equally, and so are not able to curry favour or queue-jump on the basis of their status or by using bribes. One problem with the classical perspective, however, concerns its limited attention to the social context and to human feelings.

Early work on industrial psychology and human relations, in which closer attention was paid to 'the human factor', tended to be marginalized by the dominance of scientific management and administrative principles. A major breakthrough occurred with a series of experiments at a Chicago electricity company, which came to be known as the Hawthorne Studies. Interpretations of the results of these experiments concluded that positive treatment of employees, even by simply acknowledging their presence and contribution, improved their motivation and productivity. That the potency of basic recognition of workers by managers had not been widely acknowledged prior to these studies gives a strong indication of the social distance between them. The Hawthorne Studies laid the groundwork for subsequent explorations of 'the human side of enterprise' including leadership, motivation and, more recently diverse aspects of human resource management. Even so, the core of the classical approach has remained influential, at least in contexts where change was minimal or predictable. It was only in the 1970s and early 1980s in advanced capitalist economies, as markets for commodities and finance became less stable and international competition intensified, that the classical approach was challenged by alternative design principles, such as teamworking. That, arguably, was because many organizations came under pressure to achieve increased flexibility, rapid response to the customer, more adaptive and well motivated employees and improved products with shorter life-cycles.[21] Further organizational adaptations and innovations have occurred to exploit the opportunity of the internet and other advances in information technology. Other developments, such as the opening up to capitalism of China and the ex-Soviet Union, have also prompted reflection on established designs and practices, resulting in more flexible approaches to organization design.

BRIEFCASE 2.4

Don't Forget the Context   Principles of scientific management and administration assume that there is 'one best way' of organizational design. But this 'closed systems' thinking disregards the variability of context. It suggests that the contingencies facing the retail division of a conglomerate are equivalent to those of a manufacturing division; or that the same principles are appropriately applied to the design of the financial procedures for an entrepreneurial internet firm like eBay or Google as that of a large food processing plant. Contingency means that what structure or system is viable depends upon the particular circumstances or context of its design. For organizations to be effective, this logic suggests, there must be a 'goodness of fit' between the 'structural' and 'contextual' dimensions (see Counterpoint 2.4).[22] What works effectively varies according to circumstances, which are themselves subject to change. For example, an inflexible mechanistic approach may be viable in a setting that is unchanging; but it cannot be expected to work as effectively in a different, more complex or turbulent setting. Where there is a predictable environment and the use of a routine technology, a 'classical' approach based on bureaucratic control procedures, a hierarchical structure and formal communication may be sustainable, at least so long as there is no significant change in the context. But unchanging contexts are becoming less common. For most organizations, at least some aspect of their environment is uncertain; and this uncertainty can stimulate a greater degree of innovation and flexibility where more free-flowing management processes are likely to develop. In short, and against the 'one best way' philosophy, a contingent approach suggests that the correct management approach depends on the organization's (changing) situation.

COUNTERPOINT 2.4

The claim that an approach is 'correct' should be heeded with some caution. Even if a 'good fit' between an organization and its environment is attained this does not necessarily make it 'correct' in the sense of legitimate. It would therefore be better to say that the approach is 'viable'. Whether it is 'correct' will depend upon what evaluation is made of the 'best fit'. It should not be assumed that the pragmatic test of 'best fit' is the only criteria of 'correctness'. So, for example, the 'fit' may be good but the possible negative impact upon the quality of life of employees may lead them to contest its 'correctness'.

Contemporary Organization Design

To a great extent, managers and organizations are still imprinted with the hierarchical, bureaucratic approach that arose more than a century ago. Yet numerous challenges – of globalization, diversity, ethical concerns, rapid advances in technology, the rise of e-business, a shift to knowledge and information as an increasingly important form of capital, and the growing expectations of workers for meaningful work and opportunities for personal and professional growth – prompt a questioning of the adequacy of forms of classical thinking. The perspectives of the past do not necessarily provide a road map for managing and developing today's organizations. In the contemporary context, managers are endeavouring to design and orchestrate new responses that, in general, are less mechanical and more organic in formulation.

Newtonian science suggests that the world functions as a well-behaved machine, a view that has underpinned much management thinking about organizations.[23] The science of chaos theory, in contrast, suggests that relationships in complex, adaptive systems – including organizations – are nonlinear and made up of numerous interconnections and divergent choices.[24] This is a world full of uncertainty, characterized by surprise, rapid change and confusion. Managers can't measure, predict or control in traditional ways the unfolding drama inside or outside the organization. At the same time, chaos theory suggests that randomness and disorder occur within certain larger patterns of order.

In order to make quick decisions, many organizations are being redesigned and/or developed to become so-called learning organizations. The principle of the learning organization is for communication and collaboration to be actively promoted so that everyone is engaged in identifying and solving problems, enabling the organization to continuously experiment, improve and increase its capability. The learning organization is, in principle, based on equality, open information, little hierarchy and a culture that encourages adaptability and participation, enabling ideas to bubble up from anywhere that can help the organization seize opportunities and handle crises. In a learning organization, the essential value is problem solving, as opposed to the traditional organization designed for predictable outcomes. However, as the various Counterpoints provided earlier in this chapter and in Chapter 1 imply, it is much easier to aspire to becoming a 'learning organization' than to achieve this. This is not least because it requires senior managers to release some control, and for employees to take responsibility for it without compensation or even the formal authority required to engage in problem solving.

Efficient Performance versus the Learning Organization

As managers and their staff struggle toward the learning organization, they are engaged in changing the structural dimensions of organizations. Exhibit 2.7 compares organizations designed for efficient performance with those designed for continuous learning by considering five elements of organization design: structure, tasks, systems, culture and strategy. As shown in the exhibit, all of the elements are interconnected and influence one another.

BRIEFCASE 2.5

From Vertical to Horizontal Structure The most common organizational structure, based upon classical principles, has been one in which activities are grouped together by common work from the bottom to the top of the organization. Generally, little collaboration occurs across

EXHIBIT 2.7 Two Ideal-Type Organization Design Approaches

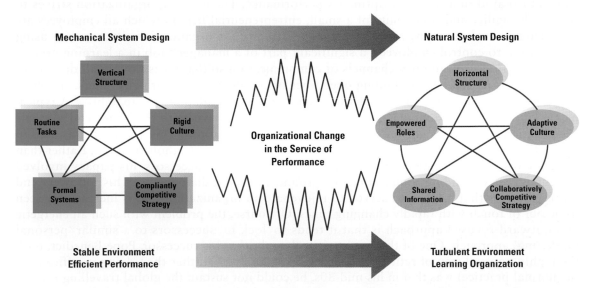

Source: Adapted from David K. Hurst, *Crisis and Renewal: Meeting the Challenge of Organizational Change*. Boston, MA.: Harvard Business School Press, 1995.

functional departments, and the whole organization is coordinated and controlled through the chain of command provided by a vertical hierarchy, with decision-making authority residing with upper-level managers. In stable conditions, this structure is consistent with cost-efficient production and in-depth skill development. In a rapidly changing environment, however, the absence of delegation results in top executives becoming overloaded with decision-making as they struggle to respond sufficiently rapidly to problems or opportunities.

In the learning organization, the vertical structure that creates distance between managers at the top of the organization and workers in the technical core is, in principle, collapsed if not disbanded. Structure is created around horizontal workflows or processes rather than departmental functions. The vertical hierarchy is dramatically flattened, with perhaps only a few senior executives in traditional support functions such as finance or human resources. Self-directed teams are the fundamental work unit in the learning organization. Boundaries between functions are eroded as teams include members from several functional areas.

From Routine Tasks to Empowered Roles   Another shift in thinking relates to the degree of formal structure and control placed on employees in the performance of their work. Recall that scientific management advocated precisely defining each job and how it should be performed. A task is a narrowly defined piece of work assigned to a person. In traditional organizations, tasks are broken down into specialized, separate parts, as in a machine. Knowledge and control of tasks are centralized at the top of the organization, and employees are expected to do as they are told. A role, in contrast, is a part in a dynamic social system. A role-holder has discretion and responsibility, allowing the person to use his or her discretion and ability to achieve an outcome or meet a goal. In principle, within learning organizations, employees play roles in teams or departments, and these roles may be continually redefined or adjusted. There are comparatively few rules or procedures, and knowledge and immediate control of tasks are located with workers rather than with supervisors or top executives. Employees are encouraged to take care of problems by working with one another and with customers.

From Formal Control Systems to Shared Information   In mechanical designs, formal systems are often implemented to manage the growing amount of complex information and to detect deviations from established standards and goals.[25] In learning organizations, in contrast, information serves a very different purpose. In principle, much information is accessible and shared in a way that optimizes performance. The learning organization strives to restore the agility and community of a small, entrepreneurial firm in which all employees are knowledgeable about many aspects of the operation of the organization. Rather than using information to control employees, a significant part of a manager's job in a learning organization is to find ways to open channels of communication so that ideas flow in all directions. A premium is placed on maintaining open lines of communication with customers, suppliers and even competitors in order to enhance their learning and adaptation capabilities. A typical means of leading by example is for managers to pay regular visits to the 'sharp end' of their organizations to gain insights into the realities of daily operations. This approach was used to great effect by the late Pope John Paul II in his leadership of the Catholic Church. Rather than remain cloistered in Rome in the tradition of many of his predecessors, his papacy involved a seemingly never-ending round of on-the-ground visits and dialogue with his followers and representatives that has helped served to rejuvenate an organization that is increasingly seen to be out of touch with rapidly changing times. Of course, the problem with such an energetic and outward-focused approach is that it tends to 'lock in' successors to a similar 'personal marketing' approach. One of the reasons it is thought that his successor, Pope Benedict, took the highly unusual step of retiring from the papacy in 2013 (rather than dying in office as is the normal practice) was that in his mid-80s, he could not sustain the global travelling routine (see Counterpoint 2.5).

COUNTERPOINT 2.5

Others have suggested that he lacked the strength to address scandals within the Vatican. His resignation may then be seen as a courageous falling upon his own sword, with the intention of those responsible for scandals and/or their cover-up being removed by his successor.[26]

From Competitive to Collaborative Strategy

In organizations designed according to classical, mechanistic principles, strategy is formulated by top managers and imposed on the organization. Top executives think about how the organization can best respond to competition and efficiently use resources. In the learning organization, in contrast, organic design principles demand the accumulated actions of an informed and empowered workforce to contribute to strategy development. If all employees are in touch with customers, suppliers and new technology, they are well placed to identify needs and solutions and participate in strategy making, and mutually beneficial insights can also be gained from partnerships with suppliers, customers and even competitors. Boundaries between organizations are becoming more diffuse, with companies participating in industry forums to exchange ideas and assessments that are of shared interest, and in forming partnerships to compete globally, sometimes joining in modular or virtual network organizations that are connected electronically.

From Rigid to Adaptive Culture

Organizations that have been highly successful in fairly stable environments – for example, where they dominate the market to produce stability – can become victims of their own success when circumstances change and their dominance fades as their culture as well as their mechanical structures are found to be ill-equipped to respond to new challenges. America's Xerox Corporation is a comparable example to that of Philips discussed in Chapter 1. Over many years, Xerox established a highly successful photocopier machine business but this failed to capitalize upon its R&D activity that had spawned such innovations as the personal computer, graphical user interface, ethernet and laser printer. Xerox was also unprepared for the entry of Japanese rivals, such as Canon and Ricoh, that competed on quality as well as price. After a disastrous diversification into insurance and financial services, the company recovered by developing digital copiers, but did not anticipate either the increased use of email or the introduction of cheap desktop printers. In an effort to reverse the tide, Xerox CEO, Paul Allaire, recruited as his successor Richard Thoman, then Louis Gerstner's right-hand man at IBM. Thoman came to Xerox as president, chief operating officer and eventually CEO, amid high hopes that the company could regain the stature of its glory years. Only 13 months later, as revenues and the stock price continued to slide, he was fired by Allaire, who had remained as Xerox chairman. Allaire and Thoman blamed each other for the failure to successfully implement their strategy. Outsiders, however, believe the failure had much more to do with Xerox's culture. It was resistant to adaptation, and some say that under Allaire it became almost totally paralyzed by politics. Thoman was brought in to shake things up. When he tried, the old guard rebelled. A management struggle developed, with the outsider Thoman and a few allies on one side lined up against Allaire and his group of insiders who were accustomed to doing things the Xerox way. Ideas and practices that helped attain success were detrimental to effective performance in a rapidly changing environment.

In a more adaptive culture ostensibly, characteristic of a learning organization, there is, in principle, greater emphasis upon openness, equality, continuous improvement and change. People are encouraged to become aware of the whole system, how everything fits together, and how the various parts of the organization interact with one another and with the environment. Treating everyone with care and respect is intended to create a climate in which people feel safe to experiment, take risks and make mistakes, all of which encourages learning. This whole system mindset aspires to minimize boundaries within the organization and with other companies. But, as we have already noted, changing in this direction can be painful and effectively resisted by groups determined to defend an approach with which they are comfortable and are better able to manipulate to their advantage. One organization that is transforming into a learning organization is Mexico's Cementos Mexicanos (Cemex), which is discussed in the *In Practice* box below.

IN PRACTICE

Cementos Mexicanos

Cementos Mexicanos (Cemex), based in Monterrey, Mexico, has been making and delivering concrete for nearly a century. But the organization is on the cutting edge of organization design, a model of what it takes to succeed in the complex environment of the twenty-first century.

Cemex specializes in delivering concrete in developing areas of the world, places where anything can, and often does, go wrong. Even in Monterrey, Cemex copes with unpredictable weather and traffic conditions, spontaneous labour disruptions, building permit snafus and arbitrary government inspections of construction sites. In addition, more than half of all orders are changed or cancelled by customers, usually at the last minute. Considering that a load of concrete is never more than 90 minutes from spoiling, those chaotic conditions mean high costs, complex scheduling and frustration for employees, managers and customers.

To help the organization compete in this environment, managers looked for both technological and organizational innovations. Leaders call their new approach 'living with chaos'. Rather than trying to change the customers, Cemex resolved to do business on the customers' own terms and design a system in which last-minute changes and unexpected problems are routine.[27]

A core element of this approach is a complex information technology system, including a global positioning satellite system and onboard computers in all delivery trucks, which is fed with streams of day-to-day data on customer orders, production schedules, traffic problems, weather conditions and so forth. Now Cemex trucks head out every morning to cruise the streets. When a customer order comes in, an employee checks the customer's credit status, locates a nearby truck and relays directions for delivery. If the order is cancelled, computers automatically direct the plant to scale back production.

Cemex also made managerial and organizational changes to support the new approach. The company enrolled all its drivers, who had an average of six years of formal schooling, in weekly secondary-education classes and began training them in delivering not just cement but quality service. In addition, many strict and demanding work rules were abolished so that workers had more discretion and responsibility for identifying and rapidly responding to problems and customer needs. As a result, Cemex trucks now operate as self-organizing business units, run by well-trained employees who think like business people. According to Francisco Perez, operations manager at Cemex in Guadalajara, 'They used to think of themselves as drivers. But anyone can deliver concrete. Now our people know that they're delivering a service that the competition cannot deliver.'

Cemex has transformed the industry by combining extensive networking technology with a new management approach that taps into the mind power of everyone in the company. People at Cemex are constantly learning – on the job, in training classes and through visits to other organizations. As a result, the company has a startling capacity to anticipate customer needs, solve problems and innovate quickly. In addition, Cemex freely shares what it knows with other organizations, even competitors, believing the widespread sharing of knowledge and information is the best way to keep the organization thriving in a world of complexity. This philosophy has helped transform a once-sleepy cement company into a global powerhouse, with over 25 000 employees on four continents, and nearly 3000 operating units in 22 countries.[28]

One priority for Cemex in the next few years will be to reduce its environmental footprint. Cement production is an energy intensive process and can also

▶

pollute the environment. Cemex has had its own share of criticism for polluting plants – particularly in the US – but has been acknowledged for its serious efforts to increase sustainability and reduce pollutive by-products in production. In 2010, the US Environmental Protection Agency gave Cemex USA an Energy Star award for the second year in a row, because of its outstanding energy management and reductions in greenhouse gas emissions. However, even pollution reduction sometimes comes with a price tag attached; the company has closed down a number of its most inefficient and polluting plants in order to meet environmental targets.

The company has been hit by the long downturn in the building sector in the Global Financial Crisis, initially in the US and Europe and more recently in China. As a result, the company embarked on a widespread divestiture programme, particularly of smaller national units such as in south-east Asia and smaller European companies like Ireland. This provided the company with more cashflow and 2015 EBITDA profits rose for the first time for several years.[29]

Summary and Interpretation

One important idea in this chapter is that organizations have been conceived as systems that either adapt to, or exert control over, the environment as a means of pursuing the goals of their dominant stakeholders. When understood in this way, different parts of the organization – identified as the technical core, technical support, administrative support and management are seen to perform key subsystem functions of production, maintenance, management, adaptation and boundary spanning.

As the context of organizations becomes more turbulent and complex, managers and organizations face a range of intertwined challenges which include coping with globalization; maintaining high standards of ethics and social responsibility; achieving rapid response to environmental changes, organizational crises or new customer expectations; shifting to a technology-based workplace; and supporting diversity. These challenges are tending to prompt a shift away from highly structured systems based on a mechanical model toward looser, more flexible systems based on a more organic model. At the very least, less rigid elements are being incorporated into structured, hierarchical systems with the intention that improved communications and responsiveness will reduce costs, improve competitiveness and thereby produce added value for shareholders. One symptom of this change is the interest in redesigning companies toward the ideal of the 'learning organization' in which there is an aspiration to develop a more horizontal structure, more empowered employees, greater sharing of information, a collaborative form of strategy and a culture that enables more rapid adaptation to changing circumstances. However, the immediate pressures "to do more with less" means that there is a defensive resistance to greater collaboration when it is experience or anticipated as damaging rather than empowering.

KEY CONCEPTS

administrative principles	chaos theory	Hawthorne Studies	stakeholder
bureaucratic organizations	classical perspective	learning organization	stakeholder approach
	contingency	open system	structural dimensions
closed system	effectiveness	role	subsystems
contextual dimensions	efficiency	scientific management	task

Discussion Questions

1   What is the difference between an open system and a closed system? Can you give an example of a closed system? How is the stakeholder approach related to the concept of an open system?

2   Use an example of an organization with which you are familiar to explain how Mintzberg's five basic parts of the organization perform the subsystem functions shown at the bottom of Exhibit 2.1. Evaluate the strengths and limitations of Mintzberg's perspective.

3   Assess the pros and cons of systems thinking for guiding management practice.

4   What is the difference between formalization and specialization? Assess the usefulness of these concepts for understanding the practice of organizing.

5   What does *contingency* mean? What are the implications of contingency theories for managers?

6   What are the primary differences between an organization designed for predictable outputs and one designed for learning and change? What challenges of management are associated with these designs? Discuss.

7   Why is shared information so important in a learning organization as compared to a predictable outputs organization? Discuss how an organization's approach to information sharing might be related to other elements of organization design, such as structure, tasks, strategy and culture.

8   What are some differences one might expect among stakeholder expectations for a nonprofit organization versus a for-profit business? Do you think nonprofit managers have to pay more attention to stakeholders than do business managers? Discuss.

9   Early management theorists believed that organizations should strive to be logical and rational, with a place for everything and everything in its place. Discuss the pros and cons of this approach for today's organizations.

Chapter 2 Workbook Measuring Dimensions of Organizations

Analyze two organizations along the dimensions shown below. Indicate where you think each organization would fall on each of the scales. Use an X to indicate the first organization and an * to show the second.

You may choose any two organizations you are familiar with, such as your place of work, the university, a student organization, your local community organization or church, or your family.

	Formalization	
Many written rules	1 2 3 4 5 6 7 8 9 10	Few rules
	Specialization	
Separate tasks and roles	1 2 3 4 5 6 7 8 9 10	Overlapping tasks
	Hierarchy	
Tall hierarchy of authority	1 2 3 4 5 6 7 8 9 10	Flat hierarchy of authority
	Technology	
Product	1 2 3 4 5 6 7 8 9 10	Service
	External environment	
Stable	1 2 3 4 5 6 7 8 9 10	Unstable

	Culture	
Clear norms and values	1 2 3 4 5 6 7 8 9 10	Ambiguous norms and values
	Professionalism	
High professional training	1 2 3 4 5 6 7 8 9 10	Low professional training
	Goals	
Well-defined goals	1 2 3 4 5 6 7 8 9 10	Goals not defined
	Size	
Large	1 2 3 4 5 6 7 8 9 10	Small
	Organizational mindset	
Mechanical system	1 2 3 4 5 6 7 8 9 10	Biological system

Questions

1 What are the main differences between the two organizations you evaluated?

2 Would you recommend that one or both of the organizations have different ratings on any of the scales? Why?

CASE FOR ANALYSIS 2.1

Developing a Human Centric Vision at Fujitsu.

This short case study will offer you the opportunity to explore three key aspects of organizational design, namely:

1 To understand the complexities of developing creative people within a company organization.

2 To examine the practical strategies to be implemented during the process of building learning organizations.

3 To explore some of the techniques needed to manage an organization in an increasingly challenging global business environment.

You will benefit by understanding the characteristics of the new intrapreneurial employees, learn how to start to build the conditions for a successful creative vision and develop an insight into how organizational development can be encouraged and sustained.

The case study will consider many of the practical and strategic challenges facing an organization as it attempts to develop creative ideas on how to motivate, manage and encourage new behaviours.

A broad definition of creativity could be the starting point and it can be defined as the examination and implementation of new thinking within an organization. Alternatively, creative new projects can be perceived as part of a contemporary managerial perspective that helps to support new innovative ideas and to breathe new life into existing business models. The original momentum that builds a successful organization has to be sustained but without a competent organizational development strategy to encourage it and to engage people across the company this may prove impossible.

The expectation will be that you have your own perspective on how organizational development can play a significant role in your organization and you are to be urged to consider how the ideas and concepts within this chapter can be effectively applied to your organisation in the future.

The ideas for improvement may start on a small scale within a strategic business unit, human resource function, operational department or country but the lessons could be shared across the whole of Fujitsu. This business has created a culture, which can adapt effectively to the changing global business environment around it. The business has an operating core built around the concept of digital transformation and has a clear set of goals and strategies, which influence behaviour across the business. The organization is quite large and multi-national but through the clever use of the concept of communities, it has developed a business which can respond and learn from its partners and customer groups. Improved performance and effectiveness are at the centre of the operations of Fujitsu and this is evidenced by the focus on knowledge management techniques and the promotion of action learning across the business. The stakeholder concept is in evidence within Fujitsu because of the development of internal and external communities, which enhance the learning process within the company and develop new collaborative projects across the globe. Fujitsu and the ICL business before in the United Kingdom were always at the forefront of contemporary organization design, leading the way in the development of learning organization, empowerment and shared information initiatives.

The case study includes a series of exercises and questions to assist you and your colleagues to consider how a new human centric vision can be identified, encouraged and developed in a more strategic manner within your organization.

Company

The search for creativity, innovation and enjoyment in Fujitsu has taken many forms and includes the desire to provide each employee with the opportunity to develop a set of skills and build a relevant knowledge base of the business environment and within the company. Fujitsu believe that technology is transforming the world. Digital technologies such as the Internet of Things and Artificial Intelligence are changing the way people work, making processes more efficient and helping create innovative new products and services.

This is stated as a digital transformation and the people within Fujitsu are empowered to help companies to achieve this objective in a creative and efficient manner.

These technologies connect businesses with new partners, enabling them to collaborate and innovate across existing boundaries. If they want to outperform the competition, today's business leaders must integrate the concept of digital transformation into every aspect of their corporate strategies and organizational design.

Fujitsu has a clear mission to assist their customers so that they can achieve digital transformation.

The business wants to be the customer's business partner, and help them on their journey of transformation.

Last year, Fujitsu began providing a digital business platform called MetaArc.

This is a cloud-based platform that enables customers to use digital technologies to grow and develop their future businesses.

They also deliver services which integrate the latest technologies on this platform, to help realize digital transformation. The company attempts to focus on their customers' business goals and work in collaborative project teams to achieve these goals.

This strategic and customer focused approach is what helps to make Fujitsu different from its competitors in the sector.

Fujitsu has been striving towards a "Human Centric" vision for some time.

This means putting people at the core of everything the company tries to achieve.

Advances in artificial intelligence are accelerating, which means that the company is focused on developing services that can be more automated in the future.

Projects

These are some of the projects that Fujitsu are pioneering, in an effort to enhance their own talent base, play a more significant role corporate social responsibility and develop new tools for the future through action learning.

Corporate Social Responsibility Projects

The Youth at Risk project is a community–based initiative within the company, which focused on the need to develop a link with the local youth and to understand their needs and refocus their energies towards society instead of against it. The involvement of seconded people from Fujitsu has greatly enhanced the development opportunities within the company and increased the confidence and enjoyment of the people involved in the initiative. The focus of improvements in enjoyment has to have a personal and corporate element and provide advantages for everyone involved in the project.

As well as community and involvement and development, Fujitsu focuses on environmental initiatives, diversity and inclusion projects, wellbeing projects for their employees across the company and high quality operating practices.

Internal & External Professional Communities

The development of many professional communities across the company has been launched to develop a greater sense of focus and an enhancement of the networking capabilities with the company. A series of communities across the business landscape of Fujitsu has helped the achievement of new business development targets within the company.

These communities are supported by the knowledge community, which can help the company to develop a specialized set of technical skills and models to assist the new venture managers in tackling complex business problems. This support activity can assist the business in developing a set of competencies that can enable a flexible and cross-functional method of working to develop. The Distinguished Fellows Scheme for example, allows the highly skilled engineers to spend time externally to the company, developing their credibility within the sector and developing a network of contacts to start the process of business development in the future.

These concepts are designed to develop the personal aspirations of everyone within these communities and to enhance the level of cross-functional cooperation that exists throughout the business. The background to these initiatives is focused on removing barriers to success and enhancing the managerial and business chances of managing complexity and the difficulties of achieving global reach.

Action Learning at Fujitsu

The introduction of action learning across the company has enhanced the enjoyment of people within the new venture and project teams. The education of people within the company has a clear link with the encouragement of these management teams to build high value customer relationships and eventually communicating with the customers' customer through expert advice and a range of innovative services focussed on digital transformation.

The challenges in this digital era: the company has to consider how technology will empower people to work more creatively and maximize their full personal potential. Fujitsu's technology and services attempt to support everyday life, helping both employees and customers to live more creative and fuller business lives.

In recent years, Fujitsu Services have won the personnel Today Intellect Award for Innovation in Career Development in recognition of its Account Management Academy. Fujitsu developed the Account Management Academy to assess its employees' future potential, rather than analyzing past performance alone and develop those people who are successful by equipping themselves with the skills needed to perform within an account management role.

Case Questions

EXERCISE 1: How would your organization define a human centric vision?

Consider some of the following questions to start the thinking process:

Q1 How does your organization define organizational development?

Q2 Can you provide 3 examples of creative actions within your human resource function that have been clearly recognized by other functions within the business as making an effective contribution to business performance?

Q3 Can you provide 3 examples of creative actions within any other functions that you consider have made a valuable contribution to business performance?

Q4 Ask an independent observer of your organization (non H.R.M.) to review the results of your analysis.

Exercise Review:

Convene a short workshop meeting for a maximum of one hour to discuss the following question:

The human resource team may lead the discussion within the meeting:

Examine the impact that effective organizational design has had on your ability to create a human centric vision within your company.

Notes

1. James D. Thompson, *Organizations in Action* (New York: McGraw-Hill, 1967), 4–13.

2. Henry Mintzberg, *The Structuring of Organizations* (Englewood Cliffs, NJ: Prentice-Hall, 1979), 215–297; and Henry Mintzberg, 'Organization Design: Fashion or Fit?' *Harvard Business Review* 59 (January–February 1981), 103–116.

3. The following discussion was heavily influenced by Richard H. Hall, *Organizations: Structures, Processes, and Outcomes* (Englewood Cliffs, NJ: Prentice-Hall, 1991); D. S. Pugh, 'The Measurement of Organization Structures: Does Context Determine Form?' *Organizational Dynamics* 1 (Spring 1973), 19–34; and D. S. Pugh, D. J. Hickson, C. R. Hinings and C. Turner, 'Dimensions of Organization Structure', *Administrative Science Quarterly* 13 (1968), 65–91.

4. Frederic Laloux (2014), *Reinventing Organizations*: A Guide to Creating Organizations Inspired by the Next Stage in Human Consciousness, Brussels, Nelson Parker.

5. Malcolm Gladwell (2000), 'The Tipping Point: How Little Things Can Make a Big Difference', New York, Little Brown. *Press Association*, 14 November, 2012, 'Great Place to Work Unveils World's Best Multinational Workplaces', Gary Hamel; March 18, 2010, 'W.L. Gore: Lessons from a Management Revolutionary', *Wall Street Journal*.

6. Matthew Curtin, Carrefour's cares, *The Edge Malaysia*, November 1, 2004; John Ryan, 'World-class Retailer –Carrefour drives down the road to domination', *Retail Week*, May 12, 2000, Pg.17; Rozenn Perrigot and Gérard Cliquet, 'Hypermarket Format: Any Future or a Real Need to Be Changed? An Empirical Study of the French, Spanish and Italian markets', paper presented at 5th International Marketing Trends Congress, Venice, 20–21 January, 2006; 'Q4 2006 Carrefour S.A. Earnings Presentation – Final', *Fair Disclosure Wire*, March 8, 2007.

7. For a description of the corporate team building activities offered by Act On Info, see their website at http://theatreeducation.co.uk/workshops-for-adults/teambuilding-events/.On sharing space, see Chris Unitt 29th November, 2010, 'Sharing office space at arts organizations in Birmingham', Created in Birmingham, available at http://www.createdinbirmingham.com/2010/11/29/sharing-officespace-at-arts-organisations-in-birmingham/. On the Arts Council of Wales and Arts NGOs resistance to cutbacks, see Abby Alford (June 30, 2010), 'Arts Council to Withdraw Funding to 32 Groups', *Western Mail*; the Arts Council of Wales investment review website at http://www.artswales.org.uk/what-we-do/funding/investmentreview, Creu Cymru, July 26, 2009, 'A position paper on theatre and arts centres across Wales', Veronica German, February 18, 2011, 'Arts Council of Wales Investment Review hits South Wales East hardest', available at http://www.veronicagerman.org.uk/tag/gwent-theatre/. National Assembly for Wales Communities and Culture Committee, February 2011, *The accessibility of arts and cultural activities in Wales*.

8. Thomas Catan, 22 June, 2011, 'Gore-Tex Faces Antitrust Probes', *The Wall Street Journal*. Mike Kessler (2012), 'Gore-Tex Under Siege from Waterproof Fabric Newcomers', *Outdoor Magazine*, April.

9. T. Donaldson and L. E. Preston, 'The Stakeholder Theory of the Corporation: Concepts, Evidence and Implications', *Academy of Management Review* 20 (1995), 65–91; Anne S. Tusi, 'A Multiple-Constituency Model of Effectiveness: An Empirical Examination at the Human Resource Subunit Level', *Administrative Science Quarterly* 35 (1990), 458–483; Charles Fombrun and Mark Shanley, 'What's in a Name? Reputation Building and Corporate Strategy', *Academy of Management Journal* 33 (1990), 233–258; Terry Connolly, Edward J. Conlon and Stuart Jay Deutsch, 'Organizational Effectiveness: A Multiple-Constituency Approach', *Academy of Management Review* 5 (1980), 211–217.

10. Charles Fishman, 'The Wal-Mart You Don't Know – Why Low Prices Have a High Cost', *Fast Company* (December 2003), 68–80.

11. Anne S. Tusi, 'A Multiple-Constituency Model of Effectiveness: An Empirical Examination at the Human Resource Subunit Level', *Administrative Science Quarterly* 35 (1990), 458–483.

12. Charles Fombrun and Mark Shanley, 'What's in a Name? Reputation Building and Corporate Strategy', *Academy of Management Journal* 33 (1990), 233–258.

13. Forest Products Association of Canada, *Annual Report 2007*, p. 16–17.

14. Rod Mickleburgh, 'There's nothing more. The town is dying,' *The Globe and Mail*, May 17, 2008, Pg. S3.

15. Joel Connelly, 'Conservationists Want to Halt Logging on Clayoquot Sound: Summer of Confrontation in British Columbia', *Seattle Post-Intelligencer*, August 30, 1993, Pg. A1.

16. 'Abitibi Bowater to stop logging in Grassy Narrows First Nation territory', Canada NewsWire, June 4, 2008.

17. Monika Winn and Charlene Zietsma (2004), 'The war of the woods: a forestry giant seeks peace', *Greener Management International* 48, 21–37.

18. B&Q policy at http://web.archive.org/web/20090106150441/http://www.diy.com/diy/jsp/aboutbandq/social_responsibility/BQSRTIMB. PDF accessed on 15 September, 2013, Hallmark at http://www.hallmark.co.uk/Global/Images/ReSPECT/SustainabilityPlatformStatement.pdf both accessed on September 15, 2013.

19. L'Express de Madagascar (January 25, 2013) 'Environnement – La gestion durable des forêts certifiée'. Communiqué de presse, 25 Janvier 2013, « VIMA Wood Industry, certifiée FCS®, poursuit son engagement pour une gestion durable des forêts ».

20. Ann Harrington, 'The Big Ideas', *Fortune* (November 22, 1999), 152–154; Robert Kanigel, *The One Best Way: Frederick Winslow Taylor and the Enigma of Efficiency* (New York: Viking, 1997); and Alan Farnham, 'The Man Who Changed Work Forever', *Fortune* (July 21, 1997), 114. For a discussion of the impact of scientific management on American industry, government and nonprofit organizations, also see Mauro F. Guillén, 'Scientific Management's Lost

Aesthetic: Architecture, Organization, and the Taylorized Beauty of the Mechanical', *Administrative Science Quarterly* 42 (1997), 682–715.

21. Amanda Bennett, *The Death of the Organization Man* (New York: William Morrow, 1990).

22. Johannes M. Pennings, 'Structural Contingency Theory: A Reappraisal', *Research in Organizational Behavior* 14 (1992), 267–309.

23. This discussion is based in part on Toby J. Tetenbaum, 'Shifting Paradigms: From Newton to Chaos', *Organizational Dynamics* (Spring 1998), 21–32.

24. Based on Tetenbaum, 'Shifting Paradigms: From Newton to Chaos', and Richard T. Pascale, 'Surfing the Edge of Chaos', *Sloan Management Review* (Spring 1999), 83–94.

25. David K. Hurst, *Crisis and Renewal: Meeting the Challenge of Organizational Change* (Boston, MA: Harvard Business School Press, 1995), 32–52.

26. 'Freeman: Will White Smoke Blow The Developing World's Way?', *Irish Independent*, April 7, 2005. Cheryl Browne, 12 February 2013, 'Pope's plan pondered', *Barrie Examiner*.

27. For more information about Cemex, see www.ssireview.org/pdf/2005SU_feature_sandoval.pdf.

28. Thomas Petzinger, *The New Pioneers: The Men and Women Who Are Transforming the Workplace and Marketplace* (New York: Simon & Schuster, 1999), 91–93; and 'In Search of the New World of Work', *Fast Company* (April 1999), 214–220; Peter Katel, 'Bordering on Chaos', *Wired* (July 1997), 98–107; Oren Harari, 'The Concrete Intangibles', *Management Review* (May 1999), 30–33; and 'Mexican Cement Maker on Verge of a Deal', *The New York Times* (September 27, 2004), A8.

29. Samantha McCaughren, Cemex set to offload Readymix, *Sunday Times*, April 27, 2014, accessed at www.thesundaytimes.co.uk/sto/news/ireland/article1404113.ece; Mexico's Cemex lifts cash flow target, may sell more assets, Reuters, Thu Mar 17, 2016, accessed at uk.reuters.com/article/mexico-cemex-idUKL2N16P0W8.

ORGANIZATIONAL PURPOSE AND STRUCTURAL DESIGN

STRATEGY, ORGANIZATION DESIGN AND EFFECTIVENESS

Starbucks Corporation

Starbucks is one of the world's best known brands. By 2012 the familiar green logo was present in 61 countries, with over 20 000 company-owned and franchised coffee shops around the world.[1] Although several other speciality coffee retailers also established themselves during the 1980s, it was Starbucks that redefined coffee drinking as the emblem of the new class of young urban professionals (yuppies).

The Starbucks phenomenon began in Seattle as a small speciality-coffee retailer, founded in 1971, and named after Captain Ahab's first mate in the book *Moby Dick*. In its early years Starbucks was better known as a coffee bean retailer than coffee shop, but once Howard Schultz took over leadership of the company in 1987, the company never looked back. Starbucks has always pursued a strategy of growth based on promoting its uniqueness. The company doesn't just sell coffee but 'the Starbucks Experience', a phrase that is routinely used in the company's promotional materials, and which is built from its six point mission statement. Developed in 1990, it emphasizes a positive work environment, respect for diversity, excellent product quality, satisfied customers, corporate responsibility and profitability. Schultz has steered Starbucks through tremendous growth, but he emphasizes the company's continuing ambitions to tap into various new markets, new customers and new products and services. Schultz's overall goal is to spur greater growth by transforming Starbucks more broadly into a retail chain rather than just a coffee shop. The company's plans for achieving that overall goal include the following:

- Expand the company's food offerings. In 2005, Starbucks began selling lunch in five new markets, bringing to 2500 the total number of stores offering lunch. Starbucks also successfully tested sales of hot breakfast at its Seattle stores, and has gradually rolled out hot breakfasts elsewhere in the United States.

- Develop the company's entertainment division into a major profit centre. The company's HearMusic brand offers a variety of ways to listen to, and buy music, from traditionally prerecorded CDs to media bars that offer customers the possibility of burning compact discs with their own selection of songs from 15 000 different albums.

- Continue store growth across the world, with 2500 openings in 2008, and an ultimate goal of 40 000 stores (20 000 in the United States and 20 000 in the rest of the world).[2]

The new goals and plans were a bold push beyond Starbucks' coffee roots. Some observers felt the company's foray into music in particular was a mistake, but Schultz and Donald (CEO) believed it fitted right in with Starbucks' strategy. 'Providing our customers with innovative and unique ways to discover and acquire all genres of great music is another way we are enhancing the Starbucks Experience', said Schultz.[3]

Despite their confidence, by early 2008, many market watchers were worried about Starbucks. On the one hand, the company continued to grow impressively fast, and the company remained very profitable. On the other hand, the company's per-store sales have flattened, and other food chains, especially McDonald's, have begun to fight back effectively. For example, McDonald's has begun offering speciality coffee at many of its stores internationally, at prices significantly below those of Starbucks.[4]

Starbucks' rapid growth beyond its original affluent yuppie target audience, into the more cost-sensitive, blue-collar market, mean the chain's revenues are particularly vulnerable to an economic downturn, such as occurred due to the sub-prime mortgage crisis that enveloped the US in 2007 and then spread around the world. During 2007, Starbucks' shares declined by 50 per cent, leading to pressure from shareholders. On January 8, 2008 Starbucks chairman Howard Schultz acted decisively. He fired Jim Donald as CEO (Donald had spearheaded Starbucks's mass-market drive) and re-assumed the position himself, simultaneously announcing store closures and a reduction in the number of openings in the next year. Schultz's keen market sense had paid off in the past. Would his swift action put Starbucks back on track? Initial market reactions were positive; investment analysts felt that Schulz would be able to recapture the Starbucks

▶

'magic'. However, that did not change the overall issues the company faced: an increasingly competitive market, especially in the US, and an enduring economic downturn.

Schulz has paid particular attention to improving the company's food offerings, navigating a tricky path between accessing the additional revenues and customers that a wider food selection can provide, and not turning into another fast food chain.

The company has taken some tough decisions: closing down unprofitable stores in the US and in Europe, although this will be balanced by opening new and often larger outlets in better locations; the company plans 1000 new US stores between 2012 and 2017.

A major part of the new growth strategy involves expanding into the rapidly growing markets in Asia, including China and India. The region 'has been a growth engine and will continue to be a growth engine despite economic uncertainty', says Jinlong Wang, the company's Asia-Pacific president. This involves not merely providing an appealing brand but creating new coffee consumers; in both countries tea has traditionally been the hot drink of choice for most. It is a strategy that appears to be reaping benefits; the company's Asia-Pacific revenues grew nearly 30 per cent in 2012 alone. The company is planning to increase the number of branches in China from 700 in 2013 to 1500 by 2015. Although Asia-Pacific is still a relatively small market (accounting for ten per cent of staff and maybe seven per cent of revenues), there is potential not just in China and India, but also new Asian Tigers such as Vietnam, where the company opened a 4000 square foot flagship outlet in Ho Chi Minh City.

Of course, Starbucks is not the only coffee company with an eye on the Asia-Pacific; Italy's Lavazza and Britain's Costa Coffee are right on Starbucks' heels, opening outlets across the region.

One area that Starbucks has to watch carefully is corporate social responsibility and corporate citizenship. Like most market leaders, the company is the target of particular scrutiny by activists, and its presence on main streets and in shopping centres around the world mean that it is easy to raise public consciousness about a problem. In comparison with other major coffee chains, Starbucks was relatively slow to acknowledge the importance of fairtrade relationships with developing country coffee suppliers; this is an area where the company continues to endure criticism. Starbucks is often faced with lobbying demands from both sides of the spectrum that can be very difficult to satisfy. In the United States in 2012, for example, the company announced that it supports same sex marriage, which delighted liberals but infuriated the Christian right; conversely, the company has angered anti-gun campaigners by permitting customers to enter its stores with concealed firearms in the US states where this is legal.

A major issue facing the company in recent years has been how to deal with accusations that it manages its tax affairs in order to minimize the tax it pays, to the detriment of the countries where it operates. In 2013, it emerged that the company's British operations had paid only £8.6 million in corporate taxes in 14 years of operations in the UK, despite having accumulated revenues of over £3 billion; an effective tax rate on revenues of less than one third of one per cent. The company apparently relied on a variety of tax reduction strategies including realizing profits in low-taxed jurisdictions even though revenues are realized in other higher taxed locations, and paying the US firm 'royalties' on each coffee sold outside the US to reflect the value of the Starbucks 'concept'. These explanations and Starbucks' offer to unilaterally pay £20 million in tax per year in 2012–2014 did not satisfy British politicians, press, or public opinion. In 2015, the European Union ruled that the sweetheart tax deals Starbucks and Italian car manufacturer Fiat had struck to pay lower taxes in certain EU countries were illegal subsidies, and ordered the companies to repay the countries concerned.[5] The tax controversy, which has also enveloped other major multinationals such as Amazon, highlights growing consumer sophistication as well as the double-edged sword that image marketing creates – it is not enough for companies to say they are good; they have to prove this is the case by their actions.[6]

Top managers are most directly responsible for positioning their organizations for success by establishing goals and strategies that can help the organization be competitive as a necessary, but not in itself sufficient, condition of being profitable. An organizational goal is a desired state of affairs or outcome that members of an organization are entreated to reach.[7] A goal represents a result or end point, generally identified by a small elite of executives, toward which it is intended that the efforts of organizational members will be directed. The goals for Starbucks in 2013 included rebalancing the company's outlets to reflect the faster-growing Asia-Pacific markets, increasing food revenues without detracting from the premium coffee focus, and rebuilding an image of corporate citizenship that has been badly affected by revelations about aggressive tax avoidance strategies. The choice of goals and strategy affects organization design, as we will discuss in this chapter.

Purpose of this Chapter

Top managers give direction to organizations. They generally exert the greatest influence in setting goals and developing the plans for their organization to attain those goals, although they may operate within a context over which they can exert limited control, at least in the short term. The purpose of this chapter is to help you understand the types of goals pursued and some of the competitive strategies managers use to reach those goals. We will examine two significant frameworks for determining strategic action and look at how strategies affect organization design. The chapter also describes the most popular approaches to measuring the effectiveness of organizational efforts. To manage organizations well, managers require a clear sense of how to identify and secure effectiveness.

The Role of Strategic Direction in Organization Design

An organization is created to achieve some purpose, which is decided by those who establish and develop it, such as the chief executive officer (CEO) and the top management team. In a for-profit business this is generally in consultation with board members, investors and creditors. It is this purpose and direction that shapes how the organization is designed and managed. Indeed, it is widely held that the primary responsibility of top management is to determine an organization's goals, strategy and design, therein adapting the organization to a changing environment.[8] Middle managers are considered to do much the same thing for major departments within the guidelines provided by top management (see Counterpoint 3.1). The relationships through which top managers typically provide direction and then design are illustrated in Exhibit 3.1.

COUNTERPOINT 3.1

One should treat with caution the tendency to represent organization design as a highly rational process which involves careful calculation and proceeds smoothly through a series of stages. In practice, the design of organizations is a messy, political process in which established routines and vested interests are challenged and defended. Uneasy, hybrid compromises are the more normal outcome. There is therefore likely to be some considerable discrepancy and tension between how the design of organizations is represented by top management – for example, as a neat if complex organization chart – and how organizations operate on a day-to-day basis.

The direction-setting process often involves some assessment of the opportunities and threats in the external environment, including the amount of change, uncertainty and resource availability. These factors are discussed in more detail in Chapter 5. Such assessments include an evaluation of internal strengths and weaknesses to define the organization's distinctive competence compared with other other organizations (e.g. competitors within the industry).[9] The assessment of the internal environment includes an evaluation of the capabilities and potential of each department and is shaped by past performance. The process of defining,

?

ONLINE
COUNTERPOINT 3.1

EXHIBIT 3.1　Top Management Role in Organization Direction, Design and Effectiveness

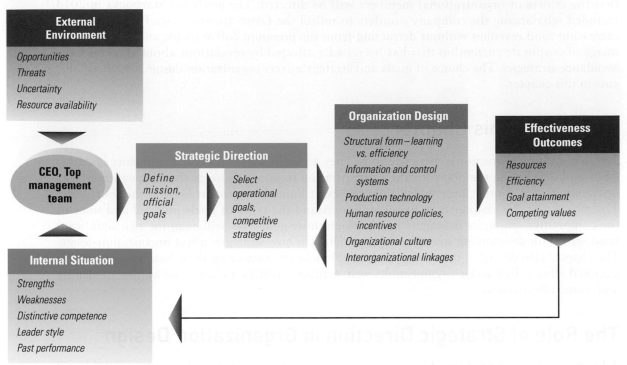

Source: Adapted from Arie Y. Lewin and Carroll U. Stephens, 'Individual Properties of the CEO as Determinants of Organization Design', unpublished manuscript, Duke University, 1990; and Arie Y. Lewin and Carroll U. Stephens, 'CEO Attributes as Determinants of Organization Design: An Integrated Model', *Organization Studies* 15: 2 (1994), 183–212.

reaffirming and/or changing the overall mission and official goals is, in principle, a matter of determining the best fit between external opportunities and threats, on the one hand, and internal strengths, including competencies, on the other. In this light, specific operational goals or strategies can be formulated to define how members of the organization are going to accomplish what is identified as their overall mission.

In Exhibit 3.1, organization design is presented as reflecting the way goals and strategies are implemented. Organization direction is seen to be achieved through decisions about structural form, including whether the design of the organization has a strong learning efficiency orientation as discussed in Chapter 2, as well as choices about information and control systems, the type of production technology, human resource policies, culture and linkages to other organizations. Changes in structure, technology, human resource policies, culture and interorganizational linkages are discussed in subsequent chapters. Also note the arrow in Exhibit 3.1 running from organization design back to strategic direction. This means that strategies are often made within the current structure of the organization, so that current design constrains or puts limits on goals and strategy.

Finally, Exhibit 3.1 illustrates, within a systems theory framework, how managers are conceived to evaluate the effectiveness of organizational efforts – that is, the extent to which the goals attributed to organizations are realized. This chart reflects the most popular ways of measuring performance, each of which is discussed later in this chapter. It is important to note here that performance measurements feed back into the internal environment, so that past performance of the organization is, in principle, taken as a point of reference when setting new goals and strategic direction for the future.

The role of top management is held to be important because managers with different backgrounds, perspectives and priorities can interpret the environment differently and develop different goals. When Daniel Vassella became CEO of the pharmaceutical multinational Novartis, formed from a merger between the Swiss-based companies Sandoz and Ciba-Geigy, he had two initial goals. First, to assure smooth integration in an industry where strong corporate cultures typically cause friction during mergers, and second, to build a long-term growth strategy. Although Sandoz and Ciba-Geigy had good reputations, they were perceived as somewhat complacent. From the outset, Vassella emphasized expanded R&D as a basis for developing new product offerings. In addition, he focused on corporate social responsibility, countering 'big pharma's' reputation as insensitive to the pharmaceutical needs of the poor in developing countries. Nevertheless, in 2014, Novartis's Japanese subsidiary was charged over its staff manipulating data during trials into a blood pressure drug,[10] (see Counterpoint 3.2).[11]

The choices top managers make about goals, strategies and organization design can have a significant impact. Goals and strategy are not fixed or immune to change. But, equally, it is important to appreciate when choices are conditioned as well as constrained. Executives do not operate autonomously. Organization design is used to implement goals and strategy and thereby influences the prospects of success. We will now discuss further the concept of organizational goals and strategy, and in the latter part of this chapter, we discuss various ways to evaluate organizational effectiveness.

COUNTERPOINT 3.2

Throughout the book we often focus on private businesses, or corporations, as if they are the only kind of organization. Of course, as we noted in Chapter 1, this is not true. Public sector and nonprofit ('third sector') organizations are an important part of the economy in almost every country of the world. Especially in Europe, the public and nonprofit sectors can be as large and important as the private sector. For example, in Germany the Catholic welfare association Caritas is the country's largest non-state employer with 350 000 staff,[12] while in most Western European countries the public sector accounts for around 40 per cent of GDP.[13] Many aspects of organization theory and design are shared between different economic sectors, but there are important differences which we try to highlight throughout the text.

Organizational Purpose

All organizations, including Novartis, Oxford University, Fiat Motors, the Roman Catholic Church, the European Commission, the local dry cleaner and the local athletics club, exist for some purpose or it may be several purposes. One major distinction is between the officially stated goals, or mission, of the organization, as communicated by spokespersons such as the CEO, and the operative goals that, in practice, are pursued within the organization by its members.

Mission

The overall, officially stated goal attributed to an organization is often encapsulated in an explicitly stated mission – the organization's reason for its existence. The mission conveys the organization's vision, shared values and beliefs. It can have a powerful impact on an organization.[14] Whether called a mission statement or official goals, the general statement of purpose and philosophy is often written down in a policy manual and/or the annual report. The mission statement for the Japanese multinational company Sumitomo is shown in Exhibit 3.2. Note how the overall vision, principles and operating guidelines are all defined.

EXHIBIT 3.2 Sumitomo's Mission Statement

STATE FARM INSURANCE

Our Mission, Our Vision and Our Shared Values

State Farm's mission is to help people manage the risks of everyday life, recover from the unexpected and realize their dreams.

We are people who make it our business to be like a good neighbour; who built a premier company by selling and keeping promises through our marketing partnerships; who bring diverse talents and experiences to our work of serving the State Farm customer.

Our success is built on a foundation of shared values - quality service and relationships, mutual trust, integrity and financial strength.

Our vision for the future is to be the customer's first and best choice in the products and services we provide. We will continue to be the leader in the insurance industry and we will become a leader in the financial services arena. Our customers' needs will determine our path. Our values will guide us.

Source: 'News and Notes from State Farm'. Public Affairs Department, 2500 Memorial Boulevard, Murfreesboro, TN 37131.

BRIEFCASE 3.1

The *mission statement* communicates to current and prospective employees, customers, investors, suppliers and competitors what the organization stands for and what it is trying to achieve. Most top leaders want employees, customers, competitors, suppliers, investors and the local community to look on them in a favourable light, and the concept of legitimacy plays a critical role.[15] The corporate concern for legitimacy is real and pertinent (see Counterpoint 3.3). Consider the accounting firm, Arthur Andersen, which was accused of obstructing justice by shredding accounting documents related to the Enron investigation. Once the previously respected global firm lost legitimacy with clients, investors and the public, it was all but dead. From 85 000 employees in 2002, by 2007 Arthur Anderson had a skeleton staff of about 200, working mainly on handling the lawsuits against the company and presiding over its orderly dissolution. In the post-Enron environment of weakened trust and increasing regulation, many organizations have sought to redefine their purpose and mission by conveying the firm's purpose in more than financial terms.[16]

COUNTERPOINT 3.3

Although most people agree that mission statements help to focus a company, they are not a panacea for unexpected business downturns, or poor management. Enron, for example, had a mission statement that promised the company would always be 'open and fair' even though corporate managers were ultimately convicted for multi-billion pound fraud![17] While some academic studies have shown companies with mission statements perform better, others have not been able to show such a link. Most likely, it is not so much the mission statement itself that helps a company succeed, but rather the benefit of focusing corporate leadership on defining the organization's purpose.[18]

Operative Goals

Operative goals describe specific measurable outcomes and are often concerned with the short run. Operative goals typically pertain to the primary tasks an organization must perform, similar to the subsystem activities identified in Chapter 2.[19] They provide direction for the day-to-day decisions and activities within departments.

Overall Performance   In for-profit organizations, overall performance goals include profitability, growth and output volume but may extend to other performance measures of reputation, corporate responsibility and so on. Profitability may be expressed in terms of net income, earnings per share or return on investment. Growth pertains to increases in revenues over time. Volume may be measured in total sales or the amount of products or services delivered. For example, in 2006 the global truck manufacturer Volvo aimed to increase sales by 10 per cent annually over a business cycle, while maintaining a focus on profitability. By 2010, with the sales growth achieved through significant expansion, the company refocused on profitability, setting specific goals annually towards the profitability objective.[20]

Government and non-profit organizations such as social service agencies or trade unions do not usually have profitability goals, but they do have goals that attempt to specify the delivery of services to clients, members or other beneficiaries within specified expense levels. The United States Internal Revenue Service has a goal of providing accurate responses to 85 per cent of taxpayer questions about new tax laws. Growth and volume goals also may be indicators of overall performance in non-profit organizations. Expanding their services to new clients is a primary goal for many social service agencies, such as the UK Samaritans, which provides helpline services to people in crisis.

Resources   Resource goals refer to the acquisition of needed material and financial resources from the environment. They may involve obtaining financing for the construction of new plants, finding less expensive sources for raw materials or hiring top-quality technology graduates. Resource goals for the French business school INSEAD include attracting top-notch professors and students. Honda Motor Company has resource goals of obtaining high-quality auto parts at low cost. For the UK's Samaritans NGO, resource goals include recruiting dedicated volunteers and expanding the organization's funding base.

EXHIBIT 3.3   Volvo Transformation Program Delivering Profit Improvement

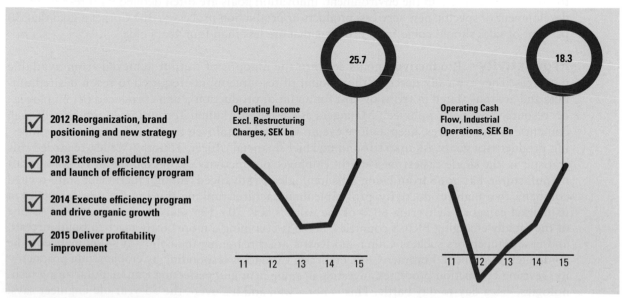

Reference: The Volvo Group Annual and Sustainability Report 2015.

Market   Market goals relate to the market share or market standing desired by the organization. An example of a market goal is Honda's desire to overtake Toyota Motor Company as the number-one seller of cars in Japan. Honda surpassed Nissan to become number two in Japan, and the Fit subcompact,[21] introduced in 2001, briefly eclipsed the Toyota Corolla as the best-selling car in that market, although the Corolla soon regained top spot.[22] In the toy industry, Canada's Mega Bloks Inc. managed to exceed its goal of 30 per cent of the North American construction toy market, and began aggressive international expansion as well as expansion of its product lines. The global giant of the industry, Denmark's Lego, has attempted to stop Mega Bloks' growth internationally[23] through both intellectual property lawsuits (mainly unsuccessful) and by refocusing on its core business.[24] The company has actually fared much better since losing its Canadian Supreme Court case against Mega Bloks in 2010, more than doubling sales by 2015.[25]

Employee Development   Employee development refers to the training, promotion, health and safety and growth of employees. It includes both managers and workers. Strong employee development goals are one of the characteristics common to organizations that regularly show up on lists of the best companies to work for. Spansion, originally a joint chip-making venture between Japan's Fujitsu and the US-based AMD and now an independent concern, has been voted best employer in Asia. Its employees, mainly based in Thailand and China, appreciated the company's commitment to employee development, even though it didn't necessarily pay the highest wages. Its Singaporean CEO, Loh Poh Chye, said, 'We are always willing to offer training to someone who's motivated, or move someone to a new department, laterally, to work across and up in a new area'. Employee development is particularly important in corporations operating internationally in very different local environments, where working cultures may vary considerably while client expectations remain high. Such is the case for international high-end hotel chains. A 2015 study of a global hotel chain operating in Azerbaijan and Kyrgyzstan in the Caucusus and Central Asia regions demonstrated the importance of setting company-wide objectives on human resource management and employee development. Despite the very different labour markets and levels of human resource development, the company's hotels in these sites were able to deliver 5-star service.[26]

Innovation and Change   Innovation goals refer to internal flexibility and readiness to adapt to unexpected changes in the environment. Innovation goals are often defined with respect to the development of specific new services, products or production processes. 3M Co. set a goal that 30 per cent of sales should come from products that are less than four years old.[27]

Productivity   Productivity goals concern the amount of output achieved from available resources. They typically describe the amount of resource inputs required to reach desired outputs and are thus stated in terms of 'cost for a unit of production', 'units produced per employee', or 'resource cost per employee'. Managers at US-based Akamai Technologies, which sells web content delivery services, keep a close eye on sales per employee to see if the company is meeting productivity goals. Akamai's founding chief financial officer, Timothy Weller, regarded this statistic as 'the single easiest measure of employee productivity'. Embraer, the Brazilian aircraft manufacturer, has gone from being a technologically advanced, though inefficient state-owned company, to a high-productivity, profitable manufacturer ranking third in the world in sales in its market category, delivering 60% of the world's new 70 - 135 seats aircraft in 2014.[28] As one of the rapidly emerging BRICS countries, Brazil is becoming a more costly place to build aircraft, and new competitors such as China and Russia are threatening the company's dominance in the commuter-jet segment. Embraer CEO, Frederico Curado, is responding by emphasizing productivity: revising production processes, investing in equipment and perfecting lean manufacturing technologies, 'It's a day-to-day battle. This is not a war, and it's over', the 55-year-old engineer says. In addition, the company is hiring staff earlier in their careers, at moderate salary levels.[29] Once the wings and landing gear are attached, each plane is dragged toward the door at two inches a minute, with workers moving along with it on a floatlike apparatus. Of course, competitors don't sit still either – Embraer's giant US rival, Boeing, has a productivity goal to push a 737 jet out of the door in five days, down from the 11 days that it currently takes.[30]

LEADING BY DESIGN

Wegmans

Supermarkets aren't typically considered great places to work. The pay is low, the hours are gruelling, and you don't get much appreciation from anyone. Most supermarkets have annual staff turnover rates of 19 to 20 per cent and as much as 100 per cent for part-timers. But the situation is different at Wegmans, an American chain of 67 stores in New York, Pennsylvania, New Jersey and Virginia. Annual staff turnover is just six per cent for full-time employees. About 6000 Wegmans workers have at least ten years of service, and more than 800 have worked at Wegmans stores for a quarter of a century.

Wegmans is one of the most successful supermarket chains in the United States. Its operating margins are about double that of the other four big chains (Albertson's, Kroger, Safeway and Ahold USA). Sales per square foot are 50 per cent higher than the industry average. An annual survey conducted by Cannondale Associates found that Wegmans beat all other retailers – even Wal-Mart – in merchandising savvy.

Employee commitment and satisfaction is an important factor in Wegmans success, and managers consider meeting goals for employee development just as important as meeting sales, profit or productivity targets. 'You cannot separate their strategy as a retailer from their strategy as an employer', says consultant Darrell Rigby, head of Bain & Company's global retail practice. Hourly wages and annual salaries at Wegmans are among the highest in the industry, but that's only a small part of the story. What really sets Wegmans apart is that it creates an environment and provides the resources to enable employees to develop to their fullest potential. The company has invested $54 million for college scholarships to more than 17 500 full and part-time employees over the past 20 years. It thinks nothing of sending employees on trips to visit wineries in California or cheesemakers in Italy. 'It's our knowledge that can help the customer', says president Danny Wegman. 'So the first pump we have to prime is our own people'. Employees are empowered to do just about anything to satisfy a customer, without checking with a higher-up. Operations chief Jack DePeters says only half-jokingly that Wegmans is 'a $3 billion company run by 16-year-old cashiers'.

Priming the pump is illustrated by the opening of a new Wegmans store in Dulles, Virginia, where the company spent $5 million on training alone. The company refuses to open a new store until everyone is fully prepared. Wegmans could have easily opened in November 2003, in time for the critical holiday sales season, but chose to wait until February. The emphasis on development over dollars pays off. Wegmans attracts high-quality employees, both for management and store positions. Shortly before he died in 2006, the then 86-year-old Robert Wegman, chairman of the company, explained why he's always emphasized employee development goals despite the high costs: 'I have never given away more than I got back.' Despite Mr Wegman's passing, the company continues to rake in best employer awards, while continuing to build revenues and profitability by cautious expansion. In 2015 the company was named by *Fortune* magazine as one of the 100 best companies to work for in America, for the eighteenth year in a row – ranking fourth overall. 'Our employees are the No. 1 reason our customers shop at Wegmans,' CEO Danny Wegman commented. 'I'm convinced there is only one path to great customer service, and that is through employees who feel they are cared about and empowered.' It was a good way for Wegmans to begin its second century in operation in 2016.[31]

The Wegmans example, and others such as Britain's John Lewis partnership (where employees actually co-own the company) demonstrates that being a good employer can be an excellent route to becoming a successful company.[32]

Successful organizations are held to use a balanced set of operative goals. Although profitability goals are important, some of today's best companies calculate that a single-minded focus on bottom-line profits may not be the best way to achieve and maintain outstanding performance. Innovation and change goals are increasingly important, even though they may initially be disruptive leading to a loss of performance measured in financial terms. Employee development goals are relevant for helping to maintain a motivated, committed workforce which can be important for corporate prosperity.

The Importance of Goals

Official goals and operative goals are important, but they serve very different purposes. Official goals and mission statements describe a value system for the organization that is frequently preoccupied with engendering legitimacy. Operative goals are often more explicit and comparatively well defined. Both kinds of goals can provide employees with a sense of direction, so that they know what they are working toward. But their motivating power can also produce negative consequences, such as bullying, impropriety and excesses of various kinds. The events at Iraq's notorious Abu Ghraib prison provide a negative illustration of the motivating power of goals. Analysts say one of the explanations for the abuse of Iraqi detainees may have been that US soldiers guarding prisoners at the Abu Ghraib prison were under so much pressure to meet quotas on the number of interrogations and intelligence reports they generated that they resorted to unethical approaches and even abuse.[33] Managers need to understand the power of goals and targets and appreciate the importance of exercising care when setting and implementing them. Another important purpose or effect of goals is to act as guidelines for employee behaviour and decision-making. Appropriate goals can place a set of constraints on behaviour and actions, including those of senior managers, so that they behave within boundaries that are acceptable to the organization and larger society.[34] Goals may also help to define the appropriate decisions concerning organization structure, innovation, employee welfare or growth. Finally, goals can provide a standard for assessment. The level of organizational performance, whether in terms of profits, units produced, degree of employee satisfaction, level of innovation or number of customer complaints, requires a basis for evaluation. Operative goals translate officially stated goals of mission into more substantive courses of action and means of measuring their attainment.

A Framework for Selecting Strategy and Design

A strategy is a plan for interacting with the competitive environment to achieve organizational goals. Some managers think of goals and strategies as interchangeable, but for our purposes, *goals* define the direction of travel, and *strategies* define how to get there. For example, a goal might be to achieve 15 per cent annual sales growth. Strategies to reach that goal might include aggressive advertising to attract new customers, motivating salespeople to increase the average size of customer purchases and acquiring other businesses that produce similar products. Strategies can include any number of techniques to achieve the goal. One important aspect of formulating strategies is choosing whether to engage in different activities from competitors or to pursue similar activities more efficiently than competitors do.[35]

Two models for formulating strategies are the Porter model of competitive strategies and Miles and Snow's strategy typology. Each provides a framework for competitive action. After describing the two models and some newer strategy concepts, we will discuss how the choice of strategies affects organization design.

Porter's Competitive Strategies

Michael E. Porter studied a number of businesses and introduced a framework describing three competitive strategies: low-cost leadership, differentiation and focus.[36] The focal strategy, in which the organization concentrates on a specific market or buyer group, is further divided into *focused low cost* and *focused differentiation*. This yields four basic strategies. To use this model, managers evaluate two factors: competitive advantage and competitive scope. With respect to advantage, managers determine whether to compete through lower cost or through the ability to offer unique or distinctive products and services that can command a premium price. Managers then determine whether the organization will compete on a broad scope (competing in many customer segments) or a narrow scope (competing in a selected customer segment or group of segments). These choices determine the selection of strategies, as illustrated in Exhibit 3.4.

Differentiation   In a differentiation strategy, organizations attempt to distinguish their products or services from others in the industry. An organization may use advertising, distinctive product features, exceptional service or new technology to achieve a product perceived as unique. This strategy usually targets customers who are not particularly concerned with price, so it can be quite profitable. Rolex watches, Tommy Hilfiger clothing and Jaguar automobiles are examples of products from companies using a differentiation strategy. Service firms such as the Nationwide Building Society (a mutual banking institution) in the UK, Four Seasons Hotels and Starbucks coffee, described in the chapter opening, can use a differentiation strategy as well.

BRIEFCASE 3.2

A differentiation strategy can reduce rivalry with competitors and fight off the threat of substitute products because customers are loyal to the organization. However, successful differentiation strategies require a number of costly activities, such as product research and design and extensive advertising.

EXHIBIT 3.4   Porter's Competitive Strategies

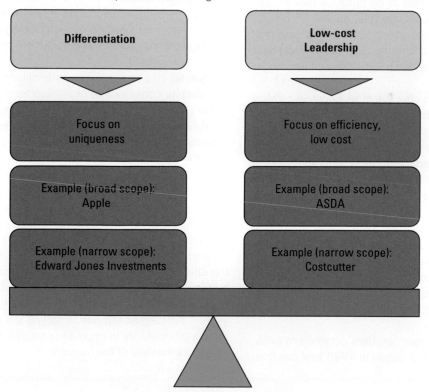

Managers Choose Which to Emphasize

Source: Based on Michael E. Porter, *Competitive Advantage: Creating and Sustaining Superior Performance* (New York: The Free Press, 1988).

IN PRACTICE

Ryanair

Fifteen or so years ago, Michael O'Leary took a trip that would change his life – and transform the Irish air carrier Ryanair into Europe's most successful, most profitable airline. O'Leary, who had been brought in as chief executive of Ryanair to save the ailing carrier, flew on American low-cost carrier Southwest Airlines and learned the tricks of running a low-cost airline.

O'Leary says of his corporate strategy: 'It's the oldest, simplest formula: Pile 'em high and sell 'em cheap ... We want to be the Wal-Mart of the airline business. Nobody will beat us on price. EVER.' And 'sell 'em cheap' he does. One industry expert says ticket prices on Ryanair are so inexpensive that it's 'nearly a no-fare carrier'. Ryanair often offers fares across Europe of less than €10 including taxes, although travellers have to be quick on their mouse buttons to catch fares like this, as well as careful to avoid a wide range of 'optional extras' and hidden but unavoidable charges such as a credit card charge for each leg of each flight for each passenger booked.

Ryanair is able to offer low fares because it keeps costs at rock bottom, lower than anyone else in Europe. The company's mantra is cheap tickets, not customer care. The carrier offers no business class, maximizes seating space, turns around an aircraft in 25 minutes rather than the 45 or so required by traditional carriers and doesn't offer travel agent commissions. Most tickets are sold over the internet, and Ryanair is the largest short-haul carrier in Europe. Instead of giving away snacks or food, Ryanair sells it. Staff costs are kept low too. In one recent year, the airline employed fewer than 2000 people to fly 24 million passengers a year, while the German carrier Lufthansa employed about 30 000 people to fly 37 million.

Ryanair's passenger numbers continue to grow. They soared from 3.9 million in 1998 to more than 24 million in 2005, nearly 50 million in 2007, and nearly 80 million in 2012.[37] However, the airline industry is increasingly competitive, other low-cost carriers are encroaching on Ryanair's territory, and soaring fuel prices worry as confident a CEO as Michael O'Leary. O'Leary still believes that Ryanair can beat anyone on price and cost control. As long as the airline keeps its disciplined approach, Ryanair will likely continue to dominate the European low-cost market.[38]

The low-cost leadership strategy is usually concerned primarily with stability rather than taking risks or seeking new opportunities for innovation and growth. A low-cost position means a company can undercut competitors' prices and still offer comparable quality and earn a reasonable profit. But when prices are already rock-bottom and the company relies upon passengers with limited disposable income, keeping flights full is a testing challenge. If flights cannot be filled, costs are already pared to the bone and novel ways of raising income are not developed, the only way to save cost is to ground the planes – something that Ryanair did at the onset of the global financial crisis in 2007/2008 – or to find ways of deriving additional revenues from existing passengers – for example, by introducing restrictive baggage allowances and then applying high penalties for exceeding them.

Ryanair has led the way in ancillary charges, and despite considerable grumbling from members of the public and more than a few run-ins with the courts and consumer protection agencies, it has actually forced not just other low-cost carriers but even the traditional airlines to follow suit. For example, in 2013 the Netherlands carrier KLM became the first of the major European 'legacy' carriers to introduce a fee for checking in luggage on European flights; subsequently other airlines like British Airways and Air France have introduced a low-fare, no-luggage category to compete with Ryanair and the other low-costs. It is estimated that airlines collected $38 billion in additional fees and charges in 2014, an increase of over 40 per cent over four years.[39] As long as Ryanair is setting the pace and forcing competitors to copy its practices, it demonstrates its mastery of the business.[40]

Low-Cost Leadership   The low-cost leadership strategy pursues strong market share by emphasizing low cost compared to competitors. With a low-cost leadership strategy, the organization aggressively seeks efficient facilities, pursues cost reductions and uses tight controls to produce products or services more efficiently than its competitors.

Focus   With Porter's third strategy, the focus strategy, the organization concentrates on a specific market or buyer group. It pursues either a low-cost advantage or a differentiation advantage within a narrowly defined market. One good example of a focused low-cost strategy is Edward Jones, a brokerage house headquartered in St Louis in America's Midwest. The firm has succeeded by building its business in rural and small-town America and providing investors with conservative, long-term investments.[41]

An example of a focused differentiation strategy is Puma, the German athletic-wear manufacturer. In 1993, when CEO Jochen Zeitz took the helm, Puma was on the brink of bankruptcy. Zeitz, then only 30 years old, revived the brand by targeting selected customer groups, especially armchair athletes, and creating stylish shoes and clothes that set design trends (see Counterpoint 3.4). Puma went 'out of its way to be different', says analyst Roland Könen. Zeitz says Puma decided to be a 'very sports-fashion brand when at the time everybody talked about sports, and sports performance and functionality. We said well it's about more.' The differentiation strategy worked and sales and profits reflected the change. Puma has been profitable every year since 1994, with sales growing faster than those of competitors. By 2016 it had 10 000 employees and operated in 120 countries worldwide.[42] Puma is ranked in the top 25 best-known brands in the US – an achievement in a country where domestic brands tend to predominate. In 2007 the company was acquired at a valuation of $5.3 billion by the French luxury brand conglomerate PPR (renamed Kering in 2013), which owns such iconic brands as Gucci and Yves St Laurent.[43]

When managers fail to adopt a competitive strategy, the organization is left with no strategic advantage, and performance almost inevitably suffers. Porter found that companies that did not consciously adopt a low-cost, differentiation, or focus strategy, for example, achieved below-average profits compared with those that used one of the three strategies. Many internet companies have failed because they did not develop competitive strategies that would distinguish them in the marketplace.[44] On the other hand, eBay and Google have been highly successful with coherent differentiation strategies. The ability of managers to devise and maintain a clear competitive strategy is one of the defining factors in an organization's success, as further discussed in this chapter's *Bookmark*.

COUNTERPOINT 3.4

Is it always a good idea to have a powerful, charismatic CEO? In this chapter we have sometimes emphasized the role of powerful CEOs, like Ryanair's Michael O'Leary, Puma's Jochen Zeitz and Starbucks' Howard Schultz. Partly this is because it is always easier to attach ideas and direction to an individual rather than to a management team as a whole.

The achievements of O'Leary, Zeitz and Schultz are real and should be acknowledged. However, strong and charismatic leadership can be a double-edged sword. Researchers are divided about the impact of charismatic leadership on profits; while some have found a positive leadership effect, others have found little or no benefit over organizations driven by bureaucratic leaders who focus on incremental change and following tried-and-true strategies. Rakesh Khurana notes in *Harvard Business Review* that, 'for all the excitement and optimism that are generated by superstar CEOs, the truth remains that the factors affecting corporate performance are varied, highly nuanced, almost frighteningly complex and certainly beyond the power of even the most charismatic leader to influence single-handedly. To pretend otherwise is to grossly oversimplify reality in the hope of finding easy answers.'

It is also important to recognize that charismatic leadership can be a force for harm as well as for good. The case of Enron is an example of the potentially negative impact of charismatic leadership. Top executives including Kenneth Lay and Jeffrey Skilling built a corporate culture that was at the same time ambitious and dynamic, and unethical and ultimately fraudulent. The company's internal culture was so dominated by this leadership that employees felt powerless to 'blow the whistle' on inappropriate business practices. Other examples of this phenomenon include Allen Stanford of the Stanford Financial Group and Bernie Ebbers of WorldCom.[45]

Some management scholars feel that the current emphasis on charismatic corporate leadership creates an environment where other 'Enrons' can emerge. Dennis Tourish and Naheed Vatcha argue that, 'the increased primacy afforded to shareholder value, the growing power of CEOs and market pressure for speedy results implies the further erosion of cultures that embrace discussion, debate and dissent'.[46] In any event, reliance upon a single individual is a source of vulnerability, especially when circumstances that have favoured his or her skills change. Perhaps success is less related to the skills *per se* but, rather, to their match with particular contingencies and opportunities. It is also worth noting that Porter's analysis makes no reference to the importance of good fit between a favoured strategy and the capacity (e.g. 'competencies') of the organization.

Miles and Snow's Strategy Typology

The Miles and Snow typology is based on the idea that managers seek to formulate strategies that will be congruent with the external environment.[47] The four strategies that can be developed to manage and exploit the external environment are the prospector, the defender, the analyzer and the reactor.

Prospector   The prospector strategy is to innovate, take risks, seek out new opportunities and grow. This strategy is suited to a dynamic, growing environment, where creativity is more important than efficiency. Historically, FedEx Corporation, the multinational courier firm, has been an innovator in both services and production technology in the rapidly changing shipping, document management and information services industry, and exemplifies the prospector strategy, as have leading high-tech companies such as Google, and more recently major players from emerging economies such as China's Xiaomi.

Defender   The defender strategy is almost the opposite of the prospector. Rather than taking risks and seeking out new opportunities, the defender strategy is concerned with stability or even retrenchment. This strategy seeks to hold onto current customers, but it neither innovates nor seeks to grow. The defender is concerned primarily with internal efficiency and control to produce reliable, high-quality products for existing customers. This strategy can be successful when the organization exists in a declining industry or a stable environment. Paramount Pictures, now a unit of media giant Viacom, has been using a defender strategy for several years.[48] Paramount turns out a steady stream of reliable hits but few blockbusters. Managers shun risk and sometimes turn down potentially high-profile films to keep a lid on costs, even if this means declining revenues but increased profits, as was the case in 2012.[49] This has enabled the company to remain highly profitable while other studios have low returns or lose money.

Analyzer   The analyzer tries to maintain a stable business while innovating on the periphery. It seems to lie midway between the prospector and the defender. Some products will be targeted toward stable, low innovation environments in which an efficiency strategy designed to keep current customers is used. Others will be targeted toward new, more dynamic environments, where growth is possible. The analyzer attempts to balance efficient production for current product lines with the creative development of new product lines. Sony Corp. illustrates an analyzer strategy

BOOKMARK 3.0

Have you read this book?

Managing Sceptically: A Critique of Organizational Fashion

BY HARVIE RAMSAY

In *Managing Sceptically*, Harvie Ramsay takes a close look at various 'innovations' in organization theory and management practice, and finds many of them to be fads that are quickly forgotten and replaced by other new, but often shallow ideas. Some past fads that Ramsay identifies include:

- *Quality circles*: this idea was imported from Japan in the 1970s, and saw its greatest popularity in the early 1980s. The idea was for groups of workers to get together to discuss ways to improve the production process. Within a few years researchers found that any short-term gains were quickly lost. Corporate productivity is embedded in a whole range of social relationships that extend into wider society, and in most cases productivity cannot be fundamentally improved by adopting a single idea from another country.

- *Total Quality Management*: a combination of American systems theory and Japanese meticulousness, TQM was intended to ensure organization-wide quality management, resulting in improved products for consumers, as well as better return to shareholders. TQM seems to have been successful mainly when combined with incentive bonuses, suggesting that it did not succeed in improving intrinsic employee motivation. By the mid-1990s, TQM seemed to be reaching the end of its life cycle.

- *Change management*: an approach that aims to structure the change process in an organization from current practices to an improved future. There are numerous change management models, which might include stages such as developing a change management strategy, enrolling senior managers as change leaders, communicating the need for change, training employees in the changed systems, coaching employees to accept and support change and approaches to sustaining the change. However, Ramsay cites one large-scale study that showed only one-third of organizations undertaking change management achieved lasting organizational strengthening.

Ramsay considers different explanations for why organizations continue to seize on new fads and fashions, given the singular lack of evidence for their success. These include the inherent contradiction in business organizations between the means to achieve improved productivity which is largely through building employee commitment, and the appropriation by shareholders of the resultant increased profits. He concludes that there is a tendency for fads to oscillate between 'rationalist' approaches such as Taylorism and 'normative' approaches, each of which generates dysfunctionalities that lead to oscillating paradigm shifts between the two norms.

Ramsay's work is several years old, but the pattern of management fads continues unabated. A highly influential and long-lasting fad for private–public partnerships was generated by David Osborne and Ted Gaebler's 1992 *Reinventing Government*. Although Osborne and Gaebler intended to strengthen public service provision, the result of applying their ideas was often state capture by private interests and the loss of universal public services. Many of the private finance schemes set up as part of the 'reinventing government' movement have proven poor value for money, and a number collapsed during the 2007–2009 global economic crisis, leaving the taxpayer holding the tab.

Source: Faranak Miraftab (2004), 'Public–Private Partnerships: The Trojan Horse of Neoliberal Development?', *Journal of Planning Education and Research*, 24, 89–101; Warwick Funnell, Robert Jupe and Jane Andrew (2009), *In Government We Trust: Market-Failure and the Delusions of Privatisation*, London, Pluto; David Walker (2008), 'Out with the outsourcers?' *Prospect*, November 20.

'*Managing Sceptically: A Critique of Organizational Fashion*', is Chapter Nine in Stewart Clegg and Gill Palmer (1996), *The politics of management knowledge*, London, Sage.

as, increasingly, does Microsoft. Sony's strategy is to defend its position in traditional consumer electronics, but also build a business in the 'integrated home entertainment' market, such as it achieved for a number of years with its Vaio computer.[50] Businesses that have become established and enjoy a degree of market domination often find it difficult to balance retention of market share in the face of more agile competitors while attempting to exploit opportunities for innovative products. Sony has never recaptured the successes of the 1980s and 1990s when its home entertainment equipment was considered the best, and its Sony Walkman introduced portable entertainment to a whole generation. Throughout the first two decades of the twenty-first century, Sony has endured cycles of declining profits, restructuring, and rounds of layoffs and retrenchment of product lines, and many analysts question the company's future prospects; the rating agency Moody's downgraded its outlook to negative amid rumours Sony would have to sell off various of its divisions. Microsoft has equally struggled to regain its dominance of the PC software market as tablet devices and cloud storage, dominated by companies like Apple, Samsung and Google, replace the traditional PC whose operating systems and productivity software are Microsoft's bread and butter. In 2013 Microsoft attempted to catch up through its Windows 8 software, which incorporated touch computing, as well as its mobile Windows phone systems. Neither strategy was entirely successful. The problem is that once a company has lost its leadership position it can be nearly impossible to regain it; it is a problem being faced by many of the first generation hi-tech companies like Microsoft, HP, Dell and Blackberry.[51]

Reactor   The reactor strategy is not really a strategy at all. Rather, reactors respond to environmental threats and opportunities in an ad hoc fashion. In a reactor strategy, top management has not defined a long-range plan, or given the organization an explicit mission or goal, so whatever actions are taken that seem to meet immediate needs. Although the reactor strategy can sometimes be successful, it can also lead to failed companies. Some large, once highly successful companies, such as Xerox and Kodak, have struggled, at least partly, because managers have failed to adopt a strategy consistent with consumer trends. In recent years, managers at McDonald's, long one of the most successful fast-food franchises in the world, have also been floundering to find the appropriate strategy. In the first decade of the 21st century, McDonald's had a string of disappointing quarterly profits as competitors continued to steal market share. Franchisees grew aggravated and discouraged by the uncertainty and lack of clear strategic direction for the future. Recent innovations, such as healthier food options and all-day breakfasts, have revived sales and profits for now, with sales up both in its US home turf and globally in 2015.[52]

The Miles and Snow typology has been widely used, and researchers have tested its validity in a variety of organizations, including hospitals, colleges, banking institutions, industrial products companies and life insurance firms. In general, researchers have found strong support for the effectiveness of this typology for organization managers in real-world situations.[53]

Emerging Concepts in Business Strategy

Strategy is a highly dynamic field. Managers – and management thinkers – are always looking for new approaches that will give them an edge over competition. Typically this involves looking at opportunities and challenges from an entirely different angle. One interesting new concept is Chan Kim and Renée Mauborgne's Blue Ocean Strategy.[54] Kim and Mauborgne divide up markets into what they call 'red oceans' and 'blue oceans'. Red oceans are market segments that are already being exploited: where strategy is geared towards finding ways to gain an edge over competitors. Although strategy is useful in these areas, as Porter and Miles and Snow discuss, ultimately the red oceans are crowded and returns on strategic innovation decline over time. By contrast, blue oceans are industries or business ideas that are not currently in existence, and so thus the size of the blue ocean market space is unknown. Concepts for products or services that meet (or even define) consumers' needs, and which are not currently in the marketplace, can take advantage of the 'blue ocean' space and generate strong profits. The authors conducted a study of business launches in 108 companies, and found that while only 14 per cent were geared to creating blue oceans, these delivered 38 per cent of total revenues and an impressive 61 per cent of total profits.

Another aspect that recent strategy thinkers have considered is the importance of strategy models in start-up companies, where the structure and philosophy imprinted on the organization at its beginning can be a key determinant of success and failure. A major Stanford University study looked at emerging hi-tech companies. James Barron and Michael Hannan, the study leaders, grouped together the differing blueprints that hi-tech entrepreneurs had in mind for their organizations as they were developing them. The five groups were star (recruiting top talent and paying highly), engineering (emphasizing professional credentials), commitment (building a strong family identity to encourage retention), bureaucracy (documented rules and systems for every eventuality), autocracy (hierarchical discipline) and companies with no clear blueprint type. Barron and Hannan found that these founding blueprints had a significant impact on success; the 'commitment' approach was the most successful model (see Counterpoint 3.5).[55]

How Strategies Affect Organization Design

Choice of strategy has implications for internal organization characteristics. In principle, organization design characteristics support the firm's competitive approach. For example, it is likely that a company wanting to grow and invent new products will look and 'feel' different from a company focused on maintaining market share for long-established products in a stable industry. Exhibit 3.5 summarizes organization design characteristics associated with the Porter and Miles and Snow strategies.

BRIEFCASE 3.3

COUNTERPOINT 3.5

The models devised by Porter and Miles and Snow, as well as the newer ideas like Blue Ocean strategy, can be analytically useful for distinguishing between different types of strategic orientation. In practice, the picture for any organization is likely to be messier, with hybrid elements and different forms of strategy being pursued for different divisions or product lines. Ultimately, the pursuit of a strategy depends upon the dispositions and capabilities of employees as much as the diagnosis of the environment of the positioning of the organization to exploit it. What type of strategy makes sense, as well as how it is pursued, will be contingent upon how managers and other employees assess the situation and their capacity to persuade others – suppliers and customers but especially investors – to support their assessment.

With a low-cost leadership strategy, managers take an efficiency approach to organization design, whereas a differentiation strategy calls for a learning approach. Recall from Chapter 2 that organizations designed for efficiency tend to have different characteristics from those designed for learning. A low-cost leadership strategy (efficiency) is associated with strong, centralized authority and tight control, standard operating procedures and emphasis on efficient procurement and distribution systems. Employees generally perform routine tasks under close supervision and control. They are not empowered to make decisions or take action on their own. A differentiation strategy, on the other hand, requires that employees be constantly experimenting and learning. Structure is more fluid and flexible, with strong horizontal coordination. Empowered employees work directly with customers and are rewarded for creativity and risk taking. Research, creativity and innovativeness are more valued than efficiency and standard procedures.

The prospector strategy requires characteristics similar to a differentiation strategy, and the defender strategy takes an efficiency approach similar to low-cost leadership. As the analyzer strategy attempts to balance efficiency and stable product lines with flexibility and learning for new products, it is associated with a mix of characteristics, as listed in Exhibit 3.5. With a reactor strategy, the organization has no direction and no clear approach to design.

EXHIBIT 3.5   Organization Design Outcomes of Strategy

Porter's Competitive Strategies	Miles and Snow's Strategy Typology
Strategy: Differentiation **Organization Design:** • Learning orientation; acts in a flexible, loosely knit way, with strong horizontal coordination • Strong capability in research • Values and incorporates mechanisms for customer intimacy • Rewards employee creativity, risk taking and innovation **Strategy:** Low-Cost Leadership **Organization Design:** • Efficiency orientation; strong central authority; tight cost control, with frequent, detailed control reports • Standard operating procedures • Highly efficient procurement and distribution systems • Close supervision; routine tasks; limited employee empowerment	**Strategy:** Prospector **Organization Design:** • Learning orientation; flexible, fluid, decentralized structure • Strong capability in research **Strategy:** Defender **Organization Design:** • Efficiency orientation; centralized authority and tight cost control • Emphasis on production efficiency; low overhead • Close supervision; little employee empowerment **Strategy:** Analyzer **Organization Design:** • Balances efficiency and learning; tight cost control with flexibility and adaptability • Efficient production for stable product lines; emphasis on creativity, research, risk-taking for innovation **Strategy:** Reactor **Organization Design:** • No clear organizational approach; design characteristics may shift abruptly, depending on current needs

Source: Based on Michael E. Porter, *Competitive Strategy: Techniques for Analyzing Industries and Competitors* (New York: The Free Press, 1980); Michael Treacy and Fred Wiersema, 'How Market Leaders Keep Their Edge', *Fortune* (February 6, 1995), 88–98; Michael Hitt, R. Duane Ireland and Robert E. Hoskisson, *Strategic Management* (St Paul, MN: West, 1995), 100–113; and Raymond E. Miles, Charles C. Snow, Alan D. Meyer and Henry J. Coleman, Jr, 'Organizational Strategy, Structure, and Process', *Academy of Management Review* 3 (1978), 546–562.

Other Factors Affecting Organization Design

Strategy is one important factor that affects organization design. Ultimately, however, organization design is a result of numerous contingencies which are discussed throughout this book. The emphasis given to efficiency and control versus learning and flexibility is conditioned by the contingencies of strategy, environment, size and life cycle, technology and organizational culture. In principle, those responsible for the design of organizations endeavour to achieve a good 'fit' with such contingencies (see Counterpoint 3.6).

COUNTERPOINT 3.6

Managers have multiple agendas that are not necessarily consistent with fitting the design of organizations to contingency factors. Assessing these factors as well as balancing them involves judgement as much as calculation. And judgements are likely to be coloured by managers' preconceptions, theories and vested interests. There is also a danger of assuming that design is the key to success when it may be that other factors – such as the capacity to dominate a market (e.g. by branding or the construction of high barriers to entry) by virtue of a monopoly position – that better account for a level of performance that is (mis)attributed to an organization's technical 'effectiveness'. For example, it is unlikely that a carrier that does not enjoy Ryanair's dominant position could derive a substantial income stream from applying the same credit card charges and excess baggage charges.

If there is minimal turbulence and therefore maximum predictability, the capacity to be adaptable or to encourage new skill development is an unnecessary cost, regardless of how employees may value it. In contrast, a rapidly changing environment may justify, managerially and technically, a more flexible structure, with strong horizontal coordination and collaboration through teams or other mechanisms. Whether this is welcomed by employees is irrelevant from this perspective unless their resistance begins to impede the implementation of a more flexible approach. In general, the demands of 'the environment' are invoked by managers to justify changes – whether in the direction of increased or reduced flexibility and learning – that are not necessarily welcomed by employees. Environments are discussed in detail in Chapters 5 and 6. In terms of size and life cycle, young, small organizations are more likely to be informal and have little division of labour, few rules and regulations and ad hoc budgeting and performance systems. Large organizations such as Coca-Cola, Sony or General Electric, on the other hand, have an extensive division of labour, numerous rules and regulations and standard procedures and systems for budgeting, control, rewards and innovation. Size and stages of the life cycle will be discussed in Chapter 10.

Likewise, in principle, design is intended to fit the workflow technology of the organization. With mass production technology, such as a traditional automobile assembly line, an emphasis upon formalization, specialization, centralized decision-making and tight control is to be expected. An e-business, on the other hand, might engender a more informal and flexible design. Technology's impact on design will be discussed in detail in Chapters 8 and 9. A final contingency affecting organization design is corporate culture. An organizational culture that values teamwork, collaboration, creativity and open communication among all employees and managers, for example, might struggle to co-exist with a tight, vertical structure and strict rules and regulations. The role of culture is discussed in Chapter 11.

Assessing Organizational Effectiveness

Understanding organizational goals and strategies, as well as the concept of fitting design to various contingencies, is a first step toward understanding organizational effectiveness. The next few sections of the chapter explore the topic of effectiveness and how effectiveness is measured in organizations.

Effectiveness is a broad concept. Effectiveness evaluates the extent to which multiple goals – whether official or operative – are attained.

Efficiency, in contrast, refers to the internal workings of the organization. Organizational efficiency is the amount of resources used to produce a unit of output.[56] It can be measured as the ratio of inputs to outputs. If one organization can achieve a given production level with fewer resources than another organization, it would be described as more efficient.[57]

Sometimes efficiency is congruent with effectiveness. In other organizations, efficiency and effectiveness are less closely related. An organization may be highly efficient but fail to achieve its goals because it makes a product for which there is weak demand. Likewise, an organization may achieve its profit goals but be inefficient.

Overall effectiveness is difficult to measure in organizations. Organizations are large, diverse and fragmented. They perform many activities simultaneously, pursue multiple goals and generate many outcomes, some intended and some unintended.[58] Managers determine what indicators to measure in order to gauge the effectiveness of their organizations. One study found that many managers have a difficult time with the concept of evaluating effectiveness based on characteristics that are not subject to hard, quantitative measurement.[59] However, top executives at some of today's leading companies are finding new ways to measure effectiveness, including the use of such 'soft' indications as 'customer delight' and employee satisfaction. A number of approaches to measuring effectiveness consider which measurements managers choose to track. These *contingency effectiveness approaches*, discussed in the next section, are based on examining which part of the organization managers consider most important to measure.

Contingency Effectiveness Approaches

Contingency approaches to measuring effectiveness focus on different parts of the organization, as shown in Exhibit 3.6. The goal approach to organizational effectiveness is concerned with the output side and whether the organization achieves its goals in terms of desired levels of output.[60] The resource-based approach assesses effectiveness by observing the beginning of the process and evaluating whether the organization effectively obtains resources necessary for high performance. The internal process approach looks at internal activities and assesses effectiveness by indicators of internal health and efficiency.

Goal Approach

The goal approach measures progress toward attainment of output goals. For example, in 2000, the United Nations set eight Millennium Development Goals to improve the quality of life in the world by the year 2015, including such targets as reducing infant mortality by two-thirds, halving the number of people suffering from hunger and ensuring all children complete basic education. By 2013, two of the goals had been met entirely, several were on track, and the UN and governments were able to focus on the few remaining where progress has been disappointing.[61]

EXHIBIT 3.6   Contingency Approaches to the Measurement of Organizational Effectiveness

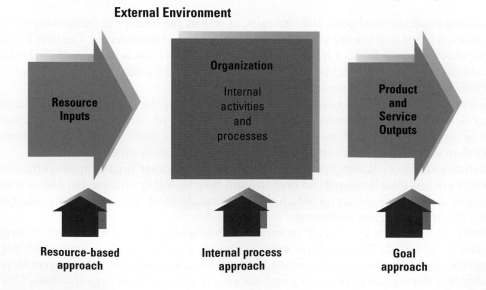

Indicators   Efforts to measure effectiveness have been more productive using operative goals than using official goals.[62] Official goals, associated with mission, tend to be abstract and difficult to measure. Operative goals, in contrast, relate to actual activities. Not unusually, there are multiple goals, as shown by a survey of US business corporations.[63] Their reported goals are shown in Exhibit 3.7. Twelve goals were listed as being important to these companies. Although the survey was conducted more than two decades ago, the 12 goals continue to be critical objectives for many for-profit organizations.

Usefulness   Business firms typically evaluate performance in terms of profitability, growth, market share and return on investment. However, identifying operative goals and measuring performance are not easy tasks. Two problems that must be resolved are the issues of multiple goals and subjective indicators of goal attainment.

Since organizations have multiple and conflicting goals, effectiveness often cannot be assessed by a single indicator. High achievement on one goal might mean low attainment of another. Moreover, as we noted earlier, there are department goals as well as overall performance goals. A full assessment of effectiveness must take into consideration several goals simultaneously.

The other issue to resolve with the goal approach is how to identify operative goals for an organization, and how to measure goal attainment. For business organizations, there are often established indicators for certain goals, such as profit or growth. However, when equivalent measures are not available for other goals some kind of assessment is frequently needed. In such circumstance, impressionistic information from customers, competitors, suppliers and employees is used in addition to intuition.

Resource-based Approach

The resource-based approach is directed to the input side of the transformation process shown in Exhibit 3.7. It assumes that organizations obtain and manage valued resources in order to be effective.[64]

EXHIBIT 3.7   Reported Goals of US Corporations

Goal	% Corporations
Profitability	89
Growth	82
Market share	66
Social responsibility	65
Employee welfare	62
Product quality and service	60
Research and development	54
Diversification	51
Efficiency	50
Financial stability	49
Resource conservation	39
Management development	35

Source: Adapted from Y. K. Shetty, 'New Look at Corporate Goals,' *California Management Review* 22, no. 2(1979), 71–79.

Indicators   Obtaining and successfully managing resources is the criterion by which organizational effectiveness is assessed. In a broad sense, indicators of effectiveness, according to the resource-based approach, encompass the following dimensions:

■ Bargaining position – the ability to obtain from the environment scarce and valued resources, including financial resources, raw materials, human resources, knowledge and technology

■ The abilities of the organization's decision-makers to perceive and correctly interpret the salient properties of the external environment (e. g. customers)

■ The ability to use tangible (e.g. supplies, people) and intangible (e.g. knowledge, corporate culture) resources in day-to-day organizational activities

■ The ability to respond appropriately to changes in the environment.

Usefulness

The resource-based approach is especially valuable when other indicators of performance are difficult to obtain. In many not-for-profit and social welfare organizations, for example, it is hard to measure output goals or internal efficiency. Regional development agencies typically market their regions on the basis of the bundle of diverse resources they have available to potential companies.[65] Amongst for-profit organizations, shared service firms, as well as shared service units within larger companies, aim to combine a range of complementary skills sets together, thus permitting the efficient centralization of specific activities for multiple internal or external clients. Shared services are part of the trend towards business process re-engineering, outsourcing and offshoring. Companies such as India's Tata Consulting Services (TCS) offer companies custom-designed solutions. N. Ganapathy Subramaniam, President of TCS's financial solutions arm, notes that his company has 'experience in consulting, business process outsourcing, engineering and IT infrastructure services and our goal is to provide clients with the right set of capabilities for the right problems at the right time'.[66]

Although the resource-based approach is valuable, it does have shortcomings. For one thing, the approach may not adequately consider the organization's link to customers, although the absence of a strong link does suggest a lack of resource in this area (of marketing) that could be remedied. Critics have argued that the resource dependency approach assumes stability in the marketplace and fails to give adequate consideration to the changing contribution and criticality of various resources as the competitive environment and customer needs change. But again, attentiveness to changing markets may be incorporated into the second element of the resource-based approach listed above.

Internal Process Approach

In the internal process approach, effectiveness is measured as internal organizational health and efficiency. An effective organization in these terms is one with a smooth, well-oiled internal process. Employees are focused and satisfied. Department activities mesh with one another to ensure high productivity. The important element in effectiveness is what the organization does with the resources it has, as reflected in internal health and efficiency. Little attention is paid to the external environment. In principle, the internal process could be very smooth yet poorly aligned to its environment, such as the shifting demands of the market, with calamitous consequences.

Indicators   Writers including Chris Argyris, Warren G. Bennis, Rensis Likert and Richard Beckhard have all worked extensively with human resources in organizations and emphasize the

IN PRACTICE

Volkswagen

Volkswagen was the first European car manufacturer to develop a genuinely mass-market vehicle, the famous VW Beetle, originally launched in 1938, and still in production in an updated version. After the end of the Second World War, Volkswagen grew rapidly, through Beetle sales, acquisition of several other European marques and global expansion. However, by the end of the 1990s the original Beetle's long run was over, and the models that replaced it had mixed reputations for consumer appeal, quality and reliability. In comparison with Toyota, Volkswagen's cars seemed tired and outdated, and the perception was reflected in Volkswagen's global sales, which fell below Toyota.

In the early years of the twenty-first century Volkswagen revamped its product line-up, and initial sales results were promising; global year-on-year sales were up 8.5 per cent in 2007. The company's new management developed an ambitious strategy to catch up with Toyota globally. In 2012, it sold over 9 million cars globally, up more than one third from 2007, and each of the company's brands and national units have been expected to set similarly ambitious targets; its US subsidiary was hoping to triple its US sales to 1 million automobiles over the next decade.

At the beginning of 2015, the outlook for Volkswagen was generally promising, and the company was back on track to challenge Toyota, an effort that was focused by the company's ambitious growth targets and assisted by problems Toyota has had with product recalls. In late 2015, however, Volkswagen's reputation for solid and trustworthy German engineering came crashing down. The problem was nitrogen oxide emissions from the company's economical diesel-fueled vehicles.

Volkswagen has long been a leader in diesel cars, which are cheaper to run than petrol-fueled cars, and have become even more competitive when fuel prices are high as had been the case for much of the first decade of the 21st century. Diesel engines also have lower emissions of certain pollutants such as carbon dioxide (CO_2). However, diesels produce other pollution including nitrogen oxide (NO) and it is debatable which type of vehicles cause more environmental harm. In response to growing concerns about diesel vehicle pollution, both the US Environmental Protection Agency (EPA) and European authorities have imposed increasingly rigorous standards on NO emissions.

For the past several years, the US EPA complained to Volkswagen that while its cars appeared to meet the new stringent emissions rules in tests, in practice on-the-road NO emissions were up to forty times worse than reported, and well beyond legal limits. It soon emerged that cars used for testing had been fitted with software that caused the vehicle to report lower than actual emissions. Within days Volkswagen was forced to admit that it had deceived the authorities and its customers. Over the next weeks the scandal deepened and intensified, as it emerged that the company had fixed test results not only in the United States but also in Europe, and that misleading pollution ratings were also being provided for CO_2 emissions on some of the company's petrol cars. The EPA threatened not to permit Volkswagen diesels from the company's 2016 range to be sold in the United States.

The scandal soon affected Volkswagen's overall prospects, and also damaged German manufacturing industry's high-quality, high-integrity image. The company had to set aside $7.3 billion to sort out the excess emissions issue, and its stock price declined by more than one-third in the days after the scandal broke. Volkswagen Group CEO Martin Winterkorn was forced to resign, and a number of other senior officials were suspended. By 2016 numerous countries in which the affected cars had been sold had opened investigations, started criminal proceedings, and blocked registration for Volkswagen diesels.

Volkswagen's official corporate goal in 2013, whilst the company was in the midst of a large scale deception of its customers, was "to offer attractive, safe and environmentally sound vehicles which can compete in an increasingly tough market and set world standards in their respective class." The Volkswagen case demonstrates that organizational mission and goals statements can be trumped by internal and external competition and profit motives, and in themselves provide little guarantee of corporate responsibility, or even attention to the long-term interests of the corporation itself.[67]

connection between human resources and effectiveness.[68] Writers on corporate culture and organizational excellence have also stressed the importance of internal processes. Results from a study of nearly 200 US secondary schools showed that both human resources and employee-oriented processes were important in explaining and promoting effectiveness in those organizations.[69]

There are seven indicators of an effective organization, as seen from an internal process approach:

1   Strong corporate culture and positive work climate

2   Team spirit, group loyalty and teamwork

3   Confidence, trust and communication between workers and management

4   Decision-making near sources of information, regardless of where those sources are on the organizational chart

5   Undistorted horizontal and vertical communication; sharing of relevant facts and feelings

6   Rewards to managers for performance, growth and development of subordinates, and for creation of cooperative work groups

7   Interaction between all parts of the organization, with conflict that occurs over projects being resolved in ways that are collectively beneficial and productive.[70]

BRIEFCASE 3.4

Usefulness   Today, many managers subscribe to the belief that committed, actively involved and satisfied employees, and a positive corporate culture, are important indicators, if not direct measures, of effectiveness. Their importance becomes evident, when, for example, a major corporation such as Boeing is found to struggle as a consequence of poor internal process. Although technical processes for building planes had improved to meet competition from Airbus and emergent smaller players like Embraer as described earlier, human relations and corporate culture at Boeing have been reported as being in some disarray. Hiring, promotion and compensation practices have been in the spotlight. Twenty-eight thousand female employees filed law suits charging that the company systematically pays women less than men. Depositions described a hostile work environment, including groping and offensive language on the part of male colleagues and bosses. CEO Harry Stonecipher was forced to resign in 2005 because of improprieties related to an affair with a female executive. These internal human resources issues, combined with reliability and safety issues as well as ethics scandals related to Boeing's external environment, have seriously damaged the company. Subsequent CEOs Alan Mullaly and Scott Carson have led a turnaround of the company's fortunes through empowering employees, re-emphasizing innovation and building a strong product strategy.[71] That said, in January 2013, the 787 Dreamliner suffered from overheating battery problems which led to regulators grounding 50 planes.[72]

In contrast to Boeing's turbulence, Four Seasons Hotels, an international luxury chain of hotels with headquarters in Toronto, Canada, has been able to maintain smooth internal processes. Treating employees well is considered key to the organization's success.[73] Workers at each hotel select a peer to receive the Employee of the Year award, which includes an expenses-paid vacation and a $1000 shopping spree. In 2016, the company was again named in the Fortune top 100 companies in the world to work for, an unbroken record since the index was founded in 1998.[74] Internal processes are particularly important for hotel chains because so many employees have contact with customers, and any one of them who is disgruntled and unfocused on customer satisfaction could potentially spoil customers' experience, a vulnerability that is increased by customer feedback websites such as Tripadvisor over which the chains have little control.[75]

The internal process approach also has shortcomings. Total output and the organization's relationship with the external environment are not evaluated. Another problem is that many aspects of inputs and internal processes are not readily or meaningfully quantifiable.

An Integrated Effectiveness Model

The three approaches – goal, resource-based, internal process – offer a distinctive perspective on organizational effectiveness. The competing values model tries to balance a concern with different kinds and aspects of effectiveness rather than focusing on one approach. The competing values model acknowledges that organizations do many things that have many outcomes.[76] It combines several indicators of effectiveness into a single framework. It is based on the assumption that there are disagreements and competing viewpoints about what constitutes effectiveness. Managers sometimes disagree over which are the most important goals to pursue and measure and stakeholders have competing claims on what they want from the organization, as described in Chapter 1.

One tragic example of conflicting viewpoints and competing interests comes from the US space agency NASA. After seven astronauts died in the explosion of the space shuttle *Columbia* in February 2003, an investigative committee found deep organizational flaws at NASA, including ineffective mechanisms for incorporating dissenting opinions between scheduling managers and safety managers. External pressures to launch on time overrode safety concerns with the *Columbia* launch. As Wayne Hale, the NASA executive charged with giving the go-ahead for the next shuttle launch, puts it, 'We dropped the torch through our own complacency, our arrogance, self-assurance, sheer stupidity and through continuing attempts to please everyone'. NASA is an extremely complex organization that operates not only with different viewpoints internally but also from the US Congress, the president and the expectations of the American public.[77]

The competing values model takes into account these complexities. The model was originally developed by Robert Quinn and John Rohrbaugh to combine the diverse indicators of performance used by managers and researchers.[78] Using a comprehensive list of performance indicators, a panel of experts in organizational effectiveness rated the indicators for similarity. The analysis produced underlying dimensions of effectiveness criteria that represented competing management values in organizations.

Indicators The first value dimension pertains to organizational focus, which is whether dominant values concern issues that are *internal* or *external* to the firm. Internal focus reflects a management concern for the well-being and productivity of employees, and external focus represents an emphasis on well-being with respect to stakeholders in the environment, such as shareholders, customers and suppliers. The second value dimension pertains to organization structure, and whether *stability or flexibility* is the dominant structural consideration. Stability reflects a management value for efficiency and top-down control, whereas flexibility represents a value for learning and change (see Chapter 2).

The value dimensions of structure and focus are illustrated in Exhibit 3.8. The combination of dimensions provides four approaches to organizational effectiveness, which, though seemingly different, are closely related. In actual organizations, these competing values can and often do exist together. Each approach reflects a different management emphasis with respect to structure and focus.[79]

A combination of external focus and flexible structure leads to an open systems emphasis. Management's primary goals are growth and resource acquisition. The organization accomplishes these goals through the subgoals of flexibility, readiness and a positive external evaluation. The dominant value is establishing a good relationship with key stakeholders in the environment to acquire resources and grow. This emphasis is similar in some ways to the resource-based approach described earlier.

The rational goal emphasis represents management values of structural control and external focus. The primary goals are productivity and efficiency. Managers strive to achieve output goals in a controlled way. Subgoals that facilitate these outcomes are internal planning and goal setting, which are rational management tools. The rational goal emphasis is similar to the goal approach described earlier.

EXHIBIT 3.8   Four Approaches to Effectiveness Values

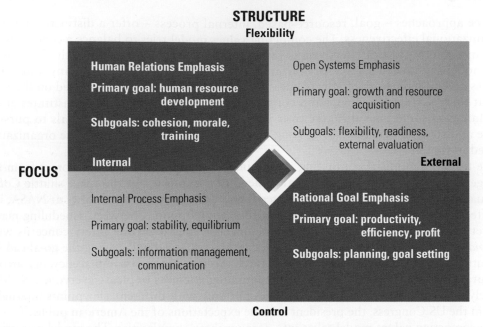

Source: Adapted from Robert E. Quinn and John Rohrbaugh, 'A Spatial Model of Effectiveness Criteria: Toward a Competing Values Approach to Organizational Analysis', Management Science 29 (1983), 363–377; and Robert E. Quinn and Kim Cameron, 'Organizational Life Cycles and Shifting Criteria of Effectiveness: Some Preliminary Evidence', Management Science 29 (1983), 33–51.

The internal process emphasis is in the lower-left section of Exhibit 3.8; it reflects the values of internal focus and structural control. The primary outcome is a stable organizational setting that maintains itself in an orderly way. Organizations that are well established in the environment and simply want to maintain their current position would affirm and support this emphasis. Subgoals include mechanisms for efficient communication, information management and decision-making. Although this part of the competing values model is similar in some ways to the internal process approach described earlier, it is less concerned with human resources than with other internal processes that lead to efficiency.

The human relations emphasis incorporates the values of an internal focus and a flexible structure. Here, management is concerned primarily with the development of human resources. Employees are given opportunities for autonomy and development. Management works toward the subgoals of cohesion, morale and training opportunities.

Usefulness   The competing values model makes two contributions: it integrates diverse concepts of effectiveness into a single perspective. Second, the model calls attention to effectiveness criteria as management values and shows how opposing values exist at the same time. It invites managers to decide which values they wish to pursue and which values will receive less emphasis (see Counterpoint 3.7). The four competing values exist simultaneously, but not all will receive equal priority.

COUNTERPOINT 3.7

It may be misleading to suggest that managers can 'decide which values they wish to pursue' as such decisions are constrained by their entrenched preconceptions, vision and priorities as well as by the pressures upon them to meet the immediate demands of investors, customers or suppliers. It is also questionable whether any organization can afford to ignore 'current productivity and profits', especially in the Anglo-American business zone where short-term profits are a primary indicator of managers' effectiveness ... and survival. It may be that a business plan for a recently established organization will focus upon getting established and gaining visibility and reputation. But it is likely that these concerns are considered to be indicators of future profitability. Immediate profitability is sacrificed in the expectation that building reputation and capability will pay future dividends. Even in the many cases where businesses are established for non-financial reasons – for example, the entrepreneur is passionate about a product or a service and/or is interested primarily in being their own boss – the survival of the business (and thus the realization of the non-financial dreams) will depend upon securing continuing external investment or generating sufficient surpluses to plough back into the development of the business.

The dominant values in an organization often change over time as organizations experience new environmental demands or new top leadership. The *In Practice* feature describes the dominant effectiveness values for the Thomson Corporation, Canada's best-known media company prior to its merger with Reuters (see feature box). The company's transformation required a strong open systems emphasis with fairly strong emphasis on human relations as well. The rational goal emphasis and internal process emphasis are much weaker. Adapting to the environment and understanding and meeting customer needs have been emphasized in recent years as many organizations have faced turbulent times and substantial opportunities for expansion.

IN PRACTICE

Thomson Reuters

When Richard Harrington took over as CEO of the Thomson Corporation in 1997, he began a process that has transformed the company from a fabled Canadian newspaper publisher into a thriving information services enterprise. The line of newspapers was sold. Managers rebuilt Thomson into an organization providing a wide variety of information products and services to four strategic market groups: Legal and Regulatory, Learning, Financial, and Science and Healthcare. In 2007, Thomson sold its Learning arm to a private equity group, Cengage, publishers of this book. By 2008, Thomson merged with Reuters to create a global leader in electronic publishing and providing integrated information solutions to corporate customers in a variety of industries.

The shift into digital information made sense. The print newspaper industry appears to be in a long, slow decline, whereas electronic information distribution is growing rapidly. However the new goals and strategy took Thomson out of the business it knew best and thrust it into a new, highly competitive environment. Financial results suffered as the company acquired new businesses, new knowledge, new skills and other resources to fit the new strategy and goals. Thomson spent several years acquiring more than 200 different businesses and melding them into a coherent whole. By 2006, both revenues and profits were back on an upwards track: revenues rose nine per cent to $1.87 billion, with profits up an impressive 57 per cent to $390 million This provided a strong platform for the merger with Reuters the next year. The merged information services giant had profits of $2.5 billion on revenues of $12.5 billion in 2014.[80]

Making the revamped company successful required a strong focus on understanding, anticipating and shaping customer needs and building good relationships with the external environment. Business unit managers were expected to thoroughly understand their potential customers, markets and competitors. At the same time, however, they also had to make the internal people changes. As a knowledge-based organization, Thomson Reuters considers employee development and a unified corporate culture fundamental to the company's success.[81]

Where uncertainties have increased and opportunities have diminished, profitablity and even survival depends more upon internal control and cost efficiency, but the balance is a dynamic one and also varies from sector to sector (see Counterpoint 3.8).

COUNTERPOINT 3.8

Is top management really able to set a clear strategic direction? We all prefer to feel that we are in control of our lives, and there is also an expectation – reflected in this chapter – that top managers will be able to fundamentally shape the direction of their companies. However, just as individuals' lives frequently take unexpected turns, the same is true of corporations and their leadership.

Sometimes in retrospect a top manager's long-term strategy may appear to be clear – and of course it is in her or his interest to represent it in such a way – but things are often much less certain on a day-to-day basis. Even the most strategy-oriented managers such as Thomson's Harrington, for example, seem to have changed direction. Thomson divested its Learning division in 2007, but earlier in Harrington's tenure he had substantially expanded Thomson Learning through acquisitions such as Macmillan Library Reference USA and Capstar, an academic testing and assessment business. Then, in late 2007, Thomson and the leading news agency Reuters agreed to merge, as discussed in the *In Practice* box, a move that could be interpreted as radically shifting Thomson's direction back towards a more traditional news focus, albeit not print newspaper publication.

Perhaps more important than the details of strategic direction is the *image* of strategic clarity and decisive leadership. Leaders such as Richard Harrington and Puma's Jochen Zeitz project an aura of competence and vision. If inconsistencies and shifts are successfully glossed over or effectively rationalized within a convincing narrative, investors are provided with a sense of assurance that the company and their human resources and financial assets are in good hands.

Summary and Interpretation

This chapter discussed organizational goals and strategies pursued to realize those goals. Goals specify the mission or purpose of an organization and its desired future state. Strategies define how the organization will reach its goals. The chapter also considered the impact of strategy on organization design and how designing the organization to fit strategy and other contingencies can lead to improved organizational effectiveness. The chapter closed with an examination of the most popular approaches to measuring effectiveness.

Organizations are widely held to exist for a well-defined purpose; and top managers are seen to define a specific mission or task to be accomplished. The mission statement, or official goals, makes explicit the purpose and direction of an organization. Official and operative goals are a key element in organizations insofar as they establish legitimacy with external groups and set standards of performance for participants.

We have cautioned against attributing excessive influence to top managers as their actions are conditioned by their specfic backgrounds and capabilities as well as the contexts, internal and external, that they seek to change and exploit. Managers develop or rationalize strategies to describe the actions they deem to be required to achieve goals. Strategies may include any number of techniques to achieve the stated goals. Two models for formulating strategies are Porter's competitive strategies and the Miles and Snow strategy typology. The formal process of organization design is represented as a process of assessing and fitting the structure of the organization to the contingencies that it faces, thereby securing enhanced organizational effectiveness.

Difficulties of defining and assessing organizational effectiveness reflect the complexity of organizations as a topic of study. No easy, simple, guaranteed measure will provide an unequivocal assessment of performance. Organizations perform diverse activities – from obtaining resource inputs to delivering outputs. Contingency approaches use output goals, resource acquisition or internal health and efficiency as the criteria of effectiveness. The competing values model aspires to provide a balanced approach that considers multiple criteria simultaneously. Organizations can be assessed by evaluating competing values for effectiveness. No approach is suitable for every organization, but proponents of each approach identify advantages that others are seen to lack.

From the point of view of managers, the goal approach to effectiveness and measures of internal efficiency may be found to be useful when credible measures are available. Factors including top-management preferences, the extent to which goals are assessed to be measurable, and the scarcity of environmental resources may influence the selection and use of effectiveness criteria. In nonprofit organizations, where internal processes and output criteria are often not quantifiable, resource acquisition may be the best available indicator of effectiveness. The competing values model of organizational effectiveness acknowledges different areas of focus (internal, external) and structure (flexibility, stability) and allows for managers to appreciate how approaches – human relations, open systems, rational goal or internal process – may be combined in order to give priority to the values to which managers subscribe and the priorities that they privilege.

KEY CONCEPTS

analyzer	goal approach	low-cost leadership	prospector
competing values model	human relations emphasis	mission	rational goal emphasis
defender	internal process approach	official goals	reactor
differentiation		open systems emphasis	resource-based approach
focus	internal process emphasis	operative goals	strategy
focus strategy		organizational goal	structure

Discussion Questions

1 Discuss the role of top management in setting organizational direction.

2 How might a company's goals for employee development be related to its goals for innovation and change? To goals for productivity? Can you identify ways these types of goals might conflict in an organization?

3 What is a goal for the class for which you are reading this text? Who established this goal? Discuss how the goal affects your direction and motivation.

4 What is the difference between a goal and a strategy as defined in the text? Identify both a goal and a strategy for a campus or community organization with which you are familiar.

5 Discuss the similarities and differences in the strategies described in Porter's competitive strategies and Miles and Snow's typology.

6 In what ways is the Blue Ocean strategy different from the approaches described by Porter, and Miles and Snow?

7 To what extent do mission statements and official goal statements provide an organization with legitimacy in the external environment?

8 Suppose you have been asked to evaluate the effectiveness of the police service in a medium-sized city. Where would you begin, and how would you proceed? What effectiveness approach would you prefer and why?

9 What are the advantages and disadvantages of the resource-based approach versus the goal approach for measuring organizational effectiveness?

10 What are the similarities and differences between assessing effectiveness on the basis of competing values versus the stakeholder approach described in Chapter 2?

11 A noted organization theorist once said, 'Organizational effectiveness can be whatever top management defines it to be'. Discuss.

Chapter 3 Workbook Identifying Company Goals and Strategies*

Choose three companies, either in the same industry or in three different industries. Search the internet for information on the companies, including annual reports. In each company look particularly at the goals expressed. Refer back to the goals in Exhibit 3.7 and also to Porter's competitive strategies in Exhibit 3.4.

	Goals from Exhibit 3.7 articulated	Strategies from Porter used
Company #1		
Company #2		
Company #3		

Questions

1 Which goals seem most important?

2 Look for differences in the goals and strategies of the three companies and develop an explanation for those differences.

3 Which of the goals or strategies should be changed? Why?

4 *Optional:* Compare your table with those of other students and look for common themes. Which companies seem to articulate and communicate their goals and strategies best?

Chapter 3 Workshop Competing Values and Organizational Effectiveness*

1 Divide into groups of four to six members.

2 Select an organization to 'study' for this exercise. It should be an organization for which one of you has worked, or it could be the university.

3 Using the exhibit 'Four Approaches to Effectiveness Values' (Exhibit 3.8), your group should list eight potential measures that show a balanced view of performance. These should relate not only to work activities, but also to goal values for the company.

4 How will achieving these goal values help the organization to become more effective? Which values could be given more weight than others? Why?

5 Present your competing values chart to the rest of the class. Each group should explain why it chose those particular values and which are more important. Be prepared to defend your position to the other groups, which are encouraged to question your choices.

*Adapted by Dorothy Marcic from general ideas in Jennifer Howard and Larry Miller, *Team Management*, The Miller Consulting Group, 1994, p.92.

JP Carpets*

By Henrik Sørensen, Aarhus University

In the spring of 1995 one of Dan Carpets' employees, Jean Pelletier, decided to start up his own business. He established JP Carpets in the small town of Val-des-Marnes. Neither the management nor the employees of Dan Carpets were surprised by his decision, because Dan Carpets had been going through a long period of problems and conflicts. Pelletier ('JP') had long voiced his dissatisfaction with what was going on in the company. As a person who emphasized working in the most appropriate and efficient manner, he simply could not live with the present situation.

After heavy criticism of Dan Carpets' management, Pelletier had reached the conclusion that its managers simply could not effectively manage the company. He believed that its (matrix) structure was totally inappropriate and had given several examples of how its working spirit was, in fact, destructive. 'We cooperate ourselves to death' was one of JP's favourite mottos.

On several occasions he had shown that the company lost orders because its employees found it more important to cooperate than to produce and deliver the carpets which its customers (primarily interior design shops, private customers or public institutions) wanted. Furthermore, the company structure with two managing directors did not function at all. Very often they gave contradictory orders and directives to the staff, and to avoid facing the ensuing problems, they simply let the employees choose their own (and sometimes more suitable) production method. As the employees did not have sufficient knowledge of the company's customers and their needs, their decisions often turned out wrong and did not stand up to reality. Both sides feeling responsible for the poor decisions, management and employees easily agreed to forget the whole matter, only to see the same problem surface again shortly afterwards.

In JP's opinion it was hard to believe that Dan Carpets' management was unaware of the company's problems, and often he saw their reactions as a sign of panic. Thus, when Dan Carpets had to deliver a major order to a large medical company last year – with the company logo printed in two colours – JP realized that no one actually knew exactly what the medical company had ordered. The product manager of the carpet division said that the medical company had ordered a carpet in two colours sharply contrasting with each other, which was an expensive production procedure. As opposed to this, the marketing manager believed that Dan Carpets was free to decide which colours to use. After three days of discussion, in which the whole order could have been produced, the two managers approached the top management and proposed that the manager losing the argument should leave the company. Top management was also unwilling to solve the conflict, saying that, 'When a company has a matrix structure, the competent managers must get used to making difficult decisions and try to find joint solutions'.

The heads of the linoleum, wooden floor and vinyl departments supported the head of the carpet department, while the functional managers for design, production and finance supported the marketing manager. A minor disagreement about the specifications of the order from the medical company had turned into a giant internal fight about who was to take decisions at the company, and ever since this fight nobody in the management group had been talking together.

The most obvious solution would have been to send the medical company a number of proposals as to how the order could be executed and let them decide. However, out of fear of not being able to deliver the order, the managing director had decided to produce the carpets in totally different colours. Subsequently his decision turned out to be disastrous: the colour composition of the carpets was very similar to a competitor's colours. When the medical company received the carpets, they sent the whole lot back to Dan Carpets. Furthermore, the medical company ordered some new carpets from one of Dan Carpets' competitors.

JP had been vocal in criticizing both the company and its management, calling their actions panicky and poorly thought through. It was clear to him that they were not able to manage the company and that another organizational structure, with a different management team, and thus a reorganization of the entire company, was needed.

*Please note this case study is entirely fictional

As time went by, Dan Carpets employees turned out to be quite reasonable. They were prepared to forget the whole matter and move on in order to make the company function despite the conflicts within the management group. On his own initiative, a member of the carpet division staff had visited the medical company to explain why everything went wrong with their order. He did not mention the ongoing conflict in the management group, but gave as explanation that the original order form had been lost, which was basically true.

Another example of the good intentions of the employees was that although the management group continued to wage war and disagree on almost everything, the employees handled all practical matters in the company. People said more or less openly that the management spent their time fighting internally while the employees made the company function. Everybody avoided asking their superiors about anything, as chances were that things would go wrong when the management group interfered. Of course this situation was untenable in the long run, and when a similar problem arose six months later, JP had had enough of the company.

He went to the managing director immediately, and in very clear terms he explained to him that the entire management of Dan Carpets was totally incompetent and incapable of managing a company of this size. 'We have pure chaos here, and although you see it, you do nothing to change the situation', he commented harshly. The managing director could only agree with him. 'I have therefore decided to start up on my own. I have hired 15 people from your carpet division, so they will be leaving Dan Carpets along with me.' JP left the managing director quite shaken and alone in his office.

JP starts his own company

The new company was established less than three months after JP's harsh exchange of words with Dan Carpets' managing director. There were no competition clauses limiting the activities of JP and his 15 new employees in their new company JP Carpets, so they immediately started competing with Dan Carpets in one of the latter's most important business areas.

Without any noticeable efforts on the part of Pelletier or his employees, a number of Dan Carpets' customers switched to JP Carpets. They simply said that Dan Carpets was too chaotic to deal with.

JP had no ambitions about making his new company too big. JP Carpets retained its original 15 employees, who got along well together. It was very strong in the manufacturing and development fields, so more and more customers found out about the qualities of JP's carpets. The company developed a skill for finding special market niches in the carpet industry.

JP Carpets had no formal structure. Staff often solved their problems by informal communication, or after Pelletier had ranted loud enough until people sat down and sorted out the issue. Having solved the problem, however, no one harboured a grudge against each other as had been the case in Dan Carpets. One major strength of JP Carpets was that whenever a customer needed a new carpet, one of the employees was appointed 'project owner' – meaning that this person followed the customer from order entry to carpet delivery. This way the customers felt that they always got custom-designed solutions, and in the event of any problems with their order, they always knew whom to contact.

Many employees felt that the main reason for JP Carpets' success was the close contact to their customers, but the only administrative member of the staff, Lise Boisvert, disagreed. She believed that the flexible way JP planned production was the secret behind JP Carpets' success.

'If we had not invested in new advanced production technologies, if we didn't have such a strong company spirit and desire to develop new products for our customers and to search for more advanced production equipment, our company would not have survived, let alone flourished', she said.

At several Friday meetings – where Jean Pelletier and his employees talked about the past week – there had been intense discussions of how JP Carpets was earning its money. Lise Boisvert had mentioned that when comparing JP Carpets with several of its large French competitors, the latter all had some advantages compared to JP. They could scope the whole market for customers, quickly shift to new products, and all had professional sales staff.

Their bureaucratic structure allowed them to enhance the efficiency of every function down to the smallest detail, unlike a small company like JP Carpets. Besides, she pointed out, as soon as a large company had sales problems because of saturation of the home market, it just started exporting – something that would have been beyond JP Carpets.

▶

JP's problems become clearer

Very few staff at JP had noticed what Lise had pointed out. This was due to several things. Lise Boisvert was the only person working in administration, which left her all alone with the administrative problems. Customers not paying their bills or suppliers not getting paid were all Lise's problem. A proper administrative department was badly needed at JP Carpets. New procedures for control and follow-up of accounts and some form of financial controls also had to be implemented as soon as possible.

The need for better financial controls was highlighted by JP Carpets' many liquidity problems in the second half of 1998. For some time a lot of expenses had had to be paid before the company could invoice its customers. This was not a sign of falling revenues, as throughout the financial year profits as a percentage of company sales were still high. However, the profit margin was falling, but only Lise Boisvert realized this.

Lise had great difficulty gaining Jean Pelletier's attention in order to explain the seriousness of their situation. She understood that she was working in an environment of almost solely male employees (including all their male jargon), and that production was considered the most important part of the company, but she could not accept that Pelletier made no effort to understand what she was telling him regarding the company accounts and financial control. 'My professional pride was hurt', she says.

She decided to quit her job. One Friday meeting when there was not much on the agenda, and everybody thought they could sit and relax over a few beers, she let loose, announcing that she intended to leave the company because of its extremely weak financial management. She said that in future she foresaw a lot of trouble between the company's employees. She knew that JP was very intent on good leadership and employee relations and hoped this would spur him into action.

JP jumped up, surprised and shocked. Lise continued talking, disclosing that JP Carpets' profits were lower than during the start-up years of the company. This made several of the employees wrinkle their foreheads, and although they normally never raised difficult company matters with JP, one of them got up and said that lately he had noticed a definite lack not only in spirit, but also in efficiency of the employees.

Suddenly JP realized that the motivation level within the JP family (as he called all the employees of the company) was declining. The company was not yet in a deep crisis, because it was still making a profit, but he was concerned because for the first time the employees were questioning his way of running the company and his style of leadership. Furthermore, Lise was right, the figures showed that profits were falling.

This whole discussion started at the same time as some of the big competitors were gearing up to take on JP Carpets, and a few, including Dan Carpets, had even prepared a coordinated competition effort against Pelletier's firm.

One of Dan Carpets' initiatives was to lower the price of its carpets, JP Carpets' sole business area, to almost the level of their production costs while raising the profit margins in other less price-sensitive product areas. This meant that Dan Carpets could offer considerably lower prices, while maintaining total company profits.

Dan Carpets had replaced its management, and the new managers had shown to be very efficient in 'cleaning up' the company in only nine months, firing all the product and functional managers, who they saw as just stirring up trouble. In organizational terms the management of the company had given up the matrix structure and divided the company into four subsidiaries, each with separate responsibility for the carpet, linoleum, wooden floor and vinyl production. They had also got rid of several employees with bad attitudes, and the company was now more customer-oriented. All four subsidiaries had introduced new advanced production facilities, using computerized inventory controls for the purchase of raw materials, so that these arrived at the company at the exact time when they were needed in the production process. Large IT supported systems also controlled deliveries to customers.

JP did not know what to do. Soon it became apparent that he was unable to effectively control the work performance of his employees. Little by little the company had grown to have 30 employees, which meant that JP no longer had the same close contact with everybody as before. Daily problems were not being solved because people had to wait until JP got the time to help them. He went from one problem to another, so much so that he felt he was functioning as the corporate 'fire extinguisher'. One consequence of all the firefighting was that no one was assessing the company's production facilities and whether they were competitive with the rest of the carpet industry.

▶

It became more and more apparent that JP was now an older man, and that he didn't have the energy to grasp the problems and deal with them. The employees were quite openly talking about a management crisis at JP Carpets, saying that if the company was to survive, 'the old man' had to resign.

JP's problems grow bigger

In January 2007 JP Carpets had an unannounced visit from the tax authorities, who had identified that there was something seriously wrong with the company's accounting. JP Carpets had few or no accounting procedures or financial controls, as Lise Boisvert had acknowledged. The result was that the company had fallen behind with its tax remittances and was liable for a hefty fine. Even JP could now see that something had to be done.

After the visit from the tax authorities everything suddenly moved very quickly. JP acknowledged that he no longer was able to effectively manage the company. One morning in March 2007 he called together all employees and told them that his life's work – JP Carpets – had for quite some time had major problems with its finances. It had outdated technology and it was being outstripped by its competitors.

JP announced that he had therefore decided to leave the daily management of the company to what he called 'a professional managing director'. A management consultancy had been recruited to find a new managing director before April 1. The employees applauded JP's decision, believing that now everything would be better.

However, they were in for a shock when on April 1 the new managing director called everybody together to tell them how he would revolutionize the company. He would take the following three measures:

1   Give the company a divisional structure and hire 30 new salesmen.

2   Introduce new technology.

3   Form a number of inter-organizational relations.

1 Give the company a divisional structure and hire 30 new salesmen

The new managing director started explaining what he planned to do in each of his three target areas. He began by confirming that he believed JP Carpets' problems were caused fundamentally by its organizational structure. 'We are in a situation where we have to begin competing with the big companies within our business area, and to do this we need a divisional structure. My reason for hiring 30 more salesmen is that I want us to be much more active in sales and marketing, not only on the home market, but also as a step towards building up an export division.

'By introducing a divisional structure we shall have a much clearer delineation of responsibilities in the company, and we all know we are in dire need of that. The daily operations of JP Carpets today are characterized by nothing but emergencies. We never seem to plan ahead. With the new structure a number of division managers will be appointed, all from outside the company.'

In his message to the employees the new managing director mentioned other advantages of a divisional structure. He also paid special attention to the role of the new top management: 'I would like the top management to be less visible in the daily running of the company than it is today, not due to lack of interest, but because it should focus its efforts on market surveillance, which needs to be much more important in our business planning. Furthermore we must be prepared to buy, merge and sell companies at the right moment, and this will be another of the top management's primary tasks.'

'We will make sure middle managers, i.e. the heads of divisions, get more responsibility, and that they are more involved in staff management than they are today. Each division will be an independent profit centre, giving the middle managers increased independence as well as greater responsibility. It will be up to each division to determine to what extent their employees should be rewarded, for instance with bonus schemes.

'The 30 new sales people will be hired and incorporated in the new divisional structure. From now on we have to compete more directly with the big companies.'

2 Introduction of new technology

'The introduction of new technology is a must. It will revolutionize the entire company,' the new managing director continued. He revealed that JP's production technology must match that of the competition, and that this would make the company's production much more flexible. 'The reason why we cannot compete with the big companies today is that we have made no investments in new technology whereas others realized many years ago that they needed to develop and implement a technology action plan. With the

►

introduction of new technology, each division will be able to quickly respond to new customer demands.

'We need to redevelop our just-in-time agreements with our suppliers, who have gradually become too lax. They claim to live up to the JIT systems but the truth is that we have built up big inventory stockpiles. This means that the suppliers can easily live up to their JIT agreements. Each division needs its own logistics manager.

'Furthermore we need to implement computer-aided manufacturing (CAM) systems within the next two years. In our construction department we should use only well-known and well-established computer-based design systems enabling us to change product lines quickly according to customer wishes.

'In our production department the entire production process needs to be automated using the CAM systems where technology supports production. This relies of course on CAD systems being used in the construction department.'

Denis Lalonde, one of the more capable employees of JP Carpets and certainly an internal candidate for one of the new middle manager positions, asked the new managing director whether he was absolutely certain that a divisional structure would be able to handle the advanced production technology. Slightly shaken by the question, the managing director answered that this was a problem they had to look into later. Lalonde spoke up again saying that it was important to make as few organizational changes as possible, and that the new director did not seem to have considered the connection between the two.

The new managing director said to Lalonde and the other employees: 'Please give me a chance. I come to JP with great ideas. Of course, I cannot give a detailed account of how everything will work right now, but I am sure we will be one of the winners in the European carpet business.' Without commenting further on Lalonde's criticism, the managing director went on to Part 3.

3 Form a number of inter-organizational relations
The new managing director pointed out that henceforth it would be vital to strengthen ties between the company and its customers, suppliers and not least its competitors. He said it was his philosophy that JP should try to manoeuvre itself into a position where it was less vulnerable to hostile actions by the big

companies. In order to do that it needed to stop challenging them directly, and instead try to show them that there is room for everybody in the industry. 'As long as you show respect towards each other, your clients and your markets, it is better to cooperate than to fight,' he said. 'You are very welcome to start spreading this message whenever you are in contact with clients, suppliers or competitors. In order to make this cooperation strategy work, we have to develop a clearer and better defined company strategy stating our basic corporate values.'

When the new managing director had presented his three proposals, about half the employees applauded enthusiastically, while the other half seemed less convinced. The director, who thought that he had made a pretty good impression, was surprised by this lukewarm reaction on the part of a good proportion of the staff.

Amelie Amyotte, another of the company's young stars, gave voice to the doubters' concerns. 'We are happy to see that something is happening in the company now, but on the other hand we are also worried. It seems strange first to introduce a divisional structure and then to introduce advanced production technology. It seems a bit ill-considered.

'If I could be a bit critical, and I think you would want me to be honest, I am very surprised to see that you want to raise such high barriers between the different divisions. What makes JP Carpets a well-run company today is the close contact between all employees, and especially between the present management and the employees. As far as I can see, you want to erect barriers not only between the employees, but also the employees and the management. In my opinion this will result in more and more serious conflicts not only between employees and management, but also among employees.

'Further, I am very worried that you are not presenting any drawbacks to all your proposals. In life change seldom brings only benefits. I think you need to be more specific about where difficulties and problems may arise. By doing that you would show us that you are realistic about possible future problems. For instance, I would like to know what disadvantages can be expected with the divisional structure, and how you propose to solve them as they arise.'

The managing director answered that he couldn't reel off all the problems which may arise, but that it was his job to foresee future problems. He came with an open and positive mindset, hoping that the

▶

employees felt the same way. It was his job to overcome resistance to change and to make sure that the company's employees exploited the potential of new organizational structures, new technology and new strategies to the full. He also needed to ensure that the employees learned to cooperate with other companies. 'Even if it has to be done by force', was the last volley he fired at the astounded employees.

Now Jean Pelletier spoke up: 'Dear friends. JP Carpets is my life's work. With your help I built up a large and profitable company. We have run into some problems which can best be solved by my retirement and the employment of a professional manager. Please support him in his work! Continue to be good employees and be constructive. The process of change we are now going through must not be jeopardized because of misguided resistance to change. I am sure the new managing director of the company will ensure that there will be a positive learning and working environment within the company.'

Now all the employees applauded their old manager, who turned and said goodbye to the new managing director. Both hoped that the company would be changed for the better, but they were also well aware of all the problems and pitfalls that lay ahead.

Case Questions

1   What were the main problems at Dan Carpets, that led JP to leave and establish his own firm?

2   Why did JP Carpets initially succeed, but ultimately run into difficulties?

3   If you were the new managing director, how would you manage Amelie Amyotte and Denis Lalonde?

4   The new managing director outlined a three-point plan. What is the rationale behind each of the points and what are the advantages and disadvantages of each?

The University Art Museum

By Peter F. Drucker

Visitors to the campus were always shown the University Art Museum, of which the large and distinguished university was very proud. A photograph of the handsome neoclassical building that housed the museum had long been used by the university for the cover of its brochures and catalogues.

The building, together with a substantial endowment, was given to the university around 1912 by an alumnus, the son of the university's first president, who had become very wealthy as an investment banker. He also gave the university his own small, but high-quality collections – one of Etruscan figurines, and one, unique in America, of English pre-Raphaelite paintings. He then served as the museum's unpaid director until his death. During his tenure he brought a few additional collections to the museum, largely from other alumni of the university. Only rarely did the museum purchase anything. As a result, the museum housed several small collections of uneven quality. As long as the founder ran the museum, none of the collections were ever shown to anybody except a few members of the university's art history faculty, who were admitted as the founder's private guests.

After the founder's death, in the late 1920s, the university intended to bring in a professional museum director. Indeed, this had been part of the agreement under which the founder had given the museum. A search committee was to be appointed; but in the meantime a graduate student in art history, who had shown interest in the museum and who had spent a good many hours in it, took over temporarily. At first, Miss Kirkoff did not even have a title, let alone a salary. But she stayed on acting as the museum's director and over the next 30 years was promoted in stages to that title. But from the first day, whatever her title, she was in charge. She immediately set about changing the museum altogether. She catalogued the collections. She pursued new gifts, again primarily small collections from alumni and other friends of the university. She organized fund raising for the museum.

But, above all, she began to integrate the museum into the work of the university.

When a space problem arose in the years immediately following World War II, Miss Kirkoff offered the third floor of the museum to the art history faculty, which moved its offices there. She remodeled the building to include classrooms and a modern and well-appointed auditorium. She raised funds to build one of the best research and reference libraries in art history in the country. She also began to organize a series of special exhibitions built around one of the museum's own collections, complemented by loans from outside collections. For each of these exhibitions, she had a distinguished member of the university's art faculty write a catalogue. These catalogues speedily became the leading scholarly texts in the fields.

Miss Kirkoff ran the University Art Museum for almost half a century. But at the age of 68, after suffering a severe stroke, she had to retire. In her letter of resignation she proudly pointed to the museum's growth and accomplishment under her stewardship. 'Our endowment', she wrote, 'now compares favorably with museums several times our size. We never have had to ask the university for any money other than our share of the university's insurance policies. Our collections in the areas of our strength, while small, are of first rate quality and importance. Above all, we are being used by more people than any museum of our size. Our lecture series, in which members of the university's art history faculty present a major subject to a university audience of students and faculty, attracts regularly three hundred to five hundred people; and if we had the seating capacity, we could easily have a larger audience. Our exhibitions are seen and studied by more visitors, most of them members of the university community, than all but the most highly publicized exhibitions in the very big museums ever draw. Above all, the courses and seminars offered in the museum have become one of the most popular and most rapidly growing educational features of the university. No other museum in this country or anywhere else,' concluded Miss Kirkoff, 'has so successfully integrated art into the life of a major university and a major university into the work of a museum.'

Miss Kirkoff strongly recommended that the university bring in a professional museum director as her

Case #3, 'The University Art Museum: Defining Purpose and Mission' (pp. 28–35), from *Management Cases* by Peter F. Drucker. © 1977 by Peter F. Drucker.

▶

successor. 'The museum is much too big and much too important to be entrusted to another amateur such as I was forty-five years ago,' she wrote. 'And it needs careful thinking regarding its direction, its basis of support, and its future relationship with the university.'

The university took Miss Kirkoff's advice. A search committee was duly appointed and, after one year's work, it produced a candidate whom everybody approved. The candidate was himself a graduate of the university who had then obtained his PhD in art history and in museum work from the university. Both his teaching and his administrative record were sound, leading to his current museum directorship in a medium-sized city. There he converted an old, well-known, but rather sleepy museum to a lively, community-oriented museum whose exhibitions were well publicized and attracted large crowds.

The new museum director took over with great fanfare in September 1981. Less than three years later he left – with less fanfare, but still with considerable noise. Whether he resigned or was fired was not quite clear. But that there was bitterness on both sides was only too obvious.

The new director, upon his arrival, had announced that he looked upon the museum as a 'major community resource' and intended to 'make the tremendous artistic and scholarly resources of the museum fully available to the academic community as well as to the public.' When he said these things in an interview with the college newspaper, everybody nodded in approval. It soon became clear that what he meant by 'community resource' and what the faculty and students understood by these words were not the same. The museum had always been 'open to the public' but, in practice, it was members of the college community who used the museum and attended its lectures, its exhibitions and its frequent seminars.

The first thing the new director did, however, was to promote visits from the public schools in the area. He soon began to change the exhibition policy. Instead of organizing small shows, focused on a major collection of the museum and built around a scholarly catalogue, he began to organize 'popular exhibitions' around 'topics of general interest' such as 'Women Artists through the Ages'. He promoted these exhibitions vigorously in the newspapers, in radio and television interviews, and, above all, in the local schools. As a result, what had been a busy but quiet place was soon knee-deep with schoolchildren, taken to the museum in special buses that cluttered the access roads around the museum and throughout the campus. The faculty, which was not particularly happy with the resulting noise and confusion, became thoroughly upset when the scholarly old chairman of the art history department was mobbed by fourth-graders who sprayed him with their water pistols as he tried to push his way through the main hall to his office.

Increasingly, the new director did not design his own shows, but brought in travelling exhibitions from major museums, importing their catalogue as well, rather than have his own faculty produce one.

The students, too, were apparently unenthusiastic after the first six or eight months, during which the new director had been somewhat of a campus hero. Attendance at the classes and seminars held at the art museum fell off sharply, as did attendance at the evening lectures. When the editor of the campus newspaper interviewed students for a story on the museum, he was told again and again that the museum had become too noisy and too 'sensational' for students to enjoy the classes and to have a chance to learn.

What brought all this to a head was an Islamic art exhibit in late 1983. Since the museum had little Islamic art, nobody criticized the showing of a travelling exhibit, offered on very advantageous terms with generous financial assistance from some of the Arab governments. But then, instead of inviting one of the university's own faculty members to deliver the customary talk at the opening of the exhibit, the director brought in a cultural attaché of one of the Arab embassies in Washington. The speaker, it was reported, used the occasion to deliver a violent attack on Israel and on the American policy of supporting Israel against the Arabs. A week later, the university senate decided to appoint an advisory committee, drawn mostly from members of the art history faculty, which, in the future, would have to approve all plans for exhibits and lectures. The director thereupon, in an interview with the campus newspaper, sharply attacked the faculty as 'elitist' and 'snobbish' and as believing that 'art belongs to the rich'. Six months later, in June 1984, his resignation was announced.

Under the bylaws of the university, the academic senate appoints a search committee. Normally, this is pure formality. The chairperson of the appropriate department submits the department's nominees for the committee who are approved and appointed, usually without debate. But when the academic senate early the following semester was asked to appoint the search committee, things were far from 'normal'. The Dean who presided, sensing the tempers in the room, tried to smooth over things by saying, 'Clearly, we picked the wrong person the last time. We will have to try very hard to find the right one this time.'

He was immediately interrupted by an economist, known for his populism, who broke in and said, 'I admit that the late director was probably not the right personality. But I strongly believe that his personality was not at the root of the problem. He tried to do what needs doing, and this got him in trouble with the faculty. He tried to make our museum a community resource, to bring in the community and to make art accessible to broad masses of people, to the Blacks and the Puerto Ricans, to the kids from the ghetto schools and to a lay public. And this is what we really resented. Maybe his methods were not the most tactful ones – I admit I could have done without those interviews he gave. But what he tried to do was right. We had better commit ourselves to the policy he wanted to put into effect, or else we will have deserved his attacks on us as "elitist" and "snobbish".'

'This is nonsense,' cut in the usually silent and polite senate member from the art history faculty. 'It makes absolutely no sense for our museum to become the kind of community resource our late director and my distinguished colleague want it to be. First, there is no need. The city has one of the world's finest and biggest museums, and it does exactly that and does it very well. Secondly, we have neither the artistic resources nor the financial resources to serve the community at large. We can do something different but equally important and indeed unique. Ours is the only museum in the country, and perhaps in the world, that is fully integrated with an academic community and truly a teaching institution. We are using it, or at least we used to until the last few unfortunate years, as a major educational resource for all our students. No other museum in the country, and as far as I know in the world, is bringing undergraduates into art the way we do. All of us, in addition to our scholarly and graduate work, teach undergraduate courses for people who are not going to be art majors or art historians. We work with the engineering students and show them what we do in our conservation and restoration work. We work with architecture students and show them the development of architecture

through the ages. Above all, we work with liberal arts students, who often have had no exposure to art before they came here and who enjoy our courses all the more because they are scholarly and not just "art appreciation". This is unique and this is what our museum can do and should do.'

'I doubt that this is really what we should be doing,' commented the chairman of the mathematics department. 'The museum, as far as I know, is part of the graduate faculty. It should concentrate on training art historians in its PhD programme, on its scholarly work and on its research. I would strongly urge that the museum be considered an adjunct to graduate and especially to PhD education, confine itself to this work, and stay out of all attempts to be "popular", both on campus and outside of it. The glory of the museum is the scholarly catalogues produced by our faculty, and our PhD graduates who are sought after by art history faculties throughout the country. This is the museum's mission, which can only be impaired by the attempts to be "popular", whether with students or with the public.'

'These are very interesting and important comments,' said the Dean, still trying to pacify. 'But I think this can wait until we know who the new director is going to be. Then we should raise these questions with him.'

'I beg to differ, Mr Dean,' said one of the elder statesmen of the faculty. 'During the summer months, I discussed this question with an old friend and neighbour of mine in the country, the director of one of the nation's great museums. He said to me: "You do not have a personality problem; you have a management problem. You have not, as a university, taken responsibility for the mission, the direction and the objectives of your museum. Until you do this, no director can succeed. And this is your decision. In fact, you cannot hope to get a good director until you can tell that person what your basic objectives are. If your late director is to blame – I know him and I know that he is abrasive – it is for being willing to take on a job when you, the university, had not faced up to the basic management decisions. There is no point talking about who should manage until it is clear what it is that has to be managed and for what.'

At this point the Dean realized that he had to adjourn the discussion unless he wanted the meeting to degenerate into a brawl. But he also realized that he had to identify the issues and possible decisions before the next senate meeting a month later.

Case Questions

1 What do you see as the fundamental problem facing the University Art Museum? Is it the selection of a new director, or something more fundamental?

2 If you were the Dean, how would you go about designing a process to decide the future direction of the University Art Museum?

3 Everyone seemed to agree that the departed director was an abrasive character. But do you think any director could have managed the museum more successfully? If so, how?

4 To what extent do you think the current problems of the University Art Museum can be traced back to the foundation of the museum in 1912?

Notes

1. http://web.archive.org/web/20090824054400/http://www.starbucks.com/aboutus/company_factsheet.pdf, accessed on September 15, 2013.

2. Starbucks Inc. Annual Report 2006, available at http://media.corporate-ir.net/media_files/irol/99/99518/reports/StarbucksAnnualReport.pdf.

3. Steven Gray, 'Starbucks Brews Broader Menu; Coffee Chain's Cup Runneth Over with Breakfast, Lunch, Music', *The Wall Street Journal* (February 9, 2005), B9; Andy Serwer, 'Hot Starbucks to Go', *Fortune* (January 26, 2004), 60–74; Jean Patteson, 'Warm Hues Hot for Fall; Call It the Starbucks Influence, as Designers Serve Colours from Latte to Espresso Spiked with Vibrant Blues', *Orlando Sentinel* (February 10, 2005), E1; 'Starbucks' Continues Successful Expansion of Music Experience', *Business Wire* (February 9, 2005), 1; and Monica Soto Ouchi, 'No Roast, Just Thanks to Can-Do Coffee Man', *Seattle Times* (February 10, 2005), A1.

4. Janet Adamy, 'McDonald's to take on a weakened Starbucks', Associated Press wire, January 7, 2008.

5. Mehreen Khan, EU rules Starbucks 'sweetheart' tax deals are illegal state subsidies: Luxembourg and Netherlands judged to have provided illegal tax breaks to the tune of €30m to corporate giants Starbucks and Fiat, *Daily Telegraph*, 21 Oct 2015, accessed at www.telegraph.co.uk/finance/newsbysector/retailandconsumer/11945013/European-Union-orders-Starbucks-and-Fiat-Juncker-Luxembourg-pay-30m-in-unpaid-taxes.html

6. Dow Jones Global News, 19 February 2013, 'Starbucks Expects to More than Double Asia Staff'. Leslie Patton, October 4, 2012, 'Starbucks CEO Sees Adding 1000 US Staff in Five Years', Bloomberg. Leslie Patton, July 12, 2012, 'Starbucks Falls After Cutting Forecast Below Estimate', *BusinessWeek*. John Geddie, Feb 14, 2012, 'Guns and Coffee: Starbucks again an open carry policy battleground', *London Times*, USA. Roxanne Escobales and Tracy McVeigh, 8 December 2012, 'Starbucks hit by UK Uncut protests as tax row boils over', *The Guardian*.

7. Amitai Etzioni, *Modern Organizations* (Englewood Cliffs, NJ: Prentice-Hall, 1964), 6.

8. John P. Kotter, 'What Effective General Managers Really Do', *Harvard Business Review* (November–December 1982), 156–167; Henry Mintzberg, *The Nature of Managerial Work* (New York: Harper & Row, 1973).

9. Charles C. Snow and Lawrence G. Hrebiniak, 'Strategy, Distinctive Competence and Organizational Performance', *Administrative Science Quarterly* 25 (1980), 317–335.

10. "Data manipulation by staff gets Novartis into legal mess in Japan", *Japan Herald*, Wednesday 2nd July, 2014, accessed at www.japanherald.com/index.php/sid/223435459

11. 'Strong R&D Medicine is the Drug of Choice for Fast-Growing Pharma', *Irish Independent*, September 9, 2004; Alison Maitland, 'A leader striving for the perfect bedside manner', *Financial Times*, November 28, 2001, page 1; David Pilling, 'What the Doctor Ordered', *Financial Times*, October 12, 1998, page 1; Bill Griffeth and Maria Bartiromo, 'Novartis: CEO and Chairman Interview', *CEO Wire* January 2, 2006.

12. Helmut K. Anheier (2002), The third sector in Europe: Five theses, Civil Society Working Paper 12, London, LSE.

13. Klein, P. (2006), *Economics Confronts the Economy*, London, Edward Elgar, p. 228.

14. Forest R. David and Fred R. David, 'It's Time to Redraft Your Mission Statement', *Journal of Business Strategy* (January–February 2003), 11–14; John Pearce and Fred David, 'Corporate Mission Statements: The Bottom Line', *Academy of Management Executive* 1, no. 2 (May 1987), 109–116; and Christopher Bart and Mark Baetz, 'The Relationship Between Mission Statements and Firm Performance: An Exploratory Study', *Journal of Management Studies* 35 (1998).

15. Mark C. Suchman, 'Managing Legitimacy: Strategic and Institutional Approaches', *Academy of Management Review* 20, no. 3 (1995), 571–610.

16. Kurt Eichenwald, 'Miscues, Missteps and the Fall of Andersen', *The New York Times* (May 8, 2002), C1, C4; Ian Wilson, 'The Agenda for Redefining Corporate Purpose: Five Key Executive Actions', *Strategy & Leadership* 32, no. 1 (2004), 21–26.

17. Chris Penttila, 'Missed Mission', Entrepreneur Magazine, May 2002, at http://www.entrepreneur.com/magazine/entrepreneur/2002/may/51106.html.

18. Fred David (1989), 'How Companies Define Their Mission', *Long Range Planning*, volume 22, 90–97; Carolyn Strong (1997), 'The question we continue to ask: How do organizations define their mission?' *Journal of Marketing Practice: Applied Marketing Science*, Volume 3, 268–283;

Jatinder Sidhu (2003), 'Mission Statements: Is it Time to Shelve Them?', *European Management Journal*, 21, 439– 446; Chris Bart (2004), 'Innovation, mission statements and learning', *International Journal of Technology Management*, 27, 544–567; Barbara Bartkus, Myron Glassman and Bruce McAfee (2006), 'Mission Statement Quality and Financial Performance', *European Management Journal*, 24, 86–94.

19. Johannes U. Stoelwinder and Martin P. Charns, 'The Task Field Model of Organization Analysis and Design', *Human Relations* 34 (1981), 743–762; Anthony Raia, *Managing by Objectives* (Glenview, Ill.: Scott, Foresman, 1974).

20. Volvo AG Annual Report 2006, page 13, at http://www.volvogroup.com/SiteCollectionDocuments/Volvo%20AB/media/publications/financial/annual%20reports/070319_volvo_engelsk_150dpi.pdf, accessed on September 15, 2013.

21. Known as the Honda Jazz in Europe.

22. Japan Automobile Dealers Association, December 6, 2006, cited at http://www.shiotsu-autotrade.jp/blog/?p=9.

23. Ivar Ekman, 'Lego braces for big changes', *International Herald Tribune*, July 2, 2005, page 9; Bernard Marotte, 'Top court quashes Lego bid against toy rival', *Globe and Mail*, November 18, 2005, B5.

24. Alex Taylor III, 'Honda Goes Its Own Way,' *Fortune* (July 22, 2002), 148–152; Joseph Pereira and Christopher J. Chipello, 'Battle of the Block Makers', *The Wall Street Journal* (February 4, 2004), B1.

25. John Kell, "Lego Says 2015 Was Its 'Best Year Ever,' With Huge Sales Jump", Fortune, March 1, 2016, accessed at fortune.com/2016/03/01/lego-sales-toys-2015/

26. Serafini, G. O., & Szamosi, L. T. (2015). Five star hotels of a Multinational Enterprise in countries of the transitional periphery: A case study in human resources management. International Business Review, 24(6), 972–983.

27. Michael Arndt, '3M: A Lab for Growth?' *BusinessWeek* (January 21, 2002), 50–51.

28. Embraer Annual Report 2014, p. 22, accessed at http://www.embraer.com.br/Documents/Relatorio-Anual/RELATORIO_ANUAL_2014_INGLES.pdf.

29. Doreen Hemlock, 'Brazilian jet maker Embraer soars', *South Florida Sun-Sentinel*, November 25, 2007; Q1 2007 Embraer-Empresa Brasileira de Aeronautica S.A. Earnings Conference Call, *Fair Disclosure Wire*, May 15, 2007.

30. Kim Cross, 'Does Your Team Measure Up?' *Business2.com* (June 12, 2001), 22–28; J. Lynn Lunsford, 'Lean Times: With Airbus on Its Tail, Boeing is Rethinking How It Builds Planes', *The Wall Street Journal* (September 5, 2001), A11.

31. Mary Chao, "Wegmans celebrates 100 years in business", Rochester Democrat and Chronicle, January 30, 2016, accessed at www.democratandchronicle.com/story/news/2016/01/30/wegmans-celebrates-100-years-business/79511060/

32. Emma Sapong, 16 January 2013, 'Wegmans ranked among best places to work for 16th straight year', *The Buffalo News*.

33. Christopher Cooper and Greg Jaffe, 'Under Fire: At Abu Ghraib, Soldiers Faced Intense Pressure to Produce Data', *The Wall Street Journal* (June 1, 2004), A1, A6.

34. James D. Thompson, *Organizations in Action* (New York: McGraw-Hill, 1967), 83–98.

35. Michael E. Porter, 'What Is Strategy?' *Harvard Business Review* (November–December 1996), 61–78.

36. Michael E. Porter, *Competitive Strategy: Techniques for Analyzing Industries and Competitors* (New York: Free Press, 1980).

37. Datamonitor, January 7, 2008.

38. Alan Ruddock, 'Keeping Up with O'Leary', *Management Today* (September 2003), 48–55; Jane Engle, 'Flying High for Pocket Change; Regional Carriers Offer Inexpensive Travel Alternative', *South Florida Sun Sentinel* (February 13, 2005), 5; 'Ryanair is Top on Net', *The Daily Mirror* (February 3, 2005), 10; and 'Ryanair Tops 2m Passengers', *Daily Post* (February 4, 2005), 21.

39. Christopher Elliott, "These 10 airlines have the highest fees", Fortune, July 14 2015, accessed at fortune.com/2015/07/14/airlines-highest-fees/

40. Ryanair Investor Relations: Passenger Traffic 2002/2013, accessed at http://www.ryanair.com/en/investor/trafficfigures. Oliver Smith, 1 Nov 2012, 'Airline "extras" continue to soar', *Daily Telegraph*. 'KLM to charge for checked baggage', *Business Traveller*, February 13 2012.

41. Richard Teitelbaum, 'The Wal-Mart of Wall Street', *Fortune* (October 13, 1997), 128–130.

42. CNN interview transcript, Puma CEO and Chairman Jochen Zeitz, September 28 2006 at http://edition.cnn.com/2006/BUSINESS/07/06/boardroom.zeitz/; Holger Elfes, 'Puma strengthens ties with its parent', *International Herald Tribune*, p. 16; 'FD (Fair Disclosure) Wire', Interim 2007 PPR (ex. Pinault Printemps Redoute) Earnings Conference Call, August 31, 2007.

43. Kevin J. O'Brien, 'Focusing on Armchair Athletes, Puma Becomes a Leader', *The New York Times* (March 12, 2004), W1.

44. Michael E. Porter, 'Strategy and the Internet', *Harvard Business Review* (March 2001), 63–78; and John Magretta, 'Why Business Models Matter', *Harvard Business Review* (May 2002), 86.

45. Martin Samociuk, Nigel Iyer and Helenne Doody (2010) *A Short Guide to Fraud Risk: Fraud Resistance and Detection*, Farnham, Gower Publishing Company; Mimi Swartz, May 21 2006, 'The Three Faces of Ken Lay', *New York Times*.

46. Dennis Tourish and Ashly Pinnington (2002), 'Transformational leadership, corporate cultism and the spirituality paradigm: An unholy trinity in the workplace?', *Human Relations*, 55, p: 147–172; Rakesh Khurana (2002), 'The Curse of the Superstar CEO', *Harvard Business Review*, 80(9), 60–67; Dennis Tourish and Naheed Vatcha (2005), 'Charismatic Leadership and Corporate Cultism at Enron: The Elimination of Dissent, the Promotion of Conformity and Organizational Collapse', *Leadership*, 1, pp. 455–480.

47. Raymond E. Miles and Charles C. Snow, *Organizational Strategy, Structure and Process* (New York: McGraw-Hill, 1978).

48. Geraldine Fabrikant, 'The Paramount Team Puts Profit Over Splash', *The New York Times* (June 30, 2002), Section 3, 1, 15.

49. Amy Cholzick, 15 November 2012, 'Viacom Profit Increases, but Movie Division Hurts Revenues', *New York Times*.

50. 'Miles and Snow: Enduring Insights for Managers: Academic Commentary by Sumantra Ghoshal', *Academy of Management Executive* 17, no. 4 (2003), 109–114.

51. Claire Atkinson, 26 October 2012, 'Shaken & stirred Sony CEO fights studio sale rumors', *New York Post*. Rex Crum, 24 January 2013, 'Microsoft May See Limited Windows 8 Traction', Dow Jones Global News.

52. Paul R. La Monica, "McDonald's sales soar thanks to all day breakfast", CNN Money, January 25, 2016, accessed at money.cnn.com/2016/01/25/investing/mcdonalds-earnings/.

53. 'On the Staying Power of Defenders, Analyzers and Prospectors: Academic Commentary by Donald C. Hambrick', *Academy of Management Executive* 17, no. 4 (2003), 115–118.

54. W. Chan Kim and Renée Mauborgne (2005), 'Blue Ocean Strategy: From Theory to Practice', *California Review of Management,* 47, 105–121; C. Kim and R. Mauborgne (2005), *Blue Ocean Strategy: How to Create Uncontested Market Space and Make the Competition Irrelevant,* Cambridge, MA, Harvard Business School Press.

55. J.N. Baron and M.T. Hannan (2002), 'Organizational blueprints for success in high-tech start-ups', *California Management Review*, Vol. 44 No.3, pp. 8–36.

56. Amitai Etzioni, *Modern Organizations*, 8; and Gary D. Sandefur, 'Efficiency in Social Service Organizations', *Administration and Society* 14 (1983), 449–468.

57. Richard M. Steers, *Organizational Effectiveness: A Behavioral View* (Santa Monica, CA: Goodyear, 1977), 51.

58. Karl E. Weick and Richard L. Daft, 'The Effectiveness of Interpretation Systems', in Kim S. Cameron and David A. Whetten, eds., *Organizational Effectiveness: A Comparison of Multiple Models* (New York: Academic Press, 1982).

59. David L. Blenkhorn and Brian Gaber, 'The Use of "Warm Fuzzies" to Assess Organizational Effectiveness,' *Journal of General Management*, 21, no. 2 (Winter 1995), 40–51.

60. Steven Strasser, J. D. Eveland, Gaylord Cummins, O. Lynn Deniston and John H. Romani, 'Conceptualizing the Goal and Systems Models of Organizational Effectiveness – Implications for Comparative Evaluation Research', *Journal of Management Studies* 18 (1981), 321–340.

61. United Nations Millennium Declaration, Resolution 55/2, September 18 2000, at http://www.un.org/millennium/declaration/ares552e.pdf; *United Nations Millennium Development Goals Report – 2007*, at http://www.un.org/millenniumgoals/pdf/mdg2007.pdf. Elizabeth Flock, 6 March 2012, 'Millennium development goals: Two down, six to go', *Washington Post*.

62. Richard H. Hall and John P. Clark, 'An Ineffective Effectiveness Study and Some Suggestions for Future Research', *Sociological Quarterly* 21 (1980), 119–134; Price, 'The Study of Organizational Effectiveness'; and Perrow, 'Analysis of Goals'.

63. Y. K. Shetty, 'New Look at Corporate Goals', *California Management Review* 22, no. 2 (1979), 71–79.

64. The discussion of the resource-based approach is based in part on Michael V. Russo and Paul A. Fouts, 'A Resource-Based Perspective on Corporate Environmental Performance and Profitability', *Academy of Management Journal* 40, no. 3 (June 1997), 534–559; and Jay B. Barney, J. L. 'Larry' Stempert, Loren T. Gustafson and Yolanda Sarason, 'Organizational Identity within the Strategic Management Conversation: Contributions and Assumptions', in *Identity in Organizations: Building Theory through Conversations*, David A. Whetten and Paul C. Godfrey, eds. (Thousand Oaks, CA: Sage Publications, 1998), 83–98.

65. Enrico Valdani and Fabio Ancarani (2001), 'Marketing Places: A Resource-Based Approach and Empirical Evidence from the European Experience', SDA Bocconi, Research Division Working Paper No. 01/55.

66. AT Kearney, Inc. (2008), *Success through Shared Services – From Back Office Functions to Strategic Drivers*, Chicago, AT Kearney, at http://web.archive.org/web/20090320034845/http://www.atkearney.com/shared_res/pdf/Shared_Services_S.pdf, accessed on September 15, 2013.; Alan Duerden, 'Commercial services strategy support', *The Banker*, December 1, 2007; Alan Rodger, 'AnalystWatch: Another Ground-Breaking Year for TCS', *Computerwire*, December 24, 2007; Elizabeth Ferrarini, 'Shared Services', *Computerworld*, November 27, 2000.

67. Brad Plumer, "Volkswagen's appalling clean diesel scandal, explained", Vox, September 23, 2015, accessed at www.vox.com/2015/9/21/9365667/volkswagen-clean-diesel-recall-passenger-cars, Michael Nienaber, "Volkswagen could pose bigger threat to German economy than Greek crisis", Reuters, September 23 2015, accessed at www.reuters.com/article/us-usa-volkswagen-germany-economy-idUSKCN0RN27S20150923, "VW Financial Services takes writedown for emissions scandal", Reuters, Mar 15, 2016, accessed at uk.reuters.com/article/us-volkswagen-financialservices-idUKKCN0WH1BO.

68. Chris Argyris, *Integrating the Individual and the Organization* (New York: Wiley, 1964); Warren G. Bennis, *Changing Organizations* (New York: McGraw-Hill, 1966); Rensis Likert, *The Human Organization* (New York: McGraw-Hill, 1967); and Richard Beckhard, *Organization Development Strategies and Models* (Reading, Mass.: Addison-Wesley, 1969).

69. Cheri Ostroff and Neal Schmitt, 'Configurations of Organizational Effectiveness and Efficiency', *Academy of Management Journal* 36 (1993), 1345–1361; Peter

J. Frost, Larry F. Moore, Meryl Reise Louis, Craig C. Lundburg and Joanne Martin, *Organizational Culture* (Beverly Hills, CA: Sage, 1985).

70. J. Barton Cunningham, 'Approaches to the Evaluation of Organizational Effectiveness', *Academy of Management Review* 2 (1977), 463–474; Beckhard, *Organization Development*.

71. Mike Lewis, 'New Boeing leader a big part of company's turnaround', *Seattle Post-Intelligencer*, September 6, 2006; James Wallace, 'Boeing leader ousted', *Seattle Post-Intelligencer*, March 8, 2005.

72. http://www.nytimes.com/2013/03/15/business/boeingpresents-fix-for-787s-battery-problems.html?_r=0

73. Roger Martin, 'How he thinks', *Canadian Business*, Winter 2007–2008, p. 78.

74. http://fortune.com/best-companies/four-seasons-hotels-resorts-70/.

75. Stanley Holmes, 'A New Black Eye for Boeing?' *BusinessWeek* (April 26, 2004), 90–92; Robert Levering and Milton Moskowitz, 'The 100 Best Companies to Work For', *Fortune* (January 24, 2005), 72–90.

76. Eric J. Walton and Sarah Dawson, 'Managers' Perceptions of Criteria of Organizational Effectiveness', *Journal of Management Studies* 38, no. 2 (2001), 173–199.

77. Beth Dickey, 'NASA's Next Step', *Government Executive* (April 15, 2004), 34.

78. Robert E. Quinn and John Rohrbaugh, 'A Spatial Model of Effectiveness Criteria: Toward a Competing Values Approach to Organizational Analysis', *Management Science* 29 (1983), 363–377.

79. Regina M. O'Neill and Robert E. Quinn, 'Editor's Note: Applications of the Competing Values Framework', *Human Resource Management* 32 (Spring 1993), 1–7.

80. Thomson Reuters 2014 Regulatory filing, accessed at https://www.google.com/finance?q=NYSE:TRI&fstype=ii&ei=F7-5VYjoFlulugSp1pWwCQ.

81. Larry Bossidy and Ram Charan, *Confronting Reality: Doing What Matters to Get Things Right* (New York: Crown Business, 2004), Chapter 9, 153–168. Thomson Reuters Annual Report, 2011.

CHAPTER 4

FUNDAMENTALS OF ORGANIZATION STRUCTURE

A LOOK INSIDE

Opel España

Opel España is the Spanish subsidiary of the global auto giant General Motors, based near the northern Spanish city of Zaragoza. While US auto manufacturers, including GM, are facing increasingly difficult market conditions in their home base due to competition from Asian car builders, global operations had been performing well, at least until the global downturn that hit manufacturing industry everywhere starting in 2007/2008. One of GM's survival strategies is based on continuing its international growth as it rebalances its activities towards growing markets outside the United States. The Zaragoza plant is GM's second largest in Europe, with over 5000 staff and annual capacity of around 450 000 vehicles, and makes the high-selling Corsa, the Meriva minivan and, since 2014, the Mokka subcompact SUV.

Consumer expectations are becoming increasingly sophisticated and differentiated. In the early days of car manufacture, Henry Ford was famously quoted as saying of his Model T, 'the customer can have any colour he wants so long as it's black'.[1] Nowadays, consumer preferences are key. Car buyers demand fashionable interiors and exteriors, technological innovation, a variety of product options to fit individual needs and high quality at reasonable prices. In addition, competition from other manufacturers has intensified, and customers have a range of high quality, competitively priced alternatives.

This increasingly demanding business environment is leading car companies to adopt various new production models, including what is termed *agile manufacturing*.[2] Agile manufacturing departs from the traditional mass production approach, focusing on highly customized manufacturing, producing vehicles as and when customers require them, rapidly changing production to meet new demands, and marketing a wide variety of products and product options to satisfy an increasingly diverse and knowledgeable customer base.

Opel España has spent considerable time and effort tailoring its physical plant, equipment, organizational structure and management systems to meet these challenges and to allow continued growth and profitability. For the launch of the fourth-generation Opel Corsa D in 2006, managers brought in experts from GM/Opel's International Technical Development Centre in Germany to design more efficient and flexible production. The strategy emphasized the need for integrated improvements. Equipment innovations included expanded use of robots in production, and new paint-spraying machinery that produces higher quality finish and fewer environmental emissions.[3] Production processes and procedures were streamlined. Central to the production redesign, however, were improvements in organizational design.

Organizational design is centred around teamwork practices designed to build empowerment, involvement and motivation of employees, from top management to the shop floor. From the beginning, the new Corsa's design was based on the integration of production, engineering and marketing managers in the development team.[4] This teamwork approach extends into the manufacturing process, where flexible manufacturing systems are based on a modular approach. The modular approach allows the end-customer to select from a wide range of standardized options so that the car that rolls off the production line is the one that the consumer has chosen. Like many other manufacturers, Opel España relies increasingly on the outsourcing of various parts of the vehicle. Again, the company is moving towards modular outsourcing, so that rather than subcontracting numerous small components, suppliers provide whole modules, such as steering assemblies, which are then incorporated into the car at the Zaragoza plant. Major suppliers, too, were involved in the Corsa design process from the earliest stage, ensuring that potential problems were smoothed out before full production began.

General Motors had originally planned to divest itself of its European plants when the parent company ran into trouble in the mid-2000s, but once the decision was made to keep its European division, it placed an emphasis on quality and efficiency. This became even more important in the wake of the economic crisis, which affected Spain particularly badly. However, the great majority of production of the Zaragoza plant is destined for export, albeit mainly within the Eurozone which remains in the doldrums a decade after the start of the 2007 global financial crisis. Like many companies, Opel España is looking at China as an export market to compensate for weak domestic markets. Volumes have gradually increased from around 265 000 in 2012 towards the plants 450 000 capacity, with a significant milestone passed in 2015 when the Zaragoza factory produced its 12 millionth car.[5]

Managers responsible for the design and redesign of organizations have used various structural arrangements with regard to the vertical and horizontal divisions of labour. Nearly every organization undergoes structural reorganization at some point to help meet new challenges or to signal the arrival of a 'new broom'. Structural changes reflect new strategies or respond to changes which, in Chapter 3, were conceived as 'contingency factors', such as environment, technology, size and life cycle, and culture. In general, the effectiveness of a directive, authoritarian management style has been increasingly criticized for its lack of responsiveness and 'agility' and there has been increased experimentation with more flexible, teamwork-based approaches in an effort to improve decision-making and put resources in places where they are assessed to produce the greatest value.[6]

Purpose of this Chapter

This chapter introduces basic concepts of organization structure. First we define a structure and provide an overview of structural design. Then, an information-processing perspective explains how information flow may be facilitated by designing vertical and horizontal linkages to achieve information flow. Basic design options are then presented, followed by strategies for grouping organizational activities into functional, divisional, matrix, horizontal, virtual network or hybrid structures. The final section examines how the application of designs depends on the organization's situation and outlines the symptoms of structural misalignment.

Organization Structure

ONLINE
COUNTERPOINT 4.1

There are three key components in the definition of organization structure:

1 Organization structure designates formal reporting relationships, including the number of levels in the hierarchy and the span of control of managers and supervisors.

2 Organization structure identifies the grouping together of individuals into departments and of departments into the total organization.

3 Organization structure includes the design of systems to ensure effective communication, coordination and integration of efforts across departments.[7]

These three elements of structure refer to both vertical and horizontal aspects of organizing. For example, the first two elements are the structural *framework*, which include the vertical hierarchy.[8] The third element pertains to the pattern of *interactions* among organizational employees.

Organization Structure Represented Visually in Organization Charts

BRIEFCASE 4.1

It isn't possible to see the internal structure of an organization the way we might see its manufacturing tools, offices or products. Although we might see employees going about their duties, performing different tasks and working in different locations, a way to show the structure underlying all this activity is through the organization chart. The organization chart is the (usually top-down) visual representation of a whole set of underlying activities and processes in an organization. Exhibit 4.1 shows a sample organization chart.

The concept of an organization chart, showing what positions exist, how they are grouped and who reports to whom, has been around for centuries.[9] Diagrams outlining church hierarchy can be found in medieval churches in Spain. However, the contemporary use of the organization chart for business stems from the Industrial Revolution, and especially from the emergence of large scale steam railways in the mid-nineteenth century. As work grew more complex and was performed by greater and greater numbers of workers, there was a pressing need to develop ways

EXHIBIT 4.1 A Sample Organization Chart

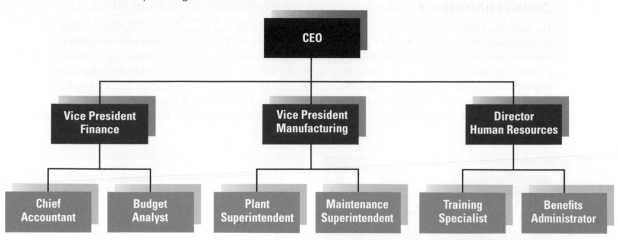

of managing and controlling organizations (see Counterpoint 4.1). One of the earliest examples of an organizational chart was in American railways, as a response to safety issues. After two passenger trains collided in Massachusetts in 1841, the public demanded better control of the operation. As a result, the Board of Directors of the Western Railroad took steps to outline 'definite responsibilities for each phase of the company's business, drawing solid lines of authority and command for the railroad's administration, maintenance and operation'.[10]

COUNTERPOINT 4.1

An organization chart is only so many lines and boxes. The organization chart indicates the structure of control but its enactment and realization depends upon the employees who provide the behaviour. Its purpose is to offer a common frame of reference that, in general and above all, asserts and reinforces a hierarchical relationship of domination between executives at the apex, managers in the middle levels and workers at the base. If all employees can be encouraged to accept this hierarchy as something that is a necessity, rather than politically imposed or expedient, then the goals of the organization determined by executives will more likely be realized through their actions. The chart is not only a technical guideline to encourage people to work together but a powerful political symbol whose acceptance implies deference to its demands.

The type of organization structure that grew out of these efforts to draw lines of command in the late nineteenth and early twentieth centuries was one in which the CEO was placed at the top and everyone else was arranged in layers down below, as illustrated in Exhibit 4.1. It indicates how thinking and decision-making are to be carried out by those at the top, and the physical work is performed by employees who are organized into distinct, functional departments where they are expected to carry out demands. This structure became increasingly entrenched in business, nonprofit and military organizations during the twentieth century. However, such a structure is not always effective, particularly in rapidly changing environments, and a variety of alternative structures have been devised to be more flexible and to increase involvement of all the organization's employees. These are typically aimed at increasing horizontal coordination and communication and encouraging adaptation to external changes. This chapter's *Bookmark 4.0* asks whether business is on the verge of a historic transformation, in which traditional forms of organizing are giving way to alternative decentralized, networked structures where more emphasis is placed on horizontal processes.

COUNTERPOINT 4.2

Decentralized structures can improve organizational flexibility and productivity. Employees' experience of decentralized structures, however, may be mixed. As decentralization increases responsibilities of line workers, employees have the chance to develop added competencies. Yet added responsibility and productivity does not necessarily come with improved salaries and job security. Are the benefits of organizational innovation being fairly shared between the company's shareholders and its employees?[11] If not, can this continue without stoking up resentment and fuelling resistance in the form of psychological distancing, withdrawal of goodwill, organized opposition, individual sabotage and so on?

BOOKMARK 4.0

Have you read this book?

The Future of Work: How the New Order of Business Will Shape Your Organization, Your Management Style and Your Life

BY THOMAS W. MALONE

Organizations are experiencing tremendous change, and Thomas W. Malone suggests in his book *The Future of Work* that they are on the verge of a fundamental shift that could be 'as important to business as the shift to democracy has been for government'. Rigid, highly centralized vertical hierarchies, he says, will essentially be a thing of the past as organizations move to flexible decentralized forms of organizing based on horizontal work processes. Command-and-control management and top-down decision-making will give way to empowered teams of employees focused on specific workflows and processes, working across organizational boundaries and making their own decisions based on up-to-the-minute information.

The Brave New World of Work

Malone describes several decentralized management structures and provides numerous examples of organizations that are experimenting with new forms of organizing and innovative management techniques. Here are some of Malone's key points about the future of work:

- *Information technology is the key driver of the transformation.* The falling cost of communication is making the distribution of power away from the corporate suite both inevitable and desirable. Outsourcing information work to India, for example, is possible because digital communication with India is so cheap, as is labour in India. In the same way, accessible information makes it possible for any lower-level employee to plan his or her work more effectively, network and get advice from people anywhere, and make good decisions based on accurate information.

- *Managers will move from command-and-control to coordinate-and-cultivate.* To coordinate is to organize work so that good things happen, whether managers are 'in control' or not. To cultivate means to bring out the best in employees with the right combination of control and freedom. W. L. Gore, the maker of Gore-Tex fabric, lets people decide what they want to do. Leaders emerge based on who has a good idea and can recruit people to work on it. AES, one of the world's largest electric power producers, coordinates and cultivates so well that it lets low-level workers make critical multimillion-dollar decisions about such things as acquiring new subsidiaries.

The Transition Years

Malone, a professor at MIT's Sloan School of Management, acknowledges that hierarchy and centralization continue to provide tremendous advantages for some companies in today's economy. In addition, for most organizations, centralized and decentralized structures and management systems will coexist well into the future. Yet, he is convinced that, ultimately, rigid hierarchical centralized structures will be consigned to the dustbin of history.

The Future of Work: How the New Order of Business Will Shape Your Organization, Your Management Style and Your Life, by Thomas W. Malone, is published by Harvard Business School Press.

Information-Processing Perspective on Structure

Exhibit 4.2 compares organizations designed for control with those designed for learning (see also Chapter 2). An *emphasis on control* is associated with specialized tasks, a hierarchy of authority, rules and regulations, formal reporting systems, few teams or task forces and centralized decision-making, which means problems and decisions are funnelled to top levels of the hierarchy for resolution. An *emphasis on learning* is associated with shared tasks, a relaxed hierarchy, few rules, face-to-face communication, many teams and task forces and informal, decentralized decision-making. Decentralized decision-making means decision-making authority is pushed down to lower organizational levels (see Counterpoint 4.3).

COUNTERPOINT 4.3

Note that the division of labour is associated with control in *the name of efficiency*, and not necessarily with the delivery of enhanced efficiency or effectiveness. At the extreme, the autocratic CEO may exert control through the micro-management of activities so that no significant decision is made without his or her agreement. Such control will likely produce a backlog of decision-making and delayed decisions that are based upon a distant and limited understanding of the specific circumstances. What is true of the autocratic CEO is also true, to a degree, of all organizations with a structure where those 'at the top' become remote from what is happening 'at the bottom'. The problems are compounded when senior management teams either assume that they are omniscient or rely upon managers who live in fear of providing unwelcome information.

Some of the most successful 'new economy' companies such as Google operate on a highly decentralized model giving employees considerable discretion to collaborate and innovate.[12] At the same time, even in a decentralized company a basic hierarchical structure usually remains in place even though it may be overlaid and obscured by an emphasis upon horizontal coordination. At the very least, shareholders require assurance that their investment is 'under control' as well as being deployed as effectively as possible by ensuring agility and responsiveness to emerging opportunities and challenges, as discussed in the Oracle case below. Increasingly, information technologies are used to monitor performance, ideally in real time, thereby facilitating centralized as well as decentralized communication to keep control of the diverse operations of global corporations. For example, Mexico's Cemex, discussed in Chapter 2, has installed computers with broadband internet connections into employees' homes, all linked to the company's intranet portal.[13]

EXHIBIT 4.2 The Relationship of Organization Design to Efficiency versus Learning Outcomes

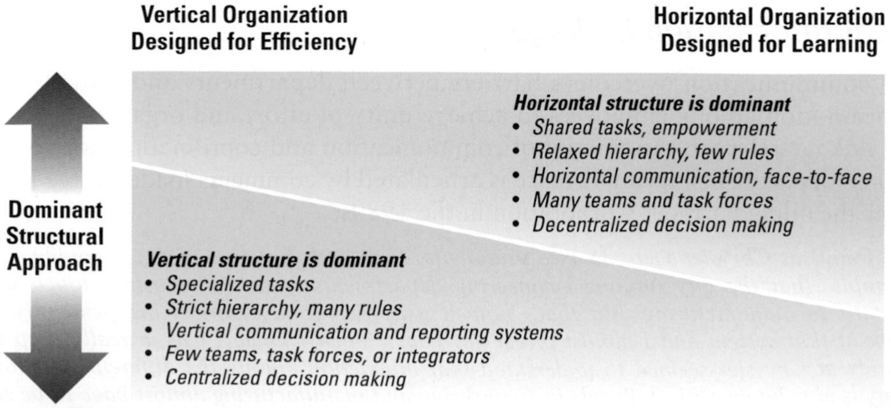

Vertical Organization Designed for Efficiency

Horizontal Organization Designed for Learning

Dominant Structural Approach

Horizontal structure is dominant
- *Shared tasks, empowerment*
- *Relaxed hierarchy, few rules*
- *Horizontal communication, face-to-face*
- *Many teams and task forces*
- *Decentralized decision making*

Vertical structure is dominant
- *Specialized tasks*
- *Strict hierarchy, many rules*
- *Vertical communication and reporting systems*
- *Few teams, task forces, or integrators*
- *Centralized decision making*

ONLINE
COUNTERPOINT 4.2

Managers are, in principle, always searching for the best combination of vertical control and horizontal collaboration, centralization and decentralization, taking advantage of communications advances to perfect interaction both vertically and horizontally.

Vertical Information Linkages

Linkage is defined as the extent of communication and coordination among organizational elements. Vertical linkages are used to coordinate activities between the top and bottom of an organization and are designed primarily for control of the organization. Employees at lower levels are expected to carry out activities consistent with top-level goals, and top executives must be informed of activities and accomplishments at the lower levels. A variety of structural devices may be used to achieve vertical linkage, including hierarchical referral, rules, plans and formal management information systems.[14]

Hierarchical Referral The first vertical device is the hierarchy, or chain of command, which is illustrated by the vertical lines in Exhibit 4.1. If a problem arises that employees don't know how to solve, it can be referred up to the next level in the hierarchy. When the problem is solved, the answer is passed back down to lower levels. The lines of the organization chart act as communication channels.

Rules and Plans The next linkage device is the use of rules and plans. To the extent that problems and decisions are repetitious, a rule or procedure can be established so employees know how to respond without communicating directly with their manager. Rules provide a standard information source enabling employees to be coordinated without actually communicating about every task. A plan also provides standing information for employees. The most widely used plan is the budget. With carefully designed budget plans, employees at lower levels can be left on their own to perform activities within their resource allotment.

Vertical Information Systems A vertical information system is another strategy for increasing vertical information capacity. Vertical information systems include the periodic reports, written information and computer-based communications distributed to managers. Information systems make communication up and down the hierarchy more efficient. Vertical information systems are an important component of vertical control at software-maker Oracle.

In today's world of corporate financial scandals and ethical concerns, many top managers are considering strengthening their organization's linkages for vertical information and control. The other major issue in organizing is to provide adequate horizontal linkages for coordination and collaboration.

Horizontal Information Linkages

Horizontal communication overcomes barriers between departments and provides opportunities for coordination among employees to achieve unity of effort and organizational objectives. Horizontal linkage refers to the amount of communication and coordination horizontally across organizational departments. Its importance is articulated by comments made by Lee Iacocca when he took over the ailing Chrysler Corporation in the 1980s:

> What I found at Chrysler were 35 vice presidents, each with his own turf ... I couldn't believe, for example, that the guy running engineering departments wasn't in constant touch with his counterpart in manufacturing. But that's how it was. Everybody worked independently. I took one look at that system and I almost threw up. That's when I knew I was in really deep trouble ... Nobody at Chrysler seemed to understand that interaction among the different functions in a company is absolutely critical. People in engineering and manufacturing almost have to be sleeping together. These guys weren't even flirting![15]

During his tenure at Chrysler (from 1997 to 2007, DaimlerChrysler[16]), Iacocca pushed horizontal coordination to a high level. Everyone working on a specific vehicle project – designers, engineers and manufacturers, as well as representatives from marketing, finance, purchasing and even outside suppliers – worked together on a single floor so they could constantly communicate.

BRIEFCASE 4.2

Horizontal linkage mechanisms often are not drawn on the organization chart, but they invariably form some element of organization structure. The following devices are structural alternatives that can improve horizontal coordination and information flow.[17] Each device enables people to exchange information.

Information Systems   A significant method of providing horizontal linkage in today's organizations is the use of cross-functional information systems. Computerized information

IN PRACTICE

Oracle Corporation

In an era of decentralization and empowerment, Larry Ellison, co-founder of Oracle, the global database management company in 1977, and CEO for over a quarter-century before he 'partially' stepped down in 2014 to become executive chairman and chief technical officer, doesn't hesitate to proclaim his belief in stronger vertical control. Oracle got in trouble some years ago because sales managers around the globe were cutting backroom deals or hammering out private, individualized compensation agreements with salespeople in different countries. Today, all the terms, including sales contracts and commissions, are dictated from the top and spelled out in a global database. All deals must be entered into the database so they can easily be tracked by top managers.

The internet plays a key part in Oracle's vertical information and control systems, by offering the power to centralize complex operations while also rapidly disseminating information all over the world. Oracle uses its own suite of internet software applications that work together on a global basis. All employees do their work via the internet, enabling the top management to carefully track, analyze and control the behaviour of each unit, manager and employee. Although many managers weren't happy with the stronger top-down control, Ellison believed it was necessary to effectively manage a sprawling global corporation that was beginning to behave more like a bunch of separate companies. In addition, the system helps to circulate and ensure implementation

of standard rules and procedures across divisions. According to Chief Marketing Officer, Mark Jarvis, this ultimately provides for greater freedom for lower levels and prevents the hierarchy from becoming overloaded. 'Once we have a standard set of global business practices', Jarvis notes, 'the [managers] can be allowed more scope for decision-making within the broad framework'.

Oracle's 2004 acquisition of PeopleSoft, as well as other, smaller acquisitions, has increased the complexity of the organization, but Oracle's top managers are focused on smooth integration through the use of vertical information systems. The company is working on developing a super-suite of software applications that combines the best features of products from Oracle, PeopleSoft and J.D. Edwards, and will allow for standardization and centralization across the enterprise. Oracle hopes that the new super-suite, dubbed Project Fusion, released in 2011 after six years of development, will allow its customers to automate an entire global infrastructure so that everything is linked and compatible and managers can get the information they need to effectively control the organization.[18] The lengthy delays encountered by Project Fusion underline the difficulties inherent in complete vertical integration.[19] Ellison has been criticized for making too many acquisitions, particularly troubled high-end computer hardware manufacturer Sun Microsystems in 2009. However, the company remains one of the Silicon Valley giants, and has prospered with its emphasis on cloud-based computing. Revenues and profits have been fairly flat in the past several years, but at nearly $40 billion in revenues and $10 billion in net income in 2015, the company is well-placed to continue responding successfully to industry transformation. Despite his announced semi-retirement, Ellison still speaks on behalf of the company, and his over $50 billion in personal wealth ranked him in 2016 the seventh wealthiest person in the world.[20]

systems can enable managers or frontline workers throughout the organization to routinely exchange information about problems, opportunities, activities or decisions. For example, Siemens uses an organization-wide information system that enables 450 000 employees around the world to share knowledge and collaborate on projects to provide better solutions to customers. The information and communications division recently collaborated with the medical division to develop new products for the healthcare market.[21]

Employees may also be encouraged to use the company's information systems in order to build relationships across the organization, aiming to support and enhance ongoing horizontal coordination across projects and geographical boundaries. In 2007, The Samaritans, a UK charity which runs telephone helplines and other services for people in emotional distress, adopted a specially tailored Customer Management System (CRM) that consolidates information about its 17 000 volunteers, its financial supporters, as well as business partners. The system permits the organization's staff to work more efficiently, making linkages between different 'customers' of the organization in a way that was not possible before. Thus, for example, its business partners could be asked to launch an appeal for volunteers within their companies. In an indication of the increasing sophistication and professionalization of charitable organizational design, in 2013 Samaritans adopted a comprehensive CRM platform, thankQ, to manage its customer relationships.[22, 23]

Direct Contact

A higher level of horizontal linkage is direct contact between managers or employees affected by a problem. One way to promote direct contact is to create a special liaison role. A liaison person is located in one department but has the responsibility for communicating and achieving coordination with another department. Liaison roles often exist between engineering and manufacturing departments because engineering has to develop and test products to fit the limitations of manufacturing facilities. At Johnson & Johnson, CEO William C. Weldon set up a committee made up of managers from research and development (R&D) and sales and marketing. The direct contact between managers in these two departments enables the company to set priorities for which new drugs to pursue and market. Weldon also created a new position to oversee R&D, with an express charge to increase coordination with sales and marketing executives.[24] Another approach is to locate people close together so they will have direct contact on a regular basis.

Task Forces

Liaison roles usually link only two departments. When linkage involves several departments, a more complex device such as a task force is required. A task force is a temporary committee composed of representatives from each organizational unit affected by a problem.[25] Each member represents the interests of a department or division and can carry information from the meeting back to that department.

Task forces can be an effective horizontal linkage device for temporary issues. They endeavour to solve problems by direct horizontal coordination and reduce the information load on the vertical hierarchy. Typically, they are disbanded after their tasks are accomplished or superceded.

Task forces have been used for everything from organizing the annual company picnic to solving expensive and complex manufacturing problems. Philips Corporation, discussed in Chapter 1, made use of multiple taskforces in its Operation Centurion to help restructure the organization as it began to face up to the need to respond to global challenges in the 1990s. The task force approach set Philips on a very long road to recovery, but in other cases, task forces have been used to give impetus to fundamentally flawed strategies. One example of a negative outcome of the task force approach was the Executive Automotive Committee formed by DaimlerChrysler CEO Jürgen Schrempp. This task force was set up specifically to identify ideas for increasing cooperation and component sharing among Mercedes, Chrysler and Mitsubishi (in which DaimlerChrysler owned a 37 per cent stake). The task force started with a product road map, showing all Mercedes, Chrysler, Dodge, Jeep and Mitsubishi vehicles to be launched over a ten-year period, along with an analysis of the components they would use, so task force members could identify overlap and find ways to share parts and cut time and costs.[26] Unfortunately, Mitsubishi was in serious trouble, both because of the languishing Japanese economy and a number of strategic errors. As Mitsubishi sank further into crisis, the logic for production integration with the company was undermined, and eventually the company was bailed out, resulting in the loss of most of DaimlerChrysler's investment, and contributing to Schrempp's departure from DaimlerChrysler.[27]

Full-time Integrator

A stronger horizontal linkage device is to create a full-time position or department solely for the purpose of coordination. A full-time integrator frequently has a title, such as product manager, project manager, programme manager or brand manager. Unlike the liaison person described earlier, the integrator does not report to one of the functional departments being coordinated. He or she is located outside the departments and has the responsibility for coordinating several departments, or even, in the case below, in integrating internal departments, suppliers and customers.

Kalmar Industries is the world's leading supplier of cargo handling equipment to ports, terminals and intermodal facilities, and is a subsidiary of the Finland-headquartered, globally present Cargotec Corporation. Kalmar provides customized cargo solutions to large scale customers, with 2014 sales of about €1.5 billion. As in many modern manufacturing enterprises, most of Kalmar's production is outsourced, with the company heavily involved in system integration, liaising closely both with suppliers and customers to ensure delivery and support of the customized product.[28] Kalmar's managers realized that although the company had strong relationships with its suppliers and customers, there were many inefficiencies due both to communications misunderstandings and logistical costs of manufacturing items in separate locations and transporting them to Kalmar for assembly. In order to respond to this issue, Kalmar established Product Supply Centres (PSCs), where key suppliers co-located their production facilities for specific Kalmar products. This approach allowed Kalmar to respond much more quickly and effectively to customers' specific requests.[29]

An integrator or integrating department can be responsible for an innovation or change project, such as coordinating the design, financing and marketing of a new product. An organization chart that illustrates the location of project managers for new product development is shown in Exhibit 4.3. The project managers are drawn to the side to indicate their separation from other departments. The arrows indicate project members assigned to the new product development. New Product A, for example, has a financial accountant assigned to keep track of costs and budgets. The engineering member provides design advice, and purchasing and manufacturing members represent their areas. The project manager is responsible for the entire project. He or she sees that the new product is completed on time, is introduced to the market, and achieves other project goals. The horizontal lines in Exhibit 4.3 indicate that project managers do not have formal authority over team members with respect to giving pay raises, hiring or firing. Formal authority rests with the managers of the functional departments.

Integrators in most companies have a lot of responsibility but little authority. The integrator has to use expertise and persuasion to achieve coordination. He or she spans the boundary between departments and must be able to get people together, maintain their trust, confront problems and resolve conflicts and disputes in the interest of the organization.[30]

Teams

Project teams tend to be the strongest horizontal linkage mechanism. Teams are permanent task forces and are often used in conjunction with a full-time integrator. When activities among departments require strong coordination over a long period of time, a cross-functional team is often the solution. Special project teams may be used when organizations have a large-scale project, a major innovation or a new product line.

Imagination Ltd, Britain's largest design firm, relies heavily upon teamwork. At the beginning of each project, Imagination puts together a team of designers, writers, artists, marketing experts, information specialists and representatives of other functional areas to carry out the entire project from beginning to end. Hewlett-Packard's Medical Products Group uses *virtual cross-functional teams*, made up of members from various countries, to develop and market medical products and

EXHIBIT 4.3   Project Manager Location in the Structure

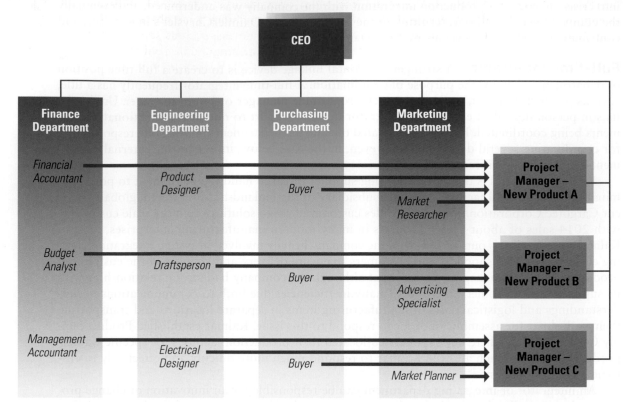

services such as electrocardiograph systems, ultrasound imaging technologies and patient monitoring systems.[31] A virtual team is one that is made up of organizationally or geographically dispersed members who are linked primarily through advanced information and communications technologies. Members frequently use online collaborative technologies to work together, rather than meeting face to face.[32]

BRIEFCASE 4.3

Volvo, the Sweden-headquartered truck manufacturer, has an enviable reputation for innovative management practices, and particularly with fostering strong teamwork. The Dutch researchers Ben Kuipers and Marco de Witte took a close look at teamwork at Volvo's cab manufacturing plant in Umeå in northern Sweden to better understand how successful teamwork develops, what they call in*Volvo*ment. They identified four dimensions to teamwork:

- Job enlargement: encouraging employee multifunctionality and thus the elimination of inefficiency within the team

- Job enrichment: the redesign of the supervision system to delegate management responsibilities to the team members

- Cooperation: members work together as a team, building on communication and a sense of shared responsibility

- High performance: the team is able to work together to resolve non-routine issues, requiring collaborative innovation.

Unlike some other studies of teamwork, Kuipers and de Witte found that these four aspects of teamwork don't occur sequentially, one after the other, but through an interconnected process. They showed that the higher the level of teamwork achieved, the better quality of product, higher productivity and employee satisfaction. Truly a win–win.[33]

Teambuilding has become so important to companies that it has spawned a whole new business opportunity in teamwork development. Many organizations hire expert companies to support the teambuilding process. Often, the teambuilding includes some physically challenging activities that require close collaboration to achieve success, such as sailing a boat together, overcoming an outdoor obstacle course or even performing a daredevil circus act. Airbus, the European aeroplane manufacturer, has management staff working in several different countries who rarely meet face to face, so building team spirit is a challenge, even with rapid advances in web-based communications. At a recent annual away day, the company hired a teambuilding company, Blue Hat, which organized a 'Da Vinci Code Challenge' in which small teams had to work together to find the famous chalice and elixir of life.[34]

Exhibit 4.4 summarizes the mechanisms for achieving horizontal linkages. These devices represent alternatives that managers can select to increase horizontal coordination in any organization. The higher-level devices provide more horizontal information capacity, although the cost to the organization in terms of time and human resources is greater. If horizontal communication is insufficient, departments will find themselves out of synchronization, resulting in inefficiency and ineffectiveness.

Organization Design Alternatives

Overall, the design of organization structure indicates required work activities, reporting relationships and departmental groupings.

Required Work Activities

Departments are created to perform tasks considered important to the company. For example, in a manufacturing company, work activities are organized into a range of functions, such as a human resource department to recruit and train employees, a purchasing department to obtain supplies and raw materials, a production department to build products, a sales department to sell products, and so forth. As organizations grow larger, their organizational structure often becomes

EXHIBIT 4.4 Ladder of Mechanisms for Horizontal Linkage and Coordination

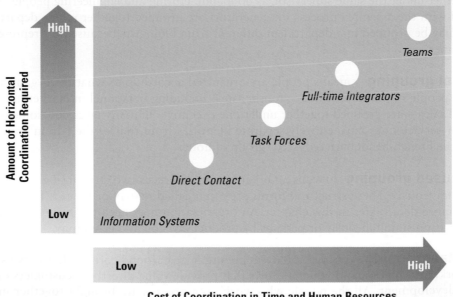

more complex as different functions are added. For example, before the 1980s many companies had large divisions ('pools') of secretarial staff. Today, most employees do much of their own administrative work so secretaries have, in effect, been replaced with information technology departments whose purpose is to deliver the smooth operation of the computers and networks used to create and transmit data within and beyond the company.

Reporting Relationships

Hierarchical reporting relationships, often called the *chain of command*, are represented by vertical lines on an organization chart. The chain of command is typically an unbroken line of authority that links all persons in an organization and shows who reports to who. Although organizations have emphasized flattening of hierarchy in recent years, this typically reflects a reduction in the number of vertical levels rather than an absence of hierarchy.

Departmental Grouping Options

Early stage companies are typically loosely structured with new functions added (and removed) on an *ad hoc* basis as the organization finds its market niche and shapes itself around the needs of operating in that niche. As the organization grows and becomes more stable, departmental groupings are typically established to provide efficiency and predictability to operations. Some options for departmental grouping, including functional grouping, divisional grouping, multifocused grouping, horizontal grouping and virtual network grouping, are illustrated in Exhibit 4.5. Departmental grouping affects employees because they share a common supervisor and common resources, are jointly responsible for performance, and tend to identify and collaborate with one another.[35] For example, a credit manager's perspective might well change if she moves from the finance department to the marketing department. As a member of the marketing department, the credit manager would work more closely with salespeople, understanding the importance of increasing sales and thus becoming more willing to see credit as a sales tool than when she was located in the finance department.

Functional grouping   places together employees who perform similar functions or work processes or who bring similar knowledge and skills to bear. For example, all marketing people work together under the same supervisor, as do manufacturing and engineering people. All people associated with the assembly process for generators are grouped together in one department. All chemists may be grouped in a department different from biologists because they represent different disciplines.

Divisional grouping   means people are organized according to what the organization produces. All people required to produce toothpaste – including personnel in marketing, manufacturing and sales – are grouped together under one executive. In many large conglomerates, some product or service lines have entirely separate identities from that of the parent company. For example, the French-headquartered Accor group of hotels.

Multifocused grouping   means an organization embraces two structural grouping alternatives simultaneously. These structural forms are often called matrix or *hybrid*. They will be discussed in more detail later in this chapter. An organization may need to group by function and product division simultaneously or perhaps by product division and geography.

Horizontal grouping   means employees are organized around core work processes, the end-to-end work, information and material flows that provide value directly to customers or support strategic development. All the people who work on a process are brought together in a group

EXHIBIT 4.5 Structural Design Options for Grouping Employees into Departments

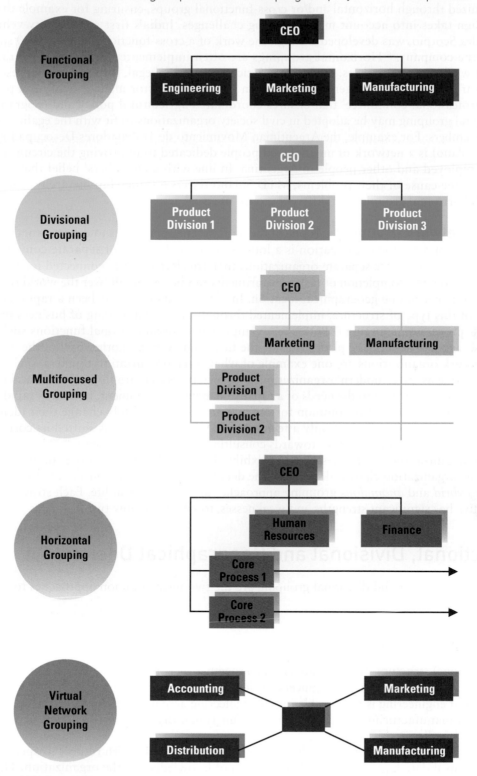

Source: Adapted from David Nadler and Michael Tushman, *Strategic Organization Design* (Glenview, IL.: Scott Foresman, 1988), 68.

rather than being separated into functional departments. Frequently, new product development is organized through horizontal and/or cross-functional groups, ensuring for example that product design takes into account manufacturing challenges. India's first sport utility vehicle, the Mahindra Scorpio, was developed through the work of a cross-functional team of 120 staff from across the company.[36] Horizontal groupings are often implemented in addition to traditional vertical working relationships. In the West African state of Senegal, for example, representatives of the various government agencies involved in agricultural sector management form part of an 'inter-professional committee' that ensures coordinated agricultural policy and programming.[37] Horizontal grouping may be adopted in civil society organizations to fit with the egalitarian ethos of the members. For example, the Argentinian Movimiento de Trabajadores Desocupados Solano (MTD Solano) is a network of unemployed people dedicated to improving the circumstances of the unemployed and other people in Argentina. In line with its members' belief that social inequality is the cause of their problems, MTD Solano rejects a leadership hierarchy and operates through horizontal groupings of different groups of social activists.[38]

Virtual network grouping is one of the more recent approaches to departmental grouping. With this grouping, the organization is a loosely connected cluster of separate components. In essence, departments are separate organizations that are electronically connected for the sharing of information and completion of tasks. Departments can be spread all over the world rather than located together in one geographical location. In recent years there has been a rapid increase in the use of this type of structure, implemented through the re-engineering of business processes. Business process outsourcing (BPO) is an example where organizational functions such as customer service can actually be placed outside the firm, and even in another part of the world. Virtual network organizations are one example of what some organization thinkers, such as David Boje, describe as 'post-modern' organizations; organizations that are fluid, flexible and infinitely reconfigurable according to the needs of a rapidly changing environment. In today's rapidly evolving environment, it is not uncommon for organizations to completely change their identity and business focus over a period of only a few years. IBM for example has shifted its core business away from computer manufacture towards consulting over the past 20 years.[39]

The organizational forms described in Exhibit 4.5 provide a range of overall options within which the organization chart is drawn and the detailed structure is designed, although as always, various *hybrid* and *anomalous* grouping approaches are found in real life. Each structural design alternative has significant strengths and weaknesses, to which we now turn.

Functional, Divisional and Geographical Designs

Functional grouping and divisional grouping are the two most common approaches to structural design.

Functional Structure

In a functional structure, activities are grouped together by common function from the bottom to the top of the organization. All engineers are located in the engineering department, and the vice president of engineering is responsible for all engineering activities. The same is true in marketing, R&D and manufacturing. An example of the functional organization structure was shown in Exhibit 4.1 earlier in this chapter.

With a functional structure, all human knowledge and skills with respect to specific activities are consolidated, providing a valuable depth of knowledge for the organization. This structure is most effective when in-depth expertise is critical to meeting organizational goals, when the organization needs to be controlled and coordinated through the vertical hierarchy, and when efficiency is important. The structure can be quite effective, especially if there is little need for horizontal coordination. Exhibit 4.6 summarizes the strengths and weaknesses of the functional structure.

The functional structure can improve economies of scale by concentrating specialists in groups in a common location and by sharing facilities. Producing all products in a single plant, for example, may strengthen a financial case for the plant to acquire the latest machinery. Constructing only one facility instead of separate facilities for each product line can reduce duplication and waste. The functional structure may also promote in-depth skill development of employees. Employees are exposed to a range of functional activities within their own department.[40]

The potential shortcoming of the functional structure is a slow response to environmental changes that require coordination across departments. The vertical hierarchy can become isolated or overloaded. Decisions pile up as top managers lack effective means of coordination across specialist functions. A functional structure may also impede innovation when this requires coordination.

Many small and medium-sized organizations in which the focus is upon core competencies, operate with a functional structure. Consider the *In Practice* case of Real Hotel Company Ltd, a medium-sized UK-based hotel chain, active in Britain and Europe. Real Hotels had made losses for several years, and in 2006 its top management decided to reorganize into a clear functional structure as one of a series of steps designed to bring the company back into the black.

Functional Structure with Horizontal Linkages

During the late years of the twentieth century, criticism of extended hierarchical structures promoted a shift toward flatter, more horizontal structures, as business activities became more complex and companies identified the potential for restructuring business processes to achieve synergies. Organizations may compensate for the vertical functional hierarchy by installing horizontal linkages, as described earlier in this chapter. Managers may improve horizontal coordination by using information systems, direct contact between departments, **BRIEFCASE 4.4** full-time integrators or project managers, task forces or teams (illustrated in Exhibit 4.3). One interesting use of horizontal linkages occurred at Karolinska Hospital in Stockholm, Sweden, which once had 47 functional departments. Even after top executives cut that down to 11, coordination was still inadequate. The team set about reorganizing workflow at the hospital around patient care. Instead of bouncing a patient from department to department, Karolinska now

EXHIBIT 4.6   Strengths and Weaknesses of Functional Organization Structure

Strengths	Weaknesses
1. Allows economies of scale within functional departments	1. Slow response time to environmental changes
2. Enables in-depth knowledge and skill development	2. May cause decisions to pile on top, hierarchy overload
3. Enables organization to accomplish functional goals	3. Leads to poor horizontal coordination among departments
4. Is best with only one or a few products	4. Results in less innovation
	5. Involves restricted view of organizational goals

Source: Adapted from Robert Duncan, 'What Is the Right Organization Structure? Decision Tree Analysis Provides the Answer', *Organizational Dynamics* (Winter 1979), 429.

envisions the illness to recovery period as a process with 'pit stops' in admissions, X-ray surgery and so forth. The most interesting aspect of the approach is the new position of nurse coordinator. Nurse coordinators serve as full-time integrators, troubleshooting transitions within or between departments. The improved horizontal coordination dramatically improved productivity and patient care at Karolinska.[41] Karolinska is effectively using horizontal linkages to overcome some of the disadvantages of the functional structure. In 2004, Karolinska merged with another large hospital. Some progress has been made in effectively integrating the hospitals, particularly in the area of IT, but integration problems remain.

In today's rapidly changing organizational environment, managers are constantly challenged to adapt and redesign organizational structures and systems to meet new operational challenges.[42] A more recent initiative involved removing 500 beds from the hospital and outsourcing them to private companies who would operate them within community-based facilities. This privatization approach to public services is being attempted in many countries, but the jury is still out as to whether it really delivers better value for money; a 2011 independent study of Swedish

IN PRACTICE

The Real Hotel Company PLC

When Michael Praeger took over as CEO of the Real Hotel Company in early 2007, he knew he had a difficult task on his hands. His previous experience with several international chains would stand him in good stead on the hotel side of the business, but the company needed radical action to halt years of poor financial performance and failed restructuring efforts.

The Real Hotel Company is a British-headquartered company with its main business operating budget to mid-range hotels. Since being founded as Friendly Hotels in the mid-1980s by the iconic hotelier Henry Edwards, in the late 1990s the company secured the European master franchise for the global chain of budget hotels, Choice Hotels International, meaning the company was operating over 300 hotels across the continent. The business almost immediately went into the red and Henry Edwards left the company he had founded. Despite a dizzying series of name changes, capital raising efforts, hotel refurbishments, attempts to sell out and even a near

bankruptcy in 2001, the business never produced satisfactory results. By the time Michael Praeger arrived, the company had already decided to exit the franchise agreement with Choice Hotels, which it successfully did in late 2006. But with the great majority of company-operated hotels now gone, the hybrid functional-geographic management structure seemed top-heavy. Furthermore, the company now needed to focus on building its own brands, which had been a lower priority while the company was trying to manage all the Choice Hotel franchises.

Praeger slimmed down the management structure, eliminating the geographic divisions in favour of functional divisions. He gave up development of Sleep Inn, a brand that had never really caught on, and focused most of the company's efforts on the new Purple Hotel label – a contemporary brand that would appeal to a younger clientele interested in value, but also style. Real Hotels invested heavily in its sales and marketing division, and pondered exiting completely from the traditional budget sector. The company now had a manageable portfolio of properties and a simple functional management structure.

In early 2008, revenues started to pick up. However, with the onset of a serious recession during 2008, all the efforts proved too little, too late, and in January 2009 Real Hotels was forced to call in the administrators. The chain was carved up, with big competitors like Travelodge picking up the most profitable properties. Was Praeger's strategy flawed, or did the global economic situation mean that the turnaround never had much chance of success?[43]

privatization initiatives sponsored by a pro-business research group concluded that it did not deliver savings.[44]

Divisional Structure

The term divisional structure is used here as the generic term for what is sometimes called a *product structure* or *strategic business units*. With this structure, divisions can be organized according to individual products, services, product groups, major projects or programmes, divisions, businesses or profit centres. The distinctive feature of a divisional structure is that grouping is based on organizational outputs.

The difference between a divisional structure and a functional structure is illustrated in Exhibit 4.7. The functional structure can be redesigned into separate product groups, and each group contains the functional departments of R&D, manufacturing, accounting and marketing. Coordination across functional departments within each product group is maximized. The divisional structure promotes flexibility and change because each unit is smaller and can adapt more flexibly to opportunities and threats. Moreover, the divisional structure *decentralizes* decision-making as the lines of authority converge at a lower level in the hierarchy. The functional structure, by contrast, is *centralized* as it forces decisions all the way to the top before a problem affecting several functions can be resolved.

EXHIBIT 4.7 Reorganization from Functional Structure to Divisional Structure at Info-Tech

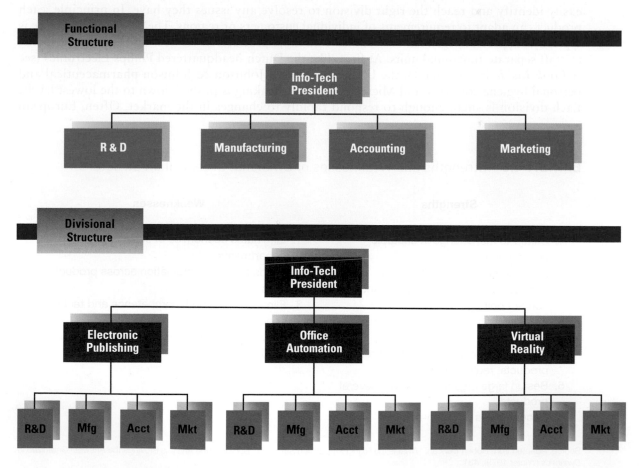

Strengths and weaknesses of the divisional structure are summarized in Exhibit 4.8. The divisional organization structure is excellent for achieving coordination across functional departments. It works well when organizations can no longer be adequately controlled through the traditional vertical hierarchy, and when goals are oriented toward adaptation and change. Giant, complex organizations such as Nestlé, General Electric and India's Tata Corporation are subdivided into a series of smaller, self-contained organizations for better control and coordination. In these large companies, the units are sometimes called divisions, businesses or strategic business units. The structure at Johnson & Johnson includes 204 separate operating units, including McNeil Consumer Products, makers of Tylenol; Ortho Pharmaceuticals, which makes Retin-A and contraceptive pills; and J & J Consumer Products, the company that manufactures globally known brands such as Johnson's Baby Shampoo and Band-Aids. Each unit is a separately chartered, autonomous company, although operating under the guidance of Johnson & Johnson's corporate headquarters.[45]

Many government organizations use a divisional structure. The British National Health Service has made extensive organizational changes in order to meet service improvement targets such as the requirement that Emergency Department patients will receive treatment within a specified time. Harrap and Gillies describe how one hospital reorganized from many small departments into five large divisions, each equipped with clear criteria for success and headed by a member of the senior management team.[46] The computer software company Microsoft uses a divisional structure to develop and market its different products.

The divisional structure has several strengths that are of benefit to Microsoft.[47] This structure is in principle responsive to fast changing, unstable conditions and can provide high product or service visibility. Each product line 'belongs' to a specific division, so customers can more easily identify and reach the right division to resolve any issues they have. In principle, each product can adapt to requirements of individual customers or regions. The divisional structure is typically adopted in organizations that have multiple products or services and enough personnel to staff separate functional units. At firms like the Dutch-headquartered Philips Electronics (see *A Look Inside* in Chapter 1), the US headquartered Johnson & Johnson pharmaceutical and personal hygiene company and Microsoft, decision-making is pushed down to the lowest levels. Each division is small enough to respond rapidly to changes in the market. Often, European

EXHIBIT 4.8 Strengths and Weaknesses of Divisional Organization Structure

Strengths	Weaknesses
1. Suited to fast change in unstable environment 2. Leads to customer satisfaction because product responsibility and contact points are clear 3. Involves high coordination across functions 4. Allows units to adapt to differences in products, regions, customers 5. Best in large organizations with several products 6. Decentralizes decision-making	1. Eliminates economies of scale in functional departments 2. Leads to poor coordination across product lines 3. Eliminates in-depth competence and technical specialization 4. Makes integration and standardization across product lines difficult

Source: Adapted from Robert Duncan, 'What Is the Right Organization Structure? Decision Tree Analysis Provides the Answer,' *Organization Dynamics* (Winter 1979), 431.

firms favour greater decentralization to both product and geographic divisions than is the case with North American corporations.

One disadvantage of using divisional structuring is the loss of economies of scale. Instead of 50 research engineers sharing a common facility in a functional structure, ten engineers may be assigned to each of five product divisions. The critical mass required for in-depth research can be lost, and physical facilities have to be duplicated for each product line. Another problem is that product lines become separate from each other, and coordination across product lines can be difficult. An executive from Johnson & Johnson said, 'We have to keep reminding ourselves that we work for the same corporation'.[48] Excessive decentralization at Philips Electronics has been blamed for depriving the company of a coherent and comprehensive response to the onslaught of Japanese electronics goods from the 1970s onwards, with the result that Philips lost its dominant position in the European market.[49]

IN PRACTICE

Microsoft

Bill Gates co-founded Microsoft in 1975 and built it into the most profitable technology company in the world. But as the company grew larger, the functional structure was just too slow and inflexible for a large organization operating in the fast-moving technology industry. Employees began complaining about the growing bureaucracy and snail's pace decision-making.

To speed things up and better respond to environmental changes, in 2002 top executives created seven business units, the Information Worker business, Microsoft Business Solutions (MBS), the Home and Entertainment Division, the Mobile and Embedded Devices Division, the Windows Client, Windows Server and the Tools group, built around the company's major products. Each division was run by a general manager and contained most of the functions of a stand-alone company, including product development, sales, marketing and finance. The division system was further streamlined three years later when the seven units were replaced by three core divisions. The Windows, MSN and Server groups became the *Microsoft Platform Products and Services Division*; the Information Worker and MBS groups were merged into the *Microsoft Business Division*; and the Mobile and Embedded Devices, and the Home and Entertainment division became the *Microsoft Entertainment and Devices Division*.[50]

What really made the new structure revolutionary for Microsoft was that the division heads were given the freedom and authority to run the businesses and spend their budgets as they see fit to meet goals. The general managers and chief financial officers for each division set their own budgets and manage their own profit and loss statements. Previously, the two top executives, Bill Gates and Steven Ballmer, were involved in practically every decision, large and small. Managers of the divisions are charged up by the new authority and responsibility. One manager said he feels 'like I am running my own little company'.

Nevertheless, Microsoft continues to lose ground to other players with very varied corporate structures, ranging from Apple, which was famously centralized in the hands of the late Steve Jobs, to Google, which operates a loose structure with substantial employee discretion. In particular, Microsoft has found it difficult to break away from its reliance on the Windows PC platform. Despite producing some attractive products in its Surface tablet and Windows Phone ranges it finds difficulty getting traction in product areas where others have already built a reputation and market dominance.

In response, in 2013, Microsoft decided to emulate Apple, dissolving its divisions and creating what it called One Microsoft. The hope is that this approach will enable the company to leverage its competitive advantages across the different product categories.[51]

It is clear that, although corporate structure is important and needs to fit with the company's competitive needs, it is only one determinant of success.[52]

From the early years of the 21st century, Microsoft began losing ground to Google. While Microsoft, with its divisional structure, had effectively countered competitive software, Google represented a new business model driven through search engine revenues. Without a coordinated approach, competitive threats can emerge from unexpected sources like this, and businesses may find themselves poorly placed even to identify the threat, let alone develop an effective response.

Companies such as Sony and Xerox have a large number of divisions and can have severe problems with horizontal coordination. It has been alleged that Sony lost out in the business of digital media products, despite its early advantage with the Walkman device, partly because of poor coordination. In the 2000s, Apple's iPod quickly captured 60 per cent of the US market versus only 10 per cent for Sony's Walkman range, a domination that Apple was then able to extend into the mobile phone and tablet categories. The digital music business depends on seamless coordination. Sony's Walkman was unable to recognize some of the music sets made with early versions of the company's SonicStage software introduced in 2001. It wasn't until version 3.4 of SonicStage that compatibility was achieved – demonstrating a disconnection with the company's division selling music downloads. By 2007, Sony had decided to wind down its music download division, having lost the battle with Apple. In response to difficulties such as this, Sony moved decisively to more effectively integrate its disparate product divisions.[53]

Unless effective horizontal mechanisms are in place, a divisional structure can be inefficient and unresponsive. One division may produce products or programmes that are incompatible with products sold by another division. Customers are frustrated when a sales representative from one division is unaware of developments in other divisions. Task forces and other linkage devices may be introduced to coordinate across divisions. A lack of technical specialization is also a problem in a divisional structure. Employees may identify with the product line rather than with a functional specialty. R&D personnel, for example, tend to be employed to undertake research to benefit a particular product line rather than basic research to benefit the entire organization.

Geographical Structure

Another basis for structural grouping is the organization's users or customers. The most common structure in this category is geography. Each region of the country may have distinct tastes and preferences. Each geographic unit includes all functions required to produce and market products or services in that region. This structure is particularly common in large NGOs, and other civil society organizations that depend upon a close connection with volunteers, supporters or clients at the local level such as the UK's Citizen's Advice Bureaux, Alcoholics Anonymous and most political parties frequently use a type of geographical structure, with a central headquarters and semi-autonomous local units. The national or international headquarters organization provides brand recognition, coordinates fund-raising services and handles some shared administrative functions, while day-to-day control and decision-making is decentralized to a greater or lesser extent to local or regional units.[54]

Multinational corporations (MNCs) often create self-contained units for different countries and parts of the world. As MNCs integrate acquisitions into corporate structure, they often move from discrete functional units that were formerly stand-alone businesses, towards geographic coordination. For example, in 2008, Kingfisher, the UK-headquartered multinational home renovation supplies retailer, best known for its B&Q stores, responded to disappointing performance in some of its units by establishing three geographic units, representing UK, France and Other Countries, each headed by a senior executive. These managers were charged with turning their region into a profit centre by strictly controlling costs and focusing on maximizing profits from existing retail space.[55] In 2015 under new CEO Véronique Laury, and while retaining the three core market areas, Kingfisher launched a new corporate strategy emphasizing greater integration of its 5 major brands, with a bigger proportion of products sold globally across the brands.[56] Some years ago, California's Apple Computer reorganized from a functional to a geographical

EXHIBIT 4.9   Geographical Structure for Apple Computer

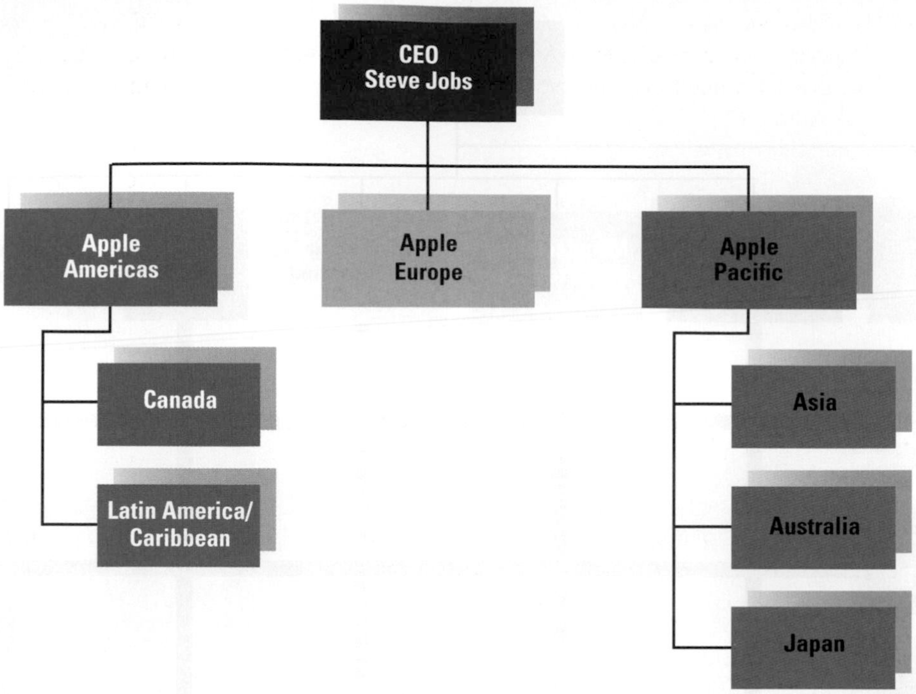

Source: Apple Computer, Inc. regions of the world, http://www.apple.com/find/areas.htm, April 18, 2000.

structure to facilitate manufacture and delivery of Apple computers to customers around the world. Exhibit 4.9 contains a partial organization structure illustrating the geographical thrust. At Apple this structure was introduced to focus managers and employees on specific geographical customers and sales targets.

The strengths and weaknesses of a geographic divisional structure are parallel to those of the divisional organization characteristics listed in Exhibit 4.8. The geographic division can adapt to specific conditions of its own country or region, and employees may identify with regional goals rather than with the overall corporate vision. Horizontal coordination within a region may be emphasized rather than linkages across regions or to the head office, and this can detract from overall corporate synergies. This is true both for national firms with regional divisions, and for multinational firms with national or regional units around the world.

Matrix Structure

Sometimes, a matrix structure is developed in an effort to give equal emphasis and attention to product and function, or product and geography. The matrix is more likely to be introduced when, say, technical expertise and product innovation and change are assessed to be of equal importance. When it is assessed that functional, divisional and geographical structures combined with horizontal linkage mechanisms are not working effectively, the matrix may be adopted as a remedy.

The matrix is a strong form of horizontal linkage as, in principle, it enables two objectives to be pursued simultaneously, as shown in Exhibit 4.10. In this structure, product managers and functional managers, for example, have equal authority within the organization, and employees

EXHIBIT 4.10   Dual-Authority Structure in a Matrix Organization

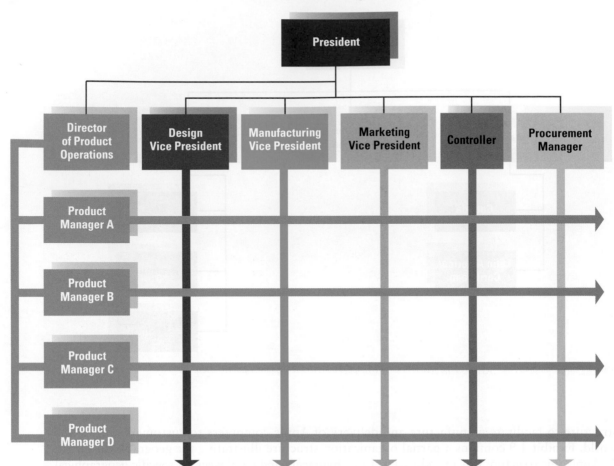

report to both of them. The matrix structure is similar to the use of full-time integrators or product managers described earlier in this chapter (Exhibit 4.3), but within the matrix structure, the product managers (horizontal) are given formal authority equal to that of the functional managers (vertical).

Conditions for the Matrix

A dual hierarchy may seem an unusual way to design an organization as it contradicts the classical principle of unity of command, but it can be a workable structure, particularly when one or more of the following conditions is met:[57]

- *Condition 1*. Pressure exists to share scarce resources across product lines. The organization is often medium sized and has a moderate number of product lines. There are pressures for the shared and flexible use of people and equipment across the product lines. For example, the organization is not large enough to assign engineers full-time to each product line, so engineers are assigned part-time to several products or projects.

- *Condition 2*. Environmental pressures exist for two or more critical outputs, such as for in-depth technical knowledge (functional structure) and frequent new products (divisional structure). The dual pressure requires sharing of power between the functional and product sides of the organization, and a dual-authority structure is needed to maintain that balance.

■ *Condition 3.* The environmental domain of the organization is both complex and uncertain. Frequent external changes and high interdependence between departments require a large amount of coordination and information processing in both vertical and horizontal directions.

In principle, a dual-authority structure can help ensure a balance between vertical and horizontal aspects of organizations.

Referring again to Exhibit 4.10, assume the matrix structure is for a clothing manufacturer. Product A is footwear, product B is outerwear, product C is night clothes and so on. Each product line serves a different market and customers. As a medium-size organization, the company must effectively use people from manufacturing, design and marketing to work on each product line. There are not enough designers to warrant a separate design department for each product line, so the designers are shared across product lines. Moreover, by keeping the manufacturing, design and marketing functions intact, it allows employees to develop the in-depth expertise to serve all product lines efficiently.

The matrix formalizes horizontal teams along with the traditional vertical hierarchy and tries to give equal balance to both. However, the matrix may shift one way or the other. Many companies have found a balanced matrix hard to implement and maintain because one side of the authority structure often dominates. For employees, serving two masters can prove a confusing and excessively demanding experience. As a consequence, two variations of matrix structure have evolved – the functional matrix and the product matrix. In a functional matrix, the functional bosses have primary authority and the project or product managers simply coordinate product activities. In a product matrix, by contrast, the project or product managers have primary authority and functional managers simply assign technical personnel to projects and provide advisory expertise as needed. For many organizations, one of these approaches becomes dominant as it accommodates established power relations and reduces conflicts arising from dual lines of authority.[58]

All kinds of organizations have experimented with versions of the matrix, including hospitals, consulting firms, banks, insurance companies, government agencies and many types of industrial firms.[59] A 2016 McKinsey study of 4000 US-based corporate employees found that the great majority have some kind of matrix reporting relationships.[60] This structure has been used by large, global organizations such as Unilever and Procter & Gamble, which fine-tune the matrix to suit their own priorities and traditions. Many chemical and pharmaceutical companies operate with various forms of the matrix structure to address the complexities of managing lengthy product portfolios in widely divergent market situations throughout the world. For example, Bayer AG, the German-based multinational, restructured in the mid-1980s from a function-based hierarchy to a three-layered matrix. The company was initially divided into six broad product areas, now streamlined down to the three areas of Healthcare, CropScience and Material-Science. A functional divisional system was also established with functions such as human resources, marketing and finance. Finally, geographic regions were established. The result was 19 interwoven units or divisions that collaborate together in multiple configurations.[61]

Strengths and Weaknesses

The matrix structure is often introduced in challenging conditions when an equality of contribution as well as close collaboration is required between, for example, product and functional elements. To be effective, the structure depends on high levels of organizational trust and mutual understanding between managers in different places in the matrix. The dual-authority structure can assist communication and coordination to cope with rapid environmental change and enables an equal balance between product and functional bosses.[62] The matrix

BRIEFCASE 4.5

EXHIBIT 4.11   Strengths and Weaknesses of Matrix Organization Structure

Strengths	Weaknesses
1. Achieves coordination necessary to meet dual demands from customers 2. Flexible sharing of human resources across products 3. Suited to complex decisions and frequent changes in unstable environment 4. Provides opportunity for both functional and product skill development 5. Best in medium-sized organizations with multiple products	1. Causes participants to experience dual authority, which can be frustrating and confusing 2. Means participants need good interpersonal skills and extensive training 3. Is time consuming; involves frequent meetings and conflict resolution sessions 4. Will not work unless participants understand it and adopt collegial rather than vertical type relationships 5. Requires great effort to maintain power balance

Source: Adapted from Robert Duncan, 'What Is the Right Organization Structure? Decision Tree Analysis Provides the Answer', *Organizational Dynamics* (Winter 1979), 429.

can facilitate discussion and adaptation to unexpected problems. It often works well in organizations of moderate size with a few product lines. Exhibit 4.11 summarizes the strengths and weaknesses of the matrix structure based on what we know of organizations that use it.[63]

A significant disadvantage of the matrix is that employees sometimes experience dual authority, reporting to two bosses and juggling conflicting demands. This can be frustrating

IN PRACTICE

CNH Global NV[64]

CNH was formed in the late 1990s through a merger of the construction and agricultural equipment companies Case and New Holland. It is the world's largest company in its market segment. One third of all combine harvesters and backhoe loaders, and one quarter of all tractors and skid steer loaders sold worldwide are built by CNH, a majority owned subsidiary of the Italian vehicle manufacturer Fiat SpA.

CNH managers wanted to benefit from the economies of scale that could be leveraged from such a large company with many common elements in its products,

while at the same time retaining the ability to tailor its products to different customer needs and desires in its different markets across the world. It aimed to achieve this through a 'multi-brand, multi-channel' strategy while establishing a global product development platform. Put simply, this meant producing a variety of lines for different markets from a few large production facilities. In order to succeed there had to be a close, interactive relationship between the marketing and sales teams on the one hand, who were close to customers, and the production experts on the other.

CNH put in place matrix accountability to structures to support this interactivity between the product and geographic managers. CNH has been largely successful in its efforts, despite facing challenging market conditions at times. The company is rated highly for employee satisfaction, despite closing several production facilities while moving towards global production platforms.

and confusing, especially if roles and responsibilities are not clearly defined by top managers.[65] Working effectively in a matrix demands excellent interpersonal and conflict-resolution skills. The matrix also forces managers to spend a great deal of time in coordinating meetings.[66] If managers do not adapt to the information and power sharing processes required to secure the benefits of the matrix, the system will underperform and fall into disrepute as employees revert to an earlier structure or develop 'work-arounds' that shadow and further disrupt the matrix. Managers must collaborate with one another rather than rely on vertical authority in decision-making. An example of a successful matrix design is discussed above.

**ONLINE
COUNTERPOINT 4.4**

Horizontal Structure

A recent approach to organizing, considered in Chapter 3, is the horizontal structure, which organizes employees around core processes. Organizations may be prompted to move toward a horizontal structure as a consequence of an intervention like total quality management or a procedure called re-engineering. Re-engineering, or *business process re-engineering*, involves the redesign of a vertical organization along its horizontal workflows and processes. A process refers to an organized group of related tasks and activities that work together to transform inputs into outputs that create value for customers.[67] Re-engineering aspires to change the way managers think about how work is done. Rather than focusing on narrow jobs structured into distinct functional departments, re-engineering emphasizes core processes that cut horizontally across the organization and involve teams of employees working together to serve customers. Examples of processes include order fulfilment, new product development and customer service.

A good illustration of process engineering is the redesign of customer services at the Vale of Glamorgan Council, a medium sized local government in Wales, UK. The council provides citizens with a range of services ranging from waste disposal to administration of planning and building regulations. In the past, citizens had to reach a specific department in order to make a complaint or arrange an appointment. It was often hard to reach the right person, and both staff and citizens wasted time leaving phone messages back and forth. After studying the problem and getting feedback from service users, the council reorganized the way it does business. Its OneVale initiative established a centralized customer contact centre in conjunction with a computerized information management system. Now, anyone needing to deal with the Council calls the contact centre, whose staff are empowered to deal with simple enquires and complaints themselves, and can set up appointments for all the Council's different departments. The council's phone lines are open late into the evening, and the Vale of Glamorgan has won awards for innovation and customer satisfaction (see Exhibit 4.12).[68]

When an organization is re-engineered to a horizontal structure, all the people throughout the organization who work on a particular process (such as customer service, claims handling or order fulfilment) have better access to one another so they can communicate and coordinate their efforts. The horizontal structure reduces the vertical hierarchy and erodes old departmental boundaries. This approach is generally facilitated by the use of information and communication technologies as well as by changing attitudes to work flexibility that have occurred in the workplace and the business environment over the past 25 years (see Counterpoint 4.4). Computerization and internet connectivity permits wide-ranging integration and coordination. Customers expect faster and better service, and employees may have the opportunity to develop new skills, and assume more responsibility. Organizations mired in a vertical mindset where each function or department operates within a separate 'silo' have a hard time meeting these challenges. Thus, numerous organizations have experimented with horizontal mechanisms such as cross-functional teams to achieve coordination across departments or task forces to accomplish temporary projects. Increasingly, organizations are shifting away from hierarchical, function-based structures to structures based on horizontal processes.

EXHIBIT 4.12   OneVale Initiative

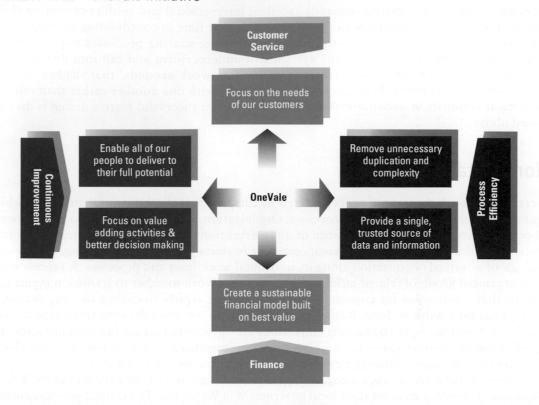

COUNTERPOINT 4.4

It would be misleading to suggest that such changes are easily or smoothly introduced or that they are always welcomed by customers or employers. Contacting call centres can be frustrating and unsatisfactory for customers and employees alike. Change is often driven by the objective of making savings rather than improving service. Or, service improvements are anticipated but an emphasis on cost reduction or a lack of vision results in poor service and disenchanted employees. Call centres can be 'designed' in various ways – at worst, there are those that mirror highly fragmented organizations, where callers wait in queues without any information and are then passed around to different employees who never give their name; and at best there are those that deal with calls promptly, courteously and are trained to manage the process – that is, take care of the handling of each call or 'case' from initial contact to its resolution.

BRIEFCASE 4.6

Characteristics

An illustration of a company re-engineered into a horizontal structure appears in Exhibit 4.13. Such an organization has the following characteristics:[69]

■ Structure is created around cross-functional core processes rather than tasks, functions or geography. Thus, boundaries between departments are obliterated.

■ Self-directed teams, not individuals, are the basis of organizational design and performance.

■ Process owners have responsibility for each core process in its entirety. For example, until the 1990s, most Britons bought houses through building societies, a kind of financial cooperative. Banks were just not set up to smoothly handle all the different elements that go in

EXHIBIT 4.13   A Horizontal Structure

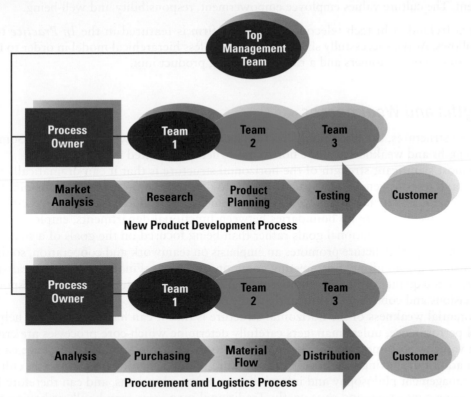

Source: Based on Frank Ostroff, *The Horizontal Organization* (New York: Oxford University Press, 1999); John A. Byrne, 'The Horizontal Corporation', *BusinessWeek* (December 20, 1993), 76–81; and Thomas A. Stewart, 'The Search for the Organization of Tomorrow', *Fortune* (May 18, 1992), 92–98.

to mortgage approval. Prospective buyers had to visit several different departments of the bank to arrange the loan, arrange the legal paperwork, obtain mortgage insurance etc., with delays of weeks if not months. As the property market became more competitive, Barclays Bank realized that if it wanted to build its mortgage business, it had to offer a comprehensive, one-stop service. It brought together all the different expertise and signing authority into a single department, allowing the process to be greatly streamlined. By 2014 the average time for Barclays to provide an offer letter was down to nine days, despite considerably tightened government requirements in the wake of the global financial crisis.[70] Barclays crystallized this new business process into its Home Finance Division. Both approvals and, crucially, profits, rose substantially, and by 2014 Barclays consolidated its position in the top five mortgage lenders in the UK.[71]

- People on the team are given the skills, tools, motivation and authority to make decisions central to the team's performance. Team members are cross-trained to perform one another's jobs, and the combined skills are sufficient to complete a major organizational task.

- Teams have the freedom to think creatively and respond flexibly to new challenges that arise.

- Customers drive the horizontal corporation. Effectiveness is measured by end-of-process performance objectives, based on the goal of bringing value to the company's stakeholders including customers and investors.

ONLINE
COUNTERPOINT 4.5

ONLINE
COUNTERPOINT 4.6

■ The culture is one of openness, trust and collaboration, focused on continuous improvement. The culture values employee empowerment, responsibility and well-being.

Avaya Ireland, a hi-tech telecommunications firm is featured in the *In Practice* text box which follows. Avaya successfully shifted to a flexible, less hierarchical model in order to meet the demands of diverse customers and a rapidly changing product mix.

Strengths and Weaknesses

As with all structures, the horizontal structure has weaknesses as well as strengths. Some of the main strengths and weaknesses of the horizontal structure are listed in Exhibit 4.14.

The most significant strength of the horizontal structure is that it can dramatically improve flexibility and responsiveness. The structure tends to direct attention toward the customer, leading to greater customer satisfaction as well as improvements in productivity, speed and efficiency. In addition, because there are no boundaries between functional departments, employees can take a broader view of organizational goals rather than being focused on the goals of a single department. The horizontal structure promotes an emphasis on teamwork and cooperation, so that team members share a commitment to meeting common objectives. Finally, the horizontal structure can improve the quality of life for employees by giving them opportunities to share responsibility, make decisions and contribute significantly to the organization.

A potential weakness of the horizontal structure is that it can harm rather than help organizational performance, unless managers carefully determine which core processes are critical for bringing value to customers. Simply defining the processes around which to organize can be difficult. In addition, shifting to a horizontal structure requires significant changes in culture, job design, management philosophy and information and reward systems, and can therefore be complicated, time consuming and thus costly. Traditional managers may baulk at having to share elements of power and authority, and find it difficult to learn to exercise leadership through team facilitation. Employees have to be trained to work effectively in a team environment, and they may be suspicious of the company's motives in dismantling overt hierarchy or hostile to its disruptive

EXHIBIT 4.14   Strengths and Weaknesses of Horizontal Structure

Strengths	Weaknesses
1. Promotes flexibility and rapid response to changes in customer needs	1. Determining core processes is difficult and time consuming
2. Directs the attention of everyone toward the production and delivery of value to the customer	2. Requires changes in culture, job design, management philosophy and information and reward systems
3. Each employee has a broader view of organizational goals	3. Traditional managers may baulk when they have to give up power and authority
4. Promotes a focus on teamwork and collaboration	4. Requires significant training of employees to work effectively in a horizontal team environment
5. Improves quality of life for employees by offering them the opportunity to share responsibility, make decisions and be accountable for outcomes	5. Can limit in-depth skill development

Sources: Based on Frank Ostroff, *The Horizontal Organization: What the Organization of the Future Looks Like and How It Delivers Value to Customers* (New York: Oxford University Press, 1999); and Richard L. Daft, *Organization Theory and Design*, 6th ed. (Cincinnati, Ohio: South-Western, 1998), 253.

IN PRACTICE

Avaya Ireland

Avaya Ireland is part of the global Avaya corporation, one of the many offspring of the giant AT&T telecommunications business that was broken up in the 1980s into smaller, more flexible and more entrepreneurial entities. Avaya specializes in manufacture of networking components, key building blocks of today's information society. Ireland is one of the main European centres for the computer industry, so Avaya Ireland had a dual advantage of location and growing demand for its product sector. Despite this positive market situation, the company languished through the 1980s and early 1990s. The company was run by a rigid functional hierarchy, with poor cross-functional communication. Costs were high compared with competitors and other subsidiaries of the Avaya group, and staff morale was poor. Avaya Ireland was in real danger of closing. In the mid-1990s top managers realized that they had to adapt to the times or the company would die. A management steering group was established to animate a process of internal dialogue, called Engaging our People. The highly inclusive, and often difficult process identified four main areas of weakness: communications, training, the manager/employee relationship and lack of teamwork. An action plan, based on the Business Excellence Model[72] was developed. Structural changes to realize the company's vision entailed replacing the rigid organizational hierarchy with cross-functional teams focused on core products, from conception, through production to end-user support. Armed with this new focus, the company was able to contain costs while improving product quality. Avaya invited customers to visit the plant and meet its new product-focused cross-functional teams. This was a highly successful initiative – customers saw that Avaya had an open culture and knowledgeable staff. Satisfaction with the company's networking products soared. In 1998 Avaya won the Irish Business Excellence overall award, and two years later a prize at the European Quality Awards as well as becoming one of the first Irish companies to be awarded ISO9001 certification. The change-driving steering group remains in place, and Avaya Ireland continues to win high marks for customer service and innovation, ranking in the Thompson Reuters top 100 for innovation for three years to 2013.[73] The company has now moved strongly into the related high-growth area of voice over internet protocol (VOIP) telephony.[74]

impact upon valued routines. Finally, because of the cross-functional nature of work, a horizontal structure can limit in-depth knowledge and skill development unless measures are taken to enable employees opportunities to maintain and build technical expertise.

Virtual Network Structure

The virtual network structure extends the concept of horizontal coordination and collaboration beyond the boundaries of the traditional organization. Many of today's organizations farm out some of their activities to other companies. Outsourcing, which means the contracting out of aspects of work (e.g. manufacturing, information technology or credit processing), to other companies is a significant trend in many industries that has implications for organization structure.[75] Accenture, for example, handles all aspects of information technology for the British food retailer J. Sainsbury's. Companies in countries such as India and Malaysia, as well as European sites such as Scotland and Eastern Europe, manage call centre and technical support for multinational corporations including financial companies, computer vendors and mobile phone companies. Entire chunks of aeroplanes manufactured by Canada's Bombardier and Brazil's Embraer are engineered and built by outside contractors, often outside Canada and Brazil respectively. Fiat Auto is involved in multiple complex outsourcing relationships with other companies handling logistics, maintenance and the manufacturing of some parts.[76]

These interorganizational relationships reflect a significant shift in organization design. An increasing number of organizations take outsourcing to the extreme and create a virtual network structure. With a virtual network structure, sometimes called a *modular structure*, the firm subcontracts many or most of its major processes to separate companies and coordinates their activities from a small headquarters organization. Nowadays fashionwear companies like Nike frequently produce none of their own clothing, focusing instead on building brand value through comprehensive marketing efforts and exercising tight control over their suppliers. The virtual network structure has become much more feasible as a result of advances in information and communication technologies.[77]

How the Structure Works

The virtual network organization may be viewed as a central hub surrounded by a network of outside specialists. Rather than being housed under one roof or located within one organization, services such as accounting, design, manufacturing, marketing and distribution are outsourced to separate companies that are connected electronically to a central office. Organizational partners located in different parts of the world may use secure networking to exchange data and information so rapidly and smoothly that a loosely connected network of suppliers, manufacturers and distributors can look and act like one seamless company. The virtual network form can also incorporate a free-market style to replace the traditional vertical hierarchy. In this case, contractors can be brought into and released from the system to meet changing needs.

With a network structure, the hub maintains control over processes in which it has difficult-to-imitate capabilities and transfers other activities – along with the decision-making for, and operational control over, those activities – to other organizations who are specialists. These organizations organize and accomplish their work using their own ideas, assets and tools.[78] The idea is that a firm can concentrate on its 'core competence' – what is key to its survival – and contract out everything else to companies with distinctive competence in those specific areas, thereby in principle enabling the organization to do more with less.[79] The network structure is often advantageous in reducing costs for start-up companies, such as Dicole, a Finnish IT firm that works with companies to implement Web 2.0 technologies, featured in the *In Practice* box below.

Strengths and Weaknesses

Exhibit 4.15 summarizes the strengths and weaknesses of the virtual network structure. One of the major strengths is that even quite small organizations can be truly global, drawing on resources worldwide to achieve the best quality and price and then selling products or services

EXHIBIT 4.15   Strengths and Weaknesses of Virtual Network Structure

Strengths	Weaknesses
1. Enables even small organizations to obtain talent and resources worldwide	1. Managers do not have hands-on control over many activities and employees
2. Gives a company immediate scale and reach without huge investments in factories, equipment or distribution facilities	2. Requires a great deal of time to manage relationships and potential conflicts with contract partners
3. Enables the organization to be highly flexible and responsive to changing needs	3. There is a risk of organizational failure if a partner fails to deliver or goes out of business
4. Reduces administrative overhead costs	4. Employee loyalty and corporate culture might be weak because employees feel they can be replaced by contract services

Sources: Based on Linda S. Ackerman, 'Transition Management: An In-Depth Look at Managing Complex Change', *Organizational Dynamics* (Summer 1982), 46–66; and Frank Ostroff, *The Horizontal Organization* (New York: Oxford University Press, 1999), Fig 2.1, 34.

IN PRACTICE

Leveraging Web 2.0

Virtual networking is made possible by new technologies, and the ever-expanding universe of virtual communication creates new opportunities almost daily. Companies small and large are exploring ways to build virtual networks and strengthen collaboration across the globe, using the boundless potential of Web 2.0, and particularly new thinking in virtual communications. This *In Practice* discusses several companies' and organizations' approaches to Web 2.0.

Dicole, a Finnish SME, works with companies to leverage Web 2.0 potential, offering a dizzying variety of potential and permutations. Dicole (www.dicole. com) has been operating for 15 years, since social media was born, and by 2013 had been working with major Finnish organizations including Nokia, auto importer VV-Auto, the Finnish state traffic agency, the Kesko food retailer and the Finnish Army.

One of the simplest forms of virtual communication is the Wiki, a word that comes from the Hawaiian for 'fast', and involves working collaboratively and in realtime on a single text. Wikipedia, the online collaborative encyclopedia, is the best known example of wiki technology, but wikis are used increasingly within companies for internal communication, and increasingly for technical documentation of work processes. As employees become more familiar with wikis, they are being used to develop product manuals and instructions for end users outside the

company. Similarly, the same technology used to create YouTube, the popular site for uploading, viewing and sharing video clips, can be used to transfer knowledge within a company quickly and cheaply. Large companies such as IBM use technology similar to that underpinning the social networking site Facebook to help employees to get to know and understand each other – over 400 000 IBM employees have their own pages on the company's 'Blue Pages', which can include photos, employees' places in the IBM hierarchy, contact information and even their own weblogs.

While many companies use versions of wikis, blogs and Facebooks, Dicole works with its customer organizations to combine the various technologies together in a tailor-made approach to virtual network communications, which it has branded Dicole Knowledge Work Environment.[80]

The concept can be taken even further through the product development technique called *crowdsourcing*, where social networking technologies are used to develop new products. Many different approaches have been tried. One example is Threadless (www.threadless.com), a Chicago-headquartered t-shirt company that invites anyone to submit t-shirt designs. If the design is selected, the designer is paid an upfront fee and a commission depending on the number of t-shirts sold with that design. By 2013, Threadless had accepted 264 055 designs from 1443 artists, and had a total 2 423 041 'community members' (customers) worldwide. Threadless's first Chief Technology Officer, Harper Reed went on to run technology for Barack Obama's successful 2012 US presidential campaign, and joined Paypal to head their software development division in 2015. Reed is not shy, either; he describes himself on his website as "Probably one of the coolest guys ever".[81, 82]

worldwide just as easily through subcontractors. The network structure also enables new or small companies to develop products or services and get them to market rapidly without huge investments in factories, equipment, warehouses or distribution facilities. The ability to arrange and rearrange resources to meet changing needs and best serve customers gives the network structure flexibility and rapid response. New technologies can be developed quickly by tapping into a worldwide network of experts. The organization can continually redefine itself to meet changing product or market opportunities. A final strength is reduced administrative over-head. Large teams of staff specialists and administrators are not needed. Managerial and

BRIEFCASE 4.7

technical talent can be focused on key activities that provide competitive advantage while other activities are outsourced.[83]

The virtual network structure also has a number of weaknesses.[84] The primary weakness is a potential lack of control associated with taking decentralization to the extreme. Managers do not have all operations under their jurisdiction and must rely on contracts, coordination and negotiation to hold things together. This can also mean increased time spent managing relationships with partners and resolving conflicts, which can be especially complex if partners are operating in different continents, many time zones away. Communications technologies have greatly reduced effective distance, but there is no substitute for face-to-face negotiations when complex, serious issues arise.

A problem of equal importance is the risk of failure if one organizational partner fails to deliver, has a plant burn down or goes out of business. Managers in the headquarters organization have to act quickly to spot problems and find new arrangements. Finally, from a human resource perspective, employee loyalty can be weak in a network organization, both because of concerns over job security and because developing a cohesive corporate culture is difficult between far-flung units or outsourced functions. Employees may feel that they could be replaced at any time by contract services. Turnover of staff may be higher because emotional commitment between the organization and employees is low. With changing products, markets and partners, the organization may need frequently to reshuffle employees to get the correct mix of skills and capabilities.

Hybrid Structure

As a practical matter, many structures in the real world do not exist in the pure forms we have outlined in this chapter. Organizations often use a hybrid structure that combines characteristics of various approaches tailored to specific strategic needs. Most companies combine characteristics of functional, divisional, geographical, horizontal or network structures to take account of the relative strengths and weaknesses of these structures in their own particular business.

BRIEFCASE 4.8

One type of hybrid that is often used is to combine characteristics of the functional and divisional structures. When a corporation grows large and has several products or markets, it typically is organized into self-contained divisions of some type. Functions that are important to each product or market are decentralized to the self-contained units. However, some functions that are relatively stable and require economies of scale and in-depth specialization are also centralized at headquarters.

Sony Europa is the European arm of the Japanese electronics giant, Sony Corporation. The company has been active in Europe since 1960 and has enjoyed success across the continent due to the famed high quality of Sony products. However, the company's involvement in Europe developed in an unplanned way, with marketing offices and manufacturing plants growing up in many different countries. Country managers, by default, became leaders of mini-empires, and there was little cross-European coordination. The weaknesses of this approach could be overlooked while Sony was growing, but as the company faced stiffer competition on both price and quality from the 1990s, company leaders realized a more strategic and coordinated approach to organizational structure was needed. Successive efforts by Sony's top management to introduce some coordination resulted in establishment of business units that grouped together consumer electronics, business and professional products and OEM products geared to industrial purchasers. While this improved coordination, each division had its own functional units such as HR, marketing and logistics, detracting from possible cost synergies and overall corporate identity. In 2002, Sony Europa's new president Mike Tsurumi established a hybrid structure which retains product divisions, but centralizes the functional areas of HR, Finance, Sales, Marketing and Infrastructure[85] (see Exhibit 4.16 as applied to Marketing). A hybrid structure such as this is often

EXHIBIT 4.16 New Structure of European Marketing Introduced During the Era of Mike Tsurumi

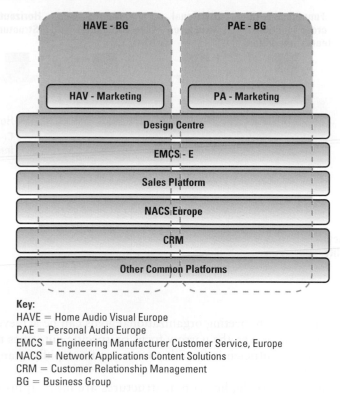

Key:
HAVE = Home Audio Visual Europe
PAE = Personal Audio Europe
EMCS = Engineering Manufacturer Customer Service, Europe
NACS = Network Applications Content Solutions
CRM = Customer Relationship Management
BG = Business Group

Prof. Paul Sparrow: http://www.lums.lancs.ac.uk/files/hr/10044.pdf

preferred over the pure functional, divisional, horizontal or virtual network structure because it can provide some of the advantages of each and overcome some of the disadvantages.

Applications of Structural Design

Each type of structure is applied in different situations and is intended to address different demands. In describing the various structures, we touched briefly on conditions such as environmental stability or change and organizational size that are related to structure. Each form of structure – functional, divisional, matrix, horizontal, network, hybrid – represents a tool that can make an organization more or less effective, depending on the exigencies of the situation and the capacity of the structure to respond effectively to their often conflicting demands.

Structural Alignment

One of the most important roles of top managers in structural design is finding the right balance between vertical control and horizontal coordination, depending on the constantly changing needs of the organization. Vertical control tends to be associated with goals of efficiency and stability, while horizontal coordination is associated with learning, innovation and flexibility. Exhibit 4.17 shows a simplified continuum that illustrates how structural approaches are associated with vertical control versus horizontal coordination. The functional structure is most appropriate when

EXHIBIT 4.17 Relationship of Structure to Organization's Need for Efficiency versus Learning

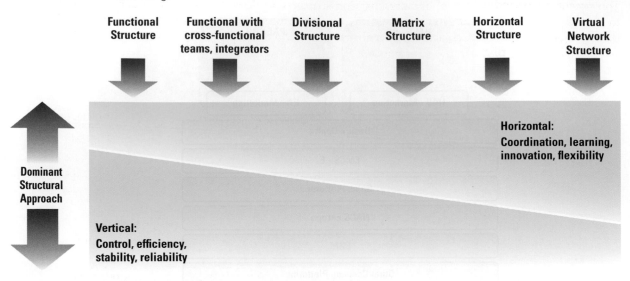

managers believe that efficiency in meeting organizational goals can be achieved through coordination by vertical hierarchy. However, the narrow focus on specific outcomes that vertical hierarchy tends to produce can be insufficiently flexible to account for rapidly changing pressures in a complex business environment.

At the opposite end of the scale, horizontal structures are more appropriate when innovation is a priority. In this case, continuous coordination among functions fosters organizational learning. The horizontal structure enables organizations to differentiate themselves and respond quickly to changes, but often at the expense of short-term efficiency. The virtual network structure offers even greater flexibility and potential for rapid response by allowing the organization to add or subtract pieces as needed to adapt and meet changing demands and challenges, as well as searching the world for lower costs and increased productivity. Exhibit 4.17 also shows how other types of structure defined in this chapter – functional with horizontal linkages, divisional and matrix – represent intermediate steps on the organization's path to cost-efficiency, innovation and learning. The exhibit does not include all possible structures, but it illustrates how organizations attempt to balance competing priorities and demands (see Counterpoint 4.5).

COUNTERPOINT 4.5

In this chapter we have presented a range of formal schemas of design. In practice, however, organizations are ongoing projects in which elements and remnants of different structures are overlapped and overlaid. The result is more of a patchwork than a 'hybrid' that is the product of successive efforts to mitigate for the limitations or weaknesses ascribed to a previous structure. Nor should it be overlooked that structures are generally imposed from the top, sometimes mainly to signal the arrival of a new CEO or management team with 'fresh ideas', and they then encounter resistance which moderates their impact and (in)effectiveness.

Symptoms of Structural Deficiency

Top executives periodically evaluate organization structure to determine whether it is appropriate to changing conditions and aspirations. Many organizations try one organization structure and then reorganize to another structure in an effort to develop a better fit between executive aspirations, internal reporting relationships and the external environment.

The following are symptomatic of structural deficiency (see Counterpoint 4.6).[86]

- *Decision-making is delayed or lacking in quality.* Decision-makers may be overloaded because the hierarchy funnels too many problems and decisions to them. Delegation to lower levels may be insufficient. Another cause of poor-quality decisions is that information may not reach the correct people. Information linkages in either the vertical or horizontal direction may be inadequate to ensure decision quality.

- *The organization does not respond innovatively to a changing environment.* One reason for lack of innovation is that departments are not coordinated horizontally. The identification of customer needs by the marketing department and the identification of technological developments in the research department must be coordinated. Organization structure also has to specify departmental responsibilities that include environmental scanning and innovation.

- *Employee performance declines and goals are not being met.* Employee performance may decline because the structure doesn't provide clear goals, responsibilities and mechanisms for coordination. The structure should reflect the complexity of the market environment and be straightforward enough for employees to effectively work within.

- *Too much conflict is evident.* In principle, organization structure is intended to enable departmental goals to combine into a single set of goals for the entire organization. When departments act at cross-purposes or departmental priorities are out of alignment with those attributed to the wider organization, it may be that the structure has incorporated insufficient horizontal linkages.

COUNTERPOINT 4.6

Although these problems may arise from 'structural deficiency' that can be corrected by the technical fix of structural redesign, the problems may also be endemic to capitalist work organizations. Decision-making may be delayed because senior managers anticipate that their jobs or career prospects are threatened by change. Innovation may be slow because it poses a threat to established 'empires' within the organization. Declines in employee performance may be associated with frustration and dissatisfaction in, ultimately, being treated as a disposable commodity or, at least, with insufficient dignity as changes are introduced (or imposed) without genuine consultation or adequate understanding of their counterproductive effects. Conflicts between individuals, groups, departments and divisions may arise from the basic understanding that responding to the demands of shareholders and/or customers is not necessarily compatible with improving the wages and conditions (e.g. pensions) of particular groups of employees.

Summary and Interpretation

Organization structure is intended to accomplish two things. It seeks to provide a framework of responsibilities, reporting relationships and groupings, and it is intended to provide mechanisms for linking and coordinating organizational elements into a coherent whole.

Managers make a strategic choice as they orient toward a traditional organization design which emphasizes vertical linkages such as hierarchy, rules and plans or toward a contemporary learning organization, which emphasizes horizontal linkages through cross-functional information systems, direct contact between managers across department lines, temporary task forces, full-time integrators and teams.

Alternatives for grouping employees and departments into overall structural design include functional grouping, divisional grouping, multifocused grouping, horizontal grouping and network grouping. With functional and divisional structures, managers also use horizontal linkage mechanisms to complement the vertical dimension and achieve integration of departments and levels into an organizational whole. With a horizontal structure, activities are organized horizontally around core work processes. A virtual network structure extends the concept of horizontal coordination and collaboration beyond the boundaries of the organization. Core activities are performed by a central hub while other functions and activities are outsourced to contract partners. The matrix structure attempts to achieve an equal balance between the vertical and horizontal dimensions of structure. Organizations rarely exist in these pure forms. Instead, hybrid or patchwork varieties evolve that incorporate more or less coherent blends of organizing activity that can be analyzed in terms of the various structural types examined in this chapter.

KEY CONCEPTS

centralized	horizontal grouping	organization structure	teams
decentralized	horizontal linkage	outsourcing	vertical information
departmental grouping	horizontal structure	process	system
divisional grouping	hybrid structure	product matrix	vertical linkages
divisional structure	integrator	re-engineering	virtual network grouping
functional grouping	liaison role	symptoms of structural	virtual network
functional matrix	matrix structure	deficiency	structure
functional structure	multifocused grouping	task force	virtual team

Discussion Questions

1 What is the definition of *organization structure*? Does organization structure appear on the organization chart? Explain.

2 How do rules and plans help an organization achieve vertical integration?

3 When is a functional structure preferable to a divisional structure?

4 Large corporations tend to use hybrid structures. Why?

5 What are the primary differences between a traditional organization designed for efficiency and a more contemporary organization designed for learning?

6 What is the difference between a task force and a team? Between a liaison role and an integrating role? Which of these provides the greatest amount of horizontal coordination?

7 What conditions usually have to be present before an organization should adopt a matrix structure?

8 The manager of a consumer products firm said, 'We use the brand manager position to train future executives'. Do you think the brand manager position is a good training ground? Discuss.

9 Why do companies using a horizontal structure have cultures that emphasize openness, employee empowerment and responsibility? What do you think a manager's job would be like in a horizontally organized company?

10 Describe the virtual network structure. Why do you think this is becoming a good structural alternative for some of today's organizations?

Chapter 4 Workbook You and Organization Structure

To better understand the importance of organization structure in your life, do the following assignment. Select one of the following situations to organize:

- A copy and printing shop
- A travel agency
- A sports rental (such as skis or snowboards) in a resort area
- A bakery.

1 Write down the mission or purpose of the organization in a few sentences.

2 What are the specific tasks to be completed to accomplish the mission?

3 Based on the specifics in number 2, develop an organization chart. Each position in the chart will perform a specific task or is responsible for a certain outcome.

4 You are into your third year of operation, and your business has been very successful. You want to add a second location a few kilometres away. What issues will you face running the business at two locations? Draw an organization chart that includes the two business locations.

5 Five more years go by and the business has grown to five locations in two cities in the same country. How do you keep in touch with it all? What issues of control and coordination have arisen? Draw an up-to-date organization chart and explain your rationale for it.

6 Twenty years later you have 75 business locations in five European countries. What are the issues and problems that have to be dealt with through organizational structure? Draw an organization chart for this organization, indicating such factors as who is responsible for customer satisfaction, how you will know if customer needs are met and how information will flow within the organization.

Adapted by Dorothy Marcic from 'Organizing', in Donald D. White and H. William Vroman, *Action in Organizations*, 2nd ed. (Boston: Allyn and Bacon, 1982), 154; and Cheryl Harvey and Kim Morouney, 'Organization Structure and Design: The Club Ed Exercise', *Journal of Management Education* (June 1985), 425–429.

Organization Structures

Scotia University

Scotia University is located in Scotland and, like most organizations, periodically re-structures its organization to better align its structure to its strategy. Universities are no different to any other organization but tend to use different terminology when it comes to organization structures. Senate is the senior academic body of the university. Legally and constitutionally it is responsible for the academic activity of the university which is teaching and research. Senate is also responsible for student conduct. The University Court is involved in the development of, and ultimately approves, the university's strategic plan. It approves any major financial decisions, such as whether or not to borrow money; it also approves the university's proposed budget.

The principal divisions are normally termed colleges, faculties or schools, with colleges being an overarching structure with direct responsibility to the University Executive or Senior Management Team. The Scotia University College of Arts contains: the School of Humanities; the School of Critical Studies; the School of Culture & Creative Arts; the School of Modern Languages & Cultures; and its graduate school. The College of Medical, Veterinary and Life Sciences contains: the School of Life Sciences; the School of Medicine; the School of Veterinary Medicine; its graduate school and seven research institutes. The College of Science and Engineering contains: the School of Chemistry; the School of Computing Science; the School of Engineering; the School of Geographical & Earth Sciences; the School of Mathematics & Statistics; the School of Physics & Astronomy; the School of Psychology; and its graduate school. The College of Social Sciences contains: the Business School; the School of Education; the School of Interdisciplinary Studies; the School of Law; the School of Social & Political Sciences; and its graduate school.

The chief executive of a Scottish university has the title Principal and Vice-Chancellor and the Chancellor is a lay-member of the university (not an employee). The Senior Management Group advises the Principal as chief executive officer of the University on matters of policy. It also advises Court and Senate on matters of strategic policy (academic and resource), and acts on a day-to-day basis to implement the policies of Court and Senate. The Senior Management Group (SMG) comprises: the Principal; Vice-Principals; Heads of Colleges; Secretary of Court; and the Director of Finance. The SMG has responsibility for ensuring that the university policies are effectively implemented and that this is done in a coordinated way across the Colleges and University Services. It has a role in developing corporate initiatives and policies, for consideration by Senate and Court. SMG maintains a watching brief on the university strategy and in particular on progress against the strategic key performance indicators (KPIs) and it takes action as required to ensure that the university is positioned to meet them. SMG also has an ongoing responsibility to monitor, assess and address risk, and in liaison with Court, update the strategic risk list annually.

The Court is the governing body of the university, and is sometimes compared to the Board of Directors of a company. Its powers have been defined over a number of years and are set out in a series of Acts of Parliament, the Universities (Scotland) Acts 1858–1966, and subsidiary regulations and ordinances. The Court has ultimate responsibility for the deployment of resources in the university and for the strategic plans of the institution. It also has a monitoring role in relation to the overall performance of the university, and it holds the Principal accountable for the effective and efficient management of the university. It is responsible for the well-being of staff. With the Senate, it is responsible for the well-being of students and for the reputation of the university. The Rector is elected by the students of the university to represent their interests. He or she is also, ex-officio, the Chairperson of the University Court, the body which administers the resources of the university. The Rector is not active in university strategy or policy-making. The role is principally as spokesperson and representative for student issues. The Rector's participation in events is entirely voluntary and depends on availability and personal choice.

Case Study Questions

1   Describe and explain the structure of Scotia University in terms of its vertical structure and illustrate with an organization chart of the Colleges.

2   How is coordination achieved in academic matters?

3   Matrix structures are often used to improve horizontal coordination and information sharing and are ideal structures for a research institute which brings together academics from across the university. Using the College of Social Sciences as your example, illustrate how a matrix organization structure could be used for a research institute in management with two research themes: business management and public management.

Notes

1. 'Henry Ford would just love Toyota: Car makers' strategy for market share', *Strategic Direction*, 2005, Vol. 21 No. 4, 25–27.

2. E. Bartezzaghi, 'The evolution of production models: is a new paradigm emerging?'*International Journal of Operations and Production Management*, 1999, Vol. 19 No. 2, 229–250.

3. 'GM updates Zaragoza plant for new Corsa'. just-auto.com, July 27, 2006.

4. Daniel Vázquez-Bustelo and Lucía Avella, 'Agile manufacturing: Industrial case studies in Spain', *Technovation*, October 2006, Vol. 26 No. 10, 1147b

5. Drew Singer, 'Opel Plant In Zaragoza, Spain Celebrates 12 Million Vehicle Milestone', May 20, 2015, accessed at http://gmauthority.com/blog/2015/05/opel-plant-in-zaragoza-spain-celebrates-12-million-vehicle-milestone/#ixzz45ERdPRIG.

6. Daniel J. Wakin, 'With Shifting Needs and Ebbing Resources, Church is Reorganizing', *The New York Times* (January 4, 2004).

7. John Child, *Organization* (New York: Harper & Row, 1984).

8. Stuart Ranson, Bob Hinings and Royston Greenwood, 'The Structuring of Organizational Structures', *Administrative Science Quarterly* 25 (1980), 1–17; and Hugh Willmott, 'The Structuring of Organizational Structure: A Note', *Administrative Science Quarterly* 26 (1981), 470–474.

9. This section is based on Frank Ostroff, *The Horizontal Organization: What the Organization of the Future Looks Like and How It Delivers Value to Customers* (New York: Oxford University Press, 1999).

10. Stephen Salsbury, *The State, the Investor and the Railroad: The Boston & Albany, 1825–1867* (Cambridge: Harvard University Press, 1967), 186–187.

11. Gideon Kunda, (1992), *Engineering Culture: Control and Commitment in a High-Tech Corporation,* Philadelphia, Temple University Press; Hugh Willmott (1993), 'Strength is Ignorance; Slavery is Freedom: Managing Culture in Modern Organizations', *Journal of Management Studies* 30, 515–552; James R. Barker (1993), 'Tightening the Iron Cage: Concertive Control in Self-Managing Teams', *Administrative Science Quarterly*, 38, 408–437.

12. Scott C. Beardsley, Bradford C. Johnson and James M. Manyika, 'Competitive advantage from better interactions', *McKinsey Quarterly*, 2006 (2), 52–63.

13. 'The Cemex Way', *The Economist*, June 16, 2001.

14. Based on Jay R. Galbraith, *Designing Complex Organizations* (Reading, MA: Addison-Wesley, 1973), and *Organization Design* (Reading, MA: Addison-Wesley, 1977), 81–127.

15. Lee Iacocca with William Novak, *Iacocca: An Autobiography* (New York: Phantom Books, 1984), 152–153.

16. In 2007 Daimler agreed to sell its Chrysler unit on to Cerebrus Capital Management: The New York Times on the Web, Micheline Maynard and Mark Landler, 'Chrysler Group to Be Sold for $7.4 Billion', *New York Times*, May 14. After Daimler demerged with Chrysler in 2007, the latter filed for bankruptcy in 2009 before coming under the majority ownership of Italian automobile manufacturer Fiat in 2011.

17. Based on Jay R. Galbraith, *Designing Complex Organizations* (Reading, MA: Addison-Wesley, 1973).

18. G. Christian Hill, 'Dog Eats Dog Food. And Damn If It Ain't Tasty', *Ecompany Now* (November 2000), 169–178; 'Country Managers: From Baron to Hotelier'; Rochelle Garner and Barbara Darrow, 'Oracle Plots Course', *CRN* (January 24, 2005), 3; and Anthony Hilton, 'Dangers behind Oracle's Dream', *Evening Standard* (February 11, 2005), 45.

19. 'Is Fusion Beyond Oracle's Reach?', *IT Week*, April 23, 2007, p. 9; Richard Waters, 'Departure of executive may delay Oracle plan', *Financial Times*, October 17, 2007.

20. Michelle Jones, 'Oracle Corporation: The Gloves Are Still Off Against Workday', Value Walk, April 5, 2016 accessed at www.valuewalk.com/2016/04/oracle-gloves-off-workday/, 'Total Cloud Revenues Up 28% but Would Have Been Up 34% in Constant Currency', Oracle Corporation press release, June 17 2015, accessed at investor.oracle.com/financial-news/financial-news-details/2015/Total-Cloud-Revenues-Up-28-but-Would-Have-Been-Up-34-in-Constant-Currency/default.aspx, http://www.forbes.com/profile/larry-ellison/

21. 'Mandate 2003: Be Agile and Efficient', *Microsoft Executive Circle* (Spring 2003), 46–48.

22. Jay Galbraith, Diane Downey and Amy Kates, 'How Networks Undergird the Lateral Capability of an Organization – Where the Work Gets Done', *Journal of Organizational Excellence* (Spring 2002), 67–78.

23. Samaritans turns to thankQ for CRM and fundraising solution, January 8, 2013, accessed at fundraising.co.uk/2013/01/08/samaritans-turns-thankq-crm-and-fundraising-solution/

24. Amy Barrett, 'Staying on Top', *BusinessWeek* (May 5, 2003), 60–68.

25. Walter Kiechel III, 'The Art of the Corporate Task Force', *Fortune* (January 28, 1991), 104–105; and William J. Altier,

'Task Forces: An Effective Management Tool', *Management Review* (February 1987), 52–57.

26. Neal E. Boudette, 'Marriage Counseling; At DaimlerChrysler, A New Push to Make Its Units Work Together', *The Wall Street Journal* (March 12, 2003), A1, A15.

27. Jeremy van Loon, July 28 2005, 'Daimler Chief Schrempp to Be Replaced by Zetsche', *Bloomberg*.

28. Mike Danilovic and Mats Winroth (2006) 'Corporate manufacturing network: from hierarchy to self-organising system', *International Journal of Integrated Supply Management*, Vol. 2, 1–2, 106–131.

29. Keith Naughton and Kathleen Kerwin, 'At GM, Two Heads May Be Worse Than One', *BusinessWeek* (August 14, 1995), 46.

30. Paul R. Lawrence and Jay W. Lorsch, 'New Managerial Job: The Integrator', *Harvard Business Review* (November–December 1967), 142–151.

31. Charles Fishman, 'Total Teamwork: Imagination Ltd.', *Fast Company* (April 2000), 156–168; Thomas L. Legare, 'How Hewlett-Packard Used Virtual Cross-Functional Teams to Deliver Healthcare Industry Solutions', *Journal of Organizational Excellence* (Autumn 2001), 29–37.

32. Anthony M. Townsend, Samuel M. DeMarie and Anthony R. Hendrickson, 'Virtual Teams: Technology and the Workplace of the Future', *Academy of Management Executive* 12, No. 3 (August 1998), 17–29.

33. Ben S. Kuipers and Marco C. de Witte (2005) 'Teamwork: a case study on development and performance', *The International Journal of Human Resource Management*, 16:2, 185–201.

34. 'Smells like team spirit', *Management Services Journal*, Winter 2005, 28–31.

35. Henry Mintzberg, *The Structuring of Organizations* (Englewood Cliffs, NJ: Prentice-Hall, 1979).

36. Dutta, S and Regani, S. (2005) 'Project Scorpio: The Making of India's First Indigenous Sports Utility Vehicle', ICFAI Center for Management Research, Case 605-005-1. Accessed at http://www.thecasecentre.org/educators/products/view?id=26630.

37. Jean Bonnal and Massimo Rossi (2005), *Understand, analyze and manage a decentralization process: The RED-IFO Model and its use*, Rome, FAO, 63–67.

38. Dina Khorasanee (2007), 'Resistance as "creation": a new sociability in Argentina', *Development in Practice*, 17, 765–774.

39. David M. Boje and Robert F. Dennehy (2008), *Managing in the postmodern world: America's revolution against exploitation*, Charlotte, IAP.

40. Based on Robert Duncan, 'What Is the Right Organization Structure?' *Organizational Dynamics* (Winter 1979), 59–80; and W. Alan Randolph and Gregory G. Dess, 'The Congruence Perspective of Organization Design: A Conceptual Model and Multivariate Research Approach', *Academy of Management Review* 9 (1984), 114–127.

41. Rahul Jacob, 'The Struggle to Create an Organization for the 21st Century', *Fortune* (April 3, 1995), 90–99.

42. 'Hur stort kan ett sjukhus bli?', *Sjukhuslakaren*, 06 / 2005, at http://www.sjukhuslakaren.se/2005/12/22/hur-stort-kanett-sjukhus-bli/.

43. 'The Real Hotel Co – Preliminary Results', *Thomson Financial News*, April 29, 2008; 'CHE Hotel Group Plc – Final Results PR Newswire UK Disclose, April 25, 2007', 'Hotel chain chairman to step down', *The Independent* (London), July 17, 1998; Damian Reece, 'Radisson and London Plaza to buy CHE', *Sunday Telegraph*, December 16, 2001, p. 2, CHE Hotels rejigs management to save 1 mln stg annually, AFX.COM, January 25, 2007; Emma Rowley, 'Hotels Group Goes Into Administration', January 21, 2009.

44. Randeep Ramesh, 19 December 2012, 'Private equity takeover lauded by the right as model for Britain: Lessons from Sweden', *The Guardian*.

45. Amy Barrett, 'Staying On Top'; Joseph Weber, 'A Big Company That Works', *BusinessWeek* (May 4, 1992), 124–132; and Elyse Tanouye, 'Johnson & Johnson Stays Fit by Shuffling Its Mix of Businesses', *The Wall Street Journal* (December 22, 1992), A1, A4.

46. Nick Harrop and Alan Gillies (2007) 'IT, culture, context: Emergency department modernisation can inform the NHS information programme', *International Journal of Public Sector Management*, 20, 272–284.

47. Based on Duncan, 'What Is the Right Organization Structure?'.

48. Weber, 'A Big Company That Works'.

49. Alan Rugman and Richard Hodgetts (2001), 'The End of Global Strategy', *European Management Journal*, 19, 333– 343: 337.

50. 'Microsoft Realigns for Next Wave of Innovation and Growth', Microsoft Corporation Press Release, September 20, 2005, accessed at http://www.microsoft.com/presspass/press/2005/sep05/09-20ExecChangesPR.mspx.

51. Gregg Keizer, 'Microsoft's focus on Windows 10 upgrades is a mistake', *Computerworld*, April 7, 2016, accessed at www.computerworld.com/article/3053524/windows-pcs/microsofts-focus-on-windows-10-upgrades-is-a-mistake.html; Nick Wingfield, 'Microsoft Overhauls, the Apple Way', New York Times, July 11, 2013, accessed at www.nytimes.com/2013/07/12/technology/microsoft-revamps-structure-and-management.html; Steve Ballmer, 'One Microsoft: Company realigns to enable innovation at greater speed, efficiency', *Microsoft News Center*, July 11, 2013 accessed at https://news.microsoft.com/2013/07/11/one-microsoft-company-realigns-to-enable-innovation-at-greater-speed-efficiency/#sm.00017mhkcyyq3crov792leh133lgx

52. Robert A. Guth, 'Midlife Correction; Inside Microsoft, Financial Managers Winning New Clout', *The Wall Street Journal* (July 23, 2003), A1, A6; and Michael Moeller, with Steve Hamm and Timothy J. Mullaney, 'Remaking Microsoft', *BusinessWeek* (May 17, 1999), 106–114.

53. Mariko Sanchanta, 'Vital signs at Sony as a talking cure takes effect', *Financial Times*, January 17, 2008, 13.

54. Maisie O'Flanagan and Lynn K. Taliento, 'Nonprofits: Ensuring That Bigger Is Better', *McKinsey Quarterly*, Issue 2 (2004), 112ff.

55. Kingfisher PLC – Final Results 2007, *Thomson Financial News*, March 27 2008.

56. Kingfisher Annual Report 2014/2015, accessed at http://www.kingfisher.com/files/reports/annual_report_2015/files/pdf/annual_report_2015.pdf

57. Stanley M. Davis and Paul R. Lawrence, *Matrix* (Reading, MA: Addison-Wesley, 1977), 11–24.

58. Erik W. Larson and David H. Gobeli, 'Matrix Management: Contradictions and Insight', *California Management Review* 29 (Summer 1987), 126–138.

59. Davis and Lawrence, *Matrix,* 155–180.
60. Michael Bazigos and Jim Harte, 'Revisiting the matrix organization', *McKinsey Quarterly*, January 2016, accessed at www.mckinsey.com/business-functions/organization/our-insights/revisiting-the-matrix-organization
61. Bayer Annual Management Report 2006, accessed at http://www.annualreport2006.bayer.com/en/bayer_management_report_2006.pdfx; Sigurt Vitols, 'Shareholder Value, Management Culture and Production Regimes in the Transformation of the German Chemical-Pharmaceutical Industry', Discussion Paper P 02–902, Wissenschaftszentrum Berlin für Sozialforschung, August 2002; *PBIRG Perspective*, Vol. 3, No. 1, 2001.
62. Lawton R. Burns, 'Matrix Management in Hospitals: Testing Theories of Matrix Structure and Development', *Administrative Science Quarterly* 34 (1989), 349–368.
63. Robert C. Ford and W. Alan Randolph, 'Cross-Functional Structures: A Review and Integration of Matrix Organizations and Project Management', *Journal of Management* 18 (June 1992), 267–294; and Duncan, 'What Is the Right Organization Structure?'
64. 'CNH Third Quarter 2007 Net Income Up 82 Percent From 2006', Marketwire, October 23, 2007; P. Morosini, H. Huber, D. Khandpur and S. Linguri (2005), 'CNH Global Construction Equipment: Building a New Global Organization Across Boundaries', ESMT European School of Management & Technology, Case number 306-136-1.
65. Carol Hymowitz, 'Managers Suddenly Have to Answer to a Crowd of Bosses' (In the Lead column), *The Wall Street Journal* (August 12, 2003), B1; and Michael Goold and Andrew Campbell, 'Making Matrix Structures Work: Creating Clarity on Unit Roles and Responsibilities', *European Management Journal* 21, No. 3 (June 2003), 351–363.
66. Christopher A. Bartlett and Sumantra Ghoshal, 'Matrix Management: Not a Structure, a Frame of Mind', *Harvard Business Review* (July–August 1990), 138–145.
67. Michael Hammer, 'Process Management and the Future of Six Sigma', *Sloan Management Review* (Winter 2002), 26–32; and Michael Hammer and Steve Stanton, 'How Process Enterprises *Really* Work', *Harvard Business Review* 77 (November–December 1999), 108–118.
68. 'Right People, Right Place, Right Time', *Excellence Wales*, Welsh Local Government Association case study, available at http://www.wlga.gov.uk/download.php?id=1135&l=1;Alaistair McLennan, 'LLPG: feel the difference!', *GeoConnexion UK News*, April/May 2007, pp 38–39; Patrick Spillane, Strategic Review of the OneVale Programme, Wales Audit Office, June 2007, accessed at https://www.valeofglamorgan.gov.uk/files/Our%20Council/Council/reports/cabinet/2007/onevale_review_appendix.pdf.
69. Based on Frank Ostroff, *The Horizontal Organization*, and Richard L. Daft, *Organization Theory and Design*, 6th ed. (Cincinnati, OH: South-Western, 1998), 250–253.
70. Barclays, The Spotlight Report, Q3 2014, page 5, accessed at https://www.home.barclays/content/dam/barclayspublic/docs/Citizenship/Reports-Publications/Q3%202014%20Barclays%20Spotlight%20Report.pdf
71. Frank Ostroff, *The Horizontal Organization*, Oxford, Oxford University Press, 1999, pp 115–130; James Tach, 'Largest lenders in 2014 reflect a competitive mortgage market', *Council of Mortgage Lenders*, September 4 2015, accessed at https://www.cml.org.uk/news/news-and-views/largest-lenders-in-2014-reflect-a-competitive-mortgage-market/
72. http://www.bqf.org.uk/efqm-excellence-model.
73. Reuters Top 100 Global Innovators, accessed at http://top100innovators.stateofinnovation.thomsonreuters.com/
74. 'Calling Time On Telcos', *Business and Finance Magazine,* October 7, 2004; Graham Dwyer and Ciaran Doyle, 'Strategic Change at Avaya Ireland', Irish Management Institute case study 302-147-1.
75. Melissa A. Schilling and H. Kevin Steensma, 'The Use of Modular Organizational Forms: An Industry-Level Analysis', *Academy of Management Journal* 44, No. 6 (2001), 1149–1168; Jane C. Linder, 'Transformational Outsourcing', *MIT Sloan Management Review* (Winter 2004), 52–58; and Denis Chamberland, 'Is It Core or Strategic? Outsourcing as a Strategic Management Tool', *Ivey Business Journal* (July–August 2003), 1–5.
76. Denis Chamberland, 'Is It Core or Strategic?'; Philip Siekman, 'The Snap-Together Business Jet', *Fortune* (January 21, 2002), 104[A]–104[H]; Keith H. Hammonds, 'Smart, Determined, Ambitious, Cheap: The New Face of Global Competition', *Fast Company* (February 2003), 91– 97; Kathleen Kerwin, 'GM: Modular Plants Won't Be a Snap', *BusinessWeek* (November 9, 1998), 168–172; and Giuseppe Bonazzi and Cristiano Antonelli, 'To Make or To Sell? The Case of In-House Outsourcing at Fiat Auto', *Organization Studies* 24, No. 4 (2003), 575–594.
77. Melissa A. Schilling and H. Kevin Steensma, 'The Use of Modular Organizational Forms'; Raymond E. Miles and Charles C. Snow, 'The New Network Firm: A Spherical Structure Built on a Human Investment Philosophy', *Organizational Dynamics* (Spring 1995), 5–18; R. E. Miles, C. C. Snow, J. A. Matthews, G. Miles and H. J. Coleman Jr., 'Organizing in the Knowledge Age: Anticipating the Cellular Form', *Academy of Management Executive* 11, No. 4 (1997), 7–24.
78. Paul Engle, 'You *Can* Outsource Strategic Processes', *Industrial Management* (January–February 2002), 13–18.
79. Don Tapscott, 'Rethinking Strategy in a Networked World', *Strategy & Business* 24 (Third Quarter, 2001), 34–41.
80. Tommi Rantanen, *University 2.0,* Helsinki, University of Technology Institute of Strategy and International Business, 2007; Teemu Arina, 'Blogs as Reflective Practice', conference, paper presented at Online Educa Berlin 2006, November 29–December 1, 2006.
81. Stuart Luman, 'Open Source Softwear', *Wired Magazine*, 13 June 2005; Mark Weingarten, 'Project Runway for the t-shirt crowd', *Business 2.0 Magazine*, June 18, 2006.
82. David Bartlett, 'Talking Point: Uberisation is coming, ready or not', *The Mercury* (Tasmania), March 10, 2016, www.themercury.com.au/news/opinion/talking-point-uberisation-is-coming-ready-or-not/news-story/119737469560450f98d6e099b0158387; http://harperreed.com/#/
83. R.E. Miles and C.C. Snow, 'The New Network Firm'; Gregory G. Dess, Abdul M. A. Rasheed, Kevin J. McLaughlin and Richard L. Priem, 'The New Corporate Architecture', *Academy of Management Executive* 9, No. 2 (1995), 7–20; and Engle, 'You *Can* Outsource Strategic Processes'.
84. The discussion of weaknesses is based on Engle, 'You *Can* Outsource Strategic Processes'; Henry W. Chesbrough and

David J. Teece, 'Organizing for Innovation: When Is Virtual Virtuous?' *Harvard Business Review* (August 2002), 127–134; Dess et al., 'The New Corporate Architecture'; and N. Anand, 'Modular, Virtual and Hollow Forms of Organization Design', working paper, London Business School, 2000.

85. Werner Braun, Mark Wilcox and Paul Sparrow, 'Sony Europe – the leadership journey: Case a: a history of change', Lancaster University Management School

Centre for Performance-led HR Case Study Series 2007 Stewart Clegg and Toyohiro Kono, 'Trends in Japanese Management: An Overview of Embedded Continuities and Disembedded Discontinuities', *Asia Pacific Journal of Management*, 19, 269–285, 2002.

86. Based on Child, *Organization*, Ch. 1; and Jonathan D. Day, Emily Lawson, and Keith Leslie, 'When Reorganization Works', *The McKinsey Quarterly*, 2003 Special Edition: The Value in Organization, 21–29.

OPEN SYSTEM
DESIGN ELEMENTS

THE EXTERNAL ENVIRONMENT

A LOOK INSIDE

Nokia

Nokia's rise, fall and restructuring ranks as one of the most dramatic in corporate history. Starting off as a forestry company in the town of Nokia, southwestern Finland, in 1865, by the mid 1980s the company had diversified into various areas ranging from rubber boots to telecommunications. It was in telecommunications and specifically mobile phones that it made its mark. In 1991 the company achieved the world's first GSM mobile phone call. From then until 1998 the company rose to become the world's biggest mobile phone company, with its 1100 model the best selling phone of all time. But by 2004, Nokia had hit serious turbulence, losing nearly a fifth of its 35 per cent global market share. Revenue growth shifted into reverse and the stock took a nosedive.

What went wrong? For one thing, Nokia was either very unlucky or showed very poor timing in its decisions on moving to advanced technologies for phones. At the beginning of the new millennium, the company decided to invest heavily in a completely new phenomenon, the smartphone. This device permitted users to surf the web, play video games, listen to music and watch movies and TV shows, something that seems commonplace in the second decade of the twenty-first century. Nokia developed some devices that were, for their time, incredibly advanced (if horrendously expensive and by today's standards, real bricks!). But the company was several years ahead of the curve. Most of all, the network infrastructure necessary to make smartphones really work was not in place, even if users of Nokia's first generation smartphones had been able to overlook some of the obvious drawbacks, like phones so big they would only fit into reinforced pockets! Although the 3G network fast enough to make intensive internet use feasible was first operationalized in 2002, it took several years before a significant proportion of the mobile phone population was connected. In fact, when the 200 millionth 3G subscriber worldwide signed up in June 2007, that still represented only 6.7 per cent of the world's mobile phone users. In other words, mass smartphone usage only became feasible from 2007 onwards at the earliest.

In the meantime, other mobile phone solutions made more sense. For the ordinary consumer, medium priced but cosmetically attractive devices now called 'feature phones' like Motorola's Razr clamshell phone introduced in 2003 – which included a camera and music player functionality – made the most sense, and sold like hotcakes in the middle years of the 2000s. For the business user, the Blackberry was the perfect device of the time. It used the internet primarily for emails – which can perform adequately with even slow, 2G connections – and was small and light.

While there is always a degree of luck in the outcome of any business decision, there are strong indications that Nokia ignored or misread what it was being told by key informants, such as the major mobile phone networks, which are the ones actually dealing with phone customers most of the time.[1] For example, Orange SA, France Telecom's wireless unit, pushed for customized phones with special features that their customers wanted, but Nokia was slow to respond. 'Their attitude was that, given their size, they didn't need to listen to us', said an executive at one European mobile operator. Analyses of Nokia's product development processes at the time suggest that it was highly centralized and perhaps therefore more inward-looking than outward-looking. Thus, perhaps, ideas that seemed good to developers and company insiders who spent their whole time thinking about mobiles were too optimistically translated to the average consumer who tends to adopt new uses for technology slowly and on a need to know basis.

These missteps allowed rivals to gobble up market share. To get Nokia back on track, its top management prioritized the introduction of a competitive range of new midrange feature phones like the Asha, slashed costs on low-end models for developing countries, and promised mobile operators to tailor phones to their specifications. From 2005, Nokia's market share rebounded sharply, as the clamshell phones went out of fashion, high end phones shrank to a pocketable size, and consumers finally warmed to the extra functionality internet phones provide. By 2007, market share was back up above 33 per cent of a much bigger global market, and the company's profit graph was rising impressively. However, the apparent good news was only a short-term respite in the death spiral of the company's mobile phone business. Nokia was increasingly ghettoized in the low end of the market, where margins are extremely thin and open to competition from low wage economies like China. Furthermore, there is plenty of evidence that in the consumer technology market, consumers will gravitate towards the newest and trendiest usable technology that they can afford. By being boxed in at the low end of the market, Nokia was setting itself up to be the trailing edge of the market the choice of consumers who weren't really choosy about their phones (and who would be very unlikely to set examples that friends and family would want to follow). The recent history of industrial development in high wage economies such as that of Finland shows that there is really only one way to succeed: by taking the high road, seeking the type of complex, innovative, high value niche which had formed the initial foundation for Nokia's success in the 1990s.

Nokia's problems were compounded because it stuck with the ageing Symbian operating system on its smartphones through to 2011, while competitors had jumped ship to Android several years previously. Thus, again, relatively impressive-looking figures (in 2009, nearly half of all smartphones shipped worldwide by all companies had Symbian OS) concealed very dark clouds on the horizon. Between 2009 and 2010 alone, Symbian market share fell from 47 per cent to 37 per cent. Years of revenue growth and consistent profits came to a shuddering halt. In 2012 the company had losses of over $3 billion, and share prices dropped 61 per cent in a single year.

Could Nokia escape its death spiral? The twin giants of iPhone – launched in 2007 and dubbed by some media wags as 'the Jesus phone' – and Android – launched in 2008 and effectively a Google initiative, have left very little room for other operating systems; a problem that has also brought Blackberry to its knees. Adopting Apple's iOS is not an option, because it is a closed system that Apple does not licence out. Android was a possibility, but it is increasingly dominated by Samsung, with other players like HTC seemingly being squeezed out. Also, the Android market is increasingly the domain of lower priced offerings such

as China's ambitious Huawei brand, which in 2013 announced what it claims is the world's fastest phone.

In February 2011, Nokia's new CEO Stephen Elop released his famous 'burning platform' memo to employees, announcing the abandonment of Symbian (Exhibit 5.1 below). Nokia's choice was effectively to link up with another 'wounded giant', Microsoft (a victim of the shift to cloud-based computing spearheaded by Google), and put all its eggs in the basket of the Windows Phone OS. The company unveiled its new Lumia series based on Windows OS in 2011, to generally positive reviews, though the Windows Phone platform was widely criticized for its relatively weak touch features and apps availability compared with the Android and iOS systems. In 2013 Windows launched version 8, integrated with the release of its overall Windows 8 computer operating system.[2] It was at this point that Nokia decided to get out of mobile phones, selling out in 2014 to Microsoft, a strategy that fit with Microsoft's desire to shift into mobile devices as Apple had so successfully done.

While the €5.44 billion Nokia received was far less than the mobile phone business had been worth a few years previously, it turned out to be a good move. By 2015 Microsoft had written off the purchase price of its investment and sharply cut back the size and ambitions of the division. The future of Windows Phones altogether seemed in the balance.

Meanwhile Nokia refocused its energies on networking equipment, successfully building a smaller but focused business, with 2015 revenues of €12.5 billion, only a quarter of its 2007/2008 peak, but with a healthy €1 billion plus profit. The company has even made plans to go back into mobiles once its no-competition deal with Microsoft expires in 2016.

While Nokia is no longer the giant household name that was as well-known as its home country, after some serious mistakes in the first decade of the 21st century, it has managed to reinvent itself and continues to be one of Finland's largest employers.[3]

Many companies, like Nokia, face tremendous uncertainty in dealing with the external environment. The only way a high-tech company like Nokia can continue to grow is through innovation, yet unless the company makes products that people want to buy, the huge investments in research and development will not pay off.

Some companies get surprised by shifts in the environment and are unable to quickly adapt to new competition, changing consumer interests or innovative technologies. The music business has been particularly impacted by the shift to digital distribution of recorded music, and hard-to-combat piracy. Iconic record stores in many countries have disappeared or been forced to

EXHIBIT 5.1 Nokia: Stephen Elop's famous 'burning platform' memo

There is a pertinent story about a man who was working on an oil platform in the North Sea. He woke up one night from a loud explosion, which suddenly set his entire oil platform on fire. In mere moments, he was surrounded by flames. Through the smoke and heat, he barely made his way out of the chaos to the platform's edge. When he looked down over the edge, all he could see were the dark, cold, foreboding Atlantic waters. As the fire approached him, the man had mere seconds to react. He could stand on the platform, and inevitably be consumed by the burning flames. Or, he could plunge 30 meters into the freezing waters. The man was standing upon a 'burning platform,' and he needed to make a choice. He decided to jump. It was unexpected. In ordinary circumstances, the man would never consider plunging into icy waters. But these were not ordinary times – his platform was on fire. The man survived the fall and the waters. After he was rescued, he noted that a 'burning platform' caused a radical change in his behaviour.

We too, are standing on a 'burning platform,' and we must decide how we are going to change our behaviour.

Over the past few months, I've shared with you what I've heard from our shareholders, operators, developers, suppliers and from you. Today, I'm going to share what I've learned and what I have come to believe. I have learned that we are standing on a burning platform. And, we have more than one explosion – we have multiple points of scorching heat that are fuelling a blazing fire around us.

For example, there is intense heat coming from our competitors, more rapidly than we ever expected. Apple disrupted the market by redefining the smartphone and attracting developers to a closed, but very powerful ecosystem.

In 2008, Apple's market share in the $300+ price range was 25 per cent; by 2010 it escalated to 61 per cent. They are enjoying a tremendous growth trajectory with a 78 per cent earnings growth year over year in Q4 2010. Apple demonstrated that if designed well, consumers would buy a high-priced phone with a great experience and developers would build applications. They changed the game, and today, Apple owns the high-end range.

And then, there is Android. In about two years, Android created a platform that attracts application developers, service providers and hardware manufacturers. Android came in at the high-end, they are now winning the mid-range, and quickly they are going downstream to phones under €100. Google has become a gravitational force, drawing much of the industry's innovation to its core.

Let's not forget about the low-end price range. In 2008, MediaTek supplied complete reference designs for phone chipsets, which enabled manufacturers in the Shenzhen region of China to produce phones at an unbelievable pace. By some accounts, this ecosystem now produces more than one third of the phones sold globally – taking share from us in emerging markets.

While competitors poured flames on our market share, what happened at Nokia? We fell behind, we missed big trends, and we lost time. At that time, we thought we were making the right decisions; but, with the benefit of hindsight, we now find ourselves years behind.

The first iPhone shipped in 2007, and we still don't have a product that is close to their experience. Android came on the scene just over two years ago, and this week they took our leadership position in smartphone volumes. Unbelievable.

We have some brilliant sources of innovation inside Nokia, but we are not bringing it to market fast enough. We thought MeeGo would be a platform for winning high-end smartphones. However, at this rate, by the end of 2011, we might have only one MeeGo product in the market.

At the midrange, we have Symbian. It has proven to be non-competitive in leading markets like North America. Additionally, Symbian is proving to be an increasingly difficult environment in which to develop to meet the continuously expanding consumer requirements, leading to slowness in product development and also creating a disadvantage when we seek to take advantage of new hardware platforms. As a result, if we continue like before, we will get further and further behind, while our competitors advance further and further ahead.

At the lower-end price range, Chinese OEMs are cranking out a device much faster than, as one Nokia employee said only partially in jest, 'the time that it takes us to polish a PowerPoint presentation.' They are fast, they are cheap, and they are challenging us.

And the truly perplexing aspect is that we're not even fighting with the right weapons. We are still too often trying to approach each price range on a device-to-device basis.

The battle of devices has now become a war of ecosystems, where ecosystems include not only the hardware and software of the device, but developers, applications, ecommerce, advertising, search, social applications, location-based services, unified communications and many other things. Our competitors aren't taking our market share with devices; they are taking our market share with an entire ecosystem. This means we're going to have to decide how we either build, catalyse or join an ecosystem.

This is one of the decisions we need to make. In the meantime, we've lost market share, we've lost mind share and we've lost time.

On Tuesday, Standard & Poor's informed that they will put our A long term and A-1 short term ratings on negative credit watch. This is a similar rating action to the one that Moody's took last week. Basically it means that during the next few weeks they will make an analysis of Nokia, and decide on a possible credit rating downgrade. Why are these credit agencies contemplating these changes? Because they are concerned about our competitiveness.

Consumer preference for Nokia declined worldwide. In the UK, our brand preference has slipped to 20 per cent, which is 8 per cent lower than last year. That means only one out of five people in the UK prefer Nokia to other brands. It's also down in the other markets, which are traditionally our strongholds: Russia, Germany, Indonesia, UAE, and on and on and on.

How did we get to this point? Why did we fall behind when the world around us evolved?

This is what I have been trying to understand. I believe at least some of it has been due to our attitude inside Nokia. We poured gasoline on our own burning platform. I believe we have lacked accountability and leadership to align and direct the company through these disruptive times. We had a series of misses. We haven't been delivering innovation fast enough. We're not collaborating internally.

Nokia, our platform is burning.

> We are working on a path forward — a path to rebuild our market leadership. When we share the new strategy on February 11, it will be a huge effort to transform our company. But, I believe that together, we can face the challenges ahead of us. Together, we can choose to define our future.
>
> The burning platform, upon which the man found himself, caused the man to shift his behaviour, and take a bold and brave step into an uncertain future. He was able to tell his story. Now, we have a great opportunity to do the same.
>
> Stephen.

Source: http://blogs.wsj.com/tech-europe/2011/02/09/full-text-nokia-ceo-stephen-elops-burning-platform-memo/) February 9, 2011.

completely change the focus of their business in order to survive. The Virgin group sold off its music stores, while US-based Tower Records, (2006) Canada's Music World (2007), and UK's HMV (2013) filed for bankruptcy,[4] and many smaller retail music chains have simply disappeared, in the wake of Spotify, Apple's iTunes and other new channels that allow music lovers to download just what they want. In the airline industry, major carriers have been pummelled by budget competitors. Belgium's flagship Sabena and Switzerland's Swissair have both gone out of business, replaced by smaller and leaner carriers; Swissair's successor was eventually purchased in 2005 by the German-based carrier Lufthansa, which also completed a buyout of Brussels Airlines, Sabena's successor, in 2011.[5] Meanwhile, during the 1990s and 2000s Ireland's Ryanair and the US budget carrier Southwest Airlines grew exponentially.[6] It is impossible for companies to avoid external shocks, but the well-structured, flexible company will be in a better position to emerge relatively unscathed from turbulence than rigid and top heavy organizations.[7]

Numerous factors in the external environment cause turbulence and uncertainty for organizations. The external environment, including international competition and events, is the source of major threats confronting today's organizations. The environment often imposes significant constraints on the choices that managers make for an organization.

Purpose of this Chapter

The purpose of this chapter is to develop a framework for assessing environments and how organizations can respond to them. First, we will identify the organizational domain and the sectors that influence the organization. Then, we will explore two major environmental forces on the organization – the need for information and the need for resources. Organizations respond to these forces through structural design, planning systems and attempts to change and control elements in the environment.

The Environmental Domain

In a broad sense the environment is infinite and includes everything outside the organization (see Counterpoint 5.1). However, the analysis presented here considers only those aspects of the

COUNTERPOINT 5.1

What is taken to be the 'environment' is always selected and interpreted by organizational members. They inevitably have particular agendas and priorities, leading them to emphasize some features and neglect others. In other words, the 'environment' is enacted, not given. In this sense, the environment is 'chosen'. But 'choice' is shaped and constrained by established agendas and perceptions that are difficult to change. Also there are numerous aspects of the 'environment' – such as fluctuations in interest rates or commodity prices – over which even the most resourceful executives can exercise very limited choice or control. Nonetheless, 'the environment' is subject to diverse interpretations or 'readings'. It is evident that, for example, Nokia executives 'read' the environment in a different way to those at Samsung. The decisions of Nokia executives (e.g. to concentrate on smartphones and neglect the middle market) effectively created an environment for other companies that successfully identified and exploited the opportunities presented to them.

EXHIBIT 5.2 An Organization's Environment

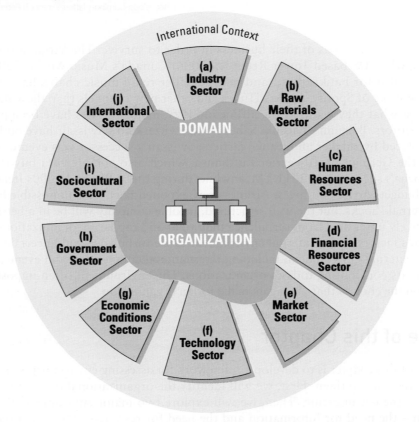

(a) Competitors, industry size and competitiveness, related industries

(b) Suppliers, manufacturers, real estate, services

(c) Labour market, employment agencies, universities, training schools, employees in other companies, unionization

(d) Stock markets, banks, savings and loans, private investors

(e) Customers, clients, potential users of products and services

(f) Techniques of production, science, computers, information technology, e-commerce

(g) Recession, unemployment rate, inflation rate, rate of investment, economics, growth

(h) City, state, federal laws and regulations, taxes, services, court system, political processes

(i) Age, values, beliefs, education, religion, work ethic, consumer and green movements

(j) Competition from and acquisition by foreign firms, entry into overseas markets, foreign customs, regulations, exchange rate

environment to which the organization is sensitive and must respond to survive. Thus, organizational environment is defined as all elements that exist outside the boundary of the organization and have the potential to affect all or part of the organization.

The environment of an organization can be understood by analyzing its domain within external sectors. An organization's domain is the chosen environmental field of action. It is the territory an organization stakes out for itself with respect to products, services and markets served. Domain defines the organization's niche and defines those external sectors with which the organization will interact to accomplish its goals.

BRIEFCASE 5.1

The environment comprises several sectors or subdivisions of the external environment that contain similar elements. Ten sectors can be analyzed for each organization: industry, raw materials, human resources, financial resources, market, technology, economic conditions, government, sociocultural and international. The sectors and a hypothetical organizational domain are illustrated in Exhibit 5.2. For most companies, the sectors in Exhibit 5.2 can be further subdivided into the task environment and general environment.

Task Environment

The task environment includes sectors with which the organization interacts directly and that have a direct impact on the organization's ability to achieve its goals. The task environment typically includes the industry, raw materials and market sectors, and perhaps the human resources and international sectors.

The following examples illustrate how each of these sectors can affect organizations:

- In the industry sector, traditional food retailers are being challenged by hypermarkets run by companies such as France's Carrefour and US-based Wal-Mart, which also carry a wide range of clothes and other non-food items that typically enjoy a higher mark-up. This shift is forcing traditional food retailers to find new ways to compete. One strategy is to focus on high-end, high quality produce, a strategy that has allowed Britain's Waitrose chain to grow profitably. Even small, highly specialized grocers have succeeded with this approach. Charlie Hicks, a greengrocer with shops in the English towns of Reigate and Bristol, 'buys only top-quality produce from specialist growers the supermarkets don't handle', and provides restaurants with 'unashamedly nice stuff'. At the 'value' end of the market, companies like Aldi and Lidl have cut heavily into traditional supermarkets' margins, with over half of British shoppers visiting one or other of the discounters in the 2014/2015 holiday season.[8,9,10]

- An interesting example in the *raw materials sector* concerns the drinks (beverage) can industry. Drinks cans were largely made from steel until the mid-1960s, when the US-based Reynolds Aluminum Company (now part of the multinational giant Alcoa) perfected the aluminium drinks can. By the mid-1980s aluminium cans dominated the drinks can market in most countries.[11,12]

- In the *market sector*, keeping up with consumers' rapidly changing preferences is a real headache for big food companies such as Nestlé SA and Kraft. Both Nestlé and Kraft have been impacted by health and ethical concerns. Nestlé has been targeted for promoting baby formula, which has been criticized as inferior to mother's milk, and unaffordable to mothers in developing countries.[13] Kraft's heyday was in the 1960s and 1970s when comfort convenience foods were widely adopted, but as concerns were raised about the nutritional value of foods like Oreo biscuits and Jell-O, Kraft was forced to introduce new eating options geared to health-conscious consumers, such as prepared salads and vitamin enhanced water. Kraft also split from its parent company Altria, in 2007, at least partly to distance itself from Altria's role as a major cigarette manufacturer.[14] Nevertheless, consumers' expressed preferences may sometimes diverge from actual spending practices – crackers, biscuits and processed cheese remain major money-spinners for Kraft. The company further tailored its offering in 2012 by splitting again, into a global snacks business renamed Mondelez and the residual US grocery business which retains the Kraft name. The rationale is that the market strategy for the fast-growing global snacks business – including brands like Cadburys and Oreo – requires different management strategies than the slower growing mainstream grocery products like Velveeta and Macaroni & Cheese.[15]

■ The *human resources sector* is of significant concern to every business. In particular, managers in companies in both developed and developing countries worry about shortages of skilled workers. Industry leaders in countries as diverse as Canada and Thailand are urging their national governments to invest heavily in education and skills in order to meet the challenges of the globalized economy. Gwyn Morgan, the former CEO of Canada's EnCana, one of the world's largest oil and gas companies, says that Canada needs to accept more highly skilled immigrants, as well as doing a better job in its education system and in training workers on-the-job.[16] Similarly, Thai business leaders have urged their government to invest more in education and skills training if the country is to achieve its ambition of becoming the 'Detroit of Asia', Asia's manufacturing hub for the automobile industry.[17,18]

■ For most companies today, in whatever country, the *international environment* is crucial. Offshoring is a major issue, with companies in both the developed economies of Europe and North America, and emerging economies throughout the world, trying to maximize the possibilities globalization provides to produce in low-cost economies and sell in high value markets. China and India have become major locales for low-cost manufacturing and service industries, respectively, although many other countries from Vietnam to South Africa are also getting in on the global restructuring of business processes. The growing strength of Asian economies, in particular, is allowing emerging economy companies like China's Huawei, Taiwan's Acer and India's Sun Pharma to establish themselves as big players and respected brand names in developed and developing country markets.[19]

General Environment

The general environment includes those sectors that might not have a direct impact on the daily operations of a firm but will indirectly influence it. The general environment often includes the government, sociocultural, economic conditions, technology and financial resources sectors (see Counterpoint 5.2). These sectors affect all organizations eventually.

COUNTERPOINT 5.2

It is analytically helpful to break down the environment into 'sectors' as this makes it easier to grasp its key elements. But it is important to appreciate how aspects of these elements are interconnected and interdependent. 'Sectors' do not exist except as a heuristic device. What exists is a complex mix of properties (e.g. natural resources, technologies) and practices, labelled 'environment'. To simplify and order this complexity, analytical tools like 'sectors' have been devised. But this way of seeing is also a way of not seeing.

Consider the following examples.

■ In the *government sector*, European Union (EU) environmental and consumer protection legislation impacts both domestic European and foreign firms. For example, one rule requires chemical makers doing business in EU countries to run safety and environmental impact tests on more than 30 000 chemicals, a process that could cost these companies more than €5 billion. Other regulations require companies to pick up the tab for recycling the products they sell in the EU. To an increasing extent, the regulatory environment is becoming global, as national governments model cutting edge practices from other jurisdictions.[20,21]

- Shifting demographics is a significant element in the *sociocultural sector*. Most developed countries have an ageing population, which affects both human resource practices and markets. Population mobility has expanded rapidly, with people drawn from poorer parts of the world to the wealthier countries of Europe and North America in search of economic opportunity. They bring their tastebuds and entertainment preferences with them, leading to market fragmentation and a plethora of niche opportunities from ethnic foods to narrowcast communications. Congolese delicacies are on sale in many Belgian supermarkets, just as British food stores now have special aisles for Polish food,[22] and in the United States, entire supermarkets have been converted to all-Hispanic *supermercados* to compete with Hispanic merchants.[23]

- General *economic conditions* often affect the way a company does business. Germany's two most celebrated daily newspapers, the *Frankfurter Allgemeine Zeitung* and the *Süddeutsche Zeitung*, expanded pell-mell during the economic boom of the late 1990s. When the economy crashed, both papers found themselves in dire financial circumstances and had to cut jobs, close regional offices, scrap special sections and cut out customized inserts.[24]

- The *technology sector* is an area in which massive changes have occurred in recent years, from digital music and video on demand to advances in cloning technology and stem-cell research. One technology having a tremendous impact on organizations is online software allowing people to easily communicate with the world through online versions of diaries, known as web logs, or *blogs*. By late 2007, one study found that 120 000 new blogs were being created each day, and in 2013, worldometer.com estimated that there are several million blog posts per day. Between 2006 and 2011 the number of blogs worldwide increased from 35 million to 173 million.[25] While most are read by few people beyond friends and family, slick and focused sites can attract thousands. While blogs remain important, social media channels including Twitter and Facebook provide ready-made platforms that both corporations and customers (happily or otherwise) use to communicate. Corporations that fail to respond to customer concerns can easily become the target of 'viral' campaigns conducted through social media and blogs that can gather together these disgruntled customers and negatively impact the corporation's image.[26]

- All businesses have to be concerned with *financial resources*, but they are 'make or break' for many entrepreneurs starting a new business. In expansionary times, capital can be relatively easy to raise, but when prospects suddenly darken, entrepreneurs can be left high and dry. In early 2007, aviation veteran and entrepreneur Tim Lee announced ambitious plans for a new Wales-based European budget airline, flyforbeans.com, copying Irish-based Ryanair's successful formula. But oil prices, one of the major cost factors for airlines, soon began to rise dramatically. Financing negotiations stalled, and in January 2013, the website address, flyforbeans.com was up for sale. Meanwhile Tim Lee moved on to another airline start-up, FastJet.com, which successfully launched in 2012, branding itself 'Africa's Low Cost Airline'.[27] In an article in 2015, the Financial Times suggested that the company should have been renamed Slowjet. This was in response to the Airline saying it was increasing their Airbus 319 "babybus" jets from three to four. However, four babybuses is a little short of the 30-strong fleet that Fastjet said in 2012 they would have by now. Pouring scorn on the venture, it is suggested that "there have been more pies in the sky than Fastjet aircraft and the shares are a fraction of what they were".[28]

International Context

As discussed earlier in this chapter, distinctions between foreign and domestic operations have become increasingly irrelevant. For example, in the auto industry, Ford first purchased Sweden's Volvo automobile manufacturing operations, then sold out in 2010 to Chinese manufacturer Zhejiang Geely Holding Group, while Germany's Daimler owned US big-three auto manufacturer Chrysler for several years until selling a majority stake to a private equity firm in 2007, and by 2012 was 61.8 per cent owned by Italy's Fiat.[29] Toyota, which has overtaken America's General Motors as the world's largest automaker, is a Japan-based company, but almost half of its worldwide production is outside Japan (see Exhibit 5.3).[30] Increasingly, corporations, no matter their home, are engaged in partnerships and alliances with other firms all around the world. These increasing global interconnections represent both opportunities and threats for organizations. The international dimension of organization theory and design will be covered in detail in Chapter 7.

The growing importance of the international sector means that the environment for all organizations is becoming extremely complex and extremely competitive. However, every organization faces uncertainty domestically as well as globally. Consider how changing elements in the various environmental sectors have created uncertainty - and opportunity - for advertising agencies such as the US-based Ogilvy & Mather.

Advertising agencies aren't the only organizations that have had to adapt to massive shifts in the environment. In the following sections, we will discuss in greater detail how companies can cope with and respond to environmental uncertainty and instability.

Environmental Uncertainty

How does the environment influence an organization? The patterns and events occurring in the environment can be described along several dimensions, such as whether the environment is stable or unstable, homogeneous or heterogeneous, simple or complex; the *munificence*, or amount of resources available to support the organization's growth; whether those resources are concentrated or dispersed; and the degree of consensus in the environment regarding the organization's

EXHIBIT 5.3   Toyota 2012 Worldwide Production Figures

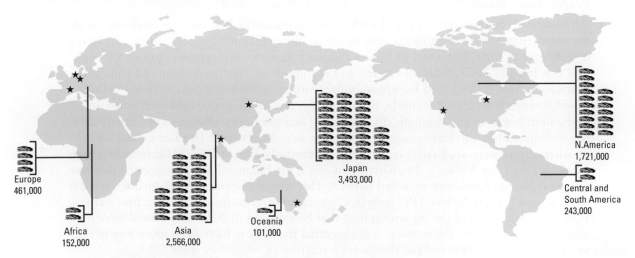

Europe
461,000

Africa
152,000

Asia
2,566,000

Oceania
101,000

Japan
3,493,000

N.America
1,721,000

Central and
South America
243,000

★ Toyota overseas manufacturing company

Source: http://www.toyota.co.jp/en/about_toyota/manufacturing/worldwide.html on July 30, 2013.

IN PRACTICE

Ogilvy & Mather

It was a sad day in the advertising industry when Ogilvy & Mather, one of the most respected advertising agencies on New York's Madison Avenue, was reduced to competing for business in a live online auction. The company had already been bought out by Britain's WPP consortium in 1989. Now its very survival seemed in doubt.

The world has changed dramatically since Ogilvy & Mather's founder David Ogilvy made deals with corporate CEOs over golf games and could reach 90 per cent of the American public with a prime-time commercial on network television. Today, agency executives frequently have to bargain with people from their client's procurement department, who are used to beating down suppliers on the price of cardboard boxes or paper bags.

The economic decline that followed the 'dot-com crash' and the September 11, 2001 terrorist attacks, led to the worst advertising recession in the United States in more than half a century. Marketing budgets were often the first to be cut. Worldwide, advertising spending declined seven per cent in 2001. US-based agencies laid off 40 000 employees, nearly 20 per cent of their workforce. Corporations began striking much less generous deals with their advertising agencies. Instead of the 15 per cent commission they used to pay on media purchases, many corporate procurement departments require agencies to itemize their labour costs and justify all the expenses they are billing the client. This knock-on effect of wider political and economic disturbances is compounded by a transformation in the communications industry. In many countries of the world, up until the 1980s, advertising agencies could reach most people through a handful of TV stations and newspapers, Now, there are hundreds of television channels catering to every conceivable taste and subgroup in the population, traditional newspapers are on the decline and a plethora of new media are cropping up. Corporations are clamouring for more innovative low-key approaches, such as product placements in video games or products integrated into television shows and music events, as well as lower-cost options such as direct mail and internet advertising. Yet many agencies have been slow to adapt, still clinging to the notion that costly primetime television commercials will pay off.

The combination of weak economic conditions, media fragmentation, new technologies and changing habits had the advertising industry reeling. As Ogilvy & Mather's longtime CEO, Shelly Lazarus, said of the first few years of the twenty-first century: 'These have not been the best years'.[31] However, the company restructured to take account of new communication technologies, and was able to bounce back, winning both awards and big new contracts around the world. Industry magazine *PR Week* said of the firm: 'Ogilvy PR is one of the few agencies that has a meaningful presence in every global region'.[32] The company has proven adept in seeking out new markets; one of its growth lines in the second decade of the twenty-first century is helping emerging Chinese brands like Haier to make a name for themselves in developed Western markets where they have hitherto been unknown. Ogilvy and Mather have also expanded their government lobbying business, although this is highly cyclical, and dependent on hot corporate and government policy issues; revenues for the Ogilvy Government Relations division rose strongly during the US debate about President Obama's healthcare reform, but fell back sharply in 2012 after legislation was enacted. The company continues to adapt to changing trends and technologies, creating the social@Ogilvy division in 2012 to focus efforts on youth and new communications channels like social media.[33,34]

intended domain.[35] These dimensions boil down to two essential ways the environment influences organizations: (1) the need for information about the environment; and (2) the need for resources from the environment. The environmental conditions of complexity and change create a greater need to gather information and to respond based on that information. The organization also is concerned with scarce material and financial resources and with the need to ensure availability of resources.

ONLINE
COUNTERPOINT 5.1

Environmental uncertainty refers primarily to those factors that an organization deals with on a regular, day-to-day basis. Recall the earlier discussion of the general environment and the task environment. Although general environmental factors – such as economic conditions, social trends or technological changes – can create uncertainty for organizations, determining an organization's environmental uncertainty generally means focusing on aspects of the *task environment*, such as how many elements the organization deals with regularly, how rapidly these elements change and so forth. To assess uncertainty, each sector of the organization's task environment can be analyzed along dimensions such as stability or instability and degree of complexity.[36] The total amount of uncertainty felt by an organization is the uncertainty accumulated across environmental sectors (see Counterpoint 5.3).

ONLINE
COUNTERPOINT 5.2

Organizations must cope with and manage uncertainty to be effective. Uncertainty is created by decision-makers not having sufficient information about environmental factors, and consequently being unable to accurately predict external changes. Uncertainty increases the risk of failure for organizational responses and makes it difficult to assess costs and probabilities associated with decision alternatives.[37] The remainder of this section will focus on the information perspective, which is concerned with uncertainty created by the extent to which the environment is simple or complex and the extent to which events are stable or unstable. Later in the chapter, we discuss how organizations control the environment to acquire needed resources.

COUNTERPOINT 5.3

If uncertainty is a result of insufficient information, it is impossible to assess its scope and significance. It is debatable if uncertainty arises from a lack of information as it is also a matter of how the available information is evaluated. If senior executives are highly risk-averse, there will never be sufficient information to overcome their intransigence and indecision. It is also questionable whether organizations can be managed on a rational basis – in the sense of waiting for information to become available in order to satisfactorily map or predict changes in the environment. Uncertainties are a function of the willingness to take risks as much as they are related to an insufficiency of information.

Simple–Complex Dimension

The simple–complex dimension concerns environmental complexity, which refers to heterogeneity, or the number and dissimilarity of external elements relevant to an organization's operations. The more external factors that regularly influence the organization and the greater number of other companies in an organization's domain, the greater the complexity. A complex environment is one in which the organization interacts with and is influenced by numerous diverse external elements. In a simple environment, the organization interacts with and is influenced by only a few similar external elements.

ONLINE
COUNTERPOINT 5.3

Aerospace firms such as Europe's Airbus and America's Boeing operate in a complex environment, as do universities. Universities span a large number of subjects or technologies and are continually buffeted by social, cultural and value changes. Universities also must cope with multiple and ever-changing government regulations, competition for top students and leading academics and scarce financial resources for many programmes. They deal with funding agencies, professional and scientific associations, alumni, parents, foundations, politicians, community residents, international agencies, donors and corporations. This large number of external elements makes up the organization's domain, creating a complex environment. On the other hand, a family-owned hardware store in a small town is in a relatively simple environment. The store does not have to deal with complex technologies or extensive government regulations. Human resources are typically not a problem because the store is run by family members and part-time help. The main external elements of real importance are a few competitors, suppliers and customers.

Stable–Unstable Dimension

The stable–unstable dimension refers to whether elements in the environment are dynamic. An environmental domain is stable if it remains the same over a period of months or years. Under unstable conditions, environmental elements shift abruptly. Environmental domains seem to be increasingly unstable for most organizations. This chapter's *Bookmark* examines the volatile nature of today's business world and gives some tips for managing in a fast-shifting environment.

ONLINE
COUNTERPOINT 5.4

Instability may occur when competitors react with aggressive moves and countermoves regarding advertising and new products, as happened with Nokia, described in this chapter's *A Look Inside*. Sometimes unpredictable events create unstable conditions. These can range from the global – ranging from the sudden spike in world oil prices and the global credit crunch that began in 2007 – to the local, such as the 2006 outbreak of salmonella poisoning in the UK, caused by unsanitary conditions in a Cadbury's manufacturing plant.[38] Today, anti-corporate and 'culture jamming' (see Adbusters and 'hate sites' on the World Wide Web, such as Ihatestarbucks. com, www.orangeproblems.co.uk, and www.killercoke.org) are an important source of instability. One estimate puts the number of anti-corporate websites on the internet at over 10 000.[39] In addition, freewheeling bloggers can destroy a company's reputation virtually overnight. Kryptonite's reputation in bicycle locks plummeted after a web log was posted claiming that the locks could be opened with a Bic pen. After 10 days of blogging, Kryptonite announced a free product exchange that would cost it about $10 million (see Counterpoint 5.4).[40]

Although environments are more unstable for most organizations today, an example of a traditionally stable environment is a public utility such as a provider of water, gas or electricity.[41] For many years, demand and supply factors for public utilities were stable, often operating either as regulated monopolies or as state-owned enterprises. Gradual increases in demand tended to occur, but were easily predicted over time. Toy companies, by contrast, typically have an unstable environment. Hot new toys are difficult to predict, a problem compounded by the encroachment of new technologies like video games. Adding to the instability for toymakers is the changing retail market, with hypermarkets like France's Carrefour and Wal-Mart/Asda undercutting even the biggest specialist toy retailers. Toy manufacture has also been impacted by internationalization of the business process, with much manufacture offshored to China and elsewhere in Asia.[42]

COUNTERPOINT 5.4

Stable environments may be a thing of the past. Even public utilities are feeling the impacts of rapid transformation in business processes, including the break-up of monopolies in the energy market. The tendency towards financialization,[43] including the ever-more innovative packaging of business components into instruments for resource mobilization and speculation, can create opacity and instability, where the line between ingenuity and criminality can seem hazy at best, as the infamous cases of Enron and Société Générale seem to demonstrate.[44]

BOOKMARK 5.0

Have you read this book?

Cradle to Cradle: Remaking the Way We Make Things

BY WILLIAM McDONOUGH AND MICHAEL BRAUNGART

In this chapter we have discussed the environment in which organizations operate, and the impact it has upon them. No environment is more important, of course, than the physical environment, where well-being is a precondition not just for successful business but for the survival of humanity. William McDonough, an American architect, and Michael Braungart, a German chemist, believe that both business and environmentalists often misunderstand the challenge of true sustainability, which they believe lies in the design process.

Working with instead of against the natural environment

To start with, say McDonough and Braungart, we need to better understand the living earth. Although environmentalists often argue that we must reduce waste, the authors point out that the natural earth itself 'wastes', except in a productive way. Most trees, for example, shed their leaves every year, but we wouldn't dream of calling this wasteful, because we understand that the dead leaves provide nutrient for rejuvenating the soil and making it fertile for new growth, from which McDonough and Braungart gleaned the principle that waste = food. Product and service design needs to build from the intelligence of natural systems, so that business and the earth can healthily co-exist.

When the City of Hannover, Germany, found out it was going to host the 2000 World's Fair, the event planners invited McDonough and Braungart to come up with a set of sustainability principles that would govern the Fair's design and operations. These Hannover principles have gone on to become a manifesto for intelligent, sustainable, industrial design:

1   Insist on rights of humanity and nature to co-exist in a healthy, supportive, diverse and sustainable way.

2   Recognize interdependence. The elements of human design interact with and depend upon the natural world, with broad and diverse implications at every scale. Expand design considerations to recognize even distant effects.

3   Respect relationships between spirit and matter. Consider all aspects of human settlement including community, dwelling, industry and trade in terms of existing and evolving connections between spiritual and material consciousness.

4   Accept responsibility for the consequences of design decisions upon human well-being, the viability of natural systems and their right to co-exist.

5   Create safe objects of long-term value. Do not burden future generations with requirements for maintenance or vigilant administration of potential danger due to the careless creation of products, processes or standards.

6   Eliminate the concept of waste. Evaluate and optimize the full life cycle of products and processes, to approach the state of natural systems, in which there is no waste.

7   Rely on natural energy flows. Human designs should, like the living world, derive their creative forces from perpetual solar income. Incorporate this energy efficiently and safely for responsible use.

8   Understand the limitations of design. No human creation lasts forever and design does not solve all problems. Those who create and plan should practice humility in the face of nature. Treat nature as a model and mentor, not as an inconvenience to be evaded or controlled.

9   Seek constant improvement by the sharing of knowledge. Encourage direct and open communication between colleagues, patrons, manufacturers and users to link long term sustainable considerations with ethical responsibility, and re-establish the integral relationship between natural processes and human activity.

One key sustainable technology is harnessing natural power, and in particular solar energy, which operated the natural world long before we developed an addiction for fossil fuel power. To an increasing extent, the search for 'alternative fuels' is focusing on solar,

▶

wind and tide energy, which are genuinely renewable, rather than bio-fuels. Crops such as palm oil deprive citizens of developing countries of crucial land on which to grow food crops, and create harmful greenhouse gas emissions when burned.

McDonough and Braungart have been involved in numerous industrial design projects that have put their principles into practice. Here are just two examples:

■ The Swiss furniture manufacturer Rohner and the textile design company DesignTex came up with a hardwearing textile for covering furniture that is both environmentally safe and so easily recyclable that it can simply be put in the ground when no longer needed, where it quickly turns into nutritious plant mulch.

■ Alain Duval of Québec, Canada's Victor Innovatex, was proud of his company's reputation for high quality textiles, but he wanted to do something of wider environmental benefit. While polyester,

a key synthetic fibre, is recyclable, the recycling process typically results in a lower value product. For example, used polyester is often turned into speed bumps to reduce traffic speed. Though this is better than throwing it straight into the landfill, it is part of a downward value spiral that is ultimately not sustainable. Victor Innovatex redesigned the polyester production process to the molecular level, choosing components that are all recyclable, as well as a catalyst that is environmentally safe. The Eco-Intelligent Polyester that came out of their research is the first infinitely recyclable polyester, a product that can be endlessly recycled into new polyester when it wears out.

William McDonough and Michael Braungart (2002), *Cradle to Cradle: Remaking the Way We Make Things,* New York, North Point Press; http://www.mcdonough.com/principles.pdf, accessed on April 14, 2009.

Framework

The simple–complex and stable–unstable dimensions are combined into a framework for assessing environmental uncertainty in Exhibit 5.4. In the *simple, stable* environment, uncertainty is low. There are only a few external elements to contend with, and they tend to remain stable. The *complex, stable* environment represents somewhat greater uncertainty. A large number of elements have to be scanned, analyzed and acted upon for the organization to perform well. External elements do not change rapidly or unexpectedly in this environment.

Even greater uncertainty is felt in the *simple, unstable* environment.[45] Rapid change creates uncertainty for managers. Even though the organization has few external elements, those elements are hard to predict, and they react unexpectedly to organizational initiatives. The greatest uncertainty for an organization occurs in the *complex, unstable* environment. A large number of elements impinge upon the organization, and they shift frequently or react strongly to organizational initiatives. When several sectors change simultaneously, the environment becomes turbulent.[46]

Beer distributors function in a simple, stable environment. Demand for beer changes only gradually. The distributor has an established delivery route, and supplies of beer arrive on schedule. Universities, home appliance manufacturers and insurance companies are also in somewhat stable, complex environments. A large number of external elements are present, but although they change, changes tend to be gradual and predictable.

Toy manufacturers are in simple, unstable environments. Organizations that design, make and sell toys, as well as those that are involved in the clothing or music industry, face shifting supply and demand. Most e-commerce companies focus on a specific competitive niche and, hence, operate in simple but unstable environments as well. Although there may be few elements to contend with – e.g. technology, competitors – they are difficult to predict and change abruptly and unexpectedly.

ONLINE COUNTERPOINT 5.5

The telecommunications industry and the airline industry face complex, unstable environments. Many external sectors are changing simultaneously. In the case of airlines, in just a few

EXHIBIT 5.4   Framework for Assessing Environmental Uncertainty

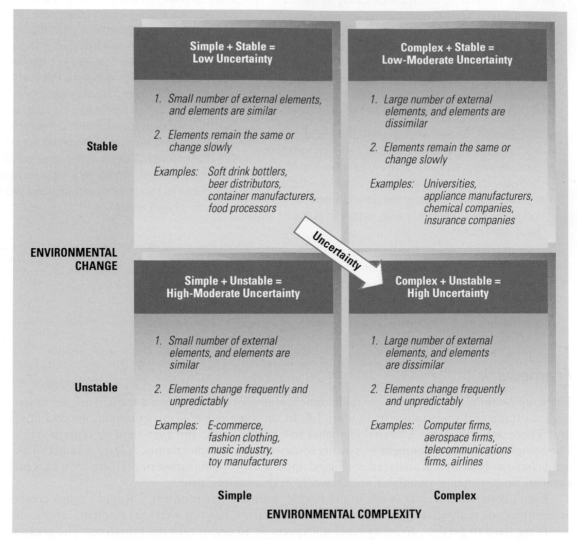

Source: Adapted and reprinted from 'Characteristics of Perceived Environments and Perceived Environmental Uncertainty,' by Robert B. Duncan, published in *Administrative Science Quarterly* 17 (1972), 313–327. Copyright © 1972 SAGE Publications.

years they have been confronted with the multiplication of security measures due to the threat of terrorism, the influx of low cost carriers like Ryanair, large tax increases on air travel and dramatic fluctuations in the price of jet fuel.[47]

Although the matrix of environmental uncertainty is undoubtedly still a useful way of understanding organizational environments, in recent years there has been an overall shift towards uncertainty throughout the business environment. As the regulatory environment has loosened, business processes can be relatively easily re-engineered and organizations need to be ready to adapt to new environments far more quickly than was the case in the past. While large corporations continue to play a major role in the global economy, organizational fluidity is becoming a necessary condition for success in most industries. So, even for example in the area of beer distribution, global logistics firms like DHL are gradually replacing specialized firms focusing only on the drinks industry. There are fewer and fewer 'safe niches' in the business world.

Adapting to Environmental Uncertainty

Once you see how environments differ with respect to change and complexity, the next question is, 'How do organizations adapt to each level of environmental uncertainty?' Environmental uncertainty represents an important contingency for organization structure and internal behaviours. Recall from Chapter 4 that organizations best equipped to face uncertainty generally have a more horizontal structure, as this encourages cross-functional communication and collaboration to adapt to environmental change. In this section we discuss in more detail how the environment affects organizations. An organization in a stable and comparatively certain environment will tend to be managed and controlled differently from an organization in an uncertain environment with respect to positions and departments, organizational differentiation and integration, control processes and future planning and forecasting. A key to organizational effectiveness and prosperity is developing an appropriate fit between the elements of internal structure and salient features of the external environment.

Positions and Departments

As the complexity and uncertainty in the external environment increases, the number of positions and departments within the organization also tends to increase, which in turn increases internal complexity. This relationship is part of being an open system. Each sector in the external environment requires an employee or department to deal with it. The human resource department deals with people who want to work for the company. The marketing department finds customers. Procurement employees obtain raw materials from perhaps hundreds of suppliers. The finance group deals with bankers and venture capitalists. The legal department works with the courts and government agencies. Most companies have added information technology departments to deal with the increasing complexity of computerized information and knowledge management systems, and many have created e-business departments to handle electronic commerce.

Government's also respond to environmental uncertainty by changing its structures. Terrorist threats have led many countries to strengthen their border controls through merging agencies that previously worked largely independently.[48]

Buffering and Boundary Spanning

The traditional approach to coping with environmental uncertainty was to establish departments or roles to buffer or absorb its effects upon the 'technical core' of organizations.[49] The technical core comprises those people who perform the production subsystem function and actually produce the product and service outputs of the organization (see Chapter 1). Buffer departments and roles support and service the technical core by taking care of the flows of materials, resources and money between the environment and the organization. They enable the technical core to function efficiently. For example, the purchasing department buffers the technical core by stockpiling supplies and raw materials. The human resource department buffers the technical core by handling the uncertainty associated with finding, hiring and training production employees.

The approach of buffering is somewhat static and defensive. Some organizations are attempting to remove or reduce the buffers in a way that exposes the technical core to the uncertain environment. Potentially, this has the benefit of adapting the core more directly to its environment as emphasis is placed upon being well-connected to customers and suppliers rather than ensuring the stability of the established technical core. For example, the American farm machinery manufacturer, John Deere, has assembly-line workers visiting local farms to determine and respond to customer concerns. The computer software industry has made involving consumers in product testing a routine activity, with 'alpha' and 'beta' versions of products under development provided free to enthusiasts in return for feedback on product flaws and areas for improvement.[50]

BRIEFCASE 5.2

Boundary-spanning roles   link and coordinate an organization with key elements in the external environment. Boundary spanning is primarily concerned with the exchange of information to (1) detect and bring into the organization information about changes in the environment; and (2) send information into the environment that presents the organization in a favourable light.[51]

Keeping in direct touch with what is going on in the environment can facilitate greater responsiveness to market changes and other developments. A study of high-tech firms found that 97 per cent of competitive failures resulted from lack of attention to market changes or the failure to act on vital information.[52] To detect and bring important information into the organization, boundary personnel scan the environment. For example, a market-research department scans and monitors trends in consumer tastes. Boundary spanners in engineering and research and development (R&D) departments scan new technological developments, innovations and raw materials. Boundary spanners prevent the organization from stagnating by keeping top managers informed about environmental changes. Often, the greater the uncertainty in the environment, the greater the importance of boundary spanners.[53]

ONLINE
COUNTERPOINT 5.6

One new approach to boundary spanning is business intelligence, which refers to the high-tech analysis of large amounts of internal and external data to spot patterns and relationships that might be significant. For example, the US company Verizon uses business intelligence to actively monitor customer interactions so that it can catch problems and fix them almost immediately.[54] Tools to automate the process have been one of the hottest areas of software development in recent years, with global spending on business intelligence software rising from $5 billion in 2007 to an estimated $50 billion in 2016. (see Counterpoint 5.5).[55]

COUNTERPOINT 5.5

Sometimes the line between business intelligence and espionage is a thin one. Verizon, along with AT&T and a host of less well-known companies, also make their expertise available, at a fee, to state intelligence services such as America's CIA. Questions have been raised about the appropriateness of outsourcing national intelligence, about whether companies involved in both business and national security intelligence-gathering have an unfair business advantage, and whether there is proper public scrutiny of privatized intelligence gathering.[56]

Business intelligence is related to another important area of boundary spanning, known as *competitive intelligence* (CI). The Strategic and Competitive Intelligence Professionals Association has its own academic journal and its membership of 3000 has more than doubled since 1997. Colleges and universities in North America and Europe are setting up degree programmes in CI to respond to the growing demand for these professionals in organizations.[57,58] Competitive intelligence gives top executives a systematic way to collect and analyze public information about rivals and use it to make better decisions.[59] Using techniques that range from internet surfing to searching through trash cans, intelligence professionals dig up information on competitors' new products, manufacturing costs or training methods and share it with top leaders.

In today's turbulent environment, many successful companies involve everyone in boundary-spanning activities. People at the grass-roots level are often able to see and interpret changes or problems sooner than managers, who are typically more removed from the day-to-day work.[60] At Canada's Cognos Corporation, which sells planning and budgeting programmes to large corporations, any of the company's 3500 employees can submit scoops about competitors through an internal website called Street Fighter. Each day, R&D and sales managers pore over the dozens of entries. Good tips are rewarded with prizes.[61,62]

The boundary task of sending information into the environment to represent the organization is used to influence other people's perception of the organization. In the marketing department, advertising and sales people represent the organization to customers. Purchasers may call on suppliers and describe purchasing needs. The legal department informs lobbyists and elected officials about the organization's needs or views on political matters. Many companies set up their own web pages to present the organization in a favourable light. For example, to counteract sites that criticize their business practices in developing countries, Nike and Shell, among many others, have created websites specifically to tell their side of the story.[63,64]

All organizations have to keep in touch with the environment. Zara, the Spain-headquartered clothing chain featured below in the *In Practice* text box, keeps its finger on the pulse of fashion, becoming the world's biggest fashion retail chain, with 2100 shops in 88 countries by 2016, only 40 years after its creation.

Differentiation and Integration

Another response to environmental uncertainty is the amount of differentiation and integration among departments. Organizational differentiation is 'the differences in cognitive and emotional orientations among managers in different functional departments, and the difference in formal structure among these departments'.[65] When the external environment is complex and rapidly changing, organizational departments become highly specialized to handle the uncertainty in their

IN PRACTICE

Zara

Amancio Ortega Gaona lives quietly in a modest apartment in La Coruña, Spain, but he has lived one of the most dramatic rags-to-riches stories in modern business. Gaona started in the rag trade at 14 as a junior assistant in a shirt store, but now owns a majority stake in Inditex, the family-controlled holding company of which Zara is the biggest asset. Gaona has succeeded in the fickle fashion business by being able to respond to changing fashions by producing new clothes lines within four to six weeks.[66] Zara's success is all the more remarkable because unlike most of its competitors (see H&M, profiled in Chapter 7), Zara outsources little of its production to low cost developing countries.

Zara's managers for each of its product lines keep their eyes peeled for new fashion opportunities, for example, copying one of singer Madonna's costumes from a major international tour and having the product on sale before the end of the tour. Sensitivity to the external environment extends to pricing policy. Rather than operating on a cost-plus basis, Zara sets its prices according to its image and market position in different countries; in Spain the company is a price leader, while in North America it is seen as a premium brand and prices are accordingly higher. Typically, Zara prices its clothes below the best known brands like Gap, but above more mass market retailers such as H&M in Europe and Old Navy in North America.

Like all successful companies, Zara knows its customers well and tailors its offer to meet their expectations, 'Zara's objective is not that consumers buy a lot but that they buy often and will find something new every time they enter the store', says a senior company manager. Unlike other fashion retailers, Zara spends very little on advertising. Instead, the company ensures it has good, highly visible high street locations. Its store managers are expected to know their customers well, their pay cheques are partly based on the accuracy of their sales predictions. The close attention Zara pays to its customers means the chain has a much lower level of new product failures, about one per cent, than the industry average of at least ten per cent.

Zara is in a difficult business, fashion tastes are notoriously fickle; the company will also need to ensure it is not blind-sided by the rapid shift to online fashion retailing through firms like Asos; in 2012 and 2013 the company quickly rolled out nationally specific online retailing websites, including in key emerging markets such as China, and by 2016 had online portals in 29 national markets.[67] Its close attention to its external environment means it is better equipped than many of its competitors to react effectively to external threats and opportunities. The shift to multi-channel delivery such as click-and-pick-up in local stores restores an advantage to companies like Zara over the pure internet play of an Asos.[68,69]

external sector (see Counterpoint 5.6). Success in each sector requires special expertise and behaviour. Employees in an R&D department thus have unique attitudes, values, goals and education that distinguish them from employees in manufacturing or sales departments.

COUNTERPOINT 5.6

A risk associated with this approach is the creation of 'silos' so that uncertainties are handled – assessed and addressed – in a fragmented manner. It can easily be assumed that some other department is handling an issue; or that wasteful duplication between departments is a consequence of a lack of coordination. To some degree the horizontal forms of communication and coordination mitigate such risks.

A study by Paul Lawrence and Jay Lorsch examined three organizational departments – manufacturing, research and sales – in ten corporations.[70] This study found that each department evolved toward a different orientation and structure to deal with specialized parts of the external environment. The market, scientific and manufacturing sub-environments identified by Lawrence and Lorsch are illustrated in Exhibit 5.5. Each department interacted with different external groups. The differences that evolved among departments within the organizations are shown in Exhibit 5.6. To work effectively with the scientific sub-environment, R&D had a goal of quality work, a long time horizon (up to five years), an informal structure and task-oriented employees. Sales was at the opposite extreme. It had a goal of customer satisfaction, was oriented toward the short term (two weeks or so), had a very formal structure, and was socially oriented.

One outcome of high differentiation is that coordination among departments becomes difficult. More time and resources must be devoted to achieving coordination when attitudes, goals and work orientation differ so widely. Integration is the quality of collaboration among departments.[71] Formal integrators are often required to coordinate departments. When the environment is highly uncertain, frequent changes require more information processing to achieve horizontal coordination, so integrators become a necessary addition to the organization structure.

EXHIBIT 5.5   Organizational Departments Differentiate to Meet Needs of Sub-environments

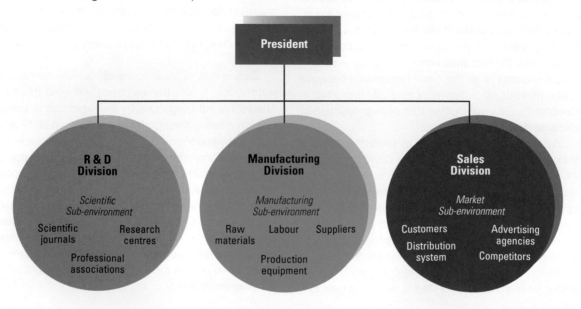

EXHIBIT 5.6 Differences in Goals and Orientations among Organizational Departments

Characteristic	R&D Department	Manufacturing Department	Sales Department
Goals	New development, quality	Efficient production	Customer satisfaction
Time horizon	Long	Short	Sort
Interpersonal orientation	Mostly task	Task	Social
Formality of structure	Low	High	High

Source: Based on Paul R. Lawrence and Jay W. Lorsch, *Organization and Environment* (Homewood, IL.: Irwin, 1969), 23–29.

Sometimes integrators are called liaison personnel, project managers, brand managers or coordinators. As illustrated in Exhibit 5.7, organizations with highly uncertain environments and a highly differentiated structure assign about 22 per cent of management personnel to integration activities, such as serving on committees, on task forces or in liaison roles.[72] In organizations characterized by very simple, stable environments, almost no managers are assigned to integration roles. Exhibit 5.7 shows that, as environmental uncertainty increases, so does differentiation among departments; hence, the organization must assign a larger percentage of managers to coordinating roles.

Lawrence and Lorsch's research concluded that organizations perform better when the levels of differentiation and integration match the level of uncertainty in the environment. Organizations that performed well in uncertain environments had high levels of both differentiation and integration, while those performing well in less uncertain environments had lower levels of differentiation and integration.

BRIEFCASE 5.3

Organic versus Mechanistic Management Processes

Another response to environmental uncertainty is the amount of formal structure and control imposed on employees. Tom Burns and G. M. Stalker observed 20 UK industrial firms and discovered that external environment was related to internal management structure.[73] When the external environment was stable, the internal organization tended to be characterized by rules, procedures and a clear hierarchy of authority. Organizations were formalized. They were also centralized, with most decisions made at the top. Burns and Stalker called this a mechanistic organization system.

In rapidly changing environments, Burns and Stalker found that the internal organization was much looser, free-flowing and adaptive. Rules and regulations often were not written down or, if written down, were ignored. People had to find their own way through the system to figure out what to do. The hierarchy of authority was not clear. Decision-making authority was

EXHIBIT 5.7 Environmental Uncertainty and Organizational Integrators

Industry	Plastics	Foods	Container
Environmental uncertainty	High	Moderate	Low
Departmental differentiation	High	Moderate	Low
Per cent management in integrating roles	22%	17%	0%

Source: Based on Jay W. Lorsch and Paul R. Lawrence, 'Environmental Factors and Organizational Integration', *Organizational Planning: Cases and Concepts* (Homewood, IL: Irwin and Dorsey, 1972), 45.

EXHIBIT 5.8   Mechanistic and Organic Forms

Mechanistic	Organic
1. Tasks are broken down into specialized, separate parts	1. Employees contribute to the common tasks of the department
2. Tasks are rigidly defined	2. Tasks are adjusted and redefined through employee teamwork
3. There is a strict hierarchy of authority and control, and there are many rules	3. There is less hierarchy of authority and control, and there are few rules
4. Knowledge and control of tasks are centralized at the top of the organization	4. Knowledge and control of tasks are located anywhere in the organization
5. Communication is vertical	5. Communication is horizontal

Source: Adapted from Gerald Zaltman, Robert Duncan, and Jonny Holbek, *Innovations and Organizations* (New York: Wiley, 1973), 131.

decentralized. Burns and Stalker used the term organic to characterize this type of management structure.

Exhibit 5.8 summarizes the differences in organic and mechanistic systems. As environmental uncertainty increases, organizations tend to become more organic, which means decentralizing authority and responsibility to lower levels, encouraging employees to take care of problems by working directly with one another, encouraging teamwork and taking an informal approach to assigning tasks and responsibility. Thus, the organization is more fluid and is able to adapt continually to changes in the external environment.[74]

The learning organization, described in Chapter 2, and the horizontal and virtual network structures, described in Chapter 4, are organic organizational forms that are used by companies to compete in rapidly changing environments. The American brand Guiltless Gourmet, which sells low-fat tortilla chips and other snack foods with healthy ingredients, shifted to a flexible network structure to remain competitive when large companies like Frito Lay entered the low-fat snack-food market. The company redesigned itself to become basically a full-time marketing organization, while production and other activities were outsourced. An 18 000 square foot plant in Austin was closed and the workforce cut from 125 to a handful of core people handling marketing and sales promotions. The flexible structure helped Guiltless Gourmet to adapt quickly to changing market conditions, but ultimately it didn't stop the company from being swallowed up by the food and consumer products giant R.A.B Holdings.[75,76]

Planning, Forecasting and Responsiveness

The whole point of increasing internal integration and shifting to more organic processes is to enhance the organization's ability to respond quickly to sudden changes in an uncertain environment. It might seem that in an environment where everything is changing all the time, planning is useless. However, in uncertain environments, planning and environmental forecasting, especially the exploration of different possible scenarios and responses, becomes *more* important as a way to keep the organization geared for a coordinated, speedy response. Japanese electronic giants such as Toshiba and Fujitsu, for example, were caught off guard by a combination of nimble new competitors, rapid technological change, deregulation, problems in Japan's banking system and the sudden end of the 1990s technology boom. Lulled into complacency by years of success, Japan's industrial electronics companies were unprepared to respond to these dramatic changes and lost billions.[77]

With increasing environmental uncertainty, planning and forecasting become more important, but also more difficult.[78] Planning can soften the adverse impact of external shifts. Organizations that have unstable environments often establish a separate planning department. In an unpredictable environment, planners scan environmental elements and analyze potential moves and countermoves by other organizations. Planning can be extensive and may forecast various *scenarios* for environmental contingencies. With scenario building, managers mentally rehearse different scenarios based on anticipating various changes that could affect the organization. Scenarios are like stories that offer alternative, vivid pictures of what the future will look like and how managers will respond. Royal Dutch/Shell Oil has long used scenario building and has been a leader in speedy response to massive changes that other organizations failed to perceive until it was too late.[79] Nevertheless, some scenarios cannot be predicted, or even if they could be predicted, there may be little a company can do in order to avoid negative outcomes except for getting out of that business and finding another. For example, no airline could have predicted the havoc that would be caused in their industry by the terrorist attack on New York's World Trade Center on September 11, 2001, the beginning of a security threat to the industry that expanded in subsequent years to attacks on airports such as the suicide bombings that closed Brussels airport for several weeks in 2016.[80]

Planning cannot substitute for other actions, such as effective boundary spanning and adequate internal integration and coordination. Organizations that are most successful in uncertain environments are those in which close attention is paid to the environment so they can spot threats and opportunities, and where intelligence is shared in a digestible and meaningful manner, thereby enabling relevant organizational members to respond swiftly and effectively.

?

ONLINE
COUNTERPOINT 5.7

Framework for Organizational Responses to Uncertainty

The ways environmental uncertainty influences organizational characteristics are summarized in Exhibit 5.9. The change and complexity dimensions are combined and illustrate four levels of uncertainty. The low uncertainty environment is simple and stable. Organizations in this environment have few departments and a mechanistic structure. In a low-to-moderate uncertainty environment, more departments are needed, along with more integrating roles to coordinate the departments. Some planning may occur. Environments that are moderate-to-high-uncertainty are unstable but simple. Organization structure is organic and decentralized. Planning is emphasized and managers are quick to make internal changes as needed. The high uncertainty environment is both complex and unstable and is the most difficult environment from a management perspective. Organizations are large and have many departments, but they are also organic. A large number of management personnel are assigned to coordination and integration, and the organization uses boundary spanning, planning and forecasting to enable a high-speed response to environmental changes.

Resource Dependence

So far, this chapter has described several ways of adapting to the lack of information and to the uncertainty associated with environmental change and complexity. We turn now to another characteristic of the organization–environment relationship that affects organizations: the importance of material and financial resources. The environment is the source of scarce and valued resources essential to organizational survival. Resource dependence means that organizations depend on the environment but strive to acquire control over resources to minimize their dependence.[81] Organizations are vulnerable if vital resources are controlled by other organizations, so there is an incentive to be as dominant and independent as possible.

Although corporate executives seek to minimize dependence, when costs and risks are high they may team up to share scarce resources and so become more competitive on a

?

ONLINE
COUNTERPOINT 5.8

EXHIBIT 5.9 Contingency Framework for Environment Uncertainty and Organizational Responses

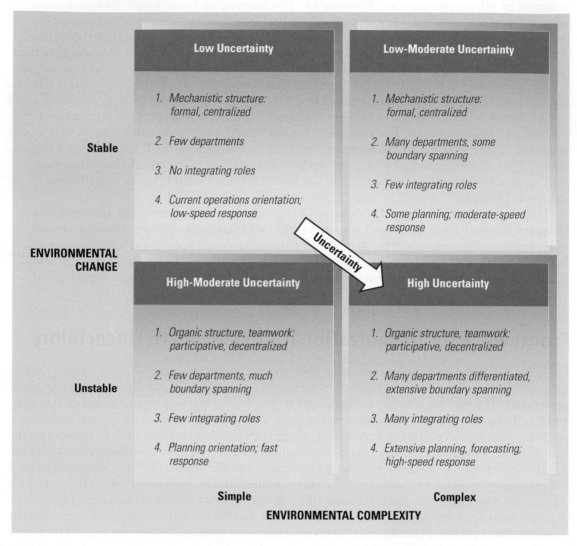

national or global basis. Formal relationships with other organizations present a dilemma to managers. They seek to reduce vulnerability with respect to resources by developing links with other organizations, but they also like to maximize their own autonomy and independence. Organizational linkages require coordination,[82] and they reduce the freedom of each organization to make decisions without concern for the goals of other organizations. Interorganizational relationships represent a tradeoff between resources and autonomy.

Once an organization relies on others for valued resources, those other organizations can influence managerial decision-making. When a large company like Samsung, Citroën or Toshiba forges a partnership with a supplier for parts, both sides benefit, but each loses some autonomy. For example, some large companies put strong pressure on their suppliers to reduce costs. Suppliers often have few alternatives but to go along with the demand.[83] In much the same way, dependence on shared resources gives advertisers considerable power over print and electronic media companies. For example, as newspapers face increasingly tough financial times, they are less likely to run stories that are critical of advertisers.

Though newspapers insist advertisers don't get special treatment, studies show that it is rare for a newspaper to severely criticize a major advertiser.[84] The American NGO Fairness and Accuracy in Reporting (FAIR) scrutinizes links between corporate advertisers and newspaper coverage.[85,86] FAIR particularly singles out the case of Wal-Mart, which has received what FAIR believes is excessively positive media coverage at the same time as it is one of the country's largest advertisers.[87] In some countries, the relationship between advertising and editorial content can be very direct; in 2003 India's biggest-circulation English-language newspaper, *The Times of India*, started accepting money from advertisers for publishing sponsored, but undeclared, editorial content.[88] As print media is increasingly replaced by electronic news portals that typically provide content for free, news outlets' reliance on advertisers has become even greater, and the line between editorial and advertisement even more blurred.

BRIEFCASE 5.4

Controlling Environmental Resources

In response to the need for resources, corporate executives try to maintain a balance between linkages with other organizations and their own independence. This balance is maintained through attempts to modify, manipulate or control other organizations.[89] To survive, managers of the focal organization often try to reach out and change or control elements in the environment. Two strategies can be adopted to manage resources in the external environment: (1) establish favourable linkages with key elements in the environment, and (2) shape the environmental domain.[90] Techniques to accomplish each of these strategies are summarized in Exhibit 5.10. As a general rule, when valued resources are scarce, executives will favour using the strategies in Exhibit 5.10 rather than go it alone. Notice how dissimilar these strategies are from the responses to environmental change and complexity described in Exhibit 5.9. The dissimilarity reflects the difference between responding, respectively, to the requirements for resources and information.

Establishing Interorganizational Linkages

Ownership   Companies use ownership to establish linkages when they buy a part of, or a controlling interest in, another company. This gives the company access to technology, products or other resources it doesn't currently have.

A greater degree of ownership and control is obtained through acquisition or merger. An *acquisition* involves the purchase of one organization by another so that the buyer assumes control. A *merger* is the unification of two or more organizations into a single unit.[91] In the steel industry, Mittal Steel merged with Luxemburg's Arcelor. Acquisition occurred when US retail giant Wal-Mart purchased Britain's Asda supermarket chain. These forms of ownership can

EXHIBIT 5.10   Organizing Strategies for Controlling the External Environment

Establishing Interorganizational Linkages	Controlling the Environmental Domain
1. Ownership	1. Change of domain
2. Contracts, joint ventures	2. Political activity, regulation
3. Cooptation, interlocking directorates	3. Trade associations
4. Executive recruitment	4. Illegitimate activities
5. Advertising, public relations	

reduce uncertainty in an area important to the acquiring company. In the past few years, there has been a huge wave of acquisition and merger activity in the telecommunications industry, reflecting the tremendous uncertainty these organizations face. The acquisition of Britain's Orange mobile phone network by France Telecom is discussed in this chapter's *In Practice* box.

Formal Strategic Alliances   When there is a high level of complementarity between the business lines, geographical positions or skills of two companies, the firms often go the route of a strategic alliance rather than ownership through merger or acquisition.[92] Such alliances are formed through contracts and joint ventures.

Contracts and joint ventures reduce uncertainty through a legal and binding relationship with another firm. Contracts come in the form of *licence agreements* that involve the purchase of the right to use an asset (such as a new technology) for a specific time and *supplier arrangements* that contract for the sale of one firm's output to another. Contracts can provide long-term security by tying customers and suppliers to specific amounts and prices. For example, the Italian fashion house Versace has forged a deal to licence its primary asset – its name – for a line of designer eyeglasses. McDonald's has successfully grown in developing countries, where traditional supplier networks might not be present. As the former Soviet Union's economy was in transition during the late 1980s, McDonald's set up operations in Moscow. At the beginning, it had to produce its own ingredients in Russia, but the company worked with emerging private suppliers to establish quality control and production reliability in return for guaranteed markets for their products.[93,94] Large retailers such as American-headquartered Wal-Mart, Britain's Tesco and France's Carrefour have gained so much clout that they can often almost dictate contracts, telling manufacturers what to make, how to make it and how much to charge for it. The changing balance of power in the production value chain has been studied by the sociologist Gary Gereffi, whose work is discussed in Chapter 7.

Joint ventures   These result in the creation of a new organization that is formally independent of the parents, although the parents will have some control.[95] In a joint venture, organizations share the risk and cost associated with large projects or innovations. AOL created a joint venture with Venezuela's Cisneros Group to smooth its entry into the Latin American online market. IBM formed a joint venture with USA Technologies Inc. to test web-enabled washers and dryers at American colleges and universities. Traditional coin-operated technology will be replaced with an IBM micropayment system that allows students to pay by swiping an ID card or pushing a code on a cell phone. They can log onto a website to see if a machine is available and have an email sent when a load is done.[96,97]

Cooptation, Interlocking Directorates   Cooptation occurs when leaders from important sectors in the environment are made part of an organization. It takes place, for example, when influential customers or suppliers are appointed to the board of directors, such as when the senior executive of a bank sits on the board of a manufacturing company. As a board member, the banker may become psychologically coopted into the priorities of the manufacturing firm. Community leaders also can be appointed to a company's board of directors or to other organizational committees or task forces. These influential people are thereby introduced to the culture and objectives of the company and are probably then more receptive to those objectives when engaged in decision-making.

An interlocking directorate is a formal linkage that occurs when a member of the board of directors of one company sits on the board of directors of another company. The individual is a communications link between companies and can influence policies and decisions. When one individual is the link between two companies, this is typically referred to as a direct interlock. An indirect interlock occurs when a director of company A and a director of company B are both directors of company C. They have access to one another but do not have direct influence over their respective companies.[98] Recent research shows that, as a firm's financial fortunes decline, direct interlocks with financial institutions tend to increase. Financial uncertainty facing an industry has also been associated with greater indirect interlocks between competing companies.[99]

Executive Recruitment   Transferring or exchanging executives also offers a method of establishing favourable linkages with external organizations. Senior officials move between government and private industry. Companies like to hire former senior officials and politicians who can both provide them advice on the processes of securing contracts or getting needed approvals, and provide introductions to key decision-making officials. For example, the former minister responsible for the British state health service, Patricia Hewitt, was hired as 'special consultant' by the world's largest chain of chemists, Alliance Boots, and the largest private owner of hospitals in the UK, in January 2008, while remaining a Member of Parliament. She also took a non-executive directorship of British Telecom (BT) having previously been instrumental, as Minister at the Department of Trade and Industry, in the creation of Ofcom, the all-in-one regulator for telecoms and the media, including the appointment of its chairman, Lord Currie.[100] Hewitt was suspended from her party caucus in the UK parliament in 2010 as a result of claims of irregularities in another of her lobbying activities.[101]

Some politicians and journalists argue that the practice of former ministers and bureaucrats lobbying for companies is inherently wrong, because it provides 'connected' companies with an unfair advantage.[102] In many countries there are rules such as a 'cooling off' period after someone leaves the public service, before they are allowed to take this type of lobbying position. The same issue arises in the private sector where companies are naturally unenthusiastic about their

IN PRACTICE

Orange and France Telecom

Worldwide, the telecommunications industry is changing perhaps more rapidly than any other industry. One of the most revolutionary of the changes in the telecom sector is 'convergence'. This describes the interweaving of broadcast, telecommunications and electronic media, and their delivery through a single modality, whether by telephone wire, by cable or increasingly, wirelessly. The opportunities and risks driven by convergence are enormous, and have led to great shake-ups in all areas of the communications industry. Convergence, in turn, has been driven by technological advances, including but not restricted to the development of the internet, wireless telecommunications and satellite broadcasting.

Mobile telephony took off in the late 1990s. An early response to expanding communications opportunities was a dramatic bidding war for mobile telephone operator licences and networks, which were seen as tremendous revenue generators. Smaller players like Britain's Orange were eyed hungrily by larger telecom operators, especially those that were lagging behind in the rush to mobile. France Telecom, which had until recently been France's state-owned telephone monopoly, had a small mobile arm but with mobiles seeming to be the wave of the future, in 2001 it pounced for Orange, with its reputation for innovation in both technology and marketing: 'This type of merger is becoming increasingly common and we expect to see many more in the coming months as the big old incumbents are forced to form partnerships with the emerging new players in order to stay ahead of the pack', said telecom veteran Gary Gibbs.[103]

Orange quickly established itself as one of the major global brands in the mobile phone industry, but with the pace of change in the sector accelerating rapidly, that was just the beginning. France Telecom continued to expand geographically, with operations in 29 countries and 263 million customers worldwide by 2016. Like its competitors, France Telecom invested heavily in digital convergence, both through acquisitions and greenfield development in broadband internet, online video gaming and television broadcasting.[104] In 2006 France Telecom decided to rebrand most of its global services under the Orange label, including Wanadoo, the largest broadband provider in Europe. Despite the dizzying pace of France Telecom's growth, many analysts wonder whether it has squeezed the creative juice out of Orange, making it a vehicle of a giant corporation, rather than quirky and innovative in the way that Apple has achieved.[105] This highlights one of the great dilemmas of mergers and acquisitions in the converged universe: size and service breadth are needed to win customers, but the price can be depersonalized service and consequently customer dissatisfaction. It's a challenge being faced throughout the telecommunications sector. Virgin Media, the full-service communications company created in 2007 through a merger between the Virgin mobile and broadband operator and NTL/Telewest Cable in the UK, faced both competitive

challenges and customer service issues;[106] in 2013 these questions began all over again as the company was acquired by competitor Liberty Global.[107] After an abortive attempt to merge their European assets in 2015, Liberty Global and Vodaphone agreed in 2016 to merge their Dutch operations.

In Britain only, Orange has tried a partnership strategy with its German counterpart T-Mobile. In 2010 they set up a joint venture under the name of Everything Everywhere (EE) which in 2012 was the first UK network to launch superfast 4G mobile broadband. Initial results were very promising. By mid-2013 nearly 700 000 UK customers were paying premium prices for the premium service, and the joint venture paid its Orange and Deutsche Telekom parent companies £159 million in dividends for the half-year. By mid-2015 EE maintained its position as the largest UK mobile phone provider with nearly one-third of the market.[108]

Source: http://www.ft.com/fastft/2016/02/16/liberty-global-vodafone-to-merge-their-dutch-operations/

executive moving to competitors with inside knowledge, and clauses are often inserted in contracts limiting managers' freedom to jump ship to a competitor. Nevertheless, as long as the practice is lawful, companies wishing to maximize their chances of winning contracts and getting projects approved will continue to hire well-connected executives. Having channels of influence and communication between organizations, both in the public and private sectors, serves to reduce financial uncertainty and dependence for an organization.

Advertising and Public Relations   A traditional way of establishing favourable relationships is through advertising. Organizations spend large amounts of money to influence the taste of consumers. Advertising is especially important in highly competitive consumer industries and in industries that experience variable demand. *The Economist* is a global publication appealing to executives looking for concise but sharp analysis of world events and business challenges. With the rise of the internet and an explosion in news sources, many magazines have faced declining circulation. However, in the decade that Helen Alexander served as CEO between 1997 and 2008, the magazine's circulation doubled, mainly by protecting its elite brand. In conjunction with the advertising agency AMV, *The Economist* built an image that encourages its readers to see themselves as intelligent and successful, a campaign that has been described as one of the best in the past 20 years. One ad says, 'It's lonely at the top, but at least there's something to read'. Alexander's successors had a solid brand to build on, which they leveraged through building the digital subscriber base for devices like the iPad, with the same marketing focus on quality. The magazine, which operates electronically behind a metered paywall, has been able to replace inevitably declining print circulation with paid digital subscriptions, with an overall readership of around 7 million by 2016.[109,110,111,112] Public relations is similar to advertising, except that stories often are free and aimed at public opinion. Public relations people cast an organization in a favourable light in speeches, in press reports and on television. Public relations attempts to shape the company's image in the minds of customers, suppliers and government officials. For example, in an effort to survive in this antismoking era, some tobacco companies have supported aggressive public relations campaigns touting smokers' rights and freedom of choice, often delivered through pseudo-independent NGOs.

Controlling the Environmental Domain

In addition to establishing favourable linkages to obtain resources, organizations often try to change the environment. We will discuss four techniques for influencing or changing a firm's environmental domain.

Change of Domain   The sectors described earlier in this chapter are not fixed. Executives determine which business they are in, the market to enter and the suppliers, banks, employees and location to use, and how this domain can be changed.[113] They can seek new environmental relationships and drop old ones. They may try to find a domain where there is little competition, no government regulation, abundant suppliers, affluent customers and barriers to keep competitors out.

Acquisition and divestment are two techniques for altering the domain. Canada's Bombardier, maker of Ski-Doo snowmobiles, began a series of acquisitions to alter its domain when the snowmobile industry declined. CEO Laurent Beaudoin gradually moved the company into the aerospace industry by negotiating deals to purchase Canadair, Boeing's De Haviland unit, business-jet pioneer Learjet and Short Brothers of Northern Ireland.[114] In 2007, Britain's Virgin Group decided to get out of the declining music retailing business by selling its Virgin Megastores, even though back in the 1980s and 1990s the stores had made founder Richard Branson's brash Virgin brand uniquely recognizable on Britain's high streets. After a management buyout the stores were rebranded Zavvi, refocusing on the expanding video games sector. Early results were positive, but eventually Zavvi fell victim to the global financial crisis, validating Branson's decision to divest the Virgin Megastores.[115]

?

ONLINE
COUNTERPOINT 5.9

Political Activity, Regulation   Political activity includes techniques to influence government legislation and regulation. Political strategy can be used to erect regulatory barriers against new competitors or to squash unfavourable legislation. The managers of corporations also try to influence the appointment to agencies of people who are sympathetic to their needs.

Microsoft has become one of the biggest and most sophisticated lobbying organizations in the world, spending $9 million in 2015[116] lobbying the US federal government alone. Microsoft has had to defend itself around the world against allegations of misusing its dominant position in computer operating system and office software. It has lobbied hard against proposed legislation in both Europe and North America that would severely restrict its ability to protect its dominant position – for example, by forcing Microsoft to 'unbundle' some of its non-core add-ons like multimedia players, and making it easier for competitors to produce software compatible with Microsoft products. One key issue on which Microsoft has lobbied successfully is for its version of 'open' office software to be certified as a global standard by the International Standardization Organization (ISO), although countries opposing Microsoft unsuccessfully appealed the 2008 decision. Once certified, Microsoft was permitted to sell its software to governments, in Europe and elsewhere, that require open software in which some of its internal code can be customized to meet customer needs and permit third-party add-ons.[117] Microsoft's lobbying effort has been global; in order to win the ISO vote against European opposition, it enlisted a number of developing country governments to become active in the organization and support its point of view.[118] Large pharmaceutical companies such as Merck and Wyeth frequently engage in political activity to influence government regulatory agency decisions regarding generic drugs or other changes that might weaken their organization's power and control.[119,120] The global retail giant Wal-Mart long steered clear of politics but in recent years has been adding lobbyists to the payroll and becoming heavily involved in political activity.

Trade Associations   Much of the work to influence the external environment is accomplished jointly with other organizations that have similar interests. In most countries, businesses have powerful associations that lobby legislators, influence new regulations and develop public relations campaigns. These exist on both a national and an industry-wide level. For example, R&D, the association of major pharmaceutical manufacturers in Canada, has engaged in a long and largely effective campaign to restrict availability of generic medications in the country, holding up the carrot of increased investment in pharmaceutical research and development, and effectively hampering development of the country's domestic generic medication industry.[121]

By pooling resources, business organizations can both fund larger lobbying campaigns than they could otherwise afford, and shield themselves from the criticism of self-interest. Small businesses are particularly dependent on industry and national associations to articulate and represent their interests, as most small businesspeople have neither the time nor the money to drop their work and lobby politicians.

Illegitimate Activities   Illegitimate activities represent the final technique companies sometimes use to control their environmental domain. Certain conditions, such as low profits, pressure from senior managers, or scarce environmental resources, may lead managers to adopt behaviours not considered legitimate.[122] Many well-known companies have been found guilty of unlawful or unethical activities. Examples include payoffs to foreign governments, illegal political contributions, promotional gifts and wiretapping. At formerly high-flying companies such as Enron and WorldCom, managers disguised financial problems through complex partnerships or questionable accounting practices. In the defence industry, the intense competition for sales of weapons systems has led some companies to do almost anything to get an edge. BAE, the major British weapons manufacturer, has made up to $2 billion dollars in payments over the past 20 years to the personal bank account of a leading member of the Saudi Arabian government, at the same time as the company secured an $80 billion contract to supply Saudi Arabia with fighter jets and other military equipment. The British government was pressured by Saudi Arabia to stop its investigation into this questionable practice, and in 2006, former Prime Minister Tony Blair decided to drop the investigation on political grounds. However, Britain's High Court ordered a full judicial review of the government's actions in 2008, stating that, 'No one, whether within this country or outside, is entitled to interfere with the course of our justice'. In addition, the United States arrested several BAE executives on suspicion of having broken American anti-corruption laws in the same matter.[123] Although 2010 settlements with the UK and US governments – costing £300 million in penalties, brought an end to the original complaints, enhanced scrutiny on the conduct of BAE unveiled a series of other allegations surrounding the company, with investigations dragging on for several years, with a long term impact on BAE's global image (see Counterpoint 5.7).[124]

One study found that companies in industries with low demand, shortages and strikes were more likely to be convicted for illegal activities, implying that illegal acts are an attempt to cope with resource scarcity. Some nonprofit organizations have been found to use illegitimate or illegal actions to bolster their visibility and reputation as they compete with other organizations for scarce grants and donations.[125]

IN PRACTICE

Wal-Mart

In the late 1990s, Wal-Mart discovered a problem that could hamper its ambitious international expansion plans – US negotiators for China's entry into the World Trade Organization had agreed to a 30-store limit on foreign retailers doing business there. Worse still, executives for the giant retailer realized they didn't know the right people in Washington to talk to about the situation.

Until 1998, Wal-Mart didn't even have a lobbyist on the payroll and spent virtually nothing on political activity. The issue of China's entry into the WTO was a wake-up call, and Wal-Mart began transforming itself from a company that shunned politics to one that works hard to bend public policy to suit its business needs. Hiring in-house lobbyists and working with lobbying organizations favourable to its goals has enabled Wal-Mart to gain significant wins on global trade issues.

In addition to concerns over global trade, Wal-Mart has found other reasons it needs government support. The company has been fighting off challenges from labour unions in the United States and elsewhere. For example, the United Food and Commercial Workers International Union helped Wal-Mart employees file a series of complaints about the company's overtime, healthcare and other policies, with the US National Labour Relations Board, leading to dozens of class-action lawsuits (in which a large group, or class, of litigants collectively bring a claim to court). Wal-Mart in turn poured millions of dollars into a campaign that presses for limits on awards in class-action suits and began lobbying for legislation that bars unions from soliciting outside retail stores. Although that legislation failed, top executives were pleased with their lobbyists' progress. Its spending on American lobbyists has risen rapidly, from $1.6 million in 2005 to $6 million in 2012, and the company makes large donations to US political parties and candidates, over $3 million in 2014 alone.[126]

Wal-Mart's lobbying activities are not restricted to the US. When the company decided it wanted to expand into the United Kingdom, it lobbied the then Prime Minister, Tony Blair, to loosen British planning regulations governing development of large new supermarkets. A few months later, Wal-Mart purchased the British chain Asda. Similarly, the company has been pressing hard, and with some success, for relaxation of India's restrictions against foreign-owned stores, seeking a share of a potentially enormous market in that emerging economy.[127] In addition to hiring lobbyists and working with other organizations, many CEOs do their own lobbying. CEOs have easier access than lobbyists and can be especially effective when they do the politicking. Political activity is so important that 'informal lobbyist' is an unwritten part of almost any CEO's job description.[128]

COUNTERPOINT 5.7

Although cases of outright fraud such as occurred at Enron are well-publicized, a wider issue relates to excessively easy-going relationships between corporations and government regulators that permits issues such as 'rogue trading' and excessively risky business strategies to flourish, especially in the financial sector whose scope is extending far beyond traditional banking to take in 'securitization' and 'marketization' of business areas such as utility and commodity markets. Particularly during economic boom periods, regulators may not be attuned to the risk of major failure, accepting overly optimistic projections by corporate executives. In retrospect, for example, the business model used by Britain's Northern Rock bank, which funded much of its mortgage lending on international money markets rather than on savings invested with the company, was highly susceptible to any general downturn in economic conditions. British regulators had quietly warned the bank, but allowed it to continue operating until the model collapsed like a pack of cards due to the credit squeeze of 2007, potentially costing British taxpayers many billions of pounds to prop up the institution.[129] Similarly, sometimes quite junior traders at financial institutions feel encouraged or even pressured to take risks in their trading portfolios. When things go badly wrong, as happened at Swiss Bank UBS in 2011, France's Société Générale in 2007, and the Singapore trading office of Barings Bank in 1995, blame is often focused on a single employee. A closer examination of this type of case usually reveals that ethical and compliance weaknesses are endemic in the corporation's culture, and that regulators are far too willing to take the word of a company's managers that all is well.[130,131]

Organization–Environment Integrative Framework

The relationships illustrated in Exhibit 5.11 summarize the two major themes about organization–environment relationships discussed in this chapter. One theme is that the amount of complexity and change in an organization's domain influences the criticality of information and hence the uncertainty felt within an organization. Greater information uncertainty is resolved through greater structural flexibility and the assignment of additional departments and boundary roles. When uncertainty is low, management structures can be more mechanistic, and the number of departments and boundary roles can be fewer. The second theme pertains to the scarcity of material and financial resources. The more dependent an organization is on other organizations for those resources, the more important it is to either establish favourable linkages with those organizations, or control entry into the domain. If dependence on external resources is low, executives can maintain a large measure of autonomy and so there is less pressure to establish linkages or control the external domain.

EXHIBIT 5.11   Relationship between Environmental Characteristics and Organizational Actions

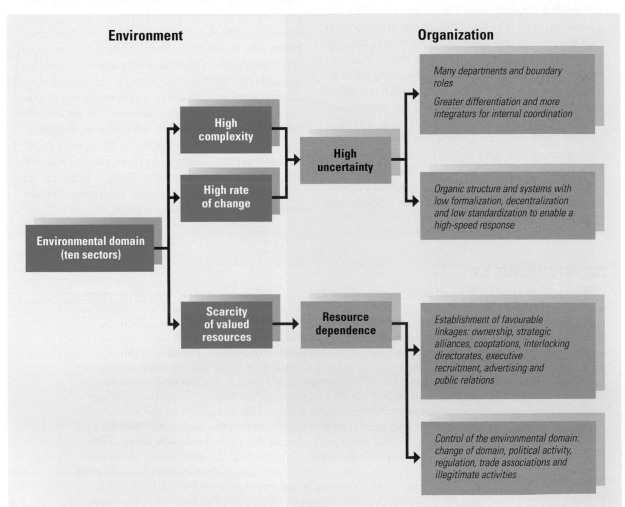

Summary and Interpretation

In this chapter, we have analyzed organizations as open social systems. All but the smallest organizations are involved with hundreds of external elements. Change and complexity in environmental domains have major implications for organization design and action. Many organizational decisions, activities and outcomes can be traced to perceived changes in the external environment.

Organizational environments differ in terms of uncertainty and can be conceptualized as stable–unstable, and simple–complex, or at least accounted for in terms of those dimensions. The creation of specific departments and functions may accordingly be justified in terms of their attentiveness to particular uncertainties.

Resources are allocated to departments in order to plan for and deal with specific environmental elements as well as to integrate diverse internal activities. Strategic alliances, interlocking directorates, executive recruitment or advertising and public relations can all serve to minimize risk and maintain a supply of scarce resources. Other measures for controlling the environment include a change of the domain in which the organization operates, political activity, participation in trade associations and perhaps illegitimate activities.

Two important themes in this chapter are that organizations both adapt to their environments and endeavour to control their effects. Such control is more feasible for large organizations that command substantial resources. But organizations with fewer but contextually critical resources may be more nimble and innovative in ways that elude the reach of their less agile competitors.

KEY CONCEPTS

boundary-spanning roles	domain	organic	simple–complex
buffering roles	general environment	organizational	dimension
business intelligence	indirect interlock	environment	stable–unstable
cooptation	integration	resource dependence	dimension
differentiation	interlocking directorate	sectors	task environment
direct interlock	mechanistic		uncertainty

Discussion Questions

1 Define *organizational environment*. Is the task environment of a new internet-based company the same as that of a government welfare agency? Discuss.

2 What are some forces that influence environmental uncertainty? Which typically has the greatest impact on uncertainty – environmental complexity or environmental change? Why?

3 Why does environmental complexity lead to organizational complexity? Explain.

4 Discuss the importance of the international sector for today's organizations, compared to domestic sectors. What are some ways in which the international sector affects organizations in your city or community?

5 Describe differentiation and integration. In what type of environmental uncertainty will differentiation and integration be greatest? Least?

6 Under what environmental conditions is organizational planning emphasized? Is planning an appropriate response to a turbulent environment?

7 What is an organic organization? A mechanistic organization? How does the environment influence organic and mechanistic structures?

8 Why do organizations become involved in inter-organizational relationships? Do these relationships affect an organization's dependency? Performance?

9   Assume you have been asked to calculate the ratio of staff employees to production employees in two organizations – one in a simple, stable environment and one in a complex, shifting environment. How would you expect these ratios to differ? Why?

10 Is changing the organization's domain a feasible strategy for coping with a threatening environment? Explain.

Chapter 5 Workbook Organizations You Rely On

Below, list eight organizations you somehow rely on in your daily life. Examples might be a restaurant, a clothing or phone store, a university, your family, the post office, the telephone company, an airline, a pizza shop that delivers, your place of work and so on. In column 1, list those eight organizations. Then, in column 2, choose another organization you could use in case the ones in column 1 were not available. In column 3, evaluate your level of dependence on the organizations listed in column 1 as Strong, Medium or Weak. Finally, in column 4, rate the certainty of that organization being able to meet your needs as High (certainty), Medium or Low.

Organization	Backup Organization	Level of Dependence	Level of Certainty
1.			
2.			
3.			
4.			
5.			
6.			
7.			
8.			

Questions

1. Do you have adequate backup organizations for those of high dependence? How might you create more backups?

2. What would you do if an organization you rated high for dependence and high for certainty suddenly became high-dependence and low-certainty? How would your behaviour relate to the concept of resource dependence?

Adapted by Dorothy Marcic from 'Organizational Dependencies', in Ricky W. Griffin and Thomas C. Head, *Practicing Management*, 2nd ed. (Dallas: Houghton Mifflin), 2–3.

Management and the External Environment

Malta and the Libyan Crisis

Fahey and Narayanan's (1986) model of the macro-environment stresses that the environment can only be understood as a system, in which each factor is related to and affects every other factor. This model offers a framework of analysis for identifying, tracking, projecting and assessing trends and patterns in the global macro-environment. It consists of four analytical stages:

- Scanning the environment to detect ongoing and emerging change.

- Monitoring specific environmental trends and patterns to determine their evolution.

- Forecasting the future direction of environmental changes.

- Assessing current and future environmental changes for their strategic and organizational implications.

Malta, a southern European country consists of an archipelago in the middle of the Mediterranean Sea. Malta covers 316m² in land, making it one of the smallest states. Malta's strategic location has been given importance over the years following a succession of powers. The country was admitted to the United Nations in 1964 and to the European Union in 2004. Malta is party to the Schengen agreement, becoming part of the Eurozone in 2008. Due to its prominent location, this strategic position has allowed Malta to develop itself as an important trading post. Geographically the distance between Malta and the nearest point on the North African Mainland is 288km. Following the Nationalist Party elected to office in 1987, relations with Libya were re-structured. The new government sought to have cordial relations and to encourage cordial ties with Libya. However military cooperation between the two countries was scrapped with no association with the Gaddafi regime. Malta's orientation was towards Europe and EU membership.

Col Muammar Gaddafi ruled Libya since 1969. Political parties were banned and his critics imprisoned, tortured and on some occasions killed. The Libyan conflict consisted of an armed conflict in the North African state of Libya fought between the forces of Col Muammar Gaddafi and those who sought to expel his government. After the overthrow of the leaders of Libya's neighbours, Tunisia and Egypt, some Libyans staged protests in February to demand change.

Key issues emerge in relation to government response to externally initiated abrupt change. As an overall strategy, the timely response of the Maltese community (as part of an international campaign) averted what could have been a potentially serious humanitarian crisis. Analysis of the data collected showed that key issues began to emerge particularly in fields of strategic management, decision-making and managerial activity. The Maltese emergency response and procedures for continuity combined to form effective operational procedures.

In terms of a change event, it was a radical change (a radical change occurred at a pivotal point), yet it did exhibit characteristics typical of a crisis (Malta's defence was at risk, a humanitarian crisis occurred, logistical impact onto the Maltese islands) as an unclear scenario evolved, sudden difficulties and shortage of time and information. There was a serious threat to the fundamental norms of a social system, which under time and pressure required making critical decisions. There was a clear point which was identified as a 'crisis point' and this helped speed up decision-making and structural formation for proper response. A gap was bridged between the recognition of a situation that was critical and response that was immediate in terms of bringing all entities together to take action, timing of response and action at the front-line.

Key objectives for public sector response through changing times require the management of ways in which agencies deliver their services and manage their performance by allocating the right quantity and quality of resources. In this case study, such actions took place to ensure that response was updated. The creation of standards for response could ensure that the goals for provision could realistically be met particularly if resource limitations are expected during a time of crisis. In many cases, it is usually a major event or crisis that provides the spark to start using lean drivers for change or demands for increased efficiency. In this case study, changing demands did call for faster processes

▶

including a reliance on resources that were prepared beforehand.

Questions

1   Could the Maltese Government have identified the threat at an earlier point in time through enhanced environmental sensitivity?

2   Which techniques can be used to identify such environmental challenges?

3   What can Governments and businesses do (if anything) to manage environmental risks?

Reference

Fahey, L. and Narayanan, V.K. (1986) *Macroenvironmental Analysis for Strategic Management, St. Paul, MN., West Publishing*.

Notes

1. Anil Hira (2012), 'Secrets behind the Finnish miracle: the rise of Nokia', *International Journal of Technology and Globalisation*, Vol. 6, 38–64; Rory Cellan-Jones, February 26, 2013, 'Nokia and Sony – in the recovery room?', *BBC News*; Jeffry Bartash, 30 November, 2011, 'Struggling Motorola back in a familiar position', *Market Watch*; *Wall Street Journal*, 9 February, 2011, 'The Burning Memo', http://blogs.wsj.com/tech-europe/2011/02/09/full-text-nokia-ceo-stephen-elops-burning-platform-memo/; C. Sabel and A. Saxenian (2008) A Fugitive Success: Finland's Economic Future, Report No. 80, Helsinki, SITRA, http://www.sitra.fi/julkaisut/raportti80.pdf; *The Economist*. July 5, 2007, 'Where would Jesus queue?'

2. Nicholas George, 'Nokia wins back market share to bolster top spot', *Financial Times,* Jan. 28, 2005 p. 21; Nokia, *Hoover Company Reports* – In-depth report, April 29, 2008; Robert Budden 'Handset prices cut in Nokia attempt to claw back sales', *Financial Times*, Apr. 29, 2004; p. 15; BBC News, 'Motorola sales close in on Nokia', July 20, 2006, accessed at http://news.bbc.co.uk/go/pr/fr/-/1/hi/business/5197946.stm.

3. Dina Bass and Adam Ewing, 'Microsoft to Cut Jobs, Take $7.6 Billion Writedown on Nokia', *Bloomberg*, July 8, 2015, accessed at www.bloomberg.com/news/articles/2015-07-08/microsoft-to-cut-7-800-jobs-as-it-restructures-phone-business; Rhiannon Williams, 'Nokia phone unit "to be renamed Microsoft Mobile"', *Daily Telegraph*, April 23, 2014, accessed at www.telegraph.co.uk/technology/nokia/10781973/Nokia-phone-unit-to-be-renamed-Microsoft-Mobile.html

4. Robert Thompson, 'As The World Turns', *Billboard*, March 8, 2008; 'Tower Records Closing; An Iconic Symbol of Music Closes', *ABC News* transcript, December 22, 2006.

5. Don Phillips, 'Switzerland clears sale of airline to Lufthansa', *International Herald Tribune*, March 23, 2005, 13.

6. Dan Milmo, 'Cheap flights boom over, says BA chief as oil hits new high', *Guardian*, 23 May 2008, p.1.

7. Paul Keegan, 'Is the Music Store Over?', *Business 2.0* (March 2004), 115–118; Tom Hansson, Jürgen Ringbeck and Markus Franke, 'Fight for Survival: A New Business Model for the Airline Industry', *Strategy + Business*, Issue 31 (Summer 2003), 78–85.

8. Matthew Boyle, 'The Wegmans Way', *Fortune* (January 24, 2005), 62–68.

9. John Vidal, 'How do you survive as a greengrocer?' *The Guardian*, June 10, 2008, g2 section, p. 3.

10. 'Half of UK shoppers visited Lidl, Aldi over Xmas', *Financial Times*, January 13, 2015, accessed at www.ft.com/fastft/2015/01/13/half-of-uk-shoppers-visited-lidl-aldi-over-xmas/

11. Dana Milbank, 'Aluminum Producers, Aggressive and Agile, Outfight Steelmakers', *The Wall Street Journal* (July 1, 1992), A1.

12. Myra Pinkham, 'Aluminium Cans – History, Development and Market' *Aluminium International Today*, April/May 2002, pp. 37–38.

13. See http://www.babymilkaction.org/resources/boycott/nestlefree.html, accessed June 18, 2008.

14. Kraft Foods Inc., *Hoover's Company Reports* – In-depth report, April 29, 2008.

15. Stephanie Strom, May 23, 2012, 'For Oreo, Cadbury and Ritz, a New Parent Company', *New York Times*.

16. Gwyn Morgan, 'Government, business must step up to ensure Canada Inc.'s recruitment success', *The Globe and Mail* (Canada), April 14, 2008, B2.

17. The Nation (Thailand), 'The government must resist the idea of an economic quick fix', March 6, 2008.

18. Aaron Bernstein, 'The Time Bomb in the Workforce: Illiteracy', *BusinessWeek* (February 25, 2002), 122.

19. Peter Svensson, 'Easing into the US market, one step at a time', The Virginian-Pilot, April 22, 2008, Pg. D5

20. 'European Union Outpaces United States on Chemical Safety', *Science Direct.com*. Retrieved May 2, 2008, from http://www.sciencedaily.com/releases/2007/01/070103110258.htm.

21. Samuel Loewenberg, 'Europe Gets Tougher on U.S. Companies', *The New York Times* (April 20, 2003), Section 3, 6.

22. Katherine Haddon, 'Top British supermarket cashes in on Polish pound', *Agence France Presse* September 11, 2006.

23. Brian Grow, 'Hispanic Nation', *BusinessWeek* (March 15, 2004), 58–70.

24. Mark Landler, 'Woes at Two Pillars of German Journalism', *The New York Times* (January 19, 2004), C8.

25. *Nielson Wire*, March 8 2012, 'Buzz in the Blogosphere: Millions More Bloggers and Blog Readers', http://blog.nielsen.com/nielsenwire/online_mobile/buzz-in-theblogosphere-millions-more-bloggers-and-blog-readers/.

26. 'Weblogs Rack Up a Decade of Posts', *BBC News*, December 17, 2007, accessed at http://news.bbc.co.uk/1/hi/technology/7147728.stm on June 18, 2008.

27. Sion Barry, 'Budget flights from Cardiff', *Western Mail*, June 11, 2007, p.1.

28. Kate Burgess, Fastject looks south to expand cut-price flights in Afica Financial Times 24 May 2015 http://www.ft.com/intl/cms/s/0/dc0aa020-008a-11e5-a908-00144feabdc0.html#axzz46C5ZK25i

29. Daimler AG (14 May 2007). 'Cerberus Takes Over Majority Interest in Chrysler Group and Related Financial Services Business for EUR 5.5 Billion ($7.4 billion) from DaimlerChrysler', press release retrieved on 6 June 2007.

30. See http://web.archive.org/web/20090222234918/http://www.toyota.co.jp/en/about_toyota/manufacturing/worldwide.html, accessed on September 15, 2013.

31. Devin Leonard, 'Nightmare on Madison Avenue', *Fortune* (June 28, 2004), 93–108; and Brian Steinberg, 'Agency Cost-Accounting Is under Trial', *The Wall Street Journal* (January 28, 2005), B2.

32. Chua Hian Hou. 'Ogilvy & Mathers Tops Ad Agency Ranking Again: Firm Retains Title on its Good Number of New Client Signings, Slew of Awards Last Year', *The Straits Times (Singapore)*. January 15, 2008; *PR Week*, '2007 ABR: Ogilvy Public Relations Worldwide The Outrider', April 23, 2007, accessed at http://www.prweekus.com/2007-ABR-Ogilvy-Public-Relations-Worldwide—The-Outrider/article/56835/ on June 18, 2008.

33. *China Daily*, 10 December, 2012, 'Chinese brands in US building name recognition'; Jenny Chan (2012), 'China's brands head west', *Campaign Magazine*, April, 44–47; T.W. Farnam, 7 February, 2013, 'Is lobbying in decline, or just redefining itself?', *The Washington Post*.

34. Stuart Elliott, 'Ogilvy & Mather Staffs Up in Social Media and Youth Marketing', *New York Times*, February 13, 2012, accessed at mediadecoder.blogs.nytimes.com/2012/02/13/ogilvy-mather-staffs-up-in-social-media-and-youth-marketing/

35. Randall D. Harris, 'Organizational Task Environments: An Evaluation of Convergent and Discriminant Validity', *Journal of Management Studies* 41, no. 5 (July 2004), 857–882; Allen C. Bluedorn, 'Pilgrim's Progress: Trends and Convergence in Research on Organizational Size and Environment', *Journal of Management* 19 (1993), 163–191; Howard E. Aldrich, *Organizations and Environments* (Englewood Cliffs, NJ: Prentice-Hall, 1979); and Fred E. Emery and Eric L. Trist, 'The Casual Texture of Organizational Environments', *Human Relations* 18 (1965), 21–32.

36. Gregory G. Dess and Donald W. Beard, 'Dimensions of Organizational Task Environments', *Administrative Science Quarterly* 29 (1984), 52–73; Ray Jurkovich, 'A Core Typology of Organizational Environments', *Administrative Science Quarterly* 19 (1974), 380–394; Robert B. Duncan, 'Characteristics of Organizational Environment and Perceived Environmental Uncertainty', *Administrative Science Quarterly* 17 (1972), 313–327.

37. Christine S. Koberg and Gerardo R. Ungson, 'The Effects of Environmental Uncertainty and Dependence on Organizational Structure and Performance: A Comparative Study', *Journal of Management* 13 (1987), 725–737; and Frances J. Milliken, 'Three Types of Perceived Uncertainty about the Environment: State, Effect and Response Uncertainty', *Academy of Management Review* 12 (1987), 133–143.

38. Calie Williams, 'Crisis management', *The Grocer*, October 6, 2007, Pg. 41.

39. David Wilson, 'See hate sites as tough love; Going online and venting anger on corporations is an extreme form of caring', *South China Morning Post*, July 5, 2005.

40. Mike France with Joann Muller, 'A Site for Soreheads', *BusinessWeek* (April 12, 1999), 86–90; D. Kirkpatrick and D. Roth, 'Why There's No Escaping the Blog'.

41. J. A. Litterer, *The Analysis of Organizations,* 2d ed. (New York: Wiley, 1973), 335.

42. Constance L. Hays, 'More Gloom on the Island of Lost Toy Makers', *The New York Times* (February 23, 2005), http://www.nytimes.com.

43. For an explanation of financialization, see Randy Martin (2002), *The Financialization of Daily Life*, Philadelphia, Temple University Press; introductory chapter available at http://www.temple.edu/tempress/chapters_1400/1615_ch1.pdf.

44. 'Former SEC Chairman Harvey Pitt speaks about illegal trading activity in France and the US', Transcript, *Wall Street Journal Report*, February 3, 2008; John Lanchester, 'Dicing with disaster', *The Guardian*, January 26, 2008, pg 31.

45. Rosalie L. Tung, 'Dimensions of Organizational Environments: An Exploratory Study of Their Impact on Organizational Structure', *Academy of Management Journal* 22 (1979), 672–693.

46. Joseph E. McCann and John Selsky, 'Hyper-turbulence and the Emergence of Type 5 Environments', *Academy of Management Review* 9 (1984), 460–470.

47. 'Prices Fuel Capacity Cuts: U.S. airlines grounding planes as costs soar, latest cutbacks in troubled domestic market', *Traffic World*, June 16, 2008, Pg. 29.

48. Rey Koslowski, 'Possible Steps Towards an International Regime for Mobility and Security', paper presented at international workshop on Global Mobility Regimes, Stockholm, June 11–12, 2004.

49. James D. Thompson, *Organizations in Action* (New York: McGraw-Hill, 1967), 20–21.

50. Alicia Buller, 'Now it's personal', *Revolution* (Brand Republic), September 3, 2007, pg. 30.

51. David B. Jemison, 'The Importance of Boundary Spanning Roles in Strategic Decision-Making', *Journal of Management Studies* 21 (1984), 131–152; and Mohamed Ibrahim Ahmad At-Twaijri and John R. Montanari, 'The Impact of Context and Choice on the Boundary-Spanning Process: An Empirical Extension', *Human Relations* 40 (1987), 783–798.

52. Michelle Cook, 'The Intelligentsia', *Business 2.0* (July 1999), 135–136.

53. Robert C. Schwab, Gerardo R. Ungson and Warren B. Brown, 'Redefining the Boundary-Spanning Environment Relationship', *Journal of Management* 11 (1985), 75–86.

54. Tom Duffy, 'Spying the Holy Grail', *Microsoft Executive Circle* (Winter 2004), 38–39.

55. 'Gartner Says Worldwide Business Intelligence Platform Market Grew 13 per cent in 2007', June 19, 2008, accessed at http://www.gartner.com/it/page.jsp?id=700410 on July 1, 2008; Karl Flinders, 'Global business intelligence spending to double in four years', *Computer Weekly*, January 07, 2013, accessed at www.computerweekly.com/news/2240175647/Global-business-intelligence-spending-to-double-in-four-years

56. Harry Hurt III, 'The Business Of Intelligence Gathering', *The New York Times*, June 15, 2008, p.5.; Tim Shorrock (2008), *Spies for Hire: The Secret World of Intelligence Outsourcing*, New York, Simon & Schuster.

57. Society of Competitive Intelligence Professionals, accessed May 4, 2008 at http://www.scip.org/content.cfm?itemnumber=2214&navItemNumber=492; http://web.archive.org/web/20110724194257/http://www.dmu.ac.uk/faculties/business_and_law/business/marketing/mk_staff_sheilawright.jsp, accessed on September 18, 2013.

58. Pia Nordlinger, 'Know Your Enemy', *Working Woman* (May 2001), 16.

59. Ken Western, 'Ethical Spying', *Business Ethics* (September/October 1995), 22–23; Stan Crock, Geoffrey Smith, Joseph Weber, Richard A. Melcher and Linda Himelstein, 'They Snoop to Conquer', *BusinessWeek* (October 28, 1996), 172–176; and Kenneth A. Sawka, 'Demystifying Business Intelligence', *Management Review* (October 1996), 47–51.

60. Edwin M. Epstein, 'How to Learn from the Environment about the Environment – A Prerequisite for Organizational Well-Being', *Journal of General Management* 29, no. 1 (Autumn 2003), 68–80.

61. 'Snooping on a Shoestring', *Business 2.0* (May 2003), 64–66.

62. Cognos Inc., Hoover's Company Records – In-depth report, April 29, 2008.

63. http://web.archive.org/web/20100128005947/http://www.shell.com/home/content/responsible_energy/sustainability_reports/dir_shell_sustainability_reports.html.

64. Mike France with Joann Muller, 'A Site for Soreheads', *BusinessWeek* (April 12, 1999), 86–90.

65. Jay W. Lorsch, 'Introduction to the Structural Design of Organizations', in Gene W. Dalton, Paul R. Lawrence and Jay W. Lorsch, eds, *Organizational Structure and Design* (Homewood, IL.: Irwin and Dorsey, 1970), 5.

66. Rhymer Rigby, 'Amancio Ortega Gaona: The shy CEO', *World Business,* 27 January 2007.

67. *News Bites – Spain*, 25 February, 2013, Inditex Group rises 1.4% with open interest rising.

68. Nirmalya Kumar and Sophie Linguri, 'Fashion Sense', *Business Strategy Review*, Summer 2006, 80–84.

69. Nick Fletcher, 'Asos shares slip despite 22% sales growth', January 14, 2016, accessed at www.theguardian.com/business/marketforceslive/2016/jan/14/asos-shares-slip-despite-22-sales-growth

70. Paul R. Lawrence and Jay W. Lorsch, *Organization and Environment* (Homewood, IL.: Irwin, 1969).

71. Jay W. Lorsch, 'Introduction to the Structural Design of Organizations', 7.

72. Jay W. Lorsch and Paul R. Lawrence, 'Environmental Factors and Organizational Integration', in J. W. Lorsch and Paul R. Lawrence, eds, *Organizational Planning: Cases and Concepts* (Homewood, IL.: Irwin and Dorsey, 1972), 45.

73. Tom Burns and G. M. Stalker, *The Management of Innovation* (London: Tavistock, 1961).

74. John A. Courtright, Gail T. Fairhurst and L. Edna Rogers, 'Interaction Patterns in Organic and Mechanistic Systems', *Academy of Management Journal* 32 (1989), 773–802.

75. Dennis K. Berman, 'Crunch Time', *BusinessWeek Frontier* (April 24, 2000), F28–F38.

76. 'R.A.B. Holdings, Inc. Announces the Purchase of Certain of the Assets of Guiltless Gourmet, Inc', *Business Wire*, November 6, 2000, accessed on June 30 2008; R.A.B. Holdings Inc. *Hoovers Company Reports – In-depth report*, April 29, 2008.

77. Robert A. Guth, 'Eroding Empires: Electronics Giants of Japan Undergo Wrenching Change', *The Wall Street Journal* (June 20, 2002), A1, A9.

78. Thomas C. Powell, 'Organizational Alignment as Competitive Advantage', *Strategic Management Journal* 13 (1992), 119–134; Mansour Javidan, 'The Impact of Environmental Uncertainty on Long-Range Planning Practices of the US Savings and Loan Industry', *Strategic Management Journal* 5 (1984), 381–392; Rosalie L. Tung, 'Dimensions of Organizational Environments', 672–693; and James D. Thompson, *Organizations in Action*.

79. Ian Wylie, 'There Is No Alternative To ...', *Fast Company* (July 2002), 106–110.

80. Trevor Maxwell, 'Legacy of 9/11 attacks: Lost innocence; Employees at Portland's jetport describe a day of terror and changes that resulted in its aftermath', *Portland Press Herald*, September 9, 2007, Pg. A1.

81. David Ulrich and Jay B. Barney, 'Perspectives in Organizations: Resource Dependence, Efficiency and Population', *Academy of Management Review* 9 (1984), 471–481; and Jeffrey Pfeffer and Gerald Salancik, *The External Control of Organizations: A Resource Dependent Perspective* (New York: Harper & Row, 1978).

82. Andrew H. Van de Ven and Gordon Walker, 'The Dynamics of Interorganizational Coordination', *Administrative Science Quarterly* (1984), 598–621; and Huseyin Leblebici and Gerald R. Salancik, 'Stability in Interorganizational Exchanges: Rulemaking Processes of the Chicago Board of Trade', *Administrative Science Quarterly* 27 (1982), 227–242.

83. Kevin Kelly and Zachary Schiller with James B. Treece, 'Cut Costs or Else: Companies Lay Down the Law to Suppliers', *BusinessWeek* (March 22, 1993), 28–29.

84. Wendy Priesnitz, 'Countering the spin', *Natural Life*, November 1, 2007, p. 34.

85. www.fair.org.

86. G. Pascal Zachary, 'Many Journalists See a Growing Reluctance to Criticize Advertisers', *The Wall Street Journal* (February 6, 1992), A1, A9.

87. Peter Hart and Janine Jackson, 'Media Lick the Hand That Feeds Them: Does Wal-Mart's money buy more than ads?', *Extra*, November/December 2005, accessed at http://www.fair.org/index.php?page=2770 on June 30, 2008.

88. Ashar, Hemal (May 11, 2004) Is this journalism? *Mid Day*, accessed at http://web.archive.org/web/20060622052800/http://ww1.mid-day.com/news/city/2004/may/83022.htm on September 15, 2013; Ninan, Sevanti (2004) 'The leader cons the reader' in Sunil K Poolani (ed) *Rape of News: The ethics (or lack of it) of selling editorial space*, pp 23-26, Mumbai: Frog Books.

89. Judith A. Babcock, Organizational Responses to Resource Scarcity and Munificence: Adaptation and Modification in Colleges within a University (Ph.D. diss., Pennsylvania State University, 1981).

90. Peter Smith Ring and Andrew H. Van de Ven, 'Developmental Processes of Corporative Interorganizational Relationships', *Academy of Management Review* 19 (1994), 90–118; Jeffrey Pfeffer, 'Beyond Management and the Worker: The Institutional Function of Management', *Academy of Management Review* 1 (April 1976), 36–46; and John P. Kotter, 'Managing External Dependence', *Academy of Management Review* 4 (1979), 87–92.

91. Bryan Borys and David B. Jemison, 'Hybrid Arrangements as Strategic Alliances: Theoretical Issues in Organizational Combinations', *Academy of Management Review* 14 (1989), 234–249.

92. Julie Cohen Mason, 'Strategic Alliances: Partnering for Success,' *Management Review* (May 1993), 10–15.

93. Adrian E. Tschoegl (2007), 'McDonald's – Much Maligned, But an Engine of Economic Development', *Global Economy Journal*, 7, article 5; George Cohon (1998), To Russia with Fries, Toronto, McLelland and Stewart.

94. Teri Agins and Alessandra Galloni, 'After Gianni; Facing a Squeeze, Versace Struggles to Trim the Fat', *The Wall Street Journal* (September 30, 2003), A1, A10; John F. Love, *McDonald's: Behind the Arches* (New York: Bantam Books, 1986).

95. Brian Borys and David B. Jemison, 'Hybrid Arrangements as Strategic Alliances'.

96. 'IBM tests Mobile Speech Applictions', IT World. Retrieved May 5, 2008, from http://www.itworld.com/ App/85/060224ibmspeech.

97. Ian Katz and Elisabeth Malkin, 'Battle for the Latin American Net', *BusinessWeek* (November 1, 1999), 194–200; 'IBM Joint Venture to Put Laundry on Web', *The Wall Street Journal* (August 30, 2002), B4.

98. Donald Palmer, 'Broken Ties: Interlocking Directorates and Intercorporate Coordination', *Administrative Science Quarterly 28* (1983), 40–55; F. David Shoorman, Max H. Bazerman and Robert S. Atkin, 'Interlocking Directorates: A Strategy for Reducing Environmental Uncertainty', *Academy of Management Review* 6 (1981), 243–251; and Ronald S. Burt, *Toward a Structural Theory of Action* (New York: Academic Press, 1982).

99. James R. Lang and Daniel E. Lockhart, 'Increased Environmental Uncertainty and Changes in Board Linkage Patterns', *Academy of Management Journal* 33 (1990), 106–128; and Mark S. Mizruchi and Linda Brewster Stearns, 'A Longitudinal Study of the Formation of Interlocking Directorates', *Administrative Science Quarterly* 33 (1988), 194–210.

100. http://www.theregister.co.uk/2008/03/13/hewitt_joins_bt/.

101. Rosa Prince, 9 December 2010, 'MPs for hire: three former Labour ministers banned from Parliament', *The Daily Telegraph*.

102. Paul Waugh, 'Ex-health secretary to work for hospital owner and Boots', *The Evening Standard*, January 18, 2008, pg B6; Simon Hoggart, 'Slasher takes on lobbyists', *The Guardian*, May 9, 2008, Pg. 14; David Craig and Peter Brooks, *Plundering the Public Sector*, London, Constable.

103. Iain S. Bruce, 'Dial M for merger', *The Sunday Herald*, June 4, 2000, Pg. 2.

104. Ekow Nelson, Rob van den Dam and Howard Kline (2008), 'A future in content(ion): Can telecom providers win a share of the digital content market?', *Journal of Telecommunications Management* 1, Pg. 125–138.

105. Robert Lester, 'Orange: In need of a brighter dawn', *Marketing Week*, December 20, 2007, Pg. 16.

106. Jon Ashworth and Rupert Steiner, 'How Branson set out to slay sky', *The Business*, March 31, 2007; Dave Bailey, 'Glitches Mar Broadband Services', *IT Week*, July 9, 2007, Pg. 26.

107. Mark Scott and Eric Pfanner, 'Liberty Global Reaches Deal for Virgin Media That May Inflame Old Rivalry', *The New York Times*, 6 February, 2013.

108. Juliette Garside, 'Everything Everywhere sees strong takeup of 4G: EE says it is on track to reach its target of 1m subscribers by Christmas', *The Guardian*, 24 July, 2013.

109. Andrew Davidson, 'The end of Alexander the great: chief of the world's top magazine quits', *The Australian*, April 28, 2008, Pg. 30; Damian Reece, A rich legacy at Economist, *The Daily Telegraph*, June 23, 2008, Pg. 5.

110. Lee Hawkins Jr. 'GM Seeks Chevrolet Revival', *The Wall Street Journal* (December 19, 2003), B4.

111. Gideon Spanier, 19 June 2012, 'Profits surge at Economist as digital gives turnover a boost', *The Independent*.

112. Economist's digital charge helps keep Private Eye at bay, February 12, 2015, accessed at www.theguardian.com/ media/2015/feb/12/economists-digital-charge-helps-keep-private-eye-at-bay; Economist readership certified at http://economistgroupmedia-1530222749.us-east-1.elb. amazonaws.com/sites/default/files/TEWA_JJ15_V2_0.pdf

113. John P. Kotter, 'Managing External Dependence'.

114. William C. Symonds, with Farah Nayeri, Geri Smith and Ted Plafker, 'Bombardier's Blitz', *BusinessWeek* (February 6, 1995), 62–66; and Joseph Weber, with Wendy Zellner and Geri Smith, 'Loud Noises at Bombardier', *BusinessWeek* (January 26, 1998), 94–95.

115. Rosie Baker, 'Sounds different', *In Store Marketing*, May 15 2008, Pg. 20; Kelly Macnamara, 'Xmas Misery For Music Store Workers', *Press Association Newsfile*, December 25, 2008.

116. Microsoft Ltd lobbying spending 2015, accessed at https://www.opensecrets.org/lobby/clientsum. php?id=D000000115.

117. Ken Schachter 'Microsoft Leads Lobbying Largesse', *Redherring.com*, April, 28 2008, retrieved May 5, 2008, from http://web.archive.org/web/20110710154943/http:// www.redherring.com/Home/24187; Kevin J. O'Brien, 'Microsoft format seen becoming a standard; Battle fought over document software', *The International Herald Tribune*, September 4, 2007, Pg. 11; Joab Jackson, 'ISO benches Microsoft OOXML', *Government Computer News*, June 11, 2008.

118. Duncan McLeod, Fear and loathing, *Financial Mail* (South Africa), May 30, 2008, Pg. 14; 'Let's Leave it Open', *Indian Express*, March 27, 2008.

119. Matthew K. Wynia, 'Public Health, Public Trust and Lobbying', *American Journal of Bioethics*, June 2007, Pg. 4.

120. Ben Worthen, 'Mr. Gates Goes to Washington', *CIO* (September 2004), 63–72; Gardiner Harris and Chris Adams, 'Delayed Reaction: Drug Manufacturers Step Up Legal Attacks That Slow Generics', *The Wall Street Journal* (July 12, 2001), A1, A10; Leila Abboud, 'Raging Hormones: How Drug Giant Keeps a Monopoly on 60-Year-Old Pill', *The Wall Street Journal* (September 9, 2004), A1.

121. Joel Caeusu, 'R&D: Patent protection attracts research to Quebec', *The Montreal Gazette*, April 24, 1999, S10; David Morley, 'Drug companies focus on profits, not people', *Victoria Times Colonist*, April 20, 2004.

122. Anthony J. Daboub, Abdul M. A. Rasheed, Richard L. Priem and David A. Gray, 'Top Management Team Characteristics and Corporate Illegal Activity', *Academy of Management Review* 20, no. 1 (1995), 138–170.

123. Nelson D. Schwartz and Lowell Bergman, 'Payload: Taking Aim At Corporate Bribery', *New York Times*, November 25, 2007, Section 3, Pg. 1; David Hencke, 'Tories join Brown in bid to block fraud investigations', *The Guardian*, April 12, 2008, Pg. 1.

124. Andrew Feinstein, 17 August, 2012, 'A trade unbounded: The SFO inquiry into the Saudi defence deal must not turn into another whitewash', *The Guardian*.

125. Barry M. Staw and Eugene Szwajkowski, 'The Scarcity-Munificence Component of Organizational Environments and the Commission of Illegal Acts,' *Administrative Science Quarterly* 20 (1975), 345–354; and Kimberly D. Elsbach and Robert I. Sutton, 'Acquiring Organizational Legitimacy through Illegitimate Actions: A Marriage of Institutional and Impression Management Theories,' *Academy of Management Journal* 35 (1992), 699–738.

126. Walmart political donations 2014, accessed at https://www.opensecrets.org/pacs/lookup2.php?strID=C00093054&cycle=2014.

127. Christopher Hope and James Hall, 'Wal-Mart did lobby Blair over Asda', *The Sunday Telegraph,* January 27, 2008, Pg. 2; 'Retail opportunities in India', *The Herald* (Glasgow), December 28 2006, Pg. 20; 'Wal-Mart keeps raising lobbying budget', *The Myrtle Beach Sun-News* (South Carolina), March 8, 2008, Pg. 2.

128. David B. Yoffie, 'How an Industry Builds Political Advantage', *Harvard Business Review* (May–June 1988), 82–89; and Jeffrey H. Birnbaum, 'Chief Executives Head to Washington to Ply the Lobbyist's Trade', *The Wall Street Journal* (March 19, 1990), A1, A16.

129. Nora Colomer, 'UK mortgage lending sees growth', *Asset Securitization Report*, November 27, 2006; Edmund Conway, 'Was stability bridge to blame for wobble?', *The Daily Telegraph*, September 24, 2007, Pg. 5.

130. *The Guardian*, 'Societe Generale scandal: Unanswered questions. Who knew what?' January 26, 2008, Pg. 4; Alex Brummer, 'Hammer Blow to City's Reputation', *The Guardian*, February 27, 1995.

131. Peter Walker, 21 November 2012, 'UBS "rogue" trader Kweku Adoboli jailed for seven years', *The Guardian*.

INTERORGANIZATIONAL RELATIONSHIPS

MAN AG

MAN Nutzfahrzeuge AG, the German-based truck, commercial vehicle and engineering equipment manufacturer celebrated its 250th anniversary in 2008, but developments since then showed how even companies with a long and impressive history can quickly be transformed by developments in a globalized economy.

The company's record of innovation is impressive, and includes the invention of the diesel engine (named after a MAN employee, Rudolf Diesel). 2007 was the company's most successful year yet, with new orders up 17 per cent, sales 19 per cent higher at €15.5 billion, and a 50 per cent increase in profits to €1.7 billion.[1] But MAN wasn't resting on its laurels. Nearly 90 per cent of the company's sales were in Europe, a mature market with relatively little room for growth. MAN began lengthy negotiations about a possible takeover of Scania, its major European competitor, but another main focus was building stronger positions outside Europe.

In 2004, MAN had established a major strategic agreement with International Truck and Engine Corp., the truck division of America's Navistar Corporation. The two companies agreed to jointly develop engines and other key components for trucks. This seemed like a perfect match because International doesn't sell in Europe, while MAN is not present in North America. Their first major collaboration, the Maxxforce big bore six-cylinder diesel engine launched in 2007, was initially such a success that it prompted the American heavy equipment manufacturer Caterpillar to abandon engine manufacture and adopt the engine as standard in its equipment. However, subsequently, Navistar proved unwilling to invest sufficiently in emissions control and the engine was caught up in a dispute with US regulators over emissions compliance.[2]

MAN also counted on expansion into the rapidly growing emerging markets of countries like India and China. In 2006 the company set up a joint venture with Force Motors, a major Indian manufacturer of commercial vehicles. By 2008 the joint venture was in production mode, with planned output of 16 to 45-tonne trucks expected to grow fourfold, from 6000 vehicles a year to 24 000 by 2010. Significantly, MAN operates a large design facility in Aurangabad, India, with over 100 design engineers. Already, some manufactured products, such as marine motors, are produced in India and shipped overseas, undoubtedly an indication of future trends in a highly competitive globalized economy. Two of MAN's competitors, Daimler Trucks and Volvo Trucks, have already set up joint venture deals with two Indian domestic vehicle manufacturers, and other companies are queuing up to sign on too.[3] MAN has also set up several joint ventures in China, though progress was slower than in India, with several joint venture (JV) deals falling through and the company eventually setting up its own manufacturing plant. MAN's efforts to expand overseas ran into trouble in 2009, when the company was accused of a widespread bribery scandal involving sales of MAN trucks in as many as 20 countries. The scandal resulted in the departure of many of MAN's top officials.

The fallout of the bribery scandal and difficulties getting anti-monopoly approvals for the Scania takeover eventually made MAN itself vulnerable for a take-over, by global automotives giant Volkswagen. Volkswagen, which has held a minority share in the company for some time, eventually lifted its stake to 55 per cent in 2011 and 75 per cent in 2012. The company also began eyeing the troubled International Trucks division of Navistar for a possible takeover but eventually dropped this in favour of finally taking a majority share in Sweden's Scania in 2014. Nevertheless, by 2016 MAN and Scania still operated as separate marques.[4] VW's long-term objective seems clear, however; to consolidate MAN with other second tier actors in the global truck industry and build its MAN division into a player big enough to leapfrog from sixth place and take on the world's two biggest players, Isuzu and Daimler AG.[5]

Managers in organizations of all sizes in all industries are rethinking how they do business in response to today's chaotic environment. One of the most widespread trends is to reduce boundaries and increase collaboration between companies, sometimes even between competitors. Today's aerospace companies, for example, depend on strategic partnerships with other organizations. The world's two giant airlines, Europe's Airbus Industrie and Boeing, the largest US aerospace company, are both involved in multiple relationships with suppliers, competitors and other organizations. Global semiconductor makers have been collaborating while competing for years because of the high costs and risks associated with creating and marketing a new generation of semiconductors. However, as the case of MAN Trucks above shows, the business of global positioning in today's consolidating global market, can lead to a dizzying series of partnerships, takeovers, mergers and break-ups.

Global competition and rapid advances in technology, communications and transportation have created amazing new opportunities, but they have also raised the cost of doing business and made it increasingly difficult to take advantage of those opportunities on their own. In this new economy, webs of organizations are emerging. A large company like France's Renault develops a special relationship with a supplier that eliminates middlemen by sharing complete information and reducing the costs of salespersons and distributors. Several small companies may be joined together to produce and market non-competing products. You can see the results of interorganizational collaboration when movies such as *War of the Worlds*, *The Incredibles* or *Star Wars: The Clone Wars* are launched. Before seeing the movie, you might read a cover story in *Hello!* or *Heat*, see a preview clip or chat live with the stars at an online site such as E! online, find action toys being given away at a fast-food franchise and notice retail stores loaded with movie-related merchandise. For some blockbuster movies, coordinated action among companies can yield millions in revenue, in addition to box-office, DVD and online streaming profits. In the new economy, organizations collaborate as teams that create value jointly rather than as autonomous companies that are in competition with all others (see Counterpoint 6.1).

COUNTERPOINT 6.1

Some care should be exercised when using the 'team' metaphor. These are alliances in which the members are very much calculating their own advantage both in joining and remaining, and in inducing and pressurizing others to cooperate. Their 'play' may be one of reciprocal exploitation rather than collective identification with the venture. As a consequence, there are issues of long-term commitment, and many of these collaborations are tentative, conditional and transitory.

Purpose of this Chapter

This chapter explores the most recent trend in organizing, which is the increasingly dense web of relationships among organizations. Companies have always been dependent on other organizations for supplies, materials and information. The question is how these relationships are managed. At one time it was a matter of a large, powerful company like Unilever or General Electric tightening the screws on small suppliers. Today a company can choose to develop positive, trusting relationships (see Counterpoint 6.2). Executives at a company like Toyota might decide to create a subsidiary such as Lexus, when they want to create a product that will achieve a decisive upmarket shift from the family cars for which the company is famous. The notion of horizontal relationships described in Chapter 4 and the understanding of environmental uncertainty in Chapter 5 are leading to the increased formation of horizontal relationships *across* organizations. Relationships are built in many ways, such as appointing preferred suppliers, establishing agreements, business partnering, joint ventures or even mergers and acquisitions.

COUNTERPOINT 6.2

A 'trusting relationship' is not necessarily something that can be 'chosen' as it involves another party whose cooperation is vital. Executives may strive to build more trusting relationships but their establishment will depend upon the willingness of the partner and also the ability to sustain trust during testing times – of market downturns, for example.

The sum total of these ideas can be daunting, because it means managers no longer can rest in the safety of managing a single organization. They have to figure out how to manage a whole set of interorganizational relationships, which is a great deal more challenging and complex.

Organizational Ecosystems

Interorganizational relationships are the relatively enduring resource transactions, flows and linkages that occur among two or more organizations.[6] Traditionally, these transactions and relationships have often been seen more as a necessary evil to obtain what an organization needs. The presumption has been that the world in business is a zero-sum game – there are simply winners and losers – in which distinct businesses thrive on autonomy and compete for supremacy. On this view, a company may be forced into interorganizational relationships, depending on its needs and the instability and complexity of the environment, but submits to this force out of weakness.

An alternative view conceives of organizations as participants in business ecosystems (see Counterpoint 6.3). An organizational ecosystem is a system formed by the interaction of a group of organizations and their environment. An ecosystem cuts across traditional industry lines. Microsoft operates in four major industries: consumer electronics, information, communications and personal computers. Its ecosystem includes millions of customers across many markets internationally, as well as hundreds of suppliers, including companies across the world such as Singapore-based Flextronics, which manufactures the Xbox under contract.[7] Cable companies like Virgin Media in the UK and Comcast in America are offering telephone service, while telephone companies like Deutsche Telekom are investing heavily in the television business.[8] Apple Computer is having greater success as an entertainment and mobile communications company with its iPhone, iPad and iTunes Music Store than it has ever had as a computer manufacturer. Apple's success grows out of close partnerships with other organizations, including music companies, consumer electronics firms, mobile phone makers, other computer companies and even car manufacturers.[9] Deutsche Telekom and Microsoft, like other business ecosystems, develop relationships with hundreds of organizations cutting across traditional business boundaries. Organizations around the world are embedded in complex networks of confusing relationships – collaborating in some markets, competing fiercely in others, with Apple and Samsung a perfect example of this contradictory phenomenon. While they slug out multi-billion lawsuits against each other, Samsung supplies the processing chips for Apple's iPhone! Indeed, research indicates that a large percentage of new alliances in recent years have been between competitors. These alliances influence organizations' competitive behaviour in varied ways.[10]

> ## COUNTERPOINT 6.3
>
> It is notable that the 'ecosystem' does not extend beyond other companies to the natural environment. There is little recognition of companies' dependence upon the biosphere or of the damage they routinely inflict upon it by externalizing their costs upon a 'party' that is unable to press charges.

Is Competition Dead?

Traditional competition, which assumes a distinct company competing for survival and supremacy with other stand-alone businesses, is increasingly displaced because each organization both supports and depends on the others for success, and perhaps for survival. However, most managers recognize that the competitive stakes are higher than ever in a world where market share can crumble overnight and no industry is immune from almost instant obsolescence.[11] A new form of competition is intensifying but it is one that involves clusters of businesses competing with other clusters.[12] The airline industry is a clear example where a number of alliances, which offer international passengers connectivity and convenience, have formed between the major players. The three largest alliances are the Star Alliance, SkyTeam and Oneworld. A more recent development is the formation of alliances between cargo airlines, such as that of SkyTeam Cargo, and WOW Alliance.

BRIEFCASE 6.1

With coevolution through an alliance or network, it is possible for members of the whole system to become stronger. Companies coevolve through discussion with each other, shared visions, alliances and managing complex relationships.

Amazon and its partners represent a business ecosystem, in which each company depends to some extent on the others and each has the opportunity to grow stronger. For example, Amazon is finding that every new retail partner has its own demands for how its products should be presented and sold. Amazon managers say they welcome the feedback because it enables them to keep improving the site. The retail partners may benefit too, because Amazon keeps a close watch on factors such as how well the retailers are managing delivery, communication and customer service. At the same time, partnerships such as that between major companies like Amazon and smaller retail partners can easily become one-sided, with the larger partner able to unilaterally change the terms of business, as Amazon did in 2013, demanding a larger take from its 'Marketplace' partners. Similarly, alliances are only as strong as the commitment of their individual members, and the WOW Alliance of cargo carriers was hurt when Lufthansa and Japan Airlines both pulled out, leaving only SAS and Singapore Airlines on board by 2010.[13] Ecosystems constantly change and evolve, with some relationships growing stronger while others weaken or are terminated.

In an organizational ecosystem, conflict and cooperation frequently exist at the same time. Procter & Gamble (P&G) and Clorox are fierce North American rivals in cleaning products and water purification, but both companies profited when they collaborated on a new cling film (called plastic wrap in North America). P&G invented a film that seals tightly only where it is pressed and won't stick elsewhere. Managers recognized the value of such a product, but P&G didn't have a cling film category. They thought a joint venture with Clorox to market the new film under the well-established Glad brand name would be more profitable than investing the time and money to establish P&G in a new product category. P&G shared the technology with Clorox in return for a 10 per cent stake in the Glad business, which P&G later boosted to 20 per cent.[14] Glad's share of the cling film market in the US shot up 23 per cent virtually overnight with the introduction of Glad Press 'n Seal. Since then, the two companies have continued the collaboration with the introduction of rubbish bags which make use of a stretchable plastic invented in P&G labs.[15] Mutual dependencies and partnerships have become a fact of life in business ecosystems. Is competition dead? Companies today may use their strength to win conflicts and negotiations, but ultimately continuing any genuine partnership demands a minimal level of cooperation.

IN PRACTICE

Amazon.com Inc.

Amazon.com was one of the earliest players in the world of online retailing, opening its virtual bookstore in 1995, before many people had even heard of the internet. Since then, Amazon has continued to evolve, from an online bookseller to an online retailer operating sales portals in Canada, the UK, Germany, Japan, France and China, as well as the original US site, with its own vast warehouses of books, DVDs, kitchen appliances and electronics. Amazon is now also a technology provider for other merchants. Today, Amazon sells everything from baby furniture to golf clubs, but its partners own and store most of the inventory. Amazon's websites serve as an online shopping mall where retailers set up shop to sell their wares to a vast global market. Amazon has partnerships with hundreds of small and large retailers, including Lovefilm, Hachette Livre and Lands End.

Amazon processes the orders and gets a cut of the sale, but retailers fill the orders from their own warehouses. The arrangement gives Amazon a way to expand into new businesses without making huge investments in inventory and developing the expertise to forecast hot products in multiple categories. As for the retailers, they get access to Amazon's global customer traffic, $100 million-plus annual spend on leading-edge technology and internet savvy, enabling them to focus on their bricks-and-mortar businesses.[16]

The partnership approach is not without its challenges. Toys 'R' Us, one of Amazon's earliest partners, sued the online firm and stopped selling its products through the company, charging that Amazon violated its contract when it began allowing other retailers to sell products that compete with Toys 'R' Us.[17] Hachette, the largest book publisher in the UK and France, was involved in a bitter and public dispute about the cut taken by Amazon, which it claimed exceeded 50 per cent of the book price, and which it said Amazon is pressing to increase even further.[18] The dispute was only concluded in late 2012, after years of litigation.[19] Some big companies, including Nike, oppose the sale of their goods on Amazon, fearing it might tarnish their premium brands. Amazon, however, insists that in the long run, the web of partnerships will benefit everyone.[20] One manufacturer that eventually agreed is Sony. Sony executives originally refused to authorize Amazon to sell Sony products, but realized they were fighting a losing battle to try and maintain control and exclusivity in the new world of internet retailing. Today, Sony products are big sellers on the site,[21] and the two companies have various collaborations to make each others' digital products available on their various platforms; for example, in 2012 Amazon Prime streaming video was made available on the PlayStation.[22]

The Changing Role of Management

Within business ecosystems managers learn to move beyond traditional responsibilities of corporate strategy and designing hierarchical structures and control systems. If a top manager looks down to enforce order and uniformity, the company is missing opportunities for new and evolving external relationships (see Counterpoint 6.4).[23] In this new world, managers think about horizontal processes in addition to vertical structures. Important initiatives are not just top down; they cut across the boundaries separating organizational units. Moreover, horizontal relationships, as described in Chapter 4, now include linkages with suppliers and customers, who become part of the team. Managers learn to see and appreciate the rich environment of opportunities that grow from cooperative relationships with other contributors to the ecosystem. As well as trying to force suppliers into low prices or customers into high prices, managers may also strive to strengthen the larger system evolving around them, finding ways to understand this big picture and how to contribute.

COUNTERPOINT 6.4

It is questionable whether these 'traditional responsibilities' are left behind. Established lines of accountability remain but are accompanied by (complexifying and sometimes contradictory) pressures to develop horizontal and collaborative processes.

In 2001 Donovan Neale-May, president of Neale-May & Partners, formed an alliance of 40 independent high-tech public relations agencies located all around the world, called GlobalFluency, to share information and market their services to acquire business that small, owner-run agencies have trouble winning on their own. 'We have companies – our own neighbours here in Colorado – that won't hire us because we don't have offices in 65 countries,' says John Metzger, CEO of a small PR firm. Now, with the power of GlobalFluency behind them, Metzger can share in accounts that once went only to large competitors. Alliance members still maintain their independence for small jobs, but by 2016, 70 partners in 40 countries could join together to pitch for regional projects or international campaigns. The E3 European Agency Network, comprised of 28 European marketing and communications firms, operates on much the same basis but with a primary focus on Europe. By 2011, E3 was ready to expand beyond Europe, taking on non-European firms as full partners for the first time, and by 2016 had six partners in Asia, North and South America.[24,25,26]

**ONLINE
COUNTERPOINT 6.1**

Interorganizational Framework

Understanding this larger organizational ecosystem is one of the most challenging areas of organization theory. The models and perspectives for understanding interorganizational relationships can be of assistance in developing horizontal management across organizations. A framework for analyzing the different views of interorganizational relationships is shown in Exhibit 6.1. Relationships among organizations can be characterized by whether the organizations are dissimilar or similar and whether relationships are competitive or cooperative. By understanding these perspectives, managers can assess their environment and adopt strategies to suit their needs. The first perspective is called resource-dependence theory, which was briefly described in Chapter 5. It describes rational ways in which dependence on the environment is reduced. The second perspective is about collaborative networks, through which dependencies upon other organizations are increased to enhance value and productivity for both. The third perspective is population ecology, which examines how new organizations fill niches left open by established organizations, and how a rich variety of new organizational forms emerges in response to the changing needs of society. The final approach is called institutionalism and explains why and how organizations legitimize themselves in the larger environment and structures are designed by borrowing ideas from each other. These four

EXHIBIT 6.1   A Framework of Interorganizational Relationships*

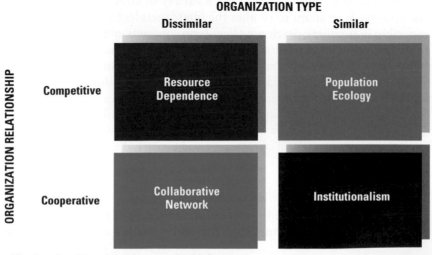

Thanks to Anand Narasimhan for suggesting this framework.

approaches to the study of interorganizational relationships are described in the remainder of this chapter.

Resource Dependence

As described in Chapter 5, resource dependence theory argues that managers in organizations try to minimize their dependence on other organizations for the supply of important resources and try to influence the environment to make resources available.[27] When threatened by greater dependence, managers will seek to assert control over external resources to minimize that dependence and so improve performance or avoid negative effects on performance.

BRIEFCASE 6.1

The amount of dependence on a resource is based on two factors. First is the importance of the resource to the organization, and second is how much discretion or monopoly power those who control a resource have over its allocation and use.[28] With an awareness of resource-dependence theory, executives may pursue strategies to reduce their dependence on the environment and learn how to use their power differences. As will be discussed below, the power differences between buyers and suppliers can be vast. Companies such as UK-headquartered Tesco or US-based Wal-Mart may be a supplier's largest, or even only customer. They often seem to hold all the cards in their relationships with suppliers, and are able to ensure the supplier meets their needs, which typically entails low price and fast, timely delivery.

COUNTERPOINT 6.5

Given their success in recent years, the buyer–supplier relationship modelled by Tesco and Wal-Mart might seem to be the preferable position vis-à-vis suppliers. However, as discussed later in this chapter, there has been some backlash against big chain domination, based on issues such as the environmental and long-term financial sustainability of this model, as well as the risk of market monopolization. There is increasing pressure on governments to regulate big chains' behaviour.[29] A recent study by Marjolein *et al.* of purchaser–supplier relationships in Holland found that the most satisfactory buyer–supplier relationships tended to occur when there was a high level of mutual dependence and interaction.[30] While awareness of the external environment is crucial, it does not necessarily follow that the best way of managing the external environment is to control it.

Resource Strategies

When resource or supply constraints are encountered, the resource-dependence perspective says they manoeuvre to maintain their autonomy through a variety of strategies, several of which were in Chapter 5. One strategy is to adapt to or alter the interdependent relationships. This could mean purchasing ownership in suppliers, developing long-term contracts, alliances or joint ventures to lock in necessary resources, or building relationships in other ways. Another technique is to use interlocking directorships, where for example boards of directors include members of the boards of supplier companies. Organizations may also join trade associations to coordinate their requirements, sign trade agreements or merge with another firm to guarantee resources and material supplies. Leaders of some organizations may engage in political actions, such as lobbying for new regulations or deregulation, favourable taxation, tariffs or subsidies, or push for new standards that make resource acquisition easier, maintain control of resources and hence reduce uncertainty.

?

ONLINE COUNTERPOINT 6.2

Power Strategies

In resource-dependence theory, the focus is upon differences of power – for example, between large, relatively independent companies with many options and small suppliers with few options.[31] With the growth of giant retail chains operating through hypermarkets, as well as online portals selling a vast range of goods, power in consumer products has shifted from vendors such as Unilever and Rubbermaid to these even bigger retailers, which can demand – and receive – special pricing deals. Companies like Carrefour, Amazon, Tesco and Wal-Mart have grown so large and powerful that they are often in a position to dictate the terms with almost any supplier. Consider Levi Strauss, which for much of its 150-year history was a powerful supplier with a jeans brand that millions of people wanted and retailers were eager to stock. 'When I first started in this business, retailers were a waystation to the consumer,' says Levi's former CEO Philip Marineau, who made the decision to supply to Wal-Mart despite the risks to his company. 'Manufacturers had a tendency to tell retailers how to do business.' But the balance of power has shifted dramatically. In order to sell to the big retailers, Levi Strauss overhauled its entire operation, from design and production to pricing and distribution. The company developed a new lower-priced brand, Levi's Signature, designed to sell through big chain stores like Wal-Mart and US, Canada and Australia-based Target stores. Levi jeans used to go from factories to a company-owned distribution centre where they were labelled, packed and sent on to retailers. Now, to meet the discount chains' need to get products fast, jeans are shipped already tagged from contract factories direct to store-run distribution centres, where they are picked up and delivered to individual stores.[32,33] When one company has greater market power over another, it can ask suppliers to absorb more costs, ship more efficiently and provide more services than ever before, frequently without a price increase. Often the suppliers assess that they have no choice but to go along, and those who fail to do so may go out of business.

The shift to selling through the big box retailers was a partial success for Levi's. Company performance, which had been lagging badly in 2003, picked up. But by 2006 Wal-Mart had cut back on the space it allocated in the store to Levi's products in favour of stocking more 'private label' jeans, which generate a higher profit margin for the retailer. One interpretation is that Wal-Mart used Levi's brand power to bring customers into the store, but once it had them there, it really wanted to sell them higher-margin goods that it sourced itself from low-cost developing countries. Levi's re-examined its strategy. First of all, it found that while the Signature concept worked well in North America and Asia-Pacific, big-box outlets like Wal-Mart were nowhere near as dominant in Europe where the opportunities and benefits of selling the lower cost brand were missing. It stopped selling Signature jeans in Europe. Second, the company found that there were greater profit opportunities in selling through its own Levi's stores. It expanded its chain – both company-owned and franchised – in the US, Europe and Asia-Pacific. Third, the company took note of the rapid growth in consumer power in developing markets in the Asia region, and decided to open 150 Levi brand stores in the region over the next few years.[34] In other words, key to Levi's resurgence was its reduction of dependence upon retail outlets over which it could exert little control. In common with other companies with well-known brands, such as Sony, Apple and Nike, it expanded through its retail outlets that also serve to promote the brand name.

Levi's counter-strategy towards Wal-Mart and the other discount retailers seemed to pay off. The company's results improved steadily between 2006 and 2008. The Signature brand declined in importance to Levi's bottom line, accounting for six per cent of sales in 2007, down from ten per cent in 2005.[35] Like many companies, Levi Strauss hoped that it would be able to gain an ever increasing share of sales in the fast-growing Asian region, and at one point planned that by 2013 the majority of its sales would be outside the US. However, like many firms, Levi Strauss underestimated the complexity of expanding across Asia. It designed a new sub-brand, Levi Denizen, to appeal to a lower price point in Asia, but tried to sell the same product across many diverse countries in Asia-Pacific, where body types and fashion tastes vary widely. Further, the Denizen brand diluted Levi's USP: its global brand recognition as an iconic product. Consumers in Asia-Pacific wanted to buy the 'real thing'. In 2012 Levi's quietly dropped Denizen (except ironically in the US where it was doing well). Asian consumers, too, also proved susceptible to the global recession; sales dropped there and in Europe, though analysts still rated the company a strong 'buy' because of the strength of its iconic brand, and by 2015 sales were rising again in both Europe and Asia.[36,37]

An ever-shifting environment is also the norm today in other industries. For decades, a few large software companies have dominated the market, creating near-monopoly situations and making it difficult for customers to choose a range of software from different vendors that will work together smoothly on their machines. Those days seem to be coming to an end, particularly in non-specialist software. Many companies are considering reducing their dependence upon Microsoft, the market-leader in operating software, in favour of open source software, notably Linux. In addition, government regulators in Europe and the United States have launched a variety of legal actions designed to force Microsoft to make its operating and office systems software more compatible with competitors' add-on products. Several governments in Europe and Asia are requiring software to be written in a standard code that can then be adapted to end-users' needs. In response, Microsoft has revised its strategy. In order to reduce the risks of being pushed out of the market, it is turning over more of its programme code to open source software developers, and is also aiming to produce its own version of open source code, allowing it to maintain an edge over its traditional competition, though not necessarily protecting it from the trend to portable devices and cloud-based software.[38] Similarly, in the rapidly growing sphere of mobile computing, the major actors, including particularly Apple and Samsung, were locked in mortal combat in the courts as well as the marketplace to determine the future characteristics of the market. However, no-one should rule out the potential for emerging actors like China's Huawei and Xiaomi, which have already badly hurt Samsung in the Chinese market, to upset the applecart. The era of secure market dominance appears to be over.[39]

Collaborative Networks

ONLINE
COUNTERPOINT 6.3

In traditional business mythology, as has often been taught in North American business schools, the relationship between organizations and their suppliers has been an adversarial one. North American companies are praised for working alone, competing with each other and believing in the tradition of individualism and self-reliance. Nowadays, this simple view of corporate independence, which may always have been an exaggeration of actual business relationships, is being challenged. The **collaborative-network** perspective is an emerging alternative to resource-dependence theory. Companies join together to become more competitive and to share scarce resources. Technology companies join together to produce next-generation products. Large aerospace firms partner with one another, and with smaller companies and suppliers, to design next-generation jets. Large pharmaceutical companies join with small biotechnology firms to share resources and knowledge and spur innovation. Consulting firms, investment companies and accounting firms may join in an alliance to meet customer demands for expanded services.[40] As companies move into their own uncharted territory, they are also racing into alliances.

Why Collaboration?

ONLINE
COUNTERPOINT 6.4

Why all this interest in interorganizational collaboration? Major reasons are sharing risks when entering new markets, mounting expensive new programmes and reducing costs and enhancing organizational profile in selected industries or technologies. Cooperation is a prerequisite for greater innovation, problem solving and performance.[41] In addition, partnerships are a major avenue for entering global markets, with both large and small firms developing partnerships across the world.

International experience shows just how effective interorganizational relationships can be. Asian countries including Japan, Korea and India have long traditions of corporate clans or industrial groups that collaborate and assist each other.[42] European companies often work together closely through cross-shareholdings, interlocking directorships, groupings of associated companies and industrial groups encompassing many different businesses.

North Americans (and US-dominated international institutions like the International Monetary Fund) by contrast have often considered interdependence a bad thing, believing it would reduce competition and hide inefficiencies. However, the experience of collaboration has shown that competition among companies can be fierce in some areas even as they collaborate in others. Interorganizational linkages provide a kind of safety net that encourages long-term investment and risk taking. Companies can achieve higher levels of innovation and performance as they learn to shift from an adversarial to a partnership mindset.[43] However, in today's quickly restructuring global business environment, partnerships and alliances can often switch rapidly, or end up in mergers and takeovers. Consider the following examples:

- Carlos Ghosn, President and CEO both of France's Renault and Japan's Nissan, has staked his career on building innovative alliances all over the world. After turning Nissan around from a near moribund position to a brief period when the company's profits were higher than Toyota, Ghosn launched a series of ever more daring alliances. These included a Nissan-branded car for the Russian market built in South Korea by a Renault-Samsung tie-up, a sub $3000 car to be built in India in conjunction with the motorbike manufacturer Bajaj, and a deal whereby Nissan would supply small cars for Chrysler to sell under its brand name, and Chrysler would build pick-up trucks for Nissan to brand and sell. Not all the projects come to fruition: the Nissan-Renault-Bajaj of India tie-up was eventually abandoned in 2012. However, Ghosn then moved on to revive the old Datsun brand as a low cost entry in emerging markets, starting with new models in India and Indonesia in 2013 and 2014, and in late 2015, the Renault Kwid priced below $4000.[44] The Chrysler alliance foundered when Chrysler decided instead to stake its future with the Italian manufacturer Fiat, but Ghosn then developed an agreement with Chrsyler's former owners, Daimler.[45] Ghosn frequently makes shareholders nervous with his bold alliances and other innovative strategies, but he points out that his Nissan-Renault tie-up is the only major automakers' collaboration that has created rather than destroyed shareholder value.[46,47]

- The German-headquartered pharmaceuticals giant Merck entered into a collaboration programme with the Indian firm Ranbaxy (now part of India's SunPharma group) for development of antiviral and anti-tuberculosis medications. Merck has established major research programmes with 44 different companies, universities and research institutions around the word in search of more effective treatments of conditions ranging from cancer to schizophrenia.[48] Other multinational pharmaceutical firms have followed Merck's strategy of partnerships with Indian manufacturers rather than using a buy-out approach. At least eight Indian firms had signed such agreements by 2012.[49]

- Turkish appliance manufacturer Arcelik – Europe's third largest appliance builder – teamed with New Zealand appliance builder Fisher and Paykel, giving Fisher and Paykel, a high quality but isolated manufacturer, access to the large and growing markets of Central and Eastern Europe, where Arcelik is strong. In return, Arcelik hoped to tie into the New Zealand firm's top notch engineering and design expertise.[50] The partnership went well for some time but eventually the rapidly growing Chinese white goods firm Haier made a play for F&P, first buying 20 per cent of the company and then eventually purchasing the company outright in 2012. Arcelik continued seeking out partnerships to expand its footprint outside its European base; in 2012 it signed a deal with India's largest air conditioner manufacturer Voltas to develop and sell a range of white goods in that country.[51]

From Adversaries to Partners

Evidence from studies of such companies as Renault, Toyota and Microsoft indicate that partnering can allow reduced cost and increased value for both parties in a predatory world economy.[52,53] Rather than organizations maintaining independence, the new model is based on interdependence and trust. A summary of this change in mindset from a traditional adversarial mindset to a partnership orientation is to be found in Exhibit 6.2. Performance measures for the partnership are loosely defined, and problems are resolved through discussion and dialogue. Managing strategic relationships with other firms has become a critical management skill, as discussed in this chapter's *Bookmark 6.0*. In the new orientation, people try to add value to both sides and believe in collaboration rather than suspicion and competition. Companies work toward equitable profits for both sides rather than just for their own benefit. The new model is characterized by lots of shared information, including electronic linkages for automatic ordering and face-to-face discussions to provide corrective feedback and solve problems. Sometimes people from other companies are on site to enable very close coordination. Partners are involved in each other's product design and production, and they invest for the long term, with an assumption of continuing relations. Partners develop equitable solutions to conflicts rather than relying on legal contractual relationships. Contracts may be loosely specified, and it is not unusual for business partners to help each other outside whatever is specified in the contract.[54]

For example, AMP, a manufacturer of electronics and electrical connectors (since bought by the US-based multinational Tyco Electronics)[55] was contacted by a customer about a broken connector that posed serious problems. It wasn't even AMP's connector, but the vice president and his sales manager went to a warehouse at the weekend and found replacement parts to get the customer back online. They provided the service with no charge as a way to enhance the relationship. Indeed, this kind of teamwork treats partner companies almost like departments of one's own organization.[56]

This new partnership mindset can be seen in a number of industries. As discussed above, Microsoft hired the Singapore-based contract manufacturer Flextronics to build but also to help design Xbox, its electronic game console.[57] Flextronics went on to build a partnership with Google; in 2012 it purchased a former Motorola mobile phone factory from Google, but continues to produce phones there for Google, as well as work closely with its larger partner on

EXHIBIT 6.2 Changing Characteristics of Interorganizational Relationships

Traditional Orientation: Adversarial	New Orientation: Partnership
Low dependence	High dependence
Suspicion, competition, arm's length	Trust, addition of value to both sides, high commitment
Detailed performance measures, closely monitored	Loose performance measures, problems discussed
Price, efficacy, own profits, limited information and feedback	Equity, fair dealing, both profit
	Electronic linkages to share key information, problem feedback and discussion
Legal resolution of conflict	Mechanisms for close coordination, people on site
Minimal involvement and up-front investment, separate resources	Involvement in partner's product design and production, shared resources
Short-term contracts	Long-term contracts
Contract limiting the relationship	Business assistance beyond the contract

Source: Based on Mick Marchington and Steven Vincent, 'Analysing the Influence of Institutional, Organizational and Interpersonal Forces in Shaping Inter-Organizational Relations', *Journal of Management Studies* 41, No. 6 (September 2004), 1029–1056; Jeffrey H. Dyer, 'How Chrysler Created an American Keiretsu', *Harvard Business Review* (July–August 1996), 42–56; Myron Magnet, 'The New Golden Rule of Business', *Fortune* (February 21, 1994), 60–64; and Peter Grittner, 'Four Elements of Successful Sourcing Strategies', *Management Review* (October 1995), 41–45.

supply chain management in Google's mobile phone ventures worldwide. When Google sold its Motorola brand to China's Lenovo in 2014, Flextronics did a deal to build phones for Lenovo in its Chennai, India plant, that opened in 2015.[58,59] Many supermarkets and other retailers rely on key suppliers to help them determine what goes on the store shelves. In a large vendor such as Procter & Gamble, for example, national data are analyzed to make recommendations for what products to offer, including not just P&G's brands, but products from its competitors as well.[60] A large British company that supplies pigments to the automobile, plastics and printing industries has a long-standing interdependent relationship with a key chemicals supplier, with the two organizations sharing information about their long-term business needs so that any changes in products or processes can benefit both sides.[61]

In this new view of partnerships, dependence on another company is seen to offer the potential to reduce risks. Greater value, it is argued, can be achieved by both parties. By being embedded in a system of interorganizational relationships, it is possible for all parties to benefit by helping each other. This is a far cry from the belief that organizations do best by being independent. Sales representatives may have a desk on the customer's factory floor, and they have access to information systems and the research lab.[62] Coordination is so intimate that it's sometimes hard to tell one organization from another. Consider, in the next *In Practice* box, how Canada's Bombardier and its suppliers were linked together almost like one organization in building the Challenger, a 'super-midsize' business jet that can comfortably fly eight passengers nonstop from coast to coast in North America.

BOOKMARK 3.0

Have you read this book?

Business as Unusual

BY ANITA RODDICK

Often in management texts there is an assumption that there is *one* best way to do business. It is clear that this is untrue, because companies that pursue very different strategies and ways of organizing are often successful in the same industry. In British retailing, for example, Asda and Waitrose have both enjoyed continuing growth, even though they follow almost diametrically opposed management styles. Asda is hierarchical and attempts to impose a uniform corporate culture, while Waitrose is employee-owned, and encourages employee individuality. They can both perform well, albeit targeting different consumer segments.

There are few more striking examples of the different paths to success than that followed by Anita Roddick. From small beginnings in the late 1970s Roddick built her Body Shop into one of the largest and most successful personal care product chains in the world, all the while determined to 'push the limits of business, to change its language, to make it a force for positive change'.

Roddick's autobiography, written not long before her untimely death in 2006, describes her own ascent to success but is above all a ringing indictment of contemporary business practices and a clarion call for change. Roddick explores some of the reasons she has been successful; these include being prepared to ignore and overcome barriers, whether unsympathetic bank managers or those who think women do not make good business leaders. She says many great entrepreneurs were outsiders; many are from immigrant communities. Others, like Roddick, suffered deprivation, whether financial or emotional; Roddick's father died suddenly when she was ten, turning her family life upside down and forcing her to decide her life path for herself. There is typically, she says, a hunger to succeed. This must translate into passion to communicate what is unique about the business, which in Roddick's case included a firm belief that Body Shop's success would contribute not merely to the financial bottom line but would also help further the social and political causes in which she believed so passionately. She underlines her frustration and disgust with mainstream business. Some examples she lists of unacceptable business practices include:

- Footloose business that abandons communities, leaving them polluted and jobless.

- The greed of corporate bosses like Disney's Michael Eisner who earned as much in one day as Third World labourers who manufacture Disney-labelled clothing would make in 166 years.

- Unfair trade agreements that allow companies to uproot well-paid, regulated jobs in the US in favour of production facilities on the Mexican side of the US-Mexico border, where labour and environmental protections are almost non-existent.

- The overwhelming impact of consumer advertising, creating a population manipulated to desire ever more ecologically unsustainable possessions, and resulting in both an ecological and a cultural monoculture.

Unlike most business leaders, who tend to demand fewer regulations (sometimes with disastrous effects such as the 2007 sub-prime crisis which was largely caused by inadequate financial regulation), Roddick's prescriptions for making business healthier included more regulation, encouraging consumer consciousness about the products they desire and buy and more responsibility on the part of business leaders. She summarizes her vision as 'spiritual business', the idea that business must act to protect and sustain the world, including 'humans, animals and the Earth itself'. She also demands that:

Any future business education programme, whether set in a local or global context, must contain the language and action of social justice, human rights, community economics and ethics, as well as the productivity of the human soul. (p. 27)

While Anglo-American business schools tend to teach students to worry only about the bottom line, Roddick emphasizes the *ethical audit*. While there are various versions of this, some only superficial, her version includes a thorough 'values report' that looks at all of Body Shop's relationships, from employees and suppliers to shareholders and to local communities.

Based on this report, Roddick's Body Shop developed and implemented an action plan to improve weak points. Another major element of the ethical audit is an environmental audit; a key objective for Body Shop in this area was aiming towards zero emissions, not just from Body Shop itself but also its suppliers and even in turn, their suppliers. An example of Roddick's preparedness to put the public good ahead of narrow business objectives was her campaign against the tyranny of the beauty business. While worries about appearance undoubtedly encourage women to buy more beauty products, including those from the Body Shop, Roddick didn't want to get rich on the basis of media and advertising industry-cultivated body insecurity. Under Roddick, the company invested heavily in campaigns warning women against the tyranny of unreasonable expectations around their bodies and self-image.

Roddick readily admits that the company has made mistakes – especially in the United States where Body Shop began by listening to marketing orthodoxy and became sucked in to mass marketing and mall culture, which made it hard for Body Shop to stand out for its unique qualities. Sales slowed in the mid-90s and franchisees started demanding even more concessions to US marketing norms such as constant price discounting. Instead of going down that slippery slope, the Body Shop stopped and looked at itself and its values. It moved out of malls, and focused on urban neighbourhood stores with their own diverse cultures and shopping environments. Bit by bit, the company's US performance improved, by sticking to its values rather than selling out to the bland sameness that has blighted so many aspects of American communities.

The bottom line of Anita Roddick's message to starting entrepreneurs: design organizations your way, with values and a mission you believe in, or don't bother doing it at all.

Business as Unusual, by Anita Roddick, is published by Anita Roddick Books

By breaking down boundaries and becoming involved in partnerships, today's companies are changing the concept of what makes an organization. The type of collaborative network illustrated by Bombardier is also being used by a growing number of automotive companies, as shown by the examples of Renault, Nissan and their partners discussed earlier in this chapter. These companies are pushing the idea of partnership further than ever before, moving somewhat toward a network approach to organization design, as described in Chapter 4.

Bombardier

In an assembly plant on the edge of Mid-Continent Airport in Wichita, a new plane is taking shape as great chunks of it are rolled in and joined together. Not counting rivets, it takes just a dozen big parts – all manufactured elsewhere – to put Bombardier's Challenger business jet (formerly called the Continental) together. Those big subassemblies come from all over the world – the engines from Phoenix in the United States, the nose and cockpit from Montreal, Canada, the mid-fuselage from Belfast, Northern Ireland, the tail from Taichung, Taiwan, the wings from Nagoya, Japan and other parts from Australia, France, Germany and Austria. When production is up to full speed, it takes just four days to put a plane together and get it in the air.

In the past, most executive-jet companies made major parts in-house. For the Challenger, which started commercial service in 2004, Canada's Bombardier instead relied heavily on suppliers for design support and the sharing of development costs and market risks.[63] The company is intertwined with about 30 suppliers, a dozen or so of which have been involved since the design stage. At one point, about 250 team members from Bombardier and 250 from outside suppliers worked together in Montreal to make sure the design was going to be good for everyone involved. Bombardier invested heavily in bringing the Challenger to market, but suppliers equalled that amount in development costs. In addition to sharing costs, the supplier companies also shared the risks. 'They haven't got a contract that says, "You're going to sell us 25 wings a year for the next 10 years". If the market's there, it's there, and if it's not, it's not,' says John Holding, who was in charge of Bombardier's engineering and product development during the development of the Challenger. The results of all the collaboration have been impressive; the Challenger is one of the most successful business jets of all time, with over half of worldwide deliveries in its sector in the latter half of the 2000s. Despite some bumps along the way that included a 2015 bailout from the Quebec, Canada government,[64] the company has continued its market dominance in the sector in the second decade of the twenty-first century, for example inking a deal in to sell up to 375 Challengers to Warren Buffet's NetJets firm over the next ten years.[65,66]

Integrating partners so that everyone benefits from and depends on the others – and managing this multinational, multicompany endeavour – is no easy task, but with development costs for a new plane reaching more than $1 billion, the partnership approach just makes sense.[67]

Population Ecology

This section introduces a different perspective on relationships among organizations. The population-ecology perspective focuses on organizational diversity and adaptation within a population of organizations.[68] A population is a set of organizations engaged in similar activities with similar patterns of resource utilization and outcomes. Organizations within a population compete for similar resources or similar customers, such as newspaper publishing organizations in Ireland.[69]

Within a population, the question asked by ecology researchers is about the large number and variation of organizations in society. Why are new organizational forms that create such diversity constantly appearing? The answer is that individual organizational adaptation is severely limited compared to the changes demanded by the environment (see Counterpoint 6.6). Innovation and change in a population of organizations take place through the birth of new forms and kinds of organizations more than by the reform and change of existing organizations. Indeed, organizational forms are considered relatively stable, and the good of a whole society is served by the development of new forms of organization through entrepreneurial initiatives. New organizations meet the new needs of society more than established organizations that are slow to change.[70]

COUNTERPOINT 6.6

What is not explained in population ecology theory is how such changes are 'demanded' by the environment. What accounts for the changes and how are the demands conveyed to organizations? Population ecology theory does not, for example, consider how environments are changed politically – by pressures being exerted upon, and by, politicians who change regulations, thereby creating or restricting existing markets and opening up new opportunities. Nor does population ecology pay attention to how organizations comprise much of the 'environment' and actively exert effects on its development. In part, budget airlines have emerged as a consequence of changes in the regulatory environment but their presence and growth has contributed greatly to the development of that environment to which established carriers have struggled to respond.

What does this theory mean in practical terms? It means that large, established organizations often become dinosaurs. As discussed in the previous chapter, many large European airlines that relied on business travellers, protected markets and nationalist loyalty have had tremendous difficulty adapting to a rapidly changing environment including the removal of national barriers to entry and the emergence of a new passenger mass market. Hence, new organizational forms such as Ryanair are emerging that fit the current environment, fill a new niche and, over time, take away business from established companies.

Why do established organizations have such a hard time adapting to a rapidly changing environment? Michael Hannan and John Freeman, originators of the population ecology model of organization, argue that there are many restrictions on the ability of organizations to change. The limitations come from heavy investment in plants, equipment and specialized personnel, limited information, established viewpoints of decision-makers, the organization's own successful history that justifies current procedures and the difficulty of changing corporate culture. True transformation is a rare and unlikely event in the face of all these barriers.[71]

New organizational forms are emerging all the time. As discussed earlier in this chapter, the advertising industry has generated alliances like E3 European Agency Network and Global Fluency, responding to the desire of small firms to trade up to bigger contracts. The same process of organizational transformation has occurred from the top down, with large advertising companies restructuring themselves as holding companies like London-headquartered WPP Group with separately incorporated and quasi-independent subsidiaries all over the world, thus getting around client concerns about potential conflict of interest when the same firm is working for competitors in the same business.[72,73] Another recent change is the development of 'corporate universities' within large companies like France's Accor, Fujitsu from Japan, Daimler and Volkswagen from Germany and Petrobras in Brazil.[74] Although the definition of corporate university is sometimes stretched to include training activities that companies have been carrying out for many years, there is little doubt that the phenomenon is important and growing. There are estimated to be more than 2000 corporate universities in North America and another 1000 in Europe. Emerging economy corporations are jumping on to the bandwagon, too; Wipro and Accenture, two Indian high-tech giants, have both opened corporate universities, as have Bank of China and China Life Insurance Company among many others in China.[75] In the UK, government has endorsed the corporate university phenomenon; the low cost airline Flybe and the rail infrastructure operator Network Rail have each been granted accreditation to award nationally recognized qualifications up to university degree level.[76,77] Some innovative companies like Google are taking the concept beyond the firm in providing university-like environments for budding outside entrepreneurs (such as Google Campus in east London, UK, established in 2012), which combine business learning with access to expert support and capital. This not only serves to build Google's image in the community but also gives the company an insight into cutting edge technology thinking.[78]

According to the population-ecology view, when looking at an organizational population as a whole, the changing environment determines which organizations survive or fail. The assumption is that individual organizations suffer from structural inertia and find it difficult to adapt to environmental changes. Thus, when rapid change occurs, old organizations are likely to decline or fail, and new organizations emerge that are better suited to the needs of the environment.

BRIEFCASE 6.3

The population-ecology model is developed from theories of natural selection in biology, and the terms *evolution* and *selection* are used to refer to the underlying behavioural processes. Theories of biological evolution try to explain why certain life forms appear and survive whereas others perish. Some theories suggest the forms that survive are typically best fitted to the immediate environment.

Some years ago, *Forbes* magazine reported a study of American businesses over 70 years, from 1917 to 1987. Have you heard of Baldwin Locomotive, Studebaker or Lehigh Coal & Navigation? These companies were among 78 per cent of the top 100 in 1917 that did not see 1987. Of the 22 that remained in the top 100, only 11 did so under their original names. The environment of the 1940s and 1950s was suitable to Woolworth, but new organizational forms like Wal-Mart became dominant in the 1980s. In 1917, most of the top 100 companies were huge steel and mining industrial organizations, which were replaced by high-technology companies such as IBM and Merck.[79] Two companies that seemed to prosper over a long period were Ford and General Motors, but in the 2000s they have gone through major crises, partly due to the emergence of global competition in the car industry. No company is immune to the processes of social change. From just 1979 to 1989, 187 of the companies on the *Fortune* 500 list ceased to exist as independent companies. Some were acquired, some merged and some were liquidated.[80] Corporate casualties in British manufacturing industry in the past 50 years have been even more dramatic.[81] Meanwhile, technology continues to change the environment. All over the world, the giant telecommunications monopolies that once decided when, and even if, we might be able to hope to have a landline telephone connection have been outpaced and often nearly eclipsed by mobile phone companies offering an ever expanding range of services on their handsets. The internet has infiltrated far beyond the office and into everyday lives of citizens; for a new generation of youth, Facebook and YouTube are every bit as important as the radio and TV were for their parents and grandparents.

Organizational Form and Niche

The population-ecology model is concerned with organizational forms. Organizational form is an organization's specific technology, structure, products, goals and personnel, which is selected or rejected by the environment. Each new organization is contingent upon finding a niche (a domain of unique environmental resources and needs) sufficient to support it.

From the viewpoint of a single firm, luck, chance and randomness play important parts in survival. New products and ideas are continually being proposed by both entrepreneurs and large organizations. Whether these ideas and organizational forms survive or fail is often a matter of chance – whether external circumstances happen to support them. A woman who started a small electronics assembly subcontracting business in Estonia in the 1990s would have had an excellent chance of success. If the same woman were to start the same business in a country with a relatively expensive manufacturing base such as the UK, the chance of success might be far less. Success or failure of a single firm thus is predicted by the characteristics of the environment rather than by reference to by the skills or strategies used by the organization.

Process of Ecological Change

The population-ecology model assumes that new organizations are always appearing in the population. Thus, organization populations are continually undergoing change. The process of change

EXHIBIT 6.3   Elements in the Population-Ecology Model of Organizations

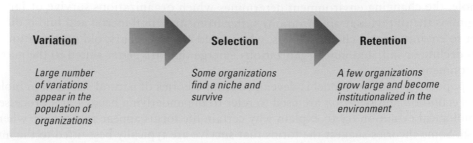

in the population is defined by three principles that occur in stages: variation, selection and retention. These stages are summarized in Exhibit 6.3.

■ *Variation*. Variation means the appearance of new, diverse forms in a population of organizations. These new organizational forms are typically initiated by entrepreneurs, established with venture capital by large corporations, or set up by a government seeking to provide new services. Some forms may be conceived to cope with a perceived need in the external environment. In recent years, a large number of new firms have been initiated to develop computer software, to provide consulting and other services to large corporations and to develop products and technologies for internet commerce. Other new organizations produce a traditional product such as steel, but do it using minimal technology and new management techniques that allow the company to survive and prosper. Lakshmi Mittal's Ispat Steel purchased declining steel plants in the former Communist bloc and turned them around by focusing on cost and appropriate markets rather than the expensive high-technology investments that more traditional Western steel producers had proposed.[82] Organizational variations are analogous to mutations in biology, and they add to the scope and complexity of organizational forms in the environment. This chapter's *Leading by Design* box describes a new organizational form conceived by a British entrepreneur to capitalize on advances in information technology and wireless text messaging.

■ *Selection*. Selection refers to whether a new organizational form is suited to the environment and can survive. Only a few variations are 'selected in' by the environment and survive over the long term. Some variations will suit the external environment better than others. Other variations fail to meet the needs of the environment and perish. When there is insufficient demand for a firm's product and when insufficient resources are available to the organization, that organization will be 'selected out'. For example, London-based Shazam, described in the *Leading by Design* box, was launched in mid-2002. If demand for the new service does not continue to grow, or if the company cannot obtain needed resources, the company will be selected out and cease to exist.

■ *Retention*. Retention is the preservation and institutionalization of selected organizational forms. Institutionalization of an organizational form means that it becomes a general norm in society. Certain technologies, products and services are highly valued by the environment. The organizational form associated with those technologies, products or services may become a dominant part of the environment. Many forms of organization have been institutionalized, such as government, schools, churches and banking institutions. McDonald's, which operates in 119 countries and provides the first job for many teenagers around the world, has become institutionalized in contemporary global life.

Institutionalized organizations like McDonald's seem to be relatively permanent features in the population of organizations, but they are not permanent in the long run. The environment is always changing, and, if the dominant organizational forms do not or cannot adapt

ONLINE
COUNTERPOINT 6.6

to external change, they will gradually diminish and be replaced by other organizations. McDonald's has had to adjust its menu to provide more healthy options, and respond to criticism about its environmental record and unhealthy fast food in order to remain on top.[83,84] The company initially did well during the global financial crisis that began in 2008, but by 2013 was being hit by the renewed vigour of competitors like Burger King.[85] British coal mines were once a highly institutionalized part of national life, but as alternative, cleaner forms of fuel came on-stream in the 1950s and 1960s, and cities started restricting use of coal fires as an anti-pollution measure, they entered a downward spiral from which they never recovered.[86]

From the population-ecology perspective, the environment is the important determinant of organizational success or failure. The organization must meet an environmental need, or it will be selected out. The process of variation, selection and retention leads to the establishment of new organizational forms in a population of organizations.

Strategies for Survival

Another principle that underlies the population ecology model is the struggle for existence, or competition. Organizations and populations of organizations are engaged in a competitive struggle over resources, and each organizational form is fighting to survive. The struggle is most intense among new organizations, and both the birth and survival frequencies of new organizations are related to factors in the larger environment. Factors such as size of urban area, percentage of

LEADING BY DESIGN

Shazam – It's Magic!

Many people have had the experience of hearing a song they like on the radio or in a dance club and waiting in vain for the DJ to identify it. Shazam, a mobile-phone music service launched in the United Kingdom in August 2002, has come to the rescue. The next time a mobile phone user hears that mystery tune, all he or she has to do is dial a four-digit number on the mobile phone, let the music play into the handset, and moments later receive a text message with the artist and song title. The user can forward a 30-second clip of the track to friends, or even download the song directly to his or her phone. The song can then be legally copied from the mobile phone to a PC and shared between multiple devices.

Shazam's magic happens through the use of a pattern-recognition software algorithm developed by the company's chief scientist. The algorithm picks out the salient characteristics of a tune and matches them against a massive music database. The company,

founded by Californian entrepreneur Chris Barton, calls the process 'tagging', and by 2012 Shazam claimed that worldwide its users had 'tagged' five billion songs, TV shows and advertisements. Users can go online and see a list of all the songs they've tagged.

Shazam's success depends on collaborative partnerships with mobile phone companies, major record labels, software companies and others. A partnership with Swiss-based SDC (Secure Digital Container) AG provides the technology that enables a complete 'tag to download' in three simple steps, allowing users to purchase music on the move. A strategic alliance with MTV Japan helped Shazam expand to about 40 million mobile phone subscribers in Japan. Deals with international mobile operators and media companies throughout the United States, Europe and Asia make Shazam's service available to more than 1 billion mobile phone users worldwide. By 2013 Shazam claimed it had 300 million users.

The mobile phone companies offer tagging as a premium service to their customers and pay Shazam a cut of the profits. Since tagging promises to drive up call times, most mobile phone companies are interested. And the record labels' interests are served by getting new music in front of consumers. Word-of-mouth recommendations are a powerful means of driving music sales, so the idea of people

▶

all over the world forwarding 30-second clips of their new songs has music companies paying attention. The service has proven to be a good predictor of future hits in Britain, so the music industry closely watches Shazam's weekly chart of tagged pre-release tracks. Shazam is the world's first in music recognition and one of the brightest new ideas in the world of technology. With multiple deals and a presence in 12 countries, it is clear that Shazam is suited to the environment and has found a solid niche. The company has gone from strength to strength, poaching some of the world's top talent to join its management and ideas team, such as Daniel Danker who developed BBC's highly successful

iPlayer platform. The company is branching out into new areas, aiming to become a one-stop shop for users to identify goods they might want to buy on media they watch, such as the fashion line Selena Gomez is wearing[87] on her recent music video, for example![88]

Sources: 'SDC Partners with Shazam to Create Simple, Secure Music Download', *M2Presswire* (February 14, 2005), 1; Steve McClure, 'Shazam Works Its Magic', *Billboard* (August 21, 2004), 60; Adam Jolly, 'Going for a Song and Growth', *Sunday Times* (June 13, 2004), 17; Michael Parsons, 'I Got Music, I Got Algorithm', *Red Herring* (May 2002), 54–57; and 'MTV and Shazam Lead Japanese Market Extending Music Recognition Offering to KDDI Subscribers and Expanding Local Music Database', *M2Presswire* (February 16, 2005), 1.

immigrants, political turbulence, industry growth rate and environmental variability have influenced the launching and survival of newspapers, telecommunication firms, railroads, government agencies, labour unions and even voluntary organizations.[89]

In the population ecology perspective, generalist and specialist strategies distinguish organizational forms in the struggle for survival. Organizations with a wide niche or domain, that is, those that offer a broad range of products or services or that serve a broad market, are generalists. Organizations that provide a narrower range of goods or services or that serve a narrower market are specialists.

In the natural environment, a specialist form of flora and fauna would evolve in protective isolation in a place like Australia, where the nearest major body of land is 2500 miles away. The flora and fauna are heavily protected. In contrast, a place like Costa Rica, which experienced wave after wave of external influences, developed a generalist set of flora and fauna that has better resilience and flexibility for adapting to a broad range of circumstances. In the business world, Amazon.com started with a specialist strategy, selling books over the internet, but evolved to a generalist strategy with the addition of music, DVDs, greeting cards and other products, plus partnering with other organizations as an online shopping mall to sell a wide range of products. A company such as the Germany-headquartered Steiff which sells high-end teddy bears,[90] would be considered a specialist, whereas Chad Valley is a generalist, marketing a broad range of toys for boys and girls up to ten years old.[91]

Specialists are generally more competitive than generalists in the narrow area in which their domains overlap. However, the breadth of the generalist's domain serves to protect it somewhat from environmental changes. Though demand may decrease for some of the generalist's products or services, it usually increases for others at the same time. In addition, because of the diversity of products, services and customers, generalists are able to reallocate resources internally to adapt to a changing environment, whereas specialists are not. However, because specialists are often smaller companies, they can sometimes move faster and be more flexible in adapting to changes.[92]

Managerial impact on company success often comes from selecting a strategy that steers a company into an open niche. Consider how Genentech has thrived after a new CEO steered it into a new niche in the pharmaceuticals industry. Genentech isn't immune from the volatility and uncertainty inherent in the industry, but managers found a niche that put the company on a solid foundation for survival over the long term. CEO Levinson chose a specialist strategy, focusing on specific therapies for relatively small subsets of patients rather than looking for one-size-fits-all blockbuster drugs.

ONLINE
COUNTERPOINT 6.7

Genentech

California-based Genentech, founded in 1976, was the world's first biotechnology firm, and its creation spurred the development of a whole new subset in the pharmaceuticals industry. A wide variety of small biotech firms have been established, with each struggling to find a niche that will enable the company to survive in the volatile, competitive world of drug development and manufacturing.

Genentech spent its early years trying to bring out blockbuster drugs and grow into a company on the scale of pharmaceutical giants like Schering-Plough or Merck. But its first potential blockbusters fizzled, and the company's fortunes dwindled. Things began to turn around when Genentech's research director, Arthur Levinson, was appointed CEO. Levinson turned the company in a new direction. Rather than betting the farm on blockbusters, Levinson chose a strategy of developing 'targeted drugs', lucrative new medicines that are aimed at small sets of patients. For example, Herceptin, Genentech's first targeted therapy launched several years ago, is a breast-cancer drug that is prescribed to only the 25 per cent of patients whose tumours reveal a specific genetic characteristic. Other targeted treatments include Rituxan, for treating an immune-cell cancer called non-Hodgkin's lymphoma, Xolair, a treatment for a type of allergic asthma, and in 2012 Pertuzumab was approved for the treatment of patients with advanced (metastatic) breast cancer.

Large drug companies are struggling in an industry that is being threatened by changes in managed care, the expiration of numerous drug patents, and the high cost of new drug development. Many have tried to compete with massive marketing campaigns to make up for the decline in blockbuster drugs. Meanwhile, Genentech is achieving remarkable success with its targeted approach. Hoffman LaRoche, the Swiss pharmaceutical major, bought Genentech in 2009 but has been careful to maintain its independence within Roche. The company recently became the top seller of branded anti-tumour drugs in the United States.[93]

Institutionalism

The institutional perspective provides yet another view of interorganizational relationships.[94] Just as companies need efficient production to survive, the institutional view argues that organizations need legitimacy from their stakeholders. The institutional perspective describes how organizations survive and succeed through ensuring congruence between an organization and the expectations from its environment, comprising norms and values from stakeholders (customers, investors, associations, boards, government, collaborating organizations). The institutional environment reflects what the greater society views as correct ways of organizing and behaving or it risks legitimacy and its social licence to exist.[95]

Legitimacy is gained when the activities of an organization are considered proper and appropriate within the environment's system of norms, values and beliefs.[96] Institutional theory points to the importance of intangible norms and values that shape behaviour, as opposed to more tangible elements, such as technology. For example, people will not deposit money in a bank unless it sends signals of compliance with norms of wise financial management. Local government encounters resistance to tax increases for funding upgraded refuse collection if residents object to aspects of the new programme.

Most organizations are concerned with legitimacy, as reflected in the various national and international surveys that rank corporations based on their reputations.[97,98] Many corporations actively shape and manage their reputations to increase their competitive advantage, and managers are searching for new ways to bolster legitimacy in the wake of ethical and financial scandals at such well-known companies as Siemens, Enron, MAN Trucks and Parmalat. Despite globalization and the presence of worldwide brands like Nike and Coca-Cola, national brands still tend to stand out at both the top and bottom of the rankings. Only Microsoft and McDonald's were mentioned consistently by respondents across Europe, Asia and North America, and McDonald's was mainly ranked poorly due to negative respondent perceptions about the quality of both its food and service. Companies that ranked highest in each country included L'Oreal in France, Porsche in Germany, Virgin Group in the UK and IKEA in Sweden.[99]

ONLINE
COUNTERPOINT 6.8

The fact that there is a payoff for having a good reputation is verified by a study of organizations in the airline industry. Having a good reputation was significantly related to higher levels of performance measures such as return on assets and net profit margin.[100]

The notion of legitimacy serves to shed light on an important question for institutional theorists. Why is there so much homogeneity in the forms and practices of established organizations? For example, visit banks, high schools, hospitals, government departments or business firms in a similar industry, in any part of the country, and they will look strikingly similar. On the other hand, when an organizational field is just getting started, such as in e-commerce, diversity is the norm. New organizations fill emerging niches. However, once an industry becomes established, there is an invisible push toward similarity based upon what emerges as a legitimate form of organization within the field. *Isomorphism* is the term used to describe this move toward similarity.

The Institutional View and Organization Design

As a result of pressure to do things in a proper and correct way, the formal structures of many organizations reflect the expectations and values of the environment rather than the demand of work activities. This means that an organization may incorporate positions or activities (equal employment officer, e-commerce division, chief ethics officer) perceived as important by the larger society to increase its legitimacy and survival prospects, even though these elements may decrease efficiency. For example, many if not most small companies set up websites, even though the benefits gained from the site are sometimes outweighed by the costs of maintaining it. Having a website is perceived as essential by the larger society today. The formal structure and design of an organization may not be rational with respect to workflow and products or services, but it will help ensure survival in the larger environment.

Organizations adapt to the environment by signalling their congruence with the demands and expectations stemming from cultural norms, standards set by professional bodies, funding agencies and customers. In this way, they obtain approval, legitimacy and continuing support. The adoption of structures thus might not be linked to actual production requirements, and might occur regardless of whether specific internal problems are solved. The institutionalist perspective draws attention to how organizational structure may be a product of conformity to established norms and values, rather than a consequence of deliberate planning.[101]

BRIEFCASE 6.4

Institutional Similarity

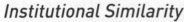

In striving for legitimacy, many aspects of structure and behaviour may be targeted toward environmental acceptance. Interorganizational relationships thus are characterized by forces that result in organizations in a similar population looking like one another.[102] Exactly how does increasing similarity occur? How are these forces realized? A summary of three mechanisms for institutional adaptation appears in Exhibit 6.4. These three core mechanisms are *mimetic forces*, which result from responses to uncertainty; *coercive forces*, which stem from overtly political influence; and *normative forces*, which result from common training and professionalism.[103]

Mimetic Forces   Most organizations, especially business organizations, face great uncertainty. It is not clear to senior executives exactly what products, services or technologies will

IN PRACTICE

Tesco

Tesco is a remarkable British success story. Despite its origins dating back to 1919, the company only really took off in the 1970s, but then grew massively in 2007 capturing 30 per cent of the British food budget (double its nearest rival Asda/Wal-Mart), and accounting for one pound in every seven spent by Britons in all shops. The company has expanded internationally with varying levels of success, with operations in 12 countries. It has increasingly moved into non-food items, moving closer to the Wal-Mart model than a traditional supermarket. Profits rose annually for many years, reaching £2.7 billion in 2007 and £3.8 billion in 2011/2012. In 2007 the company edged past US-based Home Depot to become the third largest retailer in the world.[104]

However, whereas in 2003 city analysts were quoted as saying the company had 'not put a foot wrong', from 2008 Tesco was facing a crescendo of criticism,[105] including (unusually for Britain) its own web 'hate site', www.tescopoly.com. The concerns surrounded four main issues, each connected to perceptions of the company's excessive – and arguably misused – power. The first relates to Tesco's control of land and power in the town planning process.[106] The company sometimes puts local councils under pressure to allow its stores to open even in rural areas where there is substantial local opposition. It has also been accused of banking land so that its competitors cannot expand (a claim the company vigorously denies).[107] The second issue concerns the company's relationship with producers in the UK and elsewhere. Like Wal-Mart in America, Tesco has the purchasing muscle to be able to do things its way. Some of its products are made in developing countries like Bangladesh, by workers paid very low wages.[108] It has also been accused of keeping farm produce prices so low that farmers have no choice but to follow intensive production methods, argued by animal rights campaigners to be cruel and unhygenic.[109] Tesco was one of the supermarket chains worst hit by the revelation in 2013 that some meat products were adulterated with horsemeat. Tesco has also attempted to reduce its tax burden through various offshore holding companies.[110] Finally, the company has sometimes responded aggressively to criticism, further reinforcing its image as a corporate bully.[111] Tesco remained the top UK supermarket chain, with just under 30% of the market in 2015, but its performance has been hurt by these criticisms. In 2015 the company racked up a nearly £6 billion loss. Managers are now only too aware that how the company is perceived by customers and the public plays a big role in long-term success.[112] In 2014, Dave Lewis, formerly of Unilever, took over as CEO, and in 2015 for the first time in many years, the company started retrenching, abandoning plans for new megastores, closing 43 existing supermarkets, and selling off several ancillary services such as Tesco Mobile phones and the Blinkbox music streaming service.

After many years of setting the pace as the model for supermarket development in the UK and internationally, Tesco is on the back foot. Did the company lose its grasp of its environment, or did the environment change under its feet?[113]

achieve desired goals, and sometimes the goals themselves are not clear. In the face of this uncertainty, mimetic forces, the pressure to copy or model other organizations, are in operation.

Executives observe an innovation in a firm generally regarded as successful, so the management practice is quickly copied. An example is the proliferation of Wi-Fi hotspots in cafes, hotels and airports. Starbucks was one of the first companies to adopt Wi-Fi, enabling customers to use laptops and handheld computers at Starbucks stores. The practice has rapidly been copied by both large and small companies. Many times, this modelling is done without any clear proof that performance will be improved. Mimetic processes explain why fads and fashions occur in the business world. Once a new idea starts, many organizations grab onto it, sometimes only to learn that the application is difficult and may cause more problems than it

ONLINE
COUNTERPOINT 6.9

solves. The past two decades have seen the largest merger and acquisition wave in history, but evidence shows that many of these mergers did not produce the expected financial gains and other benefits. The sheer momentum of the trend was so powerful that many companies chose to merge not because of potential increases in efficiency or profitability but simply because it seemed like the right thing to do, assisted of course by intermediaries (e.g. bank, law firms, accounting firms, etc) who stood to benefit from mergers regardless of the outcome.[114] Downsizing of the workforce is another trend that can be attributed partly to mimetic forces but also to the gains enjoyed by executives holding stock options. Despite some evidence that massive downsizing actually hurts organizations, managers perceive it as a legitimate and effective means of improving performance or, at least, of raising stock price by sending the desired message to financial markets.[115]

Techniques such as outsourcing, re-engineering, Six Sigma quality programmes and the balanced scorecard have all been adopted, often without clear evidence that they improve efficiency or effectiveness. The one certain benefit is that management's feelings of uncertainty will be reduced, and the company's image will be enhanced because the firm is seen as using the latest management techniques. A recent study of 100 organizations confirmed that those companies associated with using popular management techniques were more admired and rated higher in quality of management, even though these organizations often did not reflect higher economic performance.[116] Perhaps the clearest example of official copying is the technique of benchmarking that occurs as part of the total quality movement. *Benchmarking* means identifying which company is best at something in an industry and then duplicating the technique for creating excellence, perhaps even improving it in the process.

The mimetic process works because organizations face continuous high uncertainty, they are aware of innovations occurring in the environment and the innovations are culturally supported, thereby giving legitimacy to adopters. This is a strong mechanism by which a group of banks, or high schools or manufacturing firms begin to look and act like one another.

Coercive Forces

All organizations are subject to pressure, both formal and informal, from government, regulatory agencies and other important organizations in the environment, especially those on which a company is dependent. Coercive forces are the external pressures exerted on an organization to adopt structures, techniques or behaviours similar to other organizations. As with other changes, those brought about because of coercive forces may not make the organization more effective, but it will look more effective and will be accepted as legitimate in the environment. Some pressures may have the force of law, such as government mandates to adopt new pollution control equipment. Health and safety regulations may demand that a safety officer be appointed. The European Commission has set rules for product warranty that apply in all member states of the European Union.[117] New regulations and government oversight boards have been set up for the accounting industry following widespread accounting scandals.[118]

EXHIBIT 6.4   Three Mechanisms for Institutional Adaptation

	Mimetic	Coercive	Normative
Reason to become similar: Events:	Uncertainty Innovation visibility	Dependence Political law, rules, sanctions	Duty, obligation Professionalism – certification, accreditation
Social basis:	Culturally supported	Legal	Moral
Example:	Re-engineering, benchmarking	Pollution controls school regulations	Accounting standards, consultant training

Source: Adapted from W. Richard Scott, *Institutions and Organizations* (Thousand Oaks, CA: Sage, 1995).

Coercive pressures may also occur between organizations where there is a power difference, as described in the resource-dependence section earlier in this chapter. Large retailers and manufacturers often insist that certain policies, procedures and techniques be used by their suppliers. When Honda picked Donnelly Corporation to make all the mirrors for its US-manufactured cars, Honda insisted that Donnelly implement an employee empowerment programme. Honda managers believed the partnership could work only if Donnelly learned how to foster collaborative internal relationships.

Organizational changes that result from coercive forces occur when an organization is dependent on another, when there are political factors such as rules, laws and sanctions involved, or when some other contractual or legal basis defines the relationship. Organizations operating under those constraints will adopt changes and relate to one another in a way that increases homogeneity and limits diversity.

Normative Forces

The third reason why organizations change, according to the institutional view, is the operation of normative forces. Normative forces are pressures to change to achieve standards of professionalism, and to adopt techniques that are considered by the professional community to be up-to-date and effective. Changes may be in any area, such as information technology, accounting requirements, marketing techniques or collaborative relationships with other organizations.

COUNTERPOINT 6.7

'Normative forces' might equally be characterized as institutionalized coercive forces. Their influence is more subtle but no less potent. It might be claimed that 'normative forces' are consensual. But a moment's reflection will reveal that struggles between different groups result in particular norms being established, and which also result in these norms being challenged, defended and changed. Within organizations 'culture change' programmes are an example of how executives deploy organizational resources to introduce or strengthen particular kinds of values that are intended to have 'normative force'.

Professionals share a body of formal education based on university degrees and professional networks through which ideas are exchanged by consultants and professional leaders. Universities, consulting firms, trade associations and professional training institutions develop norms among professional managers. People are exposed to similar training and standards and adopt shared values, which are implemented in organizations with which they work. Business schools teach finance, marketing and human resource majors that certain techniques are better than others, so using those techniques becomes a standard in the field. In one study, for example, a radio station changed from a functional to a multidivisional structure because a consultant recommended it as a 'higher standard' of doing business. There was no proof that this structure was better, but the radio station wanted legitimacy and to be perceived as fully professional and up-to-date in its management techniques.

Companies accept normative pressures to become like one another through a sense of obligation or duty to high standards of performance based on professional norms shared by managers and specialists in their respective organizations. These norms are conveyed through professional education and certification and have almost a moral or ethical requirement based on the highest standards accepted by the profession at that time. In some cases, though, normative forces that maintain legitimacy break down, as they have repeatedly in the accounting

BRIEFCASE 6.5

industry and the financial sector, and coercive forces are applied to shift organizations back toward acceptable standards, or at least to convey the appearance of such a shift in order to restore legitimacy and confidence.

Summary and Interpretation

In established thinking, organizations tend to be regarded as 'closed systems' – as autonomous and separate, trying to outdo other companies. In contrast, in more recent, 'open systems' thinking, organizations are seen as part of an ecosystem. An organization may span several industries and be positioned in a dense web of relationships with other companies and agencies. Collaboration then comes to be regarded as a weapon in the armoury of competition. Organizations may compete and collaborate at the same time depending on the location and issue. In this business ecosystem, management include the development of horizontal relationships with other organizations.

Four perspectives have been developed to explain relationships among organizations. The resource-dependence perspective argues that organizations try to avoid excessive dependence on other organizations. In this view, considerable effort is devoted to controlling the environment to ensure ample resources while maintaining independence; and managers in powerful organizations gain advantage by exploiting the dependence of weaker organizations. In the collaborative-network perspective, organizations welcome collaboration and interdependence with other organizations to enhance value for both. Many executives are changing mindsets away from independence toward collaboration, often with former corporate enemies.

**ONLINE
COUNTERPOINT 6.10**

The population-ecology perspective explains why organizational diversity continuously increases with the appearance of new organizations filling niches left open by established companies. This perspective suggests that large companies usually cannot adapt to meet a changing environment; hence, new companies emerge with the appropriate form and skills to serve new needs. Through the process of variation, selection and retention, some organizations survive and grow while others perish. Executives may develop a generalist or specialist strategy to survive in the population of organizations.

The institutional perspective argues that interorganizational relationships are significantly shaped by the quest for legitimacy. Structures and activities are favoured that are perceived as valid, proper and up-to-date by external stakeholders. Techniques are copied with the consequence that organizations begin to look very similar. There are three core mechanisms that explain increasing organizational homogeneity: mimetic forces, which result from responses to uncertainty; coercive forces, which stem from power differences and political influences; and normative forces, which result from common training and professionalism.

The four perspectives offer distinct ways of making sense of organizations which may be adopted by managers to address challenges of change, competition and collaboration. Managers in organizations may be seen to struggle to reduce dependence and vulnerability; to engage in collaborative relationships with others; to capitalize on others' slowness to adapt by seizing upon openings for new organizations to flourish; and to be enabled and constrained by the requirement to secure legitimacy from the external environment.

KEY CONCEPTS

coercive forces	interorganizational	organizational	resource dependence
collaborative network	relationships	ecosystem	retention
generalist	legitimacy	organizational form	selection
institutional environment	mimetic forces	population	specialist
institutional perspective	niche	population-ecology	struggle for existence
	normative forces	perspective	variation

Discussion Questions

1 The concept of business ecosystems implies that organizations are more interdependent than ever before. From personal experience, do you agree? Explain.

2 How do you feel about the prospect of becoming a manager and having to manage a set of relationships with other companies? Discuss.

3 Assume you are the manager of a small firm that is dependent on a large computer manufacturing customer. Put yourself in the position of the small firm and describe what actions you would take to survive and succeed.

4 Many senior managers today were trained under assumptions of adversarial relationships with other companies. Assuming this to be the case, what are some of the implications and how might these be addressed in the light of the theories presented in this chapter?

5 Discuss how the adversarial versus partnership orientations work among students in class. Is there a sense of competition for grades? Is it possible to develop a partnership orientation in which your work depends on others?

6 The population-ecology perspective argues that it is desirable to have new organizations emerging and old organizations dying as the environment changes. Do you agree? Why would European countries pass laws to sustain traditional organizations and inhibit the emergence of new ones?

7 Explain how the process of variation, selection and retention might explain innovations that take place within an organization.

8 Do you believe that legitimacy really motivates a large, powerful organization such as Wal-Mart?

9 How does a concern for legitimacy result in organizations becoming more similar over time?

10 How do mimetic forces differ from normative forces? Give an example of each.

Chapter 6 Workbook Management Fads

Look up one or two articles on current trends or fads in management. Then, find one or two articles on a management fad from several years ago. Finally, surf the internet for information on both the current and previous fads.

Questions

1 How were these fads used in organizations? Use real examples from your readings.

2 Why do you think the fads were adopted? To what extent were the fads adopted to truly improve productivity and morale versus a concern to appear current in its management techniques compared to the competition?

3 Give an example in which a fad did not work as expected. Explain the reason it did not work.

Chapter 6 Workshop Ugli Orange Case

1 Form groups of three members. One person will be Dr Roland, one person will be Dr Jones and the third person will be an observer.

2 Roland and Jones will read only their own roles, but the observer will read both.

3 Role-play: Instructor announces, 'I am Mr/Ms Cardoza, the owner of the remaining Ugli oranges. My fruit export firm is based in South America. My country does not have diplomatic relations with your country, although we do have strong trade relations.'

The groups will spend about 10 minutes meeting with the other firm's representative and will decide on a course of action. Be prepared to answer the following questions:

a What do you plan to do?

b If you want to buy the oranges, what price will you offer?

c To whom and how will the oranges be delivered?

4 The observers will report the solutions reached. The groups will describe the decision-making process used.

5 The instructor will lead a discussion on the exercise addressing the following questions:

a Which groups had the most trust? How did that influence behaviour?

b Which groups shared more information? Why?

c How are trust and disclosure important in negotiations?

Role of 'Dr Jones'

You are Dr John Jones, a biological research scientist employed by a pharmaceutical firm. You have recently developed a synthetic chemical useful for curing and preventing Rudosen. Rudosen is a disease contracted by pregnant women. If not caught in the first four weeks of pregnancy, the disease causes serious brain, eye and ear damage to the unborn child. Recently there has been an outbreak of Rudosen in your state, and several thousand women have contracted the disease. You have found, with volunteer patients, that your recently developed synthetic serum cures Rudosen in its early stages. Unfortunately, the serum is made from the juice of the Ugli orange, which is a very rare fruit. Only a small quantity (approximately 4000) of these oranges were produced last season. No additional Ugli oranges will be available until next season, which will be too late to cure the present Rudosen victims.

You've demonstrated that your synthetic serum is in no way harmful to pregnant women. Consequently, there are no side effects. The Food and Drug Administration has approved production and distribution of the serum as a cure for Rudosen. Unfortunately, the current outbreak was unexpected, and your firm had not planned on having the compound serum available for 6 months. Your firm holds the patent on the synthetic serum, and it is expected to be a highly profitable product when it is generally available to the public.

You have recently been informed on good evidence that Mr R. H. Cardoza, a South American fruit exporter, is in possession of 3000 Ugli oranges in good condition. If you could obtain the juice of all 3000 you would be able to both cure present victims and provide sufficient inoculation for the remaining pregnant women in the state. No other state currently has a Rudosen threat.

You have recently been informed that Dr P. W. Roland is also urgently seeking Ugli oranges and is also aware of Mr Cardoza's possession of the 3000 available. Dr Roland is employed by a competing pharmaceutical firm. He has been working on biological warfare research for the past several years. There is a great deal of industrial espionage in the pharmaceutical industry. Over the past several years, Dr Roland's firm and yours have sued each other for infringement of patent rights and espionage law violations several times.

You've been authorized by your firm to approach Mr Cardoza to purchase the 3000 Ugli oranges. You have been told he will sell them to the highest bidder. Your firm has authorized you to bid as high as $250 000 to obtain the juice of the 3000 available oranges.

Role of 'Dr Roland'

You are Dr P. W. Roland. You work as a research biologist for a pharmaceutical firm. The firm is under contract with the government to do research on methods to combat enemy uses of biological warfare.

Recently, several World War II experimental nerve gas bombs were moved from the United States to a small island just off the US coast in the Pacific. In the process of transporting them, two of the bombs developed a leak. The leak is currently controlled by government scientists, who believe that the gas will permeate the bomb chambers within 2 weeks. They know of no method of preventing the gas from getting into the atmosphere and spreading to other islands and very likely to the west coast of North America as well. If this occurs, it is likely that several thousand people will incur serious brain damage or die.

You've developed a synthetic vapour that will neutralize the nerve gas if it is injected into the bomb chamber before the gas leaks out. The vapour is made with a chemical taken from the rind of the Ugli orange, a very rare fruit. Unfortunately, only 4000 of these oranges were produced this season.

You've been informed on good evidence that a Mr R. H. Cardoza, a fruit exporter in South America, is in possession of 3000 Ugli oranges. The chemicals from the rinds of all 3000 oranges would be sufficient to neutralize the gas if the vapour is developed and injected efficiently. You have been informed that the rinds of these oranges are in good condition.

You have learned that Dr J. W. Jones is also urgently seeking to purchase Ugli oranges and that he is aware of Mr Cardoza's possession of the 3000 available. Dr Jones works for a firm with which your firm is highly competitive. There is a great deal of industrial espionage in the pharmaceutical industry. Over the years, your firm and Dr Jones's have sued each other for violations of industrial espionage laws and infringement of patent rights several times. Litigation on two suits is still in process.

The federal government has asked your firm for assistance. You've been authorized by your firm to approach Mr Cardoza to purchase 3000 Ugli oranges. You have been told he will sell them to the highest bidder. Your firm has authorized you to bid as high as $250 000 to obtain the rinds of the oranges.

Before approaching Mr Cardoza, you have decided to talk to Dr Jones to influence him so that he will not prevent you from purchasing the oranges.

By Dr Robert House, University of Toronto.

The Project Laser Beam Multistakeholder Partnership

The date is September 2014. A project regularly described as 'transformational' and 'pioneering' was just concluding after five years. Its stakeholders must now document achievements and lessons learned.

The project - Project Laser Beam or PLB for short – had brought together UN agencies and Fortune 500 companies with governments, NGOs and local companies in Bangladesh and Indonesia. Its ambition had been to create a sustainable, replicable and scalable Public-Private Partnership model for significantly reducing under-nutrition in children.

The work was spearheaded by five key partners – the **World Food Programme** (WFP, the world's largest humanitarian agency fighting hunger worldwide), Unilever (a major consumer goods company with products sold in over 190 countries), **Royal DSM** (a global science-based company active in health nutrition and materials), the **Global Alliance for Improved Nutrition** (GAIN, a global alliance that supports public-private partnerships to increase access to the missing dietary nutrients necessary for a healthier world) and **Mondelez International Foundation** (formerly Kraft Foods Foundation, aiming to empower families and communities to lead healthier lives).

Accenture Development Partnerships, a unit within Accenture that works with the international development sector, had helped these five partners and the various other partners operating in Indonesia and in Bangladesh[1] to make the partnership as effective as possible.[2] PLB had been launched with great fanfare at the Clinton Global Initiative meeting in New York back in September 2009.

What insights had the partners gained over the past five years of working together?

The magnitude of the challenge on which they had been focused was formidable. GAIN Executive Director Marc Ameringen explained that child under-nutrition is 'one of the most pressing issues of our time' leading annually to 3.5 million child deaths and 162 million children with irreversible stunting that severely limits their potential. As Elisabeth Rasmussen, WFP Assistant Executive Director (Partnerships and Governance) put it, 'These challenges are also why we partnered with companies, governments and other organizations in 2009 to create the bold, pioneering initiative called Project Laser Beam.'

Looking back on the project, Unilever CEO Paul Polman referred to it as a 'transformational partnership' because of its multi-sector nature 'combining the expertise of leading public and private sector players .... on one of the most persistent challenges in our world.' Marc Van Ameringen from GAIN noted that 'a new approach' was required, adding that it was imperative to have the local governments work together on a common goal with the private sector, civil society and multilateral organizations. In his words, 'It is only by embracing the spirit of partnership that malnutrition can be eliminated within our lifetimes.' There was a heavy emphasis on local capacity building and local ownership of initiatives such as high-nutrient school food and home gardening initiatives.

Chris McGrath, Mondelez International Foundation External Affairs VP, spoke about the value of working with others to find and implement innovative solutions so that 'we will amplify our "listening skills" and surface new voices. Alongside these new voices, we'll bring together diverse ideas – both big and small – to deliver meaningful change.' Royal DSM, for example, has very specific expertise in micronutrients – vitamins and minerals – that can be added to staple foods; however, as CEO Feike Sijbesma remarked, 'Many effective nutritional solutions are available, but must be scaled up to reach those in need' involving, in his

1. **BRAC**, one of the world's largest international development organizations based in Bangladesh; **Consumer Association of Bangladesh (CAB)**, a non-government organization dedicated to the protection and promotion of consumers' rights and interests in the country; **Friendship**, an NGO based in Bangladesh; **GarudaFood**, an Indonesian food and beverage company; **Helen Keller International**, an international non-profit organization; **Government of Bangladesh; Government of Indonesia; JITA**, a joint venture social business of CARE and Danone; **PT Indofood Sukses Makmur**, a major Indonesian company involved in the food industry; **UNICEF**, the United Nations Children's Fund focused on children and child rights; **WaterAid**, an international non-profit organization; and **Yayasan Kegizian untuk Pengembangan Fortifikasi Pangan Indonesia**, an Indonesian nutrition foundation for food fortification.
2. https://www.accenture.com/ca-en/~/media/Accenture/Conversion-Assets/DotCom/Documents/Global/PDF/Strategy_6/Accenture-Laser-Beam-Partnership-Reduce-Child-Under-Nutrition.pdf

▶

words, 'collaboration and coordination between many parties in the form of transformational partnerships.'

WFP's Elisabeth Rasmussen noted the importance of 'investing the time and resources needed for all of us to innovate and learn how we can achieve a world with zero hunger.' As GAIN's Marc Ameringen observed, his organization had 'learnt a lot about what makes such partnerships work. Clarity of purpose, well-defined roles and good communication are critical to building trust and enabling joint innovation and action. He cited 'coordinated efforts' in both Indonesia and Bangladesh that 'built significant momentum to address malnutrition and led to concrete investments on the ground.'

The Scaling Up Nutrition (SUN) Business Network was now poised to carry the results of the project forward to a global scale.

The SUN Business Network website includes reflections on PLB achievements. The importance of further scaling up these achievements through larger platforms and initiatives is emphasized. Reference is also made to the PLB operating efficiency made possible by 'implementing a decentralized consensus-driven operating model managed by a neutral external third party,' a reference to the capabilities of Accenture Development Partnerships that facilitated relationship-building among organizations that did not typically collaborate effectively.

Case Questions:

1 Increasingly managers are faced with challenges far too complex for an organization to resolve singlehandedly. In the case of under-nutrition there are issues related to hunger, issues related to poverty and issues related to climate change, among others. The partners who collaborated on under-nutrition in Project Laser Beam had many differences – in technical expertise, organizational culture, governance structures, incentives, decision-making processes and timelines, etc. Can you identify one or two key insights that this project offers on managing highly diverse interorganizational relationships?

2 This chapter presents four distinctive perspectives on interorganizational relationships – the resource dependence perspective, the collaborative-network perspective, the population ecology perspective and the institutional perspective. How would each perspective help you to make sense of the highly diverse interorganizational relationships encompassed by Project Laser Beam?

For further information:

http://www.un.org/en/zerohunger/pdfs/Project%20 Laser%20Beam%20-%20Final%20Report.pdf

Notes

1. MAN AG, *Annual Report 2007*, Munich.
2. 'International takes wraps off MaxxForce', *Fleet Owner*, January 1, 2007, Pg. 33; 'Caterpillar Exits Engine Business Enters Work-Truck Market', *Engineering News-Record,* Vol. 260 No. 21, June 23, 2008, Pg. 97; Brezonick, Mike, 'A big step up for International: first in new family of big bore truck diesels to debut in '07; first fruits of alliance with MAN, *Diesel Progress,* Vol. 71 No. 6, June 1, 2005, Pg. 78.
3. 'Force Motors, Man To Form Heavy Trucks JV', *The Economic Times*, November 11, 2005; Roger Houghton, 'Worldwide sales for MAN trucks booming', *Business Day South Africa*, May 10, 2007, Pg. 8 'MAN to ramp up India business', *Hindustan Times*, May 9, 2008; Eliot Lobo, 'MAN goes upmarket', *Autocar Professional India*, pg. 19; Ravi Krishnan, 'Investors give thumbs down to Eicher-Volvo', *Mint*, December 11, 2007; Ammar Master, 'Daimler Trucks forms JV with Hero Group', *Mint*, December 15, 2007; 'Indian, foreign firms find symbiosis in truck market', *The Nikkei Weekly (Japan)*, November 27, 2006.
4. Sven-Erik Lindstrand, 'Scania: Sleeping Giant in Emerging VW Truck Portfolio?' *TruckingInfo*, June 2014, www.truckinginfo.com/article/story/2014/06/scania-sleeping-giant-in-emerging-vw-truck-portfolio.aspx
5. Christoph Rauwald, 5 July, 2011, 'VW Moves on Trucks – Auto Maker Takes Majority Stake in MAN in Big Step', *The Wall Street Journal*, B3; 'Volkswagen Eyeing Stake in Navistar', *Automotive World*, July 26, 2012; Daniel Schäfer, 24 November, 2009, 'Corporate shock as MAN chief quits', *Financial Times*.
6. Christine Oliver, 'Determinants of Interorganizational Relationships: Integration and Future Directions', *Academy of Management Review* 15 (1990), 241–265.
7. http://web.archive.org/web/20100205041312/http://flextronics.com/en/default.aspx, accessed on September 15, 2013.
8. Crampes, Claude and Hollander, Abraham (2006), 'Triple play time; Bundling competition in ICT industries', *Communications & Strategies*, 63, Pgs 51–71.

9. James Moore, *The Death of Competition: Leadership and Strategy in the Age of Business Ecosystems* (New York: HarperCollins, 1996); Brent Schlender, 'How Big Can Apple Get?' *Fortune* (February 21, 2005), 66–76.

10. Howard Muson, 'Friend? Foe? Both? The Confusing World of Corporate Alliances', *Across the Board* (March–April 2002), 19–25; and Devi R. Gnyawali and Ravindranath Madhavan, 'Cooperative Networks and Competitive Dynamics: A Structural Embeddedness Perspective', *Academy of Management Review* 26, No. 3 (2001), 431–445.

11. Thomas Petzinger, Jr., *The New Pioneers: The Men and Women Who Are Transforming the Workplace and Marketplace* (New York: Simon & Schuster, 1999), 53–54.

12. James Moore, 'The Death of Competition', *Fortune* (April 15, 1996), 142–144.

13. Simon Bowers, 29 March, 2013, 'Amazon faces traders' revolt over fee hikes: Third parties face huge increases to sell items via online marketplace', *The Guardian*.

14. Clorox, Hoover's Company Records – In-depth record, May 20, 2008.

15. Alice Dragoon, 'A Travel Guide to Collaboration', *CIO* (November 15, 2004), 68–75.

16. Amazon's spending in new technology increased 41 per cent to $171m in 2006 but was expected to slow down in subsequent years: Carrie Flynn 'Amazon to curtail its spending', *New York Times,* October 25, 2006, retrieved May 20, 2008, from http://www.nytimes.com/2006/10/25/technology/25amazon.html.

17. Keith Regan, 'Toys 'R' US Wins Right To End Amazon Partnership', March 3, 2006, Retrieved May 20, 2008, from http://www.technewsworld.com/story/49188.html?welcome=1211372647.

18. Edd McCracken, 'Amazon accused of squeezing publisher – Hachette says online giant is making unfair demands', *Sunday Herald*, June 8, 2008, Pg. 24.

19. Vanessa Mock and Alessandro Torello, 13 December, 2012, EU Lets Retailers Resume E-Book Discounting, *The Wall Street Journal*.

20. Doug Tsuruoka, 'Amazon Deals Have Short Shelf Life; Retailers Go Their Own Way; Unexpected competition, high cost of platform spur big store chains to cut ties', *Investor's Business Daily*, July 3, 2008

21. Nick Wingfield, 'New Chapter: A Web Giant Tries to Boost Profits by Taking On Tenants', *The Wall Street Journal* (September 24, 2003), A1, A10; and Nick Wingfield, 'Amazon's eBay Challenge', *The Wall Street Journal* (June 3, 2004), B1, B2.

22. Hayley Tsukayama, 4 April, 2012, 'Amazon Prime streaming video now available on PlayStation 3', *Washington Post*.

23. Sumantra Ghoshal and Christopher A. Bartlett, 'Changing the Role of Top Management: Beyond Structure and Process', *Harvard Business Review* (January–February 1995), 86–96.

24. Susan Greco and Kate O'Sullivan, 'Independents' Day', *Inc.* (August 2002), 76–83.

25. http://www.e3network.com/default.asp?docId=13028, accessed on July 9, 2008.

26. http://www.e3network.com/; http://www.globalfluency.us/files/GF_Agency_Profile_Feb_2016.pdf

27. J. Pfeffer and G. R. Salancik, *The External Control of Organizations: A Resource Dependence Perspective* (New York: Harper & Row, 1978).

28. Derek S. Pugh and David J. Hickson, *Writers on Organizations*, 5th ed. (Thousand Oaks, CA: Sage, 1996).

29. James Hall, 'Good For You What About Him? Britain's Powerful Supermarkets Have Been Accused of Bullying Farmers And Food Producers In Order To Keep Costs Low', *The Sunday Telegraph*, August 26, 2007; *OECD Economic Surveys – United Kingdom,* Section V. Product market competition and economic performance, 2004, Pgs 184–243.

30. Marjolein Canils and Cees Gelderman (2005), 'Purchasing strategies in the Kraljic matrix – A power and dependence perspective', *Journal of Purchasing and Supply Management,* 11, Pgs 141–155.

31. This discussion is based on Matthew Schifrin, 'The Big Squeeze', *Forbes* (March 11, 1996), 45–46; Wendy Zellner with Marti Benedetti, 'CLOUT!' *BusinessWeek* (December 21, 1992), 62–73; Kevin Kelly and Zachary Schiller with James B. Treece, 'Cut Costs or Else', *BusinessWeek* (March 22, 1993), 28–29; and Lee Berton, 'Push from Above', *The Wall Street Journal* (May 23, 1996), R24.

32. 'Fitting In; In Bow to Retailers' New Clout, Levi Strauss Makes Alterations', *The Wall Street Journal* (June 17, 2004), A1.

33. 'Levi Makes Alterations To Sew Up Wal-Mart Sales', *The State* (Columbia, SC), June 20, 2004, Pg. F3; Marquard, William, 'Leverage, invest, diversify: the supplier's bargain', *MMR*, Vol. 23 No. 20, December 11, 2006, Pgs 15–19.

34. *FD (Fair Disclosure) Wire*, Q3 2006 Levi Strauss & Co. Earnings Conference Call, October 10, 2006.

35. Ross Tucker, 'Future Face of Levi's: Women's And Overseas Seen As Keys To Growth', *Women's Wear Daily*, April 9, 2008, Pg. 1

36. Nathalie Tadena, 11 October, 2011, Levi Strauss Profit Rises 14 per cent as Sales Climb in Asia, Reuters; Jyske Bank, February 20, 2012, Levi's stands the test of time; Q3 2012 Levi Strauss and Co Earnings Conference Call, 9 October, 2012 CQ FD Disclosure; Nathalie Tadena, 10 July 2012, 'Levi's Profit Slips 38%; Sales Weaken in Asia, Europe', *The Wall Street Journal*.

37. 'Levi Strauss & Co. Announces Fourth-Quarter & Fiscal-Year 2015 Financial Results', *BusinessWire*, February 11, 2016, accessed at www.businesswire.com/news/home/20160211006340/en/Levi-Strauss-Announces-Fourth-Quarter-Fiscal-Year-2015-Financial

38. Pankaj Mishra, 'Microsoft to integrate products with Linux, rival operating tech', *MINT*, August 23, 2007; John Fontana, 'All eyes on how Microsoft pulls off ODF support; Software giant saying right things, but actions will determine if format debate headed in right direction', *Network World*, May 22, 2008, p.19; http://www.iii.org/international/rankings/ accessed on July 10, 2008.

39. Matt Warman, 3 March, 2013, 'You can't see where we'll be in five years – at least top three, maybe number one', *The Sunday Telegraph*.

40. Mitchell P. Koza and Arie Y. Lewin, 'The Co-Evolution of Network Alliances: A Longitudinal Analysis of an International Professional Service Network', Center for Research on New Organizational Forms, Working Paper 98–09–02; and Kathy Rebello with Richard Brandt, Peter Coy and Mark Lewyn, 'Your Digital Future', *BusinessWeek* (September 7, 1992), 56–64.

41. Christine Oliver, 'Determinants of Interorganizational Relationships: Integration and Future Directions', *Academy of Management Review*, 15 (1990), 241–265; Ken G. Smith, Stephen J. Carroll and Susan Ashford, 'Intra- and Interorganizational Cooperation: Toward a Research Agenda', *Academy of Management Journal*, 38 (1995), 7–23; and Ken G. Smith, Stephen J. Carroll and Susan Ashford, 'Intra- and Interorganizational Cooperation: Toward a Research Agenda', *Academy of Management Journal* 38 (1995), 7–23.

42. 'Reviving the economy by freeing corporations', *The Korea Herald*, March 19, 2008.

43. Timothy M. Stearns, Alan N. Hoffman and Jan B. Heide, 'Performance of Commercial Television Stations as an Outcome of Interorganizational Linkages and Environmental Conditions', *Academy of Management Journal* 30 (1987), 71–90; and David A. Whetten and Thomas K. Kueng, 'The Instrumental Value of Interorganizational Relations: Antecedents and Consequences of Linkage Formation', *Academy of Management Journal* 22 (1979), 325–344.

44. 'Nissan relaunches Datsun brand, to be priced under Rs 4 lakh', *Times of India*, July 15, 2013, accessed at timesofindia.indiatimes.com/business/india-business/Nissan-relaunches-Datsun-brand-to-be-priced-under-Rs-4-lakh/articleshow/21082363.cms; Greesha Sukumaran, 'Renault Kwid launched in India at Rs 2.56 lakh', *IB Times*, September 24, 2015, accessed at www.ibtimes.co.in/renault-kwid-india-launch-24-september-price-bookings-features-more-647788

45. 'Nissan calls off car project with Bajaj2', 27 September, 2012, *The Times of India*; Andjarsari Paramadith, 21 March, 2012, 'Nissan revives Datsun brand for emerging markets drive', *Reuters News*; John Reed and Bernard Simon, 24 July, 2011, 'Fiat and Chrysler drive towards full union', *Financial Times*.

46. Alex Taylor III, 'Just Another Sexy Sports Car?' *Fortune* (March 17, 2003), 76–80.

47. David Kiley, 'Ghosn: 'The U.S. Auto Market Is Not Going to Be Great Again', *Business Week Online*, April 30, 2008; Ian Rowley, 'Underwhelming News for Nissan Investors', *Business Week Online*, January 14, 2008.

48. 'Ranbaxy completes phase II trials for anti-malaria drug', The Press Trust of India July 4, 2008 Friday; http://www.biospace.com/company_profile.aspx?CompanyId=1440, accessed on July 10, 2008.

49. Deepika Amirapu, 2 May, 2012, 'Pharma MNCs GSK, Merck, Pfizer and others prefer tie-ups over acquisitions with Indian firms', *The Economic Times*.

50. 'Fisher & Paykel teams up with Turkish company', *The New Zealand Herald*, October 3, 2007.

51. Rebecca Howard, 18 October, 2012, 'Haier Poised to Buy Majority Stake in Fisher & Paykel', *The Wall Street Journal*; Writankar Mukherjee, 18 October, 2012, 'Voltas plans JV with Arcelik, to enter home appliances space', *Economic Times*.

52. David Magee, *Turnaround: How Carlos Ghosn Rescued Nissan* (London: HarperCollins, 2003).

53. Myron Magnet, 'The New Golden Rule of Business', *Fortune* (February 21, 1994), 60–64; Grittner, 'Four Elements of Successful Sourcing Strategies'; and Jeffrey H. Dyer and Nile W. Hatch, 'Using Supplier Networks to Learn Faster', *MIT Sloan Management Review* (Spring 2004), 57–63.

54. Peter Smith Ring and Andrew H. Van de Ven, 'Developmental Processes of Corporate Interorganizational Relationships', *Academy of Management Review* 19 (1994), 90–118; Jeffrey H. Dyer, 'How Chrysler Created an American *Keiretsu*', *Harvard Business Review* (July–August 1996), 42–56; Peter Grittner, 'Four Elements of Successful Sourcing Strategies'; Myron Magnet, 'The New Golden Rule of Business'; and Mick Marchington and Steven Vincent, 'Analysing the Influence of Institutional, Organizational and Interpersonal Forces in Shaping Inter-Organizational Relationships', *Journal of Management Studies* 41, No. 6 (September 2004), 1029–1056.

55. http://web.archive.org/web/20080916212843/http://www.tyco.com/livesite/Page/Tyco/Who+We+Are/History/?Accessed on September 15, 2013.

56. Magnet, 'The New Golden Rule of Business'; and Grittner, 'Four Elements of Successful Sourcing Strategies'.

57. Pete Engardio, 'The Barons of Outsourcing', *BusinessWeek* (August 28, 2000), 177–178.

58. 'Flextronics and Motorola Mobility Partner to Streamline Supply Chain Operations', 10 December, 2012, *PR Newswire*.

59. 'Lenovo to make phones in Chennai with Flextronics', *Financial Express* (India), August 18, 2015, accessed at www.financialexpress.com/article/industry/companies/lenovo-to-make-phones-in-chennai-with-flextronics/121338/

60. Andrew Raskin, 'Who's Minding the Store?' *Business 2.0* (February 2003), 70–74.

61. Marchington and Vincent, 'Analysing the Influence of Institutional, Organizational and Interpersonal Forces in Shaping Inter-Organizational Relationships'.

62. Fred R. Blekley, 'Some Companies Let Suppliers Work on Site and Even Place Orders', *The Wall Street Journal* (January 13, 1995), A1, A6.

63. 'Bombardier Challenger 300 Super Midsize Corporate Business Jet' retrieved May 21, 2008, from http://www.aerospace-technology.com/projects/bombardier/.

64. John Mulgrew, 'New order for 20 jets is "good news" for Bombardier', April 5, 2016, accessed at www.belfasttelegraph.co.uk/business/news/new-order-for-20-jets-is-good-news-for-bombardier-34598360.html

65. Marcel van Leeuwen, 'XO JET Orders and Secures Options for a Total of 80 Bombardier Challenger Jets.' September 25, 2007, retrieved May 21, 2008 from http://www.airportbusiness.com/online/article.jsp?id=14570&siteSection=1.

66. Ross Marowits, 13 June, 2012, 'Bombardier shares soar on major jet order'; 'NetJets challenger deal could be worth $9.6B', *The Toronto Star*.

67. Philip Siekman, 'The Snap-Together Business Jet', *Fortune* (January 21, 2002), 104[A]–104[H].

68. This section draws from Joel A.C. Baum, 'Organizational Ecology', in Stewart R. Clegg, Cynthia Hardy and Walter R. Nord, eds, *Handbook of Organization Studies* (Thousand Oaks, CA: Sage, 1996); Jitendra V. Singh, *Organizational Evolution: New Directions* (Newbury Park, CA: Sage, 1990); Howard Aldrich, Bill McKelvey and Dave Ulrich, 'Design Strategy from the Population Perspective', *Journal of Management* 10 (1984), 67–86; Howard E.

Aldrich, *Organizations and Environments* (Englewood Cliffs, NJ: Prentice Hall, 1979); Michael Hannan and John Freeman, 'The Population Ecology of Organizations', *American Journal of Sociology* 82 (1977), 929–964; Dave Ulrich, 'The Population Perspective: Review, Critique and Relevance', *Human Relations* 40 (1987), 137–152; Jitendra V. Singh and Charles J. Lumsden, 'Theory and Research in Organizational Ecology', *Annual Review of Sociology* 16 (1990), 161–195; Howard E. Aldrich, 'Understanding, Not Integration: Vital Signs from Three Perspectives on Organizations', in Michael Reed and Michael D. Hughes, eds, *Rethinking Organizations: New Directions in Organizational Theory and Analysis* (London: Sage, 1992); Jitendra V. Singh, David J. Tucker and Robert J. House, 'Organizational Legitimacy and the Liability of Newness', *Administrative Science Quarterly* 31 (1986), 171–193; and Douglas R. Wholey and Jack W. Brittain, 'Organizational Ecology: Findings and Implications', *Academy of Management Review* 11 (1986), 513–533.

69. G.R. Carol and M.T. Hannan (1989), 'Density Dependence in the Evolution of Populations of Newspaper Organizations', *American Sociological Review* 54, 524–541.

70. Pugh and Hickson, *Writers on Organizations*; and Lex Donaldson, *American Anti-Management Theories of Organization* (New York: Cambridge University Press, 1995).

71. Michael T. Hannan and John Freeman, 'The Population Ecology of Organizations', *American Journal of Sociology* (March 1977), 929–964.

72. Dev Kumar Boojihawon, Pavlos Dimitratos and Stephen Young (2007), 'Characteristics and influences of multinational subsidiary entrepreneurial culture: The case of the advertising sector', *International Business Review*, 16, Pgs 549–572; http://www.wpp.com/wpp/ accessed on July 11, 2008.

73. Julie Creswell, 'Cisco's Worst Nightmare (And Sun's and IBM's and Nortel's and....)', *Fortune* (February 4, 2002), 114–116.

74. John Walton (2005) 'Would the real corporate university please stand up?' *Journal of European Industrial Training*, 29, pp. 7–20; Matthias Becker, 'Driving ambition: Corporate universities are nothing new, but one manufacturer is hoping its venture will bring it academic credibility, as well as a more highly skilled workforce', *The Guardian*, September 28, 2004, Pg. 16; George Boehmer, 'German group announces corporate university to teach global goals', *Associated Press Worldstream*, August 7, 1998; Steve Coomber, 'Deans' programme goes international', *The Times*, May 14, 2008, Pg. 4.

75. 'Accenture Opens Corporate University in India', *Consulting* 29 April, 2008, accessed at http://www.consultingmag.com/articles/710/1/Accenture-Opens-Corporate-University-in-India/Accenture-Opens-Corporate-University-in-India.html on July 11, 2008; 'Wipro Technologies Bags Corporate University Xchange Award', March 28, 2008, accessed at http://www.businesswire.com/news/home/20080327005634/en/Wipro-Technologies-Bags-Corporate-University-Xchange-Award on September 15, 2013; 'Loma And China Life Establish China's Largest Corporate University', *Asia Pulse*, February 27, 2004; 'Corporate University', *China Radio International*, 3 April, 2007, Accessed at http://english.cri.cn/4026/2007/04/03/44@212015.htm on July 11, 2008.

76. 'Education – "Dumbing down" provokes fierce reaction', *Human Resources*, March 1, 2008. Pg. 7.

77. Thomas Moore, 'The Corporate University: Transforming Management Education' (presentation in August 1996; Thomas Moore is the Dean of the Arthur D. Little University).

78. Mark Prigg, February 6, 2012, 'Google sets up Campus for tech entrepreneurs', *Evening Standard*.

79. Peter Newcomb, 'No One is Safe', *Forbes* (July 13, 1987), 121; 'It's Tough Up There', *Forbes* (July 13, 1987), 145–160.

80. Stewart Feldman, 'Here One Decade, Gone the Next', *Management Review* (November 1990), 5–6.

81. Stephen Ackroyd (2006), 'Aspects of flexible, economic systems: some recent developments in the UK economy', in *Facets of Flexibility*, (eds) Skorstad E. J and Ramsdal H., Ostfold University Press, Oslo, pp 255–277.

82. Jonathan Murphy (2008), 'International financial institutions and the new global managerial order', *Critical Perspectives on Accounting*, 19, 714–740.

83. Eric Schlosser (2002), *Fast Food Nation: The Dark Side of the All-American Meal,* London, Penguin.

84. David Stires, 'Fallen Arches', *Fortune* (April 29, 2002), 74–76.

85. Julie Jargon, 9 November, 2012, 'McDonald's Is Feeling Fried', *The Wall Street Journal*.

86. Andrew Glyn and Stephen Machin (1997), 'Colliery Closures and the Decline of the UK Coal Industry' *British Journal of Industrial Relations,* Volume 35, pp. 197–214.

87. http://www.teenvogue.com/gallery/selena-gomez-kmart

88. Jason Deans, March 26, 2013, 'BBC iPlayer boss jumps ship to Shazam', *The Guardian*; Karen Kay, 31 March, 2013, 'Fancy that hat Rihanna's wearing on TV? Shazam wants to help you track it down', *The Observer*.

89. David J. Tucker, Jitendra V. Singh and Agnes G. Meinhard, 'Organizational Form, Population Dynamics, and Institutional Change: The Founding Patterns of Voluntary Organizations', *Academy of Management Journal* 33 (1990), 151–178; Glenn R. Carroll and Michael T. Hannan, 'Density Delay in the Evolution of Organizational Populations: A Model and Five Empirical Tests', *Administrative Science Quarterly* 34 (1989), 411–430; Jacques Delacroix and Glenn R. Carroll, 'Organizational Foundings: An Ecological Study of the Newspaper Industries of Argentina and Ireland', *Administrative Science Quarterly* 28 (1983), 274–291; Johannes M. Pennings, 'Organizational Birth Frequencies: An Empirical Investigation', *Administrative Science Quarterly* 27 (1982), 120–144; David Marple, 'Technological Innovation and Organizational Survival: A Population Ecology Study of Nineteenth-Century American Railroads', *Sociological Quarterly* 23 (1982), 107–116; and Thomas G. Rundall and John O. McClain, 'Environmental Selection and Physician Supply', *American Journal of Sociology* 87 (1982), 1090–1112.

90. http://www.steiffteddybears.co.uk accessed on July 11, 2008.

91. Robert D. Hof and Linda Himelstein, 'eBay vs. Amazon.com', *BusinessWeek* (May 31, 1999), 128–132; and Maria Mallory with Stephanie Anderson Forest, 'Waking Up to a Major Market', *BusinessWeek* (March 23, 1992), 70–73.

92. Arthur G. Bedeian and Raymond F. Zammuto, *Organizations: Theory and Design* (Orlando, FA: Dryden Press, 1991); and Richard L. Hall, *Organizations: Structure, Process and Outcomes* (Englewood Cliffs, NJ: Prentice-Hall, 1991).

93. David Stipp, 'How Genentech Got It', *Fortune* (June 9, 2003), 81–88.

94. M. Tina Dacin, Jerry Goodstein and W. Richard Scott, 'Institutional Theory and Institutional Change: Introduction to the Special Research Forum', *Academy of Management Journal* 45, No. 1 (2002), 45–47. Thanks to Tina Dacin for her material and suggestions for this section of the chapter.

95. J. Meyer and B. Rowan, 'Institutionalized Organizations: Formal Structure as Myth and Ceremony', *American Journal of Sociology* 83 (1990), 340–363.

96. Mark C. Suchman, 'Managing Legitimacy: Strategic and Institutional Approaches', *Academy of Management Review* 20 (1995), 571–610.

97. Jerry Useem, 'America's Most Admired Companies', *Fortune* (March 7, 2005), 66–70; and Survey Results from Harris Interactive and the Reputation Institute, reported in Ronald Alsop, 'In Business Ranking, Some Icons Lose Luster', *The Wall Street Journal* (November 15, 2004), B1.

98. Ronald Alsop, 'Corporate Reputation Survey: Best-Known Companies Aren't Always Best Liked – McDonald's Takes Pounding For Menu Items, Surly Staff; Cheers and Jeers for Microsoft', *The Wall Street Journal*, 15 November 2004 B4.

99. Grahame R. Dowling, 'Corporate Reputations: Should You Compete on Yours?' *California Management Review* 46, No. 3 (Spring 2004), 19–36; Ronald Alsop, 'In Business Ranking, Some Icons Lose Luster'.

100. Richard J. Martinez and Patricia M. Norman, 'Whither Reputation? The Effects of Different Stakeholders', *Business Horizons* 47, No. 5 (September–October 2004), 25–32.

101. Pamela S. Tolbert and Lynne G. Zucker, 'The Institutionalization of Institutional Theory', in Stewart R. Clegg, Cynthia Hardy and Walter R. Nord, eds., *Handbook of Organization Studies* (Thousand Oaks, CA: Sage, 1996).

102. Pugh and Hickson, *Writers on Organizations*; and Paul J. DiMaggio and Walter W. Powell, 'The Iron Cage Revisited: Institutional Isomorphism and Collective Rationality in Organizational Fields', *American Sociological Review* 48 (1983), 147–160.

103. This section is based largely on DiMaggio and Powell, 'The Iron Cage Revisited'; Pugh and Hickson, *Writers on Organizations*; and W. Richard Scott, *Institutions and Organizations* (Thousand Oaks, CA: Sage, 1995).

104. Tesco Annual Report 2012, available at http://www.tescoplc.com/files/reports/ar2012/files/pdf/tesco_annual_review_2012.pdf.

105. David Smith and Zoe Wood, 'Are we falling out of love with Tesco?' *The Observer*, June 29, 2008, Pg. 24.

106. 'Tesco "breaching planning laws" ', *BBC News*, August 18, 2006, accessed at http://news.bbc.co.uk/2/hi/uk_news/5261844.stm on July 11, 2008. 'Friends of The Earth: New survey spells trouble for Tesco', *M2 Presswire*, June 29, 2007.

107. James Hall, 'Size matters', *The Sunday Telegraph*, April 30, 2006, Pg. 7; 'Tesco giant crushing small traders and suppliers', *Western Mail*, April 26, 2006, Pg. 8.

108. 'Who Pays? How British Supermarkets Are Keeping Women Workers In Poverty', ActionAid, accessed at http://www.actionaid.org.uk/doc_lib/actionaid_who_pays_report.pdf on July 11, 2008.

109. Hugh Fearnley-Whittingstall, 'Kiss me chick', *The Sunday Times,* June 29, 2008, News Review; Pg.1.

110. David Leigh, 'Government outlaws tax avoidance schemes: Tesco says strategy is common practice. Offshore companies loophole to be closed', *The Guardian*, June 14, 2008, Pg. 15.

111. Jonathan Brown and Martin Hickman, 'Feathers to fly as activists target Tesco bosses', *The Independent*, June 27, 2008.

112. Julia Werdigier, 19 April, 2012, 'Tesco to Spend $1.6 Billion to Revive U.K. Business', *New York Times*.

113. Zoe Wood, 'Tesco chief unveils dramatic shakeup at troubled supermarket', *The Guardian*, January 8, 2015, accessed at www.theguardian.com/business/2015/jan/08/tesco-chief-unveils-dramatic-shake-up-troubled-supermarket

114. Ellen R. Auster and Mark L. Sirower, 'The Dynamics of Merger and Acquisition Waves', *The Journal of Applied Behavioral Science* 38, No. 2 (June 2002), 216–244.

115. William McKinley, Jun Zhao and Kathleen Garrett Rust, 'A Sociocognitive Interpretation of Organizational Downsizing', *Academy of Management Review* 25, No. 1 (2000), 227–243.

116. Barry M. Staw and Lisa D. Epstein, 'What Bandwagons Bring: Effects of Popular Management Techniques on Corporate Performance, Reputation and CEO Pay', *Administrative Science Quarterly* 45, No. 3 (September 2000), 523–560.

117. European Commission Directive on Sale of Consumer Goods and Guarantees, available at http://eur-lex.europa.eu/LexUriServ/LexUriServ.do?uri=CELEX:31999L0044:EN:HTML.

118. Jeremy Kahn, 'Deloitte Restates Its Case', *Fortune* (April 29, 2002), 64–72.

DESIGNING ORGANIZATIONS FOR THE INTERNATIONAL ENVIRONMENT

A LOOK INSIDE

H&M

H&M is a popular shopping stop for many students and other young people in Europe and around the world. The company is well-known for its competitively priced designer clothing, and has teamed up with some of the world's most famous designers. H&M is expanding aggressively; after conquering Europe in the 1980s and 1990s, the company opened stores across the USA and Canada, and is now making a crucial move into China's booming fashion clothing market. H&M is a success story, but the company faces a number of challenges, including tough competition from companies with similar strategies such as Spanish-based Zara, intellectual property battles in several key developing country markets and European Union actions to limit imports from China, where much of the company's clothing is sourced.

In 1947, the company opened its first shop in Vasteras, a medium-sized city about 100km from Stockholm. Erling Persson, H&M's founder, had visited America, and wanted to import the concept of high volume, low price that he had seen in the States. H&M has long been committed to international expansion. Like many Scandinavian retailers, the company began its internationalization in neighbouring countries, opening in Norway and Denmark in 1964. H&M came to the UK in 1976, and by the end of the 1980s had also opened stores in Switzerland, Germany and the Netherlands. In 2000 the company opened its first stores in the United States, and shortly after moved into the new accession states of the European Union. The company has expanded mainly through company-owned stores, but due to local laws has opened a small number of stores in the Gulf region as franchises. Unlike many other companies, H&M resisted opening in China's burgeoning market for a number of years, but finally opened outlets in Beijing and Shanghai in 2007, and then expanded rapidly to 318 by 2016.

H&M's ambitions to marry mass market accessibility to high design was demonstrated by the company's collaborations in 2004 and 2005 with Karl Lagerfeld and Stella McCartney. In 2004, H&M opened its 1000th store, by 2006 had about 1300 outlets worldwide, and in 2016, 3900.

H&M is careful to maintain a positive and modern corporate image. The company publishes and promotes its corporate social responsibility policy, which includes detailed policies in both the social and environmental areas, partners with UNICEF on social projects, and is part of the EU's 'Eco' label programme, which commits to a series of environmentally friendly policies. All of H&M's goods are outsourced, mainly to lower-waged countries, and as Nike and other companies have found to their cost, outsourcing brings the risk of association with unacceptable labour practices as well as broader human rights violations that take place in a number of developing countries. H&M seems well insulated against such criticism. It has a comprehensive audit system for its outsourced factories, and publishes annually a full listing of violations observed and the company's response.

Despite exceptional growth, H&M faces serious challenges. H&M is being outpaced by some other European retailers, especially Spanish-owned Inditex, the operator of the Zara chain, which has overtaken H&M as Europe's largest retailer. In the past ten years, Inditex has quintupled in size, and in 2013 had over 6000 stores worldwide, double the number of H&M, and is present in almost twice as many countries. H&M's strong concentration in Europe (with over 75 per cent of the chain's sales) could prove a limiting factor for growth, as Europe and particularly the Eurozone is a mature market with relatively slow growth rates compared with developing markets. Europe also has high and rising labour costs.

H&M's ability to insulate itself from high European costs is limited by the EU's reimposition of restrictions on clothing imports from China (the country accounts for about 30 per cent of the company's clothing items). Further, production in the new accession countries of the EU is likely to become more expensive. H&M is expanding into China, but too slowly to provide a significant balance to European activities. A strategy to open new niche stores in Europe provides the possibility for H&M to continue growing its market share in Europe despite possible saturation of its current brand. The company has moved quickly to expand its e-commerce operations across its global markets, with internet sales available across Europe and the US by 2013.

In the next few years, H&M will face the challenge of translating a rapidly growing brand into a mature marketplace anchor. Generational customer turnover will be an issue, as the managers of the British clothing retailer Marks & Spencer can testify. H&M needs to retain its current customer base as they become older and their clothing tastes change, while continuing to appeal to its high-spending youth base. One way that H&M is adapting to the need to appeal to a wide customer demographic is by launching a number of other brands with separate stores and e-commerce platforms, including COS (more upmarket), Monki (young adults), Cheap Monday (street fashion), and launched in 2013, & Other Stories, focusing on coordinated clothes and accessories.[1] The combination of fickle fashion tastes, ever-expanding offshoring opportunities and risks, the challenge of e-commerce, and a highly competitive market segment mean that H&M's managers can't rest for a moment on their past laurels.[2,3,4]

Purpose of this Chapter

This chapter considers how managers design organizations for an international environment. We begin by looking at some of the primary motivations for international expansion, the typical stages of international development and the use of strategic alliances as a means of expansion. Then, the chapter examines global strategic approaches and the application of various structural designs for global advantage. Next, we discuss some of the specific challenges global organizations face, mechanisms for addressing them, and cultural differences that influence approaches to designing and managing a global firm. The chapter takes a look at an emerging type of global organization, the *transnational model*. At the end of the chapter we examine organizational designs emerging from the changing nature of globalization such as the growth strategies adopted by *dragon multinationals* companies, typically from developing countries, whose entire business strategy is built around benefiting from global markets. Finally, we look at *value chains*, another approach to understanding how goods and services are brought to market in a globally-integrated economy.

Entering the Global Arena

ONLINE
COUNTERPOINT 7.1

As recently as 20 years ago, executives in many companies could afford to only pay limited attention to the international environment. Today, advances in communications, technology and transportation have created a new landscape with significantly lowered barriers to international competition. Products can be made and sold anywhere in the world, communications are instant and product development and life cycles are growing shorter. Few companies are protected from these developments. Few countries have large enough markets to sustain giant, innovative companies. Even in the United States, still the world's largest market for many goods and services, large companies such as Coca-Cola and Procter & Gamble rely on international sales for a substantial portion of their sales and profits. Advances in communication mean that even the smallest companies can be actively involved in international business through online business. The rapid expansion of international activities in the past few years has led some companies, especially from developing countries where markets remain quite small, to operate from the beginning with global markets in mind.

COUNTERPOINT 7.1

There is a risk of overlooking the amount of international trade – in raw materials or partially finished goods – that has existed for centuries and gathered pace during the period of industrial imperialism. The 'international environment' has always been an issue for companies involved in importing raw materials (e.g. cotton) and human resources (e.g. slaves) and exporting goods (e.g. fabrics). What has changed is the globalization of potential competitors and the opening up of new markets as a consequence of the loss of monopolies (of supply and provision) associated with colonial rule.

Motivations for Global Expansion

Economic, technological and competitive forces have combined to push many companies from a domestic to a global focus. In some industries, being successful in today's environment means succeeding on a global scale. Three primary factors motivate international expansion: economies of scale, economies of scope and cheaper production factors.[5]

Economies of Scale Building a global presence expands an organization's scale of operations, enabling it to realize economies of scale. Large international organizations are not new. During the imperial era companies like the East India Company, CFAO (The French West African Company) and Canada's Hudson's Bay Company profited from trading with imperial subjects. The Industrial Revolution was another prime motivator for both organizational growth and internationalization. Larger factories could seize the benefits of economies of scale offered by new technologies and production methods. Through large-volume production, industrial giants were able to achieve the lowest possible cost per unit of production. However, for many companies, domestic markets were soon unable to sustain the high level of sales needed to maintain enough volume to achieve scale economies. In an industry such as automobile manufacturing, for example, a company would need a tremendous share of the domestic market to achieve scale economies. Thus, organizations like Ford Motor Company became international early in their histories. Ford, for example, opened its first UK plant in 1911, only eight years after the company was founded in the USA. Economies of scale also enable companies to obtain volume discounts from suppliers, lowering the organization's cost of production.

BRIEFCASE 7.1

Economies of Scope A second factor is the enhanced potential for exploiting economies of scope. *Scope* refers to the number and variety of products and services a company offers, as well as the number and variety of regions, countries and markets it serves. Having a presence in multiple countries provides marketing power and synergy compared to the same size firm that has presence in fewer countries. For example, an advertising agency or a consultancy firm with a presence in several global markets gains a competitive edge serving large companies that span the globe. Sometimes one large multinational will generate further multinationals. Consider the case of McDonald's, which attempts to standardize its offering through the world. This creates a market opening for a supplier able to supply identical mustard and ketchup packets for its restaurants around the world. A supplier that has a presence in every country that McDonald's serves has an advantage because it provides cost, consistency and convenience benefits to McDonald's, which does not have to deal with a number of local suppliers in each country. Economies of scope can also increase a company's market power as compared to competitors, because the company develops broad knowledge of the cultural, social, economic and other factors that affect its customers in varied locations and can provide specialized products and services to meet those needs. In other words, scope may facilitate forms of learning that can be key to the development of competitive advantage in assessing and exploiting the particularities of new or emergent markets, thereby presenting products or services in ways that seem relevant and valuable.

Low-Cost Production Factors   The third major force motivating global expansion relates to factors of production. One of the earliest, and still one of the most powerful, motivations for companies to invest outside their home country is the opportunity to obtain raw materials and other resources, notably labour, at the lowest possible cost. In past centuries, slaves were imported to America and elsewhere to work on plantations, and the practice of using indentured labour continued in the Dutch colonies until 1941.[6]

Organizations have also long turned overseas to secure cheap materials that were scarce or unavailable where they were needed. Until the development of synthetic rubber in the 1930s, automobile tyres required natural rubber that could not be produced in any of the major automobile-producing companies. In the 1920s tyre companies developed rubber plantations in Brazil and Liberia, Africa, to supply rubber for tyres for the growing automobile industry, while British and Dutch companies in conjunction with their imperial governments developed new rubber plantations in Asia that eventually came to dominate the worldwide market for natural rubber.

Many companies have viewed other countries as a source of cheap labour. Textile manufacturing in Europe and North America continues to decline as companies shift more and more production to China and other East Asian countries, India, Mexico, Latin America and the Caribbean where labour costs are much lower. Software companies are setting up development centres in India and Russia, apparel and shoe companies outsource production to Asian manufacturers, and document processing for credit card and other banking applications is handled by workers in India, the Philippines and Mexico.

Other organizations have gone international in search of lower costs of capital, sources of cheap energy, reduced government restrictions or other factors that lower the company's total production costs. Companies can locate facilities wherever it is calculated to make the most economic sense in terms of needed employee education and skill levels, labour and raw materials costs, and other production factors. Automobile manufacturers such as Toyota, Ford and BMW have built plants in South Africa, Brazil and Thailand, where they can sometimes pay workers less than one-tenth of what workers earn in higher-wage, developed countries. In addition, these countries sometimes offer dramatically lower costs for factors such as land, water and electricity.[7]

Stages of International Development

No company can become a global giant overnight. The shift from domestic to global has traditionally occurred through stages of development, as illustrated in Exhibit 7.1.[8] In stage one, the domestic stage, the company is domestically oriented, but managers are aware of the global environment and may want to consider initial foreign involvement to expand production volume and realize economies of scale. Market potential is limited and is primarily in the home country. The structure of the company is domestic, typically functional or divisional, and initial foreign sales are handled through an export department. The details of freight forwarding, customs problems and foreign exchange are handled by outsiders.

In stage two, the international stage, the company takes exports seriously and begins to operate multidomestically. Multidomestic means competitive issues in each country are addressed independently of other countries; the company deals with each country individually. The predominant concern is with international competitive positioning compared with other firms in the industry. At this point, an international division has replaced the export department, and specialists are hired to handle sales, service and warehousing abroad. Multiple countries are identified as a potential market.

EXHIBIT 7.1 Four Stages of International Evolution

	I. Domestic	II. International	III. Multinational	IV. Global
Strategic Orientation	Domestically oriented	Export-oriented multidomestic	Multinational	Global
Stage of Development	Initial foreign involvement	Competitive positioning	Explosion	Global
Structure	Domestic structure, plus export department	Domestic structure, plus international division	Worldwide geographical, product	Matrix, trans-national
Market Potential	Moderate, mostly domestic	Large, multidomestic	Very large, multinational	Whole world

Source: Based on Nancy J. Adler, *International Dimensions of Organizational Behavior*, 4th ed. (Cincinnati, OH: South-Western, 2002), 8–9; and Theodore T. Herbert, 'Strategy and Multinational Organization Structure: An Interorganizational Relationships Perspective', *Academy of Management Review* 9 (1984), 259–271.

In stage three, the multinational stage, the company has extensive experience in a number of international markets and has established marketing, manufacturing or research and development facilities in several foreign countries. The organization obtains a large percentage of revenues from sales outside the home country. International operations take off, and the company has business units scattered around the world along with suppliers, manufacturers and distributors.

In the fourth and ultimate global stage, the company transcends any single country. The business is not merely a collection of domestic industries; rather, subsidiaries are interlinked to the point where competitive position in one country significantly influences activities in other countries.[9] Truly global companies no longer have a single home country, and, indeed, have been called *stateless corporations*.[10] This represents a step change from the multinational company of the 1960s and 1970s, although few companies are fully global. Most draw a major proportion of their senior staff from a single country, and tend to retain their corporate headquarters in that country, even though the bulk of their activities may be outside this traditional base.

For truly global companies, the entire world is their marketplace. Organization structure at this stage can be extremely complex and often evolves into an international matrix or trans-national model, which will be discussed later in this chapter. Companies such as Royal Dutch/Shell, Unilever and Matsushita Electric may operate in more than a hundred countries.

?

ONLINE
COUNTERPOINT 7.2

Global Expansion through International Strategic Alliances

One of the most common ways companies get involved in international operations is through strategic alliances. Companies in rapidly changing industries such as media and entertainment, pharmaceuticals, biotechnology and software might have hundreds of strategic partnerships with suppliers, partners and distributors.[11]

Typical alliances include licensing, joint ventures and consortia.[12] For example, pharmaceutical companies such as Merck, Eli Lilly, Pfizer and GlaxoSmithKline cross-license their newest drugs to one another to support industry-wide innovation and marketing and offset the high fixed costs of research and distribution.[13] A joint venture is a separate entity created with two or more active firms as sponsors. This is a popular approach to sharing development and production costs and penetrating new markets. Joint ventures may be with either customers or competitors.[14] A joint venture led by Deutsche Telekom, Sprint and Telecom France, and involving several smaller firms, serves 65 countries and functions as a single company to meet

BRIEFCASE 7.2

the telecommunications requirements of global corporations.[15] MTV Networks has joint ventures with companies in Brazil, Australia and other countries to expand its media presence globally.[16]

Manufacturing companies often seek joint ventures to achieve production cost savings through economies of scale or to distribute new technologies and products through another country's distribution channels. The 1984 agreement between Toyota and General Motors to construct a Chevrolet plant in California was Toyota's way of distributing its technology to the United States, although by 2010 the two companies went their separate ways, selling off the Fremont plant. Caterpillar Inc. and Mitsubishi Heavy Industries Ltd. established a joint venture that enabled Caterpillar to manufacture and sell in Japan and expanded Mitsubishi's export markets.[17]

Another growing approach is for companies to become involved in consortia, groups of independent companies – including suppliers, customers and even competitors – that join together to share skills, resources, costs and access to one another's markets. Airbus Industrie, for example, is a consortium made up of French, British and German aerospace companies to compete with Boeing on a global scale.[18] Consortia are longer established in other parts of the world, such as the *keiretsu* family of corporations in Japan. In Korea, these interlocking company arrangements are called *chaebol*.

A type of consortia, the global *virtual organization*, is an increasingly significant approach to meeting worldwide competition. The virtual organization refers to a continually evolving set of company relationships that exist temporarily to exploit temporary opportunities or attain specific strategic advantages. A company may be involved in multiple alliances at any one time. Oracle, an American software company highlighted in Chapter 4, is involved in as many as 15 000 short-term organizational partnerships at any time.[19] Some executives believe shifting to a consortia or virtual approach is an effective way for companies to remain competitive in the global marketplace.[20] The next *In Practice* example, STMicroelectronics NV, rapidly grew from two to 27 countries on the basis of the strength of its partnerships with customer organizations.

Designing Structure to Fit Global Strategy

As we discussed in Chapter 4, an organization's structure must fit its situation by providing sufficient information processing for coordination and control while focusing employees on specific functions, products or geographic regions. Organization design for international structure follows a similar logic, with special interest in global versus local strategic opportunities.

Model for Global Versus Local Opportunities

When organizations venture into the international domain, managers strive to formulate a coherent global strategy that will provide synergy among worldwide operations for the purpose of achieving common organizational goals. One dilemma they face is choosing whether to emphasize global integration versus national responsiveness. Managers must decide whether they want each global affiliate to act autonomously or whether activities should be standardized across countries. These decisions are reflected in the choice between a *globalization* versus a *multidomestic* global strategy.

ONLINE COUNTERPOINT 7.3

The globalization strategy means that product design, manufacturing and marketing strategy are standardized throughout the world.[21] Japanese companies took business away from European and North American competitors by developing similar high-quality, low-cost products for all countries rather than incurring higher costs by tailoring products to specific countries. Black & Decker – since 2010 part of tool conglomerate Stanley Black and Decker – became much more competitive internationally when it standardized its line of power hand tools. Frequently, large multinationals employ a global approach for some products and a locally-tailored approach for others; the world's largest food company Nestlé, for example, has both local and global brands in its portfolio.

A globalization strategy can help an organization reap economy-of-scale efficiencies by standardizing product design and manufacturing, using common suppliers, introducing products around the world faster, coordinating prices and eliminating overlapping facilities. By sharing technology, design, suppliers and manufacturing standards worldwide in a coordinated global automotive operation, Ford saved $5 billion during the first three years.[22] Even where product contents may vary by country, Nestlé can often employ a standardized packaging approach; Nescafé instant coffee's familiar jar began life in the UK but has been exported around the world.[23]

A multidomestic strategy means that competition in each country is handled independently of competition in other countries. Thus, a multidomestic strategy would encourage product design, assembly and marketing tailored to the specific needs of each country. Some companies have found that their products do not thrive in a single global market. The French rarely drink orange juice for breakfast, and in parts of Mexico laundry detergent is more likely to be used to wash dishes, not clothes. Procter & Gamble tried to standardize nappy design, but discovered that cultural values in different parts of the world required style adjustments to make the product acceptable to many mothers. For example, in Italy, designing nappies to cover the baby's navel was critical to successful sales.[24]

?

ONLINE
COUNTERPOINT 7.4

IN PRACTICE

STMicroelectronics NV

Based in Geneva, Switzerland, STMicroelectronics NV was created in 1987 by the merger of two money-losing state-owned companies: SGS Microelettronica of Italy and Thomson Semiconductors of France. Since then, the company has partnered its way to a position as the world's fifth-largest computer chip maker and a leader in one of the hottest segments of the chip industry, manufacturing a 'system-on-a-chip' that combines analogue functions (such as sound and graphics) together with digital circuitry (such as logic and memory) on a single chip. The system-on-a-chip approach opened a huge market opportunity that very few other companies were prepared to exploit.

Success for STMicroelectronics came, however, not from designing and producing the system-on-a-chip in isolation, but from developing close partnerships with customers to gain a deep understanding of their system designs and unique needs. Partnering began out of necessity, as ST needed to convince

customers to replace their complex circuit boards with its system-on-a-chip. One of the earliest major alliances was with US-based Seagate Corporation, the world's largest maker of disk drives. By understanding the company's needs, ST was able to shrink all the components on Seagate's hard disk drive onto one or two custom chips. Being able to produce smaller, cheaper and less power-hungry disk drives enabled Seagate to enter entirely new markets such as laptops and handheld computers. ST's partnership with Seagate has continued, and the company has since established similar close relationships with 12 other telecommunications, computer, automotive and consumer products companies in multiple countries. The partnership between Nokia and ST, for example, has a governance committee made up of senior executives from both companies that meets quarterly to set and measure objectives and evaluate the partnership's performance. Teams from both companies meet regularly to coordinate development, marketing and sourcing of components, and engineers participate in regular *dream days*, where they get together and create wish-list products without interference from management. The disadvantage of partnerships is that they are only as strong as their weakest member, however, and ST has been hit by Nokia's dramatic decline in the wake of the emergence of a smartphone market dominated by Apple

▶

and Samsung. Nokia's decline helped end another of ST's partnerships, a chip manufacturing JV with Ericsson which the latter decided to abandon.[25]

By taking a partnership approach, STMicroelectronics now has operations in 27 countries and is able to draw on technological expertise and market understanding from around the world. ST's top managers are working on forming alliances with partners in Asia, where it has very few, to expand its presence in that part of the world.[26]

Using strategic alliances helped STMicroelectronics move from a money-losing operation to year 2000 profits of $1.4 billion on sales of $7.8 billion, although that proved a high-water mark and while revenues continued to grow slowly, profits in subsequent years were much more modest. By 2011 revenues were over $9 billion, and profits $650 million, but by 2013 the company reported losses of almost half a billion dollars. Small profits of between $100 and $200 million per year were reported in 2014 and 2015.[27]

On the surface, STMicroelectronics seems to be close to achieving the global stage of development described in Exhibit 7.1. Over the past two decades, ST has evolved into a highly sophisticated global firm that is adept at tapping into knowledge around the world to develop innovative solutions to customers' problems. Units around the world carry the name of the city where they're located, and each is viewed as part of a unified global system.[28] The company's corporate headquarters are in Geneva, with strong regional centres in North America and Asia. Production facilities are concentrated in Europe (particularly Italy and France, the founding partners), North America and Asia, with research facilities also located on several continents. The company's core executives remain dominated, however, by nationals of Italy and France, demonstrating that truly global is very hard to achieve. Indeed analysts have argued that the company's relative slowdown over the past few years is linked to its rootedness in France and Italy, making it difficult for the company to move quickly to restructure away from its core sites and towards emerging opportunities elsewhere.[29]

Different global organization designs, as well, are better suited to global integration or national responsiveness. Recent research on more than 100 international firms based in Spain has provided further support for the connection between international structure and strategic focus.[30] The model in Exhibit 7.2 illustrates a number of structures in relation to their relevance for strategies of global integration and national responsiveness.

As indicated in Exhibit 7.2, when forces for both global integration and national responsiveness are low, simply using an international division with the domestic structure is a logical way to handle international business. For some industries, however, technological, social or economic forces may create a situation in which selling standardized products worldwide provides a basis for competitive advantage. In these cases, a global product structure is commended. This structure provides product managers with authority to handle their product lines on a global basis and enables advantage to be taken of a unified global marketplace. In other cases, competitive advantages can be gained through national responsiveness – by responding to unique demands in the various countries in which it does business. For example, people in different countries have different expectations regarding personal care products like deodorant or toothpaste. For companies in these industries, a worldwide geographic structure is appropriate. Each country or region will have subsidiaries modifying products and services to fit that locale. The advertising firm of Ogilvy & Mather divides its operations into four primary geographical regions because advertising approaches are modified to fit the tastes, preferences, cultural values and government regulations in different parts of the world.[31]

European countries frequently have stricter rules on using children for advertising than is the case in the United States, for example. In France, children are prohibited from appearing in TV advertising. In several European countries, including Norway and Sweden, TV advertising targeted at younger children is not permitted[32] In the UK, companies are prohibited from television advertising that is likely to cause children to pester their parents to purchase goods and services; in 2011 Morrisons supermarket, for example, was stopped from running ads that encouraged children to beg their parents to visit Disneyland.[33] Other regulations and even voluntary standards vary considerably around the world.

EXHIBIT 7.2 Model to Fit Organization Structure to International Advantages

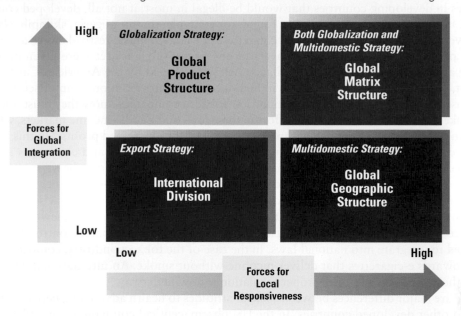

Source: Based on Christopher A. Bartlett and Sumantra Ghoshal, *Text, Cases and Readings in Cross-Border Management*, 3rd ed. (New York: Irwin McGraw-Hill, 2000), 395; Roderick E. White and Thomas A. Poynter, 'Organizing for Worldwide Advantage', *Business Quarterly* (Summer 1989), 84–89; Gunnar Hedlund, 'The Hypermodern MNC-A Heterachy?' *Human Resource Management* 25, no. 1 (Spring 1986), 9-36; and J.M. Stopford and L.T. Wells, Jr., *Managing the Multinational Enterprise* (New York: Basic Books, 1972).

EXHIBIT 7.3 Controlling Dangerous Products Internationally - Tobacco

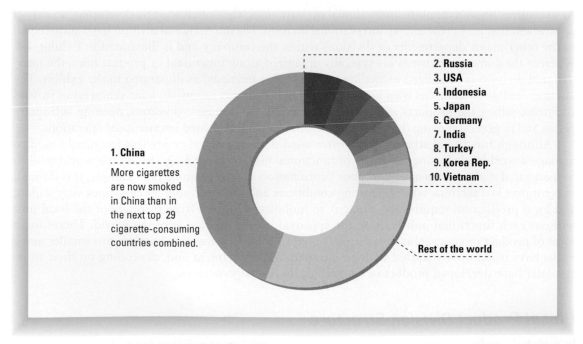

Anti-smoking organizations complain that cigarette manufacturers employ advertising techniques in developing countries that would be illegal in most, if not all, developed countries. A 2011 UK investigative newspaper report found, for example, that in Nigeria, skimpily-clad young women were employed to hand out free cigarettes; in Malawi, music festivals were advertised on cigarette packs; and in Ukraine, purchasers of one brand of cigarettes were given access to an exclusive all-night party.[34] The 2015 Tobacco Atlas, developed by the American Cancer Society, notes that, "The decline in smoking rates in high-income countries is more than offset by increased tobacco use in middle- and low-income countries. Tobacco companies know they must find replacement smokers, and focus much of their effort in these low- and middle-income markets, which have the potential for economic and demographic growth, and thus increased profits." In this as in other areas of economic activity, globalization presents both opportunities and challenges in terms of responsible corporate conduct. On the one hand, as the example of tobacco shows, unsafe products can be more easily sold in less regulated developing country markets. On the other hand, the gradual extension of protective frameworks can force companies to adopt safer practices internationally. In the case of tobacco, for example, the World Health Organization's Framework Convention on Tobacco Control (FCTC), Article 19, establishes a framework for tobacco control that states are encouraged to integrate into national laws. In the case of the tobacco industry, companies are now moving towards e-cigarettes that deliver nicotine without smoke. An international debate on the safety of these products and their proper regulation is now underway.[35]

There are major differences between societal attitudes to health advertising between the United States and other developed countries. In the US, pharmaceutical companies can widely advertise certain prescription medicines, whereas in Canada and most of Europe, this is not permitted.[36]

In many instances, such as Nestlé mentioned above, companies respond to both global and local opportunities simultaneously, in which case the global matrix structure can be used. Part of the product line may be standardized globally, and other parts tailored to the needs of local countries. We now discuss each of the structures in Exhibit 7.2 in more detail.

International Division

As executives begin to explore international opportunities, they often start by developing an export department that may grow into an international division. The international division has a status equal to the other major departments or divisions within the company and is illustrated in Exhibit 7.4. Whereas the domestic divisions are typically organized along functional or product lines, the international division is organized according to geographic interests, as illustrated in the exhibit. The international division has its own hierarchy to handle business (licensing, joint ventures) in various countries, selling the products and services created by the domestic divisions, opening subsidiary plants and in general moving the organization into more sophisticated international operations.

Although functional structures are often used domestically, they are less frequently used to manage a worldwide business.[37] Lines of functional hierarchy running around the world tend to be associated with inefficiencies and poor coordination at distant units. For example, it is difficult to centralize IT functions when operating conditions and human resources capacities vary widely, and local production requires the capacity to mobilize resources from throughout the local unit without each functional unit waiting for approval on the other side of the world. Therefore, a form of product or geographical structure is used to subdivide the organization into smaller units. Firms have traditionally started with an international department and, depending on their strategy, later have developed product or geographic divisional structures.

Global Product Division Structure

In a global product structure, the product divisions take responsibility for global operations in their specific product area. This is one of the most commonly used structures through which managers attempt to achieve global goals. That is because it provides a fairly straightforward

EXHIBIT 7.4 Domestic Hybrid Structure with International Division

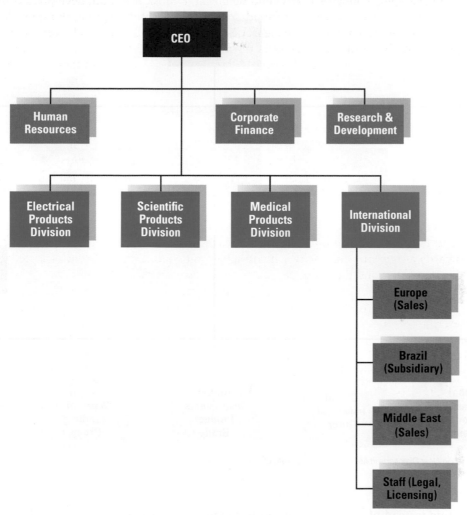

way to manage a variety of businesses and products around the world. Managers in each product division can focus on organizing for international operations as they see fit and direct employees' energy toward their own division's unique set of global problems or opportunities.[38] In addition, the structure provides top managers at headquarters with a broad perspective on competition, enabling the entire corporation to respond more rapidly to a changing global environment.[39]

With a global product structure, each division's manager is responsible for planning, organizing and controlling all functions for the production and distribution of its products for any market around the world. The product-based structure is likely to be adopted when a division handles products that are technologically similar and can be standardized for marketing worldwide (see Exhibit 7.2). Eaton Corporation, a US-based industrial manufacturer, ranked in 2015 in the world's top 100 Best Corporate Citizens for the 8th consecutive year, uses a form of *worldwide product structure*, as illustrated in Exhibit 7.5. In this structure, the automotive components group, industrial group and so on are responsible for manufacture and sale of products worldwide. In this model, the vice president international is responsible for coordinators in each region, including a coordinator for Japan, Australia, South America and northern Europe. The coordinators find ways to share facilities and improve production and delivery across all product lines sold in their region. These coordinators provide the same function as integrators described in Chapter 4. The product structure is widely used for standardizing production and sales around the globe, but it can encounter problems when the product divisions do not work well together,

EXHIBIT 7.5   Partial Global Product Structure Used by Eaton Corporation

Chairman

Law & Corporate Relations **Engineering** **President** **Finance & Administration** **International**

Regional Coordinators

Global Automotive Components Group **Global Industrial Group** **Global Instruments Product Group** **Global Materials Handling Group** **Global Truck Components Group**

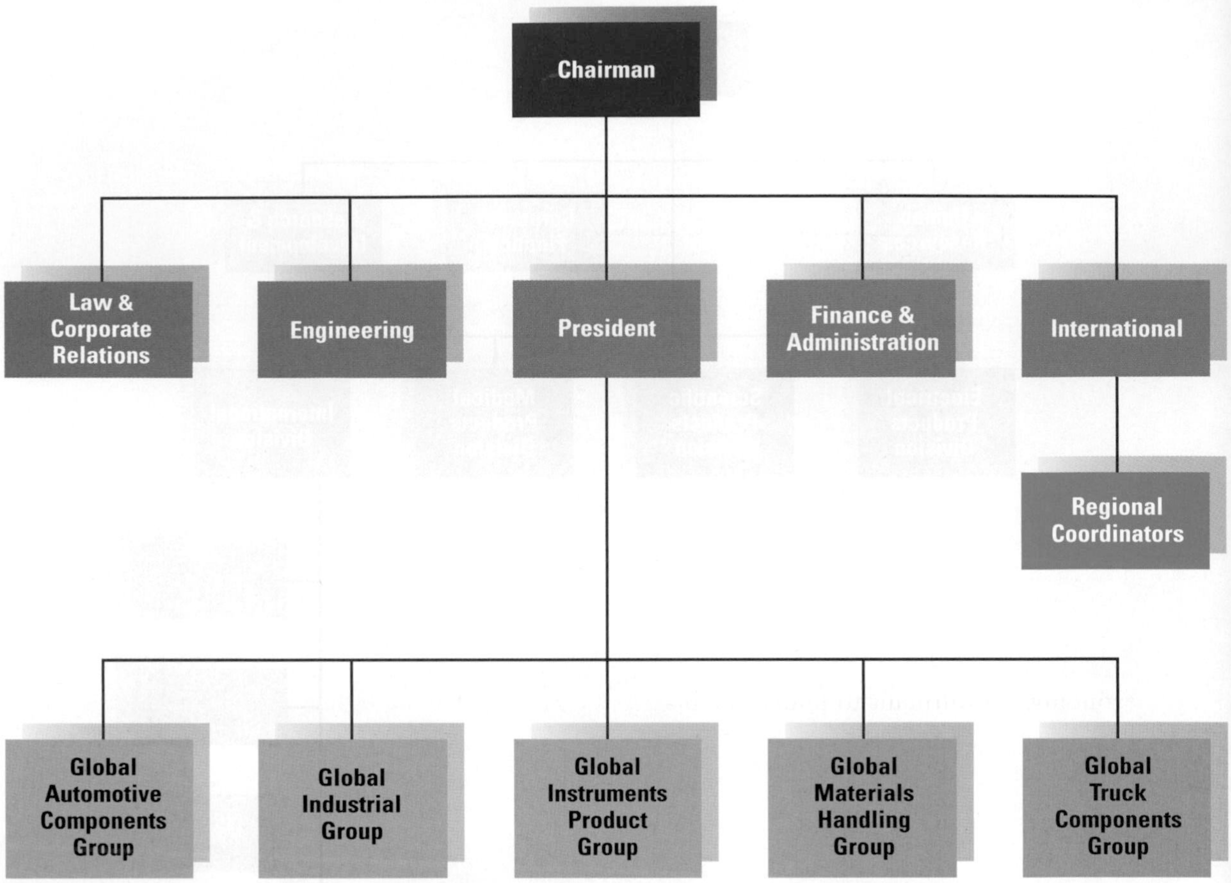

Source: *Based on New Directions in Multinational Corporate Organization* (New York: Business International Corp., 1981).

BRIEFCASE 7.3

competing instead of cooperating in some countries; and some countries may be ignored by product managers. The solution adopted by Eaton Corporation of using country coordinators who have a clearly defined role helped the company to overcome these potential problems. Like all models, Eaton's is subject to tweaking as the company develops and expands. In 2016, the group was made up of six divisions: Aerospace, Hydraulics, Truck and Automotive, and two electrical divisions, Electrical Americas, and Electrical Rest of World.[40]

Global Geographic Division Structure

A regionally-based organization tends to be developed by companies wishing to emphasize adaptation to regional or local market needs through a multidomestic strategy, as illustrated in Exhibit 7.2. The global geographic structure divides the world into geographical regions, with each geographical division reporting to the CEO. Each division has full control of functional activities within its geographical area, as shown in Exhibit 7.6.

Companies that use this type of structure have typically been those with mature product lines and stable technologies. They can find low-cost manufacturing within countries, as well as meeting different needs across countries for marketing and sales. However, several business and organizational trends have led to a broadening of the kinds of companies that use the global geographic structure.[41] The growth of service organizations has outpaced manufacturing for many years, and services by their nature occur on a local level. In addition, to meet new competitive threats, many

EXHIBIT 7.6 Global Geographic Division Structure

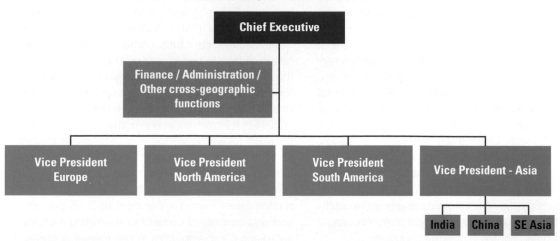

Global Geographic Division Structure

manufacturing firms are emphasizing the ability to customize their products, which requires a greater emphasis on local and regional responsiveness.

Senior management using a global geographic structure may encounter difficulties resulting from the autonomy of each regional division. Of particular importance in a globalizing economy, it is difficult to undertake planning on a global scale – such as new-product R&D – because each division acts to meet only the needs of its region. New domestic technologies and products can be difficult to transfer to international markets because each division thinks it will develop what it requires. Likewise, it is difficult to rapidly introduce products developed offshore into domestic markets; and there is often duplication of line and staff managers across regions. Companies such as Dow Chemical, Unilever (see *In Practice* box below)

IN PRACTICE

Unilever

Unilever was one of the first global conglomerates. The modern company emerged from the 1929 fusion of the British-owned Lever Brothers (founders of the famous industrial model town Port Sunlight in northern England) and the Netherlands-based Margarine Unie. Lever Brothers had been operating several factories in the United States as early as the turn of the twentieth century. Unilever, specializing in processed foods and household and beauty products, continued to grow after merger, both through brand acquisitions and brand internationalization, and was one of the 50 largest companies in the

world by 2000, with operations in approximately 100 different countries. However, unlike US-based multinational companies that have operated in a relatively stable social and political environment, European-rooted companies like Unilever have had to cope with diverse and rapidly changing operating circumstances across their national operating units.

Unilever's corporate structure is impacted by the complexities of its historical development. In essence, the company is a joint venture of two separate units, Unilever NV in the Netherlands, and Unilever PLC UK, although they are so tightly interwoven (identical boards of directors for example) as to be essentially inextricable (see chart, Unilever legal structure 2016). Unilever expanded quickly in the United States and became, with Procter & Gamble and Colgate-Palmolive, part of an oligopoly that controlled 80 per cent of the US soap market by the 1930s. The company's revenues were from an early stage geographically widely distributed, with North America, Europe and developing and emerging markets in Africa, Latin America and Asia all substantial earners. Like its American competitor Colgate-Palmolive, Unilever was organized on a global geographic basis. Today, sales in Europe, the Americas and Asia and Africa are all of approximately equal magnitude. The North American arm of the firm operated almost autonomously, the European operations reported to the Continental European Group based in Rotterdam, and the other worldwide operations to the Overseas Committee based in London. Under these geographic groupings, national companies operated with a great deal of freedom. Even in Europe during the early years of economic integration, national markets differed greatly due to tariffs, differing retail environments and a patchwork of companies holding different major household product brand names in different countries.

From the early 1960s, Unilever faced severe competition within Europe, particularly from Procter & Gamble, whose more centralized global structure was seen as permitting greater strategic purpose. Gradually, Unilever responded by attempting to centralize its European research and marketing operations, with mixed success. Transforming a company that had been assembled from numerous formerly independent companies, with high levels of decentralization, took several years. Unilever moved away from a global geographic structure towards a global matrix, a model that is discussed below. The new organizational structure, combined with the elimination of poorly performing product units, restored the company to healthy revenue and profit growth in the first years of the twenty-first century, with sales of over $50 billion and net income of nearly $8 billion in 2015.[42,43] However, wherever the balance is struck between local knowledge and centralized control, frictions need to be managed. In 2013, for example, Unilever headquarters announced it was planning to hike its royalty fee charged to subsidiaries like Hindustan Lever from 1.4 per cent to 3.15 per cent, and also centralized some of its marketing initiatives, provoking complaints from Indian market analysts.[44] At the same time that the parent company hiked its royalties, Hindustan Lever expressed a commitment to "sustainable growth" as well "positive social impact" from its Hindustan operations, and affirmed its intention to "collaborate and engage with different stakeholders including Governments, NGOs, IGOs, Suppliers, Farmers, and Distributors to tackle the challenges faced by the society."[45]

EXHIBIT 7.7 Unilever legal structure 2016

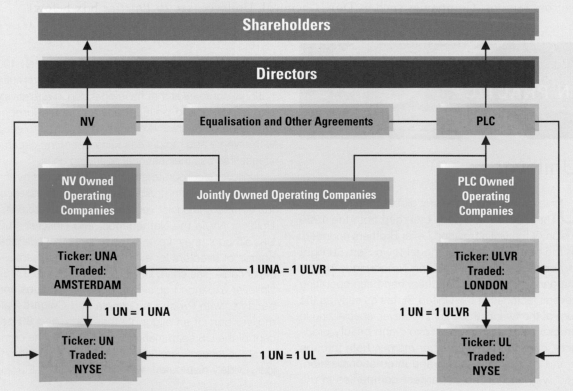

and Colgate-Palmolive find ways to take advantages of the global geographic structure while overcoming these problems. However, the emergence of global commodity chains, where different components of a single good or service's value are added in different geographic zones can present an almost insurmountable problem for businesses organized into global geographic divisions.

Global Matrix Structure

We've discussed how some companies adopt a global product division structure and have found ways to coordinate across worldwide divisions, while others favour a global geographic division structure and find ways to coordinate across geographical regions. Each of these companies emphasize a single dimension. An alternative is to devise a matrix structure to achieve vertical and horizontal coordination simultaneously along two dimensions, as discussed in Chapter 4. A global matrix structure is similar to the matrix described in Chapter 4, but for multinational corporations the geographical distances for communication are greater and coordination is more complex (Exhibit 7.8). The matrix is effective when pressure for decision-making balances product standardization and geographical localization, and when coordination to share resources is important.

Building Global Capabilities

There are many instances of well-known companies that encounter difficulties transferring successful ideas, products and services from their home country to the international domain. In the 1980s and 1990s, the British-based retailer Marks & Spencer (M&S) expanded throughout Europe and North America. By 2001 the company had decided to withdraw almost completely from overseas retailing, although by 2007 M&S relaunched its efforts, although by 2015, 90% of the company's revenues were still in the UK.[46,47,48] Wal-Mart's first foray into South America was a disaster, with the company losing $48 billion in its first two years.[49] Hundreds of companies attempted to expand into Russia after the collapse of communism. Most faced numerous unanticipated problems, and many pulled out incurring large losses.[50] Those that survived had to modify their business practices to accommodate rapidly changing rules and problems such as corruption.[51] Managers face tremendous challenges when seeking to capitalize on the opportunities that the possibility of global expansion presents.

The Global Organizational Challenge

Exhibit 7.9 illustrates the three primary segments of the global organizational challenge facing multinational organizations: greater complexity and differentiation, pressures for integration and the problem of transferring knowledge across a global firm. Organizations encounter extremely high levels of environmental complexity in the international domain. Addressing the many differences that occur among countries requires greater organizational differentiation. At the same time, managers strive to achieve coordination and collaboration among far-flung units and facilitate the development and transfer of organizational knowledge for global learning.[52]

EXHIBIT 7.8   Global Matrix Structure

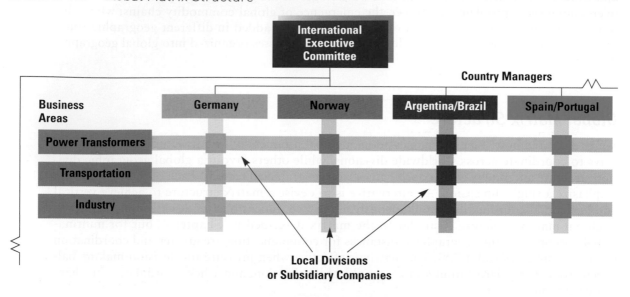

Local Divisions
or Subsidiary Companies

EXHIBIT 7.9   The Global Organizational Challenge

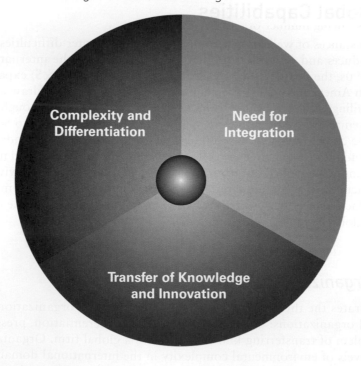

COUNTERPOINT 7.2

When considering the challenges facing executives, recall that the three segments (see Exhibit 7.9) are highly abstracted elements of highly complex practices. What managers actually do – as contrasted with what textbooks say they should be doing – is conditioned by the legacy of how the challenges have been handled in the past and the politics that constrains as well as enables what can be done today. It is likely that executives will give different amounts of emphasis and attention to the various segments. For example, some will identify knowledge transfer as a top strategic priority, whereas others will give much greater emphasis to integration. Needless to say, if each key competitor gave the same balance of emphasis to each of the segments, there would be a loss of competitive advantage to all players.

Increased Complexity and Differentiation   When organizations enter the international arena, they encounter a greater level of internal and external complexity than anything experienced on the domestic front. Companies are obliged to develop a structure to operate in numerous countries that differ in economic development, language, political systems and government regulations, cultural norms and values and infrastructure such as transportation and communication facilities. For example, although most international firms have their headquarters in wealthier, economically advanced countries, large investments are increasingly being made in emerging economies in Asia, Eastern Europe and Latin America, which offer huge new markets for their goods and services. Corporations based outside the US and Europe are quickly rising to prominence; in 2015, 98 of the Fortune 500 largest companies were based in China, second only to the US (128 companies).[53] In the area of e-commerce, the number of internet users and the amount of online sales are expanding rapidly in these emerging markets. Start-up low-cost airlines in South and South-East Asia now sell their tickets almost exclusively through the internet, whereas only a few years ago, the internet was unknown to all but a handful of the population.[54]

In addition, a growing number of global consumers are rejecting the notion of homogenized products and services, calling for greater response to local preferences. Even McDonald's, often seen as an ultimate example of standardization for a world market, has found it necessary to respond to local and national differences. In France, where some consumers have been resentful of the fast-food chain's incursion, McDonald's has boosted sales by remodelling restaurants to include features such as hardwood floors, wood-beam ceilings and comfortable armchairs, and by adding menu items such as espresso, brioche and more upscale sandwiches.[55] For religious and cultural reasons, McDonald's in India does not serve beef, the mainstay of its menu in North America and Europe.

All this complexity in the international environment is mirrored in a greater internal organizational complexity. Recall from Chapter 5 that as environments become more complex and uncertain, organizations grow more highly differentiated, with many specialized positions and departments to cope with specific sectors in the environment. Top management might set up specialized departments to deal with the diverse government, legal and accounting regulations in various countries, for example. More boundary-spanning departments might be developed to sense and respond to the external environment. In addition, organizations might implement a variety of strategies, a broader array of activities and a much larger number of products and services on an international level in order to meet the needs of a diverse market.

Integration   As organizations become more differentiated, with multiple products, divisions, departments and positions scattered across numerous countries, managers face a tremendous integration challenge. As described in Chapter 5, *integration* refers to the quality of collaboration across organizational units. The question is how to achieve the coordination and collaboration that is necessary for a global organization to reap the benefits of economies of scale, economies of scope and labour and production cost efficiencies that international expansion offers. Even in firms operating only in domestic markets, high differentiation among departments requires that more time and resources be devoted to achieving coordination because employees' attitudes, goals and work orientations differ widely. The situation is all the more complex for an international organization, whose operating units are divided not only by goals and work attitudes but by geographical distance, time differences, cultural values and perhaps even language as well. Recall the difficulties Unilever faced in coordinating its activities even in the single European market. Other companies, too, must find ways to share information, ideas, new products and technologies across the organization.

Knowledge Transfer   The third piece of the international challenge is to learn from international experiences and to leverage that learning so as to create organizational knowledge. The diversity of the international environment offers extraordinary opportunities for learning and the development of diverse capabilities. Members of organizational units in each location acquire the skills and knowledge to meet environmental challenges that arise in that particular locale. Much of that knowledge, which may be related to product improvements, operational efficiencies, technological advancements or myriad other competencies, is relevant across multiple countries, so systems are developed that promote the transfer of knowledge across the global enterprise. One good example comes from Procter & Gamble. Liquid Tide was one of P&G's most successful US product launches in the 1980s, but the product came about from the sharing of diverse international knowledge. Liquid Tide incorporated a technology for helping to suspend dirt in wash water from P&G headquarters in the United States, the formula for its cleaning agents from P&G technicians in Japan and special ingredients for fighting mineral salts present in hard water from company scientists in Brussels.[56]

COUNTERPOINT 7.3

Knowledge may be hidden deliberately in order to preserve jobs or monopolies of expertise, and not just because of cultural differences, etc. Most of the bullet points below suggest that organizations are not simply 'complex' but divided by conflicts of priority amongst different employees and interest groups. Hierarchy may facilitate managerial control but it also tends to frustrate open communication, including the sharing of knowledge.

Statements such as 'Organizations have to find ways to encourage both the development and sharing of knowledge' ring hollow when the sources of resistance to such sharing are unacknowledged or underestimated.

Most organizations tap only a fraction of the potential that is available from the cross-border transfer of knowledge.[57] There are several reasons for this:

- Knowledge often remains hidden in various units because language, cultural and geographic distances prevent top managers from recognizing it exists.
- Divisions sometimes view knowledge as power and want to hold on to it as a way to gain an influential position within the global firm.
- The 'not-invented-here' syndrome makes some managers reluctant to tap in to the know-how and expertise of other units.
- Much of an organization's knowledge is in the minds of employees and cannot easily be written down and shared with other units.

Global Coordination Mechanisms

Managers meet the global challenge of coordination and transferring knowledge across highly differentiated units in a variety of ways. Some of the most common are the use of global teams, stronger headquarters planning and control and specific coordination roles.

Global Teams   The popularity and success of teams on the domestic front allowed managers to see first-hand how this mechanism can achieve strong horizontal coordination, as described in Chapter 4, and thus recognize the promise teams held for coordination across a global firm as well. Global teams, also called transnational teams, are cross-border work groups made up of multiskilled, multinational members whose activities span multiple countries.[58] Typically, teams are of two types: intercultural teams, whose members come from different countries and meet face to face, and virtual global teams, whose members remain in separate locations around the world and conduct their work electronically.[59] Heineken formed the European Production Task Force, a 13-member team made up of multinational members, to meet regularly and come up with ideas for optimizing the company's production facilities across Europe.[60] The research unit of BT Labs has several hundred researchers spread across the United Kingdom and several other countries who work in global virtual teams to investigate virtual reality, artificial intelligence and other advanced information technologies.[61] The team approach enables technologies, ideas and learning in one country to rapidly spread across the firm via the constant sharing of information among team members.

The most advanced and competitive use of global teams involves simultaneous contributions in three strategic areas.[62] First, global teams help companies address the differentiation challenge, enabling them to be more locally responsive by providing knowledge to meet the needs of different regional markets, consumer preferences and political and legal systems. At the same time, teams provide integration benefits, helping organizations achieve global efficiencies by developing regional or worldwide cost advantages and standardizing designs and operations across countries. Finally, these teams contribute to continuous organizational learning, knowledge transfer and adaptation on a global level.

ONLINE COUNTERPOINT 7.5

Headquarters Planning
A second approach to achieving stronger global coordination is for those in headquarters to take an active role in planning, scheduling and control to keep the widely distributed pieces of the global organization working together and moving in the same direction. In one survey, 70 per cent of global companies reported that the most important function of corporate headquarters was to 'provide enterprise leadership'.[63] In the absence of a strong lead from the centre, highly autonomous divisions can begin to act like independent companies rather than coordinated parts of a global whole. When this is not desired, top management may delegate responsibility and decision-making authority in some areas, such as adapting products or services to meet local needs, while maintaining strong control through centralized management and information systems that enable headquarters to keep track of what's going on and that serve to coordinate activities across divisions and countries. Plans, schedules and formal rules and procedures can help ensure greater communication among divisions and with headquarters. They may also foster cooperation and synergy among far-flung units to achieve the goals attributed to an organization in a timely and cost-efficient way. A key role ascribed to top managers is the provision of clear strategic direction that, for example, can guide the activity of far-flung operations and help resolve competing demands from various units.

BRIEFCASE 7.4

Expanded Coordination Roles
Structural solutions may also be devised to achieve stronger coordination and collaboration.[64] Creating specific organizational roles or positions for coordination is a possible way to integrate all the elements of the enterprise to achieve a strong competitive position. In international firms, the role of top *functional managers*, for example, may be expanded to include responsibility for coordinating across countries, identifying and linking the organization's expertise and resources worldwide. In an international organization, the manufacturing manager may give priority to being aware of, and coordinating with, manufacturing operations of the company in various other parts of the world so that greater manufacturing efficiency is achieved and technology and ideas are shared across units. A new manufacturing technology developed to improve efficiency in Ford's Brazilian operations, for example, may be valuable for European and North American plants as well. Manufacturing managers are responsible for being aware of new developments wherever they occur and for using their knowledge to improve the organization. Similarly, marketing managers, human resource managers and other

functional managers at an international company are involved not only in activities for their particular location but in coordinating with their sister units in other countries.

Whereas functional managers coordinate across countries, *country managers* coordinate across functions. A country manager for an international firm coordinates all the various functional activities to meet the problems, opportunities, needs and trends in the local market, enabling the organization to achieve multinational flexibility and rapid response. The country manager in Venezuela for Unilever's national subsidiary, Unilever Andina Venezuela, is responsible for the coordination of everything that goes on in that country, from manufacturing to human resources to marketing, to ensure that activities meet the language, cultural, government and legal requirements of Venezuela. Country managers also contribute to the transfer of ideas, trends, products and technologies that arise in one country and might have significance on a broader scale.

In some organizations a formal *network coordinator* is created to coordinate information and activities related to key customer accounts. These coordinators would enable a manufacturing organization, for example, to provide knowledge and integrated solutions across multiple businesses, divisions and countries for large customers such as the France-headquartered Carrefour supermarket chain, or Wal-Mart from the US.[65] Top managers may also encourage and support informal networks and relationships to keep information flowing in all directions. Much information exchange occurs not through formal systems or structures but through informal channels and relationships. Executives can enhance organizational coordination by supporting these informal networks, giving people across boundaries opportunities to get together, develop relationships and keep in close touch.

Cultural Differences in Coordination and Control

Just as social and cultural values differ from country to country, the management values and organizational norms of international companies tend to vary depending on the organization's home country and history. Organizational norms and values are influenced by the values in the larger national culture, and these in turn influence the organization's structural approach and the ways managers coordinate and control an international firm.

National Value Systems

Many studies have attempted to determine how national value systems influence management and organizations.[66,67] Two dimensions from Hofstede's model that seem to have a strong impact within organizations are *power distance* and *uncertainty avoidance*. High power distance means that people accept inequality in power among institutions, organizations and people. Low power distance means that people expect equality in power. That is to say, they expect to be treated as equals, not as subordinates. High uncertainty avoidance means that members of a society feel uncomfortable with uncertainty and ambiguity and so are more inclined to support beliefs or programmes that promise certainty and conformity. Low uncertainty avoidance means that people have a comparatively high tolerance for the unstructured, the unclear and the unpredictable. However, as discussed in Counterpoint 7.4, Hofstede's model has been widely criticised as too static, and founded on 'national' characteristics that at best reflect only a part of individual and group identity.[68]

These value dimensions may be reflected within organizations in terms of beliefs regarding the appeal of hierarchy, centralized decision-making and control, formal rules and procedures and specialized jobs.[69] Organizations rooted in societies that value high power distance, for example, tend to be more hierarchical and centralized, with greater control and coordination from the top levels of the organization. Organizations embedded in societies in which people have a high tolerance for uncertainty may have fewer rules and formal systems, relying more on informal networks and personal communication for coordination. It is important to understand that societies often change quite rapidly, and that interpersonal communications norms are strongly affected by the type of political and economic regime in which citizens operate. Clearly, citizens living in countries ruled by

BOOKMARK 7.0

Have you read this book?

Cross-Cultural Business Behavior: Marketing, Negotiating and Managing Across Cultures

BY RICHARD R. GESTELAND

Richard Gesteland maintains that heeding the 'two iron rules of international business' is crucial to success in today's global business environment: 'In International Business, the Seller Is Expected to Adapt to the Buyer', and 'In International Business, the Visitor Is Expected to Observe Local Customs'. In his book *Cross-Cultural Business Behavior,* Gesteland explains and categorizes various cultural patterns of behaviour that can help managers follow these rules.

Logical Cultural Patterns

Gesteland outlines four major cultural value patterns, which he calls *logical patterns*, that characterize countries around the world:

- *Deal-Focused vs Relationship-Focused*. Deal-focused cultures, such as those in North America, Australia and Northern Europe, are task-oriented, while relationship-focused cultures, including those in Arabia, Africa, Latin America and Asia, are typically people-oriented. Deal-focused individuals approach business in an objective and impersonal way. Relationship-focused individuals believe in building close personal relationships as the appropriate way to conduct business.

- *Informal vs Formal*. Informal cultures place a low value on status and power differences, whereas formal cultures are typically hierarchical and status-conscious. The unconstrained values of informal cultures, such as those in the United States and Australia, may insult people from formal, hierarchical societies, just as the class-consciousness of formal groups, such as cultures in most of Europe and Latin America, may offend the egalitarian ideals of people in informal cultures.

- *Rigid-Time vs Fluid-Time*. One part of the world's societies is flexible about time and scheduling, while the other group is more rigid and dedicated to clock-time. Conflicts may occur because rigid-time types often consider fluid-time people undisciplined and irresponsible, while fluid-time people regard rigid-time folks as arrogant, demanding and enslaved by meaningless deadlines.

- *Expressive vs Reserved*. Expressive cultures include those in Latin America and the Mediterranean. Reserved cultures are those in East and Southeast Asia as well as Germanic Europe. This distinction can create a major communication gap. People from expressive cultures tend to talk louder and use more hand gestures and facial expressions. Reserved cultures may interpret raised voices and gesturing as signals of anger or instability.

A Practical Guide

Geographical-cultural differences, and the potential problems that cross-cultural communication can create, 'impact our business success throughout the global marketplace' argues Gesteland. *Cross-Cultural Business Behavior* 'is intended as a practical guide for the men and women in the front lines of world trade, those who face every day the frustrating differences in global business customs and practices'. By understanding Gesteland's logical patterns of behaviour, managers can adapt to varied cultural values and improve their chances for international success, although it is important to remember that cultural norms vary greatly within societies and can change rapidly over time. See Counterpoint 7.4.

Cross-Cultural Business Behavior: Marketing, Negotiating and Managing Across Cultures, by Richard R. Gesteland, is published by Copenhagen Business School Press.

repressive dictatorships, for example, will be cautious about criticizing authority! Communications norms may change quite rapidly after a repressive regime is replaced by a democratic one.

This chapter's *Bookmark 7.0* further examines how societal value patterns influence international organizations.

Some studies have found clear patterns of different management structures when comparing countries in Europe, the United States and Asia, although other studies have found that the firm size and type of business being conducted has a more important impact on organizational structures and management approaches.[70]

Three National Approaches to Coordination and Control

Let's look at three primary approaches to coordination and control as represented by Japanese, American and European companies.[71] It should be noted that companies in each country use tools and techniques from each of the three coordination methods. However, there are broad, general patterns that illustrate cultural differences.

Centralized Coordination in Japanese Companies
When expanding internationally, Japanese-headquartered companies have typically developed coordination mechanisms that rely on centralization. Top managers at headquarters actively direct and control overseas operations, whose primary focus is to implement strategies handed down from headquarters. The senior management teams in different country divisions tend to include some, or many Japanese nationals. This approach enables Japanese companies to leverage the knowledge and resources located at the corporate centre, attain global efficiencies, coordinate across units to obtain synergies, avoid turf battles and maintain a cohesive overall organizational vision. Top managers use strong structural linkages to ensure that managers at headquarters remain up-to-date and fully involved in all strategic decisions. However, centralization has its limits. As organizations expand and divisions grow larger, headquarters can become overloaded and decision-making slower. The quality of decisions may also suffer as greater diversity and complexity make it difficult for headquarters to understand and respond to local needs in each region. While the 'Japanese model' has proven highly effective even in various environments with deep national traditions including strong labour unions and a highly structured labour market,[72] it has sometimes encountered difficulties adapting quickly to macroeconomic and market instability.[73]

European Firms' Decentralized Approach
A different approach has typically been taken by European companies, as we saw at Unilever. Rather than relying on strong, centrally directed coordination and control, international units tend to have a high level of independence and decision-making autonomy. Companies rely on a strong mission, shared values and informal personal relationships for coordination. Thus, great emphasis is placed on careful selection, training and development of key managers throughout the international organization. Formal management and control systems are used primarily for financial rather than technical or operational control. With this approach, each international unit focuses on its local markets, enabling the company to excel in meeting diverse needs. One disadvantage is the cost of ensuring, through training and development programmes, that managers throughout a huge, global firm share goals, values and priorities. Decision-making can also be slow and complex, and disagreements and conflicts among divisions are more difficult to resolve.

The United States: Coordination and Control through Formalization
US-based companies that have expanded into the international arena have often taken a third direction. Typically, these organizations have delegated responsibility to international divisions, yet retained overall control of the enterprise through the use of sophisticated management control systems and the development of specialist headquarters staff. Formal systems, policies, standards of performance and a regular flow of information from divisions to headquarters are the primary means of coordination and control. Decision-making is based on objective data, policies and procedures, which provides for many operating efficiencies and reduces conflict among divisions and between divisions and headquarters. However, the cost of setting up complex systems, policies and rules for an international organization may be quite high. The approach also requires a larger headquarters

staff for reviewing, interpreting and sharing information, thus increasing overhead costs. Finally, standard routines and procedures don't always fit the needs of new problems and situations. Flexibility is limited when managers may pay so much attention to systems that they fail to recognize opportunities and threats in the environment.

Clearly, each of these approaches has advantages. But as international organizations grow larger and more complex, the disadvantages of each tend to become more pronounced. As traditional approaches have been inadequate to meet the demands of a rapidly changing, complex international environment, many large international companies are moving toward a new kind of organization form, the *transnational model*. This is a highly differentiated approach that is designed to address environmental complexity yet in principle offers very high levels of coordination, learning and transfer of organizational knowledge.

COUNTERPOINT 7.4

Great caution needs to be shown in associating certain types of behaviour or even certain types of organizational form with specific cultures. While differences in behaviour can be noted between countries, the origins of these differences tend to be varied and contingent on specific circumstances. Further, culture is a factor in all types of human system, not only nations. Schneider and Barsoux[74] write of 'interacting spheres of culture' in which a variety of cultural factors intersect in working relationships: industry cultures, professional cultures, national cultures, class-based culture, cultures based in ethnicity and religion, gendered cultures, etc. Thus, in an international firm, engineers from different countries may share similar working norms and practices despite the fact their 'national cultures' may appear very dissimilar.

The methodology and theoretical assumptions underlying Hofstede's research has been widely critiqued.[75] For example, his reliance on employees from a single company (IBM) introduces a major bias because of the existence of company-specific cultural norms (as noted by Schneider and Barsoux).

At worst, cultural stereotyping can lead to sweeping generalizations about human capacities and compatibilities and can lead to gross misunderstandings and a self-fulfilling prophesy of inter-civilizational conflict, whether at the level of the organization or in wider international relations. Samuel P. Huntington's thesis of the 'clash of civilizations'[76] was a key theoretical underpinning to the decision of the George W. Bush administration to unleash the United States' ill-conceived and ill-fated war against Iraq.[77]

The Transnational Model of Organization

The transnational model is an organizational form highly adapted to the character of a globalizing economy. It reflects both organizational complexity, with many diverse units, and organizational coordination, with mechanisms for integrating the varied parts. The transnational model is useful for large, multinational companies with subsidiaries in many countries that try to exploit both global and local advantages as well as technological advancements, rapid innovation and global learning and knowledge sharing. Rather than building capabilities primarily in one area, such as global efficiency, national responsiveness or global learning, the transnational model seeks to achieve all three simultaneously. Dealing with multiple, interrelated, complex issues requires a complex form of organization and structure, and a transformative approach in which innovations in one area interrelate with and leverage new ways of looking at, and developing, other aspects of the organization. The transnational model has been adopted by complex global organizations such as Philips NV, illustrated in Exhibit 7.10. Headquartered in the Netherlands, Philips has hundreds of operating units all over the world and is typical of global companies such as Unilever, Matsushita or Procter & Gamble.[78]

BRIEFCASE 7.6

The units in Exhibit 7.10 are far-flung. Achieving coordination, a sense of participation and involvement by subsidiaries and a sharing of information, knowledge, new technology and

EXHIBIT 7.10   International Organizational Units and Interlinkages within Philips NV

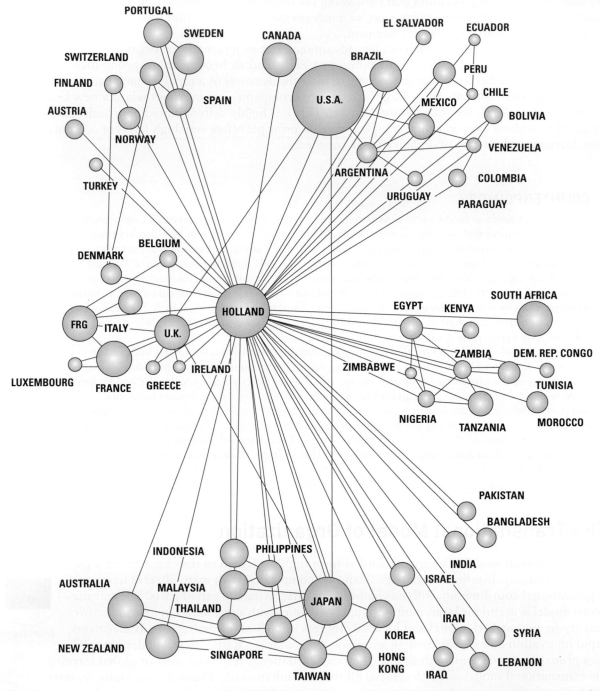

Source: Sumantra Ghoshal and Christopher A. Bartlett, 'The Multinational Corporation as an Interorganizational Network,' *Academy of Management Review* 15 (1990), 605.

customers is a tremendous challenge. Some subsidiaries may become so large that they no longer fit a narrow strategic role defined by headquarters. The transnational model addresses such challenges by creating an integrated network of individual operations that are linked together in an effort to achieve the multidimensional goals of the overall organization.[79] The management philosophy is based on *interdependence* rather than full divisional independence or total dependence of these units on headquarters for decision-making and control. Its advocates would say that the transnational model necessitates a managerial state of mind, a set of values, a shared desire to make a worldwide learning system work and a flexible and transparent structure for effectively managing such a system. Several characteristics distinguish the transnational organization from other global organization forms such as the matrix, described earlier.

1   *Assets and resources are dispersed worldwide into highly specialized operations that are linked together through interdependent relationships.* Resources and capabilities are widely distributed to help the organization sense and respond to diverse stimuli such as market needs, technological developments or consumer trends that emerge in different parts of the world. However, managers forge interdependent relationships among the various product, functional or geographic units. Mechanisms such as cross-subsidiary teams, for example, compel units to work together for the good of their own unit as well as the overall organization. Rather than being completely self-sufficient, each group has to cooperate to achieve its goals. Such interdependencies encourage the collaborative sharing of information and resources, cross-unit problem solving and collective implementation demanded by today's competitive international environment. Materials, people, products, ideas, resources and information are continually flowing among the dispersed parts of the integrated network. In addition, managers actively shape, manage and reinforce informal information networks that cross functions, products, divisions and countries.

2   *Structures are flexible and ever-changing.* The transnational operates on a principle of *flexible centralization.* It may centralize some functions in one country, some in another, yet decentralize still other functions among its many geographically dispersed operations. An R&D centre may be centralized in Holland and a purchasing centre located in Sweden, while financial accounting responsibilities are decentralized to operations in many countries. A unit in Hong Kong may be responsible for coordinating activities across Asia, while activities for all other countries are coordinated by a large division headquarters in London. The transnational requires that managers are flexible in order to reap the benefits. Some functions, products and geographic regions require more central control and coordination than others. In addition, coordination and control mechanisms are likely to change over time to meet new demands or competitive threats.

3   *Subsidiary managers initiate strategic innovations that become strategy for the corporation as a whole.* In traditional structures, managers have a strategic role only for their division. In a transnational, various centres and subsidiaries can shape the company from the bottom up by developing creative responses and initiating programmes in response to local needs and dispersing those innovations worldwide. Transnational companies recognize each of the worldwide units as a source of capabilities and knowledge that can be used to benefit the entire organization. In addition, environmental demands and opportunities vary from country to country, and exposing the whole organization to this broader range of environmental stimuli triggers greater learning and innovation.

4   *Unification and coordination are achieved primarily through corporate culture, shared vision and values and management style rather than through formal structures and systems.* The transnational is in many ways a horizontal structure. It is diverse and extended, and it exists in a fluctuating environment so that hierarchy, standard rules, procedures and close supervision are not appropriate. Achieving unity and coordination in an organization where employees come from a variety of different national backgrounds, are separated by time and geographical distance and have different cultural norms is more easily accomplished through shared understanding than through formal systems. Top leaders build a context of shared vision, values and perspectives among managers who in turn cascade these elements through all parts of the organization. Selection and training of managers emphasizes flexibility and open-mindedness. In addition, people are often rotated through different jobs, divisions and countries to gain broad experience and become socialized into the corporate culture. Achieving coordination in a transnational organization is a much more complex process than simple

centralization or decentralization of decision-making and requires shaping and adapting beliefs, culture and values so that everyone participates in information sharing and learning.

Taken together, these characteristics are intended to facilitate strong coordination, organizational learning and knowledge sharing on a broad global scale. In principle, the autonomy of organizational parts gives strength to smaller units and allows the firm to be flexible in responding to rapid change and competitive opportunities on a local level, while the emphasis on interdependency enables global efficiencies and organizational learning.

New Approaches to Global Organizational Design

Dragon Multinationals

The different stages of international organizational development described above are pertinent for international companies building from a domestic base in developed, mature economies. These companies typically have accumulated resources which they can devote to taking advantage of international opportunities. As we saw with the examples of H&M and Unilever, they often develop gradually through stages of international activity, beginning with an export division, then setting up international branches under varying degrees of headquarters supervision, before transforming themselves into the more fully-fledged global and transnational organizations described above.

In the emerging economies, particularly in the Asia-Pacific region, new types of companies have quickly grown that do not expand from a significant domestic base, but have from their beginnings depended on international and even global markets for growth. As markets in developing countries are usually relatively small, ambitious companies have little choice but to seek to expand overseas from the beginning. Other reasons for companies to skip the 'domestic' stage include heavily regulated home markets, with few opportunities for developing new businesses. These circumstances have led to the development of what the Australian business professor, John Mathews, calls dragon multinationals.[80] Companies such as Acer and Mittal Steel have exploited the developing global economy as their 'home turf' for rapid business expansion. In fact, for different reasons, both companies had to expand outside of this turf in order to become significant business organizations. India's highly regulated steel industry did not permit rapid domestic growth, so Lakshmi Mittal, the son of the owner of Ispat Industries, a medium-sized Indian steel firm, hived off a fledgling international division in 1979 and over a 15-year period transformed it into the largest steel company in the world, and ultimately led to a merger with the Luxembourg-based conglomerate Arcelor that put Mittal in charge of the Arcelor Mittal corporation.[81] Acer, founded by the Taiwanese entrepreneur, Stan Shih, exploited global trade and production networks to create a genuinely global multinational. Shih initially aimed to build his international company through acquisitions and expansion in the US, but was severely undercapitalized. On the verge of bankruptcy, in the early 1990s, Shih adopted a radically different business growth model by breaking the company down into 'cells' that network together, and with outside suppliers and marketers, to create multiple profit centres. Deliberately employing a 'fuzzy' organizational design, Acer was ready to transform itself in order to take advantage of the rapidly developing and mutating global hi-tech business (see Exhibit 7.11).

Unlike traditional multinationals that build primarily from internal resources, dragon multinationals seek to profit from external resources through three key strategies: *linkage*, *leverage* and *learning* (Exhibit 7.12). Linkage involves building partnerships and joint ventures to permit access to larger markets. Frequently, as in the case of Acer, these may begin with the dragon multinational in a subordinate role to a more well-established, often western-based multinational. Leverage entails building on global linkages to access necessary knowledge and financial resources for expansion. Learning is the commitment of the organization to improve business understanding and practice through applying knowledge gained from the repeated cycles of linkage and leverage.

Dragon multinationals can be considered one version of an emerging type of organization, the *born global*. The born global firm is one that from the outset derives competitive advantage from use

EXHIBIT 7.11 Acer's Cellular Structure

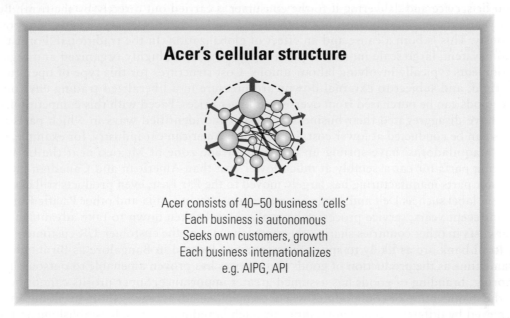

Acer's cellular structure

Acer consists of 40–50 business 'cells'
Each business is autonomous
Seeks own customers, growth
Each business internationalizes
e.g. AIPG, API

EXHIBIT 7.12 Ingredients of Success

Ingredients of success

Linkage
Links with global players drawn into collaborative networks
Acer: links with TI (DRAMs), IBM

Leverage
Technology leverage from links with advanced firms
Long-term focus: Capabilities enhancement
Securing more from contractual link than revenues

Learning
Repeated application of linkage and leverage
Enhancement of capabilities

Source: John Mathews, presentation to United Nations Industrial Development Organization Conference on Competitiveness, Mitwatersrand, South Africa, 2004.

of resources and sales in multiple countries. Born global firms usually are defined as those that begin exporting within a couple of years of their foundation, and have a global vision and strategy. The viability of the 'born global' approach is at the same time highly dependent on the type of industry and market segment. It is perhaps best viewed as one end of a continuum of contextually dependent internationalization approaches.[82]

Value Chains

The potential for dragon multinationals to succeed takes advantage of a major change in the way that business is organized internationally. Both domestic and multinational firms have always juggled with different levels of vertical integration (the extent to which the entire process of conceiving of a good or service and delivering it to the consumer is carried out directly by the firm). But, in recent years, the business process has been dis-assembled to a far greater extent than possible previously. This is both a cause and an effect of globalization. In the traditional 'Fordist' production system, large scale industrial processes take place in highly organized and regulated environments typically involving labour unions. Cost structures for this type of operation are quite rigid, and subject to external downward pressure in a liberalized trading environment where goods can be purchased from overseas at lower prices. Faced with this competition, executives have disaggregated their business processes and identified ways in which parts of the process can be conducted at lower cost. In the North American car industry, for example, plants called 'maquiladoras' have sprung up in the free trade zone of Mexico near the US border, producing parts for car assembly at much lower cost than American and Canadian factories. Computer parts manufacturing has largely moved to the Far East; even products still carrying a 'Western' label such as Dell and Apple are made primarily in China and other Pacific Rim countries. In recent years, service processes have also been broken down to take advantage of low labour costs in other countries sharing the same language as the customer. UK customers calling their local bank are as likely to speak with someone located in Bangalore as Birmingham. At the same time as the production of goods and services has proven amenable to outsourcing and offshoring, branding of goods has assumed greater importance. Super profits cannot be made from the manufacture of commodities where competitive advantage is short-lived. But they can be achieved by differentiating commodities through branding. Although establishing and maintaining a brand is risky and costly, it can transform a mundane article such as a t-shirt or piece of luggage into something prestigious and identity-enhancing. Increasingly, companies in emerging economies are attempting to build globally-recognized brands: for example Hyundai and Samsung in South Korea, Arcelor / Beko in Turkey, and Lenovo, Huawei and Haier in China.

The US economic sociologist Gary Gereffi has explored the significance of these developments in his work on global commodity and global value chains. Global chains are a way to look at the creation of value in the economic system. Gereffi notes that offshoring has gradually 'moved up the value chain'. In the 1960s and 1970s basic production began being offshored. By the 1980s developing country workers were providing basic devices such as data processing and customer service. In the 1990s, more complex tasks such as medical transcription and business accounting had moved offshore. And, in the early years of the twenty-first century there have been accelerating signs that 'top end' skilled work such as design and brand innovation are being offshored (Exhibit 7.13).

As outsourcing and offshoring have gathered pace, the complexity and variety of global value chains has increased. This has produced conflicts between corporations in developed and emerging economies as they seek to maintain the largest share of added value. Gereffi argues that there are as many as five different types of value chain, each with a different dynamic and power relationship between producers and suppliers (Exhibit 7.14).

The exhibit on the following page summarizes Gereffi's model of the five different types of value chains that are present in the global economy. These are placed on a scale according to the balance of power (or what Gereffi calls 'governance' within the value chain). In the first case, which fits the traditional model of an open market situation, power is equally balanced between many purchasers and many suppliers. Gereffi suggests that the 'captive' value chain reflects the currently dominant form, where a large retail firm such as Wal-Mart obtains most of its products from outsourced suppliers, who negotiate with the retail giant from a position of considerable disadvantage. As they are dependent on the retail giant for much if not all of their revenues, whereas the retailer can usually source from numerous other locations, they are virtually forced to do the bidding of the large retailer. Gereffi claims that it is through this mechanism that suppliers to companies like Wal-Mart have offshored much of their production to low wage countries such as China.

According to Gereffi, the ability to construct a product across territorial boundaries is a source of instability in both developed countries and emerging economies. Top corporate managers in

EXHIBIT 7.13 The Organization of Producer-driven and Buyer-driven Global Commodity Chains

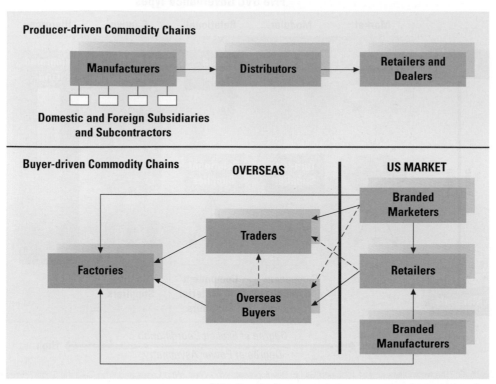

Notes: Solid arrows are primary relationships; dashed arrows are secondary relationships.
Retailers, branded marketers and traders require full-package supply from overseas factories.
Branded manufacturers ship parts for overseas assembly and re-export to the manufacturer's home market.

international businesses are therefore obliged to pay close attention to their place in the value chains, as well as the rapidly changing nature of the chains themselves, as business processes undergo rapid changes, and reputational risks, with regard to corporate social responsibilities, are increased.

Summary and Interpretation

This chapter has examined the design of organizations for complex international environments. Almost every company today is affected by significant global forces. Benefits associated with global expansion were identified as those of economies of scale, economies of scope and access to scarce or low-cost factors of production such as labour, raw materials or land. One way to become involved in international operations is through strategic alliances with international firms. Alliances include licencing, joint ventures and consortia.

Organizations have traditionally evolved through four stages, beginning with a domestic orientation, shifting to an international orientation, then changing to a multinational orientation and finally moving to a global orientation that sees the whole world as a potential market. Following this logic, they typically set up an export department, then an international department and eventually develop into a worldwide geographic or product structure. Geographic structures are most effective for organizations that can benefit from a multidomestic strategy, meaning that products and services will do best if tailored to local needs and cultures. A product structure supports a globalization strategy, which means that products and services can be standardized and sold

EXHIBIT 7.14   Five GVC Governance Types

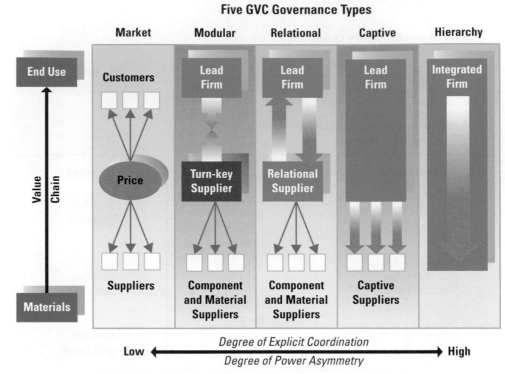

Source: Gereffi, G. 'The New Offshoring of Jobs and Global Development: Who Wins, Who Loses and Who Calls the Shots?' Presentation at Polson Institute for Global Development, Cornell University, October 28, 2005.

worldwide. Huge global firms might use a matrix structure to respond to both local and global forces simultaneously. Many firms use hybrid structures, by combining elements of two or more different structures to meet the dynamic conditions of the global environment.

Operating on a global scale is not easy. Three aspects of the global organizational challenge are addressing environmental complexity through greater organizational flexibility and differentiation, achieving integration and coordination among the highly differentiated units and implementing mechanisms for global learning and knowledge transfer. Common ways to address the problem of integration and knowledge transfer are through global teams, stronger headquarters planning and control and specific coordination roles. Diverse national and cultural values influence the approach to coordination and control. Three broad national approaches were identified: centralized coordination and control typically found in many Japanese-based firms, a decentralized approach common among European firms and the formalization approach often used by US-based international firms. In practice, most companies, no matter their home country, combine elements from each of these approaches. The transnational model, based upon a philosophy of interdependence, offers another approach to coordination where, in principle at least, members in each part of the organization are aware of, and closely integrated with, the organization as a whole so that local actions complement and enhance other company parts.

Globalization has brought new actors onto the global economic stage. Corporations from emerging economies have begun to make a substantial impact in many product and service areas. Their growth patterns tend to be different from those of traditional multinational corporations that have typically built their international business from domestic bases. For the new 'dragon multinationals', the international environment is their home territory. Their growth strategies from the beginning have been based on linkage with other international firms, the leverage of knowledge and resources from these partnerships and a rigorous approach to learning and adaptation.

A connected feature of contemporary globalization is the dissassembling and reorganization of production processes to benefit from cost and skill advantages across territorial boundaries. As different companies from different countries work together to create products and services in a value chain, corporate managers are under pressure to re-examine their company's place in the chain, the possibilities for increasing the value realization of their part of the chain, and the opportunities and threats presented by the potential for reorganizing that chain.

KEY CONCEPTS

consortia	global companies	global teams	multidomestic
domestic stage	global geographic	global value chain	multidomestic strategy
dragon multinational	structure	globalization strategy	multinational stage
economies of scale	global matrix structure	international division	power distance
economies of scope	global product structure	international stage	transnational model
factors of production	global stage	joint venture	uncertainty avoidance

Discussion Questions

1   Under what conditions should a company consider adopting a global geographic structure as opposed to a global product structure?

2   Name some companies that you think could succeed today with a globalization strategy and explain why you selected those companies. How does the globalization strategy differ from a multidomestic strategy?

3   Why would a company want to join a strategic alliance rather than go it alone in international operations? What do you see as the potential advantages and disadvantages of international alliances?

4   Why is knowledge sharing so important to a global organization?

5   What are some of the primary reasons a company decides to expand internationally? Identify a company in the news that has recently built a new overseas facility. Which of the three motivations for global expansion described in the chapter do you think best explains the company's decision? Discuss.

6   When would an organization consider using a matrix structure? How does the global matrix differ from the domestic matrix structure described in Chapter 4?

7   Name some of the elements that contribute to greater complexity for international organizations. How do organizations address this complexity? Do you think these elements apply to an online company such as eBay? Discuss.

8   Traditional values in Mexico appear to support high power distance and a low tolerance for uncertainty. What would you predict about a company that opens a division in Mexico and tries to implement global teams characterized by shared power and authority and the lack of formal guidelines, rules and structure?

9   Do you believe it is possible for a global company to achieve simultaneously the goals of global efficiency and integration, national responsiveness and flexibility and worldwide learning and knowledge sharing? Discuss.

10   What does it mean to say that the transnational model is based on a philosophy of interdependence?

11   What strategies can companies from emerging economies with limited domestic markets take in order to succeed in the global economy?

12   What are the potential benefits and dangers to a company of offshoring some of its production? What steps would a company's managers need to take in order to determine whether it should offshore, and what aspects of its business process it should offshore?

13   What are global value chains, and why are they a useful way of looking at production organization today? What might be some options managers could consider if they wanted their corporation to secure a greater proportion of the created value in a value chain?

Chapter 7 Workbook *Where is it made?*

Find three different consumer products, such as a shirt, a toy and a shoe. Try to find out the following information for each product, as shown in the table. To find this information, use websites, articles on the company from various business newspapers and magazines, and the labels on the items. You could also try calling the company and talking with someone there.

Product	What country do materials come from?	Where is it manufactured or assembled?	Which country does the marketing and advertising?	In what different countries is the product sold?
1				
2				
3				

What can you conclude about international products and organizations based on your analysis?

Chapter 7 Workshop Comparing Cultures

As a group, rent a video or a film made in another country from your own (or, alternately, go to the cinema when a foreign movie is shown). Take notes as you watch the movie, looking for similarities and differences in cultural norms compared to your own. For example, what are the similarities and differences in the following compared to your own cultural norms:

a   The way people interact with one another

b   The formality or informality of relationships

c   The attitudes toward work

d   The amount of time people spend on work vs family

e   The connection to family

f   How people have fun

Questions

1   What were the key differences you observed in the film's culture versus your own?

2   What are the advantages and disadvantages of using films to understand another culture?

Source: Copyright 2003 by Dorothy Marcic. All rights reserved.

Global Service Design at Imagination

This case study will focus on two themes:

1 The global drivers shaping the new business initiatives in Imagination.
2 The implications for organizational design of this complex business environment.

This case does not focus on the technical aspects of international business theory but rather focuses on up to date initiatives, innovation and practical perspectives. Thus, the main focus is on the examination of the changes in the global business and their effects on the development of competitive advantage within an independent communications business originally based within the UK.

The business has developed rapidly in recent years as it attempts to serve its increasingly global customer base. The company originated in London but now has operations spanning the globe in Australia, USA, Asia Pacific, Germany and more. A management team of nine key Directors run the business and the company is built on long term global partnerships across the globe including one of their most prestigious being Ford Motor Company, with one executive being given the responsibility to manage the globe relationship with the business over the long term. The Human Resource department has also grown to reflect the increasing complexities of the business and nurture an expanding group of creative innovators both internally and externally to the business.

This company has a clear motivation for growth because of the nature of their client base, which is invariably international, multinational or global in nature. They have developed by using the normal stages of international development but have moved, over more than 20 years, from domestic-based i.e. London towards a business offering global services with a flexible and global operations team and structure. This growth has been supported by a range of partnerships and alliances, which have truly operated with the concept of global and local guiding their every move. The structure of the company has needed to change with their customer base in terms of organizational structure, systems and strategic creativity in human resource management.

The company has needed to adapt and change through detailed analysis of risk and costs and a clear understanding of the need to develop appropriate organizational systems and structures to fit a complex global business environment. This structure resembles the traditional strategic business unit or divisional structure but with a strong focus on building global capabilities that can be offered to a new market, particularly in the emerging markets. The focus of the business is on managing complexity, integrating ideas and new concepts from around the globe and transferring knowledge quickly to wherever it is needed. This operation is supported by a range of global teams who are encouraged through a collaborative culture which teaches interdependence but also independence of thinking and actions across the business.

Company

Imagination is an independent creative communications company that transforms business through creativity.

The company often receives endorsements from satisfied clients who may place advertisements in leading marketing journals to explain how pleased the company was with the standard of work completed by the creative people within Imagination.

Financial performance indicators exist within the company and their increasing sales turnover and profitability over a long period has only been achieved through a clear focus on the bottom line, but their achievements are also believed to be about something else.

The question of how you would define the 'something else' is reviewed constantly and examined on the basis of whether the creativity requirements as verified by the customer or by the representative groups of customers were met. The achievement and definition of success is also discussed when the company examines the effective use of talent within the company and how their improvements, effectiveness has been welcomed by the customer. The placement of an advertisement in a marketing channel by a leading multi-national company is perhaps the ultimate example of success from Imagination's point of view.

▶

Their measurement of success appears to be based on the following:

MEASUREMENT OF SUCCESS
\
\
\

| SETTING EXACTING CREATIVE CHALLENGES | DEVELOPING GLOBAL CLIENT RELATIONSHIPS | TALENT & CLIENT DEVELOPMENT |

Imagination believes in introducing new business and strategic planning processes and understands their importance in achieving future success for themselves and their clients. This has been evidenced by their ability to hold onto one of their long-standing clients, Ford Motor Company.

The measurement of success is supported by one other factor:

The question of whether the successful new idea or concept will work effectively on a global scale and if it will enable Imagination to develop a deeper level of knowledge and experiences within new markets that can assist the company to meet the demands of an increasingly global customer base.

The key operations direction of the company is to fit within a global value chain but to maintain their independence within an increasingly interdependent business world.

Project

This is an example of how Imagination is attempting to stay one step ahead of their competitors in the communications world.

Imagination has established an Academy as a symbol of their commitment to education, creativity and commerce. It's a global initiative, celebrating and developing talent across all disciplines within the company and beyond. The Academy assists imaginers to continue to develop their careers and brings new talented people into the business at every level. This is building on the success of innovative American companies such as 3M, which recruit people from the top universities and community colleges across the United States.

The academy has partners with academic institutions to nurture future generations of talent. It was launched at UCL, London and as the first formal partnership in their global programme to connect into the centres of excellence and develop relationships with world-class universities. They launched the Imagination Academy bursary scheme with the Bartlett School of Architecture as they celebrated 175 years of academic excellence in January 2016 and sponsored the inaugural Donaldson Lecture, delivered by award-winning artist Grayson Perry CBE. Throughout 2016, the company intend to launch further bursaries for Masters-level students in Sydney, New York and Detroit.

Case Questions

1   Why should companies attempt to inhabit a world of great creative business opportunity?

2   Why are the levers of globalization so important to understand, influence and manage the implementation of a strategic talent management programme?

3   How can building strong foundations of a new organizational development strategy encourage international creativity and innovation?

Exercise 2.1

1. Highlight the main stages of employee and talent development undertaken by your organization and examine the business and human resource management challenges experienced at each stage of development.

2. Choose a global company discussed in this chapter and analyze the global employee development practices that could be adopted by the company. Consider their potential impact on future corporate performance.

3. Discuss the importance of having effective environmental scanning with your employee development team and identify improvements that could be introduced to more effectively support the talent management decisions taken by your organization.

4. How can an international business start to develop an employee development strategy that sustains creativity and competitive advantage in the volatile business environment of today?

Notes

1. http://about.hm.com/en/About/facts-about-hm/about-hm/hm-group.html

2. Data Monitor, H & M Hennes & Mauritz AB, Company Profile 735, May 2005; June 2006; Sarah Larenaudie, 'Inside the H&M Fashion Machine', *Time*, April 15, 2004, 48–51; H&M, *Facts 2006*, accessed at www.hm.com on May 3, 2008; H&M Annual Report 2005, 2006, accessed at www.hm.com/us/investorrelations/financialreports/annualreports__investorannualreports.nhtml on May 3, 2008; University of Michigan College of Human Ecology, H&M Group Review, 1998, accessed at http://web.archive.org/web/20070127021026/http://www.hed.msu.edu/internationalretailing/company/H_M/group_review.html on September 15, 2013.

3. Marcus Leroux, Katherine Griffiths,14 March, 2013, 'Zara owner to open nine stores a week as it takes on world', *The Times*.

4. Gavin Daly, 'Looking good for H&M', *Sunday Times*, April 10, 2016, accessed at www.thesundaytimes.co.uk/sto/news/ireland/Business/article1686100.ece

5. This discussion is based heavily on Christopher A. Bartlett and Sumantra Ghoshal, *Transnational Management: Text, Cases, and Readings in Cross-Border Management*, 3rd ed. (Boston: Irwin McGraw-Hill, 2000), 94–96; and Anil K. Gupta and Vijay Govindarajan, 'Converting Global Presence into Global Competitive Advantage', *Academy of Management Executive* 15, No. 2 (2001), 45–56.

6. Peter Stalker (1994), *The Work of Strangers: A Survey of International Labour Migration*, ILO, Geneva, 13.

7. Todd Zaun, Gregory L. White, Norihiko Shirouzu and Scott Miller, 'More Mileage: Auto Makers Look for Another Edge Farther from Home', *The Wall Street Journal* (July 31, 2002), A1, A8.

8. Based on Nancy J. Adler, *International Dimensions of Organizational Behavior*, 4th ed. (Cincinnati, OH: South-Western, 2002); Theodore T. Herbert, 'Strategy and Multinational Organizational Structure: An Interorganizational Relationships Perspective', *Academy of Management Review* 9 (1984), 259–271; and Laura K. Rickey, 'International Expansion – U.S. Corporations: Strategy, Stages of Development, and Structure' (unpublished manuscript, Vanderbilt University, 1991).

9. Michael E. Porter, 'Changing Patterns of International Competition', *California Management Review* 28 (Winter 1986) 9–40.

10. William J. Holstein, 'The Stateless Corporation', *BusinessWeek* (May 14, 1990), 98–115.

11. Debra Sparks, 'Partners', *BusinessWeek*, Special Report: Corporate Finance (October 25, 1999), 106–112.

12. David Lei and John W. Slocum, Jr., 'Global Strategic Alliances: Payoffs and Pitfalls', *Organizational Dynamics* (Winter 1991), 17–29.

13. Joseph Weber with Amy Barrett, 'Volatile Combos', *BusinessWeek*, Special Report: Corporate Finance (October 25, 1999), 122; and Lei and Slocum, 'Global Strategic Alliances.'

14. Stratford Sherman, 'Are Strategic Alliances Working?' *Fortune* (September 21, 1992), 77–78; David Lei, 'Strategies for Global Competition', *Long-Range Planning* 22 (1989), 102–109.

15. Cyrus F. Freidheim, Jr, *The Trillion-Dollar Enterprise: How the Alliance Revolution Will Transform Global Business* (New York: Perseus Books, 1998).

16. Ron Grover and Richard Siklos, 'When Old Foes Need Each Other', *BusinessWeek*, Special Report: Corporate Finance (October 25, 1999), 114, 118.

17. Lei, 'Strategies for Global Competition'; Sherman, 'Are Strategic Alliances Working?'

18. Debra Sparks, 'Partners', *BusinessWeek*, Special Report: Corporate Finance (October 25, 1999), 106–112.

19. Sparks, 'Partners'.

20. Kevin Kelly and Otis Port, with James Treece, Gail DeGeorge and Zachary Schiller, 'Learning from Japan', *BusinessWeek*, (January 27, 1992), 52–60; Gregory G. Dess, Abdul M. A. Rasheed, Kevin J. McLaughlin and Richard L. Priem, 'The New Corporate Architecture', *Academy of Management Executive* 9, No. 3 (1995), 7–20.

21. Kenichi Ohmae, 'Managing in a Borderless World', *Harvard Business Review* (May–June 1989), 152–161.

22. Cesare R. Mainardi, Martin Salva and Muir Sanderson, 'Label of Origin: Made on Earth', *Strategy & Business* 15 (Second Quarter 1999), 42–53; Joann S. Lublin, 'Place vs Product: It's Tough to Choose a Management Model', *The Wall Street Journal* (June 27, 2001), A1, A4.

23. Demetrakakes, P. 'Nestle's packaging wraps up the world', *Food & Drug Packaging*, October 2004.

24. Gupta and Govindarajan, 'Converting Global Presence into Global Competitive Advantage'.

25. Sam Schechner and Sven Grundberg, 18 March, 2013, 'Ericsson, STMicro End Venture', *The Wall Street Journal*.

26. Lawrence A. Fisher, 'STMicroelectronics: The Metaphysics of a Metanational Pioneer', *Strategy & Business* 28 (Third Quarter 2002), 81–89.

27. http://finance.yahoo.com/q/is?s=STM+Income+Statement&annual accessed on April 10 2016

28. Yves Doz, José Santos and Peter Williamson, *From Global to Metanational: How Companies Win in the Knowledge Economy* (Boston: Harvard Business School Press, 2001), 13–15.

29. Leila Abboud, 'Chipping Away at STMicro', *Bloomberg*, January 27, 2016, accessed at www.bloomberg.com/gadfly/articles/2016-01-27/stmicro-hamstrung-by-france-and-italy

30. José Pla-Barber, 'From Stopford and Wells's Model to Bartlett and Ghoshal's Typology: New Empirical Evidence', *Management International Review* 42, No. 2 (2002), 141–156.

31. Robert J. Kramer, *Organizing for Global Competitiveness: The Country Subsidiary Design* (New York: The Conference Board, 1997), 12.

32. Hawkes, C. 2004, 'Marketing Food to Children: The Global Regulatory Environment', Geneva, World Health Organization.

33. Mark Sweney, 27 October, 2011, 'Morrisons ad banned for targeting kids', *The Guardian*.

34. Emily Dugan, 29 May, 2011, 'Big Tobacco takes aim at the world's disadvantaged', *Independent On Sunday*.

35. American Cancer Society, The Tobacco Atlas, 2015, accessed at http://3pk43x313ggr4cy0lh3tctjh.wpengine. netdna-cdn.com/wp-content/uploads/2015/03/TA5_2015_ WEB.pdf; Daynard, R. A., & LeGresley, E. (2012). Product liability. *Tobacco control*, 21(2), 227–228; GHK Consulting (2012), 'A study on liability and the health costs of smoking', Report 2008/C6/046, accessed at ec.europa.eu/health/ tobacco/docs/tobacco_liability_final_en.pdf

36. Laura B. Pincus and James A. Belohlav, 'Legal Issues in Multinational Business: To Play the Game, You Have to Know the Rules', *Academy of Management Executive* 10, No. 3 (1996), 52–61, http://www.asa.org.uk/asa/codes.

37. John D. Daniels, Robert A. Pitts and Marietta J. Tretter, 'Strategy and Structure of US Multinationals: An Exploratory Study', *Academy of Management Journal* 27 (1984), 292–307.

38. Robert J. Kramer, *Organizing for Global Competitiveness: The Product Design* (New York: The Conference Board, 1994).

39. Robert J. Kramer, *Organizing for Global Competitiveness: The Business Unit Design* (New York: The Conference Board, 1995), 18–19.

40. Robert Wright, 5 February, 2013, 'Eaton industrial group profits dented on weak auto demand', *Financial Times*.

41. Based on Robert J. Kramer, *Organizing for Global Competitiveness: The Geographic Design* (New York: The Conference Board, 1993).

42. Fieldhouse, D. (1978) 'Unilever Overseas: The Anatomy of a Multinational', 1895–1965, Stanford, Hoover Press; Jones, G. (2005), 'Renewing Unilever: Tranformation and Tradition', Oxford, OUP; Jones, G. (2002) 'Unilever – A Case Study', HBS Case Study; Jones, G. and Miskell, P. (2005) 'European integration and corporate restructuring: the strategy of Unilever', c.1957–c.1990, *Economic History Review*, LVIII, 1, 113–139; Zurndorfer, H. (2006), 'Imperialism, Globalization, and the Soap/Suds Industry in Republican China (1912–37): The Case of Unilever and the Chinese Consumer' Global Economic History Working paper 19/06.

43. Unilver Full Year Results 2015, accessed at https:// www.unilever.com/Images/q4-2015-full-announcement_ tcm244-470010_en.pdf

44. Kala Vijayaraghavan and Ravi Balakrishnan, 28 March, 2013, 'Unilever: Losing its localised marketing mojo or playing its cards smartly', *The Economic Times*.

45. https://www.hul.co.in/investor-relations/corporate- governance/hul-policies/corporate- social-responsibility-policy/

46. 'Marks & Spencer offers international franchises', *Franchise International*, 2006, 2, p. 31.

47. Gupta and Govindarajan, 'Converting Global Presence into Global Competitive Advantage'.

48. M&S Annual Report, 2015

49. Jonathan Friedland and Louise Lee, 'The Wal-Mart Way Sometimes Gets Lost in Translation Overseas', *The Wall Street Journal* (October 8, 1997), A1, A12.

50. Robert Frank, 'Withdrawal Pains: In Paddies of Vietnam, Americans Once Again Land in a Quagmire', *The Wall Street Journal* (April 21, 2000), A1, A6.

51. Sheila Puffer, Daniel McCarthy and Anatoly Zhuplev (1998), 'Doing business in Russia: Lessons from early entrants', *Thunderbird International Business Review*, 40, 461–484.

52. The discussion of these challenges is based on Bartlett and Ghoshal, *Transnational Management*.

53. Scott Cendrowski, 'China's Global 500 companies are bigger than ever', *Fortune*, July 22, 2015, accessed at fortune.com/2015/07/22/ china-global-500-government-owned/

54. Ian Katz and Elisabeth Malkin, 'Battle for the Latin American Net', *BusinessWeek* (November 1, 1999), 194–200; and Pamela Drukerman and Nick Wingfield, 'Lost in Translation: AOL's Big Assault in Latin America Hits Snags in Brazil', *The Wall Street Journal* (July 11, 2000), A1.

55. Shirley Leung, 'McHaute Cuisine: Armchairs, TVs, and Espresso – Is It McDonald's?' *The Wall Street Journal* (August 30, 2002), A1, A6.

56. Paul Ingrassia, 'Industry is Shopping Abroad for Good Ideas to Apply to Products', *The Wall Street Journal* (April 29, 1985), A1.

57. Based on Gupta and Govindarajan, 'Converting Global Presence into Global Competitive Advantage'.

58. Vijay Govindarajan and Anil K. Gupta, 'Building an Effective Global Business Team', *MIT Sloan Management Review* 42, no. 4 (Summer 2001), 63–71.

59. Charlene Marmer Solomon, 'Building Teams Across Borders', *Global Workforce* (November 1998), 12–17.

60. Charles C. Snow, Scott A. Snell, Sue Canney Davison and Donald C. Hambrick, 'Use Transnational Teams to Globalize Your Company', *Organizational Dynamics* 24, no. 4 (Spring 1996), 50–67.

61. Jane Pickard, 'Control Freaks Need Not Apply', *People Management* (February 5, 1998), 49.

62. Snow et al., 'Use Transnational Teams to Globalize Your Company'.

63. Robert J. Kramer, *Organizing for Global Competitiveness: The Corporate Headquarters Design* (New York: The Conference Board, 1999).

64. These roles are based on Christopher A. Bartlett and Sumantra Ghoshal, *Managing Across Borders: The Transnational Solution*, 2nd ed. (Boston: Harvard Business School Press, 1998), Chapter 11, 231–249.

65. See Jay Galbraith, 'Building Organizations Around the Global Customer', *Ivey Business Journal* (September– October 2001), 17–24, for a discussion of both formal and informal lateral networks used in multinational companies.

66. Geert Hofstede, 'The Interaction Between National and Organizational Value Systems', *Journal of Management Studies* 22 (1985), 347–357; Geert Hofstede, *Cultures and Organizations: Software of the Mind* (London: McGraw-Hill, 1991).

67. Other major studies on national culture differences include Fons Trompenaars and Charles Hampden-Turner (1998), *Riding the waves of culture: understanding cultural diversity in global business*, New York, McGraw-Hill, and 'Culture, leadership, and organizations: the GLOBE study of 62 societies', by Robert J. House, Paul J. Hanges, Mansour Javidan, Peter W. Dorfman and Vipin Gupta, *Culture, Leadership, and Organizations*, London, Sage, 2004.

68. Ybema, S., & Nyíri, P. (2015). The Hofstede factor. in Nigel Holden, Snejina Michailova, Susanne Tietze (eds.) *The Routledge Companion to Cross-Cultural Management*, London, Routledge, pp. 37–48

69. This discussion is based on 'Culture and Organization', Reading 2-2 in Christopher A. Bartlett and Sumantra

Ghoshal, *Transnational Management*, 3rd ed. (Boston: Irwin McGraw-Hill, 2000), 191–216, excerpted from Susan Schneider and Jean-Louis Barsoux, *Managing Across Cultures* (London: Prentice-Hall, 1997).

70. Miller, G. (1987), 'Meta-Analysis and the Culture-Free Hypothesis', *Organization Studies*, 8, 309–326.

71. Based on Bartlett and Ghoshal, *Managing Across Borders*, 181–201.

72. James Womack, Daniel Jones and Daniel Roos (1990) *The Machine that Changed the World*, New York, Macmillan.

73. Tomasso Pardi (2005), 'Crise, effets de trajectoire et dynamiques sociales dans l'évolution de Toyota Motor Manufacturing UK', *Sociologie du travail*, 40, 188–204.

74. Susan Schneider and Jean-Louis Barsoux (2003), *Managing Across Cultures*, Harlow, FT Prentice Hall.

75. Alan M. Rugman (2009), *The Oxford Handbook of International Business*, Oxford, OUP, Pg. 773; Brendan McSweeney (2002), 'Hofstede's Model of National Cultural Differences and their Consequences: A Triumph of Faith – a Failure of Analysis', *Human Relations*, 55, 89–118; Galit Ailon (2008), 'Mirror, Mirror On The Wall: Culture's Consequences In a Value Test of its Own Design', *Academy of Management Review*, 33, 885–904.

76. Samuel P. Huntington (1996), *The Clash of Civilizations and the Remaking of World Order*, New York, Simon & Schuster.

77. Mahmood Mamdani (2004), *Good Muslim, Bad Muslim: America, the Cold War, and the Roots of Terror*, New York, Pantheon.

78. Sumantra Ghoshal and Christopher Bartlett, 'The Multinational Corporation as an Inter-organizational Network', *Academy of Management Review* 15 (1990), 603–625.

79. The description of the transnational organization is based on Bartlett and Ghoshal, *Transnational Management and Managing Across Borders.*

80. John Mathews (2002), *Dragon Multinational. A New Model for Global Growth*, Oxford, OUP.

81. Andrew Davidson, 'Billionaire's boy with ambition', *Sunday Times (London)*, April 20, 2008, Pg. 8; Stanley Reed, 'ArcelorMittal Reports Nearly $8 Billion Loss and Plans to Raise $3 Billion', *New York Times*, February 5, 2016, accessed at www.nytimes.com/2016/02/06/business/international/arcelormittal-q4-earnings.html

82. Mika Gabrielsson, V.H. Manek Kirpalani, Pavlos Dimitratos, Carl Arthur Solberg and Antonella Zucchella (2008), 'Born globals: Propositions to help advance the theory', *International Business Review*, 17, 4, 385-401

PART IV

INTERNAL DESIGN ELEMENTS

MANUFACTURING AND SERVICE TECHNOLOGIES

A LOOK INSIDE

Continental AG

Continental is one of Europe's best known automotive brands. Founded in 1871 in Hannover, the company made its name through processing rubber into various manufactured goods. 'Conti' was the first German company to produce the pneumatic tyre for bicycles, and in 1900 it provided the rubberized material from which the world's first airship was manufactured.[1] The company's association with transportation continues to the present day, and Continental remains the world's fourth-largest tyre manufacturer.

Like many European companies, Continental was deeply affected by the wars and political instability that scarred Europe in the mid-twentieth century. The Nazi war effort led to intensified research, particularly into synthetic rubber, but Germany's eventual defeat in the war and subsequent economic dislocation hampered the company in comparison with both France's Michelin and the big American tyre manufacturers.[2] Nevertheless as the economy recovered, the company shared in Germany's rising reputation for high-quality engineered goods; its rubber was fitted on iconic marques such as BMW and Mercedes. From the 1970s the pace of industrial innovation and the heat of competition sharpened. Michelin invented the radial tyre which quickly became the industry standard, and American tyre companies like Goodyear and Uniroyal pushed hard into the European market. Japanese firms like Bridgestone were not far behind, and Conti soon fell into red ink.

After some missteps, the company reorganized along divisional lines, and embarked on a growth and internationalization strategy. Continental neutralized some of its European competition through acquiring Uniroyal's European operations, and entering into a long-term tie-up with Japan's Toyo.[3] By 1992 the company had made a major shift into the North American market through acquisition of General Tire.

Conti also started moving beyond its traditional reliance on tyres, and into the wider vehicle parts market. As car manufacturers began demanding more modular parts, such as entire braking systems, Conti expanded its manufacture of brakes, both through acquisition and development of its existing operations.[4]

As vehicles became more complex, incorporating sophisticated electronics, Continental moved to capture a share of this market. Its most significant acquisition was of Siemens' automotive electronics business, which Continental bought in 2007 for €11.4 billion.[5] While vehicle electronics might seem a far cry from tyres and brakes, Continental emphasized safety as the common thread. Braking systems are increasingly based on electronics, in which Siemens was a leader, and more broadly, electronic features such as airbag controllers and radar systems also add to safety. Nevertheless, the company acknowledged that a key motivation was to diversify its product lines – into new areas such as in-car entertainment – so that it would be less dependent on a handful of car manufacturers for the bulk of its revenues.

With its many moves to adapt to the twin challenges of globalization and technological change, Continental has managed to keep growing and to remain consistently profitable. By 2015 the company's sales had reached €39 billion, with profits (EBITDA) of about €2 billion.[6] In August 2008 in a hostile takeover-bid, the privately-held German bearing-manufacturing firm Schaeffler acquired 49.9 per cent of the company, effectively a controlling stake, valuing Continental at just over €12 billion,[7] widely considered a bargain given the combined value of Conti and its recent Siemens electronics acquisition.[8] The combined company vies to become the world's largest automotive component manufacturer, competing with fellow German-based Bosch GmbH. Continental's strategy, like that of many major European firms, is to rebalance its activities and sales towards Asia, which until China's 2015–downturn was greatly outperforming European markets. The company will be hoping that Asian economies quickly bounce back (see Continental, Regional Rebalancing chart).[9] However, in the fast-changing world of European industry, last year's accolades provide no protection against this year's need to quickly change and restructure.

Globalization and technological advances have radically altered the manufacturing sector in both developed and developing countries. Where once American and European companies mainly built products for Western consumers in Western countries, now manufacturing is often carried out offshore, with the Western firm mainly concerned with assuring product quality and price competitiveness, and above all building and protecting brand value. Services have become an increasingly greater part of the economy in every developed country. Yet even services are being outsourced to locations where skilled workers can be hired for a fraction of their cost in Western Europe and North America. The restructuring of economic activity on an international and even global basis presents opportunities and challenges for companies in both developed and emerging economies. Even companies that trade on their national identities, like Britain's Reebok and Burberry, or Japan's Toyota, have been pushed by the cost factor to move to low-cost manufacturing centres outside Europe and Japan.[10,11]

The transfer of product assembly and simple services offshore was only the first step in a complex and comprehensive restructuring of the global economy. Offshoring of both manufacturing and services also causes major changes and opportunities in emerging economies. Some Western corporations such as American Express, which owns and operates a large customer call centre facility near Delhi, India, choose to establish wholly owned facilities in emerging economies.[12] Many others choose instead either to enter into joint ventures, or to subcontract part or all of a business process to local companies. This has the effect of transferring technologies and managerial competencies, as well as desperately needed funds that can be used for capital investment, into the emerging economy.

Research shows that the impact of offshoring on emerging economies varies between countries and between industries. In some countries an 'enclave' phenomenon occurs in which the most productive workers are drawn to relatively well-paying offshore jobs while the domestic-market economy remains underdeveloped. Gary Gereffi, whose value-chain theory is discussed in Chapter 7, finds that there will be winners and losers among developing countries from offshoring – with a few larger and stronger emerging economies tending to land most of the benefits.[13]

Whereas a main objective of Western companies' offshoring is to save money, ambitious emerging economy companies are always aiming to move 'up the value chain': to carry out more and more complex and sophisticated processes – whether in manufacturing or services – and eventually to develop and profit from their own process innovations. This sets the stage for a battle between established Western firms and local challengers. The very rapid emergence of Japanese and Korean strength in the automobile industry – one of the more complex and technologically intensive manufacturing challenges – showed how quickly dominance can be lost when established companies fail to adapt their technologies to meet market challenges. Now these countries are themselves being challenged by the rapid emergence of Chinese automakers. While China's rapid growth in automobile sales to become the world's largest market in 2015 was initially mainly serviced by Western and Japanese automakers, Chinese manufacturers have now secured more than 40% of the market and are themselves pressing ahead quickly with foreign expansions.[14]

This chapter explores both service and manufacturing technologies and how technology is related to organizational structure. Technology here refers to the work processes, techniques, machines and actions used to transform organizational inputs (materials, information, ideas) into outputs (products and services).[15] Technology is an organization's production process and includes work procedures as well as machinery. In recent years, connectivity and technology have become closely interwoven, as IT advances enable increasing automation and remote control of products ranging from home heating systems to self-driving cars.

An organization's core technology is the work process that is directly related to the organization's mission, such as teaching in a high school, medical services in a health clinic or manufacturing at Continental. For example, at Continental's tyre production facilities, the core

EXHIBIT 8.1 Core Transformation Process for a Manufacturing Company

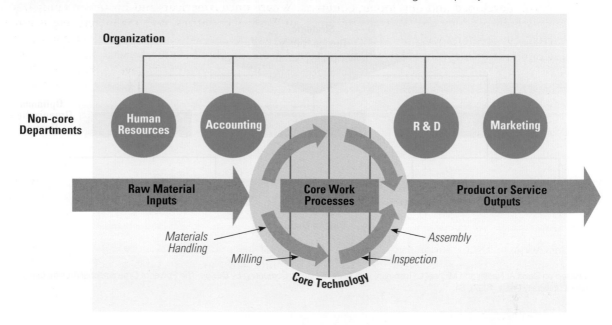

technology begins with raw materials (e.g. rubber, steel, etc.). Employees take action on the raw material to make a change in it (they process and mould the natural and synthetic rubbers), thus transforming the raw material into the output of the organization (tyres, etc.). For a service organization like DHL, the core technology includes the production equipment (e.g. sorting machines, package handling equipment, trucks, aeroplanes) and procedures for delivering packages and overnight mail. In addition, as at companies like DHL and Continental, computers and new information technology have revolutionized work processes in both manufacturing and service organizations. The specific impact of new information technology on organizations will be described in Chapter 9.

An important theme in this chapter is how core technology influences organizational structure. Understanding core technology provides insight into how an organization can be structured for efficient performance.[16]

Exhibit 8.1 features an example of core technology for a manufacturing plant. Note how the core technology consists of raw material inputs, a transformation work process (milling, inspection, assembly) that changes and adds value to the raw material and produces the ultimate product or service output that is sold to consumers. In today's large, complex organizations, core work processes vary widely and sometimes can be hard to pinpoint. A core technology can be partly understood by examining the raw materials flowing into the organization,[17] the variability of work activities,[18] the degree to which the production process is mechanized,[19] the extent to which one task depends on another in the workflow[20] or the number of new product or service outputs.[21]

A non-core technology is a work process that is important to the organization but is not directly related to its primary mission. In Exhibit 8.1, non-core work processes are illustrated by the departments of human resources (HR), accounting, research and development (R&C) and marketing. Thus, R&D transforms ideas into new products, and marketing transforms inventory into sales, each using a somewhat different work process. The output of the HR department is people to work in the organization, and accounting produces accurate statements about the organization's financial condition.

ONLINE
COUNTERPOINT 8.1

ONLINE
COUNTERPOINT 8.2

ONLINE
COUNTERPOINT 8.3

EXHIBIT 8.2 Pressures Affecting Organization Design

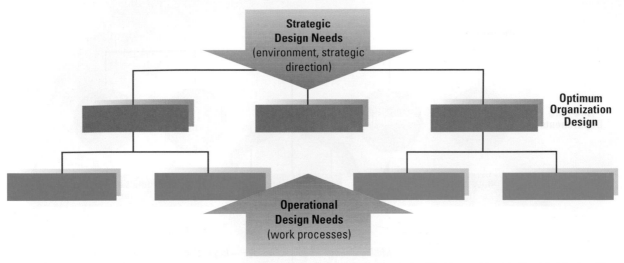

Source: Based on David A. Nadler and Michael L. Tushman, with Mark B. Nadler, *Competing by Design: The Power of Organizational Architecture* (New York: Oxford University Press, 1997), 54.

Purpose of this Chapter

In this chapter, we discuss both core and non-core work processes and their relationship to designing organization structure. The optimum organization design is based on a variety of elements, although companies and their managers never know exactly how organizational design affects productivity and profits. Exhibit 8.2 illustrates that influences affecting organization design come from both outside and within the organization. The remainder of the chapter first examines how the technology for the organization as a whole influences organization structure and design. This discussion includes both manufacturing and service technologies. Next, we examine differences in departmental technologies and how the technologies influence the design and management of organizational subunits. Third, we explore how interdependence – flow of materials and information – among departments affects structure.

BRIEFCASE 8.1

Core Organization Manufacturing Technology

Manufacturing technologies include traditional manufacturing processes and contemporary applications, such as flexible manufacturing and lean manufacturing.

Manufacturing Firms

The first and most influential study of manufacturing technology was conducted by Joan Woodward, a British industrial sociologist. Her research began as a field study of management principles in south Essex, UK. The prevailing management wisdom at the time (1950s) was contained in what were known as universal principles of management. These principles were 'one best way' prescriptions that effective organizations were expected to adopt. Woodward surveyed 100 manufacturing firms to learn how they were organized.[22] She and her research team visited each firm, interviewed managers, examined company records and observed the manufacturing operations. Her data included a wide range of structural characteristics (span of control, levels of management) and dimensions of management style (written versus verbal communications, use of rewards) and the type of manufacturing process. Data was also obtained on the commercial performance of the firms.

Woodward developed a scale and organized the firms according to technical complexity of the manufacturing process. Technical complexity refers to the extent of mechanization of the manufacturing process. High technical complexity means most of the work is performed by machines. Low technical complexity means workers play a larger role in the production process. Woodward's scale of technical complexity originally had ten categories, as summarized in Exhibit 8.3. These categories were further consolidated into three basic technology groups:

ONLINE
COUNTERPOINT 8.4

- *Group I: Small-batch and unit production.* These firms tend to be job shop operations that manufacture and assemble small orders to meet the specific requirements of customers. Small-batch production relies heavily on the human operator; it is thus not highly mechanized. Small batch production is increasingly important in a world where 'narrowcasting' is viewed as more desirable than mass market production. However, advances in technology mean that small-batch production can be viable even for relatively low cost goods. London, UK-based company, Shoes by Bryan, used partner 3D Systems' printers to launch in 2012 what he calls the world's first biodegradable 3D printed shoes, made from polylactic plastic (PLA) and entirely recyclable.[23]

- *Group II: Large-batch and mass production.* Large-batch production is a manufacturing process characterized by long production runs of standardized parts. Output often goes into inventory from which orders are filled, because customers do not have special needs. Examples include most assembly lines, such as for automobiles or LCD television monitors.

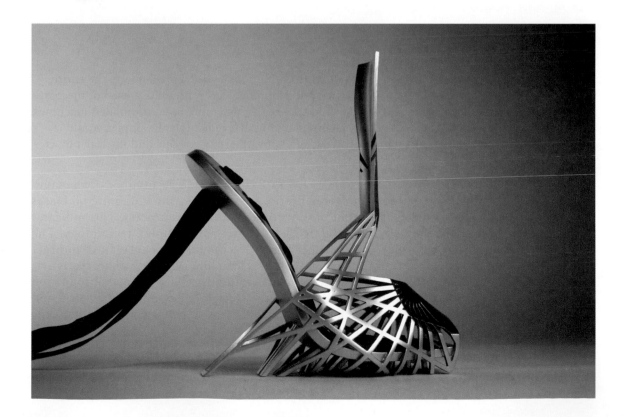

EXHIBIT 8.3   Woodward's Classification of 100 British Firms According to Their Systems of Production

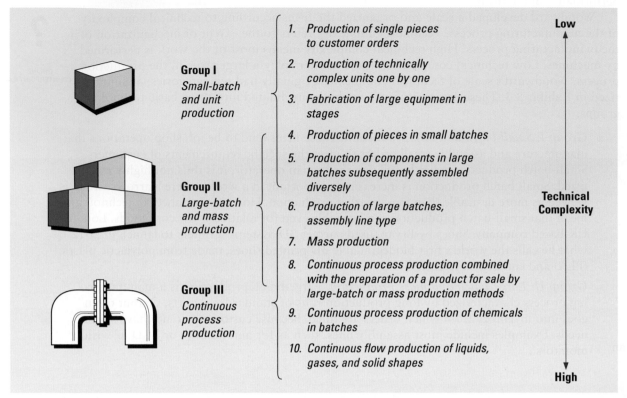

Source: Adapted from Joan Woodward, *Management and Technology* (London: Her Majesty's Stationery Office, 1958).

■ *Group III: Continuous-process production.* In continuous-process production, the entire process is mechanized. There is no starting and stopping. This represents a level of mechanization and standardization one step beyond those in an assembly line. Automated machines control the continuous process, and outcomes are highly predictable. Examples would include chemical plants, oil refineries, brewing plants, pharmaceuticals and nuclear power plants.

A few of Woodward's key findings are given in Exhibit 8.4. The number of management levels and the manager-to-total personnel ratio, for example, show definite increases as technical complexity increases from unit production to continuous process. This indicates that greater management intensity is correlated with managing complex technology. The direct-to-indirect labour ratio decreases with technical complexity because more indirect workers are required to support and maintain complex machinery. Other characteristics, such as span of control, formalized procedures and centralization, are high for mass-production technology as the work is standardized, but low for other technologies. Unit-production and continuous-process technologies require highly skilled workers to oversee and maintain the machines, and verbal communication to adapt to changing conditions. Mass production is standardized and routinized, so few exceptions occur, little verbal communication is needed and employees are less skilled.

Overall, the management systems in both unit-production and continuous-process technology are characterized as organic, as defined in Chapter 5. They are more free-flowing and adaptive,

EXHIBIT 8.4   Relationship between Technical Complexity and Structural Characteristics

Structural Characteristic	Technology		
	Unit Production	Mass Production	Continuous Process
Number of management levels	3	4	6
Supervisor span of control	23	48	15
Direct/indirect labour ratio	9:1	4:1	1:1
Manager/total personnel ratio	Low	Medium	High
Workers' skill level	High	Low	High
Formalized procedures	Low	High	Low
Centralization	Low	High	Low
Amount of verbal communication	High	Low	High
Amount of written communication	Low	High	Low
Overall structure	Organic	Mechanistic	Organic

Source: Based on *Management and Technology* by Joan Woodward (London: Her Majesty's Stationery Office, 1958).

with fewer procedures and less standardization. Mass production, however, is mechanistic, with standardized jobs and formalized procedures. Woodward's discovery about technology provided substantial new insight into the factors that produce forms of organization structure. In Joan Woodward's own words, 'Different technologies impose different kinds of demands on individuals and organizations, and those demands had to be met through an appropriate structure'.[24] In short, structure is understood to follow, or at least adapt to, technology.

Strategy, Technology and Performance

Another portion of Woodward's study examined the success of the firms along dimensions such as profitability, market share, stock price and reputation. As indicated in Chapter 3, the measurement of effectiveness is not simple or precise, but Woodward was able to rank firms on a scale of commercial success according to whether they displayed above-average, average or below-average performance on strategic objectives.

Woodward compared the structure-technology relationship against commercial success and discovered that successful firms tended to be those that had typical, or widely found, configurations of structure and technology, as shown in Exhibit 8.4. Below-average firms tended to depart from the more typical structural characteristics for their technology type. Subsequent research has broadly replicated her findings.[25]

BRIEFCASE 8.2

COUNTERPOINT 8.1

One shortcoming of this logic is that it makes no allowance for innovators who depart from standard formulae. At one moment, they may seem to be comparatively unsuccessful and this may be attributed to their deviation from 'the average of their technology', but later they may be regarded as visionary in their unusual deployment of technologies that subsequently transform the industry as they become the new 'norm'. Consider, for example, the introduction of mass or process production which initially demands a high level of investment without necessarily delivering immediate performance improvements.

What Woodward's findings suggest is that effectiveness is contingent upon an alignment of strategy, structure and technology.[26] For example, in the computer industry in the 1990s, computer makers were obliged to realign strategy, structure and technology to compete with Dell's technology innovation of direct sales, mass customization and outsourced production. Manufacturers such as IBM switched to a low-cost strategy, adopted new technology to enable them to customize PCs, revamped supply chains and began outsourcing manufacturing to other companies that could do the job more cheaply. Eventually, IBM decided that it no longer had a competitive advantage in personal computer manufacture, and sold this part of its business to China's Lenovo.[27]

In recent years it has become almost a rule of thumb that companies should farm out production. Failing to adopt appropriate new technologies to support strategy, or adopting a new technology and failing to realign strategy to match it, can lead to below par performance. Today's increased global competition results in more volatile markets, shorter product life cycles and more sophisticated and knowledgeable consumers. Retailers such as H&M, profiled in Chapter 7, do not produce any of their own merchandise. However, there are also examples of corporations, including H&M's largest competitor, Zara, that have chosen to go in the opposite direction by tightly integrating and controlling manufacturing and sales (see Chapter 5). Western firms with a high cost base have a particularly tough decision in terms of outsourcing manufacturing production. By doing so, companies benefit in the short term by the advantage of cheaper labour (known as *global labour arbitrage*) but in the longer term they may be entering into a downward spiral of cost-cutting where eventually they may well be out-competed by one of the emerging economy MNCs.

Greater structural flexibility and agility to meet these new demands has become a strategic imperative for many companies.[28] Manufacturing companies can adopt new technologies to increase their flexibility. Conversely, a highly mechanistic structure tends to hamper flexibility, so preventing the company from reaping the benefits of new technologies.[29] The technological and human systems of an organization are inextricably intertwined. This chapter's *Bookmark* provides a different perspective on technology by looking at the dangers of failing to understand the human role in managing technological advances.

Contemporary Applications

In the years since Woodward's research, new developments have occurred in manufacturing technology. Manufacturing has dropped steadily as a proportion of the gross domestic product (GDP) in Europe and North America for a number of years, although in 2004 it still represented 23 per cent of GDP in Germany, 19 per cent in Italy, 15 per cent in the UK, and 14 per cent of the GDP and 11 per cent of all employment in the United States.[30,31] Not surprisingly, the factory of today is quite different from the industrial firms Woodward studied in the 1950s. The computer industry – both for corporate and personal use – typically responds to individual customer requirements in a way that would be unthinkable for consumer electronics like television sets, for example. Often, a barebones computer system is produced in a central facility, then shipped out to a local facility for customization.[32] Sometimes this build-to-order (BTO) process involves an international partnership between two manufacturers, as in the collaboration between Hewlett Packard and Sun Moon Star to provide computers to the Taiwanese market.[33]

Computerization has had a massive impact upon continuous production processes, where processes that once required intensive (and error-prone) human supervision and intervention can now be remotely and efficiently monitored. However, it is relevant to note how continuous production requires attention not only to the core process but also to back-up systems to support that process, such as instant availability of spare parts, inventory management, etc. Syktyvkarskii LPK, a Russian paper production plant belonging to the Anglo-South African corporation Mondi Business Paper, found that despite holding large and costly inventories of spare parts, maintenance

IN PRACTICE

Crazee Things

Danny Bamping founded Crazee Things, a British games company best known for the 'Crazee Cube', a variation on the famous Rubik's cube puzzle. Until 2007, Bamping outsourced production to China, but started producing puzzles in Britain as a result of rapidly rising costs and long lag time in bringing the goods to market. Just as he was starting production in the UK, a scandal broke about safety issues affecting Chinese-made toys, such as lead found in the paint used for Mattel's Barbie dolls. He acknowledges that this was good timing for his small company, and Crazee's website now highlights British manufacture and attention to product safety and environmental standards such as a smaller carbon footprint.[34] Bamping teamed up with another British toy manufacturer to establish UK Manufacture Ltd, offering to produce toys in Britain for other toy companies.[35] Although this is a small beginning, there are increasing signs within both Europe and North America that the outsourcing urge, whether to domestic or emerging market suppliers, might be reaching its peak. In 2008, Mervyn King, governor of the Bank of England, emphasized the need for a 'rebalancing' of the economy in which manufacturing would again play an important role.[36] The same phenomenon is occurring across Europe and North America, where the automobile industry in particular is bringing more production in-house both to contain costs and to ensure quality.[37] Still, for certain products where low price and fast turnaround are necessary, even a Made-in-Britain advocate such as Bamping used a China outsourced manufacture solution, such as for his line of customized Crazee World puzzles launched in 2011, made for companies like HSBC Bank and Lloyds of London. Ultimately, however, Bamping's firm couldn't remain profitable in the face of international competition, and went out of business in 2014.[38]

engineers frequently found themselves missing critical components, resulting in production losses. They engaged the Russian IT consultants IBS to design an integrated preventative maintenance (PM) system based on the system integration platform designed by the Swiss software giant SAP. The new system ensures that maintenance planning, process monitoring and parts inventory are better coordinated. Over 200 staff from shop floor workers to top technical experts are involved in entering data into the PM system. The company estimates that computerized integration saves at least €1 million per year.[39]

Mass production manufacturing has seen similar transformations. Two significant contemporary applications of manufacturing technology are flexible manufacturing systems and lean manufacturing.

Flexible Manufacturing Systems

Most of today's factories use a variety of new manufacturing technologies, including robots, numerically controlled machine tools, radio-frequency identification (RFID), wireless technology and computerized software for product design, engineering analysis and remote control of machinery. The ultimate automated factories are referred to as flexible manufacturing systems (FMS).[40] Also called *computer-integrated manufacturing, smart factories, advanced manufacturing technology, agile manufacturing* or *the factory of the future*, FMS links together manufacturing components that previously stood alone. Thus, robots, machines, product design and engineering analysis are coordinated by a single computer.

The result has already revolutionized the shop floor, enabling large factories to deliver a wide range of custom-made products at low mass-production costs.[41] Mass customization is one effective response to the dilemma of globalization – how to benefit from the efficiencies of internationalization, while continuing to offer the customer a product that is tailored to her/him.

BOOKMARK 8.0

Have you read this book?

Inviting Disaster: Lessons from the Edge of Technology

BY JAMES R. CHILES

Dateline: Paris, France, July 25, 2000. Less than 2 minutes after Air France Concorde Flight 4590 departs Charles DeGaulle Airport, something goes horribly wrong. Trailing fire and billowing black smoke, the huge plane rolls left and crashes into a hotel, killing all 109 people aboard and four more on the ground. It's just one of the technological disasters James R. Chiles describes in his book, *Inviting Disaster: Lessons from the Edge of Technology*. One of Chiles's main points is that advancing technology makes possible the creation of machines that strain the human ability to understand and safely operate them. Moreover, he asserts, the margins of safety are drawing thinner as the energies we harness become more powerful and the time between invention and use grows shorter. Chiles believes that today, 'for every twenty books on the pursuit of success, we need a book on how things fly into tiny pieces despite enormous effort and the very highest ideals'. All complex systems, he reminds us, are destined to fail at some point.

How Things Fly Into Pieces: Examples of System Fractures

Chiles uses historical calamities such as the sinking of the *Titanic* and modern disasters such as the explosion of the space shuttle *Challenger* (the book was published before the 2003 crash of the *Columbia* shuttle) to illustrate the dangers of *system fracture*, a chain of events that involves human error in response to malfunctions in complex machinery. Disaster begins when one weak point links up with others.

- *Sultana* (American steamboat on the Mississippi River near Memphis, Tennessee), April 25, 1865.

- The boat, designed to carry a maximum of 460 people, was carrying more than 2000 Union ex-prisoners north – as well as 200 additional crew and passengers – when three of the four boilers exploded, killing 1800 people. One of the boilers had been temporarily patched to cover a crack, but the patch was too thin. Operators failed to compensate by resetting the safety valve.

- *Piper Alpha* (offshore drilling rig in the North Sea), July 6, 1988. The offshore platform processed large volumes of natural gas from other rigs via pipe. A daytime work crew, which didn't complete repair of a gas-condensate pump, relayed a verbal message to the next shift, but workers turned the pump on anyway. When the temporary seal on the pump failed, a fire trapped crewmen with no escape route, killing 167 crew and rescue workers.

- *Union Carbide (India) Ltd* (release of highly toxic chemicals into a community), Bhopal, Mahdya Pradesh, India, December 3, 1984. There are three competing theories for how water got into a storage tank, creating a violent reaction that sent highly toxic methyl isocyanate for herbicides into the environment, causing an estimated 7000 deaths: (1) poor safety maintenance, (2) sabotage, or (3) worker error.

What Causes System Fractures?

There is a veritable catalogue of causes that lead to such disasters, from design errors, insufficient operator training and poor planning to greed and mismanagement. Chiles wrote this book as a reminder that technology takes us into risky locales, whether it be outer space, up a 2000-foot tower or into a chemical processing plant. Chiles also cites examples of potential disasters that were averted by quick thinking and appropriate response. To help prevent system fractures, managers can create organizations in which people throughout the company are expert at picking out the subtle signals of real problems – and where they are empowered to report them and take prompt action.

Inviting Disaster: Lessons from the Edge of Technology, by James R. Chiles, is published by HarperBusiness.

One simple example where technology has enabled unique products to be offered to consumers is in ceramic coffee mug imaging. The advent of digital cameras has meant families the world over have many pictures they would like to keep and share with relatives. Through the internet and advances in photocopy technology, a photograph of the grandchildren can be sent across the world, printed permanently on a coffee mug, and delivered as a present to grandparents, all within a day or two.[42] Flexible manufacturing also enables small enterprises to go toe-to-toe with larger companies and low-cost offshore competitors. Flexible manufacturing is typically the result of three subcomponents:

- *Computer-aided design (CAD).* Computers are used to assist in the drafting, design and engineering of new parts. Designers guide their computers to draw specified configurations on the screen, including dimensions and component details. Hundreds of design alternatives can be explored, as can scaled-up or scaled-down versions of the original.[43]

- *Computer-aided manufacturing (CAM).* Computer-controlled machines in materials handling, fabrication, production and assembly greatly increase the speed at which items can be manufactured. CAM also permits a production line to shift rapidly from producing one product to any variety of other products by changing the instruction tapes or software codes in the computer. CAM enables the production line to quickly honour customer requests for changes in product design and product mix.[44]

- *Integrated information network.* A computerized system links all aspects of the firm – including accounting, purchasing, marketing, inventory control, design, production and so forth. This system, based on a common data and information base, enables managers to make decisions and direct the manufacturing process in a truly integrated fashion.

The combination of CAD, CAM and integrated information systems means that a new product can be designed on the computer and a prototype can be produced untouched by human hands. It becomes possible to switch quickly from one product to another, working fast and with precision, without paperwork or record keeping to bog down the system.[45]

One field that has benefited enormously from CAD and CAM is that of dentistry. In the pre-computer era, the discipline of prosthodontics – manufacture of 'false' teeth, bridges, etc., was a matter of artistic design and trial and error. Now, data from dental imaging scans can be automatically input into computers and used as a base for accurate design of needed prosthetics. This data can then be directly transferred to the manufacturing process, with an accurate finished product available much sooner, and much more likely to fit well. The success of the Swedish company, Nobel Biocare, which controls many of the best-known brands and processes in dental prosthetics, is based on effective implementation of CAD/CAM in its field.[46,47]

Some advanced factories have moved to a system called *product life-cycle management* (PLM). PLM software can manage a product from idea through development, manufacturing, testing and even maintenance in the field. The PLM software provides three primary advantages for product innovation. PLM (1) stores data on ideas and products from all parts of the company; (2) links product design to all departments (and even outside suppliers) involved in new product development; and (3) provides three-dimensional images of new products for testing and maintenance. PLM has been used to coordinate people, tools and facilities around the world for the design, development and manufacture of products as diverse as cars produced by Rolls Royce, product packaging for Procter & Gamble consumer products, and Boeing's 787 Dreamliner passenger jet.[48]

Lean Manufacturing

Flexible manufacturing is most productive in its aim to improve quality, customer service and cost cutting when all parts are used interdependently and combined with a system referred to as lean manufacturing. Lean manufacturing uses highly trained employees at every stage of the production process who take a painstaking approach to details and problem solving in order to cut waste and improve quality. It incorporates technological elements, such as CAD/CAM and PLM, but the heart of lean manufacturing is not machines or software, but people. Lean manufacturing requires changes in decision-making processes and management processes, as well as a work culture that supports active employee participation. Employees are trained to 'think lean', which means attacking waste and striving for continuous improvement in all areas.[49]

COUNTERPOINT 8.2

'Lean' manufacturing has also been described as 'mean' because in its attempts to remove all slack and waste, it intensifies work. The outcome is that workers suffer from a lack of breaks or respite from the relentless demands of the system. This shortcoming may be adequately compensated by higher wages that attract and retain personnel. But it may also take its toll on morale and goodwill, producing a workforce that lacks the energy or motivation to participate in the schemes that are key to the effective application of flexible and lean manufacturing methods.

The Toyota Production System combines techniques such as just-in-time inventory, product life-cycle management, continuous-flow production, quick changeover of assembly lines, continuous improvement and preventive maintenance with a management system that encourages employee involvement and problem solving. Any employee can stop the production line at any time to solve a problem. In addition, designing equipment to stop automatically so that a defect can be fixed is a central element of the system.[50]

Organizations that have studied and introduced the Toyota Production System have seen dramatic improvements in productivity, inventory reduction and quality. For example, MAN Nutzfahrzeuge, the truck and bus manufacturing division of the German industrial giant MAN (discussed in Chapter 6), has adopted MAN Nutzfahrzeuge Produktionssystem (MNPS), emphasizing lean thinking. Head of production systems, Marcus Schnell, says that in the cogwheel production area alone, work-in-progress fell by three-quarters, lead time by 70 per cent, and job set-up times by almost one-third. On the cylinder head assembly line, work-in-progress fell by over one-half, and productivity increased by 20 per cent.[51] Another example was at the Utah, USA plant of Sweden's Autoliv, a major global producer of vehicle safety airbags where, despite already using lean manufacturing, managers are continuing to make changes under Autoliv Production System (APS). The mantra of lean manufacturing is that there is always room for improvement.

ONLINE
COUNTERPOINT 8.5

Lean manufacturing and flexible manufacturing systems have paved the way for mass customization, which refers to using mass-production technology to quickly and cost-effectively assemble goods that are uniquely designed to fit the demands of individual customers.[52] The idea of mass customization originated in the 1990s[53,54] and was a product of a change in societal thinking towards individualism and differentiation, at the same time as this became possible through the exponential increase in the power of information technologies.[55] Various companies pioneered mass customization in their fields. Nissan Corporation of Japan coined the credo of mass customization: 'Any volume, Anytime, Anybody, Anywhere and Anything'.[56] The idea of mass customization has since expanded to products as diverse as computers, clothing, farm machinery and industrial detergents. Today, you can buy jeans customized for your body, eyeglasses moulded to precisely fit and flatter your face, uPVC windows moulded in the exact shape and size of your home, and pills with the specific combination of vitamins and minerals prescribed for an ailment.[57] In the field of computers, the American-headquartered company, Dell, used mass customization to successfully break the power of traditional PC makers like IBM and Compaq and became, for a period, the world's largest computer maker.[58] In turn Acer, featured in the *Leading by Design* box on p. 275, broke Dell's dominance by creating a new computing category of the netbook, (temporarily) meeting the IT needs of a growing and highly mobile middle class around the world.

Mass customization has taken hold across the global economy. Sixty per cent of the cars BMW sells in Europe are built to order.[59] Countless new products have been designed, based on the idea of customization. Yogurts that children take to school in their packed lunches have two pouches; one with the basic yogurt, the other containing a topping of chocolate or fudge bits that can be sprinkled on top to taste. The Sharpie pen company allows online customers to choose exactly what colour of ink they would like their pens to contain, and what message will be printed on its side. The French company Ariane Deco offers customers the chance to completely personalize their house linen, from handkerchiefs to pillowcases, to curtains.[60] Numerous national postal services now offer customers the possibility of designing their own postage stamps.[61] These latter examples suggest the direction of mass customization towards what the management futures

IN PRACTICE

Autoliv

Production supervisor Bill Webb thought he was being humble when he suggested to Toyota Motor Corp's, Takashi Harada, that his employer, automotive safety parts manufacturer Autoliv ranked around three on a scale of one to ten. He was stunned when Harada replied, 'Maybe a minus-three'. It was the opening lecture for Autoliv's education in the Toyota Production System.

Autoliv has a commanding share of the US market. Toyota was a major customer, though, and, with manufacturing defects rising, Autoliv was more than willing to accept Toyota's offer of help.

One of the first changes Harada made was to set up a system for soliciting and implementing employee suggestions, so that improvements in efficiency and safety began at the bottom. The company also made massive changes in inventory management and production processes.

At the time of Harada's comment, Autoliv was assembling airbag modules on a traditional linear, automated assembly line. The plant held about $23 million in parts – 7 to 10 days worth of inventory – in a giant warehouse. Each day, Webb pushed mountains of inventory onto the assembly floor, but since he was never sure of what was needed, he often pushed a lot of it back at the end of the day. After the introduction of lean manufacturing, software was created to track parts automatically as they were being used.

The data were communicated to the warehouse and parts were replenished just as they were needed. At the same time, the information was automatically conveyed to Autoliv's suppliers, so they could ship new stock. Inventory was cut by around 50 per cent. The assembly process was redesigned into 88 U-shaped production cells, each staffed by a handful of employees. Every 24 minutes, loud rock music signals the arrival of more parts and the rotation of each person to a different task. In addition to being trained to perform different tasks, employees are trained to continuously look for improvements in every area.

Autoliv introduced this system, which it coined the Autoliv Production System (APS), in its plants throughout the world. According to Autoliv, APS is built on a foundation of Team Work, five S,[62] Standards, Waste Elimination, TPM[63], and has three 'pillars', Just in Time, Employee Involvement and Quality First.[64]

The shift to APS lean manufacturing has paid off. Defects per million in module parts were cut dramatically, from more than 1100 in 1998 to just 16 in 2003. In that same year, Autoliv reported profits of $1 billion on revenues of $5.3 billion, and sales have continued to grow, reaching over $8 billion in 2011. 'Their plants are as good as any in the world', said Ross Robson, administrator of the Shingo Prize for Excellence in Manufacturing.[65] The company has continued to build a world class reputation for safety products, even while its one-time mentor Toyota has had its share of problems, including safety concerns. In 2012 the Euro NCAP programme, a safety rating service sponsored by European governments and consumer groups, ranked the continent's safest cars. Almost two-thirds of those selected use mainly Autoliv safety products.[66]

LEADING BY DESIGN

Acer Computers

It's not so long since the phrase 'no-one ever got fired for choosing IBM' was the watchword of the computer business around the world. Now, IBM is out of the personal computer business altogether, and the major US manufacturers such as HP and Dell are facing serious competition from Asian brands including Lenovo (the purchasers of IBM's PC business) and Acer.

Acer is truly a rags to riches story. Founder Stan Shih started the company in 1976 in Taiwan with 11 employees and a capital investment of $25 000. By 2008, Acer had become the world's largest vendor of notebook computers. The company bought Gateway, the world's fifth biggest PC manufacturer, in 2007, and is already the world's third largest PC manufacturer, with clear designs on number one spot.

Acer is one of a new type of emerging country multinationals discussed in the previous chapter, coined 'dragons' by Australian academic John Mathews. Dragon MNCs differ from traditional MNCs in several ways, including being 'born global'; they are designed from the beginning as global corporations, rather than starting with a focus on the domestic market and then gradually building overseas business.

Acer has been particularly innovative in its business structure, as noted in Chapter 6. While many MNCs have relatively decentralized organizational structures, Acer went further and spun off components of the business into separate businesses, allowing the company to leverage both outside capital and knowledge, but retain the synergies of interconnectedness. Stan Shih's second big innovation was in identifying that value is added in a creative industry such as the IT sector at both ends of what he calls the 'smiling curve' concentrated in research and design on one end, and branding on the other (see Exhibit 8.5). Manufacturing, on the other hand, tended to generate poor returns.

As a result of Shih's insight, in 2000 Acer spun-off its manufacturing facilities into a separate company,

EXHIBIT 8.5   Stan Shih's 'smiling curve' (graph by Rico Shen, 2007)

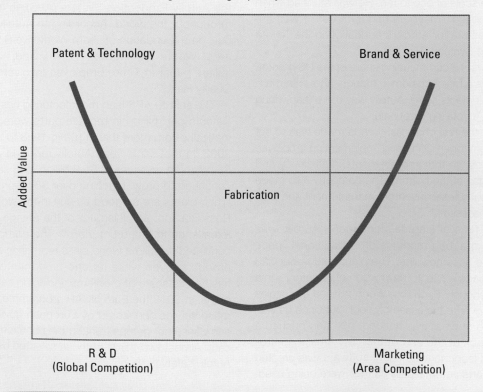

Wistron, which focuses on competitive outsourcing, while Acer concentrated on research and development and branded marketing. It was a bold move, because previously the OEM manufacturing had been seen as a cash cow which funded Acer's efforts to build its brand. Although Shih retired in 2004 the 'smiling curve' vision was successfully continued under the company's new CEO, JT Wang. The breakthrough for Acer's R&D and branding focus came in 2008 as the company established a dominant position in the rapidly emerging 'netbook' market; small, inexpensive and highly portable machines that bridge the gap between personal digital assistants (PDAs) like the Blackberry, and full-sized laptops. The timing for netbooks' entry was perfect, at the onset of a recession when consumers were looking for less expensive but still-attractive technology. Despite rival Taiwanese firm Asus having been first to mass-market a netbook, Acer's greater branding and marketing capacity allowed it to quickly catch up. By the final quarter of 2008 the company led the global market for netbooks with a 36 per cent share, and the company's long-term goal of overtaking HP as the biggest computer manufacturer in the world seemed on track, driven by organizational innovation.[67] However, like every new entrant, the netbook was most at risk from another new product category, in this case the arrival of the tablet computer, and particularly Apple's iPad. Whereas netbooks had increasingly become indistinguishable from traditional notebook computers (whose manufacturers had cut costs and prices to compete with netbooks), the tablet computer with its focus on touch screen multimedia was a truly new creature. Acer for once was caught playing catch-up. Sales and profitability figures dropped so that by 2012 the company was posting large annual losses. Stan Shih came back as chairman in 2013. Acer regrouped and refocused its strategy, betting this time on sales of its Ultrabook computer that can run for eight hours or more on one battery charge. However, it did not fundamentally alter the company's downward trajectory, now linked to the overall decline in the global PC market. In 2015 Shih admitted the company would welcome a buyout offer. Like a sports team, computer firms are only as good as their most recent results, which in Acer's case have not been good.

In 2016 the company announced a restructuring that divided the company into its 'core' computer business and what it called New Businesses including cloud computing, mobile phones and the so-called Internet of Things — the idea that devices, buildings, appliances, etc. can all be embedded with electronics and networked together.[68]

Despite its challenges would Acer's innovative organizational design carry it over this hump, or had the company's success made it complacent and driven it into a downward trajectory from which it could not escape?[69]

guru C. K. Prahalad called co-creation.[70] In co-creation, customers are integrated organically in the design process, rather than merely being 'consulted' through focus groups or similar one-off information gathering. Lego of Denmark created a web community of 1000 participants to design its new Mindstorms robot. The success of the Mindstorms project led Lego to institutionalize this process with what it calls the Lego Factory, where Lego users can design products and sell them through the Lego website.[71] When Fiat decided to develop a new version of its classic Fiat 500 car, it invited potential customers to participate in designing accessories for the car. It was overwhelmed by the response, in which over 8000 suggestions were posted, with many proposals, such as the idea of a clear glass roof, being put into production.[72,73]

Performance and Structural Implications

One key advantage of flexible manufacturing is that products of different sizes, types and customer requirements freely intermingle on the assembly line. Bar codes imprinted on a part enable machines to make instantaneous changes – such as putting a larger screw in a different location – without slowing the production process. A manufacturer can turn out an infinite variety of products in unlimited batch sizes, as illustrated in Exhibit 8.6. In traditional manufacturing systems studied by Woodward, choices were limited to the diagonal. Small batches

EXHIBIT 8.6　Relationship of Flexible Manufacturing Technology to Traditional Technologies

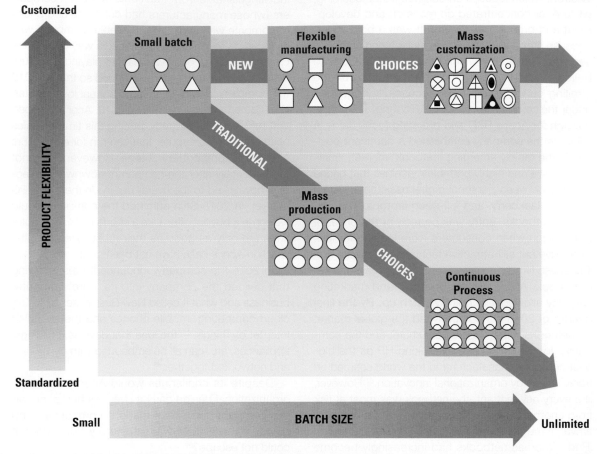

Source: Based on Jack Meredith, 'The Strategic Advantages of New Manufacturing Technologies for Small Firms', *Strategic Management Journal* 8 (1987), 249–258; Paul Adler, 'Managing Flexible Automation', *California Management Review* (Spring 1988), 34–56; and Otis Port, 'Custom-made Direct from the Plant', *BusinessWeek*/21st Century Capitalism (November 18, 1994), 158–159.

allowed for high product flexibility and custom orders, but because of the 'craftsmanship' involved in custom-making products, batch size was necessarily small. Mass production could have large batch size, but offered limited product flexibility. Continuous process could produce a single standard product in unlimited quantities. Flexible manufacturing systems allow plants to break free of this diagonal and so increase both batch size and product flexibility at the same time. When taken to its ultimate level, FMS allows for mass customization where each specific product is tailored to customer specification. This high-level use of FMS has been referred to as *computer-aided craftsmanship*.[74] Studies suggest that with FMS, machine utilization is more efficient, labour productivity increases, scrap rates decrease and product variety and customer satisfaction increase.[75]

　　Research into the relationship between FMS and organizational characteristics is beginning to emerge, and the patterns are summarized in Exhibit 8.7. Compared with traditional mass-production technologies, FMS has a narrow span of control, few hierarchical levels, adaptive tasks, low specialization and decentralization, and the overall environment is characterized as organic and self-regulative. Employees require the skills to participate in teams; training is broad (so workers are not overly specialized) and frequent (so workers are up-to-date). Expertise tends to be cognitive so workers can process abstract ideas and solve problems. Interorganizational relationships

EXHIBIT 8.7 Comparison of Organizational Characteristics Associated with Mass Production and Flexible Manufacturing Systems

Characteristic	Mass Production	FMS
Structure	Wide, many	Narrow, few
Span of control	Routine, repetitive	Adaptive, craftlike
Hierarchical levels	High	Low
Tasks	Centralized	Decentralized
Specialization	Bureaucratic, mechanistic	Self-regulating, organic
Decision-making		
Overall	Standalone	Teamwork
Human Resources	Narrow, one time	Broad, frequent
Interactions	Manual, technical	Cognitive, social
Training		Solve problems
Expertise		
	Stable	Changing
Interorganizational	Many, arm's length	Few, close relationships
Customer demand		
Suppliers		

Source: Based on Patricia L. Nemetz and Louis W. Fry, 'Flexible Manufacturing Organizations: Implications for Strategy Formulation and Organization Design', *Academy of Management Review* 13 (1988), 627–638; Paul S. Adler, 'Managing Flexible Automation,' *California Management Review* (Spring 1988), 34–56; and Jeremy Main, 'Manufacturing the Right Way', *Fortune* (May 21, 1990), 54–64.

in FMS firms are characterized by changing demand from customers – which is handled with the new technology – and close relationships with a few suppliers that provide top-quality raw materials.[76]

COUNTERPOINT 8.3

Aspects of FMS may be beneficial to employees anxious to update their skills. But lack of specialization renders them more vulnerable to replacement by other, cheaper or more pliable employees. Where there is an element of collective reward associated with teamwork, this can prove demanding and divisive. Demanding, because the pressure is on to work 'for the team' rather than exercise some discretion about the level of effort contributed. And divisive, because it can set some team members against others who are judged not to be participating sufficiently fully or not pulling their weight.

Technology alone cannot give organizations the benefits of flexibility, quality, increased production and greater customer satisfaction. FMS can become a competitive burden rather than a competitive advantage unless organizational structures and management processes are redesigned to take advantage of the new technology.[77] However, when top managers make a commitment to implement new structures and processes that empower workers and support a learning and knowledge-creating environment, FMS can help companies be more competitive.[78]

BRIEFCASE 8.3

Core Organization Service Technology

As discussed earlier, the percentage of the workforce employed in manufacturing continues to decline throughout the developed countries, while it has accelerated in emerging economies, especially in China but also increasingly in other Asian countries including Indonesia and Vietnam.

Some analysts estimate that at over 109 million, there are more than twice as many manufacturing workers in China as in all the G7 industrialized countries put together, although the trend to automation, partly driven by rising labour costs in emerging economies such as China, means that the overall number of manufacturing jobs worldwide is declining.[79,80] As manufacturing has declined particularly in developed countries, the service sector has rapidly increased in size. More than two-thirds of the European Union workforce, and almost four-fifths of the North American workforce, is employed in services, such as hospitals, hotels, parcel delivery, online services or telecommunications.[81] Service technologies are different from manufacturing technologies and this is reflected in differences of organization structure.

Service Firms

Definition Whereas manufacturing organizations pursue their primary purpose through the production of products, service organizations pursue their primary purpose through the production and provision of services, such as education, healthcare, transportation, banking and hospitality. Studies of service organizations have focused on the unique dimensions of service technologies. The characteristics of service technology are compared with those of manufacturing technology in Exhibit 8.8.

An obvious difference is that service technology produces an *intangible output*. A service often consists of knowledge and ideas rather than a physical product. A client meets with a doctor or attorney, for example, or students and teachers come together in the classroom or over the internet. A service cannot be stored, inventoried or viewed as a finished good. If a service is not

EXHIBIT 8.8   Differences between Manufacturing and Service Technologies

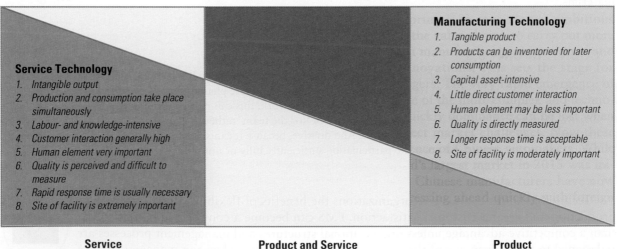

Service Technology
1. Intangible output
2. Production and consumption take place simultaneously
3. Labour- and knowledge-intensive
4. Customer interaction generally high
5. Human element very important
6. Quality is perceived and difficult to measure
7. Rapid response time is usually necessary
8. Site of facility is extremely important

Manufacturing Technology
1. Tangible product
2. Products can be inventoried for later consumption
3. Capital asset-intensive
4. Little direct customer interaction
5. Human element may be less important
6. Quality is directly measured
7. Longer response time is acceptable
8. Site of facility is moderately important

Service	Product and Service	Product
Airlines	Fast-food outlets	Soft drink companies
Hotels	Cosmetics	Steel companies
Consultants	Real estate	Automobile manufacturers
Healthcare	Stockbrokers	Mining corporations
Law firms	Retail stores	Food processing plants

Source: Based on F. F. Reichheld and W. E. Sasser, Jr, 'Zero Defections: Quality Comes to Services', *Harvard Business Review* 68 (September– October 1990), 105–111; and David E. Bowen, Caren Siehl and Benjamin Schneider, 'A Framework for Analyzing Customer Service Orientations in Manufacturing', *Academy of Management Review* 14 (1989), 75–95.

consumed immediately upon production, it disappears.[82] This typically means that service firms are *labour- and knowledge-intensive*, with many employees serving customers, in contrast to manufacturing firms that tend to be more *capital-intensive*, relying on mass production, continuous process and flexible manufacturing technologies.[83]

Direct interaction between customer and employee is generally very high with services. This direct interaction means that the *human element* (employees) becomes even more important in service firms. Most people never meet the workers who manufactured their cars, but they interact directly with the salesperson who sold them their Honda Civic or Renault Clio. The treatment received from the salesperson – or from a doctor, lawyer or hairstylist – affects the perception of the service received and the customer's level of satisfaction. The *quality* of a service is also more difficult to measure and compare than the quality of a tangible product. Another characteristic affecting customer satisfaction and perception of quality service is *rapidity of response*. When you take a friend to dinner, you want to be seated and served in a timely manner.

A final defining characteristic of service technology is that *site selection* is often much more important than with manufacturing. Services are dispersed and located geographically close to customers. For example, fast-food franchises usually disperse their facilities. Most American towns of even moderate size today have two or more McDonald's restaurants rather than one large one in order to provide service where customers want it. Penetration of fast-food chains is substantially lower in many European countries, where there are cultural and sometimes legal barriers against their expansion.[84]

In reality, it is difficult to find organizations that reflect 100 per cent service or 100 per cent manufacturing characteristics. Some service firms take on characteristics of manufacturers, and vice versa. Many manufacturing firms are placing a greater emphasis on customer service to differentiate themselves and become more competitive. Consider AESSEAL, a Bradford, UK-based manufacturer of mechanical seals for industries ranging from chemical manufacture to waste water handling, and pulp and paper production. Founder Chris Rea realized that in a business where competitors all offer similar quality products, the key to success would be strong customer service. AESSEAL achieved better customer service – and financial success – through setting an industry standard in ready availability of parts. In comparison with competitors who are able to fulfil only 95 per cent of orders immediately, AESSEAL aims for 98 per cent. Production director Richard Cook says: 'It is part of our strategy to be able to supply standard parts the next day, which is why we don't have any big hang-up about carrying stock; if the customer is in trouble that is our chance to say "we can help you" and we don't charge them a premium for quick turn times.' AESSEAL's commitment to customer service helped it to win Britain's Institute of Mechanical Engineers award for Manufacturing Excellence. The company has continued to grow both organically and through takeovers, based on its solid and customer-oriented organizational capacity. By 2016 the company employed over 1650 people worldwide in 37 countries, including 650 in the UK.[85]

In addition to the customer service component that is increasingly integrated in design of the manufacturing operations, manufacturing organizations have departments such as purchasing, HR and marketing that are based on service technology. Stockbrokers, retail stores and restaurants belong to the service sector, but the provision of a product is a significant part of the transaction. Organizations can be classified along a continuum that includes both manufacturing and service characteristics, as illustrated in Exhibit 8.7.

New Directions in Services   Service firms have always tended to provide some form of *customized output* – that is, providing a service that is responsive to specific customer demands. When you visit a hairstylist, you don't automatically get the same cut received by the previous client. The stylist cuts your hair the way you request it. However, the trend toward mass customization that is revolutionizing manufacturing is having a significant impact on the service sector as well. Customer expectations of what constitutes good service are rising.[86] Service companies such as high-end hotels combine traditional hospitality with the use of new technology to build customer loyalty. Britain's Shire group of hotels, which recently won a national award as the country's best hotel chain, has invested in its customer database to ensure that duplicates are removed, that data from all the chain's properties are consistently entered, and that customer preferences are properly recorded.[87] But successful large hotel chains don't rely on technology alone. When the Hong Kong-based Shangri-La chain, one of Asia's leading luxury hotel brands, decided to expand to North America, opening its first hotel in Vancouver, Canada, it was determined that 'traditional Asian hospitality' would be the chain's USP. Talented young hospitality professionals from North America were recruited as 'Tigers' – brand hospitality champions – and placed for training in various of the company's Asian properties, where they learned the core Shangri-La values of respect, courtesy, sincerity, helpfulness and humility.[88]

ONLINE
COUNTERPOINT 8.6

The expectation for better service is also pushing service firms in industries ranging from package delivery to banking to learn from the manufacturing sector. Japan Post, under pressure to cut a $191 million loss on operations, hired Toyota's Toshihiro Takahashi to assist in applying the Toyota Production System to the collection, sorting and delivery of mail. In all, Takahashi's team came up with 370 improvements and reduced the post office's person-hours by 20 per cent. The waste reduction was expected to cut costs by around $350 million a year.[89]

Designing the Service Organization

A feature of service technologies with a distinct influence on organizational structure and control systems is the closeness of technical core employees to the customer.[90] The differences between service and product organizations necessitated by customer contact are summarized in Exhibit 8.9.

The impact of customer contact on the design of organization structure is reflected in the use of boundary roles and structural disaggregation.[91] Boundary roles – that is roles straddling two or more kinds of activity such as manufacturing and HRM – are used extensively to reduce disruptions in the technical core. Service technology also influences internal organization characteristics used to direct and control the organization. For one thing, the skills of technical core employees typically need to be higher. In service firms, front-line employees require sufficient knowledge and awareness to handle a variety of customer problems directly and effectively. Much service work requires developed social and interpersonal skills as well as technical skills.[92]

EXHIBIT 8.9 Configuration and Structural Characteristics of Service Organizations versus Product Organizations

Structural Characteristic	Service	Product
1. Separate boundary roles	Few	Many
2. Geographical dispersion	Much	Little
3. Decision-making	Decentralized	Centralized
4. Formalization	Lower	Higher
Human Resources		
1. Employee skill level	Higher	Lower
2. Skill emphasis	Interpersonal	Technical

IN PRACTICE

Pret A Manger

'Would you like fries with that?' The standard line is rattled off by fast-food workers who have been taught to follow a script in serving customers. But at Pret A Manger, a fast-growing chain headquartered in London, England, in which McDonald's initially had a 33 per cent stake (sold to a private equity firm – Bridgepoint Capital – in 2008), you won't hear any standard lines. Employees aren't given scripts for serving customers or pigeonholed into performing the same repetitious tasks all day long. Managers want people to let their own personalities come through in offering each customer the best service possible. 'Our customers say, "I like to be served by human beings"' explains Ewan Stickley, head of employee training. Britain's *Sunday Times* ranked Pret A Manger as one of the top 50 companies to work for in the country – the only restaurant to make the cut.

Pret A Manger (faux French for 'ready to eat') operates 289 outlets (2014) in the United Kingdom and is expanding into Hong Kong and the United States.

'Nobody has ever gone to America, the home of fast food, with a concept that turned out to be a successful national chain. We think we can do that,' says chairman and CEO Andrew Rolfe. Pret's concept is based on organizing a mass-market service business around innovation rather than standardization. The menu is based on salads, fresh-made sandwiches, hot soups, sushi and a variety of yogurt parfaits and blended juices. Menu items are constantly changing, based on what sells and what customers want. Pret A Manger has built in a number of mechanisms for getting fast feedback. The CEO reviews customer and employee comments every Friday. Employees who send in the best ideas for changes to products or procedures can win up to $1500. Managers spend one day each quarter working in a store to keep in touch with customers and see how their policies affect employees.

In its native UK, Pret A Manger has been a huge hit. Translating that success to the United States is an even bigger challenge. Rather than take on the huge and diverse American market in one bite, Pret settled on the New York market, where lunch habits are fairly close to those in London. By 2016 it had 43 outlets in New York with others in Washington, Boston and Chicago. In 2012 the company opened its first store in Paris, and has expanded to 14 locations across the city. It seems surprising, but a British sandwich appears to be successfully taking on French haute cuisine![93]

Non-Core Departmental Technology

We now turn to consider departments that are not necessarily within the technical core. From a technology perspective, every department has some kind of production process consisting of a distinct technology. A large company such as Toyota Corporation has departments responsible for engineering, R&D, HR, advertising, quality control, finance and dozens of other functions. This section analyzes the nature of departmental technology in relation to departmental structure.

A framework that has been particularly influential in understanding departmental technologies was developed by Charles Perrow.[94] It has proved useful for examining a broad range of technologies which makes it directly relevant for examining their role in departmental activities.

Variety

Perrow specified two dimensions of departmental activities that are relevant to organization structure and process. The first is the number of exceptions in the work. This refers to task variety, which is the frequency of unexpected and novel events.[95] When employees encounter a large number of unexpected situations, with frequent problems, variety is considered high. When there are few problems, and when day-to-day job requirements are repetitive, technology contains little variety. Variety in departments can range from repeating a single act, such as on a traditional assembly line, to working on a series of unrelated problems or projects.

Analyzability

The second dimension of technology concerns the analyzability of work activities. When the process of transforming inputs to the department into outputs for other departments is analyzable, the work can be reduced to mechanical steps and participants can follow an objective, computational procedure to solve problems. Problem solving may involve the use of standard procedures, such as instructions and manuals, or technical knowledge, such as that in a textbook or handbook. On the other hand, some work is less readily analyzable in this sense. When problems arise, it is difficult to identify the correct solution. There is no store of techniques or procedures to tell a person exactly what to do. The cause of, or solution to, a problem is not clear, so employees rely on accumulated experience, intuition and judgement. The effective solution to a problem is then the result of wisdom and experience, and not the result of standard procedures. For example, Philippos Poulos, a tone regulator at piano maker Steinway & Sons, has an unanalyzable technology. Tone regulators carefully check each piano's hammers to ensure they produce the proper Steinway sound.[96] These quality-control tasks require years of experience and practice. Standard procedures will not tell a person how to do such tasks.

Framework

The two dimensions of technology and examples of departmental activities on Perrow's framework are shown in Exhibit 8.10. The dimensions of variety and analyzability form the basis for four major categories of technology: routine, craft, engineering and nonroutine.

Routine technologies are characterized by little task variety and the use of objective, computational procedures. The tasks are formalized and standardized. Examples include the tasks that comprise an automobile assembly line or a department in which data entry is performed.

EXHIBIT 8.10 Framework for Department Technologies

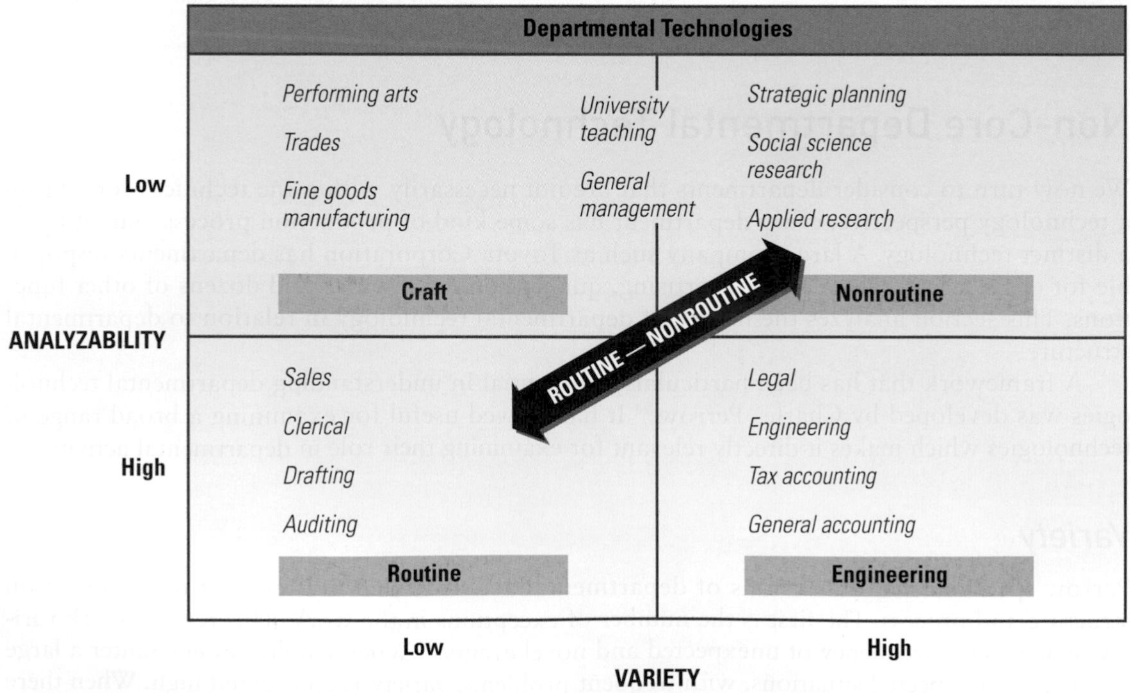

Source: Adapted from Richard Daft and Norman Macintosh, 'A New Approach to Design and Use of Management Information,' *California Management Review* 21 (1978), 82–92. Copyright © 1978 by the Regents of the University of California.

Craft technologies are characterized by a fairly stable stream of activities, but the conversion process is not analyzable or well understood. Tasks require extensive training and experience because employees respond to intangible factors on the basis of wisdom, intuition and experience. Although advances in machine technologies seem to have reduced the number of craft technologies in organizations, craft technologies are still important. For example, steel furnace engineers continue to mix steel based on intuition and experience, pattern makers at apparel firms convert rough designers' sketches into saleable garments and teams of writers for television series such as Britain's *Eastenders* or Latin America's internationally popular telenovelas (soaps) convert ideas into story lines.

Engineering technologies tend to be complex because there is substantial variety in the tasks performed. Nonetheless, many of the activities are handled on the basis of established formulas, procedures and techniques. Employees normally refer to a well-developed body of knowledge to handle problems. Many tasks within an HRM department fall into this category.

Nonroutine technologies have high task variety, and the conversion process is not analyzable or well understood. In nonroutine technology, a great deal of effort is devoted to analyzing problems and activities. Several equally acceptable options typically can be found. Experience and technical knowledge are used to solve problems and perform the work. Basic research, strategic planning and other work that involves new projects and unexpected problems are nonroutine. The blossoming biotechnology industry also represents a nonroutine technology. Breakthroughs in understanding metabolism and physiology at a cellular level depend on highly trained employees who use their experience and intuition as well as scientific knowledge. A scientist manipulating the chemical rungs on a DNA molecule has been compared to a musician playing variations on a theme.[97]

Routine versus Nonroutine   Exhibit 8.10 also illustrates how variety and analyzability can be combined into a single dimension of technology. This dimension is called *routine versus nonroutine technology*, and it is the diagonal line in Exhibit 8.10. The analyzability and variety dimensions are often correlated in departments, meaning that technologies high in variety tend to be low in analyzability, and technologies low in variety tend to be analyzable. Departments can be positioned along a single dimension of routine versus nonroutine that combines both analyzability and variety, which is a useful shorthand measure for analyzing departmental technology.

Department Design

Department technology tends to be associated with a cluster of departmental characteristics, such as the skill level of employees, formalization and pattern of communication. Definite patterns exist in the relationship between work unit technology and structural characteristics which, as we noted earlier when considering Woodward's research, tend to be associated with performance.[98]

Key relationships between technology and other dimensions of departments are described in this section and are summarized in Exhibit 8.11.

Routine technologies tend to be most strongly associated with a mechanistic structure and processes, with formal rules and rigid management processes. Nonroutine technologies are associated with a more organic structure where department management is more flexible and free-flowing. The differences can be set out in relation to the following dimensions:

BRIEFCASE 8.4

1   *Formalization.* Routine technology is characterized by standardization and division of labour into small tasks that are governed by formal rules and procedures. For nonroutine tasks, the structure is less formal and less standardized. When variety is high, as in a research department, fewer activities are covered by formal procedures.[99]

2   *Decentralization.* In routine technologies, most decision-making about task activities is centralized to management.[100] In engineering technologies, employees with technical training tend to acquire moderate decision authority because technical knowledge is important

IN PRACTICE

Health and Social Care in Northern Ireland (HSC)

In Britain, as in most other developed countries, the state of the country's health services is a matter of intense public debate. Managers and politicians are constantly tinkering with the system with the intention of achieving best outputs within limited budgets. Their efforts don't always achieve the results that were intended, but sometimes they do. One positive example comes from Northern Ireland, which as recently as 2004 had average waiting times on hospital trolleys in Accident and Emergency (A&E) wards of 24 hours or more, and more than 100 000 patients waiting for their first outpatient appointment.

Dean Sullivan, head of planning at the province's health department, says that in early 2005 a decision was made to crack the problem. The first thing the department did was to partner with the health authority in Manchester, England which had faced similar problems and dealt with them effectively. Together, they designed a three-year plan that contained four key elements: performance management, clear targets and goals, robust monitoring and sanctions in case of poor performance. He says that quality data was the foundation of the plan's success: 'When I was director of hospital services, it would take six months to get figures for waiting times from trusts.

To effect any change, you need robust monitoring arrangements and absolute clarity about what you want to achieve.'

Every Monday morning, waiting times were fed back to the Department, and action taken when they exceeded goals. The Department was empowered to move blocks of patients between semi-autonomous local health trusts, but the costs came out of the local trust's budget. Sullivan said they only had to do this once. A separate one-time only pot of money was allocated to pay for hiring doctors from elsewhere in Europe, who worked weekends and holidays to bring down the waiting list of patients. Now, people are seen immediately at A&E, and waiting times for elective surgery are down dramatically. In 2007, almost 2000 patients had been waiting more than 21 weeks for inpatient care. Within only a year, that was down to only 56.

Sullivan says it was 'not rocket science'. The key was a team of committed managers with a clear set of priorities, and the political will to make organizational changes to ensure that the key objective of reduced waiting times at all levels was met. There is still work to do in order to make the reforms sustainable; there is insufficient intermediary care for patients who can be discharged from hospital but are still not ready to stay on their own, and A&E units are still swamped by many patients who could have been safely treated by a GP.[101] Also, there is always the risk with target-oriented reforms that the exercise becomes one of 'ticking boxes' rather than really improving services. But things are going sufficiently well for now that Northern Ireland's neighbour to the south, the Republic of Ireland, studied the example of Parkland Memorial Hospital as a way of ironing out wrinkles in the Republic's healthcare system.[102]

to task accomplishment. Production employees who have long experience obtain decision authority in craft technologies as they know how to respond to problems. Decentralization to employees is greatest in nonroutine settings, where many decisions are made by employees.

3   *Worker skill level.* Work staff in routine technologies typically require little education or experience, which is congruent with repetitious work activities. In work units with greater variety, staff are more skilled and often have formal training in technical schools or universities. Training for craft activities, which are less analyzable, is more likely to be through job experience. Nonroutine activities require both formal education and job experience.[103]

4   *Span of control.* Span of control is the number of employees who report to a single manager or supervisor. This characteristic is normally influenced by departmental technology. The more complex and nonroutine the task, the more problems arise in which the

supervisor becomes involved. Although the span of control may be influenced by other factors, such as skill level of employees, it is typically smaller for complex tasks where the supervisor and subordinate interact frequently.[104]

5 *Communication and coordination.* Communication activity and frequency increase as task variety increases.[105] Frequent problems require more information sharing to reach solutions and ensure proper completion of activities. The direction of communication is typically horizontal in nonroutine work units and vertical in routine work units.[106] The form of communication varies by task analyzability.[107] When tasks are highly analyzable, statistical and written forms of communication (memos, reports, rules and procedures) are frequent. When tasks are less analyzable, information typically is conveyed face-to-face, over the telephone, or in group meetings.

Two important points are reflected in Exhibit 8.11. First, differences between departments can be clarified by reference to their workflow technology.[108] Second, structural and management processes differ based on departmental technology. Studies have found that when structure and communication characteristics did not match the technology, departments tend to be less effective[109] as employees could not communicate with the frequency required to address problems. Consider the design characteristics of health services provision in Northern Ireland, discussed in the *In Practice* box on the last page, where the reorganization of core technology brought a transformation in the delivery of key services.

EXHIBIT 8.11 Relationship of Department Technology to Structural and Management Characteristics

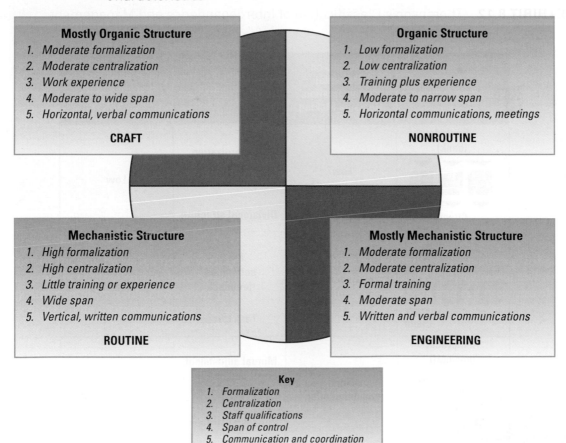

Mostly Organic Structure	**Organic Structure**
1. Moderate formalization	1. Low formalization
2. Moderate centralization	2. Low centralization
3. Work experience	3. Training plus experience
4. Moderate to wide span	4. Moderate to narrow span
5. Horizontal, verbal communications	5. Horizontal communications, meetings
CRAFT	**NONROUTINE**
Mechanistic Structure	**Mostly Mechanistic Structure**
1. High formalization	1. Moderate formalization
2. High centralization	2. Moderate centralization
3. Little training or experience	3. Formal training
4. Wide span	4. Moderate span
5. Vertical, written communications	5. Written and verbal communications
ROUTINE	**ENGINEERING**

Key
1. Formalization
2. Centralization
3. Staff qualifications
4. Span of control
5. Communication and coordination

Workflow Interdependence among Departments

Another characteristic of technology that influences structure is called interdependence. Interdependence means the extent to which departments depend on each other for resources or materials to accomplish their tasks. Where there is low interdependence, departments do their work with minimal interaction, consultation or exchange of materials with other departments. High interdependence requires the continuous exchange of resources between departments.

Types

James Thompson defined three types of interdependence that influence organization structure.[110] These interdependencies are illustrated in Exhibit 8.12 and are discussed below.

Pooled   Pooled interdependence is the most basic form of interdependence. In this form, work does not flow between units. Each department is part of the organization, but works independently. Chain restaurants or bank branches are typically examples of pooled interdependence. An outlet in Frankfurt need not interact with an outlet in Munich. Pooled interdependence may be associated with relationships within a *divisional structure*, defined in Chapter 4. Divisions or branches share financial resources from a common pool, and the performance of each division contributes to the fate of the overall organization.

Thompson proposed that pooled interdependence would exist in firms with what he called a mediating technology. A mediating technology provides products or services that mediate or

EXHIBIT 8.12   Thompson's Classification of Interdependence and Management Implications

Form of Interdependence	Demands on Horizontal Communication, Decision Making	Type of Coordination Required	Priority for Locating Units Close Together
Pooled (bank) Clients	Low communication	Standardization, rules, procedures Divisional structure	Low
Sequential (assembly line) Client	Medium communication	Plans, schedules, feedback Task forces	Medium
Reciprocal (hospital) Client	High communication	Mutual adjustment, cross-departmental meetings, teamwork Horizontal structure	High

link clients and, in so doing, allows each department to work independently. Banks, broker-age firms and real estate offices all mediate between buyers and sellers, but the offices work largely independently within the organization.

The management implications associated with pooled interdependence are quite simple. Thompson argued that managers should use rules and procedures to standardize activities across departments. If each department is required to use the same procedures and financial statements, the outcomes of all departments can be measured and compared. Very little day-to-day coordination is required among units.

BRIEFCASE 8.5

Sequential   When interdependence takes a serial form, with parts produced in one depart-ment becoming inputs to another department, it is called sequential interdependence. The effec-tiveness of the next department in the chain depends upon the performance of the preceding department. This is a higher level of interdependence than pooled interdependence as departments exchange resources and depend on others to undertake their tasks. Sequential interdependence requires the use of horizontal mechanisms such as integrators or task forces.

Sequential interdependence occurs in what Thompson called long-linked technology, which 'refers to the combination in one organization of successive stages of production; each stage of production uses as its inputs the production of the preceding stage and produces inputs for the following stage'.[111] An example of sequential interdependence comes from the shipbuilding indus-try. Until recently, ship designers made patterns and moulds out of paper and plywood, which were passed on to assembly. Mistakes in measurements or pattern mix-ups often caused errors in the cutting and assembly process, leading to delays and increased costs. American ship archi-tect, Filippo Cali, addressed this shortcoming by creating a complex software programme that serves as a link between design and assembly. The software eliminates the need for paper and ply-wood moulds by putting that crucial part of the design process inside a computer programme.[112] Another example of sequential interdependence is automobile assembly which requires engines, steering mechanisms and tyres to keep production rolling.

The management requirements for sequential interdependence are more demanding than those for pooled interdependence as it requires coordination among the linked plants or depart-ments. Extensive planning and scheduling are necessary to ensure this flow. Some day-to-day com-munication is also required to handle unexpected problems and exceptions as they arise.

Reciprocal   The highest level of interdependence is reciprocal interdependence. This exists when the output of operation A is the input to operation B, and the output of operation B is the input back again to operation A. The outputs of departments influence those departments in reciprocal fashion. Here, there is a two-way flow of materials.

Reciprocal interdependence tends to occur in organizations with what Thompson called inten-sive technologies, which provide a variety of products or services in combination to a client. Hos-pitals are an example as they provide coordinated services to patients. A patient may move back and forth between X-ray, surgery and physical therapy. A firm developing new products is another example. Intense coordination occurs between design, engineering, manufacturing and marketing in order to combine all their resources in a manner aimed to match the requirement of the customer.

Where there is reciprocal interdependence a structure that supports frequent horizontal com-munication and mutual adjustment is required.

Structural Priority

As indicated in Exhibit 8.12, because decision-making, communication and coordination problems are greatest for reciprocal interdependence, there is a case for its receiving first priority in organiza-tion structure. New product development is one area of reciprocal interdependence that is of grow-ing concern to managers as companies face increasing pressure to get new products to market fast.

Many firms are revamping the design-manufacturing relationship by closely integrating technologies discussed earlier in this chapter.[113] A horizontal structure, with linked sets of teams working on core processes, can provide the close coordination needed to support reciprocal interdependence. If reciprocally interdependent units are not located close together, coordinating mechanisms can be introduced, such as daily meetings between departments or the use of an intranet to facilitate communication. This can be challenging. The European Airbus company is a joint project of four countries: France, Germany, United Kingdom and Spain. Production of a new plan requires a complex series of negotiations about which partner is going to get what piece of the project, followed by the manufacture of the plane as a 'jigsaw' between the four manufacturing bases. Inevitably, the whole process leads to delays and added cost, as the airline industry found out in the production of the A380, the world's largest superjumbo, when delivery dates were repeatedly postponed, and the company faced losses and cancellations,[114,115] in an industry where timeliness of delivery can prove to be more important than the promise of superior product specifications.

Structural Implications

Most organizations experience various levels of interdependence, and structures emerge, or are purposefully designed, in response to these demands and other contingencies, as illustrated in Exhibit 8.13.[116] In a manufacturing firm, new product development entails reciprocal interdependence among the design, engineering, purchasing, manufacturing and sales departments. In response to this pattern of interdependence, a horizontal structure or cross-functional teams could be used to handle the back-and-forth flow of information and resources (see Counterpoint 8.4). Once a product is designed, its actual manufacture might then involve sequential interdependence,

EXHIBIT 8.13 Primary Means to Achieve Coordination for Different Levels of Task Interdependence in a Manufacturing Firm

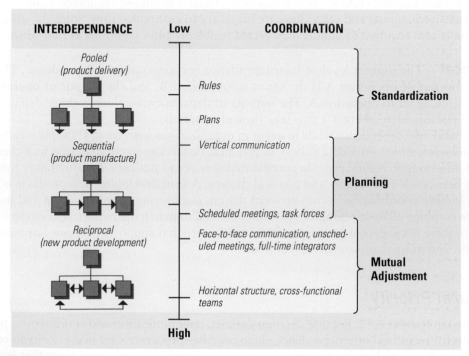

Source: Adapted from Andrew H. Van de Ven, Andre Delbecq and Richard Koenig, 'Determinants of Communication Modes within Organizations', *American Sociological Review* 41 (1976), 330.

with a flow of goods from one department to another, such as among purchasing, inventory, production control, manufacturing and assembly. The actual ordering and delivery of products approximates more closely to pooled interdependence, with warehouses working independently. Customers could place an order with the nearest facility, which would not require coordination among warehouses, except in unusual cases such as a stock outage.

COUNTERPOINT 8.4

While this design might be most consistent with the theory propounded earlier in this chapter, many other 'practical' considerations may militate against, or compromise, its application. For example, an established top-down culture of the organization may impede the development of horizontal functional teams. Even where such teams are introduced, decisions may be referred up the hierarchy.

Various new technologies can support departmental interdependence even where business processes are outsourced, or even offshored across the world. Some aspects of international business processes can speed up interdepartmental communication. For example, due to time differences, software companies can send a task to programmers in Bangalore, India to be worked on overnight, so that it can be plugged into the bigger project in Europe the next morning.[117] Medical notes and test data can be sent across the world electronically and analyzed in time to be read by a medical consultant before the next patient examination the following day.[118] In practice, however, the number of activities that can be geographically and culturally disconnected is limited by the demands of organizational interdependence, as discussed earlier in this chapter. Processes like software code writing and medical transcription might seem to require mainly *sequential* interdependence. But in practice small issues arise all the time that require minor clarifications and corrections – that is, a *reciprocal* form of interdependence. Where the different groups working on a process are co-located, this reciprocity usually means dropping into a nearby office, or having a chat at the water cooler. When one of the teams is located on the other side of the world, working in the middle of the rest of the team's night, that isn't so simple.[119] Almost without exception, managers of transnational processes state that coordination issues were more serious than they expected, and that they impose significant hidden costs.[120,121] Most complex business processes require regular yet unpredictable cross-discipline feedback. Even where technology permits real-time communication across distance, cultural differences can impose an efficiency burden, as discussed in Chapter 7.[122]

Impact of Technology on Job Design

So far, this chapter has described models for analyzing how manufacturing, service and department technologies influence structure and management processes. The concepts of job design and sociotechnical systems most directly illuminate the impact of technology on employees.

Job Design

Job design includes the assignment of goals and tasks to be accomplished by employees. Managers may intentionally change job design to improve productivity, product or service quality or worker motivation. For example, when workers are involved in performing tasks assessed to be boringly repetitive, managers may introduce job rotation, which means moving employees from job to job to give them a greater variety of tasks. Managers may also unintentionally

BRIEFCASE 8.6

influence job design through the introduction of new technologies, which can change how jobs are done and the very nature of jobs.[123]

A common theme of new technologies in the workplace is that they in some way substitute machinery for human labour. Automated teller machines (ATMs) have replaced thousands of human bank tellers, for example. In addition to replacing human workers, technology may have several different effects on the jobs that remain. Research has indicated that mass-production technologies tend to result in job simplification, which means that the variety and difficulty of tasks performed by a single person are reduced, with a potential increase in boredom and potential demotivation. More advanced technology, on the other hand, may increase levels of responsibility, recognition and opportunities for growth and development. These technologies require increased employee training and education because higher-level skills and greater competence are needed to master the new tasks. For example, ATMs took most of the routine tasks (deposits and withdrawals) away from bank tellers, freeing them up to take on less routine tasks that require higher-level skills and greater customer interaction. However, the overall number of jobs in the banking industry declined as a result of automation.[124,125]

Studies of flexible manufacturing have found that it is accompanied by the following: more opportunities for intellectual mastery and enhanced cognitive skills for workers; more worker responsibility for results; and greater interdependence among workers, enabling more social interaction and the development of teamwork and coordination skills.[126] Such developments are characterized as forms of job enrichment. Flexible manufacturing technology may also contribute to job enlargement, which is an expansion of the number of different tasks performed by an employee which include those that require additional skill sets (see Counterpoint 8.5).

ONLINE
COUNTERPOINT 8.7

ONLINE
COUNTERPOINT 8.8

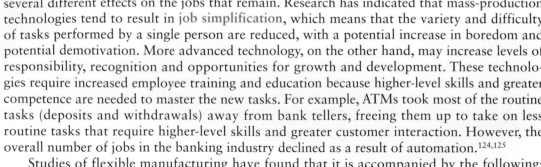

ONLINE
COUNTERPOINT 8.9

COUNTERPOINT 8.5

The dark side of enrichment and enlargement may be increased levels of stress associated with additional complexity, uncertainty and diversity. There is a tendency to emphasize the positive – less boredom, more challenge, etc. – while downplaying or disregarding the negative consequences of 'progressive' forms or job (re)design.

With advanced technology, workers have to keep learning new skills where technology is changing rapidly. Advances in *information technology*, to be discussed in detail in the next chapter, continue to exert significant effects on jobs in the service industry, including workplaces such as medical clinics, law firms, financial planners and accountants and libraries. Workers may find their jobs changing repeatedly with the introduction of new software programmes, increased use of the internet, and other advances in information technology.

Sociotechnical Systems

The sociotechnical systems approach recognizes the interaction of technical and human elements in effective job design. The *socio* element of the approach refers to the people and groups that work in organizations and how work is organized and coordinated. The *technical* element refers to the materials, tools, machines and processes used to transform organizational inputs into outputs.

Exhibit 8.14 illustrates the three primary components of the sociotechnical systems model.[127] The *social system* includes all human elements – such as individual and team behaviour, organizational culture, management practices and degree of communication openness – that can influence the performance of work. The *technical system* refers to the type of production technology, the level of interdependence, the complexity of tasks and so forth. The goal of the sociotechnical

EXHIBIT 8.14 Sociotechnical Systems Model

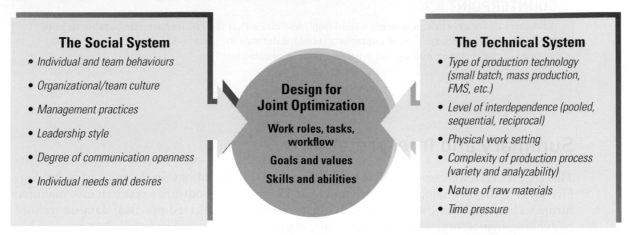

The Social System

- Individual and team behaviours
- Organizational/team culture
- Management practices
- Leadership style
- Degree of communication openness
- Individual needs and desires

Design for Joint Optimization

Work roles, tasks, workflow

Goals and values

Skills and abilities

The Technical System

- Type of production technology (small batch, mass production, FMS, etc.)
- Level of interdependence (pooled, sequential, reciprocal)
- Physical work setting
- Complexity of production process (variety and analyzability)
- Nature of raw materials
- Time pressure

Sources: Based on T. Cummings, 'Self-Regulating Work Groups: A Socio-Technical Synthesis', *Academy of Management Review* 3 (1978), 625–634; Don Hellriegel, John W. Slocum and Richard W. Woodman, *Organizational Behavior*, 8th ed. (Cincinnati, OH: South-Western, 1998), 492; and Gregory B. Northcraft and Margaret A. Neale, *Organizational Behavior: A Management Challenge*, 2nd ed. (Fort Worth, TX: The Dryden Press, 1994), 551.

systems approach is to design the organization for joint optimization where the best fit between the social and technical elements of systems is achieved. Conversely, there is a concern to avoid designs that are responsive to the human element but neglect the technical systems, or which concentrate on optimizing the technical element without regard for how human beings will use it. The sociotechnical systems approach attempts to find a sustainable balance between the capacities of employees and the technical requirements of the organization's production system (see Counterpoint 8.6).[128]

COUNTERPOINT 8.6

When expressed in this way, it is evident that 'the technical requirements of the production system' are often given priority. For example, it is decided that competitive survival depends upon changing those requirements by introducing new technical elements. Having made this decision, it is then determined how best to train and organize employees to operate the new technology. An alternative approach would be to start with the capabilities of the employees and assess which technical elements would provide the best fit so as to maximize productive capability.

One example comes from a museum that installed a closed-circuit TV system. Rather than having several guards patrolling the museum and grounds, the television could be monitored by a single guard. The technology saved money because only one guard was needed per shift, but it led to unexpected performance problems. For guards that had previously enjoyed the social interaction provided by patrolling, monitoring a closed-circuit television led to alienation and boredom. When a government agency did an 18-month test of the system, only 5 per cent of several thousand experimental covert intrusions were detected by the guard.[129] The system was ineffective because inadequate account was taken of how human beings would experience and use the new technology. Another study of paper manufacturers found that designs that put too much faith in machines and technology and pay little attention to the appropriate management of people do not achieve advances in productivity and flexibility (see Counterpoint 8.7).[130]

COUNTERPOINT 8.7

Advocates of sociotechnical systems would doubtless claim that the failures are attributable to poor application of the theory. This of course is a standard defence for people whose theories fail to take account of the complex and dynamic field of their application.

Summary and Interpretation

This chapter reviewed several frameworks and key research findings on the topic of technology. Five ideas in the technology literature stand out. The first is Woodward's research into manufacturing technology. Woodward went into organizations and collected practical data on technology characteristics, organization structure and management systems. She found clear relationships between technology and structure in the highest performing organizations that suggest how competitive advantage may be achieved by co-aligning strategy with an appropriate fit between structure and technology.

The second important idea is that there are some key differences between service and manufacturing technologies. Service technologies are characterized by intangible outcomes and direct client involvement in the production process. Service firms tend to have the fixed, machine-based technologies that appear in manufacturing organizations although some do approximate closely to their levels of standardization; hence, organization design often differs as well.

The third significant idea is Perrow's framework applied to department technologies. Understanding the variety and analyzability of a technology gives pointers to how the elements of management style, structure and process might be developed and combined to attain the most effective outcome. Routine technologies are characterized by mechanistic structure and nonroutine technologies by organic structure. Applying an incongruent management system to a department increases the risk of dissatisfaction and reduced efficiency.

The fourth important idea is interdependence among departments. The extent to which departments depend on each other for materials, information or other resources affects the amount of coordination required between them. Greater interdependence tends to increase the demands on the organization for coordination. To address these demands, design must accommodate appropriate forms of communication and coordination across departments. The trend towards business process outsourcing, including offshoring, presents challenges in maintaining interdependence across distance, that can be partially, but not fully, handled through new information and communication technologies.

The fifth important idea is that new flexible manufacturing systems are having a significant impact upon organization design. Where technologies replace routine jobs without job losses, allow employees more autonomy who want more challenges and/or responsibility, and encourage teamwork when this is not experienced as oppressive, it is probable that the new systems will be highly effective in increasing flexibility and improved response to customer demands. At the same time, there can be significant job losses, particularly at the lower end of the labour market in high-wage, 'developed' economies. Where the social conditions for introducing new technologies are less than positive with regard to job losses, interest in greater responsibility, etc., then their impact on productivity will be disappointing In this respect, sociotechnical systems theory, which attempts to design the technical and human aspects of an organization to fit one another, is highly relevant as advances in technology alter the nature of jobs and social interaction in today's manufacturing and service companies.

KEY CONCEPTS

analyzability	interdependence	long-linked technology	sequential
continuous process	job design	mass customization	interdependence
production	job enlargement	mediating technology	service technology
core technology	job enrichment	non-core technology	small-batch production
craft technologies	job rotation	nonroutine technologies	sociotechnical systems
engineering technologies	job simplification	pooled interdependence	approach
flexible manufacturing	joint optimization	reciprocal	technical complexity
systems	large-batch production	interdependence	technology
intensive technologies	lean manufacturing	routine technologies	variety

Discussion Questions

1   Where would your university or college department be located on Perrow's technology framework? Look for the underlying variety and analyzability characteristics when making your assessment. Would a department devoted exclusively to teaching be put in a different quadrant from a department devoted exclusively to research?

2   Explain Thompson's levels of interdependence. Identify an example of each level of interdependence in the university or college setting. What kinds of coordination mechanisms should an administration develop to handle each level of interdependence?

3   Describe Woodward's classification of organizational technologies. Explain why each of the three technology groups is related differently to organization structure and management processes.

4   How do flexible manufacturing and lean manufacturing differ from other manufacturing technologies? Why are these new approaches needed in today's environment?

5   What is a service technology? Are different types of service technologies likely to be associated with different structures? Explain.

6   Mass customization of products has become a common approach in manufacturing organizations. Discuss ways in which mass customization can be applied to service firms as well.

7   In what primary ways does the design of service firms typically differ from that of product firms? Why?

8   A top executive claimed that top-level management is a craft technology because the work contains intangibles, such as handling personnel, interpreting the environment and coping with unusual situations that have to be learned through experience. If this is true, is it appropriate to teach management in a business school? Does teaching management from a textbook assume that the manager's job is analyzable, and hence that formal training rather than experience is most important?

9   In which quadrant of Perrow's framework would a mass-production technology be placed? Where would small-batch and continuous process technologies be placed? Why? Would Perrow's framework lead to the same recommendation about organic versus mechanistic structures that Woodward made?

10 To what extent does the development of new technologies simplify and routinize the jobs of employees? How can new technology lead to job enlargement? Discuss.

11 Describe the sociotechnical systems model. Why might some managers oppose a sociotechnical systems approach?

Chapter 8 Workbook   Bistro Technology

You will be analyzing the technology used in three different restaurants: McDonald's, a popular national chain of your choice, and a typical local non-chain restaurant. Your instructor will tell you whether to do this assignment as individuals or in a group.

   You must visit all three restaurants and infer how the work is done, according to the following criteria. You are not allowed to interview any employees, but instead you will be an observer. Take lots of notes when you are there.

Questions

1   Is the technology used the best one for each restaurant, considering its goals and environment?

2   From the preceding data, determine if the structure and other characteristics fit the technology.

3   If you were part of a consulting team assigned to improve the operations of each organization, what recommendations would you make?

Adapted loosely by Dorothy Marcic from 'Hamburger Technology', in Douglas T. Hall et al., *Experiences in Management and Organizational Behavior*, 2nd ed. (New York: Wiley, 1982), 244–247, as well as 'Behavior, Technology and Work Design' in A. B. Shani and James B. Lau, *Behavior in Organizations* (Chicago: Irwin, 1996), M16–23 to M16–26.

Grundfos LIFELINK Water Solutions

The story begins in 2007 with a visit of the company's board chairman to Thailand where he saw first-hand the incredible struggle of the poor to get clean water. He was immediately inspired to take action by what he had observed. As he saw it, his company already had products that would readily provide part of the solution and the missing components could be either acquired or developed.

About one billion people around the world do not have access to a reliable supply of safe water. As a consequence, water-borne illnesses leading to sickness and death are commonplace in developing countries. Moreover, the time-consuming process of travelling to find water has a negative effect on productivity and often adversely affects children's school attendance. Water security is regarded as one of the top global risks today.[1] Although many organizations have worked on solutions to this life-threatening and productivity-eroding problem, water projects regularly fail to deliver the promised benefits.

Following his return from Thailand the board chairman initiated discussions in his company – Grundfos, the world's largest pump manufacturer. The plan was to design *financially sustainable* water stations for areas with little or no infrastructure and to pilot-test them in Kenya.

The challenge

Central to the project's business model is willingness by water station users to pay a minimal fee for water to cover the costs of professional servicing personnel and spare parts as well as the cost of the system. In this regard, it is crucial to build awareness among water users about the benefits for personal well-being and local entrepreneurship initiatives of a secure and uncontaminated supply of water always available to meet demand.

The evolving solution

At the outset of the project the Grundfos LIFELINK (GLL) role was primarily that of pump supplier working with NGOs familiar with local communities to handle water station site negotiations. Technology appropriate for rural Kenyan communities involved a robust solar-driven Grundfos submersible pump for pumping up groundwater combined with a storage tank and a remote monitoring system for servicing purposes as well as an automatic payment system. GLL worked on incorporating the locally popular M-Pesa mobile banking payment system and developed an automatic water dispensing system. Micro-financing would be used to cover the cost of water station installation, potentially with international aid contributions. Technicians were recruited and certified by GLL to monitor water stations remotely via the internet and carry out servicing as required.[2]

As the project evolved GLL took on a more controlling role of all facets of the operations. A decision was made to brand the project as LIFELINK and bring in a manager from Denmark. When NGOs could not successfully negotiate water station sites, GLL brought in anthropologists to design relationships with local communities, refocusing the water stations as business development projects, and to undertake negotiations with water boards. GLL further developed the payment system to produce AQtap, an intelligent water dispenser that allows users to purchase water using a smart card to which they transfer funds through the M-Pesa mobile banking system. Rapid water cleaning is now possible following the development of AQpure, a modular water treatment unit.

Where to from here?

The initial Kenyan installations provide clean water to over 100 000 people. A 'Water ATM' has been installed in Nairobi and agreements with neighbouring Uganda and India have been put into place. The project has embarked on a five-year relationship with World Vision International that has as its objective the installation of 1000 units in nine African countries. These installations will have some important environmental benefits for better management of scarce water resources. These installations are expected to build resilience to climate change and to reduce CO_2 emissions by 39 000 tonnes over their 15-year lifespan.[3] In the words of World Vision Senior Director Sean Kerrigan, 'Grundfos' technical expertise

[1] http://www.worldbank.org/en/topic/water/overview
[2] http://www.grundfos.com/market-areas/water/lifelink.html
[3] http://unfccc.int/secretariat/momentum_for_change/items/9272.php

leveraged with our on-the-ground presence in vulnerable communities has enabled us to dream big.'[4]

Fine-tuning the sustainability aspects of the business model has been a key aspect of the project's success. It offers sustainability in a number of respects – technologically with its remote monitoring and professional service and support, financially with its automatic and transparent revenue management system, environmentally with its renewable energy source and improved water management and socially with its safe and secure water service for enhanced well-being. Furthermore, its cashless, corruption-free payment system is also attractive to potential investors, such as local NGOs and international aid agencies. Awareness of the project's replicability and transformational potential are spreading. The *Momentum for Change Lighthouse Activity Award* (2015) and the *World Business & Development Award* (2012) have brought further international recognition.

The GLL business model has demonstrated that it can sustainably offer self-financing of reliable and safe water delivery for the very poor and new business opportunities are emerging in the developing world. Although further scaling up internationally would be costly with the continued presence of the Grundfos team, would continued success be possible without it?

Case Questions

1 In this chapter sociotechnical systems theory is presented. It focuses on attempts to fit together the technical and human aspects of an organization in order to deliver a product or service. What are the *human components* and the *technology components* of the Grundfos LIFELINK Project and how effectively are they interfaced?

2 You have been hired as a business consultant to advise on the scaling up of the Grundfos LIFELINK project to other countries in Africa and Asia. What advice could you offer based on testing of the business model in Kenya? Can you add any useful insights from the *In Practice* examples Pret A Manger and Health and Social Care in Northern Ireland (HSC) despite the differences in business model and context?

For further information:
Andersen, Poul Houman and Åberg, Susanne (2013), "Selling to the base of the pyramid," *Mercury Magazine*, Spring/Summer (Special Issue on the Business of Consultancies), Issue 4, pp. 58-63. Mercury Reprint 04135863.
https://www.youtube.com/watch?v=7JwwKaZUukY
https://www.youtube.com/watch?v=ItBX0NHMs7M

[4] http://www.wvi.org/clean-water-sanitation-and-hygiene-wash/article/how-mobile-technology-creating-vital-link-clean

Notes

1. http://www.conti-online.com/generator/www/us/en/continental/transport/themes/about_continental/conti_ag_history/ag_history_7_en.html accessed on August 25, 2008.
2. Paul Erker (1996) *Competition and Growth: A Contemporary History of the Continental AG*, Dusseldorf, ECON.
3. 'Toyo Ends Deal With Conti', *European Rubber Journal*, June 10, 2002.
4. *New York Times*, 'Continental A.G. in $1.93 Billion Deal', July 28, 1998.
5. *FD (Fair Disclosure) Wire*, 'Continental AG to Acquire Siemens VDO Automotive AG', July 25, 2007.
6. Annual Results 2015, accessed at http://www.continental-corporation.com/www/portal_com_de/themen/ir/news_adhoc/news/20160111_eckdaten_fyr_de.html
7. *Western Europe Automotive Insights*, 'Continental and Schaeffler Reach a Deal', September 1, 2008.
8. Christiaan Hetzner, 'Continental bidder unlikely to play nice', *International Herald Tribune*, July 28, 2008.
9. Continental AG Corporate Strategy, 2014.
10. 'Shoe giants have one foot in India', *Hindustan Times*, February 25, 2007.
11. David Williamson, 'The winners and losers of outsourcing and offshoring', *Western Mail*, September 8, 2006.
12. 'Amex jobs move to other side of world', *Star Tribune* (Minneapolis, MN), May 20, 2002.
13. Bruce A. Blonigen and Miao Wang (2004), Inappropriate Pooling of Wealthy and Poor Countries in Empirical FDI Studies, NBER Working Paper W10378; S. Kobrin (1999) 'Development after Industrialisation', in N. Hood and S. Young (eds) *The Globalization of Multinational Enterprise Activity and Economic Development,* Basingstoke, Macmillan, 133–154; Gary Gereffi and Olga Memedovic (2003), *The Global Apparel Value Chain: What Prospects for Upgrading by Developing Countries,* Vienna, UNIDO.

14. Euler Hermes Ltd., The global automotive market, Economic Outlook no.1210, August-September 2014, accessed at www.eulerhermes.com/mediacenter/Lists/mediacenter-documents/Economic-Outlook-The-global-Automotive-market-Sept14.pdf; KPMG, Global Automotive Executive Survey 2016, accessed at https://assets.kpmg.com/content/dam/kpmg/pdf/2016/01/gaes-2016.pdf

15. Charles Perrow, 'A Framework for the Comparative Analysis of Organizations', *American Sociological Review* 32 (1967), 194–208; and R. J. Schonberger, *World Class Manufacturing: The Next Decade* (New York: The Free Press, 1996).

16. Wanda J. Orlikowski, 'The Duality of Technology: Rethinking the Concept of Technology in Organizations', *Organization Science* 3 (1992), 398–427.

17. Linda Argote, 'Input Uncertainty and Organizational Coordination in Hospital Emergency Units', *Administrative Science Quarterly* 27 (1982), 420–434; Charles Perrow, *Organizational Analysis: A Sociological Approach* (Belmont, CA: Wadsworth, 1970); and William Rushing, 'Hardness of Material as Related to the Division of Labour in Manufacturing Industries', *Administrative Science Quarterly* 13 (1968), 229–245.

18. Lawrence B. Mohr, 'Organizational Technology and Organization Structure', *Administrative Science Quarterly* 16 (1971), 444–459; and David Hickson, Derek Pugh and Diana Pheysey, 'Operations Technology and Organization Structure: An Empirical Reappraisal', *Administrative Science Quarterly* 14 (1969), 378–397.

19. Joan Woodward, *Industrial Organization: Theory and Practice* (London: Oxford University Press, 1965); and Joan Woodward, *Management and Technology* (London: Her Majesty's Stationery Office, 1958).

20. Hickson, Pugh and Pheysey, 'Operations Technology and Organization Structure'; and James D. Thompson, *Organizations in Action* (New York: McGraw-Hill, 1967).

21. Edward Harvey, 'Technology and the Structure of Organizations', *American Sociological Review* 33 (1968), 241–259.

22. Based on Woodward, *Industrial Organization and Management and Technology.*

23. '3D printing puts small-scale shoe-designers back into game', *E&T Magazine*, February 2013.

24. Woodward, *Industrial Organization,* vi.

25. William L. Zwerman, *New Perspectives on Organizational Theory* (Westport, CT: Greenwood, 1970); and Harvey, 'Technology and the Structure of Organizations'.

26. Dean M. Schroeder, Steven W. Congden and C. Gopinath, 'Linking Competitive Strategy and Manufacturing Process Technology', *Journal of Management Studies* 32, No. 2 (March 1995), 163–189.

27. Steve Lohr, 'U.S. clears IBM sale to Lenovo', *The International Herald Tribune*, March 11, 2005.

28. Fernando F. Suarez, Michael A. Cusumano and Charles H. Fine, 'An Empirical Study of Flexibility in Manufacturing', *Sloan Management Review* (Fall 1995), 25–32.

29. Raymond F. Zammuto and Edward J. O'Connor, 'Gaining Advanced Manufacturing Technologies' Benefits: The Roles of Organization Design and Culture', *Academy of Management Review* 17, No. 4 (1992), 701–728; and Schroeder, Congden and Gopinath,

'Linking Competitive Strategy and Manufacturing Process Technology'.

30. Reported in Grainger David, 'One Truck a Minute,' *Fortune* (April 5, 2004), 252–258.

31. Data calculated dynamically through http://earthtrends.wri.org/ on August 26, 2008.

32. '3 Taiwan Computer Makers in BTO Operations', *Taiwan Business News*, 2 December 1997.

33. John S. McClenahen, 'Bearing Necessities', *Industry Week* (October 2004), 63ff.

34. http://web.archive.org/web/20080511193800/http://www.bedlampuzzles.com/default.asp and http://s396492048.websitehome.co.uk/crazeee/, accessed on September 15, 2013.

35. 'Toymaker hopes to boost "UK" tag appeal', *Western Morning News*, 6 December 2007.

36. Tim Webb and Heather Stewart, 'Crunch Times: Why The Future Is Made In Britain: The Factory Floor', *The Observer*, 27 April 2008.

37. Rebecca Wright, 'France's Bollore Could Invest 30 mil. Euro in Pininfarina', *Global Insight Daily Analysis*, 6 June 2008; 'Italy Antitrust OKs Fiat Group Automobiles Buy of Itca', *ANSA – English Corporate News Service*, 9 May 2007; Tom Murphy, 'Insourcing', *Ward's Auto World*, 1 May 2003.

38. Crazee Things Catalogue 2011, available at http://www.crazeethingz.com/crazee-thingz-2012-catalogue.pdf.

39. 'IBS implements Plant Maintenance Management System at Mondi Business Paper – Syktyvkarskii LPK' *SKRIN Market & Corporate News*, September 14 2006.

40. Jack R. Meredith, 'The Strategic Advantages of the Factory of the Future', *California Management Review* 29 (Spring 1987), 27–41; Jack Meredith, 'The Strategic Advantages of the New Manufacturing Technologies for Small Firms', *Strategic Management Journal* 8 (1987), 249–258; and Althea Jones and Terry Webb, 'Introducing Computer Integrated Manufacturing', *Journal of General Management* 12 (Summer 1987), 60–74.

41. Raymond F. Zammuto and Edward J. O'Connor, 'Gaining Advanced Manufacturing Technologies' Benefits: The Roles of Organization Design and Culture', *Academy of Management Review* 17 (1992), 701–728.

42. Ron Manwiller, 'Ceramic imaging's digital revolution: digital ceramic printing provides mass customization and has opened a host of new market opportunities', *Ceramic Industry*, 1 April 2008.

43. Paul S. Adler, 'Managing Flexible Automation', *California Management Review* (Spring 1988), 34–56.

44. Bela Gold, 'Computerization in Domestic and International Manufacturing'. *California Management Review* (Winter 1989), 129–143.

45. Graham Dudley and John Hassard, 'Design Issues in the Development of Computer Integrated Manufacturing (CIM)', *Journal of General Management* 16 (1990), 43–53.

46. Jeff Wise, 'Plane Dealer', *FSB* (July–August 2004), 83–84.

47. 'Nobel Biocare Holding AG – SWOT Analysis', *Global Markets Direct Company Profiles*, 4 July 2008.

48. Ibid; and Tom Massung, 'Manufacturing Efficiency', *Microsoft Executive Circle* (Winter 2004), 28–29.

49. Brian Heymans, 'Leading the Lean Enterprise', *Industrial Management* (September–October 2002), 28–33; and

Fara Warner, 'Think Lean', *Fast Company* (February 2002), 40, 42.

50. Peter Strozniak, 'Toyota Alters Face of Production', *IndustryWeek* (August 13, 2001), 46–48.

51. Malcolm Wheatley, 'Lean beacon: German industrial giant pioneers Toyota-style initiative; SAP integration to follow', *Manufacturing Business Technology*, 1 February 2008.

52. B. Joseph Pine II, *Mass Customization: The New Frontier in Business Competition* (Boston: Harvard Business School Press, 1999).

53. Rebecca Duray (2002), 'Mass customization origins: mass or custom manufacturing?', *International Journal of Operations & Production Management*, 22, 314–328.

54. Laetitia Radder and Lynette Louw (1999), 'Mass customization and mass production', *The TQM Magazine*, 11, 35–40.

55. C.W.L. Hart (1995), 'Mass customization: Conceptual underpinnings, opportunities and limits', *International Journal of Service Industry Management*, 6, 36–45.

56. Joseph B. Pine II (1999), *Mass Customization: The New Frontier in Business Competition*, Cambridge, Harvard Business Press. Cited on page 207.

57. Barry Berman, 'Should Your Firm Adopt a Mass Customization Strategy?', *Business Horizons* (July–August 2002), 51–60.

58. Antone Gonsalves, 'Acer Beats Lenovo For The World's No. 3 Computer Maker Spot: Second-place Dell was the only company in the top five to suffer a decline', *InformationWeek*, June 5, 2007.

59. Erick Schonfeld, 'The Customized, Digitized, Have-It-Your-Way Economy', *Fortune* (September 28, 1998), 115–124.

60. http://www.arianedeco.fr/, accessed on August 27, 2008.

61. These and many other examples posted by Thomas Dusart on 'La Blog de la Mass Customization', accessed at http://masscustomization.blogspot.com/ on August 27, 2008.

62. 5 S refers to five Japanese words beginning with 's' that encapsulate the philosophy underpinning lean manufacturing: *seiri, seiton, seiso, seiketsu* and *shitsuke*, signifying order, cleanliness, purity and commitment.

63. TPM–Total Productive Maintenance.

64. 'Autoliv Production System', powerpoint presentation accessed at jpsupplier.autoliv.com/asm/ASM/doc/ASM...ENG-/APS-Booklet.ppt on September 15, 2013.

65. Abrahm Lustgarten, 'Elite Factories', *Fortune,* special section, 'Industrial Management and Technology' (September 6, 2004), 240[B]–240[L].

66. 'Almost Two Thirds of all the Safety Products in Europe's Best in Class Cars Produced by Autoliv', 30 January, 2013, *Business Wire*.

67. Yeh Fang-hsun, 'Building brands key to survival for creative industry', *Central News Agency – Taiwan*, June 20, 2008; 'Acer aims to overtake HP ahead of 2011 goal', *The Toronto Star*, April 15, 2009; 'Acer expects to grab 50% share of 2009 netbook market', *Digitimes*, November 3, 2008; Stan Shih, J.T. Wang and Arthur Yeung (2006), 'Building Global Competitiveness in a Turbulent Environment: Acer's Journey of Transformation' in William H. Mobley and Elizabeth Weldon, *Advances in Global Leadership,* Bradford, Emerald Group Publishing, 201–217.

68. Jeffrey Burt, "Acer Creates 2 Major Business Groups for PCs, Cloud", e-Week, March 28, 2016, accessed at www.eweek.com/pc-hardware/acer-creates-2-major-business-groups-for-pcs-cloud.html

69. Brian Caulfield, 28 November, 2011, 'The NetBook Is Dead, The iPad Killed It, Don't Buy One', *Forbes*.

70. Geoffrey Colvin, 'Co-Creation Is Your Latest Invention', *The Washington Post*, 6 May 2008, D03.

71. Kevin O'Donnell, 'Where Do The Best Ideas Come From? The Unlikeliest Sources; Peers, Suppliers Can Spark Some Great Innovations For Marketers', *Advertising Age*, 14 July 2008.

72. Sven A. Carlsson, 'Enhancing Knowledge Acquisition through the use of ICT', *DSS2004 Conference Proceedings* (2004).

73. Marc Nohr, 'Who says that consumers know best?', *Marketing Direct*, 5 February 2008.

74. Joel D. Goldhar and David Lei, 'Variety Is Free: Manufacturing in the Twenty-First Century', *Academy of Management Executive* No. 4 (1995), 73–86.

75. Meredith, 'The Strategic Advantages of the Factory of the Future'.

76. Patricia L. Nemetz and Louis W. Fry, 'Flexible Manufacturing Organizations: Implementations for Strategy Formulation and Organization Design', *Academy of Management Review* 13 (1988), 627–638; Paul S. Adler, 'Managing Flexible Automation', *California Management Review* (Spring 1988), 34–56; Jeremy Main, 'Manufacturing the Right Way', *Fortune* (May 21, 1990), 54–64; and Frank M. Hull and Paul D. Collins, 'High-Technology Batch Production Systems: Woodward's Missing Type', *Academy of Management Journal* 30 (1987), 786–797.

77. Goldhar and Lei, 'Variety Is Free: Manufacturing in the Twenty-First Century'; P. Robert Duimering, Frank Safayeni and Lyn Purdy, 'Integrated Manufacturing: Redesign the Organization before Implementing Flexible Technology,' *Sloan Management Review* (Summer 1993), 47–56; Zammuto and O'Connor, 'Gaining Advanced Manufacturing Technologies' Benefits'.

78. Goldhar and Lei, 'Variety Is Free: Manufacturing in the Twenty-First Century'.

79. 'Manufacturing's Decline', *Johnson City Press* (July 17, 1999), 9; Ronald Henkoff, 'Service Is Everybody's Business', *Fortune* (June 27, 1994), 48–60; Ronald Henkoff, 'Finding, Training and Keeping the Best Service Workers', *Fortune* (October 3, 1994), 110–122.

80. Judith Banister (2005), 'Manufacturing employment in China', *Monthly Labor Review*, July, 11–29.

81. Antonello D'Agostino, Roberta Serafini and Melanie Ward-Warmedinger, 'Sectoral Explanations of Employment in Europe: The Role Of Services', *European Central Bank Working Paper Series* No. 625, May 2006.

82. Byron J. Finch and Richard L. Luebbe, *Operations Management: Competing in a Changing Environment* (Fort Worth, TX: The Dryden Press, 1995), 51.

83. David E. Bowen, Caren Siehl and Benjamin Schneider, 'A Framework for Analyzing Customer Service Orientations in Manufacturing', *Academy of Management Review* 14 (1989), 79–95; Peter K. Mills and Newton Margulies, 'Toward a Core Typology of Service Organizations', *Academy of Management Review* 5 (1980), 255–265; Peter K. Mills and Dennis J. Moberg, 'Perspectives on the Technology of Service Operations', *Academy of Management Review* 7 (1982), 467–478; and G. Lynn

Shostack, 'Breaking Free from Product Marketing', *Journal of Marketing* (April 1977), 73–80.

84. Rick Fantasia (1995), 'Fast Food in France', *Theory and Society*, 24, 201–243.

85. 'First Tier Focus: Service seals the deal', *Metalworking Production*, 26 September 2006.

86. Ron Zemke, 'The Service Revolution: Who Won?' *Management Review* (March 1997), 10–15; and Wayne Wilhelm and Bill Rossello, 'The Care and Feeding of Customers', *Management Review* (March 1997), 19–23.

87. Ross Bentley, 'Data with destiny', *Caterer & Hotelkeeper*, 25 August 2005.

88. Schonfeld, 'The Customized, Digitized, Have-It-Your-Way Economy'.

89. Paul Migliorato, 'Toyota Retools Japan', *Business 2.0* (August 2004), 39–41.

90. Richard B. Chase and David A. Tansik, 'The Customer Contact Model for Organization Design', *Management Science* 29 (1983), 1037–1050.

91. Ibid.

92. David E. Bowen and Edward E. Lawler III, 'The Empowerment of Service Workers: What, Why, How and When', *Sloan Management Review* (Spring 1992), 31–39: Gregory B. Northcraft and Richard B. Chase, 'Managing Service Demand at the Point of Delivery', *Academy of Management Review* 10 (1985), 66–75; and Roger W. Schmenner, 'How Can Service Businesses Survive and Prosper?' *Sloan Management Review* 27 (Spring 1986), 21–32.

93. Stephanie Clifford, 8 August, 2011, 'Pret A Manger's fresh take on fast food; British sandwich chain keeps lines short and employees energized', *International Herald Tribune*.

94. Perrow, 'A Framework for Comparative Analysis' and *Organizational Analysis*.

95. Brian T. Pentland, 'Sequential Variety in Work Processes,' *Organization Science* 14, No. 5 (September–October 2003), 528–540.

96. Jim Morrison, 'Grand Tour. Making Music: The Craft of the Steinway Piano', *Spirit* (February 1997), 42–49, 100.

97. Stuart F. Brown, 'Biotech Gets Productive', *Fortune*, special section, 'Industrial Management and Technology' (January 20, 2003), 170[A]–170[H].

98. Christopher Gresov, 'Exploring Fit and Misfit with Multiple Contingencies', *Administrative Science Quarterly* 34 (1989), 431–453; and Dale L. Goodhue and Ronald L. Thompson, 'Task-Technology Fit and Individual Performance', *MIS Quarterly* (June 1995), 213–236.

99. Gresov, 'Exploring Fit and Misfit with Multiple Contingencies'; Charles A. Glisson, 'Dependence of Technological Routinization on Structural Variables in Human Service Organizations', *Administrative Science Quarterly* 23 (1978), 383–395; and Jerald Hage and Michael Aiken, 'Routine Technology, Social Structure and Organizational Goals,' *Administrative Science Quarterly* 14 (1969), 368–379.

100. Gresov, 'Exploring Fit and Misfit with Multiple Contingencies'; A. J. Grimes and S. M. Kline, 'The Technological Imperative: The Relative Impact of Task Unit, Modal Technology and Hierarchy on Structure', *Academy of Management Journal* 16 (1973), 583–597; Lawrence G. Hrebiniak, 'Job Technologies, Supervision and Work Group Structure', *Administrative Science Quarterly* 19

(1974), 395–410; and Jeffrey Pfeffer, *Organizational Design* (Arlington Heights, IL: AHM, 1978), Chapter 1.

101. Lisa Smyth, "Almost 50% of Northern Ireland's A&E admissions were NOT emergency cases last year", *BelfastLive*, May 11, 2015, accessed at www.belfastlive.co.uk/news/health/50-northern-irelands-ae-admissions-9228742

102. 'Healthy advice from the North', *Sunday Business Post*, 27 April 2008.

103. Patrick E. Connor, *Organizations: Theory and Design* (Chicago: Science Research Associates, 1980); Richard L. Daft and Norman B. Macintosh, 'A Tentative Exploration into Amount and Equivocality of Information Processing in Organizational Work Units', *Administrative Science Quarterly* 26 (1981), 207–224.

104. Paul D. Collins and Frank Hull, 'Technology and Span of Control: Woodward Revisited', *Journal of Management Studies* 23 (1986), 143–164; Gerald D. Bell, 'The Influence of Technological Components of Work upon Management Control', *Academy of Management Journal* 8 (1965), 127–132; and Peter M. Blau and Richard A. Schoenherr, *The Structure of Organizations* (New York: Basic Books, 1971).

105. W. Alan Randolph, 'Matching Technology and the Design of Organization Units', *California Management Review* 22– 23 (1980–81), 39–48; Daft and Macintosh, 'Tentative Exploration into Amount and Equivocality of Information Processing'; and Michael L. Tushman, 'Work Characteristics and Subunit Communication Structure: A Contingency Analysis', *Administrative Science Quarterly* 24 (1979), 82–98.

106. Andrew H. Van de Ven and Diane L. Ferry, *Measuring and Assessing Organizations* (New York: Wiley, 1980); and Randolph, 'Matching Technology and the Design of Organization Units'.

107. Richard L. Daft and Robert H. Lengel, 'Information Richness: A New Approach to Managerial Behavior and Organization Design', in Barry Staw and Larry L. Cummings, eds, *Research in Organizational Behaviour*, Vol. 6 (Greenwich, CT: JAI Press, 1984), 191–233; Richard L. Daft and Norman B. Macintosh, 'A New Approach into Design and Use of Management Information', *California Management Review* 21 (1978), 82–92; Daft and Macintosh, 'A Tentative Exploration into Amount and Equivocality of Information Processing'; W. Alan Randolph, 'Organizational Technology and the Media and Purpose Dimensions of Organizational Communication', *Journal of Business Research* 6 (1978), 237–259; Linda Argote, 'Input Uncertainty and Organizational Coordination in Hospital Emergency Units', *Administrative Science Quarterly* 27 (1982), 420–434; and Andrew H. Van de Ven and Andre Delbecq, 'A Task Contingent Model of Work Unit Structure', *Administrative Science Quarterly* 19 (1974), 183–197.

108. Peggy Leatt and Rodney Schneck, 'Criteria for Grouping Nursing Subunits in Hospitals', *Academy of Management Journal* 27 (1984), 150–165; and Robert T. Keller, 'Technology-Information Processing', *Academy of Management Journal* 37, No. 1 (1994), 167–179.

109. Gresov, 'Exploring Fit and Misfit with Multiple Contingencies'; Michael L. Tushman, 'Technological Communication in R&D Laboratories: The Impact of Project Work Characteristics,' *Academy of Management Journal*

21 (1978), 624–645; and Robert T. Keller, 'Technology-Information Processing Fit and the Performance of R&D Project Groups: A Test of Contingency Theory', *Academy of Management Journal* 37, No. 1 (1994), 167–179.

110. James Thompson, *Organizations in Action* (New York: McGraw-Hill, 1967).

111. Ibid., 40.

112. Gene Bylinsky, 'Shipmaking Gets Modern', *Fortune*, special section, 'Industrial Management and Technology' (January 20, 2003), 170[K]–170[L].

113. Paul S. Adler, 'Interdepartmental Interdependence and Coordination: The Case of the Design/Manufacturing Interface', *Organization Science* 6, No. 2 (March–April 1995), 147–167.

114. Angela Jameson, 'Airbus A380 delay wipes €5bn off the value of EADS', *The Times,* June 15, 2006.

115. Mel Duvall, PLM: Boeing's Dream, Airbus' Nightmare; Product life-cycle management is helping to get Boeing's 787 off the ground, but is a key factor in Airbus' A380 delays, *CIO Insight*, 5 February 2007.

116. Christopher Gresov, 'Effects of Dependence and Tasks on Unit Design and Efficiency', *Organization Studies* 11 (1990), 503–529; Andrew H. Van de Ven, Andre Delbecq and Richard Koenig, 'Determinants of Coordination Modes within Organizations', *American Sociological Review* 41 (1976), 322–338; Linda Argote, 'Input Uncertainty and Organizational Coordination in Hospital Emergency Units'; Jack K. Ito and Richard B. Peterson, 'Effects of Task Difficulty and Interdependence on Information Processing Systems', *Academy of Management Journal* 29 (1986), 139–149; and Joseph L. C. Cheng, 'Interdependence and Coordination in Organizations: A Role-System Analysis', *Academy of Management Journal* 26 (1983), 156–162.

117. J.D. Herbsleb and R.E. Grinter (1999), 'Splitting the Organization and Integrating the Code: Conway's Law Revisited', *In Proceedings of the 21st International Conference on Software Engineering (ICSE'99)*, New York ACM Press, 85–95; Carmel, E. (1999), *Global Software Teams: Collaborating Across Borders and Time Zones*, New York, Prentice Hall.

118. Ceferino S. Rodolfo (2005), *Sustaining Philippine Advantage in Business Process Outsourcing*, Manila, Philippine Institute for Development Studies, Discussion Paper Series No. 2005-28.

119. E. Ó Conchúir, H. Holmström, P.J. Ågerfalk and B. Fitzgerald (2006) *Global Software Development: Never Mind the Problems – Are There Really Any Benefits?*, In Proceedings of the 29th Information Systems Research Seminar in Scandinavia, Helsingør, Denmark, 12–15 Aug 2006.

120. Rich Metters (2008), 'A typology of offshoring and outsourcing in electronically transmitted services', *Journal of Operations Management*, 26, 198–211.

121. Jason Cole, The Big Picture, *CIO*, 5 September 2006.

122. Anne Stringfellow, Mary B. Teagarden, Winter Nie (2008), 'Invisible costs in offshoring services work', *Journal of Operations Management*, 26, 164–179.

123. Michele Liu, Héléné Denis, Harvey Kolodny and Benjt Stymne, 'Organization Design for Technological Change', *Human Relations* 43 (January 1990), 7–22.

124. Philip Pangalos, 'One in Five Bank Jobs Will be Lost, Says Lloyds Boss – Sir Brian Pitman', *The Times*, 3 April 1995; 'Skills Review: UK Wholesale Financial Services Summary', Financial Services Skills Council, May 2007, accessed at http://www.fssc.org.uk/cgi-bin/docs.pl/1045/Skills_Review_UK_financial_services_full_report.pdf on August 28, 2008.

125. Antonia Sinden, 'The decline, flexibility and geographical restructuring of employment in British retail banks', *The Geographical Journal*, 1 March 1996, Pg 25.

126. Gerald I. Susman and Richard B. Chase, 'A Sociotechnical Analysis of the Integrated Factory', *Journal of Applied Behavioral Science* 22 (1986), 257–270; and Paul Adler, 'New Technologies, New Skills', *California Management Review* 29 (Fall 1986), 9–28.

127. Based on Don Hellriegel, John W. Slocum, Jr and Richard W. Woodman, *Organizational Behavior*, 8th ed. (Cincinnati, OH: South-Western, 1998), 491–495; and Gregory B. Northcraft and Margaret A. Neale, *Organizational Behavior: A Management Challenge*, 2nd ed. (Fort Worth, TX: The Dryden Press, 1994), 550–553.

128. F. Emery, 'Characteristics of Sociotechnical Systems', Tavistock Institute of Human Relations, document 527, 1959; William Pasmore, Carol Francis and Jeffrey Haldeman, 'Sociotechnical Systems: A North American Reflection on Empirical Studies of the 70s', *Human Relations* 35 (1982), 1179–1204; and William M. Fox, 'Sociotechnical System Principles and Guidelines: Past and Present', *Journal of Applied Behavioral Science* 31, No. 1 (March 1995), 91–105.

129. W. S. Cascio, *Managing Human Resources* (New York: McGraw-Hill, 1986), Pg 19.

130. David M. Upton, 'What Really Makes Factories Flexible?' *Harvard Business Review* (July–August 1995), 74–84.

INFORMATION TECHNOLOGY AND CONTROL

A LOOK INSIDE

The Progressive Group of Insurance Companies

The Progressive Group is the fourth largest automobile insurance group in the United States, and it just keeps growing. Not bad for a group of companies that got its start as a niche insurer for high-risk drivers and that, as recently as 1990, was only the fifteenth largest in the United States. How did a relatively small, specialized firm compete with giant insurance companies such as State Farm and Allstate in the larger market for standard and preferred auto insurance? In part, by using information technology to gain a strategic advantage.

Progressive was founded in 1937 and proved itself an innovator from the beginning, when it established the industry's first drive-in claims service. It has been innovating ever since, using technology to provide a more accurate premium rate, a better customer experience and vehicle insurance shopping information not available anywhere else.

Car insurance rates are set, in part, using information about the insurance company's past claims history. A company's ability to understand its claims experience and to use that information to ever more finely segment its customers and its pricing can help to determine its level of success. Progressive has been using technology to better understand its customers at the most granular level for a very long time, and they continue to do so – they won a prestigious award for IT innovation in 2007.[1] From the early 1990s, they began to use that understanding to more accurately price the so-called 'standard and preferred' markets segment. If Progressive was successful in accurately pricing the high-risk, or 'non-standard' segment of the market, they reasoned, why couldn't they apply that talent to the rest of the market?

Progressive introduced other technologies during the 1990s that helped the company grow from $1.2 billion in net premiums in 1990 to nearly $14 billion in 2007. First was the introduction of Immediate Response claims service, which provided the industry's first 24 hours a day, 7 days a week, in-person response to an auto crash. Using mobile technology, claims representatives would arrive wherever customers wished, write an estimate and be able to write them a cheque on the spot. Progressive has since further refined its approach. In a growing number of cities, it offers a 'concierge level' of claims service, which means that the customer need only drop off the car at a specially designated facility and pick up a rental car. The claims representative handles all aspects of the estimate, oversees the repair and inspects the repair before the customer picks up the car. The customer drives away knowing that the work is guaranteed by the shop that repaired the vehicle and by Progressive.

In the early 1990s, Progressive introduced another first – auto insurance comparison rates. Using publicly filed rates and technology, Progressive became the first, and remains the only, American auto insurance company providing consumers with comparison rates. Comparison rates were first offered by phone, but, when Progressive launched the world's first auto insurance website in 1995, the rates were available using that technology. Today, visitors to the website can buy a policy in as little as seven minutes. Customers can also use the website to manage their policies, make payments, make changes and print out additional insurance documentation.

Progressive continues to use technology to innovate, for example by making 'e-signatures' available to some of its customers. Electronic signatures eliminate most of the follow-up paperwork, allowing customers to sign applications online, authorize electronic funds transfer for payment, or sign forms to decline unwanted coverages. Progressive was one of the first advertisers to produce a 'Shazam-enabled' TV advertisement in 2011, allowing viewers to be automatically directed to Progressive's website on their mobile devices.[2]

Insurance isn't the only industry that has been transformed by information technology (IT) and the internet. Companies such as global consulting firm KPMG, TD Waterhouse, a Canadian-headquartered brokerage firm, and Factiva, part of Dow Jones and Company, which provides news, business and corporate information, have long needed to use IT effectively as a fundamental component of their businesses. But today, IT has become a crucial factor for companies in all industries, to survive and flourish in a global competitive market. Companies, both small and large, are increasingly relying on sophisticated internet-based systems to manage every link of their supply chains, from suppliers all the way through to their customers' customers.

Part of Britain's Halma group that specializes in industrial safety components, North Shields-based Elfab manufactures bursting discs – devices that provide a fail-safe pressure release – for applications such as oil and gas pipelines. It's a highly specialized business and it's crucial that customers can deal directly with knowledgeable sales staff. The problem: Elfab's customers are located all over the world. Many companies would appoint distributors in key regions, but Elfab chose to go in the other direction – setting up a worldwide freephone system so that potential customers can talk directly with someone at Elfab's offices in northern England. Sales staff speak ten different languages, so the vast majority of calls can be handled, and if there are any complex questions, the whole Elfab team is right there. It was a costly and technologically intensive solution, but ultimately it was the best answer for a specialized manufacturer like Elfab. Britain's professional association of mechanical engineers obviously agreed; they awarded Elfab their 2007 award for best customer service in a manufacturing firm, and in 2015 the company received the Queen's Award for International Trade.[3,4,5]

Quanjude, China's most famous roast duck restaurant, has been making the famous dish since 1864, during the Qing dynasty. Traditionally, the duck is cooked in a traditional wood-fired oven. But with nine company restaurants and 61 franchised outlets across the country, Quanjude faced problems of quality control. So it decided to make a giant leap forward into the computer era. In conjunction with a German company, Quanjude designed and installed computer-controlled electric ovens for many of its outlets: 'Computerized ovens, while guaranteeing quality, simplify, standardize and automate the roasting process', said the chain's general manager, Xing Ying.[6] While this solved the potential problem of uneven cooking, it disturbed some Chinese traditionalists. Seventy-seven per cent of Beijing residents surveyed by a local newspaper opposed the move, with one saying, 'We commoners not only eat Quanjude duck for its flavour, but also for the hundreds of years of tradition and culture that our ancestors left to us'.[7] Traditionalists may have more to worry about than computerized ovens, however; Beijing's diners are drooling over a competitor's successful introduction of duck burgers![8]

The rapidly growing use of IT and the internet presents not only new opportunities, but also new challenges for managers. With unlimited access to information on the internet, customers are much better informed and much more demanding, making customer loyalty harder to build.[9] In addition, the concept of electronically linking suppliers, partners and customers is forcing executives to rethink their strategies, organization design and business processes. Furthermore, IT and networking capabilities are becoming integrated into devices previously seen as simple workhorses, such as fridges and washing machines. The pace of business is moving at 'warp speed'.[10] Planning horizons have become shorter, expectations of customers change rapidly, and functionalities and new competitors spring up almost overnight. All this means managers, as well as employees throughout the organization, need quality information at their fingertips.

?

ONLINE
COUNTERPOINT 9.1

Highly successful organizations today are typically those that most effectively collect, store, distribute and use information. More than facilities, equipment or even products, it is the information a company has and how it uses it that influences its success – some would say even determines organizational survival.[11] Top managers look for ways to manage, leverage and protect what is rapidly becoming a highly valuable asset of any organization: information and knowledge.

Purpose of this Chapter

Information Technology (IT) is an essential component of successful organizations. Managers spend at least 80 per cent of their time actively exchanging information. They use this information to coordinate and galvanize action. For example, the vertical and horizontal information linkages described in Chapter 4 are designed to provide managers with relevant information for decision-making, evaluation and control. This chapter examines the evolution of IT. The chapter begins by looking at IT systems applied to organizational operations and then examines how IT is used for decision-making and control of the organization. The next sections consider how IT can add value through the use of internal coordination applications such as intranets, enterprise resource planning and knowledge management systems, as well as applications for external collaboration, such as extranets, customer-relationship management systems, e-business and the integrated enterprise. The final sections of the chapter look at possible future trends in IT innovation, and present an overview of how IT affects organization design and interorganizational relationships.

Information Technology Evolution

ONLINE
COUNTERPOINT 9.2

The evolution of IT is illustrated in Exhibit 9.1. First-line management is typically mainly concerned with well-defined problems about operational issues and past events (see Counterpoint 9.1). Top management, by contrast, deals mostly with uncertain, ambiguous issues, such as strategy and planning. As the complexity of computer-based IT systems has increased, applications have grown to support effective top management control and decision-making about complex and uncertain problems.

> ### COUNTERPOINT 9.1
>
> Many first line managers would not necessarily recognize this description – 'well-defined problems' – in much of what they face.

Initially, IT systems in organizations were applied to operations. These early applications were based on the notion of machine-room efficiency – that is, current operations could be performed more efficiently with the use of computer technology. The goal was to reduce costs by having computers take over some tasks. These systems became known as transaction processing systems (TPS), which automate the organization's routine, day-to-day business transactions. A TPS collects data from transactions such as sales, purchases from suppliers and inventory changes and stores them in a database. For example, the Greek firm Intralot specializes in setting up computerized gambling and lottery systems around the world, from Australia to Vietnam. Its system not only keeps track of the gambling on countless different events across the world, it is also sophisticated enough to pick up betting patterns which could suggest illegal manipulation of sporting events.[12,13]

In recent years, the use of data warehousing and business intelligence software has expanded the usefulness of accumulated data. Data warehousing is the use of huge databases that combine all of a company's data and allow users to access the data directly, create reports and even obtain responses to what-if questions. Building a database at a large corporation is a huge undertaking that includes defining hundreds of gigabytes of data from many existing systems, providing a means of continually updating the data, making it all compatible and linking it to other software that makes it possible for users to search and analyze the data and produce helpful reports. Software for business intelligence helps users make sense of all these data. Business intelligence refers to the high-tech analysis of a company's data in order to make better strategic decisions.[14] Sometimes referred to as data mining, business intelligence means searching out and analyzing data from multiple sources across the enterprise, and sometimes from outside sources as well, to identify patterns and relationships that might be significant.

Organizations spent over $17.9 billion on business intelligence software in 2015, a 39 per cent increase from 2012. The market is forecast to exceed $26 billion by 2020.[15,16,17] Consider how one Canadian pharmaceutical manufacturer makes profitable use of data warehousing and business intelligence discussed in the upcoming *In Practice* box.

EXHIBIT 9.1 Evolution of Organizational Applications of IT

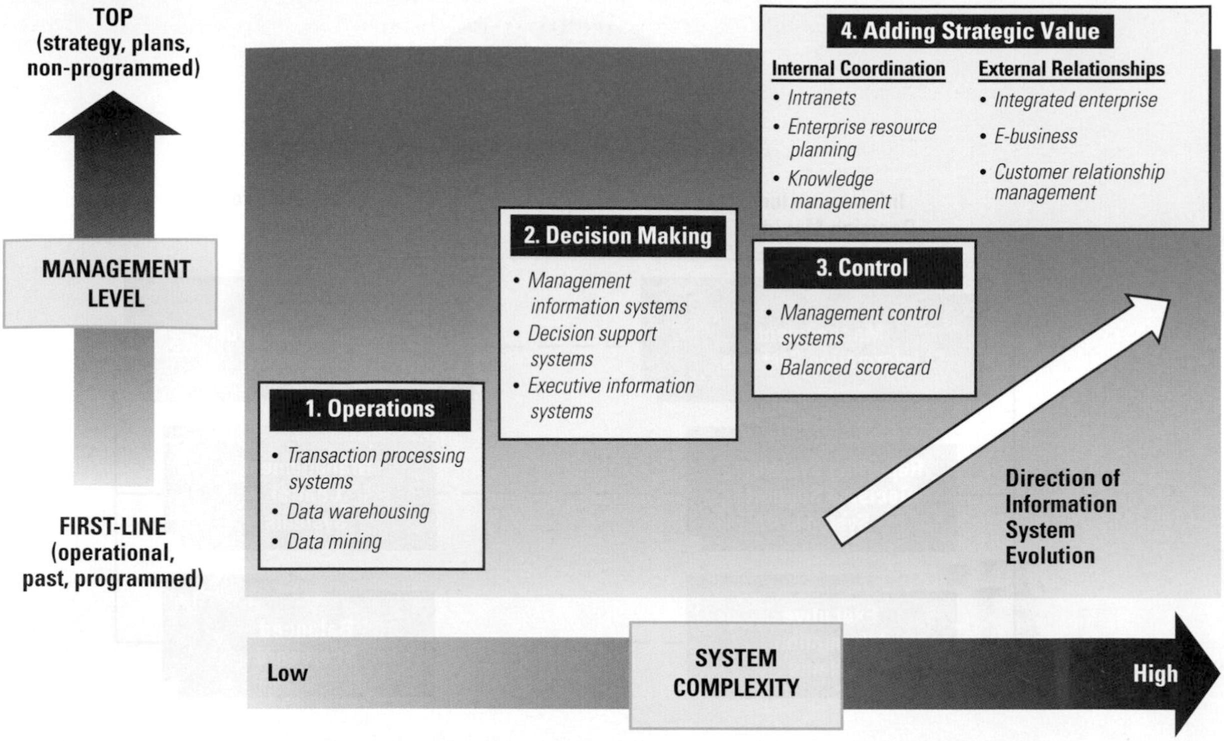

By collecting the right data and using business intelligence to analyze it, and thereby spot trends and patterns, managers such as those at Apotex are able to make better informed decisions and increase market share compared to competitors. IT has evolved to more complex systems for managerial decision-making and control of the organization, the second stage illustrated in Exhibit 8.1. Further advancements have led to the use of IT to add strategic value, the highest level of application. The remainder of this chapter will focus on these two stages in the evolution of IT.

Information for Decision-Making and Control

Through the application of more sophisticated computer-based systems, managers have tools to improve the performance of departments and the organization as a whole (see Counterpoint 9.2). These applications use information stored in corporate databases to help managers control activities and make decisions. Exhibit 9.2 illustrates one example of the various elements of information systems used for decision-making and control. In an organization, these systems are interconnected, as illustrated by the dashed lines in Exhibit 9.2. The systems for decision-making and control often share the same basic data, but the data and reports are designed and used for a primary purpose of decision-making versus control.

COUNTERPOINT 9.2

Of course, it is not the systems themselves that produce the results but, rather, the capacity of managers to obtain information that is relevant, and then to interpret it in ways that inform effective decision-making.

EXHIBIT 9.2 Information Systems for Managerial Control and Decision-Making

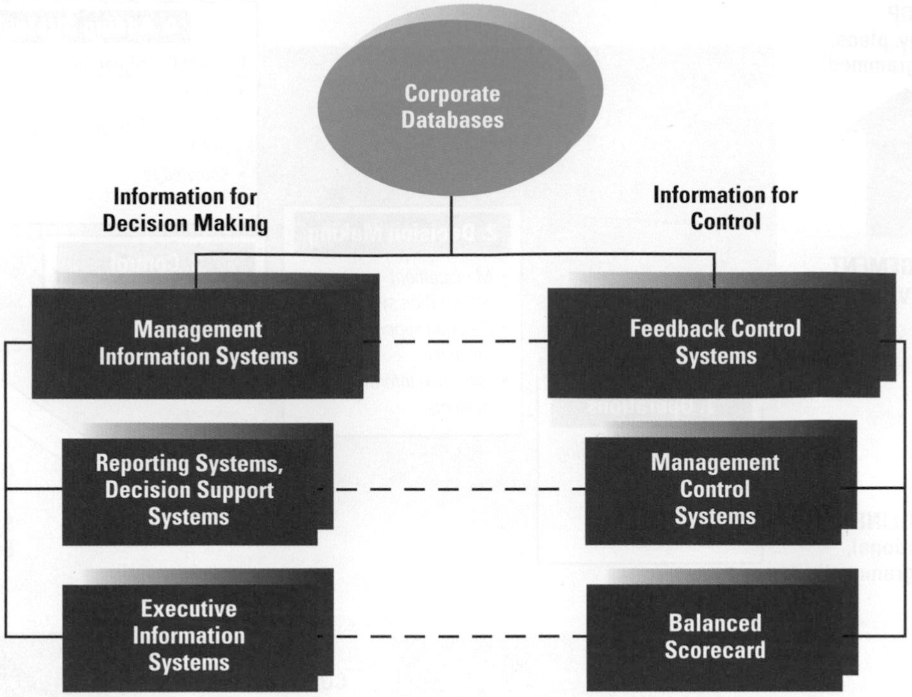

Corporate
Databases

Information for
Decision Making

Information for
Control

Management
Information Systems

Feedback Control
Systems

Reporting Systems,
Decision Support
Systems

Management
Control
Systems

Executive
Information
Systems

Balanced
Scorecard

Organizational Decision-Making Systems

BRIEFCASE 9.1

A management information system (MIS) is a computer-based system that provides informa-tion and support for managerial decision-making. The MIS is supported by the organization's transaction processing systems and by organizational and external databases. The informa-tion reporting system, the most common form of MIS, provides managers with reports that summarize data and support day-to-day decision-making. For example, when managers make decisions about production scheduling, they can review data on the anticipated number of orders within the next month, inventory levels and the availability of human resources. In the service industry, the data can be used to match pricing with demand. For example, the UK-based discount car rental agency, Holiday Autos, relies on an MIS system to balance rental prices against car availability.[18]

An executive information system (EIS) is a higher-level application that facilitates decision-making at the more senior levels of management. These systems are typically based on software that can convert large amounts of complex data into pertinent information and provide that information in a timely fashion. Often, MIS and EIS systems are combined through use of the same dataset to provide different reporting levels. SNCF, the French national railway, uses a custom-built system to provide human resource information on the company's 160 000 employees to line managers for day-to-day management and reporting purposes, as well as aggregate data on staff profiles to senior managers who can use the information to assess overall recruitment and training needs.[19]

A decision support system (DSS) provides specific benefits to managers at all levels of the organization. These interactive, computer-based systems rely on decision models and integrated databases. Using decision support software, users can pose a series of what-if questions to test possible alternatives. Based on assumptions used in the software or specified by the user, managers can explore alternatives and receive information to help them choose the option that promises to deliver the best outcome.

IN PRACTICE

Apotex, Inc.

Apotex is Canada's largest pharmaceutical company, and one of the largest generic pharmaceutical manufacturers in the world – generics are pharmaceutical products that are no longer under patent protection. Apotex exports to at least 115 countries. It is a complex and fast-changing business, with numerous twists. There are differences – sometimes subtle and sometimes large – between each country's drug patent protections, and the constant jockeying between brand-name producers (who seek to extend patent protections as long as possible) and generics (who want to be able to produce popular drugs as quickly as possible) results in frequent changes in the law and legal challenges. For example, in 2013, Apotex was party to a major case in front of the US Supreme Court arguing against patent protection actions of the major brand-name pharmaceuticals. Keeping track of subtle differences in the current legal situation, as well as overall market conditions in 115 countries, is a data management challenge. Being on top of the challenge is essential, because being first to the market with a generic product is the key to market share and financial success.

Like many companies, Apotex had various data collection systems operating in different departments. In addition, the company accesses various third-party data sources that provide additional information about market conditions and prescribing patterns in different countries. As all this information was not integrated, it couldn't easily be used for business decisions, such as deciding to produce a generic for a particular market where a brand-name drug was about to go off-patent.

To address this problem, Apotex decided to integrate its data warehousing and business intelligence using a SAP product, Business Objects XI. In addition, the company signed up for SAP's customer relationship management (CRM) package, which integrates information from pharmacists into usable information about market performance that is available to decision-makers company-wide. Michael Davidson, chief information officer of Apotex, says, 'We were able to consolidate five separate databases and manual processes onto one common platform. This enables us to effectively track marketing programmes and customer activity. The effort reduced our administrative costs and improved our visibility into customer profitability.'[20]

At Tesco, Britain's largest supermarket chain, understanding the purchasing habits of customers is key to success. One of the main tools used by Tesco to understand its customers and to retain their business is the Clubcard, a computerized card that enables customers to accumulate points that can be redeemed against future Tesco purchases or for other goods (e.g. discounted hotel deals). The card encourages customer loyalty as shoppers may choose to shop at Tesco in order to collect points, but a hidden and probably more valuable purpose of the card is to provide the company with a comprehensive profile of the customer and their shopping patterns. As Giles Pavey, an executive of the marketing firm that runs the Clubcard scheme puts it, 'It's just like standing behind someone in a checkout queue and making assumptions about their lifestyle based on what's in the trolley'.[21]

Clubcard information is subjected to sophisticated 'segmentation analysis' which identifies types of shoppers and their likely motivations when shopping. This information can be used for many purposes, including targeting advertising, setting product prices and changing the range of goods stocked by specific stores. One example of an application might be to respond to inroads being made by discount retailers like Lidl and Aldi to the 'price sensitive' segment of Tesco shoppers. Of course, Tesco could simply reduce its prices across the board in order to retain these customers, but this would be very costly, and the price cuts would be wasted on many customers who have no intention of switching to a discount retailer. However, by carefully examining the shopping patterns of the 'price sensitive' group, and applying DSS

?

ONLINE
COUNTERPOINT 9.3

modelling on likely impact of different customer retention strategies, targeted price cuts can be introduced on lines that are particularly favoured by this group. Alternatively, discount coupons could be delivered on these products, just to the 'price conscious' consumer segment.

Feedback Control Model

BRIEFCASE 9.2

Another primary use of information in organizations is for control. Effective control systems involve the use of feedback to determine whether organizational performance meets established standards. Managers set up systems for organizational control that consist of the four key steps in the feedback control model illustrated in Exhibit 9.3.

The cycle of control includes setting strategic goals for departments or the organization as a whole, establishing metrics and standards of performance, comparing metrics of actual performance to standards and correcting or changing activities as so on. Feedback control helps managers make adjustments in work activities, standards or goals to improve performance. For example, the South-African based company DigiCore provides client companies with various IT tools enabling them to manage their vehicle fleets more effectively – a high-cost operation area where lax control and poor planning can cause substantial losses. DigiCore pioneered the integration of GSM (mobile phone technology) with GPS positioning, enabling companies to track the progress of their fleets minute-by-minute. As one of the first companies in the field, DigiCore was at the forefront when fleet tracking systems became the norm. After surviving the rocky period between product development and mass sales, DigiCore has gone from strength to strength, especially in Europe where it has signed fleet management deals with large companies such as Britain's Thames Water, although it is a small player compared with global leaders Cobra, Tracker and SmarTrack. Vehicle tracking is just one type of vehicle telematics; the use of computer and positioning technology within vehicles. Many insurance firms are trialling use of in-car equipment that monitors driving patterns and thus calculates driver risk. Companies like DigiCore are in at the beginning of a technology segment that may grow substantially in the next years.[22]

EXHIBIT 9.3   A Simplified Feedback Control Model

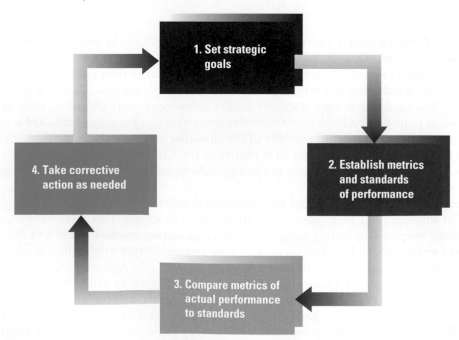

Management Control Systems

Management control systems are broadly defined as the formal routines, reports and procedures that use information to maintain or alter patterns in organization activities.[23] These control systems include the formalized information-based activities for planning, budgeting, performance evaluation, resource allocation and employee rewards. Targets are set in advance, outcomes compared to targets and variance reported to managers for corrective action (see Counterpoint 9.3). Many organizations use *executive dashboards* which enable managers to see at a glance key control indicators such as sales in relation to targets, number of products on back-order or percentage of customer service calls resolved within a specified time period.[24] Dashboard systems coordinate, organize and display the metrics that managers consider most important to monitor on a regular basis, with software automatically updating the figures. Kuwait's Vodaphone-MTC mobile phone network purchased a tailor-made Harris Corporation system monitoring software to deliver an 'executive dashboard' that provides the company's managers with graphical display of network status, usage and Key Performance Indicators (KPIs), all accessible through the web, and enabling immediate response to problems.[25,26]

ONLINE
COUNTERPOINT 9.4

COUNTERPOINT 9.3

Of course, the usefulness of these systems depends upon the reliability of the data that is input to them. Employees may have their reasons for delaying inputs or in other ways inputing data that is unreliable or even erroneous. Even when the data is complete and uncorrupted, its usefulness always depends upon its ease of accessibility, how it is interpreted and how it is then acted upon.

Exhibit 9.4 lists four control system elements that are often considered the core of management control systems: the budget and financial reports; periodic non-financial statistical reports; reward systems; and quality-control systems.[27]

The *budget* is typically used to set targets for the organization's expenditures for the year and then report actual costs on a monthly or quarterly basis. As a means of control, budgets report actual as well as planned expenditures for cash, assets, raw materials, salaries and other resources so that managers can take action to correct variances. Sometimes, the variance between budgeted and actual amounts for each line item is listed as a part of the budget. Managers also rely on a variety of other financial reports. The *balance sheet* shows a firm's financial position with respect to assets and liabilities at a specific point in time. An *income statement*, sometimes called a *profit and loss statement (P&L)*, summarizes the company's financial performance for a given time interval, such as for the week, month or year. This statement shows revenues coming into the organization from all sources and subtracts all expenses, such as cost of goods sold, interest, taxes

EXHIBIT 9.4   Management Control Systems

Subsystem	Content and Frequency
Budget, financial reports	Financial, resource expenditures, profit and loss; monthly
Statistical reports	Non-financial outputs; weekly or monthly, often computer-based
Reward systems	Evaluation of managers based on department goals and performance, set rewards; yearly
Quality control systems	Participation, benchmarking guidelines, Six Sigma goals; continuous

Source: Based on Richard L. Daft and Norman B. Macintosh, 'The Nature and Use of Formal Control Systems for Management Control and Strategy Implementation', *Journal of Management* 10 (1984), 43–66.

and depreciation. The *bottom line* indicates the net income – profit or loss – for the given time period.

Managers use periodic statistical reports to evaluate and monitor non-financial performance, such as customer satisfaction, employee performance or rate of staff turnover. For e-commerce organizations, important measurements of non-financial performance include metrics such as *stickiness* (how much attention a site gets over time), the *conversion rate*, the ratio of buyers to site visitors, and *site performance data*, such as how long it takes to load a page or how long it takes to place an order.[28] E-commerce managers regularly review reports on conversion rates, customer dropoff and other metrics to identify problems and improve their business. For all organizations, non-financial reports typically are computer-based and may be available daily, weekly or monthly. The international online auction company eBay provides a good illustration of using both financial and non-financial statistical reports for feedback control (see the *In Practice* box below).

In addition to performance measurement, eBay also uses the other control system elements listed in Exhibit 9.4 – reward systems and quality control systems. Reward systems offer incentives for managers and employees to improve performance and meet departmental goals. Managers and employees evaluate how well previous goals were met, set new goals and establish rewards for meeting the new targets. Rewards are often tied to the annual performance appraisal process, during which managers assess employee performance and provide feedback to help the employee improve performance and obtain rewards (see Counterpoint 9.4).

IN PRACTICE

eBay

Meg Whitman, CEO of eBay from 1998 until she stepped down to pursue political ambitions in 2008, had a guiding mantra: 'If you can't measure it, you can't control it'. Whitman built a company that is obsessed with performance measurement from shaky start-up to multi-billion dollar internet giant. She personally monitored performance metrics such as number of site visitors, percentage of new users and time spent on the site, as well as profit and loss statements and the ratio of eBay's revenues to the value of goods traded. Managers throughout the company also monitor performance regularly. Category managers, for example, have clear standards of performance for their auction categories (such as sports memorabilia, jewellery and watches, health and beauty, etc.). They continuously measure, tweak and promote their categories to meet or outperform their targets.

Getting a firm grip on performance measurement is essential for a company to know where to spend money, where to assign more personnel and which projects to promote or abandon. The more statistics that are available, the more early warnings managers have about problems and opportunities. But performance isn't just about numbers at eBay. Measuring customer (user) satisfaction requires a mix of methods, such as surveys, monitoring eBay discussion boards and personal contact with customers at regular live conferences.

By defining standards and effectively using financial and statistical reports, eBay managers can identify opportunities and trouble spots and move quickly to either take corrective action or take advantage of new opportunities in 'real time'. The company rebounded after encountering a sticky patch around the time of Whitman's departure. Its revenues and profits rose sharply between 2011 and 2014, driven particularly by the company's leading-edge mobile apps, as well as its payments portal PayPal, which is moving far beyond its original role of simply processing eBay purchases. PayPal is increasingly available for both online and retail purchases outside the eBay platform, and in 2015 the company spun off PayPal into a separate company. John Donahue, Whitman's replacement who continues to lead Paypal and sit on the board of eBay, says, 'We stepped on the gas with innovation. We're more technology- and innovation-driven than we've ever been. Mobile gave us the opportunity to start with a clean slate from a technology perspective.'[29,30]

COUNTERPOINT 9.4

Reward systems can also incentivize people in ways that can be unintentionally counterproductive and detrimental. One need only think of the incentivized traders in asset-backed securities whose 'exuberance' contributed directly to the financial crisis of 2008.

The final control element listed in Exhibit 9.4 is quality-control systems which managers use to train employees in quality-control methods, set targets for employee participation, establish benchmarking guidelines and assign and measure *Six Sigma* goals. For example, at eBay, Whitman used benchmarking to measure how the company's website performs compared to its peers. She found eBay's site weak in the area of adding new features, so managers have taken action to improve the site's performance in that area. Benchmarking means the process of continually measuring products, services and practices against tough competitors or other organizations recognized as industry leaders.[31] Six Sigma, originally conceived by Motorola Corporation, is a highly ambitious quality standard that specifies a goal of no more than 3.4 defects per million parts.[32] From this precise definition, Six Sigma has become a generic term for a whole set of control procedures that emphasize a relentless pursuit of higher quality and lower costs. The discipline is based on a methodology referred to as DMAIC (Define, Measure, Analyze, Improve and Control, pronounced de-MAY-ick, for short), which provides a structured way for organizations to approach and solve problems.[33]

Each of the four control systems focuses on a different aspect of the production process. The budget is used primarily to allocate resource inputs. Managers use the budget for planning the future and reducing uncertainty about the availability of human and material resources needed to perform department tasks. Computer-based statistical reports are used to control outputs. These reports contain data about output volume and quality and other indicators that provide feedback to middle management about departmental results. The reward system and quality control systems are directed at the production process. Quality control systems specify standards for employee participation, teamwork and problem solving. Reward systems provide incentives to meet goals and can help guide employee behaviour. Managers also use direct supervision to keep departmental work activities within desired limits.

BRIEFCASE 9.3

The Balanced Scorecard

In the past, most organizations tended to rely heavily upon financial accounting measures as the primary basis for measuring organizational performance and control, whereas increasingly a more balanced view, incorporating operational as well as financial measures is favoured.

The four control elements listed in Exhibit 9.4 help provide managers with a balanced view. A recent innovation additionally integrates internal financial measurements and statistical reports with a concern for markets and customers as well as employees. The balanced scorecard has been developed as a comprehensive management control system that balances traditional financial measures with operational measures relating to what are identified as critical success factors.[34] A balanced scorecard contains four major focal areas, as illustrated in Exhibit 9.5: financial performance, customer service, internal business processes and the organization's capacity for learning and growth.[35] Within these four areas, managers identify key performance indicators to be tracked. The *financial perspective* reflects a concern that the organization's activities contribute to improving short- and long-term financial performance. It includes traditional measures such as net income and return on investment. *Customer service indicators* measure such things as how customers view the organization, as well as customer retention and satisfaction. *Business process indicators* focus on production and operating statistics, such as order fulfilment or cost per order. The final component considers the organization's *potential for learning and growth*, focusing on how well resources and human capital are being managed for the company's future. Measurements include such things as employee retention, business process improvements and the introduction of new products. The components of the scorecard are designed in an integrative manner so that they complement and reinforce one another as short-term actions are linked with long-term strategic goals, as illustrated in Exhibit 9.5. Managers can use the scorecard to set goals, allocate resources, plan budgets and determine rewards.[36]

The balanced scorecard helps managers focus on the key strategic measures that define the success of a particular organization over time and communicate them clearly throughout the organization. The scorecard has become the core management control system for many corporations, including British Airways, which ties its use of the balanced scorecard to the feedback control model shown earlier in Exhibit 9.3. Scorecards serve as the agenda for monthly management meetings, where managers evaluate performance, discuss what corrective actions need to be taken and set new targets for the various elements.[37] Executive information systems facilitate use of the balanced scorecard by enabling top managers to easily track measurements in multiple areas,

EXHIBIT 9.5   Major Perspectives of the Balanced Scorecard

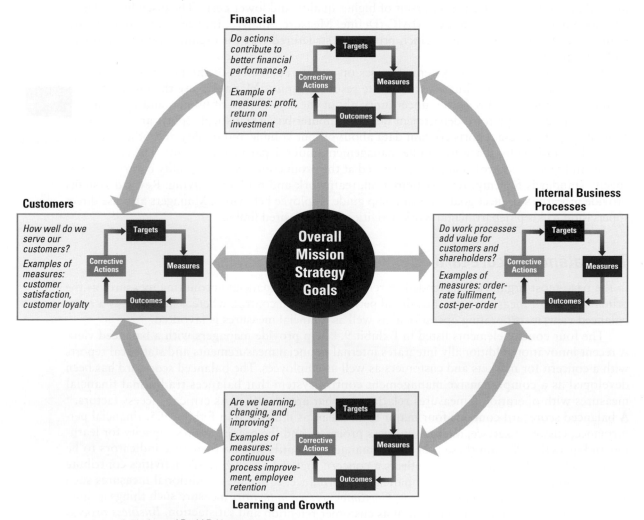

Source: Based on Robert S. Kaplan and David P. Norton, 'Using the Balanced Scorecard as a Strategic Management System', *Harvard Business Review* (January–February 1996), 75–85; Chee W. Chow, Kamal M. Haddad and James E. Williamson, 'Applying the Balanced Scorecard to Small Companies', *Management Accounting* 79, No. 2 (August 1997), 21–27; and Cathy Lazere, 'All Together Now', *CFO* (February 1998), 28–36.

rapidly analyze the data and convert huge amounts of data into clear information reports. The scorecard is not necessarily the best for all situations, and small organizations seem to have been less effective in implementing a balanced-scorecard approach. One study, for example, found that, although many small manufacturing firms measure a wide variety of non-financial factors, most did not integrate the data with other performance measures, a key feature of the balanced scorecard (see Counterpoint 9.5).[38]

ONLINE
COUNTERPOINT 9.5

COUNTERPOINT 9.5

The balanced scorecard, like any other technique or control system, is not a panacea. British Airways' use of the balanced scorecard did not prevent the disastrous opening of Terminal 5 at London Heathrow in 2008.

Terminal 5 is one of the most technologically advanced airport terminals in the world, but MPs described its opening as a 'national humiliation'. During the first five days, BA misplaced more than 23 000 bags, cancelled 500 flights and made losses of £16m.

CEO Willie Walsh revealed that IT problems and a lack of testing played a large part in the trouble. But he said the airline could have coped if IT had been the only issue. He reeled off a list of failures. Staff had not been trained properly, they were unable to park when their car parks became too full on the day of opening, staff security searches were delayed, and construction work on parts of the building was not finished when the airport opened. Unfortunately, even after the opening fiasco, Terminal 5 baggage has been beset with problems; in 2014 the IT system underpinning the baggage system failed for several days, leaving thousands of travellers without their bags for days or even weeks.[39,40]

Adding Strategic Value: Strengthening Internal Coordination

ONLINE
COUNTERPOINT 9.6

Three primary IT tools for internal coordination are intranets, enterprise resource planning (ERP) and knowledge-management systems.

Intranets

Networking, which links people and departments within a particular building or across corporate offices, enabling them to share information and cooperate on projects, has become an important strategic tool for many companies. For example, in 2008, the Irish Republic's Health Service Executive (HSE), responsible for coordinating the country's universal health-care system, consolidated its internal networks into a single intranet – Ireland's largest – that provides access to staff news, policy briefings and reports, email and contact directories for all staff and medical libraries. Existing electronic tools, such as the country's Health Atlas, which provides graphical illustrations of health challenges in different parts of Ireland, were also moved onto the intranet while also having an outward-facing web portal.[41,42]

BRIEFCASE 9.4

Networks may take many forms, but as in the case of the HSE the most common form of corporate networking is the intranet, a private, company-wide information system that uses the communications protocols and standards of the internet and the World Wide Web but is accessible only to people within the company. To view files and information, users simply navigate the site with a standard web browser, clicking on links.[43] As intranets are web-based, they can be accessed from any type of computer or workstation.

Today, most companies with intranets have moved their management information systems, executive information systems and so forth over to the intranet so they are accessible to anyone in the firm who needs them. This also enables firms to reduce the administrative costs of maintaining records, such as for absences; staff simply enter these data themselves. Cardiff University, in the UK, moved to such a self-service HR information system in 2013. In addition, having these systems as part of the intranet means new features and applications can easily be added and accessed through a standard browser.

Intranets can improve internal communications and unlock hidden information. They enable employees to keep in touch with what's going on around the organization, quickly and easily find information they need, share ideas and work on projects collaboratively. The most advanced intranets are linked into the proprietary systems that govern a company's business functions (see Counterpoint 9.6). Portable devices like smartphones and tablets (see Chapter 8) allow on-the-move employees to stay in touch anywhere in the world, downloading information and filing reports from hotel rooms and airport departure lounges, with data instantly available across the company.[44,45]

COUNTERPOINT 9.6

The usefulness of intranets depends upon the preparedness of employees to share and regularly update (rather than hoard) information, and also their willingness to use an impersonal channel rather than informal networks and word of mouth which are often richer and more nuanced in what they can provide. If information requires little interpretation or finesse, then an intranet can be useful so long as information is easy to find. Otherwise, intranets may be used infrequently and fall into disuse.

Enterprise Resource Planning

ONLINE COUNTERPOINT 9.7

Another recent approach to information management helps pull together various types of information to see how decisions and actions in one part of the organization affect other parts of the firm. A growing number of companies are setting up broad-scale information systems that take a comprehensive view of the organization's activities. These enterprise resource planning (ERP) systems collect, process and provide information about a company's entire enterprise, including order processing, product design, purchasing, inventory, manufacturing, distribution, human resources (HR), receipt of payments and forecasting of future demand.[46] An ERP system can serve as the backbone for an entire organization by integrating and optimizing all the various business processes across the entire firm.[47]

Such a system links all of these areas of activity into a network, as illustrated in Exhibit 9.6. When a salesperson takes an order, the ERP system checks to see how the order affects inventory levels, scheduling, HR, purchasing and distribution. The system replicates organizational processes in software, guides employees through the processes step-by-step, and automates as many of them as possible. For example, ERP software can automatically produce an accounts payable cheque as soon as a clerk confirms that goods have been received in inventory, send an online purchase order immediately after a manager has authorized a purchase, or schedule production at the most appropriate plant after an order is received.[48]

The world's biggest and best-known travel guidebook company, Australia-based Lonely Planet (LP), has grown from producing a stapled guide to budget travel across Asia in 1973, to selling six million guidebooks with 500 different titles a year, publishing in 14 different languages. For a long time the company just grew organically, adding new titles and publishing profits as it went along. But the sheer size of the business and its varied activities meant that important information inevitably fell off the table, and that led to costly errors. By 2003, in the wake of declining sales, Lonely Planet had to lay off staff for the first time. David Sadler, finance and operations director for Lonely Planet's Europe, Middle East and Africa (EMEA) region, was put in charge of

EXHIBIT 9.6 Example of an ERP Network

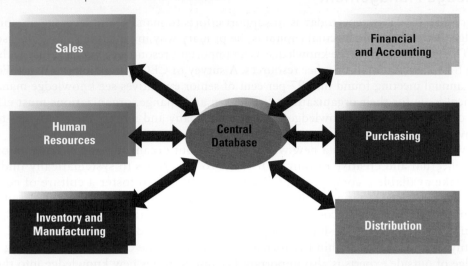

developing an ERP system that could improve efficiency by integrating information about all the company's different activities: 'Whether it's sourcing a book, developing content, managing stock, distribution or finances – trying to merge all of that into one is no easy task', says Sadler. However, Lonely Planet moved cautiously. It took more than a year identifying needs and choosing an ERP supplier – in the end choosing Swiss-based SAP. Lonely Planet decided they needed a full integration of company functions ranging from HR to print contracts, and implemented the project in stages both geographically and by enterprise functions between 2005 and 2007. The new system needed lots of ironing out, and led to further hardware investment, but it helped the company strengthen its financial controls and future planning, particularly in expanding traffic and business through the company's web portal. In October 2007, BBC Worldwide, the business arm of the British Broadcasting Corporation, bought a 75 per cent stake in Lonely Planet for around £75 million, reflecting LP's strong sales, better cost controls and improved profit margins.[49] Not bad for a company started at a kitchen table. Since being resold by BBC to NC2 Media in 2013 at a significant loss in the wake of the rise of (often free-to-access) digital alternatives like Foursquare and TripAdvisor, Lonely Planet has bounced back as customers realise they appreciate having a physical book they can flick through before and during their travels, while Lonely Planet has also made its content available electronically in various ebook formats. Piers Pickard, publishing managing director at the company, says, "If you want to search, then digital products are really good. But people don't tend to search guidebooks — they flick and browse."[50,51]

As ERP systems integrate data about all aspects of operations, managers and employees at all levels can see how decisions and actions in one part of the organization affect other parts, using this information to make better decisions. ERP can provide the kind of information furnished by transaction processing systems, as well as that provided by information reporting systems, decision support systems or executive information systems. ERP aims to weave all of these systems together so people can see the big picture and act quickly, helping the organization be smarter and more effective. ERP is not just applicable in the for-profit sector. Medecins du Monde, an international aid organization, uses an ERP system to keep precise track of expenses, supplies and needs and enable doctors and volunteers in the field to see what resources are available and where they're most urgently needed.[52] In the past, information systems required companies to invest quite heavily in hardware, as well as back-up systems in case the hardware broke down. Now, much of the storage and systems can be located in 'the Cloud'; in online storage and servers that produce the same kinds of economy of scale and specialization as did mass production in the industrial era. Many ERP systems, for example, are now cloud-based.[53]

Knowledge Management

A primary goal for IT systems today is to support efforts to manage and leverage organizational knowledge. Increasingly, intellectual capital is the primary way in which businesses measure their value.[54] Therefore, managers see knowledge as an important resource to manage, just as they manage cash flow, raw materials or other resources. A survey of CEOs attending the World Economic Forum's annual meeting found that 97 per cent of senior executives see knowledge management as a critical issue for their organizations.[55] To learn and change, organizations must effectively acquire, create and transfer knowledge across the company and modify their activities to reflect new knowledge and insight.[56]

Knowledge management is a new way to think about organizing and sharing an organization's intellectual and creative resources. It refers to the efforts to systematically find, organize and make available a company's intellectual capital and to foster a culture of continuous learning and knowledge sharing so that organizational activities build on what is already known (see Counterpoint 9.7).[57] The company's intellectual capital is the sum of its knowledge, experience, understanding, relationships, processes, innovations and discoveries. Although most of a company's knowledge is within the formal boundaries of the organization, tapping into the knowledge of outside experts is also important because it brings new knowledge into the organization that can be combined with existing knowledge to highlight problems or opportunities.[58] A variety of new software tools support collaboration and knowledge sharing through services such as web conferencing, knowledge portals, content management and the use of *wikis*, a collaboration tool. Wikis are an extension of the concept of blogs (web logs); rather than simply allowing an individual to broadcast his or her views to an online audience, as blogs do, wikis let people edit and add content to the running log.[59]

COUNTERPOINT 9.7

'Knowledge Management' can also be interpreted as the application of Taylorism to employees who work primarily with their heads rather than their hands. From this perspective, its purpose is to rationalize and systematize what had previously been the equivalent of the 'custom and practice' of the 'shopfloor'. Its consequence can be deskilling of work and degradation of work experience, with predictable consequences for morale, goodwill and staff turnover.

What Is Knowledge?   Knowledge is not the same thing as data or information, although it uses both. Data are simple, absolute facts and figures that, in and of themselves, may be of little use. A company might have data that show 30 per cent of a particular product is sold to customers in France. To be useful to the organization, the data are processed into finished *information* by connecting them with other data – for example, six out of ten of the products sold in France are bought by people over the age of 60. Information is data that have been linked with other data and converted into a useful context for specific use. Knowledge goes a step further: it is a conclusion drawn from the information after it is linked to other information and compared to what is already known. Knowledge, as opposed to information and data, always has a human factor that provides interpretations of the data. Books can contain information, but the information becomes knowledge only when a person absorbs it and puts it to use.[60]

Organizations deal with both explicit knowledge and implicit, or tacit, knowledge.[61] Explicit knowledge is formal, systematic knowledge that can be codified, written down and passed on to others in documents or general instructions. Tacit knowledge, on the other hand, is often difficult to put into words. Tacit knowledge is based on personal experience, rules of thumb, intuition and judgement. It includes professional know-how and expertise, individual insight and experience and creative solutions that are difficult to communicate

ONLINE
COUNTERPOINT 9.8

and pass on to others. Explicit knowledge may be equated with *knowing about*; tacit knowledge is equated with *knowing how*.[62]

Finding ways to transfer both explicit and tacit knowledge – the knowing about and the knowing how – across the organization is critical.[63] Although explicit knowledge can easily be captured and shared in documents and through IT systems, as much as 80 per cent of an organization's valuable knowledge may be tacit knowledge that is not easily captured and transferred.[64]

Approaches to Knowledge Management   Two distinct approaches to knowledge management are outlined in Exhibit 9.7. The first approach outlined in the exhibit deals primarily with the collection and sharing of explicit knowledge, largely through the use of sophisticated IT systems.[65] Explicit knowledge may include intellectual properties such as patents and licences; work processes such as policies and procedures; specific information on customers, markets, suppliers or competitors; competitive intelligence reports; benchmark data; and so forth. When an organization uses this approach, the focus is on collecting and codifying knowledge and storing it in databases where it can easily be accessed and reused by anyone in the organization. With this 'people-to-documents' approach, knowledge is gathered from the individuals who possess it and is organized into documents that others can access and reuse. When money management firm, Barclays Global Investors, deals with requests for proposals, for example, employees have to answer hundreds of complex questions for clients. A knowledge management system enables them to access and reuse answers to similar questions from previous proposals.[66]

Although IT plays an important role in knowledge management by enabling the storage and dissemination of data and information across the organization, IT is only one piece of a larger puzzle.[67] A complete knowledge management system includes not only processes for capturing and storing knowledge and organizing it for easy access, but also ways to generate new knowledge through learning and to share knowledge throughout the organization. As discussed in this chapter's *Bookmark 9.0*, old-fashioned paper can sometimes play just as important a role in knowledge work as computer technology.

BRIEFCASE 9.5

The second approach focuses on leveraging individual expertise and know-how – tacit knowledge – by connecting people face-to-face or through interactive media. Tacit knowledge includes professional know-how, individual insights and creativity and personal experience and intuition. With this approach, managers concentrate on developing personal networks that link people together for the sharing of tacit knowledge. The organization uses IT systems primarily for

EXHIBIT 9.7   Two Approaches to Knowledge Management

Explicit		Tacit	
Provide high-quality, reliable and fast information systems for access of codified, reusable knowledge		Channel individual expertise to provide creative advice on strategic problems	
People-to-documents approach	**Knowledge Management Strategy**	**Person-to-person approach**	
Develop an electronic document system that codifies, stores, disseminates, and allows reuse of knowledge		Develop networks for linking people so that tacit knowledge can be shared	
Invest heavily in information technology, with a goal of connecting people with reusable, codified knowledge	**Information Technology Approach**	Invest moderately in information technology, with a goal of facilitating conversations and the personal exchange of tacit knowledge	

Source: Based on Morten T. Hansen, Nitin Nohria and Thomas Tierney, 'What's Your Strategy for Managing Knowledge?' *Harvard Business Review* (March–April 1999), 106–116.

BOOKMARK 9.0

The Myth of the Paperless Office

By Abigail J. Sellen and Richard H. R. Harper

At first glance, it seems like a great idea. Get rid of all the paper that clutters desktops and put everything on computers. Especially with the proliferation of handheld gadgets, paper seems redundant. Yet paper sales increase every year because paper is woven into the fabric of our lives and organizations – and for very good reasons, argue Abigail Sellen and Richard Harper, authors of *The Myth of the Paperless Office*. Paper actually enables a certain kind of information processing, as well as supporting collaborative knowledge work. People simply can't *think* the same way when looking at a document on a computer screen.

Why Paper Persists

Sellen and Harper offer a number of reasons why paper persists. Paper has many advantages, they say, for performing certain kinds of cognitive tasks and supporting certain kinds of collaboration.

■ *Paper is flexible and easily manipulated for reading.* Most people still prefer to read newspapers or documents on paper rather than on a computer screen. The authors cite four primary reasons for this: paper allows people to flexibly navigate through documents, it facilitates the cross-referencing of more than one document at a time, it allows for easy annotation and it enables the interweaving of reading and writing. Paper allows

one to pick up a document or newspaper, flip through it, read bits here and there and quickly get a sense of the overall piece.

■ *Paper is a tool for managing and coordinating action among co-workers.* The authors cite a fascinating example of air traffic controllers who, despite the availability and use of highly sophisticated technology, continue to use paper flight strips to support a seamless teamwork, enable easy manipulation to indicate flight variations, give everyone on the team information at a glance and facilitate the rapid pace of work required in this high-pressure environment.

■ *Paper supports collaboration and sharing of knowledge.* Paper has interactional properties that are not easy to duplicate with digital media and collaborative tools. People working on collaborative documents that require the professional judgement and contributions of many people typically print drafts to read, mark up and discuss with others while flipping though the pages. Sellen and Harper argue that, without paper drafts, collaborative, iterative knowledge work is much more difficult and time consuming. Paper, they say, 'is a versatile medium that can be co-opted, shaped and adapted to meet the needs of the work'.

The Best of Both Worlds

The authors emphasize that digital technologies have their own advantages. Their point in *The Myth of the Paperless Office* is that managers should understand what paper can do and what computers can do and should know how to get the most out of each medium. 'The real issue for organizations … is not to get rid of paper for its own sake, but to have sufficient motivation to understand their own work process and the ways paper plays a role.'

The Myth of the Paperless Office, by Abigail Sellen and Richard Harper, is published by MIT Press.

ONLINE COUNTERPOINT 9.9

facilitating conversation and person-to-person sharing of experience, insight and ideas. For example, intranets are important for helping employees, especially those who are geographically dispersed, share ideas and tap into expert knowledge throughout the organization.

Organizations typically combine several methods and technologies to facilitate the sharing and transfer of both explicit and tacit knowledge. Consider the example of Toyota, the world's largest and most successful automobile manufacturer.

IN PRACTICE

Toyota Motor Corporation – developing the Prius

Toyota's success has been an inspiration to numerous other companies, as we saw in the previous chapter's discussion of the Swedish firm, Autoliv. One key element that sets Toyota apart from many other companies is its ability to make effective use of tacit knowledge. Rather than send workers on classroom courses, Toyota tends to use hands-on training, whereby employees in new plants will spend several weeks paired with workers in a longer-established facility, often followed by the experienced workers returning to the new facility to model effective work practices. The same emphasis on harvesting tacit knowledge also underpins Toyota's success in product innovation. When Toyota decided to develop a new energy-efficient car in the 1990s – which eventually became the hybrid Prius – it abandoned the traditional incremental and hierarchical approach to product development, and instead established a small team consisting of one or two experts from each area of automobile engineering expertise including body, chassis, engine, drive system and production technology. This team worked intensively together for several years, creating a sense of mutual commitment and frank dialogue. Faced with ambitious targets for fuel economy, traditional ideas that governed individual specialists' thinking about what was possible had to be abandoned. However, individual and team learning still had to be harvested and channelled. One way was achieved through emphasizing 'equal access to information'. New ideas were posted immediately on an email list open to everyone involved in the project, thus creating a dialogue around product development that spanned different expertise, and allowed tacit expertise to intermingle and produce advances in explicit knowledge. Engineers were also encouraged to think outside the box; trying out design hunches even if they were unlikely to work properly the first time. And, as Toyota product development had always emphasized, designers were encouraged to put their ideas on a single piece of paper – forcing them to making their thinking approachable to others. Finally, Toyota invested in the most advanced computer aided drafting (CAD) and computer aided engineering (CAE) systems, again encouraging team members to work together on design ideas. These various methods of knowledge harvesting enabled Toyota to produce the Prius, a revolutionary design, in only 15 months, compared with the average four years the company takes to design and produce a conventional vehicle, itself an industry-leading standard. More than a decade later, as high oil prices placed energy conservation and alternative fuels at the top of the political and business agenda, Toyota's foresight in developing the Prius seems almost clairvoyant. Through to 2015, Toyota still had a huge lead in the global hybrid segment, having sold more than three-quarters of the 10 million hybrid cars produced to date, with second place Honda lagging far behind. The company is also far ahead in the rapidly developing Chinese sales market.[68] The Prius example showed that use of leading edge technology is crucial for successful businesses, but as a support for, not in place of, human ingenuity and determination. The next tests for Toyota will be the challenge from fully-electric cars like the Tesla, as well as the integration of self-driving features being pioneered by companies like Google and Tesla. The arrival of new challengers like Google and Apple from outside the traditional automotive industry demonstrates the disruptive potential of IT.[69,70]

Adding Strategic Value: Strengthening External Relationships

External applications of IT for strengthening relationships with customers, suppliers and partners include systems for supply chain management and the integrated enterprise, customer relationship management systems and e-business organization design. The extension of corporate intranets to include customers and partners has expanded the potential for external collaboration. An **extranet** is an external communications system that uses the

ONLINE
COUNTERPOINT 9.10

internet and is shared by two or more organizations. Each organization moves certain data outside of its private intranet, but makes the data available only to the other companies sharing the extranet. For example, the British brewer Greene King set up an extranet, Pubpartners.net, available to all of the company's 1600-plus tenanted and leased pubs. Pubpartners is used not only to order products from Greene King, but also as an online information resource. The company posts useful information online, such as the rules for pubs to comply with the smoking ban in the British Isles, as well as menu and wine list guidance, marketing updates and personalized weekly sales reports.[71]

The Integrated Enterprise

BRIEFCASE 9.6

Extranets play a critical role in today's integrated enterprise. The integrated enterprise is an organization that uses advanced IT to enable close coordination within the company as well as with suppliers, customers and partners. One good example of the integrated enterprise is Corrugated Supplies of Chicago, USA, which has linked its entire factory to the internet, as described in the *Leading by Design* box. An important aspect of the integrated enterprise is *supply chain management*, which means managing the sequence of suppliers and purchasers, covering all stages of processing from obtaining raw materials to distributing finished goods to consumers.[72] For organizations to operate efficiently and provide high-quality items that meet customer needs, the company must have reliable deliveries of high-quality, reasonably priced supplies and materials. It also requires an efficient and reliable system for distributing finished products, making them readily accessible to customers.

Information Linkages   The most recent advances involve the use of computer networks or extranets to achieve the right balance of low inventory levels and customer responsiveness. Exhibit 9.8 illustrates horizontal information linkages in the integrated enterprise. By establishing electronic linkages between the organization and key partners for the sharing and exchange of data, the integrated enterprise aspires to create a seamless, integrated line stretching from end consumers to raw materials suppliers.[73] For example, in the Exhibit, as consumers purchase products in retail stores, the data are automatically fed into the retail chain's information system. In turn, the chain gives access to this constantly updated data to the manufacturing company through a secure extranet. With knowledge of this demand data, the manufacturer can produce and ship products when needed. As products are made by the manufacturer, data about raw materials used in the production process, updated inventory information and updated forecasted demand are electronically provided to the manufacturer's suppliers, and the suppliers automatically replenish the manufacturer's raw materials inventory as needed.

EXHIBIT 9.8   The Integrated Enterprise

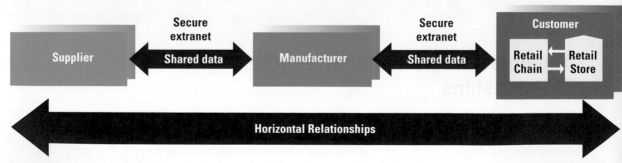

Source: Based on Jim Turcotte, Bob Silveri and Tom Jobson, 'Are You Ready for the E-Supply Chain?' *APICS – The Performance Advantage* (August 1998), 56–59.

LEADING BY DESIGN

Corrugated Supplies

Rick Van Horne had a vision. What would happen if all his plant's equipment continually fed data to the internet, where the rest of the company, as well as suppliers and customers, could keep track of what was happening on the factory floor in real time? By using a password, customers could peek into the company's internal workings at any time, calling up Corrugated's production schedules to see exactly where their orders were in the process and when they would arrive. Suppliers could tap into the system to manage their own inventory – inventory they were selling to Corrugated as well as materials stored at Corrugated's plant to sell to someone else.

It cost him millions of dollars, but Van Horne's vision became a reality, making Corrugated one of the world's first completely web-based production plants. The idea behind the system was to connect all the plant's manufacturing equipment and then link it to the web; the integrated system is available to everyone, from machinists on the plant floor to customers and suppliers off-site. Exhibit 9.9 illustrates how the system works for a customer placing an order: the customer logs onto the website and types in an order for corrugated paper precisely cut and folded for 20 000 boxes. Computers at Corrugated's factory go to work immediately to determine the best way to blend that order with numerous other orders ranging from a few dozen to 50 000 boxes. The computer comes up with the optimum schedule – that is, the one that gets the most orders out of a single roll with little leftover paper. A human operator checks the schedule on one of the numerous linked computer screens positioned around the plant and hits the Send button. Computer software directs the massive corrugators, trimmers, slitters and other equipment, which begin

EXHIBIT 9.9   Corrugated System in Action

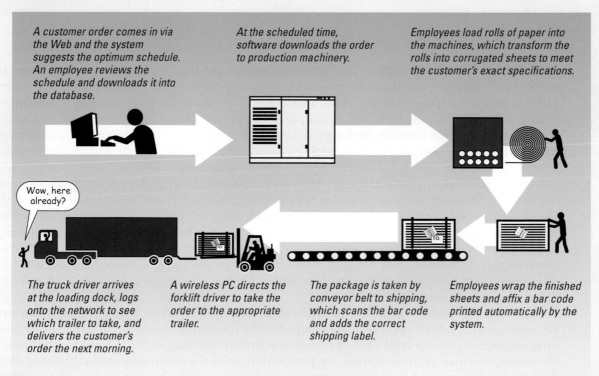

A customer order comes in via the Web and the system suggests the optimum schedule. An employee reviews the schedule and downloads it into the database.

At the scheduled time, software downloads the order to production machinery.

Employees load rolls of paper into the machines, which transform the rolls into corrugated sheets to meet the customer's exact specifications.

Wow, here already?

The truck driver arrives at the loading dock, logs onto the network to see which trailer to take, and delivers the customer's order the next morning.

A wireless PC directs the forklift driver to take the order to the appropriate trailer.

The package is taken by conveyor belt to shipping, which scans the bar code and adds the correct shipping label.

Employees wrap the finished sheets and affix a bar code printed automatically by the system.

Source: Adapted from Bill Richards, 'Superplant', *eCompany* (November 2000), 182–196.

spewing out paper orders at 250 metres per minute. Computer-controlled conveyor belts carry the order to the loading dock, where forklifts equipped with wireless PCs take the load to the designated trailer. Lorry drivers log onto the website and are told which trailer to haul to maximize their trip's efficiency. The order is usually delivered to the customer the very next day.

Today, over 80 per cent of Corrugated's orders are submitted via the internet and routed electronically to the plant floor. The system saves time and money for Corrugated by automatically scheduling special-order details and cutting out paper waste. For customers, it means faster service and fewer mix-ups. One customer, Gene Mazurek, co-owner of Suburban Corrugated Box Co., says the first thing he does each morning is log onto Corrugated's website to see what's running, what's broken, where his order is and when it should arrive. The new system has cut Mazurek's delivery time to his own customers from a week down to two days, something larger competitors can't match. 'It's 'the best thing that's ever happened so far,' says Mazurek. 'It's like Rick put his corrugating machine right inside my plant.'

In a second phase of technological upgrading, Corrugated Supplies integrated its proprietary order management system with Sage software's MAS, a standard ERP and management accounting system. This improved the Corrugated Supplies' financial controls and provided further order and financial information to customers. Corrugated has also integrated voice-over-internet-protocol (VOIP) telephone service into its data network. Not only did this result in substantial cost savings over traditional telephone service, it allowed the company's staff to answer calls outside normal office hours.

Corrugated Supplies' success has led it to expand to plants in three US states, with plans to open a large new mill in Milwaukee in 2017.[74] It found that a customized solution was required for maintaining order and productivity information across the distant sites with custom reports necessary for both senior and line managers. Corrugated worked with SWC Technology Partners in 2012 to establish a SharePoint site for each plant where a shift dashboard was deployed carrying Key Performance Indicators allowing line managers and even workers to keep real-time track of their productivity and quickly identify productivity blockage points. The system has enabled Corrugated to reduce wastage and thus improve efficiency and help the environment.[75]

Horizontal Relationships   The purpose of integrating the supply chain is for everyone to work closely together, moving in lockstep to meet customers' product and time demands. Albert Heijn supermarkets, a subsidiary of the Dutch Ahold corporation, uses extranet technologies extensively to do business both with its suppliers and its customers. The extranets are tied into a comprehensive overall business intelligence strategy. The company's suppliers can use the extranet to keep track of the company's orders, while retail customers can shop online and review purchase history. Technology also helps Albert Heijn maintain accurate distribution to its stores; it was one of the first supermarkets in the world to fully automate order picking from its distribution warehouses. The company was chosen as 'Smartest Organization in the Netherlands' by the 2008 Dutch Business Intelligence conference.[76,77] It has continued to build on its technology advantage in its To Go stores opened in 2012. Typically located in office buildings, with matching opening hours, the high tech stores use numerous display screens to advertise specials and provide customer advice. Self-service tills are also placed throughout the store, so customers just wanting to grab one item don't have to line up at the front tills. The initiative was a success, expanded to petrol station forecourts in 2016.[78,79]

As with the newer organization designs described in Chapter 4, horizontal relationships get more emphasis than vertical relationships for the integrated enterprise to work. Enterprise integration can create a level of cooperation not previously imaginable if managers approach the practice with an attitude of trust and partnership, as in the interorganizational relationships described in Chapter 6. For example, America's Wal-Mart and Procter & Gamble (P&G) started simply by sharing sales data so P&G goods could be automatically replaced as they were sold off Wal-Mart's shelves. However, this computer-to-computer exchange evolved into a horizontal relationship that had the two firms sharing customer information, shopper loyalty information and other data that provides strategic advantages for both sides of the trading partnership.[80]

Customer Relationship Management

Another approach to strengthening external relationships is through the use of customer relationship management (CRM) systems. These systems help companies track customers' interactions with the firm and allow employees to call up a customer's past sales and service records, outstanding orders or unresolved problems.[81] CRM collects in a database all the customer information that a small-town store owner would keep in his or her head – the names of customers, what they bought, what problems they've had with purchases and so forth. The system helps coordinate sales, marketing and customer service departments so that all are smoothly working together.

ONLINE COUNTERPOINT 9.11

E-Business Organization Design

CRM and the integrated enterprise are both components of e-business, a new approach to how organizations conduct their business activities. E-business can be defined as any business that takes place by digital processes over a computer network rather than in physical space. Most commonly, it refers to electronic linkages over the internet with customers, partners, suppliers, employees or other key constituents. The internet continues to transform traditional ways of doing business, helping companies in industries from banking to manufacturing to music retailing cut costs, speed innovation and enhance relationships with customers.[82] Most traditional organizations have set up internet operations to strengthen and improve these external relationships, but managers have to make a decision about how best to integrate *bricks and clicks* – that is, how to blend their traditional operations with an internet presence. In the early days of e-business, many organizations set up dot-com initiatives with little understanding of how those activities could and should be integrated with their overall business. As the reality of e-business has evolved, companies have gained valuable lessons in how to merge online and offline activities.[83]

BRIEFCASE 9.8

IN PRACTICE

Tesco.com

When Britain's number one supermarket chain, Tesco, decided to launch a dot-com operation, offering a grocery home delivery service, managers evaluated options and decided to set up an in-house division to avoid the huge start-up costs that would be required for a spin-off company. The idea was to start slowly and keep close control over the new operation to maintain profitability. Tesco managers saw their online service as just another way to attract and retain customers.

By being part of the greater Tesco enterprise, Tesco.com was able to ride on the back of the parent company, leveraging its brand, suppliers, advertising and customer database. Tesco started by offering delivery from just one store, gradually rolling out service to other areas. By integrating the new operation with the traditional stores, Tesco didn't have to build new warehouses; the internet division simply used the established warehouses and distribution systems of the chain and picked goods off supermarket shelves to fill customer orders. Using the store-based picking approach kept start-up costs low. Tesco spent no more than £150 million on its

▶

internet operation during the first four years, and the operation was profitable from the beginning. Consumer data is collected automatically, and integrated into the Clubcard scheme discussed earlier in this chapter; unlike with the physical Clubcard, however, data on customer spending patterns are collected automatically when the customer logs in, and s/he does not need to enter the Clubcard number each time. Already, in 2007, Tesco.com had grown to cover 95 per cent of the United Kingdom and was receiving 250 000 orders per week, although competition was also heating up from rival supermarkets like Sainsbury's and Asda/Wal-Mart. By 2015 online sales amounted to 5 per cent of overall UK grocery sales and were rising fast, predicted to reach 8% by 2020. The hybrid 'click-and-pick-up' approach is also gaining ground, as in the clothing sector discussed in Chapter Seven. Stores such as Morrison's that had not bothered to develop an online presence, were rushing to catch up. The next challenge is likely to come from Amazon as it expands its grocery offerings through AmazonFresh and Amazon Pantry.[84,85,86,87]

Source : http://www.theguardian.com/business/2015/dec/29/amazon-uk-boss-christoper-north-hails-pantry-grocery-expansion-supermarkets.

The range of basic strategies for setting up an internet operation is illustrated in Exhibit 9.10. In principle, there is nothing special about such operations as the same issue is confronted with the strategic options associated with engagement in any novel or non-core area of activity and expertise. At one end of the spectrum, companies can set up an in-house division that is closely integrated with the traditional business. The opposite approach is to create a spin-off company that is totally separate from the traditional organization. Many companies take a third approach that involves forging strategic partnerships with other organizations for their internet initiative. Each of these options presents distinct advantages and disadvantages.[88]

In-House Division

An in-house division offers tight integration between the internet operation and the organization's traditional operation. The organization creates a separate unit within the company that functions inside the structure and guidance of the traditional organization. This approach gives the new division several advantages which include brand recognition, purchasing leverage with suppliers, shared customer information and marketing opportunities, and distribution efficiencies. For example, Tesco developed its online grocery delivery by keeping Tesco.com closely integrated with the existing grocery chain. However, by 2013 the online business was big enough that special stores were being constructed to service online order picking alone.

Tesco's success illustrates many of the advantages of the in-house approach. A potential problem with an in-house division, however, is that the new operation might not have the flexibility and autonomy needed to move quickly in the internet world.

Spin-Off

To give their internet operations greater organizational autonomy, flexibility and focus, and to cash in on sometimes high valuations of internet stocks, many organizations have chosen to create a separate spin-off company. Many telephone companies have spun-off part or all of their internet operations, including British Telecom,[89] Portugal Telecom[90] and Hungary's Magyar Telekom.[91] Other companies have gone in the opposite direction; former Canadian publishing giant Thomson sold off most of its print publication properties to focus on electronic information delivery.[92] Advantages of a spin-off can include faster decision-making, increased flexibility and responsiveness to changing market conditions, an entrepreneurial culture and management that is totally focused on the success of the online operation. Potential disadvantages include the loss of brand recognition and marketing opportunities, higher start-up costs and loss of leverage with suppliers. The fate of internet spin-offs is also closely linked to volatile investor sentiment about high-tech stocks; for example, US appliance manufacturer Whirlpool's

EXHIBIT 9.10 The Range of Strategies for Integrating Bricks and Clicks

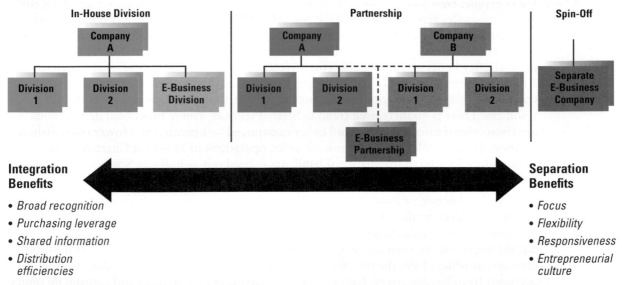

Source: Based on Ranjay Gulati and Jason Garino, 'Get the Right Mix of Bricks and Clicks', *Harvard Business Review* (May–June 2000), 107–114.

Brandwise.com spinoff, a site designed to help consumers find the best products and value, went under during a dot-com sell-off in 2000.[93]

Strategic Partnership Partnerships, whether through joint ventures or alliances, offer a middle ground, enabling organizations to attain some of the advantages and overcome some of the disadvantages of the purely in-house or spin-off options. For example, Canadian used-book distributor Abebooks acts as a portal for independent booksellers to sell their books through the internet. Although consumers can buy their books directly from Abebook's website, its books are also listed on Amazon websites across the world, as well as other major internet booksellers such as Waterstones in the UK and Buch.de in Germany, thus providing a much larger audience.[94] Another e-commerce partnership option for small and medium sized enterprises is, of course, eBay, the giant auction site discussed earlier in the chapter. More than 70 000 people in the UK alone earn a full-time living from selling on eBay.[95] It is difficult to argue with the advice of Drew Sharma, managing director of internet marketing agency, Mindfire Interactive, for smaller companies going online: 'If you can stand on the shoulders of giants, then why not?'[96] Disadvantages of partnerships include time spent managing relationships, potential conflicts between partners and a possibility that one company will fail to deliver as promised or go out of business.

IT Impact on Organization Design

Not every organization will become as heavily involved in e-business as Tesco, Corrugated Supplies or Amazon. However, advances in IT are having a tremendous impact on all organizations in every industry. Some specific implications of these advances for organization design are smaller organizations, decentralized structures, improved internal and external coordination and new network organization structures.

BRIEFCASE 9.9

1 *Smaller organizations.* Some internet-based businesses exist almost entirely in cyberspace; there is no formal organization in terms of a building with offices, desks and so forth. One or a few people may maintain the site from their homes or a rented work space.

Even for traditional businesses, new IT enables the organization to do more work with fewer people. Nowadays most customers can buy car insurance without ever speaking to an agent or sales rep. In addition, ERP and other IT systems automatically handle many administrative duties, reducing the need for clerical staff. British cattle breeder Alan Swale, who owns a renowned herd, uses the internet to sell top quality semen directly to commercial dairy herds at a reasonable cost – typically around £10 per dose – far less than if a middleman was involved.[97,98] Companies can also make use of internet and other telecommunications technologies to outsource many functions and thus use fewer in-house resources. There is an increasing trend to 'shared services' where functional departments are consolidated internationally and either outsourced or operated at a lower cost offshore location. For example, many of the back office operations of Standard Chartered, the London-headquartered international bank, are carried out in India by Scope, a subsidiary of Standard Chartered India.[99]

2   *Decentralized organizational structures.* IT enables organizations to reduce layers of management and decentralize decision-making. Information that may have previously been available only to top managers at headquarters can be quickly and easily shared throughout the organization, even across great geographical distances. Managers in varied business divisions or offices have the information to make decisions quickly rather than waiting for decisions from headquarters. Technologies that enable people to meet and coordinate online can facilitate communication and decision-making among distributed, autonomous groups of workers. In addition, technology allows for telecommuting, whereby individual workers can perform work that was once done in the office from their computers at home or other remote locations. People and groups no longer have to be located under one roof to collaborate and share information. An organization might be made up of numerous small teams or even individuals who work autonomously but coordinate electronically. Although management philosophy informs whether IT is used to decentralize information and authority or to reinforce a centralized authority structure,[100] technology tends to be used to further decentralization within centrally defined parameters.

3   *Improved horizontal coordination.* IT has the potential to improve coordination and communication within the firm. Intranets and other networks can connect people even when their offices, factories or stores are scattered around the world. The British Council, a charity established to build relationships between the UK and other countries, has invested in a comprehensive internal communications system including not just a corporate intranet, but also special software to permit 'virtual meetings', a necessity for an organization with 7900 staff in 110 countries and territories. Andrew Walker, collaboration consultant at the Council, says that, 'users are very happy as time and effort in completing projects has been reduced and travel cut through digital meetings'.[101]

4   *Improved interorganizational relationships.* IT can also improve horizontal coordination and collaboration with external parties such as suppliers, customers and partners. Extranets are increasingly important for linking companies with contract manufacturers and outsourcers, as well as for supporting the integrated enterprise, as described earlier. Exhibit 9.11 shows differences between traditional interorganizational relationship characteristics and emerging relationship characteristics. Traditionally, organizations had an arms-length relationship with suppliers. However, as we discussed in Chapter 6, suppliers are becoming closer partners, tied electronically to the organization for orders, invoices and payments. In addition, new IT has increased the power of consumers by giving them electronic access to a wealth of information from thousands of companies just by clicking a mouse. Consumers also have direct access to manufacturers, altering their perceptions and expectations regarding convenience, speed and service.

5   Studies have shown that interorganizational information networks tend to heighten integration and redefine organizational boundaries. However, the larger the system, the more

EXHIBIT 9.11 Key Characteristics of Traditional versus Emerging Interorganizational Relationships

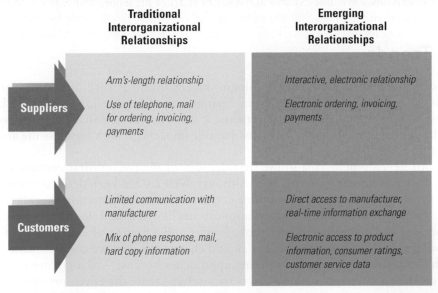

	Traditional Interorganizational Relationships	Emerging Interorganizational Relationships
Suppliers	Arm's-length relationship Use of telephone, mail for ordering, invoicing, payments	Interactive, electronic relationship Electronic ordering, invoicing, payments
Customers	Limited communication with manufacturer Mix of phone response, mail, hard copy information	Direct access to manufacturer, real-time information exchange Electronic access to product information, consumer ratings, customer service data

Source: Based on Charles V. Callahan and Bruce A. Pasternack, 'Corporate Strategy in the Digital Age', *Strategy & Business*, Issue 15 (Second Quarter 1999), 10–14.

complex and costly its implementation, with an enhanced risk of failure.[102] One example of interorganizational collaboration is the Canada Health Infoway. This project, funded by the Canadian federal government, is designed to ensure best practices in healthcare are shared across the 13 provincial and territorial healthcare systems that are responsible for operating Canada's national medicare system. In addition, the Infoway will provide early warning in case of infectious disease outbreaks. Infoway is based on the use of electronic health records (EHRs) that, when fully implemented, will give doctors instant access to Canadians' medical records when they seek treatment anywhere in the country, thus ensuring appropriate treatment.[103,104] However, Infoway has been beset by delays and cost overruns, and a decade after its initiation, is still far from complete, with many critics doubting it will ever reach its goal. Some critics argue that rather than try to build huge and complex top down systems, it is preferable to build from grassroots initiatives such as OSCAR, an open-source software developed at Montreal's McGill University, an electronic medical records system capable of tasks including disease surveillance, medication management and clinician reminders.[105]

6   *Enhanced network structures.* The high level of interorganizational collaboration demanded by a network organization structure, described in Chapter 4, would not be possible without the use of advanced IT. In the business world, these are also sometimes called *modular structures* or *virtual organizations*. Outsourcing has become a major trend, thanks to computer technology that, in principle, can tie companies together into a seamless information flow. For example, Hong Kong's Li & Fung is one of the biggest providers of clothing for retailers such as Abercrombie & Fitch, Guess, Ann Taylor, the Limited and Disney, but the company doesn't own any factories, machines or fabrics. Li & Fung specializes in managing information, relying on an electronically connected web of 7500 partners in 37 countries to provide raw materials and assemble the clothes. Using an extranet allows Li & Fung to stay in touch with worldwide partners and move items quickly from factories to retailers. It also enables retailers to track orders as they move through production and make last-minute changes and additions.[106] With a network structure, most activities are outsourced, so that different

companies perform the various functions needed by the organization. The speed and ease of electronic communication makes the network structure a viable option for companies that want to keep costs low but expand activities or market presence.

Future Trends

The rapid development of internet technologies means that it is very difficult to predict their future business impact. Just as Amazon has revolutionized bookselling, and eBay has created a whole new breed of small-time entrepreneurs, it can be expected that new technologies will emerge in the coming years that will have comparable impacts on both business life and organizational structure.[107]

One major development area in the first decades of the twenty-first century has been the emergence of what is known as Web 2.0.[108] Although Web 2.0 has been defined in different ways, basically it involves different tools for online communication, information sharing and collaboration. This ranges from virtual worlds of applications like Second Life, through YouTube with its user-generated video content, to Facebook, Twitter and a myriad of emerging platforms, most of which will quickly die, but a few will stick and change the way we communicate. These new internet vehicles differ from previous internet approaches because – to a greater or lesser extent depending on the specific application – users themselves create the environments in which they interact. Some of the applications have become enormously popular, and have attracted very high stock valuations. Facebook, for example, which had 1.6 billion users in 2016, was floated on the NASDAQ stock exchange in 2012 with an initial valuation of $104 billion. In the first year after the initial float, the company's stocks dropped about one third, so they were valued in April 2013 at $27 rather than the $38 launch price. Facebook's annual revenue of $7 billion in 2013, mainly through click-through ads, was well below the norm for a company with its level of capitalization.[109,110] However, Facebook revenues more than doubled between 2013 and 2015 to $18 billion, demonstrating the potential when companies figure out successfully how to marketize the social environment they have created.[111] Internet stocks often have very high price/revenue ratios because of the anticipation of this type of rapid and sustained growth.

Web 2.0 technologies are ingenious because much of the work is done by the users themselves; on Facebook, for example, people take the time to invite friends to join their networks, post pictures and write accounts of their current activities, and it is this user-generated content that attracts traffic to the site, with the company hoping that users will click through the advertisements that are interspersed on the Facebook pages. Such Web 2.0 applications are a distinctive form of organization in respect of the extent of user involvement in their content.

The problem Web 2.0 initiatives tend to face is how to earn revenue, the nut that Facebook is learning to crack.[112] Some Web 2.0 networking concepts have already faced a crunch; Iyomu, an adult social networking site set up by New Zealand entrepreneurs, folded in 2008 after less than a year in operation, despite attracting 100 000 users.[113] The simplest revenue generating idea is to copy Google's approach through delivering advertising at the side or bottom of the page that is derived from characteristics of the content and conversations in which the users are involved. Like Google, however, Web 2.0 companies must address accusations that the monitoring required to identify suitable advertising is an invasion of privacy. Other Web 2.0 initiatives have found niche approaches to making money. Virtual worlds can be used as a vehicle to promote specific products, such as Barbie.com, which also offers a paid 'VIP' membership to its users.[114] Indie musicians often used MySpace which, until 2008, was the biggest of the Web 2.0 domains but which has subsequently been almost completely squeezed out by YouTube and Facebook, again demonstrating the extreme fluidity of this business area.

In theory, however, the greatest value that remains to be unlocked is in the networks themselves. Long before the internet, personal social networks have been used as a business foundation – for example by cosmetics companies Avon and Mary Kay that sell through distributors' own connections. Web 2.0 communities are much larger and potentially more lucrative. Whoever discovers the key to unlock this potential, while avoiding privacy pitfalls, will have a significant impact. Wishful thinking? Possibly, but lots of people said that Google had little business potential.[115] That internet startup recorded a 40-fold increase in revenues between 2002 and 2007, from $400 million to $16 billion, $40 billion by 2012, and $75 billion by 2015.[116,117]

What comes next after Web 2.0? Some IT gurus are talking about Web 3.0. For some, Web 3.0 involves the connectivity of diverse devices, becoming known as the Internet of Things. Others relate the Next Web to the rapidly advancing autonomous analytical capacities of IT, most famously seen in the development of self-driving cars. However the next generation of IT development is defined, it is clear that it will have both business and ethical ramifications. Tesla electric car entrepreneur Elon Musk warns that, "I think we should be very careful about artificial intelligence. If I were to guess like what our biggest existential threat is, it's probably that." He argues that society urgently needs to establish a regulatory framework to ensure that humanity controls artificial intelligence in the common good.[118]

Summary and Interpretation

The information revolution has had a tremendous impact on organizations in all sectors. Operations applications are applied to well-defined tasks at lower organization levels and help to improve efficiency. These include transaction processing systems, data warehousing and data mining. Advanced computer-based systems are also used for better decision-making and control of the organization. Decision-making systems include management information systems, reporting systems, decision support systems and executive information systems, which are typically used at middle and upper levels of the organization. Management control systems include budgets and financial reports, periodic non-financial statistical reports, reward systems and quality control systems. The *balanced scorecard* technique provides managers with a more holistic view of the organization by integrating traditional financial measurements and statistical reports with a concern for markets, customers and employees.

Intranets, ERP and knowledge management systems are used primarily to support greater internal coordination, and can aid flexibility. Systems that support and strengthen external relationships include extranets and the integrated enterprise, customer relationship management and e-business. Advanced use of IT enables close coordination among a company and its suppliers, partners and customers. Customer relationship management systems help companies keep track of their customers' interactions with the organization and provide better service. To establish an e-business, companies have created an in-house division, developed a spin-off or entered a strategic partnership.

Advanced IT is having a significant impact on the design of organizations. Technology enables companies to implement a wider range of organizational design options. It has supported the growth of network organization structures in which a company subcontracts most of its major functions to separate companies that are connected electronically, but it can also enable greater coordination and centralization of decision-making. Other specific implications of advances in technology for organization design include a tendency toward smaller organizations that concentrate on their core competencies, decentralized organization structures and improved internal and external coordination.

Internet technologies are moving so fast that it is difficult to identify what will be the 'next big thing' five years, two years, or even one year down the road. One rapidly developing area is social networking, where users create their own social spaces in hosted environments. If the revenue potential of these sites can be unlocked in ethically-sound ways, they may form the basis of important new business and organizational models.

KEY CONCEPTS

balanced scorecard	e-business	information reporting	management information
benchmarking	enterprise resource	system	system
business intelligence	planning	integrated enterprise	networking
customer relationship	executive information	intellectual capital	Six Sigma
management	system	intranet	tacit knowledge
data	explicit knowledge	knowledge	Web 2.0
data mining	extranet	knowledge management	transaction processing
data warehousing	feedback control model	management control	systems
decision support system	information	systems	

Discussion Questions

1 Do you think technology will eventually enable top managers to do their jobs with little face-to-face communication? Discuss.

2 Why might a company consider using an intranet rather than traditional management and executive information systems?

3 How might an enterprise resource planning system be used to improve strategic management of a manufacturing organization?

4 Discuss some ways a large insurance company such as Progressive, described in the chapter opening, might use MIS to improve decision-making.

5 Describe how the four management control system elements discussed in the chapter might be used for feedback control within organizations. Compare and contrast this four-part system with use of the balanced scorecard.

6 Describe your use of explicit knowledge when you research and write a term paper. Do you also use tacit knowledge regarding this activity? Discuss.

7 Why is knowledge management particularly important to a company that wants to become a learning organization?

8 What is meant by the integrated enterprise? Describe how organizations can use extranets to extend and enhance horizontal relationships required for enterprise integration.

9 What are some competitive issues that might lead a company to take a partnership approach to e-business rather than setting up an in-house internet division? What are the advantages and disadvantages of each approach?

10 How might the adoption of IT affect how an organization is designed?

11 What business potential does Web 2.0 have?

TaKaDu Integrated Water Network Management

It was a chance conversation in 2008 at a technology conference in Vienna. Amir Peleg, an eight-year veteran of the Israeli Defence Forces' elite intelligence systems unit Talpiot and two IT start-up ventures, was speaking with a water engineer specialized in data collection hardware using smart water-pipe sensors. Peleg asked him what was done with the data collected. The answer? It was stored. Peleg immediately saw a business opportunity - these data could be mined to provide greatly enhanced water management.

At no point in history have concerns about a global water crisis been greater.[1] Contributing factors are increases in global population, climate change impacts and personal and industrial water requirements. Yet the problem is often argued to be one of management rather than supply.[2] Aging water system infrastructure results in water losses that can amount to 30 per cent of a water utility's supply and even 50 or 60 per cent in some instances. Faults, leaks and bursts as well as water quality, flow and level anomalies are responsible for the losses.[3] Having discovered that comparatively few entrepreneurs had been attracted to the low-tech water sector Peleg launched TaKaDu, with Hagihon, the Jerusalem Water and Wastewater Works, as the first customer for its high-tech data-driven integrated water network management.

TaKaDu incorporates data from sensors and combines it with data on weather, acoustics and GIS to produce a smart grid. Small changes to water systems, detected using patented mathematical and statistical algorithms, can be addressed before they become major problems. This software works rather like an x-ray to provide an accurate picture of extensive underground water transmission operations, pinpointing any issues that lead to 'non-revenue water.' The company aims to develop as good an understanding as possible of normal water flows in a system so that it can quickly identify and rectify abnormalities, thereby reducing water losses, repair cycles and customer complaints.

TaKaDu provides a Software-as-a-service (SaaS) business model. Public water utilities license the software on a subscription basis (a pay-as-you-go approach) with central hosting for 24/7 monitoring. No major capital investments are required for access to this very robust technology. TaKaDu has been the recipient of various awards including the World Economic Forum's Tech Pioneer Award in 2011 and the Sustainia award for the world's best sustainability innovation in 2013. Venture capital firms and companies, including ABB and 3M, have invested in TaKaDu.

Peleg is essentially rethinking the data on all aspects of utility water networks, melding them into a single interface that would allow not only better management of water systems, but also more innovation. For example, at Jerusalem's Hagihon water operations TaKaDu has helped to reduce water losses to under 10 per cent and has created opportunities for integration of other systems such as Israeli company Aquarius Spectrum that uses advanced sound equipment to detect the exact location of leaks. TaKaDu software identifies the leak location within a neighborhood and then Aquarius technology finds the specific pipe that is leaking. Another Israeli startup, Curapipe System, offers an automated leak repair system that plugs ruptures without digging.

TaKaDu has over 500 clients around the world including several in Australia of which UnityWater in southeastern Queensland is one. The partnership with UnityWater was established in 2013 at which time the utility had a non-revenue water rate of 13 per cent, a loss of about 78 litres per connection per day. In the implementation stage of the partnership with TaKaDu immediate process improvements were possible and a decision was then made to form a management group cross-cutting the organization to discuss the findings and implement further process improvements. Between 2013 and 2015 there were significant reductions in planned maintenance costs and faster reaction times to events based on more frequent data reporting back to TaKaDu. Estimated cost savings of about AUS$14 million on non-revenue

1. http://www.mckinsey.com/business-functions/sustainability-and-resource-productivity/our-insights/charting-our-water-future;
2. http://www.worldwatercouncil.org/library/archives/water-crisis/ *"There is a water crisis today. But the crisis is not about having too little water to satisfy our needs. It is a crisis of managing water so badly that billions of people - and the environment - suffer badly."* World Water Vision Report.
3. http://www.eco-business.com/videos/saving-water-smart-technology-interview-takadu-amir-peleg/

water costs and greatly improved rapport with water consumers were reported. The increase in customer confidence of 10 to 20 per cent spurred greater interest right across the organization in the potential benefits of the TaKaDu software. The UnityWater/TaKaDu partnership provided the catalyst for further broadening of the dialogue on water management strategies within the utility and created greater awareness of the potential for a more innovative approach throughout the organization.

There are reported to be about 250 000 water utilities globally of which only about 20 per cent have adopted smart systems to date. The demand for these systems is, in Peleg's words, 'growing constantly without being affected by recessions, unlike banking and telecoms.' He also notes that there is no substitute for water and that water losses will inevitably continue as the water infrastructure ages all around the world.

Case Questions:

1   As noted in this chapter IT is essential to successful organizations, with managers reportedly spending 'at least 80 per cent of their time actively exchanging information.' In what specific ways would you say that the TaKaDu software

increases opportunities for managers to enhance their information exchange process?

2   A McKinsey Survey released in May 2016 entitled "Geostrategic risks on the rise[4]" noted that the share of executives identifying geopolitical instability – both international and domestic – doubled over the two-year period 2013-2015 with the development of technologies that empower consumers and communities identified as the top priority. What arguments could you make about how TaKaDu software might help managers to address possible rises in the risks of geopolitical instability?

3   This chapter provides some examples illustrating ways in which advancements in IT are bringing about changes in the design of organizations. What key changes to organizational design do you think could be attributed to the partnership of UnityWater in Queensland, Australia, with TaKaDu?

For further information:
www.takadu.com
www.bloomberg.com/news/articles/2015-01-08/takadu-helps-israel-be-a-most-efficient-water-manager

4. http://www.mckinsey.com/business-functions/strategy-and-corporate-finance/our-insights/geostrategic-risks-on-the-rise?cid=other-eml-alt-mip-mck-oth-1605

Notes

1. 'Progressive Group of Insurance Cos. Recognized as IT Innovator', *Colorado Springs Business Journal,* June 15, 2007.
2. 'Brands Lining Up to Integrate Shazam into their Ads', 16 June, 2011, *Business Wire.*
3. 'Bursting through to take the award', *MX Magazine*, 2007, 16–17.
4. 'Award for pressure relief', *Food Trade Review*, 1 August, 2007.
5. 'North East Manufacturer Receives a Queen's Award for International Trade', May 12 2015, accessed at https://www.necc.co.uk/news/members/north-east-manufacturer-receives-a-queens-award-for-international-trade.
6. 'How can Peking duck go electric, fume Chinese', *Indo-Asian News Service*, 7 February 2008.
7. 'Purists squawk after Chinese restaurant chain switchesfrom wood ovens to electric', *National Post*, 15 January, 2008, A11.
8. 'Duck burger challenges the Chinese fast food market', March 25, 2016, Dong-A Ilbo, accessed at english.donga.com/Home/3/all/26/528409/1

9. Charles V. Callahan and Bruce A. Pasternack, 'Corporate Strategy in the Digital Age', *Strategy & Business*, Issue 15 (Second Quarter 1999), 10–14.
10. Ibid.
11. Bill Richards, 'A Total Overhaul', *The Wall Street Journal* (December 7, 1998), R30.
12. 'Intralot Signs Cooperation Agreement With Fifa's Early Warning System', *Greek Company News Bites – Stock Report*, 26 August, 2008.
13. Erik Berkman, 'How to Stay Ahead of the Curve', *CIO* (February 1, 2002), 72–80; and Heather Harreld, 'Pick-Up Artists', *CIO* (November 1, 2000), 148–154.
14. 'Business Intelligence', special advertising section, *Business 2.0* (February 2003), S1–S4; and Alice Dragoon, 'Business Intelligence Gets Smart', *CIO* (September 15, 2003), 84–91.
15. Gartner Inc, February 7, 2013, 'Gartner Says Worldwide Business Intelligence Software Revenue to Grow 7 Percent in 2013'.
16. Julie Schlosser, 'Looking for Intelligence in Ice Cream', *Fortune* (March 17, 2003), 114–120.

17. 'Business Intelligence and Analytics Software Market worth $26.78 Billion by 2020, Markets and Markets', April 2015, accessed at http://www.marketsandmarkets.com/PressReleases/business-intelligence-analytics-software.asp

18. Stephen Hoare, 'The man who went into overdrive – Positive thinking', *The Times*, 19 February, 2002.

19. 'French National Railways Improves Efficiency for Tracking 160,000 Employees Using WebFOCUS Business Intelligence', 19 August, 2008. Accessed at http://www.informationbuilders.com/news/press/release/2008/4356 on September 15, 2013.

20. 'SAP Customers Worldwide Tout Early Success With Latest CRM Offering' *PR Newswire (U.S.)*, 30 July 2008; John Mayer, 'How Apotex Integrated Business Objects Solutions into Its Existing SAP NetWeaver BI Landscape for Easier End-User Reporting', *Reporting and Analytics 2008,* accessed at http://www.scribd.com/doc/58607454/Apotex-BO-Case-Study on September 15, 2013.

21. Richard Fletcher, 'Tesco's success puts Clubcard firm on the map', *The Sunday Times*, 19 December 2004; M. Koschat, A. Ryans and S. Sequeira, 'Tesco: Keeping The Hard Discounters At Bay?', *IMD Case Study* 5-0737, 28 March, 2008.

22. Ciaran Ryan, 'DigiCore: Tight Focus And Genuine Synergies', *Financial Mail*, 11 November 2005.

23. Robert Simons, 'Strategic Organizations and Top Management Attention to Control Systems', *Strategic Management Journal* 12 (1991), 49–62.

24. Kevin Ferguson, 'Mission Control', *Inc. Magazine* (November 2003), 27–28; and Russ Banham, 'Seeing the Big Picture: New Data Tools Are Enabling CEOs to Get a Better Handle on Peformance Across Their Organizations', *Chief Executive* (November 2003), 46ff.

25. 'MTC-Vodafone Launches Harris Executive Dashboard for Service and Business Monitoring of Entire GSM/3G Network in Kuwait', *PR Newswire Europe*, 14 August, 2006.

26. Christopher Koch, 'How Verizon Flies by Wire', *CIO* (November 1, 2004), 94–96.

27. Richard L. Daft and Norman B. Macintosh, 'The Nature and Use of Formal Control Systems for Management Control and Strategy Implementation', *Journal of Management* 10 (1984), 43–66.

28. Susannah Patton, 'Web Metrics That Matter', *CIO* (November 14, 2002), 84–88; and Ramin Jaleshgari, 'The End of the Hit Parade', *CIO* (May 14, 2000), 183–190.

29. Adam Lashinsky, 'Meg and the Machine', *Fortune* (September 1, 2003), 68–78.

30. James B. Stewart, 28 July, 2012, 'Behind EBay's Comeback', *The New York Times*; April Dembosky, 28 March, 2013, 'PayPal eyes in-store retail customers', *Financial Times*.

31. Howard Rothman, 'You Need Not Be Big to Benchmark', *Nation's Business* (December, 1992), 64–65.

32. Tom Rancour and Mike McCracken, 'Applying 6 Sigma Methods for Breakthrough Safety Performance', *Professional Safety* 45, No. 10 (October 2000), 29–32; Lee Clifford, 'Why You Can Safely Ignore Six Sigma', *Fortune* (January 22, 2001), 140.

33. Michael Hammer and Jeff Goding, 'Putting Six Sigma in Perspective', *Quality* (October 2001), 58–62; Michael Hammer, 'Process Management and the Future of Six Sigma', *Sloan Management Review* (Winter 2002), 26–32.

34. 'On Balance', a CFO Interview with Robert Kaplan and David Norton, *CFO* (February 2001), 73–78; Chee W. Chow, Kamal M. Haddad and James E. Williamson, 'Applying the Balanced Scorecard to Small Companies', *Management Accounting* 79, No. 2 (August 1997), 21–27; and Robert Kaplan and David Norton, 'The Balanced Scorecard: Measures That Drive Performance', *Harvard Business Review* (January–February 1992), 71–79.

35. Based on Kaplan and Norton, 'The Balanced Scorecard'; Chow, Haddad and Williamson, 'Applying the Balanced Scorecard'; Cathy Lazere, 'All Together Now', *CFO* (February 1998), 28–36.

36. Debby Young, 'Score It a Hit', *CIO Enterprise*, Section 2 (November 15, 1998), 27ff.

37. Nils–Göran Olve, Carl-Johan Petri, Jan Roy and Sofie Roy, 'Twelve Years Later: Understanding and Realizing the Value of Balanced Scorecards', *Ivey Business Journal* (May–June 2004), 1–7.

38. William Davig, Norb Elbert and Steve Brown, 'Implementing a Strategic Planning Model for Small Manufacturing Firms: An Adaptation of the Balanced Scorecard', *SAM Advanced Management Journal* (Winter 2004), 18–24.

39. 'British Airways reveals what went wrong with Terminal 5', *Computer Weekly*, Wed 14 May, 2008 http://www.computerweekly.com/news/2240086013/British-Airwaysreveals-what-went-wrong-with-Terminal-5, accessed 2 May, 2013

40. Lizzie Porter, 'Heathrow Terminal 5 baggage: no bags for a week', *Daily Telegraph*, July 4, 2014, accessed at www.telegraph.co.uk/travel/news/Heathrow-Terminal-5-baggage-no-bags-for-a-week/

41. John Collins, 'pTools creates Ireland's largest intranet for HSE', *Irish Times*, 2 May, 2008.

42. Melanie Warner, 'Under the Knife', *Business 2.0* (January–February 2004), 84–89.

43. Wayne Kawamoto, 'Click Here for Efficiency', *BusinessWeek Enterprise* (December 7, 1998), Ent. 12–Ent. 14.

44. 'Bat keeps data on the move', *Computer Weekly*, 9 October, 2007.

45. Esther Shein, 'The Knowledge Crunch', *CIO* (May 1, 2001), 128–132.

46. Derek Slater, 'What is ERP?' *CIO Enterprise*, Section 2 (May 15, 1999), 86; and Jeffrey Zygmont, 'The Ties That Bind', *Inc. Tech* No. 3 (1998), 70–84.

47. Vincent A. Mabert, Ashok Soni and M. A. Venkataramanan, 'Enterprise Resource Planning: Common Myths versus Evolving Reality', *Business Horizons* (May–June 2001), 69–76.

48. Slater, 'What Is ERP?'

49. 'David Sadler, Lonely Planet's globetrotting finance chief –Off the beaten track', *Accountancy Age*, 6 January, 2005; Sue Sutton, 'The Lonely Planet Guide to SAP', August 2006, accessed at http://www.docstoc.com/docs/16402078/Microsoft-PowerPoint—sutton—SAUG-Presentation—Sue-Sutton on September 15, 2013; Mahesh Sharma, 'Lonely Planet strengthens its web', *The Australian*, 24 July, 2007; 'BBC Spends £75m on Lonely Planet', *Daily Mail*, 2 October 2007; Victoria Arnstein, 'Falling prices hit Lonely Planet', *The Bookseller*, 14 May,

2008, accessed at http://www.thebookseller.com/news/falling-prices-hit-lonely-planet.html on September 15, 2013.

50. Owen Thomas, 'E-Business Software: Bollinger Shipyards', *eCompany* (May 2001), 119–120.

51. Lisa Campbell, 'Lonely Planet sees profits growth', *The Bookseller*, January 2, 2014, www.thebookseller.com/news/lonely-planet-sees-profits-growth; Tom Robbins, 'Travel guidebooks come back from the brink', *Financial Times*, February 12, 2016, accessed at www.ft.com/cms/s/0/f3125754-cfe7-11e5-92a1-c5e23ef99c77.html.

52. Susannah Patton, 'Doctors' Group Profits from ERP,' *CIO* (September 1, 2003), 32.

53. Pat Garrehy, 'Manufacturing Cloud ERP – What Can We Agree Upon?', *Industrial Maintenance & Plant Operation*, 1 April, 2013.

54. Research reported in Eric Seubert, Y. Balaji and Mahesh Makhija, 'The Knowledge Imperative', *CIO Advertising Supplement* (March 15, 2000), S1–S4.

55. Andrew Mayo, 'Memory Bankers', *People Management* (January 22, 1998), 34–38; Gary Abramson, 'On the KM Midway', *CIO Enterprise*, Section 2 (May 15, 1999), 63–70.

56. David A. Garvin, 'Building a Learning Organization', in *Harvard Business Review on Knowledge Management* (Boston, MA: President and Fellows of Harvard College, 1998), 47–80.

57. Based on Mayo, 'Memory Bankers'; William Miller, 'Building the Ultimate Resource', *Management Review* (January 1999), 42–45; and Todd Datz, 'How to Speak Geek', *CIO Enterprise*, Section 2 (April 15, 1999), 46–52.

58. Vikas Anand, William H. Glick and Charles C. Manz, 'Thriving on the Knowledge of Outsiders: Tapping Organizational Social Capital', *Academy of Management Executive* 16, No. 1 (2002), 87–101.

59. Tony Kontzer, 'Kitchen Sink: Many Collaborative Options', *Information Week* (May 5, 2003), 35; sidebar in Tony Kontzer, 'Learning to Share', *Information Week* (May 5, 2003), 29–37.

60. Richard McDermott, 'Why Information Technology Inspired but Cannot Deliver Knowledge Management', *California Management Review* 41, No. 4 (Summer 1999), 103–117.

61. Based on Ikujiro Nonaka and Hirotaka Takeuchi, *The Knowledge-Creating Company: How Japanese Companies Create the Dynamics of Innovation* (New York: Oxford University Press, 1995), 8–9; and Robert M. Grant, 'Toward a Knowledge-Based Theory of the Firm', *Strategic Management Journal* 17 (Winter 1996), 109–122.

62. Grant, 'Toward a Knowledge-Based Theory of the Firm'.

63. Martin Schulz, 'The Uncertain Relevance of Newness: Organizational Learning and Knowledge Flows', *Academy of Management Journal* 44, No. 4 (2001), 661–681.

64. C. Jackson Grayson, Jr and Carla S. O'Dell, 'Mining Your Hidden Resources', *Across the Board* (April 1998), 23–28.

65. Based on Morten T. Hansen, Nitin Nohria and Thomas Tierney, 'What's Your Strategy for Managing Knowledge?' *Harvard Business Review* (March–April 1999), 106–116.

66. Kontzer, 'Learning to Share'.

67. Michael A. Fontaine, Salvatore Parise and David Miller, 'Collaborative Environments: An Effective Tool for Transforming Business Processes', *Ivey Business Journal* (May–June 2004); Mary Flood, 'Hawk Vote for California Firm Unanimous', *Houston Chronicle* (May 15, 2001), 15;

and 'Firm Finalist for Innovation,' *The Nelson Mail* (May 23, 2003), 4.

68. 'Cumulative Sales of TMC Hybrids Top 2 Million Units in Japan', November 8, 2012, TMC press release.

69. Hirotaka Takeuchi, Emi Osono and Norihiko Shimizu, 'Contradictions are the drivers of Toyota's success', Business Day (South Africa), 23 June, 2008; Japanese scholar explains use of explicit and tacit knowledge in business, Thai News Service, 22 February, 2008; Nonaka, I. and Konno, N. (1998), 'The Concept of "Ba": Building a Foundation for Knowledge Creation', *California Management Review*, 3, 40–54; Ron Sanchez, 'Tacit Knowledge versus Explicit Knowledge, Approaches to Knowledge Management Practice', Copenhagen Business School, IVS/CBS Working Paper 2004-01; Stefan Thomke and Takahiro Fujimoto (2000), 'The effect of 'front-loading' problem-solving on product development performance, *Journal of Product Innovation Management,* 17, 128–142.

70. Doug Bolton, 'Apple and Google are further ahead with their self-driving cars than previously thought, says Daimler CEO Dieter Zetsche said the two companies "can do more and know more" about the developing industry than he expected', *The Independent*, Monday 25, January 2016, accessed at www.independent.co.uk/life-style/gadgets-and-tech/news/apple-google-self-driving-autonomous-car-a6833526.html; Roger Schreffler, 'Toyota Remains Unchallenged Global Hybrid Leader', *WardsAuto*, August 20, 2014, accessed at wardsauto.com/industry/toyota-remains-unchallenged-global-hybrid-leader

71. 'All wired up', *Caterer & Hotelkeeper*, 2 August, 2007.

72. Steven A. Melnyk and David R. Denzler, *Operations Management: A Value-Driven Approach* (Burr Ridge, IL: Richard D. Irwin, 1996), 613.

73. Jim Turcotte, Bob Silveri and Tom Jobson, 'Are You Ready for the E-Supply Chain?' *APICS – The Performance Advantage* (August, 1998), 56–59.

74. Olivia Barrow, 'Corrugated materials maker looks to build $200M mill in Milwaukee area', *Milwaukee Business Journal*, October 28, 2015, accessed at www.bizjournals.com/milwaukee/news/2015/10/28/corrugated-materials-maker-looks-to-build-200m.html

75. 'Technology Succeeds with Innovation', 2013, SWC Technology Partners case study, accessed at http://www. swc.com/swc-technology-partners/success/corrugatedsupplies-company-csc-success.

76. Katherine Doherty, 'Light Speed; Distributors in Europe are achieving 99.99 percent accuracy in deliveries and reducing headcount with automated material handling systems', *Food Logistics*, 1 December, 2005. 'Long-time MicroStrategy Customer Recognized as "Smartest Organization in the Netherlands" ', *PR Newswire (U.S.)*, 28 May, 2008.

77. Sandra Swanson, 'Get Together', *Information Week* (July 1, 2002), 47–48.

78. 'Dutch supermarket Albert Heijn - convenience to go', 25 March, 2013, *Retail Week*.

79. 'Albert Heijn To Go to Receive Renewed Focus', *IGD Retail Analysis*, March 7, 2016, accessed at retailanalysis.igd.com/Hub.aspx?id=23&tid=3&nid=15015

80. Christopher Koch, 'It All Began with Drayer', *CIO* (August 1, 2002), 56–60.

81. Brian Caulfield, 'Facing Up to CRM', *Business 2.0* (August–September 2001), 149–150; and 'Customer Relationship Management: The Good, The Bad, The Future', special advertising section, *BusinessWeek* (April 28, 2003), 53–64.

82. Timothy J. Mullaney, 'E-Biz Strikes Again', *BusinessWeek* (May 10, 2004), 80–90.

83. Christopher Barnatt, 'Embracing E-Business', *Journal of General Management* 30, No. 1 (Autumn 2004), 79–96.

84. 'Tesco.com Under Fire from Rivals Over Home Deliveries', *The Evening Standard,* October 5, 2007.

85. Andy Reinhardt, 'Tesco Bets Small – and Wins Big', *BusinessWeek E.Biz* (October 1, 2001), EB26–EB32; and Patrick Barwise and Sean Meehan, 'The Benefits of Getting the Basics Right', *Financial Times* (October 8, 2004), 4.

86. Tesco PLC: Rise of online shopping drives new jobs at Tesco.com, 21 January 2013, 4-traders; AT Kearney UK, 'A Fresh Look at Online Grocery', March 2012.

87. Vanessa Henry, 'The growth potential of online shopping', *IGD*,July 14, 2015, accessed at www.igd.com/Research/Shopper-Insight/The-growth-potential-of-online-grocery/

88. This discussion is based on Ranjay Gulati and Jason Garino, 'Get the Right Mix of Bricks and Clicks', *Harvard Business Review* (May–June 2000), 107–114.

89. David L. Margulius, 'How to know when to keep great ideas in-house or launch a startup', *InfoWorld*, 4 December, 2006.

90. Emeka Obiodu, 'Portugal Telecom Spins Off PT Multimedia', *Global Insight Daily Analysis*, 12 November, 2007.

91. Magyar Telekom restructures business divisions along retail, corporate lines, *MTI – EcoNews*, 26 September, 2007.

92. Rob Ferguson, 'Thomson moves to sell all its papers except Globe – Former publishing giant concentrates on e-commerce', *The Toronto Star*, 16 February, 2000; 'Thomson hunting for new acquisitions', *The Globe and Mail*, 6 December 2006, B12.

93. 'Investors Pull the Rug Out of Brandwise.com', *The Globe and Mail (Canada)*, June 1, 2000.

94. 'In praise of … Abebooks', *The Guardian*, 5 October, 2006; Michael Gove, 'The net: not guilty of grievous harm to bookshops', *The Times*, April 24, 2007; Abebooks and Amazon pair up, *The Bookseller*, 11 October, 2002. On August 1, 2008 Amazon provisionally agreed to buy Abebooks (Amazon Acquires AbeBooks, *FinancialWire*, 3 August, 2008).

95. Richard Tyler, 'Home-based work a growing lifestyle', *Daily Telegraph*, 30 October,2007.

96. Andrew Blackman, 'A Strong Net Game', *The Wall Street Journal* (October 25, 2004), R1, R11.

97. 'Alan Swale turns to internet to improve marketing', *Dairy Farmer*, 16 October, 2006.

98. Stephanie Overby, 'Paving over Paperwork', *CIO* (February 1, 2002), 82–86.

99. 'India finance: Back office to the world', *Economist Intelligence Unit – Executive Briefing* 310, 20 February, 2003.

100. Siobhan O'Mahony and Stephen R. Barley, 'Do Digital Telecommunications Affect Work and Organization? The State of Our Knowledge', *Research in Organizational Behavior* 21 (1999), 125–161.

101. Lisa Kelly, 'Case study: The British Council', *Computing*, 7 August, 2008; *Annual Report 2007 / 2008*, British Council.

102. O'Mahony and Barley, 'Do Digital Telecommunications Affect Work and Organization?'

103. Brian Robinson, Canada to build nationwide health surveillance system, *Federal Computer Week*, 14 September 2006; http://web.archive.org/web/20081012080336/http://www.infoway-inforoute.ca/en/WhatWeDo/overview.aspx accessed on September 15, 2013; Terrence Belford, 'Physician, upgrade thyself', *The Globe and Mail*, 15 September 2006.

104. Michael A. Fontaine, Salvatore Parise and David Miller, 'Collaborative Environments: An Effective Tool for Transforming Business Processes', *Ivey Business Journal* (May–June 2004).

105. Paul Webster, 'Take two apps… And call me in the morning', *The Globe and Mail*, 30 November, 2012.

106. Joanne Lee-Young and Megan Barnett, 'Furiously Fast Fashions', *The Industry Standard* (June 11, 2001), 72–79.

107. Efthymios Constantinides and Stefan J Fountain (2008), 'Web 2.0: Conceptual foundations and marketing issues', *Journal of Direct, Data and Digital Marketing Practice*, 9, 231–244; Roman Högg, Miriam Meckel, Katarina Stanoevska-Slabeva and Robert Martignoni (2006) 'Overview of business models for Web 2.0 communities', Proceedings of GeNeMe 2006, Dresden, 28–29 September, 23–37.

108. Miltiadis D. Lytras, Ernesto Damiani and Patricia Ordonez de Pablos (eds) (2008), *Web 2.0: The Business Model*, Heidelberg, Springer Verlag.

109. Spencer E. Ante, Has Facebook's Value Taken a Hit?, *BusinessWeek*, August 5, 2008; Facebook's 100 million members shows it's out of control, U-Wire, 28 August, 2008; Dave Morin, 'We just hit 100,000,000 Facebook users!!!' accessed at http://twitter.com/davemorin/statuses/898779449 on September 4, 2008.

110. John Letzing and Scott Thurm, 'After IPO, Facebook Insiders Make $775 Million', *The Wall Street Journal*, 15 January, 2013.

111. James Brumley, 'Facebook Inc: Buying FB Stock Is Just a Matter of When', *InvestorPlace*,March 28, 2016 accessed at investorplace.com/2016/03/facebook-stock-buy-fb-when/#.Vwps6aQrJjU

112. Can social networks make money?, *Financial Express*, 22 May, 2008; McKinsey Consulting, (2007) 'How business are using Web 2.0: A McKinsey global survey', *The McKinsey Quarterly*, accessed at http://www.mckinseyquarterly.com/Marketing/Digital_Marketing/How_businesses_are_using_Web_20_A_McKinsey_Global_Survey_1913 on April 16, 2009.

113. Claire McEntee, 'Iyomu Founder Prepares To Close Site', *Dominion Post*, 19 May, 2008.

114. 'Kid-targeted virtual worlds seek impact, Revenue' *Youth Markets Alert*, 1 May, 2008.

115. Saul Hansell, 'Google's Toughest Search Is for a Business Model', *The New York Times*, 8 April, 2002; Steven Syre, 'Aggressive or Overvalued?', *The Boston Globe*, 27 July, 2004.

116. Google Financial Tables accessed at http://investor.google.com/fin_data.html on September 4, 2008.

117. Andrew Martonik, 'Google announces Q4 and FY 2015 earnings: $74.5 billion in revenue for the year, $21.3 billion for Q4', *AndroidCentral*, February 1, 2016, accessed at www.androidcentral.com/google-releases-q4-and-full-2015-earnings

118. Cade Metz, 'Elon Musk's Billion-Dollar AI Plan is about far more than saving the world', *Wired*, December 1 2015, accessed at www.wired.com/2015/12/elon-musks-billion-dollar-ai-plan-is-about-far-more-than-saving-the-world/; Emma Finamore and Kunal Dutta, 'Tesla boss Elon Musk warns artificial intelligence development is "summoning the demon"', *Independent*, October 26, 2014, accessed at www.independent.co.uk/life-style/gadgets-and-tech/news/tesla-boss-elon-musk-warns-artificial-intelligence-development-is-summoning-the-demon-9819760.html

ORGANIZATION SIZE, LIFE CYCLE AND DECLINE

A LOOK INSIDE

Interpol

Interpol, the global policing organization, operates in a complex, shifting and contested environment. Just like transnational business, transnational crime has grown in the wake of globalization and new dangers have emerged, such as the rise of international terrorism. Interpol has to work with countries from every corner of the globe, fostering cooperation among people with different cultural values, languages and legal and political systems. Moreover, it must do it all with a budget of about $100 million (2015),[1] less than what London's Metropolitan Police spends every week.[2] In the scheme of international organizations, then, Interpol is quite small; around 650 employees, including many staff loaned from national police services. It is often misunderstood; it is not a global police force but rather a knowledge network that helps national police forces to quickly access information about suspected criminals, and to work together to deal with international criminal gangs.

At its most effective, Interpol has aided in the quick capture of murderers, terrorists and other fugitives. The organization has moved during the 21st century to respond to the changing environment. In the past, if a request for assistance and information on Mohammed Atta, one of the September 11 2001 terrorist leaders, for example, came into Interpol on a weekend, too bad – the agency was closed until Monday morning. Interpol 'Red Notices' (urgent, global wanted-persons alerts) could take up to 6 months to process and were sent out by economy post to save postage costs.

When Ron Noble took over Interpol in 2001, he knew that kind of slow response had to change. In his 13 years in charge of the organization, he focused on reducing bureaucracy and transforming the agency into a modern, fast-moving organization. Keeping Interpol open 24 hours a day, 7 days a week, was one of his first changes. A policy of issuing red alerts for terrorists within 24 hours and notices for less threatening criminals within 72 hours went into effect immediately after September 11, 2001. Noble reorganized Interpol to increase speed and flexibility and to focus on the 'customer' (law enforcement groups in 179 member countries). Today, the most critical notices are translated immediately, posted online and sent via express delivery service.

The reorganization also included mechanisms for better coordination and information gathering. The goal is for Interpol to become the number one global police agency, one that coordinates and leads a multidimensional crime-fighting approach. Combatting terrorism and organized crime requires that everyone has the information they need when they need it and that local police, judicial, intelligence, diplomatic and military services all work together.

At the same time, Interpol needs to address the risk that some law enforcement agencies in repressive countries misuse Interpol's capacity to launch worldwide hunts for supposedly 'most-wanted' criminals. Interpol has been regularly criticised in recent years for doing the bidding of authoritarian regimes by agreeing to put dissidents on the Red Notice list, leading to a number of cases where it has been claimed that political dissidents have been arrested and even deported to face uncertain justice in authoritarian countries. A 2011 International Consortium of Investigative Journalists report found that at least 17 repressive countries issue 'Red Notices', a 2013 study by the charity Fair Trial found that Interpol's actions were "out of step with international asylum and extradition law", and a 2015 study by the Poland-based Open Dialogue Foundation highlighted a number of cases where Interpol maintains Red Notices issued by authoritarian governments against opponents who have been granted political asylum in third countries. Interpol needs to balance increasing efficiency with the need for transparency and respect for international human rights norms.[3]

Linked with the tricky dilemma of how to deal with police requests from unsavoury regimes, Interpol is challenged by figuring out how to respond to international terrorism. Under Ron Noble, who retired in 2014, the organization took a lead in fostering international collaboration against terrorism, but has been accused of ignoring the political motivations behind many actions of states claiming to fight terrorism, a response the scholar Mathieu Deflem has described as deriving from the inherent tendency of organizations to develop a bureaucratic rationality.

As organizations grow large and complex, they need more complex systems and procedures for guiding and controlling the organization. These characteristics can cause problems of inefficiency, rigidity and slow response time. They can also lead organizations to act according to pre-written rules, without considering the underlying moral or political issues. Every organization – from international agencies like Interpol to locally owned restaurants and hairdressing salons – wrestles with questions about organizational size, bureaucracy and control.

During the twentieth century, large organizations became widespread and bureaucracy has become a major topic of study in organization theory.[4] Most large organizations have bureaucratic characteristics, which can be very effective. These organizations provide us with abundant goods and services and accomplish astonishing feats – explorations of Mars, overnight delivery of packages to any location in the world, the scheduling and coordination of the approximately 95 000 airline flights a day worldwide (2012)[5] – that are testimony to their effectiveness. On the other hand, bureaucracy is also accused of many sins, including inefficiency, rigidity demeaning routinized work, and at worst, the inability to make appropriate moral judgments.[6]

Purpose of this Chapter

In this chapter, we explore the question of the growth of organizations, and how size relates to structure and control. In the first section, we look at the advantages of large versus small size. Then, we explore what is called an organization's life cycle and the structural characteristics at each stage. Next, we examine the historical use of bureaucracy as a means to control large organizations and compare bureaucratic control to various other control strategies. Finally, the chapter looks at the causes of organizational decline and discusses some methods for dealing with downsizing. By the end of this chapter, you should be able to recognize when bureaucratic control can make an organization effective and when other types of control are likely to prove more appropriate.

Organization Size: Is Bigger Better?

Pressures for Growth

A dream of many businesspeople is to have their company become a member of the FT Global 500 or the *Fortune* 500 lists – to grow fast and to grow big.[7] Sometimes this goal is more urgent than to make the best products or show the greatest profits. A decade ago, analysts and management scholars were heralding a shift away from 'bigness' toward small, nimble companies that could quickly respond in a fast-changing environment. Yet, despite the proliferation of new, small organizations, many of the giants such as Toyota, Procter & Gamble, Tesco and Wal-Mart have continued to grow.[8] In 2016, Tesco, for example, accounted for more than one quarter of all grocery sales in the UK, half as much again as its nearest competitor, Asda. Tesco had 300 000 employees and 3000 stores in 2013.[9] The company also holds about $25 billion worth of land for development in the UK, operates stores in 13 countries outside the UK and is the world's fourth largest retailer.[10]

Today, mega-corporations are an important part of the global business environment. Mergers have given rise to industry giants such as Nestlé, Citigroup and EE.[11] The global advertising industry is controlled by four huge agencies – London's WPP Group, Paris-based Publicis Groupe and the Omnicom Group and the Interpublic Group of Companies, both headquartered in New York.[12] These huge conglomerates own scores of companies that soak up more than half the ad industry's revenues and reach into the advertising, direct-mail marketing and public relations of every region on the planet. The growth of these agencies matches that of their clients, who are themselves growing larger and more global. Companies in all industries, from aerospace to consumer products to media, strive for growth to dominate markets and thereby expand their size and command resources to compete profitably on a global scale, to invest in new technology and to control distribution channels.[13]

Even large companies need to act nimbly to respond to rapidly changing market environments. For example, Sabanci Group, the Turkish owners of Teknosa, the country's leading chain of retail electronics shops, is facing increasing competition from European retail giants, as the country's economy integrates with Europe. Sabanci is responding on two levels. They entered into a partnership with French hypermarket giant Carrefour and at the same time invested heavily in bringing Teknosa up to international standards. They also introduced larger stores with a wider range of products that offer Turkish consumers the possibility of shopping at a familiar, trusted local retailer while enjoying the comfort and service standards that would be expected in Western Europe.[14,15] The growing capacity of emerging economy companies is demonstrated by the contrasting fortunes of Teknosa's wholly-owned electronics supermarkets, whose earnings grew 52 per cent in 2012–2013 on the back of a strong economy and consumer demand. By contrast, the Teknosa-Carrefour joint venture foundered, revenues dropping by half in the past four years, with Teknosa threatening to pull out of the alliance. Eventually, it was Carrefour that ceded ground, agreeing to reduce its share in the joint venture and leaving Teknosa in a clear controlling position. With growth in the capacity and maturity of the Turkish business sector, there has been a growing tendency for joint ventures to be bought out by the Turkish partners, as also occurred with Germany's Metro and Britain's Tesco, the latter selling out in 2015 to Turkish retail chain Beğendik.[16,17]

Whether nationally owned, part of a multinational, or a joint venture, scale is crucial to economic and political dominance in marketing-intensive companies such as Orange, Unilever, Nestlé and Procter & Gamble.[18] Greater size gives these companies power in the marketplace and thus increases revenues.[19]

**ONLINE
COUNTERPOINT 10.1**

Dilemmas of Large Size

What size organization is better poised to compete in a global environment? The arguments are summarized in Exhibit 10.1.

Large   Huge resources and economies of scale are often needed for organizations to compete globally. Only large organizations can build a massive oil and gas pipeline from Kazakhstan to Europe through the Caucasus. Only a large corporation like Airbus Industrie can build the world's first double-deck passenger aeroplane and only a large airline, such as Singapore Airlines, can afford to buy and operate it. Only a large pharmaceutical company like Germany's Bayer can invest hundreds of millions of euros developing new treatments ranging from Adalat for hypertension to new cancer treatments.[20] In addition, large organizations have the resources to be a supportive economic and social force in difficult times. In 2008, after floods in India's Bihar state killed over 1000 people and left at least 1.3 million stranded and homeless, the country's largest business conglomerate, Tata Group, sent 100 staff to work full-time on flood relief and in one week built 50 large temporary shelters.[21,22] Similarly, following the collapse of the Canadian airline Zoom in 2008, airline majors Virgin Atlantic and British Airways flew stranded holidaymakers back to the UK at greatly discounted fares, and the Baltic region's largest airline, Air Baltic, picked up travellers grounded by the failure of small Lithuanian airline Air Lituanica in 2015.[23,24,25] Large organizations also are able to get back to business more quickly following a disaster, giving employees a sense of security and belonging during an uncertain time.

Large companies are often standardized, mechanistically run and complex. The complexity offers hundreds of functional specialities within the organization to perform multifaceted tasks

EXHIBIT 10.1 Differences between Large and Small Organizations

LARGE

SMALL

Economies of scale
Global reach
Vertical hierarchy, mechanistic
Complex
Stable market
'Organization men'

Responsive, flexible
Regional reach
Flat structure, organic
Simple
Niche finding
Entrepreneurs

Source: Based on John A. Byrne, 'Is Your Company Too Big?' *BusinessWeek* (March 27, 1989), 84–94.

and to produce varied and complicated products. Moreover, large organizations, once established, can be a presence that stabilizes a market for years. Managers can join the company and still have reasonable prospects of a career reminiscent of the 'organization men' of the 1950s and 1960s. The organization can provide longevity, raises and promotions.

Small Small scale can provide significant advantages in terms of quick reaction to changing customer needs or shifting environmental and market conditions.[26] The largest transnational corporations declined in relation to the overall size of the world economy during the 1990s, though since 2000 their share of global wealth has risen again, driven to a large extent by mergers and acquisition[27] despite research which indicates that few mega-mergers live up to their expected performance levels.[28] A 2012 study found that, while smaller scale mergers can often improve economies of scale and thus subsequent performance, that the biggest 1 per cent of mergers and acquisitions tended to destroy value.[29] This chapter's *Bookmark 10.0* argues that one reason large companies sometimes fail is that top leaders become distant from the nuts and bolts of running the business. Any major strategic initiative, such as a merger, falters without careful planning as well as diligent execution.

ONLINE
COUNTERPOINT 10.2

BRIEFCASE 10.1

Despite the increasing size of many companies, small and mid-sized businesses are crucial to the economic vitality of both the developed and developing world. In the UK, for example, small businesses account for about 60 per cent of GDP.[30] Exporting is becoming a key business strategy for many small businesses around the world, such as in Sweden where the growth rate in exports for small businesses was three times as fast between 2002 and 2006 as for medium and large companies, although surveys indicated that by 2012 the proportion of Swedish small and medium sized businesses involved in exports had stalled at around 13 per cent.[31] The growth of the internet and other information technologies initially made it easier for small companies to act big, as described in Chapter 9, although consolidation and the entrance of bigger actors into the market is likely as new communications technologies mature. The growing service sector also contributes to a decrease in average organization size, as small service companies often have an advantage in better serving customers.

Small organizations typically have a comparatively flat structure and a more organic, free-flowing management style that enables entrepreneurship and innovation. Many of today's innovative drug treatments, for example, were discovered by small firms, such as Holland's PanGenetics, which focuses on developing treatments for immune diseases from the advanced research stage through to 'clinical proof of concept' – when the treatment's viability has been shown and larger companies are willing to invest in the bringing the product to market.[32] In 2009, for example, PanGenetics sold the rights to an innovative chronic pain management approach to Abbott, a US pharma major, for over $170 million.[33] To the extent that employees experience a personal involvement in small firms, this can encourage greater motivation and commitment.

Big-Company/Small-Company Hybrid   The advantages of small companies sometimes enable them to succeed and, paradoxically, grow large. Most of the firms on the *Europe's 500* list of the fastest-growing companies in Europe are relatively small and characterized by an emphasis on being fast and flexible in responding to change and emergent opportunities.[34,35] Small companies, however, can become victims of their own success as they grow large, shifting to vertical hierarchies and spawning 'organization men'. Giant companies tend to be 'built for optimization, not innovation'.[36] Big companies often become committed to their existing products and technologies and have a hard time encouraging innovation (see Counterpoint 10.1).

BRIEFCASE 10.2

COUNTERPOINT 10.1

The complexities associated with size, together with increased emphasis upon expanding the sale of existing services or goods, rather than engaging in further innovation, makes a move in the direction of bureaucracy attractive. The challenge is to consolidate to secure reliability without losing dynamism and innovation. Larger companies often rely upon acquisition to provide innovation as this allows the risks of innovation to be externalized. As we note later in this chapter, four-fifths of businesses that survive past the first year still fail within five years because they can't make the transition from the entrepreneurial stage.

One solution is what Jack Welch, the celebrated former chairman of General Electric (GE), called the 'big-company/small-company hybrid' that combines a large corporation's resources and reach with a small company's simplicity and flexibility. Stan Shih's web model of independent but interlinked businesses at Acer, discussed in Chapter 7, also combined the advantages of both small and large firms. Full-service global firms need a strong resource base and sufficient complexity and hierarchy to serve clients around the world. Size is not necessarily incompatible with speed and flexibility, as evidenced by large companies such as Google, Korea's Samsung and Britain's Virgin Group, which all continue to try new things and move quickly to change or challenge the prevailing rules or models of business.[37] The divisional structure, described in Chapter 4, is one way some large organizations strive to attain a big-company/small-company hybrid. One method is reorganizing into smaller autonomous divisions which are then empowered to think independently and imaginatively. In the 1990s Sony, facing the classic problems of inertia within a huge, successful firm, established the 'Company Within a Company System' in which divisional presidents reported to the CEO in much the same way as a CEO reports to an annual meeting. Sony's turnaround in the late 1990s is attributed to this approach, though like many organizational design changes, the impact wore off over time and the company has subsequently encountered further crises and reorganization.

BOOKMARK 10.0

Have you read this book?

In Search of Management

BY TONY WATSON

In this book Tony Watson, a UK professor of management, explores the working lives of contemporary managers. Through a case study of Ryland, a British engineering firm undergoing rapid changes in response to corporate reorganization and technological innovations, Watson explains how managers are both shaped by their environment – which they find increasingly impossible to control – and also are expected to direct their employees to meet the needs of that ever-changing environment. Watson's key concept is *strategic exchange*; the way in which humans seek both to exercise control over their own working lives while also searching for meaning and security in the external environment.

Watson's research approach is organizational ethnography. While traditionally ethnography has conjured up images of anthropologists living with exotic tribes, it is an approach increasingly used in management research and is particularly useful in understanding the dynamics and complexities of organizational culture. Watson spent a full year working as a manager inside Ryland, while also observing interactions, participating in daily routines and conducting in-depth interviews with about 60 Ryland managers.

Through the study, Watson explores the meaning of the term management, which he argues covers three different meanings; a function (the overall steering of an organization), activities (the specific actions involved in steering an organization) and the group of people responsible for steering an organization. He argues that weaknesses in the conceptualization and operationalization of the first two meanings of management are often mistakenly diagnosed as failings of the management team. As a result, managers are fired or reassigned, but the structural issues that hamper organizational effectiveness and productivity often go unaddressed.

The study shows how managers hold different and apparently conflicting attitudes to work and the company. When they look at the 'big picture' – continual workplace restructuring, job insecurity and apparent strategic incoherence – they tend to be critical or even negative about the organization. At the same time, however, they tended to be devoted to their own work and to express pride about doing a good job. Watson puts this down primarily to a basic human need for self-esteem. It is simply not sustainable for people to feel they are doing something that is not worthwhile, even if, speaking objectively, they often don't seem to be recognized for their hard work, whether this is with job security, enhanced salaries or even the sense that their ideas are valued and made use of.

Watson describes an organization that is far harder to manage than most textbooks would suggest and indeed an organization where the distinctions between 'good' and 'bad' management are far from clear. While there may be an official organizational culture, this tends to reflect a politically correct designation such as 'the learning organization', while in practice Ryland's managers acknowledged that there was also a culture of cost-cutting and layoffs that, while 'unofficial', in many ways more accurately reflected the dominant concerns of top managers in the company and its corporate parents. Beyond these overarching cultures, the organization was also segmented into various subcultures based on the divisions with which managers worked, their professional designations, their age group, etc. Therefore, organizational cohesiveness is not something that can be planned for through careful design of an organization chart of development of a strategic plan: 'productive cooperation is something that has to be striven for, in a context where conflicts and rivalries are inevitable' (p. 178). Overall, Watson found managers far more pressured and conflicted than the mythology of cool and collected Olympian leaders that is conveyed by popular media and advertising: 'The more I saw of the managers at Ryland, the more I became aware of the extent of human angst, insecurity, doubt and frailty among them'.

Watson's book seems to paint a much darker picture of organizational life than many business texts. But, really, his ethnography demonstrates that organizations cannot be abstracted from ordinary human life, which is full of contradictions, setbacks and conflict, as well as cooperation, harmony and periods of smooth sailing. Above all, organizations, made up of numerous individuals and countless different influences, are complex and ever-changing beasts. The manager will never be able to exercise absolute control, but must rather find the moments and the mechanisms whereby people can be motivated to work together to further both their own agendas and those of the organization for which they work.

In Search of Management, by Tony Watson, is published by Cengage Learning.

Another more recent approach involves selecting specific promising divisions within a company for special attention and investment, which can then foster an innovative culture throughout a large organization. In the mid-2000s, for example, the Switzerland-based engineering group ABB deliberately encouraged the growth through innovation of its Chinese subsidiary, enabling it to profit from synergy with China's dynamic economic environment with its capacity for rapid volume ramp-up.[38]

ONLINE COUNTERPOINT 10.3

The development of new organizational forms, with an emphasis on decentralizing authority and cutting out layers of the hierarchy, combined with the increasing use of information technology described in Chapter 9, can enable organizations to combine the dominance of being big with the agility of being small. The shift can even be seen in how terror-based forms of international conflict are organized, in what the social anthropologist Arjun Appadurai calls the transformation from vertebrate to cellular organization.[39,40] Appadurai notes that in contrast to the clear hierarchical structure of the nation state and its military forces, international terrorist organizations operate on a 'cellular' principle, where small groups of militants plan actions based not on the command decision-making structure of a traditional army, but through interpretation of a common set of principles that might be communicated through the internet, in religious sermons and tracts and satellite TV. In response, nation states also reorganize, carrying out their 'war on terrorism' based on smaller forces of highly skilled soldiers with access to up-to-the minute information and decentralized decision-making, unlike the First and Second World Wars, for example, which were fought with large masses of soldiers generally guided by decisions made at top levels.

Big companies also find a variety of ways to act both large and small. Australian cooperative conglomerate Wesfarmers, for example, purchased struggling Australian retailer Coles with the intention of using the advantage of size in areas such as raising capital, while turning around the chain by giving each individual store manager the autonomy to serve customers differently according to their local needs and tastes.[41,42] The company gave itself five years to turn around the Coles subsidiary, and by 2015 it was clear that the strategy had paid off, with the Coles division driving strong overall Wesfarmers results.[43] To encourage innovation, the giant corporation Royal Dutch/Shell created a strategy in its exploration-and-production division to set aside 10 per cent of the division's research budget for 'crazy' ideas. Anyone can apply for the funds and decisions are made not by managers but by a small group of nonconformist employees.[44] Small companies that are growing can also use these ideas to help their organizations retain the flexibility and customer focus that fuelled their growth.

Organizational Life Cycle

BRIEFCASE 10.3

A useful way to think about the process of organizational growth and change is the concept of an organizational life cycle.[45] This suggests that organizations are born, grow older and eventually die – either by failing or by being acquired, for example. Organization structure, leadership style and administrative systems follow a fairly predictable pattern through stages in the life cycle. Stages are sequential and follow a natural progression.

Stages of Life Cycle Development

Research on organizational life cycle suggests that organizational development is characterized by several major stages.[46] A four stage model is illustrated in Exhibit 10.2, along with the problems associated with transition to each stage. Growth is not easy. Each time an organization enters a new stage in the life cycle, it enters a new game with regard to both internal organization and the external environment.[47] For technology companies today, life cycles are getting shorter; to stay competitive, companies ranging from giants like Google to high growth companies like Holland's satnav manufacturer TomTom are seen to progress through the early stages of the cycle.

1 *Entrepreneurial stage.* When an organization is 'born', the emphasis is on creating a product or service and surviving in the marketplace. The founders tend to devote their full energies to the technical activities of production and marketing. The organization is often informal and nonbureaucratic. The hours of work are frequently long. Control is generally based on the owners' personal supervision. Growth is from a creative new product or service. For example, TomTom was founded in the early 1990s by two University of Amsterdam graduates, Peter-Frans Pauwels and Pieter Geelen. Pauwels and Geelen cut their teeth writing applications for the then popular Psion personal digital assistant (PDA). As improving technologies for handheld devices created new opportunities, they started building navigation software for PDAs, before finally realizing there was a huge market for standalone satnav devices in cars. In 2004 they launched their first TomTom device. By 2007 they were one of the fastest growing companies in Europe, built from the entrepreneurial and innovative vision of their founders.[48,49] Similarly, Apple Computer, maker of the iconic iPod, was in the entrepreneurial stage when it was created by Steve Jobs and Stephen Wozniak in Wozniak's parents' garage.

Crisis: Need for leadership. As the organization starts to grow, the larger number of employees can cause problems. The creative and technically oriented owners are confronted with management issues, but they may prefer to continue to focus their energies on making and selling the product or inventing new products and services. At this time of crisis, entrepreneurs must either adjust the design of the organization to accommodate continued growth or else bring in managers who can do so. When TomTom started to grow, they brought in Harold Goddijn, the former CEO of the early handheld computer manufacturer Psion, someone with solid experience in building a successful technology company.[50]

2 *Collectivity stage.* If the leadership crisis is resolved, the organization may then develop clearer goals and direction. Departments are established along with a hierarchy of authority, job assignments and a division of labour. At Google, founders Larry Page and Sergey Brin devoted their full energy to making sure Google provided the most powerful, fastest and simplest search engine available, then brought in a skilled manager, former Novell CEO Eric Schmidt, to run the company. Other experienced executives were hired to manage various functional areas and business units as the organization grew.[51] During this collectivity stage, employees may identify strongly with the mission of the organization and be willing to spend long hours helping the organization succeed. TomTom was in the collectivity stage during the rapid growth years from 2003 to 2008. Employees threw themselves into the business as the major product lines were established, with sales of the first TomTom device hitting 350 000.

Crisis: Need for delegation. If the new management has been successful, lower-level employees may gradually find themselves restricted by the emergence of top-down leadership. An autonomy crisis can develop as top managers, who were successful because of their strong leadership and vision, do not want to give up responsibility. Top managers want to make sure that all parts of the organization are coordinated and pulling together but middle-level managers are typically resistant to micro-management from above. During this

EXHIBIT 10.2   Organizational Life Cycle

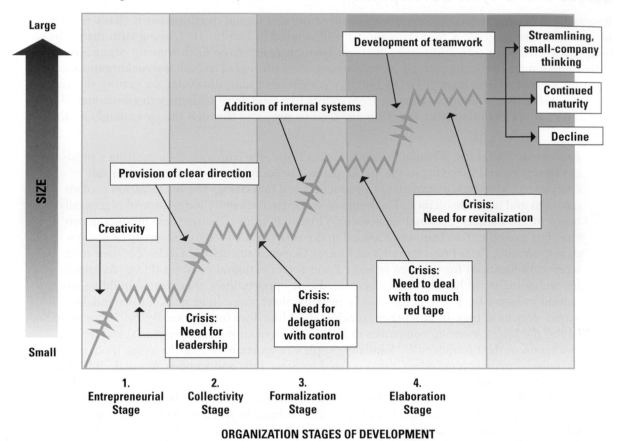

ORGANIZATION STAGES OF DEVELOPMENT

Source: Adapted from Robert E. Quinn and Kim Cameron, 'Organizational Life Cycles and Shifting Criteria of Effectiveness: Some Preliminary Evidence',
Management Science 29 (1983), 33–51; and Larry E. Greiner, 'Evolution and Revolution as Organizations Grow', *Harvard Business Review* 50 (July–
August 1972), 37–46.

phase, there is pressure to find mechanisms to control and coordinate departments without
reliance upon detailed supervision from the top.

3   *Formalization stage.* The formalization stage involves the installation and use of rules,
procedures and control systems. Communication is less frequent and more formal. Engineers, human resource specialists and other staff may be added. Top management becomes
concerned with issues such as strategy and planning and introduces systems to support
and monitor delegation of control of operations to middle management. Product groups or
other decentralized units may be formed to improve coordination. Incentive systems based
on profits may be implemented to ensure that managers work toward what is best for the
overall company. When effective, the new coordination and control systems can enable the
organization to continue growing by establishing linkage mechanisms between top management and field units.

   Crisis: Too much red tape. At this point, the proliferation of systems and programmes
may begin to stifle initiatives from middle-level executives. Middle management may resent
the intrusion of staff. Innovation may be restricted. It was at this stage of Apple's growth
that Jobs resigned from the company and a new CEO took control.

4   *Elaboration stage.* One solution to the red tape crisis is to engender a new sense of collaboration and teamwork. Managers are urged to develop skills for diagnosing problems

and working together. Social control and self-discipline can mitigate reliance upon formal controls. Managers learn to work within the bureaucracy without becoming excessively dependent upon it, or adding to it. Formal systems may be simplified and partially replaced by teams and task forces that may operate across functions or divisions of the company. Alternatively, the organization may be split into multiple divisions to maintain a small-company philosophy. Sony went through this elaboration stage of the life cycle in the 1990s.

Crisis: Need for revitalization. At some point, the organization loses momentum and enters a period of relative decline which may be temporary or terminal.[52] The organization shifts out of alignment with the environment or perhaps becomes slow moving and over-bureaucratized. To counter decline, efforts to streamline and innovate may be made. Under pressure from shareholders to revive company fortunes, top managers are often replaced. At Apple, the top spot changed hands a number of times as the company struggled to revitalize. Steve Jobs returned in mid-1997 to run the company he had founded nearly 25 years earlier. During those 25 years, Jobs had gained executive experience and management skills relevant to addressing Apple's lacklustre performance that he needed to help Apple through its problems. An older and smarter Jobs quickly reorganized the company, weeded out inefficiencies and refocused Apple on innovative products for the consumer market. Even more important, Jobs brought the entrepreneurial spirit back to Apple by moving the company in a whole new direction with the iPod music system. The iPod jump-started growth at Apple as the PC market declined. The iPod was then supplemented by the iPhone, which aimed to capture a chunk of the fast-growing mobile phone/PDA market. The iPhone was a legendary success, and was followed by the iPad, which created a largely new product category for tablet computers. Sales and profits jumped at Apple thanks to the iPod and iPhone.[53] Nevertheless, the company stumbled in 2016 as time passed from its last market-leading invention, especially after the death of the visionary Jobs, at the same time[54] as Samsung matches it glitz for glitz in the high end device market. In addition, Google and Amazon attempted to use their market muscle to force their way both into the hardware market and to dominate the growing revenue streams from internet purchases of music and apps.

Similarly, TomTom has faced a crisis because while it remains a dominant player in the standalone satnav market, smartphones nowadays have GPS integrated and many users don't bother buying a separate device. Like many companies, it has to turn itself from being a hardware company to one mainly focused on selling content and services across platforms, such as through the growing applications for internet connectivity in automobiles, with an eye to the growth of self-driving cars which will make extensive and critical use of GPS. Although by 2015 sales had declined considerably from their peak, as had revenues, share price stabilized (albeit at only one twentieth of its 2008 high), suggesting investors think TomTom has a chance of pulling off a successful reinvention of itself.[55] All mature organizations have to go through periods of revitalization or they face decline, as shown in the last stage of Exhibit 10.2.

Summary

In most countries, four-fifths of businesses that make it past the first year fail within five years because they lack the capacity to make the transition from the entrepreneurial stage.[56] The transitions can become even more difficult as organizations progress through future stages of the life cycle. Executives frequently do not successfully address the problems associated with these transitions, with the consequence that growth is restricted and so they fail or are acquired. From within an organization the life cycle crises are very real. For example, Lopez Holdings, one of the Philippines' best known conglomerates, nearly went out of business in the late 1990s after playing a leading business role in the country for one hundred years. Lopez is featured in the *In Practice* text box that follows.

Organizational Bureaucracy and Control

ONLINE
COUNTERPOINT 10.4

As organizations progress through the life cycle, they usually take on bureaucratic characteristics as they grow larger and more complex. The systematic study of bureaucracy can be traced to the work of Max Weber, a sociologist who sought to analyze and appreciate the significance of large, bureaucratic organizations in modern societies (see Counterpoint 10.2).

COUNTERPOINT 10.2

Weber was no enthusiast for bureaucracy except for its capacity to deliver 'due process' and thereby eliminate favouritism and nepotism. He was, however, interested in its significance for modern societies and therefore attempted to distil its distinctive features (see Exhibit 10.3). In principle, each client of a bureaucracy receives the same (standard, impersonal) treatment – good or bad. An important virtue of bureaucracy, Weber believed, was its removal of personal patronage and discrimination (see also below). Formalized recruitment and selection procedures increase the likelihood that employees are hired on the basis of their competence, not their skin colour, gender or personal connections. Likewise, customers can expect equal treatment, with no queue jumping or other favours. Specifically, Weber identified bureaucracy as simultaneously more efficient and more dehumanizing. Weber regarded the dehumanizing aspects as detrimental to productive, efficient organization as well as damaging to the human spirit. Critics of bureaucracy tend to emphasize the 'red tape', overlook the positive benefits of its 'impersonality' and conveniently disregard the limitations of alternatives to bureaucracy for dealing effectively and fairly with large, complex administrative tasks.

What is Bureaucracy?

Although Weber perceived bureaucracy as a potential threat to basic personal liberties, he also recognized it as the most formally rational and equitable system of organizing. He predicted the triumph of bureaucracy because of its ability to remove partiality and nepotism, and thereby deliver more efficient functioning of organizations in both business and government settings. Weber identified a set of organizational characteristics, listed in Exhibit 10.3, that typified bureaucratic organizations.

IN PRACTICE

Lopez Holdings

Lopez Holdings (formerly Benpres)[57] might not be a household name in Western Europe, but it's one of the largest and most successful business groups in the Philippines. Holdings range from television networks to water utilities, toll roads, land development and a major telephone company. In the past,

the company operated the country's first passenger airline, a steamship line and even imported double-decker buses from London, plying the streets of a provincial capital, Iloilo, in the 1930s.

The natural life cycle of corporations can be made much more complex in a developing country where business and politics are both intertwined and in conflict. Indeed, the company was built from the assets built up in a sugar hacienda that Eugenio, father of current chairman emeritus Oscar Lopez, inherited when his father, a provincial governor, was shot in a political assassination. During this *entrepreneurial* stage, the company began to transform itself from a largely agricultural undertaking into a major business

▶

player, although as expected in the classic entrepreneurial phase, there were both successes and failures. The brothers' airline was closed after it suffered too many crashes, but the company's sortie into the power business was a big success. Gradually the company moved into the *collectivity* phase. In 1961, Benpres bought out the American owners of the country's biggest electricity generator, Meralco. Under Benpres, Meralco was both profitable and produced cheap electricity that helped fuel the Philippines' economic development. Emboldened with the success, Benpres soon diversified into manufacturing electrical distribution transformers, again running an internationally competitive enterprise.

Once again, crisis came in the form of political problems. Eugenio had ambitions to create a media empire and purchased the country's biggest newspaper. Unfortunately this coincided with the rise to power of the dictator Ferdinand Marcos. Marcos took over most of the company's holdings and Eugenio fled to the US, where he died in 1975.

After Marcos himself was forced out of the Philippines, Oscar Lopez and his brothers came back to try to salvage the various arms of the company that had been seized and run into the ground. This called for a different type of leadership, capable of managing through a rebuilding of the *collectivity stage* but moving towards formalization. The Lopez brothers divided up responsibilities for the holdings and brought in a number of professional managers with the expertise needed to turn them around. By and large they were successful: the generating plants in particular were restored to full efficiency and investments made in clean technology.

But once again, Benpres fell into difficulty, this time economic rather than political. The Asian economic crisis of the late 1990s hit the Philippines particularly hard, with economic recession, declining currency and high inflation. Suddenly Benpres's debt burden became unsustainable and Benpres even had to suspend interest repayments for a while. Perhaps the company had become too secure, as can happen with the formalization stage; insufficiently attuned to the danger of sudden downturn. The crisis coincided with the death of Oscar's brother Geny, and Oscar's assumption of overall control of Benpres. Oscar's role has been mainly one of *elaboration* – emphasizing the strengthening of managerial skills and controls, rationalizing operations to ensure the business models in place were sustainable, selling off parts of the company that no longer fit a more focused business strategy. In 2010, at the age of 80, Oscar retired from daily responsibility to become Chairman Emeritus, handing the CEO role to younger brother Manuel.[58] Still it is only a matter of time before the next generation of this family-controlled corporation takes over. Will the new generation of managers launch a new phase of *revitalization*, or will the next phase in the life cycle be an end-stage, as Lawrence Miller warns in his seven-stage version of the life-cycle approach?[59]

Rules and standard procedures enabled organizational activities to be performed in a predictable, routine manner. Specialized duties meant that each employee had a clear task to perform. Hierarchy of authority provided a mechanism for supervision and control. Technical competence was the basis by which people were hired rather than friendship, family ties and favouritism. The separation of the position from the position holder meant that individuals did not own or have any inherent right to the job. Written records provided an organizational memory and continuity over time.

Bureaucracy provided many advantages over organization forms based on favouritism, social status, family connections and so on. For example, when he was appointed as commissioner of internal revenue in the Philippines some 30 years ago, Efren Plana found massive corruption, including officials hiring their relatives for high-ranking jobs and tax assessors winning promotions by bribing their superiors.[60] Likewise, Bill Browder, who made a fortune in Russia after the collapse of the Soviet Union, was eventually refused a visa to Russia because he declined to give a bribe to an Interior Ministry official.[61] The tradition of giving government posts to relatives is widespread in many countries, particularly in the developing world. As China's economy develops rapidly and integrates with the world economy, its government is trying to crack down on such nepotism,[62,63] although repeated scandals involving top Communist Party leaders between 2012 and again in 2016 connected to the offshore accounts revealed in the "Panama Papers", suggest

EXHIBIT 10.3   Weber's Dimensions of Bureaucracy

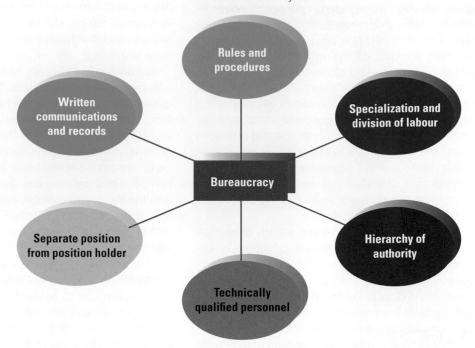

that any non-transparent, undemocratic political system is likely to generate corruption and abuse of power.[64] The logical and rational form of organization analyzed and indeed commended by Weber enables pre-bureaucratic inefficiencies to be reduced, if never entirely eliminated. In the *In Practice* feature that follows, we look at DHL, one of the largest courier companies in the world, now aiming to entrench itself as a big player in the rapidly developing third party logistics (3PL) market.

**ONLINE
COUNTERPOINT 10.5**

Bureaucratic characteristics tend to increase with large size. As DHL transitions into a global, knowledge-based logistics business, its managers are obliged to find effective ways to ensure that increased bureaucracy serves, rather than subverts, the company's business goals and does not detract from employee initiative. The new technology and emphasis on tailor-made logistics services place more demands on workers, who need flexibility and autonomy to perform well. In particular, the logistics business is moving from 3PL towards what is known as fourth-party logistics (4PL), where the logistics company carries out supply chain analysis, designs and even runs a tailor-made logistics system for the client company; DHL has quickly built a large business in this new field, for example taking over management of the large Swiss agricultural conglomerate Syngenta's transportation distribution system in 2016.[65] These types of services require flexibility, as the client and service-provider companies essentially integrate their activities in areas such as warehousing and distribution.

Size and Structural Control

BRIEFCASE 10.4

Large organizations tend to be different from small organizations along several dimensions of bureaucratic structure, including formalization, centralization and personnel ratios.

Formalization and Centralization   Formalization, as described in Chapter 1, refers to rules, procedures and written documentation, such as policy manuals and job descriptions, that prescribe the rights and duties of employees.[66] The evidence supports the conclusion

IN PRACTICE

DHL

DHL, owned by DeutschePost, the privatized German postal service, competes with America's UPS and FedEx, and Holland's TNT in the global courier market. DHL's strength is in its broad geographic coverage; customers can be pretty sure that the company will be able to deliver a package anywhere in the world, notwithstanding wars, political embargoes or mere isolation. Georgia Tech's Supply Chain and Logistics Institute proved the point with its 'Great Package Race'. For the 2007 race, they selected five out-of-the-way, dangerous, or politically isolated locations and tried to send packages to contacts in each, using DHL, UPS and FedEx. Only DHL was able to deliver to all five and at a lower overall cost than its competitors. Neither UPS nor FedEx accepted packages for Myanmar (Burma), probably due to a US government political boycott of that country. UPS lost a package to Samoa somewhere in New Zealand, perhaps because its agents told Georgia Tech that no such country as Samoa exists. FedEx failed to deliver a package to Harare, Zimbabwe, apparently because of an unpaid $1.00 customs fee – the recipient had to go and sort out the problem himself. UPS managed to get a package destined for Tikrit, the Iraq hometown of Saddam Hussein, only as far as Dubai, after which it spent a week in a warehouse in Louisville, Kentucky, before being returned to Georgia Tech. UPS even charged Georgia Tech for the package's long but fruitless journey.

In response to criticism that these delivery locations were very unusual and not a fair test of normal business flows, the Institute also sent a package from Atlanta to Singapore, a major courier destination. Again, DHL delivered before its competitors.[67]

In truth, all four of the major courier companies have remarkable capacities and excellent overall records; the results in other years' 'Great Courier Races' were less conclusive. But DHL has often come out on top when it comes to delivering to isolated international locations; its advantage is undoubtedly a network of offices in over 200 countries and its ability to deliver to 700 000 different locations. Only the state post offices can match its reach, but they lose a larger proportion of packages than DHL. International courier services are much more complex than domestic, involving not just pick-up and delivery, but customs clearance services, knowledge of different countries' rules regarding what can and cannot be carried, complexities of payment/billing when costs are incurred in several different currencies, intricacies of international insurance, etc. Such a capacity can only be sustained through a clear hierarchical accountability structure, a consistent set of rulebooks and rigid compliance to these rules. Package cut-off times have to be respected, planes have to depart and arrive on time, delivery staff have to complete their shifts on time, etc.

DHL is now aiming to turn its global reach into a competitive advantage in the rapidly expanding field of third party logistics (3PL). As companies small and large seek to globalize, they are faced with enormous logistical issues. Emerging markets typically lack the kinds of facilities taken for granted in developed countries, like good roads, secure storage facilities, consistent power supplies, transparent customs procedures, etc. The company that tries to set up a supply chain without intimate local knowledge is asking for trouble and will probably find it. Corporations with a global reach and local knowledge like DHL already have a rooted infrastructure, built on a bureaucratic structure of clear rules and operating procedures and can offer that ready-made organizational capacity for sale. DHL's Exel Supply Chain division offers services such as integrated IT solutions, warehouse operations and industry specific product distribution systems.[68]

Increasingly, the bureaucratic structure needed to manage a global logistical operation like that of DHL is intertwined with advanced informational technology systems. DHL has pioneered, for example, the use of radio frequency identification (RFID) discussed in Chapter 8, to enhance the tracking of packages,[69] and its 3PL arm has helped customers set up their own computer-based supply management systems. 3PL seems to have been a good strategy for DHL. In 2015, despite an economic slowdown in the large Chinese market, global 3PL growth for the next three years to 2018 was expected to be over 5% per year, and DHL is well-positioned to capture a good chunk of that, as one of the biggest industry actors.[70]

that large organizations are usually more formalized, as at DHL. A key reason for this is that executives in large organizations tend to rely on rules, procedures and paperwork to achieve control across large numbers of employees and departments, whereas top managers can use personal observation and informal contacts to control a small organization.[71]

ONLINE
COUNTERPOINT 10.6

Centralization refers to the level of hierarchy with authority to make decisions. In centralized organizations, decisions tend to be made at the top. In decentralized organizations, similar decisions are made at a lower level. Decentralization represents a paradox. It might seem that, in the perfect bureaucracy, all decisions would be made by the top administrator, who would have perfect control. However, as an organization grows larger and has more people and departments, decisions cannot be passed to the top because senior managers would be overloaded. Accordingly, larger organizations are often characterized by greater decentralization.[72]

Consider Honda, where in the early days Soichiro Honda and Takeo Fujisawa used to make every important decision. It was their daring insistence that the company's products could break into international markets that allowed the company to grow from tiny beginnings to become one of the world's great manufacturing enterprises. But, as Honda grew into a global automaker, the traditional, personal structure started to stand in the way of corporate development. When Honda and Fujisawa retired, the new CEO, Kiyoshi Kawashima, introduced what was called the New Honda Plan (NHP), in which leadership responsibilities would be greatly decentralized, permitting flexibility and early response to shifting circumstances in different parts of the now international firm. Under NHP, the company set up manufacturing plants around the world - a necessity. As the company continued to grow, its automobile, motorcycle and power product businesses were carved into separate autonomous divisions. The company was then further decentralized through establishment of four regional chief operating officers, for Japan, North America, Europe and the rest of the world, each having responsibility for production, research, sales and marketing.[73,74]

Personnel Ratios   Another characteristic of bureaucracy relates to personnel ratios for administrative and professional support staff. The most frequently studied ratio is the administrative ratio.[75] Two patterns have emerged. The first is that the ratio of top administration to total employees is usually smaller in large organizations,[76] indicating that organizations experience administrative economies as they grow larger. The second pattern concerns professional support staff ratios.[77] These tend to *increase* in proportion to organization size, because of the greater need for specialized skills in larger, complex organizations. The transformation of organizational structure as a result of new technology and outsourcing, and the consequent dramatic reduction in the proportion of traditional clerical staff, has significantly altered personnel structure and ratios in both the private and public sectors, although research suggests the impact varies according to the societal culture in which organizations operate, with Japanese businesses generally less affected than those in the UK and USA, for example.[78]

Exhibit 10.4 illustrates administrative and support ratios for small and large organizations. As organizations increase in size, the administrative ratio declines and the ratios for other support groups increase.[79] The net effect for direct workers is that they decline as a percentage of total employees. In summary, whereas top administrators do not make up a large proportion of employees in large organizations, they do tend to have proportionately greater overheads. In the twenty-first century, as a value chain approach to business resulted in the dismantling of many integrated organizations, many organizations outsourced administrative functions to specialized shared service organizations.[80]

ONLINE
COUNTERPOINT 10.7

Bureaucracy in a Changing World

Bureaucratic organizational characteristics have many advantages and have generally worked well in advancing the industrial age.[81] By establishing a hierarchy of authority and specific rules and procedures, bureaucracy provides an effective way to bring order to large groups of

EXHIBIT 10.4 Percentage of Personnel Allocated to Administrative and Support Activities

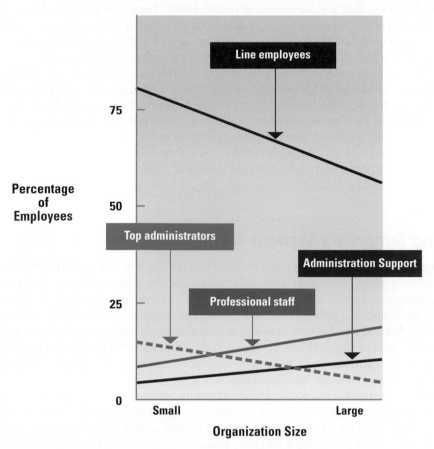

people and prevent abuses of power. Impersonal relationships are based on rules rather than the favouritism and nepotism characteristic of many preindustrial organizations. Bureaucracy provides systematic and rational ways to organize and manage tasks too complex to be understood and handled by a few individuals, thus greatly aiding the efficiency and effectiveness of large organizations.

The world is rapidly changing, however, and the machine-like bureaucratic system of the industrial age does not necessarily work well in the context of market-driven, fast capitalism in which organizations face new challenges, including rapidly changing, volatile trading environments and the rise of competitors using different, more flexible business models. Consider the difference between established airlines and their low-cost competitors and the difficulties the former have encountered either in reducing their overheads or establishing low-cost subsidiaries. At the same time, the low-cost competitors must rely upon bureaucratic procedures for their pared down operations. It is not that they operate without bureaucracy but, rather, that the bureaucracy is at once minimized and tightened by offering 'no frills'. In the process, 'exceptions' and 'outliers', such as passengers with unusual requirements, are treated in a way that is equivalent to those seeking insurance who are calculated to be bad risks. With global competition and uncertain environments, an alternative for many organizations is to minimize unproductive formalization and staff costs through outsourcing.

There are also significant differences between societies in attitudes towards bureaucracy that influence business and organizational life.[82] Some American critics have blamed government bureaucracy for intelligence, communication and accountability failures that helped lead to US disasters as diverse as the 2001 terrorist attacks, the *Columbia* space shuttle explosion, the abuses at Abu Ghraib prison and a slow response to the 2005 Hurricane Katrina devastation. 'Every time you add a layer of bureaucracy, you delay the movement of information up the chain of command ... And you dilute the information because at each step some details are taken out,' said Richard A. Posner, a federal appeals court judge who has written a book on intelligence reform.[83] However, the U.S. government Federal Emergency Management Agency was widely praised during Hurricane Sandy in 2012, demonstrating how a well-run bureaucratic organization can deliver when a comprehensive response to a complex event is required.[84] Many Europeans have tended to be more supportive of bureaucratically structured systems, believing that they are more stable and predictable and can provide better protection for the less powerful.[85] Nevertheless, at least until the onset of the global financial crisis that cast doubt on the neo-liberal model, overall global isomorphic trends still appeared to favour market-driven organizations rather than rule-driven bureaucracies.[86]

Organizing Temporary Systems for Flexibility and Innovation

How can organizations overcome the problems of bureaucracy in rapidly changing environments? Some are implementing innovative structural solutions. In organizations that have to respond rapidly to emergency or crisis situations, such as police and fire services or other emergency management agencies, an approach called the *incident command system* (ICS) has been devised. The incident command system was developed to maintain the efficiency and control benefits of bureaucracy yet prevent the problem of slow response to crises.[87] The approach is being adapted by other types of organizations to help them respond quickly to new opportunities, unforeseen competitive threats or organizational crises.

ONLINE
COUNTERPOINT 10.8

The ICS is intended to enable organizations to glide smoothly between a highly formalized, hierarchical structure effective during times of stability, and a more flexible, loosely structured one capable of responding to unexpected and demanding environmental conditions. The hierarchical side with its rules, procedures and chain of command helps maintain control and ensure adherence to rules that have been developed and tested over many years to cope with well-understood problems and situations. During times of high uncertainty, the most effective structure can be one that loosens the lines of command and enables people to work across departmental and hierarchical lines to anticipate, avoid and solve unanticipated problems, albeit within the context of a clearly understood mission and guidelines.

BRIEFCASE 10.5

Following large scale terrorist attacks in the US, Spain, India, UK and other countries in the first years of the twenty-first century, much greater attention has been paid to the management of crisis situations. For example, weaknesses in the early warning and disaster response systems dealing with the south Asian tsunami of 26 December 2004, which caused over 350 000 deaths, led to development of an Asian ICS involving international collaboration of emergency authorities.[88]

Another type of potential natural disaster is a disease pandemic in which a substantial proportion of the population would become very sick in a short period of time, overstretching the capacities of the healthcare system. Health authorities are particularly concerned about the potential for an influenza pandemic, possibly spread through infected poultry. British health authorities have developed a Pandemic Influenza Plan, which outlines the command system for such a crisis, as well as identifying the healthcare responses to different levels of pandemic. While the overall care framework is established through the ICS command structure, the Plan requires individual clinicians to make the necessary difficult local decisions about the kinds of treatment and to whom, that will be offered in a situation where the numbers of sick far exceeds the availability of beds in hospitals.[89] The Ebola pandemic of 2013 - 2016 in West Africa demonstrated the devastation that can occur when capacity and resources are not in place and able to ramp up quickly to deal with an emergent threat.

LEADING BY DESIGN

The Salvation Army

The Salvation Army has been called 'the most effective organization in the world' by a leading management scholar. One reason the organization is so effective and powerful is its approach to organizing, which makes use of the incident command system to provide the right amount of structure, control and flexibility to meet the requirements of each situation. The Salvation Army refers to its approach as 'organizing to improvise'.

The Salvation Army provides day-to-day assistance to the homeless and economically disadvantaged. In addition, the organization is involved whenever there is a major disaster – whether it be a tornado, flood, hurricane, airplane crash or terrorist attack – to network with other agencies to provide disaster relief. Long after the most desperate moments of the initial crisis have passed, the Salvation Army continues helping people rebuild their lives and communities – offering financial assistance; meeting physical needs for food, clothing and housing; and providing emotional and spiritual support to inspire hope and help people build a foundation for the future. The Army's management realizes that emergencies demand high flexibility. At the same time, the organization must have a high level of control and accountability to ensure its continued existence and meet its day-to-day responsibilities. As a former national commander puts it, 'We have to have it both ways. We can't choose to be flexible and reckless or to be accountable and responsive … We have to be several different kinds of organizations at the same time.'

In the early emergency moments of a crisis, the Salvation Army deploys a temporary organization that has its own command structure. People need to have a clear sense of who's in charge to prevent the rapid response demands from degenerating into chaos. For example, if the Army responds to a flood in Indonesia or a tornado in Oklahoma, manuals clearly specify in advance who is responsible for talking to the media, who is in charge of supply inventories, who liaises duties with other agencies and so forth. This model for the temporary organization keeps the Salvation Army responsive and consistent. In the later recovery and rebuilding phases of a crisis, supervisors frequently give people general guidelines and allow them to improvise the best solutions. There isn't time for supervisors to review and sign off on every decision that needs to be made to get families and communities re-established.

Thus, the Salvation Army actually has people simultaneously working in all different types of organization structures, from traditional vertical command structures, to horizontal teams, to a sort of network form that relies on collaboration with other agencies. Operating in such a fluid way enables the organization to accomplish amazing results. In the first month of 2013 alone, the Salvation Army helped victims of election-based violence in Kenya and ethnic strife in India, a typhoon in the Philippines and flooding in Mozambique, in addition to many more served by regular day-to-day programmes. It has been recognized as a leader in putting money to maximal use, meaning donors are willing to give because they trust the organization to be responsible and accountable at the same time as it is flexible and innovative in meeting human needs.

Sources: www.salvationarmy.org; Peter Walker and Daniel G. Maxwell (2008), *Shaping the Humanitarian World*, London, Taylor & Francis; Robert A. Watson and Ben Brown, *The Most Effective Organization in the U.S.: Leadership Secrets of the Salvation Army* (New York: Crown Business, 2001), 159–181.

The international religious charity *The Salvation Army* has long and successful experience in dealing with emergencies, from which many private and public organizations could learn. The Salvation Army's approach is discussed in the *Leading by Design* box above.

Other Approaches to Reducing Bureaucracy

A further impact of, and on, bureaucracy is the increasing *professionalism* of employees. Professionalism is defined as the length of formal training and experience of employees. More employees

ONLINE
COUNTERPOINT 10.9

need college degrees, MBAs and other professional degrees to work as attorneys, researchers or doctors at large firms like Toyota, Tesco and GlaxoSmithKline. In addition this bureaucratic process of credentialization studies of professionals shows that professional training regularizes a high standard of behaviour for employees. This is at once the product of educational bureaucracies and acts as a substitute for bureaucracy.[90] Companies extend this process when they provide ongoing formal training for *all* employees, from the front office to the shop floor, in a push for continuous individual and organizational skill acquisition. Increased training substitutes for bureaucratic rules and procedures that can constrain the creativity of employees in solving problems and increasing organizational capability.

Organizational Decline and Downsizing

Earlier in the chapter we discussed the organizational life cycle, which suggests that organizations are born, grow older and eventually die. Every organization goes through periods of temporary decline. In this section, we examine the causes and stages of organizational decline and then discuss how leaders can effectively manage the downsizing that is a reality for many companies in an era of low growth and intense competition.

Definition and Causes

The term organizational decline is used to define a condition in which a substantial, absolute decrease in an organization's resource base occurs over a period.[91] Organizational decline is often associated with some wider environmental decline – in the sense that an organizational domain experiences either a reduction in size (such as shrinkage in customer demand or erosion of a city's tax base) or a reduction in shape (such as a shift in customer demand). In general, three factors are considered to cause organizational decline.

1 *Organizational atrophy.* Atrophy occurs when organizations grow older and become inefficient and overly bureaucratized such that the ability to adapt deteriorates. Atrophy may follow a long period of success, because an organization takes success for granted, becomes attached to practices and structures that worked in the past and fails to adapt to changes in the environment.[92] For example, Blockbuster Inc., which was king of the videostore industry in the 1980s and 1990s, struggled to adapt to the new world of online film rentals and digital downloading. Blockbuster's US operations went bankrupt and were bought out by a pay TV company in 2011, the Canadian operations were closed in 2012, and the UK subsidiary itself fell into bankruptcy in 2013.[93] Companies risk becoming obsolete by sticking to patterns that were successful in the past but might no longer be effective.[94]

2 *Vulnerability.* Vulnerability reflects an organization's strategic inability to prosper in its environment. Small organizations that are not yet fully established are especially vulnerable to shifts in consumer tastes or in the economic health of the larger community. Small e-commerce companies are the first to go out of business when the technology sector goes into a downturn. Vulnerable organizations typically need to redefine their environmental domain in order to serve new industries or markets.

3 *Environmental decline or competition.* Environmental decline refers to reduced energy and resources available to support an organization. When the environment has less capacity to support an organization, managers have either to scale down operations or shift to another domain.[95] New competition increases the problem, especially for small organizations. The emergence of first Japan and the 'Asian tigers', and now China as major low cost manufacturers, has sounded the death knell for huge swathes of Western industry, ranging from home appliances to vehicle parts.[96] Of course, during generalized economic crises, such as

afflicted the global economy in the global financial crisis, environmental decline is also generalized and only a few 'counter-cyclical' industries, or those capable of making savage cuts in their costs by shedding activities or employees, are likely to prosper.[97]

A Model of Decline Stages

A model of decline stages is summarized in Exhibit 10.5. This model suggests that decline, if not countered successfully or managed effectively, can move through five stages resulting in organizational dissolution.[98]

BRIEFCASE 10.6

1 *Blinded stage.* The first stage of decline is the internal and external change that threatens long-term survival. Leaders often miss the signals of decline. The relevant antidote is the development of effective scanning and control systems, and executives willing to risk playing 'devil's advocate', that indicate when something is wrong. With timely information, alert executives can bring the organization back to top performance.

2 *Inaction stage.* The second stage of decline is called inaction in which denial occurs despite signs of deteriorating performance. Leaders may try to persuade employees that all is well. 'Creative accounting' may make things look healthy during this period. The solution is for leaders to acknowledge decline and take prompt action to realign the organization with the environment. Leadership actions may include new problem-solving approaches, increasing decision-making participation and encouraging expression of dissatisfaction to learn what is wrong.

3 *Faulty action stage.* In the third stage, leaders are forced by severe circumstances to consider major changes. Actions may involve retrenchment, including downsizing personnel. A major mistake at this stage decreases the organization's chance for a turnaround.

4 *Crisis stage.* In the fourth stage, the organization still has not been able to deal with decline effectively. There may be organization chaos, efforts to go back to basics, sharp changes, disenchantment and anger. The social fabric of the organization is eroding and dramatic actions, such as replacing top administrators and revolutionary changes in structure, strategy and culture, are necessary. Workforce downsizing may be severe.

5 *Dissolution stage.* This stage of decline is irreversible. There is a terminal loss of confidence and reputation, the loss of its best personnel and capital depletion. The only available strategy is to close down the organization in an orderly fashion and reduce the separation trauma of employees.

The *In Practice* example of Alitalia on the next page shows how failure to respond to changing circumstances in the airline industry set the company on a downward spiral towards bankruptcy. As in Alitalia's case, some of the most difficult decisions pertain to downsizing, which refers to intentionally reducing the scale of operations and often includes cutting the workforce.

ONLINE
COUNTERPOINT 10.10

Downsizing Implementation

Downsizing has become a common practice in corporations, particularly in the Anglo-Saxon business world, both in response to business downturns and as part of many change initiatives in today's organizations.[99] Re-engineering projects, mergers and acquisitions, global competition and the trend toward outsourcing have all led to job reductions.[100]

BRIEFCASE 10.7

Massive downsizing has often not achieved the intended benefits and in some cases has been harmful.[101] Studies have shown that the two major objectives of downsizing – reducing costs and increasing productivity – are achieved in only a minority of cases. Impacts on remaining employees' attitudes towards their jobs are unsurprisingly negative. The rationale for downsizing

EXHIBIT 10.5   Stages of Decline and the Widening Performance Gap

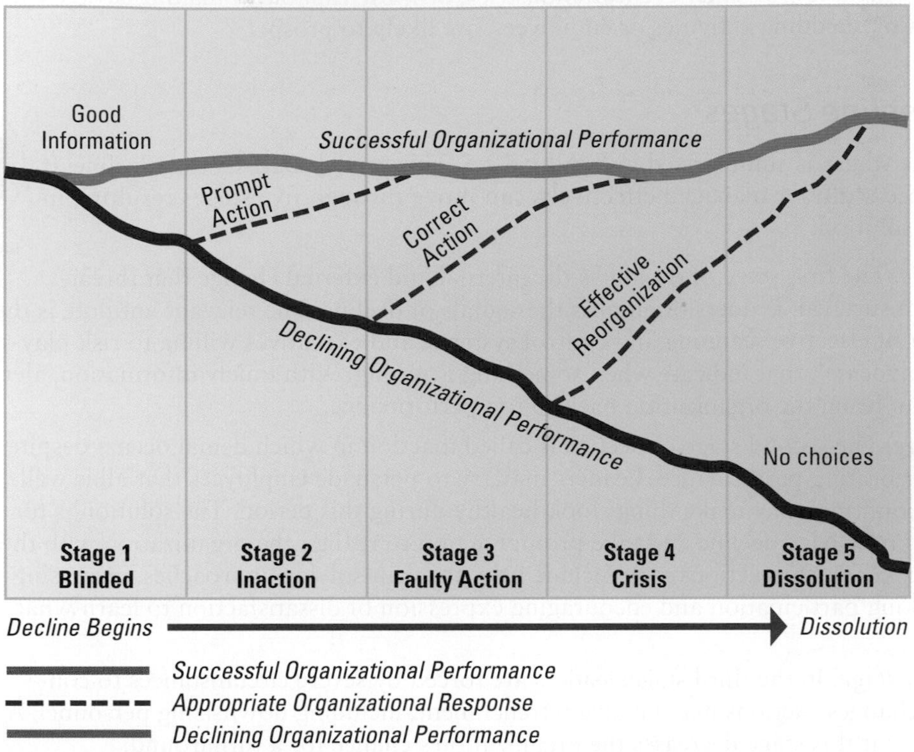

Source: Reprinted from 'Decline in Organizations: A Literature Integration and Extension', by William Weitzel and Ellen Jonsson, published in *Administrative Science Quarterly*, 34, No. 1 (March 1989). © SAGE Publications.

is often poorly thought out and is associated with excessive reliance on consultants, who have a vested interest in promoting continual organizational change. Downsizing is also associated with what van Witteloostuijn describes as 'macho management'; the idea that 'real managers make tough decisions', whether these decisions make sense or not.[102]

Nevertheless, there are times when managers have little choice but to implement downsizing strategies, whether because this is demanded by shareholders who believe it will result in increased profits, or in response to a negative market environment. A number of techniques can help smooth the downsizing process and ease tensions for employees who leave, and for those who remain.[103]

1   *Communicate more, not less.* Some executives seem to think the less that's said about a pending layoff, the better. Not so. Managers are ethically obliged to provide as much information as possible; in many jurisdictions the law also requires a lengthy notice period for impending layoffs. At US-headquartered computer networking firm 3Com Corporation, managers drew up a three-stage plan as they prepared for layoffs. First, they warned employees several months ahead that layoffs were coming. Soon thereafter, they held on-site presentations at all locations to explain to employees why the layoffs were considered necessary, and to provide as much information as they could about what employees should expect. Employees who lost their jobs were given their legal entitlement of notice.[104] Retained employees need to know what is expected of them, whether future layoffs are a possibility as well as what is being done to support co-workers who have lost their jobs.

Alitalia

Italy's economy has many post-war success stories, from the emergence of Milan as the style centre of the world, to the country's innovative car industry, to the Agip and Eni oil companies and several successful internet businesses including the international broadband operator Tiscali.

Alitalia, the country's flagship airline, is not one of those success stories. Like other European flag carriers, Alitalia was founded shortly after the end of the Second World War. In these early days of passenger aviation, the industry was dominated by state-owned carriers, of which Alitalia was one. Governments negotiated together to carve up routes between the different airlines, while fares remained high as most companies were in a near monopoly situation. It was an ideal environment and Alitalia flourished after a fashion, growing its network to encompass domestic, European and intercontinental flights. Trade unions, which had long been strong in Italian industry, were able to negotiate generous salaries and conditions. But the situation was not going to last. From the 1980s, pressure for liberalization swept across Europe and in 1992 the European Union liberalized the continent's skies, meaning any country's carrier could fly into any other country. By the end of the decade, Ryanair was spreading its low-cost wings across Europe. It was sink or swim for the national carriers. Some carriers didn't make it: Belgium's Sabena went bankrupt, followed by Swissair. Others, like British Airways, had been privatized as early as 1987 and embarked on an ambitious and generally successful restructuring, reducing the workforce to competitive levels and raising capital for new aircraft and new routes. Air France eventually joined in a successful merger with KLM, allowing the combined company to compete globally with the world's biggest airlines.

At Alitalia, the onset of competition had an enervating rather than liberating effect. The company was caught in a seemingly endless vicious cycle of squabbles about needed restructuring, union dissent and industrial action, lost revenues and worsened financial situation. The Italian government bailed out the company several times, but losses just kept mounting and the European Commission frowned upon and eventually forbade further handouts. By the new millennium, Alitalia was losing €2 million a day. The company was restructured in 2004, but the basic problems of overstaffing, poor service and endless strike disruption remained. Efforts were made to sell the company to different consortia, but these came to nothing due to union opposition and political interference.

By late 2008, the company was insolvent once again. Added to its internal problems, the price of aviation fuel had risen to hitherto unknown heights and even other, prudently-managed European carriers, were in deep trouble. Amid union and management squabbling, the planes started to run out of fuel before finally a government-backed privatization was agreed, with Skyteam alliance partner Air France-KLM holding a 25 per cent stake. However, the company's financial performance remained shaky with mounting debts, and in 2013 the company's CEO admitted Alitalia might need to give up its independent existence in order to survive. However, most potential purchasers, including Air France-KLM, were themselves in no position to take a risk on the Italian carrier. Eventually in 2015 the Gulf-based carrier Etihad bought a 49% share while the company downsized significantly and announced plans to pull out of the Skyteam Alliance. The company seemed to be heading towards absorption by Etihad.[105]

2 *Provide assistance to displaced workers.* The organization has an ethical if not a legal responsibility to help displaced workers cope with the loss of their jobs and get reestablished in the job market. The organization can provide training, innovative severance packages, extended benefits and assistance getting started in a new business or line of work. The Luxemburg-headquartered bank Dexia introduced an employee-reduction programme in 2002/2003. Rather than simply select the 8 per cent of the workforce who

were to lose their jobs, Dexia HR staff brainstormed a wide variety of options that could be offered to employees in return for agreeing to leave, ranging from support to carry out charitable projects, seed capital to start up a small business, continuation of the company's generous mortgage subsidy scheme and improved benefits for early retirement. Many employees were content to leave in return for a benefit that was relevant to their life plans, and interests and the remaining staff's morale was maintained as they could see that the company had made a real effort to minimize the downsizing programme's human impact.[106]

3   *Help the survivors thrive.* Many people experience guilt, anger, confusion and sadness after the loss of colleagues and these feelings should be acknowledged. Survivors might also be concerned about their own jobs and have difficulty adapting to the changes in job duties, responsibilities and so forth. Korea's Samsung responded creatively after having to downsize during the country's deep economic recession in the late 1990s. The company began by reducing the size and power of Samsung Restructuring Headquarters, the company's division that had been responsible for organizing the downsizing, and the company also greatly expanded the value and scope of its charitable donations, providing enhanced opportunities

IN PRACTICE

Seagram

At the end of the twentieth century, Seagram's was perhaps the best known name in the Canadian liquor trade and a highly profitable part of Montreal businessman Edgar Bronfman's business empire. However, in 2000, Bronfman decided to sell out to the French conglomerate Vivendi. Unfortunately, Vivendi, then building a global media empire, was only interested in Bronfman's pay TV holdings. As soon as it got hold of Seagram's, Vivendi cast around for a buyer. Eventually, it sold out to the British firm Diageo and the French company Pernod Ricard. This was very bad news for Seagram's staff because both companies planned to integrate Seagram's brands into their existing wine and spirits businesses, laying off all but a handful of the existing staff in the process. Ronnie Vansteenkiste, who was a senior HR staff at Seagram's, wrote about what happened next. Surprisingly, it was not as negative a story as it might have seemed at first glance.

The first positive was that Seagram's was a well run and successful operation before its sale. This made a big difference, because the existing management had the confidence of the employees. Management's first action when they found out about the likely developments was to plan various scenarios. They soon realized that winding up the Seagram division was a possibility if not a probability and they were up-front about this with the workers. Managers organized regular communications sessions where they shared their understanding of developments with their staff and they also organized sessions on 'managing change'.

Seagram's managers also knew that, while the new owners were likely to want to close down Seagram's as a separate entity, they wanted the brands they had bought to retain their positive image through the handover. This would require strong manufacturing, distribution and marketing to continue up to the moment of handover/closure. In order to reduce attrition, particularly among key staff, Seagram managers negotiated generous incentive schemes to encourage their key staff to stay on until brand handover. Managers identified staff with key skills or outstanding capacities and recommended them to the new owners. A generous layoff package was developed as soon as possible for the bulk of staff who would be leaving and a great deal of energy was put into helping to manage the emotions of the many Seagram's staff who had years of experience with the firm. The situation was not one that the Seagram's managers would have chosen, but they showed leadership and professionalism in handing it.[107]

for executives to make a tangible social contribution through volunteer activities. Eventually, of course, Samsung bounced back to become one of the global success stories of the second decade of the twenty-first century.[108,109] Another example is Seagram, featured in the *In Practice* feature above.

Summary and Interpretation

In this chapter, organizations have been seen to evolve through distinct life cycle stages as they grow and mature. Organization structure, internal systems and management issues are different for each stage of development. Growth creates crises and revolutions along the way. A major task of managers is to guide the organization through the entrepreneurial, collectivity, formalization and elaboration stages of development.

As organizations progress through the life cycle and grow larger and more complex, they generally take on bureaucratic characteristics, such as rules, division of labour, written records, hierarchy of authority and impersonal procedures. Bureaucracy is a logical form of organizing that enables firms to deploy resources in a more rational manner. However, in many large corporate and government organizations, bureaucracy has come under attack with attempts to decentralize authority, flatten organization structure, reduce rules and written records and create a small-company mindset. These companies are willing to trade the considerable benefits of bureaucracy (e.g. predictability, impartiality, elimination of nepotism) for greater responsiveness and adaptability. Many companies are subdividing to gain small-company advantages. Another approach is to incorporate an *incident command system* which promises to enable the organization to glide smoothly between a highly formalized, hierarchical approach relevant for periods of stability, and a more flexible, loosely structured orientation relevant for responding to unexpected or volatile environmental conditions.

Many organizations have stopped growing and some are declining. One of the most difficult decisions pertains to downsizing the workforce. Not only does it threaten the livelihood of those who are cast aside and unsettles those who remain, downsizing has been shown not to result in improved performance in many cases. To smooth the downsizing process, managers can communicate with employees and provide as much reliable information as possible, offer assistance to displaced workers and address the concerns of those remaining within the organization.

KEY CONCEPTS

bureaucracy	elaboration stage	formalization stage	organizational
centralization	entrepreneurial	incident command	decline
collectivity stage	stage	system	personnel ratios
downsizing	formalization	life cycle	

Discussion Questions

1 Discuss the key differences between large and small organizations. Which kinds of organizations would be better off acting as large organizations and which are best trying to act as big-company/small-company hybrids?

2 Why do large organizations tend to be more formalized?

3 If you were managing a group of professionals (e.g. a department of college professors), how might you structure the department differently than

if you were managing a department of bookkeepers? Why?

4 Apply the concept of life cycle to an organization with which you are familiar, such as a university or a local business. What stage is the organization in now? How did the organization handle or pass through phases in its life cycle?

5 Government organizations often seem more bureaucratic than for-profit organizations. Could this partly be the result of the type of control used in government organizations? Explain.

6 The incident command system has been used primarily by organizations that regularly deal with crisis situations. Discuss whether this approach seems workable for a large media company that wants to reduce bureaucracy. How about for a manufacturer of mobile phones?

7 Refer to the case study of Philips NV in Chapter 1. Try to match the historical development of Philips using the organizational life cycle approach explained in this chapter. How well does the life cycle model fit?

8 In order to address ecological sustainability, do you think a 'no growth' philosophy of management should be taught in business schools? Discuss.

Chapter 10 Workbook Control Mechanisms

Think of two situations in your life: your work and your school experiences. How is control exerted?

Questions

1 What are the advantages and disadvantages of the various controls?

2 What happens when there is too much control? Too little?

3 Does the type of control depend on the situation and the number of people involved?

Chapter 10 Workshop Windsock, Inc.

1 *Introduction.* Class is divided into four groups: Central Office, Product Design, Marketing/Sales and Production. Central Office is a slightly smaller group. If groups are large enough, assign observers to each one. Central Office is given 500 straws and 750 pins. Each person reads *only* the role description relevant to that group. *Materials needed*: plastic milk straws (500) and a box of straight pins (750).

2 *Perform task.* Depending on length of class, step 2 may take 30 to 60 minutes. Groups perform functions and prepare for a 2-minute report for stockholders.

3 *Group reports.* Each group gives a 2-minute presentation to stockholders.

4 *Observers' reports (optional).* Observers share insights with subgroups.

5 Class discussion.

   a What helped or blocked intergroup cooperation and coordination?

   b To what extent was there open versus closed communication? What impact did that have?

   c What styles of leadership were exhibited?

   d What types of team interdependencies emerged?

Roles

Central Office

Your team is the central management and administration of Windsock, Inc. You are the heart and pulse of the organization, because without your coordination and resource allocation, the organization would go under. Your task is to manage the operations of the organization, which is not an easy responsibility because you have to coordinate the activities of three distinct groups of personnel: the Marketing/Sales group, the Production group and the Product Design group. In addition, you have to manage resources including materials (pins and straws), time deadlines, communications and product requirements.

In this exercise, you are to do whatever is necessary to accomplish the mission and to keep the organization operating harmoniously and efficiently.

Windsock, Inc., has a total of 30 minutes (more if instructor assigns) to design an advertising campaign and ad copy, to design the windmill and to produce the first windmill prototypes for delivery. Good luck to you all.

Product Design

Your team is the research and product design group of Windsock, Inc. You are the brain and creative aspect of the operation, because without an innovative and successfully designed product, the organization would go under. Your duties are to design products that compete favourably in the marketplace, keeping in mind function, aesthetics, cost, ease of production and available materials.

In this exercise, you are to come up with a workable plan for a product that will be built by your production team. Your windmill must be light, portable, easy to assemble and aesthetically pleasing. Central Office controls the budget and allocates material for your division.

Windsock, Inc., as an organization has a total of 30 minutes (more if instructor assigns) to design an advertising campaign, to design the windmill (your group's task) and to produce the first windmill prototypes for delivery. Good luck to you all.

Marketing/Sales

Your team is the marketing/sales group of Windsock, Inc. You are the backbone of the operation, because without customers and sales the organization would go under. Your task is to determine the market, develop an advertising campaign to promote your company's unique product, produce ad copy and develop a sales force and sales procedures for both potential customers and the public at large.

For the purpose of this exercise, you may assume that a market analysis has been completed. Your team is now in a position to produce an advertising campaign and ad copy for the product. To be effective, you have to become very familiar with the characteristics of the product and how it is different from those products already on the market. The Central Office controls your budget and allocates materials for use by your division.

Windsock, Inc. has a total of 30 minutes (more if instructor assigns) to design an advertising campaign and ad (your group's task), to design the windmill and to produce the first windmill prototypes for delivery. Good luck to you all.

Production

Your team is the production group of Windsock, Inc. You are the heart of the operation, because without a group to produce the product, the organization would go under. You have the responsibility to coordinate and produce the product for delivery. The product involves an innovative design for a windmill that is cheaper, lighter, more portable, more flexible and more aesthetically pleasing than other designs currently available in the marketplace. Your task is to build windmills within cost guidelines, according to specifications and within a prescribed period, using predetermined materials.

For the purpose of this exercise, you are to organize your team, set production schedules and build the windmills. Central Office controls your budget, materials and specifications.

Windsock, Inc., has a total of 30 minutes (more if instructor assigns) to design an advertising campaign, to design the windmill and to produce the first windmill prototypes (your group's task) for delivery. Good luck to you all.

Adapted by Dorothy Marcic from Christopher Taylor and Saundra Taylor in 'Teaching Organizational Team-Building through Simulations', *Organizational Behaviour Teaching Review* XI(3), 86–87.

HOSPI*

By Henrik Sørensen, Aarhus University

HOSPI, a company owned by Italian entrepreneur Fabio Mussaccio, proved a success right from the start. However, in retrospect, critics in the industry claimed that it was surprising Mussaccio had not wrecked the company given his unusual approach to management.

HOSPI produces hospital equipment and the company operates in a very turbulent market. Mussaccio had understood from the start, however, that the structure of the company needed to be different from that of traditional companies. The structure had to be far more organic, with many decisions delegated to the employees of the company, because they often repay your trust by permitting the company to be far quicker on the 'trigger' than its competitors. However, many employees were not afraid to make their own decisions and sometimes were willing to 'grease the palms' of a few hospital doctors a bit too liberally in order to have their products prioritized over those of their competitors. On some occasions, Mussaccio has been accused in the media of what could be described as bribery, but each time he had weathered the storm. For example, he fired a particularly eager HOSPI sales rep, who might have gone a little too far. However, in Mussaccio's opinion you do not have to tell the media about everything you do, and he adds 'there is no need to quarrel with your employees'. So the employee who was fired was rehired shortly after in another of Mussaccio's companies. The fired employee received severance pay in HOSPI as well as a better salary in the other Mussaccio company.

In HOSPI, a strong sense of competition reigns among the employees and every employee is, so to speak, fighting with each other as well as against each other. In the course of time, this has created a highly decentralized organization that very often leads to conflicts between the individual employees; gradually an atmosphere has developed where no one is willing to take on responsibility and leadership. At the same time, many believe that as an employee they can do whatever they want because in the end Mussaccio will cover for them. This was particularly evident after the episode of the re-hired employee.

In HOSPI, there is a long series of incidents that clearly demonstrate that the organization is very much left to its own devices. Accordingly, there is limited coordination of the sales effort between the different areas, and the reports prepared by the sales manager Marta Chiabotto are rarely used for anything at all. In reality, the individual employees often define the actions that need to be taken in relation to the customers. For example, a sales rep in one district may find out from her customers that one of her colleagues is making special offers in another district.

The annual sales meeting often ends in total disaster. The original intention of the meeting was to allow the sales reps to exchange experiences, but instead it seems that each sales rep always tries to single him or herself out as the company's key salesperson, claiming that the problems in the sales division are caused by the other sales reps. If the reps eventually acknowledge that problems of some sort really exist, they inevitably think that these are to be solved by the management.

Another characteristic feature of HOSPI is that all sales reps are dissatisfied with something; and it is a standing joke in the production department that it is impossible to meet a sales rep who is not complaining about one issue or another. In other words, there are numerous problems but few solutions – compounded by the fact that Mussaccio seldom interferes.

To be fair, it should however be added that the sales team does in fact function quite well and if you ask Mussaccio it is precisely this dissatisfaction that leads employees to solve problems that emerge. But employees do not always agree with his convenient explanation. Not only do the problems faced by the sales team differ, but the team members' assessments of what is and is not a problem diverge significantly. Giuseppe Carcano – one of the most capable and proactive of the sales reps – said jokingly that the problems of the sales team depend on which of the reps feel inclined to attend the meetings. As the following example may show, there might be some truth in Carcano's statement.

For some years there were five sales reps who got along well together and also became personal friends. Of course outside work, they also discussed HOSPI, generally agreeing that since HOSPI functioned in the

*Please note this case study is entirely fictional.

way it did, they might as well try to take advantage. They decided to raise at every meeting that they considered it a huge problem for HOSPI that there was no direct relation between how well the sales reps supported each other and worked together on one hand, and the remuneration system on the other. They also complained that the division into sales districts often resulted in conflicts between the sales reps.

However, others in the sales division claimed that the districts were in fact the true strength of the company, as they were an excellent way for the individual sales rep to target his/her efforts toward the customers. They also argued that the issue of customers being aware of offers made by sales reps in other districts was hugely exaggerated.

Nevertheless, the group of friends bent Mussaccio's ears as well as the sales manager Marta Chiabotto for several years with their concerns about coordination, eventually causing the other sales reps to give up proving that it was not a problem. There were even sales reps who claimed that as long as the 'Gang of Five', as they were popularly called, concentrated on the coordination issue, which Mussaccio did not want to address, then at least they did not focus on other far more unpleasant issues. The funny thing was that when the 'Gang of Five' gradually left the company, the coordination issue sort of died out, but then there were some sales reps who drew attention to other issues instead.

As the success of HOSPI increased, Mussaccio was gradually forced to acknowledge that he had to pay more attention to the way the sales team operated. Even though he had previously always rejected the existence of problems altogether, he now admitted that things needed to change. Nevertheless he found himself in a dilemma which he was unable to solve straight away:

1   Firstly, he felt it was an important strength that the sales reps were able to negotiate directly with the customers. This meant that when the reps found themselves in a specific sales situation and had difficulties selling the products because competing companies were better or cheaper, they were able to negotiate immediately with the customers and make them an offer in order to win the order.

2   Secondly, Mussaccio felt strongly that individual employees should be able to make independent decisions in specific situations. Accordingly, he also felt that by delegating decision-making authority, management had an obligation to back up employees in case anything went wrong.

Therefore, for example, he stood by his employees who had gone too far in 'greasing the palms' of the doctors. Only on very rare occasions were the sales reps given a dressing-down. Mussaccio felt it was justifiable if a sales rep took a hasty decision to secure an order, even if it turned out later to be a bad decision. 'You rarely learn anything from your successes but you always learn something by your mistakes', was his comment.

3   Thirdly, Mussaccio believed that the fact the sales reps were making their own decisions was to a wide extent contributing to increased sales. If HOSPI didn't give the individual sales reps a wide degree of freedom to conclude the orders themselves, then many of the orders would not be obtained. However, several employees expressed their concern that the huge individual freedom hampered sharing of best practices and learning from mistakes: 'We need to have a sense of community which will allow us to learn from and discuss each other's experiences. Far too often, the individual sales rep misunderstands a customer or misinterprets what the customer wants. Furthermore, great benefits could be gained by helping each other interpret which direction the market is taking. Only if we challenge each other's views on the development will we be able to decipher the impacts of the changes and nuances of the market well enough to make us better than the rest. Great benefits can be gained by helping each other.'

New decision processes

After careful deliberation, Mussaccio decided that HOSPI's decision-making processes should be changed. In future the approach would be far more analytical. He still strongly stressed that the sales reps constituted the fulcrum of the company and that they were the ones creating the company. But the job of the sales reps changed significantly. One major change was the introduction of a number of reporting forms to be completed by the sales reps each week.

One of the new forms concerned new marketing opportunities or changed customer preferences. On this form, the sales reps were to indicate any new marketing opportunities or threats that their customer visits had given rise to during the week. The form

▶

was designed so that the sales reps would evaluate all opportunities on a scale starting from 'very easy to implement' through 'relatively easy to implement' to 'very difficult to implement'. Any threats against the company should also be categorized starting from 'significant threats with adverse impact on HOSPI' to 'threats of marginal importance to HOSPI's sales'.

These forms were then submitted to the sales manager Marta Chiabotto who examined all the forms handed in by the sales reps. Chiabotto's task then was to gather all the information obtained in a special reporting form, which was shown to Mussaccio, the production manager Edmundo Ferrari and other department managers. The management team would then consider whether the information reported by the sales reps was of such magnitude and importance that actions had to be taken.

It soon turned out the individual sales reps did not find it difficult to submit the reports and a few months after the implementation of the system, the sales manager Marta Chiabotto gained significant insight into the challenges faced by HOSPI in the market of hospital equipment.

The reporting systems proved of great value to HOSPI. One of the HOSPI sales reps reported that several of the competing companies were making a strategic alliance. He explained that the main motivation for this alliance was to increase the market share in the long run, which would be achieved through cooperation in terms of production, rationalization and reorganization of the product range, as well as through trimming the sales force. The same sales rep had also been informed by a customer that the new strategic alliance was starting to arrange large professional medical conferences and that the customer had participated in the first one himself. The theoretical topics were top class and furthermore there was an abundance of entertainment during the conference. The alliance partners competing against HOSPI had also managed to sell a fair amount of their products.

Naturally, Marta Chiabotto, the sales manager, immediately reported this information to the management team, but they disagreed among themselves about how to handle the situation. In Mussaccio's opinion, they should let the sales reps be even more aggressive than before and make sure to match or better the offers made by the competing strategic alliance at all times. Chiabotto expressed very strong reservations about this response as she pointed out

that due to their cooperation and production coordination, the companies of the strategic alliance would be far more cost-effective than HOSPI, and if they set prices close to their production costs, HOSPI would incur significant losses. Instead Edmundo Ferrari, the production manager, recommended that they copy the idea about medical conferences; but Mussaccio was very sceptical about this: 'We will not be able to compete with the strategic alliance in that context. They have more companies to share the costs of a conference whereas we would be completely on our own in bearing the costs. Furthermore, the sales reps would have to reserve part of their time for participation in the conference and they would have less time for the direct sales effort geared towards customers. As we have customers all over the country, all sales reps would have to participate, as they all want to improve their personal relations with their customers.'

The sales manager Marta Chiabotto felt that it was important not to overreact: 'We will never be able to match the companies of the strategic alliance and if I were you, Mr Mussaccio, I would take it easy. Let's just wait a few months and allow the strategic alliance time to settle and establish itself in the market. When they have done so, we will purchase one or more of the companies participating in the alliance and gain influence in this way. Later on we might merge HOSPI into the alliance and thereby maintain our market shares. It may also prove an advantage for us to let HOSPI remain independent, while at the same time we participate in the strategic alliance and gain inside information about the initiatives it is planning.'

The management group went completely silent. CEO Fabio Mussaccio, production manager Edmundo Ferrari and the sales manager Marta Chiabotto knew that HOSPI was standing at a crossroads. Not only did they face big threats in the market, the sales rep's report about the alliance had also divided the management team for the first time. And that might prove to be the biggest threat. The management team never succeeded in agreeing on a joint countermove to the competitors' strategic alliance; and when the reps were informed about the outcome of the meeting later that week, Mussaccio had to explain the situation: 'We do not agree about the measures required, but for now it will have no impact on HOSPI. I am still the one in charge and in the end I will be the one making the decision. I own HOSPI, and the only reason why no solution has been found yet is because I am considering the different views.'

However, the sales reps were not satisfied with that answer. They pointed out that a solution was urgently needed and if the management team was not able to produce something sensible, usable and durable, the sales reps would have to take matters into their own hands – just like before the reporting system was introduced.

Without saying it out loud, it actually pleased Mussaccio immensely that the sales reps wanted to take the initiative. If the sales reps took over, he could easily allow them the latitude to be much more aggressive. In this way, he would avoid the difficult discussion with his managers Edmundo Ferrari and Marta Chiabotto. The sales reps immediately started to discuss among themselves and they turned out to be divided into three groups: those who supported Mussaccio's solution, those who supported the production manager Edmundo Ferrari and those who thought that the sales manager Marta Chiabotto had suggested the best solution. So the end result was that both management and the sales reps disagreed about the actions needed.

Mussaccio was not one to give up. But at the same time he was highly affected by the fact that, for the first time in the existence of HOSPI, management and the employees were divided, and his great concern was that this division would prove the downfall of HOSPI. In the short term he particularly feared that the internal division of HOSPI would hamper the operation of the information and monitoring systems required to measure the efficiency of the company.

With management and employees divided into three roughly equal sized groups, would they be able to establish optimal decision processes and foresee conflicts? Mussaccio also feared that HOSPI was on its way into a vicious circle where the company would be unable to react efficiently to opportunities and threats posed by the market. In addition, it was obvious that both management and employees held different views on how to tackle the threats from their competitors' strategic alliance. Now when unity was most needed, they found themselves more divided than ever before.

Mussaccio feared that HOSPI was heading towards a situation where the range of the problems would increase even if they succeeded in solving some of them. Maybe management would start making the wrong decisions because it did not want to start a conflict, with the result that HOSPI would shrink away from establishing the best structure to meet the current challenges. Last but not least, he worried that his best sales reps would find jobs in the strategic alliance because they saw more opportunities there than in HOSPI.

Therefore, Mussaccio called a meeting for all employees in HOSPI – the remaining part of management and all employees in production, sales, etc. He began the meeting by saying that 'HOSPI is facing serious problems both internally within the company and externally in different markets. It is no secret that all this fuss is created by the strategic alliance. But you know that I am a man of action and that you can trust me.

'Therefore I ask you all within the next month to write down your suggested solutions on a piece of paper and send them to me. It is completely up to you whether you want to send me your personal suggestions or whether you want to work in groups to prepare a joint proposal. When I have received all the suggestions, I will pass them on to an external consultant who is independent of everybody in HOSPI, including myself. The consultant will examine all the suggestions and recommend the most appropriate solution to HOSPI's problems. Therefore I reckon that everybody in HOSPI will join forces to implement the solution suggested.'

The reaction from the employees was unmistakable. Mussaccio received a huge applause and the employees left the meeting in high spirits, well aware however that the outcome could be a solution that they had not suggested themselves. The fighting spirit and the willingness to accept the final decision were, however, obvious. Everybody wanted a stronger HOSPI, and during the month that followed suggestions poured in from the employees. Several employees submitted their own personal suggestions while also being contributors to other suggestions at the same time. At the same time, HOSPI experienced its best production and sales month ever and it was easy to imagine that HOSPI could best the strategic alliance.

Then Mussaccio hired the consultant. It came as a great surprise when the consultant completely rejected all suggestions made by the employees and chose instead to employ an analytical approach to the future decision model of HOSPI. In his analysis, the consultant chose to focus on the following issues:

1   Market conditions
2   Structure
3   Technology

▶

4   Strategy

5   Culture

Market conditions

The best way to describe the situation in HOSPI was a market with very aggressive competitors. Further, because products are sold mainly to hospitals, the number of potential sales outlets is quite small, and a single doctor may often have crucial influence on the products and suppliers chosen by a hospital. Companies producing and selling hospital equipment are often faced with numerous specific customer requirements. Often a doctor who has chosen a product from one producer meets a colleague from another hospital and they exchange experiences with respect to both products and companies. The outcome of this exchange is that one of the doctors changes his product and business preferences; therefore it is always uncertain whether the company will be able to keep a customer. In other words, the industry is characterized by major changes and frequent swapping of customers between the companies.

So far, the few companies within this line of business have found it hard to influence or control what happened in the market. The establishment of the strategic alliance should be seen as an initiative by which the competing companies are attempting to achieve a higher degree of control over the surroundings, which is not possible for HOSPI as a single company.

Structure

It is very difficult to present a precise outline of the structure in HOSPI and this lack of organizational clarity means that none of the decision-making processes are working efficiently. If the company is to function properly, it needs much greater organizational coherence and consistency between the way the company is organized and how it makes decisions.

The major challenge for the company consists, however, in determining which structure the company should aim for. It has been well-known for a long time that Edmundo Ferrari, the production manager, has been opposed to all kinds of initiatives aimed at a more organic structure. Firstly, he saw from a very early stage the dilemmas outlined by Mussaccio above; and secondly, he did not regard an organic structure to be a real structure at all. It is just a place 'where everyone does what they feel like without

coordinating anything at all' he once added, 'and consequently HOSPI is completely inefficient'.

The sales manager Marta Chiabotto, and Mussaccio himself are, however, of a completely different opinion. Fundamentally, they support a very organic structure where the individual employees to a great extent are responsible for their own actions. They believe that the sales reps should develop teams and these teams need to be able to make rapid and quite far-reaching decisions. In other words, they should not ask before they act; and should they turn out to be wrong, a solution could be found afterwards.

So it will be difficult for the top management team to agree on a basic structure, as well as to implement a clear decision-making process.

Technology

Mussaccio has invested heavily in state-of-art production equipment, and HOSPI has both CAD and CAM facilities. The production facilities of HOSPI are very flexible, with production manager Edmundo Ferrari able to switch production lines without any significant costs. HOSPI does not have separated production lines. Although the employees are divided into production teams, the different teams do not function as independent units, with products often passing through the same team several times. The teams are capable – with some quick adjustments – to change production lines. At the same time the teams do not make many independent decisions; the employees are always told what to do by the production manager, Edmundo Ferrari, and the individual teams do not make decisions before clearing them with the production manager.

Ferrari schedules production so that he always has two weeks' rolling production planned in advance. This means that the individual teams always know what to do for the next two weeks. However, sometimes they might be asked by Ferrari to produce for an urgent order.

Strategy

The strategic alliance formed by HOSPI's competitors seems likely to completely change the strategies used so far by the companies across the industry, drawing a completely new picture of how the competition will look in the future. Previously, the industry was characterized by many similar-sized competitors, and everybody was competing against everybody else. Now things would be different.

▶

In the consultant's opinion, the new strategic alliance would quite likely be offering all customers all types of products. He was also convinced that the strategic alliance would generally adopt a low-cost strategy where they would encourage the companies of the alliance that were most efficient at producing a specific product to be in charge of the production of that specific product. This would lead to low-cost advantages. Later on you would probably see a tendency to centralize the production.

The consultant believed HOSPI should abandon the strategy of producing many different products for many different segments and instead try to gain an advantage through differentiation. But the management team, especially the sales manager Marta Chiabotto was not too keen on that idea.

Chiabotto argued:

'In future, the dividing line between specialized products and cheap products will be eliminated. In the future, all companies in the industry will be able to produce everything and no one will be able to achieve the same advantages as before. All this will happen because everybody in the industry will introduce flexible production systems as we have always done.

'However, I believe we need to think in completely different terms when we plan our corporate strategy. Instead of saying that some companies will win through differentiation and others through low-cost advantages, competition in the future will involve a more progressive market approach.

'Some companies will always win by being the first on the market with new products. They win because they are able to charge an extremely high price, which will cover their R&D costs; but they run the risk that other companies in the industry will be quick to copy them. It is essential to have some concealed skills or knowledge that the other companies cannot copy easily. The companies copying them will not have nearly the same amount of R&D costs, but on the other hand they will not be able to price their products so high. I think that the big difference between the two types of companies will depend on how many of the products developed by the first type of company will later prove successful on the market.'

Then Mussaccio proposed an earlier idea of the sales manager, according to which HOSPI should not change that much but just wait for the opportunity to carry out a hostile takeover of one of the companies participating in the alliance. The consultant had been impressed by the sales manager's presentation, and also thought there was merit in the hostile takeover idea. He was starting to doubt whether his own analysis was thorough enough and his conclusions accurate.

Culture

HOSPI's culture might be the area where the consultant would be able to make the most reliable analysis. However, it was not exactly helpful that the consultant was convinced that several more or less incompatible subcultures existed in HOSPI. The most obvious contrasts existed between the production and the sales departments. In the sales department they were used to a culture with huge focus on external circumstances (the customers) and through rapid change and adaptation they had tried to meet the customers' need and requirements. Accordingly, the individual sales reps needed to understand changes in customer requirements and wishes. The consultant also noted that there had been a certain amount of turbulence in the sales team due to the new reporting systems although they had loyally followed the commands of the management. This view was immediately confirmed by the sales manager, Marta Chiabotto.

The culture of the production department was in sharp contrast. The production manager Edmundo Ferrari, and for that matter the production staff as a whole, had all come from other companies with highly traditional assembly line methods. When HOSPI introduced the flexible production system, the employees were therefore not used to planning and being in charge of the production themselves. Nor were the employees aware that efficient production at HOSPI was highly dependent on employees' initiative, commitment and active participation in day-to-day production decision-making. Therefore it had been easier for everybody that the production manager Edmundo Ferrari just took over the total responsibility. This method had suited Ferrari and the employees well. The production staff and the production manager agreed that the production department functions at its best when they were able to pre-programme and set up rules for the production processes.

Surprisingly enough, however, the consultant characterized HOSPI's culture as weak overall, to which Mussaccio in particular reacted strongly:

'So far HOSPI has been a well-functioning company and I would like to emphasize that our current

▶

problems are not caused by internal inefficiency but rather by external circumstances, because everybody else in the industry has conspired against us. But we will be fighting back.'

The consultant's and management's conclusion

Marta Chiabotto, however, responded calmly to the consultant's statement:

'I am quite convinced that we do have a strong culture, but it is not always supporting the activities that we need to perform and thus we do have problems that need to be solved. I would also like to add that I do not doubt the knowledge and experience of the consultant, but I am aware of how difficult it is to provide a clear picture of HOSPI's market conditions, structure, technology, strategy and culture. By means of the consultant's analysis, we have obtained an explanation as to why we find it so hard to introduce the right decision-making process.

'I therefore suggest that we ask the consultant to analyze our market conditions and to make some suggestions based on this analysis as to how we can organize our structure, technology, strategy and culture, which in the end will allow us to implement a decision-making process.'

Everybody agreed and the consultant began his work backed by the entire management team and the employees.

Case Questions

1 HOSPI's sales and production departments seem to have different organizational cultures. Can you describe the different characteristics? Are there reasons beyond the personalities of the sales and production manager that these different cultures should have developed?

2 How does the creation of the strategic alliance change competitive conditions for HOSPI?

3 What are the advantages and disadvantages of the organic decision-making approach that has traditionally been practiced in the sales department?

4 The consultant does not seem to have a clear idea what to do. Why do you think the company hired him?

5 Mussaccio describes himself as a man of action. Do you think that is accurate? If not, why do you think HOSPI has been a success up until now?

Notes

1. Interpol Annual Report, 2011.
2. Vivienne Walt, 'Global Alert', *Time*, 3 March, 2008; MPA Welcomes police budget that pays for even more officers on the streets of London, M2 Presswire, 14 February, 2008.
3. 'Are some countries abusing Interpol?', 19 July, 2011, *CNN Wire*; Libby Lewis, July 20, 2011, 'Interpol's Red Notices used by some to pursue political dissenters, opponents', *International Consortium of Investigative Journalists*.
4. James Q. Wilson, *Bureaucracy* (New York: Basic Books, 1989); and Charles Perrow, *Complex Organizations: A Critical Essay* (Glenview, IL: Scott, Foresman, 1979), 4.
5. *OAG Fast Facts*, October 2012.
6. Deflem, M. (2006). 'Global rule of law or global rule of law enforcement? International police cooperation and counterterrorism,' *The Annals of the American Academy of Political and Social Science*, 603, 240–251; Peter Oborne, 'The question that Interpol won't answer: why does it collaborate with totalitarians like Vladimir Putin?', *The Telegraph*, November 4, 2014, accessed at www. telegraph.co.uk/news/worldnews/europe/russia/11207965/ The-question-that-Interpol-wont-answer-why-does-it-

collaborate-with-totalitarians-like-Vladimir-Putin.html; http://www.interpol.int/About-INTERPOL/Funding; Jake Wallis Simons, 'Interpol severs ties with FIFA', *Politico*, June 12, 2015, accessed at www.politico. eu/article/interpol-severs-controversial-links-with-fifa/; Igor Savchenko, 'The Interpol system is in need of reform', *Open Dialog Foundation*, February 24, 2015 accessed at en.odfoundation.eu/a/5947,the-report-the-interpol-system-is-in-need-of-reform; Fair Trial (2013), Interpol and Human Right, Report, accessed at https:// www.fairtrials.org/wp-content/uploads/Strengthening-respect-for-human-rights-strengthening-INTERPOL5. pdf; Kathy Gilsinan, 'Interpol at 100: Does the World's Police Force Work?', *Atlantic*, May 12, 2014, accessed at www.theatlantic.com/international/archive/2014/05/ interpol-the-global-police-force-that-isnt/362086/
7. Tom Peters, 'Rethinking Scale,' *California Management Review* (Fall 1992), 7–29.
8. Jerry Useem, 'One Nation Under Wal-Mart,' *Fortune* (March 3, 2003), 65–78.
9. 'Tesco's UK Grocery Mkt Share 29.4%', 26 March, 2013, *Dow Jones Global Equities News*.

10. 'Tesco, Sainsbury's lose ground – TNS', www.just-food. com, 24 June, 2008.

11. Matt Murray, 'Critical Mass: As Huge Companies Keep Growing, CEOs Struggle to Keep Pace,' *The Wall Street Journal* (February 8, 2001), A1, A6.

12. Stuart Elliott, 'Advertising's Big Four: It's Their World Now', *The New York Times* (March 31, 2002), Section 3, 1, 10.

13. Donald V. Potter, 'Scale Matters', *Across the Board* (July–August 2000), 36–39.

14. 'Teknosa Drives Corporate Expansion Strategy', *PR Newswire*, 25 February 2008; John Ryan, Value Zeitgeist, *Retail Week*, June 13, 2008; Sabanci Holdings, *2007 Annual Report*, accessed at http://www.sabanci.com/ pdf/2007en/retail.pdf on September 10, 2008.

15. Adrian Slywotzky and Richard Wise, 'Double-Digit Growth in No-Growth Times', *Fast Company* (April 2003), 66.

16. 'Turks are unhappy with Carrefour', 26 March, 2013, *IIND*; 'Erste cuts Turkey's Teknosa to "accumulate", ups target price', 28 March, 2013, *SeeNews*.

17. 'Foreign retail chains leave Turkey amid rise in competitiveness in local players', *Hurriyet Daily News*, September 18, 2015, accessed at www.hurriyetdailynews. com/foreign-retail-chains-leave-turkey-amid-rise-in-competitiveness-in-local-players.aspx

18. Sylvester O. Monye (ed) (1999) *The Handbook of International Marketing Communications,* London, Blackwell, 56.

19. James B. Treece, 'Sometimes, You've Still Gotta Have Size', *BusinessWeek/Enterprise* (1993), 200–201 (April, 2003), 66ff.

20. Bayer AG, *Annual Report – 2006*, accessed at http://www. annualreport2006.bayer.com/en/research-anddevelopment. aspx on September 10, 2008.

21. 'Tata offers help to flood-hit Bihar', *Economic Times*, 9 September 2008; Farzand Ahmed and Amitabh Srivastava, 'Bihar's tragedy', *India Today*, September 15, 2008.

22. Alan Murray, 'The Profit Motive Has a Limit: Tragedy', *The Wall Street Journal* (September 7, 2005), A2.

23. Rod Mills, 'Long battle to get home for Zoom's weary passengers', *The Express*, August 30, 2008.

24. John A. Byrne and Heather Timmons, 'Tough Times for a New CEO', *BusinessWeek* (October 29, 2001), 64–70; and Patrick McGeehan, 'Sailing Into a Sea of Trouble', *The New York Times* (October 5, 2001), C1, C4.

25. 'Air Lituanica ceases operations; airBaltic takes over Vilnius network', *AnnaAero*, May 22, 2015, accessed at www. anna.aero/2015/05/22/air-lituanica-ceases-operations-airbaltic-takes-vilnius-network/

26. Frits K. Pil and Matthias Holweg, 'Exploring Scale: The Advantages of Thinking Small', *MIT Sloan Management Review* (Winter 2003), 33–39.

27. David Friedman, 'Is Big Back? Or Is Small Still Beautiful?' *Inc.* (April 1998), 23–28.

28. David Henry, 'Mergers: Why Most Big Deals Don't Pay Off', *BusinessWeek* (October 14, 2002), 60–70.

29. Dinara Bayazitova, Matthias Kahl and Rossen I. Valkanov (2012), 'Value Creation Estimates Beyond Announcement Returns: Mega-Mergers versus Other Mergers', UNC Business School Working Paper, available at http://papers. ssrn.com/sol3/papers.cfm?abstract_id=1502385.

30. Andy Hutson, 'It's No Time To Cry 'Timber!', *Coventry Evening Telegraph*, August 11, 2008.

31. 'Sweden: Greater growth in exports for small businesses', *Dagens Industri*, April 23, 2008. 'Swedish Small Businesses Find It Hard To Export', 16 February, 2012, *Scandinavian Companies and Markets*.

32. 'BioInnovate 2008: licensing is key to move drugs from bench to clinic in tough climate', *Pharma Marketletter*, June 10, 2008.

33. Chronic Pain; 'Abbott to Acquire Novel Investigational Biologic to Treat Chronic Pain', 25 November 2009, *Biotech Week*.

34. Entrepreneurs for Growth, *Europe's 500 – 2007*, accessed at http://web.archive.org/web/20080317043427/http:// www.europes500.com/results.html on September 15, 2013. on September 10, 2008.

35. 'The Hot 100', *Fortune* (September 5, 2005), 75–80.

36. Gary Hamel, quoted in Hammonds, 'Size Is Not a Strategy'.

37. 'The World's Most Innovative Companies', *BusinessWeek*, April 24, 2006.

38. Julian Birkinshaw, Cyril Bouquet and Tina C. Ambos (2007), 'Managing Executive Attention in the Global Company', *Sloan Management Review*, Summer 2007.

39. Arjun Appadurai (2006), *Fear of Small Numbers*, Kolkata, Seagull Press, 87–114.

40. Michael Barone, 'Not a Victory for Big Government', *The Wall Street Journal* (January 15, 2002), A16.

41. Ibid.

42. 'Coles ripe for revival', *The Courier Mail* (Australia), July 7, 2007; 'Coles posts revenue rise', *Retail Week*, August 29, 2008; Simon Evans, 'How the wolf from the west plans to revive Coles', *The Australian Financial Review,* November 7, 2007.

43. Sue Mitchell, 'Wesfarmers' net profit rises 8.3pc on strong retail growth', *Sydney Morning Herald*, August 20, 2015, accessed at www.smh.com.au/business/retail/wesfarmers-net-profit-rises-83pc-on-strong-retail-growth-20150820-gj3dey.html

44. Hammonds, 'Size Is Not a Strategy'.

45. John R. Kimberly, Robert H. Miles and associates, *The Organizational Life Cycle* (San Francisco: Jossey-Bass, 1980); Ichak Adices, 'Organizational Passages – Diagnosing and Treating Lifecycle Problems of Organizations', *Organizational Dynamics* (Summer 1979), 3–25; Danny Miller and Peter H. Friesen, 'A Longitudinal Study of the Corporate Life Cycle', *Management Science* 30 (October 1984), 1161–1183; and Neil C. Churchill and Virginia L. Lewis, 'The Five Stages of Small Business Growth', *Harvard Business Review* 61 (May–June 1983), 30–50.

46. Larry E. Greiner, 'Evolution and Revolution as Organizations Grow', *Harvard Business Review* 50 (July–August 1972), 37–46; and Robert E. Quinn and Kim Cameron, 'Organizational Life Cycles and Shifting Criteria of Effectiveness: Some Preliminary Evidence', *Management Science* 29 (1983), 33–51.

47. George Land and Beth Jarman, 'Moving beyond Breakpoint', in Michael Ray and Alan Rinzler, eds., *The New Paradigm* (New York: Jeremy P. Tarcher/Perigee Books, 1993), 250–266; and Michael L. Tushman, William H. Newman and Elaine Romanelli, 'Convergence and Upheaval: Managing the Unsteady Pace of Organizational Evolution', *California Management Review* 29 (1987), 1–16.

48. 'TomTom history: A history of innovation and categorydefining products', accessed at http://web.archive.

org/web/20080602052355/http://investors.tomtom.com/
tomtom/overview/history/ on September 15, 2013; Amy
Gilroy, Stellar Results For TomTom, Garmin In Q4, *Twice*,
February 25, 2008; Deloitte, *Stellar Performers: Technology
Fast 500 EMEA Ranking and CEO Survey 2007*, accessed
at http://www.deloitte.com/assets/Dcom-Denmark/
Local%20Assets/Documents/StellarPerformers%20
Fast%20500%202007.pdf on September 15, 2013.

49. David A. Mack and James Campbell Quick, 'EDS: An Inside
View of a Corporate Life Cycle Transition', *Organizational
Dynamics* 30, No. 3 (2002), 282–293.

50. Rhymer Rigby, 'TomTom maps the future', *World Business*,
1 June 2006.

51. Adam Lashinsky, 'Google Hires a Grown-up', *Business 2.0*
(February 2002), 22.

52. David A. Whetten, 'Sources, Responses and Effects
of Organizational Decline', in John R. Kimberly, Robert
H. Miles and associates, *The Organizational Life Cycle*,
342–374.

53. Brent Schlender, 'How Big Can Apple Get?' *Fortune*
(February 21, 2005), 67–76; and Josh Quittner with
Rebecca Winters, 'Apple's New Core – Exclusive: How
Steve Jobs Made a Sleek Machine That Could Be the
Home-Digital Hub of the Future', *Time* (January 14, 2002),
46.

54. Daisuke Wakabayashi, 'Apple Reports First Quarterly Sales
Drop Since 2003 as iPhone Stumbles', *Wall Street Journal*,
April 26, 2016, accessed at www.wsj.com/articles/apple-
reports-first-quarterly-sales-drop-since-2003-1461702629

55. Archibald Preuschat, 'TomTom Seeks New Direction;
Navigation-Tool Maker is Trying to Reposition Itself as
a Mapping-Software and Services', *The Wall Street
Journal*, 21 May, 2012; 'TomTom's (TMOAF) CEO Harold
Goddijn on Q1 2016 Results - Earnings Call Transcript',
SeekingAlpha, April 19, 2016, accessed at seekingalpha.
com/article/3966275-tomtoms-tmoaf-ceo-harold-goddijn-
q1-2016-results-earnings-call-transcript

56. Land and Jarman, 'Moving beyond Breakpoint'.

57. The current corporate structure of the Lopez Group
is documented in the company's 2012 annual
report, pages 178–184, and available at http://
www.lopez-holdings.ph/component/docman/
doc_download/430-annual-report-2012?Itemid=649.

58. Elfren Sicangco Cruz, 'The rise and fall of corporations',
BusinessWorld, August 14, 2007; Oscar M. Lopez,
'Managing Crisis The Lopez Group Way', Leadership
in Crisis Forum, Manila, July 29, 2008; '20 Business
Revolutionaries', *BusinessWorld*, 28 May 2007; 'Benpres
extends gains on anticipated debt restructuring', *AFX –
Asia*, March 11, 2003.

59. Lawrence Miller (1990), *Barbarians to Bureaucrats:
Corporate Life Cycle Strategies*, New York, CN Potter.

60. Tina Rosenberg, 'The Taint of the Greased Palm', *The New
York Times Magazine* (August 10, 2003), 28.

61. Bill Powell, 'The New Russia Threat: How The Kgb (And
Friends) Took Over Russia's Economy', *Fortune*, 15
September, 2008.

62. 'China to crack down on nepotism, official abuses', *Reuters
News*, 22 January 2007.

63. John Crewdson, 'Corruption Viewed as a Way of Life',
Bryan-College Station Eagle (November 28, 1982), 13A;
Barry Kramer, 'Chinese Officials Still Give Preference to Kin,

Despite Peking Policies', *The Wall Street Journal* (October
29, 1985), 1, 21.

64. Edward Wong, 'Xi signals his focus is tackling
corruption; China's new leader warns that not fighting
graft will "doom" party and state', *International Herald
Tribune*, 20 November, 2012; 'The Panama papers
embarrass China's leaders', *The Economist*, April
7, 2016, accessed at www.economist.com/news/
china/21696504-panama-papers-embarrass-chinas-leaders

65. 'DHL steers Syngenta's total road freight operations in
Europe', *FreightNet*, May 4, 2016, accessed at www.
freightnet.com/release/5797.htm

66. James P. Walsh and Robert D. Dewar, 'Formalization and
the Organizational Life Cycle', *Journal of Management
Studies* 24 (May 1987), 215–231.

67. 'The Great Package Race, 2007', Georgia Tech Supply
Chain & Logistics Institute, accessed at http://www2.isye.
gatech.edu/%7Ejjb/wh/package-race/2007/2007.html on
September 14, 2008; Meghan Reinke, 'The Great Package
race: Around the World in ... How Many Days?', *Ground
Support Worldwide,* 1 September, 2007; 'DHL wins "great
package race" contest' *Business Recorder,* 3 May, 2007.

68. 'DHL – SWOT Analysis', *Datamonitor Company Profiles*, 18
August 2008; Susanne Hertz and Monica Alfredsson (2003),
'Strategic development of third party logistics providers',
Industrial Marketing Management 32, 139– 149; Sean
Murphy, 'The State of the 3PL', *Supply Chain Management
Review*, 1 October, 2007.

69. Zaheeruddin Asif and Munir Mandviwalla (2005), 'Integrating
The Supply Chain With RFID: A Technical And Business
Analysis', Working Paper, Temple University School of
Business and Management, accessed at http://web.
archive.org/web/20100609113323/http://ibit.temple.edu/
programs/RFID/RFIDSupplyChain.pdf on September 15,
2013.

70. Richard Armstrong, 17 January 2013, 'Investing
in Third-Party Growth', *Journal of Commerce*;
Jeff Berman, 'Global 3PL CEOs optimistic about
future growth', *Logistics Management*, October 1,
2015, accessed at www.logisticsmgmt.com/article/
global_3pl_ceos_optimistic_about_future_growth

71. Nancy M. Carter and Thomas L. Keon, 'Specialization as
a Multidimensional Construct', *Journal of Management
Studies* 26 (1989), 11–28; Cheng-Kuang Hsu, Robert
M. March and Hiroshi Mannari, 'An Examination of the
Determinants of Organizational Structure', *American Journal
of Sociology* 88 (1983), 975–996; Guy Geeraerts, 'The
Effect of Ownership on the Organization Structure in Small
Firms', *Administrative Science Quarterly* 29 (1984), 232–
237; Bernard Reimann, 'On the Dimensions of Bureaucratic
Structure: An Empirical Reappraisal', *Administrative
Science Quarterly* 18 (1973), 462–476; Richard H. Hall,
'The Concept of Bureaucracy: An Empirical Assessment',
American Journal of Sociology 69 (1963), 32–40; and
William A. Rushing, 'Organizational Rules and Surveillance:
A Proposition in Comparative Organizational Analysis',
Administrative Science Quarterly 10 (1966), 423–443.

72. Jerald Hage and Michael Aiken, 'Relationship of
Centralization to Other Structural Properties', *Administrative
Science Quarterly* 12 (1967), 72–91.

73. Doron P. Levin, 'Honda Decentralizes Management', *The
New York Times*, 21 May, 1992.

74. Steve Lohr and John Markoff, 'You Call This a Midlife Crisis?' *The New York Times* (August 31, 2003), Section 3, 1.

75. Peter Brimelow, 'How Do You Cure Injelitance?' *Forbes* (August 7, 1989), 42–44; Jeffrey D. Ford and John W. Slocum, Jr, 'Size, Technology, Environment and the Structure of Organizations', *Academy of Management Review* 2 (1977), 561–575; and John D. Kasarda, 'The Structural Implications of Social System Size: A Three-Level Analysis', *American Sociological Review* 39 (1974), 19–28.

76. Graham Astley, 'Organizational Size and Bureaucratic Structure', *Organization Studies* 6 (1985), 201–228; Spyros K. Lioukas and Demitris A. Xerokostas, 'Size and Administrative Intensity in Organizational Divisions', *Management Science* 28 (1982), 854–868; Peter M. Blau, 'Interdependence and Hierarchy in Organizations', *Social Science Research* 1 (1972), 1–24; Peter M. Blau and R. A. Schoenherr, *The Structure of Organizations* (New York: Basic Books, 1971); A. Hawley, W. Boland and M. Boland, 'Population Size and Administration in Institutions of Higher Education', *American Sociological Review* 30 (1965), 252–255; Richard L. Daft, 'System Influence on Organization Decision-Making: The Case of Resource Allocation', *Academy of Management Journal* 21 (1978), 6–22; and B. P. Indik, 'The Relationship between Organization Size and the Supervisory Ratio', *Administrative Science Quarterly* 9 (1964), 301–312.

77. T. F. James, 'The Administrative Component in Complex Organizations', *Sociological Quarterly* 13 (1972), 533–539; Daft, 'System Influence on Organization Decision-Making'; E. A. Holdaway and E. A. Blowers, 'Administrative Ratios and Organization Size: A Longitudinal Examination', *American Sociological Review* 36 (1971), 278–286; and John Child, 'Parkinson's Progress: Accounting for the Number of Specialists in Organizations', *Administrative Science Quarterly* 18 (1973), 328–348.

78. Jonathan Morris, John Hassard and Leo McCann (2008), 'The resilience of "institutionalized capitalism": Managing managers under "shareholder capitalism" and "managerial capitalism"', *Human Relations*, 61, 687–710; Åse Gornitzka and Ingvild Marheim Larsen (2004), 'Towards professionalisation? Restructuring of administrative work force in universities', *Higher Education* 47: 455–471.

79. Richard L. Daft and Selwyn Becker, 'School District Size and the Development of Personnel Resources', *Alberta Journal of Educational Research* 24 (1978), 173–187.

80. Cathy Lazere, 'Resisting Temptation: The Fourth Annual SG&A Survey', *CFO* (December 1997), 64–70.

81. Based on Gifford and Elizabeth Pinchot, *The End of Bureaucracy and the Rise of the Intelligent Organization* (San Francisco: Berrett-Koehler Publishers, 1993), 21–29.

82. B. Guy Peters, *The Politics of Bureaucracy*, London, Routledge, 2001.

83. Scott Shane, 'The Beast That Feeds on Boxes: Bureaucracy', *The New York Times* (April 10, 2005), http://www.nytimes.com.

84. Steve Vogel, 'Officials and experts praising FEMA for its response to Hurricane Sandy', *Washington Post*, November 01, 2012.

85. John L. Campbell, John A. Hall, and Ove Kaj Pedersen (2006), *National identity and the varieties of capitalism: the Danish experience*. Montreal, McGill-Queen's Press;

Peter A. Hall and Kathleen Thelen (2009), 'Institutional change in varieties of capitalism', *Socio-Economic Review*, 7, 7–34.

86. Gili S. Drori, Yong Suk Jang and John W. Meyer (2006), Sources of Rationalized Governance: Cross-National Longitudinal Analyses, 1985–2002, *Administrative Science Quarterly*, 51, 205–229.

87. Gregory A. Bigley and Karlene H. Roberts, 'The Incident Command System: High-Reliability Organizing for Complex and Volatile Task Environments', *Academy of Management Journal* 44, No. 6 (2001), 1281–1299.

88. US Indian Ocean Tsunami Warning System (IOTWS), *Program Proceedings: Workshop On The Transition Of The US IOTWS Program To Indian Ocean Partners, December 6-7, 2007*, Bangkok, Thailand, accessed at http://apps.develebridge.net/usiotws/b/US%20IOTWS%20Transition%20Workshop%20Proceedings_Jan08.pdf on September 13, 2008.

89. Kirsty Challen, Andrew Bentley, John Bright and Darren Walter (2007), 'Mass casualty triage – pandemic influenza and critical care', *Critical Care*, 11, 212–218.

90. Philip M. Padsakoff, Larry J. Williams and William D. Todor, 'Effects of Organizational Formalization on Alienation among Professionals and Nonprofessionals', *Academy of Management Journal* 29 (1986), 820–831.

91. Kim S. Cameron, Myung Kim and David A. Whetten, 'Organizational Effects of Decline and Turbulence', *Administrative Science Quarterly* 32 (1987), 222–240.

92. Danny Miller, 'What Happens after Success: The Perils of Excellence', *Journal of Management Studies* 31, No. 3 (May 1994), 325–358.

93. Shukti Sarma, 31 January 2013, UK Blockbuster runs aground, *Retail Digital*.

94. Kris Frieswick, 'The Turning Point: What Options Do Companies Have When Their Industries Are Dying?' *CFO Magazine* (April 1, 2005), http://www/cfo.com.

95. Kim S. Cameron and Raymond Zammuto, 'Matching Managerial Strategies to Conditions of Decline', *Human Resources Management* 22 (1983), 359–375; and Leonard Greenhalgh, Anne T. Lawrence and Robert I. Sutton, 'Determinants of Workforce Reduction Strategies in Organizations', *Academy of Management Review* 13 (1988), 241–254.

96. Timothy Aeppel, 'Die Is Cast; Toolmakers Know Precisely What's the Problem: Price', *The Wall Street Journal* (November 21, 2003), A1, A6.

97. John A. Pearce II and Steven C. Michael (2006), 'Strategies to prevent economic recessions from causing business failure'.

98. William Weitzel and Ellen Jonsson, 'Reversing the Downward Spiral: Lessons from W. T. Grant and Sears Roebuck', *Academy of Management Executive* 5 (1991), 7–21; William Weitzel and Ellen Jonsson, 'Decline in Organizations: A Literature Integration and Extension', *Administrative Science Quarterly* 34 (1989), 91–109.

99. William McKinley, Carol M. Sanchez and Allen G. Schick, 'Organizational Downsizing: Constraining, Cloning, Learning', *Academy of Management Executive* 9, No. 3 (1995), 32–42.

100. Gregory B. Northcraft and Margaret A. Neale, *Organizational Behaviour: A Management Challenge,* 2nd ed. (Fort Worth, TX: The Dryden Press, 1994), 626; and

A. Catherine Higgs, 'Executive Commentary' on McKinley, Sanchez and Schick, 'Organizational Downsizing: Constraining, Cloning, Learning', 43–44.

101. Wayne Cascio, 'Strategies for Responsible Restructuring', *Academy of Management Executive* 16, No. 3 (2002), 80–91; James R. Morris, Wayne F. Cascio and Clifford E. Young, 'Downsizing after All These Years: Questions and Answers about Who Did It, How Many Did It and Who Benefited from It', *Organizational Dynamics* (Winter 1999), 78–86; Stephen Doerflein and James Atsaides, 'Corporate Psychology: Making Downsizing Work', *Electrical World* (September–October 1999), 41–43; and Brett C. Luthans and Steven M. Sommer, 'The Impact of Downsizing on Workplace Attitudes', *Group and Organization Management* 2, No. 1 (1999), 46–70.

102. James P. Guthrie and Deepak K. Datta (2008), 'Dumb and Dumber: The Impact of Downsizing on Firm Performance as Moderated by Industry Conditions', *Organization Science* 19, 108–123; Arndt Sorge and Arjen van Witteloostuijn (2004), 'The (Non)Sense of Organizational Change: An Essay about Universal Management Hypes, Sick Consultancy Metaphors, and Healthy Organization Theories', *Organization Studies,* 25, 1205–1231.

103. These techniques are based on Bob Nelson, 'The Care of the Un-Downsized', *Training and Development* (April 1997), 40–43; Shari Caudron, 'Teach Downsizing Survivors How to Thrive', *Personnel Journal* (January 1996), 38; Joel Brockner, 'Managing the Effects of Layoffs on Survivors', *California Management Review* (Winter 1992), 9–28;

Ronald Henkoff, 'Getting beyond Downsizing', *Fortune* (January 10, 1994), 58–64; Kim S. Cameron, 'Strategies for Successful Organizational Downsizing', *Human Resource Management* 33, No. 2 (Summer 1994), 189–211; and Doerflein and Atsaides, 'Corporate Psychology: Making Downsizing Work'.

104. Matt Murray, 'Stress Mounts as More Firms Announce Large Layoffs, But Don't Say Who or When' (Your Career Matters column), *The Wall Street Journal* (March 13, 2001), B1, B12.

105. 'Alitalia's Future as Independent Carrier at Stake', *Dow Jones Global News*, 11 February, 2013; '"È arrivato il sì di Ethiad", sempre più vicino l'accordo con Alitalia', *Corriere della Sera*, August 1, 2014, accessed at www. corriere.it/economia/14_agosto_01/arrivato-si-ethiad-via-libera-all-accordo-alitalia-3e4b5ce0-197b-11e4-91b2-1fd8845305fa.shtml

106. Anna Lindblom, "Dexia BIL: Working Differently", *IMD Case study* 3-1589-90.

107. Ronny Vansteenkiste (2003), 'Who Moved My Drink?: the preparation for the closure of Seagram's spirits and wine business: a personal experience' in Kenneth Paul De Meuse and Mitchell Lee Marks (eds), *Resizing the Organization,* San Francisco, John Wiley.

108. Kim Ji-hyun, 'Samsung is vanguard of corporate philanthropy: Each group affiliate undertakes unique volunteer work based on customized programs', *The Korea Herald,* 21 March 2006.

109. Caudron, 'Teach Downsizing Survivors How to Thrive'.

PART V

MANAGING DYNAMIC PROCESSES

11 Organizational Culture and Ethical Values

12 Innovation and Change

13 Decision-Making Processes

14 Conflict, Power and Politics

CHAPTER 11

ORGANIZATIONAL CULTURE AND ETHICAL VALUES

A LOOK INSIDE

Boots the Chemist

Boots. When people in the United Kingdom think of 'Boots', they are usually not thinking of sturdy footwear but rather of the local chemists and tempting shelves stocked with all kinds of health items, cosmetics and toiletries. Boots is a much-loved and trusted retail brand in the United Kingdom, but when Richard Baker took over as chief executive in 2003, the company was looking – well, a bit down at heel. Baker found himself facing one of the most difficult jobs in retailing, helping the troubled company find a way to compete with the growing power of large supermarket chains like Tesco and Asda (Baker's former employer).

Baker immediately recognized many of the problems, such as antiquated distribution and information technology (IT) systems, high costs and inefficient processes, cluttered stores and excessive headquarters personnel. But he soon realized there would be no quick fixes, because the roots of Boots's troubles went very deep, right to the heart of the organization. Indeed, the cultural values at Boots Co. Plc, he found, were woefully out of sync with today's fast-moving, competitive environment.

Baker came to Boots from Asda, which is owned by the US-based discount giant Wal-Mart. At Asda, he had been used to a culture of openness and innovation. Ideas that could promote useful change were encouraged and acted on quickly. At Boots, though, change was almost viewed as the enemy. Boots had its greatest years of success in an era when the world moved more slowly and gently. Baker felt that a 'civil service' culture had developed at the firm, with people signing on for lifetime careers and expecting to have a comfortable ride up the corporate hierarchy simply through length of service. The highly insular culture meant that outsiders and outside ideas often seemed unwelcome. With home-grown managers and a long tradition of doing things a certain way, Boots had grown culturally resistant to change. For example, one previous chairman says his efforts to encourage Boots to concentrate on aspects of the business with the most potential for long-term growth were ignored by a team of long-serving executives who tended to focus on current profits at the expense of the future.

Over the next few years, there was an overhaul of top management at Boots, and Baker took a number of steps to improve efficiency, spruce up the stores and be more price-competitive. However, the 1400-store chain continued to struggle. After a promising Christmas 2004 season, sales and profits went flat. Undeterred, Baker continued to restructure the company, culminating in an ambitious merger with the wholesale and retail druggist Alliance Unichem in 2006, and in 2007 the company was bought out by a consortium including US former nuclear scientist and billionaire, Stefano Pessina, and the famous 'corporate raiders' Kohlberg Kravis Roberts & Co (KKR). As a result of the buyout Baker left Alliance Boots, though not empty-handed; he exercised stock options worth about £13 million. The new merged company performed well into 2008, with increased sales and profits, but the enormous debt burden caused by the leveraged buyout has weighed down on the company's results ever since.

The company has changed many of its practices to increase efficiencies, from making life less comfortable for staff and managers (and worsening the employment environment in the minds of some), to its invoice procedures. Boots now requires suppliers to wait up to 75 days for payment, resulting in criticism from the British Federation of Small Businesses, which accused the company of using small businesses as an 'unofficial source of credit'.

Pessina, who took over as executive chairman, has continued his hard-driving ways, both in expanding Boots's international business into major presence in countries as diverse as Norway, Ireland, the Netherlands, Thailand and Lithuania, and in various acquisitions including a major Chinese pharmaceutical distributor. The biggest deal of all, however, saw Alliance Boots sell out to US drug store giant Wahlgreen's in 2014, creating a giant conglomerate called Walgreen Boots Alliance.

So far, Boots retains its familiar presence and look-and-feel on the UK high street. But the company is now controlled from the US, though Pessina remains CEO of the new firm – and Boots was criticized for only paying £147m tax worldwide in 2012 on sales of £23bn. Pessina himself has acquired 15% of the new shares in the new global firm, is resident in the tax haven of Monaco, and has a personal net worth estimated in 2016 at $13.7 billion.[1] The familiar high street chemist is an increasingly small – and regularly flipped – part of giant corporate empires, with a growing list of critics of its cut-throat business practices in the UK and beyond. Will it be able to continue to capture the loyalty of British shoppers?[2]

Strong cultures can have a profound impact on a company, which can be either positive or negative for the organization. For example, 3M Germany, subsidiary of the US-headquartered 3M Corporation, was chosen by *Capital* magazine as the 'best employer in Germany' three years in a row. Capital magazine said 3M had, 'credible, competent management, which treated its employees fairly and with respect, and maintained a healthy team-spirit'.[3,4] Negative cultural norms, however, can damage a company just as powerfully as positive ones can strengthen it. Consider the case of America's Enron Corp., where the corporate culture supported pushing everything to the limits: business practices, rules, personal behaviour and laws. Executives drove expensive cars, challenged employees to participate in risky competitive behaviour, and often celebrated big deals by heading off to a bar or dance club. Corporate culture at Enron ultimately led to bankruptcy and criminal convictions for top executives.[5] An internationally-widespread corporate culture in which short-term personal financial gain for executives was valued above all other values including long-term company health is widely thought to have played a key role in setting off the global financial crisis that began in 2007–2008.[6,7]

**ONLINE
COUNTERPOINT 11.1**

A related concept concerning the influence of norms and values on how people work together and how they treat one another and customers is called social capital. In organizations with a high degree of *social capital,* relationships are based on trust, mutual understandings and shared values that enable people to cooperate, and to coordinate their activities, so as to achieve organizational goals.[8] Organizations can accumulate varying levels of social capital. *Goodwill* could be viewed as a form of social capital. When relationships both within the organization and with customers, suppliers and partners are based on honesty, trust and respect, a spirit of goodwill exists and people willingly cooperate to achieve mutual benefits. A high level of social capital enables smooth social interactions and exchanges that help to facilitate smooth organizational functioning.

eBay makes use of social capital as it brings together millions of buyers and sellers, and despite tough competition from Amazon that caused a drop in revenues from 2013 onwards, continues to deliver strong earnings, with annual sales of around $8.7 billion in 2016.[9,10,11] The company harnesses and protects goodwill and trust through mechanisms that include a feedback system enabling buyers and sellers to rate one another, discussion boards that build a sense of community among site users and even regular all-day focus groups with representative buyers and sellers. Inevitably, eBay also attracts some people who abuse the system. The company has been accused by some European authorities of turning a blind eye towards unscrupulous vendors such as those who sell fake branded goods,[12] accusations that are potentially corrosive of trust and damaging for business. For this reason, the company has to balance the advantages of a free-wheeling, low-bureaucracy market with adequate buyer and seller protections. Apart from cracking down on counterfeiters, eBay successfully managed to broaden its business to include a higher proportion of fixed price transactions between buyers and sellers (including increasingly large corporations). However, like many other companies, eBay has been strongly criticized for its tax avoidance practices; in 2012 the BBC reported the company had paid only £1.2m in UK tax on sales of over £800m. Can companies like eBay, Amazon, Facebook, Google and Ikea continue to use mechanisms to avoid tax such as having headquarters in low tax jurisdictions, and still retain 'social capital' in countries where they do most of their business but do not pay much tax to help support the social safety net?[13]

Organizations also build social capital by being open and honest and cultivating positive social relationships among employees and with outsiders.

Relationships based on self-interest and subterfuge, such as those at Enron, can be devastating to a company and these traits even destabilize an entire economy, as was seen in the global financial crisis that began in 2007, when a culture of self-interested risk-taking became the norm in countless financial institutions across North America and Europe, plunging the world into its worst economic crisis since the Great Depression of the 1930s. Social capital is a relevant concept for both corporate culture and ethics, which is the subject matter of this chapter.

LEADING BY DESIGN

Different forms of capital?

Until recent years the term 'capital' described economic capital: financial resources that are needed in order to establish and develop a business. However, scholars have realized that economic capital alone is insufficient to succeed. Other inputs are needed, including human capital (the education and skills managers and employees bring with them) and social capital (the networking capacities of the people in an organization). Without human capital, economic capital will be under-utilized; machinery will not be properly maintained or deployed, high-tech companies will not develop new applications for sale, etc. But even with ample economic capital and human capital, companies will not succeed unless they can make the necessary connections. Things like building supplier networks depend on staff with contacts and good interpersonal skills. Winning contracts depends on credibility. Dealing with government regulators effectively and efficiently means being able to get along and resolve different interpretations smoothly and in the interests of your organization. These factors are examples of social capital: hard to measure, but essential to success.[14]

Purpose of this Chapter

This chapter explores ideas about corporate culture and ethical values, and it considers how these are influenced by organizations. The first section describes the nature of corporate culture, its origins and purpose, and how to identify and interpret culture through ceremonies, stories and symbols. We then examine how culture can reinforce the strategy and structural design to improve effectiveness, and then discuss the important role of culture in organizational learning and high performance. Next, the chapter turns to ethical values and social responsibility. We consider how managers implement structures and systems that influence ethical and socially responsible behaviour. The chapter also discusses how leaders shape culture and ethical values in a direction suitable for strategy and performance outcomes. The chapter closes with a brief overview of the complex cultural and ethical issues that managers face in an international environment.

?

ONLINE
COUNTERPOINT 11.2

Organizational Culture

The subject of organizational culture begs a number of questions. Can we identify cultures? Can culture be aligned with strategy? How can cultures be managed or changed? The best place to start is by defining culture and explaining how it can be identified in organizations.

What Is Organizational Culture?

Organizational culture is the set of values, norms, guiding beliefs and understandings that is shared by members of an organization and is taught to new members (see Counterpoint 11.1).[15] It represents the largely unwritten, feeling part of the organization. Everyone participates in culture, but culture generally goes unnoticed. It is often only when organizations try to implement new strategies or programmes that go against basic cultural norms and values that they come face to face with the power of culture.

COUNTERPOINT 11.1

The idea that everyone in an organization subscribes to a shared set of values, norms, etc. is contentious. Within most organizations there is diversity, so the claim of commonality could instead be seen as a form of prescriptive control: it says: 'These are the values that you should have or at least display if you are an employee of this company'. What is interesting is where the idea of a shared set of values comes from – who is it who decides what these are? The probable answer is senior managers (or perhaps consultants hired to identify the values) who select and distil from their experience what they believe or would like the values to be.

Organizational culture exists in both comparatively superficial and more deeply embedded forms, at two levels, as illustrated in Exhibit 11.1. On the surface are visible artifacts and observable behaviour – the ways people dress and act and the symbols, stories and ceremonies organization members share. The visible elements of culture may reflect or they may mask deeper values in the minds of organization members. These underlying values, assumptions, beliefs and thought processes are the less manifest, more deeply engrained aspects of culture.[16] For many years, for example, Central and Eastern Europe was dominated by the Soviet Union

EXHIBIT 11.1   Levels of Corporate Culture

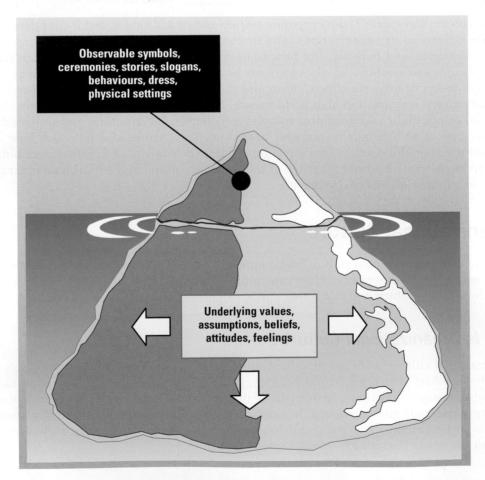

whose Communist government imposed a domineering, neo-classical architecture on new buildings, that reflected the omnipotence of the state. When capitalism re-emerged in these countries in the 1990s, early corporate architecture tended to reflect an unimaginative copy of Western-style chrome and glass structures. As a native corporate culture has emerged, local companies are beginning to demand buildings that reflect their own identities. In Hungary, for example, HungaroControl, the country's national air traffic control company, engaged a Hungarian architect to build a new headquarters which has been described as, 'a blocky, bricky slice of earthiness that departs entirely from the international model of dumb glazing and pointless form'.[17] Architecture is just one way that the attributes of culture display themselves as a patterned set of activities carried out through social interaction.[18] Those patterns can be used to interpret organizational culture.

Emergence and Purpose of Culture

Culture can, for better or worse, provide members with a sense of identity and generate in them a commitment to beliefs and values that are larger than themselves. Although ideas that become part of culture can come from anywhere within the organization, an organization's culture generally begins, at least, with a founder or early leader who articulates and implements particular ideas and values as a vision, philosophy or business strategy.

ONLINE
COUNTERPOINT 11.3

When these ideas and values are identified as a source of success, they tend to be affirmed and institutionalized, and an organizational culture emerges that reflects the vision and strategy of the founder or leader.[19] For example, Jack Ma, the founder of Alibaba, the successful Chinese B2B auction firm, worked night and day during the company's early phase to build a corporate culture different from the hierarchical tradition typical in Chinese firms. 'Alibaba's culture is no matter what you do, you have to please the customer,' says Ma. At the beginning, he says he slept only two or three hours a day, but now that the company's culture is well embedded in his team, he can play a more strategic role, 'In the past I carried an axe on the battlefield, but now I command my forces on the battlefield.'[20,21]

ONLINE
COUNTERPOINT 11.4

When cultures are purposefully constructed or shaped by managers, they are valued for performing at least two functions: (1) to integrate members so that they know how to relate to one another, and (2) to facilitate adaptation to the external environment. Internal integration means that members develop a collective identity and know-how to work together effectively (Counterpoint 11.2). It is culture that guides day-to-day working relationships and determines how people communicate within the organization, what behaviour is acceptable or not acceptable, and how power and status are allocated. External adaptation refers to how the organization meets goals and deals with outsiders. Culture helps guide the daily activities of workers to meet certain goals. It can help the organization respond rapidly to customer needs or the moves of a competitor. As discussed in this chapter's *Bookmark 11.0*, culture plays a key role in transforming an organization's performance from average to truly great.

COUNTERPOINT 11.2

This idea of culture as 'internal integration' can also be seen as indoctrination – as, for example, at Toyota or IBM. The idea of 'corporate culture' is charged with setting out how people should work together, communicate with each other, adjudicate what is acceptable and determine how allocations of status and power are made. If successful, the outcome is a group of identikit employees – like those at Enron, for example – who 'work together effectively' but become sect-like in their activities. In the absence of diversity, it is difficult to think critically or to innovate except in ways that comply with 'the culture', whatever this is dictated or designed to be. There is little possibility for gaining any distance from values that are ostensibly all-embracing and sacrosanct.

> External adaptation may also result in striving to respond to others' demands – ultimately shareholders if it is a publicly listed company – without regard to the ethics of what is done. Almost any dubious practice can be justified in the name of compliance with 'the culture' – either because it is deemed to be key to 'internal integration' or essential for 'external adaptation'.

The organization's culture also guides employee decision-making in the absence of written rules or policies.[22] Both functions of culture are related to building the organization's social capital, by forging either positive or negative relationships both within the organization and with outsiders.

Interpreting Culture

BRIEFCASE 11.1

Some of the typical and important observable aspects of culture are rites and ceremonies, stories, symbols and language.[23]

Rites and Ceremonies   Important artifacts for culture are rites and ceremonies, the elaborate, planned activities that make up a special event and are often conducted for the benefit of an audience. Managers can hold rites and ceremonies to provide dramatic examples of what a company values. These are special occasions that reinforce specific values, create a bond among people for sharing an important understanding and anoint and celebrate heroes and heroines who symbolize important beliefs and activities.[24]

ONLINE COUNTERPOINT 11.5

Four types of rites that appear in organizations are summarized below. *Rites of passage* facilitate the transition of employees into new social roles. *Rites of enhancement* create stronger social identities and increase the status of employees. *Rites of renewal* reflect training and development activities that improve organization functioning. *Rites of integration* create common bonds and good feelings among employees and increase commitment to the organization. The following examples illustrate how these rites and ceremonies are used by top managers to reinforce important cultural values.

- In a major bank, election as an officer was seen as the key event in a successful career. A series of activities accompanied every promotion to bank officer, including a special method of notification, taking the new officer to the officers' dining room for the first time and the new officer buying drinks on the Friday after his or her notification.[25] This is a rite of passage.

- Avon, the giant direct sales marketing firm that has made the 'Avon Lady' famous in 140 countries, uses awards ceremonies as a motivating tool for its army of sales consultants. For many, Avon work is a first step back into the world of business after taking time out to raise families. The company's recognition of the achievements of its sales workforce builds loyalty and commitment. At a recognition ceremony in Birmingham, UK, one award-winner, Natalie Ellis, said that, 'Avon has been a turning point in my life. I've never seen myself as an entrepreneur before, but that's exactly what this job has enabled me to become. I've really surprised myself at how much I've achieved.'[26]

- When Nigeria's Wema Bank emerged from a period of financial difficulties and necessary restructuring, the Bank's leaders organized a colourful relaunching ceremony, including a traditional royal chief, Awujale of Ijebuland, and invited key business and community leaders from the Lagos region. After the chief's speech calling for everyone to work together to support the relaunched bank, he led the invitees in impromptu dancing.[27] This is a rite of renewal.

- When new staff join the Japanese automaker Toyota, they are quickly inculcated in the Toyota Way. Everyone in every Toyota enterprise worldwide, from the humblest cleaner

BOOKMARK 11.0

Have you read this book?

Gurus, Hired Guns and Warm Bodies

SIMON BARLEY AND GIDEON KUNDA

As we shall see in Chapters 12 and 13, traditional organizational structures, with their stable hierarchies reflected in pyramid-shaped organization charts, are being challenged by various business process innovations. Technological innovations and relaxed regulation of labour markets and of trade, permit businesses to extend production process in numerous ways. The traditional workplace, such as the giant automobile plants pioneered by American manufacturers in the 1930s, is being broken up and dispersed into numerous locales, from homes – with teleworking as an increasingly common phenomenon – to across oceans, with service jobs shifted to lower cost labour areas.

Changes in the organization of production – whether of goods or services – do not merely shift the physical location of business activities, but also transform the character of organizations and the relations between people involved in production. Organizations' core activities, previously carried out by regular staff, are to an increasing extent being carried out by contractual workers.

In their book *Gurus, Hired Guns and Warm Bodies*, Barley and Kunda explore the phenomenon of contractualization of key tasks in IT firms in Silicon Valley, California, the centre of the US software industry. Their study, carried out through in-depth dialogue with 71 highly-skilled IT professionals working as contractors, reveals how the transformation in the way production is organized has led to fundamental changes in relationships between organizations and people who work for them.

Unlike many workers, Barley and Kunda's IT contractors are not obvious victims of production re-engineering. They are in high demand, enjoy high earnings and can usually work when and how they choose. Nevertheless their work lives are radically different from counterparts who have continued to work as regular staffers. To begin with, the contractors' success depends on different capacities. While technical skills are a prerequisite for both groups of workers, the contractors need different types of social capital in order to succeed (see above in this chapter for a discussion of social capital). Whereas an effective employee or manager in the firm will tend to be successful when s/he has strong social capital ties within the organization, the contractor will be more likely to be successful when s/he has looser but far more dispersed networks; what Barley and Kunda call networks with structural holes.

Similarly, contractors must guess trends for themselves and invest in learning the skills required for new IT skills so that they will profit from such trends. In short, they must *self-manage* in the absence of a traditional management structure that would in earlier times have ensured that a company's workers had up-to-date skills.

The trend to outsourcing IT professional work also creates new or expanded employment agencies that specialize in matching contractors with companies needing IT expertise for specific projects. The traditional human resource management function, previously carried out by an in-house department, thus also moves outside the organization.

Despite the advantages of greater freedom over when and where they carry out their work, the contractors had to assume responsibility for various costs that are covered by the employer in the case of the regular workforce. They are no longer covered by employee-paid benefits such as healthcare and sick leave, and it is up to them to keep abreast of new technical developments. But the differences don't stop at the financial level. Contractors told Barley and Kunda that their whole lives tended to become monetized. Because they chose when to work or not, they could put an exact price on the times they weren't working; spending time with their children, watching a sports game, etc. As a result, 'many contractors exercised their flexibility by working long hours and forgoing vacations for years at a time'. In addition, contractors tended to invest heavily in building social capital through intensive networking, another time-consuming activity on which regular employees focused much less attention.

Barley and Kunda's study suggests that the nature of work and organizations has changed drastically over the past generation, with the flattening of hierarchies, and complex organizations being dismantled in favour of leaner structures relying on short-term networks and alliances with 'free agent' consultants. This new approach does release skilled consultants from a strict 9 to 5 regimen, but ironically the self-employed consultants tended to impose far more onerous working conditions on themselves than their previous employers had done. This phenomenon of self-management appears to be a common feature in contemporary organizations; Willmott amongst others has noted the tendency for organizational discipline to be manifested through the construction of a self-motivating corporate culture rather than through the exercise of hierarchical discipline as was the case in the industrial era.[28]

Gurus, Hired Guns and Warm Bodies, by Simon Barley and Gideon Kunda is published by Princeton University Press.

to the top executives, can articulate the company's commitment to respect for people and continuous improvement. Toyota consciously builds a team spirit in which each individual feels they are respected as part of a family. From the company song to the plethora of internal clubs based on sports, hometowns, hobbies, etc.,[29] Toyota supports numerous rites of integration.[30]

ONLINE COUNTERPOINT 11.6

Stories   Stories are narratives based on events that are frequently shared among organizational employees and told to new employees to inform them about an organization. Many stories are about company heroes who serve as models or ideals for serving cultural norms and values. Some stories are considered legends because the events are historic and may have been embellished with fictional details. Other stories are myths, which are consistent with the values and beliefs of the organization but are not supported by facts.[31] Stories keep alive the primary values of the organization and provide a shared understanding among all employees (see Counterpoint 11.3). Examples of how stories shape culture are as follows:

- Stephen Denning was a manager in the African division of the World Bank, a global institution that finances development in poorer countries. He became frustrated that, while Bank staff had extensive knowledge about development issues, this was rarely disseminated to the grassroots where development workers faced challenges like the explosion of HIV/ AIDS cases. After banging his head against the wall trying to make himself heard, he attended a storytelling workshop where he learned how important it is to paint pictures that people can visualize. He started telling the (true) story of how a health worker in Zambia needed some information about AIDS, but unaware of the World Bank, which had lots of expertise located both in-country and globally, she connected to the internet and eventually downloaded information from the Centers for Disease Control in the United States. Most grassroots workers wouldn't have the initiative or technology to go that far in search of information. The story struck a chord with Bank senior staff, and within a couple of years the World Bank had set up a global Knowledge Management division, headed by Denning, that made it its business to ensure that Bank knowledge is effectively disseminated.[32]

- At 3M Corp., the story is told of a vice president who was fired early in his career for persisting with a new product even after his boss had told him to stop because the boss thought it was a stupid idea. After the worker was fired, he stayed in an unused office, working without a salary on the new product idea. Eventually he was rehired, the product was a success, and he was promoted to vice president. The story symbolizes the 3M value of persisting in what you believe in.[33]

COUNTERPOINT 11.3

One problem with corporate storytelling is that while myths can be powerful and motivate commitment and change, they can also (sometimes at the same time) be misleading and obscure alternative explanations as well as deeper underlying issues. In the case of the World Bank cited above, for example, Stephen Denning's storytelling undoubtedly played a key role in the Bank's decision to invest heavily in 'knowledge management'. The Bank even started to present itself as 'the Knowledge Bank'. But many observers have argued that the information disseminated by the Bank was often little more than self-serving propaganda designed to make the organization seem interested in eradicating global poverty, while the Bank's fiscal programmes that make up the great bulk of its development activity lead to deskilling and disinvestment in developing countries, thus actually increasing poverty.[34]

It can also be risky to follow the prescriptions of corporate mythmakers. The Harley-Davidson motorbike is famous for having turned around its image from being a heavy, unreliable monster ridden by thugs and leaking oil all over America's highways, to one of the few truly global icons of cool. Harley-Davidson executives naturally like to take credit for the turnaround, telling a story of how they had focused on quality, befriended Harley owners' groups and listened to customers' concerns and even taken to riding the bikes themselves to understand where they could be improved. Douglas Holt convincingly argues that – whether the myth had any basis in truth or not – the actions of executives had nothing to do with Harley's sudden success. Rather, by chance, Harley became a cultural icon through popular culture's mythologization of outlaw culture in movies like *Easy Rider*. Professionals with greying temples and plenty of disposable income saw an opportunity to recapture some of their fading glamour by riding these outlaw machines, and, by fluke, Harley-Davidson Company benefited from a windfall of sales and profits, even though neutral observers say the company was still badly mismanaged. The company's claim to have masterminded its success might seem harmless enough, except that when executives in other companies try to copy Harley executives' story, they typically end up failing, because that story did not account for the company's success and offers no useful lessons for other companies.[35]

Symbols   Another tool for interpreting culture is the symbol. A symbol is something that represents another thing. In one sense, ceremonies, stories, slogans and rites are all symbols. They symbolize deeper values of an organization. Another symbol is a physical artifact of the organization. Physical symbols are powerful because they focus attention on a specific item.

In recent years many Korean companies have shifted from bold, aggressive symbols, often based on the company's Roman alphabet initials, towards softer and gentler images designed to communicate a caring company. For example, the Hanwha conglomerate (formerly Hankook) started in the chemicals industry and developed product lines including military equipment and weapons. It has recently expanded into service industries including solar energy, and has adopted a new 'friendly' logo (which can be found online) with three hand-drawn circles over the company name printed in gentle, rounded letters.[36,37]

Symbols can also represent negative elements of corporate culture. At Enron, premium parking spots were symbols of power, wealth and winning at any cost. At the company's London office, executives submitted blind email bids for the limited spaces. One top manager paid £4000 to use a well-placed company spot for a year.[38]

?

ONLINE
COUNTERPOINT 11.7

Language   The final medium for influencing culture is language. Many companies use a specific saying, slogan, metaphor, motto or other form of language to convey special meaning to employees. Slogans can be readily picked up and repeated by employees as well as customers of the company. The Canadian company Rocky Mountain Soap built its image around the slogans, 'Be Kind, Be Real, Be Natural', more recently sharpening the environmental edge in the new corporate motto, 'Cleaner Bodies, Cleaner World'. There is a synergy between the company's motto and its founders' philosophy. Unlike other firms that often misuse words and images of the great outdoors in selling standard industrial products, Rocky Mountain Soap goes to tremendous lengths to remain true to the slogan. Products are developed in the company's small Rocky Mountain headquarters rather than in a distant laboratory. Only genuine natural ingredients including mountain glacier water are used, and advertising is low key and personal, such as sending customers a free bar of soap on their birthday.[39] Their environmental policy is particularly impressive, and in keeping with products that are 100 per cent natural. The products are biodegradable, do not harm watersheds or eco systems, there is minimal use of packaging which is selected with sustainability as a priority, they return to the electricity grid an equivalent amount of wind power for whatever is used in their workshop and stores, and staff are incentivized to use car-pools or bicycles.[40] The company also engages in environmental campaigns that fit with Rocky Mountain Soap's philosophy and business practices. For example, in 2012, company co-founder Karina Birch became a key organizer for the Environmental Defence NGO's 'Just Beautiful' campaign which calls for toxic ingredients to be removed from all personal care products. Birch says, 'Our company's core purpose is to remove toxins from the world. What better organization could we partner with as we pursue this never ending quest than Environmental Defence and their Just Beautiful campaign? Our goals align perfectly and my hope is that by working together we can rally enough consumers around our cause to finally propel the change that we need to see in Canada's regulations.' The company is not perfect but does try to make its environmental footprint as small as possible. How many other companies, or indeed people, could come anywhere close to making that claim?

Other significant uses of language to shape culture are as follows:

■ Before it was acquired by Oracle in a hostile takeover, which had initially been blocked by the US Department of Justice on the grounds that it would break anti-trust laws, PeopleSoft Inc. prided itself on a close-knit, family-like culture. Employees called themselves People-People, shopped at the company PeopleStore, and munched on company-funded People-Snacks. The use of this special lingo reinforced the distinctive cultural values. The loss of the culture was painful for employees, many of whom were laid off after the takeover.[41]

■ Metaphors are often used in order to 'domesticate' corporate activities. For example, when Daimler and Chrysler merged at the end of the twentieth century, phrases such as 'a marriage of equals' and 'a match dictated by chemistry' were used to describe the arrangement, encouraging staff to think positively about the merger as one built on attraction, compatibility and mutual respect. Such use of language can undoubtedly help smooth corporate restructuring, although it always runs the risk of being subverted by disaffected staff; in fact the merger was effectively a Daimler takeover, and some disgruntled Chrysler employees were heard commenting that it was 'more like a shotgun marriage'.[42,43]

ONLINE COUNTERPOINT 11.8

ONLINE COUNTERPOINT 11.9

Recall that culture comprises underlying values and assumptions and visible artifacts and observable behaviour. The slogans, symbols and ceremonies just described are artifacts that articulate underlying company values. These visible artifacts and behaviours can be used (and abused) by managers to shape company values and to strengthen organizational culture.

Organization Design and Culture

A synergistic culture can be assessed along many dimensions, such as the extent of collaboration versus isolation among people and departments, the importance of control and where control is concentrated, or whether the organization's time orientation is short range or long range.[44] Here, we will focus on two specific dimensions: (1) the extent to which the competitive environment requires flexibility or stability; and (2) the extent to which the organization's strategic focus and strength are internal or external. Four categories of culture associated with these differences, as illustrated in Exhibit 11.2, are adaptability, mission, clan and bureaucratic.[45] These four categories

EXHIBIT 11.2 Relationship of Environment and Strategy to Corporate Culture

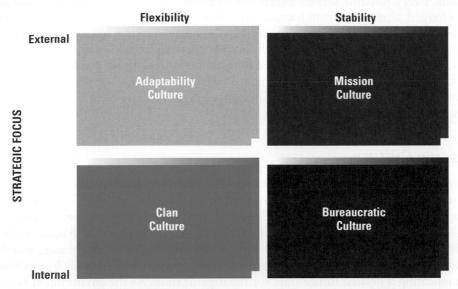

NEEDS OF THE ENVIRONMENT

Source: Based on Daniel R. Denison and Aneil K. Mishra, 'Toward a Theory of Organizational Culture and Effectiveness', *Organization Science* 6, No. 2 (March–April 1995), 204–223; R. Hooijberg and F. Petrock, 'On Cultural Change: Using the Competing Values Framework to Help Leaders Execute a Transformational Strategy', *Human Resource Management* 32 (1993), 29–50; and R. E. Quinn, *Beyond Rational Management: Mastering the Paradoxes and Competing Demands of High Performance* (San Francisco: Jossey-Bass, 1988).

relate to the fit among cultural values, strategy, structure and the environment. Each can be successful, depending on the needs of the external environment and the organization's strategic focus.

The Adaptability Culture

The adaptability culture is characterized by strategic focus on the external environment through flexibility and change to meet customer needs. The culture encourages entrepreneurial values, norms and beliefs that support the capacity of the organization to detect, interpret and translate signals from the environment into new behaviour responses. This type of company, however, doesn't just react quickly to environmental changes – it actively creates change. Innovation, creativity and risk taking are valued and rewarded.

Technology companies need to have an adaptability culture. The pace of change is so fast that any company failing to adapt quickly to competitive innovations will soon be a casualty left behind on the information superhighway. The concept of the 'real time enterprise' emerged from the high-tech sector, and reflects the goal of responding instantly to emerging issues. Partly this is possible through technology; BTexact (now part of BT Design)[46] started off as British Telecom's internal business support division but quickly became a major money-earner, helping companies reorganize their back-office functions to save money. That involves smart use of new technology to monitor blockages in processes, such as delays in transferring patient data between doctors' surgeries and hospitals. But success also requires an adaptability culture; there is no point spending money on high-tech fixes if staff are unwilling to change. Much of BTexact's work involves working with staff in institutions such as the National Health Service, training them both to use new technology and work more flexibly and efficiently.

Business models are increasingly built upon flexibility. The low-cost carrier (LCC) in the airline industry is a good example, so successful indeed that traditional full-service airlines are being priced out of short-haul and medium-haul air travel all over the world. At companies

BRIEFCASE 11.2

like Ireland's Ryanair, Hungary's WizzAir and Britain's EasyJet, routes are started up as soon as a business opportunity is sensed, and shut down again just as quickly if revenues don't meet expectations. Every possible service except the right to a random seat on the plane is 'unbundled' and charged separately, from baggage to seat selection to refreshments. A small staff team is responsible for multiple functions, with as many ancillary services outsourced as possible. The model works well in keeping down fares, although it often doesn't do as much for the companies' employees, who always need to be prepared for possible retrenchment.[47] Most e-commerce companies, such as Alibaba, Amazon and Google, as well as companies in the marketing, electronics and cosmetics industries, use this type of culture because they must move quickly to satisfy customers.

The Mission Culture

ONLINE
COUNTERPOINT 11.10

An organization concerned with serving specific customers in the external environment, but without the need for rapid change, is suited to the mission culture. The mission culture is characterized by emphasis on a clear vision of the organization's purpose and on the achievement of goals, such as sales growth, profitability or market share, to help achieve the purpose. Individual employees may be responsible for a specified level of performance, and the organization promises specified rewards in return. Managers shape behaviour by envisioning and communicating a desired future state for the organization. As the environment is stable, they can translate the vision into measurable goals and evaluate employee performance for meeting them. In some cases, mission cultures reflect a high level of competitiveness and a profit-making orientation.

Sports teams aim to build a mission culture; for their fans, success is easily measured in terms of trophies won, which in turn builds the value of the organization. Languishing teams will make special efforts to create enthusiasm and determination throughout the organization. Where they have failed to live up to their fans' expectations (which are typically on the outer limits of realism!) teams will frequently try to 'reinvent' themselves, both by calling upon a storied past and attempting to build a convincing story for the future. Cardiff City, the Welsh capital's football team, was once a major football power, but for over 50 years had languished in the lower divisions of British football. After several near misses at getting into the top flight Premier League, and losing out in several Cup Final games, Cardiff City was bought in 2010 by Malaysian businessman Vincent Tan. In 2012 the club's team colours were controversially changed from their historic blue to red, designed in part to appeal to Asian audiences where red is believed to be a lucky colour. The new image (along with a large investment in new players – see Counterpoint 11.4) didn't seem to do the club any harm on the field; in 2013 they finally made it to the Premier League. However fan discontent marred the team's stay in the Premier League and they were relegated after only a year. Eventually Tan relented and in 2015 the team's home colours reverted to the traditional blue and white. A reinvention still needs to connect with an organization's roots and tradition.[48]

COUNTERPOINT 11.4

The other, 'overlooked' key ingredient for success in the English Premier League is the financing of the club. Although teams such as Leicester City, who broke the stranglehold of the 'big four' when they won the Premier League in 2016, Stoke City and Swansea have demonstrated that the money of Manchester City and Chelsea is not the sole key to success, the capacity to buy in the best players in the world certainly helps. That said, the capacity to win or draw a football match is not dependent upon individual players but the ability of a team, including the coach, to identify and exploit the weaknesses of its opponents, in addition to the balance of good fortune in benefiting from flukes, inattentive referees, deflections and so on.

IN PRACTICE

Marks & Spencer

Marks & Spencer is a venerable British brand, but for the past few decades it has often had an image not dissimilar from that of its home country: a formerly great power whose best days seemed to be behind it. While upstart high street chains captured the imagination of Britain's youth, Marks seemed to cater to an ever greyer and staider clientele. This is an image perhaps encapsulated when the country's redoubtable 1980s Prime Minister, Margaret Thatcher, declared that M&S was where she liked to shop for her underwear. The company remained well enough loved in the UK, but when executives attempted to replicate the model overseas, the result was a resounding thud. Just because foreigners liked to watch reruns of *Fawlty Towers* and *Yes Minister* did not mean they wanted to dress in the same clothes as the shows' lead characters. When CEO, Stuart Rose, took over in 2004, the company was bleeding red ink and had retreated wounded from its forays overseas. Rose soon revamped the company's image, sharpening the pencil on prices and targeting a younger clientele to compete with chains like H&M. Exclusive designers were hired, such as Patricia Field, who had styled the clothes for the successful *Sex and the City* TV series. The 1960s model Twiggy came back to model a range of trendy clothes for mature women. By 2008, profits were once again above £1 billion, and Rose started to carefully plan another overseas venture, with the company opening its first store in mainland China in October of that year. Unfortunately that coincided with that autumn's financial and stock market meltdown. Rose left to be replaced by another prominent retail executive, Marc Bolland, formerly of Morrison's supermarkets. While the company weathered the crisis and continued building its international footprint, its fashion business constantly has to reinvent itself as fresh while retaining its core market of middle class, middle aged shoppers. In 2016 a new model connection with Alexa Chung reinvigorated its fashion credentials, but still, fashion writers pan the company's range as dowdy; "these hideous clothes are all still pretty expensive, so the idea that they're for your average, style-averse sixty something woman doesn't fly." Changing organizational culture and linked market image is extraordinarily difficult.[49,50]

The Clan Culture

The clan culture has a primary focus on the involvement and participation of the organization's members and on rapidly changing expectations from the external environment. More than any other, this culture focuses on the needs of employees as the route to high performance. Involvement and participation create a sense of responsibility and ownership and, hence, greater commitment to the organization.

In a clan culture, an important value is taking care of employees and making sure they have whatever they need to help them be satisfied as well as productive. Companies in the fashion and retail industries often adopt this culture because it releases the creativity of employees to respond to rapidly changing tastes. Wegmans, the New York, USA-based chain of supermarkets, has succeeded with a clan culture (see *Leading by Design* in Chapter 3 for more about the company). Employee commitment and satisfaction is considered key to success. Wegmans pays good wages, sends employees on learning trips and offers university scholarships for both full- and part-time employees. Employees are empowered to use their own initiative and creativity in serving customers.[51] Wegmans consistently comes near the top in polls of the best companies to work for in America, and manages at the same time to consistently make good profits.[52]

The Bureaucratic Culture

**ONLINE
COUNTERPOINT 11.11**

The bureaucratic culture has an internal focus and a consistency orientation for a stable environment. This organization has a culture that supports a methodical approach to doing business. Symbols, heroes and ceremonies support cooperation, tradition and follow established policies and practices as ways to achieve goals. Personal involvement is somewhat lower here, but that is outweighed by a high level of consistency, conformity and collaboration among members. This organization succeeds by being highly integrated and efficient.

For many years, bureaucratic cultures have suffered a bad press as the corporate environment has favoured flexibility and continuous reinvention. With the global economic troubles that began in 2008, however, some commentators began to re-evaluate this perspective. For example, in Britain, the cautious and conservative building societies – mutual associations that take in deposits from mainly small investors and lend out to home buyers – have mainly been in the decline since the 1980s, when financial services were liberalized. Many building societies converted themselves to banks. The old-time building societies operated according to strict – and 'bureaucratic' – income criteria to decide whether a person would be issued a mortgage to buy a house. In contrast, the new banks lent at ever-higher income ratios, sometimes even handing out mortgage loans of over 100 per cent of the value of the houses on which they were secured, and then went out onto the global money markets in search of cheap, but 'hot', short-term funding for those mortgages. All seemed to work well as house prices continued to rise, but when problems developed in the American financial markets and credit dried up in 2008, several of the new banks such as Northern Rock quickly went to the wall, and disaster was only averted by enormous and costly government bail-outs.[53] Similar stories of the transformation of banking into a version of high stakes gambling occurred in many countries around the world.

Culture Strength and Organizational Subcultures

Culture strength refers to the degree of agreement among members of an organization about the importance of specific values. If widespread consensus exists about the importance of those values, the culture is cohesive and strong; if little agreement exists, the culture is weak.[54]

A strong culture is typically associated with the frequent use of ceremonies, symbols, stories, heroes and slogans. Oceania in Orwell's novel *1984* offers a vivid example. Such elements are seen to increase employee commitment to the values and strategy of a company. Managers who want to create and maintain strong corporate cultures often give emphasis to the selection and socialization of employees.[55] Tech Target, a Massachusetts, USA online media company, uses a painstaking hiring process to find the kind of employees who will mesh with the company's unique values. Tech Target has an 'open-leave' policy, meaning that employees are free to come and go as they please. The culture emphasizes individual autonomy and personal responsibility; founder and CEO, Greg Strakosch, tries to hire people who are independent, achievement oriented, conscientious and capable of managing their own time.[56] With this approach, Tech Target has managed to stay ahead of the curve despite the incredibly rapid pace of innovation in the internet industry, emphasizing the use of 'big data' – the strategic use of computing power to crunch vast amounts of data to help understand markets and customers. The company continues to grow and expand internationally with 2015 sales over $100 million;[57] in 2013 Strakosch was inducted into the 'Digital Hall of Fame' at the annual *Best of the Web* awards.[58]

Culture is rarely uniform throughout the organization, particularly in large companies. Even in organizations that have strong cultures, there may be several sets of subcultures. Subcultures develop to reflect the common problems, goals and experiences that members of a team, department or other unit share. An office, branch or unit of a company that is physically separated from the company's main operations may also take on a distinctive subculture.

A mission culture may be dominant, but various departments may reflect characteristics of adaptability, clan or bureaucratic cultures. The manufacturing department of a large organization may thrive in an environment that emphasizes order, efficiency and obedience to rules, whereas the research and development (R&D) department may be characterized by employee empowerment, flexibility and customer focus. This is similar to the concept of differentiation described in Chapter 4, where employees in manufacturing, sales and research departments studied by Paul Lawrence and Jay Lorsch[59] developed different values with respect to time horizon, interpersonal relationships and formality in order to perform the job of each particular department most effectively. Differentiation is particularly common – and necessary – in multinational corporations, where companies need to respond to differing market conditions, cultural differences, regulatory environments and business climates in their operations around the world. When differentiation succeeds, whether in a national or multinational company, it can leverage maximum productivity

IN PRACTICE

Unilever Plc

Unilever products are available in every country of the world, and one household in every two across the globe has at least one Unilever product in the home. This global reach is in itself an indication of the company's success, which has been built on a far more decentralized corporate strategy than most other large multinationals. Back in 1963, Chairman George Cole put it succinctly: 'Unilever is not a ship, it is a fleet – several fleets, several hundred subsidiary companies – and the ships are of many different sizes, doing all kinds of different things, all over the place.'

Whereas other companies have focused on the biggest markets in the wealthiest countries, Unilever, with its origins in the colonial era, has been selling in developing countries since the beginning. Given wildly different consumer tastes and different-sized wallets, the only way to succeed was to give the company's national subsidiaries considerable autonomy, allowing them to develop internal cultures and business strategies suitable to the environments in which they were operating. Now that many developing countries are becoming more affluent 'emerging markets', the company's attention to these formerly small markets is paying off in spades; 38 per cent of the company's revenues came from emerging markets in 2005, more than all of Europe. India's Hindustan Unilever, for

example, is that emerging giant's largest consumer products company, with an enormous reservoir of goodwill built up over three-quarters of a century of operations. Many of India's top executives cut their teeth at Hindustan Unilever, and the company was chosen fourth-best company in the world for leadership development in 2007 in a Fortune/Hewitt Associates survey.

Nevertheless, Unilever's overall financial performance has been relatively sluggish compared with more centralized competitors like Procter & Gamble, due in part, claim critics, to an inability to draw the line between creative differentiation and local inefficiencies. Patrick Cescau, who took over as CEO in 2005, saw greater corporate coherence as one of his top priorities, 'We have to be culturally relevant, but delivering to a global strategy'. When Cescau retired in 2008, Unilever's board chose for the first time to hire its leader from outside the company, selecting as top executive Paul Polman, with a background from Procter & Gamble, further sign that the balance between differentiation and global coordination would continue to be tilted in the latter direction.[60] Results have been very positive, with sales over €50 billion in 2015, as well as profits of over $5 billion.[61,62]

Subcultures typically include the basic values of the dominant organizational culture plus additional values unique to members of the subculture. However, subcultural differences can sometimes lead to conflicts between departments, especially in organizations that do not have strong overall corporate cultures. When subcultural values become too strong and outweigh the corporate cultural values, conflicts may emerge and hurt organizational performance. Conflict will be discussed in detail in Chapter 14.

and revenues from the different capacities within the company. Poorly managed, however, it can result in culture clash or in the loss of proper systems of internal control (see Counterpoint 11.5). Where the required culture within a particular corporate subdivision varies too greatly from the corporate norm, there may be a case for spinning off that subsidiary into a separate company. The Anglo-Dutch company Unilever, featured in the *In Practice* text box above, is famous for diversity in its products, its corporate culture and its geographic reach, which at different times has proven both a help and a hindrance to the company's success.

COUNTERPOINT 11.5

This assumes that management is, or should be, in a position to control culture as if it were something that exists independently of their own activities. It may be that 'poor management' is itself a facet of the culture of the company, and one that cannot necessarily be corrected by changing the management. Ultimately, the effectiveness of 'systems of internal control', for example, will depend upon the perceived legitimacy – something that is culturally dependent.

Organizational Culture, Learning and Performance

Culture can play an important role in creating a climate that enables learning and innovative responses to challenges, competitive threats or new opportunities. A culture that encourages adaptation and change may enhance performance by energizing and motivating employees, unifying people key around goals and guiding employee behaviour so that actions are aligned with strategic priorities.

Singapore Airlines, described in the *Leading by Design* box below, has achieved phenomenal success partly because of its strong adaptive culture.[63] In *Corporate Culture and Performance*, Kotter and Heskett provided evidence that companies that intentionally managed cultural values outperformed similar companies that did not. Until recently, the culture of South Korean

LEADING BY DESIGN

Singapore Airlines

Singapore is one of Asia's many great success stories, and Singapore Airlines (SIA) is a jewel in the crown of the successful city-state located at the southern tip of the Malay Peninsula. Visitors to Singapore today almost invariably comment on its affluence, sparkling cleanliness and sense of order, but Singapore's success, like that of its flagship airline, is built on careful planning and rigorous

discipline. Singapore Airlines was created in 1972, a few years after the country achieved independence from Malaysia. From its earliest days, SIA managers focused on building the airline's competitive edge as offering uniquely high levels of customer service, building on south-east Asia's reputation for hospitality with the carefully imaged 'Singapore girl' cabin crew. At the same time, the company has always operated at a profit, unlike most other airlines in a highly volatile and competitive industry, demonstrating what one research report describes as the ability to be 'hard' while also being 'soft'. SIA aims to be at the forefront of technological change and innovation in the industry, and has been first to introduce many services that later became industry norms, such as internet booking, web and SMS check-in and a whole range of high-end services to attract and keep the lucrative business executive traveller. At the same time, the company has responded to changing social mores. As women have assumed a larger and more equal role in society, SIA faced increasing criticism from women's groups that SIA's Singapore girl was a sexist and even insulting stereotype of women. Despite denying that it was bowing to pressure, in 2007 the company put out a tender for an image revamp designed to create a more formally professional image for its cabin crew.[64] SIA is in many ways, therefore, an excellent example of the adaptive organization discussed earlier in this chapter. This adaptive approach also extends to the company's activities in corporate social responsibility (CSR) and environmental responsibility. In the post-September 11, 2001 world, Singapore Airlines worked closely with its home base Chiangi airport to become the first airline to effectively use biometrics to speed a passenger through check-in, baggage drop and security, and on to their flight within a few minutes.

As one of a handful of world-class Singaporean enterprises, SIA makes it its business not merely to practice CSR, but to be at its forefront. The airline operates a number of charitable projects in the Asia–Pacific Region, such as supporting schooling for children from low-income families in the Philippines, as well as various projects such as visiting for the elderly within Singapore. On a more strategic level, the company is invariably represented on committees for national activities such as the Singapore Compact for CSR, which ties in with the United Nations' Global Compact, and offers comprehensive CSR training for smaller and midsize Singaporean companies.[65] Like many projects in the country, the Singapore Compact is a tripartite (government, company, union) initiative.

SIA itself is majority-owned by Temasek Holdings, the Singapore government's investment holding vehicle. The biggest corporate image challenge being faced by SIA, along with other world airlines, is climate change and the argument that air travel is a significant contributor to the problem. Once again, Singapore Airlines was out in front of the issue, producing an annual environmental responsibility report for the past 7 years, and rejuvenating its fleet.[66] The company was the first in the world to acquire the huge A380 Airbus, which uses less fuel per passenger than smaller planes, but which is viewed with mixed feelings by environmental campaigners because of the additional runway infrastructure needed to support its enormous weight.

Singapore Airlines' combination of adaptive culture and attention to social and environmental values consistently push the company to the top of global rankings. The company has been ranked best airline in the world by the *World Airline Awards* three times in the past decade, and between 2007 and 2015 was never outside the top three.[67,68]

Singapore Airlines operates in a different social environment than Western companies, Singaporean society is directed by government to a much greater extent than in most Western countries, and this gives the company some advantages. For example, in the mid-1990s, when pilots were threatening industrial action, they were warned by Lee Kuan Yew, the by then 'retired' founder of Singapore, not to step too far out of line. One of the union leaders, who is not a Singaporean citizen, even had his residency permit revoked.[69] Nevertheless, overall, Singapore Airlines' high rankings for both customer service and social and environmental responsibility are well justified.

companies, such as Samsung, were typically hierarchical and male-dominated. This reflected a society that had been dominated for many years by the country's military and paternalistic business leaders. But as the country has democratized and opened to the world, values are changing along with corporate needs. With success in global markets, Korean companies have recruited international talent. Workforces are becoming more diverse, with many more women and young people in management positions. Excessive formality in addressing managers has been eliminated, salary and promotion are based on performance rather than longevity. Effective campaigns have been implemented against sexual harassment, with even senior officials disciplined. 'If men insist on the old way, they'll be in trouble,' said Cho Yoon Hee, 28, who works at Hyundai Capital, 'we women won't take it any more.[70,71]

A danger for many successful organizations is that the culture can become set, making it hard for the company to adapt as the environment changes, as we saw in the chapter-opening example of Boots, and the discussion later in this chapter on Marks and Spencer. When organizations are successful, the values, ideas and practices that helped attain success become institutionalized. As the environment changes, these values may become detrimental to, rather than productive for, future performance. The impact of a strong culture is not always positive.

Ethical Values and Social Responsibility

Corporate accounting scandals, allegations that top managers of some organizations made personal use of company funds, and charges of insider trading have blanketed the media in recent years. Top corporate managers are under scrutiny from the public as never before, and even small companies are finding a need to put more emphasis on ethics to restore trust among their customers and the community. As a consequence, of the values that make up an organization's culture, ethical values are now considered among the most important.

Sources of Individual Ethical Principles

Ethical values set standards as to what is good or bad in conduct and decision-making.[72] In any given group, organization or society there are many areas of consensus about what constitutes ethical behaviour (see Exhibit 11.3).[73] National culture, religious heritage, historical background and so forth lead to the development of societal morality, or society's view of what is right and wrong. Societal morality is often reflected in norms of behaviour and values about what makes sense for an orderly society. Some principles are codified into laws and regulations, such as laws against drunk driving, robbery or murder. In the light of the social moralities, including organizational conceptions of what is right and wrong, people develop their own ethical values – for example, by conforming doggedly to them, by completely rejecting them, or by critically engaging with them.

Laws, as well as unwritten societal norms and values, form important elements of the local environment including community, family and place of work.

It is important to acknowledge the personal quality of ethics as ethics involve a decision to act or the failure to take action (e.g. to take action to expose or challenge the wrongdoing of others). Organizational culture can exert considerable influence on such decisions, and so can encourage or impede ethical actions or promote unethical and socially irresponsible behaviour.

Managerial Ethics and Social Responsibility

ONLINE
COUNTERPOINT 11.12

BRIEFCASE 11.3

Many of the recent scandals in the news have dealt with people and corporations that broke the law. But it is important to remember that ethics goes far beyond behaviour governed by law.[74] The rule of law arises from a set of codified principles and regulations that describe how people are required to act, that are generally accepted in society and that are enforceable in the courts.[75]

The relationship between ethical standards and legal requirements is illustrated in Exhibit 11.4. Ethical standards for the most part apply to behaviour not covered by the law, and the rule of law applies to behaviour not necessarily covered by ethical standards. Current laws often reflect moral judgements, but not all moral judgements are codified into law. The morality of aiding a drowning person, for example, is not specified by law, and driving on the left- or right-hand side of the road has no moral basis; but in acts such as robbery or murder, rules and moral standards overlap.

Ethically dubious conduct in organizations is widespread. More than 54 per cent of human resource (HR) professionals polled by the US-headquartered Society for Human Resource Management and the Ethics Resource Center reported observing employees lying to supervisors

EXHIBIT 11.3 Sources of Ethical Principles and Actions

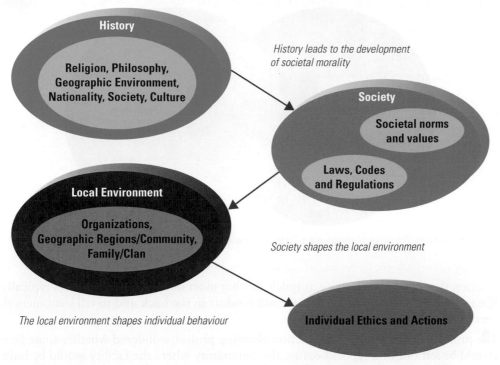

Adapted from an Exhibit provided by Susan H. Taft and Judith White. We thank them for furnishing it.

or co-workers, falsifying reports or records or abusing drugs or alcohol while on the job.[76] Many people believe that if you are not breaking the law, then you are behaving in an ethical manner, but this is incorrect. Many deviant behaviours have not been legally codified, and managers must be sensitive to emerging norms and values about those issues. It can even be the case that complying with a law (particularly in an undemocratic regime) may breach a manager's ethical standards. For example, the former apartheid government in South Africa mandated discrimination against the majority black population in various ways including through banning black people from holding certain skilled positions.[77] A manager who administered such an offensive and discriminatory policy would, in the assessment of many people, be ethically responsible but she/he would not be legally culpable for its impact on the black majority population (it might even be illegal in a certain jurisdiction *not* to discriminate). Managerial ethics are principles that guide the decisions and behaviour of managers with regard to whether they are right or wrong. The notion of social responsibility is an example of managerial ethics insofar as its ascribes an obligation to managers to make choices and take action so that the organization contributes to the welfare and interest of all organizational stakeholders, such as employees, customers, shareholders, the community and the broader society.[78]

Examples of ethical issues are as follows:[79]

■ Top executives are considering promoting a rising sales manager who consistently brings in $70 million a year and has cracked open new markets in places like Brazil and Turkey that are important to the organization's international growth. However, female employees have been complaining for years that the manager is verbally abusive to them, tells offensive jokes and throws temper tantrums if female employees don't do exactly as he says.

■ The manager of a beauty supply store is told that she and her salespeople can receive large bonuses for selling a specified number of boxes of a new product, a permanent-wave

EXHIBIT 11.4 Relationship between the Rule of Law and Ethical Standards

| Legal Requirements | Ethical Standards |

Source: LaRue Tone Hosmer, *The Ethics of Management*, 2d ed. (Homewood, IL: Irwin, 1991).

solution that costs nearly twice as much as what most of her salon customers typically use. She orders the salespeople to store the old product in the back and to tell customers there's been a delay in delivery.

■ The project manager for a construction planning project wondered whether some facts should be left out of a report because the community where the facility would be built might object if they discovered certain environmental aspects of the project.

■ An American manufacturer operating abroad was asked to make cash payments (a bribe) to government officials and was told it was consistent with local customs and the practices of firms from some European countries, despite being illegal in the United States.

ONLINE
COUNTERPOINT 11.13

As these examples illustrate, ethics and social responsibility are about making decisions. Managers make choices every day about whether, for example, to be honest or deceitful with suppliers, to treat employees with respect or disdain, and to be a good or a harmful corporate citizen. Some issues are exceedingly difficult to resolve and often represent ethical dilemmas. An ethical dilemma arises in a situation concerning right and wrong in which values are in conflict.[80] For example, for a salesperson at the beauty supply store, the value conflict is between being honest with customers and adhering to the boss's expectations. The manufacturing manager may feel torn between following local customs and being competitive with practices of a European firm, or adhering to US laws concerning bribes. When faced with such a dilemma, the temptation is to 'go along' with what others are doing, perhaps by saying 'if I don't do it, then they will' or by justifying a personally unethical action by reference to the responsibilities of parenthood, etc. which might be jeopardized by acting ethically or 'blowing the whistle'.

Does It Pay to Be Good?

ONLINE
COUNTERPOINT 11.14

As discussed earlier in the chapter, companies with high levels of social capital are more likely to enjoy long-term organizational success. One way that companies can accumulate social capital is through building a reputation for honesty, fairness and doing the right thing. Researchers have found that people prefer to work for companies that demonstrate a high level of ethics and social responsibility, so these companies can attract and retain high-quality employees.[81] Many companies now evaluate their top executives not only on the financial bottom line but also on their effectiveness in demonstrating the corporation's social responsibility.[82] Particularly in fast-growing economies, such as China, retaining capable, committed employees can be a challenge, and large firms such as Standard Chartered and Manulife Financial stress corporate integrity and social responsibility in recruitment campaigns.[83,84]

Many customers pay attention, too, and gear their purchases to companies they view as ethical. However, research shows that while most consumers will state that they have a preference for doing business with ethical companies, not all will translate that preference into actual purchasing habits, and companies designing social responsibility initiatives with a view to attracting and retaining customers would need to identify those segments of the purchasing public likely to be motivated by specific strategies.[85] At the same time, there is some research evidence that many consumers are relatively sceptical about corporations' motives for engaging in ethical activities; overall, consumers are more likely to support companies they believe have a genuine, uncompromising commitment to social responsibility rather than those that they suspect simply view it as a marketing ploy.[86,87]

?

ONLINE
COUNTERPOINT 11.15

During the Asian economic crisis of the late 1990s, PT Denpoo Mandiri Indonesia (DMI), an Indonesian appliance manufacturer, had a tough decision to make. The crisis led to a dramatic drop in the value of the Indonesian currency, the rupiah, and made appliances much more expensive to manufacture. As a result, contracts that had been signed with retailers suddenly became money-losing. Many Indonesian firms reneged on their contracts, which saved money in the short term. DMI, however, decided to bite the bullet. 'As a brand name, we must be trustworthy,' says Yeane Keet, DMI's marketing director, 'Even though we had to sell our products at a loss, we continued to honour orders already placed.' As a result, she said, the trust of retailers' in the company grew, and their loyalty to customers repaid the short term losses many times. As the crisis eased in the mid-2000s, DMI was able to expand its production and sales overseas and is now a big player in several countries in southeast Asia.[88,89]

?

ONLINE
COUNTERPOINT 11.16

Sources of Ethical Values in Organizations

Ethics in organizations is a personal as well as an organizational matter. The standards for ethical or socially responsible conduct are embodied within each employee as well as within the organization itself. In addition, external stakeholders can influence standards of what is ethical and socially responsible.

Personal Ethics

Personal values and the moral reasoning that translates these values into behaviour are an important aspect of ethical decision-making in organizations.[90]

As we discussed earlier, the historical, cultural, family, religious and community backgrounds of managers shape their personal values and provide principles by which they carry out business. Managers' behaviour is influenced by more or less conscious *ethical frameworks* that guide their decisions. Utilitarian theory, personal liberty and distributive justice are three examples of such frameworks. *Utilitarian theory* argues that ethical decisions should be made to generate the greatest benefits for the largest number of people. This framework is often consistent with business decisions because costs and benefits can be calculated in dollars, although some costs may be externalized (e.g. consumption of fossil fuels for future generations). The *personal liberty* framework argues that decisions should be made to ensure the greatest possible freedom of choice and liberty for individuals. Liberties include the freedom to act on one's conscience, freedom of speech, due process of law and the right to privacy, although this pays little attention to the unintended consequences of the protection of such liberties for public goods (e.g. unpolluted air and water). The *distributive justice* framework holds that moral decisions are those that promote equity, fairness and impartiality with respect to the distribution of rewards and the administration of rules, which are essential for social cooperation, although this begs the question of who is to determine what 'fairness', for example, means, and what kind of 'fairness' is likely to foster cooperation.[91]

Organizational Culture

Rarely can ethical or unethical business practices be attributed entirely to the personal ethics of a single manager or employee. Such practices also reflect the values, attitudes and behaviour patterns of a wider national or organizational culture. The British surfwear company Finisterre makes ethics and environmental friendliness central to its business model. Founder Tom Kay sells only renewable or recyclable fabrics, and has pulled production out of China because of that country's human rights issues, preferring to obtain his products from sources such as nuns in Colombia and a women's self-help project.[92] The company's I-spy initiative allows customers to follow the entire value chain process from design through manufacturing, to see which materials are being used with what environmental impacts, and which contractors are producing goods and in which locations with what human rights records.

Despite strong ethical commitment, small and medium-sized companies like Finisterre are constantly faced with challenges to maintain their principles in a tough economic climate. Finisterre, for example, needed a capital injection in 2010, but the investor demanded the company slash costs by moving some production to India. 'We went to India in February 2011. It wasn't the place we'd hoped for, ethically or in quality,' says Finisterre marketing director Ernest Capbert. 'But to get the ball rolling, it seemed necessary.' The investor kept demanding a bigger and bigger chunk of the company, with more and more demands that went against Finisterre's ethos. Finally Finisterre had enough, and pulled out of the deal, as well as moving production back to Europe from India. It has not been an easy ride, but the company has continued to thrive while remaining true to its principles.[93] Since 2014 it has expanded into casual 'apres-surf' gear including jeans and sweaters, managing to catch the hipster wave.[94]

Organizational culture can exert a powerful impact on personal ethics because it helps to guide employees in making daily decisions. When the culture sanctions or turns a blind eye to what employees personally regard as wrongdoing, it is much easier for employees to accommodate it or normalize it. One young Enron employee explained how he slid into unethical decisions and practices in his job: 'It was easy to get into. Well, everybody else is doing it, so maybe it isn't so bad.'[95]

Organizational Systems

Many companies have established formal ethics programmes, sometimes after facing bad publicity. For example, the British defence firm, BAE Systems, has been widely criticized for unethical conduct in various arms deals, including accusations that it paid bribes to foreign government officials to secure business. While BAE has denied acting unlawfully, it attempted to address the criticism by appointing a former Chief Justice to conduct an ethical review of the company's activities. Lord Woolf made 23 recommendations for a comprehensive ethics programme, including a comprehensive register of all the hospitality provided by the company to its clients and third parties, as well as a regular external audit of the ethics of its business activities. BAE's new CEO promised to implement all 23 recommendations within three years. The company has, however, continued to receive criticism for failing to address past conduct, demonstrating how hard it is to rebuild reputations that have been deeply damaged.[96,97]

External Stakeholders

Managerial ethics and social responsibility are influenced by a variety of external stakeholders, groups outside the organization that have a stake in the organization's performance. Ethical and socially responsible decision-making recognizes that the organization is part of a larger community and considers the impact of a decision or action on all stakeholders.[98] Important external stakeholders include government agencies, customers and special-interest groups such as those concerned with the natural environment.

Companies are legally obliged to operate within the limits of government regulations, including environmental protection requirements, workers' health and safety rules and many other laws and regulations. Numerous companies have come under investigation by financial regulatory bodies such as the Securities and Exchange Commission (SEC) in the United States and the various similar financial oversight authorities around the world for violating laws related to financial controls and accounting practices. In the wake of the global financial meltdown of 2008, the SEC launched more than 50 investigations into the subprime mortgage industry in the US, which collapse sparked worldwide financial panic. Nevertheless, there was widespread criticism that the SEC, and even more so the European regulatory authorities, acted only after the full-blown crisis had emerged.[99]

Customers, another important stakeholder group, are primarily concerned about the quality, safety and availability of goods and services. For example, fast-food restaurants such as McDonald's, Burger King and Kentucky Fried Chicken have been pressured to reduce or eliminate the presence of trans-fatty acids in their products to address growing customer concerns about health risks. Some jurisdictions such as New York in the US and Calgary in Canada have entirely banned trans fats in response to pressure from consumers and the medical profession, and in 2015 the United States mandated the phase-out of trans fats nationally by 2018.[100,101,102] In Europe, Denmark and Switzerland have put restrictions in place, virtually eliminating trans fats. The UK, in 2012, instead chose a voluntary approach of working with food companies, but this has been strongly criticized by the medical profession as unlikely to be effective. Government regulation is a crucial aspect in framing corporate ethical expectations.[103]

Special-interest groups endeavour to voice stakeholder concerns, notably about employee rights and the natural environment. The concept of *sustainable development*, a dual concern for economic growth, human well-being and environmental sustainability, has become an increasing focus of attention for business leaders. The public is no longer comfortable with organizations focusing solely on profit at the expense of the natural environment. Environmental sustainability is formally a part of strategy for companies like Canon, Unilever, Toyota, Nike and IKEA, although substantively their practices may depart dramatically from such commitment. In 2006 Toyota announced that it was committed to becoming a carbon-neutral company and producing zero emissions, and other carmakers such as BMW quickly followed suit but none has yet to come close to that goal, which many argue is pure marketing hype, as even electric cars, which do not themselves emit any emissions, produce emissions in their manufacture.[104,105]

How Leaders Shape Culture and Ethics

Values can be communicated in a number of ways – speeches, company publications, policy statements and, especially, personal actions. The introduction of formal ethics codes and training programmes, as exemplified by Enron, is however worthless if leaders do not demonstrate high standards of ethical conduct.[106]

Values-based Leadership

Leaders may strive to influence cultural and ethical values by clearly articulating a vision for organizational values that employees can believe in, communicating the vision throughout the organization and institutionalizing the vision through everyday behaviour, rituals, ceremonies and symbols, as well as through organizational systems and policies (see Counterpoint 11.6).

BRIEFCASE 11.4

Anita Roddick, the founder of the Body Shop beauty product chain who sadly died suddenly in 2007, was the pioneer of corporate social activism. Her business was phenomenally successful, with over 2000 stores in 55 countries. However, she never deviated from her commitment to sell only natural products that had not been tested on animals and to campaign for her belief in a fairer world. She sought to operationalize her values through the company; the Body Shop was one of the first companies in the world to report regularly and comprehensively on its performance in meeting its ethical and social responsibility goals. Roddick also espoused radical politics – she had no hesitation in joining protestors who shut down World Trade Organization meetings in Seattle in 1999, and was active in several campaigning NGOs including Greenpeace. Roddick's success and popularity helped to popularize corporate social responsibility in the UK and internationally.[107]

COUNTERPOINT 11.6

This presumes that employees are seeking values or a vision they can believe in. Might they not already have their own values and visions? If they are 'ethically developed', then it is probable that they will be sceptical about leaders' efforts to 'institutionalize' values which they may feel are being imposed upon them. The outcome is as likely to ferment resentment or compliance as it is to increase commitment.

Companies that fall victim to large scale employee wrongdoing are typically found to lack ethical leadership. At Société Générale, the major French bank, a junior 'rogue trader' lost nearly €5 billion in 2008 through unauthorized trades. Société Générale CEO, Daniel Bouton, initially called the errant trader a 'terrorist'. Bouton was eventually forced to step down when government and independent investigators found that internal controls were lax. The accused trader claimed that he was under pressure to deliver large trading profits, that company officials knew what he was doing, and that other traders routinely made similar financial bets. At the same time, Société Générale executives were embroiled in a court case involving alleged money laundering between Israel and France. The story was familiar to Nick Leeson, the trader whose failed financial market gambles caused the collapse of Baring's Bank 13 years earlier. Leeson claims that because of the huge profits he seemed to be making, he became a celebrity at Baring's: 'The management of the bank holds you up as an example of how they want things to be done.' British financial journalist Jules Stewart summarizes the problem: 'Due to corporate greed ... the people who should have known better turned a blind eye to what were obvious danger signals.'[108]

Employees learn about values, beliefs and goals from watching managers, just as students learn which topics are important for an exam and how to get a good grade from their teachers. To be effective values-based leaders, executives often use symbols, ceremonies, speeches and slogans that match the values. Siemens, the giant German technology group, was shaken by a bribery scandal uncovered in 2006. Apparently, for many years and in many different countries, the company had been providing illegal bribes and kick-backs to win contracts; it was a way of doing business that had become ingrained. It was crucial that Siemens act decisively to restore faith in the company. Although the previous CEO and other top managers denied wrongdoing, they stepped down. The board hired a top New York law firm as outside investigators of the scandal; their independence made it possible to dig into what had happened over a period of many years, thus fostering transparency.

In 2007 Siemens appointed Austrian Peter Loescher as its new CEO, the first time the company had chosen a non-German leader, another sign that the board was determined to mark a break with an inward-looking and self-justifying corporate culture that had hitherto marked Siemens and German industry as a whole. Loescher, former head of pharmaceutical giant Merck, quickly took several decisive steps to draw a line under the scandal. To begin with, he made clear the new rule by which Siemens was going to play: 'From Day One, what I have clearly communicated to everyone is that we have a Zero Tolerance policy; that there is absolutely no grey zone, and that Siemens stands for clean business everywhere, and at all times. So you establish this principle, and you clearly lead it from the top. And this is what both my colleagues and myself are doing every day, reinforcing this leadership principle in the organization.' Loescher also appointed a general counsel at management board level, which is responsible for compliance. All control functions were centralized (many of the bribery accusations came from different national subsidiaries), and the company's global operations in general were placed under strong central leadership, rather than the previous decentralized model that may have encouraged a 'hear no evil, see no evil' attitude towards national subsidiaries at corporate headquarters.[109] Loescher emphasized that it was not a matter of 'either' profits 'or' ethics; in fact, cleaning up the bribery scandal provided an opportunity to put the company on a more solid and sustainable business footing at the same time. By 2012 the company had been judged most ethical firm in its industry category five years in a row, while also steadily increasing profits even in the economic crisis. 'The speed of change,' said Loescher, 'was only possible because we were able to use [the bribery scandal] at the same moment to reposition the whole company.'[110] However, Siemens' improved image went along with stagnating profits and in 2013 Loescher was replaced by German executive Joe Kaeser. While the decade old corruption scandal continued to wind its way through various courts, Kaeser attracted new criticism in 2014 for visiting Vladimir Putin in Moscow, while Russia was invading neighbouring Ukraine. Was Siemens reverting to a profits before ethics policy?[111] (see Counterpoint 11.7)

Formal Structure and Systems

Structure   Managers can assign responsibility for ethical values to a specific position, as was the case with Siemens, noted above. This not only allocates organization time and energy to the problem but it also symbolizes to everyone the importance of ethics. This significance may be institutionalized in a high level ethics committee, which is a cross-functional group of executives who oversee company ethics. The committee provides rulings on questionable ethical issues and assumes responsibility for disciplining wrongdoers.

ONLINE
COUNTERPOINT 11.17

> **COUNTERPOINT 11.7**
>
> Recognizing the significance of ethics within the structure of a company can signal their importance. But it can also be a substitute, rather than an impetus, for reflection upon the institutionalized ethics of a company. To what extent do ethics codes, committees and hotlines actively encourage scrutiny of the ethics of the company's treatment of its employees or its impact upon the environment? Or could it be that these elements are introduced mainly to ensure that the company minimizes its exposure to exceptional recklessness or bad publicity?

Many large organizations have ethics departments that manage and coordinate all corporate ethics activities. These departments are headed by a chief ethics or chief compliance officer, a high-level company executive who oversees all aspects of ethics, including establishing and broadly communicating ethical standards, setting up ethics training programmes, supervising the investigation of ethical problems and advising managers on the ethical aspects of corporate decisions.[112] This position was almost unheard of 20 years ago, but recent ethical and legal problems have created a growing demand for these specialists. Between 1992 and 2016, membership in the Ethics and Compliance Association, a US-based trade group with membership on six continents, soared from only 12 companies to over 1300. There are similar business ethics associations based in Europe and Asia, as well as a global network of organizations promoting business ethics.[113,114]

Ethics offices sometimes also work as counselling centres to help employees resolve difficult ethical dilemmas. The focus is as much on helping employees make the right decisions as on disciplining wrongdoers. Many ethics offices have confidential ethics hotlines that employees can use to seek guidance as well as report questionable behaviour. One organization calls its hotline a 'Guide Line' to emphasize its use as a tool for making ethical decisions as well as reporting lapses.[115] Some organizations such as Singapore International Airlines (SIA) operate their ethics hotline in-house. SIA's ethics hotline can be reached by telephone or email 24 hours a day, and is for staff, vendors, suppliers and anyone else who deals with the airline. Other organizations such as Japan's Pioneer Corporation electronics group contract with outside organizations to run their hotline; Pioneer's is an email service run by Integrex, a Japanese firm that specializes in running ethics hotlines and similar services. The hotline at Pioneer feeds into a high-level Business Ethics Committee chaired by the company President and CEO and includes among its members company officers, division managers, board members including outside directors and corporate auditors.[116]

BRIEFCASE 11.5

Disclosure Mechanisms   A confidential hotline is an important mechanism for employees to voice concerns about ethical practices. Holding organizations accountable depends to some degree on individuals who are willing to speak up if they suspect illegal, dangerous or unethical activities. Organizations can establish policies and procedures to support and protect *whistle-blowers*. Whistle-blowing is employee disclosure of illegal, immoral or illegitimate practices on the part of the organization.[117] One value of corporate policy is to protect whistle-blowers so they will not be transferred to lower-level positions or fired because of their concerns. A policy can also encourage whistle-blowers to stay within the organization – for instance, to quietly blow the whistle to responsible managers.[118] As ethical problems in the corporate world increase, many companies are looking for ways to protect whistle-blowers as they can provide an early warning of trouble that can be addressed internally before it escapes into the media. At the same time, calls are increasing for stronger legal protection for those who report illegal or unethical business activities.[119] When there are no protective measures, whistle-blowers suffer and the company may do little or nothing to discover and root out unethical or illegal practices.

Many whistle-blowers suffer financial and personal loss to maintain their personal ethical standards. Katherine Gun, a translator at Britain's secretive General Communications Headquarters (GCHQ) was fired when she leaked an email, said to come from US authorities, that discussed a plan to arrange illegal wiretapping of United Nations delegates in order to support the US plan to invade Iraq. Gun was initially charged with breaching Britain's Official Secrets Act. The British government eventually dropped the charges. Gun went on to form the Truth-Telling Coalition, an international association devoted to protecting whistle-blowers in similar situations.[120]

Corporate whistle-blowers are often in an even weaker situation than those in the public sector. Corporations can often claim that whistle-blowers have damaged their commercial interests and/or failed to pursue all avenues within the company, even where the whistle-blower legitimately fears that complaining internally about some unethical practice will merely result in the company covering up the misdeed and getting rid of the whistle-blower. Sherron Watkins, a former executive with Enron, complained to CEO Kenneth Lay about the huge holes in company finances that were being covered up.[121] An internal enquiry was held that largely dismissed her claims, which were of course justified when the company collapsed a few months later.

Whistle-blowers are better protected in the US than in most other countries; the Sarbanes-Oxley Act of 2002, which was enacted in the wake of Enron and other corporate scandals, provides for severe criminal penalties against anyone victimizing a whistle-blower. Increasingly, companies will blow the whistle on each other when they realize that they have engaged in illegal activity, such as price-fixing, that is likely to come to light. This is because the corporate whistle-blower is often granted immunity in return for testifying against their competitors and erstwhile price-fixers. In 2007, Virgin Atlantic, Britain's second largest long-haul airline, approached the government's Office of Fair Trading with details of a scheme it had been running with British Airways, the country's biggest airline, to set the fuel surcharge charged by the two airlines, which operate a near duopoly on many routes. In return for blowing the whistle on its competitor, Virgin avoided a fine and criminal prosecution of participating executives. British Airways, on the other hand, was fined £271.5 million and four executives were charged with criminal price-fixing.[122]

Despite the obvious temptation to cover up scandal, many companies do strive to create a climate and a culture in which employees feel free to point out problems and managers take swift action to address concerns about unethical or illegal activities.

Code of Ethics
By the late 2000s, 86 per cent of the Fortune Global 200 companies had corporate codes of ethics, including 100 per cent of US-based firms, 80 per cent of European firms and over half of Asian-headquartered firms.[123] A code of ethics is a formal statement of the company's values concerning ethics and social responsibility; it clarifies to employees what the company stands for and its expectations for employee conduct. At Toyota, for example, the code of ethics is contained in two interlinked documents, the Guiding Principles of Toyota, which sets out the company's broad long-term goals, and the Toyota Code of Conduct, which outlines what is expected of employees on a daily basis; the first clause of the latter document requires employees to, 'honor the language and spirit of the law of every nation and undertake open and fair corporate activities to be a good corporate citizen of the world'.[124] The code specifies the types of behaviour expected to honour the Guiding Principles of Toyota, and encourages employees to use available company resources to help make ethical choices and decisions.[125] Codes of ethics may cover a broad range of issues, including statements of the company's guiding values, guidelines related to issues such as workplace safety, the security of proprietary information or employee privacy, and commitments to environmental responsibility, product safety and other matters of concern to stakeholders. Research comparing companies' ethics codes has found that European companies are more likely than North American to have ethics codes that go beyond strict legal compliance and mandate compliance with broader norms of ethical responsibility.[126]

Written codes of ethics clarify and formally state the company's values and expected ethical behaviour. However, it is essential that top managers support and reinforce the codes through their actions, including rewards for compliance and discipline for violations. Otherwise, a code of ethics makes no substantive contribution to ethical behaviour and indeed may act as a smoke-screen that fuels employee disaffection and cynicism. Indeed, one study found that companies with a written code of ethics are just as likely as those without a code to be found guilty of illegal activities, which suggests that, on their own, codes, committees and hotlines are not particularly effective in engendering ethical conduct.[127] Many companies that run into trouble with regulatory authorities and the formal legal system had well-developed codes of ethics. For example, the US firm Halliburton, which is accused of having bribed officials to win contracts in Nigeria, and having overcharged the US government for goods and services in Iraq, has a comprehensive code of business conduct, as does British Airways, despite its involvement in the price fixing scandal mentioned above.[128]

Training Programmes
To ensure that ethical issues are considered in daily decision-making, companies can supplement a written code of ethics with employee training programmes.[129] At GlaxoSmithKline, for example, new employees receive ethics information and training as part of their induction.[130,131]

Ethics programmes typically include some reference to frameworks for ethical decision-making, such as the approaches described earlier in this chapter. These framework formal systems and structures can be highly effective. However, they alone are not sufficient to establish and sustain ethical decision-making by company executives and staff.

Corporate Culture and Ethics in a Global Environment

Corporate culture and national culture are intertwined, as discussed in Chapter 9, and the global diversity of many of today's companies presents a challenge to managers trying to build or preserve a strong organizational culture. Employees who come from different countries often have diverse attitudes and beliefs that can make it difficult to establish a sense of community and cohesiveness based on the corporate culture. This tends to be borne out by research which suggests that national culture has a greater impact on employees than does corporate culture.[132] For example, a study of effectiveness and cultural values in Russia found that flexibility and collectivism (working together in groups), which are key values in the national culture, are considerably more important to organizational effectiveness than they are for employees working in most US-based companies.[133] Another recent study found that differences in national cultural values and preferences also create significant variance in ethical attitudes among people from different countries.[134]

Some companies have been successful in developing a broad global perspective that permeates the entire organizational culture. For example, Omron, a global electronics company that invented electronic ticket access gates, headquartered in Kyoto, Japan, has offices on six continents. Until a few years ago, Omron had always assigned Japanese managers to head them. Today, it relies on local expertise in each geographical area and blends the insights and perspectives of local managers into a global whole. Global planning meetings are held in offices around the world. In addition, Omron established a global database and standardized its software to ensure a smooth exchange of information among its offices worldwide. It takes time to develop a broad cultural mind-set and spread it throughout the company, but firms such as Omron try to bring a multicultural approach to every business issue.[135]

Building such a global culture based upon multiculturalism is a challenging task. Research has indicated that even though organizational cultures may vary widely, there are specific components that characterize a global culture. These include an emphasis on multicultural rather than national values, basing status on merit rather than nationality, being open to new ideas from other cultures, showing excitement rather than trepidation when entering new cultural environments and being sensitive to cultural differences without being limited by them.[136]

One way to foster global values is through the social audit, which measures and reports the ethical, social and environmental impact of a company's operations.[137] While many companies carry out one or other type of social audit, Social Accountability International, an NGO, has established a standardized measure, the Social Accountability 8000, or SA8000,[138] which provides a degree of consistency in measuring corporate social impact, focusing particularly on working conditions. The system is designed to work like the ISO 9000 quality-auditing system of the International Standards Organization. ISO itself has a ISO26000 social responsibility standard, which measures many of the same social impacts as part of a broader social and environmental impact standard.

Many companies are taking steps to ensure that their factories and suppliers meet SA8000 standards, especially where they operate in developing countries where formal corporate regulation may be weak or non-existent. While most companies seeking SA8000 audits are multinationals, domestic firms in emerging markets are starting to make use of the audits. China First Division Construction and Development Company, a State-owned enterprise in China which in 2012 was assessed the world's biggest construction firm,[139] became the first construction company in the country to achieve the standard. However, the standard has been criticised as a 'facade' considering that independent workers' organizations are not allowed in China and some other major emerging economies.[140,141,142]

Summary and Interpretation

This chapter has explored the importance of cultural and ethical values and how these are relevant for managing organizations. The chapter highlighted the importance of social capital and has shown how particular values contribute to it.

Organizational cultures can shape and support how employees relate to one another and learn to adapt their productive capabilities to the external environment. Culture is enacted through a variety of media and associated practices including rites and ceremonies, stories and heroes, symbols and language.

Organizational culture may reflect and reinforce, or be in tension with corporate, strategy and structure members' efforts to adapt to, or control, aspects of the environment. Ethical decision-making in organizations is shaped by many factors: personal characteristics, which include personal beliefs, moral development and reflection on the relevance of ethical frameworks for decision-making; organizational culture, which is the extent to which values, heroes, traditions and symbols inspire or subvert ethical decision-making; organizational systems, which pertain to the formal structure, policies, codes of ethics and reward systems that also focus or obscure ethical or unethical choices; and the concerns and priorities of external stakeholders, which include government agencies, customers and special interest groups.

As part of organizational culture, values-based leadership can assist in institutionalizing ethical behaviour, as may the existence of an ethics committee, disclosure mechanisms for whistle-blowing, ethics training programmes, social audits, a code of ethics, etc. However, it is salutory to recall that Enron had introduced many of these formal mechanisms including visionary leadership that proclaimed its ethicality, not least through charitable giving.

As business increasingly crosses geographical and cultural boundaries, leaders face difficult challenges in establishing ethical values which employees can readily accept. Organizations which aspire to develop global cultures face the challenge of embracing multicultural values, emphasizing merit rather than nationality, and remaining open to ideas from other cultures in a manner that is sensitive to, and respectful of, their contextual meaning.

KEY CONCEPTS

adaptability culture	ethics	legends	social audit
bureaucratic culture	ethics committee	managerial ethics	social capital
chief ethics officer	ethics hotlines	mission culture	social responsibility
clan culture	external adaptation	myths	stories
code of ethics	heroes	organizational culture	subcultures
culture	internal integration	rites and ceremonies	symbol
culture strength	language	rule of law	whistle-blowing
ethical dilemma			

Discussion Questions

1   Describe observable symbols, ceremonies, dress or other aspects of culture and the underlying values they represent for an organization where you have worked.

2   What might be some of the advantages of having several subcultures within an organization? The disadvantages?

3   Explain the concept of social capital. Name an organization currently in the business news that seems to have a high degree of social capital and one that seems to have a low degree.

4   Do you think a bureaucratic culture would be less employee oriented than a clan culture? Discuss.

5   Why is values-based leadership so important to the influence of culture? Does a symbolic act communicate more about company values than an explicit statement? Discuss.

6   Are you aware of a situation in which either you or someone you know was confronted by an ethical dilemma, such as being encouraged to inflate an expense account? Do you think the person's decision was affected by individual moral development or by the accepted values within the company? Explain.

7   Why is equality an important value to support learning and innovation? Discuss.

8   What importance would you attribute to leadership statements and actions for influencing ethical values and decision-making in an organization?

9   How do external stakeholders influence ethical decision-making in an organization? Discuss why globalization has contributed to more complex ethical issues related to external stakeholders.

10 Codes of ethics have been criticized for transferring responsibility for ethical behaviour from the organization to the individual employee. Do you agree? Do you think a code of ethics is valuable for an organization?

11 Top executives at numerous technology companies, including Nortel Networks, Sun Microsystems and Cisco, made millions of dollars from the sale of stock during the 'bubble years' of 1999–2001. When the bubble burst, ordinary investors lost 70 to 90 per cent of their holdings. Do you see anything wrong with this from an ethical standpoint? How do you think this affects the social capital of these organizations?

Chapter 11 Workbook Shop 'til You Drop: Corporate Culture in the Retail World

To understand more about corporate culture, visit two retail stores and compare them according to various factors. Go to one discount or low-end store, such as Lidl or Primark, and to one high-end store, such as Harrod's or Waitrose, or their equivalents in your country. Do not interview any employees, but instead be an observer or a shopper. Spend at least 2 hours in each store on a busy day and be very observant.

Questions

1   How does the culture seem to influence employee behaviour in each store?

2   What effect does employees' behaviour have on customers?

3   Which store was more pleasant to be in? How does that relate to the mission of the store?

Chapter 11 Workshop The Power of Ethics

This exercise will help you to better understand the concept of ethics and what it means to you.

1   Spend about 5 minutes individually answering the questions below.

2   Divide into groups of four to six members.

3   Have each group try to achieve consensus with answers to each of the four questions. For question 3, choose one scenario to highlight. You will have 20 to 40 minutes for this exercise, depending on the instructor.

4   Have groups share their answers with the whole class, after which the instructor will lead a discussion on ethics and its power in business.

Questions

1   In your own words, define the concept of ethics in one or two sentences.

2   If you were a manager, how would you motivate your employees to follow ethical behaviour? Use no more than two sentences.

3   Describe a situation in which you were faced with an ethical dilemma. What was your decision and behaviour? How did you decide to do that? Can you relate your decision to any concept in the chapter?

4   What do you think is a powerful ethical message for others? Where did you get it from? How will it influence your behaviour in the future?

Adapted by Dorothy Marcic from Allayne Barrilleaux Pizzolatto's 'Ethical Management: An Exercise in Understanding Its Power', *Journal of Management Education* 17, No. 1 (February 1993), 107–109.

CASE FOR ANALYSIS 11.1

Culture and Values

The Edam Corporation and the Edam Foundation

From its very beginnings the Edam Corporation has been a company committed to developing corporate social responsibility; building schools and houses as well as setting up sports clubs and training for its employees and the communities they live in. Since the 1970s, environmental sustainability has been high on the agenda and the organization constantly seeks ways of improving its operations, products and supply chains.

Today, the Edam Corporation drives sustainable innovation by considering the needs of people and the ecological needs of the planet. A leading proponent of the circular economy[1], the Edam Corporation is committed to helping improve the lives of people in developing countries with the formation of the Edam Foundation being a natural extension of this.

In 2015, the Edam Corporation established the Edam Foundation, a new initiative dedicated to helping enable lasting social change in disadvantaged communities through the provision and application of innovation, talent and resources provided by the Edam Corporation. Together with key non-profit partners, the Edam Foundation seeks to identify challenges where a combination of Edam expertise and partner experience can be used to create meaningful solutions that improve people's lives. The Edam Foundation provides the vehicle for the corporate social responsibility and social investment programme of the Edam Corporation and is incorporated in its document 'Edam Corporate Strategy 2015-20'.

During 2015, the Foundation developed its strategy, governance and operational structure. It established its first strategic partnerships with the International Red Cross and UNICEF with the aim of co-creating innovative solutions for disaster relief and community development and supporting social entrepreneurship. In addition to programmes with these global partners, the Edam Foundation funds local projects run by organizational sub-divisions serving diverse markets that are in line with the Foundation strategy. The Foundation also stepped up to coordinate Edam's contribution to the fight against malaria, and provided the opportunity for employees to make a donation to support the work of the Red Cross in Africa.

The Edam Foundation is also committed to improving people's lives in disadvantaged communities wherever these are located. It mobilizes Edam's expertise, innovations and global partnerships to the benefit of young and underprivileged people and communities around the world.

The Edam Foundation uses Edam's expertise and knowledge to benefit fragile parts of society, build valuable new knowledge and networks, and drive social innovation. It aims to take knowledge and experience from a community level in one country and apply them across multiple communities in numerous countries. It believes in the power of collaboration to support positive social changes towards a healthier and more sustainable future for all.

The Edam Foundation knows that when a disaster occurs, acting fast and intelligently is vital. It provides medical equipment, devises on the ground solutions as well as funds (in the event of a large scale disaster) to regions affected as quickly as possible. It donates people, products and funds to support relief efforts for natural and humanitarian disasters.

The Foundation identifies projects where Edam's expertise and innovations can make a real difference in local communities. Together with partners, the Foundation uses the Edam's technology, service and delivery innovation model and applies it solely for the facilitation of social change. The Edam Foundation is passionate about giving people the tools to build a healthier, better future for themselves. It works to provide grants, training and products that drive social innovation and enable entrepreneurship.

Questions

1 How would you evaluate the social performance of the Edam Foundation?

2 The Edam Corporation has separated some of its corporate social responsibility activities from its mainstream business activities. Do you think that this is necessary and/or desirable?

3 Can managerial ethics and corporate social responsibility sometimes be in conflict?

---

1. For an explanation of the circular economy, see https://www.ellenmacarthurfoundation.org/circular-economy.

Notes

1. http://www.forbes.com/profile/stefano-pessina/?list=billionaires

2. Marcus Leroux, 18 March, 2013, 'Boots jet-setter with a talent for alliances', *The Times*; Oliver Shah, 18 November, 2012, 'Work is the drug that keeps this Alliance Boots billionaire going', *The Sunday Times*.

3. Julia Boorstin, 'Secret Recipe: J. M. Smucker', *Fortune* (January 12, 2004), 58–59.

4. Stefan Stern, 'Old Europe fighting back', *Financial Times*, 28 May, 2008.

5. Anita Raghavan, Kathryn Kranhold and Alexei Barrionuevo, 'Full Speed Ahead: How Enron Bosses Created a Culture of Pushing Limits', *The Wall Street Journal* (August 26, 2002), A1, A7.

6. Mark C. Bolino, William H. Turnley and James M. Bloodgood, 'Citizenship Behaviour and the Creation of Social Capital in Organizations', *Academy of Management Review* 27, No. 4 (2002), 505–522; and Don Cohen and Laurence Prusak, *In Good Company: How Social Capital Makes Organizations Work* (Boston, MA: Harvard Business School Press, 2001), 3–4.

7. David Nicklaus, 'Convictions in Enron case mark end to shameful era', *St. Louis Post-Dispatch*, 28 May, 2006.

8. Eric Lichtblau, David Johnston and Ron Nixon, 'F.B.I. Struggling To Handle Wave Of Finance Cases', *The New York Times*, 19 October, 2008; Jim Mateja, 'Former Chrysler boss attacks corporate greed; World is out of whack, Lee Iacocca says in his book', *Chicago Tribune*, 27 April, 2007; Anatole Kaletsky and Robin Blackburn, 'Should capitalism be transformed?' *Prospect Magazine*, 23 October, 2008.

9. 'Fortune 1,000 Ranked within Industries', *Fortune* (April 18, 2005), F–46–F–69; Erick Shonfeld, 'eBay's Secret Ingredient', *Business 2.0* (March 2002), 52–58.

10. Michael Santoli, 'Connecting the Dots at eBay', *Barron's*, 28 April, 2012.

11. Spencer Soper and Aleksandra Gjorgievska, 'eBay Forecast Beats Estimates as Traffic Efforts Pay Off', *Bloomberg Technology*, April 16, 2016, accessed at www.bloomberg.com/news/articles/2016-04-26/ebay-sales-forecast-beats-estimates-as-traffic-efforts-pay-off

12. James Quinn, 'IBM and eBay shrug off gloom', *'The Daily Telegraph'* April 17, 2008; Pierre-Antoine Souchard, 'France Faults eBay Over Fake Goods; Website to Appeal $61 Million Court Decision Favoring Luxury Brands', The *Washington Post*, 1 July, 2008.

13. Simon Neville and Shiv Malik, 'Starbucks wake up to the smell of coffee', *The Guardian*, 12 November 2012; Harvey Morris, 'Storm in a Coffee Cup Over Corporate Tax Loopholes', *New York Times*, 26 October, 2012.

14. P. Bourdieu (1994), *Raisons Pratiques: Sur la théorie de l'action*, Paril, Seuil; Robert D. Putnam (2007) 'E Pluribus Unum: Diversity and Community in the Twenty-first Century', *Scandinavian Political Studies* 30, 137–174. For critiques of human capital and social capital see, Samuel Bowles and Herbert Gintis (1975), 'The Problem with Human Capital Theory – A Marxian Critique', *American Economic Review*, 65(2), pp. 74–82, and Ben Fine (2001), 'Social capital versus social theory: political economy and social science at the turn of the millennium', London, Routledge.

15. W. Jack Duncan, 'Organizational Culture: "Getting a Fix" on an Elusive Concept', *Academy of Management Executive* 3 (1989), 229–236; Linda Smircich, 'Concepts of Culture and Organizational Analysis', *Administrative Science Quarterly* 28 (1983), 339–358; and Andrew D. Brown and Ken Starkey, 'The Effect of Organizational Culture on Communication and Information', *Journal of Management Studies* 31, No. 6 (November 1994), 807–828.

16. Edgar H. Schein, 'Organizational Culture', *American Psychologist* 45 (February 1990), 109–119.

17. Edwin Heathcote, 'Architecture: E. Europe redefines its identity', *Financial Times*, 10 March, 2008.

18. Harrison M. Trice and Janice M. Beyer, 'Studying Organizational Cultures through Rites and Ceremonials', *Academy of Management Review* 9 (1984), 653–669; Janice M. Beyer and Harrison M. Trice, 'How an Organization's Rites Reveal Its Culture', *Organizational Dynamics* 15 (Spring 1987), 5–24; Steven P. Feldman, 'Management in Context: An Essay on the Relevance of Culture to the Understanding of Organizational Change', *Journal of Management Studies* 23 (1986), 589–607; and Mary Jo Hatch, 'The Dynamics of Organizational Culture', *Academy of Management Review* 18 (1993), 657–693.

19. This discussion is based on Edgar H. Schein, *Organizational Culture and Leadership*, 2d ed. (Homewood, IL: Richard D. Irwin, 1992); and John P. Kotter and James L. Heskett, *Corporate Culture and Performance* (New York: Free Press, 1992).

20. He Huafeng, 'Alibaba founder keeps focus on customers corporate culture', *The Wall Street Journal Asia*, 18 October, 2007.

21. Cheryl Dahle, 'Four Tires, Free Beef', *Fast Company* (September 2003), 36.

22. Larry Mallak, 'Understanding and Changing Your Organization's Culture', *Industrial Management* (March–April 2001), 18–24.

23. For a list of various elements that can be used to assess or interpret corporate culture, see '10 Key Cultural Elements', sidebar in Micah R. Kee, 'Corporate Culture Makes a Fiscal Difference', *Industrial Management* (November–December 2003), 16–20.

24. Charlotte B. Sutton, 'Richness Hierarchy of the Cultural Network: The Communication of Corporate Values' (unpublished manuscript, Texas A&M University, 1985); and Terrence E. Deal and Allan A. Kennedy, 'Culture: A New Look through Old Lenses', *Journal of Applied Behavioural Science* 19 (1983), 498–505.

25. Thomas C. Dandridge, 'Symbols at Work' (working paper, School of Business, State University of New York at Albany, 1978), 1.

26. 'Avon lady is sitting pretty after awards', *Derby Evening Telegraph*, 2 September, 2008.

27. Tunde Olofintila, 'Wema Bank – Better Days Are Here', *Daily Independent*, 23 October, 2008.

28. Willmott, H. (1993), 'Strength is Ignorance; Slavery is Freedom: Managing Culture in Modern Organizations', *Journal of Management Studies,* 30, 515–552.

29. Don Hellriegel and John W. Slocum, Jr., *Management*, 7th ed. (Cincinnati, Ohio: South-Western, 1996), 537.

30. Jack Smith, 'Driving continuous improvement', *Plant Engineering*, 1 December, 2006; Hirotaka Takeuchi, Emi Osono and Norihiko Shimizu, 'Contradictions are the drivers of Toyota's success', *Business Day* (South Africa), 23 June, 2008.

31. Trice and Beyer, 'Studying Organizational Cultures through Rites and Ceremonials'.

32. Stephen Denning, 'Telling Tales', *Harvard Business Review*.

33. Sutton, 'Richness Hierarchy of the Cultural Network'; and Terrence E. Deal and Allan A. Kennedy, *Corporate Cultures: The Rites and Rituals of Corporate Life* (Reading, MA: Addison-Wesley, 1982).

34. Jonathan Murphy (2008), *The World Bank and Global Managerialism*, London, Routledge.

35. Douglas B. Holt (2004), *How Brands Become Icons*, Cambridge, MA, Harvard Business Press, pp. 155–189.

36. 'Caring Corporations and Their Sensitive New Logos', *Chosun Ilbo*, 30 November, 2006.

37. 'FYI', *Inc.* (April 1991), 14.

38. Raghavan, Kranhold and Barrionuevo, 'Full Speed Ahead'.

39. 'Climbing the Ladder: There's more than one way to turn a regional hit into a national retail brand. How do you know which is right for you?' *National Post*, 1 February, 2007.

40. 'The owner of Rocky Mountain Soap Company joins Environmental Defence's Just Beautiful Campaign', *Canmore Leader*, 29 August, 2012.

41. David Bank, 'Fund Helps PeopleSoft ex-Workers', *The Wall Street Journal* (April 4, 2005), B4.

42. J.E. Fitzgibbon and M. Seeger (2002) 'Audiences and Metaphors of Globalization in the Daimler Chrysler Merger', *Communication Studies*, 53, 40–55.

43. Higgins and McAllaster, 'Want Innovation?'

44. James R. Detert, Roger G. Schroeder and John J. Mauriel, 'A Framework for Linking Culture and Improvement Initiatives in Organizations', *Academy of Management Review* 25, No. 4 (2000), 850–863.

45. Based on Daniel R. Denison, *Corporate Culture and Organizational Effectiveness* (New York: Wiley, 1990), 11–15; Daniel R. Denison and Aneil K. Mishra, 'Toward a Theory of Organizational Culture and Effectiveness', *Organization Science* 6, No. 2 (March–April 1995), 204–223; R. Hooijberg and F. Petrock, 'On Cultural Change: Using the Competing Values Framework to Help Leaders Execute a Transformational Strategy', *Human Resource Management* 32 (1993), 29–50; and R. E. Quinn, *Beyond Rational Management: Mastering the Paradoxes and Competing Demands of High Performance* (San Francisco: Jossey-Bass, 1988).

46. 'BT does a massive corporate re-organisation', *Public Technologies*, 25 April, 2007.

47. Helen Kelly, 'How BT Exact retrained an in-house support division with flexible skills', *Personnel Today*, 27 February, 2007; 'Management – The real story behind a real-time enterprise', *Computing*, 31 July 2003; Robert Wall and Jens Flottau, 'Turbulent Skies; Europe's low-fare sector faces uncertainty, but remains set on expansion', *Aviation Week & Space Technology*, 19 November', 2007; 'Teaching Airlines To Think More Like Marketers, Teaching Travelers To Expect Less But Pay More; Lessons to Be Had in Ancillary Revenue Creation', *M2 Presswire*, 5 December, 2007; 'Valencia Loses 750,000 Passengers And 750 Jobs As Ryanair Closes Base', *M2 Presswire*, 24 October, 2008.

48. 'Cardiff City £6m Malaysian takeover approved', *BBC Sport,* 27 May, 2010; Jon Doel, 'Enter the Dragons as City fans breathe fire over Tan talk', *The Western Mail*, 1 March, 2013; Steve Tucker, 'Are the Bluebirds right to change their identity to move forward?' *South Wales Echo*, 9 May, 2012; 'Cardiff City owner Vincent Tan agrees return to blue home kit', *BBC Sport*, January 9, 2015, accessed at www.bbc.co.uk/sport/football/30741073

49. 'Marks & Spencer's Rose faces tougher challenge', *Reuters News*, 12 May, 2008; 'Marks and sparks: Shopping in the 21st century', *The Independent*, May 27, 2007.

50. Hannah Marriott, 'Alexa Chung to collaborate with Marks & Spencer', *Guardian*, February 4, 2016, accessed at www.theguardian.com/fashion/2016/feb/04/alexa-chung-to-collaborate-with-marks-spencer-stylewatch; Hadley Freeman, 'M&S needs more than Alexa Chung – more tills, better dressing rooms and proper T-shirts', April 18, 2016, accessed at www.theguardian.com/fashion/2016/apr/18/m-and-s-alexa-chung-archive-by-alexa

51. Matthew Boyle, 'The Wegmans Way', *Fortune* (January 24, 2005), 62–68.

52. Tom Dochat, 'Wegmans grocery chain keeps it all in the family', *The Patriot-News*, 9 September, 2007.

53. BBC News, 'Northern Rock to be nationalized', 17 February, 2008, http://news.bbc.co.uk/1/hi/business/7249575.stm accessedOctober 24, 2008; David Prosser 'The Return of the Building Society: Credit Crisis, What Credit Crisis?', *The Independent,* November 23, 2007.

54. Bernard Arogyaswamy and Charles M. Byles, 'Organizational Culture: Internal and External Fits', *Journal of Management* 13 (1987), 647–659.

55. Chatman and Cha, 'Leading by Leveraging Culture'.

56. Patrick J. Sauer, 'Open-Door Management', *Inc.* (June 2003), 44.

57. Tony Silber and Bill Mickey, 'The More You Know, The More You Grow', *Folio*, January 7, 2016, accessed at www.foliomag.com/2016/the-more-you-know-the-more-you-grow/

58. 'TechTarget Recognized for Excellence in Digital Media', *Business Wire*, 16 April 2013.

59. Paul R. Lawrence and Jay W. Lorsch, *Organization and Environment* (Homewood, IL: Irwin, 1969).

60. 'Five Asian firms among global elite in leadership', *Bangkok Post*, 1 October, 2007; Simon Caulkin, 'The colossal cares of Unilever revisited', *Management Today*, September 2006; Haig Simonian and Tom Braithwaite, 'Unilever goes outside for chief', *Financial Times*, September 4, 2008;

61. Paul Sonne, Unilever Logs Hefty Sales Gain, *The Wall Street Journal Europe*, 24 January, 2013.

62. 'Unilever Full-Year 2015 Profits', accessed at https://www.unilever.com/Images/q4-2015-full-announcement_tcm244-470010_en.pdf

63. Loizos Heracleous, Jochen Wirtz and Robert Johnston, (2005) 'Kung-fu service development at Singapore Airlines', *Business Strategy Review*, Vol. 16, Issue 4, 26–31.

64. Loizos Heracleous, Jochen Wirtz and Robert Johnston (2005), 'Kung-fu service development at Singapore Airlines', *Business Strategy Review*, Winter 2005; 'Singapore Compact', http://www.csrsingapore.org/index.htmlaccessed October 28, 2008; David Fullbrook, 'Have

We Seen the Back of the Singapore Girl', *Asia Sentinel*, Friday, 9 March, 2007.

65. Penelope Phoon, 'Gaining momentum in Singapore', *The Edge Malaysia*, 7 May, 2007.

66. Singapore Airlines, Environmental Report 2007–08, http://www.singaporeair.com/saa/en_UK/docs/company_info/environment/SIA_EnvReport2007-08.pdf accessed October 28, 2008.

67. World's Best Airline Awards, www.worldairlineawards.com/Awards_2008/AirlineYear-2008.htm accessed October 28, 2008.

68. 'The World's Top 10 Airlines in 2015', *Skytrax*, accessed at www.worldairlineawards.com/Awards/worlds_best_airline.html

69. Garry Rodan, 'Singapore in 2004: Long-Awaited Leadership Transition', *Asian Survey*, January/February 2005, 45, 140–145.

70. Choe Sang-Hun, 'In South Korea, "the old way" is crumbling. Major companies lead push to abandon maleoriented, top-down business culture', *International Herald Tribune*, 25 October, 2008.

71. Tressie Wright Muldrow, Timothy Buckley and Brigitte W. Schay, 'Creating High-Performance Organizations in the Public Sector', *Human Resource Management* 41, No. 3 (Fall 2002), 341–354.

72. Gordon F. Shea, *Practical Ethics* (New York: American Management Association, 1988); Linda K. Treviño, 'Ethical Decision Making in Organizations: A Person–Situation Interactionist Model', *Academy of Management Review* 11 (1986), 601–617; and Linda Klebe Treviño and Katherine A. Nelson, *Managing Business Ethics: Straight Talk about How to Do It Right*, 2nd ed. (New York: John Wiley & Sons, Inc., 1999).

73. Thanks to Susan H. Taft, Kent State University, and Judith White, University of Redlands, for this overview of the sources of individual ethics.

74. Dawn-Marie Driscoll, 'Don't Confuse Legal and Ethical Standards', *Business Ethics* (July–August 1996), 44.

75. LaRue Tone Hosmer, *The Ethics of Management*, 2d ed. (Homewood, IL: Irwin, 1991).

76. Geanne Rosenberg, 'Truth and Consequences', *Working Woman* (July–August 1998), 79–80.

77. Frank M. Horwitz, Victoria Browning Harish Jain and Anton J. Steenkamp (2002), 'Human resource practices and discrimination in South Africa: overcoming the apartheid legacy', *The International Journal of Human Resource Management*, 13, 1105–1118.

78. N. Craig Smith, 'Corporate Social Responsibility: Whether or How?' *California Management Review* 45, No. 4 (Summer 2003), 52–76; and Eugene W. Szwajkowski, 'The Myths and Realities of Research on Organizational Misconduct', in James E. Post, ed., *Research in Corporate Social Performance and Policy*, Vol. 9 (Greenwich, CT: JAI Press, 1986), 103–122.

79. Some of these incidents are from Hosmer, *The Ethics of Management*.

80. Linda K. Treviño and Katherine A. Nelson, *Managing Business Ethics: Straight Talk about How to Do It Right* (New York: John Wiley & Sons, Inc., 1995), 4.

81. Daniel W. Greening and Daniel B. Turban, 'Corporate Social Performance as a Competitive Advantage in Attracting a Quality Workforce', *Business and Society* 39, No. 3 (September 2000), 254.

82. Alison Maitland, 'Tools to build a reputation', *Financial Times*, 20 January, 2003.

83. Andrea Li, 'Keeping staff happy key to success', *South China Morning Post*, 21 February, 2008.

84. Christopher Marquis, 'Doing Well and Doing Good', *The New York Times* (July 13, 2003), Section 3, 2; and Joseph Pereira, 'Career Journal: Doing Good and Doing Well at Timberland', *The Wall Street Journal* (September 9, 2003), B1.

85. Lois A. Mohr, Deborah J. Webb and Katherine E. Harris, 'Do Consumers Expect Companies to be Socially Responsible? The Impact of Corporate Social Responsibility on Buying Behaviour', *Journal of Consumer Affairs*, 35, 45–72.

86. Julie Pirsch, Shruti Gupta and Stacy Landreth Grau (2007) 'A Framework for Understanding Corporate Social Responsibility Programs as a Continuum: An Exploratory Study', *Journal of Business Ethics*, 70, 125–140.

87. 'The Socially Correct Corporate Business', segment in Leslie Holstrom and Simon Brady, 'The Changing Face of Global Business', *Fortune*, special advertising section (July 24, 2000), S1–S38.

88. T. Hidayat, 'Yeane Keet: If employees are happy, customers will be happy', *The Jakarta Post*, 28 May, 2008.

89. Carol Hymowitz, 'CEOs Must Work Hard to Maintain Faith in the Corner Office' (In the Lead column), *The Wall Street Journal* (July 9, 2002), B1.

90. James Weber, 'Exploring the Relationship between Personal Values and Moral Reasoning', *Human Relations* 46 (1993), 435–463.

91. Hosmer, *The Ethics of Management*.

92. Lucy Siegle, 'The Ethical Issue: Green at heart', *Observer Magazine*, 8 June, 2008.

93. Emma Haslett, 'Good Times Bad Times: Tough gig', *Management Today*, 1 May 2012.

94. Sarah Callard, 'The rise of cold-water surfing', *Telegraph*, November 15, 2014, accessed at www.telegraph.co.uk/travel/activity-and-adventure/The-rise-of-cold-water-surfing/

95. John A. Byrne with Mike France and Wendy Zellner, 'The Environment Was Ripe for Abuse', *BusinessWeek* (February 25, 2002), 118–120.

96. Matt Dickinson, Recommendations Made To BAE, *Press Association National Newswire*, 6 May, 2008; David Leigh, 'BAE Systems admits to ethical failings as investigations into corruption continue', *The Guardian*, 7 May, 2008.

97. Jennifer Bresnahan, 'For Goodness Sake', *CIO Enterprise*, Section 2 (June 15, 1999), 54–62.

98. David M. Messick and Max H. Bazerman, 'Ethical Leadership and the Psychology of Decision Making', *Sloan Management Review* (Winter 1996), 9–22; Dawn-Marie Driscoll, 'Don't Confuse Legal and Ethical Standards', *Business Ethics* (July–August 1996), 44; and Max B. E. Clarkson, 'A Stakeholder Framework for Analyzing and Evaluating Corporate Social Performance', *Academy of Management Review* 20, No. 1 (1995), 92–117.

99. 'SEC's Cox Defends Agency, Seeks More Authority', *Dow Jones News Service*, 23 October, 2008; EU Calls for Tougher Rules to Fix Crippled Financial System, *Deutsche Welle*, 1 October, 2008; EU business: Deregulation hits the buffers, *Economist Intelligence Unit*, 24 October, 2008.

100. 'New York City restaurants go trans-fat-free', *Reuters News*, 1 July, 2008.

101. Roger Parloff, 'Is Fat the Next Tobacco?' *Fortune* (February 3, 2003), 51–54.

102. 'Trans fat ban: how to tell if food contains trans fats', *The Week*, June 18, 2015, accessed at www.theweek.co.uk/64042/trans-fat-ban-how-to-tell-if-food-contains-trans-fats

103. Maeve McClenaghan, 'Analysis: Unhealthy friendships with Department of Health', *Bureau of Investigative Journalism*, November 25, 2011.

104. Toyota Motor Corporation, 'aim: zero emissions', Toyota Environmental Brochure 2006, http://www.toyota.eu/Images/Brochure_tcm416-493730.pdf accessed October 27, 2008; 'BMW unveils plans for a zero-emissions future', *Guardian Unlimited*, 27 September 2007.

105. 'The "electric cars aren't green" myth debunked', accessed at shrinkthatfootprint.com/electric-cars-green

106. Andrew W. Singer, 'The Ultimate Ethics Test', *Across the Board* (March 1992), 19–22; Ronald B. Morgan, 'Self and Co-Worker Perceptions of Ethics and Their Relationships to Leadership and Salary', *Academy of Management Journal* 36, No. 1 (February 1993), 200–214; and Joseph L. Badaracco Jr, and Allen P. Webb, 'Business Ethics: A View from the Trenches', *California Management Review* 37, No. 2 (Winter 1995), 8–28.

107. Frank Vogl, 'The proud legacy of a corporate ethics pioneer', *Financial Times*, 13 September, 2007; 'Dame Anita Roddick', *Guardian Unlimited*, 11 September, 2007.

108. Jules Stewart, 'Break the bank', *Financial Director*, 1 April, 2005; Cristina McEachern, 'Confessions of a Rogue Trader', *Advanced Trading*, 1 April, 2008; 'Societe Generale boss admits faults in control systems', *Agence France Presse*, 10 June, 2008; 'Minister faults bank controls in Societe Generale scandal', *Agence France Presse*, 4 February, 2008; 'Societe Generale scandal: Unanswered questions Who knew what?', *The Guardian*, 26 January, 2008; 'Societe Generale Scandal Presents Lessons in Operational Risk Management', *PR Newswire*, 22 February, 2008; Doreen Carvajal and James Kanter, 'Société Générale: A Quest for Glory and a Bonus Ends in Disgrace', *New York Times*, January 29, 2008.

109. 'Siemens battles bribery probes on many fronts', *Reuters News*, 8 November, 2007; Mike Esterl and David Crawford, 'Why Siemens Bribery Probe Slogs On – Decentralization, Stonewalling Make Quick Resolution Unlikely', *The Wall Street Journal*, 16 August, 2007; Michael D. Goldhaber, 'How the massive Siemens bribery scandal made U.S.–style internal investigations the new model for Europe', *American Lawyer*, 1 May, 2008; Carter Dougherty, 'The Sheriff at Siemens, at Work Under the Justice Dept's Watchful Eye', *The New York Times*, 8 October, 2008.

110. Vito J. Racanelli, 'The Culture Changer', *Barron's*, 10 March, 2012.

111. Tony Czuczka, 'Siemens CEO Rebuked as German Business Defends Putin Partnership', *Bloomberg*, March 30, 2014, accessed at www.bloomberg.com/news/articles/2014-03-30/siemens-ceo-rebuked-as-german-business-defends-putin-partnership; 'Greece indicts 13 Germans over Siemens bribery scandal', *Deutsche Welle*, March 9, 2015, accessed at www.dw.com/en/greece-indicts-13-germans-over-siemens-bribery-scandal/a-18304651

112. Alan Yuspeh, 'Do the Right Thing', *CIO* (August 1, 2000), 56–58.

113. 'Ethics & Compliance Officer Association (ECOA) Elects New Board Officers', *Business Wire*, 29 May, 2008; http://web.archive.org/web/20100210074307/http://www.theecoa.org/AM/Template.cfm?Section=Global_Ethics_and_Compliance, accessed 17 September, 2013.

114. Information in Amy Zipkin, 'Getting Religion on Corporate Ethics', *The New York Times* (October 18, 2000), C1, C10; and http://www.eoa.org, accessed April 20, 2005.

115. Treviño and Nelson, *Managing Business Ethics*, 212.

116. Karamjit Kaur, 'Ethics hotline' for SIA', *Straits Times*, 28 October, 2005; Dale Hug, 'Pioneer Opens E-Mail Based 'Business Ethics Hotline', *Japan Corporate News Network*, 13 June, 2003.

117. Janet P. Near and Marcia P. Miceli, 'Effective Whistle-Blowing', *Academy of Management Review* 20, No. 3 (1995), 679–708.

118. Richard P. Nielsen, 'Changing Unethical Organizational Behaviour', *Academy of Management Executive* 3 (1989), 123–130.

119. Jene G. James, 'Whistle-Blowing: Its Moral Justification', in Peter Madsen and Jay M. Shafritz, eds., *Essentials of Business Ethics* (New York: Meridian Books, 1990), 160–190; and Janet P. Near, Terry Morehead Dworkin and Marcia P. Miceli, 'Explaining the Whistle-Blowing Process: Suggestions from Power Theory and Justice Theory', *Organization Science* 4 (1993), 393–411.

120. Martin Bright 'Follow my lead, says whistleblower', *The Observer*, 12 September, 2004; Katharine Gun, 'The truth must out', *The Observer*; 19 September, 2004; Martin Bright, 'The woman who nearly stopped the war', *The New Statesman*, March 19, 2008.

121. Lesley Curwen, 'The corporate conscience', *The Guardian*, 21 June 2003.

122. 'British Airways executives charged over price-fixing scandal', *Guardian Unlimited*, 7 August 2008

123. Jang B. Singh (2011), 'Determinants of the effectiveness of corporate codes of ethics: An empirical study', *Journal of Business Ethics*, 101.3, 385–395.

124. 'Toyota Code of Conduct 2006', Toyota Motor Company, http://www.toyota.co.jp/en/vision/code_of_conduct/code_of_conduct.pd accessed October 28, 2008.

125. 'Setting the Standard', Lockheed Martin's website, http://web.archive.org/web/20011209081002/http://www.lockheedmartin.com/exeth/html/code/code.html, accessed September 17, 2013..

126. Cynthia Stohl, Michael Stohl and Lucy Popova, 'A New Generation of Global Corporate Codes of Ethics?', paper presented at the annual meeting of the International Communication Association, San Francisco, CA, May 23, 2007.

127. Ronald E. Berenbeim, *Corporate Ethics Practices* (New York: The Conference Board, 1992).

128. For British Airways code of conduct, see http://www.britishairways.com/cms/global/pdfs/environment/ba_corporate_responsibility_report_2008-2009.pdf, accessed September 17, 2013; and for Halliburton see http://web.archive.org/web/20080524024443/http://www.halliburton.com/Default.aspx?navid=344&pageid=731,

accessed September 17, 2013. Some of Halliburton's ethical challenges are detailed in Russell Gold, 'Halliburton Ex-Official Pleads Guilty In Bribe Case', *The Wall Street Journal*, 4 September, 2008.

129. James Weber, 'Institutionalizing Ethics into Business Organizations: A Model and Research Agenda', *Business Ethics Quarterly* 3 (1993), 419–436.

130. 'Code of conduct', GlaxoSmithKline, accessed at http://www.gsk.com/content/dam/gsk/globals/documents/pdf/Policy-Code-Conduct.pdf on September 17, 2013.

131. Landon Thomas Jr, 'On Wall Street, a Rise in Dismissals over Ethics', *The New York Times* (March 25, 2005), http://www.nytimes.com.

132. S.C. Schneider, 'National vs. Corporate Culture: Implications for Human Resource Management', *Human Resource Management* (Summer 1988), 239.

133. Carl F. Fey and Daniel R. Denison, 'Organizational Culture and Effectiveness: Can American Theory Be Applied in Russia?' *Organization Science* 14, No. 6 (November–December 2003), 686–706.

134. Terence Jackson, 'Cultural Values and Management Ethics: A 10-Nation Study', *Human Relations* 54, No. 10 (2001), 1267–1302.

135. Gail Dutton, 'Building a Global Brain', *Management Review* (May 1999), 34–38.

136. Ibid.

137. Homer H. Johnson, 'Corporate Social Audits – This Time Around', *Business Horizons* (May–June 2001), 29–36.

138. http://www.sa-intl.org, accessed October 28, 2008.

139. 'Great wall builders', *The Economist*, October 27, 2012.

140. Guan Xiaofeng, 'Building Worker Rights', *China Business Weekly*, 2 April, 2007.

141. Cassandra Kegler, 'Holding Herself Accountable', *Working Woman* (May 2001), 13; Louisa Wah, 'Treading the Sacred Ground', *Management Review* (July–August 1998), 18–22.

142. Dave Jamieson, 'Safety Inspections By Social Audit Firms For U.S. Companies Called "Façade" By Labor Groups', May 8, 2013, accessed at www.huffingtonpost.com/2013/04/23/safety-inspections-social-audit-afl-cio_n_3134930.html]

INNOVATION AND CHANGE

Purpose of this Chapter

Innovate or Perish: The Strategic Role of Change
Incremental versus Radical Change
Strategic Types of Change

Elements for Successful Change

Technology Change
The Ambidextrous Approach
Techniques for Encouraging Technology Change

New Products and Services
New Product Success Rate
Reasons for New Product Success
Horizontal Coordination Model
Achieving Competitive Advantage: The Need for
Speed

Strategy and Structure Change
The Dual-Core Approach
Organization Design for Implementing Administrative
Change

Culture Change
Forces for Culture Change
Organization Development Culture Change
Interventions

Strategies for Implementing Change
Leadership for Change
Barriers to Change
Techniques for Implementation

Summary and Interpretation

Toyota Motor Corporation

Toyota's roller-coaster ride in the car-making industry over the past decade demonstrates both the importance of innovation and the necessity of staying on top of the game across the entire corporation.

For many years, Toyota seemed to be on an unstoppable journey to the top. From small beginnings before the Second World War, and despite Japan's defeat in the war, the company gradually established a strong domestic position, and then in 1957 made a cautious entry into the American market. In early years the company specialized in low-end compact vehicles. In the early 1980s Toyota entered into the NUMMI joint venture with General Motors; for Toyota it was its first US-based plant and for General Motors, an effort to learn from Toyota's innovative lean manufacturing production system. Indeed, the basis of Toyota's inexorable rise to the top of the world motor industry was its steady stream of technological and product innovation. Toyota executives created the doctrine of *kaizen*, or continuous improvement, and the company applied it relentlessly. By the mid-2000s Toyota had taken over from General Motors as the world's biggest vehicle manufacturer.

Although big design innovations like the Prius hybrid car (see Chapter 14) can be important, Toyota knows that sweating the details is just as critical for driving innovation. Consider this: several years ago, Toyota made a small change to its production lines by using a single master brace to hold automobile frames in place as they were welded, instead of the dozens of braces used in a standard auto factory. It seemed almost insignificant in the context of the company's complex manufacturing system, yet it was a radical manufacturing innovation. That one change, referred to now as the Global Body Line system, slashed 75 per cent off the cost of retrofitting a production line and made it possible for Toyota to produce different car and truck models on a single line. The result has been billions of dollars in annual cost savings.

For developing new models, Toyota applies the concept of *obeya*, which literally means 'big room'.

To make sure all the critical factors are considered from the beginning, product development teams made up of manufacturing and product engineers, designers, marketers and suppliers hold regular face-to-face brainstorming sessions. New software programmes, including the product life cycle management software discussed in Chapter 9, also make it possible for these cross-functional teams to collaborate digitally, viewing product design changes and associated costs. That way, if a designer makes a change that conflicts with manufacturing's needs or a supplier's capability, it can be noted and adjusted immediately.

With all of these cutting edge approaches, and a strong corporate culture of improvement, the company's sudden fall from grace in the latter 2000s seems hard to fathom. It all began with growing numbers of reports of sudden uncontrolled acceleration; Toyota drivers claimed that the accelerator pedal would get stuck, with sometimes catastrophic results. One particularly horrific accident in San Diego in 2009 brought the issue to the front pages of newspapers. However, Toyota was slow to act despite evidence that the problem was caused by floor mats getting stuck under the pedal. Furthermore, the company appeared defensive in dealings with the US safety authorities investigating the problem, resting on its earlier laurels as being renowned for build quality and safety.

Problems just seemed to pile on. The company had to recall 3.8 million vehicles over the floor mat problem in 2009, and in 2010 another 1.66 million for other, different problems. By 2010, the company lost its first place in global auto sales to the resurgent GM, and in 2011 it dropped to third place after Germany's Volkswagen.

However, Toyota then demonstrated its capacity for both technical and organizational responsiveness. The company restructured to emphasize corporate social responsibility and the ability to respond quickly to crises like the floor mat issue, and for the first time, outside experts were brought in to provide advice on safety and quality control. Safety technologies were completely reworked with five new accident avoidance systems introduced in its cars. Most importantly, perhaps, the company refocused its goals away from short-term sales and profit towards long-term sustainable growth. By 2012, Toyota was once again top of the world in terms of vehicle sales, and has retained the title ever since, with sales topping 10 000 000 vehicles in 2015.[1,2,3,4]

Every company must change and innovate to survive. New discoveries and inventions quickly replace standard ways of doing things. Organizations like Toyota, Google, Apple and Unilever are searching for any innovation edge they can find. Some companies, like 3M, the maker of Post-it Notes, Thinsulate insulation, Scotch-Brite scouring pads and thousands of other products, are known for innovation. 3M's culture supports a risk-taking and entrepreneurial spirit that keeps it bubbling over with new ideas and new products. However, many large, established companies have a hard time being entrepreneurial and continually look for ways to encourage change and innovation to keep pace with changes in the external environment.

The pace of change is revealed in the fact that the parents of today's college-age students grew up without debit cards, video on demand, iPads, self-service supermarket checkout systems, smart phones and 'the cloud'. The idea of communicating instantly and for almost no cost with people around the world was unimaginable to most people as recently as a couple of decades ago.

?

ONLINE
COUNTERPOINT 12.1

Purpose of this Chapter

This chapter will explore how organizations change and how managers direct the innovation and change process. The next section describes the difference between incremental and radical change, the four types of change – technology, product, structure, people – occurring in organizations, and how to manage change successfully. The organization structure and management approach for facilitating each type of change is then discussed. Management techniques for influencing both the creation and implementation of change are also covered.

Innovate or Perish: The Strategic Role of Change

If there is one theme or lesson that emerges from previous chapters, it is that organizations run fast to keep up with changes taking place all around them. Large organizations find ways to act like small, flexible organizations. Manufacturing firms reach out for new, flexible manufacturing technology and service firms for new information technology (IT). Today's organizations position themselves to innovate and change, merely to survive, let alone prosper, in a world of increased competition.[5] As illustrated in Exhibit 12.1, a number of environmental forces condition major organizational change. Powerful forces associated with advancing technology, international economic integration, the maturing of domestic markets and the shift to capitalism in formerly communist countries have brought about a globalized economy that affects every business, from the largest to the smallest, creating more threats as well as more opportunities. To recognize and manage the threats and take advantage of the opportunities, today's companies are undergoing dramatic changes in all areas of their operations.

As we have seen in previous chapters, many organizations are responding to global forces by adopting self-directed teams and more horizontal structures that enhance communication and collaboration, streamlining supply and distribution channels and overcoming barriers of time and place through IT and e-business. Others become involved in joint ventures or consortia to exploit opportunities and extend operations or markets internationally. Some adopt structural innovations such as the virtual network approach to focus on their 'core competencies', while outside specialists handle other activities. In addition, today's organizations face a need for dramatic strategic and cultural change and for rapid and continuous innovations in technology, services, products and processes.

Incremental versus Radical Change

The changes undertaken to adapt to the environment can be evaluated according to scope – that is, the extent to which changes are incremental or radical for the organization.[6] As summarized

EXHIBIT 12.1 Forces Driving the Need for Major Organizational Change

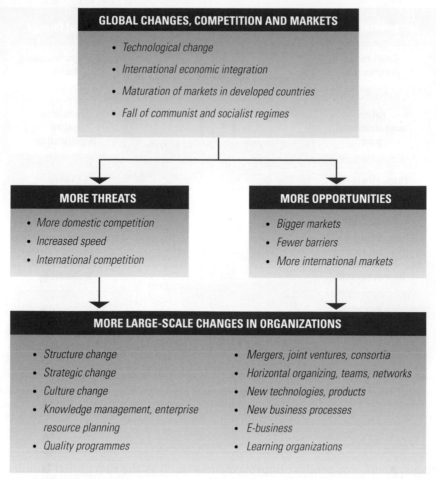

Source: Based on John P. Kotter, *The New Rules: How to Succeed in Today's Post-Corporate World* (New York: The Free Press, 1995).

in Exhibit 12.2, **incremental change** represents a series of continual progressions that maintain the organization's general equilibrium and often affect only one organizational part. **Radical change**, by contrast, breaks the frame of reference for the organization, often transforming the entire organization. For example, an incremental change is the implementation of sales teams in the marketing department, whereas a radical change is shifting the entire organization from a vertical to a horizontal structure, with all employees who work on specific core processes brought together in teams rather than being separated into functional departments such as marketing, finance, production and so forth. Although bold, transforming change receives much attention and can be powerful for an organization, recent research indicates that incremental change – the constant implementation of small ideas – more often results in a sustainable competitive advantage. At the Danish subsidiary of textile manufacturer Milliken & Co., for example, a machine supplier discovered that his company's looms were running four times faster and producing more varied products than the engineers believed was possible. The advances came via the implementation of hundreds of small changes suggested by the textile maker's front-line employees.[7] California-based Google is another company that encourages continuous incremental change, as described in the *Leading by Design* box.

For the most part, incremental change occurs through the established structure and management processes, and it may include technology improvements – such as the introduction of flexible

EXHIBIT 12.2 Incremental versus Radical Change

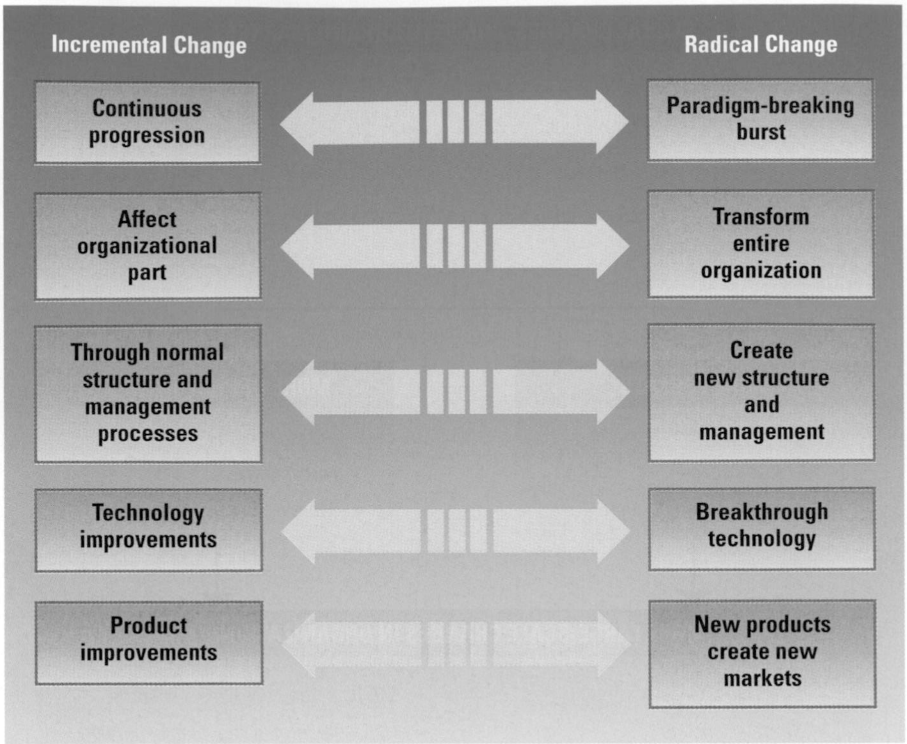

Incremental Change		Radical Change
Continuous progression	⟷	Paradigm-breaking burst
Affect organizational part	⟷	Transform entire organization
Through normal structure and management processes	⟷	Create new structure and management
Technology improvements	⟷	Breakthrough technology
Product improvements	⟷	New products create new markets

Source: Based on Alan D. Meyer, James B. Goes, and Geoffrey R. Brooks, 'Organizations in Disequilibrium: Environmental Jolts and Industry Revolutions', in George Huber and William H. Glick, eds, *Organizational Change and Redesign* (New York: Oxford University Press, 1992), 66–111; and Harry S. Dent, Jr, 'Growth through New Product Development', *Small Business Reports* (November 1990), 30–40.

manufacturing systems – or product improvements – such as the two global laundry giants Unilever and Procter & Gamble moving to concentrated detergents that wash at lower temperatures, saving energy and reducing washing costs.[8] Radical change involves the creation of a new structure and new management processes.

One example of radical change is Apple Computer, which has transformed itself from a personal computer (PC) manufacturer to a dominant force in the digital entertainment business. By creating the iPod and the iTunes online store, giving people easy, legal access to lots of songs, Apple changed the rules of the game in consumer electronics, entertainment and software.[9] Apple didn't sit back on its laurels, next introducing the iPhone and iPad. Corporate transformations and turnarounds, such as Sergio Marchionne's turnaround of Fiat[10] or Jorma Ollila's transformation of Nokia from a manufacturer of rubber boots and toilet paper to the world's biggest mobile phone manufacturer, from 1998 until overtaken by Samsung in 2012, are also considered radical change. Major turnarounds involve changes in all areas of the organization, including structure, management systems, culture, technology and products or services.

It's important not to confuse radical and rapid forms of change, although they are sometimes needed at the same time. Nokia's transformation from a sprawling multidivisional company to a cutting edge mobile telephony business took over 30 years, but it was definitely a radical transformation.[11] The company's failure to adapt quickly enough to the emergence of smartphones as the leading mobile phone market category required the company to transform once again in order to survive. In September 2013 the company announced the prospective takeover of its core mobile phone business by Microsoft, a $7 billion dollar deal that closed in 2014. The residual company is focusing on mobile network infrastructure.[12]

Strategic Types of Change

Managers can focus on four types of change within organizations to achieve strategic advantage. These four types of change are summarized in Exhibit 12.3 as products and services, strategy and structure, culture and technology. We touched on overall leadership and organizational strategy in Chapter 3 and in the previous chapter on corporate culture. Each company has a unique configuration of products and services, strategy and structure, culture and technologies that can be focused for maximum impact upon the company's chosen markets.[13]

BRIEFCASE 12.1

Technology changes are those in an organization's production process, including its knowledge and skill base, that enable distinctive competence. These changes are typically designed to make production more efficient or to produce greater volume. Changes in technology involve the techniques for making products or services such as work methods, equipment and workflow. For example, a technology change at the global courier firm DHL automatically returns details of a package's progress from handheld scanners to the company database, via Wi-fi and mobile data technology, so that vendors can instantly tell a package has been delivered.[14,15]

Product and service changes involve the product or service outputs of an organization. New products include small adaptations of existing products or entirely new product lines. New products and services are normally designed to increase the market share or to develop new markets, customers, or clients. Toyota's Hilux truck was a new product introduced to increase market share, whereas Apple's iPad was a new product that created a new market for the company. An example of a new service designed to reach new markets and customers is Korean mobile phone operator SK Telecom's introduction of technology permitting customers to view and record television programmes on their telephones.[16,17]

Strategy and structure changes pertain to the administrative domain in an organization. The administrative domain involves the supervision and management of the organization. These changes include changes in organization structure, strategic management, policies, reward systems, labour relations, coordination devices, management information and control systems and accounting and budgeting systems. Structure and system changes are usually top-down, that is, mandated by top management, whereas product and technology changes may often come from the bottom up. A system change instituted by management in a university might be a new merit pay plan. Corporate downsizing and the shift to horizontal teams are other examples of top-down structure change.

EXHIBIT 12.3 The Four Types of Change Provide a Strategic Competitive Wedge

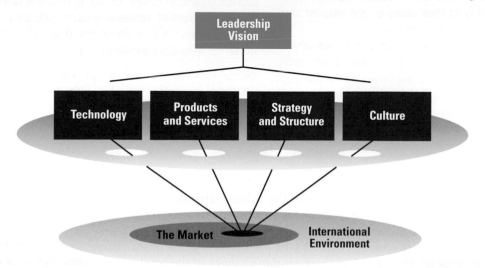

Source: Joseph E. McCann, 'Design Principles for an Innovating Company', *Academy of Management Executive* 5 (May 1991), 76–93.

LEADING BY DESIGN

Google

Google quickly became the most popular search engine on the internet with its smarter, faster approach to providing users with what they are looking for. But to maintain that success, managers knew the company needed to continuously innovate.

Then product manager Marissa Mayer suggested that the company come up with new ideas the same way as its search engine scours the web. To provide users with the best web search experience possible, Google searches far and wide, combing through billions of documents. Then it ranks the search results by relevance and zaps them to the user quickly. The idea search process works much the same way by casting a wide net across the organization. The process begins with an easy-to-use intranet. Even employees with limited technology expertise can quickly set up a page of ideas. 'We never say, 'This group should innovate and the rest should just do their jobs,' says Jonathan Rosenberg, vice president of product management. 'Everyone spends a fraction of [the] day on R&D.' The intranet has also tapped into more ideas from technologically savvy Google employees who may not be very vocal or assertive in meetings. Mayer says some engineers had lots of good ideas but were shy about putting them forth in open meetings. Now, employees can post their ideas on the intranet and see what kind of response they get.

Mayer searched the site each day to see which ideas are generating the most excitement and comments. Once a week, she sat down with a team to hash over the ideas and flesh out at least six or seven that could be fast-tracked into development. In addition to the internal search process, users continue to play a key role in innovation. Ten full-time employees read and respond to user emails and pass along ideas to project teams, who are constantly tweaking Google's service. Engineers work in teams of three and have the authority to make any changes that improve the quality of the user experience and get rid of anything that gets in the way. Moreover, Google allows any software developer to integrate its search engine into their own applications. The download is easy and the licence is free. It sounds crazy to some businesses, but Google says it 'turns the world into Google's development team'.

Google's organic approach to innovation has been highly successful. Indeed, the company is no longer just a hugely successful search engine. Google has evolved into a diverse information technology company that has put Microsoft into the shade. While Microsoft has been struggling to catch up in the game of search, Google has launched many new products ranging from Google Maps and Gmail to cutting edge mobile phones and tablets, and virtual reality devices and applications. Google has ploughed resources into numerous IT start-ups, while acquiring major internet firms like YouTube. In 2015, Google restructured itself to better manage its diverse portfolio of investments, creating a holding company called Alphabet, with subsidiaries in numerous areas including biotech, life sciences, home automation and robotics. The new organizational structure is designed to give the Google empire greater flexibility in acquiring and divesting investments.

As for Marissa Mayer, in 2012 she jumped to rival Yahoo as CEO. Unfortunately Yahoo hasn't been able to match Google's midas touch, with many of its initiatives ending in failure. By 2016 Yahoo was in the throes of massive losses and staff cutbacks, and rumours were rife that Mayer would soon be exiting the firm.[18] (See Counterpoint 12.1)

Source: Fara Warner, 'How Google Searches Itself', *Fast Company* (July 2002), 50–52; Fred Vogelstein, 'Search and Destroy', *Fortune* (May 2, 2005), 72–82; and Keith H. Hammonds, 'How Google Grows … and Grows … and Grows', *Fast Company* (April 2003), 74.

Culture changes refer to changes in the values, attitudes, expectations, beliefs, abilities and behaviour of employees. Culture changes pertain to changes in how employees think; these are changes in mind-set rather than technology, structure or products.

The four types of change in Exhibit 12.3 are interdependent – a change in one often means a change in another. New products may require changes in the production technology, or a change in structure may require new employee skills. For example, when Jong-Yung Yun took over as

COUNTERPOINT 12.1

One issue that Google will need to address, like Toyota, is the issue of corporate social responsibility. Google is undoubtedly an innovative company, but some of its approaches to its tax affairs innovate in ways that allow it to avoid paying a fair share of taxes in the jurisdictions where it operates.

In 2012 and 2013 the company was widely criticized for structuring its business affairs so as to avoid taxes. In the world of digital services, national taxation systems can often be easily circumvented. In Google's case, it paid less than one tenth of one per cent corporate taxes on UK sales of £11.5 billion, by channelling revenues through its offices in Ireland. It further reduced its UK tax exposure by asserting that most of the value of the services it provides is added in the company's headquarters in California, USA. In response to growing criticism, Google did a deal in 2016 to pay up to £130 million pounds in extra tax. While the British government hailed the deal as a breakthrough against tax avoidance, critics quickly picked apart the deal as inadequate, and pressure is mounting for a global tax regime that shuts off the use of offshore arrangements.[19]

Innovation is one of the strong points of today's fast-moving business world. It's important that such innovation is in the public interest.[20]

President and CEO of Samsung Electronics in 1996, he found the company's product division structure stood in the way of taking advantage of technological convergence. A typical case was the company's refrigerators, which had been simple machines but now included specialized semiconductors, made by another division that was not in tune with the white goods department. Over the next years Yun restructured the company to bring core divisions together.[21] The structural change was an outgrowth of the technology change.

Elements for Successful Change

Regardless of the type or scope of change, it can be analyzed as a series of stages of innovation which may overlap (see Counterpoint 12.2).[22] In the research literature on innovation, organizational change is considered the adoption of a new idea or behaviour by an organization.[23] Organizational innovation, in contrast, is the adoption of an idea or behaviour that is new to the organization's industry, market or general environment.[24] The first organization to introduce a new product is considered the innovator, and organizations that copy it are considered to adopt changes. For purposes of managing change, however, the terms *innovation* and *change* will be used interchangeably because the change process within organizations tends to be similar whether a change is early or late with respect to other organizations in the environment. Innovations typically are assimilated into an organization through a series of steps or elements. Organization members first become aware of a possible innovation, evaluate its appropriateness and then evaluate and choose the idea.[25] The key elements of successful change are summarized in Exhibit 12.4.

BRIEFCASE 12.2

COUNTERPOINT 12.2

Sequential models can be helpful in simplifying what is often a complex and even chaotic process. Innovation and change are frequently contested and resisted as they may be promoted and welcomed by some groups but viewed as a threat by others. Processes of change and innovation are often lumpy and recursive. Developments occur in fits and starts; and stages of 'awareness' and 'evaluation' are revisited as new understandings emerge and re-assessments are made.

1 *Ideas.* No company can remain competitive without new ideas; change is the outward expression of those ideas.[26] An idea is a new way of doing things. It may be a new product or service, a new management concept or a new procedure for working together in the

EXHIBIT 12.4   Sequence of Elements for Successful Change

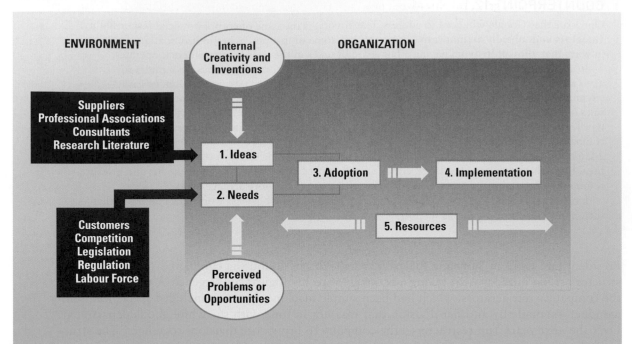

organization. Ideas can come from within or from outside the organization. Internal creativity is a dramatic element of organizational change. Creativity is the generation of novel ideas that may meet perceived needs or respond to opportunities. As discussed earlier, Google Corporation allows its engineers to spend 20 per cent of their time on projects that interest them. This has generated numerous ideas for new services, including Google Moderator, an idea management system that allows virtual collaboration on project brainstorming and idea testing.[27] At Samsung's India subsidiary, employees receive rewards for interesting innovative ideas, with extra bonuses if the innovation is implemented. The concept has been so popular that the company's 300 employees generate 1800 ideas a month.[28,29]

2 *Need*. Ideas are generally not seriously considered unless there is a perceived need for change (see Counterpoint 12.3). A perceived need for change occurs when managers see a gap between actual performance and desired performance in the organization. Managers try to establish a sense of urgency so that others will understand the need for change. Sometimes a crisis provides an undoubted sense of urgency. In many cases, however, there is no crisis, so managers have to recognize a need and communicate it to others.[30] A study of innovativeness in industrial firms, for example, suggests that organizations that encourage close attention to customers and market conditions and support for entrepreneurial activity produce more ideas and are more innovative.[31] Jeffrey Immelt, since 2000 the CEO of American-headquartered General Electric (GE), has focused on creating just those conditions at the sprawling industrial giant, which had grown in recent years largely through acquisition. By combining an emphasis on marketing, a renewed basic research effort and a company-wide focus on learning and sharing ideas, Immelt has recharged GE into a house of technological innovation, calling for constant reinvention to generate more growth from internal operations. The company has regularly been named one of the world's most innovative by business executives, and is currently investing heavily in green technologies.[32,33]

3 *Adoption.* Adoption occurs when decision-makers choose to go ahead with a proposed idea. Key managers and employees need to be in agreement to support the change. For a major organizational change, the decision might require the signing of a legal document by the board of directors. For a small change, adoption might occur with informal approval by a middle manager.

4 *Implementation.* Implementation occurs when organization members actually use a new idea, technique or behaviour. Materials and equipment may have to be acquired, and workers may have to be trained to use the new idea. Implementation is of course the most important step because without it, previous steps are to no avail. Implementation of change is often the most difficult part of the change process. Until people use the new idea, no change has actually taken place.

5 *Resources.* Human energy and activity are required to bring about change. Change does not happen on its own; it requires time, resources and energy, for both creating and implementing a new idea. Someone must develop a proposal and provide the time and effort to implement it. India's software and business process outsourcing (BPO) giant Wipro has a central innovation council that funds innovative ideas. The company has a special unit, the 'quantum innovation centre' where outside consultants help to bring new ideas to market. Each year five or six ideas are operationalized to build the range of process re-engineering services Wipro offers its clients. Wipro boss Azim Premji says, 'Analysts are saying we will do around $4 billion in revenues this year: nine to ten per cent of those revenues will come from innovation, and that's a substantial amount. We are not talking small investments; some of these projects will pay back this year, while some others the year after.'[34]

?

COUNTERPOINT 12.2

COUNTERPOINT 12.3

The 'need for change' is something that may not be perceived by all managers or employees. Some may well prefer the status quo, not just because it is familiar but because it is tried and tested. Change in itself is not necessarily a 'good thing'. It may be ill-thought through and it may have unanticipated and deleterious consequences. All too often, changes are introduced to 'make an impact', often led by a CEO who may have moved on before the full effects have been felt.

Change may be supported by 'key managers' without them agreeing that it is desirable if they anticipate that their jobs or credibility are put at risk by challenging the proposals. If this occurs, then adoption may be conditional or half-hearted. The outcome may be that the proposed change is incompletely or inadequately implemented. This may not necessarily be a 'bad thing' if the proposed idea is itself poorly thought through or if it has the effect of undermining established strengths.

One point about Exhibit 12.4 is especially important. Needs and ideas are listed simultaneously at the beginning of the change sequence. Either may occur first. Many organizations adopted the computer, for example, because it seemed a promising way to improve efficiency. The search for a vaccine against the AIDS virus, on the other hand, was stimulated by a severe need.

Technology Change

In today's business world, any company that isn't continually developing, acquiring or adapting new technology will likely be struggling to survive within a few years. However, organizations face a contradiction when it comes to technology change, because the conditions that promote new ideas are not generally the best for implementing those ideas for routine production. An innovative organization is often characterized by flexibility and empowered

BRIEFCASE 12.3

employees and the absence of rigid work rules.[35] As discussed earlier in this book, an organic, free-flowing organization is typically associated with change and is considered the most effective organization form for adapting to a highly volatile or chaotic environment.

The flexibility of an organic organization is attributed to opportunities to be creative and introduce new ideas. Organic organizations encourage a bottom-up innovation process. Ideas bubble up from middle- and lower-level employees when they have the freedom to propose ideas and to experiment. A mechanistic structure, in contrast, tends to inhibit innovation with its emphasis on rules and regulations, even though it may be the best structure for efficiently producing routine products. The challenge for managers is to combine organic and mechanistic characteristics within the organization to achieve both innovation and efficiency. To attain both aspects of technological change, an ambidextrous approach may be developed.

The Ambidextrous Approach

Recent thinking has refined the idea of organic versus mechanistic structures with respect to innovation creation versus innovation utilization. An organic structure may generate innovative ideas but is not necessarily the most effective structure for using those ideas.[36] In other words, the initiation and the utilization of change are different kinds of processes. Organic characteristics such as decentralization and employee freedom are conducive for initiating ideas; but these same conditions can make it hard to implement a change – for example, because employees are unwilling to comply. Decentralization and a generally loose structure may mean that employees can ignore the innovation.

How do executives solve this dilemma? One remedy is for the organization to use an ambidextrous approach – that is, to incorporate structures and management processes appropriate to both the creation and the implementation of innovation.[37] Another way to think of the ambidextrous approach is to consider design elements important for *exploring* new ideas versus the design elements that are most suitable for *exploiting* current capabilities. Exploration means encouraging creativity and developing new ideas, whereas exploitation means implementing those ideas to produce routine products. The organization can be designed to behave in an organic way for exploring new ideas, and in a mechanistic way to exploit and use the ideas. Exhibit 12.5 illustrates how one department is structured organically to explore and develop new ideas, while another department is structured mechanistically for routine implementation of innovations. Research has shown that an ambidextrous approach is significantly more successful in launching innovative new products or services.[38]

For example, a study of long-established Japanese companies such as Honda and Canon that have succeeded in breakthrough innovations found that these companies use an ambidextrous approach.[39] To develop ideas related to a new technology, the companies assign teams of young staff members who are not entrenched in the 'old way of doing things' to work on the project. The

EXHIBIT 12.5 Division of Labour in the Ambidextrous Organization

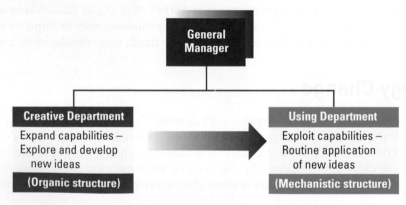

General Manager

Creative Department
Expand capabilities – Explore and develop new ideas
(Organic structure)

Using Department
Exploit capabilities – Routine application of new ideas
(Mechanistic structure)

teams are headed by an esteemed elder and are charged with doing whatever is needed to develop new ideas and products, even if it means breaking rules that are important in the larger organization for the process of implementing the new ideas.

Techniques for Encouraging Technology Change

Some of the techniques used by companies to maintain an ambidextrous approach are switching structures, creating separate creative departments, establishing venture teams and fostering corporate entrepreneurship.

Switching Structures   Switching structures occurs when, for example, managers in a predominantly mechanistic organization create an organic structure for the initiation of new ideas.[40] Some of the ways organizations have switched structures to achieve the ambidextrous approach are as follows:

- Electrolux, the Swedish home appliance maker, was facing declining sales. Its products, typically designed by the engineering department, were taking too long to get to market and were failing to capture consumers' attention. CEO Hans Straberg knew the problem needed a radical solution, and called in the chief of the Consumer Innovation division, Johan Hjertonsson. Hjertonsson had developed a reputation for radical solutions when facing up to the challenge of cheaper Chinese-made goods in the late 1990s. His approach was to abandon engineer-driven product development and instead set up cross-functional innovation teams made up of designers, engineers, marketers and salespeople working together to come up with products that excite consumers even if they are more expensive than the bog-standard imported competition. The entire company's strategy has now been revamped in order to focus on higher end, higher profit margin products, de-emphasizing lower priced, 'commoditized' products. The product development system keeps employees engaged and helps them to avoid 'silo' thinking where they become focused only on the culture and dynamics of their own divisions.[41] The company continues to perform well, and in 2011 became a big player in the emerging South American market through a buyout of the Chilean home appliance manufacturer CTI. While its ambition to take over GE's appliance business was thwarted in 2015 by US regulators who feared the combined firm would dominate the market, profitability continued to grow into 2016.[42,43]

- In 2007, the Japanese car maker Nissan opened a new innovation facility, the Nissan Advanced Technology Centre (NATC), designed to bring together R&D teams from around the company to work together more closely and more collaboratively in product development. The Centre was physically designed to encourage not only cross-functional collaboration but also to involve external engineers and visiting academics and researchers. Engineers from production factories from around the world are seconded to the centre, providing them with a different perspective on the company's business, and ensuring that nuts and bolts production issues are addressed early in the development process. The whole Centre is physically designed with an 'open' concept, for example, including 'collaboration rooms' that can accommodate up to 200 people, fitted with vehicle lifts. The facility interior is designed to permit an unobstructed view from much of the building of the testing going on in the vehicle pit-lane on the first floor, again contributing to the collaborative process. NATC is at the core of Nissan's R&D efforts, which in 2016 were focused on four priority areas; electric vehicles, self-driving cars, safety and reduced emissions.[44,45]

Both of these organizations found creative ways to be ambidextrous, establishing organic conditions for developing new ideas in the midst of more mechanistic conditions for implementing and using those ideas.

Creative Departments   In many large organizations the initiation of innovation is assigned to separate creative departments.[46] Staff departments, such as research and development (R&D), engineering, design and systems analysis, create changes for adoption in other departments. Departments that initiate change are organically structured to facilitate the generation of new ideas and techniques. Departments that then use those innovations tend to have a mechanistic structure more suitable for efficient production.

One example of a creative department is the research lab at Otsuka Pharmaceutical Company, which develops and manufactures both medicines and so-called nutraceuticals, food and drink designed to promote well-being, like its well-known sports drink Pocari Sweat. Although most big Western drug firms have switched to using robots and other high-tech tools to perform large-scale drug experiments, Japanese companies such as Otsuka are achieving success by continuing to emphasize human creativity. To get the kind of creative spirit that is willing to try new things and look for the unexpected, Otsuka's president Tatsuo Higuchi says its research labs 'put a high value on weird people'.[47] However, in its department that manufactures drugs, where routine and precision is important, a pharmaceutical company probably favours the employment of less unusual people who are comfortable following rules and standard procedures.

Another type of creative department is the idea incubator, an increasingly popular way to facilitate the development of new ideas within the organization. An idea incubator provides a safe harbour where ideas from employees throughout the organization can be developed without interference from company bureaucracy or politics.[48] The incubator gives people throughout the organization a place to go, rather than having to pitch a new idea all over the company and hope someone will pay attention. Companies as diverse as Intel India, Microsoft and Netherlands-based Philips NV use incubators to support the development of creative ideas.[49]

Venture Teams   Venture teams are a technique used to give free rein to creativity within organizations. Venture teams are often given a separate location and facilities so they are not constrained by organizational procedures. A venture team is like a small company within a large company. Numerous organizations have used the venture team concept to free creative people from the bureaucracy of a large corporation (see Counterpoint 12.4). Shell Oil established its GameChanger unit to increase innovation within the company's exploration business, providing a vehicle that channels promising employee ideas into projects funded with the parent company's capital. One of the earliest and most successful venture units is Innovacom, set up by France Telecom in 1988. Innovacom was for many years France Telecom's in-house venture capital-plus outfit, until it was eventually spun-off as an independent business in 2012. It provides capital to early-stage inventors and entrepreneurs in the fields of telecom hardware, telecom software, enterprise software and internet content and services. Innovacom was behind the start-up of such well-known internet-era companies as Kelkoo and Last Minute.com, as well as a host of less well-known but equally successful businesses.[50,51]

COUNTERPOINT 12.4

A cautionary tale about the importance of setting up venture teams early, and the need to think 'outside-the-box' of the parent business, comes from the newspaper business. Newspapers around the world have been rocked by the challenge of the internet, where information is often available free – and instantaneously. Developing an internet strategy is a matter of survival for the industry, and in most cases companies have set up internet-based operations as venture teams to explore and develop the new technology. One major challenge has been to find ways for internet operations to replace revenues from declining paper sales as readers shifted to online access. Many papers like Canada's *Globe and Mail*, the *New York Times*, and the *Irish Times* tried to charge for internet content by forcing readers to buy a subscription in the same way that they had paid for their paper copies. However, they quickly found out that the internet is a different kind of business. Readers simply went elsewhere for their news, with the result that online newspapers were in a vicious cycle of declining subscription revenues and falling readership, leading to lower advertising revenues. One-by-one they abandoned this approach, usually returning to an advertising-based revenue stream. However, advertising revenues are much lower than the amounts paper sales used to generate, so it's a dilemma internet newspaper venture groups will have to resolve soon, as the printed versions of newspapers sell fewer and fewer copies. Britain's *Telegraph* group manages to get 20 per cent of its advertising revenues from the internet, but it was one of the first major papers to go online in 1994. In recent years more and more online newspapers are going back behind paywalls again, notably led by Britain's *Times* and *Financial Times*, and the US *New York Times*.[52]

One type of venture team is called a *skunkworks*.[53] A skunkworks is a separate, small, informal, highly autonomous and often secretive group that focuses on breakthrough ideas for the business. The original skunkworks was created by America's Lockheed Martin aerospace manufacturer more than 50 years ago and is still in operation. The essence of a skunkworks is that highly talented people are given the time and freedom to let creativity reign. Michelin set up a skunkworks in Switzerland to go one step further than the Toyota Prius and develop a zeropollution car, the Hy-Light which had electric motors based in each wheel. Plans by innovative Monaco sports car manufacturer Venturi to put the vehicle into production came to nothing, but Michelin continues to innovate through its Michelin Incubators programme which encourages teams within Michelin - 'intrapreneurs' - to develop new ideas, whether innovative products like the Tweel airless tractor tyre, or existing process improvements. In 2015, 25 000 'progress ideas' were implemented, worth €15 million.[54]

A variation of the venture team concept is the new-venture fund, which provides financial resources for employees to develop new ideas, products or businesses. In order to tap into its employees' entrepreneurial urges, Lockheed Martin allows workers to take up to two years' unpaid leave to explore a new idea, using company labs and equipment and paying company rates for health insurance. If the idea is successful, the corporation's venture fund invests about $250 000 in the start-up company. One successful start-up was Genase, which created an enzyme that 'stone-washes' denim.[55]

Corporate Entrepreneurship

Corporate entrepreneurship attempts to develop an internal entrepreneurial spirit, philosophy and structure that will produce a higher-than-average number of innovations. Corporate entrepreneurship may involve the use of creative departments and new venture teams, but it also attempts to release the creative energy of all employees in the organization. Managers can create systems and structures that encourage entrepreneurship. For example, at the giant oil company BP, top executives establish contracts with the heads of all BP's business units. The unit managers are given free rein to deliver on the contract in whatever way they see fit, within clearly identified constraints.[56]

An important outcome of corporate entrepreneurship is to facilitate idea champions. These go by a variety of names, including *advocate, intrapreneur, or change agent*. Idea champions provide the time and energy to make things happen. They fight to overcome natural resistance to change and to convince others of the merit of a new idea.[57] Idea champions need not be within the organization. Some companies have found that fostering idea champions among regular customers can be a highly successful approach.[58] An example is Britain's Anglian Water, where every innovation project has a sponsor or champion who is a customer seeking a solution to a specific problem.[59] Anglian's approach has been formalized through its *Water Innovation Network*, where companies are invited to a Dragon's Den type session to pitch ideas to solve challenges facing the company. At a session in 2013, for example, companies were asked to come up with innovative approaches to deal with sewer flooding, with Anglian choosing the most promising approach for further development.[60] The business strategy of Johor Corporation (JCorp), a Malaysian state-owned regional economic development company, is built around 'intrapraneurship' with a social goal of increasing entrepreneurship among the ethnic Malay population. JCorp executives are encouraged to develop and implement business ideas in partnership with outside entrepreneurs, and can access venture funds from JCorp, which usually takes a majority ownership stake in the venture. The ventures have turned a profit overall for both JCorp and its intrapreneurs.[61,62]

Idea champions usually come in two types. The technical champion, or *product champion*, is the person who generates or adopts and develops an idea for a technological innovation and is devoted to it, even to the extent of risking position or prestige. The management champion acts as a supporter and sponsor to shield and promote an idea, such as a new project or a change of structure, within the organization.[63] The management champion sees the potential application and has the prestige and authority to get the idea a fair hearing and to allocate resources to it. Numerous studies have identified the importance of idea champions as a factor in the success of new products. US fabric and clothing manufacturer, W.L. Gore, featured in the *In Practice* box that follows, is a leading example of a company that fosters and benefits from idea champions.[64]

New Products and Services

Although the ideas just discussed are important to product and service as well as technology changes, other factors are also important. In many ways, new products and services are a special case of innovation because they are used by customers outside the organization. Since new products are designed for sale in an uncertain environment, doubts about the suitability and success of an innovation are high.

New Product Success Rate

Research has explored the enormous uncertainty associated with the development and sale of new products.[65] To understand what this uncertainty can mean to organizations, just consider such flops as Sony's Betamax video recording format, which lost out to VHS after an epic 25 year battle,[66] or IPC publishing company's *Nova* women's magazine which actually failed twice. It had been an iconic UK fashion title in the 1960s that lost readership and stopped publication in 1975, only to be revived in 2000 before failing again less than 12 months later.[67] Swiss drug manufacturer Novartis dropped $235 million in development costs for the Aurograb antibiotic before it failed its second round of clinical tests.[68] Developing and producing products that fail is a part of business in all industries. Companies spend billions on R&D for new products such as Canada's Dr Care aerosol toothpaste (that parents feared would be too popular with their children), Blue Circle Cement's abortive entry into the lawnmower market, and IBM's doomed attempt to take on Microsoft Windows with its OS/2 operating system.[69] Thousands of new products and service concepts fail each year.

IN PRACTICE

W.L. Gore

W.L. Gore a privately held American company best known as the maker of Gore-Tex fabric, is so good at innovating that it has become a major player in areas as diverse as guitar strings, dental floss, fuel cells and medical devices. Everyone at Gore is expected to become an idea champion at some time in their career with the company. Gore provides the environment for that to happen by letting employees figure out what they want to do.

Gore's employees, known as associates, don't have job titles or bosses. Rather than being assigned to tasks, people make commitments to work on projects where they think they can make the biggest contribution. That means employees tend to be 'very passionate about what they're doing', says company researcher Jeff Kolde. Kolde himself is an excellent example of an idea champion. Gore researchers had developed an improved kind of ionic membrane that separates positive and negative ions, but the company wasn't sure what to do with it. Kolde got excited about the potential use in the fuel cell industry and began sending out prototypes. The fuel cell industry got really excited too. W.L. Gore became the first commercial supplier of membrane-electron assemblies (MEAs), a critical technology for fuel cells. But Kolde first had to convince others that the project was worth their time and effort, no easy task in a new area like fuel cells. His passion for the project enabled him to recruit people from around the company, including two employees with PhDs.

Gore research associates get to spend 10 per cent of their time as 'dabble time', developing their own ideas. A senior colleague serves as a mentor and guide; if the idea is promising and the associate is passionate about it, the mentor becomes a management champion to make sure the project gets the attention and resources needed to pursue it. Gore has found that having associates recruit volunteers to work on projects turns out to be a pretty good indication of whether an innovation is likely to succeed. An example of Gore 'intrapreneurship' was the development of the Elixir guitar strings from an idea by Gore associate Dave Myers to coat strings with a polymer. The strings last longer than ordinary strings and have become a profitable niche product line for W.L. Gore.[70,71]

Experts estimate that about 80 per cent of new products fail upon introduction and another ten per cent disappear within five years (see Counterpoint 12.5). Considering that, depending on the product and the market, it can be hugely costly to successfully launch a new product, new product development is a risky, high-stakes game for organizations. Nevertheless, without new product development, companies will inevitably wither and die, and so most large, successful corporations devote energy and resources to developing new products.[72]

COUNTERPOINT 12.5

Similar figures are regularly cited for failures of organizational innovation where change programmes fail to deliver their promises. Change may be regarded as a necessity but it is also very frequently ineffective or abandoned.

- Two-thirds of Total Quality Management (TQM) programmes fail, and re-engineering initiatives fail 70 per cent of the time (Senge, 1999, pp. 5–6).[73]

- A seminal study found a 64 per cent failure rate among new technological innovations introduced into municipal public service programmes (Yin, 1978, p. vi).[74]

- Change initiatives crucial to organizational success fail 70 per cent of the time (Miller, 2002, p. 360).

- Major corporate investments in technology are not used as intended or abandoned within six months 80 per cent of the time (Gartner Group in Miller, 2002, p. 360).[75]

- Leaders of the corporate re-engineering movement report that the success rate for Fortune 1000 companies is below 50 per cent, possibly only 20 per cent (Strebel, 1996, p. 86).[76]

A survey some years ago examined 200 projects in 19 chemical, drug, electronics and petroleum laboratories to learn about success rates.[77] To be successful, the new product had to pass three stages of development: technical completion, commercialization and market success. On average, only 57 per cent of all projects undertaken in the R&D laboratories achieved technical objectives, which means all technical problems were solved and the projects moved on to production. Of all projects that were started, less than one third (31 per cent) were fully marketed and commercialized. Several projects failed at this stage because production estimates or test market results were unfavourable.

Finally, only 12 per cent of all projects originally undertaken achieved economic success. Most of the commercialized products did not earn sufficient returns to cover the cost of development and production. This means that only about one project in eight returned a profit to the company.

Reasons for New Product Success

The next question to be answered by research was, 'Why are some products – both physical products and service – more successful than others? Why has the United Arab Emirates-headquartered Thuraya satellite phone service remained profitable while US-based Iridium and Globalstar both had to declare Chapter 11 bankruptcy protection, with Motorola-backed Iridium described as one of "The 10 Biggest Tech Failures of the Last Decade" in 2009[78] (although they have both been restructured and continue to offer services)? Why did Sony's Blu-Ray format for high density data disks succeed while rival Toshiba's HD-DVD standard fall by the wayside?'[79] Further studies indicated that innovation success is often related to collaboration between technical and marketing departments. Successful new products and services seem to be technologically sound and also carefully tailored to customer needs.[80] A study called Project SAPPHO examined 17 pairs of new product innovations, with one success and one failure in each pair, and concluded the following:

1   Successful innovating companies had a much better understanding of customer needs and paid much more attention to marketing.

2   Successful innovating companies made more effective use of outside technology and outside advice, even though they did more work in-house.

3   Top management support in the successful innovating companies was from people who were more senior and had greater authority.

Thus, there is a distinct pattern of tailoring innovations to customer needs, making effective use of technology, and having influential top managers support the project. These ideas taken together indicate that the effective design for new product innovation is associated with horizontal coordination across departments.

Horizontal Coordination Model

BRIEFCASE 12.4

The organization design for achieving new product innovation involves three components – departmental specialization, boundary spanning and horizontal coordination. These components are similar to the horizontal coordination mechanisms discussed in Chapter 4, such as teams, taskforces and project managers, and the differentiation and integration ideas discussed in Chapter 5. These components can be viewed in the horizontal coordination model.

Specialization   The key departments in new product development are R&D, marketing and production. The specialization component means that the personnel in all three of these departments are highly competent at their own tasks. The three departments are differentiated from each other and have skills, goals and attitudes appropriate for their specialized functions.

Boundary Spanning   This component refers to how those departments involved with new products have excellent linkage with relevant sectors in the external environment. R&D personnel are linked to professional associations and to colleagues in other R&D departments. They are aware of recent scientific developments. Marketing personnel are closely linked to customer needs. They listen to what customers have to say, and they analyze competitor products and suggestions by distributors. For example, Charles Rolls and Tim Warrilow launched UK-based Fever-Tree in

2001 when they observed that the big drinks mixer manufacturers were focusing on high volume mixes based on cheap, artificial ingredients: the victory of company laboratories and accountants over consumer focus. Fever-Tree is named after the trees found in the Democratic Republic of Congo that are the source of the quinine that both forms the basis of tonic water and is a cure for malaria. The company developed six premium drinks mixes based on natural ingredients, and distributed through high-end bars and premium supermarkets such as the UK's Waitrose.[81] By 2015 they were selling 138 million bottles of their elixirs in 38 countries, built on a marketing pitch that emphasizes the exotic, dangerous places the founders personally visit in order to source their special, natural ingredients.[82,83]

Horizontal Coordination

This component refers to how technical, marketing and production people share ideas and information. Research people inform marketing of new technical developments to learn whether the developments are applicable to customers. Marketing people provide customer complaints and information to R&D to use in the design of new products. People from both R&D and marketing coordinate with production because new products have to fit within production capabilities so costs are not exorbitant. The decision to launch a new product is ultimately a joint decision among all three departments. Horizontal coordination, using mechanisms such as cross-functional teams, increases both the amount and the variety of information for new product development, enabling the design of products that meet customer needs and circumventing manufacturing and marketing problems.[84]

Companies such as Unilever and, W.L. Gore routinely turn to customers and other organizations for advice. Gore worked with physicians to develop its thoracic graft.[85] During development of new planes such as the Airbus A380, engineers from Airbus and the purchasing airlines worked closely with flight attendants, pilots and frequent flyers, to make sure the plane was designed for maximum functionality and customer satisfaction.[86,87]

ONLINE
COUNTERPOINT 12.2

IN PRACTICE

Unilever

Anglo-Dutch firm Unilever is one of the two giants of the global consumer products industry, along with America's Procter & Gamble. However, like many long-established and successful firms, by the beginning of the twenty-first century, Unilever was in a downward cycle of tired brands and declining profits. In 2005 then CEO Patrick Cescau launched a turnaround strategy that focused on eliminating declining brands, reducing layers of bureaucracy, investing in the more profitable emerging markets and making the company far more nimble in developing product innovations and bringing them to market.[88] Unilever sold off its North American laundry products, which had

consistently lost market share to Procter & Gamble's products on the latter's home turf.

The key to Unilever's recent successes in product innovation has been to emphasize consumer-driven product development. As noted earlier in this chapter, consumers are becoming increasingly sensitive to environmental issues. For example, breakthroughs have been achieved in concentrated liquid detergent such as *Persil Small and Mighty*, which saves energy that would have been wasted transporting the excess water in traditional more diluted detergents, as well as making it easier for the consumer to haul the product home from the supermarket.[89] Unilever is working to achieve recognition of many of its products as environmentally sound. The company is a major tea producer, and is working with the Rainforest Alliance, an environmental NGO, to have all its tea plantations in East Africa certified as environmentally and socially sustainable.[90]

The company has also successfully leveraged its decentralized structure; its products are present in about 150 countries, and product development

▶

occurs all over the globe. Whereas previously national units of Unilever worked almost independently, Cescau worked to encourage local innovation and take greater advantage of locally developed innovations.[91] One of a number of recent successes in this area has been high-calcium ice cream, which was first developed in Asian markets and then successfully introduced in Europe.[92]

Unilever has also worked closely with its advertising agencies to ensure they are producing their cutting edge campaigns for Unilever, whose products had tended to be supported by cautious, conservative advertising. Unilever long-time Chief Marketing Officer, Simon Clift, said the company and its advertising agencies were once 'a bit like a married couple who had great sex … just not with each other'. In other words, Unilever had great products that were not always backed up by great advertising campaigns, while its advertising agencies ran great campaigns, just not necessarily for Unilever. By shifting some of its accounts and restructuring its relationships with other advertising agencies, the company has produced an edgier advertising image that not only has brought several Cannes Grand Prix awards but also delivered higher sales for several products. The approach also involves careful analysis of markets. Whereas European consumers tend to appreciate racy advertisements, the same may not be true in the US, for example. A campaign for its Axe male grooming line implies that young women will lose sexual inhibition when they smell Axe products being worn by their male friends; Unilever delayed introducing its Axe line in the States at the cost of several hundred million dollars in potential revenues, partly because 'we find this overt sexual reference in advertising might not go down too well in the Bible Belt'.[93] Eventually, though, the company took the risk and introduced Axe and its 'sexy' marketing pitch in the USA. Axe's macho image built a successful brand for a number of years, but as masculine roles have become more self-aware and 'metrosexual'. In 2016 Unilever decided to relaunch the brand emphasizing individuality over macho stereotypes. It will be interesting to see how the new approach goes down in the US Bible Belt![94,95]

Innovation failures – such as Kellogg's initial efforts to introduce cornflakes to India or Chrysler Corporation's early (and in retrospect, patronizing) effort to market to women with the 'LaFemme' model car[96] – usually violate the horizontal linkage model. Employees fail to connect with customer needs and market forces or internal departments fail to adequately share needs and coordinate with one another. Recent research has confirmed a connection between effective boundary spanning that keeps the organization in touch with market forces, smooth coordination among departments and successful product development.[97]

Achieving Competitive Advantage: The Need for Speed

The rapid development of new products is becoming a major strategic weapon in the shifting international marketplace.[98] To remain competitive, companies are learning to develop ideas into new products and services incredibly fast. Whether the approach is called the horizontal linkage model, concurrent engineering, companies without walls, the parallel approach, or simultaneous coupling of departments, the point is the same – get people working together simultaneously on a project rather than in sequence. Many companies are learning to sprint to market with new products.

Time-based competition means delivering products and services faster than competitors, giving companies a competitive edge. Tekes, the Finnish government technology agency, set up RAPID, a special programme to help the country's major corporations develop products and put them on the market more quickly, essential in rapidly changing global markets. Most of the country's major corporations have benefited from the programme. Finland has been a leader in the high-tech sector, with companies regularly outstripping competitors in speed to market and thus capturing and protecting market share in highly competitive markets.[99]

Some companies use what are called *fast cycle teams* as a way to support highly important projects and deliver products and services faster than competitors. A fast cycle team is a multifunctional, and sometimes multinational, team that works under stringent timelines and is provided with high levels of company resources and empowerment to accomplish an accelerated product development project.[100,101] By using the internet to collaborate on new designs among various functional departments and with suppliers, teams at the US-headquartered plumbing accessory manufacturer Moen take a new kitchen or bath tap from drawing board to store shelf in only 16 months. The time savings mean Moen's teams can work on three times as many projects as previously and introduce up to 15 new designs a year for today's fashion-conscious consumers.[102] Similarly, as we noted in Chapter 9, Toyota used a variety of innovative team approaches to develop the innovative Prius in only 15 months, in comparison with an industry standard of four years for the development of a new car model.[103]

Another critical issue is designing products that can compete on a global scale and successfully marketing those products internationally. Companies such as the ice cream maker Häagen Dazs are trying to improve horizontal communication and collaboration across geographical regions, recognizing that they can pick up winning product ideas from customers in other countries. A new Häagen Dazs flavour, *dulce de leche*, developed primarily for sale in Argentina, quickly became a favourite in the rest of the world.[104,105]

Many new product development teams today are global teams in order to develop products that will meet diverse needs of consumers all over the world.[106] Unilever, profiled earlier in this chapter, has R&D centres globally, located in UK, US, Netherlands, China and India, which tackle challenges like how to get more mayonnaise out of a jar, a problem addressed by the 2015 launch of an Easy-Out bottle that reduces mayo left in the bottle from 13% to 3%.[107]

Strategy and Structure Change

The preceding discussion focused on new production processes and products, which are based in the technology of an organization. The expertise for such innovation lies within the technical core and specialist staff groups, such as research and engineering. This section turns to an examination of strategy and structure changes.

In the past, when the environment was relatively stable, most organizations focused on small, incremental changes to solve immediate problems or take advantage of new opportunities. However, over the past couple of decades, with globalization and technological innovations upending traditional organizational models, companies throughout the world have sought to make radical changes in strategy, structure and management processes to adapt to new competitive demands.[108] Many organizations are cutting out layers of management and decentralizing decision-making. There is a shift toward more horizontal structures, with teams of front-line workers empowered to make decisions and solve problems on their own. Some companies are breaking away from traditional organization forms and shifting toward virtual network strategies and structures. Numerous companies are reorganizing and shifting their strategies as the expansion of e-business changes the rules. Global competition and rapid technological change will likely lead to further strategy-structure realignments over the next decade. These types of changes are the responsibility of the organization's top managers, and the overall process of change is typically different from the process for innovation in technology or new products.

The Dual-Core Approach

The dual-core approach to organizational change compares administrative and technical changes. Organizations – schools, hospitals, city governments, welfare agencies, government bureaucracies and many business firms – can be conceptualized as having two cores: a

BRIEFCASE 12.5

technical core and an *administrative core*. Each core has its own employees, tasks and environmental domain. Innovation can originate in either core.

The responsibility of the administrative core includes the structure, control and coordination of the organization itself and concerns the environmental sectors of government, financial resources, economic conditions, human resources and competitors. The technical core is concerned with the transformation of raw materials into organizational products and services and involves the environmental sectors of customers and technology.[109] The point of the dual-core approach is that many organizations – especially not-for-profit and government organizations – must adopt frequent administrative changes and need to be structured differently from organizations that rely on frequent technical and product changes for competitive advantage.

Organization Design for Implementing Administrative Change

The findings from research comparing administrative and technical change suggest that a mechanistic organization structure is appropriate when there are frequent administrative changes, including changes in goals, strategy, structure, control systems and personnel.[110] In many government organizations that are bureaucratically structured, administrative changes in policy, regulations or control systems are more critical than technical changes. Organizations that successfully adopt many administrative changes often have a larger administrative ratio, are larger in size, and are centralized and formalized compared with organizations that adopt many technical changes.[111] The reason is the top-down implementation of changes in response to changes in the government, financial or legal sectors of the environment. Research into civil service reform found that the implementation of administrative innovation was extremely difficult in organizations that had an organic technical core. The professional employees in a decentralized agency could resist civil service changes. By contrast, organizations that were considered more bureaucratic in the sense of high formalization and centralization adopted administrative changes more readily.[112]

IN PRACTICE

Rio Tinto Group

Rio Tinto is one of the storied names in world mining. The company dates back to 1873 when Rothschild family companies in London and Paris came together to buy the Spanish government's Rio Tinto copper mines in southern Spain (hence the company's name). By 2008 the company was a major miner of various minerals, including bauxite, iron ore, copper and diamonds. Rio Tinto is also the world's third-largest coal producer.

As the long global boom that began in the 1990s reached a crescendo in the first years of the twenty-first century, the commodities produced by Rio Tinto

ballooned in value. Rapidly expanding economies like China and India were consuming ever-increasing quantities of metals and other minerals, and increased demand fed into higher prices. Rio Tinto expanded aggressively, including purchase of the major Canadian aluminium producer Alcan in 2007. Rio Tinto shares seemed on a one-way upwards escalator, fuelled both by commodity prices and a hostile takeover bid from rival BHP Billiton.

Suddenly, however, the bottom fell out of the market for Rio Tinto's main products. Between January and December 2008, the price of both copper and aluminium dropped by two-thirds, and iron ore by one-third. Rio Tinto's own stock price also plunged; between May and December 2008 the company's shares declined by almost 90 per cent. BHP withdrew its bid for Rio Tinto. The company's near $40 billion debt, mainly accumulated from the Alcan purchase, worried investors. Rio CEO Tom Albanese needed to do something quickly to reduce overcapacity, rein in costs, reduce debt,

▶

restage capital investments to the longer term and thus improve investor confidence. In December 2008 he announced a wide-ranging pack-age including 14 000 redundancies worldwide, a cut of more than 50 per cent in planned spending during 2009 including putting several mine projects on hold, a freeze on dividends and an asset sale to raise cash. Albanese commented, 'By taking these tough decisions now we will be well positioned when the recovery comes.' The immediate reaction of stock markets was positive, but employees and communities around the world were worried. Continuing economic uncertainty and volatile commodities prices suggest that Albanese's strategy was wise, though he personally didn't survive the downturn, being asked to resign in 2013. In 2016 iron ore prices, a major determinant of Rio Tinto stock prices, were still down 65% from a 2011 peak mainly as a result of decreased demand from China.[113,114]

The innovation approaches associated with administrative versus technical change are summarized in Exhibit 12.6. Technical change, such as changes in production techniques and innovation technology for new products, is facilitated by an organic structure, which allows ideas to bubble upward from lower- and middle-level employees. Organizations that must adopt frequent administrative changes, in contrast, tend to use a top-down process and a mechanistic structure. For example, policy changes, such as the adoption of no-smoking policies, sexual harassment policies or new safety procedures, are usually implemented through a top-down approach. Downsizing and restructuring are nearly always managed top down, for example when Danish wind-turbine manufacturer Vestas had to deal with a combination of low-cost Chinese competition and reductions in renewable energy subsidies in Western countries between 2011 and 2016. However, by remaining lean and innovative, and focusing on growing new markets for its turbines, particularly in the United States, Vestas has been able to bounce back, regaining its position as the world's largest wind turbine manufacturer and realising profits of €685 million in 2015.[115,116]

What about business organizations that are normally technologically innovative in bottom-up fashion but suddenly face a crisis and need to reorganize? Or a technically innovative, high-tech firm that must reorganize frequently to accommodate changes in production technology or the environment? Technically innovative firms may suddenly have to restructure, reduce the number

EXHIBIT 12.6 Dual-Core Approach to Organization Change

| | Type of Innovation Desired | |
	Administrative Structure	Technology
	Administrative Core	Technical Core
Direction of Change:	Top-down	Bottom-up
Examples of Change:	Strategy	Production techniques
	Downsizing	Workflow
	Structure	Product ideas
Best Organizational Design for Change:	Mechanistic	Organic

of employees, alter pay systems, disband teams or form a new division.[117] One answer is to use a top-down change process. In a top-down process, the authority for strategy and structure change lies with top management, who initiate and implement the new strategy and structure to meet environmental circumstances. This was the situation facing the Anglo-Australian mining giant, Rio Tinto Group (See *In Practice* on the preceding page), when world commodity prices fell sharply in the 2008 slump.

ONLINE
COUNTERPOINT 12.3

A study of successful corporate transformations, which frequently involve painful changes, found that managers followed a fast, focused approach. When top managers spread difficult changes such as downsizing over a long time period, employee morale suffers more and the change is much less likely to lead to positive outcomes. While analysts were surprised at the severity of Rio Tinto's cutbacks, Albanese will have been aware of best practices in corporate restructuring, and thus decided to get the bad news out of the way quickly so that morale could be rebuilt quickly and the organization could move forward.[118]

Top managers should also remember that top-down change means initiation of the idea occurs at upper levels and is implemented downward. It does not mean that lower-level employees are not educated about the change or allowed to participate in it.

Culture Change

Organizations are made up of people and their relationships with one another. Changes in strategy, structure, technologies and products do not happen on their own, and changes in any of these areas involve changes in people as well. Employees must learn how to use new technologies, or market new products, or work effectively in a team-based structure. Sometimes achieving a new way of thinking requires a focused change in the underlying corporate cultural values and norms. Changing corporate culture fundamentally shifts how work is done in an organization and generally leads to renewed commitment and empowerment of employees and a stronger bond between the company and its customers.[119]

Forces for Culture Change

A number of recent trends have contributed to a need for cultural makeovers at companies such as Marks and Spencer, IBM and DHL. Some of the primary changes requiring a shift in culture and employee mind-set are re-engineering and the move toward horizontal forms of organizing, greater employee and customer diversity, and the shift to the learning organization.

Re-engineering and Horizontal Organizing   As described in Chapter 4, re-engineering involves redesigning a vertical organization along its horizontal workflows. This changes the way managers and employees need to think about how work is done and requires greater focus on employee empowerment, collaboration, information sharing and meeting customer needs. In his book *The Re-engineering Revolution*, Michael Hammer refers to people change as 'the most perplexing, annoying, distressing and confusing part' of re-engineering.[120] Managers may confront powerful emotions as employees react to rapid, massive change with fear or anger.

In the horizontal organization, managers and front-line workers need to understand and embrace the concepts of teamwork, empowerment and cooperation. Managers shift their thinking to view workers as colleagues rather than cogs in a wheel; and workers learn to accept not only greater freedom and power, but also the higher level of responsibility that comes with them. Mutual trust, risk taking and tolerance for mistakes become key cultural values in the horizontal organization.

One of the biggest challenges in re-engineering is the shift underway in China and several other formerly communist countries in Asia, which have now adopted capitalist models. Traditionally, organizations were very hierarchical, and staff had limited opportunities to provide their input to decisions. Ironically the first generation of capitalist business leaders may even have exacerbated this attitude, as they built companies based on their own charisma and capacity to act decisively. However, as organizations mature and become more complex, effective information sharing and making best use of all the talents in the company becomes crucial. Louis Liu, a Hong Kong-based human resource management consultant, says, 'There are a lot of brilliant businessmen in the mainland. They are brilliant at doing business, but they don't even know how to hold a meeting properly. They ask their colleagues to give their report, then give each of them some verbal instructions and call that a meeting.' Gradually, though, a new generation of human resource managers is helping to foster contemporary management skills, drawing attention to the subtleties of organizational culture and not only the short term bottom line.[121]

Diversity   In many organizations, managers are engaged in implementing new recruiting, mentoring and promotion methods, diversity training programmes, tough policies regarding sexual harassment and racial discrimination and new benefits programmes that respond to a more diverse workforce. Organizations are moving beyond the concept of 'managing diversity', which emphasizes the difficulties associated with a diverse workforce, towards 'diversity leadership', where companies take a lead in fostering and supporting diversity both within and outside the organization. The Toronto, Canada office of accounting major Ernst and Young is actively involved in community programmes to support minority and immigrant youth succeed in employment. Jeanine Pereira, the firm's team development leader, says this pays off for Ernst and Young, 'We recruit worldwide, and if you can show that you help immigrants integrate into Canadian society, it is a lot easier for you to attract and retain skilled accountants from around the world.'[122]

The Learning Organization   The learning organization involves breaking down boundaries both within and between organizations to create companies that are focused on knowledge sharing and continuous learning. Recall from Chapter 1 that shifting to a learning organization involves changes in a number of areas. For example, structures become horizontal and involve empowered teams working directly with customers. There are few rules and procedures for performing tasks, and knowledge and control of tasks are located with employees rather than supervisors. Information is broadly shared rather than being concentrated with top managers. In addition, employees, customers, suppliers and partners all play a role in determining the organization's strategic direction. Clearly, all of these changes require new values, new attitudes and new ways of thinking and working together. A learning organization cannot exist without a culture that supports openness, equality, adaptability and employee participation.

As noted above, many Chinese organizations are in the process of cultural change, instituting internal reforms aimed at creating a learning organization. Zhujiang Iron and Steel Company, featured in the *In Practice* box on the next page, is a case in point.[123]

Organization Development Culture Change Interventions

Managers use a variety of approaches and techniques for changing corporate culture, some of which we discussed in Chapter 11. One method of quickly bringing about culture change is known as **organization development (OD)**, which focuses on the human and social aspects of the organization as a way to improve the organization's ability to adapt and solve problems. OD emphasizes the values of human development, fairness, openness, freedom from coercion and individual autonomy that allows workers to perform the job as they see fit, within reasonable organizational constraints.[124] In the 1970s, OD evolved as a separate field that applied the behavioural sciences in a process of planned organization-wide change, with the goal of increasing organizational effectiveness. Today, the concept has been enlarged to examine how people and groups can change to a learning organization culture in a complex and turbulent environment. Organization development is not a step-by-step procedure to solve a specific problem but a process of fundamental change in the human and social systems of the organization, including organizational culture.[125]

BRIEFCASE 12.6

IN PRACTICE

ZISCo

Zhujiang Iron and Steel Company (ZISCo) is a specialist steel producer, set up by the Chinese state in 1997 as part of its industrial upgrading programme in the country's ninth Five Year Plan. Although the company was established long after the Communist era and was organized on business rather than political lines, its operations still reflected a productivist orientation. In other words, there was an emphasis on production quantity rather than price and profit margins, and efforts to improve the bottom line were usually made through cost reduction rather than improvements to quality, leading to increased revenues. The company tended to be driven by its engineers rather than professional managers. Typically as in other Chinese firms, human resources was an underdeveloped area.

Ruoshen Zhang, president of ZISCo between 2003 and 2006, is an MBA-educated professional manager. He was well aware of modern management techniques and quickly built a reform strategy around the concept of value creation, with three elements: creating value to customers through higher quality and better marketing; to the company through

more efficient production; and to employees through remuneration and advancement opportunities tied to performance. The company introduced longer-term agreements with suppliers, a professionalized HR team, a more engaged middle management and a better system for cross-functional coordination. One of the most important innovations was investing time and resources in better understanding the customer. This paid off handsomely, as ZISCo found it could substantially reduce production waste by planning for steel offcuts to be used to make smaller parts its customers needed, rather than just being thrown in the scrap bin.

In 2006, Zhang was promoted to president of Guangzhou Iron and Steel Enterprises (GISE), ZISCo's parent company. One of his senior managers took his place. The prospects for ZISCo looked good, but Zhang was aware that he had personally driven many of the management innovations. It would be crucial in the next phase of corporate development for the whole management team to adopt a strategic orientation. The value creation approach was one step towards systematizing strategic thinking, but Zhang and his senior colleagues at GISE would need to ensure that this became a principle underlying continuous learning, rather than just a mantra repeated to satisfy senior management. The need for innovative strategic management would grow all the stronger as the Chinese construction industry was hit by the global slowdown, and with steel demand and prices at a 10 year low in 2016, steel companies across China ran up large losses.[126,127]

OD uses knowledge and techniques from the behavioural sciences to create a learning environment through increased trust, open confrontation of problems, employee empowerment and participation, knowledge and information sharing, the design of meaningful work, cooperation and collaboration between groups and the full use of human potential.

OD interventions involve training of specific groups or of everyone in the organization. For OD interventions to be successful, senior management in the organization must see the need for OD and provide enthusiastic support for the change. Techniques used by many organizations for improving people skills through OD include the following.

Large Group Intervention   Most early OD activities involved small groups and focused on incremental change. However, in recent years, there has been growing interest in the application of OD techniques to large group settings, which are more attuned to bringing about transformational change in organizations operating in complex environments.[128] The large group intervention approach[129] brings together participants from all parts of the organization – often including key stakeholders from outside the organization as well – in an off-site setting to discuss problems or opportunities and plan for change. A large group intervention might involve 50 to 500 people and last for several days. The off-site setting limits interference and distractions, enabling participants to focus on new ways of doing things. General Electric's 'Work Out' programme, an ongoing process of solving problems, learning and improving, begins with large-scale off-site meetings that get people talking across functional, hierarchical and organizational boundaries. Hourly and salaried workers come together from many different parts of the organization and join with customers and suppliers to discuss and solve specific problems.[130] The process forces a rapid analysis of ideas, the creation of solutions and the development of a plan for implementation. Over time, 'Work Out' creates a culture where ideas are rapidly translated into action and positive business results.[131]

Team Building   Team building promotes the idea that people who work together can work as a team. A work team can be brought together to discuss conflicts, goals, the decision-making process, communication, creativity and leadership. The team can then plan to overcome problems and improve results. Team-building activities are also used in many companies to train task forces, committees and new product development groups. These activities enhance communication and collaboration and strengthen the cohesiveness of organizational groups and teams.

Interdepartmental Activities   Representatives from different departments are brought together in a mutual location to expose problems or conflicts, diagnose the causes and plan improvements in communication and coordination. This type of intervention has been applied to union–management conflict, headquarters–field office conflict, interdepartmental conflict and mergers.[132] A box-storage business, which stores archived records for other companies, found interdepartmental meetings to be a key means of building a culture based on team spirit and customer focus. People from different departments met for hour-long sessions every two weeks and shared their problems, told stories about their successes, and talked about things they had observed in the company. The meetings helped people understand the problems faced in other departments and see how everyone depended on each other to do their jobs successfully.[133]

One current area in which OD can provide significant value is in spurring culture change toward valuing diversity.[134] In addition, today's organizations are continuously adapting to environmental uncertainty and increasing global competition, and OD interventions can respond to these new realities as companies strive to create greater capability for learning and growth.[135]

Strategies for Implementing Change

Managers and employees can think of inventive ways to improve the organization's technology, creative ideas for new products and services, fresh approaches to strategies and structures or ideas for fostering adaptive cultural values, but until the ideas are put into action, they are worthless to the organization. Implementation is the most crucial part of the change process, but it is also the most difficult. Change is frequently disruptive and uncomfortable for managers as well as employees. This chapter's *Bookmark 12.0* explores how managers can improve change implementation by understanding the emotional aspects of the change process. Change is complex, dynamic and messy, and implementation requires strong and persistent leadership. In this final section, we briefly discuss the role of leadership for change, some reasons for resistance to change, and techniques that managers can use to overcome resistance and successfully implement change.

Leadership for Change

One style of leadership, referred to as *transformational leadership*, is particularly suited for bringing about change. Top leaders who use a transformational leadership style enhance

BOOKMARK 12.0

Have you read this book?

The Change Monster: The Human Forces That Fuel or Foil Corporate Transformation and Change

BY JEANIE DANIEL DUCK

The change monster is lurking in every organization just waiting to gobble up unsuspecting managers who are striving to implement new strategies, accomplish reorganizations, or complete mergers. Jeanie Daniel Duck uses the term *change monster* in her book by the same name to refer to all the complex human emotions and social dynamics that emerge during major change efforts. Many managers, she says, simplify or ignore the people issues of change, a sure prescription for failure.

Mastering the Change Curve

Duck says that major organizational change typically follows a change curve – a roller-coaster ride that brings out myriad unexpected and conflicting emotions.

- *Stagnation*. This is the period during which the organization has lost direction or is moving in the wrong direction. The change monster is generally quiet – people feel comfortable and safe. However, it is the job of managers to recognize stagnation and create a sense of urgency for change.

- *Preparation*. In this stage, Duck says, 'the change monster is rudely awakened from its hibernating slumber and stretches itself, causing all kinds of emotional tremors'. This is the period during which change leaders define and refine their vision for change and begin to involve others in the change process. Emotions range from excitement and hopefulness to anxiety and betrayal. Everyone is jittery and distracted.

- *Implementation*. This phase is the actual tactical start of the change journey, and as such is the longest and typically the most painful. There is an explosion of emotions, both positive and negative, in the organization. During this phase, employees often feel in limbo. Everything has changed, and yet the changes haven't been solidified. Many people feel uncertain about their ability to function in the new environment.

- *Determination*. During this period, Duck says, the change monster is roaming the hallways, ready to do its worst damage. Many managers think the change has been accomplished and turn their attention elsewhere right at the time when reinforcement is most needed. People often exhibit *retroactive resistance*, a sort of change fatigue and a desire to revert to the old familiar patterns.

- *Fruition*. Ahhhh … the time when all the hard work pays off at last. In this phase, the changes have become a part of the accepted way of doing things. The whole organization may feel new and different. Employees have gained confidence and are optimistic and energized. The change monster has been corralled.

Coming Full Circle

It is the goal of every change initiative to reach fruition. But Duck cautions that a new period of stagnation is just around the corner. When an organization accomplishes a major change, people need to take time to bask in the success. But managers must be on guard that basking doesn't turn to napping. Managers can teach their organizations how to perpetually adapt and help them muster the will to do so. 'When an organization sees itself as a hearty band of monster slayers, change becomes a challenge they're ready to meet rather than a threat that signals retreat.'

The Change Monster: The Human Forces That Fuel or Foil Corporate Transformation and Change, by Jeanie Daniel Duck, is published by Crown Business.

organizational innovation both directly, by creating a compelling vision, and indirectly, by creating an environment that supports exploration, experimentation, risk taking and sharing of ideas.[136]

Successful change can happen only when employees are willing to devote the time and energy needed to reach new goals, as well as endure possible stress and hardship (see Counterpoint 12.6).

Having a clearly communicated vision that embodies flexibility and openness to new ideas, methods and styles sets the stage for a change-oriented organization and helps employees cope with the chaos and tension associated with change.[137] Leaders also build organization-wide commitment by taking employees through three stages of the change commitment process.[138] In the first stage, *preparation*, employees hear about the change through memos, meetings, speeches or personal contact and become aware that the change will directly affect their work. In the second stage, *acceptance*, leaders should help employees develop an understanding of the full impact of the change and the positive outcomes of making the change. When employees perceive the change as positive, the decision to implement is made. In the third stage, the true *commitment* process begins. The commitment stage involves the steps of installation and institutionalization. Installation is a trial process for the change, which gives leaders an opportunity to discuss problems and employee concerns and build commitment to action. In the final step, *institutionalization*, employees view the change not as something new but as a normal and integral part of organizational operations. The change curve, illustrated in Exhibit 12.7, is the psychological process people go through during a significant change.

COUNTERPOINT 12.6

Sadly, the way companies handled large-scale layoffs in the severe global economic recession that began in 2007 revealed that many have failed to learn the lessons outlined in this chapter about how to deal with difficult restructuring decisions. In 2008, Ford emailed about 500 Canadian staff who had recently been hired, telling them that their new jobs no longer existed.[139] In the US, RadioShack laid off 400 workers in 2007, also notifying them by email.[140] In 2008, Citigroup in the UK fired all its personal loans staff during a conference call.[141] Robbs, a shop in the British market town of Hexham, set off a fire alarm and once the workforce had assembled in the car park, informed them they no longer had jobs.[142] Few, however, could top the management consultancy Pricewaterhouse Coopers, however, which in 2003 sent a text message to 2400 employees of failed UK insurance company, The Accident Group, telling them they would not be paid and that they had lost their jobs.[143] Are such examples indicative of incompetence or simply a failure to be professional by adopting 'best practice'? An alternative interpretation is that they are symptomatic of managerial distance from, and perhaps indifference to, employees. Or it may be interpreted as managers' unwillingness to deal with the face-to-face responses of employees to such news. In another twist, the global greetings cards company Hallmark found a way to make business out of layoffs; in 2011 it launched a line of layoff sympathy cards.[144]

The pressures on organizations to change will probably increase over the next few decades. Leaders must develop the personal qualities, skills and methods needed to help their companies remain competitive. Indeed, some management experts argue that to survive the upheaval of the early twenty-first century, managers must turn their organizations into *change leaders* by using the present to actually create the future – breaking industry rules, creating new market space and routinely abandoning outmoded products, services and processes to free up resources to build the future.[145]

Barriers to Change

Leaders should expect to encounter resistance as they attempt to take the organization through the three stages of the change commitment process. It is normal for people to resist change in situations where they feel vulnerable, and many barriers to change exist at the individual and organizational levels.[146]

EXHIBIT 12.7 The Change Curve

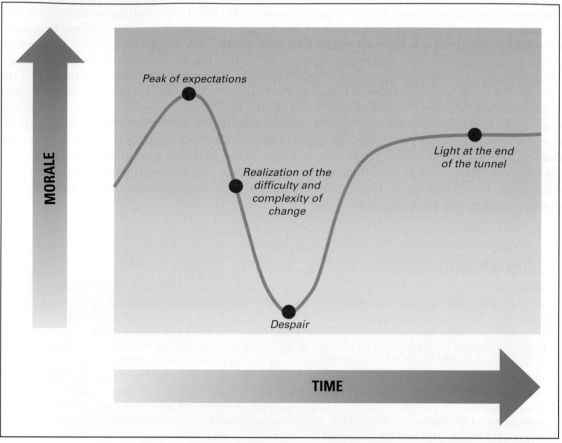

Source: Based on 'Gartner Hype Cycle: Interpreting Technology Hype', Gartner Research, http://www.gartner.com/technology/research/methodologies/hype-cycle.jsp (accessed September 17, 2013); 'The Change Equation and Curve', 21st Century Leader, http://web.archive.org/web/20111223225301/http://21stcenturyleader.co.uk/change_equation (accessed September 17, 2013); David M. Schneider and Charles Goldwasser, 'Be a Model Leader of Change', Management Review (March 1998), 41, 45; and Daryl R. Conner, *Managing at the Speed of Change* (New York: Villard Books, 1992).

1 *Excessive focus on costs.* Management may possess the mind-set that costs are all-important and may fail to appreciate the importance of a change that is not focused on costs – for example, a change to increase employee motivation or customer satisfaction.

2 *Failure to perceive benefits.* Any significant change will produce both positive and negative reactions. Education may be needed to help managers and employees perceive more positive than negative aspects of the change. In addition, if the organization's reward system discourages risk taking, a change process might falter because employees think that the risk of making the change is too high.

3 *Lack of coordination and cooperation.* Organizational fragmentation and conflict often result from the lack of coordination for change implementation. Moreover, in the case of new technology, the old and new systems must be compatible.

4 *Uncertainty avoidance.* At the individual level, many employees fear the uncertainty associated with change. Constant communication is needed so that employees know what is going on and understand how it affects their jobs.

5 *Fear of loss*. Managers and employees may fear the loss of power and status – or even their jobs. In these cases, implementation should be careful and incremental, and all employees should be involved as closely as possible in the change process.

Implementation can typically be designed to overcome many of the organizational and individual barriers to change (see Counterpoint 12.7).

COUNTERPOINT 12.7

Careful attention to implementation can reduce avoidable resistance but it is unlikely to 'overcome' it. A more realistic approach is to anticipate that change programmes will be partial in their effectiveness and will result in unintended consequences – negative as well as positive. In many situations it will simply not be possible – because of lack of resources, skills and climate – to introduce the measures suggested below under technique 5.

Techniques for Implementation

Top leaders articulate the vision and set the tone, but managers and employees throughout the organization are involved in the process of change. A number of techniques can be used to successfully implement change.[147]

BRIEFCASE 12.7

1 *Establish a sense of urgency for change.* Once managers identify a true need for change, they need to thaw resistance by creating a sense of urgency that change is really needed. Organizational crises can help unfreeze employees and make them willing to invest the time and energy needed to adopt new techniques or procedures. For example, British Airways, like all other airlines, was badly affected by the decline in air travel and oppressive security measures put in place after the September 11, 2001, terrorist attacks. Managers worked with the whole staff in order to implement necessary downsizing, and BA emerged from the crisis relatively stronger than many of its competitors.[148] However, in many cases there is no public crisis and managers have to make others aware of the need for change.

2 *Establish a coalition to guide the change.* Change managers have to build a coalition of people throughout the organization who have enough power and influence to steer the change process. For implementation to be successful, there must be a shared commitment to the need and possibilities for change. Top management support is crucial for any major change project, and lack of top management support is one of the most frequent causes of implementation failure.[149] In addition, the coalition should involve lower-level supervisors and middle managers from across the organization. For smaller changes, the support of influential managers in the affected departments is important.

3 *Create a vision and strategy for change.* Leaders who have taken their companies through major successful transformations often have one thing in common: They focus on formulating and articulating a compelling vision and strategy that will guide the change process. Even for a small change, a vision of how the future can be better and strategies to get there are important motivations for change.

4 *Find an idea that fits the need.* Finding the right idea often involves search procedures – talking with other managers, assigning a task force to investigate the problem, sending out a request to suppliers or asking creative people within the organization to develop a solution. The creation of a new idea requires organic conditions. This is a good opportunity to encourage employee participation, because employees need the freedom to think about and explore new options.[150] Belgacom, Belgium's largest telecom company, introduced

special idea management software encouraging employees to come up with ideas for new products and services, as well as more efficient practices. Wim De Meyer, Strategy and Business Development Director at Belgacom's landline department said, 'Belgacom wanted to develop a corporate culture of innovation where anyone in any job function – sales, support, field service, administration – can share their ideas and help shape the future of the company. An intelligent and creative workforce is one of Belgacom's most valued assets.'[151]

5 *Develop plans to overcome resistance to change.* Many good ideas are never used because managers failed to anticipate or prepare for resistance to change by consumers, employees or other managers. No matter how impressive the performance characteristics of an innovation, its implementation will conflict with some interests and jeopardize some alliances in the organization. To increase the chance of successful implementation, management must acknowledge the conflict, threats and potential losses perceived by employees. Several strategies can be used by managers to overcome the resistance problem:

■ *Alignment with needs and goals of users.* The best strategy for overcoming resistance is to make sure change meets a real need. Employees in R&D often come up with great ideas that solve nonexistent problems. This happens because initiators fail to consult with the intended users. Resistance can be frustrating for managers, but moderate resistance to change is good for an organization. Resistance provides a barrier to frivolous changes and to change for the sake of change. The process of overcoming resistance to change normally requires that the change be good for its users.

■ *Communication and training.* Communication means informing users about the need for change and the consequences of a proposed change, preventing rumours, misunderstanding and resentment. In one study of change efforts, the most commonly cited reason for failure was that employees learned of the change from outsiders. Top managers concentrated on communicating with the public and shareholders but failed to communicate with the people who would be most intimately involved with and most affected by the change – their own employees.[152] Open communication often gives management an opportunity to explain what steps will be taken to ensure that the change will have no adverse consequences for employees. Training is also needed to help employees understand and cope with their role in the change process.

■ *An environment that affords psychological safety.* Psychological safety means that people feel a sense of confidence that they will not be embarrassed or rejected by others in the organization. People need to feel secure and capable of making the changes that are asked of them.[153] Change requires that people be willing to take risks and do things differently, but many people are fearful of trying something new if they think they might be embarrassed by mistakes or failure. Managers support psychological safety by creating a climate of trust and mutual respect in the organization. 'Not being afraid someone is laughing at you helps you take genuine risks', says Andy Law, one of the founders of St Luke's, an advertising agency based in London.[154]

■ *Participation and involvement.* Early and extensive participation in a change should be part of implementation. Participation gives those involved a sense of control over the change activity. They understand it better, and they become committed to successful implementation. One study of the implementation and adoption of technology systems at two companies showed a much smoother implementation process at the company that introduced the new technology using a participatory approach.[155] The team-building and large group intervention activities described earlier can be effective ways to involve employees in a change process.

■ *Forcing and coercion.* As a last resort, managers may overcome resistance by threatening employees with the loss of jobs or promotions or by firing or transferring them. In other words, management power is used to overwhelm resistance. In most cases, this approach is not advisable because it leaves people angry at change managers, and the change may be sabotaged. However, this technique may be needed when speed is essential, such as when the organization faces a crisis. It may also be required for needed administrative changes that flow from the top down, such as downsizing the workforce.[156]

6 *Create change teams.* Throughout this chapter the need for resources and energy to make change happen has been discussed. Separate creative departments, new-venture groups and ad hoc teams or task forces are ways to focus energy on both creation and implementation. A separate department has the freedom to create a new technology that fits a genuine need. A task force can be created to see that implementation is completed. The task force can be responsible for communication, involvement of users, training and other activities needed for change.

7 *Foster idea champions.* One of the most effective weapons in the battle for change is the idea champion. The most effective champion is a volunteer champion who is deeply committed to a new idea. The idea champion sees that all technical activities are correct and complete. An additional champion, such as a manager sponsor, may also be needed to persuade people about implementation, even using coercion if necessary.

Summary and Interpretation

Organizations face a dilemma. Managers prefer to organize day-to-day activities in a predictable, routine manner. However, change – not stability – is the order of things, especially in today's global environment. Thus, organizations need to build in change as well as stability, to facilitate innovation as well as efficiency.

Most change in organizations is incremental, but there is a growing emphasis on the need for radical change. Four types of change – technology, products and services, strategy and structure, and culture – may give an organization a competitive edge, and managers can make certain each of the necessary ingredients for change is present.

For technical innovation, which is of concern to most organizations, an organic structure that encourages employee autonomy works best because it encourages a bottom-up flow of ideas. Other approaches are to establish a separate department charged with creating new technical ideas, establish venture teams or idea incubators and encourage idea champions. New products and services generally require cooperation among several departments, so horizontal linkage is an essential part of the innovation process.

For changes in strategy and structure, a top-down approach is typical. These innovations are in the domain of top administrators who take responsibility for restructuring, for downsizing and for changes in policies, goals and control systems.

Culture changes are also generally the responsibility of top management. Some recent trends that may create a need for broad-scale culture change in the organization are re-engineering, the shift to horizontal forms of organizing, greater organizational diversity and the learning organization. All of these changes require significant shifts in employee and manager attitudes and ways of working together. One method for bringing about this level of culture change is organization development (OD). OD focuses on the human and social aspects of the organization and uses behavioural science knowledge to bring about changes in attitudes and relationships.

KEY CONCEPTS

ambidextrous approach
change process
creative departments
creativity
culture changes
dual-core approach
horizontal coordination
    model

idea champion
idea incubator
incremental change
large group intervention
management champion
new-venture fund
organization development
organizational change

organizational innovation
product and service
    changes
radical change
skunkworks
strategy and structure
    changes
switching structures

team building
technical champion
technology changes
time-based competition
venture teams

Discussion Questions

1 How is the management of radical change likely to differ from the management of incremental change?

2 How are organic characteristics related to changes in technology? To administrative changes?

3 Describe the dual-core approach. How does administrative change normally differ from technology change? Discuss.

4 Why do organizations experience resistance to change? What steps can managers take to overcome this resistance?

5 'Bureaucracies are not innovative'. Discuss.

6 A noted organization theorist said, 'Pressure for change originates in the environment; pressure for stability originates within the organization'. Do you agree? Discuss.

7 Of the five elements required for successful change, which element do you think managers are most likely to overlook? Discuss.

8 How do the underlying values of organization development compare to the values underlying other types of change? Why do the values underlying OD make it particularly useful in shifting to a learning organization?

9 The manager of R&D for a drug company said that only five per cent of the company's new products ever achieve market success. He also said the industry average is ten per cent and wondered how his organization might increase its success rate. If you were acting as a consultant, what advice would you give him concerning organization structure?

Chapter 12 Workbook Innovation Climate

In order to examine differences in the level of innovation encouragement in organizations, you will be asked to rate two organizations. The first should be an organization in which you have worked, or the university. The second should be someone else's workplace, that of a family member, a friend or an acquaintance. You will have to interview that person to answer the questions below.

Questions

1 What comparisons in terms of innovation climates can you make between these two organizations?

2 How might productivity differ between a climate that supports innovation and a climate that does not?

3 Where would you rather work? Why?

Adapted by Dorothy Marcic from Susanne G. Scott and Reginald A. Bruce, 'Determinants of Innovative Behaviour: A Path Model of Individual Innovation in the Workplace', *Academy of Management Journal* 37, No. 3 (1994), 580–607.

Technology and Change at Universal Training

By Craig Prichard, Massey University, Palmerston North, New Zealand

Universal Training is a local authority-owned training and development services company that provides mostly public sector organizations (e.g. health, education and local authority) with training and organizational development services. Universal was 'spun off' as part of public sector changes in the early 1990s and is owned by a consortium of local authorities who remain its major clients. Universal employs about 30 staff including trainers, developers and support staff. Some work part-time or on short contracts. It has a senior management team of four. This includes Brenda, John and Carl, who manage training and development teams, and Steve, who manages a support team of eight providing IT, HR, accounts and communication support for the staff. Universal's chief executive, Harold, was the previous head of training with one of the owning local authorities and has been in the post since Universal went independent.

Typically, Universal signs long-term contracts to provide its client organizations with a range of off-the-shelf and tailored programmes. The off-the-shelf programmes typically deal with skill development areas (supervisory management, employment relations, project management and managing contracts) and statutory compliance processes such as health and safety. Tailored work includes organization development work.

Andrew is a new business studies graduate. He recently joined Universal as a junior consultant. He is the newest member of Universal's Training team, most of whom, including Sally, have more than ten years' experience with the firm. Andrew worked in the main office for about six months before going on his first 'live' job, which included a health and safety audit and training with a local authority. Since completing this assignment he was asked to update the delivery of Universal's Health and Safety courses and to investigate the use of new web-based technologies.

Sally is a 30-something trainer and organization development specialist. Sally now shares an office with Andrew. Here's Sally's account of how the change project developed.

Sally: *Before Andrew got moving he would get really frustrated and regularly tell me he was leaving. He would describe Universal as a machine designed to grind new ideas into little pieces so they can be blown away by the wind. Initially it was quite entertaining but gradually he became a real pain. I'd tell him he was taking things too personally and he should think how to work the system more effectively. I guess I was playing a kind of older sister role with him. He was particularly frustrated with his relationship with Brenda – our joint boss. Actually it was a combination of his naivety and her well honed political skills. She played him like a fish – beautifully. He'd go to see her about something and she'd say something like, 'Aarrh Andrew, just the person I want to see', which was pretty close to a bare faced lie. Then she'd say something really cuttingly sarcastic like, 'What brilliant idea do you have for me today' all with a big smile on her face – what a crocodile aye! He just didn't 'get it'. So I'd say to him 'Look, you've got two options. You can resign and go up the road to the other company that's really into these new technologies'. They had some whiz bang application for running web meetings and presentations and online quizzes, that kind of thing, and Andrew thought all this was pretty cool. Or, and this was the other option, he could get into the politics of the place and try and get the change effort moving. You'd think with his business qualification and all that, he'd have a pretty good idea what I was talking about. Well, eventually the penny seemed to drop and away he went. It was a big relief for me actually. He used to sit around complaining about what others weren't doing but now he's getting there.*

Case Questions

1. *Planning for change.* Andrew decides to take Sally's advice. Using the seven step approach identified in the 'Techniques for Implementation' in the chapter above prepare the change plan that you think Andrew would have developed for the introduction of new web-based learning technologies at Universal Training. In particular, prepare a resistance management plan that includes appropriate mix of tactics and responses to the features identified in the chapter above: *'Alignment*

with needs and goals of users', 'Communication and training', 'An environment that affords psychological safety', 'Participation and involvement' and 'Forcing and coercion'.

2. *What happened next?* In the months following the above discussion Andrew makes progress on

the change plan he devised. Imagine that Andrew has a conversation with Sally some months later in which he outlines how he worked with Brenda as part of the change process. Write that conversation.

Notes

1. John F. Burns, 'Trucks of the Taliban: Durable, Not Discreet', *The New York Times*, 23 November, 2001.

2. Robert D. Hof, 'Building an Idea Factory', *BusinessWeek* (October 11, 2004), 194–200; Brian Bremner and Chester Dawson, 'Can Anything Stop Toyota?' *BusinessWeek* (November 17, 2003), 114–122; and Norihiko Shirouzu and Jathon Sapsford, 'Heavy Load; For Toyota, a New Small Truck Carries Hopes for Topping GM', *The Wall Street Journal* (May 12, 2005), A1, A6.

3. 'Toyota CEO demands urgency as company enters better times', 27 May, 2013, *Nikkei Weekly*; Graham Dietz and Nicole Gillespie (2012), 'The Recovery of Trust: Case studies of organisational failures and trust repair', London, Institute of Business Ethics; Stephan Shakespeare and Andy Morris (2013), A Toyota Case Study: How to find 'floating' customers.

4. Yoko Kubota, 'Toyota May Take Full Control of Daihatsu in Drive to Keep Top Seat', *Wall Street Journal*, January 27, 2016, accessed at www.wsj.com/articles/toyota-retains-crown-as-worlds-top-selling-auto-maker-1453870792

5. Based on John P. Kotter, *Leading Change* (Boston, MA: Harvard Business School Press, 1996), 18–20.

6. David A. Nadler and Michael L. Tushman, 'Organizational Frame Bending: Principles for Managing Reorientation', *Academy of Management Executive* 3 (1989), 194–204; and Michael L. Tushman and Charles A. O'Reilly III, 'Ambidextrous Organizations: Managing Evolutionary and Revolutionary Change', *California Management Review* 38, No. 4 (Summer 1996), 8–30.

7. Alan G. Robinson and Dean M. Schroeder, *Ideas Are Free: How the Idea Revolution Is Liberating People and Transforming Organizations* (San Francisco: Berrett-Koehler, 2004), as reported in John Grossman, 'Strategies: Thinking Small', *Inc. Magazine* (August 2004), 34–35.

8. 'War of the whites', *Marketing Week*, 5 June 2008; http://www.unilever.co.uk/ourcompany/newsandmedia/pressreleases/2007/small_pack_mighty_profits. aspaccessed on November 24, 2008.

9. Brent Schlender, 'How Big Can Apple Get?' *Fortune* (February 21, 2005), 66–76.

10. 'The miracle of Turin – Recovery at Fiat', *The Economist*, 26 April, 2008.

11. Nokia Corporation (2008), "Nokia Firsts in Telecommunications", accessed at http://www.nokia.com/ NOKIA_COM_1/About_Nokia/Sidebars_new_concept/Nokia_firsts/Firsts.pdf on April 20, 2009.

12. Shira Ovide, 'Microsoft in $7.17 Billion Deal for Nokia Cellphone Business', *Wall Street Journal*, 3 September 2013.

13. Joseph E. McCann, 'Design Principles for an Innovating Company', *Academy of Management Executive* 5 (May 1991), 76–93.

14. 'DHL adopts new-gen Wi-Fi scanning systems', *New Zealand Transport & Logistics Business Week*, 25 January, 2007.

15. Kelly Barron, 'Logistics in Brown', *Forbes* (January 10, 2000), 78–83; and Scott Kirsner, 'Venture Vérité: United Parcel Service', *Wired* (September 1999), 83–96.

16. SanDisk, SK Telecom launch new platform for mobile TV, *Middle East North Africa Financial Network*, 13 February 2008.

17. Robert D. Hof, 'Building an Idea Factory'.

18. Adam Clark Estes, 'Google Creates Alphabet, a New Company to Rule Them All', *Gizmodo*, August 10, 2015, accessed at gizmodo.com/google-creates-alphabet-a-new-parent-company-with-ulti-1723207314; "Big Severance for Marissa Mayer if Ousted From Yahoo After a Sale", New York Times, April 29 2016, accessed at www.nytimes.com/2016/04/30/business/big-severance-for-marissa-mayer-if-ousted-from-yahoo-after-a-sale.html

19. Phillip Inman, 'Google tax deal under fire as it emerges figure included share options scheme', February 4, 2016, accessed at https://www.theguardian.com/technology/2016/feb/04/google-uk-tax-deal-share-options-scheme

20. Tom Bergin, 'How Google UK clouds its tax liabilities', *Reuters*, May 1, 2013.

21. 'The Strategist', *Latin Trade*, 1 March 2008.

22. Richard A. Wolfe, 'Organizational Innovation: Review, Critique and Suggested Research Directions', *Journal of Management Studies* 31, No. 3 (May 1994), 405–431.

23. John L. Pierce and Andre L. Delbecq, 'Organization Structure, Individual Attitudes and Innovation', *Academy of Management Review* 2 (1977), 27–37; and Michael Aiken and Jerald Hage, 'The Organic Organization and Innovation', *Sociology* 5 (1971), 63–82.

24. Richard L. Daft, 'Bureaucratic versus Non-bureaucratic Structure in the Process of Innovation and Change', in Samuel B. Bacharach, ed., *Perspectives in Organizational Sociology: Theory and Research* (Greenwich, CT: JAI Press, 1982), 129–166.

25. Alan D. Meyer and James B. Goes, 'Organizational Assimilation of Innovations: A Multilevel Contextual Analysis', *Academy of Management Journal* 31 (1988), 897–923.

26. Richard W. Woodman, John E. Sawyer and Ricky W. Griffin, 'Toward a Theory of Organizational Creativity', *Academy of Management Review* 18 (1993), 293–321; and Alan Farnham, 'How to Nurture Creative Sparks', *Fortune* (January 10, 1994), 94–100.

27. Laura He, 'Google's Secrets Of Innovation: Empowering Its Employees', *Forbes*, March 29, 2013.

28. Rajeshwari Sharma, 'Banking on ideas to grow', *Mint*, 11 June, 2007.

29. Thomas M. Burton, 'Flop Factor: By Learning from Failures, Lilly Keeps Drug Pipeline Full', *The Wall Street Journal* (April 21, 2004), A1, A12.

30. Kotter, *Leading Change*, 20–25; and John P. Kotter, 'Leading Change', *Harvard Business Review* (March–April 1995), 59–67.

31. G. Tomas, M. Hult, Robert F. Hurley and Gary A. Knight, 'Innovativeness: Its Antecedents and Impact on Business Performance', *Industrial Marketing Management* 33 (2004), 429–438.

32. Jena McGregor, '25 Most Innovative Companies: Smart Ideas for Tough Times', *BusinessWeek*, 28 April, 2008.

33. Erick Schonfeld, 'GE Sees the Light', *Business 2.0* (July 2004), 80–86.

34. Pankaj Mishra, 'Enlightened owners don't shoot themselves in the foot', *Mint*, 29 May 2007.

35. D. Bruce Merrifield, 'Intrapreneurial Corporate Renewal', *Journal of Business Venturing* 8 (September 1993), 383–389; Linsu Kim, 'Organizational Innovation and Structure', *Journal of Business Research* 8 (1980), 225–245; and Tom Burns and G. M. Stalker, *The Management of Innovation* (London: Tavistock Publications, 1961).

36. James Q. Wilson, 'Innovation in Organization: Notes toward a Theory', in James D. Thompson, ed., *Approaches to Organizational Design* (Pittsburgh, PA: University of Pittsburgh Press, 1966), 193–218.

37. Charles A. O'Reilly III and Michael L. Tushman, 'The Ambidextrous Organization', *Harvard Business Review* (April 2004), 74–81; M. L. Tushman and C. A. O'Reilly III, 'Building an Ambidextrous Organization: Forming Your Own "Skunk Works" ', *Health Forum Journal* 42, No. 2 (March–April 1999), 20–23; J. C. Spender and Eric H. Kessler, 'Managing the Uncertainties of Innovation: Extending Thompson' (1967), *Human Relations* 48, No. 1 (1995), 35–56; and Robert B. Duncan, 'The Ambidextrous Organization: Designing Dual Structures for Innovation', in Ralph H. Killman, Louis R. Pondy and Dennis Slevin, eds., *The Management of Organization*, Vol. 1 (New York: North-Holland, 1976), 167–188.

38. C. A. O'Reilly III and M. L. Tushman, 'The Ambidextrous Organization'.

39. Tushman and O'Reilly, 'Building an Ambidextrous Organization'.

40. Edward F. McDonough III and Richard Leifer, 'Using Simultaneous Structures to Cope with Uncertainty', *Academy of Management Journal* 26 (1983), 727–735.

41. Ariane Sains and Stanley Reed, 'Electrolux Redesigns Itself; Johan Hjestonsson's drive for change', *BusinessWeek*, 27 November 2006.

42. 'Electrolux acquires Chilean appliance company CTI', 22 August, 2011, accessed at http://group.electrolux.com/en/electrolux-acquires-chilean-appliance-company-cti-11433/.

43. Michael Pooler and Ed Crooks, 'GE pulls $3.3bn deal with Electrolux after regulatory opposition', *Financial Times*, December 7, 2015, accessed at www.ft.com/cms/s/0/c047bb2c-9cb4-11e5-b45d-4812f209f861.html#axzz470gmCnfE; Richard Milne, "Electrolux shares jump as profitability and forecasts power ahead", Financial Times, April 28, 2016, accessed at www.ft.com/cms/s/0/dac510a6-0d1d-11e6-9cd4-2be898308be3.html#axzz47z2wn119

44. 'Nissan opens technology centre', *Just-Auto*, 15 May, 2007.

45. Nissan Research Centre Overview, accessed at http://www.nissan-global.com/EN/NRC/OVERVIEW/

46. Judith R. Blau and William McKinley, 'Ideas, Complexity, and Innovation', *Administrative Science Quarterly* 24 (1979), 200–219.

47. Peter Landers, 'Back to Basics; With Dry Pipelines, Big Drug Makers Stock Up in Japan', *The Wall Street Journal* (November 24, 2003), A1, A7.

48. Sherri Eng, 'Hatching Schemes', *The Industry Standard* (November 27–December 4, 2000), 174–175.

49. Carl Mortished, 'Philips changes the mood with bold move into the bedroom', *The Times*, 6 September, 2008; 'Nurture your inner entrepreneurs', *Computer Weekly*, 11 December 2007; PP Thimmayya and J Padmapriya, 'Intel India logs in inhouse entrepreneurial ventures', *The Economic Times*, 29 November, 2007.

50. Julian Birkinshaw and Susan A. Hill (2005), 'Corporate Venturing Units: Vehicles for Strategic Success in the New Europe', *Organizational Dynamics*, 34, 247–257; Michel Ferrari (2008), 'Strategic spin-off: a new incentive contract for managing R&D researchers, *The Journal of Technology Transfer*, Volume 33, Number 6.

51. Christine Canabou, 'Fast Ideas for Slow Times', *Fast Company* (May 2003), 52.

52. Manfreda Cavazza, 'Can online save newspapers?', *Media Week*, 2 September, 2008; Peter John Meiklem, 'Good Times for one Irish editor … but are the storm clouds gathering?', *Sunday Herald*, 8 June, 2008.

53. Christopher Hoenig, 'Skunk Works Secrets,' *CIO* (July 1, 2000), 74–76.

54. Elaine Chen, 'Starting up innovation: How your company can empower intrapreneurs', *TechBeacon*, June 16, 2015, accessed at techbeacon.com/starting-innovation-how-your-company-can-empower-intrapreneurs

55. Phaedra Hise, 'New Recruitment Strategy: Ask Your Best Employees to Leave', *Inc.* (July 1997), 2.

56. Daniel F. Jennings and James R. Lumpkin, 'Functioning Modeling Corporate Entrepreneurship: An Empirical

Integrative Analysis', *Journal of Management* 15 (1989), 485–502; and Julian Birkinshaw, 'The Paradox of Corporate Entrepreneurship', *Strategy & Business,* issue 30 (Spring 2003), 46–57.

57. Jane M. Howell and Christopher A. Higgins, 'Champions of Technology Innovation', *Administrative Science Quarterly* 35 (1990), 317–341; and Jane M. Howell and Christopher A. Higgins, 'Champions of Change: Identifying, Understanding, and Supporting Champions of Technology Innovations', *Organizational Dynamics* (Summer 1990), 40–55.

58. Peter F. Drucker, 'Change Leaders', *Inc.* (June 1999), 65–72; and Peter F. Drucker, *Management Challenges for the 21st Century* (New York: HarperBusiness, 1999).

59. Stuart Crainer and Des Dearlove, 'Water Works', *Management Review* (May 1999), 39–43.

60. 'Innovative ideas pitched to Anglian Water at WIN event', 2 April 2013, *Water Briefing*, accessed at http://waterbriefing. org/home/technology-focus/item/7210-innovative-ideas-pitched-to-anglian-water-at-win-event.

61. Dalila Abu Bakar, 'The intrapreneur way', *Malaysian Business*, 1 February, 2007.

62. Thomas J. Peters and Robert H. Waterman, Jr., *In Search of Excellence* (New York: Harper & Row, 1982).

63. Peter J. Frost and Carolyn P. Egri, 'The Political Process of Innovation', in L. L. Cummings and Barry M. Staw, eds, *Research in Organizational Behavior*, Vol. 13 (New York: JAI Press, 1991), 229–295; Jay R. Galbraith, 'Designing the Innovating Organization', *Organizational Dynamics* (Winter 1982), 5–25; and Marsha Sinatar, 'Entrepreneurs, Chaos and Creativity – Can Creative People Really Survive Large Company Structure?' *Sloan Management Review* (Winter 1985), 57–62.

64. See Lionel Roure, 'Product Champion Characteristics in France and Germany', *Human Relations* 54, No. 5 (2001), 663–682 for a recent review of the literature related to product champions.

65. Ann Harrington, 'Who's Afraid of a New Product?' *Fortune* (November 10, 2003), 189–192.

66. 'Bye-bye, Betamax', *The Japan Times*, 8 September 2002.

67. Claire Billings, 'IPC closes *Nova* magazine after 12 months', *Brand Republic*, 3 May, 2001.

68. 'Novartis plans $235M charge after dropping drug', *Associated Press*, August 29, 2008.

69. Paul B. Carroll and Chunka Mui, '7 Ways to Fail Big', *Harvard Business Review*, Vol. 86 Issue 9, pp. 82-9; Paul B. Carroll and Chunka Mui (2008), *Billion-Dollar Lessons: What You Can Learn from the Most Inexcusable Business Failures of the Last 25 Years*, Knoxville TN, Portfolio; Sangita Joshi. 'Getting the recipe right', *Business Line*, 13 November, 2003; Robert McMath and Thomas Forbes (2000), *What Were They Thinking?: Marketing Lessons I've Learned from Over 80,000 New Products*, New York, Times Books.

70. Christopher Power with Kathleen Kerwin, Ronald Grover, Keith Alexander and Robert D. Hof, 'Flops', *BusinessWeek* (August 16, 1993), 76–82; Modesto A. Maidique and Billie Jo Zirger, 'A Study of Success and Failure in Product Innovation: The Case of the U.S. Electronics Industry', *IEEE Transactions in Engineering Management* 31 (November 1984), 192–203.

71. Chloe Green, 'Why the innovative spirit should be ingrained and cultural, not departmentalized', *Information Age*, November 17, 2015, accessed at www.information-age. com/it-management/strategy-and-innovation/123460513/ why-innovative-spirit-should-be-ingrained-and-cultural-not-departmentalised

72. Cliff Edwards, 'Many Products Have Gone Way of the Edsel', *Johnson City Press* (May 23, 1999), 28, 30; Paul Lukas, 'The Ghastliest Product Launches', *Fortune* (March 16, 1998), 44; Robert McMath, *What Were They Thinking? Marketing Lessons I've Learned from Over 80,000 New-Product Innovations and Idiocies* (New York: Times Business, 1998).

73. P. Senge (1999). *The dance of change.* New York: Currency Doubleday.

74. R. K. Yin (1978). *Changing urban bureaucracies: how new practices become routinized.* Santa Monica: Rand Corporation.

75. D. Miller (2002). Successful change leaders: What makes them? What do they do that is different?, *Journal of Change Management,* 2(4), 359–368.

76. P. Strebel (1996). Why Do Employees Resist Change? *Harvard Business Review*, 74(3), 86–92.

77. Edwin Mansfield, J. Rapaport, J. Schnee, S. Wagner and M. Hamburger, *Research and Innovation in Modern Corporations* (New York: Norton, 1971); and Antonio J. Bailetti and Paul F. Litva, 'Integrating Customer Requirements into Product Designs', *Journal of Product Innovation Management* 12 (1995), 3–15.

78. 'The 10 Biggest Tech Failures of the Last Decade', *Time*, May 14, 2009, accessed at content.time.com/time/specials/ packages/article/0,28804,1898610_1898625_1898640,00. html

79. 'Blu-ray aplasta a HD- DVD en el mercado japonés de grabadoras', *Gaceta de los Negocios*, 19 January 2008.

80. Shona L. Brown and Kathleen M. Eisenhardt, 'Product Development: Past Research, Present Findings, and Future Directions', *Academy of Management Review* 20, No. 2 (1995), 343–378; F. Axel Johne and Patricia A. Snelson, 'Success Factors in Product Innovation: A Selective Review of the Literature', *Journal of Product Innovation Management* 5 (1988), 114–128; and Science Policy Research Unit, University of Sussex, *Success and Failure in Industrial Innovation* (London: Centre for the Study of Industrial Innovation, 1972).

81. 'Brand innovators', *Marketing Week*, 24 April 2008.

82. Rebecca Lynne Tan,'Risking their lives for cocktails', *Straits Times*, 13 May, 2013.

83. FeverTree Annual Report 2015, accessed at http:// fevertree2.d3r-cdn.com/pdfs/original/1089-2015-ar-final-2016-03-21-.pdf

84. Brown and Eisenhardt, 'Product Development'; Dan Dimancescu and Kemp Dwenger, 'Smoothing the Product Development Path', *Management Review* (January 1996), 36–41.

85. Ann Harrington, 'Who's Afraid of a New Product?' *Fortune* (November 10, 2003), 189–192.

86. 'Riding on the A380', *Channel NewsAsia*, 16 October, 2007.

87. Melissa A. Schilling and Charles W. L. Hill, 'Managing the New Product Development Process', *Academy of Management Executive* 12, No. 3 (1998), 67–81; and J. Lynn Lunsford and Daniel Michaels, 'New Orders; After Four

Years in the Rear, Boeing Is Set to Jet Past Airbus', *The Wall Street Journal* (June 10, 2005), A1, A5.

88. Deborah Ball, 'Unilever's sales, margins increase', *The Wall Street Journal*, 2 August, 2007.

89. 'War of the whites', *Marketing Week*, 5 June 2008.

90. Toby Webb, 'Unilever's CEO: Social innovation and sustainability the only game in town', *Ethical Corporation*, 30 May, 2007.

91. Andrew Saunders, 'Britain's Most Admired Companies: Tough Times turn Tables', *Management Today*, 1 December, 2008.

92. 'Innovation helps Unilever take the cream', *Citywire*, 3 May 2007.

93. 'CCFC to Unilever: Ax the Axe Campaign if You Care about "Real Beauty"', accessed at http://web.archive.org/web/20120514015423/http://commercialfreechildhood.org/pressreleases/axtheaxe.htm on September 17, 2013.

94. Andrew Newman, 'Shaving Below a Man's Neck, if That's What She Wants', *The New York Times*, 26 March, 2013.

95. Jennifer Faull, Axe wants to give men their own Dove moment in first global brand campaign, *The Drum*, January 13, 2016, accessed at www.thedrum.com/news/2016/01/13/axe-wants-give-men-their-own-dove-moment-first-global-brand-campaign

96. Matt Haig (2003), *Brand failures*, London, Kogan Page.

97. Kenneth B. Kahn, 'Market Orientation, Interdepartmental Integration, and Product Development Performance', *The Journal of Product Innovation Management* 18 (2001), 314–323; and Ali E. Akgün, Gary S. Lynn and John C. Byrne, 'Taking the Guesswork Out of New Product Development: How Successful High-Tech Companies Get That Way', *Journal of Business Strategy* 25, No. 4 (2004), 41–46.

98. John A. Pearce II, 'Speed Merchants', *Organizational Dynamics* 30, No. 3 (2002), 191–205; Kathleen M. Eisenhardt and Behnam N. Tabrizi, 'Accelerating Adaptive Processes: Product Innovation in the Global Computer Industry', *Administrative Science Quarterly* 40 (1995), 84–110; Dougherty and Hardy, 'Sustained Product Innovation in Large, Mature Organizations'; and Karne Bronikowski, 'Speeding New Products to Market', *Journal of Business Strategy* (September–October 1990), 34–37.

99. 'Rapid Product Development – RAPID 1996–1999', Government of Finland, Tekes, accessed at www.tekes.fi/en/document/43371/rapid_evaluointi_pdf on September 17, 2013.

100. V.K. Narayanan, B. Kemmerer, F.L. Douglas, and B. Guernsey (2003), 'The Social Construction of Organizational Capabilities: A Multilevel Analysis' in Bala Chakravarthy, Strategic Management Society, Guenter Mueller-Stewens and Peter Lorange, *Strategy Process: Shaping the Contours of the Field*, Oxford, Blackwell, 137–163.

101. V. K. Narayanan, Frank L. Douglas, Brock Guernsey and John Charnes, 'How Top Management Steers Fast Cycle Teams to Success', *Strategy & Leadership* 30, No. 3 (2002), 19–27.

102. Faith Keenan, 'Opening the Spigot', *Business-Week e.biz* (June 4, 2001), EB17–EB20.

103. Steve Konicki, 'Time Trials', *Information Week* (June 3, 2002), 36–44.

104. http://www.haagen-dazs.co.uk/collection/pints/index.htmaccessed on December 15, 2008.

105. David Leonhardt, 'It Was a Hit in Buenos Aires – So Why Not Boise?' *BusinessWeek* (September 7, 1998), 56, 58.

106. Edward F. McDonough III, Kenneth B. Kahn and Gloria Barczak, 'An Investigation of the Use of Global, Virtual, and Colocated New Product Development Teams', *The Journal of Product Innovation Management* 18 (2001), 110–120.

107. Squeezing more Hellmann's from every bottle, *Unilever*, August 17, 2015, accessed at https://www.unilever.co.uk/about/innovation/latest-news/squeezing-more-hellmanns-from-every-bottle.html

108. Raymond E. Miles, Henry J. Coleman, Jr and W. E. Douglas Creed, 'Keys to Success in Corporate Redesign', *California Management Review* 37, No. 3 (Spring 1995), 128–145.

109. Richard L. Daft, 'Bureaucratic versus Nonbureaucratic Structure'; Robert W. Zmud, 'Diffusion of Modern Software Practices: Influence of Centralization and Formalization', *Management Science* 28 (1982), 1421–1431.

110. Richard L. Daft, 'A Dual-Core Model of Organizational Innovation'; Zmud, 'Diffusion of Modern Software Practices'.

111. Fariborz Damanpour, 'The Adoption of Technological, Administrative, and Ancillary Innovations: Impact of Organizational Factors', *Journal of Management* 13 (1987), 675–688.

112. Gregory H. Gaertner, Karen N. Gaertner and David M. Akinnusi, 'Environment, Strategy and the Implementation of Administrative Change: The Case of Civil Service Reform', *Academy of Management Journal* 27 (1984), 525–543.

113. Tanalee Smith, 'Rio Tinto to cut 14,000 jobs to cope with slump', *Associated Press*, 10 December, 2008; 'Rio to axe 14,000 and cut spending', *The Gold Coast Bulletin*, 11 December, 2008; Tom Jennemann, 'Alcan in focus as Rio slashes debt, cuts jobs', *Metal Bulletin News Alert Service*, 10 December 2008; Vivek Tulpule, *Commodity markets report*, London, Rio Tinto, December 2008.

114. Clyde Russell, 'Rio, BHP investors may be too cautious on iron ore rally', *Globe and Mail*, May 5, 2016, accessed at www.theglobeandmail.com/globe-investor/investment-ideas/rio-bhp-investors-may-be-too-cautious-on-iron-ore-rally/article29887487/

115. Nicolas Rolander, 'Vestas CEO Aims to Keep Lead in Australian Wind-Energy Market', 9 April 2013.

116. Vestas 2015 Annual Report, accessed at https://www.vestas.com/~/media/vestas/investor/investor%20pdf/financial%20reports/2015/fy/160209_ca_uk_annual%20report%202015.pdf

117. Claudia Bird Schoonhoven and Mariann Jelinek, 'Dynamic Tension in Innovative, High Technology Firms: Managing Rapid Technology Change through Organization Structure', in Mary Ann Von Glinow and Susan Albers Mohrman, eds, *Managing Complexity in High Technology Organizations* (New York: Oxford University Press, 1990), 90–118.

118. Stan Pace, 'Rip the Band-Aid Off Quickly', *Strategy & Leadership* 30, No. 1 (2002), 4–9.

119. Benson L. Porter and Warrington S. Parker, Jr, 'Culture Change', *Human Resource Management* 31 (Spring–Summer 1992), 45–67.

120. Quoted in Anne B. Fisher, 'Making Change Stick', *Fortune* (April 17, 1995), 122.

121. May Chan, 'Put staff through paces: Companies in the mainland need to train their next generation of leaders to compete', *South China Morning Post*, 27 September, 2008.

122. Trevor Phillips, 'A diverse workforce makes business sense', *Financial Times*, 21 July 2008; 'Diversity Management is out: Diversity Leadership is in', *Canada NewsWire*, 29 April, 2008.

123. 'Brief introduction of Zhujiang Steel', accessed at http://web.archive.org/web/20080828164444/http://www.gise-zis.com/english/english.htm on September 17, 2013; Huang, X., 'Strategic Management at Zhujiang Iron And Steel Company', Case 307-392-1, Asia Case Research Centre, The University of Hong Kong.

124. W. Warner Burke, 'The New Agenda for Organization Development', in Wendell L. French, Cecil H. Bell, Jr. and Robert A. Zawacki, *Organization Development and Transformation: Managing Effective Change* (Burr Ridge, IL: Irwin McGraw-Hill, 2000), 523–535.

125. W. Warner Burke, *Organization Development: A Process of Learning and Changing*, 2nd ed. (Reading, MA: Addison-Wesley, 1994); and Wendell L. French and Cecil H. Bell, Jr., 'A History of Organization Development', in French, Bell and Zawacki, *Organization Development and Transformation*, 20–42.

126. Zhang Bolin, 'Sad China industry mantra: Make steel, lose money; China's mighty steel firms are in slump that shows no sign of easing', *MarketWatch*, 19 March, 2012.

127. Anurag Viswanath, 'China laying off millions: Why it will be a huge test of political tenacity', *Financial Express* (India), accessed at www.financialexpress.com/article/fe-columnist/china-to-lay-off-millions-a-test-of-political-tenacity/245824/

128. French and Bell, 'A History of Organization Development'.

129. The information on large group intervention is based on Kathleen D. Dannemiller and Robert W. Jacobs, 'Changing the Way Organizations Change: A Revolution of Common Sense', *The Journal of Applied Behavioral Science* 28, No. 4 (December 1992), 480–498; Barbara B. Bunker and Billie T. Alban, 'Conclusion: What Makes Large Group Interventions Effective?' *The Journal of Applied Behavioral Science* 28, No. 4 (December 1992), 570–591; and Marvin R. Weisbord, 'Inventing the Future: Search Strategies for Whole System Improvements', in French, Bell and Zawacki, *Organization Development and Transformation*, 242–250.

130. J. Quinn, 'What a Workout!' *Performance* (November 1994), 58–63; and Bunker and Alban, 'Conclusion: What Makes Large Group Interventions Effective?'

131. Dave Ulrich, Steve Kerr and Ron Ashkenas, with Debbie Burke and Patrice Murphy, *The GE Work Out: How to Implement GE's Revolutionary Method for Busting Bureaucracy and Attacking Organizational Problems – Fast!* (New York: McGraw-Hill, 2002).

132. Paul F. Buller, 'For Successful Strategic Change: Blend OD Practices with Strategic Management', *Organizational Dynamics* (Winter 1988), 42–55.

133. Norm Brodsky, 'Everybody Sells', (Street Smarts column), *Inc. Magazine* (June 2004), 53–54.

134. Richard S. Allen and Kendyl A. Montgomery, 'Applying an Organizational Development Approach to Creating Diversity', *Organizational Dynamics* 30, No. 2 (2001), 149–161.

135. Jyotsna Sanzgiri and Jonathan Z. Gottlieb, 'Philosophic and Pragmatic Influences on the Practice of Organization Development, 1950–2000', *Organizational Dynamics* (Autumn 1992), 57–69.

136. Bernard M. Bass, 'Theory of Transformational Leadership Redux', *Leadership Quarterly* 6, No. 4 (1995), 463–478; and Dong I. Jung, Chee Chow and Anne Wu, 'The Role of Transformational Leadership in Enhancing Organizational Innovation: Hypotheses and Some Preliminary Findings', *The Leadership Quarterly* 14 (2003), 525–544.

137. Ronald Recardo, Kathleen Molloy and James Pellegrino, 'How the Learning Organization Manages Change', *National Productivity Review* (Winter 1995/96), 7–13.

138. Based on Daryl R. Conner, *Managing at the Speed of Change* (New York: Villard Books, 1992), 146–160.

139. Linda Diebel, 'Layoff by email: Ford's latest innovation', *Toronto Star*, July 28, 2008.

140. 'RadioShack lays off employees via e-mail', *USA Today*, March 2, 2007.

141. 'You're fired – by conference call', *The Evening Standard (London)*, May 21, 2008.

142. Sathnam Sanghera, 'There really is no easy way to say this', *The Times*, May 3, 2008.

143. 'Dealing with mass redundancies', *Contract Journal*, June 13, 2007; 'Bust company sacks workers by text', *BBC News,* 30 May, 2003, accessed at http://news.bbc.co.uk/1/hi/business/2949578.stm on April 20, 2009.

144. Adriana Barton, 'Hallmark introduces job-loss sympathy cards', *The Globe and Mail*, September 27, 2011.

145. Drucker, *Management Challenges for the 21st Century*; Tushman and O'Reilly, 'Ambidextrous Organizations'; Gary Hamel and C. K. Prahalad, 'Seeing the Future First', *Fortune* (September 4, 1994), 64–70; and Linda Yates and Peter Skarzynski, 'How Do Companies Get to the Future First?' *Management Review* (January 1999), 16–22.

146. Based on Carol A. Beatty and John R. M. Gordon, 'Barriers to the Implementation of CAD/CAM Systems', *Sloan Management Review* (Summer 1988), 25–33.

147. These techniques are based partly on John P. Kotter's eight-stage model of planned organizational change, Kotter, *Leading Change*, 20–25.

148. Burke Warner (2008), *Organization Change: Theory and Practice*, London, Sage Publications; 'Change: well begun is half done', *Financial Express*, 13 January, 2006.

149. Everett M. Rogers and Floyd Shoemaker, *Communication of Innovations: A Cross Cultural Approach*, 2d ed. (New York: Free Press, 1971); Stratford P. Sherman, 'Eight Big Masters of Innovation', *Fortune* (October 15, 1984), 66–84.

150. Richard L. Daft and Selwyn W. Becker, *Innovation in Organizations* (New York: Elsevier, 1978); and John P. Kotter and Leonard A. Schlesinger, 'Choosing Strategies for Change', *Harvard Business Review* 57 (1979), 106–114.

151. 'Belgacom Standardizes on Imaginatik's Idea Central Global to Foster Culture of Innovation', *Business Wire*, 19 October, 2004.

152. Peter Richardson and D. Keith Denton, 'Communicating Change', *Human Resource Management* 35, No. 2 (Summer 1996), 203–216.

153. Edgar H. Schein and Warren Bennis, *Personal and Organizational Change via Group Methods* (New York: Wiley, 1965); and Amy Edmondson, 'Psychological Safety and Learning Behavior in Work Teams', *Administrative Science Quarterly* 44 (1999), 350–383.

154. Diane L. Coutu, 'Creating the Most Frightening Company on Earth; An Interview with Andy Law of St. Luke's', *Harvard Business Review* (September–October 2000), 143–150.

155. Philip H. Mirvis, Amy L. Sales and Edward J. Hackett, 'The Implementation and Adoption of New Technology in Organizations: The Impact on Work, People, and Culture', *Human Resource Management* 30 (Spring 1991), 113– 139; Arthur E. Wallach, 'System Changes Begin in the Training Department', *Personnel Journal* 58 (1979), 846– 848, 872; and Paul R. Lawrence, 'How to Deal with Resistance to Change', *Harvard Business Review* 47 (January–February 1969), 4–12, 166–176.

156. Dexter C. Dunphy and Doug A. Stace, 'Transformational and Coercive Strategies for Planned Organizational Change: Beyond the O.D. Model', *Organizational Studies* 9 (1988), 317–334; and Kotter and Schlesinger, 'Choosing Strategies for Change'.

DECISION-MAKING PROCESSES

A LOOK INSIDE

Oroton Group

Every Australian woman, and most of their partners, knows about Oroton handbags. Founded in Sydney 70 years ago by Boyd Lane, Oroton became a household fashion name in the early 1950s with the introduction of its iconic mesh handbags. The company continued to expand in the intervening years, selling through the major Australian department store David Jones, opening a chain of more than 30 company stores in Australia and New Zealand and even briefly venturing into the US market. Oroton gradually expanded its range of fashion accessories, selling jewellery, watches, purses and wallets and make-up accoutrements. Oroton also began accumulating Australian franchises of global retail brands, including the Canadian shoe outlet Aldo and the American preppie clothiers Polo Ralph Lauren. In addition, the company picked up several well-respected Australian brand outlets such as Morrissey, named after Peter Morrissey, the country's best known fashion designer, and designer of uniforms to Australia's flagship airline Qantas. Although Oroton group went public in 1987, the Lane family continued to play a key management role, with the founder's grandson Ross Lane holding managing director and CEO positions until 2006.

Despite the value of the Oroton brand in Australasia, the company's efforts at expansion enjoyed mixed success. Oroton pulled out of the US market back in 1997 after poor trading results. From the early 2000s, Aldo shoe stores performed poorly, and results were disappointing at Morrissey. In 2006, as the Australian retail market tightened, the company dipped into the red, and the board realized something needed to be done. A strategic review was ordered, which concluded that the company's different brands lacked synergy, and management focus was dissipated between too many different endeavours. The company underwent a significant restructuring and downsizing. Sally Macdonald, a Harvard MBA, former executive with US retailer, Banana Republic, came on board, first as a management consultant with Boston Consulting Group working on the restructuring, then

directly as group CEO. The company focused on the strong Oroton and Polo/Ralph Lauren brands, while a tough decision was made to sell off Aldo and Morrissey.

Internally, several Lane family members stepped off the board, and Ross Lane moved up to Chairman, leaving day-to-day decisions in Macdonald's hands. Headquarters staff were cut significantly in line with the focused, slimmed-down company. A performance-based pay structure was introduced, and several lower performing stores closed, but a new flagship shop in Sydney was opened, along with an online sales portal. Despite the tough decisions, innovative thinking was encouraged in the company, with improved communication and a less hierarchical structure. Headquarters was redesigned on an open plan concept, and a 360-degree staff feedback system introduced.

The early results were very promising. The company was back in the black in 2007 despite the upheaval. In FY 2007–2008 profits doubled to A\$16 million. Like-for-like sales were up 20 per cent in the Oroton stores and 17 per cent at Polo/Ralph Lauren. Profits continued to rise, reaching almost A\$40 million in 2012/2013. New international licensing agreements were signed for the Oroton bags, including in the lucrative Japanese market. However, restructuring is no cure for a bleak overall business environment. With its share price already affected by stagnating profits, they tumbled by 20 per cent when the company was to lose its licence to sell Polo/Lauren goods in Australia in 2013. The Lauren business represented almost half of the company's sales. Despite generally positive assessments of her seven years at the helm, Sally Macdonald stepped down, to be replaced by Mark Newman, perhaps ironically formerly head of the Polo/Lauren department.

It has been a difficult transition. Initially Oroton tried to replace Polo/Lauren with a link up with US menswear brand Brooks Brothers, but the joint venture was a failure. Oroton then refocused on its high-end handbags while pursuing mid-market shoppers through a deal with the US Gap brand that's particularly strong in children's wear. There has been a slow uptick. Although sales in 2016 were about the same as five years earlier, profits are less than half the figures earlier in the decade.

One area that Oroton will need to address is scrutiny of human rights and working conditions in its developing country supply chain. The company was given a poor 'D+' rating on supply chain transparency in a major 2016 Australian NGO report on working conditions in the outsourced fashion sector, whereas Zara, for example, rated an 'A'. Consumers increasingly insist on transparent ethical standards, especially from companies that operate at the top end of the market.

Oroton is a survivor, and its ability to weather changing fashion trends demonstrates organizational flexibility and durability, but its history over the past decade demonstrates today's firms can never take success for granted.[1]

Every organization grows, prospers or fails at least in part as a result of decisions by its managers, and decisions can be risky and uncertain, without any guarantee of success. Sometimes, decision-making is a trial-and-error process, in which top managers continue to search for appropriate ways to solve complex problems. At Oroton, the management team continue to evaluate the market environment and adjust the company's strategies to deal with the environment. Decision-making is carried out amid constantly changing factors, unclear information and conflicting points of view. The 2002 decision to merge two American IT giants Hewlett-Packard (HP) and Compaq, for example, was highly controversial. Former HP CEO Carly Fiorina and her supporters believed it was essential for HP's future success, but other managers and board members argued that it was insane to risk HP's printer business and move the company more deeply into the highly competitive computer world. Fiorina's side ultimately won out, but results of the merger were disappointing. Hewlett-Packard's board ousted Fiorina in early 2005, partly due to issues related to the Compaq merger. Her replacement as CEO, Mark Hurd, faced his own challenges, with managers, consultants and observers offering different, often conflicting, views of what was needed to get HP back on track. He had to take tough decisions, initially cutting the company's workforce by 10 per cent and in late 2008 announcing a further 24 600 redundancies worldwide over the next three years in a bid to improve the company's focus and bottom line.[2,3] Nevertheless, by 2010, even though HP was selling more personal computers than any other company worldwide,[4] Hurd was forced out in a sexual harassment scandal. The company brought in former eBay chief Meg Whitman to put the company back on track.[5]

Many organizational decisions turn out to be serious mistakes. The acquisition of Britain's venerable BHS department store chain by TopShop owner Sir Philip Green in 2000 ended in him selling out for £1 in 2015, but not before more than £423 million had been paid out in dividends. The company collapsed only a year after Green sold out, with huge pension liabilities, and sparked off government and parliamentary enquiries.[6]

Britain's RBS banking group, for example, embarked on a highly ambitious expansion strategy under CEO Fred Goodwin. Under Goodwin's leadership what had been a mid-size Scottish bank briefly made it into the ranks of the world's ten largest banks. Through a combination of acquisitions, including the much larger NatWest Bank, and ruthless cost-cutting (for which he earned the title Fred the Shred), RBS became fast-growing, highly profitable but also highly-leveraged. The final chapter in the expansion was the £46 billion buyout in 2007 of Dutch banking major ABN-Amro, in alliance with Belgium's Fortis and Spain's Santander banks. Goodwin announced that the deal had catapulted his bank, 'to the top of the premier league', but the US subprime mortgage crisis was already beginning to shake credit markets, and it was not long before he was being openly criticized. RBS shares slumped from over £7 in early 2007 to less than 50 pence by the time the company was forced to accept partial nationalization by the UK government in late 2008 in order to avoid total collapse. Goodwin was forced to resign, telling shareholders he was 'extremely sorry' for the errors he and fellow managers had made.[7,8] Eventually, in 2012, the British government made the highly unusual decision to strip him of the knighthood he had been awarded in 2004 for services to banking.[9]

The problems at RBS and much of the rest of the British banking sector pale in comparison with problems in the Icelandic business sector that emerged in 2008. All major Icelandic banks collapsed as a result of being heavily over-leveraged when the credit crunch hit in 2008. In 2007 alone they had made loans equivalent to nine times the size of the entire Icelandic economy, and it was anticipated that the failure of the banks would cost the Icelandic state more than 80 per cent of the country's annual GDP. Furthermore, the crisis badly hit several business empires that had grown enormously in an era of easy credit and infectious ambition among Iceland's business leaders. Largest amongst these groups is Baugur, a retail empire with worldwide holdings, but concentrated in the UK, where it owned all or part of many household names including House of Fraser, Iceland supermarkets, Hamley's and Moss Bros. Britain's *Financial Times* describes Baugur's plight: 'The Icelandic banks highly leveraged their borrowings to holding companies [such as Baugur] to make leveraged acquisitions of companies that were dependent on leveraged consumers and that's why it unravelled so quickly.' By the end of 2008, much of Baugur's once mighty retail empire was on the selling block, a victim of overambition, and in early 2009 Baugur had to seek bankruptcy protection.

Yet managers also make many successful decisions every day. NXP Electronics, a chip manufacturer spin-off from Philips, built its business during 2008 despite the global slowdown, through a series of astute partnerships and product development strategies, particularly expanding into the fast-growing wireless technology sector.[10] Meg Whitman made eBay a model of what an internet company should be, by keeping the company focused on nurturing its community of buyers and sellers; as noted above, she has a new challenge since being brought in to lead HP in 2012, one that she continued to struggle with four years later. In 2015 she split the company in two, HP Inc focusing on the personal computer business and Hewlett Packard Enterprises working with B2B services including networking and consulting.[11] At Japan's Nissan, Carlos Ghosn implemented structural, management and product changes that transformed the company from being directionless and debt-ridden into one of the most dynamic and profitable automakers in the world, among other things introducing in 2010 the Nissan Leaf, the world's first mass-produced zero-emissions car.[12] And Ed Robinson and Matt Smith of Britain's Viral Factory pioneered the viral advertising concept, successfully skating the boundaries of the permissible in edgy ads for companies such as Diesel jeans and Trojan condoms.[13]

?

ONLINE
COUNTERPOINT 13.1

Purpose of this Chapter

At any time, members of an organization may be engaged in identifying problems and implementing alternatives for hundreds of decisions. Managers and organizations somehow muddle through these processes.[14] The purpose here is to analyze these processes to learn what decision-making is actually like in organizational settings. Decision-making processes can be thought of as the brain and nervous system of an organization. Decision-making is the end use of the information and control systems described in Chapter 9. Major decisions are made about organization strategy, structure, innovation and acquisitions. This chapter explores how organizations can and should make decisions about these issues.

The first section defines decision-making. The next section examines how individual managers make decisions. Then several models of organizational decision-making are explored. Each model is used in a different organizational situation. The final section in this chapter combines the models into a single framework that describes when and how they should be used and discusses special issues, such as decision mistakes.

Definitions

Organizational decision-making is formally defined as the process of identifying and solving problems. The process has two major stages. In the problem identification stage, information about environmental and organizational conditions is monitored to determine if performance is satisfactory and to diagnose the cause of shortcomings. The problem solution stage is when alternative courses of action are considered and one alternative is selected and implemented.

BRIEFCASE 13.1

Organizational decisions vary in complexity and can be categorized as programmed or nonprogrammed.[15] Programmed decisions are repetitive and well defined, and procedures exist for resolving the problem. They are well structured because criteria of performance are normally clear, good information is available about current performance, alternatives are easily specified and there is relative certainty that the chosen alternative will be successful. Examples of programmed decisions include decision rules, such as when to replace an office photocopier, when to reimburse managers for travel expenses or whether an applicant has sufficient qualifications for an assembly-line job. Many companies adopt rules based on experience with programmed decisions. For example, a rule for large hotels staffing banquets is to allow one server per thirty guests for a sit-down function and one server per forty guests for a buffet.[16]

ONLINE
COUNTERPOINT 13.2

Nonprogrammed decisions are novel and poorly defined, and no procedure exists for solving the problem. They are used when an organization has not seen a problem before and may not know how to respond. Clear-cut decision criteria do not exist. Alternatives are fuzzy. There is uncertainty about whether a proposed solution will solve the problem. Typically, few alternatives can be developed for a nonprogrammed decision, so a single solution is custom-tailored to the problem.

COUNTERPOINT 13.1

It may be potentially misleading to say that nonprogrammed decisions are always novel or poorly defined: they may have been seen before; they may be amenable to definition. What makes them 'nonprogrammed' is the absence of any predetermined, systematic way of proceeding. That may be because there is no strong inclination to develop a procedure or because there is a conflict, manifest or latent, over how to proceed.

Many nonprogrammed decisions involve strategic planning, because uncertainty is great and decisions are complex. One example is the situation faced by water utility organizations both in the private and public sectors. The pipes and other infrastructure have to be replaced on a regular basis, and every utility has an upgrading schedule. However, unexpected problems such as pipe breaks can occur at any time, even where company projections suggest the infrastructure is not due for repair or renewal. The problem may be a single fault due, for example, to poor installation, which can simply be repaired with focus then restored to planned upgrading elsewhere in the system. Alternatively it could, however, reflect a bigger problem that will require diversion of resources from previously-planned upgrading. Utility and other companies responsible for complex infrastructure need to have strategies for dealing with unexpected difficulties which are inevitable in complex systems.[17] The Metronet consortium that was contracted by London Underground to rehabilitate and maintain part of London's ageing Underground system was hit by numerous nonprogrammed issues ranging from ballooning staffing costs to unexpectedly difficult engineering challenges. The company had inadequately planned for such unforeseen challenges and folded, resulting in losses both for its investors and the state-owned Transport for London organization that had contracted the private–public partnership (PPP) project.[18,19]

Particularly complex nonprogrammed decisions have been referred to as 'wicked' decisions, because simply defining the problem can turn into a major task. Wicked problems are often associated with manager conflicts over objectives and alternatives, rapidly changing circumstances and unclear linkages among decision elements. Managers dealing with a wicked decision may hit on a solution that merely proves they failed to correctly define the problem to begin with.[20]

Today's managers and organizations are dealing with a higher percentage of nonprogrammed decisions because of the rapidly changing business environment. As outlined in Exhibit 13.1,

EXHIBIT 13.1 Decision-Making in Today's Environment

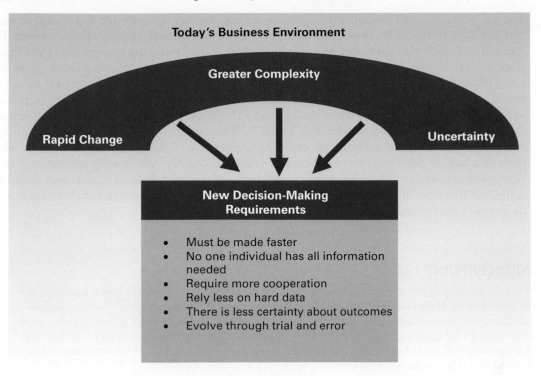

Today's Business Environment

Greater Complexity

Rapid Change

Uncertainty

New Decision-Making Requirements

- Must be made faster
- No one individual has all information needed
- Require more cooperation
- Rely less on hard data
- There is less certainty about outcomes
- Evolve through trial and error

Source: Based on John P. Kotter, *Leading Change* (Boston, MA: Harvard Business School Press, 1996), p. 56.

today's environment has increased both the number and complexity of decisions that have to be made and has created a need for new decision-making processes. Managers in fast-changing e-business departments, for example, often have to make quick decisions based on very limited information. Another example is the impact of globalization. The trend toward business process outsourcing to low-wage countries has managers in most Western countries struggling with complex decisions concerning the advantages and disadvantages of moving part or all of their operations offshore. These decisions include not only strict cost–benefit analysis but also ethical considerations about working conditions in developing countries and the impacts of job losses in the company's home environment. These issues can reflect poorly on the company's image. For example, the sports apparel company Reebok has been sharply criticized in Canada – where ice hockey has the same exalted status as football in much of the rest of the world – for moving production of hockey jerseys to China and other low-cost Asian countries. In fact, almost all of the athletic footwear for which Reebok (now owned by German sportswear giant Adidas) is most famous is manufactured in low cost Asian countries – China (51 per cent of total footwear production), Indonesia (21 per cent), Vietnam (17 per cent) and Thailand (7 per cent).[21]

Individual Decision-Making

Individual decision-making by managers can be described in two ways. First is the rational approach, which suggests how managers should try to make decisions. Second is the bounded rationality perspective, which describes how decisions actually have to be made under severe time and resource constraints. The rational approach is an ideal managers may work towards but never reach.

Rational Approach

ONLINE
COUNTERPOINT 13.3

ONLINE
COUNTERPOINT 13.4

The rational approach to individual decision-making stresses the need for systematic analysis of a problem followed by choice and implementation in a logical, step-by-step sequence. The rational approach was developed to guide individual decision-making because many managers were observed to be unsystematic and arbitrary in their approach to organizational decisions.

Although the rational model is an ideal not fully achievable in the real world of uncertainty, complexity and rapid change highlighted in Exhibit 13.1, the model does help managers think about decisions more clearly and rationally. Managers should use systematic procedures to make decisions whenever possible. When managers have a deep understanding of the rational decision-making process, it can help them make better decisions even when there is a lack of clear information. Military organizations typically aim to use rational decision-making in order to handle complex problems quickly and decisively, although paradoxically, the decision of a state's leaders to go to war is frequently an irrational decision with disastrous consequences.

COUNTERPOINT 13.2

What the rational approach struggles to model is the complex interdependency and interaction of different factors. It also tends to assume a non-dynamic context so that seemingly 'ideal' solutions are calculated for circumstances that, as a consequence of change, no longer exist. Often so-called tacit knowledge based upon experience can be more instructive than additional amounts of information that can simply flood the process. A sub-optimal quick decision is often more effective than a delayed decision that is accompanied by increased uncertainty and lack of direction.

According to the rational approach, decision-making can be broken down into eight steps, as illustrated in Exhibit 13.2.[22]

1 *Monitor the decision environment.* In the first step, a manager monitors internal and external information that will indicate deviations from planned or acceptable behaviour. He or she talks to colleagues and reviews financial statements, performance evaluations, industry indices, competitors' activities and so forth. Increasingly, environmental monitoring is supported by specialist software. For example, Switzerland's Cablecom was becoming increasingly concerned by the proportion of customers it was losing. As Federico Cesconi, Cablecom's director of business intelligence noted: 'It's very difficult to win back customers after they've left you. And in Europe, the win-back rate is only about 10 per cent to 15 per cent. So, our intent was to assess the satisfaction of every single customer.'

2 *Define the decision problem.* The manager responds to deviations by identifying essential details of the problem: where, when, who was involved, who was affected and how current activities are influenced. For Cablecom, this might mean defining whether customers are lost early in their relationship with the company, what groups have customers with the highest and lowest levels of 'churn', etc. Cablecom's data analysis found that complaints to customer contracts started rolling in after about nine months on average, and customers were mostly lost in the 12- to 14-month period.

3 *Specify decision objectives.* The manager determines what performance outcomes should be achieved by a decision.

4 *Diagnose the problem.* In this step, the manager digs below the surface to analyze the cause of the problem. Additional data might be gathered to facilitate this diagnosis. Understanding the cause enables appropriate treatment. For Cablecom, the problem seemed to be a combination of excessively pressuring sales pitches, and a lack of follow-up response to complaints.

EXHIBIT 13.2 Steps in the Rational Approach to Decision-Making

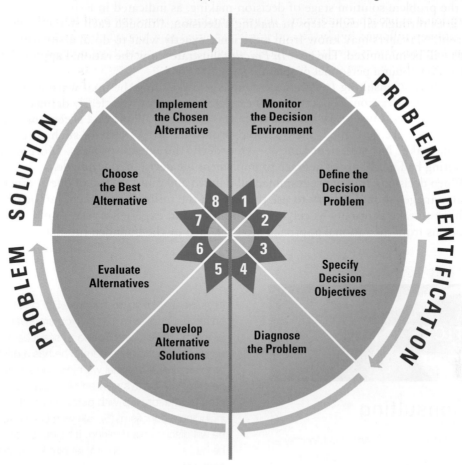

5 *Develop alternative solutions*. Before a manager can move ahead with a decisive action plan, he or she must have a clear understanding of the various options available to achieve desired objectives. The manager may seek ideas and suggestions from other people. Cablecom's options included ensuring sales pitches also incorporated attractive new product offers, and following up customer complaint calls to see if the customer was now satisfied.

6 *Evaluate alternatives*. This step may involve the use of statistical techniques or personal experience to gauge the probability of success. The merits of each alternative are assessed, as well as the probability that it will reach the desired objectives.

7 *Choose the best alternative*. This step is the core of the decision process. The manager uses his or her analysis of the problem, objectives and alternatives to select a single alternative that has the best chance for success. At Cablecom, decisions were made both to roll out new product offerings such as personal video recorders (PVR) and an online video library that can be delivered through cable's superfast broadband connection.

8 *Implement the chosen alternative*. Finally, the manager uses managerial, administrative and persuasive abilities and gives directions to ensure that the decision is carried out. The monitoring activity (step 1) begins again as soon as the solution is implemented. For Cablecom's Federico Cesconi, the decision cycle is a continuous process, with new decisions made daily, based on monitoring the environment for problems and opportunities.[23]

The first four steps in this sequence are the problem identification stage, and the next four steps are the problem solution stage of decision-making, as indicated in Exhibit 13.2. A manager normally goes through all eight steps in making a decision, although each step may not be a distinct element. Managers may know from experience exactly what to do in a situation, so one or more steps will be minimized. The next *In Practice* illustrates how the rational approach is used to make a decision about a personnel problem.

In the Alberta Consulting *In Practice* example below, issuing the final warning to Joe DeFoe was a programmed decision. The standard of expected behaviour was clearly defined, information on the frequency and cause of DeFoe's absence was readily available and acceptable alternatives and procedures were described. The rational procedure works best in such cases, when the decision-maker has sufficient time for an orderly, thoughtful process. Moreover, Alberta Consulting had mechanisms in place to implement the decision, once made.

When decisions are nonprogrammed, ill-defined and piling on top of one another, the individual manager should still try to use the steps in the rational approach, but he or she often will have to take shortcuts by relying on intuition and experience (see Counterpoint 13.3). Deviations from the rational approach are explained by the bounded rationality perspective.

ONLINE COUNTERPOINT 13.5

IN PRACTICE

Alberta Consulting

1   *Monitor the decision environment*. It is Monday morning, and Joe DeFoe, Alberta's accounts receivable supervisor, is absent again.

2   *Define the decision problem*. This is the fourth consecutive Monday DeFoe has been absent. Company policy forbids unexcused absenteeism, and DeFoe has been warned about his excessive absenteeism on the last two occasions. A final warning is in order but can be delayed, if warranted.

3   *Specify decision objectives*. DeFoe should attend work regularly and establish the invoice collection levels of which he is capable. The time period for solving the problem is two weeks.

4   *Diagnose the problem*. Discreet discussions with DeFoe's co-workers and information gleaned from DeFoe indicate that DeFoe has a drinking problem. He apparently uses Mondays to dry out from weekend benders. Discussion with other company sources confirms that DeFoe is a problem drinker.

5   *Develop alternative solutions*. (1) Fire DeFoe. (2) Issue a final warning without comment.

(3) Issue a warning and accuse DeFoe of being an alcoholic to let him know you are aware of his problem. (4) Talk with DeFoe to see if he will discuss his drinking. If he admits he has a drinking problem, delay the final warning and suggest that he enrol in Alberta's new employee assistance programme for help with personal problems, including alcoholism. (5) Talk with DeFoe to see if he will discuss his drinking. If he does not admit he has a drinking problem, let him know that the next absence will cost him his job.

6   *Evaluate alternatives*. The cost of training a replacement is the same for each alternative. Alternative 1 ignores cost and other criteria. Alternatives 2 and 3 do not adhere to company policy, which advocates counselling where appropriate. Alternative 4 is designed for the benefit of both DeFoe and the company. It might save a good employee if DeFoe is willing to seek assistance. Alternative 5 is primarily for the benefit of the company. A final warning might provide some incentive for DeFoe to admit he has a drinking problem. If so, dismissal might be avoided, but further absences will no longer be tolerated.

7   *Choose the best alternative*. DeFoe does not admit that he has a drinking problem. Choose alternative 5.

8   *Implement the chosen alternative*. Write up the case and issue the final warning.[24]

COUNTERPOINT 13.3

'Intuition' and 'experience' are not helpfully characterized as 'short cuts'. It might be more relevant to call rational decision-making 'long-winded' and 'clunky'.

Bounded Rationality Perspective

The point of the rational approach is that managers should try to use systematic procedures to arrive at good decisions. When organizations are facing little competition and are dealing with well-understood issues, managers generally use rational procedures to make decisions.[25] Yet research into managerial decision-making shows that managers often are unable to follow an ideal procedure. Many decisions must be made very quickly. Time pressure, a large number of internal and external factors affecting a decision, and the ill-defined nature of many problems make systematic analysis virtually impossible. Managers have only so much time and mental capacity and, hence, cannot evaluate every goal, problem and alternative. The attempt to be rational is bounded (limited) by the enormous complexity of many problems. There is a limit to how rational managers can be. For example, an executive in a hurry may have a choice of 50 ties on a rack but will take the first or second one that matches his suit. The executive doesn't carefully weigh all 50 alternatives because the short amount of time and the large number of plausible alternatives would be overwhelming. The manager simply selects the first tie that solves the problem and moves on to the next task.

Constraints and Trade-offs   Not only are large organizational decisions too complex to fully comprehend, but several other constraints impinge on the decision-maker, as illustrated in Exhibit 13.3. For many decisions, the circumstances are ambiguous, requiring social support, a shared perspective on what happens and acceptance and agreement. For example, the decision to outsource production to low labour cost countries is typically based on a limited cost benefit analysis of savings that can be realized by replacing high cost in-house staffing with lower cost contracted labour overseas. However, moving parts of the business process not only outside the company, but also outside the home country business environment greatly increases the unknowns.[26] Trust between the contracting parties is typically limited, especially in the critical early stages of outsourcing, and can rarely be fully replaced by comprehensive contract terms and conditions. Trust is built up over time through close working interaction which is difficult to replicate in distant outsourced units.

ONLINE
COUNTERPOINT 13.6

BRIEFCASE 13.2

Numerous other unknowns can impinge on the outcomes of an outsourcing strategy, ranging from currency exchange risk (for example, the British pound lost 10 per cent of its value against the US dollar immediately after the country's electorate surprisingly voted to leave the European Union in June 2016) to end-user resistance (particularly in the case of outsourced call centres). Finally, some analysts argue that outsourcing leads inherently to *asymmetric power relationships*, with the supplier often in the ascendancy over the outsourcing organization. UK academic Chris Lonsdale believes that it is 'risible' to think that British National Health Service (NHS) commercial managers, for example, each responsible for managing hundreds of service contracts, can effectively foresee issues likely to arise in each of the contracts. In contrast, the supplier companies to the NHS are often multinationals with highly professional sales and marketing teams able to structure advantageous contracts and skate over potential pitfalls.[27]

Even in cases where the outsourcing strategy is well-planned and generally successful, such as Danish medical supplies company Coloplast, which decided to outsource volume production to Hungary mid-2000s, managers can be surprised by the number of unexpected challenges that arose. These ranged from inefficiencies caused by the location of the distribution warehouse close to the Danish headquarters, meaning goods produced in Hungary had to be transported all the

EXHIBIT 13.3   Constraints and Trade-offs during Nonprogrammed Decision-Making

Bounded Rationality:
Limited time, information, resources to deal with complex, multidimensional issues

Trade-off

Trade-off

Trade-off

Personal Constraints:
Personal desire for prestige, success; personal decision style; and the desire to satisfy emotional needs, cope with pressure, maintain self-concept

Trade-off

Decision/ Choice:
Search for a high-quality decision alternative

Organizational Constraints:
Level of: agreement, shared perspective, cooperation or support; corporate culture and structure, ethical values

Trade-off

Source: Adapted from Irving L. Janis, *Crucial Decisions* (New York: Free Press, 1989); and A. L. George, *Presidential Decision Making in Foreign Policy: The Effective Use of Information and Advice* (Boulder, CO: Westview Press, 1980).

way to northern Europe for centralized distribution, to the complexity of transferring tacit knowledge underpinning the production process.[28] Managerial decisions, small and large, are made in the context of imperfect knowledge, and of bounded rationality.[29] Nevertheless, a well-managed firm like Coloplast can adapt to the unexpected. By 2013, Coloplast's Hungarian plants accounted for two-thirds of the company's profits and the company was also ranked among the world's best employers. In 2015 Forbes ranked Coloplast the 33rd most innovative company in the world, while the company continued to expand its manufacturing base in Hungary.[30,31]

ONLINE COUNTERPOINT 13.8

Corporate culture and ethical values also influence decision-making, as discussed in Chapter 11. In the best cases, such as at the late Anita Roddick's Body Shop, companies have primary goals of improving the world while enhancing the lives of employees and customers. Managers also often make decisions within a context of trying to please upper managers, people who are perceived to have power within the organization, or others they respect and want to emulate.[32] Personal constraints – such as decision style, work pressure, desire for prestige, or simple feelings of insecurity – may constrain either the search for alternatives or the acceptability of an alternative. All of these factors constrain a perfectly rational approach that should lead to an obviously ideal choice.[33] Even seemingly simple decisions, such as selecting a job on graduation from college, can quickly become so complex that a bounded rationality approach is, in practice, used. Graduating students have been known to search for a job until they have two or three acceptable job offers, at which point their search activity rapidly diminishes. Hundreds of firms may be available for interviews, and two or three job offers are far short of the maximum number that would be possible if students made the decision based on perfect rationality.

The Role of Intuition   The bounded rationality perspective is often associated with intuitive decision processes. In intuitive decision-making, experience and judgement rather than sequential logic or explicit reasoning are used to make decisions.[34] Intuition is not arbitrary or irrational because it is based on years of practice and hands-on experience, often stored in the subconscious. When managers use their intuition based on long experience with organizational issues, they more rapidly perceive and understand problems, and they develop a gut feeling or hunch about which alternative will solve a problem, speeding the decision-making process.[35] The value of intuition for effective decision-making is supported by a growing body of research from psychology, organizational science and other disciplines.[36] Indeed, many universities are offering courses in creativity and intuition so business students can learn to understand and use these processes.

In a situation of great complexity or ambiguity, previous experience and judgement are needed to incorporate intangible elements at both the problem identification and problem solution stages.[37] A study of manager problem-finding showed that 30 of 33 problems were ambiguous and ill-defined.[38] Bits and scraps of unrelated information from informal sources resulted in a pattern in the manager's mind. The manager could not prove a problem existed but knew intuitively that a certain area needed attention. A too-simple view of a complex problem is often associated with decision failure.[39] Intuition plays an increasingly important role in problem identification in today's fast-paced and uncertain business environment.

ONLINE
COUNTERPOINT 13.1

Intuitive processes are also used in the problem solution stage. Executives frequently make decisions without explicit reference to the impact on profits or to other measurable outcomes.[40] As we saw in Exhibit 13.3, many intangible factors – such as a person's concern about the support of other executives, fear of failure and social attitudes – influence selection of the best alternative. These factors cannot be quantified in a systematic way, so intuition guides the choice of a solution. Managers may make a decision based on what they sense to be right rather than on what they can document with hard data. A 2006 survey of American CEOs found that six in ten acknowledge that 'gut feeling' is highly influential in their decision-making, while a 2011 study by a team led from the University of Alberta in Canada found that first instincts were usually the best guide to setting goals.[41] Similar results have been found in New Zealand and elsewhere.[42,43]

COUNTERPOINT 13.4

It may be a mistake to conflate a sense of 'what is right' with 'gut feeling'. 'Gut feeling' is as likely to be accommodating of self-interest or with staying in the comfort zone as it is with taking decisions that turn out to be 'right'.

Take the case of Austrian motorbike manufacturer KTM Fahrrad GmbH. Stefan Pierer took over in 2002 as CEO of the company after it emerged from bankruptcy. Once he had put the company back on its feet he took a leap into the unknown, steering KTM, long famous for its off-road models, into the competitive world of street bikes. The gut decision has been a huge success; by 2015 KTM was Europe's biggest motorbike manufacturer on the back of two decades of consistent revenue growth.[44] Street bikes now make up almost one-third of KTM's revenues. Pierer says, 'When it comes to really serious business decisions I ultimately rely on my intuition. It's sometimes the case that rational arguments speak for or against something, but then somehow the decision still won't leave me in peace. I wake up in the night and have the feeling that I should do it differently after all.'[45] Pierer has continued to make bold decisions. He is moving emphasis towards fast-growing Asian markets through a partnership with Indian bike manufacturer Baja which has a 48 per cent stake in the firm. It is a partnership that has been a great success, and the joint venture announced plans to focus on expansion in Indonesia, a huge motorbike market, in 2016.[46] At the same time KTM purchased high-end BMW subsidiary Husqvarna of Sweden, acquiring a valuable marque and top-notch engineering.[47] However, there are also many examples of intuitive decisions that turned out to be complete failures.[48] This chapter's *Bookmark* discusses how managers can give their intuition a better chance of leading to successful decisions.

Managers may walk a fine line between making arbitrary decisions without careful study, and relying obsessively on numbers and rational analysis.[49] Remember that the bounded rationality perspective and the use of intuition apply particularly to nonprogrammed decisions. The novel, unclear, complex aspects of nonprogrammed decisions mean hard data and logical procedures are not available. One study of executive decision-making found that managers simply could not use the rational approach for nonprogrammed decisions, such as when to buy a computed tomography (CT) scanner for an osteopathic hospital or whether a city had a need for and could reasonably adopt an enterprise resource planning system.[50] In those cases, managers had limited time and resources, and some factors simply couldn't be measured and analyzed. Trying to quantify such information could cause mistakes because it may oversimplify decision criteria. Intuition can also balance and supplement rational analysis to help organization leaders make better decisions. Geoff Travis, founder of Rough Trade, the British indie record label, relied on his intuition, his innate feel for 'the next thing' in music, to build a successful label that also freed young musicians from the suffocating control of the big record companies.[51]

Organizational Decision-Making

Organizations are composed of managers who make decisions using both rational and intuitive processes; but organization-level decisions are not usually made by a single manager. Many organizational decisions involve several managers. Problem identification and problem solution involve many departments, multiple viewpoints and even other organizations, which are beyond the scope of an individual manager.

The processes by which decisions are made in organizations are influenced by a number of factors, particularly the organization's own internal structures and the degree of stability or instability of the external environment.[52] Research into organization-level decision-making has identified four primary types of organizational decision-making processes: the management science approach, the Carnegie model, the incremental decision process model and the garbage can model.

BRIEFCASE 13.3

BOOKMARK 13.0

Have you read this book?

Blink: The Power of Thinking without Thinking

BY MALCOLM GLADWELL

Snap decisions can be just as good as – and sometimes better than – decisions that are made cautiously and deliberately. Yet they can also be seriously flawed or even dangerously wrong. That's the premise of Malcolm Gladwell's *Blink: The Power of Thinking without Thinking*. Gladwell explores how our 'adaptive unconscious' arrives at complex, important decisions in an instant – and how we can train it to make those decisions good ones.

Sharpening Your Intuition

Even when we think our decision-making is the result of careful analysis and rational consideration, Gladwell says, most of it actually happens subconsciously in a split second. This process, which he refers to as 'rapid cognition', provides room for both amazing insight and grave error. Here are some tips for improving rapid cognition:

- *Remember that more is not better.* Gladwell argues that giving people too much data and information hampers their ability to make good decisions. He cites a study showing that emergency room doctors who are best at diagnosing heart attacks gather less information from their patients than other doctors do. Rather than overloading on information, search out the most meaningful parts.

- *Practice thin-slicing.* The process Gladwell refers to as *thin-slicing* is what harnesses the power of the adaptive unconscious and enables us to make smart decisions with minimal time and information. Thin-slicing means focusing on a thin slice of pertinent data or information and allowing your intuition to do the work for you. Gladwell cites the example of a Pentagon war game, in which an enemy team of commodities traders defeated a US Army that had 'an unpredented amount of information and intelligence' and 'did a thoroughly rational and rigorous analysis that covered every conceivable contingency'. The commodities traders were used to making thousands of instant decisions an hour based on limited information. Managers can practise spontaneous decision-making until it becomes second nature.

- *Know your limits*. Not every decision should be based on intuition. When you have a depth of knowledge and experience in an area, you can put more trust in your gut feelings. Gladwell also

cautions to beware of biases that interfere with good decision-making. *Blink* suggests that we can teach ourselves to sort through first impressions and figure out which are important and which are based on subconscious biases such as stereotypes or emotional baggage.

Conclusion

Blink is filled with lively and interesting anecdotes, such as how firefighters can 'slow down a moment' and create an environment where spontaneous decision-making can take place. Gladwell asserts that a better understanding of the process of split-second decision-making can help people make better decisions in all areas of their lives, as well as help them anticipate and avoid miscalculations.

Blink: The Power of Thinking without Thinking, by Malcolm Gladwell, is published by Little, Brown.

Management Science Approach

The management science approach to organizational decision-making is the analogue to the rational approach by individual managers. Management science came into being during the Second World War.[53] At that time, mathematical and statistical techniques were applied to urgent, large-scale military problems that were beyond the ability of individual decision-makers.

Mathematicians, physicists and operations researchers used systems analysis to develop artillery trajectories, antisubmarine strategies and bombing strategies such as salvoing (discharging multiple shells simultaneously). Consider the problem of a battleship trying to sink an enemy ship several miles away. The calculation for aiming the battleship's guns should consider distance, wind speed, shell size, speed and direction of both ships, pitch and roll of the firing ship and curvature of the earth. Methods for performing such calculations using trial and error and intuition are not accurate, take far too long and may never achieve success.

This is where management science came in. Analysts were able to identify the relevant variables involved in aiming a ship's guns and could model them with the use of mathematical equations. Distance, speed, pitch, roll, shell size and so on could be calculated and entered into the equations. The answer was immediate, and the guns could begin firing. Factors such as pitch and roll were soon measured mechanically and fed directly into the targeting mechanism. Today, the human element is completely removed from the targeting process. Radar picks up the target, and the entire sequence is computed automatically.

Management science yielded success for many military problems. This approach to decision-making diffused into corporations and business schools, where techniques were studied and elaborated. Today, many corporations have assigned departments to use these techniques. The computer department develops quantitative data for analysis. Operations research departments use mathematical models to quantify relevant variables and develop a quantitative representation of alternative solutions and the probability of each one solving the problem. These departments also use such devices as linear programming, Bayesian statistics, PERT charts and computer simulations.

Management science is an excellent device for organizational decision-making when problems are analyzable and when the variables can be identified and measured. Mathematical models can contain a thousand or more variables, each one relevant in some way to the ultimate outcome. Management science

LEADING BY DESIGN

Rough Trade

It all started because Geoff Travis couldn't find the Rough Trade records that he liked, back in 1976 when big labels were king and if you didn't fit their formula you didn't have a chance. Travis set up a small record store and stocked it with his kind of music, alternative, edgy material. He freely admits he was lucky, because musical taste was on the cusp of a revolution. The musical lull of the early 1970s was about to be shaken up by the advent of punk. Travis started by selling his huge collection of alternative music records he had bought while hitchhiking across America the previous year, where bands like the Ramones had already started to shake things up. His West London location turned out to be at the epicentre of the European scene, 'The Clash lived up the road, and The Sex Pistols would come in trying to sell us all the records they'd nicked from somewhere else', Travis recalls.

It wasn't long before Travis's friends who owned similar stores across London started to source hard-to-find music through him, and soon he formed the core of a national network of independent record stores and the myriad fledgling labels that were producing singles by new artists. Rough Trade records was born two years later in 1978, with early successes like The Fall and Stiff Little Fingers. The first band Rough Trade chaperoned to the big time was The Smiths, and by 2008 some of the names featuring on the label's 30-year anniversary tour were The Strokes, Belle & Sebastian, Arcade Fire and Jarvis Cocker.

Rough Trade has seen its ups and downs. In the early 1990s the distribution arm of the business folded, and Travis sold off the record label in order to ensure artists, who risked losing desperately needed record sales revenues in the bankruptcy, would be paid. But after working for another label for a while, Travis bought Rough Trade back and relaunched it in 2000. Since then the company has picked some up-and-coming indie bands like British Sea Power, the Palma Violets, Warpaint and Alabama Shakes, while continuing as home to bands like The Strokes, Jarvis Cocker and Pulp. Record stores have come back into vogue with the hipster generation, and Rough Trade has highly successful record stores-cum-concert venues in both London and New York. Underpinned by Travis's firm commitment to choose bands according to his intuition, rather than a prepackaged marketing formula, Rough Trade looks set to continue ploughing its own furrow for years to come.[54,55]

techniques have been used to correctly solve problems as diverse as finding the right spot for a church camp, test-marketing the first of a new family of products, drilling for oil and radically altering the distribution of telecommunications services.[56] The *In Practice* example on the next page describes how Germany's Labour Agency, the Bundesagentur für Arbeit used management science techniques to set up its Virtual Labour Market (VAM).

Despite the positive outcomes, VAM's development had its share of controversy, which is very common in a complex system. Cost overruns in the final development phase led to allegations of corruption in awarding contracts. An enquiry showed this was not the case but that more could have been done to keep costs closer to original estimates.[57]

Management science can accurately and quickly solve problems that have too many explicit variables for human processing. This system is at its best when applied to problems that are analyzable, are measurable and can be structured in a logical way. Increasingly sophisticated computer technology and software programmes are allowing the expansion of management science to cover a broader range of problems than ever before. For example, most large retailers, including Zara, Marks & Spencer and Gap, use software to analyze current and historical sales data and determine when, where and how much to mark down prices. Airlines and hotel chains now use yield management software to set prices according to factors such as passenger load and occupancy rates, respectively. The success of European low-cost carrier Ryanair is based to a significant extent on sophisticated use of yield management systems. Passengers booking well in advance for unseasonal destinations, such as seaside resorts in midwinter, can snag rock-bottom fares of a few euros, but those wishing to travel at short notice on well-subscribed flights can expect to pay top prices.[58] Former Ryanair executives Jim McMahon and Seamus Moriarty set up an aviation consultancy that specializes in helping other airlines to take best advantage of yield management systems to maximize their seat revenues.[59,60] Yield management pricing is now being used in many different sectors from car rentals to do-it-yourself equipment rental. Railway companies across Europe now use yield management with positive results; France's state-owned SNCF railway company first introduced the system for its high-speed TGV trains and then extended the approach to its regional TER services.[61]

Companies often seek to address potential negative customer sentiment when considering using yield management.[62] This can take various forms. Customers who have paid top prices for a holiday package may well feel ripped-off if they find that fellow travellers who booked at the last minute paid far less than they did. Further, customers are aware that costs to provide a service such as a hotel room tend to be similar despite tariffs varying widely according to load factors. Loyal customers who always use a particular company may object if they suddenly find they have to pay an exorbitant rate for a service because they are using it at a popular time, and will be more likely to 'counter-attack' by searching for a cheaper alternative with another company. Finally, yield management introduces a complexity to travel planning that can be irritating; SNCF's yield management has been widely criticised on these grounds by French rail passengers.[63] Yield management can thus damage customer loyalty, another important weapon in a company's competitive arsenal.[64]

Management science has, to go along with its successes, produced many failures.[65] In recent years, many banks have begun using computerized scoring systems to rate those applying for credit, but some argue that human judgement is needed to assess an individual's real creditworthiness. Many analysts place part of the responsibility for the global credit system meltdown of 2007–2008 on banks' withdrawal from personal relationships with their clients in favour of outsourced models where companies – frequently based in offshore locations such as India or elsewhere – were paid to identify potential borrowers through telephone canvassing. Although a rudimentary financial qualification assessment was conducted, usually on the telephone, the loan-originating companies were most interested in getting their fee for finding a customer. Banks and other financial institutions then 'securitized' these loans by packaging them up in bundles which were then assigned a market value based on the supposed solidity of the underlying security – such as customers' houses. These financial instruments were then swapped amongst the banks and sold off to various investors in an increasingly complex series of arrangements. The complexity of the system was such that banks and other investors lost track of the underlying value of the securities. Investors and banks panicked when it became clear that the house price boom in countries like the US and UK was coming to an end and that significant numbers of customers could not afford to repay their loans and mortgages. Banks knew that many of the bundled loans and mortgages they held were sure to be worthless, but did not know which ones. The credit explosion turned overnight into a credit freeze and numerous financial institutions in Europe, the USA and the rest of the world, either went bankrupt or had to be bailed out at enormous cost to taxpayers.[66] The computerized infrastructure that managed the credit system, from customer credit assessment through to loan bundling and securitization, appeared sophisticated but obscured the absence of adequate internal and external oversight.

The dangers of complex, poorly understood, poorly regulated, computerized financial markets are also demonstrated by the collapse of Bernard L. Madoff Investment Securities in late 2008.[67] Madoff, a former chairman of the NASDAQ stock exchange and highly regarded figure in US financial circles, concocted a scheme in which he purported to manage investors' funds using a complex and secretive computerized investment model. In fact it appears he paid existing investors

Germany's Virtual Labour Market[68]

Despite the successes of the German economy in the post-war period, by the mid-2000s the country was still faced with stubbornly high levels of unemployment, particularly among youth. At the same time, as in most countries, employers continued to say that they could not find the right people to fill certain positions. The German government labour agency responsible for helping unemployed people get matched with work opportunities, the Bundesagentur fur Arbeit (BfA), set about developing an IT-based system that would match workers with available opportunities. The new system consists of internal and external online portals, with links to private firms' HR departments, as well as commercial and government employment services. VerBIS, the intranet (internal) portal, supports the 100 000 counsellors and placement workers located in BfA's employment offices throughout Germany. These internal users make about 40 million hits on the portal every day.

VAM has helped BfA to improve the quality and efficiency of its work. Its centralized database of all job opportunities in Germany makes it a useful resource not only for the unemployed but for employed workers seeking better jobs. The system has substantially reduced the time taken to match qualified candidates against available employment opportunities, with about 800 000 jobs posted and 5.5 million job seekers registered at any one time. Over two million job matches are identified every week. In addition, the system maintains updated records of all workers seeking employment, which can be accessed by any BfA counsellor across the country. This contrasts positively with the previous system where personnel files were held by individual counsellors, with information frequently being lost when counsellors changed or the jobseeker moved.

The internet side of the VAM provides new services both to employers and jobseekers. Employers can directly enter information about positions available, and for the first time job seekers can access a nationwide database of positions available, either from home through an internet connection, or at one of the terminals located in all BfA offices. The system helps job seekers take greater control over their job search, and reduces the time BfA workers have to devote to each case.

The new system is part of labour market reforms that the German government has put in place in an effort to reduce long-term unemployment. It is linked to training and social benefits databases and thus helps ensure people receive the benefit to which they are entitled. The more efficient matching service gets people back into the workforce more quickly, thus improving government finances. But the most important aspect of the system is the help it provides for people seeking rewarding work. Markus Michel, formerly unemployed, worked with his BfA placement agent to find his current job using the system's enhanced matching technology – it is a position requiring skills which he had acquired by self-study but for which he had no formal qualification: 'I would have fallen through the cracks [before] because the only possible job search would have been the search for a job title'.

Germany's dynamic approach to tackling unemployment has reaped dividends. By 2016 the country, had the second lowest overall level of unemployment in the EU at 4.2%, a 35 year low, as well as youth unemployment of 7.7 per cent compared with 15 per cent in 2005. This despite the global recession that hit in 2008 and led to record youth unemployment in many EU countries and an average EU rate in 2016 of 23.8 per cent.[69,70] The virtual labour market concept has been adopted in other countries, including the UK.[71]

their dividends using new investors' resources, as well as leaching off substantial amounts of money to his own account. The US Securities and Exchange Commission, which should have overseen his activities, failed to detect the fraud despite numerous tip-offs. Once the final tallies were made, losses were expected to exceed $25 billion, and the incident sent shockwaves through stock markets already depressed by the impacts of the credit meltdown described above.[72,73]

Apart from complexity and the consequent tendency for lack of transparency, another problem with the management science approach is that quantitative data are not rich and do not convey tacit knowledge, as described in Chapter 9. Informal cues that indicate the existence of problems have to be sensed on a more personal basis by managers.[74] The most sophisticated mathematical analyses are of limited value if the important factors cannot be quantified and included in the model. Such things as competitor reactions, consumer tastes and product warmth are qualitative dimensions. In these situations, the role of management science is to supplement manager decision-making. Quantitative results can be given to managers for discussion and interpretation along with their informal opinions, judgement and intuition. The final decision typically includes both qualitative factors and quantitative calculations.

Carnegie Model

The Carnegie model of organizational decision-making is based on the work of Richard Cyert, James March and Herbert Simon, who were all associated with Carnegie-Mellon University in Pittsburgh, USA.[75] Their research helped formulate the bounded rationality approach to individual decision-making, as well as provide new insights about organizational decisions.

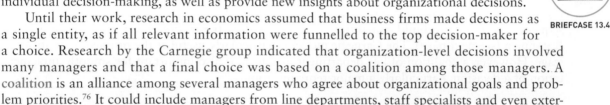

BRIEFCASE 13.4

Until their work, research in economics assumed that business firms made decisions as a single entity, as if all relevant information were funnelled to the top decision-maker for a choice. Research by the Carnegie group indicated that organization-level decisions involved many managers and that a final choice was based on a coalition among those managers. A coalition is an alliance among several managers who agree about organizational goals and problem priorities.[76] It could include managers from line departments, staff specialists and even external groups, such as powerful customers, bankers or union representatives.

Management coalitions are needed during decision-making for two reasons. First, organizational goals are often ambiguous, and operative goals of departments are often inconsistent. When goals are ambiguous and inconsistent, managers will naturally tend to disagree about problem priorities. They must bargain about problems and build a coalition around the question of which problems to solve.

COUNTERPOINT 13.5

While attention to coalition building is undoubtedly important, it requires a close appreciation of what enables coalitions to be built. How, for example, is credibility and legitimacy established? To what extent do coalitions represent the outcome of established power relations? What kinds of 'solutions' are simply never contemplated because those occupying privileged positions have effectively closed them off? Coalition building does not mean that the resulting decisions are better ones, only that they have been agreed by a dominant coalition. What is probable is that the decision broadly reflects the preconceptions, fears, hopes and values of the coalition members.

The second reason for coalitions is that individual managers intend to be rational but function with human cognitive limitations and other constraints, as described earlier. Managers do not have the time, resources or mental capacity to identify all dimensions and to process all information relevant to a decision. These limitations lead to deliberative, coalition-building behaviour. Managers talk to each other and exchange points of view to gather information and reduce ambiguity. People who have relevant information or a stake in a decision outcome are consulted. Building a coalition will lead to a decision that is supported by interested parties.

The process of coalition formation has several implications for organizational decision behaviour. First, decisions are made to *satisfice* rather than to optimize problem solutions. Satisficing means accepting a satisfactory rather than a maximum level of performance, enabling managers to achieve several goals simultaneously. In decision-making, the coalition will accept a solution that is perceived as satisfactory to all coalition members. Second, managers are concerned with immediate problems and short-run solutions. They engage in what Cyert and March called *problemistic search*.[77]

Problemistic search means managers look around in the immediate environment for a solution to quickly resolve a problem. Managers don't expect a perfect solution when the situation is ill-defined and conflict-laden. This contrasts with the management science approach, which assumes that analysis can uncover every reasonable alternative. The Carnegie model says that search behaviour is just sufficient to produce a satisfactory solution and that managers typically adopt the first satisfactory solution that emerges. Third, discussion and bargaining are especially important in the problem identification stage of decision-making. Unless coalition members perceive a problem, action will not be taken.

The decision process described in the Carnegie model is summarized in Exhibit 13.4. The Carnegie model points out that building agreement through a managerial coalition is a major part of organizational decision-making. This is especially true at upper management levels. Discussion and bargaining are time consuming, so search procedures are usually simple and the selected alternative satisfices rather than optimizes problem solution. When problems are programmed – are clear and have been seen before – the organization will rely on previous procedures and routines. Nonprogrammed decisions, however, require bargaining and conflict resolution. The consequences of failing to build a coalition are illustrated by the *In Practice* case of Encyclopaedia Britannica (see next page). The Carnegie model is particularly useful at the problem identification stage. However, a coalition of key department managers is also important for smooth implementation of a decision, particularly a major reorganization.

Incremental Decision Process Model

BRIEFCASE 13.5

Henry Mintzberg and his associates at McGill University in Montreal, Canada, have approached organizational decision-making from a different perspective. They identified 25 decisions made in organizations and traced the events associated with these decisions from beginning to end.[78] Their research identified each step in the decision sequence. This approach to decision-making, called the incremental decision process model, places less emphasis on the political and social factors described in the Carnegie model, but tells more about the structured sequence of activities undertaken from the discovery of a problem to its solution.[79]

EXHIBIT 13.4 Choice Processes in the Carnegie

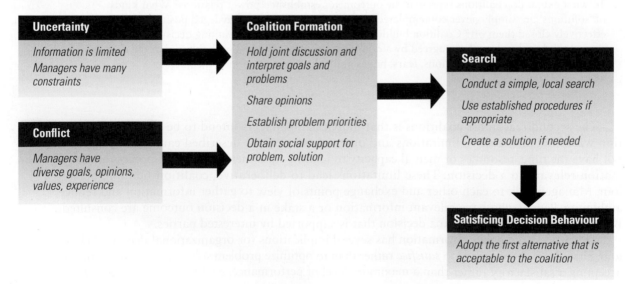

Sample decisions in Mintzberg's research included choosing which jet aircraft to acquire for a regional airline, developing a new supper club, developing a new container terminal in a harbour, identifying a new market for a deodorant, installing a controversial new medical treatment in a hospital and firing a star radio announcer.[80] The scope and importance of these decisions are revealed in the length of time taken to complete them. Most of these decisions took more than a year, and one third of them took more than two years. Most of these decisions were nonprogrammed and required custom-designed solutions.

One discovery from this research is that major organization choices are usually a series of small choices that combine to produce the major decision. Thus, many organizational decisions are a series of nibbles rather than a big bite. Organizations move through several decision points and may hit barriers along the way. Mintzberg called these barriers *decision interrupts*. An interrupt may mean an organization has to cycle back through a previous decision and try something

IN PRACTICE

Encyclopaedia Britannica

For most of its 231-year history, the *Encyclopaedia Britannica* has been viewed as an illustrious repository of cultural and historical knowledge. Generations of students and librarians relied on the *Britannica* – but that was before CD-ROMs and the internet became the study tools of choice. Suddenly, the 32-volume collection of encyclopedias, stretching four feet on a bookshelf and costing as much as a personal computer, seemed destined to fade into history.

When Swiss-based financier Joseph Safra bought Britannica, he discovered one of the reasons. For nearly a decade, managers had bickered over goals and priorities. Some top executives believed the company needed to invest more in electronic media, but others supported Britannica's traditional direct-to-home sales force. Eventually, the company's Compton unit, a CD-ROM pioneer now being used by millions of consumers, was sold, leaving Britannica without any presence in the new market. In the 1980s, Microsoft had approached Britannica to develop a CD-ROM encyclopedia; when it didn't work out, Microsoft went with Funk & Wagnalls and developed Encarta. Microsoft arranged to have Encarta preinstalled on PCs, so the CD-ROM was essentially free to new PC buyers. When Britannica finally came out with its CD-ROM version, however, it was priced at a staggering $1200. The squabbling among managers, owners and editors about product development,

pricing, distribution and other important decisions contributed to the company's decline.

The first step in Safra's turnaround strategy was to install a new top management team, led by one of his longtime advisors. The team immediately coalesced around the important problem of establishing a presence in the world of electronic media. With this goal, the company rushed out a revamped, lower-cost CD-ROM package and launched the Britannica.com website, which allows users to call up encyclopedia entries online as well as get a list of links to related websites. The team also created a separate digital media division to focus on new product development, such as for wireless web technology. Managers are looking toward the wireless web as the best route to a successful future and have teamed up with numerous wireless carriers and licensed Britannica's content to other websites. In 2012, Britannica made the final leap, announcing it was to abandon print publication altogether. The company has shifted to an online subscriber model, both for 50 000 customers who pay $70 a year, and 450 000 who are subscribed through services bundled through telecom and internet providers. The company is successful, but still has to worry both about free competitors (notably, Wikipedia), and the rapidly changing systems of delivering knowledge online. The company has expanded its on-site advertising, with subscriber revenue dropping from 95% to 75% of Britannica's income between 2012 and 2014.[81]

Building a coalition focused on common goals rather than having managers pushing and pulling in different directions got Britannica off the critical list by helping it cross the bridge to the digital era. Now, managers are in the process of evaluation to see what new decisions need to be made to help the company thrive in the digital world.[82,83]

new. Decision loops or cycles are one way the organization learns which alternatives will work. The ultimate solution may be very different from what was initially anticipated.

The pattern of decision stages discovered by Mintzberg and his associates is shown in Exhibit 13.5. Each box indicates a possible step in the decision sequence. The steps take place in three major decision phases: identification, development and selection.

Identification Phase   The identification phase begins with *recognition*. Recognition means one or more managers become aware of a problem and the importance of making a decision. Recognition is usually stimulated by a problem or an opportunity. A problem exists when elements in the external environment change or when internal performance is perceived to be below standard. In the case of firing a radio announcer, comments about the announcer came from listeners, other announcers and advertisers. Managers interpreted these cues until a pattern emerged that indicated a problem had to be dealt with.

The second step is *diagnosis*, in which more information is gathered if needed to define the problem situation. Diagnosis may be systematic or informal, depending upon the severity of the problem. Severe problems do not allow time for extensive diagnosis; the response must be immediate. Mild problems are usually diagnosed in a more systematic manner.

?

ONLINE
COUNTERPOINT 13.9

Development Phase   In the development phase, a solution is shaped to solve the problem defined in the identification phase. The development of a solution takes one of two directions. First, *search* procedures may be used to seek out alternatives within the organization's repertoire of solutions. For example, in the case of firing a star announcer, managers asked what the radio station had done the last time an announcer had to be let go. To conduct the search, organization participants may look into their own memories, talk to other managers or examine the formal procedures of the organization.

The second direction of development is to *design* a custom solution. This happens when the problem is novel so that previous experience has no value. Mintzberg found that in these cases, key decision-makers have only a vague idea of the ideal solution. Gradually, through a trial-and-error process, a custom-designed alternative will emerge. Development of the solution is a groping, incremental procedure, building a solution brick by brick.

Selection Phase   The selection phase is when the solution is chosen. This phase is not always a matter of making a clear choice among alternatives. In the case of custom-made solutions, selection is more an evaluation of the single alternative that seems feasible.

Evaluation and choice may be accomplished in three ways. The *judgement* form of selection is used when a final choice falls upon a single decision-maker, and the choice involves judgement based upon experience. In analysis, alternatives are evaluated on a more systematic basis, such as with management science techniques. Mintzberg found that most decisions did not involve systematic analysis and evaluation of alternatives. *Bargaining* occurs when selection involves a group of decision-makers. Each decision-maker may have a different stake in the outcome, so conflict emerges. Discussion and bargaining occur until a coalition is formed, as in the Carnegie model described earlier.

When a decision is formally accepted by the organization, *authorization* takes place. The decision may be passed up the hierarchy to the responsible hierarchical level. Authorization is often routine because the expertise and knowledge rest with the lower-level decision-makers who identified the problem and developed the solution. A few decisions are rejected because of implications not anticipated by lower-level managers.

Dynamic Factors   The lower part of the chart in Exhibit 12.5 shows lines running back toward the beginning of the decision process. These lines represent loops or cycles that take place in the decision process. Organizational decisions do not follow an orderly progression from recognition through authorization. Minor problems arise that force a loop back to an earlier stage.

EXHIBIT 13.5 The Incremental Decision Process Model

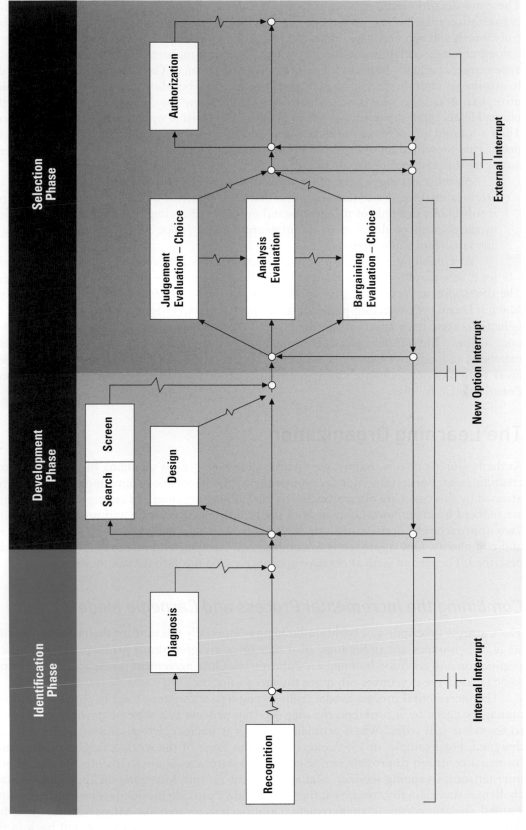

Source: Adapted and reprinted from 'The Structure of Unstructured Decision Processes' by Henry Mintzberg, Duru Raisinghani and Andre Theoret, published in *Administrative Science Quarterly* 21, No. 2 (1976), 266, by permission of The *Administrative Science Quarterly*. Copyright c 1976 Cornell University.

These are decision interrupts. If a custom-designed solution is perceived as unsatisfactory, the organization may have to go back to the very beginning and reconsider whether the problem is truly worth solving. Feedback loops can be caused by problems of timing, politics, disagreement among managers, inability to identify a feasible solution, turnover of managers or the sudden appearance of a new alternative. For example, when a small Canadian airline made the decision to acquire jet aircraft, the board authorized the decision, but shortly afterwards, a new chief executive was brought in who cancelled the contract, recycling the decision back to the identification phase. He accepted the diagnosis of the problem but insisted upon a new search for alternatives. Then a foreign airline went out of business and two used aircraft became available at a bargain price. This presented an unexpected option, and the chief executive used his own judgement to authorize the purchase of the aircraft.[84]

ONLINE
COUNTERPOINT 13.10

As most decisions take place over an extended period of time, circumstances change. Decision-making is a dynamic process that may require a number of cycles before a problem is solved. An example of the incremental process and cycling that can take place is illustrated by the decision of global razor manufacturer Gillette (since 2005 a Procter & Gamble subsidiary) to create a new razor.

At Gillette, the identification phase occurred because executives were aware of the need for a new razor and became alert to the idea of using three blades to produce a closer shave. The development phase was characterized by the trial-and-error custom design leading to the Mach3. During the selection phase, certain approaches were found to be unacceptable, causing Gillette to cycle back and redesign the razor, including using thinner, stronger blades. Advancing once again to the selection phase, the Mach3 passed the judgement of top executives and board members, and manufacturing and marketing budgets were quickly authorized. This decision took more than a decade. Gillette's decision-making process for its new razors is discussed in the *In Practice* which follows.

The Learning Organization

At the beginning of this chapter, we discussed how the rapidly changing business environment is creating greater uncertainty for decision-makers. Managers in organizations that are particularly affected by this trend are often attracted to the learning organization concept. These organizations are marked by much uncertainty at both the problem identification and problem solution stages. Two approaches to decision-making have evolved to help managers cope with this uncertainty and complexity. One approach is to combine the Carnegie and incremental process models just described. The second is an alternative approach called the garbage can model.

Combining the Incremental Process and Carnegie Models

The Carnegie description of coalition building is especially relevant for the problem identification stage. When issues are ambiguous, or if managers disagree about problem severity, discussion, negotiation and coalition building are appropriate. Once agreement is reached about the problem to be tackled, the executives can move toward a solution.

The incremental process model tends to emphasize the steps used to reach a solution. After managers agree on a problem, the step-by-step process is a way of trying various solutions to see what will work. When problem solution is unclear, a trial-and-error solution may be designed. For example, in 1999, executives from three of the world's largest music companies formed a coalition to provide online consumers with a legal alternative to the digital piracy of internet song-swapping services. Making the joint venture MusicNet an appealing choice was a challenge. As originally conceived, the service didn't provide music lovers with the features they wanted, so managers took an incremental approach to try to make MusicNet more user-friendly. After a brief period of success, MusicNet, now part of MediaNet Digital, fell back in the face

IN PRACTICE

Gillette Company

The Gillette Company (now a Procter and Gamble subsidiary) uses incremental decision-making to perfect the design of razors such as the Mach3 family of razors. While searching for a new idea to increase sales in Gillette's mature shaving market, researchers at the company's British research lab came up with a bright idea to create a razor with three blades to produce a closer, smoother, more comfortable shave (recognition and diagnosis). Ten years later, the Mach3 reached the market, after thousands of shaving tests, numerous design modifications and a development and tooling cost of $750 million, roughly the amount a pharmaceutical firm invests in developing a blockbuster drug.

The technical demands of building a razor with three blades that would follow a man's face and also be easy to clean, had several blind alleys. Engineers first tried to find established techniques (search, screen), but none fitted the bill. Eventually a prototype called Manx was built (design), and in shaving tests it greatly outperformed Gillette's Sensor Excel, the company's best-selling razor at the time. However, Gillette's CEO insisted that the razor had to have a radically new blade edge so the razor could use thinner blades (internal interrupt), so engineers began looking for new technology that could produce a stronger blade (search, screen). Eventually, the new edge, known as DLC for diamond-like carbon coating, would be applied atom by atom with chip-making technology (design).

The board gave final approval for production of the Mach3 to begin in the fourth quarter of 1997. The new razor was introduced in the summer of 1998 and began smoothly sliding off shelves. Gillette recovered its huge investment in record time. Gillette then started the process of searching for the next shaving breakthrough all over again, using new technology that can examine a razor blade at the atomic level and high-speed video that can capture the act of cutting a single whisker. The company has continued to move ahead in increments and rolled out its five-bladed Fusion in 2006. Fusion became Procter & Gamble's fastest growing brand ever, while Mach3 in its various permutations, as well as the earlier Sensor, continue to sell well to loyal consumers unwilling to pay the premium prices for Gillette's newest products, and tempted by increasing publicity for lower-cost alternatives. At the same time, the company has continued to expand at the top end with innovations like 2014's ProGlide Flexball.[85,86,87]

of increased competition. The music industry is still casting about for effective responses to illegal file-sharing. For several years music companies tried a combination of negotiating legal file-sharing contracts with various providers including Apple's iTunes, and legal action against people illegally sharing their files through 'torrent' software. In late 2008 the biggest industry association, the Recording Industry Association of America, decided to discontinue the lawsuit strategy, which had created some bad publicity for the industry without significantly affecting the illegal file-sharing problem. Instead, the US and European music industry has shifted its focus to internet service providers (ISPs). ISPs also don't like illegal file-sharing as it uses up a huge amount of internet bandwidth, although they naturally want to avoid having to act as 'police' by blocking users or passing on details about their customers to the authorities. Instead of launching lawsuits, the music industry identifies abusers and contacts their ISP, who can issue warnings and even cut abusers' internet service altogether. The music and film industries have backed up the pressure on ISPs by obtaining court injunctions to block filesharing services, though ISPs often push back against too much regulation.[88,89] Intellectual property protection still varies substantially between countries, as do the strategies industry associations and individual recording industry companies use to combat piracy. As one executive put it, 'This is a business of trial and error'.[90]

The two models do not disagree with one another. They describe how managers make decisions when either problem identification or solution is uncertain. The application of these two models to the stages in the decision process is illustrated in Exhibit 13.6. When both parts of the decision process are simultaneously highly uncertain, which is often the case in learning organizations, managers find themselves in a difficult position. Decision processes in that situation may be a combination of Carnegie and incremental process models, and this combination may evolve into a situation described in the garbage can model.

Garbage Can Model

The garbage can model is not directly comparable to the earlier models because it deals with the pattern or flow of multiple decisions within organizations, whereas the incremental and Carnegie models focus on how a single decision is made. The garbage can model assists in considering the whole organization and the frequent decisions being made by managers throughout.

Organized Anarchy　　The garbage can model was developed to explain the pattern of decision-making in which managers experience extremely high uncertainty. Michael Cohen, James March and Johan Olsen, the originators of the model, called the highly uncertain conditions an *organized anarchy*, which is an extremely organic organization.[91] Organized anarchies do not rely on the normal vertical hierarchy of authority and bureaucratic decision rules. They result from three characteristics:

1 *Problematic preferences.* Goals, problems, alternatives and solutions are ill-defined. Ambiguity characterizes each step of a decision process.

2 *Unclear, poorly understood technology.* Cause-and-effect relationships within the organization are difficult to identify. An explicit database that applies to decisions is not available.

3 *Turnover.* Organizational positions experience turnover of participants. In addition, employees are busy and have only limited time to allocate to any one problem or decision. Participation in any given decision will be fluid and limited.

An organized anarchy is characterized by rapid change and a collegial, nonbureaucratic environment. No organization fits this extremely organic circumstance all the time but many organizations exhibit such features from time to time and executives find themselves in positions of making decisions under unclear, problematic circumstances. The garbage can model is useful for understanding the pattern of these decisions.

Streams of Events　　The unique characteristic of the garbage can model is that the decision process is not seen as a sequence of steps that begins with a problem and ends with a solution.

EXHIBIT 13.6　　Decision Process when Problem Identification and Problem Solution Are Uncertain:

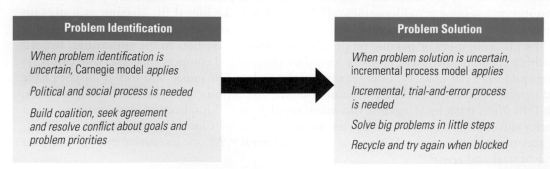

Problem Identification	Problem Solution
When problem identification is uncertain, Carnegie model *applies*	*When problem solution is uncertain,* incremental process model *applies*
Political and social process is needed	Incremental, trial-and-error process is needed
Build coalition, seek agreement and resolve conflict about goals and problem priorities	Solve big problems in little steps
	Recycle and try again when blocked

Indeed, problem identification and problem solution may not be connected to each other. An idea may be proposed as a solution when no problem is specified. A problem may exist and never generate a solution. Decisions are the outcome of independent streams of events within the organization. The four streams relevant to organizational decision-making are as follows:

1 *Problems*. Problems are points of dissatisfaction with current activities and performance. They represent a gap between desired performance and current activities. Problems are perceived to require attention. However, they are distinct from solutions and choices. A problem may lead to a proposed solution or it may not. Problems may not be solved when solutions are adopted.

2 *Potential solutions*. A solution is an idea somebody proposes for adoption. Such ideas form a flow of alternative solutions through the organization. Ideas may be brought into the organization by new personnel or may be invented by existing personnel. Participants may simply be attracted to certain ideas and push them as logical choices regardless of problems. Attraction to an idea may cause an employee to look for a problem to which the idea can be attached and, hence, justified. The point is that solutions exist independent of problems.

3 *Participants*. Organization participants are employees who come and go throughout the organization. People are hired, reassigned and fired. Participants vary widely in their ideas, perception of problems, experience, values and training. The problems and solutions recognized by one manager will differ from those recognized by another manager.

4 *Choice opportunities*. Choice opportunities are occasions when an organization usually makes a decision. They occur when contracts are signed, people are hired or a new product is authorized. They also occur when the right mix of participants, solutions and problems exists. Thus, a manager who happened to learn of a good idea may suddenly become aware of a problem to which it applies and, hence, can provide the organization with a choice opportunity. Match-ups of problems and solutions often result in decisions.

With the concept of four streams, the overall pattern of organizational decision-making takes on a random quality. Problems, solutions, participants and choices all flow through the organization. In one sense, the organization is a large garbage can in which these streams are being stirred, as illustrated in Exhibit 13.7. When a problem, solution and participant happen to connect at one point, a decision may be made and the problem may be solved; but if the solution does not fit the problem, the problem may not be solved.

Thus, when viewing the organization as a whole and considering its high level of uncertainty, one sees problems arise that are not solved and solutions tried that do not work. Organization decisions are disorderly and not the result of a logical, step-by-step sequence. Events may be so ill-defined and complex that decisions, problems and solutions act as independent events. When they connect, some problems are solved, but many are not (see Counterpoint 13.6).[92]

COUNTERPOINT 13.6

The garbage can model illuminates the messy, disorderly quality of much complex decision-making. What it does not do is account for the role of power brokering in the process of proposing solutions, making choices and even ensuring that decisions are not made or indefinitely deferred. In other words, in common with other decision-making approaches discussed in this chapter, including the Carnegie school, it does not shed much light on how power operates to define what and how problems are identified or ignored, and what possible solutions are considered or excluded.

EXHIBIT 13.7   Illustration of Independent Streams of Events in the Garbage Can Model of Decision-making

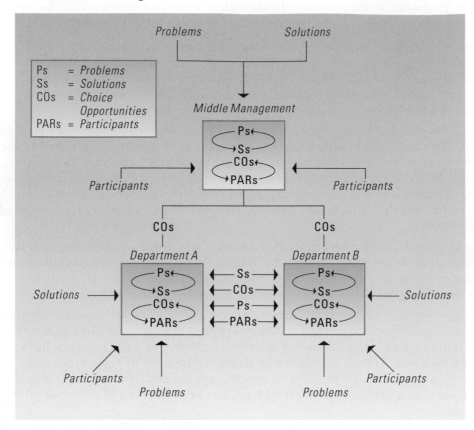

Consequences   There are four specific consequences of the garbage can decision process for organizational decision-making:

1   *Solutions may be proposed even when problems do not exist.* A manager might be sold on an idea and might try to sell it to the rest of the organization. An example was the adoption of computers by many organizations during the 1970s. The computer was an exciting solution and was pushed by both computer manufacturers and systems analysts within organizations. The computer did not solve any problems in those initial applications. Indeed, some computers caused more problems than they solved, although eventually, of course, computers became integral to most business processes.

2   *Choices are made without solving problems.* A choice such as creating a new department may be made with the intention of solving a problem; but, under conditions of high uncertainty, the choice may be incorrect. Moreover, many choices just seem to happen. People decide to quit, the organization's budget is cut, or a new policy bulletin is issued. These choices may be oriented toward problems but do not necessarily solve them.

3   *Problems may persist without being solved.* Organization participants get used to certain problems and give up trying to solve them; or participants may not know how to solve certain problems because the technology is unclear. A university in Canada was placed on probation by the American Association of University Professors because a professor had been denied tenure without due process. The probation was a nagging annoyance that the administrators wanted to remove. Fifteen years later, the nontenured professor died. The probation continues because the university did not acquiesce to the demands of the heirs of

the association to re-evaluate the case. The university would like to solve the problem, but administrators are not sure how, and they do not have the resources to allocate to it. The probation problem persists without a solution.

4 *A few problems are solved.* The decision process does work in the aggregate. In computer simulation models of the garbage can approach, important problems were often resolved. Solutions do connect with appropriate problems and participants so that a good choice is made. Of course, not all problems are resolved when choices are made, but the organization does move in the direction of problem reduction.

The effects of independent streams and the rather chaotic decision processes of the garbage can model can be seen in many organizational processes, including the ways United Nations peacekeeping missions are agreed upon and organized, discussed in the next *In Practice* box.

In the exceptionally complex environment of global governance, a garbage can decision-making model is likely to develop. However the fact that it has worked passably well for international peacekeeping in recent years is no guarantee it will succeed in the future. Success is dependent on a combination of a fluid decision-making environment, openness to policy alternatives, and effective policy 'champions' or entrepreneurs. As the international environment shifts and the United Nations changes over time, the decision-making arena may be less open to experimentation, or worse, policy entrepreneurs may pull less positive options out of the 'primeval policy soup', as was the case with American neoconservatives' attempts to enforce democratic transitions in the Middle East through US military power.[93]

Contingency Decision-Making Framework

This chapter has covered several approaches to organizational decision-making, including management science, the Carnegie model, the incremental decision process model and the garbage can model. It has also discussed rational and intuitive decision processes used by individual managers. Each decision approach is a relatively accurate description of the actual decision process, yet all differ from each other. Management science, for example, reflects a different set of decision assumptions and procedures than does the garbage can model.

One reason for having different approaches is that they appear and have purchase in different organizational situations. Two characteristics of organizations that condition the use of decision approaches are (1) problem consensus and (2) technical knowledge about the means to solve those problems.[94] Analyzing organizations along these two dimensions suggests which approach will be used to make decisions.

IN PRACTICE

United Nations Peacekeeping

The United Nations organization was created in the aftermath of the Second World War as a means to ensure international cooperation, thus avoiding the bloody military disasters of the two great wars of the twentieth century. The UN has many different functions and agencies, dealing with issues as diverse as child poverty, economic development, democratic governance and the environment. However, the UN is perhaps most famous for its 'blue helmet' peacekeeping operations in various troubled parts of the world. During the Cold War, peacekeeping missions were relatively infrequent, small scale, emphasized neutrality between the conflicting parties, and primarily involved monitoring of the situation. Between 1947 and 1988 only 13 missions were undertaken.

As the Cold War ended, the UN became much more active, and much more proactive, stretching traditional peacekeeping principles of consent, neutrality and limited use of force. In only seven years after 1988, 27 missions were organized, more than double the total in the previous 30 years. Furthermore, the new, 'second generation' missions tended to get directly involved in the *enforcement* of peace agreements. The UN started to take an active role in building state institutions after conflict.

Although the change in the UN's role has been generally welcomed as preferable to the Cold War era when human suffering through conflict often went unaddressed because of the stand-off between the US and USSR, until recently there has been little analysis of how this change actually came about. Michael Lipson, a Montreal academic, analyzed the processes underlying the shift to second generation peacekeeping and found that the 'garbage can model' provided a good explanation.

As discussed above, the garbage can model applies in situations of 'organized anarchy'. The UN, with its 190-plus member states and complex decision-making processes, is a classic organized anarchy. During the Cold War this anarchy was tempered, because many states owed allegiance to one or other of the superpowers, meaning that the balance of forces in decision-making was fairly consistent.[95] As the Soviet bloc disintegrated, this certainty of voting patterns disappeared. Although the Americans expected to assume a dominant role, this didn't happen, as states realized they no longer needed the protective umbrella of a superpower, and made their choices more independently. The UN organization itself is not a unitary actor, with its various commissions, agencies and authorities each having their own missions, mandates and particular interests. The UN as a whole, therefore, encounters *problematic preferences*.

The UN also has to deal with *unclear technology* (remember that technology in organization science refers to the way decisions are made). Although in theory an organizational chart could be drawn, in practice decisions are made through ever-changing processes and alliances. Boutros Boutros-Ghali, former UN Secretary-General, admitted that he did not really understand the intricate workings of the organization. Finally, the UN in recent years has had very *fluid participation*. The number of state-members of the UN increased significantly as countries like the former USSR, Yugoslavia and others broke up into smaller units, each with a UN seat. Within the UN administration, waves of internal restructuring have continually changed the bureaucratic dynamics, so that a clear hierarchical decision-making process is absent.

When deciding what to do about conflicts in various parts of the world, the 'organized anarchy' of the UN has been faced with *ambiguity* on several levels, in which 'alternative interpretations or perspectives on the situation are available, and the basis for choosing among them is unclear'. UN decision-makers were unsure about, 'the nature and causes of interstate, ethnic and civil conflicts, the nature of post-Cold War order, the role of the United Nations, and the implications for peacekeeping'.[96] Although the number of conflicts globally has not increased since the end of the Cold War, the expectation that the UN will deal effectively with them has increased greatly.

In the absence of a rational method for deciding *how* to act effectively, UN policy makers dipped into what one analyst calls the 'policy primeval soup'.[97] This soup is made up of all the different peacekeeping options that have been tried, or even proposed and discarded in the past, of international organizations. For example, in planning for the first 'second generation' peacekeeping effort in post-apartheid Namibia at the end of the 1980s, officials looked back as far as the United Nations' predecessor, the League of Nations, which had been given a mandate to govern the disputed Saar region between France and Germany after the First World War. They also explored ambitious earlier UN peacekeeping missions such as in the Congo in the 1960s.

Whereas most of these efforts had been classified as failures, post-Cold War optimism about the possibilities for peace and democratic transformation meant that a mutation and recombination of ideas from the 'policy soup' could be tried by the UN's Transition Assistance Group (UNTAG) for Namibia. The successful outcome of the Namibia transition was an impetus for further peacekeeping interventions that included activities like overseeing disarmament, demobilization and reintegration (DD&R), humanitarian relief and working to develop the political foundations for new state institutions like governments and parliaments. In the late 1980s and early 1990s, these new peacekeeping approaches were tried in various countries including Cambodia, Nicaragua, Haiti, El Salvador and Angola.

▶

Not all the 'second-generation' peacekeeping initiatives tried by the UN have been successful; the long-running failure to establish a stable government in Somalia, and the inability to bring about sustainable peace in the eastern Democratic Republic of Congo are cases in point. However, on the whole, a more active and intense involvement of the UN in not only monitoring peace agreements but also through helping in rehabilitation and building stable post-conflict institutions, has reduced the dangers of violence reigniting, and has improved the lives of people affected by conflict.

Problem Consensus

Problem consensus refers to the agreement among managers about the nature of a problem or opportunity and about which goals and outcomes to pursue. This variable ranges from complete agreement to complete disagreement. When managers agree, there is little uncertainty – the problems and goals of the organization are clear, and so are standards of performance. When managers disagree, organization direction and performance expectations are in dispute, creating a situation of high uncertainty. Problem uncertainty frequently occurs over competing visions for the use of scarce natural resources. For example, several different interests conflicted over use of a mountainous area in Switzerland. Recreational users wanted access to skiing and hiking opportunities, which would generate tourism revenues. The area was also the site of an important international highway, and there was pressure from road planners and users to expand the road. Finally, environmentalists felt that this fragile area with unique biodiversity needed to be left alone to protect its habitat. Advocates for all three positions could be found within the local government.[98]

?

ONLINE COUNTERPOINT 13.11

Problem consensus tends to be low when organizations are differentiated, as described in Chapter 5. This would apply where different departments within the same government have different missions, as in the Swiss case above. Recall that uncertain environments cause organizational departments to differentiate from one another in goals and attitudes to specialize in specific sectors. This differentiation leads to disagreement and conflict, so managers must make a special effort to build coalitions during decision-making. For example, the American space agency NASA has been criticized for failing to identify problems with the *Columbia* space shuttle that might have prevented the February 2003 disaster. Part of the reason was high differentiation and conflicting opinions between safety managers and scheduling managers, in which pressure to launch on time overrode safety concerns. In addition, after the launch, engineers three times requested – and were denied – better photos to assess the damage from a piece of foam debris that struck the shuttle's left wing just seconds after launch. Investigations now indicate that the damage caused by the debris may have been the primary physical cause of the explosion. Mechanisms for hearing dissenting opinions and building coalitions can improve decision-making at NASA and other organizations dealing with complex problems.[99]

Problem consensus is especially important for the problem identification stage of decision-making. When problems are clear and agreed on, they provide clear standards and expectations for performance. When problems are not agreed on, problem identification is uncertain and management attention must be focused on gaining agreement about goals and priorities.

Technical Knowledge about Solutions

Technical knowledge refers to understanding and agreement about how to solve problems and reach organizational goals. This variable can range from complete agreement and certainty to complete disagreement and uncertainty about cause–effect relationships leading to problem solution. For example, international organization managers disagreed with each other about how to achieve some of the Millennium Development Goals, as discussed in Chapter 3. On the universal education goals, World Bank and International Monetary Fund managers argue that the problem is that teachers are too costly, and they have put pressure on developing country governments to introduce low-priced contract teachers. Experts at UN agencies like the United Nations Childrens Fund (UNICEF) and UNESCO believe that this will be counterproductive in producing more education but of a lower standard, and that holistic approaches employing community empowerment and lifelong learning strategies will have a better long-term result.[100] The disagreement about causes and solutions has led to conflicting policy implementation in developing countries.

When means are well understood, the appropriate alternatives can be identified and calculated with some degree of certainty. When means are poorly understood, potential solutions are ill-defined and uncertain. Intuition, judgement and trial and error become the basis for decisions.

Contingency Framework

Exhibit 13.8 describes the contingency decision-making framework, which brings together the two dimensions of problem consensus and technical knowledge about solutions. Each cell represents an organizational situation that is appropriate for the decision-making approaches described in this chapter.

Cell 1   In cell 1 of Exhibit 13.8, rational decision procedures are used because problems are agreed on and cause–effect relationships are well understood, so there is little uncertainty. Decisions can be made in a computational manner. Alternatives can be identified and the best solution adopted through analysis and calculations. The rational models described earlier in this chapter, both for individuals and for the organization, are appropriate when problems and the means for solving them are well defined.

Cell 2   In cell 2, there is high uncertainty about problems and priorities, so bargaining and compromise are used to reach consensus. Tackling one problem might mean the organization must postpone action on other issues. The priorities given to respective problems are decided through discussion, debate and coalition building.

Managers in this situation should use broad participation to achieve consensus in the decision process. Opinions should be surfaced and discussed until compromise is reached. The organization will not otherwise move forward as an integrated unit. In the Swiss mountain region case, a strategy was developed so that the interests of the different users of the area could be reconciled.

The Carnegie model applies when there is dissension about organizational problems. When groups within the organization disagree, or when the organization is in conflict with constituencies (government regulators, suppliers, unions), bargaining and negotiation are required. The bargaining strategy is especially relevant to the problem identification stage of the decision process. Once bargaining and negotiation are completed, the organization will have support for one direction.

Cell 3   In a cell 3 situation, problems and standards of performance are certain, but alternative technical solutions are vague and uncertain. Techniques to solve a problem are ill defined and poorly understood. When an individual manager faces this situation, intuition will be the decision guideline. The manager will rely on past experience and judgement to make a decision. Rational, analytical approaches are not effective because the alternatives cannot be identified and calculated. Hard facts and accurate information are not available.

The incremental decision process model reflects trial and error on the part of the organization. Once a problem is identified, a sequence of small steps enables the organization to learn a solution. As new problems arise, the organization may recycle back to an earlier point and start over. Eventually, over a period of months or years, the organization will acquire sufficient experience to solve the problem in a satisfactory way.

EXHIBIT 13.8 Contingency Framework for Using Decision Models

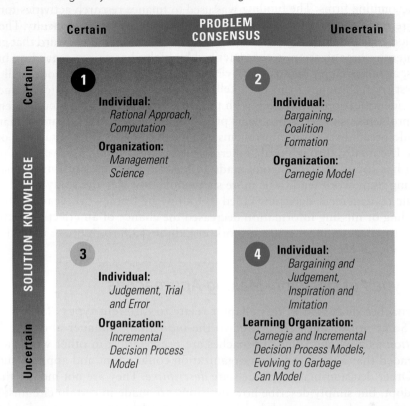

The UK-based Pret A Manger fast food chain, featured in Chapter 8, provides an example of a cell 3 situation. Co-founders Julian Metcalfe and Sinclair Beecham didn't know exactly what format would work best. They wanted something more flexible than a traditional plate service, and eventually came up with a winning idea, the boxed take-out, an approach long popular in Japan with its 'Bento boxes'. They also tried all kinds of different fillings before realizing that, actually, customers wanted a lot of choice, unlike many fast-food chains that focus on a few staples.[101]

The situation in cell 3, of senior managers agreeing about problems but not knowing how to solve them, occurs frequently in business organizations. If managers use incremental decisions in such situations, they will usually eventually acquire the technical knowledge to accomplish goals and solve problems.

Cell 4 The situation in cell 4, characterized by high uncertainty about both problems and solutions, is difficult for decision-making. An individual manager making a decision under this high level of uncertainty can employ techniques from both cell 2 and cell 3. The manager can attempt to build a coalition to establish goals and priorities and use judgement, intuition or trial and error to solve problems. Additional techniques, such as inspiration and imitation, also may be required. Inspiration refers to an innovative, creative solution that is not reached by logical means. Inspiration sometimes comes like a flash of insight, but – similar to intuition – it is often based on deep knowledge and understanding of a problem that the unconscious mind has had time to mull over.[102] Imitation means adopting a decision tried elsewhere in the hope that it will work in this situation.

For example, in one university accounting department, faculty members were unhappy with their current circumstances but could not decide on the direction the department should take. Some faculty members wanted a greater research orientation, whereas others wanted greater orientation toward business firms and accounting applications. The disagreement about goals was compounded because neither group was sure about the best technique for achieving its goals. The ultimate solution was inspirational on the part of the dean. An accounting research centre was established with funding from major accounting firms. The funding was used to finance research activities for faculty interested in basic research and to provide contact with business firms for other faculty. The solution provided a common goal and unified people within the department to work toward that goal.

When an entire organization is characterized by high uncertainty regarding both problems and solutions, as in learning organizations, elements of the garbage can model will appear. Managers may first try techniques from both cells 2 and 3, but logical decision sequences starting with problem identification and ending with problem solution will not occur. Potential solutions will precede problems as often as problems precede solutions. In this situation, managers should encourage widespread discussion of problems and idea proposals to facilitate the opportunity to make choices. Eventually, through trial and error, the organization will solve some problems.

Research has found that decisions made following the prescriptions of the contingency decision-making framework tend to be more successful. However, the study noted that nearly six of ten strategic management decisions failed to follow the framework, leading to a situation in which misleading or missing information decreased the chance of an effective decision choice.[103] Managers can use the contingency framework in Exhibit 13.8 to improve the likelihood of successful organizational decisions.

Different Types of Decision-Making Approaches

**ONLINE
COUNTERPOINT 13.12**

The approaches discussed in this chapter relate to different types and levels of decision-making. Some approaches are geared to the *individual* manager and others apply to an *organization* as a whole. Some approaches are *prescriptive*; in other words an approach is recommended that a manager or an organization could adopt and apply in suitable circumstances. Other decision-making models are *descriptive*. They are not models that a company should adopt, but simply describe how decisions are made in certain circumstances. To give a couple of examples, a rational decision-making model applies to an *individual* and is *prescriptive*; it is a model a manager can choose to follow. On the other hand, the garbage can model applies to an *organization*, and is *descriptive*; organizations do not choose to apply a garbage can model; it just happens, as discussed in the example of United Nations peacemaking operations. Exhibit 13.9 categorizes the different models we have discussed in this chapter according to the individual/organization and prescriptive/descriptive criteria.

EXHIBIT 13.9   Summary of decision-making models

Approach	Individual or Organizational	Prescriptive or descriptive
Rational	Individual	Prescriptive
Bounded rationality	Individual	Descriptive
Management Science	Organizational	Prescriptive
Carnegie	Mainly organizational	Descriptive
Incremental	Organizational	Descriptive
Combining Carnegie and incremental	Organizational	Descriptive
Garbage can	Organizational	Descriptive
Contingency	Individual	Prescriptive

Dirk Akkermans, Assistant Professor, Department of International Economics and Business, Faculty of Economics and Business, University of Groningen, the Netherlands.

Special Decision Circumstances

In a highly competitive world beset by global competition and rapid change, decision-making seldom fits the traditional rational, analytical model. Today's managers have to make high-stakes decisions more often and more quickly than ever before in an environment that is increasingly less predictable. For example, interviews with CEOs in high-tech industries found that they strive to use some type of rational process, but the uncertainty and change in the industry often make that approach impossible or unsuccessful. The way these managers actually reach decisions is through a complex interaction with other managers, subordinates, environmental factors and organizational events.[104]

Three issues of particular concern for today's decision-makers are coping with high-velocity environments, learning from decision mistakes and avoiding escalating commitment.

BRIEFCASE 13.7

High-Velocity Environments

In some industries today, the rate of competitive and technological change is so extreme that market data are either unavailable or obsolete, strategic windows open and shut quickly, perhaps within a few months, and the cost of poor decisions is company failure. Research has examined how successful companies make decisions in these high-velocity environments, especially to understand whether organizations abandon rational approaches or have time for incremental implementation.[105]

A comparison of successful with unsuccessful decisions in high-velocity environments found the following patterns:

- Successful decision-makers tracked information in real time to develop a deep and intuitive grasp of the business. Two to three intense meetings per week with all key players were usual. Decision-makers tracked operating statistics about cash, scrap, backlog, work in process and shipments to constantly feel the pulse of what was happening. Unsuccessful firms were more concerned with future planning and forward-looking information, with only a loose grip on immediate happenings.

- During a major decision, successful companies began immediately to build multiple alternatives. Implementation of alternatives sometimes ran in parallel before they finally settled on a final choice. Companies that made decisions slowly developed just one alternative, moving to another only after the first one failed.

- Fast, successful decision-makers sought advice from everyone and depended heavily on one or two savvy, trusted colleagues as counsellors. Slow companies were unable to build trust and agreement among the best people.

- Fast companies involved everyone in the decision and tried for consensus; but if consensus did not emerge, the top manager made the choice and moved ahead. Waiting for everyone to be on board created more delays than was warranted. Slow companies delayed decisions to achieve a uniform consensus.

- Fast, successful choices were well integrated with other decisions and the overall strategic direction of the company. Less successful choices considered the decision in isolation from other decisions; the decision was made in the abstract.[106]

When speed matters, a slow decision is as ineffective as the wrong decision. As we discussed in Chapter 12, speed is a crucial competitive weapon in a growing number of industries, and companies can learn to make decisions quickly. To improve the chances of a good decision under high-velocity conditions, some organizations stimulate constructive conflict through a technique called point–counterpoint, which divides decision-makers into two groups and assigns them different, often competing responsibilities.[107] The groups develop

ONLINE
COUNTERPOINT 13.13

and exchange proposals and debate options until they arrive at a common set of understand-ings and recommendations. Groups can often make better decisions because multiple and diverse opinions are considered. In the face of complexity and uncertainty, the more people who have a say in the decision-making, the better. At the leading computer chip maker Intel Corp., the decision-making process typically involves people from several different areas and levels of hierar-chy, 'jousting with one another about the pros and cons of this or that', says Craig Barrett, board chairman of Intel from 1998-2005.[108]

In group decision-making, a consensus may not always be reached, but the exercise gives everyone a chance to consider options and state their opinions, and it gives top managers a broader understanding. Typically, those involved support the final choice. Once a decision has been made at Intel, for example, it is everyone's responsibility to be involved and commit, even if they disagree. As Barrett says, 'No backbiting, no second-guessing. We make a decision, we charge ahead.'[109]

Decision Mistakes and Learning

Organizational decisions result in many errors, especially when made in conditions of great uncer-tainty. Managers simply cannot accurately determine or predict which alternative will solve a problem. In these cases, the organization must make the decision – and take the risk – often in the spirit of trial and error. If an alternative fails, they can learn from it and try another alternative that better fits the situation. Each failure provides new information and insight. The point for managers is to move ahead with the decision process despite the potential for mistakes. 'Chaotic action is preferable to orderly inaction'.[110]

In some organizations, managers are encouraged to instil a climate of experimentation to facilitate creative decision-making. If one idea fails, another idea should be tried. Failure often lays the groundwork for success, such as when technicians at 3M developed Post-it Notes based on a failed product – a not-very-sticky glue.

Stanley Kalms (properly speaking, Lord Kalms of Edgware), whose Dixon's Retail (before 2010, DSGi) group is the largest electronics retailer in Europe, freely acknowledges that many of his efforts have fallen flat. Since his dad started out with a single small photography shop in Southend, UK, the evolving family-led company has constantly tried new business angles. Many of his initiatives worked, but others haven't. Kalms was the first retailer to focus heav-ily on marketing products from the burgeoning Asian electronics industry back in the 1970s, when sturdy but costly German brands like Leica and Grundig still ruled European markets. Freeserve, his early entry into internet service providers (ISPs), also paid off handsomely when he sold out to French giant Wanadoo in 2000 for £1.65 billion. But the 1987 purchase of Silo, one of the early US 'big box' retailers, was a failure, and he bailed out in 1993 shortly before the US chain went under.[111] The acquisition of the UK's biggest electronics chain, Curry's, in 1984, has been a success, but the shift to online purchasing in the early 2000s forced Dixon's Retail to cut back on its retail presence and try to quickly build online success against internet specialists like Amazon. The Europe-wide recession that began in 2008 hit Dixon's Retail hard, with the company running up substantial losses in four of the five years between 2008 and 2012. However, the company looks to be weathering the storm, and in the process has seen off two major competitors; American chain Best Buy, which tried to break into the UK market, but gave up in 2011, while long term rival Comet went bankrupt in 2012. In 2014 Dixon's merged with mobile phone retailer Carphone Warehouse, creating a dominant technology retailer. Ini-tial results were positive, with profits of £77 million announced in 2015. Kalms has stepped aside from day-to-day involvement in the company while remaining Honorary President, but the Dixon's empire still seems to be staying true to his motto: 'Bend the rules! Rules are for bending. There are only two rules that should never be bent: say what you mean, mean what you say; and don't steal.'[112,113,114]

Only by making mistakes can managers and organizations go through the process of decision learning and acquire sufficient experience and knowledge to perform more effectively in the future. Sinclair Beecham of Pret A Manger says, 'It's important not to kill ideas in the making. We've made zillions of mistakes, yet making and recognizing mistakes is the way we've gone forward.'

Escalating Commitment

A much more dangerous mistake is to persist in a course of action when it is failing, a tendency referred to as **escalating commitment**. Research suggests that managers often continue to invest time and money in a solution despite strong evidence that it is not working. Two explanations are given for why managers escalate commitment to a failing decision. The first is that they block or distort negative information when they are personally responsible for a negative decision. In some cases, they continue to throw good money after bad even when a strategy seems incorrect and goals are not being met.[115]

BRIEFCASE 13.8

A second explanation for escalating commitment to a failing decision is that consistency and persistence are valued in contemporary society. Consistent managers are considered better leaders than those who switch around from one course of action to another. Even though organizations learn through trial and error, organizational norms value consistency. These norms may result in a course of action being maintained, resources being squandered and learning being inhibited. Escalating commitment is a common issue where a company has already sunk a lot of money, and particularly managers' passion, into a business idea. Guy Laliberté, founder of the world famous Cirque du Soleil circus in Québec, Canada, had long dreamed of having an iconic headquarters building in the circus's home town of Montreal.[116] In conjunction with the provincial lottery agency, Loto Quebec, Laliberté drew up plans for a huge Cirque-themed casino and hotel, which would be the centrepiece of a redevelopment of the city's rundown waterfront area. However, the proposal drew strong criticism from anti-poverty groups, whose objections included fears the casino would worsen gambling problems among the poor. Cirque du Soleil had no financial downside on the project, but the bad publicity was one of the first big threats to the company's positive reputation. Despite strong backing from Montreal's business community, after a couple of years of wrangling, Laliberté decided to pull out. It was a big blow to the company's development strategy and to Laliberté's ego; he had even restructured Cirque and hired a top private sector manager to execute the company's shift beyond a circus into operator of entertainment complexes. But ultimately, Laliberté had identified a dangerous escalating commitment to a losing project, and pulled the plug in time.

Failure to admit a mistake and adopt a new course of action is far worse than an attitude that tolerates mistakes to encourage learning. The next time Cirque du Soleil had a chance to develop an entertainment complex, this time in Miami, they quickly identified the same type of barriers that they had seen in Montreal, and decided to end their involvement much earlier in the process.

Based on what has been said about decision-making in this chapter, one can expect companies to be ultimately successful in their decision-making by adopting a learning approach toward solutions. They will make mistakes along the way, but they will resolve uncertainty through the trial-and-error process.

Summary and Interpretation

The most important idea in this chapter is that most organizational decisions are not made in a logical, rational manner. Most decisions do not begin with the careful analysis of a problem, followed by systematic analysis of alternatives, and finally implementation of a solution. On the contrary, decision processes are characterized by conflict, coalition building, trial and error, speed and mistakes. Managers operate under many constraints that limit rationality; hence, intuition and hunch often are the criteria for choice.

Another important idea is that individuals make decisions, but organizational decisions are not made by a single individual. Organizational decision-making is a social process. Only in rare circumstances do managers analyze problems and find solutions by themselves. Many problems are not clear, so widespread discussion and coalition building take place. Once goals and priorities are set, alternatives to achieve those goals can be tried. When a manager does make an individual decision, it is often a small part of a larger decision process. Organizations solve big problems through a series of small steps. A single manager may initiate one step but should be aware of the larger decision process to which it belongs.

The greatest amount of conflict and coalition building occurs when problems are not agreed on. Priorities must be established to indicate which goals are important and what problems should be solved first. If a manager attacks a problem other people do not agree with, the manager will lose support for the solution to be implemented. Thus, time and activity should be spent building a coalition in the problem identification stage of decision-making. Then the organization can move toward solutions. Under conditions of low technical knowledge, the solution unfolds as a series of incremental trials that will gradually lead to an overall solution.

A novel and challenging decision-making approach is the garbage can model. This model describes how decision processes can seem almost random in highly organic organizations. Decisions, problems, ideas and people flow through organizations and mix together in various combinations. Some problems may never be solved, but many are, and this enables the organization to move toward maintaining and improving its level of performance.

Finally, decisions may have to be taken quickly which means staying in immediate touch with operations and the environment. In an uncertain world, mistakes will be made, through processes of trial and error. Encouraging trial-and-error incrementalism can facilitate organizational learning. Unwillingness to change from a failing course of action can, on the other hand, have serious negative consequences for an organization. Norms for consistency and the desire to prove one's decision correct can lead to continued investment in a useless course of action.

KEY CONCEPTS

bounded rationality perspective	garbage can model	management science approach	problem identification
Carnegie model	high-velocity environments	nonprogrammed decisions	problem solution
coalition	imitation	organizational decision-making	problemistic search
contingency decision-making framework	incremental decision process model	organized anarchy	programmed decisions
decision learning	inspiration	point–counterpoint	rational approach
escalating commitment	intuitive decision-making	problem consensus	satisficing
			technical knowledge

Discussion Questions

1 When you are faced with choosing between several valid options, how do you typically make your decision? How do you think managers typically choose between several options? What are the similarities between your decision process and what you think managers do?

2 A professional economist once told his class, 'An individual decision-maker should process all relevant information and select the economically rational alternative'. Do you agree? Why or why not?

3 Do you think intuition is a valid way to make important business decisions? Why or why not? Can you

think of a time when you used intuition to make a decision?

4   The Carnegie model emphasizes the need for a political coalition in the decision-making process. When and why are coalitions necessary?

5   What are the three major phases in Mintzberg's incremental decision process model? Why might managers recycle through one or more phases of the model?

6   An organization theorist once told her class, 'Organizations never make big decisions. They make small decisions that eventually add up to a big decision.' Explain the logic behind this statement.

7   How would you make a decision to select a building site for a new waste-treatment plant in the Philippines? Where would you start with this complex decision, and what steps would you take? Explain which decision model in the chapter best describes your approach.

8   Why should managers in high-velocity environments be encouraged to worry more about the present than the future? Discuss.

9   Describe the four streams of events in the garbage can model of decision-making. Do you think those streams are independent of each other? Why?

10 Why are decision mistakes usually accepted in organizations but penalized in college courses and exams that are designed to train managers?

Chapter 13 Workbook Decision Styles

Think of some recent decisions that have influenced your life. Choose two significant decisions that you made and two decisions that other people made. Fill out the following table, using Exhibit 13.8 to determine decision styles.

Questions

1   How can a decision approach influence the outcome of the decision? What happens when the approach fits the decision? When it doesn't fit?

2   How can you know which approach is best?

Adapted by Dorothy Marcic from 'Action Assignment' in Jennifer M. Howard and Lawrence M. Miller, *Team Management* (Miller Consulting Group, 1994), 205.

CASE FOR ANALYSIS 13.1

Policy Models, Rationality, Deliberative Approaches and Co-production in Government Decision Making

Governments globally are concerned about the ways in which public policy decisions are taken and are often placed in a dilemma between making the best use of public funds through rational decision-making and the need to maintain the popular support of the public through consensus seeking decision-making.

Policy models help to promote a better understanding of the nature of policy. If policy-makers pursued and were capable of complete rationality they would produce "perfect" policies. However, most policy-makers are not capable of complete rationality, and many have developed more incremental approaches to policy-making. A useful approach to policy models is to divide them into three types:

a. Ideal Type
This does not exist in real life, but can help understanding and explanation by exploring underlying ideas or concepts (such as "rationality").

b. Descriptive Model
This relates to a real-life situation, and its purposes are those of description, exploration and understanding.

c. Prescriptive Model
This relates to what is desirable. It is concerned with what ought to be rather than with what is.

Most policy theorists employ models which emphasise the process of policy making and the cyclical nature of that process over time. Some models are prescriptive, some are descriptive. Certain theorists use a "mixed model" which combines both descriptive and prescriptive elements. Simon's approach is to consider rationality as a prescriptive idea but then to argue that more policy-makers should move towards the rational policy model. Lindblom believes that incrementalism is the way policy is formulated, and argues that it should remain so.

The value of public policy models is that they are based on studies of decision-making in a public services context unlike many of the contemporary 'business-like' management decision-making techniques. Government decision-takers try to combine the best of public policy analysis with business-like approaches contextualised for the public sector.

The concept of evidence-based policy and decision is now a standard of best practice in Government. Increased public scrutiny and accountability has created a heightened awareness of the need for politicians and decision makers to have a range of evidence to support policy development and decision-making in the public sector.

Deliberative methods are commonly described as a hybrid between consultation and research. They aim to involve stakeholders in decision-making in a meaningful way by providing an opportunity for participants to find out more about an issue, consider relevant evidence and discuss this evidence with other participants before presenting their views. Involvement in deliberative methods has been seen as potentially more satisfying and beneficial for participants. In addition, there is an increasing interest in openness, accountability, stakeholder involvement and co-ownership of governmental decisions.

Common methods include **Citizens Juries** or **Panels** where Jurors or Panelists hear from a variety of experts and cross-examine them about the topic and present their findings as a report and/or an oral presentation at the end of the event. **Consensus** Conferences also facilitate discussion between the public and experts and usually last for several days. The media play a key part in this decision-making process and are invited to attend the event. **Deliberative Workshops** are similar to focus groups although there is more time devoted to the deliberation of the decision. Another approach **is Deliberative Polling** which is a quantitative assessment of people's opinions before the deliberation. Participants are then provided with in-depth information on the subject matter, participate in discussions and have the opportunity to ask questions. After deliberation participants' opinions are measured once again and any differences between the two are highlighted. **Deliberative Mapping** combines quantitative and qualitative methods to assess how participants rate different policy options against a set of defined criteria. The emphasis

▶

of the process is not on integrating expert and public voices but understanding the different perspectives each offer to a policy process.

Co-production is a relationship where professionals and citizens share power to design, plan and deliver support together, recognizing that both partners have vital contributions to make in order to improve quality of life for people and communities. Genuine co-production is not involvement, consultation and engagement – it goes further than seeking people's advice or asking their opinion and then reverting back to the state to deliver.

Co-production relates to the generation of human and social capital and to strengthening the 'core economy', and sees these aims as the central roles of all public services. It therefore has potentially transformative implications for the way public services are delivered and how the public sector thinks about power, resources, responsibility, accountability and outcomes.

Questions

1 Is governmental decision-making programmed or non-programmed? Explain your answer.

2 What would be the disadvantages of pure rationality in government decision-making?

3 What are the advantages and disadvantages of public involvement in governmental decision-making?

Notes

1. 'CEO Sally Macdonald quits Oroton shortly after profit warning', *Australian Business Review*, August 14, 2013, accessed at www.theaustralian.com.au/business/companies/ceo-sally-macdonald-quits-oroton-shortly-after-profit-warning/story-fn91v9q3-1226696848532; Esther Han, 'Oroton, Pumpkin Patch and Lorna Jane shamed for low transparency of supply chains', *Sydney Morning Herald*, April 20, 2016, accessed at www.smh.com.au/business/consumer-affairs/oroton-pumpkin-patch-and-lorna-jane-shamed-for-low-transparency-of-supply-chains-20160420-goauoh.html; Sue Mitchell, 'Oroton first-half profit rebounds 73 per cent', *Sydney Monring Herald*, March 17, 2016, accessed at www.smh.com.au/business/retail/oroton-firsthalf-profit-rebounds-73-per-cent-20160316-gnktq9.html; Gershon Nimbalker, Jasmin Mawson and Claire Harris, The 2016 Australian Fashion Report, Baptist World Aid Australia, accessed at www.baptistworldaid.org.au/assets/Be-Fair-Section/FashionReport.pdf

2. Carol J. Loomis, 'Why Carly's Big Bet Is Failing', *Fortune* (February 7, 2005), 50–64; David Bank and Joann S. Lublin, 'For HP, No Shortage of Ideas; Turnaround Experts Offer Wide Range of Conflicting Strategies', *Asian Wall Street Journal* (February 14, 2005), M5; and James B. Stewart, 'Common Sense: Finding a New CEO Won't Help Unless HP Finds New Products', *The Wall Street Journal* (February 23, 2005), D3.

3. 'Hewlett Packard Company', *Hoover's Company Reports – In-Depth Report*, November 10, 2008, HP anuncia mais 9000 despedimentos na Europa, *EuroNews*, 25 September, 2008.

4. 'PC sales down 7%, Dell toppled in the US', *Guardian Unlimited*, April 16, 2009.

5. George Anders, June 10, 2013, 'The Reluctant Savior Of Hewlett-Packard', *Forbes;* Ashlee Vance, August 9, 2010, 'Oracle Chief Faults H.P. Board for Forcing Hurd's Resignation', *The New York Times*.

6. 'Sir Philip Green has big questions to answer over BHS', *The Observer*, May 1, 2016, accessed at https://www.theguardian.com/business/2016/may/01/philip-green-bhs-big-questions-answer-parliament

7. 'A year on from ABN Amro Goodwin is facing flak', *Birmingham Post*, 24 April, 2008; Moody's downgrades ratings of Royal Bank of Scotland to Aa1/B', *Moody's Investors Service Press Release*, 27 June, 2008; Erikka Askeland 'RBS admits 'deal too far' as shareholders vote for bail-out', *The Scotsman*, 21 November, 2008; 'Fred is shredded', *Irish Independent*, 18 October, 2008; Victor Mallet, 'Still standing', *Financial Times*, 16 December, 2008.

8. Adam Horowitz, Mark Athitakis, Mark Lasswell and Owen Thomas, '101 Dumbest Moments in Business', *Business 2.0* (January–February 2005), 103–112.

9. *BBC News*, 31 January, 2012, 'Former RBS boss Sir Fred Goodwin to lose knighthood'.

10. 'NXP Named by Business Watch as One of the Top Ten Fast Reaction Companies of 2008', *ENP Newswire*, 12 December 2008.

11. Quentin Hardy, 'Meg Whitman Seeks Reinvention for HP as It Prepares for Split', *New York Times*, October 30, 2015, accessed at www.nytimes.com/2015/10/31/technology/meg-whitman-seeks-reinvention-for-hp-as-it-prepares-for-split.html

12. Saul Hansell, 'Meg Whitman and eBay, Net Survivors', *The New York Times* (May 5, 2002), 17; Michael V. Copeland and Owen Thomas, 'Hits (& Misses)', *Business 2.0* (January–February 2004), 126; Carlos Ghosn, 'Saving the Business without Losing the Company', *Harvard Business Review* (January 2002), 37–45.

13. 'The top ten viral ad campaigns: Adverts so good people choose to watch them? Send them to their friends, even?', *Times Online*, July 25, 2007; Claire Beale, 'Can you create a buzz around a sex toy without saying what it is?', *The Independent*, 29 September, 2008.

14. Charles Lindblom, 'The Science of "Muddling Through,"' *Public Administration Review* 29 (1954), 79–88.

15. Herbert A. Simon, *The New Science of Management Decision* (Englewood Cliffs, NJ: Prentice-Hall, 1960), 1–8.

16. Paul J. H. Schoemaker and J. Edward Russo, 'A Pyramid of Decision Approaches', *California Management Review* (Fall 1993), 9–31.

17. P. Torterotot, M. Rebelo, C. Werey and J. Craveiro (2004), 'Rehabilitation of water networks: analysis of the decision-making processes', paper presented at 4th IWA World Water Congress – Marrakech, 19–24 September.

18. Dan Milmo, 'Tube repairs at risk as cost overrun hits £750m', *Guardian*, 19 April, 2007; Pippa Crerar, 'Tube Partnership Investigated Over Metronet Collapse', *The Evening Standard*, 29 August, 2007.

19. Rick Brooks, 'Sealing Their Fate; A Deal with Target Put Lid on Revival at Tupperware', *The Wall Street Journal* (February 18, 2004), A1, A9.

20. Michael Pacanowsky, 'Team Tools for Wicked Problems', *Organizational Dynamics* 23, No. 3 (Winter 1995), 36–51.

21. 'Canada's National Sport not so Canadian', *Canada NewsWire*, 27 November, 2008; 'New goal for NHL Jerseys', *The Hamilton Spectator*, 29 November, 2008.

22. Earnest R. Archer, 'How to Make a Business Decision: An Analysis of Theory and Practice', *Management Review* 69 (February 1980), 54–61; and Boris Blai, 'Eight Steps to Successful Problem Solving', *Supervisory Management* (January 1986), 7–9.

23. Christopher Hosford, 'Cablecom mines text to satisfy clients', *B to B*, 14 July, 2008; Cablecom offers new services, *Inside Satellite TV*, 27 August, 2008; 'Cablecom brings out HD PVR', *Broadband TV News,* 5 November, 2008.

24. Adapted from Archer, 'How to Make a Business Decision', 59–61.

25. James W. Dean Jr and Mark P. Sharfman, 'Procedural Rationality in the Strategic Decision-Making Process', *Journal of Management Studies* 30 (1993), 587–610.

26. Michelle Perry, 'Outsourcing – Scrutinised, demonized', *Accountancy,* 22 January, 2007; Nancy Feig, 'Transformational Outsourcing: Strategies for the 21st Century', *Bank Systems + Technology*, 1 August, 2007; 'The recipe for success', *Computer Weekly*, 10 July, 2007; 'Outsourcing is making its mark', *Computing*, 7 November, 2007; Ephraim Schwartz, 'Painful lessons from IT outsourcing gone bad', *InfoWorld Daily News*, 25 August, 2008.

27. Chris Lonsdale (2006), 'Risk Mitigation and Outsourcing: Alternative Models for Managing Supply Risk', in Peter Barrar and Roxane Gervais (eds), *Global Outsourcing Strategies: An International Reference on Effective Outsourcing Relationships,* London, Gower.

28. Bo Nielsen, Torben Pedersen and Jacob Pyndt (2008), 'Coloplast A/S: Organizational Challenges in Offshoring', Case 9B08M031, London ON, Richard Ivey School of Business.

29. Farnaz Fassihi, Greg Jaffe, Yaroslav Trofimov, Carla Anne Robbins and Yochi J. Dreazen, 'Winning the Peace; Early US Decisions on Iraq Now Haunt American Efforts', *The Wall Street Journal* (April 19, 2004), A1, A14.

30. MTI-EcoInfo, 8 March, 2013, 'Ötmilliárdos fejlesztés a Coloplast magyarországi gyáraiban'; Colorfast, *Corporate Responsibility Report, 2011/2012*, Humlebaek, Colorfast, accessed at http://www.coloplast.com/Documents/CSR/Coloplast_CR_Report_2012.pdf.

31. Richard Higgs, 'Coloplast doubles size of Hungarian medical products plant', *Plastics News*, April 27, 2015, accessed at www.plasticsnews.com/article/20150427/NEWS/150429927/coloplast-doubles-size-of-hungarian-medical-products-plant; Coloplast, accessed at http://www.forbes.com/companies/coloplast/

32. Art Kleiner, 'Core Group Therapy', *Strategy & Business*, issue 27 (Second Quarter, 2002), 26–31.

33. Irving L. Janis, *Crucial Decisions: Leadership in Policymaking and Crisis Management* and (New York: The Free Press, 1989); and Paul C. Nutt, 'Flexible Decision Styles and the Choices of Top Executives', *Journal of Management Studies* 30 (1993), 695–721.

34. Herbert A. Simon, 'Making Management Decisions: The Role of Intuition and Emotion', *Academy of Management Executive* 1 (February, 1987), 57–64; and Daniel J. Eisenberg, 'How Senior Managers Think', *Harvard Business Review* 62 (November–December 1984), 80–90.

35. Sefan Wally and J. Robert Baum, 'Personal and Structural Determinants of the Pace of Strategic Decision Making', *Academy of Management Journal* 37, No. 4 (1994), 932–956; and Orlando Behling and Norman L. Eckel, 'Making Sense Out of Intuition', *Academy of Management Executive* 5, No. 1 (1991), 46–54.

36. Gary Klein, *Intuition at Work: Why Developing Your Gut Instincts Will Make You Better at What You Do* (New York: Doubleday, 2002); Milorad M. Novicevic, Thomas J. Hench and Daniel A. Wren, '"Playing By Ear … In an Incessant Din of Reasons": Chester Barnard and the History of Intuition in Management Thought', *Management Decision* 40, No. 10 (2002), 992–1002; Alden M. Hayashi, 'When to Trust Your Gut', *Harvard Business Review* (February 2001), 59–65; Brian R. Reinwald, 'Tactical Intuition', *Military Review* 80, No. 5 (September–October 2000), 78–88; Thomas A. Stewart, 'How to Think with Your Gut', *Business 2.0* (November 2002), accessed at http://cognitive-edge.com/uploads/articles/49_Thinking_with_your_Gut_(T_Stewart_article_in_Bus_2).pdf on September 17, 2013; Bill Breen, 'What's Your Intuition?' *Fast Company* (September 2000), 290–300; and Henry Mintzberg and Frances Westley, 'Decision Making: It's Not What You Think', *MIT Sloan Management Review* (Spring 2001), 89–93.

37. Thomas F. Issack, 'Intuition: An Ignored Dimension of Management', *Academy of Management Review* 3 (1978), 917–922.

38. Marjorie A. Lyles, 'Defining Strategic Problems: Subjective Criteria of Executives', *Organizational Studies* 8 (1987), 263–280; and Marjorie A. Lyles and Ian I. Mitroff, 'Organizational Problem Formulation: An Empirical Study', *Administrative Science Quarterly* 25 (1980), 102–119.

39. Marjorie A. Lyles and Howard Thomas, 'Strategic Problem Formulation: Biases and Assumptions Embedded in Alternative Decision-Making Models', *Journal of Management Studies* 25 (1988), 131–145.

40. Ross Stagner, 'Corporate Decision-Making: An Empirical Study', *Journal of Applied Psychology* 53 (1969), 1–13.

41. Sarah G. Moore, Melissa J. Ferguson and Tanya L. Chartrand (2011), 'Affect in the Aftermath: How the Implicit Pursuit of a Goal Influences Implicit Evaluations', *Cognition & Emotion*, 25(3), 453–65.

42. 'CEOs More Likely to Rely on Intuition than Metrics When Making Business Decisions', *Business Wire*, November 6, 2006; Jabulani Sikhakhane, 'Managers can benefit from an overlooked resource: the gut', *The Star*, 6 September, 2007; 'SME Survey: Gut feeling rules in small businesses', *The Independent Financial Review*, 21 February 2007.

43. Reported in Eric Bonabeau, 'Don't Trust Your Gut', *Harvard Business Review* (May 2003), 116ff.

44. Kirby Garlitos, 'KTM Edges Out BMW, Sells Record 158,760 Motorcycles In 2014', *TopSpeed*, January 26, 2015, accessed at www.topspeed.com/motorcycles/motorcycle-news/ktm-edges-out-bmw-sells-record-158-760-motorcycles-in-2014-ar167309.html

45. Hamish Cooper, 'KTM's rocket for the road', *The Courier-Mail* (Australia), 19 April, 2008; Kurt Matzler, Franz Bailom and Todd A. Mooradian 'Intuitive Decision Making', *MIT Sloan Management Review*, October 1, 2007.

46. 'Bajaj Auto, KTM to extend network in Indonesia', *Economic Times* (India), April 8, 2016, accessed at economictimes.indiatimes.com/industry/auto/news/industry/bajaj-auto-ktm-to-extend-network-in-indonesia/articleshow/51743584.cms

47. Lijee Philip and Ketan Thakkar, 1 February, 2013, 'KTM promoter Stefan Pierer's Pierer Industrie buys out 100 per cent stake in BMW's Husqvarna brand', *The Economic Times*.

48. Bonabeau, 'Don't Trust Your Gut'.

49. Ann Langley, 'Between "Paralysis by Analysis" and "Extinction by Instinct,"' *Sloan Management Review* (Spring 1995), 63–76.

50. Paul C. Nutt, 'Types of Organizational Decision Processes', *Administrative Science Quarterly* 29 (1984), 414–450.

51. Brian Boyd, 'Magic maker', *Irish Times*, 8 October, 2007; David Sinclair, 'Rough Trade: The label that changed music history', *The Independent*, 8 September, 2006; Fiona Shepherd, 'Rough diamonds', *The Scotsman*, 25 November, 2008; Nadine Mcbay. 'Roughing it around Britain', *Metro*, 25 November, 2008.

52. Nandini Rajagopalan, Abdul M. A. Rasheed and Deepak K. Datta, 'Strategic Decision Processes: Critical Review and Future Decisions', *Journal of Management* 19 (1993), 349–384; Paul J. H. Schoemaker, 'Strategic Decisions in Organizations: Rational and Behavioural Views', *Journal of Management Studies* 30 (1993), 107–129; Charles J. McMillan, 'Qualitative Models of Organizational Decision Making', *Journal of Management Studies* 5 (1980), 22–39; and Paul C. Nutt, 'Models for Decision Making in Organizations and Some Contextual Variables Which Stimulate Optimal Use', *Academy of Management Review* 1 (1976), 84–98.

53. Hugh J. Miser, 'Operations Analysis in the Army Air Forces in World War II: Some Reminiscences', *Interfaces* 23 (September–October 1993), 47–49; Harold J. Leavitt, William R. Dill and Henry B. Eyring, *The Organizational World* (New York: Harcourt Brace Jovanovich, 1973), Chap. 6.

54. Richard King, 23 March 2012, 'Film & Music: There is a light that never goes out', *The Guardian*; http://www.roughtraderecords.com/.

55. 'Rough Trade Records: 10 Releases That Make It One Of The Best Indie Labels In The World', *New Musical Express*, March 16, 2015, accessed at www.nme.com/photos/rough-trade-records-10-releases-that-make-it-one-of-the-best-indie-labels-in-the-world/372524#/photo/1; Dorian Lynskey, 'The rise, fall and rise again of Rough Trade', *The Observer*, November 23, 2013, accessed at www.theguardian.com/music/2013/nov/23/rough-trade-new-york-store

56. Stephen J. Huxley, 'Finding the Right Spot for a Church Camp in Spain', *Interfaces* 12 (October 1982), 108–114; James E. Hodder and Henry E. Riggs, 'Pitfalls in Evaluating Risky Projects', *Harvard Business Review* (January–February 1985), 128–135.

57. 'Labour Agency report on creating "virtual labour market"', *German News*, 3 November 2004, accessed at, http://web.archive.org/web/20050222100004/http://www.germnews.de/archive/dn/2004/11/03.html on September 17, 2013.

58. Alistair Osborne, 'Ryanair protests too much', *Daily Telegraph*, 7 June, 2007.

59. 'Ex-Ryanair duo set up aviation consultancy', *Irish Independent*, 18 January, 2008.

60. Julie Schlosser, 'Markdown Lowdown', *Fortune* (January 12, 2004), 40; Christina Binkley, 'Numbers Game; Taking Retailers' Cues, Harrah's Taps Into Science of Gambling', *The Wall Street Journal* (November 22, 2004), A1, A8.

61. 'Les TER, prochain chantier de la politique tarifaire de la compagnie ferroviaire', *Les Echos*, 29 October, 2008.

62. Barry Berman (2005), 'Applying yield management pricing to your service business', *Business Horizons*, 48, 169–179.

63. François Delétraz, 'SNCF: Les tarifs les plus complexes d'Europe', *Le Figaro*, March 30, 2015, accessed at www.lefigaro.fr/voyages/2015/03/26/30003-20150326ARTFIG00327-sncf-politique-tarifaire-ultra-compliquee-et-amendes-en-rafale-pour-les-usagers-un-peu-perdus.php

64. Peter Jarvis (2002), 'Introducing yield management into a new industry', *Journal of Revenue and Pricing Management*, Vol. 1, 67–75; Jochen Wirtz, Jeannette Ho, Pheng Theng and Paul Patterson, 'Yield Management: Resolving Potential Customer and Employee Conflicts' (2001), Working Paper 0126, National University of Singapore Business School.

65. Harold J. Leavitt, 'Beyond the Analytic Manager', *California Management Review* 17 (1975), 5–12; and C. Jackson Grayson, Jr, 'Management Science and Business Practice', *Harvard Business Review* 51 (July–August 1973), 41–48.

66. Larry Elliott and Dan Atkinson (2008), *The Gods That Failed: How Blind Faith in Markets Has Cost Us Our Future*, London, Bodley Head; 'The foreclosure epidemic: the costs to families and communities of the predictable mortgage meltdown: an interview with Allen Fishbein', *Multinational Monitor*, 1 May, 2007.

67. Amir Efrati, 'The Madoff Fraud Case: Scope of Alleged Fraud Is Still Being Assessed', *The Wall Street Journal*, 18 December, 2008; Marcy Gordon, 'Madoff fraud case raises questions about SEC's scrutiny of operations, response to alarms', *Associated Press Newswires*, 13 December,

2008; 'The Madoff Fraud Case: Victims of Scandal Reflect on Shocking Turnabout', *The Wall Street Journal*, 20 December, 2008.

68. The Computerworld Honors Program, 'Germany's Labour Agency (Bundesagentur für Arbeit): Virtual Labour Market (VAM)', accessed at http://www.cwhonors.org/viewCaseStudy.asp?NominationID=204 on December 23, 2008.

69. Bettina Kohlrausch (2012), 'Youth Unemployment in Germany: Skill Biased Patterns of Labour Market Integration', Berlin, FES; Ingrid Melander and Nicholas Vinocur (2013), 'Germany warns of 'revolution' as youth unemployment threatens to tear Europe apart', *National Post*, May 13, http://business.financialpost.com/2013/05/28/germany-warns-of-revolution-as-youth-unemploymentthreatens-to-tear-europe-apart/

70. Unemployment statistics, March 2016, Eurostat, accessed at ec.europa.eu/eurostat/statistics-explained/index.php/Unemployment_statistics

71. Rajeshree Sisodia, 'Jobless welcome hi-tech option', *The Journal* (Newcastle, UK), 21 February, 2003.

72. James Auger, 'Madoff Fraud Scandal Further Undermines Confidence in US. Financial System, Regulation', *Global Insight Daily Analysis*, 15 December, 2008.

73. David Wessel, 'A Man Who Governs Credit Is Denied a Toys 'R' Us Card', *The Wall Street Journal* (December 14, 1995), B1.

74. Richard L. Daft and John C. Wiginton, 'Language and Organization', *Academy of Management Review* (1979), 179–191.

75. Based on Richard M. Cyert and James G. March, *A Behavioural Theory of the Firm* (Englewood Cliffs, NJ: Prentice-Hall, 1963); and James G. March and Herbert A. Simon, *Organizations* (New York: Wiley, 1958).

76. William B. Stevenson, Joan L. Pearce and Lyman W. Porter, 'The Concept of "Coalition" in Organization Theory and Research', *Academy of Management Review* 10 (1985), 256–268.

77. Cyert and March, *A Behavioural Theory of the Firm*, 120–222.

78. Based on Henry Mintzberg, Duru Raisinghani and André Théorêt, 'The Structure of "Unstructured" Decision Processes', *Administrative Science Quarterly* 21 (1976), 246–275.

79. Lawrence T. Pinfield, 'A Field Evaluation of Perspectives on Organizational Decision Making', *Administrative Science Quarterly* 31 (1986), 365–388.

80. Mintzberg et al., 'The Structure of "Unstructured" Decision Processes'.

81. L. Gordon Crovitz, 'Information Age: Can Britannica Rule the Web?', 20 March, 2012, *The Wall Street Journal Europe*, p. 17.

82. Pui-Wing Tam, 'One for the History Books: The Tale of How Britannica Is Trying to Leap from the Old Economy Into the New One', *The Wall Street Journal* (December 11, 2000), R32; and Richard A. Melcher, 'Dusting Off the *Britannica*', *BusinessWeek* (October 20, 1997), 143–146.

83. Robert Channick, 'Encyclopaedia Britannica sees digital growth, aims to draw new users', *Chicago Tribune*, September 10, 2014, accessed at www.chicagotribune.com/business/ct-britannica-digital-0911-biz-20140910-story.html

84. Ibid., 270.

85. 'Gillette Fusion Case Study Demonstrates Developing a $1US Billion Brand', *Business Wire*, August 1, 2008; William C. Symonds, 'Gillette's 5 Blade Wonder', *Business Week*, September 15, 2005.

86. William C. Symonds with Carol Matlack, 'Gillette's Edge', *BusinessWeek* (January 19, 1998), 70–77; William C. Symonds, 'Would You Spend $1.50 for a Razor Blade?' *BusinessWeek* (April 27, 1998), 46; and Peter J. Howe, 'Innovative; For the Past Half Century, "Cutting Edge" Has Meant More at Gillette Co. Than a Sharp Blade,' *Boston Globe* (January 30, 2005), D1.

87. Kevin Roose, 'Gillette's New Razor Is Everything That's Wrong With American Innovation', *New York*, April 18, 2014, accessed at nymag.com/daily/intelligencer/2014/04/gillettes-razor-everything-wrong-with-america.html

88. Garrett Downing, 'Music-sharing lawsuits ending; Illegal downloading still will draw warning', *The Columbus Dispatch*, 23 December, 2008; 'Will warning file-sharers curb their behaviour?', *New Media Age*, 31 July, 2008; Sean Crotty, 'Why file sharers should beware', *Daily Post (Liverpool)*, 23 September, 2008; John McKinlay, 'Filesharers under fire', Silicon.com, 3 September, 2008.

89. Josh Halliday, 'British ISPs will block The Pirate Bay within weeks', *Guardian*, https://www.theguardian.com/technology/2012/apr/30/british-isps-block-pirate-bay

90. Anna Wilde Mathews, Martin Peers and Nick Wingfield, 'Off-Key: The Music Industry Is Finally Online, but Few Listen', *The Wall Street Journal* (May 7, 2002), A1, A20; and http://www.musicnet.com.

91. Michael D. Cohen, James G. March and Johan P. Olsen, 'A Garbage Can Model of Organizational Choice', *Administrative Science Quarterly* 17 (March 1972), 1–25; and Michael D. Cohen and James G. March, *Leadership and Ambiguity: The American College President* (New York: McGraw-Hill, 1974).

92. Michael Masuch and Perry LaPotin, 'Beyond Garbage Cans: An AI Model of Organizational Choice', *Administrative Science Quarterly* 34 (1989), 38–67.

93. Francis Fukuyama (2007), *America at the Crossroads: Democracy, Power, and the Neoconservative Legacy*, New Haven, CT, Yale University Press; Arthur A. Goldsmith (2008), 'Making the World Safe for Partial Democracy? Questioning the Premises of Democracy Promotion', *International Security*, 33, 120–147.

94. Adapted from James D. Thompson, *Organizations in Action* (New York: McGraw-Hill, 1967), Chap. 10; and McMillan, 'Qualitative Models of Organizational Decision Making', 25.

95. William M. Newmann (1998), 'Foreign policy decision making, garbage cans and policy shifts: the Eisenhower administration and the "Chances for Peace" speech' *American Review of Public Administration*, 28, 187–212.

96. Michael Lipson (2007), 'A 'Garbage Can Model' of UN Peacekeeping', *Global Governance* 13, 79–97, p. 96.

97. John Kingdon (1993), 'How do issues get on public policy agendas?', in John Kingdon (ed.) *Sociology and the Public Agenda*, London, Sage, 40–50.

98. Johannes Heeb and Karin Hindenlang (2008), 'Negotiating Landscape in the Swiss Alps: Experience with Implementation of a Systemic Landscape Development Approach', *Mountain Research and Development*, 28, 105–109.

99. Beth Dickey, 'NASA's Next Step', *Government Executive* (April 15, 2004), 34ff; and Jena McGregor, 'Gospels of Failure', *Fast Company* (February 2005), 61–67.

100. Jonathan Murphy (2008), *The World Bank and Global Managerialism*, London, Routledge, 108–117,

101. Dave Waller, 'From little acorns', *Management Today*, July 1, 2007, p.42.

102. Mintzberg and Wheatley, 'Decision Making: It's Not What You Think'.

103. Paul C. Nutt, 'Selecting Decision Rules for Crucial Choices: An Investigation of the Thompson Framework', *The Journal of Applied Behavioural Science* 38, No. 1 (March 2002), 99–131; and Paul C. Nutt, 'Making Strategic Choices', *Journal of Management Studies* 39, No. 1 (January 2002), 67–95.

104. George T. Doran and Jack Gunn, 'Decision Making in High-Tech Firms: Perspectives of Three Executives', *Business Horizons* (November–December 2002), 7–16.

105. L. J. Bourgeois III and Kathleen M. Eisenhardt, 'Strategic Decision Processes in High Velocity Environments: Four Cases in the Microcomputer Industry', *Management Science* 34 (1988), 816–835.

106. Kathleen M. Eisenhardt, 'Speed and Strategic Course: How Managers Accelerate Decision Making', *California Management Review* (Spring 1990), 39–54.

107. David A. Garvin and Michael A. Roberto, 'What You Don't Know about Making Decisions', *Harvard Business Review* (September 2001), 108–116.

108. Janes Surowiecki, *The Wisdom of Crowds: Why the Many Are Smarter Than the Few and How Collective Wisdom Shapes Business, Economies, Societies and Nations* (New York: Doubleday, 2004); Doran and Gunn, 'Decision Making in High-Tech Firms'.

109. Doran and Gunn, 'Decision Making in High-Tech Firms'.

110. Karl Weick, *The Social Psychology of Organizing*, 2d ed. (Reading, MA: Addison-Wesley, 1979), 243.

111. Matt Roush, 'How Fretter fell: 'Whole bunch of things' led to demise of appliance icon,' *Crain's Detroit Business*, December 2, 1996.

112. Dave Waller, 'Stanley Kalms turned an ailing photographic studio into Dixons, the mighty consumer electronics chain', *Management Today*, 1 November, 2007; Charlotte Hardie, 'Voices of experience', *Retail Week*, 5 September, 2008; 'Dixons through the ages', *Daily Telegraph*, 6 April, 2006; James Hall, 'Whatever happened to dear old Dixons?' *The Sunday Telegraph*, 8 April, 2007; James Hall, 'It's time to recharge the batteries', *The Sunday Telegraph*, 3 June, 2007.

113. Neil Craven, 'We fought off Best Buy – By Getting Better', *The Mail on Sunday*, 27 November, 2011; Sarah Butler, 'Dixons benefits from Comet's demise', *The Guardian*, 18 January, 2013.

114. Ashley Armstrong, 'Dixons Carphone sales to top £10bn in maiden results since marriage', *Telegraph*, July 11, 2015, accessed at www.telegraph.co.uk/finance/newsbysector/retailandconsumer/11731645/Dixons-Carphone-sales-to-top-10bn-in-maiden-results-since-marriage.html

115. Helga Drummond, 'Too Little Too Late: A Case Study of Escalation in Decision Making', *Organization Studies* 15, No. 4 (1994), 591–607; Joel Brockner, 'The Escalation of Commitment to a Failing Course of Action: Toward Theoretical Progress', *Academy of Management Review* 17 (1992), 39–61; Barry M. Staw and Jerry Ross, 'Knowing When to Pull the Plug', *Harvard Business Review* 65 (March–April 1987), 68–74; and Barry M. Staw, 'The Escalation of Commitment to a Course of Action', *Academy of Management Review* 6 (1981), 577–587.

116. Konrad Yakabuski, 'The Greatest Canadian Company on Earth; From hippies on stilts to global champion', *Globe and Mail*, 31 August, 2007; James Mennie, 'Tourism, business boards ready to roll dice on new casino locale', *The Montreal Gazette*, 13 October, 2005.

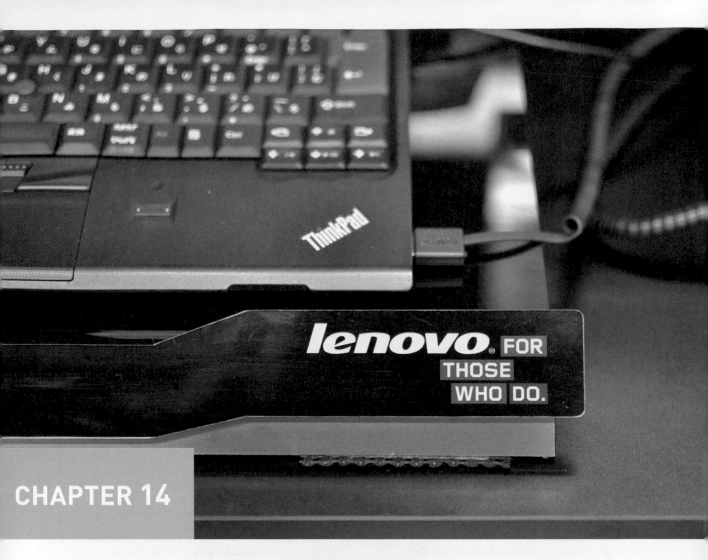

CONFLICT, POWER AND POLITICS

Lenovo

In 2005, the Chinese computer manufacturer Lenovo shocked the IT world when it purchased IBM's personal computer business for about $1.3 billion. IBM, which was focused increasingly on IT consulting services, had been losing market share to personal computer (PC) manufacturing specialists like Dell. Lenovo, which is part-owned by the Chinese state, had been growing rapidly since being set up by the Chinese Academy of Sciences in 1984. By the time of the IBM takeover it was the ninth biggest PC manufacturer in the world, while IBM was third biggest. Nevertheless, many industry-watchers were sceptical. Lenovo's strength was in the Chinese market where it sold low-end machines, whereas IBM was best known for its high-end machines, particularly the ThinkPad range which was popular with high-flying global executives. Furthermore, would Lenovo, until the IBM purchase almost unknown in the West, be able to hold on to IBM's best employees, who were used to the prestige and privileges associated with working for one of the top global corporations? Many of the big computer firm mergers have faced big problems, as we saw in the previous chapter with HP and Compaq, where the two firms cannibalized each other's sales and morale and profits plummeted. HP CEO, Carly Fiorino, the mastermind of that merger, paid for those problems with her job. Indeed, at the beginning, things were shaky at Lenovo. Online computer user forums were full of stories (probably mainly mythological) about how the quality of the ThinkPad machines had gone down as soon as Lenovo (or, 'the Chinese') took over. A major sale of computers to the US defence department was scrapped by the US government, supposedly due to security concerns. Former IBM staffers were nervous, wondering what corporate culture their new bosses would bring along with them.

Indeed, there were huge differences in the ways the two firms were managed. The Chinese firm had been used to operating with military-like discipline. Twice a day calisthenic exercises were broadcast over the loudspeaker system at Lenovo with staff expected to stop work and do their stretches. Managers arriving late to meetings had to stand at the front of the meeting room with their head bowed for a full minute while their colleagues watched in silence. On the other hand, Chinese executives felt their American colleagues tended to wastefully hog meeting time: 'The Americans would just talk and talk,' says Qiao Jian, a vice president of human resources, 'Then they'd say "How come you don't want to add value to this meeting?"'

Lenovo brought in William Amelio, a top American computer executive as CEO in an effort to convince American corporate purchasers that nothing had changed from the old days when it was famously said that 'Nobody ever got fired for buying IBM'. Amelio, himself a former 18-year IBM veteran, had previously been Dell VP for the Asia region. Along with company president, Yang Yanqing, he decided to tackle the cultural issues head-on organizing a cultural audit of employees. As they suspected, they found that former IBM employees often didn't really trust their new Lenovo colleagues, while the Lenovo managers found the new American staff undisciplined, used to being let off the hook too easily for missing targets or blowing deadlines.

Problems often originated in communication. 'Westerners tend to speak first, then listen and Easterners tend to listen, then speak,' said the company's head of HR, Ken diPietro. But while the former IBM executives said they valued straight talk and communicating openly, the Chinese staff didn't see things that way. A Chinese colleague told Mr Amelio: 'You know what straight talk really means in China? It means an excuse for Westerners to be rude.' The incident helped bring home to Amelio that trust is required for effective communication. A workshop dubbed 'East Meets West', was organized which addressed topics including Western and Eastern history and religion. It was a great success and has been expanded into a four-day programme for all Lenovo managers.

A problem of differing attitudes to targets and deadlines was addressed by delving into different management practices in the two firms. 'The China side was a rigorous, metrics-driven, fact-based organization – very edgy' said Amelio. 'They would put goals in place and do whatever it took to achieve them. They would argue hard at the start as to where the goal post should be. But once the goal post was set, they would make sure commitments were kept.' On the other hand, in the old IBM business, 'Typically, the finance department would hand targets to the team that would usually be 120 per cent of what was actually do-able. So a culture started to build up where if you could explain why you couldn't do 120 per cent and 90 per cent was good enough, you were OK. But that's insidious. You don't keep a performance-based culture when that kind of mentality starts to seep through an organization.' So the whole firm, including the former IBM team, moved to a performance-based culture that sets realistic targets but also ensures people are accountable for what they say they are going to do.

The salary structure in the merged business was also carefully examined. At IBM, sales staff had been paid about 80 per cent in base salary, with around 20 per cent for performance, whereas at Lenovo most salary was performance-related. When the companies were integrated, the Chinese Lenovo managers often found they were making far less than staff they supervised who had come over from IBM. The salary structure was brought into alignment, although this has to be balanced against the much lower cost of living in China compared with the US.

Overall, the massive effort put into ironing out conflicts and misunderstandings helped to build a successful organization. Lenovo continued to grow its business and avoided the disastrous mistakes of the HP-Compaq merger. However, problems still exist. The company still has a double personality: as a mass market, consumer brand in China, and an up-market, enterprise-oriented brand in the West. Lenovo, like all its competitors, faces tough market conditions in the light of economic slowdown including in its home China market, but the company continues to perform well overall and demonstrates strategic nimbleness, holding on to the number one spot in worldwide computer sales in 2016, albeit in a shrinking market. The culture of dialogue and common understanding of, and across, cultures both within and beyond the company, will remain one of the keys to Lenovo's continuing success.[1,2,3]

All organizations are a complex mix of individuals and groups with different backgrounds and perspectives and pursuing various goals and interests. Conflict is a natural and inevitable outcome of the close interaction of people who may have diverse opinions and values, pursue different objectives and have differential access to information and resources within the organization (see Counterpoint 14.1). Individuals and groups will use power and political activity to handle their differences and manage conflict.[4]

COUNTERPOINT 14.1

This conception of conflict could also be seen, however, as reducing it to the opinions and values of individuals instead of appreciating how such differences arise – for example, as a consequence of occupying different positions in the hierarchy or because they come from different social or cultural backgrounds. In other words, individual differences in *organizations* are often understandable by paying attention to differences within and between *societies*.

Too much conflict can be harmful. However, conflict can also be a positive force because it challenges the status quo, encourages new ideas and approaches, and leads to change.[5] Some degree of conflict occurs in all human relationships – between friends, romantic partners and teammates, as well as between parents and children, teachers and students and bosses and employees. Within organizations, individuals and groups frequently have different interests and priorities. Managers in all organizations regularly deal with conflict, and struggle with decisions about how to get the most out of employees, enhance job satisfaction and team identification and realize high organizational performance.

ONLINE
COUNTERPOINT 14.1

Purpose of this Chapter

In this chapter we discuss the nature of conflict and the operation of power and political tactics to manage and reduce conflict among individuals and groups. The notion of conflict has appeared in previous chapters. In Chapter 4, we considered horizontal linkages such as task forces and teams that encourage collaboration among functional departments. Chapter 5 introduced the concept of differentiation, which means that members of different departments may pursue different goals and have different attitudes and values. Chapter 11 discussed the emergence of subcultures and in Chapter 13, coalition building was proposed as one way to resolve disagreements among departments.

The first sections of this chapter explore the nature of intergroup conflict, some characteristics of organizations that contribute to conflict, and the use of a political versus a rational model of organizing to manage conflicting interests. Subsequent sections examine individual and organizational power, the vertical and horizontal sources of power for managers and other employees and how power is mobilized to attain organizational goals. We also discuss some tactics managers can use to facilitate collaboration among people and departments.

Intergroup Conflict in Organizations

Intergroup conflict can be analyzed in relation to group identification, observable group differences and frustration. First, employees have to perceive themselves as part of an identifiable group, such as a department.[6] Second, there has to be a group difference of some form. Groups may be located on different floors of the building, members may have different social or educational backgrounds or members may work in different departments with different responsibilities within the organization. The ability to identify oneself as a part of one group and to observe differences in comparison with other groups is a necessary but not sufficient condition for conflict.[7]

The third ingredient is frustration. Frustration means that if one group achieves its goal, the other will not; it will be blocked. Frustration need not be severe and only needs to be anticipated to set off intergroup conflict. Intergroup conflict will appear when one group tries to advance its position in relation to other groups. Intergroup conflict can be defined as the behaviour that occurs among organizational groups when participants identify with one group and perceive that other groups may block their group's achievements or expectations.[8] In the chapter opening *A Look Inside*, managers from the two halves of the new Lenovo company found communication frustrating. This was not merely because of different styles of dialogue, but also because the two companies had pursued different business strategies and because the former Lenovo executives had inferior compensation packages compared with former IBM staff, even though the pre-merger Lenovo business had been more profitable than the IBM PC operation. Conflict is similar to competition but more severe. Competition is rivalry among groups in the pursuit of a common prize, whereas conflict presumes frustration of goal achievement.

Intergroup conflict within organizations can occur horizontally across departments or vertically between different levels of the organization.[9] The production department of a manufacturing company may have a dispute with quality control because new quality procedures reduce production efficiency. Teammates may argue about the best way to accomplish tasks and achieve goals. Workers may clash with bosses about new work methods, reward systems or job assignments. Another typical area of conflict is between groups such as unions and management, franchise owners and headquarters, and managers and investors. For example, Germany's Deutsche Telekom has been involved in conflicts for several years with staff over job cuts and restructuring aimed at making the privatized company more competitive.[10] Australia's Bank of Queensland, which sold off branches to owner-managers as franchises, ended up in court as many of the franchisees lost money, even as the Bank itself was turning record profits. Also in Australia, the investor Souls

Private Equity wrote off the entire value of its A$18.8 million investment in 24 per cent of the country's Krispy Kreme doughnut chain because it felt the company's aggressive store opening policy was unwise given the global recession, even as CEO John McGuigan insisted that, 'We are just getting on with the game and running the business. We have a different degree of confidence in current performance.'[11]

Conflict can also occur between different divisions or business units within an organization, such as between the auditing and consulting units of big firms such as PricewaterhouseCoopers and Deloitte.[12] In global organizations, conflicts between regional managers and business division managers, among different divisions or between divisions and headquarters are common because of the complexities of international business, as described in Chapter 7.

Sources of Conflict

Some specific organizational characteristics can generate conflict. These sources of intergroup conflict include goal incompatibility, differentiation, task interdependence and limited resources. These characteristics of organizational relationships are determined by the contextual factors of environment, size, technology, strategy and goals and organizational structure, which have been discussed in previous chapters. These characteristics, in turn, help shape the extent to which a rational model of behaviour, rather than a political model of behaviour, is deployed in accomplishing objectives.

Goal Incompatibility   Goal incompatibility is probably the greatest cause of intergroup conflict in organizations.[13] The goals of each department reflect the specific objectives members are trying to achieve. The achievement of one department's goals often interferes with another department's goals. University security staff, for example, have a goal of providing a safe and secure campus. They can achieve their goal by locking all buildings on evenings and weekends and not distributing keys. Without easy access to buildings, however, progress toward the science department's research goals will proceed slowly. On the other hand, if scientists come and go at all hours and security is ignored, the security team's goals for security will not be met (and valuable property of the university might be stolen).

Exhibit 14.1 shows examples of goal conflict between typical marketing and manufacturing departments. Marketing strives to increase the breadth of the product line to meet customer tastes for variety. A broad product line means short production runs, so manufacturing has to bear higher costs.[14] Other areas of goal conflict are quality, cost control and new products or services. Designers of Indian car manufacturer Tata's Nano car, which was aimed at making car ownership affordable for the burgeoning middle classes in developing countries, had to cut corners in order to break the 100 000 rupee (about $2500 at the time) barrier. For example, the car lacked some basic features which are considered standard and even legally required in developed countries, such as air bags, side impact beams and anti-lock brakes. In 2014, the car achieved zero stars (out of four) in the German Global New Car Assessment Programme (Ncap), dealing a potentially fatal blow to plans to expand to European and North American markets.[15,16] Not only do these safety issues make it impossible to sell the car in countries with higher safety standards than India, they may also create an image problem within India, where those moving up from motorbikes to cars want a vehicle that not only gets them around but is both safe and not perceived as a cheap alternative to a 'real' car. By 2015, six years after launch, the Nano's sales in India were sliding badly and total sales since launch of 260 000 were well below initial expectations.[17,18]

Differentiation   *Differentiation* was defined in Chapter 4 as 'the differences in cognitive and emotional orientations among managers in different functional departments'. Departments or

EXHIBIT 14.1 Marketing-Manufacturing Areas of Potential Goal Conflict

Goal Conflict	MARKETING versus MANUFACTURING	
	Operative Goal is Customer Satisfaction	Operative Goal is Production Efficiency
Conflict Area	Typical Comment	Typical Comment
1. Breadth of product line	'Our customers demand variety.'	'The product line is too broad – all we get are short, uneconomical runs.'
2. New product introduction	'New products are our lifeblood.'	'Unnecessary design changes are prohibitively expensive.'
3. Product scheduling	'We need faster response. Our customer lead times are too long.'	'We need realistic commitments that don't change like wind direction.'
4. Physical distribution	'Why don't we ever have the right merchandise in inventory?'	'We can't afford to keep huge inventories.'
5. Quality	'Why can't we have reasonable quality at lower cost?'	'Why must we always offer options that are too expensive and offer little customer utility?'

Source: Based on Benson S. Shapiro, 'Can Marketing and Manufacturing Coexist?' *Harvard Business Review* 55 (September–October 1977), 104–114; and Victoria L. Crittenden, Lorraine R. Gardiner, and Antonie Stam, 'Reducing Conflict between Marketing and Manufacturing,' *Industrial Marketing Management* 22 (1993), 299–309.

divisions within an organization often differ in values, attitudes and standards of behaviour and these subcultural differences lead to conflicts.[19] Consider an encounter between a sales manager and a research and development (R&D) scientist about a new product:

> The sales manager may be outgoing and concerned with maintaining a warm, friendly relationship with the scientist. He may be put off because the scientist seems withdrawn and disinclined to talk about anything other than the problems in which he is interested. He may also be annoyed that the scientist seems to have such freedom in choosing what he will work on. Furthermore, the scientist is probably often late for appointments, which, from the salesman's point of view, is no way to run a business. Our scientist, for his part, may feel uncomfortable because the salesman seems to be pressing for immediate answers to technical questions that will take a long time to investigate. All the discomforts are concrete manifestations of the relatively wide differences between these two men in respect to their working and thinking styles.[20]

A lack of trust within the organization can magnify these natural differences and increase the potential for conflict among departments and with top managers, as a new CEO discovered at Guidant (now part of Boston Scientific) (see Counterpoint 14.2). Her solution was to build a new culture of honesty, as discussed in this chapter's *Leading by Design*, although as the subsequent Counterpoint shows, the new culture did not necessarily extend to the company's disclosures to doctors and patient users of the company's devices (see Counterpoint 14.3).

COUNTERPOINT 14.2

Lack of trust is often associated with conflict. Lack of trust indicates a lack of respect for the other person or group which, in turn, indicates doubts about the legitimacy of their claims or even their existence. If executives are not willing openly to share all information with employees, what does this say about trust? What does it say about divergent or convergent interests?

LEADING BY DESIGN

Managing Dynamic Processes

Guidant[21] (now part of Boston Scientific) was the darling of the medical devices industry. The company, established by US pharmaceutical giant Eli Lilly, reached $100 million in sales within five years of launching its first product and revolutionized the field of angioplasty by producing one innovation after another. But when Ginger Graham took over as president and CEO of the medical device manufacturer, she realized that something was terribly wrong. Even though top managers were still touting Guidant's strong internal and external relationships as key to the company's success, the reality was that these relationships were increasingly marked by conflict and discord rather than harmony and cooperation.

When Graham gave her first address to the company, she decided to tell the truth: 'I've always heard about what a wonderful company Guidant is,' she began, 'but frankly, that's not what I see. What I see is deteriorating morale, disillusioned customers and finger-pointing. I see a place where R&D and manufacturing are practically at war. You folks in sales blame manufacturing. R&D blames marketing. We're all so busy blaming each other that nothing gets done.' The response of employees – standing and cheering their approval – confirmed Graham's suspicions. People just wanted to hear that someone at the top knew the truth and was willing to admit it. From that moment, Graham began building a culture at Guidant in which everyone feels free to tell the truth without fear of negative consequences.

Guidant established a number of practices fostering open and honest communications. To start, Graham reversed the top-down communication structure in an immediately visible way. Each top manager was assigned a coach from lower ranks of the organization. The coaches were trained to ask questions and gather specific information from everyone throughout the organization about the manager's openness and honest communication skills. Managers met with their coaches once a quarter. As it had support from the top, the coaching programme worked to close the communication gap between managers and employees. Managers also began sharing all information with employees – good and bad – and asking for their help in solving company problems. Employees who went above and beyond the call of duty to meet organizational goals were recognized and rewarded.

Rallying everyone around company goals rather than departmental goals helped alleviate much of the tension and conflict between departments. The war between R&D and manufacturing, however, had become so entrenched that stronger methods were needed.

Even though it cost the company dearly, Graham shut down product development altogether while representatives from R&D, manufacturing, clinical and marketing worked with a professional facilitator to confront the issues head-on and come up with a new approach to product development. The process meant that no new products went out of the door for 18 months, but the results were worth it. The company repeatedly launched innovative new products every year, produced enough to supply the entire market in a matter of weeks, completed clinical studies in record-setting time and improved quality while cutting costs.

Source: Ginger L. Graham, 'If You Want Honesty, Break Some Rules', *Harvard Business Review* (April 2002), 42–47.

COUNTERPOINT 14.3

Organizational culture also affects how a company will behave towards its clients or customers. In the case of Guidant there also appear to have been problems in its external conduct. In the mid-2000s the company had to defend itself against accusations it did not properly warn doctors and patients of flaws in its heart devices, implicated in at least one death. The issue, which led to a large recall, also helped force the sale of Guidant to Boston Scientific. In turn Boston Scientific has struggled to resolve problems both with Guidant's devices and the conduct of its sales team. The company had to make an out of court settlement with the US federal government to end a lawsuit claiming it had paid kickbacks to doctors to use its heart devices, and recalls of devices continued through at least 2009.[22] Forbes magazine described Boston Scientific's acquisition of Guidant as "the (second) worst deal ever".

Task interdependence   Task interdependence refers to the dependence of one unit on another for materials, resources or information. As described in Chapter 8, *pooled interdependence* means there is little interaction; *sequential interdependence* means the output of one department goes to the next department; and *reciprocal interdependence* means that departments mutually exchange materials and information.[23]

Generally, as interdependence increases, the potential for conflict increases.[24] In the case of pooled interdependence, units have little need to interact. Conflict is at a minimum. Sequential and reciprocal interdependence require employees to spend time coordinating and sharing information. Employees must communicate frequently and differences in goals or attitudes will surface. Conflict is especially likely to occur when agreement is not reached about the coordination of services to each other. Greater interdependence means departments often exert pressure for a fast response because departmental work has to wait on other departments.[25]

BRIEFCASE 14.1

Limited Resources   Another major source of conflict involves competition between groups for what members perceive as limited resources.[26] There is limited money, physical facilities, staff resources and human resources to share among departments. In their desire to achieve goals or expand empires, groups want to increase their resources. This throws them into conflict. Managers may develop strategies, such as inflating budget requirements or working behind the scenes, to obtain a desired level of resources.

Resources symbolize power and influence within an organization. The ability to obtain resources enhances prestige. Departments typically believe they have a legitimate claim on additional resources. However, exercising that claim results in conflict. For example, in almost every organization, conflict occurs during the annual budget exercise.

Rational versus Political Model

The sources of intergroup conflict are listed in Exhibit 14.2. The degree of goal incompatibility, differentiation, interdependence and conflict over limited resources influences whether a rational or political model of behaviour predominates within the organization.

EXHIBIT 14.2   Sources of Conflict and Use of Rational versus Political Model

Sources of Potential Intergroup Conflict	Rational Model		Political Model
• Goal incompatibility • Differentiation • Task interdependence • Limited resources	Consistent across participants	Goals	Inconsistent, pluralistic within the organization
	Centralized	Power and control	Decentralized, shifting coalitions and interest groups
	Orderly, logical, rational	Decision process	Disorderly, result of bargaining and interplay among interests
	Norm of efficiency	Rules and norms	Free play of market forces; conflict is legitimate and expected
	Extensive, systematic, accurate	Information	Ambiguous; information used and withheld strategically

When goals are in alignment, there is little differentiation, departments are characterized by pooled interdependence and resources seem abundant, managers can rely upon a rational model of organization, as outlined in Exhibit 14.2. As with the rational approach to decision-making described in Chapter 13, the rational model of organization is not fully achievable in the real world. That is because it assumes common agreement on an organization's objectives that is highly unlikely in all but the smallest organization (see Counterpoint 14.4). In the rational organization, behaviour is not random or accidental. Goals are clear and choices are made in a logical way. When a decision is needed, the goal is defined, alternatives are identified and the choice with the highest probability of success is selected.[27] The opposite view of organizational processes is the political model, also described in Exhibit 14.2. When, as in the political model, groups have separate interests, goals and values, disagreement and conflict are normal. Groups will engage in the push and pull of debate to decide goals and reach decisions. Information is ambiguous and incomplete. Typically, rational and political processes co-exist in organizations. Jeff Bezos, the founder and CEO of global online bookseller Amazon.com, emphasizes a rational approach to planning and decision-making, based upon evidence rather than opinion, whenever possible. 'The great thing about fact-based decisions,' he says, 'is that they overrule the hierarchy. The most junior person in the company can win an argument with the most senior person with a fact-based decision.' For decisions and situations that are complex, ill-defined and controversial, however, Bezos uses a political model, discussing the issues with people, building agreement among senior executives and relying on his own judgement.[28]

COUNTERPOINT 14.4

For some observers, there is a tendency to regard the rational model as non-political. But if 'rational' decisions are always guided by assumptions and values that fill in for missing information, don't they shade into political decisions? Also, how often is a rational decision made *post hoc*? That is to say, rationality is invoked to justify the decision rather than to make it. When Bezos says that there are 'fact-based decisions', he is arguably referring to the kinds of facts that he is prepared to recognize and endorse – that is, facts that are usable in a way that he judges to be good (e.g. for securing his position, or for the profitable growth of the company). Politics is indeed 'needed to accomplish objectives' and the most potent form of politics is that which appears to be non-political or 'rational'.

Managers may strive to adopt rational procedures but will find that 'politics' is needed to accomplish objectives.

Power and Organizations

Power is an intangible force in organizations. It cannot be seen, but its effect can be felt. *Power is often defined as the potential ability of one person (or department) to influence other people (or departments) to carry out orders[29]* or to do something they would not otherwise have done.[30] Other definitions stress that power is the ability to achieve goals or outcomes that power holders desire.[31] The achievement of desired outcomes is the basis of the definition used here: Power is the ability of one person or department in an organization to influence other people to bring about desired outcomes. It is the potential to influence others within the organization with the goal of attaining desired outcomes for power holders.

Power exists only in a relationship between two or more people and it can be exercised in either vertical or horizontal directions. The source of power often derives from an exchange relationship in which one position or department provides scarce or valued resources to other departments. When one person is dependent on another person, a power relationship emerges in which the person with the resources has greater power (see Counterpoint 14.5).[32]

ONLINE
COUNTERPOINT 14.2

When power exists in a relationship, the power holders can achieve compliance with their requests. Powerful individuals are often able to get bigger budgets for their departments, more favourable production schedules and more control over the organization's agenda.[33]

COUNTERPOINT 14.5

It could also be argued that the person or group with the greatest power is the person who is least vulnerable to the dependency of others. The person or group who is commonsensically seen to have the most power is not ultimately powerful if s/he depends upon others to sustain that power or is obliged to ensure others' subjugation in order to maintain that power. Consider the example of the football owners and managers in the following paragraph. The owners are desperate for results and silverware. They have the resources. But they are dependent upon managers and ultimately the players to realize their dreams.

As an illustration, consider how power has shifted in the game of football. Seasoned team managers, who typically base their decisions on instinct and experience, are losing power to wealthy owners who purchase teams and tend both to estimate their own capacities very highly and to expect very rapid results (and returns on their investments). For example, venerable Edinburgh, Scotland football team Heart of Midlothian, purchased in 2005 by Lithuanian multi-millionaire Vladimir Romanov. When Romanov took over, the team was riding high in the Scottish Premier League. He soon fired the company's chief executive and replaced him with his own son, Roman. Manager George Burley was fired after 12 games in charge despite the team being top of the league! In less than ten years, the Romanovs went through ten managers. They also loaded the company with debt borrowed from Lithuanian banks that they controlled. By 2012 Hearts was in freefall, with players' wages and government tax bills unpaid. In 2013 the club went into administration, and with the points penalty deducted by the Scottish League, fell into the country's second division. The next year, the club was brought out of administration by local Edinburgh businesswoman Ann Budge, who has put the club back on an even financial and footballing keel; the club was immediately promoted back to the Scottish Premier League, and finished third in the league its first year back in 2015–2016.

There are numerous examples in British football, and a number of other countries, of narcissistic – and sometimes overtly corrupt – owners destroying longstanding and deeply rooted clubs. Some consider this phenomenon a particularly visible example of a trend towards unsustainable, crisis-prone and debt-driven business practices in the wider global economy.[34]

Individual versus Organizational Power

In popular literature, power is often described as a personal characteristic, and a frequent topic is how one person can influence or dominate another person.[35] You probably recall from an earlier management or organizational behaviour course that managers have five sources of personal power.[36] *Legitimate power* is the authority granted by the organization to the formal management position a manager holds. *Reward power* stems from the ability to bestow rewards – a promotion, raise or pat on the back – to other people. The authority to punish or recommend punishment is called *coercive power. Expert power* derives from a person's greater skill or knowledge about the tasks being performed. The last, *referent power,* is derived from personal characteristics: people admire the manager and want to be like or identify with the manager out of respect and admiration. Each of these sources may be used by individuals within organizations.

Power in organizations, however, is often the result of structural characteristics.[37] Organizations are large, complex systems that contain hundreds, even thousands, of people. These systems have a formal hierarchy in which some tasks are more important regardless of who performs them. In addition, some positions have access to greater resources or their contribution to the organization is more critical. Thus, the important power processes in organizations reflect larger organizational relationships, both horizontal and vertical.

Power versus Authority

Anyone in an organization can exercise power to achieve desired outcomes, though of course the amount of power that individuals hold in an organization varies substantially. Toyota executive, Takeshi Uchiyamada, grasped his opportunity to drive change when he was put in charge of organizing the company's various research centres. He became interested in the possibilities for developing a fuel-efficient car and in 1996 was appointed chief engineer of the team developing the new Prius, which was released in December 1997. The car has shifted the paradigm of automobile development away from bigger and faster to cleaner and greener.[38] As a result, Uchiyamada is viewed within Toyota and throughout the global automobile industry as the leader of a transport revolution.[39] In 2013, after Toyota had faced a number of setbacks including major product recalls, Uchiyamada was made chairman of the whole company in an attempt to return the company to its glory as world number one in terms of both sales and reputation. In 2015 Toyota was back at the front of the pack, once again the world's largest automaker, and judged to have the best corporate reputation.[40,41]

The concept of formal authority is related to power but is narrower in scope. Authority is also a force for achieving desired outcomes, but only as prescribed by the formal hierarchy and reporting relationships. Three properties identify authority:

ONLINE COUNTERPOINT 14.3

BRIEFCASE 14.2

1   *Authority is vested in organizational positions.* People have authority because of the positions they hold, not because of personal characteristics or resources.

2   *Authority is accepted by subordinates.* Subordinates comply because they believe position holders have a legitimate right to exercise power.[42] In most organizations around the world, employees accept that supervisors can legitimately tell them what time to arrive at work, the tasks to perform while they're there and what time they can go home.

3   *Authority flows down the vertical hierarchy.*[43] Authority exists along the formal chain of command and positions at the top of the hierarchy are vested with more formal authority than are positions at the bottom.

Organizational power can be exercised upward, downward and horizontally in organizations. Formal authority is exercised downward along the hierarchy and is the same as legitimate power. In the following sections, we will examine vertical and horizontal sources of power for employees throughout the organization.

Vertical Sources of Power

All employees along the vertical hierarchy have access to some sources of power. There are four major sources of vertical power: formal position, resources, control of decision premises and information and network centrality.[44]

Formal Position   Certain rights, responsibilities and prerogatives accrue to top positions. People throughout the organization accept the legitimate right of top managers to set goals, make decisions and direct activities. Thus, the power from formal position is sometimes called *legitimate power*.[45] Senior managers routinely use symbols and language to perpetuate their legitimate power (see Counterpoint 14.6). For example, many large corporations have private jet aircraft for the use of their top executives. Canada's Bombardier, the market leader in corporate and private jets, predicted that the global market for corporate jets will almost double from 12 800 to 24 800 jets between 2007 and 2017. The jets not only allow executives to get around their empires more quickly than by commercial carrier, but also demonstrate the corporate power and wealth in their control.[46]

COUNTERPOINT 14.6

Sometimes the line between legitimate displays of authority and unreasonable excess can be hard to define. For example, money managers for the super-rich are expected to show their own style and class in order to attract clients and make them feel at ease. Russ Prince, who runs a consultancy that studies the habits of the super-rich, says, 'If you want to deal with the super-rich, it is important to have some measure of success of your own. A man in a mansion is not going to take advice from a man who lives in a hovel.' Global banking giant Citigroup's Todd Thomson, who headed the company's wealth management division, took this advice at face value. He had the division's boardroom decked out in marble flooring and polished wood cabinets, and installed a tropical fish tank, Persian rugs and a wood-burning fireplace in his 50th floor office overlooking New York's Central Park. Unfortunately for Thomson, by 2007 Citigroup's finances were already starting to tighten in advance of the global credit crunch, and the company's top managers decided he had gone too far, firing him for lack of judgement.[47] Thomson's case was not unique. Merrill Lynch's CEO, John Thain, spent $1.2m of company funds to refurbish his office, including a waste paper basket costing over $1000.

The amount of power provided to middle managers and lower-level participants is mainly built into the organization's structural design. The allocation of power to middle managers and staff is important because power enables employees to be productive. When job tasks are non-routine and when employees participate in self-directed teams and problem-solving task forces, this encourages flexibility and the exercise of discretion. Access to powerful people and the development of a relationship with them can, in addition, provide a strong base of influence.[48] For example, in some organizations an administrative assistant to the president might have more power than a department head because the assistant has access to the senior executive on a daily basis and can act as a gate-keeper.

By designing tasks and interactions along the hierarchy, everyone can exert more influence. Winnipeg, Canada-based haulage company Bison Transport has grown over the past 20 years from just 18 trucks to over 1000, based on employee empowerment at all levels of the organization. 'Throughout our business we endeavour to train people to make good decisions and we then allow and encourage them to make good decisions, so there's an empowerment for the driver to decide when the truck moves,' says Don Streuber, the company's president and CEO. The company management is committed to genuinely listen to its employees and use their input to improve the organization. 'Our employees have expressed concerns about our commitment to the environment', says Mr. Streuber. Management took note – and worked with staff to push through modifications to vehicles and driving practices. Bison has been recognized with a special award from the US Environmental Protection Agency for its commitment to sustainability and environmental responsibility, in addition to being named one of Canada's 50 best managed companies for 15 years consecutively, and a host of other awards, including being voted best large North American haulier to drive for in 2016, by the Truckload Carriers Association (TCA).[49,50]

Resources Organizations allocate huge amounts of resources. Buildings are constructed, salaries are paid and equipment and supplies are purchased. Each year, new resources are allocated in the form of budgets. These resources are allocated downward from top managers. In most cases, top managers control the resources and, hence, can determine their distribution. Resources can be used as rewards and punishments, which are additional sources of power. Resource allocation also creates a dependency relationship. Lower-level participants depend on top managers for the financial and physical resources needed to perform their tasks. Top management can exchange resources in the form of salaries and bonuses, personnel, promotions and physical facilities for compliance with the outcomes they desire. The board of PCCW, Hong Kong's largest telecommunications firm, was concerned that the company's shares lagged well behind the local Hang Seng stock market index, limiting shareholder value. Therefore, a new bonus scheme was drawn up in 2007 that tied executive directors' and senior managers' bonuses to the company's share value as well as to internal goals such as numbers of subscribers and revenue per customer. Initial results were positive, with the company outperforming the Hang Seng during the first half of 2007. However, the shares slumped again during 2008, suggesting the stock price-linked bonus scheme had not worked.[51]

During the global economic downturn beginning in 2007–2008, considerable negative attention was focused on the impact of bonus schemes, particularly in the financial sector, which rewards short-term performance over long-term viability. In the UK, bankers received £13.2 billion in bonuses in the first five months of 2008, when only a few months later the British government was forced to implement a huge bailout package including partial privatization of several banks in order to avoid the total collapse of the country's banking system. Richard Lambert, head of Britain's employer association the CBI, singled out the bonus culture as a main cause of the global financial crisis, saying that it 'has encouraged some employees to take spectacular short-term risks, confident that if things work out well they will reap huge rewards and that if they don't they won't be around to pay the price.'[52]

Control of Decision Premises and Information

Control of decision premises means that top managers place constraints on decisions made at lower levels by specifying a frame of reference and guidelines for decision-making. In one sense, top managers make big decisions, whereas lower-level participants make small decisions. Top management decides which goal an organization will try to achieve, such as increased market share. Lower-level participants then decide how the goal is to be reached. In one company, top management appointed a committee to select a new marketing vice president. The CEO provided the committee with detailed qualifications that the new vice president should have. He also selected people to serve on the committee. In this way, the CEO shaped the decision premises within which the marketing vice president would be chosen. Top manager actions and decisions such as these place limits on the decisions of lower-level managers and thereby influence the outcome of their decisions.[53]

ONLINE
COUNTERPOINT 14.4

The control of information can also be a source of power. Managers in today's organizations recognize that information is a primary business resource and that by controlling what information is collected, how it is interpreted and how it is shared, they can influence how decisions are made.[54] In many of today's companies, especially in learning organizations, information is openly and broadly shared, which increases the power of people throughout the organization (see Counterpoint 14.7).

COUNTERPOINT 14.7

Even in the most 'enlightened' and 'progressive' of 'learning organizations', it is doubtful that all information is openly shared or even available to consult. The limited availability of this information, despite the existence of intranets and so on, is perhaps indicative of the limited trust and significant social distance that exists between different groups of employees. It is this distance that recurrently impedes and undermines cooperation.

Top managers generally have access to more information than other employees do. This information can be released as needed to shape the decision outcomes of other people. In one organization, Clark Ltd, the senior information technology (IT) manager controlled information given to the board of directors and thereby influenced the board's decision to purchase a sophisticated computer system.[55] The board of directors had formal authority to decide from which company the system would be purchased. The management services group was asked to recommend which of six computer manufacturers should receive the order. Jim Kenny was in charge of the management services group and Kenny disagreed with other managers about which system to purchase. As shown in Exhibit 14.3, other managers had to go through Kenny to have their viewpoints

EXHIBIT 14.3   Information Flow for Computer Decision at Clark Ltd.

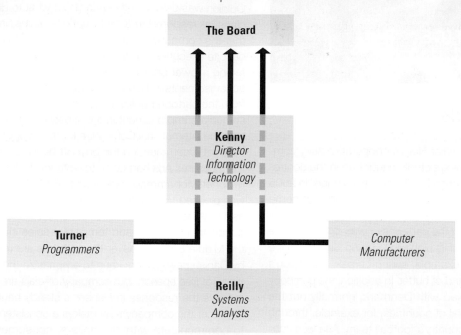

Source: Andrew M. Pettigrew, *The Politics of Organizational Decision-Making* (London: Tavistock, 1973), 235.

heard by the board. Kenny shaped the board's thinking toward selecting the system he preferred by controlling information given to them.

Control of information can also be used to shape decisions for self-serving, unethical and even illegal purposes. For example, at Hollinger International, Inc., which owned major newspapers around the world including the UK *Daily Telegraph*, Canada's *National Post*, the *Chicago Sun-Times* and Israel's *Jerusalem Post*, the board approved a series of transactions that allowed Canadian-born CEO, Conrad Black, and his colleagues to improperly draw off millions of dollars from the company for personal gain. Although the board has been criticized for its lax governance, directors insisted that their decisions were based on false, skewed or misleading information provided by Black. Black was eventually convicted of fraud and obstruction of justice by a US court and sentenced to six and a half years in prison, fined US$125 000 and ordered to pay $6.1 million in restitution.[56,57]

Middle managers and lower-level employees may also have access to information that can increase their power. A secretary to a senior executive can often control information that other people want and will thus be able to influence those people. Top executives depend on people throughout the organization for information about problems or opportunities. Middle managers or lower-level employees may manipulate the information they provide to top managers in order to influence decision outcomes.

Network Centrality   Network centrality means being centrally located in the organization and having access to information and people that are critical to the company's success. Top executives are more successful when they put themselves at the centre of a communication network, building connections with people throughout the company. Sir Howard Stringer, the CEO of Sony, is known as a skilled corporate politician who builds trust and alliances across different divisions and hierarchical levels. Stringer has been praised for his ability to network with almost everyone. He needs these political skills to understand the sprawling Sony empire and get the various divisions working together. 'He's the only one I know who can manage the Japanese [electronics side] and the show-bizzers [entertainment side],' said a former head of Sony Pictures Entertainment.[58]

IN PRACTICE

Arla Foods

Arla Foods, a major Nordic cooperative dairy company, was unexpectedly caught up in the controversy over publication in a Danish newspaper in 2005 of cartoons of the Prophet Mohammed that some Muslims found offensive. Although Arla had absolutely nothing to do with the cartoons, it was drawn into the dispute because of its high profile brand identities in the Middle East, for example, selling Lurpak, the region's most popular brand of butter. In addition, the company is closely identified with Denmark, normally not the most controversial of countries, for example, through sponsoring the country's football team. Arla was subjected to a boycott in which 50 000 stores in 20 Muslims countries pulled its products, action that was soon costing the company $1.8 million a day in lost sales.

Opinion was divided within Arla about what to do. Finn Hansen, responsible for international sales, insisted that the company needed to respond to the boycott, despite executives at Arla and other Danish firms preferring a lower profile. The company printed two large advertisements in Saudi newspapers distancing itself from the cartoon publication. Although there was little immediate improvement in the situation, a few weeks later the International Committee for the Support of the Prophet recommended the boycott be lifted, praising the measures Arla had taken to distance itself from the Prophet Mohammad caricatures. By 2008, Hansen was pleased to note that 'our position is just as good as it was before the Mohammad crisis'. There are still occasional flare-ups and temporary sales slumps in the Middle East whenever the cartoons are reprinted by Danish newspapers keen to emphasize the importance of free speech, but company officials are happy to leave the response in Hansen's steady hands. He says that the company now makes a consistent effort to communicate with its retailers, consumers and employees in the Middle East, so that 'Everyone knows that Arla has nothing to do with these drawings' and boycott talks quickly fade away.[59,60]

One of the barriers that women face in moving into middle and senior management is a tendency to be excluded from these traditional work networks that often rotate around male-focused activities including drinking, golf and following professional sports. Effective programmes have been established in several countries to encourage women to network both within and outside their organizations. For example, a pilot partnership between Britain's Treasury ministry and the international accounting and consultancy firm PricewaterhouseCoopers (PwC) brought together ten middle managers each from the two organizations to network together and informally mentor each other. The group strategized ways they could build networks where they could demonstrate their capacities within their organizations and beyond. The initial pilot was a success and several further rounds were launched involving women middle managers from different ministries and private companies. Tina Hallett, PwC partner in charge of women-in-work initiatives, who coordinated the firm's participation in the project, chairs PwCwomen, an internal network with 900 members – even including some men. Hallett says she got involved in organized networking because: 'I'd got to a reasonably senior level and I wanted to help other people to maximize their potential'.[61]

Employees may also exercise more power when their jobs are related to current areas of concern or opportunity. When a job pertains to pressing organizational problems, power is more easily accumulated. For example, managers at all levels who possess crisis leadership skills have gained power in today's world of international tensions and misunderstandings, major natural disasters and economic uncertainty.

Employees like Arla's Finn Hansen increase their network centrality by becoming knowledgeable and expert about certain activities or by taking on difficult tasks and acquiring specialized knowledge that makes them indispensable to managers above them. People who show initiative, work beyond what is expected, take on undesirable but important projects and show interest in learning about the company and industry often find themselves with influence. Physical location also helps because some locations are in the centre of things. Central location lets a person be visible to key people and become part of important interaction networks.

People   Top leaders often increase their power by surrounding themselves with a group of loyal executives.[62] Loyal managers keep the top leader informed and in touch with events and report possible disobedience or troublemaking in the organization. Top executives can use their central positions to build alliances and exercise substantial power when they have a management team that is fully in support of their decisions and actions.

This works in the opposite direction too. Lower-level people have greater power when they have positive relationships and connections with higher-ups. By being loyal and supportive of their bosses, employees sometimes gain favourable status and exert greater influence.

Although it is usual for senior executives to surround themselves with loyal employees, and for staff to cultivate positive relationships with their superiors, this all too often degenerates into sycophancy, where subordinates publicly agree with their superiors even when they privately know that errors are being made. Many recent corporate collapses and scandals have their origins in a culture of top management inability to encourage and accept constructive criticism from subordinates.[63]

At Lenovo, the chapter-opening *A Look Inside,* a healthier approach was adopted. As we saw, senior company officials emphasized building open lines of communication as a means to break down barriers between the mainly Chinese continuing Lenovo employees and the former IBM staff who joined them after the takeover. An additional positive effect of this approach is that staff are encouraged to make constructive criticism of company directions, even when this implies criticism of other managers. Then CEO, William Amelio, told his managers, 'You have to make sure you tell me what's not working well … if I find out later on that something was busted and you didn't include it … we have a problem.' As an example, during one senior management meeting in 2008, several participants were shocked that consumer sales boss Liu Jun sharply questioned Gerry P. Smith, Lenovo's head of supply chain, about shortages of the popular new netbook PCs. Although the tone was a little inappropriate and Jun later apologized, putting it down to poor English, Smith says 'I sat there and smiled and took it', and the incident left apparently no hard feelings.[64]

Horizontal Sources of Power

Horizontal power pertains to relationships across departments or divisions. All vice presidents are usually at the same level on the organization chart. Does this mean each department has the same amount of power? No. Horizontal power is not defined by the formal hierarchy or the organization chart. Each department makes a unique contribution to organizational success. Some departments will have greater say and will achieve their desired outcomes, whereas others will not. For example, Charles Perrow surveyed managers in several industrial firms.[65] He bluntly asked, 'Which department has the most power?' among four major departments: production, sales and marketing, R&D and finance and accounting. Partial survey results are given in Exhibit 14.4.

In most firms, sales had the greatest power. In a few firms, production was also quite powerful. On average, the sales and production departments were more powerful than R&D and finance, although substantial variation existed. Differences in the amount of horizontal power clearly occurred in those firms. Today, IT departments have growing power in many organizations.

Horizontal power is difficult to measure because power differences are not defined on the organization chart. However, some initial explanations for departmental power differences, such as those shown in Exhibit 14.4, have been found. The theoretical concept that explains relative power is called strategic contingencies.[66]

?

ONLINE
COUNTERPOINT 14.5

EXHIBIT 14.4   Ratings of Power among Departments in Industrial Firms

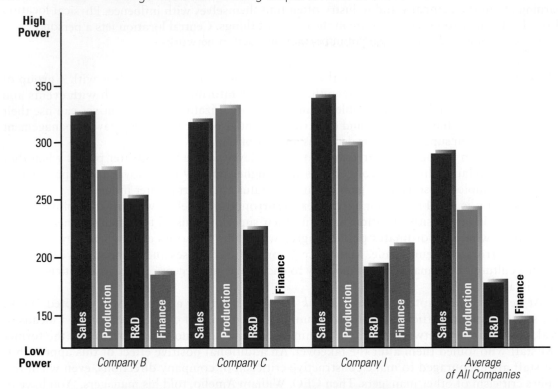

Source: Charles Perrow, 'Departmental Power and Perspective in Industrial Firms,' in Mayer N. Zald, ed., *Power in Organizations* (Nashville, TN: Vanderbilt University Press, 1970), 64.

Strategic Contingencies   Strategic contingencies are events and activities both inside and outside an organization that are essential for attaining organizational goals. Departments involved with strategic contingencies for the organization tend to have greater power. Departmental activities are important when they provide strategic value by solving problems or crises for the organization. For example, if an organization faces an intense threat from lawsuits and regulations, the legal department will gain power and influence over organizational decisions because it copes with such a threat. If product innovation is the key strategic issue, the power of R&D can be expected to be high.

ONLINE
COUNTERPOINT 14.5

The strategic contingency approach to power is similar to the resource dependence model described in Chapters 5 and 6. Recall that organizations try to reduce dependency on the external environment. The strategic contingency approach to power suggests that the departments most responsible for dealing with key resource issues and dependencies in the environment will become most powerful.

Power Sources   Jeffrey Pfeffer and Gerald Salancik, among others, have been instrumental in conducting research on the strategic contingency theory.[67] Their findings indicate that a department rated as powerful may possess one or more of the characteristics illustrated in Exhibit 14.5.[68] In some organizations these five power sources overlap, but each provides a useful way to evaluate sources of horizontal power.

1   Dependency. Interdepartmental dependency is a key element underlying relative power. Power is derived from having something someone else wants. The power of department A over department B is greater when department B depends on department A.[69] Materials,

EXHIBIT 14.5 Strategic Contingencies that Influence Horizontal Power among Departments

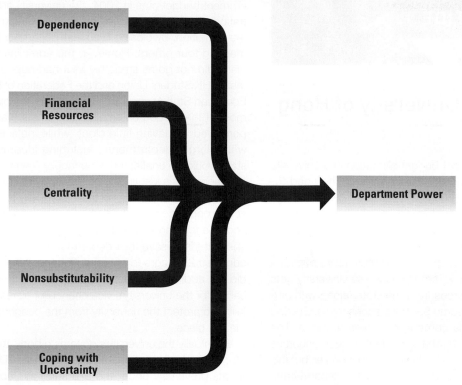

information and resources may flow between departments in one direction, such as in the case of sequential task interdependence (see Chapter 8). In such cases, the department receiving resources is in a lower power position than the department providing them. The number and strength of dependencies are also important. When seven or eight departments must come for help to the engineering department, for example, engineering is in a strong power position. In contrast, a department that depends on many other departments is in a low power position. Likewise, a department in an otherwise low power position might gain power through dependencies. If a factory cannot produce without the expertise of maintenance workers to keep the machines working, the maintenance department is in a strong power position because it has control over a strategic contingency.

2   **Financial resources.** There's a new golden rule in the business world: 'The person with the gold makes the rules'.[70] Control over resources is an important source of power in organizations. Money can be converted into other kinds of resources that are needed by other departments. Money generates dependency; departments that provide financial resources have something other departments want. Departments that generate income for an organization have greater power. Exhibit 14.4 showed sales as the most powerful unit in most industrial firms. This is because salespeople find customers and bring in money, thereby removing an important problem for the organization. An ability to provide financial resources also explains why certain departments are powerful in other organizations, such as universities.

In their study of the budgeting process at the University of Illinois in the USA, Pfeffer and Salancik concluded that, 'Power derived from acquiring resources is used to obtain more

IN PRACTICE

Chinese University of Hong Kong

You might expect budget allocation in a university to be a straightforward process. The need for financial resources can be determined by such things as the number of undergraduate students, the number of graduate students and the number of faculty in each department.

In fact, resource allocation at most universities is a highly political process. The Chinese University gets most of its resources from the state, along with students' fees and some business sponsorship. Beyond that, some funds come from research grants. The larger departments, that provide the most resources to the university, tend to have the most power, but this is complicated because some smaller departments, like Religion, provide a lot of 'service' courses to students from other departments. In addition, departments with high quality students bring prestige to the institution which is helpful in funding negotiations.

When the Chinese University faced substantial government budget cuts in 2004, the university administration decided to take the opportunity to restructure the institution, by closing five small departments and merging four others. However, the administration's plans did not go as smoothly as it had hoped. Both the CUHK Student Union and the Federation of Higher Education Staff Associations argued that the plan put most of the burden on small departments that were perceived as having little clout, while inefficiencies within larger departments, including incompetent staff, would be unaffected. One faculty member said, 'Management is just finding an easy way to cope with the budget cuts, picking on staff least likely to put up strong opposition. They could have cut the salaries of underperforming staff instead.' After students threatened sit-ins to save their departments, the university administration agreed on consultations. When these did not address their concerns the students started calling for the university's vice chancellor to resign for failing to protect the university from the budget cuts in the first place.

Eventually the university's governing body, the senate, backed down on many of the changes. Departments previously under the axe such as Japanese Studies were allowed to access external support to continue operations, while others slated for merger, such as Religion, were allowed to continue offering specialized degrees.[72]

resources, which in turn can be employed to produce more power – the rich get richer'.[71] The case of the Chinese University, discussed in the above *In Practice* box, confirms their conclusion, but only up to a point. While larger departments were initially in a stronger position to demand resources than smaller ones, a determined fightback by the smaller departments, supported by students' and faculty organizations, was able to ensure the pain of budget cuts was spread more evenly across the institution than the university administration initially intended.

3 **Centrality.** Centrality reflects a department's role in the primary activity of an organization.[73] One measure of centrality is the extent to which the work of the department affects the final output of the organization. For example, the production department is more central and usually has more power than staff groups (assuming no other critical contingencies). Centrality is associated with power because it reflects the contribution made to the organization. The corporate finance department of an investment bank generally has more power than the stock research department. By contrast, in the manufacturing firms described in Exhibit 14.4, finance tends to be low in power. When the finance department has the limited task of recording money and expenditures, it is not responsible for obtaining critical resources, nor for producing the products of the organization. Today, however, finance departments have greater power in many organizations because of the greater need for controlling costs.

4   Nonsubstitutability. Power is also determined by *nonsubstitutability,* which means that a department's function cannot be performed by other readily available resources. Similarly, if an employee cannot be easily replaced, his or her power is greater. If an organization has no alternative sources of skill and information, a department's power will be greater. This can be the case when management uses outside consultants. Consultants might be used as substitutes for staff people to reduce the power of staff groups.

The impact of substitutability on power was studied for programmers in computer departments.[74] When computers were first introduced, programming was a rare and specialized occupation. Programmers controlled the use of organizational computers because they alone possessed the knowledge to programme them. Over a period of about ten years, computer programming became a more common activity. People could be substituted easily, and the power of programming departments dropped, although the power of computer network planners grew as companies began depending on more and more complex IT systems.

5   Coping with Uncertainty. Elements in the environment can change swiftly and can be unpredictable and complex. In the face of uncertainty, little information is available to managers on appropriate courses of action. Departments that reduce this uncertainty for the organization will increase their power.[75] When market research personnel accurately predict changes in demand for new products, they gain power and prestige because they have reduced a critical uncertainty. But forecasting is only one technique. Sometimes uncertainty can be reduced by taking quick and appropriate action after an unpredictable event occurs.

ONLINE
COUNTERPOINT 14.7

Departments can cope with critical uncertainties by (1) obtaining prior information, (2) prevention, and (3) absorption.[76] *Obtaining prior information* means a department can reduce an organization's uncertainty by forecasting an event. Departments increase their power through *prevention* by predicting and forestalling negative events. *Absorption* occurs when a department takes action after an event to reduce its negative consequences. Consider the *In Practice* from the British healthcare industry on the next page.

BRIEFCASE 14.3

Due to the risks of cost overrun, the contract negotiating and legal teams at the state-run National Health Service (NHS) were in a high power position. They coped with a critical uncertainty by obtaining prior information and through prevention. However, room for absorption after problems appeared – including cost delays and the pullout of key contracts – was limited, as the NHS was caught between ballooning costs and delays on the one hand, and the refusal by contractors to continue working unless their additional costs were covered on the other hand.

It is more difficult to know what was happening internally at Accenture and Fujitsu, as private corporations' business matters are closed to public scrutiny. But in all likelihood the political attractiveness of gaining these huge and prestigious contracts drove corporate leaders to agree to contracts without adequate prior information and prevention. Healthcare IT experts within the firms, like Fujitsu's Andrew Rollerson, probably realized early on that the project would be problematic and a potential big money loser. The fact Rollerson spoke out publicly about the problems and was disciplined suggests his views were not heard within the company early enough. Eventually, however, Fujitsu's beancounters must have put down their feet and insisted on a contract renegotiation. When that didn't happen, Fujitsu reluctantly pulled out.

Horizontal power relationships in organizations change as strategic contingencies change, as for example Fujitsu came to confront the financial black hole the NPfIT project had become.

In a healthcare system dealing with a major health crisis, the communications department might gain power, for example, by soothing public fears and keeping people informed about the health department's efforts to control the spread of disease. As another example, in the late 1990s the World Bank, which provides developing countries with development financing, faced major criticism from civil society activists who said that many of the projects it supported made things worse for poor people in developing countries, even though the World Bank's overall mandate is to reduce global poverty. The Bank was put into crisis mode until its external relations

NHS and the National Programme for IT[77]

The British National Health Service (NHS) is one of the longest-operating universal health service systems in the world. Every British citizen is entitled to comprehensive healthcare coverage, in most cases without any charge. Although the NHS is operated as a public service, many services have always been provided by private contractors, including, for example, groups of doctors operating family practice clinics. In recent years the process of outsourcing has expanding with many ancillary services such as IT support being tendered to outside companies. So, when the NHS decided it needed to establish a new computer network for the whole service, including a comprehensive patient database that would allow service providers anywhere in England to access a patient's full medical records, it decided to outsource the project to a number of private service suppliers. The project, begun in 2004, is called the National Programme for Information Technology (NPfIT). It quickly became the world's largest non-military IT project, with a total cost possibly exceeding £20 billion.[78]

There are a number of different departments and interests involved in decision-making for such a project. Politicians from outside the NHS had ultimate authority over the institution and were clearly enthusiastic about the concept of 'joined-up services'. However, they were perhaps naïve about the challenges involved in making a coordinated IT system work in such a large institution with numerous legacy systems being used, and the potential for substantial resistance from GPs and other staff more concerned with day-to-day patient care than the long-term potential of IT. The NHS established a special unit, Connecting for Health (CfH), which would be responsible for implementing NPfIT. This unit included NHS internal IT experts who were very supportive of the project and would be responsible for designing the overall system architecture. However CfH also contained a Central Commercial Team (the 'beancounters') responsible for drawing up the contracts with outside contractors and monitoring their performance.

The relationship between government services and outside contractors is often fraught with difficulties, especially when, as in the case of the NHS, the systems being outsourced are extremely complex and difficult to specify. Cost overruns are common, and critics frequently accuse outside contractors of fleecing the public purse with unnecessary expenditures and frequent demands for contract amendments and increased payments.[79] These criticisms greatly strengthened the power of the beancounters. They ensured that the NPfIT contracts were tightly worded, with tough penalties for failure to deliver, and payments made only once the patient records and other data systems were operational. As the head of NPfIT, Richard Granger, put it, the system 'shifted a vast amount of the risk associated with the project to service providers, which have to demonstrate that their systems work before being paid'. Four main contracts were signed with outsourcing consultants, including one with Accenture valued at about £2 billion and another with Fujitsu worth about £1 billion.

Perhaps predictably, the project ran into difficulties from an early stage. The complexity of the system led to difficulty meeting the needs of all stakeholders. There were more legacy computer systems in place than the contractors expected, and folding them into the new NPfIT proved very time consuming. Integration of the various elements of the new IT system was much more complex than had been anticipated. Some of the expert IT subcontractors that the contractor companies like Accenture and Fujitsu had hired were unable to produce operational software.

Due to the tight contracts that had been signed, the cost of the implementation delays fell on the contractors and subcontractors. By 2006, Accenture had already lost £400 million, even though it was by far the most successful of the contractors in putting its parts of the IT systems into place. Accenture's bosses decided to cut their losses and negotiated a pull-out from the contract, avoiding most of the very heavy penalties that could have been assessed. By 2007, Fujitsu also found itself in difficulties. Its project chief was suspended for telling an industry conference of his concerns: 'It isn't working, and it isn't going to work,' said Andrew Rollerson. 'There is a belief that the national programme is somehow going to propel transformation in the NHS simply by delivering an IT system. Nothing could be further from the truth. A vacuum, a chasm, is opening up.' In 2008 Fujitsu tried to renegotiate its contract with the NHS, but without success. It, too, pulled out, saying, 'In the end the terms the NHS were willing to agree to we could not have afforded... There was a limit beyond which we could not go.' The result was that only two main contractors remained. This seriously weakens the bargaining position of the NHS, because the remaining contractors know that the NHS's options are limited, and that the government cannot afford the embarrassment of allowing the project to fail. Richard Granger left NPfIT in 2008 amid rumours he was exhausted by the enormity of the project and the delays and cost overruns. The project limped along for a couple of years but was eventually scrapped in 2011 after another negative report from the UK parliament's watchdog Public Account Committee.[80]

The strength of the NHS beancounters in the NPfIT process derived from the NHS's legitimate need to control costs on an extremely complex project. But did the rigid focus on payment-for-results mean that the real stakeholders – patients and healthcare providers – didn't get their concerns heard, and thus resisted participating in it? Or was the project simply too ambitious to ever succeed?[81,82]

(communications) department embarked on an extensive, costly and substantially effective campaign to build links with civil society and to improve the image of the organization.[83] As in the World Bank example, the communications department can gain power by helping the organization present a positive side to the story and counteract the arguments of protestors. Departments that help organizations cope with new strategic issues will have greater power.

Political Processes in Organizations

Politics, like power, is intangible and difficult to measure. It is hidden from view and is hard to observe in a systematic way. Two surveys uncovered the following reactions of managers toward political behaviour.[84]

ONLINE COUNTERPOINT 14.8

1 Most managers have a negative view toward politics and believe that politics will more often hurt than help an organization in achieving its goals.
2 Managers believe that political behaviour is common in practically all organizations.
3 Most managers think that political behaviour occurs more often at upper rather than lower levels in organizations.
4 Political behaviour arises in certain decision domains, such as structural change, but is absent from other decisions, such as handling employee grievances.

Based on these surveys, politics seems more likely to occur at the top levels of an organization and around certain issues and decisions. Moreover, managers do not approve of political behaviour (see Counterpoint 14.8). The remainder of this chapter explores more fully what political behaviour is, when it should be used, the type of issues and decisions most likely to be associated with politics, and some political tactics that may be effective.

COUNTERPOINT 14.8

An alternative possible explanation of managers' aversion to references to 'politics' is that it undermines their sense of professionalism and authority. Instead of the image of impartial, rational professionalism which they like to project, managers are portrayed as 'political fixers'. Yet, the rough and tumble of management is all about coping with uncertainty and endeavouring to 'fix' problems on the basis of limited information, often with an eye to how it will play with the boss, and ultimately with regard to how it will be received by shareholders.

Definition

Power has been described as the available force or potential for achieving desired outcomes (see Counterpoint 14.9). *Politics* is the use of power to influence decisions in order to achieve those outcomes. The exercise of power and influence has led to two ways to define politics – as self-serving behaviour or as a widespread organizational decision process. The first definition emphasizes that politics is self-serving and involves activities that are not sanctioned by the organization.[85]

COUNTERPOINT 14.9

What these definitions tend to overlook is how power becomes institutionalized – notably in social and organizational hierarchies. Simply occupying an elevated position in a hierarchy provides access to resources and a degree of legitimacy. Much is done routinely that serves to reproduce this position. At the same time, there is always the possibility that the institution will be challenged – by competitors or from within by resistance or incompetence. So whatever power is vested in institutions and hierarchical position, it is dependent upon subordinates' ability and willingness to reproduce their dependence. Paradoxically, it is the person or group that is least dependent upon others that has the greatest (personal or collective) power.

In this view, politics involves deception and dishonesty for purposes of individual self-interest and leads to conflict and disharmony within the work environment. This dark view of politics is widely held by laypeople, and political activity certainly can be used in this way. Recent studies have shown that workers who perceive this kind of political activity within their companies often have related feelings of anxiety and job dissatisfaction. Studies also support the belief that inappropriate use of politics is related to low employee morale, inferior organizational performance and poor decision-making.[86] This view of politics explains why managers in the aforementioned surveys did not approve of political behaviour.

Although politics can be used in a negative, self-serving way, the appropriate use of political behaviour can serve organizational goals.[87] The second view sees politics as a widespread organizational process for resolving differences among organizational interest groups.[88] Politics is the process of bargaining and negotiation that is used to overcome conflicts and differences of opinion. In this view, politics is similar to the coalition-building decision processes defined in Chapter 13.

ONLINE
COUNTERPOINT 14.9

Political behaviour can be either a positive or a negative force. Politics is the use of power to get things accomplished – good things as well as bad. Uncertainty and conflict are natural and inevitable, and politics is the mechanism for reaching agreement, whether by unforced consent or through coercion. Politics allows decisions to be made that otherwise might be stalemated or unsolvable.

When is Political Activity Used?

BRIEFCASE 14.4

Three **domains of political activity** (areas in which politics plays a role) in most organizations are structural change, management succession and resource allocation.

Structural reorganizations strike at the heart of power and authority relationships. Reorganizations such as those discussed in Chapter 4 change responsibilities and tasks, which can also affect the underlying power base from strategic contingencies. For these reasons, a major reorganization can lead to an explosion of political activity (although of course reorganizations are themselves often the outcome of political activity!).[89] Managers may actively bargain and negotiate to maintain the responsibilities and power bases they have. Mergers and acquisitions also frequently create tremendous political activity. Organizational changes such as hiring new executives, promotions and transfers have great political significance, particularly at top organizational levels where uncertainty is high and networks of trust, cooperation and communication among executives are important.[90] Hiring decisions can generate uncertainty, discussion and disagreement. Managers can use hiring and promotion to strengthen network alliances and coalitions by putting their own people in prominent positions.

The third area of political activity is resource allocation. Resource allocation decisions encompass all resources required for organizational performance, including salaries, operating budgets, employees, office facilities, equipment, use of the company aeroplane and so forth. Resources are so vital that disagreement about priorities exists, and political processes help resolve the dilemmas.

Using Power, Politics and Collaboration

One theme in this chapter has been that power in organizations is not primarily a phenomenon of the individual. It is related to the resources that departments command, the role departments play in an organization and the environmental contingencies with which departments cope. Position and responsibility, more than personality and style, determine a manager's influence on outcomes in the organization.

Power is exercised through the individual political behaviour of individuals, however. Individual managers seek agreement about a strategy to achieve their departments' desired outcomes. Individual managers negotiate decisions and adopt tactics that enable them to acquire and use power. In addition, managers develop ways to increase cooperation and collaboration within the organization to reduce damaging conflicts.

In one study, HR executives, who were not seen as having centrality to the firm's mission, took a low-key approach to try to influence others, whereas finance executives, who had a more central and powerful position, used harder, more direct influence tactics.[91] The following sections briefly summarize various tactics that managers can use to increase the power base of their departments, political tactics they can use to achieve desired outcomes, and tactics for increasing collaboration. These tactics are summarized in Exhibit 14.6.

Tactics for Increasing Power

Four tactics for increasing power for the organization are as follows:

1 *Enter areas of high uncertainty.* One source of departmental power is to cope with critical uncertainties.[92] If department managers can identify key uncertainties and take steps to remove those uncertainties, the department's power base will be enhanced. The contracting and legal teams in the NHS example above initially enhanced their power through promising to remove uncertainties with a tough negotiating strategy. In a manufacturing plant, uncertainties could arise from stoppages on an assembly line, from the quality demanded of a new product, or from the inability to predict a demand for new services. Once an

EXHIBIT 14.6 Power and Political Tactics in Organizations

Tactics for Increasing the Power Base	Political Tactics for Using Power	Tactics for Enhancing Collaboration
1. Enter areas of high uncertainty. 2. Create dependencies. 3. Provide scarce resources. 4. Satisfy strategic contingencies. 5. Make a direct appeal.	1. Build coalitions and expand networks. 2. Use confrontation and negotiation. 3. Schedule intergroup consultation. 4. Enhance legitimacy and expertise. 5. Create superordinate goals.	1. Create integration devices. 2. Assign loyal people to key positions. 3. Control decision premises. 4. Practice member rotation.

uncertainty is identified, the department can take action to cope with it. By their very nature, uncertain tasks will not be solved immediately. Trial and error will be needed, which is to the advantage of the department. The trial-and-error process provides experience and expertise that cannot easily be duplicated by other departments.

2 *Create dependencies.* Dependencies are another source of power.[93] When the organization depends on a department for information, materials, knowledge or skills, that department will hold power over others. This power can be increased by incurring obligations. Doing additional work that helps out other departments will obligate the other departments to respond at a future date. The power accumulated by creating a dependency can be used to resolve future disagreements in the department's favour. An equally effective and related strategy is to reduce dependency on other departments by acquiring necessary information or skills. IT departments have created dependencies in many organizations because of the rapid changes in this area. Employees in other departments depend on the IT unit to master complex software programmes, changing use of the internet and other advances so that they will have the information they need to perform effectively.

3 *Provide scarce resources.* Resources are always important to organizational survival. Departments that accumulate resources and provide them to an organization in the form of money, information or facilities will be powerful. University departments with the greatest power tend to be those that obtain external research funds for contributions to university overhead. Likewise, sales departments are powerful in industrial firms because they bring in financial resources.

4 *Satisfy strategic contingencies.* The theory of strategic contingencies says that some elements in the external environment and within the organization are especially important for organizational success. A contingency could be a critical event, a task for which there are no substitutes, or a central task that is interdependent with many others in the organization. An analysis of the organization and its changing environment will reveal strategic contingencies. To the extent that contingencies are new or are not being satisfied, there is room for a department to move into those critical areas and increase its importance and power.

In summary, the allocation of power in an organization is not random. Power is the result of organizational processes that can be understood and to a degree predicted. The abilities to reduce uncertainty, increase dependency on one's own department, obtain resources and cope with strategic contingencies all enhance a department's power.

Political Tactics for Using Power

The use of power in organizations requires both skill and willingness. Many decisions are made through political processes because rational decision processes do not fit. Uncertainty or disagreement is too high. Political tactics for using power to influence decision outcomes include the following:

1 *Build coalitions and expand networks.* Coalition building means taking the time to talk with other managers to persuade them to your point of view.[94] Most important decisions are made outside of formal meetings. Managers discuss issues with each other and reach agreement. Effective managers are those who huddle, meeting in groups of twos and threes to resolve key issues.[95] Effective managers also build networks of relationships across hierarchical and functional boundaries. Networks can be expanded by (1) reaching out to establish contact with additional managers and (2) coopting dissenters. A research project found that the ability to build networks has a positive impact on both employees' perception of a manager's effectiveness and the ability of the manager to influence performance.[96] Establishing contact with additional managers means building good interpersonal

relationships based on liking, trust and respect. Reliability and the motivation to work with, rather than exploit, others are part of both networking and coalition building.[97] The second approach to expanding networks, cooptation, is the act of bringing a dissenter into one's network. One example of cooptation involved a university committee whose membership was based on promotion and tenure. Several professors who were critical of the tenure and promotion process were appointed to the committee. Once a part of the administrative process, they could see the administrative point of view. Cooptation effectively brought them into the administrative network.[98]

2 *Assign loyal people to key positions.* Another political tactic is to assign trusted and loyal people to key positions in the organization or department. Top managers as well as department heads often use the hiring, transfer and promotion processes to place in key positions people who are sympathetic to the outcomes of the department, thus helping to achieve departmental goals.[99] Top leaders frequently use this tactic, as we discussed earlier. However, this can backfire if people are chosen more for their loyalty than their capacities. For example, the Australian-born media baron, Rupert Murdoch, has appointed his son James to senior positions within the News Corp. empire.[100] Initially James Murdoch gained a reputation as a savvy businessman with a mind of his own, but the wisdom of the appointment was later put into doubt as he was dragged into the phone hacking scandal that resulted in the closing of the company's British tabloid *The News of the World* and numerous arrests of News Corp journalists. By 2012 James had been forced to resign from several key positions in the family media empire.[101] Similarly, the sons of late British media mogul, Robert Maxwell, were in senior company positions when their father died mysteriously leaving behind a collapsing business empire. An inquiry found Kevin 'bears a heavy responsibility in respect of many of the events leading to the business collapse' which left hundreds of workers without company pensions.[102] When he became CEO at US investment bank Merrill Lynch & Co., Stan O'Neal removed a whole generation of top talent and moved in other managers who supported his vision and goals for the organization. O'Neal was eventually forced to leave Merrill Lynch after the bank lost at least $3.7 billion in bad investments on sub-prime mortgages. The bank came close to failing and had to be taken over by the Bank of America to avoid bankruptcy.[103,104]

3 *Control decision premises.* To control decision premises means to constrain the boundaries of a decision. One technique is to choose or limit information provided to other managers. A common method is simply to put your department's best foot forward, such as selectively presenting favourable criteria. A variety of statistics can be assembled to support the departmental point of view. A university department that is growing rapidly and has a large number of students can make claims for additional resources by emphasizing its growth and large size. Such objective criteria do not always work, but they are a valuable step.

Decision premises can be further influenced by limiting the decision process. Decisions can be influenced by the items put on an agenda for an important meeting or even by the sequence in which items are discussed.[105] Items discussed last, when time is short and people want to leave, will receive less attention than those discussed earlier. Calling attention to specific problems and suggesting alternatives also will affect outcomes. Stressing a specific problem to get it – rather than problems not relevant to your department – on the agenda is an example of agenda setting.

4 *Enhance legitimacy and expertise.* Managers can exert the greatest influence in areas in which they have recognized legitimacy and expertise. If a request is within the task domain of a department and is consistent with the department's vested interest, other departments will tend to comply. Members can also identify external consultants or other experts within the organization to support their cause.[106] For example, a financial vice president in a large retail firm wanted to fire the director of HR management. She hired a consultant to

evaluate the HR projects undertaken to date. A negative report from the consultant provided sufficient legitimacy to fire the director, who was replaced with a director loyal to the financial vice president.

5 *Make a direct appeal.* If managers do not ask, they seldom receive. Political activity is effective only when goals and needs are made explicit so the organization can respond. Managers should bargain aggressively and be persuasive. An assertive proposal may be accepted because other managers have no better alternatives. Moreover, an explicit proposal will often receive favourable treatment because other alternatives are ambiguous and less well defined. Effective political behaviour requires sufficient forcefulness and risk taking to at least ask for what you need to achieve desired outcomes.

BRIEFCASE 14.5

This chapter's *Bookmark 14.0* describes some basic psychological principles that underlie successful political influence tactics. Managers can use this understanding to assert influence and get things done within the organization. When managers ignore political tactics, they may find themselves failing without understanding why. This is partly the reason Tim Koogle failed to accomplish a key acquisition at Yahoo! (see the In Practice case example below).

Tactics for Enhancing Collaboration

Power and political tactics are important means for getting things done within organizations. Most organizations today have at least moderate inter-unit conflict. An additional approach in many organizations is to overcome conflict by stimulating cooperation and collaboration among departments to support the attainment of organizational goals. Tactics for enhancing collaboration include the following:

1 *Create integration devices.* As described in Chapter 4, teams, task forces and project managers who span the boundaries between departments can be used as integration devices. Bringing together representatives from conflicting departments in joint problem-solving teams is an effective way to enhance collaboration because representatives learn to understand each other's point of view.[107] Sometimes a full-time integrator is assigned to achieve cooperation and collaboration by meeting with members of the respective departments and exchanging information. The integrator has to understand each group's problems and must be able to move both groups toward a solution that is mutually acceptable.[108]

Teams and task forces reduce conflict and enhance cooperation because they integrate people from different departments. Integration devices can also be used to enhance cooperation between labour and management, as the example of German-based car manufacturer Volkswagen and union IG Metall demonstrates (the *In Practice* box two pages on).

Labour–management teams, which are designed to increase worker participation and provide a cooperative model for solving union–management problems, are used at many companies throughout the world. For example, in 2006 Transnet, the South African state company responsible for the country's national airline, railways and ports, set up teams with the industries' main trade unions in order to work out a restructuring plan that would meet the needs of the country, company, workers and transport users.[109]

2 *Use confrontation and negotiation.* Confrontation occurs when parties in conflict directly engage one another and try to work out their differences. Negotiation is the bargaining process that often occurs during confrontation and that enables the parties to systematically reach a solution. These techniques bring appointed representatives from the departments together to work out a serious dispute. For example, in 2006 and 2007, Chilean copper miners were engaged in disputes with their employer, Codelco, over wages and labour conditions, which they eventually resolved after tough negotiations.[110,111]

BOOKMARK 3.0

Have you read this book?

Against Management

BY MARTIN PARKER

Throughout this book we have talked about management as something that is inevitable and important, indeed pivotal in the life of organizations. Managers are presented as able to build a great organization, or lead an organization to ruin, depending on their capacities and their ability to select the right organization theory and design strategies. But actually, do managers really have as much power as we often imagine, and even if they do, is it desirable for the world to be 'managed'?

In this provocative and influential book, Martin Parker takes aim at the idea that perfecting management is a desirable goal. He argues that managerialism is a dogmatic ideology, insisting that only markets run by professional managers can efficiently organize human interaction. In fact, the actual results of this system are often dehumanizing. He says 'organizations are getting too big to be human', they are offering an 'increasingly homogenized set of choices for consumers,' and they have constructed a world in which the artifice of brands has become more important and more valuable than the products upon which the brand logo is applied.

Parker is critical of efforts to humanize managerial capitalism originating from within business schools. For example, he argues that the field of 'business ethics' when taught in business schools is a figleaf that covers up the need for a deeper political debate about what kind of a society we want to construct, and what types of organizations are needed in order to facilitate a more human-oriented society. In general, he believes that academia, which emphasizes the importance of a mythological 'neutrality', is less effective than civil society campaigners in identifying and rooting out the negative features of business activity.

Given the importance of organizations in many people's lives, Parker explores whether they could play a more positive, holistic role if they were stripped of their managerialist focus on market efficiency. He speculates about the possibility of 'orgunities': organizations that would act as places of spiritual belonging and of productive enterprise. Of course, organizations are exclusive institutions with entry criteria and the ever-present possibility of enforced exit. Thus, transferring citizenship to them from the universal level of the state could restrict rather than enhance freedoms, an issue Parker somewhat skates over.

Ultimately, Parker argues for 'demanagerialization' of society, so that the normative goals of organizations would be as important as their 'efficiency', which is currently measured solely from the point of view of their success in generating profits. He calls for an expansion of grassroots, community level organizations that would meet local needs, such as quality childcare and environmentally sustainable transportation. Rather than devoting themselves to a single corporate identity, people should be encouraged to nurture our multifaceted identities, through multiple and decentred community memberships.

Parker's critique may seem radical and his solutions Utopian. It is important, however, that we keep open the possibility for alternative ways of thinking about organizations and also that we are open to criticism when organizations stray far from their ultimate purpose, which is to serve the needs of people.[112]

Against Management by Martin Parker, is published by Polity.

Confrontation and negotiation involve some risk. There is no guarantee that discussions will focus on a conflict or that emotions will not get out of hand. However, if members are able to resolve the conflict on the basis of face-to-face discussions, they will find new respect for each other, and future collaboration becomes easier. The beginnings of relatively permanent attitude change are possible through direct negotiation.

Confrontation and negotiation are more likely to be successful when managers engage in a *win–win strategy*. Win–win means both sides adopt a positive attitude and strive to

IN PRACTICE

Yahoo!

In late March of 2000, Yahoo! began negotiating to buy online auction leader eBay Inc. Tim Koogle, Yahoo!'s CEO at the time, was fully in support of the deal, believing it would enable the company to beef up its e-commerce revenues and bring needed new blood to the increasingly insular Yahoo! culture. But the deal never happened, and while Yahoo!'s fortunes flagged, eBay's revenues and net income continued to climb.

What happened? Jeffrey Mallett, Yahoo!'s president, opposed the acquisition of eBay, and he used political tactics to quash it. Koogle had always been a consensus-style manager. He believed the top leaders would debate the pros and cons of the acquisition and arrive at the best decision. In addition, he felt sure the merits of the eBay deal would ultimately win the day. But Mallett, who insiders say was already angling to take over the CEO job, began courting co-founders

Jerry Yang and David Filo. Eventually, he convinced them that the eBay culture was a poor fit with Yahoo!. With Koogle outnumbered, the deal fell apart. A former Yahoo! manager called it management by persuasion.

By failing to build a coalition, Koogle allowed Mallett to control this important decision. It's only one example of several that ultimately led to Koogle being pushed out. Despite Mallett's political moves, he was passed over for the top job in favour of an outsider, who board members felt could turn the struggling company around. Koogle took the decision to seek a new CEO calmly and blamed himself for not keeping a closer eye on Mallett.[113] However, Yahoo! performance continued to disappoint and Mallett himself resigned not long after. Ten years later the company remains one of the big IT names, but sales have stagnated and Yahoo! has never achieved the predominant position its early successes suggested. In 2012 the company hired former Google executive, Merissa Meyer as CEO, hoping to import some of Google Inc's market leading gold dust. However by 2016 there was no sign of an upturn, with Yahoo's core business valued at almost nothing and widespread demands for Mayer to step down. Meanwhile, eBay continues to go from strength to strength.[114,115]

resolve the conflict in a way that will benefit each other.[116] If the negotiations deteriorate into a strictly win–lose strategy (each group wants to defeat the other), the confrontation will usually be ineffective. The differences between win–win and win–lose strategies of negotiation are shown in Exhibit 14.7. With a win–win strategy – which includes defining the problem as mutual, communicating openly and avoiding threats – understanding can be changed while the dispute is resolved.

One type of negotiation, used to resolve a disagreement between workers and management, is referred to as **collective bargaining**. The bargaining process is usually accomplished through a union and results in an agreement that specifies each party's responsibilities for the next several years, as with the contract between VW and IG Metall.

3 *Schedule intergroup consultation.* When conflict is intense and enduring, and department members are suspicious and uncooperative, top managers may intervene as third parties to help resolve the conflict or bring in third-party consultants from outside the organization.[117] This process, sometimes called *workplace mediation,* is a strong intervention to reduce conflict because it involves bringing the disputing parties together and allowing each side to present its version of the situation. The technique has been developed by such psychologists as Robert Blake, Jane Mouton and Richard Walton.[118]

Department members attend a workshop, which may last for several days, away from day-to-day work problems. This approach is similar to the organization development (OD) approach described in Chapter 12. The conflicting groups are separated, and each group

IN PRACTICE

Volkswagen and IG Metall

Germany has risen from catastrophic defeat in the second World War to become Europe's pre-eminent manufacturing centre. This success is built on a unique system of labour–management cooperation called codetermination in which workers are entitled to significant representation in company decision-making processes. One of the strongest partnerships has been at the automaker Volkswagen, the world's third largest automobile maker.

Like other major automakers, Volkswagen has gone through a series of highs and lows, depending on the strength of the company's product offer, as well as competitors' strategies. In contrast with other European car companies which have tended to engage in mass layoffs, VW has usually been able to agree on less radical measures with IG Metall, the major union representing most German VW workers. For example, when the company came close to bankruptcy in 1993 and 1994, workers agreed on a package of reduced salaries and short-hours working in order to save costs. Again, in 2004, as VW attempted to restructure in order to respond to heightened competition from Asian carmakers, the union was able to agree on a pay freeze in return for seven years job security.

Beginning in the 1980s, Volkswagen has acquired a number of foreign automakers, including Spain's SEAT, and Skoda from the Czech Republic. VW workers worried that their jobs would be at risk given these countries' lower labour costs. However, the company and union agreed on setting up first a European Works Council including representation from workers and management across the company's European plants, and then a World Works Council including representation from the company's plants overseas, including in Latin America where VW is a major player. The international works councils have not removed all frictions between management and workers over attempts to reduce costs by moving production to lower wage countries, but Volkswagen has maintained a much higher proportion of its manufacturing capacity within Germany and other high wage European countries than is the case for many other companies.

The cooperative approach is constantly under threat, however, given globalization and pressures to lower costs. In 2009, Porsche, traditionally much less sympathetic to unions, took effective control of Volkswagen, although through 2013 the new management and IG Metall were able to hammer out collective agreements covering wages and benefits giving small pay raises up to 2015; there will be further tests of the union-management relationship in light of the financial hit the company has taken in the 2015 emissions scandal.[119] Not all of the good relationships between management and union representatives were built on an entirely honourable foundation, however; evidence emerged that the company had paid for prostitutes for works council members on a junket to Brazil.[120,121]

is invited to discuss and make a list of its perceptions of itself and the other group. Group representatives publicly share these perceptions, and together the groups discuss the results.

Intergroup consultation can be quite demanding for everyone involved. Although it is fairly easy to have conflicting groups list perceptions and identify discrepancies, exploring their differences face-to-face and agreeing to change is more difficult. If handled correctly, these sessions can help department employees understand each other much better and lead to improved attitudes and better working relationships for years to come.

4 *Practice member rotation.* Rotation means that individuals from one department can be asked to work in another department on a temporary or permanent basis. The advantage is that individuals become submerged in the values, attitudes, problems and goals of the other department. In addition, individuals can explain the problems and goals of their original departments to their new colleagues. This enables a frank, accurate exchange of views and information. Rotation works slowly to reduce conflict but is very effective for changing the underlying attitudes and perceptions that promote conflict.[122]

EXHIBIT 14.7 Negotiating Strategies

Win–Win Strategy	Win–Lose Strategy
1. Define the conflict as a mutual problem.	1. Define the problem as a win–lose situation.
2. Pursue joint outcomes.	2. Pursue own group's outcomes.
3. Find creative agreements that satisfy both groups.	3. Force the other group into submission.
4. Be open, honest and accurate in communicating the group's needs, goals and proposals.	4. Be deceitful, inaccurate and misleading in communicating the group's needs, goals and proposals.
5. Avoid threats (to reduce the other's defensiveness).	5. Use threats (to force submission).
6. Communicate flexibility of position.	6. Communicate strong commitment (rigidity) regarding one's position.

Source: Adapted from David W. Johnson and Frank P. Johnson, *Joining Together: Group Theory and Group Skills* (Englewood Cliffs, NJ: Prentice-Hall, 1975), 182–183.

5 *Create shared mission and superordinate goals.* Another strategy is for top management to create a shared mission and establish superordinate goals that require cooperation among departments.[123] Studies have shown that when employees from different departments see that their goals are linked together, they will openly share resources and information.[124] To be effective, superordinate goals must be substantial, and employees must be granted the time and incentives to work cooperatively in pursuit of the superordinate goals rather than departmental subgoals.

Summary and Interpretation

The central message of this chapter is that conflict, power and politics are endemic to organizing. Differences in goals, backgrounds and tasks can throw groups into conflict. Managers use power and politics to manage and resolve conflict. Two views of organization were presented. The rational model of organization assumes that organizations have specific goals and that problems can be logically solved. The other view, the political model of organization, is the basis for much of the chapter. This view assumes that the goals of an organization are not specific or agreed upon. Departments have different values and interests, so managers come into conflict. Decisions are made on the basis of power and political influence. Bargaining, negotiation, persuasion and coalition building decide outcomes.

The chapter also discussed the vertical and horizontal sources of power. Vertical sources of power include formal position, resources, control of decision premises and network centrality. In general, managers at the top of the organizational hierarchy wield more power than people at lower levels. However, positions all along the hierarchy can be designed to increase the power of employees. As organizations face increased competition and environmental uncertainty, top executives are finding that empowering middle managers and lower-level employees can help the organization be more competitive. Research into horizontal power processes has revealed that certain characteristics make some departments more powerful than others. Such factors as dependency, resources and nonsubstitutability determine the influence of departments.

Managers can use political tactics such as coalition building, expanded networks and control of decision premises. Tactics for enhancing collaboration include integration devices, confrontation and negotiation, intergroup consultation, member rotation and shared mission and superordinate goals.

KEY CONCEPTS

authority	domains of political	nonsubstitutability	sources of intergroup
centrality	activity	political model	conflict
collective bargaining	financial resources	political tactics for using	strategic contingencies
competition	intergroup conflict	power	tactics for enhancing
confrontation	labour–management	power	collaboration
coping with uncertainty	teams	power sources	tactics for increasing
decision premises	negotiation	rational model	power
dependency	network centrality		

Discussion Questions

1 Give an example from your personal experience of how differences in tasks, personal background and training lead to conflict among groups. How might task interdependence have influenced that conflict?

2 A noted expert on organizations said that some conflict is beneficial to organizations. Discuss.

3 In a rapidly changing organization, are decisions more likely to be made using the rational or political model of organization? Discuss.

4 What is the difference between power and authority? Is it possible for a person to have formal authority but to exercise little power? Discuss.

5 In Exhibit 14.4, R&D has greater power in company B than in the other firms. Discuss possible strategic contingencies that give R&D greater power in this firm.

6 State University X receives 90 per cent of its financial resources from the state and is overcrowded with students. It is trying to pass regulations to limit student enrolment. Private University Y receives 90 per cent of its income from student tuition and has barely enough students to make ends meet. It is actively recruiting students for next year. In which university will

students have greater power? What implications will this have for professors and administrators? Discuss.

7 A bookkeeper at HealthSouth Corp., which is currently embroiled in a financial scandal, tried for several years to expose fraud in the organization's accounting department, but he couldn't get anyone to pay attention to his claims. How would you evaluate this employee's power? What might he have done to increase his power and call notice to the ethical and legal problems at the firm?

8 The engineering college at a major university brings in three times as many government research dollars as does the rest of the university combined. Engineering appears wealthy and has many professors on full-time research status. Yet, when internal research funds are allocated, engineering gets a larger share of the money, even though it already has substantial external research funds. Why would this happen?

9 Which do you believe would have a greater long-term impact on changing employee attitudes toward increased collaboration – intergroup consultation or confrontation and negotiation? Discuss.

Chapter 14 Workbook How Do You Handle Conflict?

Think about how you typically handle a dispute with a team member, friend, or co-worker, and then answer the following statements based on whether they are True or False for you. There are no right or wrong answers, so answer honestly.

		Mostly False	Mostly True
1.	I feel that differences are not worth arguing about.	____	____
2.	I would avoid a person who wants to discuss a disagreement.	____	____
3.	I would rather keep my views to myself than argue.	____	____
4.	I typically avoid taking positions that create a dispute.	____	____
5.	I try hard to win my position.	____	____
6.	I strongly assert my opinion in a disagreement.	____	____
7.	I raise my voice to get other people to accept my position.	____	____
8.	I stand firm in expressing my viewpoint.	____	____
9.	I give in a little if other people do the same.	____	____
10.	I will split the difference to reach an agreement.	____	____
11.	I offer trade-offs to reach a solution.	____	____
12.	I give up some points in exchange for others.	____	____
13.	I don't want to hurt others' feelings.	____	____
14.	I am quick to agree when someone I am arguing with makes a good point.	____	____
15.	I try to smooth over disagreements by minimizing their seriousness.	____	____
16.	I want to be considerate of other people's emotions.	____	____
17.	I suggest a solution that includes the other person's point of view.	____	____
18.	I combine arguments into a new solution from ideas raised in the dispute.	____	____
19.	I try to include the other person's ideas to create a solution they will accept.	____	____
20.	I assess the merits of other viewpoints as equal to my own.	____	____

Scoring and interpretation: Five categories of conflict-handling strategies are measured by these 20 questions: avoiding, dominating, bargaining, accommodating and collaborating. These five strategies reflect different levels of personal desire for *assertiveness or cooperation*. The higher your score for a strategy, the more likely that is your preferred conflict-handling approach. A lower score suggests you probably do not use that approach.

Dominating Style (my way) reflects a high degree of assertiveness to get one's own way and fulfil one's self-interest. Add one point for each Mostly True for items 5-8: _____.

Accommodating Style (your way) reflects a high degree of cooperativeness and a desire to oblige or help others as most important. Add one point for each Mostly True for items 13-16:_____.

Avoiding Style (no way) reflects neither assertiveness nor cooperativeness, which means that conflict is avoided whenever possible. Add one point for each Mostly True for items 1-4:_____.

Bargaining Style (half way) reflects a tendency to meet half way by using a moderate amount of both assertiveness and cooperativeness. Add one for each Mostly True for items 9-12:_____.

Collaborating Style (our way) reflects a high degree of both assertiveness and cooperativeness to meet the needs of both parties. Add one for each Mostly True for items 17-20:_____.

Questions

1 Which strategy do you find easiest to use? Most difficult?

2 How would your answers change if the other party to the conflict was a friend, family member or co-worker?

3 How do you feel about your approach to handling conflict? What changes would you like to make?

Closing Tuatech Web Design

By Craig Prichard, **Department of Management, Massey University, Palmerston North, New Zealand**

Tuatech is a software company based in Auckland, New Zealand, with a global reputation in computer graphics. The firm was founded in the mid-1990s by two software engineers and a technology manager. The technology manager brought with him to the new firm a successful website design and development practice. In Tuatech's early years the web design business was highly profitable and provided much of the early capital for software development. Since then the website design and hosting business has lost ground to larger and more specialized web agencies. The company's software products have, meanwhile, received international acclaim and significant licensing contracts have been signed with global software houses. In mid-2006 the former technology manager, who had overseen the company's operations, including its web design office, sold his share of the business to the two other directors and retired. In response the directors promoted the company's web sales person to the post of web design unit manager. This new manager struggled to adjust to his new role. He continued to book work for the design team but conflicts erupted between himself and some members of the unit's six staff (four developers, a graphic designer and a part-time trainer). The performance of the web design group plummeted. The manager resigned abruptly in the midst of these difficulties. Realizing that they were out of their depth, the company's two directors successfully advertised and appointed both a new manager for the web design business, Radha Singh, and a new general manager for the firm, Sam Little. Both new managers started work on the same day.

Sam worked previously as a technology services manager for a large public sector organization. He was determined to make a success of his work with the much smaller but highly regarded Tuatech.

Before he started work he developed, for his own use, an analysis and plans for the firm that included notes on how he might deal with the web design unit. Sam identified significant weaknesses in the performance of the design group – for which Radha was to become responsible. In the first two weeks on the job he put a lot of time into getting to know and supporting Radha. He then introduced Radha to the owners of another web design company in the local area, Mana Web Design, whom he knew were looking for new staff. Sam also discussed whether Mana Web Design would be able to take on any new work that Tuatech's web design office received – the firm was enthusiastic. Two weeks later Sam met with Tuatech's two directors for their regular monthly meeting. At that meeting Sam announced that Radha had resigned her position as manager of the firm's web design studio and taken a position with Mana Web Design. The directors were surprised.

'Really, she's gone?' said Brendon.

'Yes, unfortunately. She left yesterday,' replied Sam.

'Oh, dear! Just a month in the job,' said Peter, Tuatech's other director. 'Those guys can be trouble. Is Haiden up to his old tricks, then?'

'It's complicated,' said Sam. 'Gender differences, cultural background. As you know Radha's a recent migrant. She struggled with some of our less endearing local customs. She tried to get on with the staff, they might have overwhelmed her a bit; I offered some ideas but didn't want to meddle too much.'

Brendon interrupted: 'What concerns me right now are all these complaints from customers the web group has been accumulating. Everything is running late, they have promised a heap and delivered next to nothing, and do we also have some cash flow problems as well?'

'Yes,' said Sam. 'There's some urgency there.'

Sam followed up: 'I've done some analysis using a systems approach I picked up a little while back. We seem to have three options: battle through, appoint another manager or shut the unit down. I'd like to run over the analysis and then perhaps we could agree a final decision late next week. In the meantime I need to meet the design group, let them know we are considering options, and get their input – they might have some good ideas! Also I'm going to get some advice

A number of details of the case have been changed to protect both the identity of the firm and those involved.

▶

from a local HR consultant about restructuring and redundancy – just so that we don't get into hot water.'

Under New Zealand employment law any efforts by managers or owners to make changes to employees' jobs and work arrangements must be discussed with those potentially affected by these changes BEFORE formal decisions are made. Sam's move to discuss the options, but not the final decision, with the directors, and then to hold formal meetings with employees over the issue, is in line with these provisions.

After his meeting with the directors Sam sent individual letters about the first meeting to all the members of the web design team. Present at the Monday meeting were the developers (Haiden, Chandra, Jin and Reese), the graphic artist (Jen) and the trainer (Georgia). Sam took along Janine, the directors' secretary, to take notes. When he and Janine entered the room the design staff were sitting in silence.

Haiden suddenly stood up, smiling. 'And here comes our new boss,' he said. 'Can we have a big round of applause for Sam, the saviour of Tuatech web design and development, hip hip hooray!' The design team turned and watched Sam and Janine walk toward them and sit at the large table around which they had gathered.

'Thanks, Haiden,' said Sam, unfazed at the sarcasm. 'I'll get straight to it.'

Sam told the group that there had been a significant decline in the number of new web design and support customers and a reduction in the number of new initiatives from existing customers. In response the directors were reluctant to continue financing the deficit in this operation and were considering making positions in the web services group redundant. However, the directors were very keen to hear any options and suggestions the web group could table.

Each of the meetings with the web group was difficult and heated at times as tempers flared. The closure process took 18 months to run its course and concluded in mid-2008 with two redundancies. During that period three of the web design team moved to Mana Web Design where they work with Radha as their manager.

Case Questions

1 Do you think the decision to shut down the unit was handled well?

2 Radha's departure from Tuatech seems to have been a pivotal moment. Why did Tuatech's web design unit perform poorly when Radha managed it, while she seemed to be successful in the same position at Manha Web Design?

3 Are there lessons for Tuatech in this case study that it should apply to other departments within the company?

Selecting a New Dean for a University Faculty

By Tuomo Peltonen, University of Oulu

Veijo Karhila is sitting in his professorial office. He has to make a difficult decision whether to run for the dean of the faculty of economics at the Lakeside University. Things have escalated quickly since his colleague Kari Miettinen was chosen as the new vice-rector for the whole university. Miettinen had acted as the dean of the faculty for many years and now has to step down because it is not acceptable to hold a double position in the university hierarchy. In fact, Miettinen has been the only dean the faculty has had since its inauguration about ten years ago. He was recently elected for another three-year post as the other professors were reluctant to take the task, fearing the responsibilities it carries with it. But now the situation has changed. Veijo Karhila knows that he and the rest of the marketing department will not accept Matti Virtanen, a colleague from economics, to be selected as the new dean. Yet, running for the post means that he has to engage with the other groups of the faculty to secure the required support. Becoming a dean would mean a farewell to the life of a regular department professor and a new challenge in an administrative task. At the same time he knows that, in reality, as the head of the largest department he has no other option but to run for the leadership of the faculty.

Lakeside is a relatively large university in the middle of Finland. It is governed in a similar way to all the other Finnish universities, namely by a combination of bureaucracy and representative democracy. The university is composed of faculties, which all have a faculty council that is formally charged with making most of the administrative decisions. Some operative issues such as the grading of dissertations are handled at the departmental level. In addition, there is a university board that decides on the overall strategy of the organization. The university board is chaired by the rector of the university, who is normally a tenured professor. Typical for the Finnish system is the absence of professional managers in the governing bodies. The faculty council consists of representatives of different employee groups, who participate as elected officials in the decision-making. Thus, for example, the dean of the faculty, one of the tenured professors, works in a position of trust rather than in a dedicated managerial position. Faculty council consists of three segments representing three different personnel groups: professors, other faculty staff and students. Members are elected democratically among each group represented in the council. Professors have the biggest single number of seats in each council but they do not have the majority, meaning that for controversial issues there is a need to build coalitions across three representative groups.

The faculty of economics is the smallest of the five faculties within the Lakeside University. It is organized into four departments: economics, accounting, management and marketing. Professor of Economics, Kari Miettinen, has been the head of the faculty for some ten years. He is also the oldest of the tenured professors. In recent years, the economics department has been suffering from a loss of students at the same time as accounting and marketing have grown in size. Marketing makes up almost half of the faculty in terms of number of staff. The management department is a more fragmented unit, where several miniature disciplines are organized into an administrative whole. There is an informal division between different disciplines that reflects their methodological and scientific preferences: economics, accounting and finance, all based on quantitative research approaches, reside on the second floor whereas more qualitatively oriented marketing and management occupy the third floor. Yet at the same time there are differences between individual subject areas within each floor that in turn illustrate substantial divergences in orientations towards research and teaching. Marketing and accounting are for example more practice-oriented than economics, which tends to focus on broader macroeconomic issues and methodology. However, despite these divisions the faculty was enjoying a relatively stable working climate. Difficult issues were normally negotiated before they were allowed to escalate into visible conflicts. The dean exerted his leadership in questions that required conciliation between diverging interests.

Things started to roll when Dean Kari Miettinen was chosen as the vice-rector of university. He had to step down from the office of the faculty dean, leaving the rest of the staff a couple of weeks to fill the

▶

position. Quite soon, Matti Virtanen, another professor from economics, announced his willingness to run for dean-ship. Virtanen was known to be close to Dean Miettinen, both professionally and socially. This announcement was met with a response from the marketing department that they would not accept a situation where both vice-rector, still influential in his new role, and the new dean, would represent economics and the quantitative disciplines. Professors from the management department were also reluctant to accept Virtanen as the new dean, fearing that a bias in decision-making would result.

However, despite opposition from the marketing discipline, Veijo Karhila, the head of the marketing department, was not keen to run for deanship because of his other ongoing projects and commitments. At the same time it was he who would be the obvious counter-candidate for Virtanen. It took some time for Karhila to make up his mind about the candidacy. As he hesitated, his colleagues at the management department made an effort to try and convince him that his candidacy was needed. Only after one of the professors indicated that unless Karhila stands for office, he will be running instead, Karhila made up his mind and announced that he will be running for deanship.

Important decisions were normally primed before the faculty council sessions in an informal meeting of professors. The routine was to form a consensus around an issue that was then pursued in the formal council sessions so as to avoid unnecessary conflict. This time there was no consensus in the meeting. Both Matti Virtanen and Veijo Karhila insisted on staying as candidates for the post. They both assured everyone that they had the needed support from the faculty council members. The meeting ended without any solution to the competition between the rival candidates and their support groups. The atmosphere was becoming increasingly tense as the faculty began dividing into two opposing camps each supporting the different agenda of each of the candidates.

At this point, the coalition behind Veijo Karhila activated. Virtanen had a group of supporters in the faculty council. They would probably vote for him. However, there were a number of uncertain members, including professors and students, who had not decided on who to vote for. Management department professors, keen to support the runner from the marketing department, started lobbying individual council

members who had been relatively neutral in many other issues, propagated openly for Karhila. Some hesitating professors were persuaded to support Karhila. The main argument was that selecting Virtanen would lead to a power imbalance in favour of a small clique that did not represent the collective will of the faculty.

It soon became evident that the students would hold the balance of power in the selection. Student members come from different disciplines but they also represent the more general student voice in matters related to teaching and the treatment of students by the staff. Some of the students were hesitant about who to promote. They had been satisfied with the current dean who was seen to be easy to access. Students would have liked to see the same trend continue with the new dean. In this sense, Virtanen would be an attractive candidate. Karhila, instead, was viewed as somewhat less student-friendly although his accomplishments in the development of the faculty were widely appreciated.

With Karhila being limited in his negotiating power with the students, a management department professor turned directly to one of the student members of the council he knew. The student was in a key position as an active member of the student union. The management department professor expressed the fears among the faculty that the selection of Virtanen would mean a fracture in the harmonious relations between the different departments within the faculty. Karhila would bring stability. In addition to talking directly to a student, supporters of Karhila asked a former colleague of theirs to make an additional plea to the student. The former colleague and the key student were kinsfolk.

There was also a series of manoeuvres on the other side. Virtanen had contacted several council members to talk about his potential support in case of a ballot. He was especially active among some of the members representing the non-professorial staff in the second group. The group consisted of lecturers and administrative faculty members. Many of these were in support of Virtanen who they viewed as more impartial than Karhila, who was in the eyes of many a slightly authoritarian leader. Non-professorial staff work under the supervision of professors, and it is the nature of this hierarchical relationship that affects the way in which professors are evaluated as leaders. Virtanen and his supporters wanted to see faculty being run on the basis of jointly agreed rules

▶

and regulations rather than on the whims of the few professors each pursuing their own narrow academic and disciplinary agenda. There were also concerns about the marketing department taking over other departments on the issues related to the contents of research and teaching as well as in how academic work was to be organized in the faculty. Some older lecturers in particular were afraid of the possible restructurings that would make them obsolete, as new degree programmes would be introduced to replace the traditional curricula.

Karhila and his coalition, instead, perceived Virtanen and his supporters as defenders of their own vulnerable position. They thought that the opposing group was on the losing side as the faculty was evolving from an economics department into a modern business school. In their eyes, the rival group just wanted to use bureaucratic rules and regulations to delay the reforms that were in any way necessary in the near future. There was, for example, a widespread belief that Virtanen was running for deanship to be able to retreat from the departmental or operative problems looming ahead. The group itself wanted to emphasize the freedom of academic research in the face of what was seen as an intensifying bureaucratization of university life. Some also perceived the tendency to lean on the formal administrative principles as an attempt to control those academics that are active in consulting, management education and other extra-departmental tasks.

Then the council meeting day came. There was a lot of tension in the air as the two candidates presented themselves. Both had prepared a short formal programme speech outlining how they would develop faculty. Brief discussion was followed by a ballot. The votes were counted and with a slight surprise in his face, the administrative clerk announced the result. Karhila had received eight votes and Virtanen five, meaning that Karhila was elected as the new dean of the faculty. As the meeting dissembled, many open questions were left in the air. The supporters of Virtanen were baffled with the result. They noticed that some of the regular student members were missing and deputy members had been called to participate in the meeting. Perhaps there was a secret conspiracy between the students and the coalition that had turned the result in the favour of Karhila. Suspicions of foul play abounded. Similarly, the supporters of the new dean reflected later on the events of the day, sharing their feelings about the ideas of the opposing camp. The coalition was particularly disoriented about the way in which Virtanen displayed his eagerness to move from a faculty job to a full-time administrative position. This confirmed to them the belief that Virtanen was not defending the interests of the faculty as a whole. They were convinced that the right candidate had won.

As the Election Day came to a close, many were wondering about what exactly had happened during the preceding weeks. How was it possible that a smallish university unit was suddenly transformed into a battleground between opposing viewpoints and groups? And how were the participants of this political drama to go on in their daily work now, as the illusion of unity was so severely broken? Nobody knew just how the workplace would function after the dust settled and life at the faculty would return to business as usual. One thing was sure: these divides would affect the relations between individual members of the faculty community for years to come.

Case Questions

1   How would you explain the emergence of division in the case organization? What were the background social and cultural structures accounting for the surfacing of different interest groups within the faculty?

2   What kinds of political tactics did the different interest groups pursue in order to influence faculty council decision-making? How would you describe the effectiveness of various tactics used?

Notes

1. Amit Roy Choudhury, ' Lessons from the cultural divide', Business Times Singapore, 11 October, 2008; Karlin Lillington, 'Learning about Lenovo', Irish Times, 25 July, 2008; Rick Newman, 'Lenovo's Great Leap', U.S. News & World Report October 15, 2007; Jane Spencer and Loretta Chao, 'Lenovo goes global, with bumps', The Wall Street Journal Asia, 5 November, 2008; 'The IBM/ Lenovo Deal: Victory For China?', Knowledge@Wharton, accessed at http://knowledge.wharton.upenn.edu/ article.cfm?articleid=1106 on January 5, 2009; Rebecca Buckman, 'Lenovo Gets Its Yin-Yang On; The new face of globalism means having an office everywhere and nowhere', Forbes, 22 December, 2008; Venkatesha Babu, 'Lenovo is at a Tipping Point', Business Today, 22 April, 2007; Elaine Chan, 'Chen crosses cultures to make Lenovo global', South China Morning Post, 21 April, 2008.

2. Owen Fletcher, 'Lenovo to Reorganize, Taps Ex-Acer Leader', The Wall Street Journal, 6 January, 2012.

3. 'Lenovo tops PC market as shipments fall 10% in Q1: Gartner', Times of India, April 12, 2016, accessed at timesofindia.indiatimes.com/tech/tech-news/Lenovo- tops-PC-market-as-shipments-fall-10-in-Q1-Gartner/ articleshow/51792517.cms

4. Lee G. Bolman and Terrence E. Deal, Reframing Organizations: Artistry, Choice and Leadership (San Francisco: Jossey-Bass, 1991).

5. Paul M. Terry, 'Conflict Management', The Journal of Leadership Studies 3, No. 2 (1996), 3–21; and Kathleen M. Eisenhardt, Jean L. Kahwajy and L. J. Bourgeois III, 'How Management Teams Can Have a Good Fight', Harvard Business Review (July–August 1997), 77–85.

6. Clayton T. Alderfer and Ken K. Smith, 'Studying Intergroup Relations Imbedded in Organizations', Administrative Science Quarterly 27 (1982), 35–65.

7. Muzafer Sherif, 'Experiments in Group Conflict', Scientific American 195 (1956), 54–58; and Edgar H. Schein Organizational Psychology, 3rd ed. (Englewood Cliffs, NJ: Prentice-Hall, 1980).

8. M. Afzalur Rahim, 'A Strategy for Managing Conflict in Complex Organizations', Human Relations 38 (1985), 81–89; Kenneth Thomas, 'Conflict and Conflict Management', in M.D. Dunnette, ed., Handbook of Industrial and Organizational Psychology (Chicago, IL: Rand McNally, 1976); and Stuart M. Schmidt and Thomas A. Kochan, 'Conflict: Toward Conceptual Clarity', Administrative Science Quarterly 13 (1972), 359–370.

9. L. David Brown, 'Managing Conflict among Groups', in David A. Kolb, Irwin M. Rubin and James M. McIntyre, eds, Organizational Psychology: A Book of Readings (Englewood Cliffs, NJ: Prentice-Hall, 1979), 377–389; and Robert W. Ruekert and Orville C. Walker, Jr, 'Interactions between Marketing and R&D Departments in Implementing Different Business Strategies', Strategic Management Journal 8 (1987), 233–248.

10. Mike Esterl, 'Deutsche Telekom, Union Clash', Wall Street Journal, September 12, 2008.

11. Giles Parkinson, 'Is Krispy getting Kremed?', Business Spectator, 23 September, 2008.

12. Nanette Byrnes with Mike McNamee, Ronald Grover, Joann Muller and Andrew Park, 'Auditing Here, Consulting Over There', BusinessWeek (April 8, 2002), 34–36.

13. Thomas A. Kochan, George P. Huber and L. L. Cummings, 'Determinants of Intraorganizational Conflict in Collective Bargaining in the Public Sector', Administrative Science Quarterly 20 (1975), 10–23.

14. Victoria L. Crittenden, Lorraine R. Gardiner and Antonie Stam, 'Reducing Conflict between Marketing and Manufacturing', Industrial Marketing Management 22 (1993), 299–309; and Benson S. Shapiro, 'Can Marketing and Manufacturing Coexist?' Harvard Business Review 55 (September–October 1977), 104–114.

15. Peter Wells, 'Finding Nano: the significance of Tata's long awaited one lakh car', Automotive World, 15 January, 2008; Hiroshi Kotani, 'Tata's Nano raises hopes, eyebrows', Nikkei Weekly, 21 January, 2008.

16. Philip Oltermann and Paige McClanahan, 'Tata Nano safety under scrutiny after dire crash test results', Guardian, January 31, 2014, accessed at www. theguardian.com/global-development/2014/jan/31/ tata-nano-safety-crash-test-results

17. Business Day, 'Crank corner', 18 April, 2013; Santanu Choudhury and Anirban Chowdhury, 'Tata Motors Profit Drops 37%, but Tops Forecast', The Wall Street Journal, 29 May, 2013.

18. 'Sales of Tata Nano, world's cheapest car, set to hit six- year lows', Indian Express, March 5, 2015, accessed at indianexpress.com/article/business/business-others/sales- of-tata-nano-worlds-cheapest-car-set-to-hit-six-year-lows/

19. Eric H. Neilsen, 'Understanding and Managing Intergroup Conflict', in Jay W. Lorsch and Paul R. Lawrence, eds, Managing Group and Intergroup Relations (Homewood, IL: Irwin and Dorsey, 1972), 329–343; and Richard E. Walton and John M. Dutton, 'The Management of Interdepartmental Conflict: A Model and Review', Administrative Science Quarterly 14 (1969), 73–84.

20. Jay W. Lorsch, 'Introduction to the Structural Design of Organizations', in Gene W. Dalton, Paul R. Lawrence and Jay W. Lorsch, eds, Organization Structure and Design (Homewood, IL: Irwin and Dorsey, 1970), 5.

21. Jonathan D. Rockoff, 'Boston Scientific Issues Big Recall of Its Implantable Defibrillators', 16 March, 2010, The Wall Street Journal; Barry Meier, 'Inquiry Arranged by Guidant May Aid Lawsuits and Critics', 22 March, 2006, New York Times, p. 4.

22. Guidant went through several name changes since being formed, originally Cardiac Pacemakers Inc., then Advanced Cardiovascular Systems, and finally Guidant, now part of Boston Scientific. We have used Guidant throughout for the sake of simplicity; Shawn Tully, "The (second) worst deal ever", Fortune, October 5 2006, accessed at archive.fortune.com/magazines/fortune/fortune_ archive/2006/10/16/8390284/index.htm

23. James D. Thompson, Organizations in Action (New York: McGraw-Hill, 1967), 54–56.

24. Walton and Dutton, 'The Management of Interdepartmental Conflict'.

25. Joseph McCann and Jay R. Galbraith, 'Interdepartmental Relations', in Paul C. Nystrom and William H. Starbuck,

eds, *Handbook of Organizational Design*, Vol. 2 (New York: Oxford University Press, 1981), 60–84.

26. Roderick M. Cramer, 'Intergroup Relations and Organizational Dilemmas: The Role of Categorization Processes', in L. L. Cummings and Barry M. Staw, eds, *Research in Organizational Behavior*, Vol. 13 (New York: JAI Press, 1991), 191–228; Neilsen, 'Understanding and Managing Intergroup Conflict', and Louis R. Pondy, 'Organizational Conflict: Concepts and Models', *Administrative Science Quarterly* 12 (1968), 296–320.

27. Jeffrey Pfeffer, *Power in Organizations* (Marshfield, MA: Pitman, 1981).

28. Alan Deutschman, 'The Mind of Jeff Bezos', *Fast Company* (August 2004), 53–58.

29. Robert A. Dahl, 'The Concept of Power', *Behavioral Science* 2 (1957), 201–215.

30. W. Graham Astley and Paramijit S. Sachdeva, 'Structural Sources of Intraorganizational Power: A Theoretical Synthesis', *Academy of Management Review* 9 (1984), 104–113; Abraham Kaplan, 'Power in Perspective', in Robert L. Kahn and Elise Boulding, eds, *Power and Conflict in Organizations* (London: Tavistock, 1964), 11–32.

31. Gerald R. Salancik and Jeffrey Pfeffer, 'The Bases and Use of Power in Organizational Decision-Making: The Case of the University', *Administrative Science Quarterly* 19 (1974), 453–473.

32. Richard M. Emerson, 'Power-Dependence Relations', *American Sociological Review* 27 (1962), 31–41.

33. Rosabeth Moss Kanter, 'Power Failure in Management Circuits', *Harvard Business Review* (July–August 1979), 65–75.

34. Alison Campsie, 'Hearts debts: taxes, wages and £185 for a poppy wreath', *The Herald* (Scotland), August 1, 2013, accessed at www.heraldscotland.com/news/13116418. Hearts_debts__taxes__wages_and___185_for_a_poppy_wreath/; Jamie Ranger, 'A rich man's playground: what does the future hold for club ownership in the British game?', *FourFourTwo*, December 8, 2015, accessed at www.fourfourtwo.com/features/rich-mans-playground-what-does-future-hold-club-ownership-british-game; Jonathan Freedland, 'In the Premier League the endgame of rampant capitalism is being played out', *Guardian*, October 18, 2011, accessed at www.theguardian.com/commentisfree/2011/oct/18/premier-league-rampant-capitalism; David Conn, 'What is it that attracts US investors to the multi-million-pound EPL?', *Guardian*, December 23, 2015, accessed at www.theguardian.com/football/blog/2015/dec/23/everton-us-investors-john-moores-charles-noell; Bi, Y. (2015). Integration or resistance: the influx of foreign capital in British football in the transnational age. *Soccer & Society*, 16(1), 17–41

35. Examples are Robert Greene and Joost Elffers, *The 48 Laws of Power* (New York: Viking, 1999); Jeffrey J. Fox, *How to Become CEO* (New York: Hyperion, 1999).

36. John R. P. French, Jr and Bertram Raven, 'The Bases of Social Power', in *Group Dynamics*, D. Cartwright and A. F. Zander, eds (Evanston, IL: Row Peterson, 1960), 607–623.

37. Ran Lachman, 'Power from What? A Reexamination of Its Relationships with Structural Conditions', *Administrative Science Quarterly* 34 (1989), 231–251; and Daniel J. Brass, 'Being in the Right Place: A Structural Analysis of Individual Influence in an Organization', *Administrative Science Quarterly* 29 (1984), 518–539.

38. 'Leading engineer behind the Toyota Prius hybrid car', *EE Times*, 28 October, 2005, accessed at http://www.eetimes.com/document.asp?doc_id=1157796 on September 17, 2013.

39. 'Leading a global revolution', *New Zealand Herald*, 3 November, 2007; 'Toyota engineers reflect as Prius approaches 10th birthday', *The Japan Times*, 22 May, 2007.

40. Yoshio Takahashi and Yoree Koh, 'Toyota Shakes Up Top Ranks – Amid Executive Changes, the Japanese Auto Maker Intends to Add Outsiders to Board for First Time', *The Wall Street Journal*, 7 March, 2013.

41. 'Toyota Remains Most Valuable Global Automotive Brand', *BusinessWire*, October 6, 2015, accessed at www.businesswire.com/news/home/20151006006661/en/TOYOTA-Remains-Valuable-Global-Automotive-Brand-Interbrand; "Toyota world No. 1 again", Japan News, April 26 2016, accessed at the-japan-news.com/news/article/0002904655

42. A. J. Grimes, 'Authority, Power, Influence and Social Control: A Theoretical Synthesis', *Academy of Management Review* 3 (1978), 724–735.

43. Astley and Sachdeva, 'Structural Sources of Intraorganizational Power'.

44. Jeffrey Pfeffer, *Managing with Power: Politics and Influence in Organizations* (Boston, MA: Harvard Business School Press, 1992).

45. Robert L. Peabody, 'Perceptions of Organizational Authority', *Administrative Science Quarterly* 6 (1962), 479.

46. 'Corporate Jet Market Forecasted to Double in 10 Years', *Maeil Business Newspaper*, 22 July, 2008.

47. Stephen Foley, 'The new masters of the universe', *The Independent*, 26 February, 2007; Siobhan Kennedy, 'Ex-Citigroup boss tells of "smear campaign"', *The Times*, 8 November, 2007; Dominic Rushe, 'Money honey brings down bank high-flyer', *The Sunday Times*, 28 January, 2007; 'Citigroup Announces Departure of Head of Global Wealth Management Division', *M2 Presswire*, 23 January, 2007.

48. Richard S. Blackburn, 'Lower Participant Power: Toward a Conceptual Integration', *Academy of Management Review* 6 (1981), 127–131.

49. 'On the right road with safety focus', *National Post*, 21 July, 2008; 'Bison Transport is not only one of Canada's Best Managed Companies, but also the nation's safest fleet', *Canadian Transportation and Logistics*, 1 April, 2008

50. 'Grand Prize Winners Announced in Truckload Carriers Association/Overdrive/TruckersNews.com Driver of the Year Contests,' March 9, 2016, accessed at www.truckload.org/index.php?bid=1445&archiveyear=2016&nid=564

51. Frederick Yeung, 'PCCW links executive bonuses to share price incentive seeks to end years of underperformance', *South China Morning Post*, 1 June 2007; '$1.9bn plan to take PCCW private', *Financial Times,* 4 November, 2008.

52. David Teather, 'What credit crunch? City bankers receive pounds 13bn bonuses this year', *The Guardian*, 26 May 2008; Mark Milner, 'Brown and City regulator clamp down on bonuses', *The Guardian*, 14 October, 2008.

53. Pfeffer, *Power in Organizations*.

54. Erik W. Larson and Jonathan B. King, 'The Systemic Distortion of Information: An Ongoing Challenge to Management', *Organizational Dynamics* 24, No. 3 (Winter 1996), 49–61; and Thomas H. Davenport, Robert G. Eccles and Laurence Prusak, 'Information Politics', *Sloan Management Review* (Fall 1992), 53–65.

55. Andrew M. Pettigrew, *The Politics of Organizational Decision-Making* (London: Tavistock, 1973).

56. 'A chronology of events in the Conrad Black fraud case', *The Canadian Press*, 3 March, 2008; Stephen Foley, 'Lord Fraud: Conrad Black faces jail after being convicted on four counts of fraud and obstruction', *Belfast Telegraph*, 14 July, 2007.

57. Robert Frank and Elena Cherney, 'Paper Tigers; Lord Black's Board: A-List Cast Played Acquiescent Role', *The Wall Street Journal* (September 27, 2004), A1.

58. Lorne Manly and Andrew Ross Sorkin, 'At Sony, Diplomacy Trumps Technology', *The New York Times* (March 8, 2005), http://www.nytimes.com.

59. Andrew Higgins, 'Cartoon puts Danish firms on the spot – Hit by Muslim fury, businesses weigh sales against values', *The Wall Street Journal Europe*, 14 February, 2006; 'Arla Products Back In Saudi Stores After Boycott Lifted', *Dow Jones International News*, 6 April, 2006; 'Arla Foods and the Cartoon Crisis', Richard Ivey Business School Case Study 9B08M005, 13 February, 2008; 'When markets melt away – Consumer boycotts', *The Economist*, 11 February, 2006; Martin Burlund, 'Denmark's Arla yet to see Prophet cartoon boycott', *Reuters News*, 4 March, 2008.

60. 'Tien jaar na de Mohammed-cartoons: een overzicht', *RTLNieuws*, February 21, 2015, accessed at www.rtlnieuws.nl/nieuws/buitenland/tien-jaar-na-de-mohammed-cartoons-een-overzicht

61. Mark Hunter, 'Where women want to work', *The Times*, 8 October, 2008; Carol Lewis, 'Life's all about making connections', *The Times,* 4 October, 2006; Roland Gribben, 'Sisters are doing it for themselves, *The Daily Telegraph,* 6 September, 2007.

62. Astley and Sachdeva, 'Structural Sources of Intraorganizational Power'; and Noel M. Tichy and Charles Fombrun, 'Network Analysis in Organizational Settings', *Human Relations* 32 (1979), 923–965.

63. Aoife White, 'Fortis falls hard after trying to fly too high', *Associated Press Newswires*, 29 September, 2008; Clive Horwood, 'Board stupid', *Euromoney*, 1 February, 2008; Ruth Sunderland, 'Inside the minds of men who want to get rich quick', *The Observer*, 21 December, 2008.

64. Rebecca Buckman, 'Lenovo Gets Its Yin-Yang On; The new face of globalism means having an office everywhere and Nowhere', *Forbes*, 22 December, 2008.

65. Charles Perrow, 'Departmental Power and Perspective in Industrial Firms,' in Mayer N. Zald, ed., *Power in Organizations* (Nashville, TN: Vanderbilt University Press, 1970), 59–89.

66. D. J. Hickson, C. R. Hinings, C. A. Lee, R. E. Schneck and J. M. Pennings, 'A Strategic Contingencies Theory of Intraorganizational Power', *Administrative Science Quarterly* 16 (1971), 216–229; and Gerald R. Salancik and Jeffrey Pfeffer, 'Who Gets Power – and How They Hold onto It: A Strategic-Contingency Model of Power', *Organizational Dynamics* (Winter 1977), 3–21.

67. Pfeffer, *Managing with Power*; Salancik and Pfeffer, 'Who Gets Power'; C. R. Hinings, D. J. Hickson, J. M. Pennings and R. E. Schneck, 'Structural Conditions of Intraorganizational Power', *Administrative Science Quarterly* 19 (1974), 22–44.

68. Carol Stoak Saunders, 'The Strategic Contingencies Theory of Power: Multiple Perspectives', *Journal of Management Studies* 27 (1990), 1–18; Warren Boeker, 'The Development and Institutionalization of Sub-Unit Power in Organizations', *Administrative Science Quarterly* 34 (1989), 388–510; and Irit Cohen and Ran Lachman, 'The Generality of the Strategic Contingencies Approach to Sub-Unit Power', *Organizational Studies* 9 (1988), 371–391.

69. Emerson, 'Power-Dependence Relations'.

70. Pfeffer, *Managing with Power*.

71. Salancik and Pfeffer, 'Bases and Use of Power in Organizational Decision-Making', 470.

72. Teddy Ng, 'University denies giving in to students', *The Standard*, 25 February, 2004; Linda Yeung, 'Students consulted in Chinese U rejig', *South China Morning Post*, 7 February, 2004; Linda Yeung, 'Chinese U minnows face 2 mauling under strict budget constraints', *South China Morning Post*, 17 January, 2004; May Chan, 'CUHK students want head to stand down', *South China Morning Post*, 21 February, 2004; Marek Kwiek (2006) 'Academic Entrepreneurship vs Changing Governance and Institutional Management Structures at European Universities' (a theme paper for the European Commission EUEREK project).

73. Hickson et al., 'A Strategic Contingencies Theory'.

74. Pettigrew, *The Politics of Organizational Decision-Making*.

75. Hickson et al., 'A Strategic Contingencies Theory'.

76. Ibid.

77. Laton McCartney, 'Prescription for Disaster', *CIO Insight*, 13 November, 2006.

78. Nic Fleming, 'Bill for hi-tech NHS soars to £20 billion', *Daily Telegraph*, 12 October, 2004.

79. Allyson M. Pollock (2005), *NHS Plc: The Privatisation of Our Health Care*, London, Verso; David Craig and Richard Brooks, *Plundering the Public Sector*, London, Constable.

80. Brian Brady and Jonathan Owen, 'Where does all our money go?', *Independent On Sunday*, 10 January, 2010; 'Government to scrap NPfIT NHS IT programme today', 22 September, 2011, *ComputerworldUK*.

81. Mark Ballard, 'NPfIT champion suspended after speaking out', *The Register*, 8 March, 2007; Lucy Sherriff, 'Fujitsu man condemns NPfIT as failure', *The Register*, 13 February, 2007; Simon Bowers, 'Accenture to quit NHS technology overhaul', *The Guardian*, 28 September, 2006; 'Accenture feels the squeeze on NHS contracts', *E-Health Insider*, 8 April, 2005; Chip Means, 'Fujitsu ends contract with NHS IT project', *Healthcare I.T. News EU*, 30 May, 2008; Paul Crompton (2007), 'The National Programme for Information Technology – An Overview', *Journal of Visual Communication in Medicine*, 30, 72–77; Nick Heath, 'The 10 projects at the heart of NHS IT', Silicon.com, 10 November, 2008; John Oates, 'NHS IT: what went wrong, what will go wrong', *The Register*, 30 May, 2008; Laton McCartney, 'Prescription for Disaster', *CIO Insight*, 13 November, 2006; Jane Hendy et al. (2005), 'Challenges to implementing the national programme for information technology (NPfIT)', *British Medical Journal*, 331, 331–336; The National Programme for IT in the NHS, 'Procurement approach document', NHS, 2003; 'Accenture's NHS losses grow as NPfIT delays mount', *E-Health Insider*, 29 March, 2006; Nicholas Timmins, 'NHS narrows down field for £2.3bn IT contracts', *Financial Times*, 6 August, 2003; Rosalie Marshall, Outlook for NHS IT is far from healthy, *Computing*, 13 November, 2008; UK National Audit Office, 'NHS Connecting for Health Process Capability Appraisal',

report CR050700, 28 April, 2005; Second full NAO review of NPfIT to be carried out, E-Health Insider, 26 April, 2007.

82. Barbara Martinez, 'Strong Medicine; With New Muscle, Hospitals Squeeze Insurers on Rates', *The Wall Street Journal* (April 12, 2002), A1; James V. DeLong, 'Rule of Law: Just What Crime Did Columbia/HCA Commit?' *The Wall Street Journal* (August 20, 1997), A15; and Lucette Lagnado, 'House Panel Begins Inquiry into Hospital Billing Practices', *The Wall Street Journal* (July 17, 2003), B1.

83. Jonathan Murphy (2008), *The World Bank and Global Managerialism*, London, Routledge, pp. 76–98. 93. Pfeffer, *Power in Organizations*. 94. Ibid. 95. Stephen Brook, 'Murdochs make the headlines', *Guardian Unlimited*, 14 July, 2008.

84. Jeffrey Gantz and Victor V. Murray, 'Experience of Workplace Politics', *Academy of Management Journal* 23 (1980), 237–251; and Dan L. Madison, Robert W. Allen, Lyman W. Porter, Patricia A. Renwick and Bronston T. Mayes, 'Organizational Politics: An Exploration of Managers' Perception', *Human Relations* 33 (1980), 79–100.

85. Gerald R. Ferris and K. Michele Kacmar, 'Perceptions of Organizational Politics', *Journal of Management* 18 (1992), 93–116; Parmod Kumar and Rehana Ghadially, 'Organizational Politics and Its Effects on Members of Organizations', *Human Relations* 42 (1989), 305–314; Donald J. Vredenburgh and John G. Maurer, 'A Process Framework of Organizational Politics', *Human Relations* 37 (1984), 47–66; and Gerald R. Ferris, Dwight D. Frink, Maria Carmen Galang, Jing Zhou, Michele Kacmar and Jack L. Howard, 'Perceptions of Organizational Politics: Prediction, Stress-Related Implications and Outcomes', *Human Relations* 49, No. 2 (1996), 233–266.

86. Ferris et al., 'Perceptions of Organizational Politics: Prediction, Stress-Related Implications and Outcomes'; John J. Voyer, 'Coercive Organizational Politics and Organizational Outcomes: An Interpretive Study', *Organization Science* 5, No. 1 (February 1994), 72–85; and James W. Dean, Jr. and Mark P. Sharfman, 'Does Decision Process Matter? A Study of Strategic Decision-Making Effectiveness', *Academy of Management Journal* 39, No. 2 (1996), 368–396.

87. Jeffrey Pfeffer, *Managing with Power: Politics and Influence in Organizations* (Boston, MA: Harvard Business School Press, 1992).

88. Amos Drory and Tsilia Romm, 'The Definition of Organizational Politics: A Review', *Human Relations* 43 (1990), 1133–1154; Vredenburgh and Maurer, 'A Process Framework of Organizational Politics'; and Lafe Low, 'It's Politics, As Usual', *CIO* (April 1, 2004), 87–90.

89. Madison et al., 'Organizational Politics'; Jay R. Galbraith, *Organizational Design* (Reading, MA: Addison-Wesley, 1977). 2 Office, New Baby', *New York Times*, July 17, 2012.

90. Gantz and Murray, 'Experience of Workplace Politics'; Pfeffer, *Power in Organizations*.

91. Harvey G. Enns and Dean B. McFarlin, 'When Executives Influence Peers, Does Function Matter?' *Human Resource Management* 4, No. 2 (Summer 2003), 125–142.

92. Hickson et al., 'A Strategic Contingencies Theory'.

93. Pfeffer, *Power in Organizations*.

94. Ibid.

95. V. Dallas Merrell, *Huddling: The Informal Way to Management Success* (New York: AMACON, 1979).

96. Ceasar Douglas and Anthony P. Ammeter, 'An Examination of Leader Political Skill and Its Effect on Ratings of Leader Effectiveness', *The Leadership Quarterly* 15 (2004), 537–550.

97. Vredenburgh and Maurer, 'A Process Framework of Organizational Politics'. Business: VW's Woes Mount Amid Claims Of Sex Junkets for Union Chiefs – Scandal Rocks Auto Giant As Its Luxury Push Fades; New Blow to Germany Inc.,' *The Wall Street Journal*, 17 November, 2005; BBC News, 'IG Metall deal averts VW strike', accessed at http://news.bbc.co.uk/1/hi/business/3978405.stm on January 7, 2009; Ian Greer and Marco Hauptmeier (2008), 'Political Entrepreneurs and Co-Managers: Labour Transnationalism at Four Multinational Auto Companies', *British Journal of Industrial Relations*, 46, pp. 76–97; Paul Newton, 'VW and IG Metall Agree to Continue Restructuring Talks', *Global Insight Daily Analysis*, 14 July, 2006; Jack Ewing, 'Volkswagen Rolls the Dice on Tennessee', *Der Spiegel Online*, http://web.archive.org/web/20060109130047/http://www.fes.or.kr/Industrial_Relations/Vw-de.htm on January 7, 2009; 'VW taken over by Porsche; Luxury car maker's move sends stocks soaring', *Vancouver Province*, 7 January 2009.

98. Pfeffer, *Power in Organizations*.

99. Ibid.

100. Stephen Brook, 'Murdochs make the headlines', *Guardian Unlimited*, 14 July, 2008.

101. Dan Sabbagh and Dominic Rushe, 'James Murdoch steps down as BSkyB chairman as hacking scandal deepens', *The Guardian*, 3 April, 2012.

102. 'Maxwell inquiry indicts son and bank', *Irish Times*, 31 March, 2001.

103. Bank of America to buy Merrill Lynch for 50 billion, *Agence France Presse*, 15 September, 2008; Dominic Walsh and Suzy Jagger, 'Morgan Stanley takes Dollar 3.7bn sub-prime hit', *The Times*, 8 November, 2007.

104. Ann Davis and Randall Smith, 'Merrill Switch: Popular Veteran Is In, Not Out', *The Wall Street Journal* (August 13, 2003), C1.

105. Pfeffer, *Power in Organizations*.

106. Ibid.

107. Robert R. Blake and Jane S. Mouton, 'Overcoming Group Warfare', *Harvard Business Review* (November–December 1984), 98–108.

108. Blake and Mouton, 'Overcoming Group Warfare'; Paul R. Lawrence and Jay W. Lorsch, 'New Management Job: The Integrator', *Harvard Business Review* 45 (November–December 1967), 142–151.

109. 'Transnet strike off as unions agree to talk', *FT Now*, 25 March, 2006; Transnet, Unions Sign Restructuring Accord, South African Press Association, 16 May, 2006.

110. 'Chile Codelco reaches wage agreement with workers', *Reuters News*, 21 February, 2007; Paul Harris, 'Codelco Norte union threatens strike', *Metal Bulletin News Alert Service*, 21 February, 2007; 'Codelco Norte Closes Negotiations With Unions', *Corporate Chile*, December 21, 2006.

111. White, et al., 'UAW Is Facing Biggest Battles in Two Decades'.

112. N. Klein, (2000), No Logo: No Space, No Choice, No Jobs: Taking Aim at the Brand Bullies, London, Flamingo; J. Murphy, (2004), 'Managerialism Meets its Nemesis', Organization, 11, 315–319. Against Management by Martin Parker, is published by Polity.

113. Ben Elgin, 'Inside Yahoo!' BusinessWeek (May 21, 2001), 114–122.

114. Claire Cain Miller, 'Yahoo Chief's Challenge? Corner Office, New Baby', New York Times, July 17, 2012.

115. Geoff Colvin, 'Yahoo's Marissa Mayer Faces a Steady Stream of Crises', Fortune, January 6, 2016, accessed at fortune.com/2016/01/06/yahoo-marissa-mayer-rahm-emanuel-crisis-management/; Geoff Colvin, 'Marissa Mayer May Be Running Out of Options at Yahoo', Fortune, December 2015, accessed at fortune.com/2015/12/01/marissa-mayer-yahoo-2/

116. Robert R. Blake, Herbert A. Shepard and Jane S. Mouton, Managing Intergroup Conflict in Industry (Houston: Gulf Publishing, 1964); Doug Stewart, 'Expand the Pie before You Divvy It Up', Smithsonian (November 1997), 78–90.

117. Patrick S. Nugent, 'Managing Conflict: Third-Party Interventions for Managers', Academy of Management Executive 16, No. 1 (2002), 139–155.

118. Blake and Mouton, 'Overcoming Group Warfare'; Schein, Organizational Psychology; Blake, Shepard and Mouton, Managing Intergroup Conflict in Industry; and Richard E. Walton, Interpersonal Peacemaking: Confrontation and Third-Party Consultations (Reading, MA: Addison-Wesley, 1969).

119. Associated Press Newswires, 'Volkswagen workers win two-stage raise of 3.4 and 2.2 percent as company faces tough market', 28 May, 2013.

120. Stephen Power and Matthew Karnitschnig, 'Risky Business: VW's Woes Mount Amid Claims Of Sex Junkets for Union Chiefs – Scandal Rocks Auto Giant As Its Luxury Push Fades; New Blow to Germany Inc.,' The Wall Street Journal, 17 November, 2005; BBC News, 'IG Metall deal averts VW strike', accessed at http://news.bbc.co.uk/1/hi/business/3978405.stm on January 7, 2009; Ian Greer and Marco Hauptmeier (2008), 'Political Entrepreneurs and Co-Managers: Labour Transnationalism at Four Multinational Auto Companies', British Journal of Industrial Relations, 46, pp. 76–97; Paul Newton, 'VW and IG Metall Agree to Continue Restructuring Talks', Global Insight Daily Analysis, 14 July, 2006; Jack Ewing, 'Volkswagen Rolls the Dice on Tennessee', Der Spiegel Online, 11 December, 2008; 'Declaration on Social Rights and Industrial Relationships at Volkswagen', accessed at http://web.archive.org/web/20060109130047/http://www.fes.or.kr/Industrial_Relations/Vw-de.htm on January 7, 2009; 'VW taken over by Porsche; Luxury car maker's move sends stocks soaring', Vancouver Province, 7 January 2009.

121. Richard Milne, 'IG Metall union's nominee signals VW's road out of trouble', Financial Times, December 9, 2015, accessed at www.ft.com/cms/s/0/d455c240-9e57-11e5-b45d-4812f209f861.html; 'VW calls for "measured" pay settlement', DNA India, April 26, 2016, accessed at www.dnaindia.com/money/report-volkswagen-has-no-right-to-use-emissions-scandal-crisis-to-deny-wage-hike-to-workers-union-2206418

122. Neilsen, 'Understanding and Managing Intergroup Conflict'; McCann and Galbraith, 'Interdepartmental Relations'.

123. Neilsen, 'Understanding and Managing Intergroup Conflict'; McCann and Galbraith, 'Interdepartmental Relations'; Sherif et al., Intergroup Conflict and Cooperation.

124. Dean Tjosvold, Valerie Dann and Choy Wong, 'Managing Conflict between Departments to Serve Customers', Human Relations 45 (1992), 1035–1054.

INTEGRATIVE CASES

Luxurious Goat Milk Products: Working with Local Culture – RojaAHP

Kim Maya Sutton

Jade Hochschule Wilhelmshaven, Germany

This case study is fictional for educational purposes. All people except President Rouhani are fictional; RojaAHP is also fictional. Any likeness to persons or organizations is purely coincidental.

Hannah woke up with a start that morning in September of 2016, convinced she'd slept in. She had to get up, get ready, meet the Abdarschi, find a taxi, make it to town and all of that in just … wait – only 5am? She sighed and placed her head back on the linen sheet she used to fend off some of the night heat. In the last five years, the one thing she had not gotten used to was the heat.

Hannah Williams (*14 October 1984 in Al Fashir, Sudan)

Born to US American parents, a general logistician and a nurse who both worked for Doctors Without Borders, Hannah Williams was more of a miracle than anything else, said her grandmother Dotty: 'Your parents always met so briefly. He clearly heard my wish for another little one in the family to whom I could tend.' Hannah grew up with Dotty in her old plantation house in Kentucky and until she turned 5, she only saw her mum and dad on special occasions. One dismal day in 1989, her world turned into a whirlwind that had not stopped since. Dotty died, and her mother showed up to home-school her while working part-time in the field. They lived in foreign countries on 9-12 month assignments. (MSF UF, 2016)

Hannah got used to this lifestyle, learned languages quickly, and was particularly fascinated with Middle Eastern cultures. The beauty of Damascus with the strong bazaar colours and smells, the strange sizzling noises at the Dead Sea and the beautiful ruins of Karnak Temple in Luxor sparked an interest in her. This is where she would live when she was an adult, she decided. When her parents retired to a quiet life back on the Old Plantation, Hannah went to Cologne, Germany, to study pharmaceutical chemistry. At a student party in 2004, she met her later husband, Philip, and their future business partner, Ali, who studied engineering and management.

Ali Turani (* 02 April 1984 in Tehran, Iran)

Ali grew up with the traditional Persian values. He was also very interested in everything Western. When in 1994, the opportunity arose to stay with a distant uncle in Germany, his parents gave him as much money and jewellery as they could spare and sent their only son to study, knowing he'd come back and bring new knowledge to help his country later. Ali learned German easily, soaked up all the information like a sponge, and concluded German high school with honors. He worked in a Persian restaurant to earn his living and took up internships where he could. With very structured days, he knew exactly when to study, work, enjoy culture. As a Shiite, he did not consume alcohol and was always a role model for his fellow students. It was tough for Philip to convince his friend to join the party in the first place.

Philip Albers (*12 March 1982 in Cologne, Germany)

His mother a publisher and his father a forensic doctor, Philip followed in his father's admiration for Ernest Hemingway's writings. His dream was to become a correspondent in troubled areas, war-torn countries, and to help with his journalistic work. Let the world know what was really happening!

When he met Hannah, that dream was pushed into a corner by his desire to marry this outstanding exuberant woman, to move around the world with her and take any writing assignment that presented itself.

The Trio

Hannah finished her Master of Science in Pharmaceutical Science and Chemistry in Loughborough, UK in 2008 (LBORO 2016), Philip graduated one year later with a Master of Arts in Publishing from University College London, UK (UCL 2016). Ali graduated with a Master of Engineering in Technical Management from the University of Applied Sciences in Cologne (RFH 2016). They saw each other regularly during this time and Hannah and Philip married in Gretna Green only a few weeks after graduation with Ali as their groomsman. In 2009, Haryette Albers was born in Guatemala during a volunteer stay at Casa Guatemala. Hannah and Philip stayed another 6 months (Casa Guatemala 2016) and then moved on to La Antigua to discover this city inspired by the Italian Renaissance. (UNESCO 2016) They stayed with locals and were fully immersed in this traditional, Catholic society where rules and laws seemed to regulate just about anything (The Hofstede Centre 2016), and yet where the people were spirited, hospitable, forgiving and ever-friendly towards foreigners.

Dozens of Skype conferences from the small internet café La Parada in La Antigua, long emails and months of planning later, their plan was finalized.

RojaAHP

Their start-up would produce fine cosmetics with goat milk and saffron, luxurious and sensual. Hannah had already devised some recipes. They would need carrier oils, shea butter, emulsifiers, fragrances, some other additives, saffron and goat milk. The idea was to use solely organic, sustainable ingredients and to source the ingredients at fairly low cost. Goat population in Iran was increasing (Valizadeh 2010), and they were sure most other ingredients could also be sourced locally.

It was clear from the beginning that RojaAHP would tolerate no child labour or animal testing; instead, they would provide a safe place for women to work. Their long-term goal was to also provide on-site childcare facilities so that women would have an easy time finding employment with them while not having to worry about their offspring. Workers in Iran receive wages of about 10 mio Rial (something like 300 Euros) per month; the other employees would be paid around 60 mio Rial per month.

Hannah read in a German newspaper in 2010 that women in Tehran spend two billion dollars on cosmetics. Some institute had found out that women spend 1% of their monthly income and even Iranian men use anti-age creams, expensive aftershaves and face masks. (Borgstede 2010)

They decided to set up their headquarter in Isfahan, in an abandoned factory Ali was hoping to buy for very little money. A distant uncle had connections to the previous owner. Apart from very few expected local sales, they'd transport their luxurious goods with trucks to Tehran and distribute via local perfumeries, stores and hotels. Once possible, they would expand and export to the Netherlands, Germany and the UK.

2011

February

Hannah was so excited. She was finally here, in Tehran! Her parents had left her the Old Plantation and her lawyer had secured a fine deal when he sold it to some celebrity. With high spirits and only a suitcase with the bare necessities, she strode out of Tehran Mehrabad Airport. She pulled the hijab somewhat tighter around her face, holding it with one hand. Ali had warned her not to wear it too loosely. Suddenly, two women with chador approached her from a small group of people and addressed her; while she turned to look at them, her hijab came loose and a blond wisp of hair escaped. One of the women inhaled sharply and her tone turned sharp. In her life, Hannah had learned several bits of several languages, but this fast, guttural Farsi made no sense to her. She responded in slow, regulated American, "I am sorry but I do not understand you? My name is Hannah Williams. I am an American!" When the old woman stared at her, it occurred to Hannah that she was in trouble. Her attire was not suitable enough, her voice sounded frantic, and thus probably cheeky, and she had promptly forgotten any Farsi Ali had taught her.

1.0

A younger woman also in chador stepped out of the same group of people, pulling several pins out of her Hijab without loosening it.

She offered the extra pins to Hannah and whispered in broken English, "These two women are with the Committee for the Promotion of Virtue and the Prevention of Vice. They say you must wear better clothing. Hijab not tight enough. Blouse too tight." Hannah was alarmed. Apart from the pashmina she had bought in Florence, she had brought nothing else to cover up her curves – she'd planned to go shopping on the bazaar first thing to get the proper colours and fabric. "I don't have anything else except this!" Hannah added, pulling out her pashmina. The young woman nodded, grabbed the cashmere scarf and draped it around Hannah. A rapid battle of words ensued between the women until finally, the young one said, "They say you can leave. Consider this a warning. Go and buy proper clothes soon. If they catch you again, you promise in writing to never do again. Then they know your name and all!" All Hannah could muster at this point was a teary-eyed, "Merci bien! Motsahkerm!" (Dehghan 2016)

2011

March

When Hannah arrived in Isfahan, she could barely contain her excitement. She was going to meet Haryette and Philip at the small furnished apartment Ali had rented for them. Allegedly, it belonged to some uncle who was currently doing business in Dubai—they'd decided to not ask too many questions as the place seemed to come at a reasonable price and the pictures Ali showed them looked beautifully oriental, as far as Philip was concerned.

The weather was pleasant when the driver dropped Hannah off at the address she'd provided him in writing. Even after her four-week crash course in modern Farsi, she still did not feel secure enough to actually speak without embarrassing herself or her dialog partner. "Ghabel nadare," said the driver when Hannah offered him the bundle of Rial bills Ali had recommended for the trip south. She recognized it as, "No need to pay," and thought Ali had taken care of it already or the driver was from Isfahan anyway or whatever. So she left the car with her duffle bag and small traditional-looking tote bag full of goodies for Haryette. It was noisy on this road so she jumped when the driver's voice appeared right in her ear shouting something about an insult to his whole family and shameful Americans. Shaking, she handed over the bills, wondering why he'd said "Ghabel Nadare" in the first place. She still had so much to learn.

The grand opening ceremony was in the late afternoon one week later. Philip and Hannah left the house together, once again with a driver Ali had organized. This time, he assured them, they would not have to pay. This was their company driver. A small bill would be fine, not too much and just enough to show appreciation. He'd also explained that "Ghabel Nadare" was one of those complicated Taroofs only Iranians could really fully understand. A mixture of generosity, a deeply ingrained desire to help and be humane coupled with the very actual need to sustain made it hard for foreigners to understand when this small gesture was meant in all earnest and when it was more of a conversation starter, maybe the beginning of a delicious bartering session.

Mount Soffeh was visible this day behind the factory and the entire staff were standing in front, waiting for the managers.

Mariam, the 48 years old forelady Philip and Hannah had met for lunch the week before, was standing in the middle of the arrangement, dressed in a white Hijab, tunic, pants and manteaux with their logo on it – a purple desert rose. To either side of her stood 35 female workers, all dressed in the same outfit, albeit in blue. 'Hierarchy differentiation.' Hannah decided to ask Ali about this later.

In a much smaller row before the workers stood the other staff members. 31-year-old Armin from Tehran exhibited his western attitude even today: blue jeans, sneakers, Abercrombie and Fitch T-Shirt, and a baseball cap. A designer stubble completed his noncompliant looks. He seemed perfect for local marketing and sales tasks. Next to him, 58-year-old Arian from Isfahan stood bolt upright: full beard, dark slacks, dark blue button down shirt, loafers. He too seemed the right pick for the task: finances, negotiations with banks, sponsors and business partners.

Somewhat to the side stood 38-year-old Mohammad from Tehran; his long moustache, dusty pants, shirt and boots immediately gave him away as the trucker. With him stood five other men in similar apparel, looking sceptical.

"The contrast between Isfahan being more traditional and Tehran more modern could not have been put into better words than these two men managed to portray in their starkly contrasting appearance," whispered Philip to Hannah. She nodded as she stepped out of the car and almost collided with Mustafa, the Abdarschi who was balancing a tray with tea glasses. 'Luckily, I did not make him drop anything,' she thought, smiled at him and went straight for Mariam. Somehow shifting Haryette to her left hip, she extended her right hand to shake the other woman's hand. When Mariam did not reciprocate, she quickly pretended that she'd wanted to just swipe the sweat from her forehead. There was no emotion in the older woman's eyes.

Somewhat taken aback after having met Mariam a few days ago where she was rather personable, Hannah assumed this was a display of power. To remove herself from the awkward situation, she turned around and went straight for Mustafa, loudly saying, "I really could use one of those lovely teas. It's warm today."

Philip noticed Arian and Mustafa both flinch but he could not imagine why. It was warm for March. Mustafa skillfully poured the hot tea into a glass, looked her straight in the eyes, and asked if she wanted sugar. She shook her head, smiled pleasantly and hoped desperately that she'd managed *Aberu*, the Persian concept of saving face. (Gorges 2005)

2012

May

Hannah and Philip had just come back from a meeting with a local supplier. They had asked the older man for a break in their payments. Sales were not going as well as they'd hoped; Armin had so far only been able to convince a handful of boutiques in Tehran to sell their products and most of them wanted a 30% cut of the price received. They had not managed to convince the supplier and after telling Ali about their meeting, they were ashamed about their apparent dilettantism in regards to intercultural understanding.

Ali was raging, "You cannot just waltz in there, Hannah, and try to shake the man's hand! I thought you knew better by now!"

"Well, yes, but I thought since he's our business partner—"

"Business partner. Business partner! He is, but you are still a woman and this is Isfahan! You sit in the background, only regulate internal affairs. You can accompany Philip, but you cannot speak, shake hands, take over. It just doesn't work here! Mr Hashemi would not even have told Philip what went wrong; he'll probably call me later to ask that Hannah never does this again."

"But Philip doesn't know the details, he—"

"Then brief him! For the last time, you are going to ruin us if you keep this up!"

"But Ali, I am a modern Western woman and I do not want to follow these archaic rules! I just cannot see why I should!"

"Hannah. Stop your backtalk. You must respect the Persian culture. You came to this country, wanting to work here so adapt! If you speak with such an impertinent tone with our business partners, I am not surprised we are not getting anywhere. In future, I am going to go to these meetings! End of discussion."

2013

March

After Ali had taken over negotiations with business partners and also re-briefed Armin, sales in Tehran had picked up and even some perfumeries in Isfahan now carried their soaps and crèmes. The factory was running two shifts, one from 6am to 12:30pm and one from 2:30pm to 8:30pm. The long pause was meant to alleviate stress in the summer and create something like the South American siesta. Of course, the factory was closed on Fridays and it was also not operational Saturdays and Sundays, although there was always the option to work 24/6 should the demand increase.

They'd had a number of applications from teenagers hoping to work in the factory but Ali had turned them all down. "It's better to hire more mature women. They work better and there will be no rumours that Philip and I … well, you know."

Hannah had been meeting with Mariam regularly and the older woman had done a great job in coaching Hannah. She now understood that she could be just as influential if she briefed Philip and stayed in her research area of the factory, working on new recipes and products. She'd come to trust Arian with the finances: securing loans from Iranian banks, finding local sponsors, keeping a balance, etc.

She'd also reviewed how to behave when invited to a dinner event with business partners. Hannah used to speak her mind and would have just liked to say, "I don't like lamb." Mariam had taught her *Mehman nawazi*, Persian hospitality which dictated this was not a very good idea. Together, they thought of a better way of avoiding an insult: eat something before going to such dinners and then say, in case something was served that she deemed inedible, "It looks delicious but I am not very hungry today; maybe the heat is giving me trouble."

When inviting business partners to her house, Hannah had to offer the guests food first before she served herself. She also learnt to understand Tarofs to be much more complicated than the book "Not without My Daughter" by Betty Mahmoody suggested. They were not just empty promises and compliments, but a complex of highly ritualized behaviours. They could be compliments, gifts, offers and good behaviour. If Persians offer each other compliments or gift, there's always Tarof

1.0

at work. An example that Mariam gave Hannah was that if a business partner showed up to her house uninvited and right around dinner time, she was supposed to offer him to join the family dinner. He would know that this offer could not possibly be meant seriously but would consider the offer an act of courtesy. He would turn down the invitation several times and the conversation would be very polite and complicated. In the end, both guest and host would save face. (Gorges 2005)

2016

February

The Iranian Parliament proposed a bill to lower working hours for women from 44 to 36 hours. Primarily, women with children and disabled partners were supposed to profit from this regulation, receiving full compensation for less work. The discussion that had been going on for 10 years received new ammunition with this bill. Women's rights activists became more than ever concerned that employers will hire even less women than before. (fh 2016)

RojaAHO reacted immediately. Within their on-site kindergarten, they set up a day-care facility for the elderly. RojaAHP workers who had someone to take care of could bring them along and drop them off in the Rose-Center. In a rotation system, one family member would be with them every day so the elderly saw the familiar faces. Seven women signed up for the model immediately and the relief was noticeable in their productivity instantaneously. Another benefit appeared after a few weeks: both generations in the intergenerational care facility profited from the new situation. The elderly laughed more than before, amused by the children playing, and the children learned the old values and stories.

April

Finally, the sanctions against Iran were lifted! RojaAHP could now begin to export to Western Europe. Everything had long been set up: trucks from a subcontractor were to take the goods 930 kilometres south to Bandar Abbas, where they were to be loaded onto MSC freight containers. MSC takes the AE10-route straight from Bandar Abbas to Rotterdam via the Suez Canal and several stops on the way. (WPS 2016) Well aware of the difficult route they chose, RojaAHP had selected Asian Insurance Company for their most conclusive freight insurance, including general average, standard cargo, war risk and piracy. Asia Insurance Company (2016)

Of course, they would still send many trucks up the Utubahne 7 to Tehran even though the standard traffic jam getting into the metropolis was not just a nuisance to the drivers, but particularly in the summer time, also a challenge to the cooling system in the trucks.

RojaAHP set up a new decision-making system. Workers were prompted to think of ways to improve the facilities. Suggestions were discussed in small work groups and whenever possible, implemented. This empowerment also raised productivity.

September

Hannah had learned Farsi so well she was now able to negotiate with the authorities much better than anyone else at RojaAHP. Somehow, the people in administration reacted better to her now than to Ali or Philip. So, whenever they had something to file or discuss, Hannah had their driver take her and he waited or went shopping while she took care of business. Mariam had done a fine job – Hannah almost seemed to understand their subtleties of culture better than they did themselves. Her success was primarily due to her increased perception though; she noticed the smallest flinch in people immediately and then, with a charismatic smile and her almost accent-free Farsi explained how she was still learning and a foreigner... people loved her for it and her standing and reputation increased.

Weekly, they received about a dozen applications for worker positions and they were very proud to now get international applications for internships. Marketing, logistics, social media manager were the most requested types of work. Armin was setting up for their first intern to arrive at the end of the month. As a mechanical engineering student, he'd be looking at the factory processes; his focus was on finding where manufacturing processes could be improved, whether lean manufacturing was possible and how their manufacturing compared in an international context. The student would be sharing a flat with Armin. Luckily, the young man spoke Farsi so no translator would be necessary.

The government congregation sent by President Rouhani arrived just on time. *IRIB*, the Islamic Republic of Iran Broadcasting, had sent an outside broadcasting van and the newspaper *Donya e eqtesad* (Donya e eqtesad 2016) had sent two reporters (one from the UK and one from Tehran) alongside a photographer. RojaAHP had been selected for a government grant. Someone from the Ministry of Labour and Social Affairs would present them with the certificate today. They had also been informed that they'd receive a tax break. All this for the simple and persistent following of their original goals: sustainable and luxurious cosmetics, locally sourced ingredients, sustainable jobs and humane working conditions for women in Iran. This was a tremendous honour to a company run mainly by foreigners, which is why it created such a hype. The media were incredibly supportive, though. IRIB would film their facilities on-site and report on their success within just five years; *Donya e eqtesad* had already begun interviewing some of their key employees and would run a set of feature articles.

Most likely, this would result in higher sales numbers and another reputation push. Soon, Hannah, Philip and Haryette could go on to new adventures and let RojaAHP work on its own.

Questions

1. Discuss the issues that RojaAHP was facing and which measures they had to take to eliminate them. How did the corporate culture and the owners' underlying values clash with the national culture?
2. Which ethical principles does RojaAHP follow and how did/does this contribute to their corporate strategy and success?
3. Describe the stakeholder groups of RojaAHP and discuss their influence. Which problems can you foresee coming from which groups and which solutions do you propose to RojaAHP?

References

Asia Insurance Company (2016). Notification Porta|Freight. [online] Available at: <http://www.bimehasia. com/%D8%B1%D8%B4%D8%AA%D9%87-%D9%87%D8%A7-%D9%88-%D8%B7%D8%B1%D8%AD-%D9%87%D8%A7%DB%8C-%D8%A8%DB%8C%D9%85%D9%87-%D8%A7%DB%8C/%D8%AD%D9%85%D9%84-%D9%88-%D9%86%D9%82%D9%84/%D8%B4%D8%B1%D8%A7%DB%8C%D8%B7-C>.

Borgstede, M. (2010). *Frauen liegen bei Kosmetikkonsum weltweit vorn*. [online] Available at: <http://www. welt.de/lifestyle/article7388703/Frauen-liegen-bei-Kosmetikkonsum-weltweit-vorn.html>.

Casa Guatemala (2016). *Casa Guatemala: Volunteer*. [online] Available at: <http://www.casa-guatemala.org/volunteer/>.

Couchsurfing (2016). *Stay with Locals and Make Travel Friends*. [online] Available at: <https://www.couchsurfing.com/>.

Dehghan, S. K. (2016). *Influx of morality police to patrol the streets of Tehran*. [online] Available at: <http://www.theguardian.com/world/2016/apr/20/influx-of-morality-police-to-patrol-the-streets-of-tehran>.

Donya e eqtesad (2016). [online] Available at: <http://donya-e-eqtesad.com/>.

Eckert, M. (2015). *Gründen im Iran: "Die Sanktionen haben auch Vorteile"|impulse*. [online] Available at: <https://www.impulse.de/unternehmen/gruenden-im-iran-die-sanktionen-haben-auch-vorteile/2061241.html>

Fh (2016). *Verkürzte Arbeitszeit für Frauen – Iran Journal*. [online] Available at: <http://iranjournal.org/news/verkuerzte-arbeitszeit-fuer-frauen>.

Gorges (2005). *Kulturstandards im Iran*. [online] Available at: <https://www.ihk-krefeld.de/de/media/pdf/international/interkulturelle_kompetenz/interkulturelle_kompetenz/iran_kulturstandards.pdf>.

LBORO (2016). *Pharmaceutical Science and Medicinal Chemistry | Postgraduate Study – 2016 | Loughborough University*. [online] Available at: <http://www.lboro.ac.uk/study/postgraduate/programmes/departments/chemistry/pharmaceutical-science-medicinal-chemistry/>.

MSF USA (2016). *General Logisticians*. [online] Available at: <http://www.doctorswithoutborders.org/work-us/work-field/who-we-need/general-logisticians>.

RFH (2016). *Technical Management (M.Eng.) – Rheinische Fachhochschule Köln*. [online] Available at: <http://www.rfh-koeln.de/studium/studiengaenge/ingenieurwesen/technical_mgmt/index_ger.html>.

Simple Eden (2016). *Natural Body Care Products Made From Goat Milk*. [online] Available at: <http://www.simply-eden.com/collections/>.

The Hofstede Centre (2016). *Countries – Geert Hofstede*. [online] Available at: <https://geert-hofstede.com/countries.html>.

UCL (2016). *MA in Publishing*. [online] Available at: <https://www.ucl.ac.uk/publishing/studies/ma-in-publishing> [Accessed 4 December 2014].

UNESCO (2016). *Antigua Guatemala – UNESCO World Heritage Centre*. [online] Available at: <http://whc.unesco.org/en/list/65 >.

Valizadeh, Reza (2010). Iranian Sheep and Goats at a Glance. [online] Available at: <https://pooya.um.ac.ir/ResearchDocuments/papers/1013463.pdf >.

WPS Mediterranean Shipping Company (MSC) (2016). *World Port Source* [online] Available at: <http://www.worldportsource.com/shipping/Mediterranean_Shipping_Company_MSC__46.php >.

INTEGRATIVE CASE 2.0

'Box-Ticking' in Organizations: Lessons of the Nimrod Disaster

Helga Drummond
University of Liverpool

Introduction

On 2nd September 2006, Nimrod XV230 was on a routine flight over Afghanistan. At 11:11:33, about one and a-half-minutes after mid-air refuelling, the crew received two warnings of fire on the aircraft:

11:12:26 the aircraft depressurised.

11:13:45 the camera operator reports *'"we have flames coming from the rear of the engines on the starboard side"'*.

11:14:10 MAYDAY transmitted. Aircraft diverts to Kandahar airfield.

11:16:54 another plane spots Nimrod descending in flames.

11:17:39 Nimrod disintegrates in mid-air. All fourteen personnel on board killed (The Nimrod Review 2009: Ch. 1).

Nimrod XV230 suffered a so called 'normal accident' (Perrow 1999, 2011 a). That is, in a tightly coupled system, a failure in one component triggers a rapidly escalating chain of events culminating in catastrophe. A system is tightly coupled where, 'Processes happen very fast and can't be turned off, the failed parts can't be isolated from other parts,' (Perrow 1999: 4). The fire started in an unprotected and inaccessible zone of the aircraft. Although the crew behaved impeccably once the fire was discovered, carrying out the correct emergency drills, they had no hope of being able to control the blaze. The fuselage disintegrated rapidly causing the wings and then the tail to break away. The crash was unsurvivable (The Nimrod Review 2009: Ch. 1).

Fire needs three things: flammable material, oxygen and temperature above the point of ignition. The fire was most probably caused by a small leak from a fuel coupling or pipe within the No. 7 Tank Dry Bay - where the wing joins the fuselage, port and starboard. Leaking fuel found an ignition source - probably an exposed surface. This hazard (subsequently referred to as H73) had lain dormant, hidden behind a maze of pipes, pulleys, ducts and wiring, invisible during routine maintenance, since the aircraft entered service in 1969.

That fatal flaw of co-proximity of fuel and an ignition source might have been spotted when the Safety Case for the aircraft was compiled just two years earlier. It is a matter of record that the Safety Case did not draw attention to H73. In fact, the official enquiry into the disaster describes the Safety Case as a 'lamentable' document, essentially a 'box ticking' exercise containing numerous errors and omissions (The Nimrod Review 2009: 10). Yet it was signed off by the Ministry of Defence. What went wrong? Moreover, why were two subsequent "near misses" with the aircraft not acted upon?

What follows examines how the Nimrod Safety Case was constructed and what lessons can be learned from the disaster. The main theme is how safety devices that are a means to an end can become an end in themselves.

Enquiries into the disaster

First a word on materials: there were two official enquiries into the loss of Nimrod XV 230. The Ministry of Defence Board of Inquiry (2007) investigated the immediate causes. The Board discovered deficiencies in the Nimrod Safety Case, prompting a second independent enquiry into the wider aspects of the disaster (The Nimrod Review 2009). The present study draws on the latter as it subsumes the findings of the Board of Inquiry.

The Nimrod Review (2009) was conducted over twenty months. It examined thousands of documents, some dating back to the 1930s and interviewed hundreds of witnesses of all ranks from many organizations in the UK and abroad. The Review team (including technical advisors appointed by the Ministry of Defence) also travelled in a Nimrod (The Nimrod Review 2009: 7). The resultant report is extremely detailed (585 pages). It examines the history of the aircraft and maintenance regime; the detailed layout and condition of the interior, the construction of the Nimrod Safety Case and subsequent events.

Emphatically, the case study that follows does not attempt to tell the whole of the Nimrod story. It is immensely long and complex. However, the Report is a public document so the reader can easily access evidence cited in the presented study (including photographs, worksheets and pro-formas) in order to check the interpretation and read additional detail.

THE NIMROD DISASTER
Background: "Intrinsic high level of confidence"

Safety Cases were introduced in the UK after the Piper Alpha disaster in 1988. An oil rig owned by Occidental Petroleum caught fire, killing 167 men, leaving only 61 survivors. According to Ministry of Defence guidance for outside contractors, a Safety Case should address four questions. One, what could go wrong? Two, how bad could it be? Three, what has been done? Four, what can be done if it happens? (The Nimrod Review 2009: 181 see reference to White Booklet). The overarching aim is to ensure that all important hazards are reduced to 'as low as reasonably practicable'.

Formal work on the Nimrod Safety Case began in 11 April 2001. Three organizations were involved: The Nimrod Integrated Project Team (IPT) from the Ministry of Defence; BAE Systems as contractors; and QinetiQ acting as independent advisors to the Nimrod IPT though not appointed as such. From the start the Ministry of Defence made it clear that the budget for the exercise was extremely limited compared to what had been spent on other aircraft.

The first question during initial discussions between BAE Systems and the Nimrod IPT was whether a full blown Safety Case was necessary given Nimrod's limited life expectancy (the aircraft was already flying well past its 'out of service' date) and apparently good safety record. For instance, the Executive Summary of the Nimrod Safety Plan referred to an: 'intrinsic high level of corporate confidence' in Nimrod, but noted, 'there is currently a lack of structured argument and supporting evidence formally recorded and maintained ... to support the requirements of forthcoming legislation.' (The Nimrod Review 2009: 196).

Defining requirements: A "high level of corporate confidence"

One option considered early on involved using an Implicit Safety Case to construct an Explicit Safety Case. The idea was apparently inspired by Ministry of Defence regulations that allowed an aircraft built to design principles current at the time; that has received the necessary flight clearances, and operated satisfactorily, to stand surrogate for an Explicit Safety Case provided there is nothing to contradict that information (The Nimrod Review 2009: 177).

The idea was dropped because it did not meet legal requirements. However, it was the genesis of a shared understanding that given '"the high level of corporate confidence"' the compilation of the Safety Case would mainly involve seeking out documentation, ('structured evidence'), to support the claim – a reflection of the evolving consensus that Nimrod was basically safe and therefore the Nimrod Safety Case would mainly involve documenting the fact (The Nimrod Review 2009: 10). In other words, the exercise would involve demonstrating presumed safety rather than looking for gaps in safety.

"There does not appear to be any significant concern...."

The Nimrod Safety Case was constructed in two main phases[1]. Phase One (November 2002 to April 2003) involved a physical inspection of the aircraft's systems and zones. Six BAE Systems engineers inspected their allotted zones looking for potential hazards. The details of that exercise need not concern us except that the fire/explosion risk that eventually caused the disaster

---

[1]This is necessarily an abridged and simplified account.

was recorded. Recall, fire needs three things: flammable material, oxygen and temperature above the point of ignition. The worksheet pertaining to H73 is labelled, *'Multiple systems in very close proximity.'*[2] The hazard description for the starboard side reads: *In an area closely packed with flight control cables and pulleys, hydraulic services, unprotected electrical cables and hot air ducting there exists a potential for hot air, fuel and hydraulic leaks and possible fire.*

Initial Probability: Remote (The Nimrod Review: 2009: 204).

The entry for the port side is similar except that the hazard is classified merely as 'improbable'; that is, a much lower level of concern. Yet the two hazards were almost identical.

Phase Two of the Nimrod Safety Case involved assessing and mitigating each of the 105 hazards identified in Phase One down to 'improbable'. This was a desk-based exercise, involving different engineers from Phase One – except for two. What follows are just a few examples of how the exercise unfolded.

Firstly, for Zone 113, engineers recommended a design investigation to consider, *'The probability of system failure resulting from the identified foul/chafing hazard'*.

Yet the overall hazard was deemed 'improbable' *'... not considering the above foul/chafing hazard'* (The Nimrod review: 2009: 296). ...

In other words, the target rating of 'improbable' was achieved by bracketing a potential hazard.

Secondly, engineers working on Phase Two found some of their photographs hard to understand. They assumed, however, that if any serious hazards were present, they would have revealed themselves long ago. For instance, the entry for H3 reads, *'There does not appear to be any significant concern ... if there was any major shortcoming ... it would have surfaced by now'* (The Nimrod Review 2009: 295).

Thirdly, engineers working from manuals frequently used formulaic phrases like, 'It is assumed that appropriate crew drills have already been considered in dealing with such an event,' and 'Emergency procedures and general airmanship are provided for the crew to address the failure as appropriate' (The Nimrod Review 2009: 29). Yet these phrases were used where there was no published drill because the zones were inaccessible.

H73: "Further analytical techniques are considered necessary"

The engineer assigned to H73, Witness R knew little about Nimrods. He assumed that the Cross Feed duct only became hot during engine starts on the ground (The Nimrod Review 2009: 191). In fact, it was used routinely to re-start engines in flight, for example, after loitering. Moreover, Witness R assumed that the duct insulation was adequate, *'The Bleed ducting is insulated and so surface temperatures will be below bleed air temperatures'* he wrote (The Nimrod Review 2009: 289).

Witness R made this assessment aided by photographs. The photographs (The Nimrod Review 2009: 207), however, do not show the gaps in the insulation on the starboard side - or the deterioration.

The pro-formas used by engineers became highly repetitive. For instance:

Section 6 runs to an impressive 18 paragraphs, each ostensibly analyzing one of the 18 *'key potential hazards'* ... giving the semblance of detailed and careful analysis.... But on closer inspection ... the paragraphs are largely repetitive of one another and thin on real analysis (The Nimrod Review 2009: 287).

Witness R agreed with The Nimrod Review that those eighteen aforementioned paragraphs could be condensed into a single sentence namely ... *'From in-service data, the potential for fuel/hydraulic pipe leakage is given as Improbable'* (The Nimrod Review 2009: 287 bold omitted).

Under pressure to meet the deadline, Witness R requested and was allowed to use data from the Nimrod MRA4 to assess risks. The data gave a standard probability rating for fuel pipe and coupling failures as one in approximately 66 Nimrod years. That meant the risk could automatically be classified as 'Improbable' without further examination or analysis (The Nimrod Review 2009: 291). But Nimrod MRA4 was new. It had little in common with older Nimrods.

Besides, RAF maintenance data told a different story. Specifically, between 1983 and 2006 there had been a four-fold increase in the number of leaks from fuel couplings in Nimrods. Moreover, since 2000 there had been about thirty-eight leaks on fuel couplings a year on older Nimrods including XV230 (The Nimrod Review 2009:

---

[2]Unless otherwise stated, italics are in original.

278). But this cumbersome and difficult to access database was not utilized by engineers working on the Nimrod Safety Case. Moreover, anyone with experience of working on Nimrod would have known that fuel leaks were by no means uncommon. But there was no significant operator involvement in the exercise.

In addition, between 1980 and 1982 the cracking of ducts was regularly discussed at meetings of the Nimrod Structural Integrity Working Party (The Nimrod Review 2009: 156). Moreover, in the 1990s a series of hot air leaks caused concern – even though no damage resulted (The Nimrod Review 2009: 137). Ominous incidents had also occurred with other aircraft. For example, in 2002 a Tornado suffered multiple control failures forcing the crew to eject as the aircraft plunged into a river. The crash was caused by fuel dripping through an incorrectly installed seal onto a hot pipe (The Nimrod Review 2009: 154). None of this information was supplied to engineers working on the Nimrod Safety Case. The assessment for H73 simply said, *'From in-service data the potential for fuel pipe leakage is given as improbable'* (The Nimrod Review 2009: 289).

The exercise was also dogged by personality clashes between junior and senior ranks within BAE that delayed the exercise for months. In the end, BAE Systems ran out of time. Consequently forty-three out of 105 hazards were left with probability ratings 'unclassified' and status of the hazard 'open' with the caption, *'Further analytical techniques are considered necessary in order to categorise the risk ...'* (The Nimrod Review 2009: 226). All had a potential severity rating of catastrophic. H73 was one of them.

The Customer Acceptance Conference and Sign Off: Symbols and Semiotics

A Customer Acceptance Conference was held on 31st August and 1st September 2004. It is a matter of record that BAE Systems did not draw attention to gaps in the Safety Case. Moreover, the Conference saw the data base containing the worksheets and pro-formas for one hazard (H 54) by way of demonstration, with attendees huddled round a small computer screen (The Nimrod Review 2009: 228). Otherwise, the Conference mainly consisted of PowerPoint presentations plus a written report. Moreover, the executive summary, conclusions and appendices were missing, scheduled to follow in the final delivery of documentation a few weeks later. Secondly, the Nimrod Project Team had earlier signalled

that they wanted 'no surprises' (The Nimrod Review 2009: 213).

The minutes of the conference state that the documentation had been confirmed by an 'an independent review' by BAE Systems Airworthiness function. It subsequently transpired, however, that the reviewer had been asked only to 'cast an eye' over the documentation (The Nimrod Review 2009: 229). It is a matter of record that BAE Systems did not highlight the number of hazards left 'open'. Nor did the Nimrod IPT ask penetrating questions (The Nimrod Review 2009: 229). At the end of the conference all attendees were asked if they supported completion. When QinetiQ's representative demurred as they had not seen the full documentation, they were 'booed out' (The Nimrod Review: 2009: 238). Junior engineers resolved to present a united front. So they kept quiet at the Conference, "'schtum"' (Nimrod Review 2009: 235) hoping that the customer would not raise awkward questions.

No such questions were asked. The final documentation arrived about three weeks later. The Executive Summary concluded, ***'The aircraft type is deemed acceptably safe to operate and maintain within specified contexts has been deemed as having been achieved'*** (The Nimrod Review 2009: 242 bold in original).

However, the text of Executive Summary noted in red, *'This abstract should be read in conjunction with ANNEX B and ANNEX C to this report.'* (The Nimrod Review 2009: 241). Identified hazards are then mentioned, followed by, *'For the Status of these hazards, refer to Annex B of this report. In relation to ... recommendations made against all identified hazards remaining open (qty 43) refer to ANNEX C of this report.'* (The Nimrod Review 2009: 242 underlining deleted).

The statement concludes, 'Subject to [Nimrod] IPT consideration of the above mentioned recommendations, all potential safety hazards ... have been appropriately addressed.' (The Nimrod Review 2009: 242.

Furthermore, whereas the Executive Summary refers to the top level goal as 'been deemed' to have been achieved; the Conclusions state, *'is considered* as having been demonstrated as having been achieved' (The Nimrod Review 2009: 243 underlining added).

As regards H73, Annex C stated:

From the photographic evidence ... it appears that there are potentials for fire hazards.... Further investigation is required to confirm that the potential loss due to contamination of the various services in the zone ... would not be a hazard to the aircraft. Further analytical techniques are considered

2.0

necessary in order to categorise the risk of the specific fire/explosion hazard.' (The Nimrod Review 2009: 244).

It is not clear who, if anyone in the Nimrod IPT or senior management read beyond the statement in bold. Again, it is a matter of record that the Safety Case was signed off.

Missed chances

On 22 November 2004, unknown to the crew, a corroded hot air duct in No. 7 Dry Tank Bay on Nimrod XV227 disintegrated. The Nimrod IPT sent a suite of papers to BAE Systems who were investigating the incident to attach to the Nimrod Safety Case (The Nimrod Review 2009: 319). Nine months later in August 2005, a fatigued duct (H66) on Nimrod XV229 failed (The Nimrod Review 2009: 320). That too was treated as an isolated incident.

Implications for Practice

The Nimrod Safety Case took four years to complete. The aircraft caught fire and crashed within six minutes. Yet no one apparently had the slightest premonition of disaster. Before discussing implications for practice, it is important to mention that there were other contributory causes of disaster, not least the dilution of the RAF airworthiness regime and sheer pressure of work on the Nimrod IPT (The Nimrod Review 2009).

The first lesson is that certification ('*deemed acceptably safe to operate*') does not mean safe. Certification simply means that doubts and argument have been officially banished. Engineers were still debating the risks with rocket seals even as spaceship Challenger was being launched. The problems were officially filed as solved (Starbuck and Milliken 1988). But the rocket exploded seconds later, killing everyone on board. More recently, the collapsed Rana Plaza clothing factory in Bangladesh that killed over 1000 people in the worst industrial accident since Bhopal was officially certified by government building supervisors. In the present story, 'independent review' meant no more than 'cast eye over'. Like a Mayfair address, certification may be more symbol than substance (Pfeffer 1981 discusses the role of symbols in organizations).

To be more precise, bureaucracy can only operate by proxy:

> Bureaucratic modes of organization are not geared to deal with factual realities; they deal with what is symbolically acceptable as evidence, which usually

means a piece of paper carrying an appropriate signature, date and so on. The important requirement for the bureaucrat to take action is that the action can be shown to be symbolically correct (Morgan, Frost and Pondy, 1983: p. 9).

The piece of paper or artefact is a condensation symbol – it presents information in a very concentrated form. But it is also potentially referential, that is capable of structuring perceptions and emotions (e.g., Edelman, 1970). In other words, symbols can lie.

To understand how and why symbolic evidence of performance may lie, it is necessary to look behind the scenes. Organizations issue templates (including Safety Case forms) to guide action and reduce the need for constant referral. But actors have to decide how to interpret them and decide rules of relevance. For example, what counts as information and what information counts (Brown, 1978; Garfinkel, 1967). According to Garfinkel, actors can exercise considerable discretion about how to approach tasks like compiling Safety Cases so long as the results are symbolically satisfying.

Symbolically satisfying means the resultant report looks the part. That is, all doubts and messy inconsistencies eliminated or smoothed away by skilful use of language. Inevitably, therefore, a gap exists between the document (representation) and reality. That gap, if it is sufficiently wide, can become the 'explosive boundary' (Taleb, 2007: p. xxv) from which disaster springs.

One way of resolving doubt is to assume that because something has not happened in the past, it will not happen in the future. But probabilities can change in ways that are almost imperceptible as systems, people and hardware change (Starbuck and Milliken 1988). Insulation wears away. Corporate memory erodes as minutes disappear into deep archives. In a dynamic environment, past success offers no guarantee of future safety.

Limitations of audits

The Nimrod Review (2009: 261) concludes that if the Nimrod Safety Case had been audited (as required by the Nimrod Safety Plan) deficiencies would have been exposed. Perhaps: but audits too are more symbol than substance. To be more precise, audits are part of the organization ceremonial – rituals of verification (e.g., Power 1997) that provide reassurance by not looking too hard (Pfeffer 1981). For example, hospitals are audited on the number of patients treated, not on the number cured. Schools are audited on whether they have strategies in place to deal with bullying, not whether those strategies actually work. Barings, Enron and Lehman's were all audited by household names. More importantly, the Nimrod IPT had itself passed an audit in 2004 (Nimrod Review 2009: 399). Audits have their place, but they guarantee nothing except maybe to lull us into a false sense of security.

Indirect causes of disaster

Analyzing disaster in complex organizations is like peeling the layers off an onion. To understand how disaster unfolds, it is necessary to look at contributory factors as well as proximate ones. Nimrod was flying well past its 'out of service' date because of equipment procurement delays. Research has shown that waiting begets waiting (e.g., Rubin and Brockner, 1975). It is therefore important to institute protocols for managing ageing systems and technology. Just as pipe couplings, insulation and seals degrade; so does information. Recall, the Nimrod Safety Case got underway in 2001. By then, twenty years had passed since concerns about cracked ducts emerged. Knowledgeable people move on. Data bases decay and fall into disuse. Minutes of meetings disappear into deep archives. Organizations need systems for keeping safety critical information in view – no matter how old it may be.

Making sense of weak signals

Weak signals frequently foreshadow disaster. Weak signals refer to, 'Seemingly random or disconnected … information that at first appears to be background noise but can be recognized as part of a significant pattern,' (Schoemaker and Day, 2009: p. 86).

Treating weak signals as weak is the easiest way to miss them. Organizations too may be culpable. For example, before 9/11 US some intelligence agencies knew about foreign nationals paying for flying lessons in cash and showing no interest in learning how to take off or land a plane (e.g., Bazerman and Watkins, 2008). Staff working in silos never shared this potentially telling information. Similarly, the near loss of Nimrod XV227 contradicted the theory that Nimrod was safe. Furthermore, it pointed directly at the innate fire/explosion risk. The opportunity to avert disaster was lost because by referring the incident for BAE Systems to investigate, the Nimrod Project Team ended up out-sourcing their thinking.

By reacting strongly to surprises, organizations can forestall disaster. A surprise is anything that is unexpected. Expectations are theories of the world liable to be contradicted by experience (Weick and Sutcliffe 2001 discuss surprise). Conceptually, near misses are disasters but for chance (Weick and Sutcliffe 2001). (If Nimrod XV227's fuel tanks had been full, the aircraft might have been lost altogether.) Treat them so.

Using the strengths of bureaucracy

Symbolic does necessarily mean no substance (Pfeffer, 1981). One reason why disasters are relatively rare is that safety systems usually deliver something. Audits identify some weaknesses. Safety cultures prevent some accidents. Safety cases highlight some hazards. The trick is to use the strengths of bureaucracy (not least the ability to capture, store and manipulate data) to detect weak signals and act upon them in a timely fashion.

The science of risk

Strictly speaking risk cannot be managed and controlled because it resides only in our imagination (Barki 2011, Drummond 2011, 2012: Ch. 4). The danger with risk assessments, risk registers and all the other paraphernalia associated with risk is that it too can lull us into a false sense of security. Systems of risk management purport to take unknown hazards and bring them under control by breaking them down into apparently manageable pieces, and classifying and quantifying them (Drummond 2011). As the Nimrod story shows, risk exists as organizations define it. Moreover, that definition may be highly self-serving.

What is not?

Busy executives rarely read beyond the executive summary. Nimrod had been flying for almost forty years. Yet the Safety Case appeared to give the old, time-served aircraft a clean bill of health. The lesson is that if there are no surprises, if all the information seems to point one way, and particularly if it appears to confirm what managers already know, believe to be true and want to hear, that may indicate a confirmation trap. Confirmation traps refers to our innate tendency as human beings to unconsciously seek out and focus attention upon information that seems to confirm our pre-conceived views whilst downplaying disconfirming data (Bazerman and Wattkins 2008 Ch: 4, Drummond 2012 Ch. 1). The cure is to

2.0

2.0

look for small inconsistencies. Busy executives should ask themselves, 'what I am not hearing?'

Operator involvement

It is not clear why there was no operator involvement in the construction of the Nimrod Safety Case as originally planned. Had there been such involvement, many mistakes might have been avoided. People with intimate knowledge and experience of the aircraft might have compensated for the loss and degradation of information. They would certainly have known that fuel leaks were by no means rare. Such engagement is time-consuming. However, it is an essential, not a luxury.

Normal deviance

Yet not even operator involvement guaranteed safety. Recall, Nimrod operators regarded fuel leaks as inevitable. The idea was to prevent them reaching an ignition source by tracing possible leak paths. But leaking fuel has a habit of seeping uncontrollably. The point is, treating dangerous occurrences as 'normal' events – 'that's always happening' can blind organizations to danger. For example, one reason alleged rape and sexual assault by the late Jimmy Savile were never investigated properly was the police mind-set, 'Jim gets lots of complaints'. Disaster theorists call it normalized deviance, that is, where danger stares us in the face yet no one acts because this is how things have always been.

Final thoughts

We see what we expect (Weick 1995). The Safety Case was not the only missed opportunity to avert disaster. Between 1969 and 2006 many engineers worked in No. 7 Dry Tank Bay. But nobody apparently noticed the dangerous positioning of the fuel pipes. The Nimrod Review (2009: 156) concludes that no one saw it because no one was looking for it.

There is another plausible possibility. Perhaps someone, possibly more than one person, of the myriad engineers and technicians who came and went over the years did notice the fatal flaw, recognized it, but did nothing. It is a sad reality of organizational life that it would have been much easier to rationalize the hazard as 'improbable', than rock the boat. Research has consistently shown that people tend to discount outcomes with small probabilities - even those

with potential to cause catastrophe (e.g., March and Shapira 1987; Taleb 2008; Allison and Zelikow 1999: xii). For instance, Japan's seawall was just a bit bigger than the largest tsunami experienced in the last 1000 years; a design 'Based on probabilistic thinking, not thinking about what is possible,' (Perrow (2011 b: 47). Similarly, the Nimrod disaster should remind us that 'Improbable' does not mean 'Impossible'. There may be an 'awesome crack' (Allison and Zelikow 1999: xii) between the two – like a tiny gap in the insulation.

References

Allison, G. and Zelikow, P. (1999) *Essence of Decision: Explaining the Cuban Missile Crisis*, New York, Longman.

Barki, H. (2011) 'Managing illusions of control,' *Journal of Information Technology, 26*, 280-281.

Bazerman, M. H. and Watkins, M. D. (2008) *Predictable Surprises, The Disasters You Should Have Seen Coming and How to Prevent Them,* Boston, Harvard Business Press.

Brown, R. H. (1978) 'Bureaucracy as praxis: toward a political phenomenology of organizations', *Administrative Science Quarterly, 23*, 365-382.

Drummond, H. (2011) 'MIS and illusions of control: analysis of the risks of risk management,' *Journal of Information Technology, 259-267.

Drummond, H. (2012) *The Economist Guide to Decision-Making,* Economist Publications in association with Profile, London.

Edelman, M. (1970) *The Symbolic Uses of Politics,* Chicago, University of Illinois.

Garfinkel, H. (1967) *Studies in Ethnomethodology,* Polity, Cambridge.

March, J. G., Shapira, Z. (1987) 'Managerial perspectives on risk and risk taking,' *Management Science, 33,* 1404-1418.

Ministry of Defence (2007) *Board of Inquiry into the Accident Involving Nimrod MR2 XV230,* www.mod.uk.

Morgan., G. P., Frost, P. J., and Pondy, R. L. (1983) 'Organizational symbolism'. In L. R. Pondy., P. J. Frost, G. Morgan, G. and T. C. Dandridge, (eds.) *Organizational Symbolism,* London: JAI, pp. 3-35.

Perrow, C. (1999) *Normal Accidents: Living With High Risk Technologies,* Princeton, Princeton University Press.

Perrow, C. (2011) *The Next Catastrophe: Reducing Our Vulnerabilities to Natural, Industrial and Terrorist Disasters,* Princeton, Princeton University Press.

Pfeffer, J. (1981) 'Management as symbolic action: the creation and maintenance of organizational paradigms.' In L. L. Cummings and B. M. Staw (Eds.), *Research in Organizational Behavior,* Greenwich, JAI Press, 1-52.

Power, M. (1997) *The Audit Society,* Oxford, Oxford University Press.

Reason, J. (1997) *Managing the Risks of Organizational Accidents,* London, Ashgate.

Rubin J. Z., and Brockner, J. (1975) Factors affecting entrapment in waiting situations: the Rosencrantz and

Guildenstern effect, *Journal of Personality and Social Psychology*, 31: 1054-1063.

Schoemaker, P. J. H. and Day, G. S. (2009) 'How to make sense of weak signals', *MIT Sloan Management Review,* 50, 81-89.

Starbuck, W. H. and Millken F. J. (1988) 'Challenger: fine-tuning the odds until something breaks,' *Journal of Management Studies, 25*, 319-340.

Taleb, N. (2008) *The Black Swan: The Impact of the Highly Improbable,* London, Penguin. Penguin, London.

The Nimrod Review: An Independent Review into the Broader Issues surrounding the loss of RAF Nimrod MR2 Aircraft XV230 in Afghanistan in 2006 (Charles Haddon-Cave QC), London, TSO, 2009.

Weick, K. E. (1995) *Sense Making in Organizations*, Beverly Hills, Sage.

Weick, K. E. and Sutcliffe, K. M. (2001) *Managing the Unexpected: Assuring High Performance in an Age of Complexity,* San Francisco, Jossey-Bass.

Further Reading

2.0

Bazerman, M. H. and Watkins, M. D. (2008) *Predictable Surprises, The Disasters You Should Have Seen Coming and How to Prevent Them,* Boston, Harvard Business Press.

Drummond, H. (2012) *The Economist Guide to Decision-Making,* Economist Publications in association with Profile, London.

Perrow, C. (1999) *Normal Accidents: Living With High Risk Technologies,* Princeton, Princeton University Press.

Perrow, C. (2011) *The Next Catastrophe: Reducing Our Vulnerabilities to Natural, Industrial and Terrorist Disasters,* Princeton, Princeton University Press.

Reason, J. (1997) *Managing the Risks of Organizational Accidents,* London, Ashgate.

Weick, K. E. and Sutcliffe, K. M. (2001) *Managing the Unexpected: Assuring High Performance in an Age of Complexity,* San Francisco, Jossey-Bass.

INTEGRATIVE CASE 3.0

Onward to the Customer of One; from Debt Collectors to Customer Service Agents at New Zealand's Inland Revenue

Craig Prichard

Massey University, New Zealand

The global financial crisis knocked a hole the size of Antarctica in the New Zealand Government's tax budget. After years of surpluses, the dive into the red came as a shock. It wasn't long before Government ministers were telling the country's tax collector, Inland Revenue (IR), that no tax defaulter was to be left unturned in the search for cash.

This was just the green light that David Udy, IR's head of Collections, had been looking for. What he had in mind however was not a campaign of house calls on painters, builders and musicians – IR's traditional targets. He was toying with something much bigger, hairier and rather more monstrous; the kind of organizational change that would have New Zealand's most traditional civil servants trembling in their gumboots.

In fact, what the GFC had offered up, in the form of a growing bubble of uncollected tax, was a chance to set New Zealand's biggest debt collection agency on a genuinely 180-degree new course. A course that in the end would turn income, sales and business taxes into 'products', tax defaulters into the IR's customers, and turn IR's traditional hard-bitten tax collectors into empathetic customer service agents on a quest to see the world from where their customers saw it and to walk briefly in their shoes.

But infusing a core state service like Inland Revenue with the smarts expected of a high-end retailer or personal banker would be no Sunday stroll among the filing cabinets. Collections, as the service became known at its launch in 2012, has hundreds staff who, as Udy

admits, did not come to work at Inland Revenue expecting change. They came looking for a stable routine and reliable workplace.

Questions

1. **What caused the Global Financial Crisis?** The GFC had multiple causes. Some point to a US housing market price bubble and people's inability to cover their loans. Others identify the failure of financial markets regulation and consequent failure, or threat of failure, of key financial institutions that had invested and traded in questionable financial assets that underpinned the house price bubble. Others take a more system-based view and put the blame with capitalism as a system that is inherently unstable and from time to time passes through periods of severe contraction. In such periods, speculative investments fails, capital accumulation slows or goes in reverse, wiping away huge amounts of value and plunging economies into long term recession and austerity.

2. **For many the Global Financial Crisis was a disaster. But for a change manager was it a problem or an opportunity?** An opportunity! To paraphrase change management guru John Kotter, there's nothing quite so useful as a good crisis and in 2009 the economic shock of the GFC was obvious and palpable. A 'good' crisis, however, is one that leads to the questioning of existing practices, and creates a sense

of urgency and energy that things must be done differently in response. The challenge is how to direct and organize that energy.

3. **What impact might years of Government surpluses have had on Inland Revenue's ability to collect unpaid taxes?** Years of surpluses meant certain classes of tax debt were taking either a very long time to be collected, or were not being collected at all (written off). In some instances, it took two years before the first letter requesting payment was going to a defaulter, and the rate of default was increasing beyond the rate that Inland Revenue could collect it. In 2009 the New Zealand Government's Auditor General told Inland Revenue that this simply had to change. For David Udy, the key problem was that collectors just didn't understand their tax debtors and consequently these 'customers' were not getting the right service attention in the right way at the right time. It was this, he said, that had to change.

4. **What tactics, strategies, advice and support are needed to make the kind of change that David Udy had in mind?** Alongside a three-fold increase in tax collecting personnel, a new computer system and a new organizational structure, the change process involved multiple rounds of workshops over a five-year period. At its core the project is a traditional organizational development process where IR staff were given a method for solving the organization's problems. Organized and run by the consulting company *Assured*, IR staffers produced elaborate murals, maps and drawings that contextualized their organization in its environment, identified the drivers for change, the key blockers, challenges and their 'desired future state'. The difference between the current and desired future states then creates the guiding narrative of the change journey and its key 'transition points'.

Customer workshops

If truth could be told David Udy, New Zealand's tax debt collecting supremo, is a bit of a comic. In another life he might have even made a good living in stand-up. Thankfully his witty turns of phrase, his dry self-effacing moments of hilarity, have not gone to waste. They have carried the day more than once during long, grinding,

sometimes intense workshops around the country where Udy and his consulting support team worked to drag battle-hardened tax collectors through a set of what Udy calls his 'come to Jesus' moments; transition points when the doubters, sceptics and unbelievers joined in the 'change journey'.

'We were in Tauranga[1]. We were having this heated conversation. 'Why do I want to know who the customers were', they asked. 'It's bloody simple really', I was saying. 'I want to be able to tell the Commissioner we understand our business. So I want you to tell me who the customers are when dealing with this particular product[2]'. After applying lots of pressure on this person, he then said – *it's men, white, they work in white vans with a ladder on top.* Good, write that down, that is the customer! It is that mix of patience and keeping the pressure on until people express.

For Udy the 'white vans with ladders on top' is a fine 'Come to Jesus' moment. A transition point when the struggling staffer edged toward becoming a customer-centric believer. A moment when the loyalty civil servant 'unwrapped the onion', as Udy would say, and began to regard defaulting tax payers as Collection's service customers.

But back in the beginning, back in 2010, everyone was a doubter. Even Udy's senior staff didn't take him seriously. 'Let's humour David', they were saying. 'It would all blow over'. But Udy was no pushover and through months and months of their scheduled two day monthly workshops, first with his senior group, then cascading out across the organization, the 'doubters' passed through these obligatory points of passage, their own ' Jesus' moments, and they joined the fold.

'You've got to have faith and have patience early only. The people I inherited were more 'doing people', so you had to structure conversations in the right way so people could see the tangible links back to their reference points.

'One of the tyrannies we have today is that we want results too quickly and we don't understand that we are dealing with people. It takes time. You've got to have faith and have patience early on. 'We had to be very clear to give people permission to

---

[1] A small New Zealand city on the East Coast of the North Island about two hours from Auckland famous for its surf beaches and surrounding Kiwi Fruit Orchards.

[2] In the new language of the change project a 'product' is a particular tax collecting form e.g. goods and services tax, company tax, pay-as-you-earn income tax.

3.0

think differently. In the beginning we'll just humour David because he's not going away.'

But becoming a believer doesn't happen overnight, David admits.   The average IR staffer will take years to unlearn deeply ingrained thinking and practice. David Udy is clearly a patient man, but he is also, as his staff mentioned, no quitter, nor is he easily satisfied. He is unlikely to be entirely satisfied for example with the effort to see tax defaulters as 'men with vans with ladders on the top'. The desired future state goes further - to a point where the service knows their 'customers' so well, so intimately, so completely, that they will have just the right conversation at the right time so the outstanding tax is paid.

Question: Is there more to the change project than a set of workshops? Inland Revenue's face-to-face workshop sessions, facilitated by consulting company Assured, were just one part of the project. Alongside it was the installation of a brand-new customer centric IT system and a tripling of the core staff, each selected on an explicit set of person qualities, and trained in such a way that they took for granted the new customer-central mantra. To underwrite this mantra, to bed in this new relationship with debtors, all IR staff, senior managers included, had to, as Udy put it, 'eat their own dog tucker'. Now dog tucker is not a forced meal of meagre rations (a few old dry bones and biscuits). The 'dog's tucker' in this case was the new customer-centic debt collection computer system that everyone at Inland Revenue, David Udy and his senior group of managers included, had to learn to operate. Everyone had to be certified on the new system, and through this everyone had to come to terms with not just the meaning of customer-centric relations to tax debtors, but the very means by which those new meanings were to be used.

But what really oiled the wheels of the Inland Revenue was money. Collections, as it became in 2012, received regular Government funding injections and grew staff numbers three-fold. The service's 2009 staff complement of just 300, who were struggling to deal with the top 30 000 defaulting cases each year, was tripled to over 900 staff by 2014 and that year Collections dealt with more than 530 000 debt cases.

Question: What job does the consultant do in this process? *Assured,* a company owned by veteran NZ change consultant Grant Wallace, provided a wraparound

support service for the Inland Revenue Change process over the full five-year period. They came and went during that time, running workshops and supporting the change leaders. Their approach involves building a robust and increasingly detailed narrative and technical repository to support the organization's shift to a desired future state. Their change approach melds aspects of John Kotter's classic eight element change method using visual artefacts and compelling change stories.

'What I think Grant's crew and the whole process is really good at is using questions to dig deeper into problems. Tell us more, they say. We generate huge lists, but the really important thing was, you realise there are no barriers, just a series of constraints to deal with. You could actually watch the light bulbs going on in people's heads – bugger it, I am going to make a difference.'

Three times to Jesus; transition points

But back in 2009 David Udy's first effort to turn this most traditional, hierarchical and aged of government agencies into a customer-obsessed youngster began in earnest with a simple six question survey of his immediate staff. The aim was to draw his senior group toward their first 'come to Jesus' transition. He asked: Who they were, what did they do, what was the most important issue they were facing then and there, what irked them the most, and what keeps you up at night? He fed the answer back to the group and they showed how the group shared common problems and common concerns – which suggested that they had something to gain from working together.

As Udy puts it: 'The first transition was 'yes, we will play, we can see the benefit'. The second transition point occurred when one person out of the group brought a problem to the table, and that person didn't have an answer for it. They were saying: 'We say we are going to do this, but when I look at the world this way, I see all these problems'. And I was thinking: 'YES' hugs and kisses, we've actually got people on the journey now'. From this, the group was then able to describe the current state, what they wanted to be different, and to draw the first draft of the first journey maps - which was the third transition point.[3]

---

[3]*Assured's* approach involves extensive use of visual media to mobilize and record the change process. It employs a seasoned artist who turns the participant's simple sketches into elaborate, wall-sized drawings of an organization's change journey using metaphors and cartoon images to elaborate the visual narrative. For an example of one of these drawings see the ' http://www.wpma.org.nz/about/renewing-nz/ (part of work *Assured* did for New Zealand's Wood Processors and Manufacturers Association (WPMA).

David then told the group that they were going to use this question-asking methodology to work out how they were going to frame up their business to work better. In effect he was saying: 'do you want to come on the journey'?

'Now what we were saying is that you can't be half-hearted. You have to be for it but if you're not, that's okay, put your hand up and we can sort it out. No-one got out at that point. Everyone decided they would come for the journey because ultimately everyone is passionate about trying to make a difference. If you can frame that right, most human beings will come for the ride'.

Why are the transitions so important? A change agent can only show and guide, ultimately those involved have to make some kind of choice, they have to make a decision about where they stand and what they were going to do next. And that can be uncomfortable for some. A customer centric approach means creating a strong sense of empathy and understanding for the services 'customers'.

'The big thing you have got to get your head around is that it is a different way of thinking. You have got to reframe your own thinking first if you are going to lead this. To me it starts with, 'do you want to make a difference to customers?' If so, then here is a model that figures out what services meet those customer needs. Those three questions – who are your customers, what do they want and why do they want it? – if we could answer the why a lot of people get into debt, we would be home and hosed. That is the big thing we are still working on.'

David Udy led the process. But the seeming success of IR collection's four-year change programme was not simply down to his wit and brilliance. As David tells it, a whole battalion of forces and factors conspired to initiate and amplify the need, direction and commitment to change at Collections. Each of the small wins bought further help and support that in turn amplified and extended the work until Collections had surpassed it's collection budget and was, according to Udy, the apple in the commissioner's eye, with a full 20 awards in recent years for excellence.

Onward to the customer of one

3.0

In truth though, change is simply a set of departure lounges. The 'white vans with ladders on the top' statement is just one of many starts. The utopia for David Udy's Inland Revenue, the place they are heading, and at which they will likely never arrive, is a place where tax collectors know enough about their 'customers' so they can have exactly the right conversation at the right time with the right outcome for the wider goal - the social and economic well-being of New Zealand. David has a little mantra that evokes this taxman's new nirvana, something he has probably said a million times already: 'Onward to the customer of one'.

Final Questions

1. What is meant by David Udy's phrase a 'Onward to the customer of one'?
2. What role might the phrase play in the Inland Revenue change project?
3. Does moving to a 'customer of one' raise any ethical or moral issues?
4. None of David Udy's reporting managers decided against going 'on the journey'. All (seemingly) became true believers and passed through the three 'come to Jesus' transition points. Drawing on your reading of power relations and political tactics in chapter 13, why did none bail out?
5. Inland Revenue's change project is an elaborate multi-year Organization Development programme (see chapter 11). Why was this approach particularly suited to this organization and what might be some of challenges of using it in other types of organizations?
6. Why would seemingly frivolous and light hearted phrases like 'Come to Jesus' and 'Eat your own dog tucker' be important in serious and expensive change projects such as the one described above? Discuss using Chapter 10's presentation of different organization cultures and subcultures?

INTEGRATIVE CASE 4.0

Changing the Culture at Trans-Gen PLC: What's wrong with Senior Management?

Anni Hollings
Staffordshire University

Trans-Gen PLC (TrG) is a design and manufacturer of protection and control systems for electrical transmission and distribution networks. It is part of a bigger division of a dual-country-owned major employer. The Division is supported throughout the world by more than 60 industrial and commercial units employing more than 14 000 and has a turnover in excess of €1500M. The British unit of TrG is located in a small county town in the North Midlands. The unit still enjoys a dominant position in many of the world's markets, a position not shared by some units in the Division which have seen their markets diminish.

TrG prides itself on its international reputation, and provides a number of client-centred services to ensure its reputation and market position remain dominant. The client-responsive services are:

- Research and Development. The group continuously analyzes the needs of its customers, enabling it to design and perfect products best suited to the specifications of international markets.

- Applications Expertise. All units provide applications teams which are at the disposal of customers to match their requirements to the specific features of the product range. Using various state-of-the-art techniques, the applications teams can replicate all known faults to ensure the correct match of protection relays to system requirements.

- Training. The Group is renowned throughout the world for the quality of its customer training courses which vary from annual sessions to several weeks of general theory and practical work on protection and control systems, to dedicated programmes on specific products.

- Quality Assurance. The Group has always attempted to manufacture equipment which meets or exceeds the highest industry standards. In response to these standards becoming ever more stringent, the Group has implemented a total quality assurance and enhancement approach to ensure the excellence of its products.

- After Sales Service. Since the reliability of power systems worldwide is becoming increasingly vital, a rapid and effective response to potential problems is essential. The Group's after-sales service teams are capable of meeting every known need including on-site commissioning, the supply of components and all stages of maintenance.

- Commercial Establishment. A network of representatives, agents and manufacturing capability in more than 120 countries exists to ensure that the lines of communication between the Group and its customers are as short as possible.

In 2011, TrG embarked on a programme of change which incorporated the integration of various dimensions of quality including the technical perspective of perceived quality, human-focused quality management and intelligent quality management. The company wanted to ensure that technical, social and sustainable facets of quality were integrated into all decisions regarding a delivery of a superior product and service.

Previously there had been two other attempts at 'Total Quality'. Both these attempts had been driven by middle-management without the commitment of senior managers. Failure for these attempts was attributed to this lack of commitment and involvement from the top. It meant that the workforce had been introduced to some of the ideas and principles of TQM, which had resulted in TQM being perceived negatively based upon experience of ambivalence and disenfranchisement by senior employees.

Any third attempt must prove to be successful otherwise there would be serious implications for the sustainability of growth and profits. Being reputed as an organization that was rooted in best practice, quality products and services were perceived as useful strategic tools to achieve economic and financial success and stability. The introduction of changes in working practices through which the company could secure its future was also tied into the acceptance that electronic developments had meant that TrG products had lost their uniqueness. The strategic response was to change the organizational emphasis from being product driven to service driven. Service and customer loyalty to TrG were to be marketed as the unique selling point which would ensure competitive advantage.

The Managing Director was the champion of the change programme. He had been a strong supporter of the ideas of TQM and was convinced the approach would be appropriate for TrG. He contracted a consultancy to conduct an employee and customer attitude survey to establish the need, or otherwise, for TrG to embark on a major programme for change. 40% of the employees were included, selection being by random sample based on every 5th person on the 'head-count' list. The results of the surveys were fed back to the senior management team over a two-day workshop conducted by the consultants. Recommendations were made to implement and pursue a programme which would see TrG applying the principles and best practices of contemporary quality management.

The consultants identified several areas of frustration for employees and customers. Employee comments drew attention to the perceptions that:

- standards were inconsistent and that there was an emphasis on quantity rather than quality,
- there were too many systems and products,
- there were frequent component shortages,
- the organization was fragmented with too many departments 'doing their own thing',
- there was no sense of direction from 'the hierarchy' and that 'they' were too remote,
- there were too many barriers to getting things done,
- there was very little awareness of what was going on for most of the time.

Customer comments highlighted problems with:

- lead-times, with products taking too long to make and deliver meaning that delivery dates were often meaningless;
- liaison, which was often variable and feedback was often slow;
- persistent and minor problems with otherwise good quality products, but providing enough irritation for customers to seek alternative suppliers.

The general statement which TrG used to sum up the surveys was that:

"We are good but we need to improve to get ahead".

The rationale for the introduction of new ways of working based upon a culture change into TrG was established. The communication to internal and external stakeholders stated that:

"All companies are dependent upon their customers and stakeholders, survival and growth depend on continuing to meet their needs. Satisfied customers help create more demand which in turn help provide more growth and sustained investment. TrG recognizes that our customers are searching to improve their performance and that as a supplier, TrG must respond and collaborate with its customers in order to outperform our competitors".

Secondary to this, the company communicated to its employees:

"We also wished to continue to grow, become more proactive to change, build on the improvement culture that already exists and solve long-standing problems".

"The new approach to quality will provide the new stimulus which will assist us towards expanding our continuous improvement goal".

In October 2011 the MD decided that the programme of change would be promoted under the heading of *Delivering the Future through Total Quality*. A TQ Coordinator was appointed; this was a part-time role for a member of the senior management team and was given to the Chief Accountant, who was fully supportive of the Managing Director's initiative and the ideas which underpinned a total quality agenda. A full-time TQ Manager was appointed whose role was to coordinate, monitor and progress all TQ-related activity on behalf of the company, key elements of which were training and communication.

Also the Company Steering Group(CSG) and Functional Steering Groups (FSG) were formed. The CSG comprised the Management Team and the TQ Manager with the Managing Director in the chair. The FSGs comprised the departmental heads of that function, plus a part-time facilitator with the functional head in the chair. The part-time TQ facilitators were to perform a role similar to that of the TQ Manager but with a functional focus and in support of their chairperson. There were five functional steering groups established.

During late 2011 a series of workshops were conducted designed to provide awareness of the new approach and to communicate the survey results. The audience was all middle management to supervisory level. The workshops were led by the TQ Manager with a representative from the consultancy in a facilitator role. The workshops covered an agenda which was essentially informative, with topics including, 'What is our approach to quality', 'How to gain commitment' and 'Gaining improvements'. During these workshops participants were asked to consider possible projects for improvement.

The role and influence of the external consultant was very important. Deliberately designed not to be intrusive, he was 'at hand' throughout the workshops to provide advice and support to the TQ Manager; he was also contracted on a 'retainer' to provide a mentoring role to the TQ Manager on what turned out to be fortnightly discussion and review sessions.

In January 2012 a vision statement was formulated and initial improvement projects were selected. The vision statement was presented and proposed the following:

"We believe that our future growth and prosperity lie in providing products and services which please our customers and outperform our competitors. Simply, we aim to be the best. We shall achieve this by working closely together and using the undoubted skill of everyone here to challenge and improve everything we do."

By January 2012, five company-wide projects had been identified, which were designed to promote multi-disciplinary teamworking and short-term success. There were several functional projects which were to achieve short-term success within specific location areas and gain greater employee response to, and awareness of, what could be achieved. The five company-wide projects were selected directly as a result of the top and second level management awareness sessions; employee involvement at that time was negligible. They were chosen to cover a good cross-section of external issues which concentrated on customer satisfaction and included reducing lead-times, improving modification and repair turnaround times, and improving the company

image; internal issues which addressed company performance, particularly product range rationalisation; and people issues which were intended to highlight the value of people to the company and focused on personal appraisals.

The FSGs, who had ownership of the functional projects, identified projects which covered a wide range of activities, but the choice was heavily influenced by the external consultants who suggested projects which could be statistically measured. This was, in part, a reflection of the consultant's own practice paradigm, which was essentially operations management and therefore efficiency dominated; and in part, consistent with TrG's known base of expertise and unlikely to present any complications in terms of analysis and interpretation.

Team leaders were selected by the CSG and the relevant FSGs as appropriate, and teams of six to eight multi-disciplined groups of people were chosen by the team-leader in consultation with interested parties. Training was given to all project teams on the Key Principles of the new ways of working which were:

- To give the customers what they want when they want it.
- To work as suppliers and customers to each other to improve our service.
- To explore and try out better ways of doing things.
- To strive to do things right first time, every time.
- To measure how we are doing and agree improvement targets.
- To take advantage of training.
- To foster effective communication.

Best Practice Tools and Techniques included:

- Teamworking
- Running Effective Meetings
- Uses of Delegation
- The Problem-solving Process
- Action/Work Planning
- Report Writing
- Telephone Techniques
- Making Presentations.

The training was managed and led by the TQ Manager, who, prior to taking up the role, had been the Training Manager. It was an activity he enjoyed and had earned a considerable reputation as a very effective learning facilitator. He was intent on using his own skills and sphere of influence to demonstrate the principles in practice, consequently he spent a considerable amount of time on ensuring that the material and learning programme reflected best practice. His drive and energy throughout this programme was well received and people responded positively to him.

The training was under the general title of the 'Business Improvement Programme'. The emphasis was on employees communicating more effectively, becoming more involved, showing a greater willingness to suggest and accept change, identifying and solving problems, and through thinking of ways to reduce waste. For the TQ Manager the main message was one of 'empowerment' a principle and concept to which he was deeply committed. In the publicity, Total Quality was presented as the 'cornerstone' of customer satisfaction, team spirit, job security and job satisfaction.

The Business Improvement Programme incorporated four other general elements which were activated over the next 12 months:

- Process Reviews
- Personal Change
- Communication
- Improvement Monitoring.

The process reviews were considered to be a medium to long-term exercise to be conducted by the senior management team. However, an initial review was conducted to compare the organization structure with the main business processes and the key tasks performed by each of the functions. The review required a critical analysis of the interaction between the functions and highlighted several areas of concern in relation to anomalies in practice, gaps of information and overlaps of responsibility. The review also involved establishing better customer/supplier relationships and customer satisfaction measures. The customer/supplier network brought the concept of the internal customer into the arena with emphasis being given to the notion of work colleagues as suppliers or receivers of 'products'.

To support changes in behaviour and attitudes to reflect the new values underpinning the new ways of working a programme called 'Personal Change' was used to introduce a redesigned personal appraisal scheme linked to a revamped performance management strategy. The initial intention was to cover 250 employees from the Managing Director downwards, which essentially covered the management. In introducing the new scheme care was taken to ensure that appropriate training was received by all involved as either an appraiser or appraisee. Personal development

and improvement were seen as key factors of the overall continuous improvement message, with appraisal being the vehicle through which individuals could be reviewed in the context of the improvement projects, and guided with regard to future requirements.

Improved organizational communications were regarded as being a critical feature of the Business Improvement Programme and a variety of communication methods were adopted or revamped to reflect the ideas of greater involvement.

Interactive total quality awareness sessions were conducted with 700 personnel in small groups of 15–20 people. These were led by the TQ manager and covered 40% of the workforce. The majority of shop-floor employees did not attend. The sessions were used to generate information about 'real' problems at all levels of the organization and inform projects in specific areas and functions. The purpose of these projects was to ensure a greater sense of ownership with the improvements taking place, more personal involvement because these projects would have direct relevance to the group, which, in turn would encourage the employees to demonstrate the 'will' to help colleagues in solving problems that were seen to be of a shared concern.

Specific Information Bulletins were produced for company-wide circulation and posted on special Bulletin Boards. These gave updated information on the progress of the projects with the company-wide projects receiving general circulation and more specific projects promoted as appropriate.

In November 2012 a purpose designed in-house publication entitled *Feedback* was introduced. This was a free publication for all employees and provided information of a general nature about total quality developments, details about project progress and indication of what might happen in the future. This was edited by the TQ manager and encouraged all employees to contribute. *Feedback* was published bi-monthly. In the first edition it contained the TQ Statement which was signed by all members of the Senior Management Team. However, the original promoter of the change, the Managing Director, had been promoted to a Group Board position and his position was being held by a 'caretaker' Managing Director, who was not interested in taking on the job on a permanent basis.

The edition gave an explanation of the TQ motif that the Company was adopting. The triangular style was said to symbolize the overall concept of the programme because 'Total' meant that it involved everyone and everything that TrG did, 'Quality' covered both products and service to colleagues and customers, and that it was a 'Programme' that would demand commitment and effort over many years. The underlying message was that change did not come about easily and that success would only be achieved through engaged employees helping each other to make continuous improvements.

A Facilitator Group comprising the Functional Group Heads and the TQ Manager met every month to communicate progress, share experiences, discuss problems and formulate new initiatives.

Following the review of 2013, the objectives for the following two years were published. These were to:

- Improve company performance through streamlining and improving the product range, simplifying key business processes, establishing effective performance measures for all stages of every main process, applying new production techniques to give higher product quality standards, developing supplier relationships and implementing joint performance monitoring, reducing costs and adding value, and improving interdepartmental service.

- Improve customer satisfaction, through reducing lead times, improving delivery reliability, improving modifications and repair response times and turnaround times, reducing development lead-times, and improving the customer complaint response times. It was also part of the communication exercise to improve communication and consultation with the marketplace through every means possible.

- The 'People' objectives covered training and communications with statements made about ensuring that people had the right tools and the right training for a given job, that the company was committed to investing in the large training requirement, that needs were being identified and prioritized to business requirements and, that all employees were to be exposed to the Business Improvement awareness sessions by June 2014.

After two years of running the programme, fewer than 25% of the employees had been given any formal opportunity to learn about, and discuss the change programme, although bulletins and the magazine had kept people informed of what was happening. A new Chief Executive was in post. Claims of success were being made about several of the projects and the objectives for the next two years were essentially more of the same.

The TQ Manager realized that if the new ways of working were to succeed it was essential that they were incorporated into the general activities which everyone undertook. Despite the claims of success, the project teams had tended to divorce the new approach from the day-to-day activities by taking people from their functional base to do a 'special' task. However, the TQ manager was confident that the infrastructure was in place and, although slowly, the message was permeating throughout the company. He was also anxious to progress the awareness sessions so that everyone had been given the same information and that everyone was fully informed about what was expected of them.

During 2014 the role of Quality Coordinator was given to a new member of the board of directors, the Quality and Management Information Systems Director. He was previously the General Manager of a Division within TrG. He was a stalwart supporter of TQ principles and someone who had achieved considerable success with several projects in his previous posts. The new TQ Coordinator, whilst competent and pleasant did not offer the TQ Manager the inspiration that he had previously enjoyed. As the 'new-boy' on the senior management team the Quality and MIS Director was a junior member with a portfolio that was yet to be proved.

Other changes were made to the senior management team during the year resulting from the retirement of the Marketing Director, who was replaced by the promoted Marketing Manager, and the position of Sales Director was given to the promoted Sales Manager. The important effect of these appointments was that the age profile of the senior management team dropped significantly, with the average dropping from the high 50s to mid-40s. The Managing Director became one of the older members of the team. There were now nine members of the senior management team covering: Personnel, Manufacturing, Marketing, Sales, Finance, Engineering, Quality and MIS, and Business Development. All were men, and all but the Personnel Director had spent the majority of their careers with TrG.

Throughout 2014 the company continued to pursue the objectives identified in the projects, but there was clear evidence that some middle managers in key positions of influence were expressing their scepticism. This was no more so than in the main production section. Traditionally, the production area had been dominated by work-study specialists and members of the Institute of Management Services and the values and techniques were hard to dispel, particularly when both shared an ideology of continuous improvement. The message which tended to dominate was one of 'no change'. Change was seen as being unnecessary, the company was seen as being successful and this was breeding complacency.

It was decided to re-structure certain production sections and introduce 'cellular manufacturing' as part of the business processes project. It was felt 'cells' would encourage greater teamworking and participation. The 'cells' were introduced on an incremental basis meaning that some sections were operating as a 'cell' whilst others were still operating along the traditional functional/divisional lines. The decision to choose one section over another reflected both appropriateness of the tasks being undertaken and the responsiveness of the individuals involved to adopt the new working practices.

For the TQ Manager, cells offered a route to empowerment, for the Manufacturing Director, cell manufacturing provided a vehicle through which participants would have to discuss problems and issues together; for the shop-stewards, there was not enough mutual trust and respect between management and the shop-floor for the majority of people to want to become involved. At supervisory level the response was of ambivalence, based on an assumption that because the employees are conscientious, they would always work to the best of their ability.

The operatives showed far more enthusiasm for 'cells' than at any other level. 'Cells' were seen as providing scope for job variety and seeing the whole operation, as well as providing opportunities for participation in decisions which affected production. It was recognized that there was an element of de-skilling, but variety made up for that. The jobs were much more interesting; as operatives they were no longer just 'nuts and bolts' and could take a pride in the finished product.

There was also a high degree of 'self-importance' expressed by the operatives. The general feeling was that it was the workforce which had the foresight to make things happen and that it was the commitment of the workforce to each other that ensured the success of the initiatives. It was agreed that senior management was too remote to have any impact on the way that the day to day operations were conducted.

Engagement was not universal, some employees expressed complete disenchantment, but their negative response was not attributable to the new initiatives, more of a general dissatisfaction with the company as a whole. These operatives would not have voiced their opinion in the public arena, all agreed that outright opposition would be the route to 'choosing your way out of a job'!

Throughout the first six months of 2014, the TQ Manager maintained a high profile and was able to energize and encourage people to become involved in the new ideas. He adopted a strategy of persuasion and inspiration, partly because that strategy reflected both his beliefs and value system but mainly because he had absolutely no authority to tell people what to do. As the year progressed, the lack of authority began to wear heavily on him. Unable to generate the energy for change at Board level, he felt that many of his initiatives were being frustrated. Unable to 'force' his ideas through in those areas where resistance was endangering the potential achievements, he began to feel that his personal credentials were being put at risk. Knowing that the TQ Manager was unable to insist that the new working methods be adopted, several middle managers used that knowledge as a ploy to reinforce their own preferred operating methods.

These reflected the traditional works-study paradigm. Most of the manufacturing managers had developed their specialist knowledge through this particular career route. The knowledge and skills underpinning management services had been highly valued by the Company. For some, the language of 'quality' was difficult to differentiate between that which reflected the 'Quality Control/Assurance' perspective and that which embraced the philosophy of the new ways of working. The result was the messages became blurred as several managers were reinterpreting the TQ messages in terms of their own frame of reference.

Unfortunately, the closeness of the two narratives merely served to frustrate the change process and create tension between people in positions of influence. Despite the tendency to describe everyone as pulling in the same direction, it was clear that this was not the case and no-one was more aware of this than the TQ Manager. The TQ Manager was emerging as both 'hero' and 'villain'. To the operatives, the Trades Union officials, and those at junior levels of management, the Improvement Programme was the TQ Manager. To others less well disposed to what the programme was seeking to achieve, the TQ Manager was an interference in the primary requirement of getting the job done.

At senior management levels, the achievements that had been made were described largely in terms of themselves and their ability to manage. Whilst on the one hand they acknowledged the change programme, on the other, they were reluctant to acknowledge its impact. Interpretations of why projects had been successful lacked consensus. Several 'camps' appeared with the Manufacturing Director and the Managing Director being seen as leaders, key players and significant influencers of policy, but not necessarily in a joint capacity; and the HRM Director pursuing his own direction. The lack of unity at the senior level was commented on by

4.0

the majority of employees. This disunity was accepted as 'a fact of life at TrG'.

The credibility of the programme experienced a serious blow when the company announced the need to make 150 employees redundant. The reason given was a fall in actual orders against expected sales. The management considered that they were 'lucky' and had demonstrated foresight in ensuring that there were temporary staff who would be laid-off and that the substantive workforce would not be affected except by those who would choose to go. This proved to be 'cold comfort' to the employees who saw the action as just he 'tip of the iceberg'.

The Business Improvement Programme was now interpreted in different ways. It had been sold to the employees as the vehicle through which TrG would establish market dominance, implying that it was to secure employment. Yet, within the first year of operation across all levels it had proved necessary to lose employees. The shop-floor accepted the situation with a degree of resignation, as long as there were no enforced redundancies then things were seen as being all right.

The TQ Manager drove the change message even harder, picking up on the faltering morale and the drop in general complacency as employees realised their jobs were not secure and the company was not 'invincible'. More people began to accept that there was a need to ensure that customers were given quality products and quality service. The TQ Manager was convinced that there was a greater team ethos emerging with people actively cooperating with each other. In some respects, the negative experiences that the TQ Manager had been through were now acting as a challenge and he became more energized.

In January 2015 the senior management held their annual Business Review, held over two days with the TQ Manager being present on Day 1. Different managers gave feedback sessions on the progress of projects towards the major company objectives. The Managing Director was obsessive about timings and despite the development of some critical and analytical discussion, they were not allowed to proceed beyond the allotted time period. The HR Director chose to take an unusual stance during these presentations. Despite the significant implications for HRM for all the projects, and the communications project specifically, the involvement of the HRM Director was minimal. He chose not to participate cooperatively in the presentations and allowed the MIS and Quality Director to dominate the feedback on the progress of the Internal Communications project.

The Quality and MIS Director reported that the awareness exercise had now been presented to 1250 of the 1600 employees, and that the 350 remaining employees would be dealt with over the next 10 weeks. He then went on to introduce the new strategic project group that was to assess *the motivational values of sharing power*. The members of the strategic group were to be himself, the HRM Director, the TQ Manager - who was to act as coordinator, and the Chief Accountant. The group was to use an external consultancy, particularly in the area of Team Briefing, and was to survey the whole workforce, to which the HRM Director responded:

"We know what we know, there is a need for certain members of the departments to have communication training. Business communications are by and large restricted to criticizing or demanding greater effort from our employees. The supervisors are kept 'in the dark' regarding the company's and departments' success and the leaders act like overlords. The leaders fail to understand the complexity of their demeanour. Information is provided on a need to know basis leaving the elite with control of information. There is inter-departmental rivalry and secrecy and the organization structure doesn't allow answers to be given, and we don't give a damn because we don't give answers. The perception is that there is not a lot going on, except on a local basis. Notice boards are the least effective way of giving information, people are not interested in what is going on elsewhere."

For the first time in the proceedings the HRM Director had made a significant contribution and he knew its impact had not been lost. His authority challenged anyone to contradict him, which they did not, and he had 'the floor'. He continued then with his view on the training programme:

"The training objective was a bit 'iffy' anyway. We had identified the training plans off the back of appraisal, but to be brutally honest, the procedures which have been demanded by, for example ISO 9001, have overtaken TQ. Complying with ISO 9001 requires a large negative stick really, rather than the TrG TQ approach. We need some revised objectives and I have initiated a pilot programme of competency-based training and development plans. I have started with the Instruments Department and they have stuck with us. There was a difference of expectation between HR and Instruments but now they have a better application of HR techniques, for example the use of job descriptions including a list of competencies. We have also identified a new appraisal process based on comparison between what the job needs and what the job holder has which will allow an individual career plan to emerge. This approach should allow us to meet the requirements of ISO 9001. I chose Instruments because they were people who wanted to cooperate. I anticipate that the SHRD Plan will be in budget by July and that the pilot will be completed in March and the main programme in place by July."

The impact on the Senior Management group was profound. The Manufacturing Director raised points for debate, others got defensive and in some cases abusive, but the HRM Director was self-assured and uncompromising. The impact on the TQ Manager was palpable. By seemingly criticizing the Senior Management the HR Director had 'poured scorn' on much of the Programme, by linking it to ISO 9001, the implication was that those in charge did not know what they were doing. He returned to his seat, his authority and expertise in tact and his domain untouched. The TQ Manager stood to give an account of what he had been doing and did so without enthusiasm and seemingly sapped of all energy. His presentation was lacklustre and comprised of a series of statistics, estimable in themselves but now without impact.

In the early part of 2015 the TQ Manager lost his main supporter at Board level. The resignation of the Chief Accountant was to serve yet another blow to the increasingly frustrated TQ Manager. As one of the oldest serving members of the senior management team, and a leading protagonist of Business Improvement from its earliest inception at TrG, the Chief Accountant had played an invaluable part in the successes of the Programme and in supporting the TQ Manager. His had been a sympathetic and powerful voice at Board level, and his influence would be missed. His contribution to the Programme had also been recognized and acknowledged at other levels, particularly with the operatives and supervisory levels. He was unusual amongst his senior management colleagues in as much as he was known to the shop-floor. The only other senior manager to gain personal recognition was the Manufacturing Director who achieved almost mythical status - an image he was careful not to disabuse and a personal strategy he was keen to pursue.

The isolation of the TQ Manager was completed by the resignation of the consultant who had maintained

constructive communication sessions with him. Before leaving TRC he gave an account of his views on how the company had progressed. He had been involved since 2011 and reviewed the success around the three objectives of customer focus, challenging over-wasteful working and developing a working environment where everyone feels able to challenge what they do and in so doing all contribute to the company's success.

He believed that the TQ banner had contributed in part to the improvement in the company's performance. He identified the annual objective setting and review process; the fact that the company had become increasingly more measured; the introduction of a new management structure to control improvement activities; project teams which had been set up to tackle large and small issues; the initiation of the review of the management of key processes; and the attempt to improve communications. His praise was not, however, fulsome. He commented on how the business success had been counter-productive to the change. He noted how some people still questioned why there was a need to change. He had observed how many people still regarded the TQ programme as a project-based programme and that they did not see TQ as being integral to their every-day activities. Most serious of all was his observation that the philosophy of Total Quality was not yet ingrained into the organizational culture and that too many employees were still to see an impact of TQ on their working environment.

Whilst his comments were an attempt to stimulate interest, they did little to help counter the criticism the HRM Director had implied. He presented his belief that the principles of TQ could not be compromised and that if the company was to be successful then it needed to embrace changes relating to improving customer service, changes in the way work was undertaken with a quicker move towards cell working, and changes to the way that people are managed particularly the way they are developed and encouraged to participate. In essence, more of what had been introduced right at the beginning of the programme.

Whilst to those who understood TQ and what it attempted to achieve, the message was one of hope and encouragement that the process was ongoing and evolving. To those who had yet to discover the programme and experience its impact, the message was damning, had nothing been achieved? Had they been doing it wrong all along? There were now all sorts of conflicting messages being circulated and the TQ Manager found himself experiencing more barriers to the easy passage

4.0 of the introduction of a programme to which he was passionately committed.

Questions

1. What problems were caused by the different narratives on change, especially between the production managers and the TQ manager?
2. What does the case demonstrate about the role a senior management team should play in organizational-wide change programmes?
3. What could the TQ Manager have done differently?

Further reading

Carolin Abrell-Vogel, Jens Rowold, (2014) "Leaders' commitment to change and their effectiveness in change – a multilevel investigation". Journal of Organizational Change Management, Vol 27, Iss: 6 pp. 900–921.

Elizabeth Briody, Tracy Meerwarth Peter, Robert Trotter (2012) "A story's impact on organizational culture change". Journal of Organizational Change Management, Vol 25, Iss: 1 pp. 67–87.

Albert Weckenmann, Goekhan Akkasoglu, Teresa Werner , (2015) "Quality management – history and trends", The TQM Journal, Vol. 27 Iss: 3, pp. 281–293.

R.P. Mohanty, B.P. Sethi, (1996) "TQM -a comparative approach", Work Study, Vol. 45 Iss: 1, pp. 13–19.

INTEGRATIVE CASE 5.0

Blood on the Gatepost: Family Conflicts in the New Zealand Farming Industry[1]

Craig Prichard
Massey University (New Zealand)

In the pre-dawn dark on July 8, 2010 farm manager, Scott Guy, left his house and began the short drive to work. As he reached the dark country road at the end of his drive just outside the town of Feilding in New Zealand central North Island he discovered, to his surprise, that the gate had been shut. He stopped his ute and went to swing the gate open leaving the motor running and headlights on to light his way. As he reached the gate a lone assailant stepped into the light and fired twin shotgun blasts to his throat and chest. Within seconds Scott Guy was dead. It would take police nine months to lay a murder charge. After a highly public investigation they charged Ewen Macdonald, Guy's fellow farm manager and brother-in-law, with the killing.

At the time of his death, 31-year-old Guy had a lot going for him. His wife was expecting their second child, they had just finished building a new house on land that was part of his father's farm, the couple had been given a 10 per cent share in the family farming business valued at NZ$285 000, and he was earning a NZ$100 000-a-year salary as a farm manager. Meanwhile the dairy industry was booming. Strong global demand for protein and particularly the high volumes and good prices paid for baby milk powder by China's burgeoning middle class was flowing back to good returns to farmers.[2,3]

In the last 20 years the value, scale and reach of New Zealand's dairy food exporting industry had increased dramatically. But its core organizational structure had changed little. While corporate-style dairy organizations had increased in number, the family-based owner-operator remained the industry's dominant format. The key difference between today and 20 years ago is that the average New Zealand dairy farm is a multi-million dollar business. To keep ahead and to take full advantage of the good times, farmers have taken on more land, more cows, more advanced technologies, more debt and more labour. The average New Zealand farm is now milking nearly 400 cows – twice the number it was milking back in 1997 – and is no longer a one-person operation with occasional needs for family labour. Farms such as those run by Bryan Guy and his family, which milks 720 cows on about 300 hectares, and requires multiple part-time and full-time staff, have led the change. Managers and farm workers are required not just to milk production animals, but to rear replacement stock and harvest

---

[1]Unless otherwise stated this case is based on the daily update files from the court case: http://www.stuff.co.nz/dominion-post/news/7043739/Scott-Guy-murder-case-Live-updates.

[2]This wave of prosperity had bought swathes of new dairy farms into the industry, many of them converted sheep farms in New Zealand's South Island. This has added nearly 600 000 hectares to the dairy land and a million more cows during the 2000s, bringing the national herd to around 4.5m productive animals. New Zealand exports almost all of it dairy production. The industry contributes 25 per cent of the country's export earning, almost all of it through Fonterra, the country's largest company and the world's largest dairy exporter. Fonterra employs about 20 000 people around the world and is a cooperative owned by 10 500 dairy farmers including Scott Guy's father, Bryan Guy.

[3]The inflation adjusted payout to farmers per kilogram of milk solids (the industry currency) reached $8 in 2007–2008 and again in 2010-2011 (Dairy Statistics, 2012). In that year average milk solids production per cow hit 364 kgs and the price of land climbed by 8 per cent.

5.0   forage crops to feed hungry cows. But as with any change, not everyone was going in the same direction. And things don't always go to plan.

Rivalry and Conflict

Two farm consultants who gave evidence at Ewen's murder trial described Bryan Guy and his dairy manager, Ewen Macdonald, as 'high achievers, superb driven farmers, with hard working employees'. They said the farm's milk solid output (the unit of measurement for dairy farm production) was significantly higher than other farms in the area and it was 'one of the best-run operations they had seen'. Ewen had been working for Bryan Guy since the mid-1990s when he joined the farm from school at 16. Bryan told the court on day seven of the trial that Ewen was 'very keen and diligent and good with farm management'. During the late 1990s Bryan got involved in dairy industry governance and Ewen took on more responsibility. He eventually became dairy manager. Along the way Ewen had married Anna, Bryan Guy's youngest daughter, and they began raising four children on the farm.

Scott Guy was by all accounts a likeable, easy going, traditional young man. When he left school he went to work as a stockman on farms in New Zealand and later Australia. His mother told the court that as a youngster he had little interest in dairy farming. When he lost his job in Hawkes Bay in 2003 his father came to the rescue, creating a position for him as farm manager back on the family farm alongside his brother-in-law. Anna Guy told the court that she had her doubts about the partnership: 'two's company, three's a crowd', she said.

Scott and Ewen had been mates when they were younger. They had flatted together and Scott had been Ewen's best man at his wedding. But they were competitive and Nikki Guy, Scott's older sister, told the court that the farm wasn't big enough for the two of them. Farm consultant Simon Redmund, who had visited the Guy Farm over a ten-year period, said Ewen was 'streets ahead' of Scott Guy in farming skill. He had also spoken to Macdonald about becoming manager of another farm as a way to further his career but it did not come to anything. In retrospect perhaps Ewen might have taken this offer seriously.

Scott came to resent his brother-in-law's influence, ability and approach to farming. He told a meeting in 2006 that there were 'too many bosses' on the farm. He confided in his younger brother Callum. Callum told the court that Scott thought Ewen was trying to take over the farm and that he wanted to work on his own with their father. Scott was also upset that his sister and her husband had moved into the family home when their parents moved to nearby Feilding and he told his younger brother that he wasn't happy that he and his wife Kylee had the same 10 per cent share in the farm as Ewen and his sister, Anna.

In response to these tensions Bryan Guy called a series of meetings. He discussed work arrangements and gave each man separate responsibilities on the farm. But the grumbles continued. In 2009 Scott put his frustration on the table. He announced at a family business meeting, much to everyone's surprise, that he wanted to inherit the farm, and that Ewen should work for him. He also said that his sister, Anna (Ewen's wife), did not deserve the farm shareholding as she had not worked on the farm. The announcement shocked the rest of the family. At the police interview more than a year later Macdonald said this announcement 'completely blew me away'.

While Bryan and Joanne Guy explained to Scott that he would not be inheriting the farm, and the plan was that they would all work together, Macdonald began to fear that he was being squeezed off the farm. Macdonald's fears were further heightened in early 2010 when Bryan Guy began introducing his son to the farm's accounting system. He told the court that Scott was the obvious choice to take on this job. He gave Scott authority to sign cheques so that if something happened to his father he would know how to do it. He said he wanted to get Macdonald involved as well but had not shown him how it worked.

Macdonald's concerns were further raised a little while later when Bryan and Joanne Guy returned from a business seminar. They were discussing plans to use some of the land for other purposes including developing a recreational lake. Mrs Guy told the court that her daughter, Anna, had said that Ewen 'was a bit worried that suddenly the dairy side of it might fall over and they might be out of the picture'.

Throughout the period Macdonald became increasingly critical of Scott's work performance. There were issues over the quality of the calves Scott was rearing, the amount of time spent with his wife and new baby, and claims that he wasn't pulling his weight on the farm. These tensions boiled over into a public spat in September 2009. Nikki Guy told the court that Scott left milking early to attend a function at the Palmerston North fashion boutique she and her mother owned. She said that later 'Ewen kind of told him off for leaving early and Scott didn't appreciate that. Scott said "... I'm not going to sit here and listen to that shit" and he left'.

Anger and Violence

While the occasional heated meeting, verbal spat, disagreement over the allocation of work and responsibility might be regarded as normal organizational events, the trial of Ewen Macdonald for the murder of Scott Guy brought to light an entirely hidden, darker and more sinister side to Macdonald's frustrations.

Scott Guy's death in July 2010 had been preceded by a series of unexplained local crimes seemingly directed at Scott Guy and his family. In 2008 the old house that Scott was relocating to make way for his new dwelling was destroyed in an arson attack as it sat on a transporter. And a year later the almost completed new home was damaged by vandals who caused more than $20 000 worth of damage to internal walls and fittings. The most disturbing aspect of the attack was the obscene graffiti scrawled in paint on the walls, directed at Scott's wife Kylee.

While Macdonald denied he murdered Scott Guy, he admitted to police that he had caused the arson, the damage and the graffiti. While Macdonald initially denied involvement, they forced a confession after his accomplice Callum Boe admitted the offences. Here is a transcript of the interview.[4]

Macdonald admits torching the house and trucks and then

Police: The next thing on the timeline is clearly what?

EM: Graffitti (Police: Damage to the house) yeah (tell me what happened there). Callum and I did it (why was that?) arrh that probably was directed I guess yes. (had Kylee done something to you, Ewen?) nah nah (cos the wording on the wall, can you remember) bitch slapper or something (how did you write that) with a paintbrush (when did you do it) on that night, before we went on that trip to Ruakaka.

Police: What was going on in your mind.

EM: Nothing, just doing it.

Police: Was there some jealousy about Scott having a new house?

EM: Not about the house it was probably just you know I had sort of about the whole, wasn't a fair partnership, I was sort of having to flog my guts, work my arse off.

Police: That was about seven months after that meeting when Scott vented saying that he wanted to take control.

EM: Yip

Police: And you told us that everything was fine. But was it fine?

EM: Nah I was still holding a bit of a grudge. I yeah yeah I was disappointed that it wasn't a fair partnership.

Police: In what way wasn't it fair though?

EM: What with the hours I had to work and I didn't get to spend as much time at home with the kids whereas Scott got a lot more home time. To me it felt like I was working my arse off and it wasn't equal, the hours work and yeah.

Police: Why did you use the bikes to go up there [to the house to burn it]?

EM: I guess no lights, no motors and no one would hear us and you can leave them out of the way if someone goes past.

EM: I also said that I wouldn't take someone's life, I'm not that extreme.

Police: You said if we find the person responsible for the arson and the damage then we find the murderer. Ewen we have found the person responsible for the arson and the damage.

EM: Yeah but I'm not the murderer.

EM: It makes sense; it makes sense from your investigation.

Police: Given that, do you think you are going to walk out of here today not being charged with murder.

EM: I'd say you are going to charge me with murder but I'm not guilty.

Despite these admissions and the history of conflict between the two men Ewen Macdonald was found not guilty by a jury of killing Scott Guy after a 20-day trial. The defence argued that there was no credible evidence linking Macdonald to the scene of the murder, and a series of other possible suspects and circumstances that the crown had been unable to rule out. Defence lawyer Greg King told the court in his summing up that while there were problems between the two men, and Macdonald had done dreadful things to Scott's property, there was a big difference between destroying property and killing Scott Guy.

[4]See full interview and related links here: http://www.3news.co.nz/Ewen-Macdonalds-first-police-interview-Part-2 VIDEO/tabid/423/articleID/258281/Default.aspx

5.0

King said there were unexplained tyre marks at the scene, a reliable report of a sedan speeding up Aorangi Road away from Guy's house around the time of the killing, and a cigarette box at the scene that may have come from a local burglary. There was also no link between the farm gun, the alleged murder weapon, and the killing. The farm gun had to be manually loaded and witnesses reported three quick blast discharges. King told the crown that 'Everything you have said is wrong'.

In his summing up the crown prosecutor focused on the resentment and the family conflict over the farm. Prosecutor Ben Vanderlolk told the jury that Scott Guy's sense of entitlement at inheriting the farm 'got into Macdonald's head. No one knows the depth of his resentment'. Despite efforts to resolve the issue of shareholding and housing, Macdonald was still not happy. To him everything was in place to accommodate Scott and Kylee Guy, and the family meeting before the shooting led him to believe that further disruption was coming his way. Both men had wildly divergent plans and they were never on the same page. Macdonald felt that his family's security was being threatened and this led to offensive and destructive activity. The prosecutor claimed that Guy's murder was the results of an 'intense, personal hatred' that Macdonald developed out of fear that he would be forced off the Feilding farm should Guy inherit it.

Popular opinion paints Macdonald as a 'blimmin' psycho'.[5] But the extent of Macdonald's undisclosed and after-dark activities went beyond the house attacks and was a surprise to many, including Bryan and Joanne Guy. But Macdonald's wider offending was withheld from the jury. The defence had claimed these were unrelated and therefore prejudicial to the case. As well as the vandalism, arson and wilful damage to Scott Guy's house, Macdonald was also involved in deer poaching expeditions that, when he was caught, led to a string of property damage offences. These 'missions' as Macdonald referred to them, included visiting two farms in the lower Manawatu about 100 times over a two-year period to poach deer.[6] During one mission Macdonald and his colleague Boe were caught. While this seems to have been dealt with privately between Macdonald's father Kerry and the property owner, it fuelled a revengeful and destructive rampage by Macdonald and Boe that involved killing 19 calves with a hammer, emptying a vat containing 16 000 litres of milk and burning down a 100-year-old duck shooting shelter. While reference to these charges was ruled inadmissible by the trial judge, Macdonald pleaded guilty to these offences, and served most of a five-year jail term (with three failed attempts at early parole). He was released in late 2015'.[7]

The Third Party

The trial focused on the events leading up to the murder and the relationship between Macdonald and Guy. But there was always a third party involved. The evidence, of course, showed that Bryan Guy only wished to do the best by his children. But there was some conflict here. Bryan appeared to have been caught between the demands of developing a successful business - that demanded a wide range of skills and abilities - and developing a business where their family featured prominently as owners and managers. While not directly related to the murder, these two objectives created some of the conditions that informed the trial. In a series of media interviews that followed Macdonald's non-guilty verdict, Bryan Guy responded to questions about what he might have done differently. In one interview he made the following comment:

> Yes, we knew when we took the boys in as partners and their wives as partners on the farm that a lot of businesses and not just farming businesses, but particularly a lot of family farming businesses, don't always work well when you get brothers or fathers and sons working together. So because we were so aware of that we thought, well, we would make sure that we were going to make it work, and we did think that we had put a lot of effort in. We had got a lot of really good advice, we had done a lot of planning with it, we thought we had been talking to everyone about how things were working. But yeah so obviously we didn't do it quite right. So you do wonder. But it's no good beating

---

[5]See, for example, media commentator Bryan Edward's comments on the case (http://brianedwardsmedia.co.nz/2012/08/why-the-jury-in-the-scott-guy-murder-trial-should-have-been-privy-to-all-the-facts-about-ewen-macdonald/) accessed February 7, 2012.

[6]Details are here: http://www.nzherald.co.nz/nz/news/article.cfm?c_id=1&objectid=10824508

[7]Macdonald applied three times for early release before the Parole Board granted his application in 2015. In previous attempts the board noted that Macdonald had 'not yet addressed his personality traits which lead him to offend and that more treatment could be required to help him do so' (see report here: http://www.stuff.co.nz/national/crime/63262948/ewen-macdonald-denied-parole)

5.0

ourselves up about it we just have to move on and look to the future.[8,9]

Globally, family businesses dominate many economies. In the US 80 per cent of corporations are either controlled or owned by one family and contribute up to 60 per cent of that nation's GDP (Collins, 2012:5). In New Zealand the assets of about three quarters of the 30 000 farming units are held in family trusts. A recent ANZ Bank survey of 750 of these farmers found that 91 per cent regarded the farm as a family business and 71 per cent were looking to pass this on to the next generation.[10]

Put differently we might say that a very large portion of New Zealand's export earning assets are located in owner-operators, family businesses, most of which will be passed to that family's next generation. Bryan Guy had a plan as to how he was going to do this. But from the case above at least it is clear that no shortage of plans, consultant reports, and meetings, acts of generosity, fairness and efforts to create equitable distribution of work, jobs, shareholding and rewards can always quell the tension and conflict that families harbour. Of course conventional corporate or cooperative businesses are not without their patrilineal and sibling-type rivalries. But at least in such instances the conflict between biological

and symbolic succession is to some degree avoided and family blood is unlikely to be found on the gatepost.

Questions

1. From the case suggest three further steps that Bryan Guy might have taken to strengthen and develop the family business and that would also have avoided or reduced the tension and conflict between Scott Guy and Ewen Macdonald.
2. Discuss the extent that traditional gendered identities and relations underpin the conflict on the Guy farm.
3. Identify, using your answers to (1) and (2), the relative strengths and weaknesses of family and corporate ownership and control of business organizations.

References

Collins, L., Fakoussa, R., Seaman, C., Otten, D., Tucker, J., Grisoni, L. and Graham, S. (2012) *The Modern Family Business: Relationships, Succession and Transition,* London: Palgrave Macmillan.

Dairy NZ (2012J NZ *Dairy Statistics 2011-12,* Hamilton, NZ: Dairy NZ.

[8]See full report here: http://www.3news.co.nz/Support-helped-Scott-Guys-parents/tabid/309/articleID/269773/ Default.aspx

[9]Bryan and Joanne Guy sold the family farm at the end of 2015. When interviewed, they said that 'succession plans changed when Scott was killed'.

[10]See full press release here: http://www.anz.co.nz/resources/5/4/5466d3804c694734a90eff6f4f40a049/POBB_agri_press_release.pdf

COUNTERPOINTS – RECOMMENDED SUPPLEMENTARY READING

The following books are recommended for exploring the alternative perspectives in the Counterpoints that appear in *Organization Theory and Design* and its accompanying web-based materials. Common to these texts is their location within a broad, alternative approach to the study of management and organization known as critical management studies (CMS) which forms one of the divisions within the Academy of Management (see http://aom.org/DIG/).

Textbooks range from introductory (little previous specialist knowledge required) to advanced (substantial specialist knowledge required). Edited collections contain previously published material including journal articles and extracts from books that can be variable in their level of difficulty. Handbooks provide state-of-the art reviews and tend to be comparatively advanced. In addition to these sources, articles published in good (tightly refereed) academic journals are a relevant resource for advanced students. The recommended texts generally have indexes which can be searched for key words. Google Scholar (www.scholar.google.com/) is a useful tool for searching for relevant articles and books; the number of citations received by a book or an article, when taking into account its date of publication, can provide an indication of a text's influence and scholarly standing.

Textbooks

Introductory

Knights, D. and Willmott, H.C. (2012), 2nd ed., *Introducing Organizational Behaviour and Management*, Andover: Cengage Learning
Wilson, F.M. (2003), *Organizational Behaviour and Gender*, Aldershot: Gower/Ashgate.

Intermediate

Barry, J., Chandler, J. and Clark, H. (2009), 2nd ed., *Organizational Behaviour: A Critical Text*, Andover: Cengage Learning
Clegg, S.R, Pitsis, T. and Kornberger, M. (2011), 3rd ed., *Managing and Organizations: An Introduction to Theory and Practice*, London: Sage
Fulop. L., Linstead, S. and Lilley, S. (2004), *Management and Organization: A Critical Text*, London: Macmillan Palgrave
Grey, C. (2013), 3rd ed., *A Very Short Fairly Interesting and Reasonably Cheap Book About Studying Organizations*, London: Sage
Hatch, M-J. with Cunliffe, A. (2006), 3rd ed., *Organization Theory: Modern, Symbolic, and Postmodern Perspectives*, Oxford: Oxford University Press
Thompson, P. and McHugh, D. (2009), 4th ed., *Work Organizations: A Critical Approach*, London: Palgrave Macmillan

Advanced

Alvesson, M. and Willmott, H.C. (2012), 2nd ed., *Making Sense of Management*, London: Sage
Jackson, N. and Carter, P. (2004), 2nd ed., *Rethinking Organizational Behaviour: A Poststructuralist Framework*, London: Prentice-Hall
McAuley, J., Duberley, J. and Johnson, P. (2013), 2nd ed., *Organization Theory: Challenges and Perspectives*, London: FT Prentice-Hall

Edited collections

Alvesson, M. and Willmott, H.C. (2003), *Studying Management Critically*, London: Sage
Clark, H., Chandler, J. and Barry, J. (1994), *Organizations and Identities: Text and Readings in Organizational Behaviour*, Andover: Cengage Learning
Knights, D. and Willmott, H.C. (2010), *Organizational Analysis*, Andover: Cengage Learning

Handbooks

Alvesson, M., Bridgman, T. and Willmott, H.C. (2011), *Oxford Handbook of Critical Management Studies*, Oxford University Press
Barry, D. and Hansen, H. (2008), *The Sage Handbook of New Approaches in Management and Organization*, London: Sage
Clegg, S., Hardy, C., Lawrence, T. and Nord, W.R. (2006), *The Sage Handbook of Organization Studies*, London: Sage

GLOSSARY

A

adaptability culture a culture characterized by strategic focus on the external environment through flexibility and change.

administrative principles a closed systems management perspective that focuses on the total organization and grows from the insights of practitioners.

ambidextrous approach a characteristic of an organization that can behave in both an organic and a mechanistic way.

analyzability a dimension of technology in which work activities can be reduced to mechanical steps and participants can follow an objective, computational procedure to solve problems.

analyzer a business strategy that seeks to maintain a stable business while innovating on the periphery.

authority a force for achieving desired outcomes that is prescribed by the formal hierarchy and reporting relationships.

B

balanced scorecard a comprehensive management control system that balances traditional financial measures with operational measures relating to an organization's critical success factors.

benchmarking process whereby companies find out how others do something better than they do and then try to imitate or improve on it.

boundary spanning roles activities that link and coordinate an organization with key elements in the external environment.

bounded rationality perspective how decisions are made when time is limited, a large number of internal and external factors affect a decision and the problem is ill-defined.

buffering roles activities that absorb uncertainty from the environment.

bureaucracy an organizational framework marked by rules and procedures, specialization and division of labour, hierarchy of authority, technically qualified personnel, separate position and incumbent and written communications and records.

bureaucratic control the use of rules, policies, hierarchy of authority, written documentation, standardization and other bureaucratic mechanisms to standardize behaviour and assess performance.

bureaucratic culture a culture that has an internal focus and a consistency orientation for a stable environment.

bureaucratic organization a perspective that emphasizes management on an impersonal, rational basis through such elements as clearly defined authority and responsibility, formal recordkeeping and uniform application of standard rules.

business intelligence high-tech analysis of large amounts of internal and external data to identify patterns and relationships.

C

Carnegie model organizational decision-making involving many managers and a final choice based on a coalition among those managers.

centrality a trait of a department whose role is in the primary activity of an organization.

centralization refers to the level of hierarchy with authority to make decisions.

centralized decision-making is limited to higher authority.

change process the way in which changes occur in an organization.

chaos theory a scientific theory that suggests that relationships in complex, adaptive systems are made up of numerous interconnections that create unintended effects and render the environment unpredictable.

chief ethics officer high-level company executive who oversees all aspects of ethics, including establishing and broadly communicating ethical standards, setting up ethics training programmes, supervising the investigation of ethical problems and advising managers in the ethical aspects of corporate decisions.

clan culture a culture that focuses primarily on the involvement and participation of the organization's members and on rapidly changing expectations from the external environment.

classical perspective assumes that there is one best way to organize and manage based upon rational principles, whether applied to the design of work, as exemplified in Taylor's scientific management, or the design of organizational structures, and articulated in Fayol's thinking on administration.

closed system a system that is autonomous, enclosed and not dependent on its environment.

coalition an alliance among several managers who agree through bargaining about organizational goals and problem priorities.

code of ethics a formal statement of the company's values concerning ethics and social responsibility.

coercive forces external pressures such as legal requirements exerted on an organization to adopt structures, techniques or behaviours similar to other organizations.

collaborative network an emerging perspective whereby organizations allow themselves to become dependent on other organizations to increase value and productivity for all.

collective bargaining the negotiation of an agreement between management and workers.

collectivity stage the life cycle phase in which an organization has strong leadership and begins to develop clear goals and direction.

competing values approach a perspective on organizational effectiveness that combines diverse indicators of performance that represent competing management values.

competition rivalry between individuals or groups over a valued material or symbolic resource.

confrontation a situation in which parties in conflict directly engage one another and try to work out their differences.

consortia groups of firms that venture into new products and technologies.

contextual dimensions traits that characterize the whole organization, including its size, technology, environment and goals.

contingency a theory meaning one thing depends on other things; the organization's situation dictates the management approach.

contingency decision-making framework a perspective that brings together the two organizational dimensions of problem consensus and technical knowledge about solutions.

continuous process production a completely mechanized manufacturing process in which there is no starting or stopping.

cooptation occurs when leaders from important sectors in the environment are made part of an organization.

coping with uncertainty a source of power for a department that reduces uncertainty for other departments by obtaining prior information, prevention and absorption.

core technology the work process that is directly related to the organization's mission.

craft technology technology characterized by a fairly stable stream of activities but in which the conversion process is not analyzable or well understood.

creative departments organizational departments that initiate change, such as research and development, engineering, design and systems analysis.

creativity the generation of novel ideas that may meet perceived needs or respond to opportunities.

culture the set of values, guiding beliefs, understandings and ways of thinking that are shared and are taught to new members as correct.

culture changes changes in the values, attitudes, expectations, beliefs, abilities and behaviour of employees.

culture strength the degree of agreement among members of an organization about the importance of specific values.

customer relationship management systems that help companies track customer interactions with the firm and allow employees to call up a customer's past sales and service records, outstanding orders or unresolved problems.

D

data the input of a communication channel.

data mining software that uses sophisticated decision-making processes to search raw data for patterns and relationships that may be significant.

data warehousing the use of a huge database that combines all of an organization's data and allows users to access the data directly, create reports and obtain answers to 'what-if' questions.

decentralized decision-making and communication are spread out across the company.

decision learning a process of recognizing and admitting mistakes that allows managers and organizations to acquire the experience and knowledge to perform more effectively in the future.

decision premises constraining frames of reference and guidelines placed by top managers on decisions made at lower levels.

decision support system (DSS) a system that enables managers at all levels of the organization to retrieve, manipulate and display information from integrated databases for making specific decisions.

defender a business strategy that seeks stability or even retrenchment rather than innovation or growth.

departmental grouping a structure in which employees share a common supervisor and resources, are jointly responsible for performance and tend to identify and collaborate with each other.

dependency one aspect of horizontal power: when one department is dependent on another, the latter is in a position of greater power.

differentiation the cognitive and emotional differences among managers in various functional departments of an organization and formal structure differences among these departments.

direct interlock a situation that occurs when a member of the board of directors of one company sits on the board of another.

divisional grouping a grouping in which people are organized according to what the organization produces.

divisional structure the structuring of the organization according to individual products, services, product groups, major projects or profit centres; also called *product structure* or *strategic business units.*

domain an organization's environmental field of activity.

domains of political activity areas in which politics plays a role. Three such domains are structural change, management succession and resource allocation.

domestic stage the first stage of international development in which a company is domestically oriented while managers are aware of the global environment.

downsizing intentionally reducing the size of a company's workforce by laying off employees.

dragon multinationals multinational enterprises (MNEs) originating from the Asia-Pacific region, notably those that have become leading firms in their sector.

dual-core approach an organizational change perspective that identifies the unique processes associated with administrative change compared to those associated with technical change.

E

e-business any business that takes place by digital processes over a computer network rather than in physical space.

economies of scale achieving lower costs through large volume production; often made possible by global expansion.

economies of scope achieving economies by having a presence in many product lines, technologies or geographic areas.

effectiveness the degree to which an organization achieves its goals.

efficiency the amount of resources used to produce a unit of output.

elaboration stage the organizational life cycle phase in which the red tape crisis is resolved through the development of a new sense of teamwork and collaboration.

electronic data interchange (EDI) the linking of organizations through computers for the transmission of data without human interference.

empowerment the delegation of power or authority to subordinates; also called *power sharing*.

engineering technology technology in which there is substantial variety in the tasks performed, but activities are usually handled on the basis of established formulas, procedures and techniques.

enterprise resource planning (ERP) sophisticated computerized systems that collect, process and provide information about a company's entire enterprise, including order processing, product design, purchasing, inventory, manufacturing, distribution, human resources, receipt of payments and forecasting of future demand.

entrepreneurial stage the life cycle phase in which an organization is born and its emphasis is on creating a product and surviving in the marketplace.

escalating commitment persisting in a course of action when it is failing; occurs because managers block or distort negative information and because consistency and persistence are valued in contemporary society.

ethical dilemma when each alternative choice or behaviour seems undesirable because of a potentially negative ethical consequence.

ethics the code of moral principles and values that governs the behaviour of a person or group with respect to what is right or wrong.

ethics committee a group of executives appointed to oversee company ethics.

ethics hotline a telephone number that employees can call to seek guidance and to report questionable behaviour.

executive information system (EIS) interactive systems that help top managers monitor and control organizational operations by processing and presenting data in usable form.

explicit knowledge formal, systematic knowledge that can be codified, written down and passed on to others in documents or general instructions.

external adaptation the manner in which an organization meets goals and deals with outsiders.

extranet private information network.

F

factors of production supplies necessary for production, such as land, raw materials and labour.

feedback control model a control cycle that involves setting goals, establishing standards of performance, measuring actual performance and comparing it to standards and changing activities as needed based on the feedback.

financial resources control over money is an important source of power within an organization.

flexible manufacturing systems (FMS) using computers to link together manufacturing components such as robots, machines, product design and engineering analysis to enable fast switching from one product to another.

focus an organization's dominant perspective which may be internal or external.

focus strategy a strategy in which an organization concentrates on a specific regional market or buyer group.

formalization the degree to which an organization has rules, procedures and written documentation.

formalization stage the phase in an organization's life cycle involving the installation and use of rules, procedures and control systems.

functional grouping the placing together of employees who perform similar functions or work processes or who bring similar knowledge and skills to bear.

functional matrix a structure in which functional bosses have primary authority and product or project managers simply coordinate product activities.

functional structure the grouping of activities by common function.

G

garbage can model model that describes the pattern or flow of multiple decisions within an organization.

general environment includes those sectors that may not directly affect the daily operations of a firm but will indirectly influence it.

generalist an organization that offers a broad range of products or services and serves a broad market.

global company a company that no longer thinks of itself as having a home country.

global geographical structure a form in which an organization divides its operations into world regions, each of which reports to the CEO.

globalization strategy the standardization of product design and advertising strategy throughout the world.

global matrix structure a form of horizontal linkage in an international organization in which both product and geographical structures are implemented simultaneously to achieve a balance between standardization and globalization.

global product structure a form in which product divisions take responsibility for global operations in their specific product areas.

global stage the stage of international development in which the company transcends any one country.

global teams work groups made up of multinational members whose activities span multiple countries; also called *transnational teams*.

global value chains the set of activities – including design, production, marketing, distribution and support – which comprise the process from the conception to the use of a product or service. Often these occur across multiple firms and geographical locations.

goal approach an approach to organizational effectiveness that is concerned with output and whether the organization achieves its output goals.

H

Hawthorne Studies a series of experiments on worker productivity begun in 1924 at the Hawthorne plant of Western Electric Company in Illinois; attributed employees' greater output to managers' increased interest in them during the study.

heroes organizational members who serve as models or ideals for serving cultural norms and values.

high-velocity environments industries in which competitive and technological change is so extreme that market data is either unavailable or obsolete, strategic windows open and shut quickly and the cost of a decision error is company failure.

horizontal coordination model a model of the three components of organizational design needed to achieve new product innovation: departmental specialization, boundary spanning and horizontal linkages.

horizontal grouping the organizing of employees around core work processes rather than by function, product or geography.

horizontal linkage the amount of communication and coordination that occurs horizontally across organizational departments.

horizontal structure a structure that virtually eliminates both the vertical hierarchy and departmental boundaries by organizing teams of employees around core work processes; the end-to-end work, information and material flows that provide value directly to customers.

human relations model emphasis on an aspect of the competing values model that incorporates the values of an internal focus and a flexible structure.

hybrid structure a structure that combines characteristics of various structural approaches (functional, divisional, geographical, horizontal) tailored to specific strategic needs.

I

idea champions organizational members who provide the time and energy to make things happen; sometimes called *advocates, intrapreneurs* and *change agents.*

idea incubator safe harbour where ideas from employees throughout the organization can be developed without interference from company bureaucracy or politics.

imitation the adoption of a decision tried elsewhere in the hope that it will work in the present situation.

incident command system developed to maintain the efficiency and control benefits of bureaucracy yet prevent the problems of slow response to crises.

incremental change a series of continual progressions that maintain an organization's general equilibrium and often affect only one organizational part.

incremental decision process model a model that describes the structured sequence of activities undertaken from the discovery of a problem to its solution.

indirect interlock a situation that occurs when a director of one company and a director of another are both directors of a third company.

information that which alters or reinforces understanding.

information reporting systems the most common form of management information system, these computerized systems provide managers with reports that summarize data and support day-to-day decision-making.

inspiration an innovative, creative solution that is not reached by logical means.

institutional environment norms and values from stakeholders (customers, investors, boards, government, etc.) that organizations try to follow in order to please stakeholders.

institutional perspective an emerging view that holds that under high uncertainty, organizations imitate others in the same institutional environment.

integrated enterprise an organization that uses advanced information technology to enable close coordination within the company as well as with suppliers, customers and partners.

integration the quality of collaboration between departments of an organization.

integrator a position or department created solely to coordinate several departments.

intellectual capital the sum of an organization's knowledge, experience, understanding, processes, innovations and discoveries.

intensive technologies a variety of products or services provided in combination to a client.

interdependence the extent to which departments depend on each other for resources or materials to accomplish their tasks.

intergroup conflict behaviour that occurs between organizational groups when participants identify with one group and perceive that other groups may block their group's goal achievements or expectations.

interlocking directorate a formal linkage that occurs when a member of the board of directors of one company sits on the board of another company.

internal integration a state in which organization members develop a collective identity and know how to work together effectively.

internal process approach an approach that looks at internal activities and assesses effectiveness by indicators of internal health and efficiency.

internal process emphasis an aspect of the competing values model that reflects the values of internal focus and structural control.

international division a division that is equal in status to other major departments within a company and has its own hierarchy to handle business in various countries.

international stage the second stage of international development, in which the company takes exports seriously and begins to think multidomestically.

interorganizational relationships the relatively enduring resource transactions, flows and linkages that occur among two or more organizations.

intranet a private, company-wide information network that uses the communications protocols and standards of the internet but is accessible only to people within the company.

intuitive decision-making the use of experience and judgement rather than sequential logic or explicit reasoning to solve a problem.

J

job design the assignment of goals and tasks to be accomplished by employees.

job enlargement the designing of jobs to expand the number of different tasks performed by an employee.

job enrichment the designing of jobs to increase responsibility, recognition and opportunities for growth and achievement.

job rotation moving employees from job to job to give them a greater variety of tasks and alleviate boredom.

job simplification the reduction of the number and difficulty of tasks performed by a single person.

joint optimization the goal of the sociotechnical systems approach, which states that an organization will function best only if its social and technical systems are designed to fit the needs of one another.

joint venture a separate entity for sharing development and production costs and penetrating new markets that is created with two or more active firms as sponsors.

K

knowledge a conclusion drawn from the interpretation of information that has been linked to other information and compared to what is already known.

knowledge management the efforts to systematically find, organize and make available a company's intellectual capital and to foster a culture of continuous learning and knowledge sharing so that organizational activities build on existing knowledge.

L

labour–management teams a cooperative approach designed to increase worker participation and provide a cooperative model for union-management problems.

language slogans, sayings, metaphors or other expressions that convey a special meaning to employees.

large-batch production a manufacturing process characterized by long production runs of standardized parts.

large group intervention an approach that brings together participants from all parts of the organization (and may include outside stakeholders as well) to discuss problems or opportunities and plan for change.

lean manufacturing uses highly trained employees at every stage of the production process, who take a painstaking approach to details and continuous problem-solving to cut waste and improve quality.

learning organization an organization in which everyone is engaged in identifying and solving problems, enabling the organization to continuously experiment, improve and increase its capability.

legends stories of events based in history that may have been embellished with fictional details.

legitimacy the general perspective that an organization's actions are desirable, proper and appropriate within the environment's system of norms, values and beliefs.

level of analysis in systems theory, the subsystem on which the primary focus is placed; four levels of analysis normally characterize organizations.

liaison role the function of a person located in one department who is responsible for communicating and achieving coordination with another department.

life cycle a perspective on organizational growth and change that suggests that organizations are born, grow older and eventually die.

long-linked technology the combination within one organization of successive stages of production, with each stage using as its inputs the production of the preceding stage.

low-cost leadership a strategy that tries to increase market share by emphasizing low cost when compared with competitors' products.

M

management champion a manager who acts as a supporter and sponsor of a technical champion to shield and promote an idea within the organization.

management control systems the formalized routines, reports and procedures that use information to maintain or alter patterns in organizational activity.

management information system (MIS) a comprehensive, computerized system that provides information and supports day-to-day decision-making.

management science approach organizational decision-making that is the analog to the rational approach by individual managers.

managerial ethics principles that guide the decisions and behaviours of managers with regard to whether they are morally right or wrong.

mass customization the use of computer-integrated systems and flexible work processes to enable companies to mass produce a variety of products or services designed to exact customer specification.

matrix structure a strong form of horizontal linkage in which both product and functional structures (horizontal and vertical) are implemented simultaneously.

mechanistic an organization system marked by rules, procedures, a clear hierarchy of authority and centralized decision-making.

mediating technology the provision of products or services that mediate or link clients from the external environment and allow each department to work independently.

meso theory a new approach to organization studies that integrates both micro and macro levels of analysis.

mimetic forces under conditions of uncertainty, the pressure to copy or model other organizations that appear to be successful in the environment.

mission the organization's reason for its existence.

mission culture a culture that places emphasis on a clear vision of the organization's purpose and on the achievement of specific goals.

multidomestic a strategy aimed *either* at maximizing local responsiveness by customizing products or services to local conditions and preferences *or* at achieving economies of scale and reducing overheads by selling similar products and services in multiple countries.

multidomestic company a company that deals with competitive issues in each country independent of other countries.

multidomestic strategy one in which competition in each country is handled independently of competition in other countries.

multifocused grouping a structure in which an organization embraces structural grouping alternatives simultaneously.

multinational stage the stage of international development in which a company has marketing and production facilities in many countries and more than one-third of its sales outside its home country.

myths stories that are consistent with the values and beliefs of the organization but are not supported by facts.

N

negotiation the bargaining process that often occurs during confrontation and enables the parties to systematically reach a solution.

network centrality top managers increase their power by locating themselves centrally in an organization and surrounding themselves with loyal subordinates.

networking linking computers within or between organizations.

new-venture fund a fund that provides financial resources to employees to develop new ideas, products or businesses.

niche a domain of unique environmental resources and needs.

non-core technology a department work process that is important to the organization but is not directly related to its central mission.

nonprogrammed decisions novel and poorly defined, these are used when no procedure exists for solving the problem.

nonroutine technology technology in which there is high task variety and the conversion process is not analyzable or well understood.

nonsubstitutability a trait of a department whose function cannot be performed by other readily available resources.

normative forces pressures to adopt structures, techniques or management processes because they are considered by the community to be up-to-date and effective.

O

official goals the formally stated definition of business scope and outcomes the organization is trying to achieve; another term for *mission*.

open system a system that must interact with the environment to survive.

open systems emphasis an aspect of the competing values model that reflects a combination of external focus and flexible structure.

operative goals descriptions of the ends sought through the actual operating procedures of the organization; these explain what the organization is trying to accomplish.

organic an organization system marked by free-flowing, adaptive processes, an unclear hierarchy of authority and decentralized decision-making.

organization development a behavioural science field devoted to improving performance through trust, open confrontation of problems, employee empowerment and participation, the design of meaningful work, cooperation between groups and the full use of human potential.

organization structure designates formal reporting relationships, including the number of levels in the hierarchy and the span of control of managers and supervisors; identifies the grouping together of individuals into departments and of departments into the total organization; and includes the design of systems to ensure effective communication, coordination and integration of efforts across departments.

organization theory a macro approach to organizations that analyzes the whole organization as a unit.

organizational behaviour a micro approach to organizations that focuses on the individuals within organizations as the relevant units for analysis.

organizational change the adoption of a new idea or behaviour by an organization.

organizational culture a complex of norms, values and ways of doing things that are ascribed to an organization or its members, often by senior managers or observers who have a vested interest in representing it in a uniform way that disregards and obscures the existence of multiple (e.g. occupational) cultures and conflicting values.

organizational decision-making the organizational process of identifying and solving problems.

organizational decline a condition in which a substantial, absolute decrease in an organization's resource base occurs over a period of time.

organizational ecosystem a system formed by the interaction of a community of organizations and their environment, usually cutting across traditional industry lines.

organizational environment all elements that exist outside the boundary of the organization and have the potential to affect all or part of the organization.

organizational form an organization's specific technology, structure, products, goals and personnel.

organizational goal a desired state of affairs that the organization attempts to reach.

organizational innovation the adoption of an idea or behaviour that is new to an organization's industry, market or general environment.

organizational politics activities to acquire, develop and use power and other resources to obtain one's preferred outcome when there is uncertainty or disagreement about choices.

organizations social entities that are goal-directed, deliberately structured activity systems linked to the external environment.

organized anarchy extremely organic organizations characterized by highly uncertain conditions.

outsourcing to contract out certain corporate functions, such as manufacturing, information technology or credit processing, to other companies.

P

personnel ratios the proportions of administrative, clerical and professional support staff.

point–counterpoint a decision-making technique that divides decision-makers into two groups and assigns them different, often competing responsibilities.

political model a definition of an organization as being made up of groups that have separate interests, goals and values in which power and influence are needed to reach decisions.

political tactics for using power these include building coalitions, expanding networks, controlling decision premises, enhancing legitimacy and expertise and making a direct appeal.

pooled interdependence the lowest form of interdependence among departments, in which work does not flow between units.

population a set of organizations engaged in similar activities with similar patterns of resource utilization and outcomes.

population ecology perspective a perspective in which the focus is on organizational diversity and adaptation within a community or population or organizations.

power the ability of one person or department in an organization to influence others to bring about desired outcomes.

power distance the level of inequality people are willing to accept within an organization.

power sources there are five sources of horizontal power in organizations: dependency, financial resources, centrality, nonsubstitutability and the ability to cope with uncertainty.

problem consensus the agreement among managers about the nature of problems or opportunities and about which goals and outcomes to pursue.

problem identification the decision-making stage in which information about environmental and organizational conditions is monitored to determine if performance is satisfactory and to diagnose the cause of shortcomings.

problem solution the decision-making stage in which alternative courses of action are considered and one alternative is selected and implemented.

problemistic search occurs when managers look around in the immediate environment for a solution to resolve a problem quickly.

process organized group of related tasks and activities that work together to transform inputs into outputs that create value for customers.

product and service changes changes in an organization's product or service outputs.

product matrix a variation of the matrix structure in which project or product managers have primary authority and functional managers simply assign technical personnel to projects and provide advisory expertise.

programmed decisions repetitive and well-defined procedures that exist for resolving problems.

prospector a business strategy characterized by innovation, risk-taking, seeking out new opportunities and growth.

R

radical change a breaking of the frame of reference for an organization, often creating a new equilibrium because the entire organization is transformed.

rational approach a process of decision-making that stresses the need for systematic analysis of a problem followed by choice and implementation in a logical sequence.

rational goal emphasis an aspect of the competing values model that reflects values of structural control and external focus.

rational model a description of an organization characterized by a rational approach to decision-making, extensive and reliable information systems, central power, a norm of optimization, uniform values across groups, little conflict and an efficiency orientation.

reactor a business strategy in which environmental threats and opportunities are responded to in an ad hoc fashion.

reasons organizations grow growth occurs because it is an organizational goal, it is necessary to attract and keep quality managers or it is necessary to maintain economic health.

reciprocal interdependence the highest level of interdependence, in which the output of one operation is the input of a second, and the output of the second operation is the input of the first (for example, a hospital).

re-engineering redesigning a vertical organization along its horizontal workflows and processes.

resource dependence a situation in which organizations depend on the environment but strive to acquire control over resources to minimize their dependence.

resource-based approach an organizational perspective that assesses effectiveness by observing how successfully the organization obtains, integrates and manages valued resources.

retention the preservation and institutionalization of selected organizational forms.

rites and ceremonies the elaborate, planned activities that make up a special event and often are conducted for the benefit of an audience.

role a part in a dynamic social system that allows an employee to use his or her discretion and ability to achieve outcomes and meet goals.

routine technology technology characterized by little task variety and the use of objective, computational procedures.

rule of law that which arises from a set of codified principles and regulations that describe how people are required to act, are generally accepted in society and are enforceable in the courts.

S

satisficing the acceptance by organizations of a satisfactory rather than a maximum level of performance.

scientific management a classical approach that claims decisions about organization and job design should be based on precise, scientific measurement and procedures.

sectors subdivisions of the external environment that contain similar elements.

selection the process by which organizational variations are determined to fit the external environment; variations that fail to fit the needs of the environment are 'selected out'.

sequential interdependence a serial form of interdependence in which the output of one operation becomes the input to another operation.

service technology technology characterized by simultaneous production and consumption, customized output, customer participation, intangible output and being labour intensive.

simple–complex dimension the number and dissimilarity of external elements relevant to an organization's operation.

Six Sigma quality standard that specifies a goal of no more than 3.4 defects per million parts; expanded to refer to a set of control procedures that emphasize the relentless pursuit of higher quality and lower costs.

skunkworks separate, small, informal, highly autonomous and often secretive group that focuses on breakthrough ideas for the business.

small-batch production a manufacturing process, often custom work, that is not highly mechanized and relies heavily on the human operator.

social audit measures and reports the ethical, social and environmental impact of a company's operations.

social capital the quality of interactions among people, affected by whether they share a common perspective.

social responsibility management's obligation to make choices and take action so that the organization contributes to the welfare and interest of society as well as itself.

sociotechnical systems approach an approach that combines the needs of people with the needs of technical efficiency.

sources of intergroup conflict factors that generate conflict, including goal incompatibility, differentiation, task interdependence and limited resources.

specialist an organization that has a narrow range of goods or services or serves a narrow market.

stable–unstable dimension the state of an organization's environmental elements.

stakeholder any group within or outside an organization that has a stake in the organization's performance.

stakeholder approach also called the *constituency approach,* this perspective assesses the satisfaction of stakeholders as an indicator of the organization's performance.

standardization a policy that ensures all branches of the company at all locations operate in the same way.

stories narratives based on true events that are frequently shared among organizational employees and told to new employees to inform them about an organization.

strategic contingencies events and activities inside and outside an organization that are essential for attaining organizational goals.

strategy the current set of plans, decisions and objectives that have been adopted to achieve the organization's goals.

strategy and structure changes changes in the administrative domain of an organization, including structure, policies, reward systems, labour relations, coordination devices, management information control systems and accounting and budgeting.

structural dimensions descriptions of the internal characteristics of an organization.

structure the formal reporting relationships, groupings and systems of an organization.

struggle for existence a principle of the population ecology model that holds that organizations are engaged in a competitive struggle for resources and fighting to survive.

subcultures cultures that develop within an organization to reflect the common problems, goals and experiences that members of a team, department or other unit share.

subsystems divisions of an organization that perform specific functions for the organization's survival; organizational subsystems perform the essential functions of boundary spanning, production, maintenance, adaptation and management.

switching structures an organization creates an organic structure when such a structure is needed for the initiation of new ideas.

symbol something that represents another thing.

symptoms of structural deficiency signs of the organization structure being out of alignment, including delayed or poor quality decision-making, failure to respond innovatively to environmental changes and too much conflict.

system a set of interacting elements that acquires inputs from the environment, transforms them, and discharges outputs to the external environment.

T

tacit knowledge knowledge that is based on personal experience, intuition, rules of thumb and judgement, and cannot be easily codified and passed on to others in written form.

tactics for enhancing collaboration techniques such as integration devices, confrontation and negotiation, intergroup consultation, member rotation and shared mission and superordinate goals that enable groups to overcome differences and work together.

tactics for increasing power these include entering areas of high uncertainty, creating dependencies, providing resources and satisfying strategic contingencies.

task a narrowly defined piece of work assigned to a person.

task environment sectors with which the organization interacts directly and that have a direct effect on the organization's ability to achieve its goals.

task force a temporary committee composed of representatives from each department affected by a problem.

team building activities that promote the idea that people who work together can work as a team.

teams permanent task forces often used in conjunction with a full-time integrator.

technical champion a person who generates or adopts and develops an idea for a technological innovation and is devoted to it, even to the extent of risking position or prestige; also called *product champion.*

technical complexity the extent of mechanization in the manufacturing process.

technical knowledge understanding and agreement about how to solve problems and reach organizational goals.

technology the tools, techniques and actions used to transform organizational inputs into outputs.

technology changes changes in an organization's production process, including its knowledge and skills base, that enable distinctive competence.

time-based competition delivering products and services faster than competitors, giving companies a competitive edge.

transaction processing systems (TPS) automation of the organization's routine, day-to-day business transactions.

transnational model a form of horizontal organization that has multiple centres, subsidiary managers who initiate strategy and innovations for the company as a whole and unity and coordination achieved through corporate culture and shared vision and values.

U

uncertainty occurs when decision-makers do not have sufficient information about environmental factors and have a difficult time predicting external changes.

uncertainty avoidance the level of tolerance for and comfort with uncertainty and individualism within a culture.

V

values-based leadership a relationship between a leader and followers that is based on strongly shared values that are advocated and acted upon by the leader.

variation appearance of new organizational forms in response to the needs of the external environment; analogous to mutations in biology.

variety in terms of tasks, the frequency of unexpected and novel events that occur in the conversion process.

venture teams a technique to foster creativity within organizations in which a small team is set up as its own company to pursue innovations.

vertical information system the periodic reports, written information and computer-based communications distributed to managers.

vertical linkages communication and coordination activities connecting the top and bottom of an organization.

virtual network grouping organization that is a loosely connected cluster of separate components.

virtual network structure the firm subcontracts many or most of its major processes to separate companies and coordinates their activities from a small headquarters organization.

virtual team made up of organizationally or geographically dispersed members who are linked through advanced information and communications technologies. Members frequently use the internet and collaborative software to work together, rather than meeting face-to-face.

W

Web 2.0 introduced in 2004, Web 2.0 technology is distinguished by the capacity to offer a much improved level user interaction making websites more dynamic and interconnected so that information is easier to share (e.g. social networking, blogs, etc).

whistle-blowing employee disclosure of illegal, immoral or illegitimate practices on the part of the organization.

SUBJECT INDEX